A NEW CIVILIZATION

The "Hidden" History of the Catholic Church,
Freemasonry, and Non-Human Intelligences

GABRIEL PIEDRA, Th.D.

by His Blood
Cover: Emily Coscolla

TABLE OF CONTENTS

INTRODUCTION--- 9

CHAPTER 1
European Freemasonry against the Jesuits and the temporal power
of the Papacy --- 15
The Papacy, the Jesuits, and the Freemasons: for freedom of conscience ---- 15

CHAPTER 2
"The Clash of Civilizations"-The Vatican vs. Freemasonry and the
United States of America, part 1 ------------------------------------ 21
Historical hostility between Freemasonry and the Jesuits -------------------- 21
Background and long-term consequences of the Masonic Congress of the
Allied Nations --- 24
The Society of Jesus and its various factions amid the uniformity of the
order -- 34
The League of Nations, the Vatican, and the Jesuits' Conspiracy ------------ 36

CHAPTER 3
"The clash of civilizations" - Concordats with the enemy --------------- 47
The Vatican and Nazi Germany --- 47
The relationship between the Papacy and Italian Fascism -------------------- 53
Pius XII and Franco's Spain -- 57
Nazism and the Ukrainian Catholic Army ---------------------------------- 61
Ante Pavelić, the Croatian Catholic Church and the Independent State of
Croatia -- 62

CHAPTER 4
"The Clash of Civilizations"-The Vatican vs. Freemasonry and the
United States of America, part 2 ------------------------------------ 93
France, the Jesuit conspiracy against Freemasonry, and the League of
Nations -- 93
The French post-war era, Catholicism and Freemasonry ---------------------- 108
From the League of Nations to the United Nations. The consistent role of
intercontinental Freemasonry, the United States, and a United and
democratic Europe -- 117
The CIA and its attempts to bring democracy to the Roman Catholic
Church: the journey towards the Second Vatican Council -------------------- 122
The Second Vatican Council: the United States and Freemasonry for more
modernist Popes -- 127
Vatican II, Freemasonry, the United States, the Revolution of 1968, and the
transformation of the Roman Catholic Church ------------------------------ 135

The relationship between the US secret services, Freemasonry, the anti-communist struggle, and Americanism in Italy ------------------------------- 142
Expansion of the Masonic presence in the Roman Catholic Church --------- 144
The transformation of the Catholic Church and its role
in world geopolitics -- 149
Freemasons and prelates for the conquest of the Catholic Church: Vatican
II and post-conciliar period --- 152

CHAPTER 5
John Paul II and the American Century ------------------------------------ 171
John Paul II, Ronald Reagan, and the fall of Communism --------------------- 171
The Balkan War and the indirect promotion of Catholic interests through
U.S. and NATO support --- 180

CHAPTER 6
War on terror: the U.S.-Vatican crusade against Islam -------------------- 191
George W. Bush and the extreme Christian right in the U.S. ------------------ 191
U.S. "crusade" plans against Islam and Vatican support ----------------------- 204
Organizations, people, and other facts related to the Iraq invasion ---------- 222
Blackwater and military evangelism in Iraq ------------------------------------- 230
Detention centers --- 236
The "black sites" spreading to the world...-------------------------------------- 240
Afghanistan and more...-- 245

CHAPTER 7
Attempts to establish a theocracy, the spies, and more "black sites"-- 253
Attempt to establish martial law --- 253
U.S. spying system on civilians and terrorists --------------------------------- 259

CHAPTER 8
"My name is Jorge Bergoglio"--- 261
From Bergoglio to Francis, Pontiff of the Roman Catholic Church
a. His role during the Argentine dictatorship ----------------------------------- 261
b. The military chaplains of the Society of Jesus endorsed by Bergoglio and
a history of torture and kidnapping --- 269
c. Jorge Mario Bergoglio and Commander Emilio Eduardo Massera --------- 271
d. A renewed Bergoglio - from conservatism to liberation theology,
freemasonry and mysticism -- 272
e. Ambiguities and cover-ups in the 21st century ------------------------------- 276

CHAPTER 9

The resurgence of the papacy: a pope from the end of the world ------ 279
Still in the 21st century: among Freemasons, "contactees" and "prophecies"- 279
Malachi Martin, and Lucifer at the Vatican ------------------------------- 282
Satanism in the Vatican and inside the U.S. Catholic Church under
Cardinal Bernardin -- 283
Malachi Martin and *The Last Pope* --------------------------------------- 288
Towards a new papal election: the candidacy of Jorge Bergoglio and the
Sankt Gallen group--- 294
Road to abdication, part one -- 312
Road to abdication, part two -- 314
An agenda driven under the mastery of ambiguity: Background ------------ 325
Action -- 328
On the Independent State of Croatia------------------------------------- 337
Superstar pope -- 338

CHAPTER 10

Pope Francis and Freemasonry --- 343
A Mason pope, very well received by freemasons -------------------------- 343
Catholic Church and Freemasonry during Francis' papacy ------------------ 353
Pope Francis' ambiguities about his attitude towards Freemasonry -------- 354

CHAPTER 11

The new "Holy Alliance" -- 357
New U.S.-Vatican alliance: influences and the alliance between Obama and
Pope Francis -- 357
Pope Francis' address to the European Parliament (brief account) -------- 371
Accelerated ecumenism --- 373
Pope Francis' visit to the U.S. Congress -------------------------------- 375
Pope Francis and the UN Agenda
a. Brief History of the Climate Change Agenda --------------------------- 382
b. The UN surrenders to the Catholic Church ----------------------------- 385
The Paris Agreements on COP21 and some of their ratifications ----------- 395
Sunday rest decrees in the world -- 398
Events related to the evolution of global solutions
to peace and prosperity --- 402

CHAPTER 12

**The Pope and H. Clinton. Trump and the resurgence
of Christian fascism** -- 405
Context – "Catholic Spring" --- 405
George Soros, the Vatican, and the U.S. Catholic Church endorsing Hillary
Clinton for president in 2016 --- 406
Insights and other early facts about the 2016 presidential election and its
aftermath --- 410

Attempts to install a right-wing catholic-protestant theocracy --------------- 412
Lurking danger -- 434

CHAPTER 13
Biden and Francis, the Pandemic and the opportunity for The Great Reset --- 447
Biden's strongly Catholic administration and its relationship with
the Holy See -- 447
President Biden's Background and Relationship with Pope Francis ---------- 449
COVID-19 --- 452
COVID-19 and 'the new normal' --- 461
A new post-COVID-19 world order led by the Vatican through
the Great Reset --- 466
Fratelli Tutti -- 471

CHAPTER 14
French Freemasonry and the Holy See in the 21st Century --------------- 475
French Freemasonry and the Holy See in the 21st Century ------------------- 475

CHAPTER 15
Donald Trump and the resurgence of Christian fascism - part 2 -------- 483
The new age of fascism -- 483
A Catholic-evangelical far-right under Trump --------------------------------- 488
Precedents to the U.S. Capitol Attack on January 6, 2021 -------------------- 495
Assault on the Capitol on January 6, 2021 ------------------------------------ 504
Several extreme right-wing groups and the Christian and Catholic far-right
in the January 6 manifestation --- 508
Peril: the post-January 6 era -- 514
Dangers on the horizon-1 --- 516
Dangers on the horizon-2 --- 524

CHAPTER 16
Schism in the Catholic Church and the resistance against Pope Francis --- 527
Schism under Francis' papacy --- 527
Conservative U.S. Catholic plot against Pope Francis ------------------------ 532
Conservative and international Catholic conspiracy against Pope Francis -- 537
Powerful resistance against Pope Francis and the support for Trump ------- 545

CHAPTER 17
A last papacy? -- 561
A U.S. pope or a pope sympathetic to the far-right? -------------------------- 561

CHAPTER 18

The Secret - concealment about non-human intelligences -------------- 565
Sign, Grudge, and Blue Book projects ------------------------------------ 565
Significant sighting cases and the U.S. government cover-up ---------------- 565
A worldwide phenomenon --- 573
UFO crash retrieval and reverse engineering program ---------------------- 576
"The beginning of the end" -- 592
Major revelations -- 599
Recovered and examined remains of 'UAPs' and additional revelations ----- 605
Bills and laws for the declassification of programs on UAP technology,
including their pilots-- 606
National Defense Authorization Act 2022 -------------------------------- 606
David Grusch --- 608
Whistleblowers of UFO crash retrieval and reverse engineering program --- 612
Unidentified Anomalous Phenomena Disclosure Act of 2023 ---------------- 614

CHAPTER 19

Origins and intentions of the non-human phenomenon ----------------- 617
Particularities of the phenomenon in the present time ---------------------- 617
Long-standing characteristics of the phenomenon ------------------------- 618
Cases of the "gods" in more modern times ------------------------------- 620
"Satan," Lam, and 'modern' music -------------------------------------- 623
"Somber" and future effects --- 629

CHAPTER 20

The Holy See, non-human forces, and the future of humanity ---------- 631
Introduction --- 631
Supernatural events in the Catholic Church and the UFO phenomenon ---- 633
The Catholic Church, the authentic apparitions of Fatima
and Freemasonry -- 634
Catholic Church's thoughts on the possibility of extraterrestrial life --------- 641
The people's advocate Daniel Sheehan and the Jesuits, the Vatican, and
Project Blue Book --- 647
Jorge Mario Bergoglio's influences on UFOs and non-human entities:
1. The Jesuit priest and astronomer Benito Segundo Reyna ------------------- 651
2. Ángel Cristo Acoglanis, Pedro Romaniuk, Solari Parravicini, Pope
Francis, UFOs and "extraterrestrials," and the future of the Roman Catholic
Church -- 653
The Andes, home of "the gods": The Mapuches, the case of the Jesuits,
Bergoglio and Solari Parravicini -------------------------------------- 661
The prophecy of the then Cardinal Bergoglio --------------------------- 666
Dr. Edgard Mitchell, John Podesta, revelation, *extraterrestrial* contact, and
the Vatican -- 667

When the phenomenon seems to especially favor both ultra-conservative
Catholicism and progressive Catholicism ------------------------------------ 674
1. The "Virgin of Revelation," "our Lady of Fatima," and Pope Pius XII's
UFO apparitions --- 674
2. The Garabandal apparitions, Spain -------------------------------------- 677
3. The Medjugorje apparitions in Bosnia-Herzegovina ---------------------- 679
4. Chris Bledsoe and the UAP phenomenon -------------------------------- 682
Bledsoe and "the lady" --- 683
"The dead" warn of an assassination attempt on Pope Francis --------------- 684
International Organization for the Destiny of the World: the Vatican,
Freemasons, military, prelates, politicians, others, and John Podesta -------- 684

INTRODUCTION

Ignatius of Loyola, the founder of the Society of Jesus - the Jesuits - in 1540 and whose order was the most powerful defender of the papacy, employed the following reasoning:

"Unity prevails over conflict, the whole is greater than the part, time is greater than space, realities are more important than ideas."[1]

Jesuit Juan Carlos Scannone tells us about the use of the elements mentioned by Pope Francis: "when Jorge Bergoglio was Provincial, in 1974, he already used them; and I have heard him mention them to illuminate different situations that were dealt with in that area."[2] Bergoglio made use of these elements on several occasions and has even done so during his papacy. He did so extensively in *Evangelii Gaudium*.[3] Pope Francis would make use of this scheme in helping the poor and the most disadvantaged, but also in the unity of ideologies; although trying "not to violate" Catholic doctrine. In turn, he would do so influenced, which is well documented, by Masonic ideals and by what he considers superior non-human intelligences to unify humanity for a common good that is presumed to be ideal.

Malachi Brendan Martin, a Jesuit and renowned scholar, wrote that for centuries, the Jesuits have been considered the main and undisputed champions of the Catholic Church and the papacy in preserving and promoting its authority, both politically, educationally, and religiously.[4]

In a book from the Georgetown University Press, from the Society of Jesus, we read about the Society's past:

"A rich historical literature now details the rapid expansion of the Jesuits into almost every corner of the globe in the first generations after Ignatius of Loyola, with Francis Xavier in Japan, Pedro Martínez in Havana, and José de Acosta in Peru before 1600. If Catholicism is the world's first global institution, then the Jesuits were indispensable to its geographical spread away from Europe. These Jesuits link the Age of Discovery to the Catholic variant of the Republic of Letters."[5]

The Society of Jesus quickly won the affection of the popes and large sectors of the Catholic Church, but also many enemies. Among them, Freemasonry.

---

[1] Horacio Verbitsky, Vigilia de armas (Tomo 3). Del Cordobazo de 1969 al 23 de marzo de 1976: Historia política de la iglesia católica (Editorial Sudamericana, 2013), op. cit.
[2] Aldo Duzdevich, Salvados por Francisco: Cómo un joven sacerdote se arriesgó para ayudar a perseguidos por la dictadura (Grupo Editorial Random House, Argentina, 2019), op. cit.
[3] Barrett Turner (2017), Pacis Progressio: How Francis' Four NewPrinciples Develop Catholic Social Teachinginto Catholic Social Praxis, Journal of Moral Theology, Vol. 6, No. 1, pp. 117-125.
[4] Malachi Martin, The Jesuits: The Society of Jesus and the Betrayal of the Roman Catholic Church (Simon & Schuster, New York, 1987), p. 28; David I. Kertzer, Prisoner of the Vatican: The Pope's Secret Plot to Capture Rome from the New Italian State (Houghton Mifflin Company, New York, 2004), p. 88.
[5] Thomas Banchoff and José Casanova, Editors, The Jesuits and Globalization: Historical Legacies and Contemporary Challenges (Georgetown University Press, Washington, DC, 2016), p. 131.

Freemasonry is an organization that admits men of all religions among its members. Therefore, one of its requirements is the belief in a supreme being. They believe in brotherhood, moral discipline, and helping others.

The lodges are composed of Masonic members, but their temples are also called lodges, which have a series of religious symbols where syncretism is strongly present. Their ceremonies are also loaded with symbolism, all of which communicate the thinking and values of the organization.

Among its members are lay Catholics, priests, even bishops and cardinals, as well as a wide range of lay people and leaders of different Christian denominations. But it also includes Jews, non-traditional Muslims, and others.

It should be noted that Freemasonry has its origins in the influence of the Benedictine Cluniac monks, who were in Jerusalem during the Crusades (1096 and 1291), the well-known religious military expeditions promoted by the Catholic Church and the Catholic Western powers to reconquer Jerusalem from the Muslim presence.[6]

The origin of Freemasonry is very much, but not only, centered on the symbolism of the Temple of Solomon in Jerusalem. Thus, Masonic history tells us that the Benedictine Cluniac monks were very interested in the Temple of Jerusalem. The *fratres conversi* and the *fratres barbati* marched with their Benedictine masters to Jerusalem, to reconquer the Temple which they read in the works of Bede as well as in the Ordinary Gloss of Walafrid Strabon. Their chests contained the commentaries of the great Benedictine exegetes on the Temple of Solomon, as well as the architectural manuals of Vitruvius and Theophilus. But they also knew about Hiram Abif, the builder of the temple.[7]

The monks, primarily of the Benedictine Order, developed the art of construction during the Middle Ages. The apogee of Romanesque and Gothic constructions, of abbeys and cathedrals, coincided with the historical process framed by the Crusades and in the times of the Cluniac Order, when the lodges of Benedictine builders adopted this symbology.[8]

The allegorical basis of operative Masonic symbolism was established by the Benedictine monks of the Carolingian Empire.[9] As documented and quoted by the journalist and Mason Edward R. Callaey, the Masons inherited from the Benedictine monks: "A body of religious doctrine constructed by allegories pointing to a rule of morality, to a sublimated vision of the act of building, to a conscience identified with the empire of the spiritual forces of Catholic thought." Thus, the Masons remained dependent on Catholic doctrine until the end of the 14th century, which is evident in the documents, constitutions, and manuscripts that are very important in Masonic historiography.[10]

In the 18th century, the regular clergy provided content to the Masonic high degrees, maintaining a high Catholic background around the Templar metaphor.[11]

---

[6] Eduardo R. Callaey, El Otro Imperio Cristiano: De la Orden del Temple a la Francmasonería (Ediciones Nowtilus, S.L., Madrid, 2005), p. 78.

[7] Ibid.

[8] Ibid, pp. 40, 12, 41.

[9] Ibid, p. 176.

[10] Ibid, p. 96.

[11] Ibid, p. 176.

Benedictine monks, Augustinians, and Jesuits formed a consistent group within the lodges; and the "philosophical" development that arose from this to the Masonic systems and rites of the second half of that century, is very remarkable.[12]

Freemasonry has had a great influence since the 18th century, being lovers of freedom, of free thought, they were staunch enemies of the Catholic Church and the Jesuits, who did not respect freedom of conscience and religion, fighting against the progressivism of the nations. The lodges have had and still have a lot of influence at the political and social level up to certain levels, but depending on the place, the same as the papacy and the Society of Jesus.

But since the 1930s, an understanding began between the Jesuits and the Masons, with a high level of relationship until the present day, with exceptions but also with secret designs, which reaches a climax at the present.

The coincidence of the above with what is happening today, where a more progressive Roman Catholicism is confronting a much more traditional one in unprecedented ways, and where a very progressive United States is confronting a much more conservative one also without precedent, coincides in turn with an intensely growing interest, fundamentally in the United States, in revealing what is behind the unidentified anomalous phenomenon or UAP; as UFOs are usually called today. These historical concurrences do not necessarily all come together under a cherished design, but they are not without their consequences when they meet.

We are talking about the most influential and powerful religion on Earth, as well as the most powerful country on the planet, at the time of an unprecedented revelation in the history of the world about non-human intelligences behind the UAP phenomenon.

Now, it is true that many conspiracy theories abound against the Jesuits[13] and the Masons;[14] even of both institutions conspiring for the same purpose.[15] But these supposed plots also exist about the UAPs, although not everything is unreal.

For example about the Jesuits, I do not believe in the "Monita Secreta" (Secret Instruction of the Jesuits), or in the "Extreme Oath of the Jesuits," nor that the Jesuits sank the Titanic; nor that they are behind the assassination of U.S. President John F. Kennedy. As well as many other excessively extravagant and overloaded claims of speculation due to highly imaginative, horrible, and irresponsible connections. As in any good religious organization, I believe there are members of the Society of Jesus who are highly honorable, as well as others who are not. In fact, I greatly admire the dedication, drive, charisma, intellect, and wisdom of so many Jesuits.

Additionally, I do not subscribe to the allegations that the Masons control world governments and the world economy, or that they conspired to create three world wars.

---

[12] Ibid.

[13] Jim McDermott (June 14, 2022), The uncomfortable truths behind crazy Jesuit conspiracy theories, America Magazine; Andrew Heath Fink (2020), *The Importance of Conspiracy Theory in Extremist Ideology and Propaganda* (Publication No. 1115) [Ph.D. dissertation, Leiden University, The Netherlands]; Thomas Milan Konda, Conspiracies of Conspiracies: How Delusions Have Overrun America (The University of Chicago Press, Chicago, 2019), pp. 23, 36, 37, 40, 211.

[14] Emily McGee (2020), "Meeters in Secret: The History of Freemasonry and Its Influence on Conspiracy Culture in the United States," Scholars Day Conference. 28; Michael Barkun, A Culture of Conspiracy: Apocalyptic Visions in Contemporary America (University of California Press, 2003), pp. 126-140; Loïc Nicolas (2015). Jésuites, Juifs, francs-maçons : la rhétorique au service de la conspiration. Diogène, 249-250, 75-87.

[15] Thomas Milan Konda, Conspiracies of Conspiracies: How Delusions Have Overrun America (The University of Chicago Press, Chicago, 2019), p. 211.

We must say that there have been Masons who greatly honor the humanitarian principles of their institution, just as there are Masons who are not honorable.

In general, the positive sense of living, of helping others that Masons possess, is admirable. Indeed, both Jesuits and Masons tend to be very respectful of others as well as open to the ideas of others, without creating sides of "truth."

Finally, I also do not believe that "extraterrestrial" beings control world governments.

I am a staunch enemy of conspiracy theories. Connecting events with characters and organizations of various kinds, and from there concluding a conspiracy against society and/or governments of all kinds, has done and continues to do considerable damage to much of humanity. Even circumstantial evidence that seems to indicate as too plausible a conspiracy, may turn out under rigorous investigation, not to be a reality. Something that has been demonstrated time and time again.

Therefore, what should matter to us are rigorously documented facts. Where guessing has no place, but conclusive evidence.

But another problem is at the opposite extreme. We refer to the radical rejection of certain statements, just because they seem too extraordinary to be taken seriously. While it is true that some things should be rejected out of hand because they carry all the hallmarks of falsehood, this is not always the case.

There are rigorously documented works such as that of John Dickie,[16] which, while departing from conspiracy theories, even accepts that the influence of the Freemasons has shaped the modern world.

However, not everything rests on imagination and the desire to find conspiracies where they do not exist. To trace the veracity or otherwise of any claim, we must set aside bias. Therefore, while we should ignore empty or non-evidence-based claims, there must be a serious responsibility in dealing with information, whether it be through documents or even through different people supplying it to us. When something is communicated, it may affect the recipient in some way, and we are responsible for the results of what we share: whether it is serious or not.

While I have almost always been very open and unprejudiced to reports and investigate if they deserve credit, it is not true that I was always so objective to hear some things that I rejected outright as absurd, until with further investigation, the evidence hit me in the face. So after so long, I had to give up... and finally, after much digging and consulting, I had to conclude as authentic many things that seemed implausible to me.

Thus, to this day, although the Vatican issued in mid-November 2023 a reminder of the prohibition for Catholics to belong to Freemasonry, with the signature of Pope Francis,[17] the truth is that at the same time, the pope has largely supported relations with the organization, as well as the membership of Catholics in Freemasonry... However, this goes further. We have been able to confirm it by data and due to various sources within Freemasonry and others. But these apparent Vatican contradictions are part of what the Vatican has been for too long, particularly during the present papacy.

---

[16] John Dickie, The Craft: How the Freemasons Made the Modern World (Hodder & Stoughton, 2021).

[17] L'Osservatore Romano (November 17, 2023), La fe católica es irreconciliable con la masonería, L'Osservatore Romano; Cortes, Mons. Julito. (November 13, 2023). [Foglio di Udienza con il Santo Padre. Richiesta di Sua Ecc.za Mons. Julito Cortes, Vescovo di Dumaguete (Filippine) circa il "best pastoral approach" riguardo all'adesione alla massoneria da parte di fedeli cattolici.]

I ask the reader to be open-minded and take the documentation seriously. The following is an essay that deals with the struggle for civilization from the late 18th century to the present; in a battle to transform political, social, economic, and even religious thought and action. It is the battle for civilization where the Roman Catholic Church, Freemasonry, the United States, and even the interest for the unknown; for forces or intelligences beyond our human understanding behind the UFO or UAP phenomenon, lead a struggle along a path that seems confusing, but is reaching an unprecedented climax although with certain historical resemblances. It is a driving force from which we should not remain indifferent. And where reason, under the dominion of authentic human charity, is imperative for the search for truth, for the sake of the good of our destiny as human beings and what that means.

CHAPTER

1

European Freemasonry against the Jesuits and the temporal power of the Papacy

The Papacy, the Jesuits, and the Freemasons: for freedom of conscience

It is true that the primary documents do not show that the Society of Jesus was founded to combat Protestantism,[1] but it is also true that when the first Jesuits arrived in Germany in 1540 and wrote in shock at the conditions of the religious environment, Protestantism became a substantial issue for the Jesuits. In addition, Pope Julius III declared in 1550 the "defense of the faith" as an additional area of responsibility for the Society.[2]

Another enemy of the papacy was European Freemasonry. By the year 1735 or even earlier, "the main European Lodges were avowed enemies of papal centralized jurisdiction and Roman Catholic dogmatic teaching."[3]

In this context and during the pontificate of Pope Clement XIII, the open offensive against the Society of Jesus became more latent, provoking an almost total inactivity in the Vatican's intelligence services, then known as the Holy Alliance (The Entity, starting in 1936). Eric Frattini, a renowned Spanish journalist, points out that the monarchs Ferdinand VI of Spain, Joseph I of Portugal, Frederick II of Prussia, Leopold in Tuscany, Joseph II of Austria, Charles III, first in Naples and then in Spain, were wary of the growing and influential power of the Jesuit order. Frattini writes: "The king's ministers attacked the Jesuits for their conservative education, their extremism in defending Church intervention in political affairs, and especially their evident subservience to the Holy See."[4]

European Freemasonry is undoubtedly, in the context of the Enlightenment of the eighteenth century, very outstanding, being that the most powerful European statesmen necessarily belonged to the Lodge. In fact, the principal advisors of the Bourbon princes and the Count of Aranda, royal advisor in Spain, were Masons. Also the Marquis of Pombal, royal advisor in Portugal; the Minister of Tillot and the Duke of Choiseul in France; as well as Prince von Kaunitz, and Gerard von Swieten at the court

---

[1] Jorge Cañizares-Esguerra, Robert Aleksander Maryks, R.P. Hsia, Encounters between Jesuits and Protestants in Asia and the Americas (Brill, 2018), p. 1.

[2] Markus Friedrich, The Jesuits: A History (Princeton University Press, 2022), ob. cit.

[3] Malachi Martin, The Jesuits: The Society of Jesus and the Betrayal of the Roman Catholic Church (Simon & Schuster, New York, 1987), p. 213.

[4] Eric Frattini, The Entity: Five Centuries of Secret Vatican Espionage (St. Martin's Press, New York, 2008), p. 119.

of Maria Theresa of Austria.[5] Choiseul had written to Joseph of Austria: "I know the pains they [the Jesuits] have taken […] to spread darkness over the surface of the earth, and to dominate and confuse Europe from Cape Finisterre to the North Sea."[6]

The ultra-conservative Jesuit, Malachi Martin, wrote of the Masons, "They saw in the Jesuits "the sworn enemies of Freemasonry," the "most cunning enemies of tolerance," and "the worst corruptors of freedom.""[7]

The Jesuit order knew in great detail from letters, documents, and other reports at the time who was plotting their destruction. The best way to end the papacy for the Freemasons was by eradicating the Jesuits.[8]

The war was formally declared, although by both sides through secret plans and actions. The Holy Alliance, the Vatican's intelligence service, with Neri Corsini as its head, drafted in 1733 the first major report on Freemasonry, which was delivered to Pope Clement XII and incited him to ratify a new Constitution in the Papal State on January 14, 1734, where all its citizens were forbidden to take part in Masonic rites on pain of death and confiscation of all their property. For Clement XII, Freemasonry prevented the full approach of the individual to religion, putting his loyalty to the secret society, but not to God.[9]

Since 1733, an English-speaking Jacobite Masonic lodge had been operating in Rome, but in 1737 the lodge was closed and its officers were arrested by the Papal Inquisition.[10] This was because the Holy Alliance gave the pope an additional report on the increasingly threatening Masonic presence within the Catholic Church.[11] The following year, Clement XII published *In Eminenti*- the first papal bull against Freemasonry; therefore, foreign Masons continued to meet secretly.[12]

The different European countries antagonistic against the Order began to expel the Jesuits. Then, the Grand Master of Malta, following the Portuguese, French, and Spanish actions, signed the order of expulsion of the Society of Jesus and its members on April 22, 1768, apparently forced by his commitments with the Kingdom of Naples. The same year, the Duchy of Parma followed suit against the Society of Jesus. Pope Clement XII formally protested, issuing several bulls against such measures, but this action only provoked the French troops to occupy Avignon and the county of Venaissin. Naples subsequently occupied the papal cities of Benevento and Pontecorvo. Parma threatened the pope with invading the Papal State if he did not withdraw the bulls and condemnations. In January 1769, the ambassadors of Spain, France, and Naples in Rome formally asked Pope Clement XIII for the total suppression of the

---

[5] Malachi Martin, The Jesuits: The Society of Jesus and the Betrayal of the Roman Catholic Church (Simon & Schuster, New York, 1987), p. 213.

[6] Ibid.

[7] Ibid.

[8] Ibid.

[9] Eric Frattini, The Entity: Five Centuries of Secret Vatican Espionage (St. Martin's Press, New York, 2008), p. 117.

[10] Nicolas Laos, Freemasons, World Order, and Mind Wars: The Great Reality of Memphis-Misraim Masonry (Algora Publishing, New York, 2016), p. 83.

[11] Eric Frattini, The Entity: Five Centuries of Secret Vatican Espionage (St. Martin's Press, New York, 2008), p. 117.

[12] Nicolas Laos, Freemasons, World Order, and Mind Wars: The Great Reality of Memphis-Misraim Masonry (Algora Publishing, New York, 2016), p. 83.

Society of Jesus. Although the pope prepared to resist, he died a few days later of apoplexy.[13]

The efforts promoted by the European Freemasons of the mentioned nations gave their fruits when finally the new pope –anti-Jesuit- Clement XIV, published on November 2, 1773, his *Dominus ac Redemptur*, suppressing the Society of Jesus.[14] But Catherine of Russia and Frederick of Prussia refused to promulgate the papal decree.[15]

Faced with these events, the Masons of the antagonistic countries and other nations, who knew of the great power of the Jesuits, saw their designs of liberation almost fulfilled not only on the fate of the Society and its plans to strengthen the papacy but also on the Masonic attempts to disappear the last institution in the decades to come. The papacy saw that its effective intelligence service, the Holy Alliance, was greatly diminished since the Jesuits formed the bulk of the papal spies.[16]

Father Lorenzo Ricci, who was then the general of the Society of Jesus, along with his most faithful collaborators, were escorted on September 23 of that year to the castle of Sant'Angelo in Rome, where they were severely confined.[17]

With the suppression of the order, the Papal States of Avignon, Venaissin, Benevento, and Pontecorvo were restored.[18]

On February 15, 1775, Giovanni Angelo Braschi was elected as the new pope, taking the name Pius VI. He reigned during most of the convulsive era of the French Revolution,[19] that would change the destiny of Europe.

For its part, a permanent lodge was founded in Rome in 1787, but was closed by the Inquisition in 1789, the same day that Count Alessandro di Cagliostro - pseudonym of the occultist Giuseppe Balsamo - was arrested and taken prisoner in the Castle of Sant'Angelo to be sentenced to death for being a Freemason; but his sentence was changed by Pius VI to a life of confinement in the same prison.[20] This, being that Cagliostro was invited by painters and sculptors of the French Academy in Rome to attend meetings of their lodge, trying to establish his own. But according to Pius VI, Freemasonry and revolution were practically synonymous. Not for nothing did the French Academy in Rome express support for republicanism, so the presence of Cagliostro in the lodge "Amis Sincères" instigated the pope to give a hard lesson to the said French Freemasons and their new leader;[21] whom he not only accused of being a Mason, but also a sorcerer, a heretic, a blasphemer - either against God, the Virgin

[13] Eric Frattini, The Entity: Five Centuries of Secret Vatican Espionage (St. Martin's Press, New York, 2008), p. 120.

[14] Malachi Martin, The Jesuits: The Society of Jesus and the Betrayal of the Roman Catholic Church (Simon & Schuster, New York, 1987), p. 216; Paul Shore (2020), The Years of Jesuit Suppression, 1773–1814: Survival, Setbacks, and Transformation, Brill Research Perspectives in Jesuit Studies, 2(1), pp. 1-25.

[15] Malachi Martin, The Jesuits: The Society of Jesus and the Betrayal of the Roman Catholic Church (Simon & Schuster, New York, 1987), p. 217.

[16] Eric Frattini, The Entity: Five Centuries of Secret Vatican Espionage (St. Martin's Press, New York, 2008), p. 120

[17] Ibid, p. 122.

[18] Ibid.

[19] Ibid, p. 124.

[20] Nicolas Laos, Freemasons, World Order, and Mind Wars: The Great Reality of Memphis-Misraim Masonry (Algora Publishing, New York, 2016), p. 83.

[21] Ibid.

Mary, the saints, and all Catholicism; as well as forgery, swindling, calumny and sedition.[22]

Cardinal Giovanni Battista Caprara, then head of the Holy Alliance, together with his agents, began to notice clear anti-clerical movements in France.[23]

The French Revolution, which began in May 1789 and lasted until November 1799, had many anti-clerical Masonic supporters who hated the papacy and who also fought against Masons who were supporters of the belief in God and religion, such as the regular lodges.[24] The French Catholic Church suffered vigorous persecution and was later abolished.[25] Previously, relations between revolutionary Paris and the papacy had been broken in March 1791.[26]

Agents of the Holy Alliance, for its part, who recovered the Catholic alliance with Louis XVI to continue his loyalty to the papacy, tried to save his life from the revolutionaries, but the king was caught and guillotined several days later.[27]

Things then became very difficult for the papacy, particularly after Pius VI's protests about all that had happened, provoked French hostilities by dispossessing the Holy See of several papal states and many valuable material goods.[28]

On December 28, 1797, a crowd gathered in front of the residence of the French ambassador to the Vatican to demand the proclamation of the Republic. But a contingent of papal guards forced their way in. Then, one of them, who was a former member of the "Black Order," which was part of the counter-espionage of the Holy Alliance, assassinated the French general Mathurin-Léonard Duphot, who, having been one of the trusted men and one of the best strategists of the great general Napoleon Bonaparte, provoked him to order in retaliation General Berthier to launch his troops to conquer Rome.[29] In this way, in 1798, Berthier captured Pope Pius VI during the French occupation of Italy. He stripped the supreme pontiff of the "Fisherman's Ring," who was then taken out of Italy on a tortuous journey and imprisoned in Valencia, France, where he died in 1799.[30]

It was not only in Europe that the power of Catholicism and the Jesuits was greatly diminished, but also in the Americas. Historically, the three Americas achieved independence from the Spanish crown thanks to Freemasonry. The greatest liberators of America, Miranda, Simón Bolívar, and José de San Martín, were Masons. In fact, from Spain, the Count of Aranda, who was a Freemason, as well as many other members of the court and King Charles III of Spain, expelled the Jesuits from the

---

[22] Corrado Augias, The Secrets of Italy: People, Places, and Hidden Histories (Rizzoli Ex Libris, Park Avenue South, New York, 2014), p. 69.

[23] Eric Frattini, The Entity: Five Centuries of Secret Vatican Espionage (St. Martin's Press, New York, 2008), p. 125.

[24] Eduardo R. Callaey, El Mito de la Revolución Masónica: La verdad sobre los masones y la Revolución Francesa, los Iluminados y el nacimiento de la masonería moderna (Ediciones Nowtilus, 1st edition, 2007), op. cit.

[25] Roger Price, The Church and the State in France, 1789-1870 (Palgrave Macmillan, Aberystwyth, Reino Unido, 2017), op. cit.

[26] Eric Frattini, The Entity: Five Centuries of Secret Vatican Espionage (St. Martin's Press, New York, 2008), p. 125.

[27] Ibid, p. 126.

[28] Ibid, p. 127.

[29] Ibid, pp. 130, 131.

[30] Michael J. Schuck, That They Be One: The Social Teaching of the Papal Encyclicals, 1740-1989 (Georgetown University Press, Washington, D.C., 1991), p. 6.

American territories of the Spanish colonies to limit the Catholic power in the region.[31] Dr. Antonio Las Heras, an Argentine Masonic historian, tells us:

"I can tell you that the independence of all America: North America, Central America, and South America, is the result of the work of Masons in their lodges. And of a universal Masonic plan."[32]

Thus came Latin American independence from the hegemony of Spain, for the establishment of republican and liberal ideals throughout the vast region.[33]

But let us return now to Rome, on March 14, 1800, when Luigi Barnaba Chiaramonti was elected pope, bearing the name Pius VII.[34]

Faced with the wave of European anti-Catholicism and the proclaimed new republics of those years that threatened the papacy, the pope needed a much larger contingent to confront it; so in 1814 he restored the Society of Jesus.[35] That same year coincided with a slowdown in the contemporary globalization process due in large part to the Napoleonic wars.[36] As the Jesuits forged their network anew, they confronted a new wave of antagonism both in Europe and around the globe, especially in France, parts of southern Europe, and Latin America.[37]

After the French invasion of 1809, Freemasonry flourished in Rome, but a new wave of suppression was launched by Pope Pius VII precisely in 1814[38] when he restored the Jesuit order.

The nineteenth century was a turbulent one for the survival of Catholicism, with a revolutionary France condemning it and a papal see poised to fight back to regain its temporal power.[39] Moreover, the Jesuits were the undisputed champions of Catholicism in attempting to regain temporal power from the papacy, with Pope Pius IX as the last pontiff of the Papal States.[40]

What this has to do with the present is the great historical journey that spans, not only but particularly, from the dawn of the Great War (1914-1918), when a new democratic future was dawning in Europe. The future of Roman Catholicism was threatened as its temporal power was to be further undermined.

What would the Jesuits do, and what strange powers, unknown to most, have been hiding behind such attempts? An unbiased understanding and analysis of historical

---

[31] Dalila Zaritzky (Producer) Rodrigo H. Vila (Director). (2012), El Complot de los Masones. (Cinema 7 Films / History Channel). Note: unless otherwise indicated, it'll be the same source.

[32] Ibid.

[33] Ibid.

[34] David I. Kertzer, The Popes Against the Jews: The Vatican's Role in the Rise of Modern Anti-Semitism (Vintage Books, New York, First edition, 2002), p. 297.

[35] David I. Kertzer, Prisoner of the Vatican: The Pope's Secret Plot to Capture Rome from the New Italian State (Houghton Mifflin Company, Park Avenue South, New York, 2004), p. 88.

[36] Thomas Banchoff and José Casanova (editors), The Jesuits and Globalization: Historical Legacies and Contemporary Challenges (Georgetown University Press, Washington, DC, 2016), p. 229.

[37] Ibid, p. 111.

[38] Nicolas Laos, Freemasons, World Order, and Mind Wars: The Great Reality of Memphis-Misraim Masonry (Algora Publishing, New York, 2016), p. 83.

[39] Frank J. Coppa, Politics and the Papacy in the Modern World (Greenwood Publishing Group, Westport, CT, 2008), pp. 6, 7.

[40] David I. Kertzer, Prisoner of the Vatican: The Pope's Secret Plot to Capture Rome from the New Italian State (Houghton Mifflin Company, Park Avenue South, New York, 2004), pp. 87, 88.

information can help us to have a better outcome for our future as human beings, in the face of the invitation of historical progress that is presented to us.

CHAPTER

2

"The Clash of Civilizations" -The Vatican vs. Freemasonry and the United States of America, part 1

Historical hostility between Freemasonry and the Jesuits
Let us go back for a few moments to the 17th and 18th centuries, the era of the Enlightenment, which according to Milan Zafirovski was characterized by the following:

"Alternatively, the Enlightenment's principle of human reason constitutes a countervailing force against oppression, subjugation, and the subversion of democracy and free civil society, namely the abuse of political and other social power. Hence, it functions as the antidote to the old "poison" of the pre-Enlightenment like medievalism and feudalism precisely defined by extreme oppression, subjugation, and the destruction or perversion of human liberty, dignity, and life in the form of tyranny, especially its theocratic variant in "godly society" a la the respublica Christiana [to the Christian republic]."[1]

Historically, it can be stated as true "the manifest and direct inheritance [...] observing that individual liberties and rights, such as "Universal Rights of Man" come from "the French Revolution."[2]

Voltaire, who died in 1778 and therefore before the French Revolution, but who sowed part of the seeds of it, was a French writer, historian, and philosopher of the Enlightenment, whose period, which had influences and effects on a global scale,[3] was of formidable importance. He was also a radical anticlerical Freemason who belonged to the Freemasonry of the Grand Orient of France.

A witness of the two Masonic solemnities at which Voltaire presided, published his reflections three years later in a writing which had great success both in France and abroad.[4] Look at its effects concerning the Jesuit novitiate in the *Tableau de Paris*, whose author was the Masonic Brother Mercier, a member of the Neuf Sœurs Lodge,

---

[1] Milan Zafirovski, The Enlightenment and Its Effects on Modern Society (Springer, New York, 2011), p. 144.

[2] Ibid, pp. 143, 144.

[3] Sebastian Conrad, Enlightenment in Global History: A Historiographical Critique, *The American Historical Review*, Volume 117, 4 Edition, October 2012.

[4] Louis Amiable, Une loge maçonnique d'avant 1789, la loge des Neuf Sœurs, étude critique (Paris: Former bookstore Germer Baillière & Cie, Félix Alcan, 1897), p. 89.

and who in 1778 was a lawyer in the Parliament of Paris, from where we quote extensively:[5]

"O change! O instability of human things! Who would have said that lodges of Freemasons would be established in the Rue Pot-de-Fer, in the novitiate of the Jesuits, in the very rooms where they discussed theology; that the Grand Orient would succeed the Society of Jesus; that the philosophical lodge of the Nine Sisters would occupy the meditation room of the sons of Loyola; that M. de Voltaire would be received as a Freemason in 1778, and that M. de La Dixmerie would address to him these happy verses...."

"That only in the name of the illustrious brother
Every Freemason triumphs today
If he receives light from us.
The world receives it from him.

"That his eulogy and his apotheosis would be celebrated with the greatest pomp in the same place where St. Francis Xavier was invoked?

"Oh, inversion! The venerable one sitting in the place of Fr. Griffet, the Masonic mysteries taking his place! I dare not finish. When I am under these vaults inaccessible to the rude rays of the sun, girded with the august apron, I seem to see all these Jesuit shadows wandering about, casting angry and desperate glances at me. And there I saw Brother Voltaire enter, to the sound of instruments, in the same room where he had so often been theologically cursed. It was the will of the great Architect of the Universe. He was praised for having fought fanaticism and superstition for sixty years; for it was he who put to death the monster that others had wounded. The monster carries the arrow in its sides; it may turn upon itself for some time yet, exhaling the last efforts of its impotent rage; but it must fall at last and satisfy the Universe.

O Jesuit, would you have guessed all this, when your father de la Chaise was wrapping his august penitent in his most dangerous lies, and when others of the same robe were inspiring his barbarous intolerance, his low and narrow ideas, his attacks on the liberty and dignity of man? You have been the obstinate enemies of the beneficent light of philosophy; and the philosophers rejoice, in your houses, at your rapid fall! The Freemasons, sustained on the basis of charity, tolerance, and universal benevolence, will still exist when your names no longer awaken more than the idea of pursuing selfishness."[6]

Edgar Quinet, influential French historian and intellectual, wrote in the 18th century that, "The school of the Society of Jesus threatened to liquidate liberty after liberty, even before its appearance."[7] He also stated:

"Now I see well that it is not only the spirit of the Revolution, as I said before, that is at stake. What else, then? Well, the very existence of the spirit of France, as it has

---

[5] Ibid; quoting T. II, p. 154 (ninth edition, Amsterdam, 1782, in-8). The first edition dates from 1781.
[6] Ibid, pp. 89, 90.
[7] MM. Michelet and Quinet, The Jesuits (Longman, Brown, Green, and Longmans, Paternoster-Row, London, Fourth edition, 1848), p. 113.

always been, and two incompatible things struggling for dominance: either Jesuitism must abolish the spirit of France, or France abolish the spirit of Jesuitism."[8]

Gustave Mesureur, the Grand Master of the Grand Lodge of France, expressed himself in the first issue of the magazine "Le Symbolisme," of the Freemason Oswald Wirth in 1912:

"It should also be remembered that Freemasonry has always been, if not the enemy of the Catholic Church, at least the counterweight of its political influence in society, that it is a force that was not useless and that was not disdained even by the legitimist and imperialist governments to curb the demands of the clergy and moderate the invasion of the Jesuits; the violent and repeated attacks of the current clerical press against the Freemasons show us that nothing has changed and that the battle continues."[9]

The Enlightenment, the French Revolution, and radical anti-clerical Freemasonry were responsible for the misfortune -as mentioned in the previous chapter -of the papacy in February 1798, when Napoleon's armies took Rome and imprisoned Pope Pius VI.

And the fighting and accusations would continue over the years.

But what was the reaction of the Catholic Church to all the democratic movements which, as we shall see, were directed by the United States towards Europe? What we are about to tell, we believe, is an astonishing story.

More than a century after the beginning of the French Revolution, the Society of Jesus, with the support of the Vatican, extended its long arm to the Masons to apparently find bridges of understanding. In fact, the journalists Galeazzi and Pinotti, rightly say that the Jesuits would be one of the conduits of Masonic infiltration in the Vatican and a bridge of dialogue with the forces of modernization, generically qualified as "leftists" or in any case progressive.[10] This, however, entailed a design that was discovered decades later by some French Freemasons who regretted their contact and dialogue with the Jesuits. Much has happened when the Catholic Church has tolerated Freemasonry when it has served its ends. Giuliano Di Bernardo, former Grand Master of the Grand Orient of Italy, tells us about the relationship between the two institutions:

"The relationship between the Church and Freemasonry is very old. And historically there have always been Masonic lodges within the Catholic Church. The Church has considered Freemasonry as a resource since its origins in the early eighteenth century, and in its early days considered it useful in repairing the Anglican schism. From 1717 to 1738, a situation arose in which the Church hoped to change the state of religious affairs in England through Freemasonry. Mostly in an attempt to bring the Anglican Church back into the Church of Rome."[11]

---

[8] Ibid, p. 98.

[9] Jean-Laurent Turbet (May 25, 2013), Le Printemps de l'Anti-France manifeste devant le Grand Orient de France, Le Blog des Spiritualités: https://www.jlturbet.net/article-le-printemps-de-l-anti-france-manifeste-devant-le-grand-orient-de-france-118036189.html Accessed on February 15, 2024.

[10] Giacomo Galeazzi, Ferruccio Pinotti, Vaticano Massone: Logge, denaro e poteri occulti: il lato segreto della Chiesa di papa Francesco (Piemme, 2014), op. cit.

[11] Ibid; Interview by Ferruccio Pinotti to Prof. Giuliano Di Bernardo.

Since then, there has been a continuous interlocution between the Catholic Church and Freemasonry, in which the Jesuits have played a central role.[12]

Inversely, what plans did Freemasonry have to counter attempts at papal supremacy in Europe and the rest of the world?

Background and long-term consequences of the Masonic Congress of the Allied Nations[13]

Eduardo R. Callaey, a well-known Argentine Masonic journalist and historian, wrote in his documented work:

.".."] in the 19th century, the armies of the world - royalist and independence armies - almost all under the command of Freemasons, would change the geopolitical map of the West and prepare it for the great leap towards progress. The foundations of the New World Order, which is not in vain attributed to the Freemasons, would be laid. Behind those armies would come the lodges, and with them progress, education, and hope."[14]

Argentine Freemasonry made its pronouncement in 1873:

"Our time is one of transition: the old world is crumbling; but on its ruins, we must build anew, and instead of waiting for this work to begin with the bloodshed that one day produced the wars of Northern Europe, under the pretense of religious strife; instead of new horrors coming to disturb the world, like those of France in 1793 and 1871, let us advance from our tents: Let us interpose ourselves between the sword of the slashers and the ravages of the passionate, or of the ignorant, and if it is true that our mission is one of beneficence and peace, let us break down the fence of fears and make our order the determined champion of social equality."[15]

The Grand Orient of France tried, after 1877, to re-establish and protect its international relations. In the year 1896, it already maintained diplomatic relations with the Supreme Council of France of the REAA, the Scottish Symbolic Grand Lodge, the Grand Orient of Argentina, the Grand Orient of Belgium, the Grand Orient of Brazil, the Supreme Council of Cuba, the Symbolic Grand Lodge of Hungary, the Grand Orient of Italy, the Supreme Council of Luxembourg, the Scottish Symbolic Grand Lodge of Mexico, the Grand Orient of the Netherlands, the Grand Lodge of Peru, the Grand Orient of Peru, the Grand Lodge of the Netherlands, the Grand Lodge of Peru, Grand Orient Lusitano (Portugal), Swiss Alpine Grand Lodge, Grand Orient of Uruguay, Supreme Council of Colombia, Supreme Council of the Dominican Republic,

---

[12] Ibid.

[13] Some sources on Freemasonry: John Dickie, The Craft: How the Freemasons Made the Modern World (PublicAffairs, New York, 2020); James Wasserman, The Secrets of Masonic Washington: A Guidebook to Signs, Symbols, and Ceremonies at the Origin of America's Capital (Destiny Books, Rochester, Vermont, 2008); David Ovason, The Secret Architecture of Our Nation's Capital: The Masons and the Building of Washington, D.C. (Perennial/HarperCollins, First edition, edition EPub, 2012).

[14] Eduardo R. Callaey, Masones, caballeros e Illuminati: El gran complot (Editorial Masónica, Asturias, Spain, 2014), op. cit.

[15] H∴ Pedro Piqueras (May 30, 1873), Crónica local, Revista Masónica Americana, Num. 14, Year 1°, p. 440.

Grand Orient of Egypt, Grand Orient of Greece, Grand Orient of Spain, Grand Orient of Haiti and the Grand Orient of France.[16]

A new meeting of Freemasons from all over the world was held in The Hague in 1896. Another one in 1900 in Paris, on the occasion of the Universal Exposition, and which was rejected by England. Then, the delegates of the Masonic powers in the congress unanimously condemned the method of war and proposed an international arbitration to solve the conflicts between nations (the League of Nations was already taking shape).

In September 1902, a World Congress was convened in Geneva with 31 Masonic obediences participating, among which was the Grand Orient of France. The following year, the International Bureau of Masonic Relations (IBMR) was created, which was soon disturbed by European crises and the emergence of various threats. However, hostility towards Germany faded for a few years, with the Masons at the forefront of the peace movement. Years later, in 1907, three thousand French and German Freemasons met in the heart of the Vosges, at the Schucht Pass, overcoming the resentments and the spirit of revenge linked to the painful territorial question of Alsace-Lorraine. On July 1, 1914, the Grand Orient of France submitted to the consideration of the lodges the Franco-German relations and asked: "Could not Alsace-Lorraine become autonomous and a link between France and Germany?" However, on August 3 of that year, war was declared (1st World War). The Great War put the reborn Masonic relations between France and Germany to the test. And in December, the Grand Orient of France denounced the German Masons who "dishonor our beautiful Institution," while the Grosslogenbund (the organ of the German Masonic obediences) made it known in 1915, that it "rejects any community with the degenerate secret societies which abuse the respected name of Freemasonry."

Almost three years later, with the entry of the United States into the war on the side of the Entente (France, United Kingdom, Russia, Italy, and Japan) against the Central Powers (Germany, Austria-Hungary, the Ottoman Empire, and Bulgaria), the Grand Orient de France and the Grand Lodge of France were recognized by the Grand Lodges of Alabama, Iowa, Louisiana, Minnesota, New Jersey, and Rhode Island. The leading role of French Freemasonry as a peacemaker was notorious for much of American Freemasonry.

Months earlier, from January 14-16, 1917, a Conference of the Masonic Societies of the Allied Nations was held, which was organized jointly by the Ile-de-France lodges of the Grand Orient of France and the Grand Lodge, and "with the participation of the Grand Masters of Portugal and Italy, as well as Belgian and Serbian delegations."

"A manifesto from the Freemasonry of the Allied powers to the Freemasons of the neutral powers stated that "war for peace, war for the security of peaceful nations, war against militarism" was "the only way to make our ideas triumph"; "the victory of the Allies will be the victory of pacifism."

The conference was attended by 1500 Freemasons and concluded with this message: "Our aim is to work for a free Europe and a free World;" "our mission is to liberate nations and men." It concluded with a banquet at the Cercle républicain, where the

---

[16] Alain Bauer, Jean-Claude Rochigneux, Les relations internationales de la franc-maçonnerie française (Armand Colin, 2010), op. cit. Note: unless otherwise indicated, it'll be the same source.

delegates paid homage to "the soldiers of the brave allied armies who fight, suffer and die, and who endure the greatest hardships not for conquest, but for the triumph of the Masonic ideal of progress, justice, and protection of the weak, the oppressed and all those who form the great brotherhood of man."

For its part, the Vatican was concerned about the popularity in European circles of American Catholics who sought to unite liberalism and their religion.[17] In fact, "A key figure here was the priest and founder of the Paulist Fathers, Isaac Thomas Hecker, who famously argued that the time had come for Catholics to accept modernity, liberty, and Republicanism."[18] Pope Leo XIII considered the doctrine of Church-State separation held by the United States to be heretical.

But in the fall of 1915, the year after the outbreak of the Great War, Germany and the Vatican pressured the United States to stop supplying arms and aid to the Entente and to promise not to join the war. Pietro Gasparri, the Vatican Secretary of State, instructed the apostolic delegate to the United States that it was imperative to force the U.S. President to embrace neutrality. He stated "This war is a crime against mankind, and it will last as long as the United States sends arms, ammunition, and money" and continues to show its "lack of neutrality" in supporting France, Russia, and Great Britain."[19] For the Vatican, the United States not entering the war was crucial. And the fact that President Woodrow Wilson was a Protestant compounded the papacy's concern. They feared that a new secular, democratic, and anti-Catholic order would be created.

At the end of May 1917, Archbishop and Apostolic Nuncio to Germany, Eugenio Pacelli (future Pope Pius XII), undertook his first major diplomatic mission when he traveled from Italy to Germany. As he made his journey, he prayed to the Virgin Mary and rehearsed his first speech to the Germans. The train pulled into Munich on May 25, with a crowd thronging the station eager to welcome the new papal ambassador to Bavaria. These were dark times: more than 1.5 million German soldiers had already died in the Great War, with the streets of Munich crowded with widows, fatherless children, and wounded veterans. Pacelli did not wait to explain to the city's inhabitants and rulers why he was there: the fate of the Catholic Church had been in the balance since the late 19th century, with the pope's status as sovereign being called into question by the unification of Italy, with the Papal States having been torn apart. He noted that this was compounded by the pan-European culture wars led by liberals and socialists who professed false gods or none at all. Both groups had attempted to transform the European continent. They questioned whether church and state should work together for the spiritual flourishing of individuals. And new laws were passed separating church and state, reducing the church's right to intervene publicly.

[17] Giuliana Chamedes, A Twentieth-Century Crusade: The Vatican's Battle to Remake Christian Europe (Harvard University Press, Cambridge, Massachusetts, 2019), p. 21.

[18] Ibid; citing Claude Fohlen, "American Catholicism and European Catholicism: The convergence de l'Américanisme," Revue d'histoire moderne et contemporaine 34 (1987): 215-230; y Scott Appleby, Church and Age Unite! The Modernist Impulse in American Catholicism (South Bend, IN: University of Notre Dame Press, 1992).

[19] Ibid, p. 20; citing Jean Jules Jusserand, dispatch no. 581, and the British ambassador in Paris, September 4, 1915, Archives of the French Ministry of Foreign Affairs, Paris, Paix 1914–1920, vol. 2. Quoted in Annie Lacroix- Riz, Le Vatican, Europe et le Reich: De la Première Guerre mondiale à la guerre froide, 1914–1945 (Paris: Armand Colin, Nouvelle édition refondue, 2010), 527.

Historian Giuliana Chamedes documents that Pacelli's message to the Bavarians, who were facing a tough decision, was: "Would they join hands with the central government of the Roman Catholic Church and help "reconstruct human society on the solid ground of Christian justice [and] Christian law"? Or would they step aside and participate in the continent's capture by the Church's enemies?"[20] Pacelli was then, one of dozens of papal diplomats who were carrying the gospel of concordat diplomacy throughout Europe; both East and West.

When the archbishop witnessed the outbreak of the Great War in July 1914, he saw it as a warning of what could happen when populations turned away from Catholic teachings and ceased to respect the Church's mission. When the United States joined the war in April 1917, for papal diplomats this was part of a plan to further reduce the power of the Catholic Church in Europe "and to buoy secular, liberal, and Freemason movements instead." We shall see that such fears of the Catholic Church were not unfounded.[21]

After U.S. President Woodrow Wilson's announcement to join the war to make the world "safe for democracy," papal officials like Pacelli expressed their unease: they believed it paved the way for an anti-clerical uprising.[22] In response, "papal officials and mainstream Catholic newspapers and journals closely bound to the pope ratcheted up their attacks against the United States."[23]

Pacelli saw in the American meddling a carefully laid plan to "meddling in matters European" and transform the continent's identity forever: to capture Europe and "Americanize the whole world, making it Freemason so as to liberate it from its servitude to the Kaiser, the pope, and the priesthood."[24] He claimed that President Wilson was engaged in "a tendentious attempt to mislead public opinion."[25]

In the face of all this, "papal diplomats began meticulously compiling massive photography binders depicting Allied bombings of churches, which were presented as proof of the fundamentally antireligious and "profanatory" aims of the "liberal powers" under the United States' sway."[26]

It was a moment of great awakening for the papacy, which motivated Pope Benedict XV to move from defense to offense. During the war, he presented "the Vatican as an international actor equipped with its own detailed solution to the European crisis."[27] At

---

[20] Ibid, p. 15; quoting Eugenio Pacelli, *Gesammelte Reden: Erster Apostolischer Nuntius beim Deutschen Reich* (Berlin: Buchverlag Germania, 1930), 26; Epigraph: Matthias Erzberger, Parere sul miglior modo di risolvere la Questione Romana (n.p.: n.p., 1920), 7.

[21] Ibid, p. 2.

[22] Giuliana Chamedes, Note: *Same.*

[23] Ibid, p. 22; citing For the horrified reaction of the powerful Vatican Secretary of State, see, for example, Pietro Gasparri, Diary, II, 65, April 7, 1917. See also Benedict XV, speech before the "Opera della preservazione della Fede," Nov. 22, 1915; Ad Beatissimi Apostolorum; "I discorsi degli statisti alleati e l'appello di pace del Papa," Civiltà Cattolica, Feb. 2, 1918, 194; and numerous articles in Osservatore Romano: Jan. 19, 1919; Feb. 14, 1919; June 12, 1920.

[24] Ibid, p. 2; citing to Eugenio Pacelli a Pietro Gasparri, Munich, December 20, 1918. ASV, A.E.S., Baviera, terzo periodo. 1918-1921, pos. 67, ff. 15-18.

[25] Ibid, p. 22; citing Eugenio Pacelli to Pietro Gasparri, Munich, September 6, 1917, ASV, A.E.S., Stati Ecclesiastici, 1914-1921, pos. 1317, fasc.470, vol. 4, f. 242; and Pacelli to Gasparri, Munich, December 20, 1918, ASV, A.E.S., Baviera, terzo periodo, 1918-1921, pos. 67, ff. 15-18. For Pacelli's message, which included Wilson's texts in English and German, see ASV, Arch. Nunz. Monaco 410, fasc. 4, f. 16.

[26] Ibid; citing to SV, A.E.S., Germania 415, June-July 1918 folder. Cited in Fattorini, *Germania e Santa Sede*, 91-92.

[27] Ibid, p. 23.

the height of the conflict, he announced that the Holy See had its peace agreement to reorder European international society and keep liberals and socialists at bay. Chamedes documents:

"This peace plan called for the overturning of secular visions of world order, and rested on the re-Christianization of European states via the embrace of national self-determination and international law."[28]

Benedict XV asked his papal ambassadors/nuncios to other nations to lead the initiative. Like Pacelli, they traveled by train and ship amid the conflict to promote the papacy and provide the rulers of European nations with ways to oppose the liberal and socialist movements. To do this, the papal representatives were asked to use the concordat, which was a bilateral treaty that would bind the Catholic Church and the nation-state under international law. This gave legitimacy and other advantages to the emerging political leaders and the newly constituted nation-states to consolidate their claims to territorial sovereignty. In this way, they would oppose the influence of liberalism and the rise of left-wing revolution. In turn, such treaties "would greatly expand the Vatican's control over everything from education to family law, from press freedom to the organization of local churches."[29]

"By making religious instruction in public schools mandatory, giving the Church jurisdiction over a range of civil-law matters, and increasing monies funneled from the state to the Church, the treaties spelled out relationships of tight Church–state collaboration. The papal use of law thus aimed to be, borrowing from Clifford Geertz's phrasing, "constructive of social realities rather than merely reflective of them."[30]

Chamedes again, when quoting:

"The internationalism of the pope is a constant menace for the existence and the prosperity of the nation," an Italian Freemason announced in 1916, soon after his country's entry into the Great War. His concern was with the papacy's close dealings with the German and Habsburg empires—dealings that, he feared, would "sow trouble in the conscience of the faithful."[31]

Benedict XV defined his strategy in dialogue with the Central Powers. As the Austro-Hungarian Empire crumbled, the relationship with the German Empire became increasingly important for the Holy See. However, numerous powers tried to curry favor with the pope during the war. He responded with suspicion to the efforts of France, Italy, and Great Britain, but welcomed Germany. Especially since the Germans had numerous diplomatic representatives in the Vatican and a close relationship with

---

[28] Ibid, p. 3.

[29] Ibid.

[30] Ibid; citing to Clifford Geertz, "Local Knowledge: Fact and Law in Comparative Perspective," en su Local Knowledge: Further Essays in Interpretive Anthropology (New York: Basic Books, 1983), 167–234, at 232.

[31] Ibid, p. 17; citing Grand Master Mason Ferrari, in a circular of December 1916, quoted in Matthias Erzberger, Souvenirs de guerre (París: Payot, 1921), 169.

28

the Jesuit headquarters in Rome. Germany also had very good relations with Italy, and the Italian clergy dominated the Vatican. Moreover, the German church successfully confronted its liberal and socialist adversaries; and it successfully resisted efforts to separate church and state.

In 1917, a year before the end of World War I, the Grand Orient of France convened the Congress of Freemasonry of the Allied and Neutral Nations to be held on June 28-30 of the same year. An official document speaks of the details[32] in which Masonic representations from France, Italy, Spain, Switzerland, Belgium, Serbia, Argentina, the United States, and a delegation from Costa Rica participated.[33] That document tells us, from where we quote several important paragraphs:

"This Masonic Congress of Allied and Neutral Nations has come at the right time. We all know the disasters of the past; we must now build the happy city of the future. It is to undertake this truly Masonic work that we have invited you here...

What are we facing? This war, unleashed by the military autocracies, has become a formidable dispute in which the democracies have organized themselves against the despotic military powers.....

It is therefore absolutely indispensable to create a supranational authority, whose aim will not be to suppress the causes of conflicts but to resolve peacefully the differences between nations.

Freemasonry, working for peace, intends to study this new organism, the League of Nations. Freemasonry will be the agent of propaganda for this conception of universal peace and happiness. That, my Most Illustrious Brethren, is our work. Let us set to work."[34]

Let's see other illustrative paragraphs:

"We are invited to triumph in the work which was undertaken by the Holy Alliance, because of its principles, which are contrary to our own, and through the universal but guaranteed reconciliation of men, to manifest the proof of our principles. We shall crown the work of the French Revolution.
[...]
"The more one studies the present situation, the more one realizes that the abdication of the Hohenzollerns [the royal German dynasty] is the means to achieve the League of Nations. It is not for us, my brothers, to define or demarcate the conditions of peace... but we can at least indicate the four principal points which we consider necessary:(1) The return to France of Alsace-Lorraine;(2) The reconstitution of Poland by the reunification of its three separate parts;(3) The independence of Bohemia;(4) In principle, the liberation or unification of all the nations now oppressed by the political and administrative organization of the Habsburg Empire into States which those nations will elect by referendum...."[35]

---

[32] Congrès des maçonneries des nations alliées et neutres les 28, 29 et 30 juin 1917 (Grand Orient de France : Grande Loge de France).
[33] Ibid, pp. 4-6.
[34] Ibid, op. cit.
[35] Ibid, op. cit.

The text continues:

"The whole destiny of Europe and the new humanity is involved in the resolution of this problem of nationality. After the failure of the German plan will come the Federation of the United States of Europe, by freedom and by right.
How, then, will this end be achieved?
In the first place, by the suppression of all despotism... and in the second place, by the regulation of international conflicts employing arbitration."[36]

Now, three additional paragraphs reveal:

"This Congress sends to Mr. Wilson, President of the United States, the homage of its admiration and the tribute of its recognition for the great services he has rendered to Humanity.
It declares that it is pleased to collaborate with President Wilson in this work of international justice and democratic fraternity, which is the proper ideal of Freemasonry,
And affirms that the eternal principles of Freemasonry are entirely in harmony with those proclaimed by President Wilson for the defense of civilization and the liberty of the peoples....."[37]

Later we will see that it was in that congress that the idea of creating the League of Nations (created in 1919) was born, which in turn was the precursor of the United Nations (UN/1945), as well as the creation of the European Community, later called the European Union.

Moving forward, in August 1917, Benedict XV published a peace plan that was drawn up in dialogue with German politicians and which was intended to present the Vatican as an international actor with its own detailed solution to the European crisis.[38] With that, he hoped to counter the American plan for Europe. Emperor Wilhelm II applauded and encouraged the papal work. The head of the Catholic Church expressed his readiness to take up the challenge, mediate peace negotiations, and to put an end to the war. The peace plan and papal encyclicals insisted that it was neither "prudent" nor "safe" for "governments or states to separate themselves from the holy religion of Jesus Christ, from which their authority receives such strength and support."[39] Soon after the publication of the papal plan, it became a focal point in a lively debate, and, by the end of August, the peace plan was endorsed by all the leaders of the Central Powers. Neutral countries such as Spain and Belgium praised the proposal, as did the Christian Democrats of other nations, such as those of Italy. The papal nuncio to Germany, Eugenio Pacelli, translated "the declarations of celebration with extreme speed and sent them to Rome." But not everyone shared the enthusiasm: Italy and France as countries rejected it. Especially since France had the influence of the Grand Orient of France on

---

[36] Ibid, op. cit.
[37] Ibid, op. cit.
[38] Giuliana Chamedes, A Twentieth-Century Crusade: The Vatican's Battle to Remake Christian Europe (Harvard University Press, Cambridge, Massachusetts, 2019), p. 23.
[39] Ibid, p. 24; citing to Benedict XV, Ad Beatissimi Apostolorum (November 1, 1914), §11, available online at http://w2.vatican.va/content/benedict-xv/en/encyclicals/documents/hf_ben-xv_enc_01111914_ad-beatissimi-apostolorum.html.

its side. Woodrow Wilson's Secretary of State, concerned, asked American ambassadors abroad for opinions on the pope's plan. Wilson sent his reply to Pope Benedict XV on August 27: while applauding the papacy's commitment to peace, he advised the pope to abandon his naive hope of goodwill from the Central Powers and to allow the German Empire to retain its former borders: peace would come until those empires forged their own nation-states. The letter was widely circulated internationally. The Germans reacted negatively, and in January 1918, Wilson presented his first set of peace objectives where instead of endorsing a Vatican-inspired international order, he called for the spread of democracy, particularly in the former territories of the Russian and German empires.[40]

In the Vatican, negative reactions were not long in coming, particularly from the Jesuits.

It should also be noted that a secret document from the Vatican Archives in 1918 reveals a Masonic plot to destroy the Throne and the Altar (the relationship between the State and the Catholic Church).

Dr. Michael Hesemann found in the archives of the Apostolic Nunciature in Munich a handwritten letter dated November 8, 1918, from the Archbishop of Cologne, Cardinal Felix von Hartmann, addressed to Archbishop Eugenio Pacelli, Apostolic Nuncio in Germany and future Pope Pius XII. The letter alluded to information that Emperor Wilhelm II of Germany had just received and that he wanted to transmit to the pope with the help of von Hartmann.[41] The most important extracts from this letter:

"Your Excellency,

"His Majesty the Emperor just has let it be known to me "that, according to news that came to him yesterday, the Grand Orient has just decided first to depose all Sovereigns – first of all him, the Emperor – then to destroy (?) the Cathol.[olic] Church, to imprison the pope, etc and, finally, to establish on the ruins of the former bourgeois society a world republic under the leadership of American Big Capital. The German Freemasons are purportedly loyal to the [German] Emperor (which is to be doubted!) and they informed him about it. Also England wants to preserve the current bourgeois order. France and America, however, are said to be under the full influence of the Grand Orient [Freemasonic Lodge]. Bolshevism is said to be the external tool to establish the desired conditions. In the face of such a great danger which threatens in addition to the Monarchy, also the Catholic Church; it is thus important that the German episcopacy be informed and that also the pope be warned." So far the message of His Majesty. I have believed myself to be duty-bound to pass it on to Your Excellency, and I have to leave it up to Your judgment whether You wish to pass this message on to Rome. The stormy demand of the [German] Social Democrats that the Emperor should abdicate gives a certain confirmation to this message. May God protect us and His Holy Church in this terrible turmoil! [....] With utmost devotion and being at His Excellency's disposal, Cardinal Felix de [von] Hartmann."[42]

---

[40] Ibid, pp. 23, 24.
[41] Maike Hickson (May 11, 2017), Secret 1918 Vatican Archive Document Reveals Freemasonic Plot to Destroy Throne and Altar, One Peter 5.
[42] A.S.V., Arch. Nunz. Monaco d.B. 342, fasc. 13, p. 95-96; cited in Ibid.

Indeed, 1917 was the year of the Russian revolution that culminated in massive persecution of the Church, but it was also the year of the entry of the United States into World War I when the two superpowers that would shape the history of the 20th century for the next 74 years were born.[43]

A day later, the November Revolution broke out in Germany, prompting the abdication of Emperor Wilhelm II.[44] Now, although the emperor claimed that there was an international conspiracy hatched by the Austro-Hungarian empire in league "with the Vatican, the Wittelsbachs, the Jesuits, the Freemasons and World Jewry,"[45] not everything can be relegated to conspiracy-mongering. We cannot involve a Jewish-Antisemitic conspiracy, which is out of the picture... as well as other elements mentioned. The emperor supported the Vatican but had his own later ideas.

Dr. Richard B. Spence, professor of history at the University of Idaho, did excellent research through many state documents located in different historical archives, where he found the plans of the United States to overthrow Czarist Russia and make it a target of world democracy, especially after World War I. He also found the plans of the United States to overthrow Czarist Russia and make it a target of world democracy, especially after the First World War.[46] Such documentation, to cite just a few sources, he gathers from *The New York Times*; from the archives of Columbia, Stanford, Yale, and Cambridge Universities; the U.S. Department of Justice's Bureau of Investigation (forerunner of the FBI); the U.S. State Department; the U.K. Foreign Office; the U.S. Army and Navy intelligence services; as well as Russian state archives, among others.

He documents that big oil companies, banks, investment houses, railroad tycoons, steel magnates, shipping companies, construction companies, tycoons like the Rockefellers, and individual companies like Armor Meat Packing, Anaconda Copper, International Nickel, International Harvester, Singer Sewing Machine, General Electric, Crane-Westinghouse, AT&T, and Allied Machinery, which became a wholly owned A subsidiary of American International Corporation (AIC), a speculative consortium of Wall Street high rollers with 9 vice presidents and 24 directors headquartered near other business interests in the Equitable Building at 120 Broadway in lower Manhattan, because of their overwhelming greed and desire for big profits, were linked with the Russian revolutionaries as early as 1905, with organizations such as the Russian-Asian Bank, the American-Russian Chamber of Commerce and others both inside and outside Russia. Likewise, offices of insurance agents, export-import merchants, charities, arms and munitions dealers, foreign diplomats, and others, all near 116 Broadway and 140 Broadway; as well as the New York Federal Reserve and the American Red Cross, joined in support of the overthrow of the regime of Tsar Nicholas II.[47]

---

[43] Deborah Castellano Lubov (May 10, 2017), Interview With German Historian and Author Dr. Michael Hesemann on Fatima, Letter #18, 2017: Fatima at 100, Inside the Vatican.

[44] Maike Hickson (May 11, 2017), Secret 1918 Vatican Archive Document Reveals Freemasonic Plot to Destroy Throne and Altar, One Peter 5.

[45] John C. G. Röhl, Wilhelm II: Into the Abyss of War and Exile, 1900-1941 (Cambridge University Press, 2014), p. 1214, 1233. See also the writings of Friedrich Wichtl: they contain truths, but also exaggerations. See on the problematics of such conspiracy theories: Rogello Aragón (May./Nov. 2015), "La más formidable secta": la Primera Guerra Mundial como parte de la conspiración Judeo-Masónica (o de los excesos de la interpretación histórica), REHMLAC vol.7 n.1.

[46] Richard B. Spence, Wall Street and the Russian Revolution: 1905-1925 (Trine Day LLC, Walterville, OR, 2017), op. cit.

[47] Ibid.

After the Russian Revolution (1917), the same interests, encouraged by the administration of then-President Woodrow Wilson, granted heavy private loans to Russian banks. All to take over Russian resources and further empower the United States.

Only briefly, Spence mentions a sector of American Freemasonry involved in Russian democracy.[48]

The U.S. State Department, the intelligence services, and the CFR were involved in selling the idea of support for the Bolsheviks.[49]

Indeed, the role of Russian Freemasonry in the Provisional Government was extremely significant. Kuskova, one of the founders of Russian political Freemasonry, argued that it was created by the same individuals who later founded the Liberation Union (*Soiuz osvobozhdeniia*), the organization of Russian liberals and radicals that was instrumental in bringing about the 1905 Revolution;[50] from which American interests would work.[51] Of the Masonic forces that joined, there were Trudovik Kerenskii (who was secretary of the Masonic Supreme Council from mid-1916), and the radicals who participated in Masonic political organization after 1910, too many to name here. Charles Richard Crane was an American businessman with powerful political connections and in alliance with Freemasonry, who supported the Kerenskii revolution.[52] The strategy of the organization, according to a document dated November 10, 1955, that recalls the previous decades, was "to restore the Union of Liberation and to work underground for the liberation of Russia."[53] In early 1914, the Moscow Masons, Konovalov, Morozov, Nekrasov, Prokopovich, Skvortsov-Stepanov, and Volkov, created the Information Committee (*Informatsionnyi komite*), a front organization to provide closer contacts between liberal and socialist parties.[54] The Masons' efforts intensified with World War I, as they gathered support throughout Russia.[55] By early 1916, the political-masonic organization joined the growing number of opposition groups.[56]

A certain Papas was a Freemason, occultist, and a secret agent of the French government to secure the Franco-Russian alliance, as well as an emissary of French Freemasonry in the organization of French lodges.

Alexander Kerenskii, who was secretary general of the Grand Orient of Russia from 1916 to July 1917, participated in the meetings of the Russian duma or parliament, where all the liberals were Masons of the Grand Orient of Russia, Spence tells us.

When the revolution succeeded, there was a transition to provisional power where the Masons had a large presence.[57] Alexander Kerenskii was Minister-President of the Russian Provisional Government. While Nikolai Nekrasov, the original secretary

---

[48] Ibid.

[49] Ibid.

[50] Norton, B. (1983). Russian Political Masonry and the February Revolution of 1917. International Review of Social History, 28(2), 244; citing Kuskova a Dan, November 14, 1958.

[51] Richard B. Spence, Wall Street and the Russian Revolution: 1905-1925 (Trine Day LLC, Walterville, OR, 2017), op. cit.

[52] Norton, B. (1983). Russian Political Masonry and the February Revolution of 1917. International Review of Social History, 28(2), 251.

[53] Ibid; citing a Kuskova a Vol'skii, November 10, 1955.

[54] Ibid, pp. 251, 252.

[55] Ibid, p. 252.

[56] Ibid, p. 253.

[57] Ibid, p. 253-257.

general of the Grand Orient, was vice-president. However, this provisional government was overthrown in the October Revolution of 1917 by the Bolsheviks.

Russian Freemasons continued their activities in exile, mainly in French lodges and Russian lodges in France.

As the Bolsheviks were more in line with American ambitions, the Americans supported them. For example, in less than four years, the Bolsheviks expropriated the Russian economy from its former owners, collapsing it and stripping the country of gold and valuables, most of which ended up in the West.[58]

But with Lenin's death in early 1924, Stalin and Trotsky were in a battle for control of the Communist Party; with Wall Street becoming involved in the battle raging in Moscow. But Stalin prevailed in December 1925 and launched a policy where Russia would cease to be a "raw materials appendage of world capitalism,"[59] ceasing to be influenced by the United States.

The Society of Jesus and its various factions amid the uniformity of the order
Before delving into the continuity of these important historical events, we must establish a clarifying picture of the Jesuits that does not allow for confusion. Thus, despite the Vatican's plans with its peace plan during the Great War and the support of the Jesuits, the Society of Jesus was not unanimous about which factions to support during the military conflict. Włodzimierz Ledóchowski, the General of the Society, strove to sustain Jesuit solidarity across battle lines during World War I, but the patriotism of Jesuits belonging to their respective countries involved in the war betrayed that commitment: many Jesuits went to the battlefield supporting Wilhelm II, but many others to nations fighting against Germany, such as France and the United States.[60]

Strangely enough, Ledóchowski always expressed support for France during the conflict. However, it was for convenience, because it was in the field of faith: the best interests and the preservation of the unity of the Catholic Church in Europe compelled him to develop closer ties with allied countries (France and Russia).[61]

However, years later, the Jesuit provinces of France and Belgium had internal resistance to the strong condemnation of communism by Pius XI and pushed by the Jesuit general. The concern of both provinces was to present a more positive response to the threat of communism.[62]

Ledóchowski, on the other hand, was very conservative; to such an extent that he did not agree with the more progressive order of the Catholic Church in the countries where it developed, such as France and the United States. For example, he disagreed with the majority position of the French clergy in defending the French Jesuits Pierre Teilhard de Chardin, Henri Bouillard, and Henri De Lubac, because of their departure

---

[58] Richard B. Spence, Wall Street and the Russian Revolution: 1905-1925 (Trine Day LLC, Walterville, OR, 2017), op. cit.
[59] Ibid.
[60] John T. McGreevy, American Jesuits and the World How an Embattled Religious Order Made Modern Catholicism Global (Princeton University Press, New Jersey, 2016), pp. 174-176.
[61] Chenaux, P. (2018). Father Włodzimierz Ledóchowski (1866–1942): Driving Force behind Papal Anti-Communism during the Interwar Period, *Journal of Jesuit Studies*, 5(1), pp. 55, 56.
[62] Ibid, p. 70.

on critical points from Catholic doctrine and their militant progressivism.[63] The popes, passing through Pius X, Benedict XV, in short, disagreed, for example, with defending de Chardin and strongly pressured the French clergy to retract. Something the clergy disagreed with.[64] Although Pope Benedict XV and his Secretary of State supported Germany, they disagreed with German ambitions on the one hand.[65] But that does not mean that they were in full agreement with the Allies (France, the United Kingdom, Russia, Italy, Japan, and the United States). But the overwhelming majority of the Roman Curia, the Italian Catholic clergy and laity in general, were in favor of the Central Powers; and there was also a crisis between the Roman Curia and France, because of the many Catholic modernist intellectuals in the country.[66]

With Benedict XV dead and Cardinal Ratti elected as Pope Pius XI, he enlisted the help of American Jesuit John La Farge - without notifying the Jesuit general - one of the editors of the Jesuit magazine *America*, to develop a new encyclical directly condemning European anti-Semitism ("Humani Generis Unitas").[67] The pope requested it because La Farge was the Jesuit pioneer of racial justice in the United States, and who would come to support civil rights marches in the United States.[68] La Farge, naturally, sought advice from Ledóchowski, who was deeply anti-Semitic, and who said that La Farge should be assisted by two Jesuits - one German and one French.[69]

After finishing the work, they gave the draft directly to the General of the Jesuits and not to Pius XI. Months went by, and one month before the death of Pius XI, already seriously ill, the Jesuit general sent the encyclical to the pope, who was unable to publish it...[70]

LaFarge was progressive on religious tolerance, as was Jesuit John Courtney Murray, who would later help draft the decree on religious freedom proclaimed during the Second Vatican Ecumenical Council.[71]

At the same time, the Jesuit general disagreed with the opening of Fordham University to non-Catholic students.[72]

Thus, as is naturally known, not all Jesuits agree with what other members of their Society say or do, even to the point of profound disagreement.[73]

---

[63] Ralph M. McInerny (editor), New Themes in Christian Philosophy (University of Notre Dame Press, Indiana, 1968), pp. 180-182; Robert Nugent, Silence Speaks: Teilhard de Chardin, Yves Congar, John Courtney Murray, and Thomas Merton (Paulist Press, New York/Mahwah, NJ, 2011), pp. 14-17.

[64] Robert Nugent, Silence Speaks: Teilhard de Chardin, Yves Congar, John Courtney Murray, and Thomas Merton (Paulist Press, New York/Mahwah, NJ, 2011), pp. 14-17.

[65] John Pollard, The Papacy in the Age of Totalitarianism: 1914-1958 (Oxford University Press, 2014), pp. 38, 39.

[66] Ibid, p. 39.

[67] Gary Wills, Papal Sin: Structures of Deceit (Image Books/Doubleday, New York, 2000), p. 30.

[68] James T. Keane (17 de enero, 2023), The life and legacy of John LaFarge, a Jesuit pioneer for racial justice, America Magazine.

[69] Gary Wills, Papal Sin: Structures of Deceit (Image Books/Doubleday, New York, 2000), p. 30.

[70] Ibid, p. 31.

[71] Lafontaine, R. (2007). Lonergan's Functional Specialties as a Model for Doctrinal Development: John Courtney Murray and The Second Vatican Council's "Declaration on Religious Freedom." Gregorianum, 88(4), 780–805; The New York Times (June 13, 1966), La Farge Institute Names Director, The New York Times, p. 45.

[72] Thomas J. Shelley, Fordham, A History of the Jesuit University of New York: 1841-2003 (Fordham University Press, 2016), p. 192.

For all these differences and nuances, as we shall see, the approaches of the Jesuits and some other French clerics to French non anti-clerical Freemasonry must be considered with great care. We shall see that this outward action of rapprochement, although it was a plot that began in the Vatican and was directed at France, to destabilize French Freemasonry and the policy of that country to slow down and even contain the efforts of the United States and Europe for a world order that threatened to undermine and even disappear the sense of existence of the Catholic Church in the world, not everyone saw and sees things in the same way.

Although not all were in cahoots and there were and are differences, the plan as a whole continues.

Those are two contrasting and opposing ways of seeing the world but through dissimulation.

The League of Nations, the Vatican, and the Jesuits' Conspiracy

On the Vatican's plans to counter the efforts described, while papal treaty diplomacy was very successful "first in Eastern Europe and then in Central and Western Europe;" Benedict XV realized that by legal agreements alone he could not regain all of Europe. The concordats were made without consulting the will of the people, which forced them to follow a new set of legal restrictions. Therefore, after the Great War, the Vatican decided to invest in an unprecedented way in the institutions and practices of civil society; creating, expanding, and centralizing youth organizations. It invented groups and communication networks for Catholic workers and peasants. It also ensured that lay activism was regularly supervised and monitored by parish priests, bishops, and even the Holy See itself. This was a struggle for freedom and civilizational identity.[74]

Despite these efforts, the secular movements continued to gain ground. And precisely with the advent of Bolshevism.[75]

Within weeks, the more Western leftist radicals staged their uprisings in Vienna, Budapest, Milan, and Munich. But they were violently suppressed. In 1919, however, Russian revolutionaries and their European comrades founded the Communist International, or Comintern, heralding an imminent and powerful wave of uprisings. The Comintern became a truly internationalist force with activities in Eastern and Western Europe and in non-Western countries struggling to free themselves from imperial rule. All these movements were a direct challenge to Catholic transnational activism. The papacy saw it as a direct result of the shortcomings and errors of the Paris agreement that ended the Great War.[76]

"A new generation of right-wing ethno-nationalists— active in Poland, Germany, Austria, Italy, and Spain—agreed. They condemned the League of Nations and the Comintern in the same breath, leaning on repurposed anti-liberal and anti-Semitic motifs. In the 1930s the papacy, in dialogue with these groups and terrified by the

---

[73] Joaquim Fernandes y Fina d'Armada, El Secreto de Fátima: La historia oculta de las misteriosas apariciones y la conspiración de los jesuitas (Ediciones Nowtilus S.I., Madrid, 2007), pp. 260-263; James Bernauer S.J., Jesuit Kaddish: Jesuits, Jews, and Holocaust Remembrance (University of Notre Dame Press, Notre Dame, Indiana, 2020).

[74] Giuliana Chamedes, A Twentieth-Century Crusade: The Vatican's Battle to Remake Christian Europe (Harvard University Press, Cambridge, Massachusetts, 2019), pp. 3, 4.

[75] Ibid, p. 4.

[76] Ibid.

Comintern, launched a far-reaching anticommunist campaign. The little-studied campaign was a historic first for the Church. The Vatican's response to liberalism was primarily legal and diplomatic in nature, but its response to communism, which emerged from the battle against liberalism, was an ambitious cultural crusade carried forward by newly formed Catholic grassroots organizations, mass media instruments, and specially dedicated papal institutions. Its aim was to enlist the masses and send the message that communism was the earthly face of Satan himself."[77]

The Catholic International was the most ambitious pre-Cold War anti-communist project, using the media to promote Catholicism and create new transnational communities of belonging. It forged boundaries between and within European states.[78]

It called for the expulsion of communists from the body politic, making the papal crusade to sanction discrimination and violence, while freely referring to several racist creeds "(including the anti-Semitic myth of Judeo-Bolshevism) and doing little to curb the rise of right-wing extremism." Thus a common internationalist identity was forged for European Christians.[79]

Giuliana Chamedes tells us about Catholic Internationalism:

"Born at the height of World War I, its purpose was to use new and technologically advanced means to centralize power and glue members to Rome, even as it provided an infrastructure for increased sociability within national bounds. As one of the pope's flagship journals announced, the pope was the heart of the undertaking—"If Moscow's Comintern is at the head of the Communist International, [then] Rome is the center of the Catholic International!" Participant observers concurred that the Catholic Church had "achieved an internationality beyond the wildest dreams of socialists or cosmopolitan theorists," and that Rome had become "the seat of the mightiest *Internationale* the world has ever seen."[80]

Catholic intellectuals in countries such as Poland, France, Austria, and Germany for years forged transnational connections after World War I. With Catholic information and exchange networks, they helped consolidate Christian Democratic parties and push forward European integration plans under Catholicism. With Catholic networks of information and exchange, they helped consolidate Christian Democratic parties and push forward plans for European integration under Catholicism. But the Vatican would extend its influence first in Eastern Europe: Poland, Latvia, Lithuania, and Estonia.[81]

In this regard, it was a prelate, Eugenio Pacelli, who after the defeat of the Central Powers in the Great War, developed the new model of Vatican concordats with other nations that would give Roman Catholicism an advantage and dominance in those countries. As we said, thus counteracting secular plans in Europe. Benedict XV used the Eastern countries mentioned above as "guinea pigs." The Holy See rehearsed its

---

[77] Ibid, p. 5.

[78] Ibid.

[79] Ibid.

[80] Ibid, p. 6; citing *Lettres de Rome*, 1, n° 1 (May 1935): I, Roman Archives of the Jesuit Order (ARSI), Jesuit Center for Social Communication (hereafter cited as JESCOM), the Private Library of Father Ledóchowski.; Stephen J. Brown, "Catholic Internationalism," Studies: An Irish Quarterly Review 14, no. 55 (1925): 476-479.

[81] Ibid, pp. 8, 14.

plans for reordering international affairs. Encouraged by its success in Eastern Europe, the Holy See government would soon export the concordats to Central and Western Europe. This modus operandi would continue for almost forty years.[82]

Likewise, the American Catholic press would be numerous and very critical of the attempts to create the League of Nations and the participation of the United States in the process.[83] The League would be considered Masonic and, the Catholic press stressed that only the Catholic Church was capable of bringing Europe to peace and uniting the nations.[84] It recommended in turn that the United States bring God to the nation for its "true" prosperity.[85]

In addition to the implementation of concordats with the Holy See and criticism of the United States and the League of Nations, there were additional plans. Being that papal dreams of European dominance were threatened in a very real way with the intervention of the United States and European and American Freemasonry to shape Europe, it was through the urging of Pope Benedict XV and Włodzimierz Ledóchowski, the general of the Jesuit order, that a vast plan was devised to interfere against the dreams of European democracy pushed by the American nation and the Freemasons. The Vatican and the Society of Jesus would start in France.

While French Jesuits and Dominicans developed a more progressive theology beginning in the 1930s and 1940s, influenced by Belgium, which would play a key role in modernizing the Catholic Church and eventually inspire many of the changes that took place during and after the Second Vatican Council,[86] the truth is that in their different ways of thinking, this progressivism insists on placing the Catholic Church as the most influential moral power in the political and social life of the world.

Yves Le Roy de La Brière was a French Jesuit priest, influential theologian, and author, who stated in 1932:

"If the jurists and heads of state of the nineteenth and early twentieth centuries - the anticlericals and simple liberals - could return to earth... they would find it hard to believe what they see and hear. They would return to crouch in their graves rather than remain the impotent witnesses of this collapse of their beloved work of legislative secularization."[87]

La Brière was of monarchist thought and supported the traditional Catholic doctrine of the union of Church and State: where papal teaching influenced governments.[88]

---

[82] Ibid, pp. 32, 33.

[83] Zacharewicz, M. M. (1956). The Attitude of the Catholic Press Toward The League of Nations. Records of the American Catholic Historical Society of Philadelphia, 67(2/4), 88–104.

[84] Ibid, pp. 93-96.

[85] Ibid.

[86] Sarah Shortall, Soldiers of God in a Secular World: Catholic Theology and Twentieth-Century French Politics (Harvard University Press, Massachusetts, 2021).

[87] Giuliana Chamedes, A Twentieth-Century Crusade: The Vatican's Battle to Remake Christian Europe (Harvard University Press, Cambridge, Massachusetts, 2019), p. 34; citing R. P Yves de la Brière, Études et paix (Paris: Flammarion, 1932), 603.

[88] Michael Sutton, Nationalism, Positivism and Catholicism: The Politics of Charles Maurras and French Catholics 1890-1914 (Cambridge University Press, Cambridge, 2002), p. 223.

Thus, according to La Brière, as we read from 1911, the Catholic Church had the right to demand the state to force religion through laws.[89]

During World War I, La Brière actively and courageously supported Benedict XV's efforts to negotiate the compromised peace, in opposition to the American plan. But when the war ended, Henri-Marie Baudrillart, a priest and rector of the Institut Catholique de Paris (Catholic Institute of Paris), created a chair on "Christian principles of international law" or international law, which he entrusted to La Brière, who "ironically" became "a tireless advocate of international peace and the League of Nations."[90] Even so, such apparent support was a plan to destabilize the ideals of the League of Nations through Catholic influences coming from the Vatican. For La Brière, after the French Revolution and the advent of the modern secular state, the question of the Church's support for civil authority had necessarily to be expressed in different terms, but ultimately, that right was not to be relinquished.[91] The change of terms had to occur to hide the traditional governmental model of the Vatican to avoid resistance. Thus, according to the Jesuit, for the Catholic Church to play its role in achieving its ends through the State, it must necessarily conform in some way to the established circumstances. La Brière wrote a book in 1918 on The League of Nations showing support, but noting that the papal design for peace was the ideal.[92] The Jesuit,

"Gradually, it achieved an international audience and tried to go beyond the ideals of the League of Nations, adding a spiritual dimension rooted in the Christian tradition from St. Augustine to Luigi Taparelli d'Azeglio [Jesuit]."[93]

It was decided that the A.P. or Action Populaire (Popular Action- a Jesuit association and magazine), would come back into existence. And that it would do so in Reims as in the past, with a small office in Paris that would facilitate the personal contacts indispensable for the organism's function on a national scale.[94] The Society of Jesus would make efforts to counteract the "anti-Christian, secularist, socialist, communist" movements bent on "promoting their own plans for the transformation of society and also, in fact, for the elimination of religion."[95]

In the meantime, La Brière and other Jesuits would try to influence the League of Nations to open up the horizons of the Church in Europe and the rest of the world.

---

[89] Ibid, pp. 216, 217; citando a La Briere, 'A propos d'une lettre de M. Imbart de la Tour', 138. 45 P. Imbart de la Tour, 'L'Emploi de la force au service de la vraie religion: reponse aux "Etudes" ', Etudes, 129(1911), 858-62.

[90] Michael Sutton, en Ibid, p. 213 Y Charles E. O'Neill, en Ibid.

[91] Ibid, p. 214.

[92] Yves de La Brière, La "Société des Nations"?: Essai historique et juridique: Moyen-Age, "Grand Dessein" de Henri IV, politique de l'équilibre, concert Européen, lois et sanctions internationales, chimères et utopies, rôle international de la Papauté (Beauschesne), op. cit. Véase asimismo Yves de La Brière, L'organisation internationale du monde contemporain et la papauté souveraine (Editions Spes, Paris, 1927).

[93] Charles E. O'Neill, S.I., Joaquín M.a Domínguez, S.I., Diccionario histórico de la Compañía de Jesús: Infante de Santiago-Piatkiewicz (Institutum Historicum, S.I., Roma, Universidad Pontificia Comillas, Madrid, 2001), p. 2237.

[94] P. Droulers, Le père Desbuquois et l'Action Populaire: Dans la gestation d'un monde nouveau (1919-1946) (Presses de l'Université Grégorienne, Rome, 1981), p. 8.

[95] Ibid, p. 7.

It should be noted that the A.P. received an express letter and a gift from Benedict XV on December 16, 1918. It was on November 11, less than a month before, that the armistice signed at Le Francport took place, ending the Great War. It was then that Gustave Desbuquois, another French Jesuit priest, left for Reims to begin the task described above; but the place was in ruins, so he moved temporarily to Paris.[96] Desbuquois would forge ties with leading French Freemasons, to undermine the influence of Freemasonry in France as well as in European social reconstruction, and to shape the League of Nations as envisaged by La Brière. And as we shall see later, the vital task of forging ties and influence with French Freemasons would be passed on to another Jesuit.

As Oscar L. Arnal documents so well, "Immediately after the war, French Catholics also joined the conservative National Bloc." This coalition of right-wing parties meant "for them the continuation of national pride, distrust of the League of Nations and territorial gains against the defeated Germans."[97]

"One [bishop] described the Wilsonian league as a utopian creation "inspired" by theories of J.-J. and the Declaration of the Rights of Man," while others [bishops] insisted upon a relentless bellicosity toward Germany."[98]

In this regard, the Paris Peace Conference as mentioned elsewhere, which was held from January 1919 to January 1920 to export democracy to the European continent, had Woodrow Wilson as its protagonist.[99] Pope Benedict XV was excluded. And Achille Ratti (future Pope Pius XI) and his assistant expressed themselves in the Jesuit magazine *Civiltà Cattolica*, denouncing Wilson and liberal internationalism, echoing the words of Cardinal Gasparri, expressed in the official Vatican newspaper, *L'Osservatore Romano*, "that Wilson in person bore the final and ultimate "responsibility" for the "odious offense" of excluding the pope from the meeting."[100] We read verbatim that, "The Vatican daily synthetically noted that the world's populations now faced a stark choice between the "light of Rome" and the "moral nullity" [nullismo morale] of Paris, whose "menacing darkness" lurked ready to swallow Europe whole."[101]

Giuliana Chamedes:

"In Rome, the Paris Peace Treaties were promptly written off as the opposite of instruments of peace—as settlements that "represented a colossal failure of human judgment and expertise." If only the "weak and unheeded voice of humanity," as

---

[96] Ibid, p. 8.

[97] Oscar L. Arnal, Ambivalent Alliance: The Catholic Church and the Action Française, 1899-1939 (University of Pittsburgh Press, Pittsburgh, Pa, 1985), p. 90.

[98] Ibid.

[99] Giuliana Chamedes, A Twentieth-Century Crusade: The Vatican's Battle to Remake Christian Europe (Harvard University Press, Cambridge, Massachusetts, 2019), pp. 52, 53.

[100] Ibid, p. 53; citing Padre Rosa, "La guerra fratricida in Italia e il 'grido di pace' del Papa," *Civiltà Cattolica*, August 19, 1922; Giuseppe Angelini, "Responsabilità?," *Osservatore Romano*, May 15, 1919. The latter article was actually written by Gasparri, as documented in his *Memorie*. See *Il cardinal Gasparri e la questione romana (con brani delle memorie inedite)*, ed. G. Spadolini (Florence: Le Monnier, 1972), 227–231.

[101] Ibid; citing "Le vie dei popoli," *Osservatore Romano*, 30 de octubre, 1920.

channeled by the pope, had been invited to Versailles, all would have been otherwise."[102]

In 1919, Bishop W. H. Nolens, chairman of the Dutch delegation to the first International Labour Conference (of the League of Nations) in Washington, mentioned in his speech and in private the absence of moral forces, particularly religious ones, "which he considered essential to the dynamism and effectiveness of the work undertaken." Also at the second conference, held in Genoa in 1920, the bishop spoke with Arthur Fontaine, President of the Council of the International Labor Organization [ILO- of the League of Nations], and with Albert Thomas, the director of the organization. Thomas showed himself - we read - "convinced of the desirability of having the support of the Vatican, "in the interest of labor" and also as a means of obtaining "a more secure collaboration on the part of Catholics, workers, and employers"; and he asked Nolens to run "for our Genoa plan" and its implementation."[103]

Likewise, in September 1921, shortly before the third conference to be held in Geneva, Nolens wrote extensively to Pietro Gasparri, the Vatican's Cardinal Secretary of State, to whom he had been discussing the project since the autumn of 1920. But since the ILO had official status and was linked to the League of Nations, the Holy See was to be admitted on an equal footing with the other governments; but under pressure from the Italian government it had been kept out of the Peace Conference and the League of Nations itself.[104] As a provisional intermediate solution, Nolens suggested perhaps "a special deputy to the Bureau in Geneva."[105] We also read:

"Moreover, in 1920, at the Semaine Sociale in Caen, Zamanski proclaimed the faith of French social Catholics in the necessity and future of the ILO, and in July 1921, the C.I.S.C., an international Christian trade union organization, made official contact with the ILO through a visit to Geneva to Thomas, who showed great support. At the end of July 1922, Thomas sent his close collaborator Paul Devinat to represent him at the Semaine Sociale in Strasbourg (every year he had the ILO officially represented). From October 1923, letters were exchanged between Devinat and Bishop Vanneufville, correspondent in Rome of La Croix, and with E. Duthoit, President of the Semaines Sociales Francaises (French Social Week)."[106]

Duthoit and Albert Thomas met in Paris on May 12, 1924, and, at the end of that month, Thomas, accompanied by Devinat, was received at the Vatican by Bishop Borgongini-Duca, Secretary for Extraordinary Ecclesiastical Affairs.[107]

---

[102] Ibid; citing "Dove sono i responsabili?," *Osservatore Romano*, November 6, 1919. For similar views, see also "Un'altra illusion," *Osservatore Romano*, November 9, 1919; and "L'irresponsibilità della guerra e della pace falsa," *Osservatore Romano*, 22 de noviembre, 1919; Angelini, "Di chi la colpa?," *Osservatore Romano*, March 18, 1920.

[103] P. Droulers, Le père Desbuquois et l'Action Populaire: Dans la gestation d'un monde nouveau (1919-1946) (Presses de l'Université Grégorienne, Rome, 1981), p. 124.

[104] Ibid, pp. 124, 125.

[105] Ibid, p. 125.

[106] Ibid.

[107] Ibid, pp. 125, 126.

Certainly, not everything would please the papacy. In July, Pius XI made it known, for general diplomatic reasons, that he was not in favor of the Holy See joining as an official member of a League of Nations body.[108]

Oscar Arnal states:

"Pius XI advocated international collaboration under the arbitration of the Vatican instead of the League of Nations, which was considered to be inspired by some heretical notions. Cooperation between the League of Nations and the Holy See required the supremacy of the latter over the former. Moreover, concordats with the various conservative powers were to be used together with the League of Nations to curb the Bolshevik threat and preserve social order."[109]

Now, Thomas, without giving up and ignoring the Vatican's true intentions, together with church leaders approached the idea of an unofficially delegated ecclesiastical presence. On behalf of Thomas, Tessier asked the Jesuit Father Desbuquois, who understood the importance of such Catholic collaboration at the international level, to provide someone, naming one of the best-prepared members of his team.[110] Thus, from the A. P., Desbuquois chose the Jesuit priest André Arnou, who, as one of its members, was called to join the ILO - International Labor Office - in Geneva.[111] Although his participation was that of a simple advisor, with no official or unofficial representation of the Holy See, something supported by the General of the Jesuits, Ledochowski.[112] This was followed by a significant collaboration of the Catholic missions in the ILO at the instigation of the Jesuits and accepted and promoted by Thomas. Many Catholics from all countries worked in a private capacity for the ILO and the League of Nations on human rights issues, advocating against forced labor in the still-existing colonies.[113]

The way in which this was set in motion, generated acceptance "for his broadmindedness and competence, in an environment dominated by socialists and agnostics, Protestants and Jews, who at first were astonished by the presence of this priest and Jesuit, and where the administrative authorities were not very favorable to him." Thus, the Jesuit "worked intensely on documentation, correspondence and relations, and drew up dossiers, most of which were included in the Director's reports to the annual meeting of the ILO."[114] Several of the speeches given by Albert Thomas to Catholic organizations were prepared by Arnou, in favor of human rights.[115] Now, it should be noted that while this was being done, the Society of Jesus and the Catholic Church were concealing their intentions, although not so underhandedly..... But it is worth noting that the discourse of the Catholic Church at the level of the League of Nations, through the ILO, very much reflects the progressive model of the time in defense of human rights. But the Jesuits, on the other hand, were secretly working in

---

[108] Ibid, p. 126.
[109] Oscar L. Arnal, Ambivalent Alliance: The Catholic Church and the Action Française, 1899-1939 (University of Pittsburgh Press, Pittsburgh, Pa, 1985), p. 168.
[110] P. Droulers, Le père Desbuquois et l'Action Populaire: Dans la gestation d'un monde nouveau (1919-1946) (Presses de l'Université Grégorienne, Rome, 1981), p. 126.
[111] Ibid, p. 124, 126.
[112] Ibid, p. 126.
[113] Ibid, p. 127.
[114] Ibid.
[115] Ibid; also compare with page 130.

sympathy with right-wing totalitarian movements in Europe, as will be seen in due course. It was a double face, so that the Jesuits were the papacy's arm par excellence to reach out to the progressive secular world, "becoming like them," to win them over... However, not all Jesuits and other clergy would see things the same way. Regarding the conspiracy, however, it would not be fully understood particularly today, by the most conservative ecclesiastical forces at all levels and by the laity.

Meanwhile, in France, the ground was being prepared to destroy every element contrary to the Church. In this regard, we read:

"The collective letter of the French hierarchy, published early in 1924, reflected a patriotic ideology designed to warm the heart of any devoted integral nationalist. All loyal citizens were urged to beware of internationalist doctrines contrary to both "nature and religion," likely a reference to both bolshevism and the Wilsonian ideas embodied in the new League of Nations."[116]

To better understand the forces of French Catholicism and its role in Vichy France as Hitler's puppet, we must look a little further into history. Let us begin with the French National Catholic Federation (NCF) formed in February 1925, which was characterized by extreme nationalism, social Catholicism, anti-Masonry, anti-Marxism, and rejection of political democracy.[117] Led by General Édouard de Castelnau, some three million joined the NCF. Castelnau was unaware of the intense Fascist clerical propaganda program. Both the NCF and Catholic Action were made up of many Jesuits.[118] In the prologue of a book on the NCF, the priest Janvier recorded the act of consecration that the general read, from which some fragments are quoted:

"Sacred Heart of Jesus, The chiefs and representatives of French Catholics, prostrating themselves now before you, have assembled and organised the National Catholic Federation (N.C.F.) to re-establish your reign over this land... All of us, those who are present and those who are absent, have not always been irreproachable... We carry the burden of the crimes the French nation committed against you... It is then with the view to repair and expiate that we present to you, today, our desires, intentions and unanimous resolution to re-establish over the whole of France your sacred and royal sovereignty, and liberate the souls of her children from a sacriligious teaching... We will not flinch any more before this fight for which you condescended to arm us. We want everything to be bent before and devoted to your service...

"Sacred Heart of Jesus, we beseech you, through the Virgin Mary, to receive the homage..."[119]

He then proceeds to enumerate what they described as the crimes of France:

"Fatal words and general directives: socialism is condemned... liberalism is condemned... Leo XIII showed that the freedom of worship is unjustifiable. The pope also showed that the freedom of speech and expression cannot be justifiably

---

[116] Oscar L. Arnal, Ambivalent Alliance: The Catholic Church and the Action Française, 1899-1939 (University of Pittsburgh Press, Pittsburgh, Pa, 1985), p. 90.
[117] Ibid, p. 117, 118.
[118] Edmond Paris, The Secret History of the Jesuits (Chick Publications, Ontario, Calif. 1982), p. 221.
[119] Ibid, pp. 221, 222.

accorded... So, the freedom of thought, press, teaching and worship, considered by some as rights natural to man, cannot possibly be given...

"We must," said Pius XI, "re-instate these teachings and regulations of the Church."[120]

For the Social Week of 1926 in Le Havre on "The Problem of International Life," Jesuit Debouquois was asked to speak on "The Church and International Life." Despite the criticisms, he took pains to make it feel favorable to the League of Nations.[121]

"Referring to the principle of collaboration between Church and State, which he had developed the previous year, he showed that collaboration between the Church and international society is also necessary and fruitful, respecting the "natural and providential variety of human groups."[122]

Desbuquois stressed the importance of collaboration and respect between the different denominations and henceforth engaged in efforts to bring France and Germany closer together, something that Pope Pius XI personally encouraged.[123]

Nonetheless, some of the means of the Jesuits in France would not be seen as positive by Pius XI. Thus, in the fall of 1926, La Brière met with the pope in a private audience where a solution to the official Catholic position on Action Française other than condemnation was discussed. The Action Française was an extreme right-wing monarchist political movement that was denounced as atheist, agnostic, anti-Christian, and anti-Catholic. The pope was concerned about the question of its moral and religious influence. To avoid the danger of linking the group to politics, the pope recommended on December 20 of the same year that Catholics unite in a national Catholic federation to defend religious liberties.[124]

Many French Jesuits had to be reprimanded for joining the Action Française.[125]

Moreover, in the audience with the pope, he let the French Jesuit know that the Holy See was not interested in a permanent seat in the League of Nations, given the claimed superiority of the Apostolic See. At the same time, Pius XI hoped to gain the support of those Catholics who had worked for positive collaboration, with the aim of becoming involved in deliberations where ecclesiastical interests were at stake.[126]

The following year or 1927, Franz von Papen, private chamberlain to the pope and with whom the Nazi government's Reichskonkordat would be signed with the Holy See in 1933, in what would be a breakthrough in French affairs and support for French Catholicism, said:

---

[120] Ibid, p. 222; citing to Georges Viance, "La Federation nationale catholique," foreword by the R.P. Janvier (Flarnrnarion, Paris, 1930), pp. 186-188.

[121] P. Droulers, Le père Desbuquois et l'Action Populaire: Dans la gestation d'un monde nouveau (1919-1946) (Presses de l'Université Grégorienne, Rome, 1981), p. 319.

[122] Ibid.

[123] Ibid, p. 320.

[124] Charles E. O'Neill, S.I., Joaquín M.a Domínguez, S.I., Diccionario histórico de la Compañía de Jesús: Infante de Santiago-Piatkiewicz (Institutum Historicum, S.I., Rome, Universidad Pontificia Comillas, Madrid, 2001), p. 2237.

[125] Ibid, pp. 194-202.

[126] Lucia Ceci, The Vatican and Mussolini's Italy (Brill, Leiden; Boston, 2017), p. 125.

"Our first meeting took place in 1927, when a German delegation, to which I had the honour to belong, came to Paris, for the "Social Week of the Catholic Institute," under the presidency of Monseigneur Baudrillart.

This was indeed a fruitful first contact as it marked the start of a long exchange of visits between important personalities from France and Germany. "On the French side, the RR. FF. Delattre (Jesuit), de la Briere (Jesuit) and Denset (Jesuit)... were present at these conferences."[127]

He added that at times, "this conference of Catholics reached superhuman heights of greatness."[128]

The large number of concordats that Pius XI established with other European countries was staggering. But the most controversial were with Benito Mussolini's fascist Italy; with Hitler's Nazi Germany; with Franco's Spain; with Salazar's Portugal; and with the puppet Vichy regime in France. All of these were totalitarian states. But the rest were: Latvia (1922), Bavaria (1924), Poland (1925), Romania (1927), Lithuania (1927), Czechoslovakia (1928), Prussia (1929), Baden (1932), Austria (1933), and Yugoslavia (1935), as well as the partial agreements with France in 1924 and 1926, and with Portugal and Ecuador (1937). Due to the very nature of such alliances, the Holy See did not enter into the merits or demerits of the political regimes, but adapted itself to the *de facto* situations, placing the interests of the Catholic Church at the forefront.[129]

Beginning in 1922 and for the rest of the decade, Vatican diplomacy tried various ways to establish official relations with the Soviet government. This was despite the assassination of several Catholic priests by that government.[130] The Jesuits knew what was brewing.

Years later, in 1932, the General of the Jesuits, Ledochowski, decided to withdraw Arnou from Geneva, lacking Catholic representation in the League of Nations.[131] This, due to rivalries of ideas and influence concerning Arnou, which provoked denunciations from the conservatives and, "above all, unofficial political pressure on the Holy See by the French government and also by the Italian fascist government, for hostility to trade union and international action." For this reason, on February 13, 1932, Ledochowski wrote that "given the present circumstances, it seems more prudent that neither Father Arnou nor any Jesuit should henceforth be in the service of the League of Nations;" specifying that these reasons did not come from Arnou. But at the insistence of filling the vacancy, Ledochowski sent the Jesuit Danset, who was in Buenos Aires on mission and who took Desbuquois' place in Geneva in February 1934. But despite his enormous work, after a year he had to resign; he later died in Paris.[132]

He was succeeded by the Jesuit priest Albert Le Roy at the beginning of 1936.[133]

---

[127] Edmond Paris, The Secret History of the Jesuits (Chick Publications, Ontario, Calif. 1982), p. 222; citing Franz von Papen: "Memoires" (Flarnmarion, Paris, 1953), p. 91; Andre Guerber: "Himmler et ses crimes" (Les Documents Nuit et Jour, Paris, 1981).

[128] Ibid, p. 169.

[129] Lucia Ceci, The Vatican and Mussolini's Italy (Brill, Leiden; Boston, 2017), p. 125.

[130] Ibid, pp. 125, 126.

[131] P. Droulers, Le père Desbuquois et l'Action Populaire: Dans la gestation d'un monde nouveau (1919-1946) (Presses de l'Université Grégorienne, Rome, 1981), p. 132.

[132] Ibid, p. 129.

[133] Ibid, p. 130.

About all these efforts, what about the Vatican's concordats with the different European countries and their effects on the citizenry to counteract the attempts to democratize the old continent? That remains to be seen.

CHAPTER

3

"The clash of civilizations"
- Concordats with the enemy

The Vatican and Nazi Germany

The continued struggle of the Catholic Church to survive and continue its longed-for recovery of dominion would be seen with the concordats it would have with various countries in Europe and others.

From 1931 to 1933, anti-Communist Catholics in close contact with the Holy See began to send more worrisome notes that Communism was on Germany's doorstep. Conservative political figures also made the same claims to papal diplomats.[1]

Around this time, in January 1933, German Chancellor Kurt von Schleiger and German President Paul von Hindenburg resigned. Since the conservative old guard to which they belonged was losing power, they thought of collaborating with the Nazi Party to survive. Paul von Hindenburg appointed Adolf Hitler Reich Chancellor. Within five months, the National Socialist Party established a dictatorship and swept away German democracy.[2] Nevertheless, these events did not worry the German Catholic hierarchy, which was focused on the influence of communism in Germany. Cardinal Eugenio Pacelli asked the German and Bavarian bishops by letter whether they thought it appropriate for the Holy Office to issue a condemnation of communism and the German organizations that spread it, but the answer was that such a condemnation would be superfluous since Hilter was doing much to combat it.[3]

"Following the Reichstag fire, the new chancellor had severely limited freedom of the press, political meetings, and marches, and the right to electoral campaigning. On March 23 the Reichstag passed the Enabling Act, which abolished democracy and the constitutional state."[4]

The bishops' concern, however, focused on whether the Reichstag fire had been set by the Communists to overthrow the state, as Hitler claimed. They asked the Holy See, therefore, to applaud Hitler's bold actions, rather than mourn the loss of German democracy.[5]

At the beginning of 1933, Eugenio Pacelli, the future Pope Pius XII, stated during an audience with Pius XI, that "Hitler is the first (and only) statesman who has to date

---

[1] Giuliana Chamedes, A Twentieth-Century Crusade: The Vatican's Battle to Remake Christian Europe (Harvard University Press, Cambridge, Massachusetts, 2019), p. 140.
[2] Ibid.
[3] Ibid, p. 141.
[4] Ibid.
[5] Ibid.

spoken publicly against communism. Until now only the pope had done so."[6] Just three days later, in a meeting with French Ambassador François Charles-Roux, Pius XI modified his opinion of Hitler, especially since he believed him to be "an ally against Bolshevism."[7] He made similar statements on March 13 to the cardinals during a consistory and also in private.[8] In the middle of the month, the German bishops stated that they were willing to retract the condemnation of National Socialism "if the new government demonstrates in fact that the fears of the bishops were unfounded," and "if in addition the new government continues to remain strong in the battle against advancing Bolshevism and public immorality."[9]

"On March 23, the day when he gave German democracy its final blow with the Enabling Act, Hitler also engaged in moves modeled on Mussolini's courting of the Holy See. Hitler delivered a speech in which he asserted that Christianity was "the most important factor in the maintenance of [Germany's] national identity." In an apparent tiptoe away from his commitment to a fusion of Protestantism and Catholicism in a "positive Christianity," the German chancellor promised to honor the Holy See's concordats with individual German states, maintain government support of Catholic schools, and uphold religious education in public, while simultaneously doing battle with "atheistic organizations" undermining the Christian churches. The rights of the churches, he said, would "not be infringed upon." Hitler promised to "maintain and further friendly relations with the Holy See."[10]

Precisely, the bishops' conference in Fulda formally lifted the ban on Catholic membership in the National Socialist party.[11] We also read that:

"In response, five days later, the Fulda bishops' conference formally lifted the existing ban on Catholic membership in the National Socialist party. "The occasion for this revision," the German nuncio reported to Pius XI, "was offered by the serene speech delivered last Thursday in the Reichstag by the head of the government [Hitler], but the real determining cause, I believe, is to try to do something about the attitude of growing sympathy of the Catholic masses, young and old, for the new regime." (The Bishop of Linz, Johannes Maria Gföllner, was not so impressed, and immediately reissued the existing prohibitions against Austrian Catholics joining the Nazi party.)"[12]

---

[6] Ibid; citing Audience of March 4, 1933, ASV, A.E.S., Stati Ecclesiastici, quarto period, pos. 430a, fasc. 348, f. 3, as reprinted in Ludwig Volk, *Das Reichskonkordat vom 20. Juli 1933* (Mainz: Matthias-Grünewald- Verlag, 1972), 65, note 24.

[7] Ibid, p. 142; quoting Charles-Roux to Paul-Boncour, March 7, 1933, reprinted in Volk, *Das Reichskonkordat*, note 25.

[8] Ibid; citing Faulhaber to the Bavarian episcopate, March 24, 1933, in Bernhard Stasiewski, ed., *Akten deutscher Bischöfe über die Lage der Kirche, 1933–1945,* vol. 1, *1933–1934* (Mainz: Matthias Grünewald-Verlag, 1968), 16–18.

[9] Ibid.

[10] Ibid; citing Hitler's declaration upon introducing the Enabling Act in Parliament on March 23, 1933, as reprinted in Hubert Gruber, *Katholische Kirche und Nationalsozialismus, 1930–1945: Ein Bericht in Quellen* (Paderborn: Schöningh, 2006), 34.

[11] Ibid; citing: For more on this episode, see Eugene Jones, "Franz von Papen, Catholic Conservatives, and the Establishment of the Third Reich, 1933–1934," *Journal of Modern History* 83 (June 2011): 272–318.

[12] Ibid; citing Ibid and other sources.

Nevertheless, Pius XI was satisfied with Hitler's statement of March 23, as was *L'Osservatore Romano*, underlining especially the German Chancellor's double commitment to concordats and anti-Communism.[13] But on April 1, Pius XI informed the nuncio in Berlin that he knew of the anti-Semitic excesses in Germany, and that it would be a good idea for him to find a way to say or do something. Exactly one week later, the Holy See was considering the idea of potential concordat negotiations with the Reich. Although the central government of the Holy See remained suspicious of Nazism, they concluded that Nazism, as well as Italian fascism, could be "righted" and "domesticated" to ensure the victory of Catholicism. On April 15 of that year - 1933 - negotiations for the concordat were underway, even though on April 1 "the Nazi regime announced the first nationwide boycott targeting Jewish businesses and professionals." A week later, a law restricting employment in the civil service to "Aryans" followed: many Jews were dismissed from their jobs. Almost no one in the hierarchy and members of the German Catholic Church lodged protests against the treatment of Jews. Attention focused on the concordat and the rights of Catholics.[14]

Pacelli was the Vatican Secretary of State under Pius XI. He believed that the Catholic Church could survive and be united in the modern world only by reinforcing papal authority through law enforcement.[15] The cardinal would be the protagonist in the signing of the Reichskonkordat (Concordat between the Holy See and the German Reich).[16] It must be considered that while Hitler, who had recognized in his *Mein Kampf* that a confrontation with the German Catholic Church would be disastrous and that the Church should not interfere with the State, while the Chancellor gave a positive public view of it, privately vowed to completely eradicate Christianity from Germany.[17] He was trying to manipulate the power of the churches to his advantage.[18]

The German Center Party (Catholic) was extremely powerful and so was the Catholic influence in Germany. It waged war against the National Socialist Party and the Catholics who belonged to the party.[19]

However, the Concordat between the Holy See and the German Reich was signed on July 20, 1933, by Cardinal Secretary of State Eugenio Pacelli on behalf of Pope Pius XI and German Vice Chancellor Franz von Papen on behalf of President Paul von Hindenburg and the German government. Hitler was still chancellor of Germany.

Pacelli believed that Germany would not respect the concordat, although not all articles at once; but he knew that the concordat created the legal basis for resistance to the regime and would at least preserve the Church despite persecution.[20]

Nevertheless, we will find many German clergymen supporting the German invasion of Europe in what was World War II.[21]

---

[13] Ibid, pp. 142, 143; citing Audience with Pacelli of March 25, 1933, ASV, A.E.S., Stati Ecclesiastici (quarto periodo), pos. 430a, fasc. 348, f. 15, as cited in Wolf, *Pope and Devil*, 165.

[14] Ibid, p. 143.

[15] John Cornwell, Hitler's Pope: The Secret History of Pius XII (Penguin Books, New York, 2002), p. 85.

[16] Ibid, p. 130

[17] Ibid, pp. 105, 106.

[18] Ibid, p. 106

[19] Ibid, pp. 106-108.

[20] Frank J. Coppa, Editor, Controversial Concordats: The Vatican's Relations with Napoleon, Mussolini, and Hitler (The Catholic University of America Press, Washington, D.C., 1999), pp. 187, 188.

[21] Karlheinz Deschner, God and the Fascists: The Vatican Alliance with Mussolini, Franco, Hitler, and Pavelic (Prometheus Books, New York, 2013), op. cit.

On the role of Pius XII during World War II, David Kertzer has produced the most rigorous analysis to date on the subject. While he has had solid criticisms on some historical aspects, these do not respond to the pope's interest in advancing Catholicism in Germany and the countries of Europe under the aegis of the Holy See, as well as of the governments adhering to the pacts with it.[22]

On March 4, 1939, just two days after Pacelli's election to the papacy, bearing the name Pius XII, he asked the German ambassador, Diego von Bergen, to see him the next day.[23] Through the ambassador, Hitler sent Pope Pius XII a telegram of congratulations. The Italian Catholic press echoed the Führer's message, which was considered a clear sign that he wanted to work with the new pope for the improvement of relations.

Pius XII asked the German ambassador to thank the Führer for his good wishes.

The next day, the pope wrote directly to Hitler, expressing the hope that, as pope, he would be able to restore harmonious relations between Church and State in the German Reich. The pope also instructed the Vatican newspaper *L'Osservatore Romano* to cease all criticism of the German government.

The pope was not very sympathetic to the Jews. The Serbian historian Vladimir Umeljic quotes a letter of Pacelli's from 1919 when he was nuncio in Munich:

"... In the middle of the room was a gang of suspicious-looking young women, Jewish, like all the other Jews here. They behaved provocatively and ambiguously, and the head of this female human scum was Levi's partner. She was a Russian woman, a Russian Jewess, a divorcee, she was responsible for all that.... This Levi is a young woman of about 30 or 35 years old, also Russian or Russian Jewess.... Pale, dirty, with the eyes of a drug addict, with a hoarse, vulgar and repulsive voice.... Her face looks intelligent and insidious at the same time..."[24]

Pius XII did not sympathize with the Jews, as we shall see unless they were converted to Catholicism.

On March 14 of the same year, German forces entered Czechoslovakia and occupied Prague the following day.[25] This occurred while the pope was approaching the Führer to try to relax pressure on the German Catholic Church. Hitler's ambassador to the

[22] David I. Kertzer, The Pope at War: The Secret History of Pius XII, Mussolini, and Hitler (Oxford University Press, Oxford, Reuno Unido. First edition, 2022); Matteo Luigi Napolitano (June 21, 2022), On the already-public negotiations between the Holy See and Germany, Vatican News; John L. Allen Jr. (June 28, 2022), ¿La defensa que hace el Vaticano del Papa Pío XII, es también sobre el Papa Francisco?, Angelus; Matteo Luigi Napolitano (January 8, 2021), Pius XII, the New Vatican Archives, and the "hypologists", The Catholic World Report; The New York Times (August 31, 2020), Archivos desclasificados brindan nuevas pistas sobre el rol del Papa Pío XII ante Adolf Hitler y el el nazismo, Clarín; Avi Holzman (March 30, 2023), David Kertzer, Vatican Historian, speaks about the Pope's role during World War II, Student Life.

[23] David I. Kertzer, The Pope at War: The Secret History of Pius XII, Mussolini, and Hitler (Oxford University Press, Oxford, Reuno Unido. First edition, 2022), op. cit. Note: unless otherwise indicated, it'll be the same source.

[24] Telegraf (April 10, 2020), "Hitlerov papa" koji je ćutao na Holokaust: Šta će spisi iz Vatikana otkriti o Stepincu?, Telegraf.

[25] David I. Kertzer, The Pope at War. The Secret History of Pius XII, Mussolini, and Hitler (Oxford University Press, Oxford, United Kingdom. First edition, 2022), op. cit. Note: unless otherwise indicated, it'll be the same source.

Vatican, alerting Berlin about the pressure Pius XII was facing to protest the invasion, wrote that fortunately "the Pope has declined these requests very firmly. He has given those around him to understand that he sees no reason to interfere in historic processes in which, from the political point of view, the Church is not interested."[26]

Kertzer tells us:

"From the first days of his papacy, Pius XII decided it was best to tread a careful path. He was committed to maintaining the church's mutually beneficial collaboration with Italy's Fascist government and was eager to reach an understanding with Nazi Germany. But at the same time he had to avoid antagonizing the Catholic faithful elsewhere, especially in the United States, on whose financial support the Vatican depended. Above all, his aim was to safeguard the church and thereby protect its God-given mission of saving souls.

At the heart of the pope's strategy was a decision to allow wide latitude to each country's church hierarchy in supporting its nation's rulers and policies, including making war. In this way, the church could enjoy good relations with governments anywhere in the world, regardless of their political nature, as long as they in turn supported the church's institutional interests."

When war broke out in the months that followed, the pope carefully crafted his statements to be seen by both sides as supportive of their cause.

At the time, the United States and Britain were frustrated by the formalization of official ties between the Vatican and Japan (1942), the third Axis country, but the Holy See said there was "insufficient evidence" of Japanese atrocities.[27] British intelligence concluded that the Catholic Church, throughout a dozen Middle Eastern countries, had developed pro-fascist and pro-Axis tendencies, which dominated its spiritual functions.[28]

During World War II, the Wehrmacht, or unified armed forces of Nazi Germany, recruited more than 17,000 Catholic priests and seminarians. Although some served as chaplains in the German army, the vast majority were aides in field hospitals, stretcher-bearers, radio telegraphers, or general infantry; depending on their level of ordination. "They served in all theaters, from Norway to North Africa and from France to the easternmost stretches of the embattled Soviet Union." Their participation in the conflict in German uniform, laden with Nazi insignia, was justified because it was part of their religious vocation of service to others.[29] In fact, a secret appendix to the Reichskonkordat included such positions. It was not reported to the German bishops until early in the war.[30] But it should be noted that their sense of patriotic duty and national sentiment did not lead them to support Nazism. Lauren Faulkner Rossi, comments that "they willfully misunderstood or ignored some of the war's goals, perhaps a necessary precondition of their support." Their deliberate support occurred in June 1941, when Germany invaded Soviet Russia, dramatically escalating the war.

---

[26] Ibid; citing Bergen to Foreign Ministry, Berlin, March 22, 1939, DGFP, series D, vol. 6, n. 65.

[27] Gerald Posner, God's Bankers: A History of Money and Power at the Vatican (Simon & Schuster Paperbacks, New York, 2015), p. 90.

[28] Ibid, pp. 90, 91.

[29] Lauren Faulkner Rossi, Wehrmacht Priests: Catholicism and the Nazi War of Anihilation (Harvard University Press, Cambridge, Massachusetts – London, England, 2015), p. 1.

[30] Ibid, pp. 69, 70.

When the regime resumed its attempts to limit the Church's wartime ministry, even then there was a decree summarily discharging all Jesuits serving in the army.[31] The bishops had sent a formal letter to the pope, declaring that the war was "in a new phase, maybe in its end- stage."[32]

"They quickly issued a pastoral letter urging Catholic Germans, both soldiers on the Eastern Front and civilians back home, to stand firmly against Bolshevism, "of which we German bishops have warned German Catholics, and called them to vigilance in countless pastoral letters, between 1921 and 1936."

Some bishops also saw the invasion of the Soviet Union as an opportunity to protest state- directed harassment of the Church in Germany."[33]

For Pope Pius XII, even before his election, Germany's mission was crucial to defeat communism.[34] But the pope gave a single veiled denunciation of German aggression in his 1939 encyclical, when the army attacked Catholic Poland: without mentioning names and in softened words.[35]

During the conflict, the German church saw it as imperative to protect Jewish converts to Catholicism, although, for the Nazis, Jewish converts were still Jews.[36]

"For every clergyman who openly resisted— the Jesuits Rupert Mayer and Alfred Delp; Bernhard Lichtenberg, provost of Berlin's Catholic cathedral; Cardinal August von Galen, bishop of Münster; Konrad von Preysing, bishop of Berlin— there was a "brown priest," such as Albanus Schachleiter or Philipp Haeuser, who touted Nazi ideology and promoted antisemitism. Most fell between these two poles, choosing to work within the political circumstances without displaying either open fervor or contempt for Nazism."[37]

The German Christian churches supporting Hitler, to a lesser or greater extent, had among the Catholic Church clergymen who openly supported him and those who also resisted him.[38] There were also lay Catholics who resisted the Führer.[39]

---

[31] Ibid, p. 55.

[32] Ibid; citing Salutation of the German bishops to Pius XII, 24 June 1941, in *Akten DB V* (Volk), 455.

[33] Ibid.

[34] Ibid, pp. 14, 15.

[35] Ibid, p. 54.

[36] Ibid, p. 57.

[37] Ibid, p. 7.

[38] Anthony J. Sciolino, The Holocaust, the Church, and the Law of Unintended Consequences: How Christian Anti-Judaism Spawned Nazi Anti-Semitism (iUniverse, Inc., Bloomington, IN, 2014); Robert P. Ericksen, Complicity in the Holocaust: Churches and Universities in Nazi Germany (Cambridge University Press, 2012); Robert P. Ericksen, Susannah Heschel (editors), Betrayal: German Churches and the Holocaust (Augsburg Fortress, Minneapolis, MN, 2nd edition, 1999); Kevin Spicer, Hitler's Priests: Catholic Clergy and National Socialism (Northern Illinois University Press, 2008); Kevin Spicer, Resisting the Third Reich: The Catholic Clergy in Hitler's Berlin (Northern Illinois University Press, 2004).

[39] Peter Bartley, Catholics Confronting Hitler: The Catholic Church and the Nazis (Ignatius Press, San Francisco, 2016).

The relationship between the Papacy and Italian Fascism

The dictator of Fascist Italy, Benito Mussolini, had some good relations with Pius XI and subsequently with his successor, Pope Pius XII. *Il Duce* took them particularly under his premise and with disagreements with the Vatican. But even if the Vatican did not agree with all the policies of Fascist Italy, it exploited the system to its advantage by recovering the Papal States with the Lateran Pacts signed on February 11, 1929.

Like Mussolini, Pope Pius XI was authoritarian. He counted on the clergy, particularly the Jesuit order, led by Włodzimierz Halka Ledóchowski, its general; who would not tolerate accusations against Mussolini and fascism; and was an avid anti-Semite who saw in the Rothschild dynasty a great Jewish conspiracy.[40]

Under the anxiety of the papacy of Pius XI, the Italian Catholic clergy, the Jesuits, and Eugenio Pacelli, Protestants were a constant concern.[41] Harvard historian Kevin J. Madigan tells us, mentioning prelates, one of them a Jesuit:

"Tinti and Tacchi Venturi feared the political motives of the United States, the country from which many of the Protestant missionaries—especially Methodists, Baptists, and Adventists—were being disgorged. In one of his letters Tinti tells Tacchi Venturi an anecdote by way of illustrating the real and present danger of American imperial ambitions."[42]

The worries of Pius XI and Pacelli were calmed when the Italian authorities intervened, especially with the consecrated Adventist missionaries who preached in the Italian villages.[43]

However, the struggles for supremacy between the papacy and the Fascist government were energetic. Although Mussolini greatly favored the Catholic Church in society and government in Italy, he claimed that Fascism was the leading facet of the country, something that greatly annoyed Pius XI, who dreamed of the return of the primacy of Catholic society and politics in Italy.[44]

In June 1929, because of Mussolini's parliamentary speeches, Pius XI was furious; and in a meeting in his library with De Vecchi, the Italian ambassador to the Vatican, he informed him - in the ambassador's words - in "harsh, resentful, often crude and cutting," that "Things can't go on this way," he warned, shaking his head, "they absolutely cannot go on this way"." "Your behavior offends the Church and its head. I went out to meet Italy with an open heart and in payment for your loyalty Signor Mussolini has shot us in the back with a machine gun." David Kertzer documents:

"Riffling through papers on his desk, the pope pulled out reports of recent mistreatment of local Catholic Action chapters. In some areas, officers had been roughed up, and people had been told that good Italians did not join Catholic Action."

---

[40] David I. Kertzer, The Pope and Mussolini: The Secret History of Pius XI and the Rise of Fascism in Europe (Random House, LLC, New York, 2014), op. cit.

[41] Kevin Madigan, The Popes against the Protestants: The Vatican and Evangelical Christianity in Fascist Italy (Yale University Press, 2021), op. cit.

[42] Ibid.

[43] Ibid.

[44] David I. Kertzer, The Pope and Mussolini: The Secret History of Pius XI and the Rise of Fascism in Europe (Random House, LLC, New York, 2014), op. cit. Note: unless otherwise indicated, it'll be the same source.

De Vecchi tried to defend the government, but Pius XI, striking the table with the palm of his hand, said, "I don't want to hear this!" After two and a half hours of meeting, the pope told De Vecchi before leaving: "Tell Signor Mussolini, in my name, not to confuse his friends with his enemies and vice versa, for confusion of that kind would limit the place that he will have in history..... And," added the pope, "tell him that every day, in my prayers, I ask the Lord to bless him."

Both Pius XI and Mussolini traded power to protect themselves. Both the Vatican and Fascist Italy shared conspiracy theories against the Jews. Pius XI saw in Mussolini the man Providence had chosen for that time. Mussolini gave great power to the Italian Catholic Church, ordering crucifixes to be placed on the walls of schools, in every courthouse and hospital. He also subsidized Catholic schools and granted millions of lire for the restoration of churches damaged during the Great War.

The publication of newspaper columns disparaging the pope or the Catholic Church was prohibited.

Both the Vatican newspapers, *L'Osservatore Romano* and *La Civiltà Cattolica*, praised Mussolini and urged Italian Catholics not to rise up in protest against the Fascist government, but to support it.

Nevertheless, Mussolini hated the clergy and thought that his favor to the Church served as a strategic means to gain more power, due to the great influence of Catholicism in Italy. The Jesuit priest Tacchi Venturi was for years an intermediary between the Italian dictator and the pope. About Tacchi Venturi, the pope wrote to *Il Duce* that he was "a good Jesuit and a good fascist." Venturi had once told Mussolini that there was "a plot" against him by the League of Nations, which was - according to him – "dominated by Jews and Freemasons".

In mid-September, at another meeting between Pius XI and the Italian ambassador, the latter told the pope that Mussolini was displeased with his words; and he was sending word to him that he had better keep quiet and settle things through diplomatic channels. But in reply, Pius XI struck the desk with his hand and remarked: "So you don't want me to speak, you don't want me to say that which it is my duty to say?"

The ambassador replied:

"That's not exactly what I mean, Holiness," responded De Vecchi. "I know the person on the other side and my advice is meant only to aid the common good."

The Pope's response:

"For the common good," Pius repeated. "Let me tell you how I will proceed from now on to satisfy you on certain occasions. I will open this window"—here the pope, his voice rising, pointed with his finger to the window behind his desk—"and I will shout so that everyone in Saint Peter's Square can hear me!"

De Vecchi was momentarily speechless. "That's what I will do," the pope repeated, "whether you like it or not, Mr. Ambassador!"

In another meeting between the two in the fall (November 15, 1929), the pope was more furious and again complained against the treatment Catholic Action was receiving; and he repeatedly pounded his fist on his desk. The Pope said: "Rome is mine"; to which De Vecchi replied: "Rome, is the capital of Italy, home of His Majesty the king and the government."

"Rome," replied the pontiff, "is my diocese."

"Certainly," agreed the ambassador, "in matters of religion—"

"Yes," the pope interrupted, "all the rest is just a matter of keeping the streets clean."

Now, despite the assaults, attacks, and deaths perpetrated by the Fascist authorities against critics of the government, the Vatican went ahead in its support of fascism. Pius XI would say of Mussolini that the protection of Jesus Christ was with him.

In 1934, faced with the threat of military hostilities between Italy and Ethiopia, the Pope was concerned about the possibility of Mussolini's invasion of the African country. However, other sectors of the Catholic Church differed. For example, Italy's most influential Catholic newspaper, L'Avvenire d'Italia of Bologna, echoing the Fascist press, said that the Ethiopians were pagan barbarians and that war would bring civilization and Christianity to the savages.

Subsequently, Pius XI and the Vatican Secretary of State, Cardinal Eugenio Pacelli, and others, justified the invasion of Ethiopia on the grounds that Italy had the right to claim by virtue of agreements. Or, in other words, a simple Mandate over the peripheral regions of the Ethiopian Empire. Therefore, according to Pacelli in a letter to King George V of Great Britain, Mussolini's demands were reasonable.

Even with the good relations between the Vatican and Ethiopia, the Italian clergy misrepresented the situation of that nation, demeaning without restraint the emperor, his government, and the Ethiopian Orthodox Church. They demonized Ethiopian citizens, giving the invasion a false moral purpose.[45] No wonder, since at the beginning of 1935, the Italian clergy considered the campaign against Ethiopia as a Catholic crusade.

Although the clergy of other countries asked Pope Pius XI to condemn the Italian attempts at aggression against Ethiopia, he remained silent. However, the overwhelming majority of the Italian clergy (who supported Il Duce) invoked the support of Italian Catholics for the aggression. On July 13 of that year, the Parisian newspaper Le National reported that Pius XI ordered "that the Palatine Guards must fulfill, at the present moment, all their military obligations." The following day, Le Temps confirmed the information and added: "The Pope is pleased with the Italian action in Africa, for the success of the Italian army would assure to the Catholic Missions in Ethiopia supremacy over the Coptic [sic] Clergy."[46] Furthermore, Pius XI made a statement referring to the Ethiopians at the time of the Italian Lazarist Jacobis as "recently converted Catholics, heretics, Muslims and pagans."[47]

Referring to the principal financial advisor to the Holy See concerning the military conflict:

"[…] it is well attested that Pius XI, to whom Nogara reported regularly, permitted the Vatican banker to acquire substantial holdings in Italy's major arms and

---

[45] Ian Campbell, Holy War: The Untold Story of Catholic Italy's Crusade Against the Ethiopian Orthodox Church (C. Hurst & Co., Londres, 2021), op. cit.

[46] Ibid.

[47] Ibid; citando a GIOVAGNOLI, A., 2008, pp. 243–4, citando Discorsi di Pio XI, D. Berletto, Città de Vaticano, Libreria Editrice Vaticana, 1985, vol. III, pp. 361–2.

munitions factories. According to one published source, Nogara acquired 'a munitions plant that supplied arms for the Italian army's invasion of Ethiopia'."[48]

However, the pope seemed to be reeling, since after declaring in August that this would be an unjust invasion, which reached the ears of the then-Italian ambassador to the Vatican, Giuseppe Talamo, the pope's text to be published was changed in sections sensitive to the Italian government.[49]

But the following month, on September 13, Pacelli informed *Il Duce* in writing that the pope would not stand in the way of the invasion.[50]

"And to reinforce the message that the soldiers were doing God's work, yet another media campaign was launched, in which picture postcards were produced in their thousands, showing Christ or the Virgin Mary hovering over the troops to guide them into Ethiopia, which was now being projected as some sort of Promised Land."[51]

However given the comparatively favorable environment of the Ethiopian Catholic Church, and that the invasion would jeopardize the work of the Catholic clergy in that country, Pius XI belatedly tried to dissuade Mussolini on the grounds that it could be detrimental to him and Italy.[52]

One day before the invasion, on October 2, 1935, cardinals, archbishops, and bishops as standard bearers supported by abundant Italian government and Catholic propaganda and by the ringing of church bells throughout the country, celebrated that the Italians announced the invasion.[53]

On October 3, 1935, with Catholic priests blessing the Italian troops, 110,000 soldiers began hostilities. The Ethiopian troops were defeated; thousands of their citizens were massacred (1935-1936).[54]

The celebration of the Italian Catholic Church and the Fascist state was immense.

The following year, Mussolini announced in December 1937 Italy's withdrawal from the League of Nations.[55]

On January 9, 1938, two thousand priests and 60 bishops marched in solemn procession through the streets of Rome, preceded by carabinieri and a military band, to

---

[48] Ibid; citing LO BELLO, N., 1969, p. 72.

[49] David I. Kertzer, The Pope and Mussolini: The Secret History of Pius XI and the Rise of Fascism in Europe (Random House, LLC, New York, 2014), op. cit. Note: unless otherwise indicated, it'll be the same source.

[50] Ian Campbell, Holy War: The Untold Story of Catholic Italy's Crusade Against the Ethiopian Orthodox Church (C. Hurst & Co., Londres, 2021), op. cit.; citing Pacelli to Mussolini, 14 Sept. 1935, ASMAE, AISS, *busta* 56, *fasc* 1, sf 1c, cited in KERTZER, D.I., 2014, p. 218. Kertzer notes that according to an informant (ACS, DAGR, *busta* 1320, *informatore* n. 52, Roma, 12 Sept. 1935), the pope sent his envoy Tacchi Venturi on a secret mission to England to lobby local Catholics to support the invasion, but that no evidence has yet come to light to suggest that the trip actually took place. KERTZER, D.I., 2014, p. 456.

[51] Ibid.

[52] Ibid.

[53] Ibid.

[54] David I. Kertzer, The Pope and Mussolini: The Secret History of Pius XI and the Rise of Fascism in Europe (Random House, LLC, New York, 2014), op. cit.; Ian Campbell, Holy War: The Untold Story of Catholic Italy's Crusade Against the Ethiopian Orthodox Church (C. Hurst & Co., Londres, 2021), op. cit.

[55] David I. Kertzer, The Pope and Mussolini: The Secret History of Pius XI and the Rise of Fascism in Europe (Random House, LLC, New York, 2014), op. cit. Note: unless otherwise indicated, it'll be the same source.

lay laurels on the tombs of the heroes of the Fascist Revolution of the so-called Battle of the Wheat. The *blessing of God* was invoked by the Archbishop of Udine, Monsignor Giuseppe Nogara at the Palazzo Venezia.

For that event, which also honored Mussolini, Cardinal Raffaele Rossi, secretary of the Curia office responsible for matters affecting the clergy, had sought advice from Vatican Secretary of State Pacelli about bishops seeking advice on attending the event. Pacelli informed him that he saw no objection to clerics participating in the event. But before receiving Pacelli's letter, Cardinal Rossi sent a consultation from another bishop, who felt that the invitations should not be accepted.

David I. Kertzer reports:

"The cardinal had put Pacelli in an awkward position, for allowing a journalist to convene Italy's bishops was undeniably unseemly. Pacelli consulted the pope, who agreed that such an invitation "did not merit being accepted." Yet neither the pope nor Pacelli was eager to offend the Duce."

With Pope Pius XI dead and Pacelli elected to the papacy under the name of Pius XII, Mussolini summoned the Jesuit priest Tacchi Venturi to continue to act as an intermediary between him and the pope.[56] Mussolini's requests to Pius XII were: to help in dealing with Spain, for as Spanish dictator Francisco Franco successfully concluded his war to overthrow the leftist Spanish government, the nation's Catholic clergy needed to offer him their unwavering support. Likewise, the Duce had a request for Croatia; for Mussolini feared that Hitler had that country in mind among his plans. It was therefore important for the pope to make it clear to the Croatian Catholic clergy that his sympathies were with Italy. The third request was for the Latin American Catholic clergy to combat American influence in Latin America and to urge their governments to strengthen ties with Fascist Italy since the American nation was trying to weaken the "Latin Catholic mentality" by "Protestant penetration."

Subsequently, Tacchi Venturi informed Mussolini that Pius XII was unhappy that the anti-Semitic racial laws enacted in the previous months were being used against Jewish converts to Catholicism. The pope wanted "to see that all the descendants of mixed marriages, baptized in infancy, and brought up as Christians, be recognized as Aryans." Mussolini said he would take care of the matter.

Pius XII and Franco's Spain

Wishing to begin his relations with the Italian dictator positively, Pius XII acted swiftly on Mussolini's requests. For example, he sent a personal telegram to General Francisco Franco to grant him his blessing and express his gratitude to God for "the victory of Catholic Spain." Franco responded with satisfaction to Pius XII's message, praising what he called "the complete victory achieved by our arms in the heroic crusade against the enemies of Religion, of the Fatherland and of Christian civilization."

But let's go further back in time. Franco relentlessly persecuted Freemasons, Jews, communists, anarchists, and trade unionists. And he committed genocide through the

---

[56] David I. Kertzer, The Pope at War: The Secret History of Pius XII, Mussolini, and Hitler (Oxford University Press, Oxford, Reuno Unido. Primera edición, 2022), op. cit. Note: unless otherwise indicated, it'll be the same source.

use of torture, with 296 concentration camps and mass graves.[57] Almost a million Spanish people passed through the concentration camps, among them dead and exiled.[58]

The general, who was deeply Catholic and wanted to rescue the Spanish Catholic culture, had said on July 20, 1936, in an order sent to his generals: "You will organize concentration camps with the disturbing elements, which you will employ in public works, separated from the population."[59]

He also pointed out: "In a civil war, a systematic occupation of territory, accompanied by a necessary cleansing, is preferable to a rapid defeat of enemy armies that leaves the country infested with adversaries."

Questioned by journalist Jay Allen:

"[Franco] There will be no compromise or truce, I will continue to prepare my march towards Madrid. I will advance! I will take the capital. I will save Spain from Marxism, whatever the cost.

"[Allen] Does that mean you will have to kill half of Spain?

"[Franco] I repeat, whatever it takes."

Some of the words of his generals, such as Emilio Mola, were: "It is necessary to propagate an atmosphere of terror. We have to create an impression of domination... Anyone who is an open or secret defender of the Popular Front must be shot." He subsequently stated: "Dialogue? Never! This war has to end with the extermination of the enemies of Spain [...]. I want to defeat them to impose my will on them, which is yours, and to annihilate them."

General Juan Yagüe said: "Whoever resists, you know what you have to do: to jail or to the wall, it doesn't matter (laughter and applause). We have proposed to redeem you and we will redeem you, whether you want it or not. We do not need you for anything; elections, there will never be again, why do we want your votes? First, we are going to redeem those on the other side; we are going to impose our civilization on them since they don't want it by hook or by crook..."

The words of General Gonzalo Queipo de Llano: "I repeat that the words pardon and amnesty will be erased from the dictionary. These people will be pursued like wild beasts until they all disappear [...]"

"José María Pemán Pemartín, intellectual and propagandist of the rebels: "Spanish! Cleanse this land of the hordes that have no Homeland and no God".

The tremendously cruel Franco regime, with all its atrocities, would also be defined by the heartless theft of children from women's prisons.[60]

---

[57] Carlos Hernández de Miguel, Los campos de concentración de Franco: Sometimiento, torturas y muerte tras las alambradas (Penguin Random House Grupo Editorial, 2019).

[58] Juan Miguel Baquero, El país de la desmemoria: Del genocidio franquista al silencio interminable (Roca Editorial, 2019).

[59] Carlos Hernández de Miguel, Los campos de concentración de Franco: Sometimiento, torturas y muerte tras las alambradas (Penguin Random House Grupo Editorial, 2019). Note: unless otherwise indicated, it'll be the same source.

[60] Javier Rodrigo, Hasta la raíz: violencia durante la Guerra Civil y la dictadura franquista (Alianza Editorial, 2008), p. 27.

Now, on the role of the Catholic Church itself, two months after the outbreak of the Civil War, the bishop of Salamanca declared that the military rebellion was a crusade.[61] In fact, in the summer of 1937, the Vatican recognized Franco's government, later sending a nuncio to the nation.

For his part, Isidro Gomá, Cardinal Primate of Spain during the Civil War, explained: "It is indeed convenient for the war to end. But it should not end with a compromise, a settlement, or a reconciliation. Hostilities must be taken to the extreme of achieving victory at the point of the sword. Let the Reds surrender, since they have been defeated. No pacification other than that of arms is possible. To organize peace within a Christian constitution, it is indispensable to extirpate all the rottenness of secular legislation." This cardinal and Franco's intentions were supported by Pacelli years before he became pope: when he was Vatican Secretary of State.

On May 10, 1937, Franco had told Cardinal Gomá that given that all the bishops were on his side, to publish "a letter that, addressed to the episcopate of the whole world, with the request that it be reproduced in the Catholic press, could put the truth in its proper place." The Collective Letter of the Spanish episcopate supporting the military rebellion after a year of war was dated July 1, 1937. Gomá communicated Franco's request to Eugenio Pacelli. The Secretary of State responded in a letter on July 31, noting that "With the keenest interest I have seen the aforementioned Collective Letter, appreciating the noble sentiments that have inspired it." But he wrote that he preferred that it not be published, because the unanimity of the whole episcopate was desirable, since two bishops did not want to sign it.[62] Moreover, it was desirable that the Letter be written in less energetic tones.

The letter was made with the conditions requested by the Vatican Secretary of State. Thus, on March 8, 1938, Pacelli sent Gomá a letter praising the Spanish document, according to Pacelli's own words, "for the noble sentiments in which it is inspired, as well as the high sense of justice of these Excellency Bishops in absolutely condemning evil, from whatever quarter it may come."[63] But, as the well-known journalist Peter Eisner wrote:

"[...] the pope turned down Pacelli's requests that the Vatican be more supportive of Generalissimo Francisco Franco in Spain. Pacelli saw Spain as a clear confrontation between good—the Nazi and Fascist-backed Nationalists—and bad—the Soviet-supported Spanish government. Pius did not see the dispute in such stark terms—he never accepted or trusted Franco and questioned Franco's ties to the Nazis."[64]

The support of the Spanish Catholic Church for Franco's dictatorship was overwhelming.[65]

---

[61] Carlos Hernández de Miguel, Los campos de concentración de Franco: Sometimiento, torturas y muerte tras las alambradas (Penguin Random House Grupo Editorial, 2019). Note: unless otherwise indicated, it'll be the same source.

[62] Hilari Raguer (July 2, 2017), La carta de los obispos españoles que incomodó al Vaticano, El País.

[63] Ibid.

[64] Peter Eisner, The Pope's Last Crusade: How an American Jesuit Helped Pope Pius XI's Campaign to Stop Hitler (HaperCollins, Nashville, Tennessee, United States, 2013), op. cit.

[65] Xosé Chao Rego, Iglesia y franquismo: 40 años de nacional-catolicismo (1936-1976) (tresCtres Editores, Galicia, Spain, 1st edition, 2007).

The Spanish Jesuits, supported by the general of their Society, Włodzimierz Ledóchowski, supported Franco's regime and sought a single Spain. The Jesuits became under Franco a "corporate symbol of the intended national and Catholic revolution."[66]

"In May 1938, in the midst of the war, Franco repealed the 1932 decree, returned to the Society [of Jesus] all the properties seized by the Republic and part of the patrimony seized by Carlos III in 1772. As a sign of gratitude, the then-general of the Society, Father Ledochowski, added the name of the Generalissimo to those of the founders and great benefactors of the Society, and later, in 1943, Father Magni, Vicar General, sent the Generalissimo a document in which the Society thanked him for the immense benefit of the return of all the goods that the revolution had taken from it. In this document - known as the "Letter of Brotherhood" - he was informed that he was to be "a participant in all the Masses, prayers, penances and works of zeal that by the grace of God are and will be done in our provinces of Spain"."[67]

On May 20, 1939, with the announcement of church bells, the Victory of Madrid parade was held, which was a military exhibition organized by Franco's general government to celebrate the triumph obtained in the recently ended Spanish civil war.[68]

"Franco had given the Church the monopoly of education and an extraordinary power in the control and censorship of spectacles, books, and customs. Franco's first act after the Victory parade in 1939 was to preside over a solemn tedeum in the church of Santa Barbara in Madrid: Franco and Cardinal Gomá, primate of the Spanish Church, consecrated Spain to the Catholic cause."[69]

Pope Eugenio Pacelli, already Pius XII, acted with concern in supporting Franco's dictatorship. Even years after the end of World War II. On August 27, 1953, the concordat between Spain and the Holy See was signed.[70] In this way, the adhesion of the Spanish people to the chair of St. Peter was shown.[71]

But Pius XII also granted the Spanish dictator the highest decoration and honor bestowed by the Holy See: the Supreme Equestrian Order of the Militia of Our Lord Jesus Christ (Order of Christ).[72] With it, Franco was rewarded for his most important services to the Church.[73] The text, dated December 21, 1953, read in part:

---

[66] Charles E. O'Neill, S.I., Joaquín M.a Domínguez, S.I., Diccionario histórico de la Compañía de Jesús: Infante de Santiago-Piatkiewicz (Institutum Historicum, S.I., Roma, Universidad Pontificia Comillas, Madrid, 2001), p. 1290.

[67] Luis Felipe Utrera-Molina Gómez (June 11, 2018), Compañía de Jesús y Memoria histórica, ABC Opinión.

[68] Juan Pablo Fusi, Franco: Autoritarismo y poder personal (Taurus, 2011), op. cit.

[69] Ibid.

[70] Xosé Chao Rego, Iglesia y franquismo: 40 años de nacional-catolicismo (1936-1976) (tresCtres Editores, Galicia, España, 1st edition, 2007), pp. 161, 162.

[71] Rafael Rabasco Ferreira, La representación pontificia en la Corte española: Historia de una ceremonia y diplomacia (Editorial Sanz y Torres S.L., 2017), p. 240.

[72] Ibid; citing LA VANGUARDIA ESPAÑOLA, El Nuncio de Su Santidad el Papa presentó las credenciales a su Excelencia el Jefe del Estado, wednesday, December 23, 1953.

[73] Ibid.

"Pope Pius XII to our beloved son Francisco Franco Bahamonde, Head of the Spanish State. Greetings and apostolic blessing.

We remember with how much solemnity and attendance of the faithful the International Eucharistic Congress was celebrated last year in Barcelona, to which we know that the civil authorities lent enthusiasm and collaboration.

Moreover, on the occasion of the recent Concordat celebrated between this Apostolic See and the Spanish nation, we have congratulated ourselves for the happy conclusion of the same and for your adhesion to the Chair of St. Peter, which was very evident in the elaboration of such an important agreement. In this way, the necessary relations that always existed between the Roman Pontiffs and the Spanish Nation have been shaped for common fruit and usefulness.

We know that this is also your feeling and that of the Catholic Spanish people, through the informal letters which you have sent us, and for which we thank you most expressly.

For these and other reasons, wishing to give you a sign of our benevolence, by these our Letters we elect, constitute, and name you Knight of the Militia of Jesus Christ and we admit you to our Supreme Order of the aforementioned knights."[74]

The ceremony was held on Friday, February 26, 1954, in the chapel of the Palacio de Oriente.[75] The distinction was presented to Franco by the newly appointed nuncio of the Holy See in Spain, Monsignor Ildebrando Antoniutti.[76]

But the Second Vatican Council, convoked by Pius XII's successor, Pope John XXIII, and concluded by Paul VI in December 1965, irritated Franco. The results of the Council pushed most of the Spanish bishops to move away from their twinning with the Franco dictatorship, where some held representative positions. The Council contributed to the collapse of National Catholicism, considering the Roman Church as a "perfect society" and the only religion of the State.[77]

Nazism and the Ukrainian Catholic Army

The Nazis coveted the support of the Vatican in September 1942 to subdue the Soviet-dominated Ukraine. Pius XII, although reluctant to this appeal because it meant more pressure to make concessions to the German army, which had already murdered many Ukrainian Greek Catholic priests, finally accepted some concessions despite a protest that the Holy See itself sent to the Ukrainian prelates.[78] Almost 800,000 Ukrainian Jews were murdered and their executioners needed new destinies. The Ukrainian unit was called the "Galician Police Division" before it was formally accepted by the SS.[79]

It was Gustav Otto Wächter, the Nazi governor of Galicia, who directed the massacre against the Jews.[80] German supply lines were then threatened by Soviet partisan

---

[74] Xosé Chao Rego, Iglesia y franquismo: 40 años de nacional-catolicismo (1936-1976) (tresCtres Editores, Galicia, España, 1st edition, 2007), p. 166.

[75] Rafael Rabasco Ferreira, La representación pontificia en la Corte española: Historia de una ceremonia y diplomacia (Editorial Sanz y Torres S.L., 2017), p. 241.

[76] Danilo Albin (August 26, 2018), El Vaticano nunca retiró la condecoración que entregó a Franco por sus "servicios" a la Iglesia, Público.

[77] Juan G. Bedoya (December 7, 2005), El concilio que irritó a Franco, El País.

[78] Mark Aarons y John Loftus, Unholy Trinity: The Vatican, The Nazis, and The Swiss Banks (St. Martin's Griffin, New York, 1998), pp. 173-180.

[79] Ibid, p. 180.

[80] Ibid.

resistance. Wächter, therefore, recognized that he had to win the sympathies of the civilian population that helped the partisans, so his centerpiece was the five million Catholic Uniates, three and a half million of whom were concentrated precisely in the region of Galicia.

Archbishop Andrey Szepticky, their religious leader, prepared the way by blessing the SS Galicia Division; whereby the Ukraine now had its fighting force with Uniate Catholic chaplains, in what soon became a Catholic army on a crusade against the "Godless Bolsheviks." Bishop Bučko rejoiced at the preservation of anti-Russian nationalism; and the seeds of cooperation sown by the Lavitrano Catholic Mission, were paying off when only three months after he concluded his work, "the Vatican floated a story in the *New York Herald Tribune* and the *Washington Post* about Pius XII's post-war hopes for Europe." Pius XII favored an anti-Communist Central European Confederation of Catholic states stretching "from the Baltic to the Black Seas." This was Pius XI's dream Catholic Intermarium being realized by his successor.[81] The U.S. War Department did not look favorably on dreams of Catholic supremacy in the region, arguing for the freedom of the peoples to govern themselves democratically.[82]

In 1942, the Congregatio pro Ecclesia Orientali, charged with sending trained Jesuits to the Soviet Union with the mission of reuniting the Russian Orthodox Church and the Catholic Church as soon as possible, was led by its secretary, Cardinal Tisserant.[83] The Congregation was actively preparing a missionary network of Uniates. Jesuit priests were sent in disguise to Soviet territory to provide intelligence reports on the prospects of religious reunification.[84]

However, the Vatican's dream was severely discontinued when the SS Galicia was virtually destroyed at the Battle of Brody in 1944.[85] Subsequent attempts through Stepan Bandera and others even after the war, were to no avail.[86]

Ante Pavelić, the Croatian Catholic Church and the Independent State of Croatia
The family of the future dictator of Croatia, Ante Pavelić, was devoutly Catholic. His uncle Milan was a Jesuit, and would later become beloved by the so-called ustasha assassins – more about them latter - thanks to his poem "Pod Okom Božjim" (Under the Eye of God).[87]

It was at the Episcopal school in Travnik, where Pavelić received his first formal education, and where a delegation of the Society of Jesus arrived to run the minor and major seminary in Travnik with the institute of theology and philosophy in Sarajevo. One of the seminary's first prominent students, was Ivan Šarić, future vicar apostolic of Bosnia and a staunch advocate of ustasha doctrine. He was followed by Pavelić, and years later, by Krunoslav Draganović, who would become a priest, Šarić's secretary,

---

[81] Ibid, p. 181.
[82] Ibid, pp. 181, 182.
[83] Ibid, pp. 182, 183.
[84] Ibid, p. 183.
[85] Ibid, p. 186.
[86] Ibid, pp. 186-207.
[87] Pino Adriano y Giorgio Cingolani, Nationalism and Terror: Ante Pavelić and Ustasha Terrorism from Fascism to the Cold War (Central European University Press (CEU Press), Budapest-New York, 2018), pp. 5, 6.

and after World War II the organizer of the Vatican escape routes that were used by ustasha and Nazi war criminals to reach the southern seas.

These three Croats, originally from Bosnia-Herzegovina, would place the Ustaše cause at the center of their lives.[88] Both Pavelić and Draganović would fight for what they considered the return of the vanished Croatia, which for them was founded on Catholicism by history.[89]

Bosnia was influenced by Franciscan priests in the 14th century, being sent from Rome as inquisitors to extirpate the so-called heresy from the Bosnian church. The Franciscans were accused of performing forced conversions to Catholicism, and those who refused lost their possessions and were forced to be banished or die.[90]

In the 19th century, the ultranationalist and overtly clerical Croatian Party of Rights, founded by Ante Starčević and Eugen Kvaternik around 1860, held the primacy of the Croatian race over all Balkan peoples and the existence of "an "eternal and natural Croat right" to absolute state sovereignty."[91] They also believed that:

"Serbs, dubbed "Slavoserbs" by Starčević, were doubly slaves, for their name came from the Latin words *sclavus* and *servus*. Slavoserbs were a corrupt, greedy, deceitful, and dishonest people, for whom there was no remedy other than the use of the stick. 20 Jews were "a race lacking, with few exceptions, all morals and a homeland. To allow Jews to take part in public life is like throwing mud into a glass of pure water— it makes all the water murky."[92]

After his studies in Travnik, Pavelić went to Zagreb to continue his education at Franz Joseph University and joined the student association of the Croatian Party of Rights; whose leadership he soon assumed.[93]

For its part, the Serbian Orthodox Church formed the undisputed majority in the Balkan region, followed by the Catholic Church. Although the state offered everyone freedom of religion and respected all religious communities, it especially favored the Serbian Orthodox Church as the religion of the king.[94]

The rights of the Catholic Church would be the subject of an agreement with the Holy See, beginning in 1920, but which stalled without the government of Belgrade being forced to do so. This, was because the Ministry of Religion was in the hands of the Orthodox, so the Catholic episcopate had to submit to the decisions of the central power.[95]

Regarding all those aspects mentioned about the belief in "the primacy of the Croatian race" over the other Balkan peoples,[96] and the contempt towards Serbs and the competition against the Serbian Orthodox Church, would be the central background of the atrocities that would be committed in Ante Pavelić's Croatia from 1941-1945.

---

[88] Ibid, p. 6.
[89] Ibid, pp. 6, 7.
[90] Ibid, p. 9.
[91] Ibid, p.12.
[92] Ibid, p. 13.
[93] Ibid, pp. 13, 14.
[94] Ibid, p. 30.
[95] Ibid.
[96] Ibid, p. 12.

The city of Zagreb, the capital of Croatia, was a thriving center with a strong Catholic press, particularly thanks to the Jesuits and the Franciscans. But it was also home to several Catholic associations. The special favor for the Orthodox Church, however, led to prejudice and undermined the Catholic Church in various ways.[97]

"In December 1925, Monsignor Bauer, the archbishop of Zagreb and primate of Croatia, went to Belgrade with a delegation of high ecclesiastics to present King Alexander and the government with a memorandum on "all matters concerning religious persecution, education, stipends, the agrarian question, and so forth." The king and government did not receive the representatives of the Catholic episcopate. Once back in Zagreb, the latter denounced the central authority's deafness by issuing a document that was broadly circulated by the Catholic press."[98]

Various Italian interests that were at stake in the Balkan region began to take shape with the cooperation of Pavelić and Mussolini, who established contact from 1925 onwards and with the interest of creating an independent Croatia.[99]

When the Serbian empire learned of the attempts to disintegrate it because of the desire to establish an independent Croatia, in early 1930, in what was labeled as a year of dictatorship, "the Catholic hierarchy and masses of devout Croats were very worried," since Belgrade was passing laws restricting Catholic associations; and a law allowing lay people to teach religion classes, something that had previously been the prerogative of priests.[100]

Antun Bauer, former Primate of Croatia and Archbishop of Zagreb, protested vigorously, pointing out that Pius XI's encyclical issued in December 1929, affirmed the primacy of the Catholic Church in the education of youth. The Serbian minister of religion asked Monsignor Bauer in Belgrade to make a public declaration of loyalty to the Karađorđević dynasty and the Belgrade regime. But Bauer refused and reaffirmed his loyalty to the pope. Back in Zagreb, Bauer secretly informed "one of the heads of the Croatian opposition" [led by Pavelić] that the clergy was "united" in endorsing him, with the sole exception of the bishop of Djakovo, Monsignor Akšamović, who had yet to speak either for or against him." The Vatican secretly externalized that it was fully on the side of the clergy, but to avoid the possibility of not reaching an agreement soon with Yugoslavia, it kept the strictest silence.[101] However, La Civiltà Cattolica, which is the newspaper of the Jesuits in the Vatican, openly and vigorously criticized the persecution against Catholicism in the Kingdom of Yugoslavia, causing Belgrade to mitigate some of the measures. It was then that a powerful Catholic movement emerged in Zagreb with several Catholic organizations to defend its position.[102]

In 1930, the Ustaša, or Ustasha organization was born; chaired by the poglavnik (leader or commander), Ante Pavelić and seeking Croatian independence.[103] It reads:

---

[97] Ibid, p. 32.
[98] Ibid.
[99] Ibid, pp. 34-38.
[100] Ibid, pp. 65, 66.
[101] Ibid, p. 66.
[102] Ibid, p. 67.
[103] Ibid, p. 70.

"Anti-Serbian sentiments were well summarized by Pavelić's maxim: "A head for a tooth, ten heads for one." The sacredness of the struggle was set in stone in the Ustasha motto "Bog i Hrvati" (God and the Croats)."[104]

In Croatia, Alojzije Stepinac, Archbishop of Zagreb and Primate of the Croatian Catholic Church since 1937, was preparing the atmosphere. Before speaking of Stepinac's role, we will refer to his letter to the Ban (title of local rulers) of Croatia, then Ivan Šubašić. Stepinac intervened against "left-leaning persons" in public office and complained about a citizen who was a Jew and a communist.

He saw it as his duty to help denounce those on the left to the authorities so that they could intervene:

"I think it is my duty to inform you about the matter of Mr. Jove Magovac, who has been removed from the post of commissioner in Koprivnica. Yesterday he was at my house and complained bitterly that he was neither morally nor materially, neither guilty nor obliged to suffer. Morally, because the will of the people, who are completely left-wing, as he and a large part of the population think, is eliminated."[105]

Also, the archbishop denounced a Jewish citizen who replaced Magovac, stating: "And he was replaced by the Jew Hiršl, responsible for disciplinary reasons for communism..."[106] Likewise:

"I am free to attach an excerpt from a letter from an excellent HSS official from those parts, so you can see how 95% of the population de facto thinks.
[...]
One thing is certain, and that is that the communists have firmly raised their heads and think that the time has come, that both the Croatian Banovina and all civilian orders be stabbed in the back [...].
I ask Mr. Bane to consider this only as confidential private information."[107]

But in the autumn of 1939, Stepinac gave the following instruction to the priests of Croatia:

"If followers of the Jewish and Serbian Orthodox religions who are in danger of death come to you and ask you to convert to the Catholic faith, hospitably welcome them in order to save their lives. Then do not ask them to follow the Catholic doctrine first. For the Serbian Orthodox are already Christians like us and the Jewish religion is the religion from which Catholicism arose. The mission that Christians must fulfill and the role they must play is first and foremost to save people. When these times of madness and barbarism pass, those who have converted out of conviction will remain

---

[104] Ibid.
[105] Stepinac, Alojzije, Arzobispo de Zagreb. Letter to Ivan Šubašić, Ban de Croacia. November 11, 1939. Publicly provided by Domagoj Margetić and Danko Vasović, of the old state archives.
[106] Ibid.
[107] Ibid.

in the Catholic Church, while the others - when the danger has passed - will return to their religion."[108]

But the contradictions would be patent during those fatal years, as will be seen later.

For his part, Pavelić began to have a favorable environment for his plans in Croatia through the Catholic Church.

The Serbian government began hostilities against the ustasha movement and sought Ante Pavelić to eliminate him.[109]

Under the pseudonym A. S. Mrzlodovski, Pavelić published in July 1938 the pamphlet *Errors and Horrors: Communism and Bolshevism in Russia and in the World*, whose most cited sources came from hundreds of pages of the Jesuit magazine *La Civiltà Cattolica*; as well as from the newspaper *Lettres de Rome*, edited by the Jesuit priest Joseph Ledit.[110] The only hope, according to Pavelić, rested in fascism and Nazism.[111]

Due to the already growing tensions, Belgrade tried to make peace with Zagreb but without success.[112] Apparently, Pavelić used foreign Yugoslav ecclesiastics sympathetic to the separatist movement, particularly Franciscan priests.[113] Pavelić, who had been in Borgo Ognissanti 32, in the Franciscan convent with Ghirlandaio's The Last Supper visiting a friar, was receiving special help from Franciscans in Italy.[114] Adriano and G. Cingolani:

"From within the Florentine convent, a center of Franciscan missions, Justin Medić continued to scheme for the return to "Sacred Croatia." "Franciscans not only spread Ustasha ideals from churches to numerous villages," Zagreb's newspaper Hrvatski Narod wrote in 1941, they also allowed Croatian fighters to meet with Ustasha leaders in monasteries "during the toughest period of the struggle." To avoid giving friars all the credit, the reverend Dragutin Kamber, a collaborator of Archbishop Šarić, would later boast: "For the most part, we Croatian Catholic priests were among those who prepared the advent of independent Croatia."[115]

José Manuel de Castells Tejón wrote that "Pius XII always showed a very special predilection for the Ustashis, whom he had already described in 1939 as "outposts of Christianity" and" he would receive "on several occasions their delegations and their leader (whom he congratulated), covering them with honors."[116]

---

[108] Dr. Hans Jansen, Pius XII: Chronologie van een onophoudelijk protest (Kampen: Editorial Kok, 2003), p. 88.

[109] Pino Adriano and Giorgio Cingolani, Nationalism and Terror: Ante Pavelić and Ustasha Terrorism from Fascism to the Cold War (Central European University Press (CEU Press), Budapest-New York, 2018), pp. 71-73.

[110] Ibid, p. 151.

[111] Ibid, pp. 151, 152.

[112] Ibid, p. 152 et seq.

[113] Ibid, pp. 155-157.

[114] Ibid, p. 157.

[115] Ibid; citing Laurière, *Assassins au nom de Dieu*, 80.

[116] Juan Manuel de Castells Tejón, Tan lejos de Dios: Delitos y falsedades de la iglesia que Francisco quiere reformar (Intermedio Editores S.A.S, 2014), ob. cit.

In the summer of 1940, the threat of the German offensive to the west seemed imminent, as did the inevitability of Italy's joining Germany in the military conflict.[117]

In an attempt to curb Mussolini's aggressive attempts, Pius XII, through *L'Osservatore Romano*, congratulated Mussolini at every opportunity for his peace initiatives; which irritated him. In the last week of 1940, the Italian dictator said in a mocking tone that the Vatican was the "chronic appendicitis of Italy."[118] Thus, in the first week of May, the Fascists beat street vendors offering *L'Osservatore Romano*, taking away copies which they publicly burned. The Pope became the target of Fascist fury, and, on May 3, he received information from Josef Müller, the German agent who served as Oster's courier in the conspiracy to depose Hitler, that Germany would attack Holland and Belgium. The Vatican Secretariat of State alerted the nuncios of both nations, but agents intercepted the messages and Mussolini was given notice of the pope's private warnings. In Berlin, this information became known; which ended up displeasing Italy and Germany.[119]

Then Paris and London pressured Pius XII to condemn the May 10, 1940, invasion of Holland, Belgium, and Luxembourg and to do everything possible to prevent Italy's entry into the conflict. The Vatican Secretary of State, Domenico Tardini, drafted a papal statement condemning the invasion, but Pius XII ruled out such a speech because it might infuriate the Germans. So he sent telegrams to the sovereigns of the three invaded countries, expressing sympathy and affection for the suffering. But London and Paris regretted that the pope did not make a direct denunciation of the aggression. When the text of the messages was published in *L'Osservatore Romano*, it enraged the fascists, who stoned the car that was driving Pius XII to Mass by shouting: "Death to the pope! Down with the pope!" Pius XII did not venture into the streets again until the fall of Mussolini.[120] In June, the Italian dictator announced that the country would join the war.[121]

Despite these setbacks, the military penetration of the Balkans led to a triumph for Catholicism in the region much appreciated by Pius XII. Adolf Hitler would invade Yugoslavia on April 6, 1941, and when the Wehrmacht penetrated Zagreb on April 10, 1941, Croatian fascists declared Croatian independence.[122] John Cornwell explains:

"The following day, Italy and Hungary (another Fascist state) joined forces with Hitler for their share of the Yugoslav cake. By April 12 Hitler had issued his plan for a partitioned Yugoslavia, granting "Aryan" status to an independent Croatia under Ante Pavelic, who had been awaiting developments under the auspices of Mussolini in Italy. Pavelic's group, the Ustashe (from the verb *ustati*, meaning "to rise up"), had opposed the formation of the South Slav kingdom of Yugoslavia after the First World War and had planned disruption and sabotage from the safe haven of Italy: it was Pavelic who had plotted the assassination of King Alexander in 1934. Mussolini had

---

[117] John Cornwell, *Hitler's Pope: The Secret History of Pius XII* (Penguin Books, New York, 2002), p. 241.
[118] Ibid.
[119] Ibid, p. 242.
[120] Ibid, pp. 242, 243.
[121] Ibid, pp. 243, 246.
[122] Ibid, p. 248.

granted Pavelic use of training camps on a remote Aeolian island and access to Radio Bari for propaganda broadcasts across the Adriatic."[123]

On April 10, 1941, at 1 p.m., in Zagreb, Slavko Kvaternik proclaimed the birth of the Independent State of Croatia under the leadership of Ante Pavelić,[124] who declared the same day:

"It is the duty of the Ustashi movement to ensure that the Independent State of Croatia is ruled always and everywhere only by Croatians, so that they are the sole master of all the real and spiritual good in their own land. Within Croatia there can be no compromise between the Croatian people and others who are not pure Croats; Ustashi must extinguish all trace of such people."[125]

Two days later, on April 12, Alojzije Stepinac paid homage to General Slavko Kvaternik, congratulating him on the independence of Croatia. Four days later, the archbishop was received by Ante Pavelić. Stepinac welcomed him to the new regime, showing his satisfaction with the emergence of the new independent Croatian state.[126] That sentiment was expressed in a circular sent to the clergy on April 28, where the Croatian state was described as "an ancient and ardently desired dream." The "Creator" himself was credited, since behind what had happened "it was easy to see the hand of God at work..."[127]

"As a result, osmosis had taken place elevating Ustasha hierarchs to leading positions within the Catholic Action organization and the Crusaders' group (Križari). Meanwhile, in their monasteries, Franciscans of Bosnia-Herzegovina housed clandestine meetings of the members of the Ustasha organization. The archbishop of Sarajevo, Ivan Šarić, had openly sided with the Ustasha on a number of issues right from the beginning. The archbishop and his collaborators, Krunoslav Draganović and Franjo Kralik, formed a closeknit group released from Stepinac's authority both for historical reasons and on account of the Catholic Church's hierarchical structure."[128]

Avro Manhattan:

"The sundry semimilitary, illegal terrorist movements were likewise screened by the mantle of religion. Most of them were affiliated with Catholic organizations under the direct supervision of Catholic Action, which was strictly controlled by the Catholic Hierarchy—e.g. the Brotherhood of the Crusaders, with about 540 societies

---

[123] Ibid, pp. 248, 249.
[124] Pino Adriano and Giorgio Cingolani, Nationalism and Terror: Ante Pavelić and Ustasha Terrorism from Fascism to the Cold War (Central European University Press (CEU Press), Budapest-New York, 2018), p. 174.
[125] David Yallop, The Power and the Glory: Inside the Dark Heart of Pope John Paul II's Vatican (Constable & Robinson Ltd, London, 2007), op. cit.
[126] Pino Adriano and Giorgio Cingolani, Nationalism and Terror: Ante Pavelić and Ustasha Terrorism from Fascism to the Cold War (Central European University Press (CEU Press), Budapest-New York, 2018), p. 181.
[127] Ibid; citing Talpo, *Dalmazia,* 315.
[128] Ibid, p. 182.

and 30,000 members; the Sisterhood of the Crusaders, with 452 societies and 19,000 members; the Catholic Student Associations, Domagoj, and such like."[129]

It was then that the most gruesome massacres began. Thus, during a typical act of atrocity, in the same month of April, a gang of ustashas gathered 331 Serbs in Otočac and were forced to dig their own graves before being hacked to death. The local Orthodox priest was forced to recite prayers for the dying while his son was brutally murdered. The priest was then terribly tortured.[130]

On April 16, Stepinac was informed by Pavelić that he would "show no tolerance towards the Orthodox Church," after which the archbishop noted in his diary that the *poglavnik* "was a sincere Catholic."[131] On the same day, the ustasha militia and the Germans burned the largest synagogue in Sarajevo and destroyed its large bookstore and archives.[132]

Archbishop Stepinac's epistle of April 28, noted:

"Honorable brethren, since we know the men who are in charge of the destiny of the Croatian people, we are deeply convinced that our mission will have great understanding and support. Therefore, respond to my call to a sacred work to protect and improve the Independent State of Croatia."[133]

On the same date, 250 Serbs were massacred in Bjelovar; and in the churches of Croatia, a pastoral letter of Stepinac was read from the Catholic pulpits calling the clergy and the faithful to collaborate with the efforts of their *poglavnik*.[134] Similarly, Ustashi storm troopers arrested 250 Orthodox peasants, including Stevan Ivankovitch and Orthodox priest Bozin, after surrounding the villages of Gudovac, Tuke Brezovac, Klokocevac, and Bolac in the Bjelovar district. After taking them all to a field, they were ordered to dig their own graves and, once done, their hands were tied behind their backs and they were pushed alive into the graves.[135]

Adriano and Cingolani tell us:

"On 30 April, a law decree "On Croatian Citizenship" went into effect. This piece of legislation established that the right to citizenship belonged only to those who could claim Aryan descent: "Jews and Serbs are not citizens of the Independent State of Croatia, though they may live in the state. [...] Only Aryans enjoy political rights." The decree clarified that the state's ultimate aim was the elimination of nonAryan national identities. Use of Cyrillic was forbidden throughout the state, and the tax

[129] Avro Manhattan, The Vatican's Holocaust: The Most Horrifying Religious Massacre of the 20th Century (Ozark Books, Springfield, United States, 1986), p. 23.
[130] Carlo Falconi, The Silence of Pius XII (Little, Brown, 1965), p. 278.
[131] Juan Manuel de Castells Tejón, Tan lejos de Dios: Delitos y falsedades de la iglesia que Francisco quiere reformar (Intermedio Editores S.A.S, 2014), ob. cit.
[132] Pino Adriano and Giorgio Cingolani, Nationalism and Terror: Ante Pavelić and Ustasha Terrorism from Fascism to the Cold War (Central European University Press (CEU Press), Budapest-New York, 2018), p. 189; citing Scotti, *Ustascia tra il fascio e la svastica*, 82.
[133] Krsto Skanata (Producer) Krsto Skanata (Director). (1993), Bog i Hrvati. (Dunav Film).
[134] Juan Manuel de Castells Tejón, Tan lejos de Dios: Delitos y falsedades de la iglesia que Francisco quiere reformar (Intermedio Editores S.A.S, 2014), ob. cit.
[135] Avro Manhattan, The Vatican's Holocaust: The Most Horrifying Religious Massacre of the 20th Century (Ozark Books, Springfield, United States, 1986), p. 44.

Serbian citizens residing in Croatia paid the patriarchate—the Orthodox clergy's main means of sustenance—was abol- ished. Other similar measures followed: all schools run by the Ortho- dox clergy were shut down; the term "Serbian Orthodox religion" was forbidden, and replaced with "Greek–Oriental religion"; finally, citizens of Serbian ethnicity were compelled to wear a colored band on their right arm. As tersely stated by the minister of education Mile Budak, "one-third [of the Serbian Orthodox] will be expelled, one-third killed, and one-third converted to Catholicism."[136]

The *Catholic Weekly* of Croatia May 11, 1941:

"The image of the Blessed Virgin Mary appeared as an omen, crossing the skies of our new, young, and free Croatia. The Mother of God is coming to visit Croatia. She wants to take under her veil the young, newborn Croatia to mark exactly one thousand years of Catholicism of the Croatians. She comes to us again, to take her ancient place on our flag of freedom. The Croatian God and the Mary of the old days are resurrected. Christ and the Croatians are marching together again, through history."[137]

Dreadful atrocities would occur in the years to come. Avro Manhattan recounts in his book, *The Vatican's Holocaust*:

"Victims were executed in groups without trial on bridges and then thrown into the river. In May 1941 the Ustashi besieged Glina. Having gathered together all the Orthodox males of over fifteen years of age from Karlovac, Sisak and Petrinja, they drove them outside the town and killed 600 of them with guns, knives and sledge hammers."[138]

The first official protest to reach the Vatican about the massacres occurred on May 17 and was sent by the expatriate government of Yugoslavia and addressed to the Vatican Secretary of State, denouncing the massacres of Serbs in Croatia, Bosnia-Herzegovina, and Vojvodina, begging the Holy See to act.[139] Likewise, another document, personally signed by King Peter II of Yugoslavia and addressed to Pius XII: "In the alleged independent state of Croatia, Serbs are doomed to extermination. In order to make the extermination faster and more effective, one of the most brutal and hideous laws in the eyes of the civilized world, the one against Jews, is being equally applied to the Serbian population. Never before had a Christian people been humiliated and persecuted to such an extent by an authority also professing to be Christian. I appeal to Your Holiness to place my people, the victim of the most unjust violence,

[136] Pino Adriano y Giorgio Cingolani, Nationalism and Terror: Ante Pavelić and Ustasha Terrorism from Fascism to the Cold War (Central European University Press (CEU Press), Budapest-New York, 2018), pp. 189, 190.

[137] Krsto Skanata (Producer) Krsto Skanata (Director) (1993), Bog i Hrvati (Dunav Film).

[138] Avro Manhattan, The Vatican's Holocaust: The Most Horrifying Religious Massacre of the 20th Century (Ozark Books, Springfield, United States, 1986), p. 41.

[139] Pino Adriano and Giorgio Cingolani, Nationalism and Terror: Ante Pavelić and Ustasha Terrorism from Fascism to the Cold War (Central European University Press (CEU Press), Budapest-New York, 2018), p. 202.

under the protection of your high authority."[140] Other denunciations followed.[141] But the pope did not act.

Let us now look at an apparent contradiction, as shown in a letter dated May 16, 1941, from Stepinac to Pope Pius XII, where he refers to the racial laws in the Independent State of Croatia, mentioning them as the "laws against the Jews" as a means to appease the Nazis:

"It is obvious by now, the pressure from the Germans, which is strongly felt in the laws against Jews, although they claim that they do not want to interfere in the internal affairs of the Croatian state. In fact, the racist law passed these days must be attributed to strong pressure from Germany, because I know from personal meetings with the people who govern the country that they do not intend to keep the law in full force for long. It is much less bad if the Croats were to pass this law than if the Germans were to take all power into their hands. In that case, we would suffer the fate of the Slovenes."[142]

Stepinac, writing to Minister Artuković, had shown him his disagreement with that legislation, showing that it was preferable for the Croats to take the racial laws into their own hands in order to avoid worse treatment of the Jews. How to explain this in light of Stepinac's prejudices towards the Jews? Simply he was in favor of better treatment of the Jews than the Germans would give them, but conservative Catholic doctrine would prevent him from considering the Jews in full equality with the rest. The same letter tells us about the Serbs and the Orthodox:

"Since the government is Catholic, there is a great increase in the conversion of Jews and schismatic Orthodox (by this term Stepinac refers to Orthodox Serbs) to Catholicism. We must be very careful in receiving them since material interests are at stake [...] The future is in God's hands, no one knows. We fear the sinister influence of National Socialism in our country. But the sincere desire of today's rulers in Croatia to strengthen the teaching of the Catholic Church imposes on us the obligation to help and support them with the full loyalty and strength at our disposal."[143]

"Schismatics" was a term used not pejoratively for centuries; and Stepinac refers here to the fact that the motives for the conversions of Jews and Orthodox should be examined: that they should be sincere. But the Archbishop says that the desire of the rulers in Croatia is sincere, in strengthening Catholic teaching.[144] With this in mind, let us even remember when Stepinac wrote in his diary that Ante Pavelić was a sincere Catholic, in response to being told by the *poglavnik* that he would not tolerate the Serbian Orthodox Church. This tells us that sincere conversions did not imply that "heresy" was tolerated.

---

[140] Ibid; citing ADSS, vol. 4, doc. 393, 597-98.
[141] Ibid.
[142] Jure Krišto (March 26, 2021), Krišto: Klasić dokumente ne čita pažljivo, a 'zločince' prosuđuje po unutarnjoj matrici, Bitnonet: https://www.bitno.net/academicus/znanost/jure-kristo-hrvoje-klasic-alojzije-stepinac/; accessed May 29, 2023.
[143] Ibid.
[144] Ibid.

But there are other apparent contradictions. It is worth noting what historian Esther Gitman says about the relationship between the archbishop and the *poglavnik*:

"The relationship between Pavelić and Archbishop Stepinac was tense on several accounts: first, the Archbishop did not participate in the welcome extended to Pavelić at the Zagreb railroad station on April 13, 1941; second, no "Te Deum" was sung at the cathedral on the occasion of Pavelić's birthday. The animosity between the two was also recognized in Pavelić's conduct; he attended services at the Zagreb Cathedral only once in four years, and, even on that occasion, he was not greeted at the entrance by Stepinac. Another issue of contention was Stepinac's active discouragement of the clergy from joining the Ustaše movement. Stepinac stated that to join was a political act and contrary to the tradition that maintained neutrality."[145]

Gitman uncovered hundreds of original documents from Croatian archives, and spoke with numerous survivors from Ante Pavelić's era in Croatia, demonstrating how Stepinac saved hundreds of Croatian Jews (even as early as 1938 he denounced Nazism and anti-Semitism).[146] But is this enough to say that he had no involvement in the crimes committed in the New Independent State of Croatia?

But historian John Cornwell documents that in 1940, Stepinac told Prince Paul regent of Yugoslavia: "The most ideal thing would be for the Serbs to return to the faith of their fathers, that is, to bow the head before Christ's representative, the Holy Father. Then we could at last breathe in this part of Europe, for Byzantinism has played a frightful role in the history of this part of the world." Also for Pacelli, the separated Christian brethren should "see the error of their ways and return to full union with the Pope and Rome."[147] All these statements, put in perspective, do not show a great tolerance of either Stepinac or Pacelli towards Orthodox Christians. Moreover, we will see that Stepinac himself participated in these massacres.

In the middle of May, Ante Pavelić was received by Benito Mussolini in Italy.[148] Stepinac arranged a private audience between the *poglavnik* and Pope Pius XII.[149]

The Vatican pondered such a meeting since they could not ignore his embarrassing past - particularly since "the court of Aix-en-Provence had sentenced him to death in absentia for the killing of King Alexander."[150] That is why the Secretary of State turned to Stepinac, who in turn had put the crucial question to *Poglavnik*, whose response was:

---

[145] Esther Gitman (2006), A Question of Judgement: Dr. Alojzije Stepinac and the Jews, Review of Croatian History, Vol. II No. 1, p. 51.

[146] Esther Gitman, When Courage Prevailed: The Rescue and Survival of Jews in the Independent State of Croatia 1941-1945 (Paragon House, St. Paul, MN. First Edition, 2011); Esther Gitman, Alojzije Stepinac - Pillar of human rights (Krscanska sadasnjost, 2019). See also Robin Harris, Stepinac: His Life and Times (Gracewing, 2016).

[147] John Cornwell, Hitler's Pope: The Secret History of Pius XII (Penguin Books, New York, 2002), p. 265; citing Steinbger, «Types of Genocide», p. 178.

[148] Pino Adriano and Giorgio Cingolani, Nationalism and Terror: Ante Pavelić and Ustasha Terrorism from Fascism to the Cold War (Central European University Press (CEU Press), Budapest-New York, 2018), p. 186.

[149] Retchkiman, Golda (2020) "The Ustaše and the Roman Catholic Church in the Independent State of Croatia," Occasional Papers on Religion in Eastern Europe: Vol. 40 : Ed. 1 , Article 9, p. 82.

[150] Pino Adriano y Giorgio Cingolani, Nationalism and Terror: Ante Pavelić and Ustasha Terrorism from Fascism to the Cold War (Central European University Press (CEU Press), Budapest-New York, 2018), p. 186.

"My Excellency," the poglavnik had answered, "my conscience is absolutely calm and tranquil. I am responsible for this fact to the same extent that any Croat is."[151] Endorsed by Stepinac, that revelation dispelled all doubts, and the pope resolved to grant - it was May 18, 1941 - Pavelić a private audience "in his capacity as a Catholic personage, not as a political man"[152] William Phillips, the American ambassador in Rome, met with the Vatican Secretary of State, Giovanni Battista Montini, to learn the official line regarding that meeting.[153] In surprising justification for the audience with a convicted terrorist and murderer, Montini explained that the pope, as head of the Church, could not refuse to receive Catholics when asked.[154] Pavelić was received as a private individual and not as head of the Independent State of Croatia. When Anthony Eden, British Foreign Secretary heard of the audience, he complained to Monsignor Godfrey, the apostolic delegate: "I am much disturbed by this reception, and cannot accept the Vatican's description of M. Pavelitch as a statesman. In my view, he is a regicide. It is incredible that His Holiness should receive such a man."[155] The British ambassador to Italy, Sir D'Arcy Osborne, who also protested the meeting, was told by the pope that Pavelić was a 'much maligned man' who was not responsible for the death of King Alexander in 1934.[156]

Just weeks before the reception with the pope, as we have seen, the Pavelić regime began massacring the enemies of the ustashi and passing laws depriving Serbs and Jews of their rights.[157]

Pavelić, together with a state delegation from the Independent State of Croatia, was received at the private bookstore of Pius XII.[158] The Croatian delegation included the most important ustasha representatives - Mile Budak, Andrija Artuković, Mirko Puk, Ivo Petrić, Jozo Dumandžić and Mladen Lorković.[159] Poglavnik promised, "that Catholi- cism would inspire the Croatian people's conduct and legislation." Likewise, during the meeting, *poglavnik* referred to the matter of the Vatican's recognition of the new Croatian state. But Pius XII informed him that the practice of the Holy See "prevented him from speaking for or against the new state until a peace treaty was in place clearly defining all territorial matters."[160]

---

[151] Ibid, pp. 186, 187.

[152] Ibid, p. 187.

[153] Robert B. McCormick, Croatia Under Ante Pavelić: America, the Ustaše and Croatian Genocide (I.B. Tauris & Co Ltd, Lóndres-New York, 2014), p. 68.

[154] Ibid, pp. 68, 69.

[155] Ibid, p. 69.

[156] Ibid; David Yallop, The Power and the Glory: Inside the Dark Heart of Pope John Paul II's Vatican (Constable & Robinson Ltd, London, 2007), op. cit.

[157] Ibid.

[158] Pino Adriano and Giorgio Cingolani, Nationalism and Terror: Ante Pavelić and Ustasha Terrorism from Fascism to the Cold War (Central European University Press (CEU Press), Budapest-New York, 2018), p. 187.

[159] Vuković Slobodan V. (2004), Uloga Vatikana u razbijanju Jugoslavije, Sociološki pregled, vol. 38, issue 3, p. 430.

[160] Pino Adriano and Giorgio Cingolani, Nationalism and Terror: Ante Pavelić and Ustasha Terrorism from Fascism to the Cold War (Central European University Press (CEU Press), Budapest-New York, 2018), p. 187. Note: There is a facet of that meeting that is little known, if proven true: Dušan Đaković, during the preparation of his master's thesis in the 1980s - The Serbian Question in Croatia - received from the Historical Archive in Gospić the "Jadovno Field" file (pillar over 2 meters and with about 60 thousand folded papyrus sheets) containing, among other things, the statement of an ustasha tried after the end of the war for crimes committed during the war. He described where the ustashas got the idea to throw Serbs,

The real reason the Vatican did not recognize the independent state of Croatia was because they feared potential repercussions from the Allies, particularly the United States and Great Britain.[161]

The following month, in a letter to the pope dated June 14, Stepinac advocated that the Holy See recognize the Independent State of Croatia. He mentioned the disappointment of the state leadership that it had not yet happened. In addition, the archbishop mentioned to Pius XII the statements of representatives of the Croatian authorities recalling the millions of Croatian lives perished in defense of Catholicism, adding, "These are the sentiments of the Most Holy Father which fill the soul of Poglavnik Pavelić and other members of his government." Taking advantage of the kind of struggle being waged in Croatia, he wrote: "I have no doubt, Holy Father, that here a desperate life-and-death struggle is being waged between the schism presented in the Serbs and the Catholicism presented in the Croats."[162] Zagreb historian Hrvoje Klasić says about the letter:

"It is equally interesting how Stepinac experiences the developments related to the behavior of the members, up to the war of the strongest Croatian political party, HSS: "The fact is that Dr. Maček has more supporters in Croatia. Some of the supporters fled the country, some are members of the Yugoslav government in emigration. But a healthy part of Maček's party immediately joined the ranks of the boss." The procedure of this "healthy part" of the HSS for Stepinac is a guarantee of the success of the new state, because: "although it is obvious that among Poglavnik's supporters not everything is as one would wish, it should be taken into account and evaluated the fact that Pavelić is a true believing practicing Catholic, and that he wants to create, despite the enormous problems, a Catholic state in Croatia."[163]

Gypsies, and Jews into the wells. Precisely, he relates that Pavelić, Budak, and a certain Maric, from Lika, who was Pavelić's companion and advisor shortly after the creation of the Independent State of Croatia, with the papal nuncio in Zagreb, had gone to visit Pope Pius XII. Discussing how to kill as many of them as possible with as few clues as possible, Pius XII asked them where they would hide the corpses if they happened to live in Finland, to which his guests replied that by throwing them into the lakes that abound in that country. But Pius XII suggested that "since you live in Croatia, where there are no lakes as in Finland, throw them in the escarpments of Lika." There was also talk that detainees from all camps in the area of the Independent State of Croatia, would be transported to Jadovno, where they would be thrown alive or dead on the escarpments of the Velebit mountain range; and that such an arrangement began to materialize immediately.

Đaković gave the dossier to Gospić professor Miloš Počuča, whose relatives ended up in the Velebit escarpments, from where it was taken in December 1991 due to his wife's account. If this archive is not physically destroyed, it could currently be in the Lika Museum in Gospić, according to Mr. Đaković.

[161] Retchkiman, Golda (2020) "The Ustaše and the Roman Catholic Church in the Independent State of Croatia," Occasional Papers on Religion in Eastern Europe: Vol. 40 : Ed. 1 , Article 9, p. 83; citing to citing Carl Savich, "The Vatican Role in the Ustasha Genocide in the Independent State of Croatia," Serbianna, November 11, 2011, accessed October 12, 2019, http://serbiana.com/analysis/archives/1182

[162] Hrvoje Klasić (March 24, 2021), Donosimo dijelove pisama koje je Alojzije Stepinac slao papi Piju XII., RTL Digital: https://net.hr/danas/hrvatska/ekskluzivno-objavljujemo-dijelove-stepincevih-pisama-o-ustasama-pavelicu-srbima-i-rasnim-zakonima-o-kojima-prica-porfirije-i-citava-hrvatska-875fb2d2-b1c7-11eb-8038-0242ac13003b; accessed May 29, 2023.

[163] Ibid.

From the letter, which is extensive, we quote one more excerpt:

"It is in the great interest of the Serbian schismatics to enter the Catholic Church. Surely they do it under the impression that the government supports Catholicism. But there is no denying that they are being driven out by all the misery of the schismatic church... I believe that if Poglavnik Pavelic were to head the government for 20 years, the schismatics would be completely liquidated from Croatia"[164]

About this segment of the letter, it is said that Stepinac saw in the decadence of the Serbian Orthodox Church a sign that Catholic stability would attract them, which is understood by "liquidating" the schismatics.[165] But it is difficult to arrive at this interpretation since it is difficult to conceive of a liquidation of Orthodox by their mere conversion to Catholicism. Add to this, the content of the words of Pius XII in his meeting with Ante Pavelić and his delegation, as well as Stepinac's role in the massacres at Jasenovac, as we shall see later.

At the same time, in the same letter, Stepinac speaks about the need to expel the schismatics (Orthodox Serbs) and informs the pope that he spoke with Ante Pavelić and Slavko Kvaternik about the transfer of 200 thousand Slovenians to Croatia; and the same number of Serbs "transferred" to Serbia, Action which would be equal to human resettlement.[166] Stepinac tells him about the decisions taken by the Croatian government with the Nazis.[167] Similarly, the Serbs are not asked their opinion.

But there is also a document that sheds more light on this subject. In a letter of April 23, 1941, from Archbishop Stepinac to the Minister of the Interior, Andrija Artuković, he says: "On the occasion of the announced adoption of anti-Jewish laws, I have the honor to warn you of the following: there are good Catholics who are of Jewish race and who converted from Jewish religious law out of conviction...there are among them those who stood out as good Croatian nationalists. I think it would be good if these converts were taken into account when passing the necessary laws." For such a reason, when Stepinac went so far as to complain about the inhumane treatment of Jews in a letter to Ante Pavelić on June 21 of the same year, he did so without protesting other anti-racial laws; even though he spoke out against anti-Semitism and cruelties later on. Thus, Stepinac did not ask Pavelić to repeal the racial laws, but "that the sending to the camps be done in such a way that they could prepare the most necessary things."

When the archbishop mentions to the *poglavnik* "that the Ustasha in Glina shot 260 Serbs without trial or investigation," pointing out that "according to Catholic morality,

[164] Ibid.

[165] Dr. Jure Krišto (April 6, 2021), Bitno.net, 01.04.2021, ANALIZA PISAMA KARDINALA STEPINCA (2) Krišto: Rečenice kojima je Stepinac zaključio pismo Papi sadrže cijelu povijest njegovog odnosa prema ustašama: http://www.veritas.org.rs/bitno-net-01-04-2021-analiza-pisama-kardinala-stepinca-2-kristo-recenice-kojima-je-stepinac-zakljucio-pismo-papi-sadrze-cijelu-povijest-njegovog-odnosa-prema-ustasama/; accessed May 29, 2023.

[166] Hrvoje Klasić (March 30, 2021), NOVI DETALJI O STEPINČEVIM PISMIMA: / Što je o logorima, Židovima i 'nearijevcima' pisao Paveliću i Artukoviću; Je li moglo drugačije?, Play Digital: https://net.hr/danas/hrvatska/novi-detalji-o-stepincevim-pismima-sto-je-o-logorima-zidovima-i-nearijevcima-pisao-pavelicu-i-artukovicu-i-je-li-mogao-napraviti-drugacije-e38422fa-b1c7-11eb-ae00-0242ac150016; accessed May 29, 2023.

[167] Mario Jareb (April 4, 2021), Jareb za Narod.hr: 'Duboko problematično' Klasićevo insinuiranje - osvrt na tumačenja dvaju Stepinčevih pisama, Narod HR.

this is not allowed," he asked him that "no Serb should be killed in the whole territory of the NDH, if his/her guilt for which he/she deserved death is not proven."[168]

Stepinac thought of giving them the opportunity for conversion; especially, as we shall see, in the face of the looming loss of the War to the Allied powers.

On August 3, 1941, knowing of the terrible persecutions in Croatia, Pius XII sent Giuseppe Ramiro Marcone as a delegate or emissary of the Holy See, with the rank of Visitor of Croatia.[169] Ramiro Marcone was seen with Ante Pavelić, as well as with leading religious, political, and military ustasha leaders.[170] A CIA document reveals that the apostolic visitation lasted throughout the war.[171]

What continued in Croatia were forced conversions to Catholicism, deportations, and mass extermination of Jews, Serbs, and Gypsies.

Cambridge University historian Jonathan Steinberg relates:

"Serbian and Jewish men, women and children were literally hacked to death. Whole villages were razed to the ground and the people driven into barns to which the *Ustaši* set fire. There is in the Italian Foreign Ministry archive a collection of photographs of the butcher knives, hooks and axes used to chop up Serbian victims. There are photographs of Serb women with breasts hacked off by pocket knives, men with eyes gouged out, emasculated and mutilated."[172]

By the same month of May, forced conversions of Orthodox to Catholicism began.[173] These were characterized by mass ceremonies, where ustasha militiamen and Catholic priests baptized hundreds of Serbs at a time.[174] For many Serbian Orthodox Christians, conversion to Catholicism became the only way to avoid annihilation.[175]

The ustasha squads went through all Serb-inhabited villages, carrying out indiscriminate roundups that were usually carried out at night.[176] Families were taken to prisons or concentration camps.[177]

---

[168] Hrvoje Klasić (March 30, 2021), NOVI DETALJI O STEPINČEVIM PISMIMA: / Što je o logorima, Židovima i 'nearijevcima' pisao Paveliću i Artukoviću; Je li moglo drugačije?, Play Digital: https://net.hr/danas/hrvatska/novi-detalji-o-stepincevim-pismima-sto-je-o-logorima-zidovima-i-nearijevcima-pisao-pavelicu-i-artukovicu-i-je-li-mogao-napraviti-drugacije-e38422fa-b1c7-11eb-ae00-0242ac150016; accessed May 29, 2023.

[169] Pino Adriano and Giorgio Cingolani, Nationalism and Terror: Ante Pavelić and Ustasha Terrorism from Fascism to the Cold War (Central European University Press (CEU Press), Budapest-New York, 2018), pp. 82, 83.

[170] Ibid, p. 83; citing Carl Savich, "The Vatican Role in the Ustasha Genocide in the Independent State of Croatia," Serbianna, November 11, 2011, accessed October 12, 2019, http://serbiana.com/analysis/archives/1182

[171] U.S. CIA (_/_/_). Peinding release of Ambassador Eizenstats Vol. II Report on WW II victim gold. Washington, DC: United States Government Printing Office, p. 2.

[172] Jonathan Steinberg, All or Nothing: The Axis and the Holocaust, 1941-43 (Taylor & Francis e-Library, 2005), p. 28.

[173] Pino Adriano and Giorgio Cingolani, Nationalism and Terror: Ante Pavelić and Ustasha Terrorism from Fascism to the Cold War (Central European University Press (CEU Press), Budapest-New York, 2018), p. 191.

[174] Ibid, pp. 191, 192.

[175] Ibid, p. 192.

[176] Ibid.

[177] Ibid; citing Alexander, *Church and State in Yugoslavia since 1945*, 23.

The atrocities were not confined to these camps, as many executions and mass murders in the summer of 1941 occurred particularly in Bosnia-Herzegovina and in Krajina, a Serb-majority region of Croatia.[178] In June, an ustasha squad accompanied by two Catholic priests arrived in Opuzen, in the Dalmatian hinterland, surrounded 450 Serbs, and massacred them.[179]

Goldstein recounts, "On 1 July, Vjekoslav-Maks Luburić "led a group of Ustasha in the village of Suvaj, where they killed at least 173 people, mostly women, children and seniors, for the youth had already fled to the mountains. Luburić's expedition continued in the villages of Bubanj and Osredak, and in three days' time between 279 and 330 people were killed."[180] By the end of the month, at least 1800 Serbs were killed in Lika.[181]

General Furio Monticelli commented: "Remaining inactive spectators, we feel like accomplices to these acts of violence and brutality, which will certainly be condemned by history."[182] The Germans were also affected, as reflected in a June 1941 report, in which the military plenipotentiary in Zagreb, Edmund Glaise von Horstenau, recounted that during the previous weeks, both in the countryside and in the cities, he expressed that the ustasha were "raging mad."[183] The following month:

"Horstenau drew attention to the "utterly inhuman treatment" to which Serbs living in Croatia were being subjected on account of the Ustasha's blind and bloody fury. And he added that even among Croats no one could feel safe in that land, for the Croatian revolution was "by far the harshest and most brutal of all the different revolutions" he had ever "been through at more or less close hand since 1918."[184]

Pino Adriano and Giorgio Cingolani, rightly point out that: "the list of atrocities committed by the Ustasha in the summer of 1941 is endless, the details often blood-curdling."[185] They continue by stating that "In Korenica, hundreds of Serbs were tortured and mutilated: nose and ears cut off, eyes pulled out, limbs broken; some were forced to hold red-hot bricks, dance barefoot on barbed wire, wear crowns made of nails; others were tortured with needles driven under their fingernails or matches lit under their noses."[186]

Ljubo Jednjak, the sole survivor of the mass murder in Glina, a village south of Zagreb, on the banks of its river, recounts that on May 14, 1941, the 700 residents of the village, who were mostly farmers and small estate owners, were gathered in the local Orthodox church to celebrate their conversion to Catholicism through baptism.[187] Before the function, a unit of ustasha soldiers burst in and asked everyone to show their

[178] Ibid, p. 193.
[179] Ibid; citing MAE, Gabinetto Ministro e Segreteria generale 1923-1943, b. 1493, f. 3, Notizie dalla Dalmazia relative alla situazione in Croazia, August 22, 1941.
[180] Ibid; citing Goldstein, *Hrvatska 1918-2008*, 266.
[181] Ibid.
[182] Ibid; citing MAE, Gabinetto Ministro e Segreteria generale 1923-1943, b. 1493, f. 3, Situazione politica in Tenin, June 16, 1941.
[183] Ibid, p. 194.
[184] Ibid.
[185] Ibid.
[186] Ibid; citing Paris, *Genocidio nella Croazia satellite*, 120.
[187] Ibid.

"conversion certificates."[188] But only two had them, so they were expelled. The massacre began immediately, starting with Orthodox priest Bogdan Opačić, followed by most of the residents. The few who were not killed were locked in the church, which was set on fire.[189]

Towards the end of the summer, the Vatican received, through Branko Bokunm, a report of the atrocities committed by the Pavelić regime, complete with eyewitness accounts of Catholics and chilling photographs. However, the Vatican, with Pope Pius XII, said about the massacres they received information about a week later, that it was just communist propaganda.[190]

Also, the presence of Catholic priests was classic in these atrocities. Their involvement was so extensive that it was difficult to imagine an ustasha squadron without a priest, particularly a Franciscan friar leading and inciting the killings.[191] Catholics were called upon from the pulpits to persecute the Serbs.[192]

"Many monasteries served as hubs for Ustasha activity and as weapon depots for operative agents, while ordinary citizens were being incited to persecute Serbs from the pulpits of their local churches. In July, Ivo Guberina, a key player in the Catholic Action organization and the chaplain to Pavelić's personal guard, wrote that Croatia would free itself of all its poisons by any means necessary, including the sword."[193]

Many Franciscan priests took an ustasha oath in front of a crucifix, a gun, a knife, and a hand grenade. Siroki Brijeg was an ustasha criminal center in Herzegovina, a Catholic church where many creators of ustasha ideology were recruited, as well as ustasha murderers.[194]

Pope Pius XII appointed Archbishop Alojzije Stepinac as military vicar of the Croatian army, who blessed the ustasha troops before the massacres. The unit had a syndic, who was a priest whose duty was to look after the soldiers and encourage them in looting and crimes. Through newspapers and radio, a bloodthirsty hatred against the Serbs was inflamed. Srećko Perić, a Franciscan priest, sent a message from the altar of the Catholic church in Gorica, near Livno in April 1941: "Croatian brethren! Go and massacre all Serbs. First, kill my sister who is married to a Serb, then kill all the others. When you finish the job, come to my church, I will confess you and give you communion. All your sins will be forgiven."[195]

Mile Budak, the main Ustaše ideologue, said on July 13, 1941: "The Ustashi movement is based on religion. Therefore our acts stem from our devotion to religion and to the Catholic Church."[196]

---

[188] Ibid, pp. 194, 195.

[189] Ibid, p. 195.

[190] Ibid, p. 203.

[191] Ibid, p. 195; citing Falconi, *Il silenzio di Pio XII*, 382.

[192] Krsto Skanata (Producer) Krsto Skanata (Director) (1993), Bog i Hrvati (Dunav Film).

[193] Pino Adriano and Giorgio Cingolani, Nationalism and Terror: Ante Pavelić and Ustasha Terrorism from Fascism to the Cold War (Central European University Press (CEU Press), Budapest-New York, 2018), p. 195; citing Paris, *Genocidio nella Croazia satellite*, 125.

[194] Krsto Skanata (Producer) Krsto Skanata (Director) (1993), Bog i Hrvati (Dunav Film).

[195] Ibid.

[196] Edmond Paris, Genocide in Satellite Croatia, 1941-1945: A Record of Racial and Religious Persecutions and Massacres (Chicago: American Institute for Balkan Affairs), ob. cit.

Friar Dionizije, Franciscan cleric appointed director of the Religious Department of the Ustacha regime: "In those regions yonder, I arranged for everything to be cleared away, everything from a chicken to an old man, and should that be necessary, I shall do so here too, since it is not sinful nowadays to kill even a seven year-old child, if it is standing in the way of our *Ustashi* order… Pay no heed to my religious vestments, for you should know that when the necessity arises, I take into my hands a machinegun and exterminate everybody down to the cradle, everybody who is opposed to the *Ustashi* State and Government."[197]

Perić immediately gathered all Serbs in Livno and took them to Koprivnica (between Bugojno Kupres), where they were brutally tortured and then murdered.[198] By August 20, 1941, more than 5600 adults, women and children were killed. And the friars of the Gorica monastery assisted the Franciscan in killing and torturing the Serbs. Perić also ordered that all the men of the village of Golinjevo be thrown into a karst well in the Tušnica mountain. Men, women, and children from Gornji and Donji Rupljanje were thrown into a well in the Klanacka forest. Also, the aforementioned Franciscan priest ordered the slaughter of Serbs, about two hundred, in the school in Celebić. By his order, more than three hundred women and children from Chaprazlija were killed. And several hundred Serbs were thrown into a forest at the Dikuša well.

The message of Udbina's coadjutor in the magazine of the Sarajevo archbishopric was that "while men of the cloth had worked for religion seizing the cross and breviary thus far, the time was now ripe for them to hold the gun and rifle." It was no coincidence, being that Archbishop Ivan Šarić was among the most enthusiastic supporters of the ustasha regime.[199] Nicknamed the "Hangman of the Serbs," he had said that the elimination of the Jews was a "renewal of human dignity." Catholic priests served as Ante Pavelić's private bodyguards.[200]

Similarly, Miroslav Filipović-Majstorović, a Franciscan priest from the Petrićevac monastery near Banja Luka, with the help of other monks and priests, personally directed the murders of Orthodox Christians in several Serbian villages.[201] Known as the "Friar of Satan," he spearheaded and himself participated in merciless mass murders,[202] where cruelty surpasses fiction, both from children to adults. He organized gruesome massacres in several villages in the region of Banja Luka (today in Bosnia-Herzegovina).[203] Before February 1942, for example, he led the assault on the villages of Motike and Sergovac in Drakulić, together with his lieutenant, priest Zvonimir Brekalo. Encouraged by Filipović, the ustashas massacred 2302 people.[204] He was

---

[197] David Yallop, The Power and the Glory: Inside the Dark Heart of Pope John Paul II's Vatican (Constable & Robinson Ltd, London, 2007), op. cit.

[198] Krsto Skanata (Producer) Krsto Skanata (Director) (1993), Bog i Hrvati (Dunav Film).

[199] Pino Adriano and Giorgio Cingolani, Nationalism and Terror: Ante Pavelić and Ustasha Terrorism from Fascism to the Cold War (Central European University Press (CEU Press), Budapest-New York, 2018), p. 195.

[200] Gerald Posner, God's Bankers: A History of Money and Power at the Vatican (Simon & Schuster Paperbacks, New York, 2015), p. 89.

[201] Pino Adriano and Giorgio Cingolani, Nationalism and Terror: Ante Pavelić and Ustasha Terrorism from Fascism to the Cold War (Central European University Press (CEU Press), Budapest-New York, 2018), p. 196; citing Novak, *Magnum Crimen*, 637-38; Alexander, The Triple Myth, 76.

[202] Ibid.

[203] Milan Bulajić, Jasenovac: The Jewish Serbian Holocaust (the Role of the Vatican) in Nazi-Ustasha Croatia (1941-1945) (University of Michigan, 2002), p. 169.

[204] Ignacio Montes de Oca, Ustashas: El ejército nazi de Perón y el Vaticano (Sudamericana, 2013), op. cit.

director of the cruelest Croatian concentration camp, Jasenovac; where tens of thousands of victims died mercilessly.[205] For that reason, the friar was also nicknamed "Devil of Jasenovac."[206] Following the advice of the priest D. Juric, Filipovic let more than 2000 Orthodox children die while the camp was under his command. Special camps for children were established in many parts of Croatia.[207] On the night of August 29, 1943, four Franciscan priests, Miroslav Filipović, Petar Brzica, Mile Friganović, Ante Zrinusic, and another religious surnamed Spika, held a competition to see who would kill the most prisoners but without using firearms; Brzica having won with 1360 kills.[208] Filipović committed heinous crimes for which in 1945 he was sentenced to death.[209] Three ustasha officers, who were also Franciscan priests, were Filipović's deputies. [210]

"Father Bozidas Bralo, Sarajevo's chief of security, was responsible for enforcing the country's anti-Semitic legislation. And a popular priest, Father Dyonisy Juricev, wrote in a leading newspaper that it was no longer a sin to kill Serbs or Jews so long as they were at least seven years old. The role played by clerics in the killings helped absolve ordinary Catholics from being afflicted by a troubled conscience."[211]

Although Filipović was suspended by the papal legate in Zagreb in 1942 for excessive crimes,[212] this was due solely to the lack of mercy shown by the Franciscan priest to those who should have had a chance to convert to Catholicism.

Three bishops and hundreds of Orthodox priests were killed, and up to 299 Serbian churches were looted and destroyed.

Ignacio Montes De Oca:

"Since in Pavelić's Croatia there was no clear separation between the earthly and the religious, it was not unusual for priests to be put in charge of the administration of entire regions. The towns of Zepce, Karlovac, Ogulin, and Doboj were among the districts in which ustasha priests concentrated civil, military, and religious power. In Knin, the brutal Father Simic was the governor and head of the local ustasha gangs."[213]

About other positions, in *Novi List*, No. 54 in 1941, the election of Stjepan Lukic to the post of logorni pobocnik (aide-de-camp) of the Zepce camp was reported. Dragutin

---

[205] Michael Phayer, The Catholic Church and the Holocaust, 1930-1965 (Indiana University Press, Bloomington, IN, 2000), p. 38; Egon Berger, 44 Months in Jasenovac (Sentia Publishing Company, 2016), ob cit.

[206] Gerald Posner, God's Bankers: A History of Money and Power at the Vatican (Simon & Schuster Paperbacks, New York, 2015), p. 89.

[207] Avro Manhattan, The Vatican's Holocaust: The Most Horrifying Religious Massacre of the 20th Century (Ozark Books, Springfield, United States, 1986), p. 45.

[208] Ignacio Montes de Oca, Ustashas: El ejército nazi de Perón y el Vaticano (Sudamericana, 2013), op. cit.

[209] Andriana Benčić Kužnar, Danijela Lucić and Stipe Odak (eds.), Jasenovac Concentration Camp: An Unfinished Past (Routledge, New York, NY, 2023), ob. cit.

[210] Gerald Posner, God's Bankers: A History of Money and Power at the Vatican (Simon & Schuster Paperbacks, New York, 2015), p. 89.

[211] Ibid.

[212] Sergej Županić (April 20, 2018), Njih 600 bježalo je iz Jasenovca od fra Sotone, Express.

[213] Ignacio Montes de Oca, Ustashas: El ejército nazi de Perón y el Vaticano (Sudamericana, 2013), op. cit.

Kamber, a Jesuit priest in Doboj as well as an avowed ustashi, was elected in April of that year to the post of commander of the Ustashis for the Doboj district, with all political and civil powers concentrated in his hands.[214] He ordered the murder of 300 Orthodox Serbs in the locality and the court-martial of 250 more, most of whom were shot.[215]

On May 25, 1941, the Catholic newspaper *Katolicki List*, published an article entitled "Why are the Jews being persecuted?" It justified the genocide by the usual accusations, and ended by attributing to "God": "The movement to rid the world of the Jews is a movement for the rebirth of human dignity. The Almighty and Wise God is behind this movement." In this way, many priests and friars carried out murders, and it is estimated that half of the twenty extermination camps of the Ustaše had priests as commanders.[216]

"Additionally, the Croatian Church profited from the genocide by receiving the lion's share of the property confiscated from the Orthodox Church. Another source of income was the forced conversion of thousands of Serbs, forced to renounce their Orthodox religion at knifepoint. Each convert had to pay the Church 180 dinars and write a letter of thanks to the bishop of Zagreb, Alojzije Stepinac."[217]

Additionaly, it is documented that: "The Catholic monks and priests who participated in the massacres were mostly military chaplains for the Ustasha militia, and eluded, at least in part, the control of Catholic authorities."[218]

The BBC in London issued a report on February 16, 1942, clear enough:

"The worst atrocities are being committed around the Archbishop of Zagreb. The blood of brethren is flowing in streams. Orthodox are being forced to convert to Catholicism and we do not hear the Archbishop's voice preaching rebellion. Instead, he is reported to be taking part in Nazi and fascist parades."[219]

Avro Manhattan gives a non-exhaustive account of the 1941-1943 murders, telling us that in March 1943, inmates of the Djakovo camp were intentionally infected with typhus, killing 367 people. On September 15, 1941, every inmate of the Jasenovac camp who was unable to work - between 600 and 700 - was killed. One thousand women were killed in the Stara Gradiska camp. At the end of 1942, of the 5,000 Orthodox Serbs taken to the Jasenovac camp, 2,000 were killed on the way, while the

---

[214] Avro Manhattan, The Vatican's Holocaust: The Most Horrifying Religious Massacre of the 20th Century (Ozark Books, Springfield, United States, 1986), p. 69.

[215] Ibid, p. 80.

[216] Juan Manuel de Castells Tejón, Tan lejos de Dios: Delitos y falsedades de la iglesia que Francisco quiere reformar (Intermedio Editores S.A.S, 2014), ob. cit.

[217] Ibid.

[218] Pino Adriano y Giorgio Cingolani, Nationalism and Terror: Ante Pavelić and Ustasha Terrorism from Fascism to the Cold War (Central European University Press (CEU Press), Budapest-New York, 2018), p. 196.

[219] Juan Manuel de Castells Tejón, Tan lejos de Dios: Delitos y falsedades de la iglesia que Francisco quiere reformar (Intermedio Editores S.A.S, 2014), op. cit.; citando a John Cornwell, op. cit., pp. 283-284.

rest were transferred to Gradina, where on August 28 they were executed by hammering.[220]

In 1941, in the Krapje camp, 4,000 prisoners were murdered; while in the Brocice camp in November of that year, 8,000 prisoners were murdered. In the same way, from December 1941 to February 1942, in Velika Kosutarica, in Jasenovac, 40 thousand Orthodox Serbs were massacred. In the summer of 1942 in the Jasenovac camp, about 66 thousand Orthodox Serbs brought from the villages of Bosnian Marches, among them 2 thousand children, were massacred.[221]

"Mass deportations and mass executions, mainly in isolated small towns and villages, were well-planned operations. As a rule, the procedure was a simple one. Ustashi authorities summoned groups of Serbs under the pretext of recruitment for military service or public works. Once rounded up, they were surrounded by detachments of armed Ustashi, taken outside the village, and executed."[222]

As in Bosnia-Herzegovina, in the mountainous regions of Upper Dalmatia, women and children were taken to remote places to be massacred.[223] Morber, a Catholic priest, invited the Serbs to convert to the Catholic religion in the village of Stikade in Lika. But the reluctance of those who accepted caused the Ustashis to surround and massacre them with rifles and sledgehammers and throw their bodies into a ditch.[224] Avro Manhattan quotes an article from *The News Chronicle* of January 3, 1942:

"**180,000 die in Serb Terror.** Mass murders of men, women and children are described by the Archbishop of the Serbian Orthodox Church in a document which has reached the Yugoslav Legation in London. It is the most ghastly record of bestiality yet compiled during the present war.... In the village of Korito, the Archbishops records, 163 peasants were tortured, tied into bundles of three and thrown into a pit. Some were found still alive, so the Ustashi threw in bombs to finish them off..."

"...266 bodies are consigned to this pit. Subsequently petrol was poured into it and set alight. More than 600 people were killed in and around Krupa between July 25th and 30th. Most of them had been cut to pieces with knives, axes and scythes. In one place, four Orthodox Serbs were crucified on the doors of their houses, tortured and finally killed with knives," reported the Daily Telegraph (3rd January 1942). "It is suggested that the names (of the criminals) should go before an international court of justice to be set up after the war..."[225]

For his part, according to Dr. Slavenko Terzić, the Archbishop of Zagreb, Alojzije Stepinac, was an intermediary between the Nazi spies and the Vatican. The Soviet People's Commissariat for Internal Affairs (NKVD), retains among its documentation a statement by German SS commander Dr. Karl Neuhaus that Stepinac, for 270 thousand

---

[220] Avro Manhattan, The Vatican's Holocaust: The Most Horrifying Religious Massacre of the 20th Century (Ozark Books, Springfield, United States), p. 86.
[221] Ibid, p. 48.
[222] Ibid, p. 52.
[223] Ibid.
[224] Ibid, p. 128.
[225] Ibid.

Reichsmarks (German Imperial Marks), allowed German Secret State Police (SD) agent Franz Heger to reach Pope Pius XII in order to influence his decisions. Neuhaus was a senior National Socialist party official, and from 1942, worked in the Reich Security Main Office as head of the church department in the First Operational Directorate of the Secret State Police. Testifying before the NKVD in 1945, Neuhaus stated that cooperation between the SD and Stepinac began in 1941. Stepinac entrusted Heger with the task of organizing commercial visits to the church in Marija Bistrica, where, according to the Catholic Church, there were miracle-working icons.

Stepinac gave written recommendations to Heger to pass on to Pius XII, who became very close.

The Archbishop of Croatia, called the Serbs the greatest danger to the nation, supporting hostilities against them. Kaše, Hitler's deputy, testified at the trial that Stepinac openly suggested to him that the Germans forcibly expel 240,000 Serbs from Slovenia alone.

With the consent and under the supervision of the papal legate Giuseppe Ramiro Marcone, Stepinac convened a new Episcopal Conference in Zagreb on November 17-20, 1941, which was dedicated to the conversion of the Serbian Orthodox to Catholicism.

About the archbishop, the testimony of Mr. Vasa Kondić, who was from the Podkozar village of Sladinja and who was imprisoned in the Jasenovac extermination camp when he was only seven years old, is important. He recounts that in Jasenovac, the worst murderers and torturers were Catholic priests. In 1941, Stepinac arrived at the camp, where Maks Luburić and Kondić carried out hundreds of deaths of women and children. There, Stepinac also carried out terrible deaths against countless children.

Anka Mećava Mišljenović, a survivor of that time, tells of being in Jastrebarsko, a concentration camp for Serbian children run by nuns, where in a crowded church, they were all converted to Catholicism. Stepinać himself was present there. Many of the children and their families were killed.[226]

Furthermore, before and around this time, it is recognized that the Vatican was not opposed to forced conversions to Catholicism. For example, on February 6, 1942, Pope Pius XII privately received 206 ustashis members in uniforms and blessed them, symbolically supporting their actions of forced conversions and the systematic killing of Orthodox "schismatics." In fact, two days later - February 8 - Rusinović, the ustasha envoy to the Holy See, kept a report which said, among other things, "The Holy See rejoices (at the forced 'reconversion')." [227]

On January 1, 1943, Pius XII sent a telegram to Ante Pavelić thanking him for his good wishes, noting, "For all that you have expressed to US both in your own name and that of the Croatian Catholics. We thank you and joyfully send the apostolic benediction to you and to the Croatian people." In March of the same year, during the anniversary of the enthronement of Pius XII, there was also another exchange of good wishes.[228]

---

[226] Anka Mećava Mišljenović (February 1, 2010), Anka Mećava Mišljenović, February 1, 2010, Belgrade, Jasenovac Research Institute: https://www.jasenovac.org/what-was-jasenovac/survivor-testimonies/anka-mecava-misljenovic-february-1-2010-belgrade/; accessed July 13, 2023.

[227] Vuković Slobodan V. (2004), Uloga Vatikana u razbijanju Jugoslavije, Sociološki pregled, vol. 38, issue 3, p. 430.

[228] Donald J. Beswick (September 5, 1977), Ustashi and the Pope, Salient. Official Newspaper of Victoria University of Wellington Students Association. Vol 40 No. 22, op. cit.

A memo from Stepinac dated May 18, 1943, begs Pope Pius XII to preserve the "Independent State of Croatia," stating:

"In bringing peace to the world, think, Holy Father, of the Croatian nation, ever faithful to Christ and to you. The young Croatian State, born in circumstances more terrible and difficult than any other state for many centuries, struggling desperately for its survival, shows with all this at every opportunity that it wants to remain faithful to its great Catholic traditions and to ensure better and clearer prospects for the Catholic Church in that corner of the globe. Otherwise, its destruction or fatal reduction: thousands of the best Croatian believers and priests would willingly and gladly sacrifice their lives to avoid this terrible possibility. Not only would those 240,000 converts of Serbian Orthodoxy be destroyed, but also the entire Catholic population of so many territories with all their churches and monasteries..."[229]

The following month, on June 5, 1943, Ante Pavelić sent the pope his congratulations; to which Pius XII responded cordially, "Praying God for the happiness of the Croatian people."[230] Pavelić visited Rome then and Pius XII was afraid to receive him for fear of offending the Allies, and yet he received him.[231]

However, a setback would come: on the occasion of a massacre committed by the ustashis in early 1943, Stepinac gave a sermon in the cathedral of Zagreb raising his voice against such crimes, so in revenge, the ustashis would shoot thirty peasants from his home village of Krašić, including his brother Maksim, without the knowledge of the archbishop.

According to the documents, the Zagreb archbishop's protests were prompted by Vatican pressure, which in that year assumed that the defeat of Hitler's coalition had begun;[232] and believed that the ustasha government in Croatia would be replaced. In this way, they wanted to escape unscathed from the post-war international condemnation.

"Stepinac had officially criticized the government's policies more than once, particularly its racial policies. Yet his attacks on the Ustasha leaders and his relations with the partisans did not seriously undermine his conviction that the regime's faults were greatly outweighed by its merits. These included the war on abortion, the ban

---

[229] Editorial Board, Secret Documents on Relations between the Vatican and the Ustasha ND, Library of the Society of Croatian Journalists, Zagreb, 1952; Vojislav Gaćinović, Date - 1961, Paris, France, p. 101.

[230] Donald J. Beswick (September 5, 1977), Ustashi and the Pope, Salient. Official Newspaper of Victoria University of Wellington Students Association. Vol 40 No. 22, ob. cit.

[231] John Pollard, The Papacy in the Age of Totalitarianism, 1914-1958 (Oxford University Press, Oxford, OX, UK, 2014), p. 347; Michael Phayer, Pius XII, the Holocaust, and the Cold War (Indiana University Press, Bloomington, IN, 2008), p. 219.

[232] Pino Adriano and Giorgio Cingolani, Nationalism and Terror: Ante Pavelić and Ustasha Terrorism from Fascism to the Cold War (Central European University Press (CEU Press), Budapest-New York, 2018), p. 252. For a reason Vatican Radio warned the French people in that same month of June 1943, where we quote the response of Pétain's government, "he who makes a distinction between Jews and other men is unfaithful to God and is in conflict with God's commands." The impact of any statement, however, was limited. A censorship order to the press said, "No mention is to be made of the Vatican protest to Marshal Pétain in favor of the Jews." Pope St. John Paul II (2000), A Response to 'The Vatican and the Holocaust', Catholic Culture/Catholic League (November, 2000).

on all pornography, the abolition of Masonry, decrees against blasphemy, the Christian education of soldiers, and increased endowments for divinity schools."[233]

The Vatican's idea, which was pushed through Archbishop Stepinac, was to change the Ustasha government in Croatia and bring to power Maček's HSS party, allowing the nation (being ostensibly anti-fascist) to maintain the borders of the Independent State of Croatia. It is not by chance that in a report of May 8 of that year (days before the aforementioned letter) from Abbot Ramiro Marcone to the Secretary of State, he shows "the efforts of the Croatian episcopate in favor of the Orthodox Serbs and Jews in the territory of the NDH." In addition to "another dossier, much more exhaustive, in defense of the Orthodox and non-Christians in Croatia, addressed by the Archbishop of Zagreb to Cardinal Maglione [...]" and where "The representative of the Apostolic See in Croatia reminds the Vatican Secretariat of State of the partial activities of the Orthodox clergy before and at the time of the attack on Yugoslavia. Abbot Ramiro Marcone points out that the Catholic episcopate and clergy in the new state are committed to respect universal human and Christian principles."[234] All this meant double-dealing on the part of the Vatican, especially since they were assured at the time that the Serbs were sending propaganda about massacres committed against them; and that instead, it was the Serbs themselves who were massacring Catholics.[235] We must remember that Stepinac's protests against the severity applied to Serbs and Jews from 1941 and subsequent years,[236] was in line with his philosophy of allowing them a sincere conversion to Catholicism.

In March 1944, Pope Pius XII sent the following telegram to Ante Pavelić: "The wishes which you and the Croatian people have expressed to Us, upon the occasion of the fifth anniversary of Our Pontificate, are very dear to Us, and We pray that God may bless you with His most gracious gifts."[237]

Although, indeed, the figures of the killings in Croatia are often manipulated for political reasons, the available documentation leaves no doubt about the number of victims from 1941 to 1945.[238] German archives show that by September 6, 1941, 200,000 Serbs had been killed.

A report of February 17, 1942, states 300,000 murders. While on September 16 of the same year, it is said that several hundred thousand.

By September 27, 1943, 400,000 deaths were reported. A later report put the figure at 500,000. Another document shows that on March 16, 1944, between 600,000 and 700,000 people were reported massacred. A later report shows 750,000. A gradual increase in victims can be seen near the end of the war. These sources from the German archives, cross-checked with the Italian Fascist, Croatian, and Serbian ones, confirm the number of victims claimed by Ante Pavelić's Croatia.

---

[233] Ibid, p. 252; citing ADSS, vol. 9, doc. 130, 220-22.

[234] Franjo Šanjek (December 18, 1997), Dr. Alojzije Stepinac i Nezavisna Država Hrvatska u svjetlu nadbiskupova dossiera Svetoj Stolici (1943.), Croatica Christiana Periodica; Vol.21, No. 40, pp. 98, 99.

[235] Ibid, pp. 100, 101.

[236] Michael Phayer, Pius XII, the Holocaust, and the Cold War (Indiana University Press, Bloomington, IN, 2008), pp. 12, 13.

[237] Donald J. Beswick (September 5, 1977), Ustashi and the Pope, Salient. Official Newspaper of Victoria University of Wellington Students Association. Vol 40 No. 22, ob. cit.

[238] Vladimir Umeljić (November 7, 2011), Vladimir Umeljic: Comment on: Jasenovac is being used for political interests, Јадодовно 1941. - Jadovno 1941. Note: unless otherwise noted, this is the same source.

Sometime later, as a result of the defeat of Nazi Germany, resulting in the fall of ustashi Croatia in 1945, Ante Pavelić and many ustasha criminals went on the run.[239] After consultations with Rome, Stepinac and Ante Pavelić set in motion a joint plan that would prevent their model state from crumbling as was happening to fascist Europe around them. They planned to prevent the Yugoslav government from dispersing the Ustashis armies and to persuade the Allies to occupy Yugoslavia to prevent the Central Government from seizing the Independent State of Croatia. Convinced that the Vatican would use its influence among the Great Powers to save them, Stepinac and Ante Pavelić desperately set about implementing their new policy. In the meantime, they began to reorganize the Ustashi armies to prevent the Ustashi collapse of Croatia, as well as resist and if possible destroy the new Yugoslav Central Government.[240] Stepinac summoned his bishops to a conference on March 24, 1945, to obtain the use of the spiritual authority of the Church for the promotion of political and military designs. Backed by the majority of the bishops, the archbishop issued a pastoral letter, first praising Ante Pavelić, after which they attacked the Yugoslav National Liberation movement. Next, they "ordered all Croats to help the Ustashi bands to fight the Yugoslav troops."[241]

Domagoj Margetić, a Croatian journalist, ended up in 2006 in custody by the government of the then Prime Minister of Croatia, Ivo Sanader, for publishing highly classified documents.[242] Although he was sentenced to three months in prison, as he was a heart patient, he was detained in the Zagreb prison hospital. He was placed in a room with Dinko Šakić, the last commandant of the Jasenovac concentration camp. He had near his bed a picture of himself on horseback with Ante Pavelić, as well as a lot of iconography around the room. Šakić was then close to 80 years old.

A part of Šakić's memoirs written in a dark red notebook and whose minutes were signed by Pavelić, Šakić, Luburić, and Stepinac, describes the last days of the Independent State of Croatia and a meeting then with Ante Pavelić, Maks Luburić, and Dinko Šakić himself with Cardinal Alojzije Stepinac, who invited them to the meeting. Stepinac told them, on behalf and at the expense of the English, that through the English secret services they were guaranteed to escape safely. Pavelić agreed to that plan, after which a number of works of art and valuables that were mostly stolen from Jewish, Serbian, and Gypsy families in the territory of the Independent State of Croatia, were stored in the treasury of the Zagreb Cathedral and even a record was made.[243]

Avro Manhattan comments that, "At the end of April, 1945, Pavelić, with the full consent of Stepinac, ordered the burial, in the Franciscan monastery in Zagreb Cathedral city, the Capitol, of thirty-six chests of plundered gold and valuables—rings, jewelry, gold watches, gold dentures, gold fillings which had been wrenched from the

---

[239] Avro Manhattan, The Vatican's Holocaust: The Most Horrifying Religious Massacre of the 20th Century (Ozark Books, Springfield, United States, 1986), pp. 24, 29.

[240] Ibid, p. 138.

[241] Ibid, p. 139.

[242] (July 2, 2017), INTERVJU: Domagoj Margetić o antifašizmu, Titu, Paveliću, Londonu i Berlinu, GLOBAL CIR TELEVIZIJA: https://www.youtube.com/watch?v=tzi_n_N1QzM; accessed May 31, 2023. Note: unless otherwise noted, this is the same source.

[243] Ignacio Montes de Oca, Ustashas: El ejército nazi de Perón y el Vaticano (Sudamericana, 2013), op. cit.

jaws of victims whom the Ustashi had massacred—and about two truckloads of silver."[244]

Ignacio Montes de Oca points out:

"In May 1944, the ustashas deposited 80 million dollars of the time in gold and 403 million in cash of the same currency in the Swiss National Bank. In August of the same year, a new deposit of $1.1 million was recorded in the same account. New deposits were made in the following months until an unspecified amount was reached."[245]

Quoting Uki Goñi, we are told that "the USSR government transferred to the financial system managed by the Vatican 2.4 tons of gold and an undetermined amount of foreign currency from 1944 until the end of the war." And "that it is possible to document the shipment of 789 ponds of gold to the Swiss National Bank in May of that year and 1 ton the following August."[246]

It is also known that in July 1945, the Swiss authorities returned to the Yugoslav government 1.33 tons of gold in 121 ingots that the ustasha regime had hidden in its banks. Pavelić himself deposited in the Vatican coffers an approximate total of 882 pounds of gold that served for his accommodation and of the ustashas hidden in Rome in the near future.

It is known that "Pavelić still had about 200 million Swiss francs, which were then deposited in accounts controlled by the Holy See."

Šakić writes that Pavelić never received the aforementioned assurances from the British government through Stepinac. These negotiations, discussions, and agreements were very detailed.[247]

The British government pressured its secret services so that they, in turn, pressured Tito in Yugoslavia to get London to protect Stepinac; apparently returning the favor for all that the archbishop did in various mediations and for the British.

Pavelić fled Croatia in May 1945.[248] The Catholic priest Krunoslav Draganović spent a fortune on the escapes of Pavelić and many ustasha criminals.[249] As revealed by priest Milan Simcic, who was Draganović's secretary, in the post-war period "every move made around the ustashas had the support of Pope Pius XII, who was informed by Bishop Montini about every important detail in this plot, including the route of the Croatian treasury."

From his hiding place in Austria, Pavelić mid-year ordered his new corps of fighters called *krizari* (the crusaders) to an offensive in Croatia against Tito's troops. The

---

[244] Avro Manhattan, The Vatican's Holocaust: The Most Horrifying Religious Massacre of the 20th Century (Ozark Books, Springfield, United States, 1986), p. 141.

[245] Ignacio Montes de Oca, Ustashas: El ejército nazi de Perón y el Vaticano (Sudamericana, 2013), op. cit. Note: unless otherwise indicated, it is the same source.

[246] Ignacio Montes de Oca, Ustashas: El ejército nazi de Perón y el Vaticano (Sudamericana, 2013), op. cit. Note: unless otherwise indicated, it is the same source.

[247] (July 2, 2017), INTERVJU: Domagoj Margetić o antifašizmu, Titu, Paveliću, Londonu i Berlinu, GLOBAL CIR TELEVIZIJA: https://www.youtube.com/watch?v=tzi_n_N1QzM; accessed May 31, 2023. Note: unless otherwise noted, this is the same source.

[248] Uki Goñi, The Real Odessa: How Peron Brought The Nazi War Criminals To Argentina (Granta Books, 2022), ob. cit.

[249] Ignacio Montes de Oca, Ustashas: El ejército nazi de Perón y el Vaticano (Sudamericana, 2013), op. cit. Note: unless otherwise indicated, it is the same source.

krizari were made up of ustasha soldiers and officers whose action against Yugoslavia had been named months earlier, "Operation April 10." Most of the *Krizari* had light weapons, but some arms and ammunition were supplied to them by the Allies, in the interest of fighting communism.

"Pavelić left in the hands of Vjekoslav Luburić the command of Operation April 10. By that time, Luburić had set up his ustasha station in Franco's Spain.

Ustasha Kavran was appointed camp commander and his staff was headed by Ljubo Miloš, Luburić's brother-in-law, who had served as an officer in the Jasenovac and Lopeglova concentration camps."

In October of that year (1945), Pavelić ordered Luburić to commission Colonel Ustasha Erik Lisak -Pavelić's former head of public security- to travel clandestinely to Croatia to organize resistance against Tito's communist regime. Lizak had been appointed commander of the Krizari in Croatia.

In the following days, General Ante Moskov, Pavelić's wartime chief of custody, infiltrated into Croatia to reinforce Lisak's work. But also Luka Grgić, an ustasha lieutenant, and Ante Vrban, former commandant of the Stara Gradiška and Slana concentration camps, where he murdered Serb and Jewish children with Zyklon B poison gas, joined them in the expedition.

Lisak was received in Zagreb on September 19 by Archbishop Stepinac, who launched a network of shelters in Croatian Catholic Church properties for the first krizari groups. Stepinac's commitment to them was sealed in the Croatian Curia building, in a ceremony over which he presided and at which the flag of the new version of the ustasha militia was enshrined.

The Croats, meanwhile, were assisted by British and American agents in Italy in their attempts to destabilize the Tito regime. Many of the Krizari collaborated as spies and informers for the West. Lewis Perry, a British intelligence colonel, helped the Krizari to Yugoslavia to carry out their operations. And Srecko Rover was one of the closest Croatians to the British spy.

Catholic convents and monasteries in Croatia were used as shelters by the Krizari as they planned attack operations against Tito's communist government.

The radio network that the Catholic Church had to link its congregations in Croatia was used by Pavelić to communicate with the Krizari. The network "was based in the command set up by his men inside the Vatican premises in Rome."

Yugoslavia asked Italy and the Vatican numerous times to stop the activities of the Krizari. But the response was silence or refusal to take responsibility for these activities. The headquarters for the operations was the College of San Girolamo in Rome.

Ten days before the final collapse and after "hasty consultations with the Vatican […] Ante Pavelić asked a trusted friend to take hold of the reins of Ustashi Government. His name? Archbishop Stepinac."[250] When the regime fell on November 8, 1945, Ustashi Croatia disintegrated, so Stepinac reconsecrated the strength of the

---

[250] Avro Manhattan, The Vatican's Holocaust: The Most Horrifying Religious Massacre of the 20th Century (Ozark Books, Springfield, United States, 1986), pp. 139, 140.

Ustashi Crusaders with a decree in his chapel. After the act, he received "a pledge from Ustashi intellectuals" to fight to the end for the liberator of ustashi Croatia."[251]

But in April 1946, because of the failure of the Krizari and the Croatian Catholic Church against the Tito regime, Pavelić decided to move to Rome, coming under the direct protection of the Vatican.[252] Later that month, Pavelić was detected at the Collegio Pio Pontificio and then tracked down at the College of San Girolamo, a Catholic seminary where at least a hundred Croats were taking refuge. A group of ustashas bodyguards protected Pavelić from Tito's agents. To avoid his arrest, Vatican officials provided Pavelić with a car with Holy See diplomatic plates that granted him absolute immunity as he drove around the Italian capital to meet with his supporters. Faced with the pressure of hiding Pavelić in the Roman center, Vatican authorities moved him in May 1946 to the Villa of Castel Gandolfo, the summer residence of the popes, where the former pro-Nazi president of Romania was also staying.

Already in June, Pavelić attempts to escape to South America from Spain with a Spanish passport under the false name of Pedro Gronner, which was given to him by Krunoslav Draganović. When he arrived in Austria, he changed his identity again, presenting documents that credited him as the Spanish priest Pedro Gomez, ostensibly a "Spanish minister of religion." The OSS, the predecessor of the American CIA, searched for him throughout his journey through various monasteries and churches of the Jesuit order.

"However, the Vatican's espionage system discovered, most likely with the help of its American contacts, that the OSS agents who were unaware of the protection Poglavnik was receiving were setting a trap to capture him as soon as he arrived in Spain. Warned in time, the ustasha returned to Vatican lands, where he began to look for another escape route."

During the following months, Pavelić was a guest in other buildings of the Holy See, and by January 1947, OSS agents in Rome followed him to the Dominican monastery of Santa Sabina. In March they saw him at the Vatican college on Via Gioacchino Belli, and then elsewhere.

Subsequently, the OSS learned that he and his ustashas were again hiding in San Girolamo College and other Vatican-controlled buildings. We read again that:

"In May 1947, U.S. Secretary of State George Marshall received a secret memorandum from Vincent La Vista, his military attaché in Rome, in which he accused the Vatican of being the main force behind the mass escape of war criminals and gave a detailed account of the Church personalities involved and the responsibility of Pius XII in its operation. [...]
[...] the escape route to Latin America was not a mere improvisation but a grand conspiracy put together by extremely powerful actors. There it is described in detail of the role of Draganović and twenty-one other high-ranking Vatican officials throughout Europe."

---

[251] Ibid, p. 29, 142.
[252] Ignacio Montes de Oca, Ustashas: Perón's Nazi Army and the Vatican (Sudamericana, 2013), ob. cit. Unless otherwise indicated, from here on it is the same source.

Draganović had a daily working relationship with Cardinal Pietro Fumasoni Biondi, in charge of the Congregation of Propaganda Fide. Another regular visitor to the cardinal was James Jesus Angleton, representative of U.S. counterintelligence in Rome and Dulles' man within the secret service operating in Rome.

Vincent La Vista, a Foreign Service officer in Rome, verified the existence of two antagonistic groupings within the Western regimes.

When Pavelić was about to be caught, Angleton requested permission from the State Department to carry out the arrest. But in July 1947, he was told that Operation Circle was to be aborted and that the Ustaše criminals were to be left under Vatican protection.

William Gowen, a U.S. agent who was looking for Pavelić and confirmed to me the role of several of these criminals, relates that Giovanni Montini (future Pope Paul VI), later complained to Angleton about the investigations conducted by the OSS, arguing that his men broke into Vatican buildings that enjoyed diplomatic immunity.

A few years later, Pavelić and many Ustaše and Nazi criminals managed to flee to South America, particularly Argentina with the help of Vatican intelligence agents. The operation of escape of war criminals by the Vatican was Operation Monastery.[253] Alois Hudal was a key bishop in the operation, to which Pope Pius XII provided the funds for its operation, according to Monsignor Bayer himself, who was in charge of the Nazi fugitives in the operation.[254]

Stepinac, for his part, was arrested in September 1946, provoking a harsh reaction from Pius XII and the Vatican's enraged international appeal for "justice."[255] The Croatian archbishop was put on trial by Tito's communist government; along with many other priests and ustasha criminals, he was found guilty.[256] He said at the trial that he opposed forced conversions to Catholicism, saying that he "could not" be responsible for what other dioceses did without his consent.[257] He spent five years in Lepoglava prison and was then transferred to house arrest, confined to his home parish of Krašić.[258] He passed away on February 10, 1960.[259]

A Croatian-born revisionism about events during the Independent State of Croatia insists that there were no massacres and that Jews were treated well. It further claims that there were mostly concentration camps against Croats. But thorough historical research disproves these attempts.[260] A recent case, for example, was the promotion of

[253] Eric Frattini, The Entity: Five Centuries of Secret Vatican Espionage (St. Martin's Press, New York, 2008), pp. 281, 282.

[254] Philippe Sands, The Ratline: The Exalted Life and Mysterious Death of a Nazi Fugitive (Vintage Books, 2022), p. 229; Uki Goñi, The Real Odessa: How Perón Brought the Nazi War Criminals to Argentina (Granta Books, 2022), ob. cit.

[255] Avro Manhattan, The Vatican's Holocaust: The Most Horrifying Religious Massacre of the 20th Century (Ozark Books, Springfield, United States, 1986), p. 150-152.

[256] Alexander, S. (1978). Archbishop Stepinac reconsidered. Religion in Communist Lands, 6(2), 76-88.

[257] Jozo Tomasevich, War and Revolution in Yugoslavia, 1941-1945: Occupation and Collaboration (Stanford University Press, Stanford, California, 2001), pp. 578, 579.

[258] Marcus Tanner, Croatia: A Nation Forged in War (Yale University Press, 1997), p. 186.

[259] Jozo Tomasevich, War and Revolution in Yugoslavia, 1941-1945: Occupation and Collaboration (Stanford University Press, Stanford, California, 2001), p. 562.

[260] Ivo Goldstein (August 21, 2021), A collage of lies: the Croatian right's Holocaust revisionism, The Jerusalem Post; Jelena Prtorić (June 3, 2020), Why won't Croatia face its past? New Internationalist; N1 Zagreb (September 1, 2019), Simon Wiesenthal Centre urges Croatia to ban Jasenovac revisionist works, N1; Anja Vladisavljevic (January 25, 2019), Holocaust Revisionism Widespread in Croatia, Warns Report,

a book by Josip Pečarić, a professor of mathematics at the University of Zagreb; and Stjepan Razum, a Catholic priest employed by the Croatian State Archives. The promotion of the book "The Lie of Jasenovac" was given on January 17, 2019, in the hall of the Jesuit Church, or Church of the Sacred Heart of Jesus in Zagreb. This church regularly performs funeral masses for Ante Pavelić. The publisher of the book has published other revisionist works lacking historical rigor, and those doing such work advocate the inclusion of the Independent State of Croatia.[261]

Baron Avro Manhattan met Mrs. Eleanor Roosevelt, wife of the late President of the United States at a private dinner in Upper Brook Street, Mayfair, London.[262] When asked if she had heard of the ustashi crimes, she replied:

"One of the worst, if not the worst, crimes of the war." was her prompt reply. "I heard of them in the winter of 1941-2. Neither I nor my husband at first believed them to be true."

"I did not believe them either," the present author commented. "I assumed them to be propaganda."

"We thought the same," replied Mrs. Roosevelt. "The Catholic lobby was the most successful at the White House for years."[263]

When he asked Mrs. Roosevelt why these Catholic atrocities were not as well known as the Nazi ones, she replied:

"Nazi Germany is no more," replied Mrs. Roosevelt. "The Catholic Church is still here with us. More powerful than ever. With her own Press and the World Press at her bidding. Anything published about the atrocities in the future will not be believed…."[264]

Stepinac was beatified on October 3, 1998, by Pope John Paul II during his visit to Croatia.[265]

It would be foolish to generalize the Croatian people, so here we refer specifically to those who adhered to the ustasha teachings and participated in one way or another in the intolerance that occurred during World War II. After talking for hours with a friend who is a descendant of several victims of the most horrible cruelties committed during the Independent State of Croatia, and sharing with me testimonies and additional information about numerous survivors, I can say that it is gratifying to know that there is hope, faith, and love within those who witnessed the unimaginable.

Balkan Transitional Justice; Goldstein, I., & Goldstein, S. (2002). Revisionism in Croatia: The case of Franjo Tudman. East European Jewish Affairs, 32(1), 52-64.

[261] Portal Novosti (January 7, 2019), Promocija revizionističke knjige u crkvenoj dvorani, Portal Novosti.

[262] Avro Manhattan, The Vatican's Holocaust: The Most Horrifying Religious Massacre of the 20th Century (Ozark Books, Springfield, United States, 1986), p. 133.

[263] Ibid.

[264] Ibid.

[265] David Yallop, The Power and the Glory: Inside the Dark Heart of Pope John Paul II's Vatican (Constable & Robinson Ltd, London, 2007), op. cit.

CHAPTER

4

"The Clash of Civilizations" -The Vatican vs. Freemasonry and the United States of America, part 2

France, the Jesuit conspiracy against Freemasonry, and the League of Nations
Mildred J. Headings stated in 1949 that the Catholic Church is the largest in France and claimed to teach the only true religion. But the French Church also denounced Freemasonry.

The Catholic party tried in the past to influence the French regime, and in the first period of the Third Republic (the whole period was from 1870 to 1940), many Catholics organized with anti-republican elements to overthrow it. Consequently, Republicans and Freemasons contended to make the political, administrative, and educational state organization republican and democratic only through the expulsion of Catholics from such spheres.[1]

The French Freemason Albert Lantoine, referring to the Jesuit Hermann J. Gruber and on the relations between Jesuits and Freemasons, wrote:

"In June 1928, notable Freemasons, among them the Secretary General of the Grand Lodge of New York, Ossian Lang, and the Viennese philosopher Dr. Kurt Reichl, met in Aachen with the Jesuit who had once proved to be the most inflexible adversary of the "sect," Father Gruber. [...] the meeting had, however, this remarkable result: "Both sides showed themselves willing to greatly restrict their mutual polemics and to refrain in particular, in the future, from any hateful and fact-distorting imputations."[2]

We further read that the previous year, Gruber defended in a reply to Brother Mason Dr. Kurt Reichl, whose most characteristic passages are:

"I absolutely share your point of view and find also that the exchange of views between Catholics and Freemasons, in which are at stake not only the higher interests of all men individually, but also those of all nations and peoples and those of all mankind, must be conducted with due seriousness and in the spirit of a truly Christian or truly humanitarian love... allowing oneself to be guided by the sole ambition of making objective truth triumph in the interest of all."[3]

---

[1] Mildred J. Headings, French Freemasonry Under the Third Republic (The Johns Hopkins Press, Baltimore, 1949), p. 122.
[2] Albert Lantoine, Lettre Au Souverain Pontife (Editions Du Symbolisme, 16, rue Ernest-Renan (xv^c), 1937), p. 59.
[3] Ibid, pp. 59, 60.

For his part, Lantoine stated that, "We do not believe that Fr. Gruber, in his letter, as well as in his meeting with the Masons in Aachen, obeyed his personal inspiration. A Jesuit does not and cannot allow himself such initiatives. He had behind him the leaders of his Order, and I dare to hope, an even more brilliant Authority. Indeed, far from denying such a policy, *La Civiltà Cattolica* of Rome and the *Etudes* of Paris supported him with the delicacy of tact demanded by the "profession.""[4] Now, we wonder why precisely Rome and Paris. We noted that it was from the Grand Orient of France and from the French government that support was pouring in for the United States to democratize all of Europe; the survival of the Catholic Church being thus threatened.

For their part, the Jesuits of France took certain actions in an attempt to influence the nation not to be a benefactor of American purposes on the European continent; and for Catholicism to regain its power and place as it had for most of its history.

We will now look at another chapter in the resistance of the Society of Jesus. Pierre-Joseph Berteloot, a French Jesuit priest, with visiting cards entitled to the A.P./Popular Action of the Society, "from one step to another gained access to the most diverse circles and personalities; Desbuquois encouraged and advised him in his contacts, very secret, with right-wing Freemasons, in particular with the historian Albert Lantoine, whose prejudices against Catholicism he tried to overthrow."[5] In this way, Lantoine had many other contacts with ecclesiastics.[6]

The collaboration between Berteloot and Desbuquois resulted in a covert conspiracy of the Jesuits against French Freemasonry to stop the cooperation with the United States to democratize Europe and remove papal powerful influence.

Thus, in 1934, Berteloot, through the journal *Études* and his friendship with Lantoine, who wrote at his request his famous *Lettre au Souverain Pontife* -Letter to the Sovereign Pontiff- in Paris in 1937, supported a rapprochement and pacification between the Catholic Church and Freemasonry. Therefore, Berteloot wrote the titles: *La Franc-Maçonnerie et l'Eglise Catholique, Perspectives de pacification* (Freemasonry and the Catholic Church, Perspectives of pacification/Paris, 1947); *Les Francs-Maçons devant l'Histoire* (Freemasons before History/Paris, 1949) and *Jésuite et Franc-Maçon. Souvenirs d'une amitié* (Jesuits and Freemasons. Memories of a friendship/Paris, 1952).[7] The *Revue de Paris* published on September 15, 1938, Berteloot's response to the offers of truce from the Freemasons. Alluding to the Catholic origins of Freemasonry, "Berteloot asked the sincere Masons if they would have the courage to return Freemasonry to its primitive purity." That question provoked astonishment and some anger among Masons and the Catholic Church. While Lantoine was accused of having sold out to the Jesuits, Berteloot was reproached for having

---

[4] Ibid.

[5] P. Droulers, Le père Desbuquois et l'Action Populaire: Dans la gestation d'un monde nouveau (1919-1946) (Presses de l'Université Grégorienne, Rome, 1981), p. 45, note 24.

[6] Jean-Laurent Turbet (July 24, 2007), "Lettre au Souverain Pontife," d'Albert Lantoine, Le Blog des Spiritualités.

[7] Charles E. O'Neill, S.I., Joaquín M.a Domínguez, S.I., Diccionario histórico de la Compañía de Jesús: Infante de Santiago-Piatkiewicz (Institutum Historicum, S.I., Rome, Universidad Pontificia Comillas, Madrid, 2001), p. 2561.

become a Masonic instrument. Nevertheless, several Masonic publications approved of Lantoine's initiative.[8]

Victor Dillar, another Jesuit priest, established contact in Vichy during the Nazi occupation with several Freemasons; among them were Lehman, Yves Marsaudon - a close friend of Roncalli, future Pope John XXIII and a Freemason -, and the Count of Foy, who were members of the Supreme Council of France (Ancient and Accepted Scottish Rite). Joining forces with Jesuit Victor Dillard, they organized a group of "libres-penseurs- et libres-croyants," (free-thinkers and free-believers) as they called it in the intimacy with fine humor. They aimed to bring together all men of goodwill, and Dillard regularly attended these colloquiums where numerous Freemasons and sympathizers were not lacking.[9]

Eduardo R. Callaey, historian and Argentinean Mason, says that in 1937, a member of the Supreme Council of the 33rd Degree of the Ancient and Accepted Scottish Rite of France, Albert Lantoine, "after having maintained for years a deep dialogue with his Jesuit friend, Fr. Joseph Berteloot, transmitted his famous *Letter to the Sovereign Pontiff*" (to Pope Pius XII) in which he proposed *"a truce of God"*: the end of a long era of war and dissent, since *"Freemasonry and the Church had a common heritage to save...."*[10]

The Church did not acknowledge receipt of the letter, but many Catholics and Masons sought to overcome the conflict by preserving each side's respective identity.[11]

Part of the letter reads as follows:

"There is as much purity and as much grandeur in the word of the philosophers as in that of the Redeemer. The light-infused in the ruins of the Parthenon remains as lively as the flaming chorus of the cathedrals. Therefore, to avert the avalanche of the barbarians, your God should make a chain with the gods. For behold, the time is coming when the "mouth of darkness" spoken of in Scripture will be opened. It is about to engulf both the grace of Sleep and the virtue of Thought.
[...]
Possessed by the spirit of examination, we are servants of Satan. You, possessors of truth, are servants of God. These two masters complement each other. They need each other. You are pressing the Power to exterminate Freemasonry. Beware! On that day, in the words of Meleager, your murderous mouths will "burst into tears," for the death of Satan will mark the agony of your Death."[12]

Lantoine once said of the words "servants of Satan": "I was wrong, I didn't use quite the correct term. I should have said servants of Lucifer."[13]

---

[8] J. A. Faucher, A. Ricker, Histoire de la Franc-Maçonnerie en France (Nouvelles Editions Latines, Paris, 1967), p. 426.

[9] Charles E. O'Neill, S.I., Joaquín M.a Domínguez, S.I., Diccionario histórico de la Compañía de Jesús: Infante de Santiago-Piatkiewicz (Institutum Historicum, S.I., Rome, Universidad Pontificia Comillas, Madrid, 2001), p. 2561.

[10] Eduardo R. Callaey, El Otro Imperio Cristiano: De la Orden del Temple a la Francmasonería (Ediciones Nowtilus, S.L., Madrid, 2005), p. 217.

[11] Ibid.

[12] Albert Lantoine, Lettre Au Souverain Pontife (Editions Du Symbolisme, 16, rue Ernest-Renan (xvc), 1937), pp. 168, 169, 170.

[13] Vicomte Léon de Poncins, Freemasonry and the Vatican: A Struggle for Recognition (EWorld Inc., New Edition, 1994), ob. cit.

Michel Dumesnil de Gramont, Grand Master of the Grand Lodge of France, wrote in his work La Maconnerie et l'Eglise Catholique (pp. 9-12), referring critically to Lantoine: "Catholicism now appeals to him as a protector of the noblest spiritual ideals, and even, as Antonio Coen thought, as the champion of freedom of thought." He expressed in turn that "Lantoine would like French Masonry to accompany him in his pilgrimage towards Rome."[14]

Berteloot strove to demonstrate that the lodges were strongly impregnated with Catholicism, beginning with the guilds of stonemasons dominated by monks, until the 18th century, and later giving way to English Protestantism. With this, he wanted to prove to the Catholics that Freemasonry was not an enemy of Catholicism, but he did not influence so much the Grand Orient of France; but to the Scottish Rite of the Grand Lodge. The Jesuit convinced some Masonic personalities, such as Mr. Marc Rucart, affiliated to a third rite - the Human Right - who would go to Rome in 1949 to visit the Pope.[15]

In those years, Nazi Germany, Fascist Italy, Franco's Spain, and the USSR would persecute Freemasonry.[16] France would face the same problems.

But the truth is, there were hidden intentions within the Society of Jesus in France to get closer to the French Freemasons. On the eve of World War II, Berteloot appealed for a "truce" between French Freemasonry and the Catholic Church. By then, France was threatened from within by communist propaganda, and from outside by the greed of dictatorial governments (Nazi Germany and Fascist Italy). Because of this danger, Berteloot implored that the collaboration and unity of all French people was absolutely necessary. That unity included Freemasonry. His request was published on September 15, 1938, in the *Revue de Paris*.[17] Thus, because of the growing dangers, both internal and external, facing the French state, some French Freemasons, among them Jean Richard Bloch, Antonio Coen, André Lebey, Albert Lantoine, Cauwel, and F. Varache, encouraged at that time a common front composed of Masonic and religious organizations. In this regard, Lantoine called attention to the fact that Jesuit Joseph Berteloot, considered a prominent Catholic, noted the lack of essential opposition between faith and reason, and asked if it would not be possible to cease the war between Freemasonry and Catholicism. Lantoine added that dignitaries of the Catholic Church were trying to avoid polemics against Freemasonry. Masons were also asked to remain silent on matters causing dissension between the two factions.[18] The Catholic Church, through Berteloot, saw in common with Freemasonry that opposing extremes (right and left) were not acceptable (incidentally, a position similar to that of Pope Francis), and would join forces against all repression; although some Masons were more inclined toward Bolshevism.[19] Lantoine, for his part, called for the spiritual forces to unite with the Masons in the face of the red danger (communism).[20] For the Freemason, "faith and thought and the forces represented by the church and

---

[14] Ibid.

[15] Le Monde (April 27, 1950), Les origines catholiques DE LA FRANC-MAÇONNERIE, Le Monde.

[16] Alain Bauer, Jean-Claude Rochigneux, Les relations internationales de la franc-maçonnerie française (Armand Colin, 2010), op. cit.

[17] Robert A. Graham (January 14, 1956), Apostle to the Freemasons, America Magazine, p. 423.

[18] Mildred J. Headings, French Freemasonry Under the Third Republic (The Johns Hopkins Press, Baltimore, 1949), p. 277; quoting *B. G. L.*, May, 1936, pp. 441-445.

[19] Ibid, pp. 277, 278.

[20] Ibid, p. 278.

Freemasonry [...] find the surest refuge in the democracies."[21] M. Coen, one of the most active Masons promoting a union between these factions, indicated that Freemasonry addressed those whom the church did not reach and that, therefore, the actions of Catholicism and Freemasonry complemented each other. He pointed out that both the Catholic Church and Freemasonry drew from the same spiritual forces: Judaism, the Greek heritage, and the writings of the Church Fathers; asking Masons to try to understand Catholicism beyond what was regularly associated at certain periods with some political groupings. He stressed the work of social betterment and his support for moral elevation, in the achievement of the Masonic ideals, and that what mattered was the betterment of man and not the means.[22]

Naturally, even when all these efforts were made, there was resistance by some Masons who questioned a Masonic alliance with the Catholic Church. They argued that a compromise between freethought and Catholicism was impossible. And that an alliance between non-Catholic religions and Catholicism was also doubtful.[23] After recalling the long list of encyclicals against Freemasonry, De Gramont requested that the initiative of appeasement come from the Catholic Church.[24] Other Masons warned against an alliance with the "enemy of progress", and mentioned "Spain in an effort to prove that Roman Catholicism awaited a favorable opportunity to execute "such a plan in France."[25] They were referring to the Franco government's repression of pro-Catholicism, which persecuted and crushed Freemasonry.

As for other voices more favorable to Catholicism, Marcel Caulwel, one of the Masons closest to Berteloot, requested that the Bible be restored in Masonic temples.[26]

On February 1, 1939, both the Grand Orient of France and the National Grand Lodge of France, responsible for restoring Anderson's Constitutions to their lodges, wrote to U.S. President Roosevelt (also a Mason),[27] through their Grand Masters and on behalf of both obediences, to thank him for his efforts to maintain peace; and to express their concern about the danger threatening Europe from Germany, stating that he was the only person with the authority to request a conference for all interested states to meet and address the situation.[28] The previous year, the U.S. Jesuit weekly, *America*, published that American Freemasons were rather conservative and not "not rabidly anti-Catholic."[29] But that Freemasonry was undergoing a "most insidious change" by being endangered by "a most secret penetration of the [Grand] Orient of Paris;" particularly in New York and Washington, D.C.[30] The American Jesuits were well

---

[21] Ibid; quoting *B. G. L.*, July, 1938, p. 196 (an excerpt from *Le Symbolisme*, June, 1938).

[22] Ibid.

[23] Ibid.

[24] Ibid, p. 279; citing *B. G. L.*, May, 1936, pp. 441-452; *ibid*, March, 1939, pp. 59-66; *ibid*, May, 1939, pp. 97-110.

[25] Ibid; citing *Bulletin Mensuel des Ateliers Supérieurs*, November, 1935, pp. 165-170; *B. G. L.*, May, 1938, pp. 130-133.

[26] Ibid; xiting *B. G. L.*, March, 1938, pp. 91-94.

[27] William D. Moore, Masonic Temples: Freemasonry, Ritual Architecture, and Masculine Archetypes (The University of Tennessee Press, Knoxville, 2006), p. xviii; Áine Cain and Abby Jackson (February 19, 2018), 20 US presidents who belonged to shadowy secret societies, Insider.

[28] Mildred J. Headings, French Freemasonry Under the Third Republic (The Johns Hopkins Press, Baltimore, 1949), pp. 279, 280; quoting *B. G. L.*, March, 1937, pp. 65-67.

[29] Paul A. Fisher, Behind the Lodge Door: Church, State and Freemasonry In America (TAN Books, Charlotte, North Carolina, 1994), p. 192; quoting America, April 30, 1938, "Commentary" section, p. 74.

[30] Ibid.

aware that the Grand Orient of France was the least sympathetic obedience to French Catholicism and the Vatican; as well as the biggest booster of contacts with American Freemasons for European democracy.

On the other hand, German aggression was about to threaten France. We will quote the words of Francois Tenand:

"A clever and persistant propaganda campaign began in favour of a "Petain dictatorship"...

"In 1935, Gustave Herve published a pamphlet which we are going to examine... The tract is entitled "We need Petain"... its foreword is an enthusiastic apology of the "Italian recovery" and "the even more amazing recovery of Germany", also an exaltation of the wonderful chiefs who were the authors of these recoveries. Now what about our own French people?... There is a man around whom we could gather... We also have a providential man... Do you want to know his name? It is Petain".

"We need Petain", for the homeland is in a dangerous position; and not only the homeland, but Catholicism also: "Christian civilisation is condemned to death if a dictatorial regime is not set up in every country"...

"Listen: "In peace time, a regime can only be swept away by a coup d'Etat if it is willing or if it has no support from the army and administrations. The operation can be a success only through a war and especially a defeat".[31]

After clearly alluding to Mussolini in Italy and Hitler in Germany, the dictator for France had to be Petain. Oscar Arnal writes: "Like it or not, French Catholicism was compelled to coexist with a secular republican state, and it did so, with some reluctance, until the "divine miracle" of Philippe Pétain."[32]

He was seen as someone who would recover the homeland and save Catholicism from the forces that threatened it in the country. The following year, in 1936, Canon Coube wrote that "The Lord who brought forth Charlemagne and the heroes of the Crusades can still raise up saviours... Amongst us, there must be men whom He has marked with His seal and who will be revealed when his time has come... Amongst us, there must be men of the cloth who are the workmen in the great national restorations. But what are the necessary conditions they need to accomplish this mission? Natural qualities of intelligence and character; also supernatural qualities that is to say obedience to God and His Law is just as indispensable, as this political work is moral and religious before anything else. These saviours are men with generous hearts who work only for the glory of God..." In fact, Francois Ternand said that Petain's name was not a secret among clerics and fascists.[33]

---

[31] Edmond Paris, The Secret History of the Jesuits (Chick Publications, Ontario, Calif. 1982), p. 158; citing Francois Tenand, "L' Ascension politique du Marechal Petain", (Ed. du livre francais, Paris 1946, pp. 40 ss).

[32] Oscar L. Arnal, Ambivalent Alliance: The Catholic Church and the Action Française, 1899-1939 (University of Pittsburgh Press, Pittsburgh, Pa, 1985), p. 96.

[33] Edmond Paris, The Secret History of the Jesuits (Chick Publications, Ontario, Calif. 1982), p. 158; citing Canon Coube: "Sainte Therese de l'Enfant Jesus et les crises du temps present", (Flammarion, Paris 1936, pp.165 ss). Imprimatur: 11th of January 1936.

98

Some former traitors who were collaborators of the Nazi regime and in sympathy with Catholicism, were Deat (hidden after the war in a convent of San Vito, near Turin until his death), Bucard and Doriot.[34] The French Freemason Edmond Paris tells us:

"Here is the secret report of agent 654 J.56, working for the German Secret Service, who sent these revelations to Himmler: "Paris, 5th of July 1939. "I can declare that, in France, the situation is now in our hands. Everything is ready for J day and all our agents are at their posts. Within a few weeks, the police force and military system will collapse like a pack of cards".

Many secret documents relate that the traitors had been chosen a long time before. Men like Luchaire, Bucard, Deat, Doriot... and Abel Bonnard (of the French Academy)"[35]

Andre Guerber detailed the payments that the German S.R. granted to the above-mentioned. [36]

French Catholic Action produced a generation of dictators on the model of Leon Degrelle; with men like Deat, Bucard, and Doriot, who was the agent No. 56 BK of the German secret service, and was also the most appreciated by the archbishopric and his supporters.[37]

When Germany invaded France in 1940, Marshal Philippe Pétain finally seized power in the country. With that, he sent Charles Huntziger to sign an armistice with the Germans on June 22 of the same year.

On July 10, 569 parliamentarians voted in favor of granting full powers to Pétain, against 80 not in favor, assuming full dictatorial powers, and united in his person the powers of president and prime minister, being designated "head of the French State." With that decision, came the capitulation of the Third Republic, being replaced by the Vichy regime, which was the puppet state in part of the French territory and all its colonies. The new government established from the beginning a collaborationist state with the Nazi regime, and therefore totally oppressive. The Vichy government not only persecuted Jews but also outlawed Freemasonry.[38]

During the occupation, the rector of the Catholic Institute of Paris, Cardinal Braudillart, said on July 30, 1941: "Hitler's war is a noble enterprise undertaken for the defence of European culture." The Archbishop of Paris, Cardinal Suhard, set an example to the whole bishopric by his full collaboration, as did the nuncio, Monsignor Valerio Valeri.[39]

---

[34] Loyd E. Lee (editor), World War II: Crucible of the Contemporary World: Commentary and Readings (M.E. Sharpe, 1991), p. 98; John Hellman, Knight-Monks of Vichy France: Uriage, 1940-1945 (McGill-Queen's University Press, 1993), p. 192.

[35] Edmond Paris, The Secret History of the Jesuits (Chick Publications, Ontario, Calif. 1982), p. 157; Andre Guerber: "Himmler et ses crimes" (Les Documents Nuit et Jour, Paris, 1981).

[36] Ibid.

[37] Ibid.

[38] Pierre Chevallier, Histoire de la Franc-Maçonnerie française. 3 La Maçonnerie: Eglise de la République (1877-1944) (Librairie Athène Fayard, 1975), ob. cit.

[39] Edmond Paris, The Secret History of the Jesuits (Chick Publications, Ontario, Calif. 1982), p. 159, and note 102.

Despite the persecution against the Masons, the lodges continued to work clandestinely. In the presence of the Consul General of the United States, an initiation was held in the crypt of a church near Cusset.[40]

An important fraction of Catholics involved in the French Resistance and certain Freemasons enrolled in the same fight against the common enemy led them to consider transcending their mutual opposition and to conclude an alliance. Or at least a modus vivendi.[41] Thus, on an unspecified date, there was a meeting in Toulouse between the Catholic resistance fighter Henri Frenay and the leader of the Droit Humain lodge, Marc Rucart. At the latter's request, he wanted his interlocutor to arrange an interview with Cardinal Gerlier, Primate of the Gauls. Rucart told him, in a dialogue which we transcribe below:

"You must know that I hold a high rank in Freemasonry... but Pétain has banished us from the nation. The anti-Masonic laws condemn many of our friends to misery. This would suffice to make you understand the feelings that I have towards Pétain, his regime, and the National Revolution... Add to this that I have just come out of prison. I spent almost a year in Fresnes... Have you ever been in prison?
- No, fortunately for me...
- Yes, of course. But I can't think of a better place to reflect. Not only did I think a lot, but I read a lot, especially the Old and New Testaments, and I even studied them. I even studied them. You seem surprised...?
- Yes, I didn't think the Bible could be the bedside book of a Masonic worshiper, but as a Catholic I am delighted. Has the divine light enlightened you?
- It would be too much to say, but after all," he replies with a smile, "perhaps it was the Holy Spirit who inspired the reflections that followed my reading.... Between Masonic morality and the Gospels, I found a great common denominator. Suddenly, the battles waged by the Church and the Lodges, undoubtedly necessary and legitimate fifty years ago, seem to me today derisory, anachronistic, and harmful. I would like to try to appease the old quarrels, to build a bridge between Freemasonry and the Catholic Church, to prepare together reconciliation, or at least understanding and tolerance..."

Marc Rucart then asked Henry Frenay if he could arrange an interview with Cardinal Gerlier to discuss the matter. On his return to Lyon, Frenay informed Father Chaillet, the Cardinal's secretary, of the former minister's wish. The message was passed on, but Frenay expressed that "I will never know if the meeting between the two men took place." But what was going on behind the scenes was impressive: Charles Riandey was a Catholic Freemason who participated in the plot of the French clergy, particularly with the Jesuits, to influence and destroy Freemasonry and re-establish French Catholic power.

---

[40] J. A. Faucher, A. Ricker, Histoire de la Franc-Maçonnerie en France (Nouvelles Editions Latines, Paris, 1967), p. 433.

[41] Pierre Chevallier, Histoire de la Franc-Maçonnerie française. 3 La Maçonnerie: Eglise de la République (1877-1944) (Librairie Athène Fayard, 1975), ob. cit. Note: unless otherwise indicated, this is the same source.

Riandey came from a very conservative Catholic family, and expressed that in "the social milieu to which my family belonged, we rather professed an aversion to Freemasonry."[42]

But let us look at his actions on the eve of the German invasion of France and during its occupation: the deputy bishop of Paris, Monsignor Beaussart, had brought in 1938 to Pope Pius XI the Masonic report on the French episcopate: with 17 cardinals, archbishops and bishops who were enrolled in the lodges. By then, Beaussart had excellent relations with Charles Riandey, who was Sovereign Grand Commander of the Masonic Supreme Council on Avenue de Villiers, as well as its Grand Chancellor. Such an exceptional relationship was due to the plot planned against the Masons.

In 1941, Monsignor Beaussart intervened on behalf of Riandey with the pro-Nazi authorities of Vichy and Paris so that he would not be disturbed in his official position as Secretary General of the City Hall of the 18th district of Paris because of his status as a Freemason. Incidentally, the said town hall persecuted Jews as well as Frenchmen who were against the pro-Nazi French government.[43] Before delving into the details, let's look at a first episode: the parish priest of Saint-Eloi wrote to Riandey: "It seems that a controversy about your name is feared. I dare say that this is not possible. One does not attack what one respects."[44] At that time, Riandey was working as Secretary General of the 12th District of Paris, when he was summoned for his Masonic quality, on Avenue Hoche by Dr. Pfannstiel.[45] But the clergy of the 12th district wished to keep Riandey in his post.[46] However, he lost his functions after the publication of the law of August 11, 1941, against Freemasonry.[47] Then, Bishop Beaussart and Father Courbe, provincial of the Jesuits in Vichy, intervened on his behalf.[48] He was released, after which he was informed by the head of the service of the German secret society that the clerics helped him.[49] Again, thanks to them, and four months later, Riandey was appointed Secretary General of the City Council of the 18th district of Paris.[50] There he maintained the best relations with the clergy, particularly with the provincial of the Society of Jesus, Monsignor Courbe, who was also rector of the Sacré-Coeu basilica.[51]

---

[42] Jean-Laurent Turbet (May 7, 2021), Charles Riandey, les juifs, les autres et... lui, Le Blog des Spiritualités: https://www.jlturbet.net/2021/05/charles-riandey-les-juifs-les-autres-et.lui Accessed February 4, 2024.

[43] La Maçonne (October 20, 2016), Charles Riandey, antisémite ?, Overblog: https://lamaconne.over-blog.com/2016/10/charles-riandey-antisemite.html Accessed February 4, 2024; Pierre Chevallier, Histoire de la Franc-Maçonnerie française. 3 La Maçonnerie: Eglise de la République (1877-1944) (Librairie Athène Fayard, 1975), ob. cit.

[44] Félix Bonafé, Le Souverain Grand Commandeur Charles Riandey (FeniXX réédition numérique, 1975), ob. cit.

[45] Alain Bernheim, 33° (2017),Charles Riandey and the Supreme Council for France, Herodom, Volume 25, p. 110.

[46] Félix Bonafé, Le Souverain Grand Commandeur Charles Riandey (FeniXX réédition numérique, 1975), ob. cit.

[47] Alain Bernheim, 33° (2017),Charles Riandey and the Supreme Council for France, Herodom, Volume 25, p. 110.

[48] Ibid; citing Bonafé 1975, 23-24.

[49] Pierre Chevallier, Histoire de la Franc-Maçonnerie française. 3 La Maçonnerie: Eglise de la République (1877-1944) (Librairie Athène Fayard, 1975), ob. cit.

[50] Alain Bernheim, 33° (2017),Charles Riandey and the Supreme Council for France, Herodom, Volume 25, p. 110.

[51] Félix Bonafé, Le Souverain Grand Commandeur Charles Riandey (FeniXX réédition numérique, 1975), ob. cit.

Monsignor Beaussart intervened on his behalf with the pro-Nazi authorities of Vichy and the capital, so that he would not be bothered because he was a Freemason. Incidentally, as we said, the said district persecuted Jews as well as Frenchmen who were against the pro-Nazi French government.[52] Riandey received Pétain in early 1944 when he arrived at the Bichat hospital at the bedside of the wounded after the Allied bombing raids.[53]

The Catholic Church enjoyed great influence and favor with the puppet Vichy government ruled by Pétain, being an accomplice of Nazism in World War II.

For his part, Riandey's fascist tendencies are well established.

He was vehemently anti-Semitic; stating that he could not stand Jewish names, as well as the Jewish invasion of Freemasonry.

But going back in time, besides Riandey's good relations with the clergy, how did he view French Freemasonry? He believed that it was being punished by Nazism because it departed from a spiritual approach. A "punishment" he said it surely deserved...[54] For him, the spiritual approach came from Catholicism, even though he claimed to be against what he called colonialism whether Catholic, Protestant, or Jewish in the lodges.[55] However, that was lip service. Riandey went so far as to write in Paris, on January 29, 1942, in support of the collaborationist government:

"I have always sought to exalt Catholics and Masons towards a renewal, a rejuvenation of their common spiritual background, so that our civilization may not die of starvation and that France may occupy in the world the place and role it assigns to its own genius. I am honored to have found myself in communion on this point with a good number of ecclesiastics and laymen."[56]

Wrote Freemason Jean-Laurent Turbet about Riandey: "Of course, if Freemasonry had been what he wanted it to be: Catholic, reactionary, anti-democratic, for Vichy and collaborator, "perhaps" it would not have suffered (but even that is not certain)."[57]

But Riandey's role in his collaboration with the French clergy in the plot against Freemasonry, particularly with the Jesuits, has not yet been described. We shall see it by citing the pertinent documentation.

Earlier, the editors of *Esotérisme, gnoses & imaginaire symbolique: mélanges offerts à Antoine Faivre*, explained:

"Finally, what about the Jesuits? If I do not believe with Bode that the sectarians of Ignatius were the masters of Freemasonry, I do not doubt that they tried to infiltrate and control it, and if, for the eighteenth century, we lack documentary evidence, the

[52] La Maçonne (October 20, 2016), Charles Riandey, antisémite ?, Overblog: https://lamaconne.over-blog.com/2016/10/charles-riandey-antisemite.html Accessed February 4, 2024; Pierre Chevallier, Histoire de la Franc-Maçonnerie française. 3 La Maçonnerie: Eglise de la République (1877-1944) (Librairie Athène Fayard, 1975), ob. cit.

[53] La Maçonne (October 20, 2016), Charles Riandey, antisémite ?, Overblog: https://lamaconne.over-blog.com/2016/10/charles-riandey-antisemite.html Accessed on February 4, 2024

[54] Jean-Laurent Turbet (May 7, 2021), Charles Riandey, les juifs, les autres et... lui, Le Blog des Spiritualités: https://www.jlturbet.net/2021/05/charles-riandey-les-juifs-les-autres-et.lui Accessed February 4, 2024.

[55] Ibid.

[56] Ibid.

[57] Ibid.

testimony of J. Corneloup is of great value for our time. It should be recalled that in 1943 the two main Masonic powers in France, the Grand Orient and the Grand Lodge, drew up a project to unify French Freemasonry. The project failed. At the same time that the principal dignitaries of the Supreme Council of the Scottish Rite - Riandey and Cauwel - were negotiating with the representatives of the Grand Orient and its Grand College, underhandedly, there were talks with the Reverend Fathers Berteloot and Gorce - Jesuit and Dominican respectively - to constitute a Masonry that was frankly clerical or, more precisely, whose ideology would have been controlled by Rome."[58]

Just before his death, the Freemason Marcel Cauwel - who was close to the Jesuit Berteloot - informed the Freemason Corneloup of his remorse for allowing himself to be influenced by members of the Society of Jesus: "I leave the fact to the reflections of those who consider the existence of a Jesuit influence in 15th century Freemasonry, especially concerning the High Degrees, to be implausible./ A close examination of the letters shows that the conversations between the Scots and the Jesuits were directed to a more ambitious goal than the conversations that, for example, Wirth, Lantoine, and I had had before the war, with Fr. Berteloot and Fr. Gorce (Dominican). It was then only a question of seeking to create a climate of appeasement, putting an end, on both sides, to the unjustified accusations, of the campaigns of mutual defamation. Now it was a union of spiritual forces, pushed to the point of collaboration between the Catholic Church and Freemasonry - a sentence of Riandey even contains these words: "to merge" - under the benevolent gaze, it seems, of an accomplice State [...]."[59]

Let us now look at some brief extracts from letters of the distressed Marcel Cauwel sent to Corneloup, the first of which speaks of a commitment of Cauwel to Berteloot for a rapprochement and collaboration between Freemasonry and Catholicism to prepare for peace on earth:

"1. From Cauwel to Berteloot, June 1st 1943: "[...] It will be up to the spiritual forces, by their approach, their 'cordial understanding', their trusting collaboration, to prepare peace on earth among all men of goodwill, giving thanks to God in the highest heavens."[60]

One of the letters in Cauwel's possession was written by Mason Charles Riandey to Berteloot, which is disturbing.

Behind the back of the Sovereign Grand Commander, René Raymond, Riandey initiated negotiations at a distance with Pierre Laval through Joseph Berteloot, for the creation of a Catholic Freemasonry and to distance itself from the Jews. If truth be told, Riandey and Cauwel, when approaching Pétain and Laval, had the idea of a "state Freemasonry."[61] Since 1942, Laval was Prime Minister of France, an accomplice of Nazism and an ultra-right Catholic. Pétain himself was a Catholic. All of which

---

[58] Richard Caron, Joscelyn Godwin, Wouter J. Hanegraaff & Jean-Louis Vieillard-Baron (eds.), Esotérisme, gnoses & imaginaire symbolique: mélanges offerts à Antoine Faivre (Peeters, Bondgenotenlaan, Leuven, Belgium, 2001), p. 466.

[59] Ibid, pp. 466, 467.

[60] Ibid, p. 467.

[61] La Maçonne (October 20, 2016), Charles Riandey, antisémite ?, Overblog: https://lamaconne.over-blog.com/2016/10/charles-riandey-antisemite.html Accessed on February 4, 2024

demonstrates the solid connections both of the French clergy with the Nazi puppet government, as well as of the Jesuits. The dreamed state Freemasonry, controlled by the Jesuits and with the plan to unify the two most powerful Masonic branches in France, was intended to be influenced and controlled by Rome.

On March 19, 1943, Riandey wrote to Berteloot in the face of Germany's potential defeat: "Obviously we have to plan for a turbulent period because the speculators and the Jews will recover."[62]

For his part, the repentant Cauwel, as indicated above, shared the compromising correspondence with Corneloup before his death.

Charles Riandey's astonishing letter to Berteloot:

"2. From Riandey to Berteloot. June 5, 1943: "[...] In response to these wishes, I open a parenthesis to say that not only is it not difficult for me to obtain from my group the acceptance of these principles, but that their essential purpose is to promote them in a clear spirit of close obedience. They are, moreover, in conformity with those elaborated by the Grand Convent Ecot-sais of Lausanne in 1875, which affirmed the belief in God and the immortality of the soul./ I add that we are a goodly number who have never admitted in the past to deviate from them and that we are determined to obtain, by all appropriate tactics, that reconstruction be carried out on these bases, and that it will only benefit whoever accepts them. [...] The current upheavals offer the institutions a unique opportunity to realign themselves with the essential foundations. They must seize it. If they miss the opportunity (sic), they will never have it again. [...] The Catholic Church is by far the foremost of these institutions. The others were born only of delays or reluctance in the past to adapt to contrasting movements. Now the example must be set. I am convinced that the others - myself in particular - will be happy to walk with her [the Catholic Church], or even to mingle with her, if she moves resolutely towards the new and broad horizons opened up."[63]

Note that the letter is clear that Freemasonry was to mingle or walk side by side with the Catholic Church. Riandey affirmed that many Masons were with him and that the principles by which they would be governed in conformity with those elaborated by the Grand Convent Ecot-sais de Lausanne in 1875, "affirmed the belief in God and the immortality of the soul." But this is not true, according to the same documents of the Grand Convent.[64]

Moreover, Riandey mentioned that only those who accept such principles would benefit.

It was further argued that advantage should be taken of existing upheavals to bring institutions into line "with the essential foundations." This referred to the hostilities

[62] Jean-Laurent Turbet (May 7, 2021), Charles Riandey, les juifs, les autres et... lui, Le Blog des Spiritualités: https://www.jlturbet.net/2021/05/charles-riandey-les-juifs-les-autres-et.lui Accessed February 4, 2024.

[63] Richard Caron, Joscelyn Godwin, Wouter J. Hanegraaff & Jean-Louis Vieillard-Baron (eds.), Esotérisme, gnoses & imaginaire symbolique: mélanges offerts à Antoine Faivre (Peeters, Bondgenotenlaan, Leuven, Belgium, 2001), p. 467.

[64] Jean-Laurent Turbet (May 7, 2021), Charles Riandey, les juifs, les autres et... lui, Le Blog des Spiritualités: https://www.jlturbet.net/2021/05/charles-riandey-les-juifs-les-autres-et.lui Accessed February 4, 2024.

generated by Nazism in France. And there was talk of seizing that opportunity, or they would not have it again.

Moreover, the Jesuit Provincial, Bishop Courbe, had the special mission of handling the entire process in the utmost secrecy.

We quote directly with the editors' commentary citing the letters:

"Comeloup gives other letters which perfectly demonstrate that in the margins of the official negotiations between the Grand Orient and the Grand Lodge, Charles Riandey and Marcel Cauwel were negotiating with representatives of the Society of Jesus, who were certainly in cahoots with certain representatives of the Vichy government and were considering the possibility of a Masonic order that would "merge" with the *corpus christi*. It is worth citing one last document, attached by Cauwell to this epistolary exchange. Corneloup, in order to appease the debate, crosses out the names and positions of three representatives of the Supreme Scottish Council:

"The Supreme Council of the Grand Lodge of France has conceived the project of reconstructing in France a State Freemasonry with the authorization and support of the Vichy public authorities.

The project began to be executed in October 1943.

The main instigators are:
- Mr. X., 33c (quality)
- Mr. Y..33c (quality)
- Mr. Y., 33c (quality), member of the Synarchie d'Empire movement, also called Synarchie, most of whose members were part of the ministerial cabinets created by Marshal Pétain.

Its instigators began by sounding out some of their colleagues likely to adhere to their plan. They managed to gather a number of 33rd-degree Masons to create a Workshop for each degree:
1° Blue Lodge
2° Lodge of Perfection
3° Chapter
4° Philosophical Council
5° Consistory
6° Sovereign Court
7° Supreme Council

After these first successful approaches, the instigators contacted the Provincial of the Jesuits in Lyon (November 1943). Following this meeting, they requested an audience with Mr. Pierre Laval, who received them shortly thereafter in Vichy and granted them his authorization as Minister of the Interior.

Such a revival of French Freemasonry, even after the assurances of a conservative spirit with which the operation was surrounded, has produced very different shocks in the opinion of the ruling parties.

So far, the occupying authorities have granted it only an indifference tinged with suspicion. They have not, however, prevented the emergence of a movement which, on the other hand, was not unfavorable to them [...]."[65]

---

[65] Richard Caron, Joscelyn Godwin, Wouter J. Hanegraaff & Jean-Louis Vieillard-Baron (eds.), Esotericism, gnoses & imaginaire symbolique: mélanges offerts à Antoine Faivre (Peeters,

The renewal of French Freemasonry, clandestinely promoted by the Society of Jesus, sought to renew Freemasonry and make it the "legitimate and regular heir of their common spiritual and material heritage." It was intended to merge the Grand Orient of France and the Grand Lodge of France, by eliminating everything that was considered anti-Christian. Through this scheme, it was proposed to use such Masonry to unite all of France. Had it succeeded, the Society of Jesus could have subverted the plans of French Freemasonry in its support of a united democratic Europe that diminished Catholic power. But there was no agreement on the plan.[66]

The regular French Masonic unity with the United Grand Lodge of England had and has had enormous challenges.[67]

This tells us that the French Jesuits were not far from the right wing. Thus, we can glimpse a way of acting that hid the purpose of controlling Freemasonry. There was also a certain transformation within French Freemasonry which, despite its various adjustments, continues to have a certain influence to this day, as we shall see.

In addition, as the editors quoted above say: "The enterprise failed; but the endorsement of the Provincial of the Jesuits in Lyon, the allusion of Father Berteloot in his correspondence with Riandey to "the enterprise in progress," is a clear indication that certain dignitaries of the Supreme Council of the rue de Puteaux did not frown upon the creation of a State Freemasonry that the Society of Jesus would have controlled de facto."[68]

Because of the agitation in the Vichy government to this project, it came to an end, and Pétain had an article published criticizing Freemasonry to calm the spirits of the citizenry.[69]

Charles Riandey, under his cloak of duplicity, kept silent on these facts in his Confessions d'un Grand Commandeur de la Franc-Maçonnerie (Confessions of a Grand Commander of Freemasonry), Monaco 1989.[70]

At the beginning of 1944, in January or February, and under the interested eye of the Jesuits, effective negotiations began between a representative of the Catholic hierarchy and representatives of Freemasonry near the Neuilly Bridge, at the home of a clergyman.[71] The physician and Freemason, Peloquin, attended as a dignitary the meeting in which a representative of the hierarchy participated, the president of the Catholic Youth, the president of the Christian Democracy, Albert Bayet, a member of the Ligue des droits de l'homme (the League of Human Rights) and Bellanger, a

---

Bondgenotenlaan, Leuven, Belgium, 2001), pp. 467, 468; citing J. Corneloup, *Un document capital: Histoire et causes d'un échec*, Paris 1976, 76-83.
[66] Alain Bauer, Jean-Claude Rochigneux, Les relations internationales de la franc-maçonnerie française (Armand Colin, 2010), ob. cit.
[67] Ibid.
[68] Richard Caron, Joscelyn Godwin, Wouter J. Hanegraaff & Jean-Louis Vieillard-Baron (eds.), Esotérisme, gnoses & imaginaire symbolique: mélanges offerts à Antoine Faivre (Peeters, Bondgenotenlaan, Leuven, Belgium, 2001), pp. 468, 469.
[69] La Maçonne (October 20, 2016), Charles Riandey, antisémite ?, Overblog: https://lamaconne.over-blog.com/2016/10/charles-riandey-antisemite.html Accessed on February 4, 2024
[70] Richard Caron, Joscelyn Godwin, Wouter J. Hanegraaff & Jean-Louis Vieillard-Baron (eds.), Esotérisme, gnoses & imaginaire symbolique: mélanges offerts à Antoine Faivre (Peeters, Bondgenotenlaan, Leuven, Belgium, 2001), p. 469.
[71] Pierre Chevallier, Histoire de la Franc-Maçonnerie française. 3 La Maçonnerie: Eglise de la République (1877-1944) (Librairie Athène Fayard, 1975), ob. cit.

member of the Ligue de l'enseignement (League of Education). Part of the conversation:

" ... The priest proposed a truce, asking Freemasonry - for I will only speak of it - to cease its attacks on the Church. To which, after having returned the ball to the Church's court, Brother [Mason] Peloquin replied: "... If you will cease to strike, I may ask our [Masonic] brethren... to cease striking in their turn."

A common note was drafted and agreed to be presented to the hierarchy, in which "only a truce is mentioned."

However, at the second meeting, the Masons were asked to use their influence with whomever they could to maintain the subsidies granted by the Vichy government to the free (Catholic) school; but the Masons said "no." In the face of the refusal, the prelate asked to think about consulting the hierarchy. Already at the third meeting, the Catholic representatives said: "If the subsidies are not maintained, the Catholic Church will consider itself persecuted." To which the Masons replied: "No, there is no persecution. If we prevented them from worshiping or recruiting people, yes, we would persecute them. But by taking away a subsidy that is not theirs, no." The priest, who seemed embarrassed to have personally accepted that conception, said that the Church wanted to get paid; that it's a matter of money. That made Peloquin break off the talks. But two months later, he received another invitation, however, he said it was impossible to turn back. The Masons also noted that this was a sign that the Catholic Church was willing to accept advantages from the government, even if it was immoral.

Marius Lepage, venerable of the lodge of Volney de Laval - of the Grand Orient of France (GOF), strove to maintain a spiritualist current (very different from the GOF) in the tradition of Wirth and Lantoine, with whom we saw that Berteloot had very good relations. For the Catholic Church, that current represented a Masonic tendency to be forgiven. Especially since Monsignor Richaud intervened on his behalf with the Vichy authorities during the occupation to avoid his dismissal, when his name was published in the *Journal Officiel* on the list of Freemasons. However, Lepage was not so obfuscated before those who made themselves disciples of Berteloot, for he did not forget that the Jesuit took off his mask in a letter to the Freemason Oswald Wirth during the occupation when he expressed his satisfaction at seeing Freemasonry finally destroyed.[72] Nor did he forget that Berteloot wanted to assist the Freemason Camille Savoire on his deathbed, taking advantage of it to take the documents of the Grand Prior of the Gaufes.[73] Not for nothing, "After the defeat, both in Vichy and in the occupied zone, there were anti-Jewish Catholic Masons, often of a long tradition, such as Faÿ, Vallat, Coston, Henriot, etc., who promoted and ensured the anti-Masonic measures."[74]

---

[72] J. A. Faucher, A. Ricker, Histoire de la Franc-Maçonnerie en France (Nouvelles Editions Latines, Paris, 1967), p. 464.

[73] Ibid, pp. 464, 465.

[74] Rousse-Lacordaire, Jérôme. " Bulletin d'histoire des ésotérismes ," Revue des sciences philosophiques et théologiques, vol. 95, no. 3, 2011, p. 711.

Joseph Berteloot campaigned for a "rapprochement" with Freemasonry after World War II.[75] But he died in 1955. Wirth died in 1943.

The French post-war era, Catholicism and Freemasonry

After the liberation of France, the government asked the Vatican to withdraw at least 30 bishops and archbishops who were deeply committed to the Vichy government, but the Vatican finally withdrew only three of them.[76] The Catholic newspaper *La Croix*, which through the archbishops urged the French youth to collaborate in the victory of Germany, was criticized.[77] A certain "Artaban" published on December 13, 1957:

"In 1944, 'La Croix' was prosecuted for having favoured the enemy and brought before the Court of Justice in Paris; the case was put in the hands of Judge Raoult who dismissed it. The affair was discussed at the Chamber, on the 13th of March 1946 (see J.O. Parliamentary Debates, pages 713-714) and it was learned, then, that M. de Menthon, minister for Justice and thorough at purging the French press, had spoken in favour of 'La Croix'.

In fact, "the voice of pontifical thought"—as Pius XII called it, in 1942, when sending it his blessing—was the only one exempted from the general measures taken to suppress all the newspapers published during the occupation, even though, as 'Artaban' reminds us:

"'La Croix' received instructions from the German Lieutenant Sahm and, in Vichy, from Pierre Laval."[78]

Suhard, the Archbishop of Paris, who had been the leader of the clergy collaborators, decided to celebrate undisturbed the Te Deum victory of the Allies at Notre Dame on August 25, 1944. But when General de Gaulle returned to Paris, he refused to meet with the Cardinal for the occasion, as the latter was openly accused of collaborationist tendencies.[79]

In contrast, according to the "France-Dimanche" of December 26, 1948, on the anniversary of his entry into the priesthood, Suhard received a letter signed by Pope Pius XII congratulating him, among other things, for his role during the occupation.[80]

In August of that year, in Bad Hofgastein, a meeting took place between the Cardinal of Vienna, Theodor Innitzer, and the Austrian Grand Master Scheichelbauer: the Cardinal's objective was to verify the Masonic beliefs on atheism. And four years later, there was contact between Austrian Freemasonry and the Vienna nunciature, something that Pius XII rejected.[81]

We know that Pius XII, seeing that the Axis powers would lose the war, sent notifications to the clergy in the various countries of the conflict, so that many turned in

---

[75] La Maçonne (October 20, 2016), Charles Riandey, antisémite ?, Overblog: https://lamaconne.over-blog.com/2016/10/charles-riandey-antisemite.html Accessed February 4, 2024; Robert A. Graham (January 14, 1956), Apostle to the Freemasons, America Magazine, p. 423.

[76] Edmond Paris, The Secret History of the Jesuits (Chick Publications, Ontario, Calif. 1982), p. 159.

[77] Ibid.

[78] Ibid.

[79] Ibid, p. 161.

[80] Ibid.

[81] Giacomo Galeazzi, Ferruccio Pinotti, Vaticano Massone: Logge, denaro e poteri occulti: il lato segreto della Chiesa di papa Francesco (Piemme, 2014), ob. cit.

favor of resistance against the Nazis, as was the documented example of the Jesuits and the Dominicans between 1941-43.[82]

What became of Charles Riandey? When the Allied troops arrived to liberate Paris, Riandey conveniently joined the Masonic resistance group Patriam Recuperare; for which he was arrested by the Gestapo on June 14, 1944; and then deported on August 21 to the Buchenwald camp. More than one hundred Freemasons were executed there; and many more elsewhere. Riandey was liberated on April 11, 1945, with the arrival of the U.S. troops.[83] Thus, under a cloak of innocence, he was not accused of collaborationism.

From 1950, Riandey was Grand Orator of the Supreme Council of France. He also was again elected Federal Councillor of the Grand Lodge of France, becoming its Grand Chancellor (in charge of foreign affairs) on September 17, 1953.[84] That same day, his Convent voted to make it obligatory to take the oath on the Three Great Lights. This "allowed Grand Master Louis Doignon to present, on May 16, 1954, the candidacy of the Grand Lodge to the Convention of Luxembourg." In October, with the agreement of the Grand Master, Riandey entered into confidential negotiations with Pierre Chéret, Grand Master of the French National Grand Lodge. On these negotiations:

"These led to the drafting of preparatory protocols, after which official bilateral talks (May 26 - September 13, 1955) resulted in a proposal for a merger between the two obediences*. The magnitude of the sacrifices required of the Grand Lodge of France was such that, at the Federal Council meeting of November 26, 1955, this project was withdrawn from the agenda of the Convent scheduled for January 14 and 15, 1956, a decision taken unanimously by those present, including Riandey. On September 8, 1956, the Grand Lodge of France was admitted as a member of the Luxembourg Convention."

Riandey, as outgoing Grand Chancellor and Federal Councilor, presented the last report to the Convent of the Grand Lodge of France on September 20, 1956, recommending "to the 204 members present that they ratify this accession unanimously."

We must emphasize that the above-mentioned attempts to unite Masonic obediences responded to the Jesuits' plans to control French Freemasonry and, in turn, to influence the direction of the United States and the United Nations - successor to the League of Nations - in Europe.

---

[82] John Hellman, Knight-Monks of Vichy France: Uriage, 1940-1945 (McGill-Queen's University Press, 1993), p. 125.

[83] Richard Caron, Joscelyn Godwin, Wouter J. Hanegraaff & Jean-Louis Vieillard-Baron (eds.), Esotérisme, gnoses & imaginaire symbolique: mélanges offerts à Antoine Faivre (Peeters, Bondgenotenlaan, Leuven, Belgium, 2001), p. 469; citing Lucien Sabah, Une police politique de Vichy: le Service des Société Secrètes, Paris 1996, 272-273; Félix Bonafé, Le Souverain Grand Commandeur Charles Riandey (FeniXX réédition numérique, 1975), ob. cit.; La Maçonne (October 20, 2016), Charles Riandey, antisémite ?, Overblog: https://lamaconne.over-blog.com/2016/10/charles-riandey-antisemite.html Accessed February 4, 2024; Jean-Laurent Turbet (May 7, 2021), Charles Riandey, les juifs, les autres et.... lui, Le Blog des Spiritualités: https://www.jlturbet.net/2021/05/charles-riandey-les-juifs-les-autres-et.lui Accessed February 4, 2024.

[84] Eric Saunier (editor), Encyclopédie de la franc-maçonnerie (Le Livre de Poche, 2002), ob. cit. Note: unless otherwise indicated, this is the same source.

In February 1959, talks began between the Grand Orient of France, the Grand Lodge of France, and the French National Grand Lodge to create a United Grand Lodge of France. But the plan failed four months later. In September, "the Convent of the Grand Lodge of France decided to suspend relations with the Grand Orient of France and the Grand Orient of Belgium."

After the death of Grand Commander Jacques Maréchal, Riandey was elected as his successor by the Supreme Council on May 26, 1961.

Months later, the Grand Lodge of France sent its Federal Council to resume tripartite talks, "but the conditions imposed by the French National Grand Lodge made it impossible." Several Masonic obediences suspended relations with the Grand Lodge of France: the United Grand Lodges of Germany in 1960 and the Grand Lodge of Belgium in 1964. In the latter year, Riandey was the author of the foreword to the work of the Mason and personal friend of the nuncio and future Pope John XXIII, Yves Marsaudon, namely, L'Oecuménisme vu par un franc-maçon de tradition (Ecumenism as seen by a traditional Mason).

For their part, the year after the first cessation of relations with the Masonic obediences, the Jesuits entered the scene somewhat less underhandedly. Just when the Second Vatican Council was being prepared, in 1961, the Mason Lepage wanted to invite a priest to his lodge, something he probably discussed with the superior of the Trappist monastery that served as "canonical advisor" to the Volney lodge. So he spoke to his friend, Catholic lawyer and writer Alec Mellor, who specialized in the study of Masonic subjects. So Mellor suggested the Jesuit Michel Riquet.[85] It should be noted that Riquet had his first encounters with Freemasonry from 1936 until the war, with ties with Freemasons in the cabinets of Henry Sellier and Marc Rucart, Ministers of Public Health and Social Security respectively. When Riquet joined the Resistance in September 1940, he renewed his relations with Freemasonry. During the war, in a meeting with Joseph Berteloot, the latter brought Riquet closer to Freemasonry, a time when Berteloot revealed his true scheme.[86]

Likewise, Major Gamas, a former deportee as well as a member of the Supreme Council of the Scottish Rite and a devout Catholic, contributed to bringing Michel Riquet closer to Freemasonry.[87]

Mellor then visited him and asked:

"- Would you be willing to talk about atheism in a Masonic lodge, Father?
- Why not? but my superiors would have to agree.

"Then a strange negotiation took place. Marius Lepage talks with the Bishop of Laval.

"- Father Riquet remains under the authority of the general of the Jesuits if he agrees...observes the prelate."[88]

---

[85] J. A. Faucher, A. Ricker, Histoire de la Franc-Maçonnerie en France (Nouvelles Editions Latines, Paris, 1967), p. 465.

[86] Eric Saunier (editor), Encyclopédie de la franc-maçonnerie (Le Livre de Poche, 2002), ob. cit.

[87] Ibid.

[88] J. A. Faucher, A. Ricker, Histoire de la Franc-Maçonnerie en France (Nouvelles Editions Latines, Paris, 1967), p. 465.

Subsequently, Alec Mellor met with the general of the Jesuits, the Belgian Jean Baptiste Janssens, who said yes, but that Riquet should take responsibility for what happened if he agreed.[89]

In 1961, Riquet appeared before a group of five hundred Masons stressing that Freemasonry and Catholics are "separated brothers."[90]

The conference provoked quite strong reactions from many lodges of the GOF/Grand Orient of France, leading initially to the suspension of Marius Lepage and his summons before the disciplinary authorities of the obedience, before being acquitted in the first instance on September 23, 1961. Then came the appeal lodged by the Council of the Order, and finally on December 18, 1961.[91] But Lepage resigned from the GOI for other reasons in 1963.[92]

In February 1964, Riandey met secretly with the Grand Master of the French National Grand Lodge, Ernest Van Hecke, to try again for an alliance. As we shall see a little later, Riandey was interested in a rapprochement and formalization with the United Grand Lodge of England, which had some links with Rome through the Jesuits.

But apart from Riandey, and faced with the isolations of the aforementioned obediences, it was decided to resume contacts with the Grand Orient of France in 1964, and a meeting was held on April 15 "which resulted in a treaty of fraternal alliance."[93] Informed of the talks with the GOF, Riandey tried unsuccessfully to disrupt them, because it did not obey his plans. But the fraternal alliance was unanimously adopted on September 7 by the General Assembly of the Grand Orient of France and ratified on September 17, 1964, by the Convent of the Grand Lodge of France by 140 votes in favor and 82 against." Riandey did not see in the alliance with the Grand Orient of France such a background as he desired with the alliance, so a new plan was devised. When the treaty was ratified, Riandey "promoted the creation of a new Grand Lodge in which he imagined he could gather 3,000 to 4,000 Masons who had left the Grand Lodge of France." Thus, in October 1964, Riandey again met secretly with the leaders of the French National Grand Lodge, while "Hofman traveled to London to explain the French situation as he perceived it to the Grand Secretary of the United Grand Lodge, Sir James Stubbs, and the Grand Commander, R. L. Loyd."

On November 27, Riandey sent a message to all members of the Supreme Council of France, urging them to resign from the Grand Lodge of France by January 31, 1965, or face dismissal. By this time, the United Grand Lodge of England had adherents among the Jesuits near the Vatican and even within the apostolic palaces. And about Jesuit involvement in the Catholic Church's rapprochement with Freemasonry, the Grand Commander of the Scottish Rite in the United States, Luther Smith, said that "during a

---

[89] Ibid.

[90] NC (June 9, 1961), Dialogue Of Masons, Catholics?, The Monitor; Volume CIII, Number 10, p. 1; Paul A. Fisher, Behind the Lodge Door: Church, State and Freemasonry In America (TAN Books, Charlotte, North Carolina, 1994), p. 195; citing America, April 22, 1961, "Commentary" section, "Priest And Freemason," p. 168.

[91] Alain Bernheim, Marius Lepage, vol. 65, coll. " Travaux de la Loge nationale de recherche Villard de Honnecourt ," 2007a, pp. 242-250.

[92] Ibid, pp. 254-258.

[93] Eric Saunier (editor), Encyclopédie de la franc-maçonnerie (Le Livre de Poche, 2002), ob. cit. Note: unless otherwise indicated, this is the same source.

visit to Rome, Italy, in 1957, he found that a Masonic group sponsored by Jesuits was attempting to organize there."[94]

A few months later, on December 18, when the members of the Supreme Council met in session and learned that His Grand Commander (Riandey) was in secret contact with the French National Grand Lodge, they demanded that he resign his office.[95]

Three days later, Grand Commander Hofman arrived in Paris. He met with Riandey and Van Hecke, and worked out with the latter a seven-point plan which Riandey accepted on December 22. The story goes on to tell us that:

"In a letter dated December 24, Hofman informed the Grand Commander of the Southern Jurisdiction of the United States, Luther Smith, of the results of his trips to London and Paris and proposed to reconstitute and "re-constitute" the Supreme Council of France. On January 18, 1965, Hofman wrote to Riandey: "What is absolutely necessary is...that you be [sic] reinstated at Van Hecke." Riandey agreed, and his "reinitiation" by the Grand Master of the French National Grand Lodge took place on February 9."

The story continues:

"On February 13, in Amsterdam, Riandey and several other members of the Grand Lodge of France, who had in the meantime been regularized by the French National Grand Lodge, were initiated or reinitiated in all the degrees of the Rite up to the 33°. Riandey became an active member of the Supreme Council of the Netherlands, charged on behalf of the Grand Commanders of the two American jurisdictions and those of Canada and the Netherlands "to reconstitute in France... a regular Supreme Council," which he immediately carried out. This Supreme Council "for France" was "consecrated" on April 24, 1965, in Paris by a delegation of the Supreme Council of the Netherlands."

Undoubtedly, Riandey longed at all costs for the regularization of the Scottish orthodoxy of the Supreme Council of France when no one questioned it, as Corneloup wrote in 1968.

The Jesuit Riquet maintained almost exclusive relations with the French National Grand Lodge, with which Lepage was affiliated.

Riquet implemented a positive appreciation of regular Freemasonry by intervening with Bishop Etchegaraym, then secretary of the French Bishops' Conference; and later by serving as an intermediary between the French National Grand Lodge and the Vatican.

"Finally, unofficially in 1970 and officially in 1972, he obtained from the Sacred Congregation for the Doctrine of the Faith, then presided over by Cardinal Seper, to endorse the restrictive interpretation of canon 2335 of the 1917 Code of Canon Law: members of Masonic lodges who conspire against the Church and the legitimate civil

---

[94] New Age, November, 1957, "Grand Commander's Visitation," p. 685; quoted in Paul A. Fisher, Behind the Lodge Door: Church, State and Freemasonry In America (TAN Books, Charlotte, North Carolina, 1994), p. 194.

[95] Eric Saunier (editor), Encyclopédie de la franc-maçonnerie (Le Livre de Poche, 2002), ob. cit. Note: unless otherwise indicated, this is the same source.

powers are excommunicated. Even more so when the new version of the Code of Canon Law (1983) eliminates all reference to Freemasonry, Mr. Riquet sees in it the culmination of his work."

Michel Riquet ultimately contributed to bringing Catholics and Masons closer together.

When France's most powerful Freemason, Michel Baroin, died in an accident in February 1987, Riquet said that Baroin was not an enemy of the church; and offered his respects. Also, the cardinal archbishop of Paris authorized a Catholic church funeral for Baroin.[96]

In summary, and as stated in Diccionario histórico de la Compañía de Jesús (Historical Dictionary of the Society of Jesus):

"Berteloot's legacy was taken up in Belgium by Fr. Michel Diericks, whose interesting posthumous work *Freimaurerei, die Grosse Unbekkante, Ein versuch zu Einsicht und Würdigung* (Frankfurt-Hamburg, 1968) is preserved; and in Paris by Fr. Michel Riquet, whose activity in the field of Freemasonry became more notable since he delivered (1961) his polemical lecture at the Volney lodge in Laval. His frequent contacts with high members of French Freemasonry, his abundant articles in the press, his book *Les Franc-Maçons* (Paris, 1968), and his direct pastoral action with a large group of Catholic Masons served as an endorsement for different Masonic obediences to invite him to speak in their respective lodges in an atmosphere of détente, an index of appreciation and recognition of the work of understanding and rapprochement carried out by Riquet."[97]

To this, we must add the role of Charles de Gaulle, who was a conservative Catholic and who had led the French resistance against Nazi Germany. He presided over the Provisional Government of the French Republic from 1944 to 1946 to re-establish democracy in France. He prevailed in the Cold War and promoted Franco-German reconciliation. He was also President of France from 1959-1969.

A special CIA report of August 16, 1963, noted that the main obstacle to the U.S.-sponsored European political union was the refusal of the French partners to accept the Gaullist concept (of President Charles De Gaulle) of a Paris-dominated "European Europe" as a competitor to Washington-style European unity.[98] De Gaulle had an antipathy for the "technocrats" in Brussels.[99] Given his disdain for "supranationalism and integration", he was labeled by the CIA as "the ardent anti-integrationist";[100] although he accepted some market issues of the same.[101] With this, de Gaulle did not look very favorably on the plans of the U.S. government, and by extensión U.S.

---

[96] Martin Short, Inside the Brotherhood: Further Secrets of the Freemasons (HarperCollins Publishers, London, 1990), pp. 164, 165.

[97] Charles E. O'Neill, S.I., Joaquín M.a Domínguez, S.I., Diccionario histórico de la Compañía de Jesús: Infante de Santiago-Piatkiewicz (Institutum Historicum, S.I., Rome, Universidad Pontificia Comillas, Madrid, 2001), p. 2561-2562.

[98] U.S. CIA (November 28, 1948). EUROPEAN UNION: STATUS AND PROSPECTS, Chargé d'Affaires, Washington, DC: U.S. Government Printing Office, pp. 1-3.

[99] Ibid, pp. 4, 5.

[100] Ibid, pp. 6, 7.

[101] Ibid, p. 6.

Freemasonry, French and European Freemasonry in general, of its democratic form for the continent. British historian Elie Kedourie commented:

"The European movement seems thus to have come to another of its major turning points--with De Gaulle in the key role. Integration cannot proceed without France, and only De Gaulle is in position to bring about another rapid advance. Assuming De Gaulle desires sorne kind af European union, bis chances of achieving it any time soon would seem to depend on his willingness to accept a somewhat more modest role in it for France and on his defining a generally acceptable basis for the union's relations with the United States."[102]

The neuralgic aspect of this revelation is that, as we said, De Gaulle was a conservative Catholic.[103] His father, Henri De Gaulle, was a product of Jesuit education, becoming himself a teacher in Jesuit schools. Both he and his wife were fervent Catholics and monarchists. Precisely, Henri De Gaulle believed that the French Revolution of 1789 and the Protestant Reformation were essentially satanic. He was one of the subscribers to the newspaper of the ultra-nationalist movement, *Action française*. His son Charles continued to read it until the 1930s. He was raised Catholic, but his loyalty to Catholicism was tied to his loyalty to his country.

Charles, like his brothers, attended Catholic schools and the pre-conciliar Jesuit imprint remained with him throughout his life.[104] He referred to the Jesuits as "his Jesuits" when he met Jesuit General Pedro Arrupe in Rome in 1967. Some members of de Gaulle's ministry throughout the 1960s, such as Interior Minister Roger Frey, held regular meetings with priests such as Jesuit theologian and future Cardinal Jean Daniélou - one of the most influential theologians of Vatican II, but without abandoning doctrinal orthodoxy - to maintain discreet communications with influential church figures. De Gaulle strove to establish cordial relations with the Holy See. He knew John XXIII from his time as nuncio to France and was also sympathetic to Paul VI. Although he paid close attention to the debates and discussions at the Second Vatican Council, while he supported the Council's reforms and the opening of a conversation with modernity, he was not without doubts. He did not agree with the more progressive positions of the Council. Interestingly, French Jesuits were open to Vatican II, but without departing from the doctrinal orthodoxy of Catholicism (with some exceptions). And De Gaulle was friends with several of these Jesuits. As we shall see, it was part of the plan.

The Society of Jesus underwent radical changes that would distinguish it from almost all other sectors of the Catholic Church. They took Vatican Council II very seriously;[105] with the then General of the Society, the Spanish Jesuit priest Pedro Arrupe. But that did not lead them to renounce their ambitions for the glory of Catholicism in the world. But this time with a more modernist vision, without

---

[102] Ibid, p. 1.
[103] Elie Kedourie (January 1993), De Gaulle, Commentary Magazine. Note: unless otherwise indicated, this is the same source.
[104] Dr. Samuel Gregg (Nov. 8, 2020), The Faith of Charles De Gaulle, The Catholic World Report. Note: unless otherwise noted, this is the same source.
[105] Ricardo de la Cierva, Oscura Rebelión en la Iglesia: Jesuitas, teología de la liberación, carmelitas, marianistas y socialistas: la denuncia definitiva (Plaza & Janes Editores, S. A., Barcelona, Spain. First edition, 1987), pp. 697-709.

renouncing the cultural element of the Church, but not so drastically in order to reach the secular world. Again, not all of them think alike.

French Catholics got most of what they wanted in de Gaulle: nationalism, social conservatism, and an end to anti-clerical legislation.[106] Although in 1943 he abolished Vichy's illegal anti-Masonic laws, de Gaulle disliked the Freemasons - apparently particularly the Grand Orient of France.[107]

Nevertheless, before he became president, a month before the Allied invasion of France on D-Day, the American CIA's predecessor, the OSS, created a newsletter for its director entitled, "The Jesuits and De Gaulle," which discussed an article written by American Jesuit John LaFarge Jr. in *America* magazine entitled "And What of de Gaulle?" LaFarge's opinion was of interest to the OSS because, in 1944, public opinion and the American Catholic Church were ambivalent about the role de Gaulle might play in France's future. The U.S. espionage organization was also interested because the American Jesuits argued that since de Gaulle was anti-Communist, he deserved the support of the Church.[108] For the OSS, the French Catholic Church and de Gaulle were of concern to U.S. democratic plans in Europe. LaFarge believed that the American government and Catholic interests should unite to help de Gaulle "maintain an effective position against any Communist attempt to dominate the resistance movement and thereby seize power in postwar France."[109]

His party, *Rassemblement du peuple Français*, founded in April 1947, was disapproved by the U.S. government because of de Gaulle's nationalist ideas.[110] A CIA document dated June 2, 1947, noted the intelligence agency's concern that the Catholic Church was speculated to be supporting General de Gaulle and his party. The report indicated that the entire Catholic Church was expected to oppose the party; and "that the hostility of the Jesuits would lead the rest of the church against de Gaulle." That all the Jesuits," the document continued, "do not felt so strongly about de Gaulle;" and the Jesuit priest Chaillet, who met de Gaulle on April 28, 1947, said he would have to wait sometime to decide whether to support him. However, there were many indications in Paris that the Catholic Church was solidly behind de Gaulle and the party. A large Catholic social and youth organization meeting glorified de Gaulle as a national hero, amid enthusiastic applause from the audience.[111]

But de Gaulle understood "Europe as a key geographical and historical construction." He wanted the European states to unite to cooperate closely to increase their power, especially that of France.[112] As we documented, de Gaulle ensured that France was in a position to join the Common Market and by demanding the

---

[106] Roy P. Domenico and Mark Y. Hanley (eds.), Encyclopedia of Modern Christian Politics (Greenwood Press, Westport, Connecticut, 2006), Volume 1, A-K, p. 455.

[107] Jasper Ridley, The Freemasons: the most powerful society on earth (Ediciones B, S. A., Barcelona, 2014), ob. cit.; quoting Grand Orient to De Gaulle, 18 October 1944, ibid, III, pp. 399-400.

[108] Charles R. Gallagher, S.J. (2018), Decentering American Jesuit Anti-Communism: John LaFarge's United Front Strategy, 1934-39, Journal of Jesuit Studies 5, p. 98.

[109] Ibid; citing Interoffice memo, T/3 to Dewitt C. Poole, May 5, 1944, microfiche, int-12fr-807, Foreign Nationalities Branch Files, u.s. Office of Strategic Services (Bethesda, md: University Publications of America, 1988).

[110] Raymond Aron, The United States and the World: 1945-1973 (Routledge, New York, 2017), p. 83.

[111] U.S. CIA (June 2, 1947). Speculation Regarding Church Support of General de Gaulle, Washington, DC: U.S. Government Printing Office.

[112] Éric Anceau, "De Gaulle and Europe," Encyclopédie d'histoire numérique de l'Europe [online], ISSN 2677-6588, published on 22/06/20, accessed on 14/03/2023. Permalink : https://ehne.fr/en/node/12243.

establishment of the Common Agricultural Policy (CAP). His vision was a Europe of sovereign states.

Faced with these facts, the Grand Orient of France was very concerned about de Gaulle's nationalist tendencies, while they were co-constructing a united Europe where nationalism would be left behind (as we will see below).[113]

The Freemasons feared above all, "a Christian democratic Europe dominated by the Vatican that would turn its back on secularism."[114]

Now, as a result of the work of the Jesuits and Riandey, we cite, as Jean-Laurent Turbet tells us, that many Catholics frequented the lodges, including priests and some bishops. And that there were "prelates such as Daniel Pézeril, auxiliary bishop of Paris, Jean-Charles Thomas, bishop of Versailles or André Collini, archbishop of Toulouse or Father Michel Riquet, Jesuit, initiated a positive dialogue and promoted fruitful and friendly exchanges."[115] For what purpose?

The Diccionario histórico de la Compañía de Jesús (Historical Dictionary of the Society of Jesus) highlights:

"In other countries such as the United States, Canada, Spain, Germany, etc., some Jesuits on a personal level, either from the University, historical research, or direct pastoral action, have been equally important in a recent search for mutual understanding and rapprochement between two institutions that had traditionally been considered not only antagonistic but incompatible and bitter enemies.[116]

In short, France has a stronger anticlerical tradition than Italy. The French Revolution, inspired by Masonic notions and by Freemasons such as Diderot, Voltaire, and Lafayette, led French Freemasonry to attack Catholics and Catholicism ever since. But in 1948, the main French Masonic order, the Grand Orient of France, had a small 'regular' rival: the Grande Loge Nationale Française (GLNF). This had the backing of the regular Grand Lodges abroad, including those of England, Ireland, and Scotland. The Archbishop of Paris, in 1969, was in favor of Catholic membership in this Masonic lodge. Ernest van Hecke, Grand Master of the GLNF, asked Paul VI in 1971 to end the ban on regular Freemasonry.[117]

Also, Töhötöm Nagy, a Hungarian Jesuit priest who became a Freemason after emigrating to Argentina, reaching the highest degrees, longed to break the prejudices of the Masons against the Jesuits and vice versa. He wrote to Pope Paul VI to have the Catholic Church rescind its ban on Catholics joining Freemasonry.[118]

---

[113] Denis Lefebvre (2007), Traités de Rome. Un demi-siècle d'Europe sous le regard des frères, Dans Humanisme 1(N° 276), pp. 32, 33.

[114] Ibid, p. 32, 33.

[115] Jean-Laurent Turbet (March 22, 2007), Eglise/Franc-maçonnerie : le retour des vieux démons, par Romano Libero, théologien, Le Blog des Spiritualités.

[116] Charles E. O'Neill, S.I., Joaquín M.a Domínguez, S.I., Diccionario histórico de la Compañía de Jesús: Infante de Santiago-Piatkiewicz (Institutum Historicum, S.I., Rome, Universidad Pontificia Comillas, Madrid, 2001), p. 2562.

[117] Martin Short, Inside the Brotherhood: Further Secrets of the Freemasons (HarperCollins Publishers, London, 1990), p. 154.

[118] Dr. Töhötöm Nagy, Jesuitas y Masones: Con una carta abierta a Su Santidad Paulo VI (Edición del autor, Buenos Aires, 1963).

From the League of Nations to the United Nations. The consistent role of intercontinental Freemasonry, the United States, and a United and democratic Europe

Regarding the transition from the League of Nations (1919) to the United Nations (UN, in 1945), writes Milton Arrieta López, a specialist and Mason of the highest degree:

"The Declaration of the Rights of Man and of the Citizen of 1789 constituted a progressive norm and can be considered as a direct precedent of the Universal Declaration of Human Rights that the United Nations would subscribe in 1948, whose responsible and promoter was Henri Laugier, initiated in Freemasonry on July 24, 1911, in the Lodge Les Étudiants of the Grand Orient of France." We also read that "Laugier was Under-Secretary General of the UN and Chairman of the Commission on Human Rights, appointed by the Economic and Social Council (ECOSOC) of the United Nations for the preparation of the International Bill of Human Rights."[119]

Historian Ludovic Tournès, for the *Journal of Modern European History* on the role of the Rockefeller Foundation in the United States:

"The Rockefeller Foundation played an important role in the transition from the League of Nations to the United Nations through its collaboration with two international organisations. The first was the Economic, Financial and Transit Department (EFTD) of the LoN. By financing its move to the United States and all of its work during the Second World War, the RF would allow it to make a major contribution to the reorganisation of the global economic order after 1945. The second organisation was the United Nations Relief and Rehabilitation Administration (UNRRA), which the RF provided with staff, working methods, and a network of contacts around the world. The RF was thus deeply involved in the redefinition of the overall structure of the system of international organisations during WWII."[120]

Masonic plans to implement the European Community were in the making. Dr. Marian Mihaila, Assistant Grand Master of the National Grand Lodge of Romania, comments that at the beginning of the 20th century, the great European Masons took up the idea of creating the European Community: Aristide Briand, French Minister of Foreign Affairs and delegate to the League of Nations, proposed on August 18, 1929, the creation of a European federal structure, whose plan was drawn up on May 1, 1930. Seventeen days later, it was taken to the League of Nations for examination.[121] Briand was Prime Minister of France and a member of the Grand Orient of France; initiated in the Lodge Le Trait d'Union de Saint Nazaire. He was the first to defend the idea of The United States of Europe in a speech on September 5, 1929, at the 10th Assembly of the League of Nations.[122] Marian Mihaila comments:

---

[119] Milton Arrieta López (2018), La República Universal de los Masones. Un ideal para la paz perpetua, Opción, Año 34, No. 87, p. 899.
[120] Ludovic Tournès (2014), Tournès, L. (2014). The Rockefeller Foundation and the Transition from the League of Nations to the UN (1939-1946). Journal of Modern European History, 12(3), p. 340.
[121] Marian Mihaila, Ph.D (Fall 2006), 'European Union and Freemasonry', Masonic Forum Magazine, ob. cit.
[122] SOULAGES, LAMANT, 1995: 197-198; quoted in Milton Arrieta López (2018), The Universal Republic of the Masons. An ideal for perpetual peace, Opción, Year 34, No. 87, p. 903.

"The adepts of the idea of a united Europe are grouped – as I have shown before - in the Pan-European Movement whose supporter was also a mason, Count Richard N.C. Kalergi [...] He was encouraged and financed by a series of American masons who wanted to create thus, according to the American model (the first masonic state in history) the United States of Europe.

"Being stopped during WWII, in August 1946 the masons take up again their secular dream: they create the European Union of Federalists."[123]

On September 19 of the same year - in Mihaila's words - "the mason Churchill" made a speech declaring himself in favor of the creation of the United States of Europe. He indicated the urgency for France and Germany to unite. Robert Schuman's plan was skillfully conceived by Jean Monnet, deputy secretary general of the League of Nations; and by Etienne Hirsch, Paul Reuter, and Pierre Uri, his close associates.[124] Mihaila continues:

"Many of them are members in the European Union Chain (Chaine d'Union Europeenne - C.U.E.), a Freemasons' group with representatives especially in Belgium, Germany, the Netherlands, Switzerland and France. CUE wants to reunite the European Freemasons irrespective of nationality, obedience, religious and philosophic ideas, race and language. In order to achieve its objective it organizes meetings of the Freemasons, when the problems of future Europe are discussed."[125]

From May 7-11, 1948, the Hague Congress, or Congress of Europe was held, attended by hundreds of delegates from all over Europe and observers from Canada and the United States. It was organized by Brugman, Duncan Sandys, and Józef Retinger, to discuss ideas on the development of European political cooperation. It was chaired by Winston Churchill and was attended by 713 delegates with nearly half British and half French.[126] It voted to create a "Council of Europe" and launch a "European Movement" to coordinate groups promoting European integration "to 'break down national sovereignty by concrete practical action in the political and economic spheres'."[127]

Denis Lefebvre, writing for *Dans Humanisme* of Editions du Grand Orient de France, wrote that after the Hague Congress, the Grand Orient of France proposed to its lodges to study in September: "Is European civilization in decline? Its causes. Its remedies." More than 40% of the lodges that debated the subject, concluded that the answer was the European federation, as "the first step towards a world government with a universal language and a generalized currency."[128]

---

[123] Marian Mihaila, Ph.D (Fall 2006), 'European Union and Freemasonry', Masonic Forum Magazine, ob. cit.

[124] Ibid.

[125] Ibid.

[126] Christopher Booker, Richard North, Great Deception: Can the European Union survive? (Bloomsbury, New York, Third Edition, 2016), ob. cit.

[127] Ibid; citing Boothby, Lord (1978), Boothby - Recollections Of A Rebel (London, Hutchinson), p. 264.

[128] Denis Lefebvre (2007), Traités de Rome. Un demi-siècle d'Europe sous le regard des frères, Dans Humanisme 1(N° 276), p. 32.

Also, shortly after the congress, Retinger and Sandys traveled to the United States to gain support for their campaign for European unity.[129] There they met William J. (Wild Bill) Donovan, one of the founders of the CIA in 1947, and his colleague Allen Dulles, who would later become head of the CIA. Both, in the words of Booker and North, "had recently joined in support of Coudenhove to form a Committee for a Free and United Europe." However, Coundenhove was abandoned. The American Committee on United Europe (ACUE) was then formed. ACUE was a conduit for covert CIA funding, which was augmented by contributions from private foundations such as the Ford Foundation and the Rockefeller Institute. In this way, the desire for a united Europe was promoted by the U.S. State Department. ACUE funding was secretly channeled over the next few years to a number of individuals and organizations working for European integration. They ranged from politicians such as Paul-Henri Spaak, as well as trade unions, and influential British magazines such as Lord Layton's *The Economist*. And like the intellectual monthly *Encounter*. Nevertheless, ACUE had as its main beneficiary of funding the European Movement; which was kept afloat between 1949 and 1960 almost entirely from the 4 million dollars supplied by the CIA. Such contributions accounted for between one-half and two-thirds of the Movement's income.

At this time, the so-called "Father of Europe," Jean Monnet, who had also been Deputy Secretary General of the League of Nations (1919-1923) and was a founder of the ACUE, was in secret contact with U.S. agencies in helping to achieve European integration. As an example, a letter from the Ford Foundation written to Monnet on January 8, 1965 explains:

"Dear Mr. Monnet

"We have today sent our check for $150,000 to The Chase Manhattan Bank for deposit to the account of the Centre de Documentation du Comite d'Action pour les Etats-Unis d'Europe No. 8060656.

"This remittance represents payment of our grant to the Center of Documentation of the Action Committee for the United States of Europe over a two-year period for continued support of its program of policy research on European unification and an Atlantic partnership. The terms of this grant were set forth in Mr. McDaniel's letter to you dated December 15, 1964.

"We would appreciate receiving an acknowledgement of this payment when you receive notifice from the bank."[130]

The Schuman Declaration (French Foreign Minister Robert Schuman) of May 9, 1950, which would set the tone for Franco-German reconciliation leading to the European Community, was drafted by U.S. Secretary of State Dean Acheson at a

---

[129] Christopher Booker, Richard North, Great Deception: Can the European Union survive? (Bloomsbury, New York, Third Edition, 2016), ob. cit. Note: unless otherwise noted, this is the same source.

[130] MacLeod, Norman W. Assistant Secretary of the Ford Foundation. Letter to Monnet, Jean. President of the Documentation Center of the Action Committee for the United States of Europe. January 8, 1965; quoted in Philippe de Villiers, J'ai tiré sur le fil du mensonge et tout est venu (Fayard, Paris, 2019), ob. cit.

meeting at Foggy Bottom.[131] Schuman's chief of staff said, "It all began in Washington."[132]

A U.S. government memorandum dated July 26 of that year and signed by General William J. Donovan, head of the wartime OSS (U.S. Office of Strategic Services), the forerunner of the CIA, reveals the campaign to promote a fully-fledged European parliament.[133]

The administration of President Harry Truman, a Freemason, bullied the French, even as the president threatened to cut off Marshall Plan aid to rebuild a war-torn Europe - all in a furious meeting with resisting French leaders in September 1950. His goal was for the French to reach a modus vivendi with Germany in the early post-World War II years. [134]

A CIA document from the U.S. Senate indicates France's rejection of the European Defense Community (EDC) on August 30, 1954:

"Yet the circumstances attending the death of EDC and the birth of Western European Union were such as to give pause to the United States. In our quest for peace, freedom and security, we must necessarily assess our future European policies in the light of European thought patterns observable in the past. It was necessary, therefore, to examine the underlying factors in French policy and public opinion which led to the rejection of EDC while gaining at least tentative acceptance of the decisions reached later in London. One of the first questions to come to an American mind was whether the overriding needs of Western security might induce France to subordinate her historic fear and distrust of Germany to an accord by which both nations might achieve greater safety against Soviet Russia encroachment."[135]

The special envoy, Julius Klein, said: "with the Mendes-France group, held extended discussions with some of the Premier's closest advisers, with opposition parliamentarians, with French and American journalists and with American diplomatic and military officials." [136]

The issue of the Soviet threat was a good impetus that came from 1951 in talks between American and French representatives. Because of this, Germany could not be left in a military vacuum, which prompted the French to present a plan devised by René Pleven and Jean Monnet.[137]

The ACUE was the key front for the CIA and was chaired by Donovan, who provided in 1958 53.5% of the European movement's funds; whose board included Walter Bedell Smith and Allen Dulles, CIA directors in the 1950s, as well as a caste of former OSS officials who were also in the CIA.

---

[131] Ambrose Evans-Pritchard (April 27, 2016), The European Union always was a CIA project, as Brexiteers discover, The Telegraph.
[132] Ibid.
[133] Ibid.
[134] Ibid.
[135] Senate (September-October 1954 - 1965). Report on European Mission by Brigadier General Julius Klein. Washington, DC: United States Government Printing Office, p. 4.
[136] Ibid.
[137] Ibid.

The documentation shows that some of the "founding fathers" of European integration were treated as hired hands; prevented from finding alternative financing that would break the dependence on Washington.[138]

The United States wanted an additional market to get rid of its excess production capacity.[139]

French politician Philippe de Villiers documents, citing state documents:

"Monnet wanted to build a Europe in line with American objectives: institutional, commercial, and cultural. He urged his compatriots in his adopted homeland: "You must help us to create a common European market of 150 million consumers like yours," or again: "The ultimate aim of the ECSC is to contribute to the creation of the United States of Europe."
[...]
Confidential exchanges of letters [...] between Monnet and Acheson, the Secretary of State, reveal that, for the Americans, "The United States is a "European power".[140]

In March 1957, the Treaties of Rome were signed, which gave birth to the European Union. The Freemasons of the Grand Orient of France participated in the debates and took their place, with their methods and vision of the world. They welcomed the signing of the Treaties and the birth of the Common Market, one of the great achievements of the government of Guy Mollet, a socialist politician and French Freemason of the Grand Orient of France. Indeed, the Convent of the Grand Orient of France of September 1958, indicated that "this organization, required by the current situation, conforms to the secular principles of the Masonic order." Although in 1958 they expressed their doubts because of what they considered progressive deviations.[141]

In 1965, concerning the construction of a united Europe, they requested that "consultations be undertaken with a view to making flexible and progressive arrangements for the long-term functioning of the confederal institutions." That year they also called for the merger of the executives of the various communities (achieved in April), and for the European Parliament to be elected by universal suffrage, which became effective until 1979.[142]

Additional CIA documents, in addition to the essays examined, show the deep interest of U.S. intelligence in a democratic Europe according to the sights of the United States.[143]

---

[138] Ambrose Evans-Pritchard (April 27, 2016), The European Union always was a CIA project, as Brexiteers discover, The Telegraph.

[139] Philippe de Villiers, J'ai tiré sur le fil du mensonge et tout est venu (Fayard, Paris, 2019), ob. cit.

[140] Ibid; citing Confidential: "The United States is a "European Power," AMK 23/1/26 in Letter from Jean Monnet to Dean Acheson, AMK C 23/1/28.

[141] Denis Lefebvre (2007), Traités de Rome. Un demi-siècle d'Europe sous le regard des frères, Dans Humanisme 1(N° 276), pp. 30, 32.

[142] Ibid, p. 32.

[143] U.S. CIA (April 7, 1948). Report of Allegedly Revived "OSS" Activities in Europe, and of CIA "Consideration" of Arming American-Sponsored European Undergrounds, Donovan and Hillenkoetter Mentioned by Name; U.S. CIA (August 14, 1964), EUROPEAN UNION: HOW FAR, HOW SOON? Washington, DC: United States Government Printing Office; U.S. CIA (November 15, 1971). Intelligence Memorandum: European Community Inches Toward More Political Unity. Washington, DC: United States Government Printing Office; U.S. CIA (November 10, 1983). Trends in Machinery Trade Flows Between The United States and Western Europe. Washington, DC: United States Government Printing Office.

De Villiers, among others, wrote a profuse essay full of documents: letters, notes, facsimiles, etc., from a large number of U.S. government archives and organizations on the subject.[144]

The CIA and its attempts to bring democracy to the Roman Catholic Church: the journey towards the Second Vatican Council

The Bilderberg Group was created by Jozef Retinger, who was a supporter of the anti-Nazi resistance in Poland and a CIA-funded activist for European unification.[145] The growing distrust between Western Europe and the U.S. in the early 1950s was closed due to the common concern of communism and the Soviet Union. Indeed, the West's response to communism was the topic discussed at the first Bilderberg meeting in Holland in 1954. On the agenda of later meetings were The European Defense Community and Communist infiltration in various Western countries. Retinger wrote that the Bilderberg was a factory of initiatives, allowing a person or group to develop it even further.

Charles Jackson, who helped establish the U.S. branch of the Bilderberg, helped provide a useful connection between those ideas and those capable of translating them. Jackson had experience in clandestine warfare, having been responsible for General Eisenhower's psychological warfare department in North Africa and London. After World War II, Jackson became vice president of Time, Inc. and chairman of the CIA-funded National Committee for a Free Europe, controlled by Radio Free Europe. But also, as an effective instrument of the Cold War, he supported the Pro Deo Movement, the identity of which we shall see below.

Pro Deo (International University of Social Studies) was a university founded in 1945 with an American vocation located in Rome, with students from all continents trained as future leaders of freedom to support the building of a free world. It was established through the vision of its rector, Belgian-born Dominican priest Felix A. Morlion.[146] Morlion got his start in espionage and propaganda in pre-World War II Belgium, where his Catholic Press Center campaigned against moral decadence in the cinema and Communist infiltration of the nation's industry.[147] The founding of the "Pro Deo (For God) Information and Publication Center" took place in Brussels, Belgium, in 1932, sparking a movement to fight totalitarian ideologies in Western Europe with Catholic-led opinion campaigns.[148] Morlion came into contact with Britain's secret intelligence service (MI6), who were interested in his anti-communism and his contacts with Catholic dissidents in Nazi-ruled Germany.[149]

William J. Donovan, the head of the U.S. intelligence services (OSS-predecessor of the CIA), funded Morlion's activities during the war, referring to them as his

---

[144] Philippe de Villiers, J'ai tiré sur le fil du mensonge et tout est venu (Fayard, Paris, 2019), ob. cit.

[145] Philip Willan (Aug. 12, 2015), Calvi drama wrapped in a Cold War intelligence web, The Italian Insider. Note: unless otherwise noted, this is the same source.

[146] Freedom's Future Leaders, The American Council for the International Promotion of Democracy Under God (C.I.P.) Inc. (1957), ob. cit.

[147] Philip Willan (Aug. 12, 2015), Calvi drama wrapped in a Cold War intelligence web, The Italian Insider.

[148] Aubourg, Valérie. « « A Philosophy of Democracy under God » : C.D. Jackson, Henry Luce et le mouvement Pro Deo (1941-1964) », Revue française d'études américaines, vol. no 107, no. 1, 2006, p. 30.

[149] Philip Willan (Aug. 12, 2015), Calvi drama wrapped in a Cold War intelligence web, The Italian Insider.

122

"psychological warfare activities in the United States in 1941-1944 with other anti-totalitarian leaders."[150]

After the German invasion in 1940, Morlion, wanted by the Gestapo, was helped to escape to Portugal by Donovan, where the Dominican reconstituted the international Pro Deo center in Lisbon that year.[151] But then he was brought to greater safety in New York in 1941, around an American Catholic International Press (CIP), which "offered a press service, a biweekly bulletin and courses on the principles of democracy."[152]

After the liberation of Rome in 1944, Donovan moved Morlion there, where in November, Pope Pius XII asked him to found a training structure called the School of Mass Media as the nucleus of the instrument of democratic anti-communist coordination.[153] Pius XII was unaware of the democratic operations of U.S. intelligence that would involve spying on the Vatican in order to "democratize" it.

Pro Deo was dedicated to the fight against communism in Italy. The university trained for years leaders who in turn instructed the actors of the "civic committees" created by Luigi Gedda, president of the Italian Catholic Action. Also, with the discreet but abundant financial support of the U.S. government, they played a decisive role in the electoral victory of the Christian Democracy in 1948.[154] The same documented source adds:

"But it is much more original than a simple anti-communist ally. Pro Deo was linked to the "Catholic Action" movement launched in the 1920s and 1930s by Pope Pius XI to re-establish the Church's influence in society, and which was particularly successful in Belgium and the Netherlands, former Spanish possessions where the campaigns of the Counter-Reformation and the influence of the Congregatio de Propaganda Fide had been very rigorous. As a counterpoint to Catholic Action, Morlion tried to reconcile modern communication techniques with the evangelical message, convinced that the Christian reconquest of the masses could only succeed by developing an adapted propaganda based on cinema, press and radio. As a commentator in a major Catholic newspaper, De Standaard, he created in 1931 the Press Film Documentation (DOCIP), which became an international center in 1933 and played an important role in Catholic Film Action. He was also involved in the development of a Catholic Press Center in 1934, which became international in 1939 and drew the ire of Goebbels. His experience, summarized in 1944 in *The Apostolate of Public Opinion* (Morlion), is an

---

[150] « International University of Social Studies Pro Deo », Rome, Italy, enclosure to a letter from Morlion to S. Segal, April 3, 1957, CDJP Box B6 Pro Deo-1957 (5); quoted in Ibid.

[151] Aubourg, Valérie. « « A Philosophy of Democracy under God » : C.D. Jackson, Henry Luce et le mouvement Pro Deo (1941-1964) », Revue française d'études américaines, vol. no 107, no. 1, 2006, p. 30; Philip Willan (August 12, 2015), Calvi drama wrapped in a Cold War intelligence web, The Italian Insider.

[152] Morlion, "The International Alliance for Democracy Under God," n.d. [1962], 4-6, CD Jackson Papers, Eisenhower Library, Abilene, KS. [1962], 4-6, CD Jackson Papers, Eisenhower Library, Abilene, KS (ci-dessous CDJP) Box 84 Pro Deo-1962 (2); quoted in Aubourg, Valérie. « « A Philosophy of Democracy under God » : C.D. Jackson, Henry Luce et le mouvement Pro Deo (1941-1964) », Revue française d'études américaines, vol. no 107, no. 1, 2006, p. 30.

[153] Aubourg, Valérie. « « A Philosophy of Democracy under God » : C.D. Jackson, Henry Luce et le mouvement Pro Deo (1941-1964) », Revue française d'études américaines, vol. no 107, no. 1, 2006, p. 30.

[154] Ibid, pp. 30, 31; citing « Short History of the International University of Social Studies "Pro Deo" » [written by Morlion], appended to a letter from Morlion to H. Schmiddy, Oct. 31, 1960, CDJP Box 85 Pro Deo 1960 (1).

excellent reflection on the techniques of propaganda and organization which he considered indispensable for the Church."[155]

But this underwent a transformation, for when the Dominican was in New York, he noticed that democracy and faith were mutually reinforcing.[156]

Morlion had founded the Pro Deo University with the help of the then Undersecretary of State for Ordinary Affairs, Giovanni Battista Montini, the future Pope Paul VI.[157]

Some important aspects about Montini: about Freemasonry, he once confided to Morlion: "When the time is ripe, peace will be made between the Church and Freemasonry. I am sure that we will arrive at it: the Church will lift the excommunication and the Freemasons will do their part by laying down their arms. But it will take time. Time and prudence."[158]

Earlier, in 1942 and as Vatican Secretary of State, Montini organized on behalf of Earl Brennan of the OSS, an espionage network that used the Vatican diplomatic structure to send maps of the Japanese war industry to Washington (codenamed Project Vessel).[159]

He also allowed the escape of Nazi criminals, fascists, and Croatian Ustashas, having under his supervision the office that issued documents for expatriation. The so-called "Operation Monastery."[160]

Now, Morlion operated with his core of spies in an anti-communist function and established close relations with the American Mediterranean Academy of Giovanni Francesco Alliata di Montereale, a Mason of the Grand Lodge Alam.[161]

Morlion's anti-communist activities made him a natural ally of the Italian Masonic lodge P2 of Licio Gelli and Roberto Calvi.[162] Don Ennio Innocenti, former Secretary of the Ecumenical Commission of the Vicariate of Rome, Chaplain of the Archconfraternity Aurigarum, and Member of the Presbytery of the Patriarchal Vatican Basilica, had said that "Among the Jesuits, there has existed for a long time an attitude of sympathy with the Masons." He mentioned that according to two papal nuncios and some friends, they point out that the American episcopate spoke of Masonic infiltration in their midst; as well as in the Catholic churches of the United States.[163]

---

[155] Ibid.

[156] Aubourg, Valérie. « « A Philosophy of Democracy under God » : C.D. Jackson, Henry Luce et le mouvement Pro Deo (1941-1964) », Revue française d'études américaines, vol. no 107, no. 1, 2006, pp. 30, 31.

[157] Norman Cousins, The Improbable Triumvirate: An Asterik to the History of a Hopeful Year, 1962-1963 (W. W. W. Norton & Company, Inc., New York. First Edition, 1972), pp. 10, 11.

[158] Roberto Fabiani, I massoni in Italia (L'espresso, 1978), ob. cit.

[159] Andrea Montella (August 23, 2010), Biografia di Toni Negri, Potere Operaio, Superclan - Uomini, culture, tecniche dell'eversione imperialista, Storia Veneta.

[160] Ibid.

[161] Ibid.

[162] Philip Willan (Aug. 12, 2015), Calvi drama wrapped in a Cold War intelligence web, The Italian Insider.

[163] Tatiana Santi (June 14, 2017), Rivelazioni sull'infiltrazione massonica nella Chiesa, Sputnik.

In addition, Pro Deo had the American support of Henry Luce, the influential head of Time-Life, Inc., the famous newspaper empire.[164] CD Jackson was Luce's correspondent in Europe on the subject, including when Luce was appointed President Eisenhower's Cold War advisor. So was Luce's wife, as U.S. ambassador to Rome.[165]

Through Henry Luce and CD Jackson (with close contacts with the OSS and Allen Dulles), American analysis was given to Pro Deo using the religious element that shaped the worldview of a certain American elite, with the role of religion in the Cold War and religious networks as influential tools reinforcing American foreign policy.[166]

Luce wrote about shaping the "American century," and did not hesitate to use his magazines to support the Republican party and spread his worldview: "The United States must commit itself to saving Europe, securing a dominant position in international relations to spread its model there and to fight vigorously against communism throughout the world."[167]

The Pro Deo University programs, run in Rome and supported by U.S. intelligence, were developed by an interfaith board of trustees and faculty from eleven countries. With Christian, Jewish, Muslim, Hindu, and Buddhist students. [168]

The institution also received guidance from a U.S. Council made up of Catholics, Protestants, and Jews.[169] An important report reads:

"The purpose of the University—"to train freedom's future leaders" —arose, fundamentally, out of the chaotic conditions throughout Europe after World War II. The free nations could not survive without stable political and economic frameworks. For this reason "Pro Deo" established Schools of Political Science, Economic and Business Administration, Industrial and Labor Relations, Mass Communications Media (the press, radio and TV), Commercial and Diplomatic Languages, and Graduate Schools of Applied Social Sciences and Public Opinion—all conducted along the lines of social science research as carried on by the larger American universities."[170]

The Pro Deo University was financed by the CIA itself and by the president of Fiat, Vittorio Valetta, who was a Bilderberger or member of the Bilderberg Group. In this way, Morlion provided US intelligence with information on the Vatican and a worldwide network of correspondents.[171]

Not surprisingly, the Vatican was suspicious of Pro Deo's activities, which fizzled out in 1955 when Luce, Jackson, and others provided further assistance to the university. Jackson discussed Pro Deo with U.S. Secretary of State John Foster Dulles

---

[164] Aubourg, Valérie. « « A Philosophy of Democracy under God » : C.D. Jackson, Henry Luce et le mouvement Pro Deo (1941-1964) », Revue française d'études américaines, vol. no 107, no. 1, 2006, pp. 29, 31.

[165] Ibid, p. 29.

[166] Ibid, pp. 29, 30.

[167] Ibid, p. 31.

[168] Freedom's Future Leaders, The American Council for the International Promotion of Democracy Under God (C.I.P.) Inc. (1957), ob. cit.

[169] Ibid.

[170] Reginald M. Durbin, O.P. (Winter, 1959), Some modern Dominican apostolates, Dominicana, Vol. XLIV, No. 4, p. 391.

[171] Philip Willan (Aug. 12, 2015), Calvi drama wrapped in a Cold War intelligence web, The Italian Insider.

while receiving a favorable report from the U.S. Embassy in Rome, then under Clare Boothe Luce, who converted to Catholicism in 1946 and with great attention to Pro Deo. With the approval of Allen Dulles, director of the CIA, Jackson made a $25,000 contribution in late 1955 and channeled other payments through Frederick Dolbeare,[172] vice president for Free Europe.

A letter from C.D. Jackson to Allen Dulles, reveals the importance of continuing to support Pro Deo even financially to strengthen and continue its anti-communist operations. But he also stressed the importance of Vatican support against European communist forces because of prelates in key positions in European countries; and indicated that several candidates for the papacy were key, such as the conservative Cardinal Siri, whom they would try to manipulate for their goals if elected pope at the next conclave.[173] Although Siri was not considered the ideal candidate for the papacy by the Americans.

Valérie Aubourg documented the planning:

"Eventually, Jackson entrusted the secretariat and part of the CIP's activities to Ethel Schroeder, vice president of the International Advisory Council, a CIA front organization, and, from 1956, of Free Europe Press, a branch of RFE (Matthews 423). For his part, Luce struck a deal with Valletta to raise the necessary $320,000 (200 million lire) in additional funds, using the Time, Inc. network."[174]

Jackson used Pro Deo as a source of information on Vatican thinking to be used for the State Department.[175] Morlion sent some reports on the matter, and, as a result, discreet CIA-funded "special projects" were arranged.[176] Henry Luce went on to express:

"In this way, the Catholic Church, dedicated to the worldwide struggle against communism, could participate educationally beyond the simple training of priests, and identify with the tremendous need in Europe for a spirit of Christian religion within social, industrial and economic progress, rather than alongside it."[177]

Luce believed that in Europe "the struggle for freedom has too often been anti-religious and religion has been too often opposed to freedom."[178]

---

[172] Aubourg, Valérie. « « A Philosophy of Democracy under God » : C.D. Jackson, Henry Luce et le mouvement Pro Deo (1941-1964) », Revue française d'études américaines, vol. no 107, no. 1, 2006, p. 34.

[173] Jackson, C. D. Letter to Mr. Allen Dulles. Director of the CIA. December 10, 1956.

[174] Aubourg, Valérie. « « A Philosophy of Democracy under God » : C.D. Jackson, Henry Luce et le mouvement Pro Deo (1941-1964) », Revue française d'études américaines, vol. no 107, no. 1, 2006, p. 34; citing Morlion, Note, 11 Sept., 1956.

[175] "The New Orientation of Vatican International Policies," 6 Oct. 1955, CDJP Box 86 Pro Deo 1955 (1) and "International Relations Studies 1," sent 15 Dec. 1957 by Morlion to Jackson, CDJP Box 84 Pro Deo 1958 (3); H. Luce à H. Ford, 19 Nov. 1955, CDJP Box 87 Pro Deo 1955 (1); citing Ibid, p. 36.

[176] "The New Orientation of Vatican International Policies," 6 Oct. 1955, CDJP Box 86 Pro Deo 1955 (1) and "International Relations Studies 1," sent 15 Dec. 1957 by Morlion to Jackson, CDJP Box 84 Pro Deo 1958 (3); quoted in Ibid.

[177] H. Luce à H. Ford, 19 Nov. 1955, CDJP Box 87 Pro Deo 1955 (1); quoted in Ibid.

[178] Luce, "The Great Liberal Tradition," June 18, 1953 (Jessup 126); quoted in Ibid.

We will return later to Morlion and Pro Deo, Luce, and Jackson, as well as others, in their links with the CIA to try to democratize the Catholic Church at the time of the Vatican II popes: John XXIII and Paul VI.

The Second Vatican Council: the United States and Freemasonry for more modernist Popes

What was the Second Vatican Ecumenical Council? Salvador Aragonés comments that "it was the most important religious event of the 20th century." The Catholic Church convened a Council for 1962, at the initiative of Pope John XXIII, so that the Church could open up to the world, to all men and women, and make a general examination of conscience to adapt the exposition of the Gospel Message to modern times. The Council would be closed by his successor, Pope Paul VI on December 8, 1965.[179]

It had a colossal impact on what Catholicism became and its relations with the world. It involved the other Christian churches, particularly the Orthodox.[180]

The Council's message embraced every burning issue in the world. From the arms race, to peace, to the proclamation that the dignity of every person in the world is equal before God, without distinction of any kind; and calling for the fulfillment of human rights for all individuals.[181]

The well-known Catholic political scientist and writer, George Weigel, wrote that Vatican II "was the most important Catholic event in half a millennium." Adding that its "achievements were many and notable; it was also followed by ecclesiastical upheavals that continue to roil the Church today."[182]

Eamon Duffy, a distinguished Catholic historian, likewise called the council the most significant religious event of the last 500 years.[183] Andrew Brown wrote of the Council, that when the 2,600 bishops gathered in Rome to reinvent the church for the modern era "finished, the largest religious denomination in the world was quite unrecognisable."[184]

What changed that was so dramatic? A brief list tells us:

1. The Catholic liturgy changed from Latin to vernacular languages, especially for the Scripture readings at Mass. With the priest facing the people.[185] This made the Mass understandable to the language of the people, and more simple and understandable.

The new Mass was named Novus Ordo Missae in 1969 by Paul VI.

2. Likewise, through the decree Unitatis Redintegratio, ecumenism was declared a good movement; Catholics were encouraged to be part of it and Eastern Christians and Protestants were referred to as "separated" brethren. Protestants were no longer considered heretics.

3. Likewise, the declaration Dignitatis Humanae recognized for the first time the rights of conscience of each individual to religious freedom, declaring that it was the

---

[179] Salvador Aragonés (6 de diciembre, 2015), ¿Por qué el Concilio Vaticano II fue y es tan importante?, Aleteia.
[180] Ibid.
[181] Ibid.
[182] George Weigel (September 30, 2022), What Vatican II Accomplished, The Wall Street Journal.
[183] Andrew Brown (October 11, 2012), How the second Vatican council responded to the modern world, The Guardian.
[184] Ibid.
[185] Catholic Register staff (Oct. 8, 2012), What changed at Vatican II, The Catholic Register. Note: unless otherwise noted, this is the same source.

responsibility of states to protect it. Therefore, the state was to be neutral in religion. Thus, the Second Vatican Ecumenical Council defended the separation of Church and State. Unlikely in the history of Roman Catholicism.

4. Likewise, according to Nostra Aetate, Jews are not to be considered as rejected or cursed by God.

5. Likewise, the council declared that the Catholic Church does not reject anything true and holy from other religions.

6. For its part, the decree Perfectae Caritatis points out that sisters, brothers, and priests of religious orders should rediscover the original purpose of their religious order and adapt it to the modern world.

7. The ordination of a code of canon law was also adopted, which was revised and written, but promulgated until 1983 by Pope John Paul II.

How did it all start?

With the death of Pope Pius XII in 1958, U.S. agents hoped that Giovanni Battista Montini - the future Pope Paul VI - would move closer to the papal throne; something that eventually happened.[186]

Montini was another beneficiary of CIA largesse. The payments made to him reveal one aspect of the agency's why people become radical. The archbishop had a long association with Western governments and their intelligence agencies.[187] Moreover, Montini's work was CIA-Masonry-Vatican in the late 1950s.[188] He would have to wait until 1963 when he became pope.[189]

Meanwhile, another CIA favorite, Cardinal Angelo Giuseppe Roncalli -future Pope John XXIII-, was an ideal candidate for the papacy. But let's take a look at his life. He was born on November 25, 1881.[190]

In short, in his life, he modified Catholic orthodoxy in doctrinal and social matters. He became involved in 1913 with socialist societies in Europe that were trying to agitate the people, "inciting them to riot against the public authorities." Roncalli supported Nicolo Rezzara, one of his parishioners who advocated social progress and civil strikes, outlining a memorandum with his plans for justice, peace, and freedom. For his part, Cardinal Giuseppe De Lai, secretary of the Consistorial Congregation, suspected Roncalli of being a modernist and took a close look at his activities. In 1924, Roncalli was released from his teaching post at the Lateran University, being accused of modernism; and he continued to be observed.

Also, being the ecclesiastical representative for Bulgaria, he told the faithful during his first sermon in Sofia to forget their prejudices against the Orthodox.

He was also appointed Vicar Apostolic and Apostolic Delegate to Turkey and Greece in 1944, the year in which he was elected Apostolic Nuncio to France. During

---

[186] David Wemhoff, John Courtney Murray, Time/Life, and The American Proposition: How the CIA's Doctrinal Warfare Program Changed the Catholic Church (Wagon Wheel Press of Presence LLC, New Edition, 2022), Volume 1, ob. cit.

[187] William Blum, Killing Hope: US Military & CIA Interventions since World War II (Zed Books London, London, 2004), p. 120.

[188] Ferdinando Imposimato, La Repubblica delle stragi impunite (Newton Compton Editori, 2013), ob. cit.

[189] William Blum, Killing Hope: US Military & CIA Interventions since World War II (Zed Books London, London, 2004), p. 120.

[190] Francis Radecki, CMRI, Rev. Dominic Radecki, CMRI, What Has Happened to the Catholic Church? (St. Joseph's Media, 1994), ob. cit. Note: unless otherwise noted, this is the same source.

his nunciature in that country, the movement of worker priests grew considerably. Priests went to the factories participating in strikes and protests, trying to fight for the workers. Many of the priests joined Communist-controlled unions, causing scandal to the workers who belonged to Catholic unions. As a result, the Jesuit and Dominican superiors withdrew their priests from the field in 1954. Most of the priests returned to their parishes, but the rebels left the factories and married.

On January 15, 1953, Roncalli, who was already archbishop, was elected patriarch of Venice and made cardinal on October 29 of the same year.

A little more than four years later, on February 1, 1957, the 32nd Congress of the Italian Socialist Party was held in Venice; and Roncalli called the socialists brethren; and invited them to visit him in the palace.

He also paid a cordial visit to the communist mayor at the Venice town hall, conveying his best wishes.

But Roncalli would also be related to Freemasonry. On this aspect, let us look at the testimony of Franco Bellegrandi, who was chamberlain to popes from the end of the pontificate of Pius XII until the pontificate of Paul VI. He was a professor of modern history at the University of Innsbruck in Austria and for a time served as a correspondent for *L'Osservatore Romano*, the Vatican's official newspaper. In his work *Nikita Roncalli*, he wrote that in 1950:

"His Eminent Highness, Prince Chigi Albani della Rovere, then Grand Master of the Sovereign Military Order of Malta, had received in the office of the Grand Magisterium in Rome, a letter from Cardinal Canali, heavy as a rock: Pius XII, protector of the Order, had just learned, with great sorrow, that the Minister of the Order of Malta in Paris was a Freemason. They hurried, in the Magistral Palace of the Via dei Condotti, to rummage through the file of Baron Marsaudon, recently appointed in place of Count Pierredon, who had been retired."[191]

Under the strictest reserve, the Vatican arranged for the Order of Malta to send immediately to Paris someone it could trust to investigate the delicate discovery in depth. A professed chaplain of the same Order, Monsignor Rossi Stockalper, who was also a canon of Santa Maria Maggiore, was chosen. Leaving immediately for Paris, he had been advised to begin the investigation with the Jesuit priest Joseph Berteloot. Already covered in this chapter as a conspirator with the French Jesuits against the League of Nations and French Freemasonry.

Berteloot being consulted with the strictest discretion, confirmed to Stockalper that Yves Marsaudon was a Freemason, of the "thirty-third degree," as well as a life member of the Council of the Grand Lodge of the Scottish Rite. The shock this caused Stockalper, made him take out his handkerchief, wipe his forehead and polish his glasses. He then asked Berteloot if a namesake had led them to make a mistake, to which the Jesuit immediately took a document from his file and read Marsaudon's full civil status, confirming that he was a Mason.

Stockalper then asked Berteloot, "How is it possible, Father, that you have kept such a secret?" His reply was, "It is not my business to keep the archbishopric informed, nor

---

[191] Franco Bellegrandi, Nichitaroncalli: Controvita di un Papa (International E.I.L.E.S., First Edition, 1994), ob. cit.; Roger Peyrefitte, Knights of Malta (Criterion Books, Inc., New York, 1959), ob. cit.; Note: unless otherwise noted, this is the same source.

the Nunciature, nor the Order of Malta. My task is to keep the Society of Jesus informed."

The monsignor replied, "Very well. But why didn't the Society of Jesus pass the information on to them?"

Berteloot: "The Society of Jesus practices prudence. It only passes on information if it considers it makes sense to do so; and only, of course, if it is asked. The Archbishopric and the Nunciature have their own intelligence services, and one might suppose that they have more reason to make their information available to you. Monsignor Roncalli and Monsignor Feltin will be happy to look into the matter further."

Stockalper went to see the Archbishop of Paris, Monsignor Feltin, from whom he obtained information. Feltin in turn sent Stockalper to his vicar general, Monsignor Bohan, who knew Baron Marsaudon better. After having more detailed information and with a heavy heart, Stockalper went to number 10, President Wilson Avenue, which was the residence of Nuncio Angelo Roncalli, the future Pope John XXIII. The monsignor tactfully asked Roncalli for information about Marsaudon. The nuncio, between a smile and a joke, had the monsignor return to the secretary of the nunciature Bruno Heim, who finally told Stockalper that Freemasonry was like "one of the last forces of social conservation in today's world, and, therefore, a force of religious conservation." With enthusiastic judgment, he referred to Baron Marsaudon as the one who made Roncalli understand the transcendent value of Freemasonry. As a result, the nuncio supported and approved his appointment as minister of the Order of Malta in Paris. Heim added that "the nunciature in Paris was working in great secrecy to reconcile the Catholic Church with Freemasonry."

Roger Peyrefitte, in the 1959 version of his book on the Knights of Malta, also referred to this account, which was first written in the French language (1957); having obtained information from solid sources.

For his part, Roncalli's progressive conditions are not the only thing that moved him closer to Freemasonry. He even was a Freemason and well-known to the French Jesuits. Carlos Vázquez Rangel, the Grand Commander of the Supreme Council of Mexican Freemasonry and president of the National Confederation of Liberal Organizations, told the Mexican magazine *Proceso*, published on October 10, 1992, that the Bishop of Cuernavaca, Sergio Mendez Arceo, was a Freemason. He revealed that the two worked together in the lodge. Arceo was in charge of presenting at the Second Vatican Council "an initiative to revoke the papal bull of Clement V in which Catholics were forbidden to belong to Freemasonry, under penalty of being excommunicated." That interdict was repealed, among other things, because "the then Pope John XXIII was also a Freemason, as was his successor, Paul VI" - he pointed out.[192] Rangel further said: "It was in Paris that the profane Angello Roncalli and Giovanni Montini were initiated, on the same day, into the august mysteries of the brotherhood. That is why it is not strange that much of what was achieved in the Second Vatican Council, of John XIII, is based on the Freemasonic principles and postulates."[193]

---

[192] La Redacción (October 10, 1992), Como secretario de Gobernación, castigaba a Prigione con cinco horas de antesala, Proceso.
[193] Ibid.

The very famous Mexican Grand Master Alfonso Sierra Partida also reported, in his book *La Masonería en el Mundo Contemporáneo* (*Freemasonry in the Contemporary World*), published in 1972, how he tried to publish, but without success, in several newspapers in Mexico City, the copy of the presumed initiation act in a Masonic lodge in Paris, where the initiation of Angello Roncalli is recorded.[194] Due to the refusal of the press, Alfonso Sierra ordered copies that circulated profusely in Mexican Masonic circles.[195]

There is also the testimony of the then Grand Master of the Grand Orient of Italy, the lawyer Virgilio Gaito, who expressed himself on three occasions about John XXIII's membership in Freemasonry.[196] His first time was in an interview with Fabio Andriola, published in *L'Italia Settimanale* on January 26, 1994, where he said: "It is said that John XXIII was initiated into Freemasonry when he was nuncio in Paris. I relate what I was told. After all, in his messages, I grasped many aspects that are really Masonic."[197]

The second time was in an interview with Giovanni Cubeddu, which appeared in the February 1994 issue of *30 Giorni:*

"Pope John XXIII, moreover, seems to have been initiated in Paris and to have participated in the work of the Istanbul Workshops. Then, when I heard the ecclesiastical hierarchies speak in homilies of man as the center of the Universe, I was moved to tears."[198]

Gaito revealed to Italian journalists Giacomo Galeazzi and Ferruccio Pinotti that the Greek Masonic brothers were the ones who told him about John XXIII's membership in Freemasonry.[199]

With all this in consideration, let us look at what happened years later, shortly before Roncalli was elected pope: in September 1958, about seven or eight days before the conclave that would elect the successor to Pius XII, Bellegrandi was informed by Count Sela that while he was at the Orope Sanctuary, while attending one of the dinners at the home of the Belorussian industrialist Attilio Botto, he noticed one of the guests, known to be a high Masonic authority in contact with the Vatican. While driving the Count home, he indicated to the latter that "…The next pope will not be Siri, as is being whispered in some Roman circles because he is too authoritarian a cardinal. They will elect a conciliatory pope. The choice has already fallen on the patriarch of Venice Roncalli."

Count Sela asked in surprise: "Elected by whom?" the answer was: "By our Masonic representatives in the Conclave." The Count asked, "Are there Masons in the Conclave?" "Certainly," was the reply; "the Church is in our hands." Sela asked in

---

[194] Eduardo Seleson (June, 2010), Los papas masones, Boletín Informativo "Piedra en Bruto," Año 11 - N° 11, p. 11 [Eduardo Seleson 32°(October, 1993), Los papas masones, Publicación Oficial de la Gran Logia del Rito de York en Bolivia, p. 11] [Alfonso Sierra Partida, La Masonería Frente Al Mundo Contemporáneo (Editorial Masónico Menphis, México, D. F., 1972), ob. cit.]

[195] Ibid.

[196] Carlo Alberto Agnoli, La Massoneria alla conquista della Chiesa (E.I.L.E. S, 1996), p. 41.

[197] Ibid.

[198] Ibid.

[199] Giacomo Galeazzi, Ferruccio Pinotti, Vaticano Massone: Logge, denaro e poteri occulti: il lato segreto della Chiesa di papa Francesco (Piemme, 2014), ob. cit.

perplexity, "Who, then, rules in the Church?" [...] "No one can say where the upper steps are. The steps are hidden."

It should be noted that a secret telegram from the U.S. State Department, dated October 11, 1958, and sent from Rome to the U.S. Secretary of State, revealed the interest in a more modern pope:

"During conversation with embassy officer, Vatican source expressed personal view next pope will be "elected" outside conclave by agreement between cardinals. Source said Pius XII elected this manner and recalled that as cardinals were entering 1939 conclave card Pizzardo called him aside and asked him to prepare biographical sketch of Pacelli. Added he consulted with Msgr. Montini and both decided, for obvious reasons, not to go ahead with Pizzardo's request.

"Speculating on Pius XII successor source said College may very well choose an old cardinal whose short pontificate may be devoted entirely to the re-organization of the Roman curia left by deceased pope in "deplorable state." Source indicated election of Siri, Ruffini, Ottaviani would be "misfortune for Church" since these three cardinals have an unrealistic approach to great problems facing world today. Source said election of anyone of three could depend on influence of American cardinals and volunteered suggestion U.S. authorities would do well exercise discreetly "their own influence on certain American cardinals."[200]

Roncalli was elected pope on October 28, 1958, taking the name John XXIII.[201] We will see below the good relations of this papacy with the United States.

About his election, it should be added that years later the French Cardinal Eugène Tisserant, a prominent member of the Roman Curia, referred to it in a letter dated March 12, 1970:

"The election of the present Pontiff [Paul VI] was made quickly. It was the previous one, that of John XXIII, that could have been discussed since the sessions were numerous. I do not see how the information about the ballots could have been given out by anyone after the Conclave. Secrecy has been imposed more clearly than ever. It is laughable, in any case, to say that any cardinal would have been elected. You will understand that I can say no more."[202]

In the French newspaper *Juvénal*, on September 25, 1964, appeared an interview granted to the aforementioned Yves Marsaudon, the minister of the Supreme Council of France for Scottish Rite Freemasonry, to Jean-André Faucher, which the Pauline Father Rosario Esposito reproduces in his book entitled "Le Grandi Concordanze tra Chiesa e Massoneria" ("The Great Concordances between the Church and Freemasonry"). We reproduce the most remarkable part:

---

[200] U.S. State Department (October 11, 1958). From Rome, Zellerbach. To the Secretary of State. Washington, DC: United States Government Printing Office.
[201] John Booty, The Church in History (Morehouse Publishing, New York, 2003), p. 171.
[202] Tisserant, Eugène, Cardinal. Letter to Dear Sir__. March 12, 1970.

132

"Faucher: "Did you get to know Pope John well?"

"Marsaudon: "I was very close to Archbishop Roncalli, Apostolic Nuncio in Paris. He received me several times at the Nunciature, and on several occasions he came to my house in Bellevue in Seine-et-Oise. When I was appointed Minister of the Order of Malta, I expressed my perplexities to the Nuncio about my Masonic membership. Monsignor Roncalli formally confirmed to me that I remain in Freemasonry."

"Faucher: "Did you see him again after his elevation to the tiara [papacy]?"

"Marsaudon: "Yes, he received me at Castel Gandolfo in my capacity as Minister Emeritus of the Order of Malta and gave me his blessing renewing his encouragement for a work of rapprochement between Churches, as well as between the Church and Freemasonry tradition."[203]

When the Second Vatican Council began in 1962, convened by John XXIII the previous year, it declared John the Baptist and John the Evangelist as the special patron saints of the council; both of whom are the same patron saints of Freemasonry.[204]

John XXIII died on June 3, 1963.[205]

On the eve of the conclave that would elect his successor (Cardinal Montini, under the name of Paul VI), between the first and second sessions of the Second Vatican Council, in the late morning of June 18, a secret meeting was held in a large villa in Grottaferrata, a few kilometers from Rome.[206] It was promoted by two cardinals who were among the protagonists of the Council: Josef Frings, from Cologne. And Giacomo Lercaro, from Bologna. Also in attendance were many cardinals who played a prominent role in the Council; and who were also "great electors" of Cardinal Montini: Cardinals Liénart, Léger, Alfrink, Kònig, Suenens, among others. The owner of the villa was a collaborator of Cardinal Lercaro: Umberto Ortolani, a Masonic businessman who twenty years later would be accused of being the puppet master of the Masonic lodge P2 of Licio Gelli and sentenced to 12 years in prison for the bankruptcy of Banco Ambrosiano. Ortolani was already partially introduced in the Vatican for his work in the civic committees with Luigi Gedda.

Italian journalist Ignazio Ingrao tells the story (He does not believe in a conspiracy):

"The lawyer Ortolani," as the Archbishop of Bologna calls him in his Letters of the Council 1962-1965, is also very active outside the ecumenical assembly: he organizes lunches, dinners, and meetings at his home in Rome and at his villa in Grottaferrata with prelates, observers, and experts, which Lercaro never misses. When the cardinal arrives from Bologna, "the lawyer" runs to pick him up at the station or airport and keeps him up to date with news from the sacred Roman palaces. He even has a chapel built in his villa in Grottaferrata, which Lercaro unfailingly blesses. Ortolani could

---

[203] Carlo Alberto Agnoli, La Massoneria alla conquista della Chiesa (E.I.L.E. S, 1996), p. 39; citing Nardini Ed, 1987, p. 391.

[204] Michael J. Matt (August 18, 2015), Patron Saints of Vatican II...and Freemasonry?," The Remnant Newspaper.

[205] John Booty, The Church in History (Morehouse Publishing, New York, 2003), p. 171.

[206] Ignazio Ingrao, Il Concilio Segreto: Misteri, intrighi e giochi di potere dell'evento che ha cambiato il volto della Chiesa (Editions Piemme, 2013), ob. cit. Note: unless otherwise indicated, it is the same source.

also be very generous: to the Archbishop of Bologna he donated numerous works of art, including a bronze statue of Giacomo Manzù portraying him with the miter on his head; to the Jesuits, he donated the tabernacle of the chapel of Villa Malta, home of the fortnightly magazine "La Civiltà Cattolica." In 1963 he was also conferred the title of "Gentleman of His Holiness," which, twenty years later, would disappear from the Pontifical Yearbook, when the P2 scandal had already broken out and Ortolani was under an international arrest warrant."

Ortolani himself confirms the meeting as host, where the election of Montini was discussed. Some preferred Cardinal Lercaro. But Giulio Andreotti confirms that the preference at that meeting was to vote for Montini. Paul VI rewarded Ortolani's hospitality, naming him a gentleman of His Holiness.[207]

Licio Gelli, the Grand Master of P2, indicated regarding Paul VI:

"Yes, of course, I met Pope Montini. I sent him a bed with a pure gold lacquered structure and a special mattress. I have a very good and magnificent memory of Paul VI," Venerable P2 related. "We had a brief conversation, then the Pope asked me - we were sitting in front of a small table - "Can you write your address on a piece of paper? You never know...." I had it typed.[208]

Jacques Mitterrand, former Grand Master of the Grand Orient of France, after comparing the reactionary Pius XII with John XXIII and Paul VI, wrote about the new post-conciliar mentality:

"Something has changed in the Church. The answers given by the pope [sic; Paul VI - JKW] to such burning questions as the celibacy of the clergy and birth control are fiercely contested within the Church. Some bishops, some priests, and members of the laity have questioned the word of the Supreme Pontiff himself. In the eyes of the Mason [he] who discusses dogma is already a Mason without an apron."[209]

About both popes, ecumenism and Freemasonry, French Freemason Yves Marsaudon, the aforementioned personal friend of John XXIII since his time as nuncio to France, wrote in his book L'Oecuménisme vu par un franc-maçon de tradition (Ecumenism as seen by a traditional Freemason):

"To the memory of Angelo Roncalli, priest, archbishop of Messembria, apostolic nuncio in Paris, cardinal of the Roman Church, patriarch of Venice, pope under the name of John XXIII, who has deigned to grant us his blessing, his understanding, and his protection."[210]

---

[207] Los Milenarios, El Vaticano Contra Dios (Ediciones B, S.A., Barcelona, Spain, 1999), ob. cit.

[208] Giacomo Galeazzi, Ferruccio Pinotti, Vaticano Massone: Logge, denaro e poteri occulti: il lato segreto della Chiesa di papa Francesco (Piemme, 2014), ob. cit.

[209] Lefebvre, p. 182.

[210] Yves Marsaudon, L'oecuménisme vu par un Franc-Maçon de tradition (Editions Vitian, Paris, 1964), ob. cit.

134

"To the pope of peace, to the father of all Christians, to the friend of all men, to his august continuator, His Holiness Pope Paul VI."[211]

"Catholics [...] must not forget that all roads lead to God. And they will have to accept that this courageous idea of freethought, which we can truly call a revolution, which springs from our Masonic lodges, has spread magnificently over the dome of St. Peter's.
 [...]
It can be said that ecumenism is the legitimate child of Freemasonry."[212]

"The sense of universalism that reigns these days in Rome is very close to our raison d'être, therefore, we cannot ignore the Second Vatican Council and its consequences [...] With all our hearts, we support the revolution of John XXIII."[213]

Marsaudon, referring to the evolutionary theology of the French Jesuit Pierre Teilhard de Chardin, hoped that the concept of God to prevail would be that of "a conjunction of science and mysticism in a now possible agreement." Thus arriving at a "metaphysical relativism" situated "at a level so far removed from dogmas that one no longer has anything at all."[214]

Vatican II, Freemasonry, the United States, the Revolution of 1968, and the transformation of the Roman Catholic Church

After 1945, in the context of the Cold War, the United States developed its foreign policy in Italy through Freemasonry. The Vatican exploited these channels for its investments in the United States. The banker Florio Fiorini said: "The link between Vatican finances and the American world became a strong factor in Italy after the war. It is intertwined with the existing relations between the industrial world of the North and French Masonic finance on the one hand and Central European finance on the other."[215]

Regarding John XXIII's relations with the United States, we read that financier Florio Fiorini, who personally knew Cardinal Francis Spellman of New York, indicated about his relationship with the pope:

"[...] a man of great financial mind, who allowed John XXIII to leave his investments in Italy and transfer the Vatican's enormous financial resources to America. Do you think that today the American Catholic Church is the fourth largest real estate power in the United States? [...] high-level class action lawyers know that the Church has huge real estate holdings."[216]

Valérie Aubourg, a French ethnologist and professor, comments that "the ambition to develop a modern democratic vision" with the support of the Catholic Church in

---

[211] Ibid.

[212] Ibid.

[213] Ibid.

[214] Ibid.

[215] Giacomo Galeazzi, Ferruccio Pinotti, Vaticano Massone: Logge, denaro e poteri occulti: il lato segreto della Chiesa di papa Francesco (Piemme, 2014), ob. cit.

[216] Ibid.

encouraging social reforms to invigorate resistance to communism, clearly coincided with the objectives of the U.S. government of John F. Kennedy and his Alliance for the Progress of Latin America. This period corresponded to the action of the new Pope John XXIII, who was "concerned with ecumenical dialogue and the adaptation of the Church to the modern world, convoked the Second Vatican Council in 1962." The Pope also encouraged Catholic action in favor of social progress and against "false ideologies" by taking up "in May 1961 in Mater et Magistra the message of the famous encyclical Rerum Novarum and extending it to the problem of underdevelopment in the world." Thus, the "concerns of Washington and the Vatican converged in 1961-62."[217]

Felix Morlion, the Dominican priest and president of Pro Deo University linked to the CIA, approached Vatican diplomacy in the early 1960s when John XXIII was pope.[218]

According to Morlion himself, Pro Deo was a "private Atlantic pact for democracy under God," based on a new alliance between "the largest moral community in the world, centered in Rome," and "the largest democratic nation in the world, the United States."[219] The priest used Pro Deo as a policy of openness to the pontiff; with the support of the powerful Cardinal Augustin Bea, president of the Secretariat for Promoting Christian Unity, one of the preparatory bodies of the Second Vatican Council and organizing since 1962 inter-Christian and later ecumenical meetings: the so-called Agape meetings with the congratulations of those close to Pope John XXIII.[220]

Felix Morlion was working on a book about John XXIII, although the pope's ideas had not yet burst into the world with full force. Both Morlion and the United States admired John XXIII's belief in the principles of fraternalism and world understanding, as well as the warmth of his personality. He was shaping up to be a democratic pope. But it was months later, with the encyclical Pacem in Terris, that the pope reached his historic peak.[221] Morlion felt the emotion of the profound changes that were brewing under that papacy:

"You must believe me," Father Morlion said, "when I tell you that dramatic ideas are shaping up and all the world will come to acclaim and love this gentle man. Pope John. He is not arbitrary or fixed. He has a profound respect for people of all faiths. He wants to help save the peace."[222]

Here we return to Henry Luce, the powerful U.S. businessman who owned Time-Life, as well as Charles Douglas (C.D.) Jackson, who was a psychological warfare advisor to the U.S. government and a senior executive of Time Inc. In June 1961,

---

[217] Aubourg, Valérie. « « A Philosophy of Democracy under God » : C.D. Jackson, Henry Luce et le mouvement Pro Deo (1941-1964) », Revue française d'études américaines, vol. no 107, no. 1, 2006, p. 38.
[218] Ibid, p. 40.
[219] Morlion, « The International Alliance for Democracy Under God », CDJP Box 84 Pro Deo 1962 (2), 2, and its original, less sober version, dictated by Morlion, CDJP Box 85 Pro Deo 1962 (9), 2-3, 6; quoted in Ibid.
[220] Aubourg, Valérie. « « A Philosophy of Democracy under God » : C.D. Jackson, Henry Luce et le mouvement Pro Deo (1941-1964) », Revue française d'études américaines, vol. no 107, no. 1, 2006, p. 39.
[221] Norman Cousins, The Improbable Triumvirate: An Asterik to the History of a Hopeful Year, 1962-1963 (W. W. Norton & Company, Inc., New York. First Edition, 1972), p. 11.
[222] Ibid.

confident of the new face of the Vatican under John XXIII, and after consultation with the State Department, U.S. leaders created a branch of the CIP/Center of Information Pro Deo in Rome.

C.D. Jackson assumed the presidency of the U.S. CIP with three vice presidents: "one Protestant (Luce), one Catholic (Gerald L. Carroll, of the Michael P. Grace II Trust, a small Catholic foundation, also chairman of the Steering Committee of the Catholic Interracial Council of New York), and one Jewish (Alan M. Stroock)."

In November 1962, to relieve the overburdened Jackson, Henry Luce was appointed chairman of the board, with Peter Grace taking over the chairmanship. Prestigious personalities from the business world were added to the CIP board of directors: "Marcel Rand of *Remington-Rand*, J. Bolton of *Standard Oil*, James Farley of *Coca-Cola International Corp*, John Bugas, vice president of *Ford Motor Co*, Arthur Watson, president of *IBM World Trade Corp*, David Rockefeller, and Eric Johnston, president of the *Motion Picture Association of America*."[223]

C.D. Jackson was received by Pope John XXIII in the summer of 1962, "for whom massive support for Pro Deo University would help anchor American influence in the European Community."[224] Thurston Davis, then editor-in-chief of the American Jesuit magazine, *America*, was somewhat puzzled by Pro Deo's ecumenical ideology.[225] One of the exceptions to the new face that the Society of Jesus was developing for years.

But the pro-American and more progressive Jesuit, John Courtney Murray, who was involved in the project with his links to the CIA, was struggling to instill in the Catholic Church the American proposal. On February 27, 1962, he wrote to Clare Boothe Luce, Henry Luce's wife, who was ambassador to Rome that the object of this historical argument is to show that, just as the institution of the Church-State owes its genesis to the special structure of a social-historical situation, it also depends for its justification on the peculiarities of this situation. If the situation is altered, the argument in favor of the institution is undermined.[226]

Murray was the editor of the Jesuit journal *Theological Studies* at Woodstock Seminary in New York, where he was a professor. He wrote the address "The American Proposition," which was delivered by Henry Luce at Pro Deo University in Rome.

Likewise, Robert Blair Kaiser, a Time magazine journalist, received $20,000 a month from Luce to host parties in his spacious Rome apartment for participants and journalists who were part of the Second Vatican Council. Kaiser and his wife "often host 50 or 100 journalists and monsignors, priests, and bishops and diplomats, sometimes during the week, sometimes on the weekend" to share information and "to provide a space where the agenda of a 'more open Church' could be freely discussed." Journalists from the Jesuit weekly *America* met regularly. Jesuits and other prelates "thought (and said out loud) that the Church was overloaded with excess baggage, myth, superstition, and nonsense. With him, they voted on all the important reforms of

---

[223] Aubourg, Valérie. « « A Philosophy of Democracy under God » : C.D. Jackson, Henry Luce et le mouvement Pro Deo (1941-1964) », Revue française d'études américaines, vol. no 107, no. 1, 2006, p. 39.
[224] Ibid.
[225] Ibid, p. 41.
[226] David Wemhoff, John Courtney Murray, Time/Life, and The American Proposition: How the CIA's Doctrinal Warfare Program Changed the Catholic Church (Wagon Wheel Press of Presence LLC, New Edition, 2022), Volume 1, ob. cit.

Vatican II, most of which tended to make the Church less Roman – and more Catholic…"[227]

U.S. leaders recognized that the triumph of the American proposition on the European continent depended largely on the dismantling of the Roman Catholic Church's commitment to the anti-naturalistic, anti-Thomistic commitment to the social kingship of Christ in its doctrine. As well as the weakening of the dogmatic defenses surrounding it.[228] For this reason, John Courtney Murray was the leading apologist for religious liberty as "the best possible shield for the Faith" in the Catholic world. By the late summer of 1949, Murray had engaged Protestants in their own magazines to talk about church and state, and thus religious liberty. For his part, Henry Luce published Murray's thinking in his magazine. Thus, from 1950 to 1952, a crucial debate took place within the Catholic Church about the relationship of Church and State; and, of course, religious liberty. Details of the debate were presented for the first time in American journals and media. Jesuits Murray and Gustave Weigel, as well as writers for *America* magazine, played a decisive role in favor of Americanism. However, there were many other Catholic dignitaries in favor of the idea. Indeed, that time was when U.S. government agencies engaged in psychological warfare to establish American ideals in particular ways. For example, Dr. Edward P. Lilly, an official specializing in the history of 20th-century political and psychological warfare, designed and implemented the U.S. Government's Ideological Doctrinal Warfare Program. Lilly directed and coordinated plans to infiltrate Christianity, Hinduism, Buddhism, and Islam to further American ideology. In the case of Catholicism, they used priests as tools of fomentation. Murray's ideas of religious freedom were successful when they were proposed in 1965 at Vatican II under the papacy of Paul VI. The more Americanized and progressive Catholic dialogue in the United States angered many U.S. Catholics, as did the advances of progress under John XXIII and later under Paul VI at Vatican II. Nevertheless, many Catholics were successfully influenced.

But there were other agents and actions taken to fulfill the objectives of democratizing the Roman Catholic Church:

A Jesuit priest by the name of Robert Leiber, who was a close advisor to Pope Pius XII until his death, was then the head of the Vatican's intelligence services, called the Entity. However, Leiber had been trained by the U.S. FBI;[229] and was a supporter of Murray's efforts. Leiber was also a source of intelligence for the Americans.[230] He thus had a dual role: to help the Church progress but under American ideals.

Both Jesuits and other American theologians used *America* magazine to attack the Vatican's more orthodox and intransigent positions on Church and State.[231]

---

[227] Maike Hickson (May 14, 2021), Report: Time magazine gave journalist $20,000 per month to host progressivist parties during Vatican II, LifeSite News.

[228] David Wemhoff, John Courtney Murray, Time/Life, and The American Proposition: How the CIA's Doctrinal Warfare Program Changed the Catholic Church (Wagon Wheel Press of Presence LLC, New Edition, 2022), Volume 1, ob. cit. Note: unless otherwise noted, this is the same source.

[229] Eric Frattini, The Entity: Five Centuries of Secret Vatican Espionage (St. Martin's Press, New York, 2008),

[230] David Wemhoff, John Courtney Murray, Time/Life, and The American Proposition: How the CIA's Doctrinal Warfare Program Changed the Catholic Church (Wagon Wheel Press of Presence LLC, New Edition, 2022), Volume 1, ob. cit.

[231] Ibid.

For her part, Marie-Louise, Jean Monnet's older sister and the aforementioned founding father of Europe, was assigned to the United States and had the status of "consecrated laywoman." She worked for "Catholic Action in independent circles" and later became the only woman auditor of the Second Vatican Council.[232]

So many operations occurring behind the scenes and in a public manner would achieve much of the designs of freedom and democracy that Americans longed for in the Roman Catholic Church. We cannot skip over additional Pro Deo actions during these years. Thus, add that Pro Deo used American teaching methods and textbooks. The objectives of that university were supported by the American Council for the International Promotion of Democracy Under God, based in the United States. Its directors were recommended without racial or religious discrimination.[233]

In 1958, Pro Deo's Institute of International Relations initiated "a coordinated program of social research and sponsored a series of conferences on American psychological strategy and communications. It introduced a seminar on the 'Challenge to American Democracy' conducted by American experts." The greatest concepts taught through Pro Deo were: the inviolability of human dignity and human rights. The ideals of justice and fraternity, are based on the Fatherhood of God. And the creativity of individual entrepreneurship.[234]

Morlion subsequently worked more closely with the CIA, U.S. Ambassador Mary Luce, three NATO countries, and the Dominican order; to impede the Italian Communist party and to maintain and expand a flow of American democratic ideals into Italy.[235]

Pro Deo was one of the CIA's most important contacts for advancing the U.S. agenda in the Vatican. Indeed, it was "always a crossroads of meetings between CIA men, high prelates, and big industrialists." Morlion was photographed by Mino Pecorelli's "Mondo d'Oggi," where he appeared with three CIA agents and Christian Democrat ministers Giuseppe Spataro and Mariano Rumor. So, it is known that Morlion was a CIA agent.

The U.S. government was advancing the operation not only with Pro Deo, but also with the Freemasons in Italy. There was an alliance between the Vatican and Freemasonry, directly with the P2 lodge which was regulated by the Grand Orient of Italy. The alliance bore fruit in financial terms.[236]

Also, in the late 1960s, Morlion established contact with Yves Gerin Serac's Aginter press in Lisbon, who was one of the major provocateurs, being an expert in anti-communist covert operations.[237]

It should be noted that Americans United for Separation of Church and State (AU), born in 1948 and having as its first director Glenn L. Archer, who was also a Mason

---

[232] Philippe de Villiers, J'ai tiré sur le fil du mensonge et tout est venu (Fayard, Paris, 2019), ob. cit.; citing Éric Roussel, *Jean Monnet, op. cit.*

[233] Freedom's Future Leaders, The American Council for the International Promotion of Democracy Under God (C.I.P.) Inc. (1957), ob. cit.

[234] Ibid.

[235] Andrea Montella (August 23, 2010), Biografia di Toni Negri, Potere Operaio, Superclan - Uomini, culture, tecniche dell'eversione imperialista, Storia Veneta.

[236] Ferdinando Imposimato, La Repubblica delle stragi impunite (Newton Compton Editori, 2013), ob. cit.

[237] Andrea Montella (August 23, 2010), Biografia di Toni Negri, Potere Operaio, Superclan - Uomini, culture, tecniche dell'eversione imperialista, Storia Veneta.

and a Shriner,[238] fought against Catholic interference in the affairs of the U.S. government.[239]

"Mr. Archer and his organization also charged in 1955 that U.S. Catholic cardinals who vote for a new pope violate U.S. laws and should forfeit their citizenship. He said U.S. law barred a citizen from taking part in a foreign election."[240]

Rob Boston wrote in Church & State:

"Not everyone was pleased to see the sudden appearance of a group committed to defending church-state separation on the national stage. Christian nationalism wasn't the powerful political movement it is today, but the hierarchy of the Roman Catholic Church often butted heads with AU. Church leaders sought taxpayer support for its network of private religious schools, worked to ban artificial birth control and advocated for censorship of books, films and other materials they believed cast religion in a poor light – all stands AU opposed.

"These battles were spirited, and the church hierarchy sometimes accused Archer of anti-Catholicism. It was highly ironic, therefore, in 1960 when Archer found himself defending John F. Kennedy against the clergy of Kennedy's own church. During his presidential campaign, Ken-nedy had vowed to oppose tax funding of religious schools, a stance he emphasized in an exchange of letters with Archer. Kennedy's position angered the church hierarchy, but Archer pointed out that it was in line with the Constitution."[241]

Thus, with all this in mind, we see that the numerous movements in favor of the American Project advanced fervently at the Second Vatican Council.

A tumultuous debate on religious freedom took place during the third session of the Council.[242] The American Jesuit magazine, *America*, documents:

"As the final session opened on September 14, 1965, two opposing and irreconcilable "sides" were lined up against one another. The traditionalist side, led by Cardinal Alfredo Ottaviani, was a powerful minority who argued the state was obligated, through its officials, to worship God according to the Catholic religion. Reformers, following the thought of John Courtney Murray, S.J., argued the church could and should support religious freedom in secular states. Both sides saw the question as a matter of speaking the truth about God and the church and morality; for these men, the stakes could not be higher."

---

[238] The Washington Post (Nov. 20, 2002), Glenn L. Archer, Sr., The Washington Post; William L. Fox, Lodge of the Double-Headed Eagle: Two Centuries of Scottish Rite Freemasonry in America's Southern Jurisdiction (University of Arkansas Press, 1997), ob. cit.

[239] The Washington Post (Nov. 20, 2002), Glenn L. Archer, Sr., The Washington Post.

[240] Ibid.

[241] Rob Boston (March 1, 2022), Americans United's Founding Father: Meet Glenn L. Archer, AU's First Executive Director, Church & State Magazine.

[242] Barry Hudock (November 19, 2015), The Fight for Religious Freedom: John Courtney Murray's role in 'Dignitatis Humanae', America Magazine. Note: unless otherwise noted, hereafter is the same source.

140

America published on January 9, 1965, an article by John Courtney Murray defending religious freedom. It was also published in Italian and German newspapers and, months later, *L'Osservatore Romano* published an article by the prominent French theologian and Jesuit, Charles Boyer, of the Gregorian University; in which he defended Murray's thesis.

Supporters and opponents reviewed the religious freedom text the bishops received in June. Joseph Ritter, the cardinal of St. Louis, Missouri, wrote a letter to the entire U.S. episcopate asking for support for the outline. Coetus Internationalis Patrum, a bishops' interest group opposed to the draft, invited the world's bishops to provide their mailing addresses in Rome during the upcoming council session to receive advice on how to vote. Cardinal Giuseppe Siri wrote to Paul VI complaining that if the new document were promulgated, it would "especially benefit religious indifferentism."

Murray and the U.S. bishops prepared a series of coordinated interventions for the fourth session of the Council, which covered all the cardinal points. On September 15, the text was debated, with U.S. bishops defending it for the next few hours, with one bishop commenting, "The voices are the voices of the United States bishops; but the thoughts are the thoughts of John Courtney Murray!" Then came the opposing voices, with the influential Cardinal Ernesto Ruffini saying that the state was obliged through its officials to worship God according to the Catholic religion.

The debate was heated and of great interest, until Monday, September 20, the fourth day of the debate, when Cardinal Josef Beran spoke in favor of the document on religious freedom. Beran had been imprisoned by the Nazis during the Second World War in the Theresienstadt and Dachau concentration camps. After four years of freedom, being elected bishop of Prague, he was imprisoned in 1949 by the communist regime until 1963. His government then prevented him from exercising his ministry. He was later appointed as a cardinal by Paul VI, after moving to Rome. Beran's intervention was catalytic:

"Standing for the first time before his brother bishops, who knew well the suffering he had endured for his fidelity, Beran reminded them of the burning of the Czech priest Jan Hus in the 15th century and the forced conversions of Czech Protestants in the 17th century. These events, he said, "left a certain wound hiding in the hearts of the people" and damaged the church's credibility. He called on the church to repent and said that "the principle of religious freedom and freedom of conscience must be set forth clearly and without any restriction flowing from opportunistic considerations."

Other important voices continued to defend the document. But the fight for the Church's traditional position was strong, and Protestant observers were concerned. Paul VI, who supported the document, called for a vote.

On Tuesday at 10:30 am, after several interventions in favor of the document, the vote was 1997 in favor, 224 against, and one null. The bishops responded with joy and applause. On Wednesday morning, the *London Times* called the decision "a great event in the history of Catholicism and in the history of freedom." Archbishop Karol Wojtyla (future Pope John Paul II) also spoke in favor.

After the arduous work on the final document, on December 7, 1965, the last session of the Council, "Dignitatis Humanae," or the Declaration on Religious Freedom, was born. The work of Murray, Time Inc., and the CIA, and by extensión, American Freemasonry, French, and others. Murray criticized conservative clerics' claims of

Masonic infiltration of the Vatican, as well as their adherence to absolute fidelity to papal teachings, on September 9, 1953, when criticizing a document: "I think it quite shocking to find out that Freemasonry has penetrated the Curia, and I tremble for your 'security'! Seriously, it is a bit alarming to see abroad in the Church the mentality represented by this document. In a way, the most astonishing statement was… where there is mention of 'absolute fidelity to the teachings of the Popes and of St. Thomas, which is the same thing.' I happen to be acquainted with some of the South American literature on Maritain, and some of it borders closely on the vicious. However, it is somehow instructive to read this kind of literature. It makes one realize more and more the necessity of serenity and charity in controversy."[243]

Murray wrote that he found more support for his views on religious freedom in Europe than in American theological circles (despite support for freedom from U.S. clerics).

The relationship between the US secret services, Freemasonry, the anti-communist struggle, and Americanism in Italy

About the links between the American secret services, Freemasonry, the anti-communist struggle, and Americanism in Italy, the United States clandestinely recruited for the state security apparatus even Fascists and other ultra-right-wingers defeated after World War II. All to fight against communism. The pro-fascist selection was not political but for intelligence purposes. The United States also founded the Christian Democratic Party (CDP), which was crammed with collaborationists, royalists, and unreconstructed fascists.[244] But it dominated in the Italian presidency and parliament for several years (the 50s).[245]

During the 1960s, the head of the P2 Masonic Lodge, Licio Gelli (pro-Fascist) and the CIA manipulated Italian politics to keep the Communists out of power. Frank Gigliotti, CIA agent and American Masonic Lodge Freemason, personally recruited Gelli and instructed him to install a parallel anti-Communist government in Italy in close collaboration with the CIA station in Rome.[246] Gigliotti was president of the "Agitation Committee" created in the United States to respond to the appeal launched by the Masons of the Grand Orient of Italy, involved in the controversial work of reappropriation of the Palazzo Giustiniani Masonic house confiscated during the Fascist period. The American Masons sponsored the compromise between the Grand Orient of Italy and the Italian State, which was signed on July 7, 1960.[247]

That same year, the American Masons also "intervened through Gigliotti in the operation of unification of the Supreme Council of the Most Serene Grand Lodge of the ALAM of the Sicilian Prince Giovanni Alliata di Montereale (whose name will be linked to the events of the Borghese coup, to those of the "Rosa dei Venti" and Mafia organizations), which later led to Lodge P2, with the Grand Orient."[248]

---

[243] Donald E. Pelotte, John Courtney Murray: Theologian in Conflict (Paulist Press, New York, 1976), p. 65, note 51.

[244] Daniele Ganser, NATO's Secret Armies: Operation Gladio and Terrorism in Western Europe (Frank Cass, New York, 2005), p. 64.

[245] Ibid, pp. 64, 67.

[246] Ibid, p. 73.

[247] Parliamentary Committee P2 (Sept. 8/26, 2023), Frank Gigliotti, l'agente della Cia massone vicino ai cugini italiani, Domani.

[248] Ibid.

On the other hand, Ted Shackley, CIA director of covert operations in Rome, introduced Gelli to Alexander Haig, Nixon's military advisor in the 1960s.[249] Both Haig and Nixon's national security advisor, Henry Kissinger, authorized Gelli in the summer of 1969 to recruit four hundred high-ranking Italian and NATO officers into his lodge. Gelli's contacts with the United States remained excellent throughout the Cold War.[250]

As a sign of trust and respect, Licio Gelli was a guest in 1974 at Gerald Ford's U.S. presidential inauguration ceremonies; and again in 1977 at Jimmy Carter's inauguration ceremony. Likewise, when Reagan became President of the United States in 1981, Gelli was seated in the front row in Washington.[251]

Later, Antonio Bellocchio, the Communist member of the Anselmi Commission, declared: "We have come to the definite conclusion that Italy is a country of limited sovereignty because of the interference of the American secret service and international freemasonry." Bellocchio lamented that at the time of the Reagan administration, Italian parliamentarians shied away from investigating the P2 lodge's links to the United States. "'If the majority of the commission had been prepared to follow us in this analysis they would have had to admit that they are puppets of the United States of America, and they don't intend to admit that ever." It was concluded in the investigation that although Masonic lodges exist in Germany, Spain, France, Argentina, Australia, Uruguay, Ireland, Greece, Indonesia, and most of the rest of the countries of the world, the headquarters of the Masons were in the United States and had 5 million members.[252]

During the Italian First Republic, the anti-communist parallel government of the Propaganda Due/P2 lodge, and the anti-communist parallel army Gladio (code name for the clandestine armed resistance operations of the so-called Stay Behind Network planned by the Brussels Treaty Organization, and later by NATO), both financed by the United States, cooperated closely. After the discovery of P2, Licio Gelli escaped arrest by fleeing to South America. After the end of the Cold War, he was pleased to confirm that the secret army was made up of staunch anti-communists, many from the ranks of the mercenaries who fought in the Spanish Civil War; and many others from the fascist Salo republic. The organization was well-built. Had the communist force grown in Italy, the United States would have helped Italy, triggered another war and generously supplied them with weapons from the air. Gelli recounted that the gladiators were paid well, as the U.S. spent a lot of money on the network: "The Americans paid them large sums of money, the equivalent of an excellent salary. And they guaranteed the financial support of the families in case the Gladiator was killed."[253]

This is also since the revival of Italian Freemasonry after the war was encouraged by the British and Americans, with the emergence of lodges in the face of the advance of

[249] Daniele Ganser, NATO's Secret Armies: Operation Gladio and Terrorism in Western Europe (Frank Cass, New York, 2005), pp. 73, 74.
[250] Ibid, p. 74.
[251] Ibid.
[252] Ibid. quoting: In an interview with Willan. Quoted in Willan, Puppetmasters, p. 55. 64; Igel, Andreotti, p. 229; The New Statesman, September 21, 1984.
[253] Ibid, p. 75; citing Hugh O'Shaughnessy: Gladio. Europe's best kept secret; The Observer, June 7, 1992; Gentile, Gladio, p. 28.

the Allied armies as the fascist persecution of Freemasons came to an end.[254] A secret service report on Italian Freemasonry highlights the influence of British and American Freemasonry on Italian lodges.

Philip Willan wrote: "A secret service report on 'Freemasonry in Italy' highlighted the influence of British and American freemasonry on Italian lodges. 'Washington's policy is to direct European states towards interests and objectives that fall into the United States' orbit, concerned as it is not to lose Western Europe and to counteract Moscow's attempts to engineer the break-up of NATO.'"

Furthermore, the American Masonic presence coincided with the military presence of NATO. Giuseppe D'Alema indicated that U.S. lodges have been established at all NATO bases in Italy. The Grand Orient of Italy owed a special debt of gratitude to the U.S. government when they intervened to help the GOI recover Palazzo Giustiniani.

Operation Gladio, directed by the American CIA and British MI6 to stop the Soviet invasion of Western Europe through elite secret paramilitary armed forces stationed in various capitalist countries, was managed and concealed by NATO. The countries where it was carried out were Austria, Belgium, Denmark, France, Germany, Greece, Italy, Luxembourg, the Netherlands, Norway, Portugal, Spain, Sweden, Switzerland, Turkey, the United Kingdom and the United States.

Expansion of the Masonic presence in the Roman Catholic Church
It is known of the strong infiltration of Freemasonry in the Vatican, at least since 1949, during the reign of Pius XII. A time when the infiltrated Freemasons were even able to obtain for a person, or even a family, a private audience with the pontiff. This was when the pope could only be approached by heads of state, ambassadors, and, with difficulty, the cardinals of the Curia.[255] However, the greatest influence was seen during and after the Second Vatican Council.

José Antonio Ferrer Benimeli, a Jesuit priest and specialist in Freemasonry, said:

"It is easy that the wars gave birth to the desire for tolerance, peace, and fraternity, that is, true ecumenism, which two centuries later would be consecrated and canonized by the Second Vatican Council, and which curiously is reflected in the distinctive titles of the lodges, in which not only the names of the saints are frequent, but also those referring to friendship and fraternal union."[256]

The more or less official contacts of the Catholic Church with Freemasonry flourished almost everywhere. Here are some examples: the Dutch Capuchin Wildiers reported on the French Jesuit Teilhard de Chardin in front of a Lodge in Amsterdam in 1962.[257]

The Bishop of Cuernavaca, Sergio Mendez Arceo, who was a Mason, made repeated attempts to eliminate the enmity between the Church and the lodges. And we read that the Grand Lodge of Haiti addressed the pope on May 26, 1962, begging him to end the

---

[254] Philip Willan, Puppetmasters: The Political Use of Terrorism in Italy (Authors Choice Press, New York, 1991, 2002), ob. cit. Note: unless otherwise noted, this is the same source.
[255] Los Milenarios, El Vaticano Contra Dios (Ediciones B, S.A., Barcelona, Spain, 1999), ob. cit.
[256] José Antonio Ferrer Benimeli, S.J., Masonería, Iglesia, Revolución e Independencia (Editorial Pontificia Universidad Javeriana, Bogotá, D. C., First edition: January 2015), pp. 24, 25.
[257] Giacomo Galeazzi, Ferruccio Pinotti, Vaticano Massone: Logge, denaro e poteri occulti: il lato segreto della Chiesa di papa Francesco (Piemme, 2014), ob. cit.

enmity; as did Helmke, the Grand Master of the Grand Lodge of Austria who wrote to Cardinal Franz König.[258]

Rosario Esposito, a Pauline priest as well as a professor at several pontifical universities and a great promoter of the agreement between the Catholic Church and Freemasonry, revealed that Paul VI continued and encouraged rapprochement with Freemasonry.[259] He did so through public meetings in a spirit of ecumenical fraternity in the period 1969-1977; and between exponents of the Catholic Church and very high dignitaries of Freemasonry. The protagonists of the approaches were Rosario Esposito and Don Miano, of the Secretariat for non-believers; as well as Monsignor Alberto Ablondi, president of the Special Commission for Ecumenism (Mason of the important Pecorelli and *Panorama* lists), and with the Jesuit priest Giovanni Caprile, of *La Civiltà Cattolica* magazine.[260] Giordano Gamberini, the Grand Master of the Grand Orient of Italy, participated on the side of the Freemasons.[261]

It is worth noting that Esposito, in an interview with the Masonic newspaper *Corriere Partenopeo*, professed himself "a Mason to the depths of his spirit," and added that, "I am so in solidarity with them, I share everything: the Constitutions, the Landmarks, the Ancient Duties: I am totally with them."[262]

We noted elsewhere in this book that the Pauline wrote in *The Masonic Review* of July 1978, and in a message already quoted, that Monsignor Giovanni Montini had told the Dominican Felix Morlion, that "Not a generation will pass without peace being made between the two societies."[263]

Esposito indicated that Montini's decision was more a decision than a prediction; when he became pope, he implemented it in the pre-announced terms.[264] That Paul VI was very open to Freemasonry is also attested by Giulio Mazzon, personal secretary of the partisans of ANPI, candidate for Grand Master, and great friend of Virgilio Gaito.[265]

In this regard, journalists Giacomo Galeazzi and Ferruccio Pinotti state:

"During the pontificate of Paul VI, there were numerous public handshakes between heads of Freemasonry and important cardinals: the Americans Richard Cushing, Terence Cooke, John Cody and John Joseph Krol, the Austrian Franz König, the Dutch Bernard Alfrink, the French Maurice Feltin, Francois Marty and Roger Etchegaray, the Chilean Raúl Silva Henríquez, the Brazilians Aloisio Lorscheider, and Paulo Evaristo Arns, in short, almost all the leaders of the progressive wing of the Council. In Italy, Bishops Dante Bernini, of Albano, and Alberto Ablondi, of Livorno, participated in the meetings between delegations of the Catholic Church and Freemasonry. And in the Vatican, the Cardinal Prefect of the former Holy Office, the

---

[258] Ibid.

[259] Carlo Alberto Agnoli, La Massoneria alla conquista della Chiesa (E.I.L.E. S, 1996), pp. 41, 42; citing Father Rosario Esposito "Le grandi concordanze tra Chiesa e massoneria," cit. p. 420.

[260] Ibid, p. 42.

[261] Ibid, quoting J. A. Ferrer, G. Caprile. "Massoneria e Chiesa Cattolica," ediz. Paoline cit. pp. 125-127.

[262] Ibid, quoting "Corriere Partenopeo," year XIII, n. 5, July 1991.

[263] Ibid, pp. 42, 43; citing J. A. Ferrer, G. Caprile "Massoneria e Chiesa Cattolica," p. 91.

[264] Ibid.

[265] Giacomo Galeazzi, Ferruccio Pinotti, Vaticano Massone: Logge, denaro e poteri occulti: il lato segreto della Chiesa di papa Francesco (Piemme, 2014), ob. cit.

Croatian Franjo Seper, the predecessor of Joseph Ratzinger, was pulling the strings."[266]

But what thoughts were there during the time of Paul VI among the Masons? Henry C. Clausen, Sovereign Grand Commander of the Supreme Council of the Scottish Rite of the American Southern Jurisdiction, wrote in 1976 that many of the Catholic friends of the Masons reject as alien to America the medieval fulminations against Freemasonry; noting how much they have in common: they accept the standards of American democracy, recognize that they have "a pluralistic system in a new and permanent form of relationship between religion and government, and call upon their church leaders to stop attacks upon Masonry and Masonic ceremonies." He said they hoped for winds of freedom that would create a friendly and tolerant atmosphere, which is the climate Masons seek as men of goodwill in the nation. Clausen also mentioned as an example the Rev. John A. O'Brien, Ph.D., who speaking in 1973 at a luncheon sponsored by the Chicago Lawyers Shrine Club (of the Masons),[267] noted:

"As a Roman Catholic, a research professor of theology at the University of Notre Dame, and a priest for more than half a century, I want to pay a long overdue tribute to the Freemasons for the distinguished contribution which they have made to the civic, commercial, scientific, cultural and spiritual life of our nation. They have given us some of our greatest presidents, generals, legislators, statesmen, citizens and patriots. If that rich and many-faceted contribution were withdrawn, our nation would be impoverished indeed.
"During a priestly ministry of more than fifty years, many of my closest and dearest friends have been Masons, and I count their friendship as a pearl beyond all price."[268]

Clausen also referred to the attempts in the Vatican to liberalize the restrictive provisions of canon law, because since the codification of canon law in the Codex Juris Canonici, papal bulls and briefs would be only personal expressions.[269] All of the above was part of the change brought about by Paul VI and the Second Vatican Council.
Cardinal John Willebrands, Secretary for Christian Unity, also addressed representatives of the DeMolay Masonic Order during their 50th anniversary when visiting the Vatican:

"It is a pleasure and an honor for me to welcome you-at the request of the Secretariat of State-in the house of the Holy Father. The Holy Father is taking a short and necessary vacation in his residence at Castel Gandolfo, preparing at the same time for his journey to Africa. Therefore he can now receive only on Wednesdays....
"So we fulfill the commandments given in the book of Deuteronomy (6,5), and quoted by Christ in the gospel of Mark (12,29): 'Hear, O Israel: the Lord our God, the Lord is one; and you shall love the Lord your God with all your heart and with all your soul and with all your mind and with all your strength,' and Christ adds to this first commandment the second, which we find also in the book Leviticus (19,18): 'You

---

[266] Ibid.
[267] Henry C. Clausen, Clausen's Commentaries on Morals and Dogma (The Supreme Council, 33, Ancient and Accepted Scottish Rite of Freemasonry, Second Edition, 1976), p. 190.
[268] Ibid, p. 191.
[269] Ibid.

shall love your neighbor as yourself',' and concludes: 'there is no other commandment greater than these'."[270]

The cardinal continued:

"This inspiration animates the Order of DeMolay and therefore you as its members, in your service to humanity, especially of the sick, the abandoned, the invalids, etc.

"May I, as the President of the Secretariat for Promoting Christian Unity, express my gratitude and joy that the membership of the Order includes Catholics and Protestants and Jews in a great cooperation for the benefit of humanity.

"I congratulate you particularly on the occasion of the 50th anniversary of the Order and I pray that the Lord of Hosts may bless you in all your noble work."[271]

All this tells us of a Pope Paul VI who had an enormous interest in Masonic circles and in turn their friendship with Roman Catholicism. It is not surprising that there was so much rapprochement between the two institutions during his papacy. We will now look at additional revealing examples.

Richard Cushing, Cardinal Archbishop of Boston and who appears in the Masonic list of journalist Mino Pecorelli, held in 1965 and 66, two conferences in Masonic lodges. He also participated along with other prelates in convivial meetings "with exponents of Freemasonry; Cardinal Avelar Brandão Vilela (1912-1986), archbishop of Sào Salvador de Bahia, who even celebrated a Christmas Mass on December 26, 1975 for the members of the Libertade Masonic Lodge of his city and their families, and by Cardinal Paulo Evaristo Arns, who in 1976 was conferred "a high Masonic honor.""[272]

Years earlier, in 1974, German Freemasons increased pressure for direct dialogue with the Catholic episcopate in Germany, which occurred between 1974 and 1980.[273] In 1976, Cardinal Terence Cooke addressed three thousand Masons at a Masonic Dedication Breakfast in New York:

"I lament that in bygone days in many places, due to some extent to a failure to communicate, there was at times an estrangement between your ancestors and some clerics, of all faiths... Whatever happened in the past should not stand between us and the future. Your invitation to me is a joyful event on the road of friendship between the Masons and the Catholics of America."[274]

Likewise, Cardinal Cody of Chicago did his best to put an end to the Church's conflict with Freemasonry.[275]

---

[270] Ibid, pp. 191, 192.

[271] Ibid, p. 192.

[272] Carlo Alberto Agnoli, La Massoneria alla conquista della Chiesa (E.I.L.E. S, 1996), p. 33; citing La citazione è tratta dal quindicinale Sì sì no no, del 30 novembre 1992, p. 7; cf. J. Ferrér-Benimeli, G. Caprile, Massoneria e Chiesa cattolica, p. 116; cf. P. R. Esposito, op. cit, p. 36; cf. J. Ferrér-Benimeli, G. Caprile, op. cit., p. 148.

[273] Giacomo Galeazzi, Ferruccio Pinotti, Vaticano Massone: Logge, denaro e poteri occulti: il lato segreto della Chiesa di papa Francesco (Piemme, 2014), ob. cit.

[274] Martin Short, Inside the Brotherhood: Further Secrets of the Freemasons (HarperCollins Publishers, London, 1990), p. 156; quoting New Liberty Magazine.

[275] Giacomo Galeazzi, Ferruccio Pinotti, Vaticano Massone: Logge, denaro e poteri occulti: il lato segreto della Chiesa di papa Francesco (Piemme, 2014), ob. cit.

But equally, sinister characters such as Bishop Paul Marcinkus, president of the IOR or Vatican Bank and who appears as a Freemason in the Pecorelli list, collaborated closely with the powerful Propaganda 2.[276]

Another Freemason of Paul VI's time was the powerful Cardinal Agostino Casaroli, who appears on the list.[277] Additionally, the Pauline priest Rosario Esposito, in his work Le Grandi Concordanze tra Chiesa e Massoneria (*The Great Concordances between the Church and Freemasonry*), published by the Masonic publishing house Nardini of Florence in 1987, reported that on October 20, 1985, Cardinal Casaroli, on the occasion of the celebrations of the fortieth anniversary of the UN, celebrated in St. Patrick's Cathedral in New York, a wide-ranging homily that "testifies that the concordances between the Church and Freemasonry can be considered as acquired de facto."[278]

In a letter from Casaroli (Masonic name, Pasa) to the Grand Master of the Grand Orient of Italy, Lino Salvini, dated March 14, 1974, he wrote about the bishops appointed in the countries of the East:

"I think it is totally useless to insist on a subject of which I am more convinced than you are of the VV.AA., namely, that of a highly distensive policy with all the countries of the East, to the point that not only pro-Communist bishops were appointed, but also pro-Communist priests were ordained.

"My behavior toward you, as you well know, has always been loyal and faithful. But we cannot run the risk of ruining such a peacefully accomplished work by a clumsy and hasty action in our inner camp.

"You know my program, and you also know well my closest collaborators, which you yourselves have given me. All it takes is a lot of patience and trust. Verbally the rest."[279]

What other Masons were in very high positions? Cardinal Jean Villot, who was Secretary of State under Paul VI, John Paul I, and John Paul II until he died in 1979, denied in a letter dated October 31, 1976, to the French magazine *Lectures Françaises*, that he had any relationship with Freemasonry.[280] This is because the magazine had published in its 1976 issue, the list of Masonic clerics, which included Villot himself.[281] However, after his death, the book *Vie et perspectives de la franc-maçonnerie traditionnelle ("Life and Perspectives of Traditional Freemasonry")* by Jean Tourniac, Grand Orator of the National Grand Lodge of France, was found among his belongings. The cover of the book contained two handwritten dedications to Villot, one from the author and the other from the Grand Master of the lodge.[282]

---

[276] Carlo Alberto Agnoli, La Massoneria alla conquista della Chiesa (E.I.L.E. S, 1996), p. 15; citing 30 Giorni, 11 November 1992, p. 16.

[277] Ibid, p. 22.

[278] Ibid; citing cf. P. R. Esposito, Le Grandi Concordanze tra Chiesa e Massoneria, p. 210.

[279] Pass. Letter to the Venerable Grand Master. March 14, 1974.

[280] Carlo Alberto Agnoli, La Massoneria alla conquista della Chiesa (E.I.L.E. S, 1996), pp. 28, 29.

[281] Ibid, p. 28.

[282] Ibid, p. 29.

It should be noted that Villot's theological positions and ideals were remarkably in agreement with those of Cardinals Suenens, Poletti, Casaroli, Bishop Gottardi of Trent, and others, who appear next to his name in the lists of *Introibo, Panorama,* and *Policy Observer.*[283]

Suenenes (listed as a Freemason),[284] being a progressive cardinal of Belgium and a Vatican II priest, declared that "Vatican II is the French Revolution in the Church."[285]

For his part, Cardinal Franz König, authorized Archbishop of Vienna-Austria, with Cardinal Suenens and others, was one of the main promoters of the conciliar innovations.[286] Aldo Mola, the then official historian of Italian Freemasonry, said based on a "very high and excellently informed Justinian dignitary," that Koenig was a member of a covert Roman lodge to which belonged "Cesare Merzagora, Marcello Saccucci, Giuseppe Caradonna, Luigi Preti, Eugenio Cefis, Guido Carli, Enrico Cuccia, Michele Sindona, along with other celebrities and well-known people."[287] The Italian magazine *Il Borghese* of August 15, 1976, referred to König's presumed affiliation with Freemasonry. The Cardinal, together with the Deputy Grand Master of Austrian Freemasonry, Dr. Kurt Baresch, was the promoter of the commission that approved in great secrecy the Lichtenau Declaration of July 5, 1970;[288] which stated that, contrary to the official position of the Catholic Church, Freemasons did not represent a threat to it. It also recommended that canonical penalties against Freemasons be abolished and recommended further dialogue between Catholics and Freemasons. This declaration was drafted and signed by a mixed Catholic and Masonic commission, which begins with an invocation to the Great Architect of the Universe.[289]

Much more can be said, but with these examples, it is enough to see the openness of the papacy, particularly during Paul VI, to Freemasonry. Now, about some certainty of Montini as a Freemason, what we can say is that if he was, he was not prepared for such drastic changes in the Church of which he was the leader, as we shall see more. Thus, the plans of the Jesuits and the ecclesiastical hierarchy involved in the conspiracy were in turn pitted against Masonic desires to participate in the transformation and control of the Catholic Church. It was, and is, a power struggle for the destiny and identity of civilization as a whole.

The transformation of the Catholic Church and its role in world geopolitics
The power of the Catholic Church was considerably diminished by the American interference in the European countries where Gladio and others operated; but also by the interference suffered by the Freemasons and American agents during the aforementioned Second Vatican Ecumenical Council. The historian Giuliana Chamedes, says about the results of Vatican II and the great cultural changes of the 60s:

---

[283] Ibid.

[284] Ibid, p. 31.

[285] Lefebvre, p. 100, in Vennari, p. 26; quoted in Ted Flynn, Hope of the Wicked: The Master Plan to Rule the World (MaxKol Communications, Inc. 2000), p. 149.

[286] Carlo Alberto Agnoli, La Massoneria alla conquista della Chiesa (E.I.L.E. S, 1996), p. 31.

[287] Ibid; citing cf. A. Mola, Storia della Massoneria italiana dalle origini ai nostri giorni, Bompiani Ed., 1992, p. 744. We have corroborated: Aldo A. Mola, Storia della Massoneria italiana dalle origini ai nostri giorni (Grupo Editoriale Fabbri, Bompiani, Sonzogno, Etas S.p.A, 1992), p. 744.

[288] Ibid.

[289] Ibid.

"The 1960s are my endpoint because this decade marked a decisive caesura in papal diplomacy. The changes introduced by the Second Vatican Council began the work of upending the interwar papal crusade against communism and liberalism, while the sweeping social and cultural changes of these years did the rest of the work. For the first time in decades, the central government of the Catholic Church renounced the concordat project and began to question its investment in the nation-state as the linchpin of international order. At the same time, the pope tentatively apologized for the ethno-nationalism, anti-Semitism, and racism that its internationalist crusade had helped unleash. But this reorientation—important as it was—proved incomplete. Despite all the innovations of the 1960s, the Church struggled to provide a convincing answer to the burning question of what *should* constitute the proper relationship between Church and state. It eschewed the project of robustly defining a new vision for the international order. And it did not clearly delineate who, or what, were the Church's core enemies (if liberalism and communism no longer were). As a result of these shortcomings and the companion success of competing internationalist movements in mobilizing millions of Catholics in Europe, Church membership hemorrhaged. By the 1970s the number of practicing Catholics in Europe had dipped dramatically, and although papal activity certainly did not disappear, it had taken stock of this profound shift by jettisoning its interwar praxis and shifting its emphasis to other parts of the globe."[290]

Andrew Brown comments that the dramatic changes brought about by the Council had serious consequences for the evangelizing and political strength of Catholicism. For example, in the ten years following the Council, 100,000 men left the priesthood worldwide. For once the walls of custom and reverence that surrounded them were broken down, there seemed to be nothing to hold them back. The 1970s also produced an explosion of sexual abuse of minors, as was seen in later figures. Cloistered orders of nuns were emptied. And bold theologians were beginning to question papal infallibility.[291] The church saw its influence in the states weakened, although it retained much of its strength.

Even Pope Paul VI was alarmed; and when he made his famous statement on June 29, 1972, that "the smoke of Satan has entered the temple of God," he was referring to the post-Vatican II period as a day of clouds, storms, and darkness. Paul VI continued to implement it but with less enthusiasm and more warnings.[292]

Even though the reforms on the Mass were causing a disaster in the faith, Paul VI imposed himself authoritatively, as reflected in the private meeting he had with the Catholic theologian Jean Guitton in November 1976.[293]

His message of June 29, 1972, described here in part, and from where we quote extensively:

---

[290] Giuliana Chamedes, A Twentieth-Century Crusade: The Vatican's Battle to Remake Christian Europe (Harvard University Press, Cambridge, Massachusetts, 2019), p. 12.
[291] Andrew Brown (October 11, 2012), How the second Vatican council responded to the modern world, The Guardian.
[292] Rembert G. Weakland, A Pilgrim in a Pilgrim Church: Memoirs of a Catholic Archbishop (Wm. B. Eerdmans Publishing Co., Grand Rapids, Michigan, 2009), p. 214.
[293] Jean Guitton, Paolo VI segreto, cit., pp. 144, 145; quoted in Antonio Socci, The Fourth Secret of Fatima (The Sphere of Books, 2012), ob. cit.

"Referring to the situation of the Church today, the Holy Father says he has the feeling that "the smoke of Satan has entered the temple of God through some crack. There is doubt, uncertainty, uneasiness, dissatisfaction, confrontation. We no longer trust the Church, we trust the first profane prophet who comes to speak to us from some newspaper or some social movement to seek him out and ask him if he has the formula for true life. And we already feel we are his lords and masters. Doubt has entered our consciences, and it has done so through windows that should have been opened to the light.

[...]

This state of uncertainty also reigns in the Church. It was believed that after the Council there would come a sunny day for the history of the Church. Instead, a day of clouds, of storm, of darkness, of searching, of uncertainty has arrived. We preach ecumenism and we distance ourselves more and more from others. We try to dig chasms instead of filling them.

How did this happen? The pope confided to those present his thought: that there was the intervention of an adverse power. His name is the devil, that mysterious being to whom the Letter of St. Peter also alludes. Many times, moreover, in the Gospel, on the lips of Christ himself, there is mention of this enemy of mankind. "We believe - observes the Holy Father- "in something preternatural that has come into the world precisely to disturb, to stifle the fruits of the Ecumenical Council, and to prevent the Church from bursting into a hymn of joy at having regained full self-awareness."[294]

He also agreed in his dialogues with Jean Guitton:

"I had an intense call to live in the world, to be a layman, as they say today. I did not feel led to the clerical life which, at times, seemed to me static, closed, more interested in preserving than in promoting, implying the renunciation of earthly tendencies to the extent of its condemnation of the world. However, if one had those feelings, could one become a priest in the twentieth century? If I feel this way, it means that I am called to another state, where I would fulfill myself more harmoniously, for the common good of the Church."[295]

"I noticed how secular his thinking was. He was not a cleric, but a layman who had suddenly been promoted to the papacy."[296]

There are many other sources on the Second Vatican Council, which tell us about the great changes of the Council and its history.[297]

---

[294] Paolo VI (June 29, 1972), IX anniversario dell'incoronazione di Sua Santità, solennità dei Santi Apostoli Pietro e Paolo, Dicastero per la Comunicazione - Libreria Editrice Vaticana, pp. 4, 5.

[295] Jean Guitton, Diálogos con Pablo VI (Ediciones Encuentro, S.A., Madrid, 2014), p. 273.

[296] Jean Guitton, Paul VI secret (Desclée De Brouwer, 1979), p. 18.

[297] See for example, among the many books on the subject: Rev. Ralph M. Wiltgen, S.V.D., The Inside Story of Vatican II: A Firsthand Account of the Council's Inner Workings (TAN Books, Cahrlotte, North Carolina, 2014); Matthew L. Lamb, Matthew Levering (eds.), Vatican II: Renewal within Tradition (Oxford University Press, Inc., 2008); Matthew L. Lamb & Matthew Levering (eds.), The Reception of Vatican II (Oxford University Press, 2017); George H. Tavard, Vatican II and the Ecumenical Way (Marquette University Press, Milwaukee, Wisconsin, 2006); Gerd-Rainer Horn, The Spirit of Vatican II: Western European Progressive Catholicism in the Long Sixties (Oxford University Press, First Edition,

Papal internationalism, until the 1960s and 1970s, consisted of celebrating and promoting an alternative, exclusively Catholic European international order that was neither liberal nor communist (nor Protestant or Jewish, according to his thinking), actively resisting alternative forms of identity. But although Catholic internationalism was then widely rejected, it found new advocates in the 20th century and continued to call for the deprivatization of religion: in a recent period spanning from the papacy of John Paul II to that of Benedict XVI, where Catholic internationalism returned to the fore, and the Catholic crusade to influence European politics, law, and society.[298]

But how did Masonic interference occur during Vatican II? A pope so inclined to Freemasonry, as Paul VI, did not expect what would happen with Masonic interference in the Vatican and its results for Catholicism worldwide, as we will see below; as we go back years before he became pope, until we reach the papacy of Wojtyla.

Freemasons and prelates for the conquest of the Catholic Church: Vatican II and post-conciliar period

From before the Second Vatican Council and after it, Masonic clerics mobilized for internal changes in the Roman Catholic Church to bring it into line with the modern world. It is not surprising that Monsignor Joseph C. Fenton, writing in a letter dated January 23, 1961, to Redemptorist priest Francis J. Connell indicated: "It is clear to us that [Bishop Antoinino] Romeo is right and that there is.... [a] world-wide movement against orthodoxy in the Church."[299] We will see the main protagonists of this history, and sometimes going back to previous years to know the history of some particular character, until we see the historical whole more fully. We emphasize that we obtained copies of the letters and others from Dr. Franco Adessa, who worked with the now-deceased priest Luigi Villa, to whom Pope Pius XII entrusted the task of safeguarding the Catholic Church from Freemasonry; particularly from its infiltrators. Pius XII placed Luigi Villa under the protection of Cardinals Alfredo Ottaviani, Prefect of the Holy Office, Pietro Parente, and Pietro Palazzini.[300]

We will begin with Monsignor Pasquale Macchi, who was Pope Paul VI's personal secretary from 1954.[301] Macchi had connections with disgraced figures in the Milanese financial world since the 1950s; such as Roberto Calvi and Michele Sindona, two members of the P2/Propaganda Due Masonic lodge. Sindona made a fortune as a tax evasion agent for the Mafia, acquiring a number of banks at the end of the decade. He also befriended Cardinal Montini (future Pope Paul VI). Already in the 1960s, Macchi introduced Sindona and Calvi to the world of Vatican finance, where another associated P2 figure, Umberto Ortolani, as we have already seen, was close to Cardinal Lercaro, thus bringing him closer to the center of Paul VI's affairs.

2015); Piotr H. Kosicki (editor), Vatican II: Behind the Iron Curtain (The Catholic University of American Press, Washington, D.C., 2016).

[298] Ibid.

[299] David Wemhoff, John Courtney Murray, Time/Life, and The American Proposition: How the CIA's Doctrinal Warfare Program Changed the Catholic Church (Wagon Wheel Press of Presence LLC, New Edition, 2022), Volume 1, ob. cit.

[300] Raymund Maria (October 20, 2022), Is Masonic infiltration responsible for the widespread apostasy among Catholic clergy?," LifeSiteNews.

[301] H.J.A. Sire, Phoenix from the Ashes: The Making, Unmaking, and Restoration of Catholic Tradition (Angelic Press, Kettering, Ohio, 2015), ob. cit. Note: unless otherwise noted, this is the same source.

Likewise, Paul Marcinkus, archbishop and also a member of P2, enjoyed the favor of Pope Montini from the beginning of his pontificate. Marcinkus was a compadre of Monsignor Macchi and, in 1971, the former was appointed president of the IOR (Vatican Bank), which was being used by Sindona to transfer huge sums of money from his Italian banks to Switzerland, which accompanied currency speculation.

Macchi was a member of the "Vatican Lodge" since 1958. His Masonic name was Mapa. Some letters reveal the Masonic plans in the Vatican and the interest in the election of a pope chosen by them. Something we will see later.

When Giordano Gamberini was Grand Master of the Grand Orient of Italy, a mason clergyman, Monsignor Francesco Marchisano, sent some letters to Gamberini about a plan to take over the priestly seminaries in the Italian regions of Piedmont and Lombardy. Numerous Freemasons had already infiltrated these seminaries. Marchisano had been appointed on May 4, 1961, as Supernumerary Private Camerlengo; and on May 7 of the following year, as head of the Office for the Seminaries. Again, in 1961, he was president of the Pontifical Commission for the Cultural Heritage of the Church. Between June 3, 1969, and October 6, 1988, he served as Undersecretary of the S.C. for Seminaries and Universities.

The first letter was dated May 23, 1961. He wrote that he received with great joy through Brother Mapa (Monsignor Pasquale Macchi) the assignment to "organize silently in all Piedmont and Lombardy the way to break the studies and discipline in the Seminaries." He wrote that he would need many collaborators, especially from the faculty.[302]

So, on September 12, 1961, in another letter addressed to Gamberini, Marchisano pointed out that after having approached and contacted the Masonic brothers Pelmi (Michele Pellegrino, future Archbishop of Turin) and Bifra (Franco Biffi, rector of the Lateran), he returned to Mapa to present the first work plan: Marchisano recommended starting with the disintegration of the curricula by insisting that the new professors teach a different theology and a different philosophy.[303]

Pellegrino was made a Mason on May 2, 1960, while Biffi's date is August 15, 1959.

In another letter, dated October 14 and the year very fuzzy, Macchi wrote to Giordano Gamberini informing him of a meeting he had with the Masons Pelmi, Mapa, Bifra, Salma, Buan, Algo, and Vino, where he concluded:

"At the meeting, last night, F.F. [Fellow Freemasons] Pelmo, Mapa, Bifra, Salma, Buan, Algo, and Vino were present, I was able to conclude that:
"- first of all, experiences must be initiated in some seminaries in Italy, those of Trento and Turin, or the one in Udine where we have a good number of FF;
- secondly, we must spread our concept of freedom and dignity of the human person in all seminaries, without any hesitation on the part of superiors or any law. A capable press is necessary.

At this point, a meeting with all of you is urgently needed to decide how to act and to whom to entrust the various tasks."[304]

[302] Frama (Monsignor Francesco Marchisano). Letter to Illustrious and Venerable Grand Master (Corrado Mastrocinque). May 23, 1961.
[303] Frama. Letter to the Grand Master. September 12, 1961.
[304] Frama (Monsignor Francesco Marchisano). Letter to Illustrious and Venerable Grand Master (Giordano Gamberini). October 14 [Year not clear].

Of the names not yet identified, let's say that Salma is Salvatore Marsili, who was abbot O.S.B. of Finalpia and was made a Freemason on July 2, 1963. Algo is Alessandro Gottardi, Archbishop of Trento who became a Freemason on June 13, 1959. Vino is Virgilio Noè, Master of Ceremonies and Mason since April 3, 1961. Buan is Monsignor Annibale Bugnini, who was secretary of the commission that worked on the reform of the Catholic liturgy following the Second Vatican Council.

Again, Marchisano addressed Gamberini on January 4, 1969, informing him that he had just received Mapa's communication about his [Marchisano] appointment as cardinal, "obtained through You through all Your mighty ways."[305]

Regarding the concepts of freedom and human dignity mentioned in the letter of October 14, these were taken up by the Jesuits and other American clerics, all of which were more in tune with the new modernity. To this end, they separated their colleges and universities from the Magisterium of the Church. Regarding the consequences and relations of the Second Vatican Council with liberal social movements, both in the United States and in France, let us say that two years after the Council closed, in July 1967, the Jesuit priest Vincent O'Keefe, being president of Fordham University, together with the priest Theodore M. Hesburgh, rector of the University of Notre Dame, organized a meeting of all the presidents of the Catholic Universities in the United States, in Land O' Lakes in Wisconsin. They signed at the meeting the Land O' Lakes Declaration, which expressed the independence of their Catholic universities and colleges from all authority and bond of fidelity to the Magisterium of the Church. That declaration was made in order to modernize the universities and to carry the vision of Vatican II.[306] The background papers, which did much to shape the document, were prepared by several clergy - half of them Jesuits: George N. Shuster, John Tracy Ellis, Michael P. Walsh, S.J., Thomas Ambrogi, S.J., Paul C. Reinert, S.J., Neil G. McCluskey, S.J., William Richardson, S.J., John E. Walsh, C.S.C., Larenzo Roy and Lucien Vachon. And most of the final editing was done by Jesuit Robert J. Henle.

Archbishop Carlo Maria Viganó has cited several statements of some defenders of Vatican Council II, exposing its connection with the social revolution of the 60s of the previous century, explaining:

"What I wish to emphasize is the close connection between the rebellion of the ultra-progressive clergy — with the Jesuits in the lead — and the education of generations of Catholics, who were formed according to the modernist ideology flowing into the Council, which served as a premise not only for '68 revolution in the political sphere, but also for the doctrinal and moral revolution in the ecclesial sphere. Without Vatican II, we would not have had the student revolution that radically changed life in

---

[305] Frama (Cardinal Francesco Marchisano). Letter to the Grand Master (Giordano Gamberini). January 4, 1969.

[306] John I. Jenkins, C.S.C. (July 11, 2017), The document that changed Catholic education forever, America Magazine; Stephen Beale (July 17, 2017), Land O'Lakes 50 Years Later: How the Statement Affected Academia, National Catholic Register; Wilson D. Miscamble, C.S.C., American Priest: The Ambitious Life and Conflicted Legacy of Notre Dame's Father Ted Hesburgh (IMAGE, New York, 2019), p. 123.

the Western world, the vision of the family, the role of women and the very concept of authority."[307]

Of the revolution of 1968 in France, he said that the protagonists of the Second Vatican Council themselves noted a relationship with the famous student protests of '68, both from a historical and sociological point of view.[308] And he quotes Ratzinger (late Pope Emeritus Benedict XVI):

"Adherence to a utopian anarchistic Marxism ... was supported on the front lines by university chaplains and student associations who saw in it the dawn of the realization of Christian hopes. The guiding light is to be found in the events of May 1968 in France. Dominicans and Jesuits were at the barricades. The intercommunion carried out at an ecumenical Mass at the barricades was considered a kind of landmark in salvation history, a kind of revelation that inaugurated a new era of Christianity."[309]

Note the mention of Jesuits and Dominicans in this revolution.
René Laurentin, one of the *periti* or experts of the council:

"The demands of the May '68 movement largely coincided with the council's grand ideas, particularly in the council's Constitution on the Church and the World. To a certain extent, Vatican II was already a protest against the Curia by a group of bishops who were trying to create an institutionally prefabricated council."[310]

Alvaro Calderon, an Argentine theologian, also wrote:

"If there is anything that immediately stands out to those who study the Second Vatican Council, it is the change, in a liberal sense, of the concept of authority. The pope stripped himself of his supreme authority in favor of the bishops (collegiality); the bishops stripped themselves of their authority in favor of theologians; theologians gave up their science in favor of listening to the faithful. And the voice of the faithful is nothing more than the fruit of propaganda."[311]

Agostino Giovagnoli, professor of contemporary history at the Catholic University of Milan, stated that the links between the Second Vatican Council and the revolution of '68 are deeper than previously thought. He tells us that, "The protest of 1968 intersected in different ways with an evolution of the Italian Catholic world that had already been going on for some time." Giovagnoli recounts that the Jesuit historian

---

[307] Marco Tosatti (September 14, 2020), Marco Tosatti Interviews Abp. Carlo Maria Viganò: Why you can't be a Catholic and a Democrat, Church Militant: https://www.churchmilitant.com/news/article/interview-by-marco-tosatti-with-abp-carlo-maria-vigano Accessed February 25, 2024.
[308] Ibid.
[309] Joseph Ratzinger, *Les principes de la théologie catholique*, Téqui, Paris 1985, p. 433. Note: we have eliminated the italics from the quoted statements. Quoted in Ibid.
[310] René Laurentin, *Crisi della Chiesa e secondo Sinodo episcopale*, Morcelliana, Brescia 1969, p. 16; quoted in Ibid.
[311] Álvaro Calderón, *La lámpara bajo el celemín. Cuestión disputada sobre la autoridad doctrinal del magisterio eclesiástico desde el Concilio Vaticano II*, Ed. Rio Reconquista, Argentina 2009; quoted in Ibid.

Michel de Certeau, who participated in the "French May" in Paris, wrote that in 1968 "the word was pronounced as in 1789 the Bastille was taken."[312]

It has been said that Vatican II got rid of a Church enclosed in organizational and institutional schemes that marginalized it, thus inviting the Catholic Church to listen to the world and to itself.[313] Bishop Jacques Noyer, emeritus of Amiens, tells us:

"I am convinced that the spirit that inspired the preparation, celebration and implementation of the Second Vatican Council is a great opportunity for the Church and the world. It is the Gospel offered to the men of today. Deep down, May '68 was a spiritual movement, even a mystical one, consistent with the dream of the Council."[314]

All this is very important, in terms of the influence of Freemasonry on the Roman Catholic Church and the social progressive movements in different parts of the world, but we must go further. In addition to the above, let us return to the Masonic infiltration of the Vatican and the changes in Catholicism on a global scale. Another of the Masonic clergy, the best known and one of the most involved in the image of Catholicism and its openness to the world and other Christian communities, was Monsignor Annibale Bugnini. What did he get involved in and what actions did he take? Bugnini was secretary of the commission that worked on the reform of the Catholic liturgy that followed the Second Vatican Council. Thus, the rite that brought about the most important changes to the image of Roman Catholicism was that of the Mass, with the purpose of reaching out to the Protestant communities. The reasons for this were given by Bugnini and Paul VI. The Monsignor said in 1965:

"The 7th prayer bears the title: 'For the unity of Christians' (not 'of the Church', which has always been one). It no longer speaks of "heretics" and "schismatics," but of "all the brethren who believe in Christ" [...].

Scholars will reflect on and emphasize the biblical and liturgical sources from which the new texts, chiseled by the study groups of the "Consilium" derive or draw their inspiration. How can we not lament, for example, the "ad sanctam matrem Ecclesiam catolicam atque apostolicam revocare dignetur" of the seventh prayer? And yet, love for souls and the desire to facilitate by every means the path of union for separated brethren, removing every stone that could constitute, even remotely, a stumbling block or cause of discomfort, have induced the Church also to these painful sacrifices. In the confidence that common prayer will hasten the day when the whole "family of God," united "in the integrity of faith and the sign of charity," will be able to sing "with one voice," "with one accord," the Easter Alleluia of resurrection and life."[315]

---

[312] Giovanna Pasqualin Traversa (April 26, 2018), Il Sessantotto. Agostino Giovagnoli (storico): "Profondo legame con il Concilio che ne ha anticipato alcuni tratti," Società per l'Informazione Religiosa - SIR Spa.

[313] Ibid.

[314] John-Henry Western (Sept. 14, 2020), Archbishop Viganò hints he believes God will deliver the election to President Trump, LifeSiteNews; quoting José Antonio Ureta (2018), Il Maggio '68 e il Concilio Vaticano II, Rivista TFP.

[315] A. Bugnini (March 19, 1965), Le "Variationes" ad alcuni testi della Settimana Santa, L'Osservatore Romano, No. 65, p. 6.

156

Jean Guitton, a personal friend of Paul VI, went so far as to say of the pope's intention:

"J. Guitton : [...] I do not think I am wrong in saying that the intention of Paul VI and of the new liturgy that bears his name is to ask the faithful for greater participation in the Mass, to give more prominence to Scripture and less prominence to all that is, some say magical, others say consubstantial, transubstantial consecration, which is the Catholic faith. That is to say, Paul VI had the ecumenical intention of erasing, or at least correcting, or at least softening what was too Catholic, in the traditional sense, in the Mass, and to bring the Catholic Mass closer, I repeat, to the Calvinist Mass."[316]

At Bugnini's invitation,[317] six Protestant ministers were involved in the realization of the New Mass through their various contributions. A. Raymond George (Methodist), Ronald Jaspar (Anglican), Massey Shepherd (Episcopalian), Friedrich Künneth (Lutheran), Eugene Brand (Lutheran), Max Thurian (Calvinist Taizé Community).[318] L'Osservatore Romano of April 23, 1970, mentioned the ministers as collaborators of the new Mass.

One of the six, Ronald Jaspar, described to British Catholic writer Michael Davies how the Protestant contributors made their contributions, which were often applied verbatim.[319]

Protestant publications stated that they could use the New Mass in their services.[320]

Bugnini was commissioned by Paul VI for the reforms of the Roman rite mass, which would pass under numerous omissions and would be given in the language of each country; allowing greater use of musical styles and musical instruments.[321]

Louis Bouyer, in his memoirs on the Second Vatican Council, referred to "the maneuvers of the mealy-mouthed scoundrel [...] the Neapolitan Vincentian, Bugnini, a man as bereft of culture as he was of basic honesty [...]" He recounted the "subterfuge Bugnini used to obtain what was closest to his heart, or, I should say, what the men who have to be called his handlers managed to pass through him."[322]

Bouyer wrote on the subject:

"On several occasions, whether the scuttling of the liturgy of the dead or even that incredible enterprise to expurgate the Psalms for use in the Divine Office, Bugnini ran into an opposition that was not only massive but also, one might say, close to unanimous. In such cases, he didn't hesitate to say: "But the Pope wills it!" After that, of course, there was no question of discussing the matter any further.

---

[316] Yves Chiron, François-Georges Dreyfus, Jean Guitton, Entretien sur Paul VI (Nivoit, 2011), pp. 27, 28.
[317] Charles Thedore Murr, Murder in the 33rd Degree: Gagnon's Investigation of Freemasonry in the Vatican (Charles T. Murr, 2022), ob. cit.
[318] Referenced by Louis Tofari (August 30, 2013), What About those Six Protestants and the New Mass, The Remnant.
[319] Ibid.
[320] Ibid; quoting Jean Guitton, who cites a Protestant publication in the December 10, 1969 issue of La Croix; M.G. Siegvalt (Protestant professor of dogmatic theology) in La Croix on November 22, 1969.
[321] Charles Thedore Murr, Murder in the 33rd Degree: Gagnon's Investigation of Freemasonry in the Vatican (Charles T. Murr, 2022), ob. cit.
[322] Louis Bouyer, The Memoirs of Louis Bouyer: From Youth and Conversion to Vatican II, the Liturgical Reform, and After (Angelic Press, Ohio, 2015), ob. cit.

Yet, one day when he had made use of that argument I had a lunch appointment with my friend Msgr. Del Gallo, who as privy Chamberlain had a flat right above the papal apartments at the time. As I was coming back down—after the siesta, of course—and came out of the lift onto the Cortile San Damaso, Bugnini in person was emerging from the staircase on his way in from the Bronze Gate. At the sight of me, he didn't just turn pale: he was visibly aghast. I straightaway understood that, knowing me to be *notus pontifici*, he supposed I had just been with the pope. But in my innocence I simply could not guess why he would be so terrorized at the idea that I might have had an interview with the pope regarding our affairs.

I would be given the answer, though weeks later, by Paul VI himself. As he was discussing our famous work with me, work which he had finally ratified without being much more satisfied with it than I was, he said to me: "Now why did you do [x] in the reform?" [...] Naturally, I answered: "Why, simply because Bugnini had assured us that you absolutely wished it." His reaction was instantaneous: "Can this be? He told me himself that you were unanimous on this!"[323]

This tells us that although Paul VI wanted a Mass that would bring Protestants closer together, he did not agree with the drastic changes proposed by Bugnini.

The changes introduced by the monsignor to the Mass created a liturgical revolution that would do serious damage to Catholic traditionalism. Catholic priest Charles T. Murr explains that several members of the committees formed under Bugnini, who served as experts during Vatican II, regretted their participation in the work of liturgical reform. Bugnini's Masonic affiliation could explain much of what was against the Church's tradition, liturgically, doctrinally, and morally.[324]

Before continuing, let us note first of all that since the end of 1968, the Vatican counter-espionage, the *Sodalitium Pianum* (SP), had been investigating various members of the Roman Curia for possible infiltration by Freemasons. When in 1971 the head of the SP was summoned before Paul VI, who received a thick dossier with names, dates, and places with every connection of Freemasonry in the various dicasteries of the Vatican State, he ordered the end of the investigation and ordered the report to be deposited in the Secret Archives.[325]

Peruvian-Spanish journalist Eric Frattini tells us:

"The *Sodalitium Pianum's* list of Masons included such illustrious cardinals as Augustín Bea, secretary of state during the papacies of John XXIII and Paul VI; Sebastiano Baggio, prefect of the Sacred Congregation of Bishops; Agostino Casaroli, secretary of state during the papacy of John Paul II; Achille Lienart, Archbishop of Lille; Pasquale Macchi, Pope Paul VI's private secretary; Salvatore Pappalardo, Archbishop of Palermo; Michele Pelligrino, Archbishop of Turin; Ugo Poletti, vicar of the diocese of Rome; and Jean Villot, Pope Paul VI's secretary of state."

---

[323] Ibid.

[324] Charles Thedore Murr, Murder in the 33rd Degree: Gagnon's Investigation of Freemasonry in the Vatican (Charles T. Murr, 2022), ob. cit.

[325] Eric Frattini, The Entity: Five Centuries of Secret Vatican Espionage (St. Martin's Press, New York, 2008),

For his part, although Bugnini himself denied being a Freemason,[326] the evidence dismisses that claim.

First of all, his name appears in the list of Masonic prelates of the Italian journalist Mino Pecorelli. But one of the strongest pieces of evidence comes from Charles T. Murr, the Catholic priest who collaborated closely with Cardinal Edouard Gagnon in the dangerous mission that Paul VI entrusted to him: to investigate the Vatican Curia to detect the presence of Freemasonry.[327]

Bugnini was Assistant Secretary of the Sacred Congregation for Divine Worship. And Gagnon received confirmation from an earlier investigation that Bugnini was a Freemason. That investigation began when Bugnini once left his briefcase in a meeting room in one of the curial departments at the Vatican. Then, a priest opened the briefcase to find out the identity of the owner; finding documents that implicated Bugnini as a member of Freemasonry. The priest took the briefcase and the documents to Cardinal Dino Staffa, then Prefect of the Apostolic Signatura.[328] Later, two highly respected cardinals, Staffa himself as well as Silvio Oddi, met with Paul VI and presented him with very serious documentation.[329] It was found that two high-ranking members of the Roman Curia, Cardinal Sebastiano Baggio, prefect of the Sacred Congregation for Bishops, and Bishop Annibale Bugnini, were active Freemasons. In office since 1973, Baggio decided who would become the bishops of the Catholic Church. The bishops appointed by the cardinal reflected his convenient ideological views labeled as progressive. Their values departed from Catholic orthodoxy and opposed the central authority of Rome, favoring a compromising dialogue with the world; something supported by Freemasonry, as both cardinals told Paul VI.

Staffa and Oddi insisted to Paul VI that he dispense with his Secretary of State, Jean Villot, in dealing with this matter because of his ties to the accused. The pope turned the situation over to the only man who enjoyed his full confidence, Archbishop Giovanni Benelli, the Vatican's Assistant Secretary of State. By papal mandate, the archbishop "set out to double- and triple-check the authenticity of the documents; to verify them and verify them again." The pope instructed Benelli to be very quick about it.

Paul VI and Benelli agreed to say nothing to Villot about the serious allegations until the proper investigator could be identified and an official announcement of the investigation made. Benelli told the pope, "Certainly, I share your desire for secrecy on this entire matter [...] however, how can it be successfully executed in absolute secrecy?" After a recommendation from Benelli to work with two collaborators mentioned by him, the pope authorized Archbishop Donato Squicciarini and the beneficiary of the pope's benefice, Mario Marini.

It took Benelli months to conduct the investigation, "but through vast international diplomatic networking and after extensive examination of the evidence, he knew much

---

[326] Louis Bouyer, The Memoirs of Louis Bouyer: From Youth and Conversion to Vatican II, the Liturgical Reform, and After (Angelic Press, Ohio, 2015), ob. cit., note 101: quoting a letter to the Editor written by Bugnini in *Homiletic and Pastoral Review* 80 (May 1980): 4-6, cited in his *Reform*, 92-93.

[327] Charles Thedore Murr, Murder in the 33rd Degree: Gagnon's Investigation of Freemasonry in the Vatican (Charles T. Murr, 2022). Compare: Dr. Robert Moynihan (July 16, 2009), Letter from Rome, #20, 2009, A Dying Cardinal, Inside the Vatican Magazine.

[328] Joseph Shaw (Summer 2020), Bugnini's Briefcase, Mass of Ages, Issue 204, p. 41.

[329] Charles Thedore Murr, Murder in the 33rd Degree: Gagnon's Investigation of Freemasonry in the Vatican (Charles T. Murr, 2022). Note: unless otherwise noted, this is the same source.

more about Baggio and Bugnini than he cared to know, and more about the two than they themselves did." The Archbishop obtained further evidence of Baggio's and Bugnini's membership in French and Italian Freemasonry.

Many lists of Masonic prelates had already been leaked to the press.[330] For example, the *Panorama* list of August 10, 1976.[331] Those lists circulated for months in the Vatican, so some cardinals asked for clarity.[332] So Paul VI, through Benelli, entrusted the investigation of that list (especially - again - Bugnini) to Interpol and General Mino; and two months later, the commander of the Benemérita and Interpol delivered their dossier in which Archbishop Annibale Bugnini and "Cardinals Sebastiano Baggio, Jean Villot, Ugo Poletti (vicar of Rome), Paul Marcinkus deus ex machina of the IOR (Institute for the Works of Religion), Agostino Casaroli and dozens of other religious were confirmed as affiliated to Freemasonry."[333]

In mid-1977, Giuseppe Siri, the Cardinal Archbishop of Genoa, asked Mino for new and deeper investigations of the *Panorama* list.[334] But from intercepted phone calls to Licio Gelli, it was revealed that he had been discussing the succession of General Mino, who died shortly afterward - October 31 - in suspicious circumstances.[335]

The list would have been compiled from documents photocopied at the headquarters of the Grand Orient of Italy by a young employee, the nephew of a friar, who in the presence of his uncle handed everything over to Monsignor Benelli, then deputy Secretary of State.[336]

Now, after Benelli gave the report to Pope Paul VI, Bugnini had a rocky fall, when the pontiff merged the two liturgical dicasteries into one, leaving Bugnini without a job. Paul VI decided to make him apostolic nuncio in Uruguay, but Bugnini protested in writing, stating that he had no diplomatic training or experience and did not speak Spanish. Wanting to know what was going on, the pope declined to answer him and offered him instead to be nuncio in Iran (where there was no Catholic presence), which he accepted and began in January 1976[337] until his death.

Dr. Alice von Hildebrand, in a 2001 interview with *Latin Mass* magazine and reprinted in *Christian Order* in 2007, referred to a conversation of Bishop Gagnon with Don Luigi Villa of the diocese of Brescia, where he told him about his research for the pope.[338] Villa would have access to letters from Annibale Bugnini to Italian Freemasonry, and vice versa.

Documentation of Bugnini's affiliation with Freemasonry, of which Cardinal Silvio Oddi had copies, was given to me by one of several sources in Rome who knew Oddi and was part of the research on clerical Masons. The evidence has been the subject of

---

[330] Carlo Alberto Agnoli, La Massoneria alla conquista della Chiesa (E.I.L.E. S, 1996), ob. cit.

[331] Ibid, p. 3.

[332] Ibid, p. 15; citing 30 Giorni, 11 November 1992, p. 30 et seq.

[333] Ignazio Ingrao, Il Concilio Segreto: Misteri, intrighi e giochi di potere dell'evento che ha cambiato il volto della Chiesa (Editions Piemme, 2013), ob. cit.; Carlo Alberto Agnoli, La Massoneria alla conquista della Chiesa (E.I.L.E. S, 1996), p. 15; quoting 30 Giorni, of 11 November 1992, p. 32.

[334] Carlo Alberto Agnoli, La Massoneria alla conquista della Chiesa (E.I.L.E. S, 1996), p. 15; citing 30 Giorni, 11 November 1992, pp. 34, 35.

[335] Ibid, pp. 15, 16.

[336] Ibid, p. 16; citing Il Sabato, August 10, 1991, p. 21 et seq.

[337] Joseph Shaw (Summer 2020), Bugnini's Briefcase, Mass of Ages, Issue 204, pp. 40, 42.

[338] Dr. Robert Moynihan (July 16, 2009), Letter from Rome, #20, 2009, A Dying Cardinal, Inside the Vatican Magazine.

debate for many years, but the sources we have cited and others have confirmed the authenticity of the documents.

The following is a summary of the letters. The first one is dated July 14, 1964, to Monsignor Bugnini (Buan) by the Masons of the Grand Orient of Italy,[339] when it was its Grand Master Giordano Gamberini. Firstly, Bugnini (Buan) was informed: "of the commission that the Council of Brothers has established for you in agreement with the Grand Master and the Princes Assistants to the Throne." Second, he was charged to adhere to the program of Rocca, the ex-priest: "It will be necessary to assimilate a new religion: new dogma, new rite, new priesthood through the naturalization of the Incarnation." Another aspect was that the Church authorities had to approve the decisions of the base.

By changing rites and languages and confronting priests, bishops, and cardinals, the consolidation of Roman Catholicism would be weakened, since its strength lies in the unity of ritual and ecclesiastical authority.

Finally, Bugnini was asked to choose "among the clergy the most suitable and secret elements and to communicate them to us immediately so that we can approach them and negotiate." It was added: "All this must take place within a decade." Finally, he was informed that his salary of 500 thousand lire per month could be increased and doubled depending on progress. –"You are embraced by the Brothers of the Council united to the Grand Master."

Bugnini replied days later, on July 27. He addressed Grand Master Gamberini and the councilors, thanking them for commissioning him to carry out Brother Rocca's program:

"Your letter of the 14th compels me first of all to thank you for the confidence you place in me for the entire execution of Brother Rocca's program. In particular:

"1) I have already chosen the collaborators whom I will personally introduce to you and whom you will hire according to specific tasks: they are experts in the various subjects and professors in the various Pontifical Roman Athenaeums.
2) My task will be very easy and achievable inasmuch as I have as intimates Cardinal LERCARO and Paul VI himself, who gives me the utmost confidence in everything so that he will never suspect my relations with you. I will do everything possible so that the priest (... illegible) becomes papal master of ceremonies: then everything will be easier.
3) The desacralization will have to be done step by step: for this reason, I beg you to be understanding with me. Protestant and Orthodox elements must be introduced into the Catholic liturgy under the guise of ecumenism: then the way will be open for everything. All this takes time, but in ten years we will achieve it."[340]

On April 6, 1967, Buan/Bugnini wrote to Giordano Gamberini and the Councilors:

"As I had promised, the way has been cleared for profanation with the official publication of the Instruction on Sacred Music of March 5.

---

[339] On behalf of the Council of Brothers. Letter to "Buan." July 14, 1964. Note: unless otherwise indicated, this is the same source.
[340] Buan. Letter to the Grand Master. July 21, 1964.

As you may have noticed, this is a deliberately very ambiguous and convoluted document. Although, in fact, it reaffirms certain traditional principles, almost in passing and so as not to give too much away, I have struggled to emphasize certain points:

    1) the preeminent part of the people

    2) the vernacular language, rather than the official language

    3) the role of women, who can also form a schola cantorum on their own

    4) the different degrees of participation, so that the previous system is broken and fractioned, to the point that no one sings or participates anymore.

    5) the freedom of different genres of composition and instruments.

More could have been done, but, as I have already said verbally, there is the serious difficulty of the Congregation of Rites, whose secretary is a bitter enemy of mine: Antonelli. They should, through our Brother Assistants to the Throne, have that Congregation abolished and put me in Antonelli's place. But we will talk about this verbally." [341]

A correspondence from Bugnini, dated July 2, 1967, notes that "the degrees of profanation are advancing at a good pace. In fact, another Instruction has come out, the application of which began on June 29." [342] Claiming that victory was assured, he wrote:

"(1) the vernacular language is sovereign in the whole liturgy, even in its essential parts

2) sacred ornaments are increasingly being reduced

3) maximum freedom of choice of the different forms up to private creativity and.... to chaos!

4) genuflections, kisses, bows, ceremonies, ritual prescriptions... are suppressed.

[...]

I fought bitterly and had to resort to every trick in order to get it approved by the Pope, against my enemies in the Congregation of Rites. Fortunately for us, we immediately found support including from the friends and brothers of Laus University, who are faithful." [343]

A last letter, dated October 22, 1973, from Bugnini to the Grand Master (then Lino Salvini) and to the Deputies:

"With reference to your letter of 17 c.m. I will tell you that I perfectly understand your concern for the harm that the Holy Year may cause. But I want to inform you immediately that I have promptly gathered together our following confreres: Erba, Fragi, Mani, Gigi, Chie, Monda, Mago, Saba, Bigi, Gica, Pinpi, Salma and Lube. All of them are among our most faithful theologians.

"They have the task of studying how to diminish as much as possible the importance and the necessity of the Holy Year, in such a way that neither the clergy nor the people feel it. They will think of organizing conferences and congresses and

---

[341] Buan. Letter to the Grand Master. April 6, 1967.

[342] Buan. Letter to the Grand Master and Councilors. July 2, 1967.

[343] Ibid.

162

distributing a wide press among the young clergy, easily vulnerable on certain issues. They will surely hold a conference in Assisi to launch ideas against the Holy Year."[344]

Unfortunately we do not have the letter of October 17, but we do have the identities of the Masonic prelates, which are: **Erba:** Balducci Ernesto (5/16/1966; Matr. 1452/3) (Piarist religious); **Fragi:** Franzoni Giovanni (5/2/1965; Matr. 2246/47); **Mani:** Mancini Italo (3/18/1968; Matr. 1551/142) (Chaplain to His Holiness); **Gigi:** Girardi Giulio (9/8/1970; Registration 1471/52); **Chie:** Chiavacci Enrico (7/2/1970; Registration 121/34) (Professor of Morals University of Florence); **Monda:** Mongillo Dalmazio (2/16/1969; Registration 2145/22) (Dominican, Professor of Morals at the Angelicum in Rome); **Mago:** Gozzini Mario (5/14/1970; Registration 31/11); **Saba:** Acquaviva Sabino (12/3/1969; Registration 275/69) (Professor of Sociology); **Bigi:** Bianchi Giovanni (10/23/1969; Registration Number 2251/11); **Gicap:** Caputo Giuseppe (11/15/1971; Registration Number 6125/63); **Pimpi:** Pinto Pio Vito (4/2/1970; Registration Number 3317/42) (secretary. in charge Supreme Tribunal Signatura Apostolica); **Salma:** Marsili Salvatore (7/2/1963; Matricola 1278/49) (abbot O.S.B. of Finalpia); **Lube:** Bettazzi Luigi (5/11/1966; Matricola 1347/45) (Bishop of Ivrea).

After verifying the documentation, Benelli informed the pope that although Bugnini and Baggio were the heavyweights in the scandal, they were only *"the tip of the iceberg."* After showing his findings to the pope and explaining them at length, Paul VI did not say a word, but he was very concerned.[345] Benelli at the time recommended a thorough, impartial and independent investigation by Archbishop Édouard Gagnon. Pope Paul agreed. And before Staffa died, he gave Gagnon all the evidence of Bugnini and Baggio's membership in Freemasonry.[346] Eric Frattini tells us:

"In early January 1974, the supreme pontiff ordered the heads of the Holy Alliance and *Sodalitium Pianum* to meet with him in his private dining room. The three men met for about three and a half hours. No one else knew what was said or how, but during this meeting Paul VI asked his intelligence directors to put in motion what became known as "Operation *Nessun Dorma*" (Let no one sleep).

The goal of this operation was to assemble a broad report revealing the needs and deficiencies of all Vatican departments and detailing accusations of corrupt behavior by Vatican officials. Although the investigation itself was assigned to the Holy Alliance, the task of writing the final report fell to Archbishop Édouard Gagnon and Monsignor Istvan Mester, the head of the Congregation for the Clergy."[347]

Eric Frattini continues:

"For months, Holy Alliance agents walked kilometer after kilometer of Vatican hallways, questioning and interrogating all the officials of the many papal departments. In a few weeks, the pope's spies had hundreds of accusations of

---

[344] Buan. Letter to the Grand Master and Deputies. October 22, 1973.
[345] Charles Thedore Murr, Murder in the 33rd Degree: Gagnon's Investigation of Freemasonry in the Vatican (Charles T. Murr, 2022).
[346] Ibid.
[347] Eric Frattini, The Entity: Five Centuries of Secret Vatican Espionage (St. Martin's Press, New York, 2008),

irregularities and crimes committed by bishops and cardinals. Finally, Monsignor Gagnon, as president of the commission, spent three months organizing all the material the Holy Alliance had collected. The voluminous report exposing hidden activities within the curia bore the title *Nessun Dorma*, the same as the Holy Alliance operation. Holy Alliance and S.P. agents kept watch over it every night."[348]

Gagnon's work cost him sleepless nights.[349] At the time, the Vatican Secretary of State, Jean Villot, was very suspicious of the inquiry. Strangely enough, Gagnon's dossier disappeared, and he found his stay infringed upon by strangers..... Eventually, he suffered the ransacking of his private rooms, office break-ins, and death threats. It took him a long time to redo the report of hundreds of pages. Priest Charles Murr took Gagnon to various appointments and helped him on several occasions to organize the information and documents received concerning the Apostolic Visitation (the investigation itself). He had boxes full and ended up reading all the documents.

On May 15, 1978, the Assistant Secretary of State, Archbishop Agostino Casaroli, telephoned Gagnon informing him that it was "almost" certain that his audience with Paul VI would take place the following day. But Jean Villot had obstructed such an audience many times. Everyone in the Vatican knew about it and was anxious.

Once Gagnon was received by Paul VI, he showed him the confirmation of Sebastiano Baggio as a Freemason on page 4, indicating that: "…In 1972, Secretary of State, Cardinal Jean Villot [...] "*à lutter farouchement [fought tooth and nail]* for this man - one of his closest friends and political allies - to be named Prefect of the Sacred Congregation for Bishops! Holy Father!" [...]"

"A Freemason naming every new bishop in the world! And every new archbishop, given a metropolitan See, and many of them guaranteed a cardinal's hat and a vote in the next papal election!"

He jointly added: "Shortly before he died [...] Cardinal Staffa asked to speak with me. He told me that in 1972, and again in 1975, in his capacity as Prefect of the Supreme Tribunal of the Apostolic Signatura he and Cardinal Oddi came to speak with Your Holiness about this very man and Archbishop Annibale Bugnini. They supplied Your Holiness with evidentiary documentation to verify these extremely serious accusations. I include copies of the same in my report. They indicated that both men were and, I presume, still are, Freemasons with powerful Masonic connections — and that many of those connections, Holy Father, lead straight to the Institute for the Works of Religion [the Vatican Bank]."

After two hours, being visibly tired, the pope told Gagnon: "[...] You have before you a tired old man… who stands at the threshold of death and prepares himself, these days, to meet his Creator… and to answer for his many sins and faults… [...]We beg you to guard all of this, your invaluable research [...] you will please take this entire matter to our younger and stronger successor…" Regarding the succession of Paul VI to the papacy, the rector magnifico of the Pontifical Lateran University, who was discovered to be a Freemason, drew the attention of Vatican counter-espionage in the 1970s for his strange and sudden displacements in Italy and abroad. In the summer of 1974, assuming a false identity and dressed in civilian clothes, he met with two people

---

[348] Ibid.
[349] Charles Thedore Murr, Murder in the 33rd Degree: Gagnon's Investigation of Freemasonry in the Vatican (Charles T. Murr, 2022). Note: unless otherwise noted, this is the same source.

in the restaurant of a hotel in Genoa, where he was recorded by the secret service through a device placed under the table. The whispered conversation, which was badly recorded, was deciphered with great difficulty, revealing that the final period of Paul VI's pontificate would be in February 1975. Then the subject of the conclave was discussed and the names of the candidates to be nominated were mentioned: Sebastiano Baggio, Ugo Poletti, and Jean Villot.[350] All of them were Freemasons.

At that time, Paul VI was not suffering from an illness that condemned him to death. The weekly *Tempo* published an article confirming the confidential story, pointing out a plot against the pope, since a typed sheet of tissue paper arrived at his desk, informing him of the danger and mentioning the names of Cardinal Baggio and Monsignor Annibale Bugnini.[351] Masons who did not see in Paul VI the promise they longed for.

But after the death of Paul VI, on August 6, 1978, the *Rivista Massonica* published an article by the former Grand Master of the GOI, Giordano Gamberini: "[...] for us it is the death of the one who brought down the sentence of Clement XII and his successors. [...] the first time that the head of the greatest western religion dies, not in a state of hostility towards the Freemasons."[352]

A further Masonic reaction is seen in a letter from Cardinal Sebastiano Baggio, president of the Congregation for Bishops, to Grand Master Lino Salvini and the Assistants, dated August 8, 1978:

"Following the sudden death of Paul VI, two important situations arise that I wish to communicate to you:

"The first has already been excellently solved by MAPA: it is a matter of saving all the secret documents useful and necessary to us that Pope [Paul] VI had jealously locked up in his study. MAPA left Castelgandolfo that same night and carried out the urgent and secret operation. These documents will be delivered to you shortly.

The second is even more serious: the succession of Pope [Paul] VI, for which you have promised me all your work, mobilizing all your forces so that my faithful work will be rewarded. I do not give you any advice, knowing perfectly well your ability. I only wait with confidence.[353]

In those days, the *Euroitalia* news agency also published, on August 17 and 25, the names of four papal candidates who were Freemasons. It did so with the full names, the number, and the date of inscription, listing 113 names of ecclesiastics and eight other influential personalities in the Catholic environment. In addition to this, on September 12, the then renowned Italian journalist, Mino Pecorelli, published in the magazine *Osservatore Politico* an article entitled *"La Gran Loggia Vaticana"* [*"The Grand*

---

[350] Los Milenarios, El Vaticano Contra Dios (Ediciones B, S.A., Barcelona, Spain, 1999), ob. cit.

[351] Ibid.

[352] Carlo Alberto Agnoli, La Massoneria alla conquista della Chiesa (E.I.L.E. S, 1996), p. 44; citing J. Ferrer Benimeli, G. Caprile, "Massoneria e Chiesa cattólica" cit. p. 91; Giacomo Galeazzi, Ferruccio Pinotti, Vaticano Massone: Logge, denaro e poteri occulti: il lato segreto della Chiesa di papa Francesco (Piemme, 2014), ob. cit.

[353] SB (Sebastiano Baggio). Letter to the Grand Master and Assistants. August 8, 1978.

Vatican Lodge"][354] Although not all of the list was reliable, some names have been verified.

The late English journalist David Yallop, commented on Pecorelli's revelations, that he was a repentant member of P2, with a bitter feud with his former Grand Master Licio Gelli.[355]

Pecorelli believed that publishing the list of Vatican Freemasons would put Gelli in a very serious situation; particularly since many of the names on the list were good friends of Gelli and Ortolani.[356]

It should be added that before the conclave that would elect Cardinal Luciani as the successor of Paul VI, the rumor circulated that several of the main *papavili* were Freemasons.[357]

For his part, the priest Mario Marini, who was also aware of the Vatican intelligence investigation and was a close friend of Cardinal Gagnon, of Murr, and of Cardinal Dino Staffa, was worried about the upcoming conclave.[358] He told Staffa and Gagnon: "My recurring nightmare [...] is having to pledge obedience to the new pontiff, and having to kiss the Fisherman's Ring on the hand of the first Freemason Pope!"[359]

Sebastiano Baggio saw his hopes frustrated, being elected Cardinal Albino Luciani to the papacy on August 26, 1978, taking the name of John Paul I.

Giovanni Benelli, who made the first inquiry into Freemasonry in the Vatican, was elected Secretary of State, but would not accept until Sebastiano Baggio was removed from the Congregation for Bishops.

One day, the following exchange took place between John Paul I and Cardinal Felici Pericle:

"'Eminence, the revision of Canon Law that has preoccupied so much of your time, did the Holy Father envisage a change in the Church's position on Freemasonry?'

'There have been over the years various pressure groups. Certain interested parties who urged a more "modern" view. The Holy Father was still considering the arguments when he died.'

Felici went on to indicate that among those who strongly favoured a relaxation of the canon rule that declared that any Roman Catholic who became a Freemason was automatically excommunicated, was Cardinal Jean Villot."[360]

For his part, John Paul I, being informed by Benelli of Freemasonry in the Vatican, kindly received Édouard Gagnon on September 25, 1978, who, after informing the pope of the investigation, John Paul I kept Gagnon's documentation and said he would

---

[354] Carlo Alberto Agnoli, La Massoneria alla conquista della Chiesa (E.I.L.E. S, 1996), p. 15; citing 30 Giorni, 11 November 1992, p. 4.
[355] David Yallop, In God's Name: An Investigation into the Murder of Pope John Paul I (Constable & Robinson Ltd., London, 2007), ob. cit.
[356] Ibid, p. 185.
[357] Ibid.
[358] Charles Thedore Murr, Murder in the 33rd Degree: Gagnon's Investigation of Freemasonry in the Vatican (Charles T. Murr, 2022). Note: unless otherwise noted, this is the same source.
[359] From the testimony of numerous Freemasons, we saw that John XXIII was a Freemason. But as we have already said, whether Paul VI was or not, he did not expect such a radical transformation of Catholicism and that Freemasonry itself would dominate too much the Vatican system.
[360] David Yallop, In God's Name: An Investigation into the Murder of Pope John Paul I (Constable & Robinson Ltd., London, 2007), ob. cit.

address the situation directly. He would first take up the case of Baggio, who met with the pope on the night of September 27 (1978). The Swiss guards reported angry voices, after which Baggio left, slamming the door. A few hours later, Pope Luciani died... in very mysterious circumstances.

Let us now look at a letter from Baggio dated October 2 of the same year (four days after the pope's death):

"Let me express to you all my regret and disappointment: unfortunately I must admit that you have not at all worked promptly and astutely for my election.

Now that the inept elected has suddenly passed away, I hope they will move with another strategy so that, if my name cannot succeed at all, at least one of our loyalists will be elected.

I hope I will not be disappointed this second time as well. That would be very serious, as the danger of a foreigner or a conservative looms over us. Attention."[361]

After the October conclave, Giovanni Benelli was there to ensure that there would not be a Masonic pontiff.[362]

Again, Baggio's optimism was ruined, as Polish Cardinal Karol Wojtyla was elected, taking the name John Paul II.

By then, the dispute between Mino Pecorelli and Licio Gelli took a turn. Gelli wanted to bribe Pecorelli to keep quiet. But the journalist demanded more money, to which Gelli refused. Pecorelli then published the first of what was to be a series of articles on the Propaganda Due Lodge. It revealed that Gelli, as a former Nazi ex-Fascist hierarch and ally of the Communists, also had close relations with the CIA. The P2 members concluded that Pecorelli had betrayed them, so Gelli telephoned Pecorelli's offices in Rome, suggesting that they have dinner together for a peaceful discussion, to which the journalist agreed.[363]

However, at 9:15 p.m. on the evening of March 20 (1979), Pecorelli left his office and walked to his car, parked a short distance away, to attend the dinner with Gelli, but was murdered in his car with two bullets and in the style of the Sicilian Mafia.[364] Propaganda Due was very powerful in Italy.

We will now go back a few weeks, returning to Gagnon's research. On February 6, 1979, the archbishop had an audience with the new pope, John Paul II to show him the research.[365] But the brief meeting was disastrous. As a result, Gagnon wrote his resignation as president of the Pontifical Commission for the Family, and two days later, he left Rome for the jungles of Colombia to serve the poor.

In early 1981, the Italian secret police informed Pope Wojtyla that, in a raid on the Masonic Grand Lodge Propaganda Due (P2), they had uncovered a Masonic plot to bankrupt the Vatican. In May, an assassination attempt was made on John Paul II, who was then fighting for his life in the Gemelli Hospital.

---

[361] SB (Sebastiano Baggio). Letter to the Grand Master and Assistants. October 2, 1978.

[362] Charles Thedore Murr, Murder in the 33rd Degree: Gagnon's Investigation of Freemasonry in the Vatican (Charles T. Murr, 2022), ob. cit.

[363] David Yallop, In God's Name: An Investigation into the Murder of Pope John Paul I (Constable & Robinson Ltd., London, 2007), ob. cit.

[364] Ibid.

[365] Charles Thedore Murr, Murder in the 33rd Degree: Gagnon's Investigation of Freemasonry in the Vatican (Charles T. Murr, 2022), ob. cit. Note: unless otherwise noted, this is the same source.

Suspecting that Masons were involved, the first two words uttered after regaining speech were, "F-i-nd G-a-g-n-o-n…"

Agostino Casaroli, the secretary of state, tracked him down, and Gagnon returned to Rome, meeting with the pope. John Paul II seemed much more interested in the results of the investigation than the last time they spoke. When he asked Gagnon to return to Rome, the bishop had two conditions: the removal of Sebastiano Baggio from the Congregation for Bishops, and the removal of Bishop Paul Marcinkus from the Vatican Bank (the IOR).

Released from office in 1984, Baggio was replaced by African Cardinal Bernard Gantin, who was a friend and protégé of Giovanni Benelli. Baggio was appointed President of the Pontifical Commission for Vatican City State; described by the press as a degradation (he died in 1993).

Gagnon was named a cardinal on May 25, 1985.

Benelli was asked to serve as Vatican secretary of state in 1982, agreeing willingly. But ten days after his private audience with the pope, he died of a massive heart attack.

Monsignor Luigi Marinelli, who was a member of the Congregation for the Oriental Churches at the time of John Paul II,[366] and worked for 45 years in the Vatican,[367] had published a book that even brought him to the pontifical tribunal; while the Tribunal of the Rota wanted to sequester the book from all of Italy.[368] Marinelli wrote that for 20 years (1979), during the papacy of Wojtyla, Freemasonry was "on the verge of overcoming the levels of security," camping "as mistress and chief" in the Vatican; "and awaits the moment when it manages to reach the best levers of power and command."[369] All with the disapproval of John Paul II, who thought he could not do anything at all.

Thus, in the nineties, well over two-thirds of the highly placed prelates in the Vatican belonged to Freemasonry: cardinals, bishops of prestigious dioceses, or prefects of important dicasteries and others as heads of cordades.[370]

Regarding the relationship between the Jesuits and Freemasonry, we will go in parts. During the aforementioned pontificate, Monsignor Marinelli wrote about the Rotary Club and the Lions Club:

"[…] the Jesuit magazine La Civiltà Cattolica showed without the slightest hint of doubt that, due to their Masonic derivation, they [the Rotarians and Lions] maintain close contacts with the sect. There was an intense controversy about the veracity of that statement until the Grand Master Giordano Gamberini, in the Masonic magazine Hiram [Bimonthly organ of the Grand Orient of Italy, founded in 1870. Editorial Erasmo] of February 1, 1981, officially confirmed that both Rotarians and Lions derive from and converge in Freemasonry, writing: "Melvin Jones, Master Mason of Chicago, was one of the founders of the Lions, and also its general secretary and treasurer until 1917. In the Lions, the Masonic origin is also evident even in the crest

[366] Eduardo Febbro (1999), El libro negro del Vaticano, Página 12, p. 25.
[367] Obituary (October 25, 2000), Luigi Marinelli, 73, Critic of the Vatican, The New York Times, Section B, p. 11.
[368] Eduardo Febbro (1999), El libro negro del Vaticano, Página 12, p. 25.
[369] Los Milenarios, El Vaticano Contra Dios (Ediciones B, S.A., Barcelona, Spain, 1999), ob. cit.
[370] Ibid.

chosen by the association. The Rotary Club had also maintained almost identical relations with Freemasonry."[371]

The following year, in 1982, the Jesuit priest Federico Weber was elected for the first time to the prestigious position of district governor of the Rotary district of Sicily-Malta, without being barred from doing so by his superiors in the Society of Jesus. Even many cardinals, generously rewarded and encouraged by the late Cardinal Baggio, consider themselves honored when Rotary officials invite them to inaugurate new venues or the social course and offer them "the opportunity to appear with their learned lectures and to participate in exquisite banquets."[372]

Also during John Paul II, Opus Dei and the Masons were vying for power in the Vatican. Cardinal José Rosalio Castillo Lara, elected in 1990 by the Polish pope as President of the Pontifical Commission for Vatican City State, as well as President of the Administration of the Patrimony of the Holy See, was also rumored to be a Mason. He was also a member of the supervisory commission of cardinals of the Vatican Bank.[373]

In addition, Cardinal Achille Silvestrini (prefect of the Congregation for Oriental Churches, and one of the heads of the Vatican Masonic clan), Cardinal Pio Lagui (prefect of the Congregation for Catholic Education), Cardinal Camillo Ruini (vicar general of Rome), and Monsignor Celestino Migliore (undersecretary for relations with the States) were also Masons.[374]

A protégé of Achille Silvestrini, Monsignor Romeo Panciroli, was also a Freemason.[375] He had become an official of the Pontifical Council for Social Communications in 1964; became undersecretary on January 7, 1970, and secretary on September 24, 1973. On June 3, 1976, Paul VI appointed him interim director of the Holy See Press Office. He was appointed director on September 5 of the same year. Under John Paul II, Panciroli held several important posts abroad. But in 1999, he served in various positions in the Vatican Secretariat of State.

It was documented that during the papacy of John Paul II, that many Masonic clergy were members of the "Vatican Lodge." Which is branched in the Apostolic Palace and which is a power confraternity where several cardinals also belong.[376] It bears the name of Loggia Ecclesiae,[377] which Pier Carpi, journalist and close friend of Gelli, said in an interview to the *European* on December 12, 1987, and with the title *"In St. Peter's Lodge,"* that it operated in the Vatican and reported directly to the Duke of Kent, the Grand Master of the Grand Mother Lodge of England. Gelli defined the Loggia Ecclesiae as "more powerful" and composed "only (by) cardinals and high prelates."[378]

Carlos Vázquez Rangel, Grand Commander of the Supreme Council of Mexican Freemasonry, told the Mexican magazine *Proceso* about the Vatican in 1992:

---

[371] Ibid.

[372] Ibid.

[373] Disciples of Truth, Lies and crimes in the Vatican: the truth about the triple murder in the Swiss Guard's quarters (Ediciones B, 200), p. 67.

[374] Ibid.

[375] Ibid, p. 142.

[376] Ibid, p. 66.

[377] Carlo Alberto Agnoli, La Massoneria alla conquista della Chiesa (E.I.L.E. S, 1996), p. 31.

[378] Ibid, p. 32.

"Certainly, you will find many reactionaries there, but you will also find many Masonic brothers: in the eight blocks that form the territory of the Vatican there are four Masonic lodges. Some of the high officials of the Vatican are Masons. They belong, as we do, to the Scottish Rite, but independently. Even in countries where the Church cannot act, they carry out their work through the lodges, secretly."[379]

Ironically, Cardinal Silvio Oddi, one of the denouncers before Paul VI of Archbishop Bugnini's Masonic affiliation, took part in the drafting of two letters written by the Grand Master of the Grand Orient of Italy to John Paul II: the first in 1993 and the second on February 1, 1996. The message was to put an end to the Catholic Church's enmities with Freemasonry. Intriguingly, Oddi worked for several years with Roncalli (future John XXIII and Freemason) when he was nuncio in Paris. Relations between the two were excellent even when Roncalli was pope, and Oddi knew perfectly well the Masonic milieu during those years.[380]

John Paul II was not a Freemason, but in Vaticano Massone we read that a former CIA agent confessed to the theologian -former Dominican- Matthew Fox, that "former Cardinal Karol Wojtyla, Archbishop of Krakow, was 'our man' in Poland for decades;" and that "right-wing clerics and the CIA pushed him quickly to the papal throne."[381]

John Paul II "chose the Dominican Georges Cottier as theologian of the Pontifical Household, author of an essay entitled Regards catholiques sur la franc-maçonnerie in which the high prelate hoped for dialogue and collaboration between the Church and Freemasonry in the great challenges to which all humanity is called, including the problems of peace and war."[382] John Paul II was not the great candidate longed for by the Freemasons, although he was the candidate of the pro-Reagan conservatives against the Soviet Union, as we will see below.

---

[379] La Redacción (October 10, 1992), As Secretary of the Interior, he punished Prigione with five hours of anteroom, Proceso.
[380] Giacomo Galeazzi, Ferruccio Pinotti, Vaticano Massone: Logge, denaro e poteri occulti: il lato segreto della Chiesa di papa Francesco (Piemme, 2014), ob. cit.
[381] Ibid.
[382] Ibid.

170

CHAPTER

5

John Paul II and the American Century

John Paul II, Ronald Reagan, and the fall of Communism

In the late 1970s, discussions between the United States and the Vatican about the situation in Poland were conducted by the national security advisor under Jimmy Carter, Zbigniew Brzezinski, as well as Cardinal Josef Tomko, head of Vatican propaganda and former head of the Vatican's counter-espionage service, *Sodalitium Pianum*.[1]

Under Jimmy Carter and John Paul II, Tomko and Brzezinski designed "Operation Open Book," whose operation was to flood Eastern Europe as well as Soviet territories such as Ukraine and the Baltic states with anti-Communist books.[2] The CIA and the Vatican Intelligence Service (The Entity) would carry out the plan using priests practicing in those regions.[3]

Thus, through the Reagan-John Paul II alliance during the 1980s, communism fell in 1991 through the collaboration of the CIA and the Vatican Entity.

Edmundo Morris, who was Ronald Reagan's personal biographer:

"Leaders who are secretive and unknown do better than those who utterly reveal themselves. Reagan and the pope understood that."[4]

Weeks before his swearing-in as the new President of the United States on January 20, 1981, Ronald Reagan made strategic contacts between Washington and the Vatican, between him and Pope John Paul II, and between CIA Director William Casey and the head of the Entity, Monsignor Luigi Poggi.[5]

According to Reagan and his advisors, the Catholic Church was the perfect counterweight to communism.[6]

Paul Kengor writes:

"The Holy Father surely was aware also that Reagan had surrounded himself with Catholics on his staff, some of whom were fundamental to his growing efforts against the Soviet Union: Bill Casey, Bill Clark, and Clark's predecessor at the NSC, Dick

---

[1] Eric Frattini, The Entity: Five Centuries of Secret Vatican Espionage (St. Martin's Press, New York, 2008), p. 326.
[2] Ibid.
[3] Ibid.
[4] Carl Bernstein and Marco Politi, His Holiness: John Paul II and the History of Our Time (Penguin Books, Nueva York, 1997), p. 380.
[5] Eric Frattini, The Entity: Five Centuries of Secret Vatican Espionage (St. Martin's Press, New York, 2008), p. 326.
[6] Ibid, p. 327.

Allen. Secretary of State Al Haig was Catholic (Haig's brother was a Jesuit priest). Reagan's chief speechwriter, Tony Dolan, was Catholic, a student of Latin and Aquinas."[7]

Carl Bernstein and Marco Politi wrote that Reagan and John Paul II secretly exchanged letters in 1981 and 1982, both about Poland and about the prospects for a wide-ranging arms deal between the United States and the Soviets.[8]

Reagan had ordered CIA Director William Casey and U.S. Ambassador-at-Large and former CIA Deputy Director Vernon Walters, a whole world of intelligence reports to the Vatican on Poland and every place the pope visited where he was fulfilling his evangelical mission.[9]

For his part, Casey had been educated by the Jesuits and had assumed a deep attachment to the Virgin Mary; he also manifested his devotion with statues of Jesus and Mary throughout his Long Island home. These were things Casey had in common with the pope, besides having supported Franco during the Spanish Civil War, for although the Falange was fascist, its members were Catholics who fought the communists. But they also shared support for right-wing dictatorships.[10] Casey's widow, Sophia, said Casey and John Paul II "would ask each other to pray about things," including Poland."[11]

John Paul II had the first of a series of meetings with him on April 7, 1981.[12]

In that month, after receiving a refusal from Lech Walesa (leader of the Solidarity trade union, who protested in Poland and was supported by the CIA and the Entity) of a possible negotiation, the Polish Prime Minister Wojciech Jaruzelski prepared to impose martial law with tanks. It was then that a letter from Leonidas Brezhnev addressed to Jaruzelski was intercepted by the Entity's intelligence agent codenamed "Gull," who was Colonel Ryszard Kuklinski, also a CIA mole, who passed thirty-five thousand pages of secret documents to US intelligence. This letter called for firmness against what happened or, "otherwise, we will take care of it."[13]

Reagan's special ambassador, Vernon Walters, who also visited the pope regularly, met with him for the first time on November 30.[14]

Walters showed John Paul II a series of satellite photos showing columns of tanks heading toward Gdansk.[15]

Two weeks after the imposition of martial law (Dec. 13) in communist Poland, Reagan appointed William Clark, who was "the Catholic conscience of the

[7] Paul Kengor, A Pope and a President: John Paul II, Ronald Reagan, and the Extraordinary Untold Story of the 20th Century (Intercollegiate Studies Institute, 2017), ob. cit.

[8] Carl Bernstein and Marco Politi, His Holiness: John Paul II and the History of Our Time (Penguin Books, Nueva York, 1997), p. 355.

[9] Ibid, 381.

[10] David Yallop, The Power and the Glory: Inside the Dark Heart of Pope John Paul II's Vatican (Constable & Robinson Ltd, London, 2007), op. cit.

[11] Seth G. Jones, A Covert Action: Reagan, the CIA, and the Cold War Struggle in Poland (W. W. W. Norton & Company, 2018), ob. cit.

[12] David Yallop, The Power and the Glory: Inside the Dark Heart of Pope John Paul II's Vatican (Constable & Robinson Ltd, London, 2007), op. cit.

[13] Abate Faria (April 29, 2021), L'Entità e l'operazione recupero del "Gabbiano," Filodiritto.

[14] David Yallop, The Power and the Glory: Inside the Dark Heart of Pope John Paul II's Vatican (Constable & Robinson Ltd, London, 2007), op. cit.

[15] Abate Faria (April 29, 2021), L'Entità e l'operazione recupero del "Gabbiano," Filodiritto.

administration," as national security advisor.[16] After martial law was declared, Reagan wrote to John Paul II asking him to "draw on the great authority that you and the church command in Poland to urge General Jaruzelski" to negotiate peacefully with Solidarity.[17] To support the Solidarity Union and put pressure on Jaruzelski, the leader asked the pope to use his persuasion throughout the West and his influence with the Catholic Church.[18] The pope agreed to use his power on the moral plane.[19]

On June 7, 1982, a summit meeting between the Vatican and the United States was held at the Vatican itself. The secret alliance between the two countries took place.[20]

For fifty minutes, and in the papal study, the U.S. president and John Paul II proposed, and we quote, "that the collapse of the Soviet empire was inevitable, more for spiritual than for strategic reasons, and that the world built at Yalta not only should not but could not to stand."[21]

Reagan announced the next day at the Palace of Westminster in London, the end of the Soviet Union, which was prey to a great revolutionary crisis in which Poland, then under martial law but magnificently irreconcilable with repression, was the linchpin. There would be repeated outbursts against repression in Eastern Europe, and he predicted that "the Soviet Union itself is not immune to this reality." Reagan and John Paul II had commented on this among themselves.[22]

John Paul II and Reagan would later admit that the Soviet system was already in decline and that all they did was to shake it up so that it would collapse.[23]

Both would use their enormous power to bring about radical change in the world, which they both believed was inspired by God with the collapse of communism to install Christian ideals. Carl Bernstein and Marco Politi write - we paraphrase - that almost as soon as the Solidarity movement was instituted, Ronald Reagan considered the union to be an elemental crack in the Iron Curtain, and that Poland, the Polish Pope Wojtyla, and Lech Walesa, were the instruments mysteriously chosen by God to shake the planet.[24] And they add that:

"Both believed in the power of the symbolic act as well as in the role of divine Providence, particularly after both had been shot by assassins within six weeks of each

---

[16] Carl Bernstein and Marco Politi, His Holiness: John Paul II and the History of Our Time (Penguin Books, Nueva York, 1997), p. 355.

[17] Seth G. Jones, A Covert Action: Reagan, the CIA, and the Cold War Struggle in Poland (W. W. Norton & Company, 2018), ob. cit. Citing Letter from Ronald Reagan to His Holiness, John Paul II, December 17, 1981. Available from the National Security Council, Executive Secretariat, NSC: Heads of State Files, The Vatican, Box 41, Ronald Reagan Presidential Library.

[18] Citing Letter from Ronald Reagan to His Holiness, John Paul II, December 29, 1981. Available from the National Security Council, Executive Secretariat, NSC: Heads of State Files, The Vatican, Box 41, Ronald Reagan Presidential Library.

[19] Memorandum from Dennis Blair to William P. Clark, Subject: Letter from the Pope to the President, January 7, 1982. Available from the National Security Council, Executive Secretariat, NSC: Heads of State Files, The Vatican, Box 41, Ronald Reagan Presidential Library. See also Letter from Ronald Reagan to His Holiness, John Paul II, February 23, 1982. Available from the National Security Council, Executive Secretariat, NSC: Heads of State Files, The Vatican, Box 41, Ronald Reagan Presidential Library.

[20] Carl Bernstein and Marco Politi, His Holiness: John Paul II and the History of Our Time (Penguin Books, Nueva York, 1997), p. 355.

[21] Ibid, pp. 355, 356.

[22] Ibid, p. 356.

[23] Ibid.

[24] Ibid.

other and survived. In the first minutes of their meeting both agreed that they had been saved by God them to play a special role in the destiny of Eastern Europe. "Look at the evil forces that were put in our way and how Providence intervened," Reagan said, and the pope agreed."[25]

For both leaders, the pope's resources were based on the intelligence services of the Holy See, the Entity, headed by Archbishop Luigi Poggi.

Gordon Thomas tells us that Poggi "was the natural heir to the world of secret papal politics, with special responsibility for gathering intelligence from Communist Europe"; and that in the Vatican he was called "the pope's spy."[26]

Indeed, the Solidarity movement in Poland led by Lech Walesa, was financed by the IOR or Vatican Bank led by Paul Marcinkus with the help of Poggi and the Entity, and the CIA led by Casey.[27]

We point out that Solidarity was the largest Christian trade union protest movement in Communist Europe, which opened the various breaches that would lead to the collapse of the Soviet Union. Since John Paul II and his top advisors saw that if Solidarity were to win in Poland, a shock wave would spread to Ukraine, the Balkans, Latvia, Lithuania, Estonia, and perhaps Czechoslovakia, something that Reagan understood would be the end of communism and the Cold War.[28]

Jan Nowak, head of the Polish-American Congress, was the liaison for new joint operations between the CIA and the Entity, maintaining a constant flow of information between Warsaw and the Vatican, and from the Vatican to Washington.[29] But Nowak also financed and shipped money to Poland to fund clandestine media, printing presses, photocopiers, and the like.[30]

The apostolic delegate in Washington, Archbishop Pio Laghi, was also visited by CIA Director William Casey, as well as by William Clark, Assistant to the President for National Security Affairs. But Cardinal John Krol of Philadelphia also made an appearance, as Reagan needed to know all the facets of the intelligence operation mounted by The Entity in Poland.[31]

"In the spring of 1981, relations between the White House and the Vatican were very fluid, especially in regard to Poland and Central America. William Casey, Vernon Walters, William Clark, and Zbigniew Brzezinski, on the U.S. side, and Monsignor Luigi Poggi and Cardinals Pio Laghi, John Krol, and Agostino Casaroli on the Vatican side became a sort of shock force whose only responsibility was to support the Solidarity union in its struggle against the communist government in Warsaw."[32]

---

[25] Ibid, p. 357.

[26] Gordon Thomas, Gideon's Spies: The Secret History of the Mossad (Thomas Dunne Books, St. Martin's Press, New York, 2015, Seventh Edition, Revised and Updated), p. 227.

[27] Eric Frattini, The Entity: Five Centuries of Secret Vatican Espionage (St. Martin's Press, New York, 2008), p. 339.

[28] Ibid, p.327.

[29] Ibid, p. 328.

[30] Ibid, citing Zbigniew Brzezinski, The Grand Failure: The Birth and Death of Communism in the Twentieth Century (Scribner Publishers, New York, 1989), ob. cit.

[31] Eric Frattini, The Entity: Five Centuries of Secret Vatican Espionage (St. Martin's Press, New York, 2008), p. 328.

[32] Ibid.

174

Vernon Walters sent more and more abundant reports each time Reagan traveled to Rome to meet secretly with Pope John Paul II; these included Poland, Central America, terrorism, Chile, Chinese military power, Argentina, liberation theology - or the health of Leonid Brezhnev, Pakistani nuclear ambitions, Ukraine, or the situation in the Middle East.[33] Poland was naturally a focus of attention in U.S.-Vatican relations: such as Polish refugees in the U.S., the role of Solidarity, martial law, and sanctions.[34]

John Paul II received substantial written reports from agents of the Entity, who in turn passed them on to Luigi Poggi in the presence of Cardinal Agostino Casaroli.[35]

An agent of the Entity, Polish Jesuit Kazimierz Przydatek was commissioned by Poggi to organize a group of Polish priests to infiltrate the unionists and trade unionists. Henceforth, Przydatek was Walesa's shadow and the Vatican's best informant on Polish affairs. Przydatek persuaded Walesa to bring Tadeusz Mazowiecki, editor of the Catholic newspaper *Wiez*, and Catholic historian Bronislaw Geremek into the leadership of Solidarity. From then on, the movement was under the control of the Catholic Church.[36]

Seth G. Jones documents:

"In terms of spycraft, the CIA entrusted only a few Catholic officials— always working through surrogates—to bring money and material into Poland as part of QRHELPFUL. Catholic Church officials were not subject to border controls and could carry money and equipment into Poland with little risk of being searched. These individuals likely had no idea they were carrying CIA money or contraband, since they weren't getting it directly from CIA case officers. Case officers like Celia Larkin were prohibited from working directly with clergy.
[...]
For the CIA, a successful QRHELPFUL covert action program meant understanding the power of the Catholic Church in Polish society and cajoling church leaders to support Solidarity. But the CIA didn't need to convince the Vatican to help. Most Catholic officials were already on their side."[37]

By 1983, the vast majority of Catholic officials either supported Solidarity or looked the other way to ignore underground activities: "A clandestine network of nuns and priests provided money, distributed literature, offered sanctuary, and delivered material to the Solidarity underground," write Richard Breitman and Norman J.W. Goda. Also assisting the union were the Bishop's Palace in Kraków, St. Martin's Church in Warsaw, and St. Bridget's Church in Gdańsk.[38]

---

[33] Ibid, pp. 328, 329.
[34] Seth G. Jones, A Covert Action: Reagan, the CIA, and the Cold War Struggle in Poland (W. W. W. Norton & Company, 2018), ob. cit.
[35] Eric Frattini, The Entity: Five Centuries of Secret Vatican Espionage (St. Martin's Press, New York, 2008), p. 324.
[36] Ibid, p. 325.
[37] Seth G. Jones, A Covert Action: Reagan, the CIA, and the Cold War Struggle in Poland (W. W. Norton & Company, 2018), ob. cit. Citing Letter from Ronald Reagan to His Holiness, John Paul II, December 17, 1981. Available from the National Security Council, Executive Secretariat, NSC: Heads of State Files, The Vatican, Box 41, Ronald Reagan Presidential Library.
[38] Ibid.

During that decade, the so-called Prolog magazine as a CIA operation for many years, expanded its operations to other Soviet countries and included Soviet Jewish dissidents; something that was considered impressive.[39]

Employees of both Prolog, Radio Liberty, and Radio Free Europe interviewed tens of thousands of travelers from the Soviet bloc to the West. Such contacts and networks were important later that decade, when high-ranking members of the Ukrainian Soviet cultural establishment became leaders of the Rukh (Ukrainian People's Movement for Reconstruction); nationalist émigrés adopted a distinct strategy of hostility to members of that establishment; and distrusted the Ukrainian democratic opposition. Indeed, by its outreach to other Soviet satellites, Prolog supported the Polish Solidarity movement,[40] which would eventually bring about the subsequent collapse of the Soviet Union.

Prolog also worked through the London-based Ukrainian Press Agency with left- and right-wing opposition groups in Central and Eastern Europe, as well as Polish, Hungarian, and Czech groups.[41]

Both the expansion of CIA covert action through Prolog in Soviet countries, as well as the U.S. Department of Defense, wanted the supported groups to be malleable, as they did not want them to become extremist and violent.[42]

An additional infusion of funds under President Ronald Reagan allowed Prolog to inject $3.5 million into Soviet Ukraine, which was invested to:

"[...] publications, finances and technology, including computers, printers, camera's, video equipment, photocopiers, fax machines, tape recorders, and printing machines which had a great impact upon sustaining and increasing anti-regime activities and opposition groups in the late 1980s in the final push towards Ukrainian Independence."[43]

The CIA provided a diversion in Geneva at the first meeting between Gorbachev and President Reagan: anti-Soviet demonstrations, rallies, exhibitions, and more. Prolog employees and freelancers organized press conferences and met with journalists to publicize the Soviet occupation of Afghanistan, the 1986 Chernobyl nuclear accident, and the lack of human rights in Soviet Ukraine.[44]

In September 1984, Josyf Slipyj, the major archbishop of the Ukrainian Greek Catholic Church, died. He was buried in Rome, where John Paul II went to pay his last respects.[45]

---

[39] Richard Breitman and Norman J.W. Goda, Hitler's Shadow: Nazi War Criminals, U.S. Intelligence, and the Cold War (National Archives, 2012), p. 90; citing FY 1982 Renewal of Activity PDDYNAMIC, NARA, RG 263, E ZZ-19, B 59, QRPLUMB, v. 4.

[40] Taras Kuzio, U.S. support for Ukraine's liberation during the Cold War: A study of Prolog Research and Publishing Corporation, Communist and Post-Communist Studies xxx (2012), p. 56.

[41] Ibid, p. 59.

[42] Ibid.

[43] Ibid, p. 61.

[44] Ibid.

[45] (September 23, 1984), Patriarch Josyf I buried in Rome, The Ukrainian Weekly, Vol. LII, No. 39, pp. 2, 4.

Ronald Reagan spoke out:

"It is with deep sense of loss that I acknowledge the death of Josyf Cardinal Slipyj, major archbishop of the Ukrainian Catholic Church, and extend my condolences to Ukrainians throughout the world.

When we remember Cardinal Slipyj's 18 years in Soviet prison camps, when we reflect that he was condemned to the gulag because he refused to betray his Church, we see the power and strength of the human spirit brought clearly Into focus.

[...]

Cardinal Slipyj's commitment to God and the freedom of men was unshakable, despite punishment and exile for his beliefs. Because of his inspired life, he has long been a symbol of the strength of God and human spirit. He will remain such, cherished not only by Ukrainians, but by men and women of good will in all nations."[46]

On September 16, while visiting Canada, Pope John Paul II was greeted by Ukrainian Catholics at the Cathedral of St. Volodymyr and Olha, which is the seat of the Greek Catholic Church of Canada. In his address in Ukrainian, the pope praised Ukrainian Christians for their heroism in maintaining their faith in communist-occupied Ukraine. He said: "In you 1 embrace in the charity of Christ all the people of your homeland, together with their history, culture, and the heroism with which they lived their faith."[47]

He also noted that the Ukrainian Catholic Church, through its distinctive Byzantine rite, could serve as a bridge to the Russian and Ukrainian Orthodox Churches. Therefore, he said, Ukrainian Catholics were in a privileged position to help bring about reconciliation between Eastern and Western Christians. In the same month, ten thousand demonstrators took to the streets of Washington D.C. to protest against the Russification of Ukraine. The demonstrators were Ukrainian Americans who demonstrated at the Shevchenko monument, a march to the Soviet embassy, and a rally in Lafayette Park, right in front of the White House.[48]

The CIA reported in October 1985 that an underground magazine, *The Chronicle of the Ukrainian Catholic Church*, was a good source of information on the activities of Ukrainian Catholics and the regime's tactics to try to discredit the Catholic Church and its leaders.[49]

"The increased activism on the part of Ukrainian Catholic revealed by The Chronicle is part of a larger burgeoning of religion taking place in the USSR today. Ukrainian Catholic activism, however, poses special problems for the regime, because of the Ukrainian church's ties to Rome and historical association with Ukrainian national feeling. Over the past several years, the onset of unrest in Poland and the election of a Slavic Pope have increased regime concern that external influences could spur greater dissent among Ukrainian Catholics.

---

[46] Ibid, p. 2.

[47] Ibid, p. 3.

[48] Ibid, p. 3, 1.

[49] U.S. CIA (October 17, 1985). Religious Dissent and The Chronicle of the Ukrainian Catholic Church, DC: U.S. Government Printing Office, p. 1.

"The regime has reacted to the Chronicle's appearance by harshly repressing most of those known to be involved in its publication. Ukrainian Catholicism has such a large popular base in Western Ukraine, however, that continued agitation among the church's adherent is likely. This activism will continue to be a thorn in the refime's side, impeding efforts to Sovietize and Russify Western Ukraine."[50]

The Central Intelligence Agency report said that in recent years, the communist regime had increased its efforts to liquidate the Ukrainian Catholic Church, "probably reflecting increased official concern about Ukrainian susceptibility to Papal and Polish influences."[51] The CIA, which supported such moves from abroad with the Vatican Entity led by Luigi Poggi, saw in Poland and Ukraine nations whose religious awakening was extremely important in destabilizing the communist regime, which was extremely concerned with what was happening and with the election of Pope John Paul II:

"Because of the religious, ethnic, and cultural affinity between Western Ukraine and Poland, the Soviet regime has always been sensitive to the problem of a spillover of political and religious influences. Soviet fears of contagion intensified with the onset of unrest in Poland in 1979. Reporting from Western Ukraine in 1980-81 indicated a high level of interest--especially among young people--in developments in Poland, which Ukrainians were able to follow by watching Polish television. Scattered strikes reportedly occurred in several Western Ukrainian cities during this period.

"The election of a Polish Pope in 1979 contributed to the concern of Soviet authorities, who have been apprehensive that Pope John Paul II's vocal support of the Uniate Church would open the door to increased external influences on Ukraine. The Pope increased Radio Vatican's broadcasting time in Slavic languages, appointed East Europeans to several important positions in the Vatican hierarchy, and in 1979 sent a letter of support to the head of the Uniate Church. In his most recent statement on the subject, in early October, Pope John Paul II told a synod of the Ukrainian Catholic Church in exile that the Ukrainian Church "was, and is, unjustly treated and persecuted" and that as a fellow Slav he shared its leaders' grief."[52]

At the end of the decade, one of the signs that the ice was broken was the coming out of hiding of the Ukrainian Greek Catholic Church, as happened with numerous demonstrations in Lviv and Kiev, and even in Moscow; so the state persecuted them, but in turn the local authorities in western Ukraine began to return their temples. The Kremlin was still trying to stop the process, but after Gorbachev's meeting with John Paul II, the persecution stopped completely and the mass return of the Greek Catholic churches began. When the first ones were returned in 1989, it was an occasion for the faithful of the Roman Catholic Church to demand local councils and executive committees to reclaim the churches closed during the Soviet era. The church began to revive and, in 1990, thousands of rallies in Lviv and student hunger strikes in Kiev,

---

[50] Ibid, pp. 1, 2.
[51] Ibid, p. 2.
[52] Ibid, p. 3.

178

with the Revolution on Granite, the chain of unity and the proclamation of Ukrainian state sovereignty.[53]

All these events were aimed at awakening the Polish and Ukrainian people's zeal for freedom.

It is not superfluous to add that William Wilson, Ronald Reagan's personal representative to the Holy See, took an interest with John Paul II, for example, in the lobbying that unconditionally favored the Chilean military dictatorship of Pinochet and the Argentine military junta, U.S. policies on many other South American issues, the Middle East, the financing of Afghan rebels, and the situation of the Catholic Church in Ukraine and Poland.[54]

However, the operations in Lithuania and Ukraine, which provoked widespread discontent with Gorbachev on the part of Catholics in those countries, led the Russian president to consider in 1990 that through private conversations with John Paul II, he could smooth his way with them.[55] Gorbachev *promised* Wojtyla that he would let him visit the Soviet Union, so the pontiff helped him to appease the Catholics in the Baltic countries and the Ukraine.[56]

Moscow made a last attempt to suppress the protests and return to the old order, but that would hasten the collapse of the Soviet Union. Subsequently, the opening of churches everywhere began.[57]

On the other hand, the information obtained by the Entity was shared with the CIA, thus supporting trade union movements and other mass protest movements in the then regions belonging to the Soviet bloc, which could not hold out any longer and collapsed on December 25, 1991.

The upheaval in Poland caused shock waves that spread to Ukraine, the Balkans, Latvia, Lithuania, Estonia, and Czechoslovakia.[58]

A secret Soviet government document had defined the problem with Pope John Paul II:

"The Vatican "now use[s] religion in the ideological struggle against Socialist lands" and seeks "to increase religious fanaticism against the political and ideological principles of the socialist societies. The Vatican, above all, disseminates this new propaganda, which constitutes a change in policy."

With the election of Pope Wojtyla, the document continues, "the characteristics of Vatican and Catholic Church policies in different regions of the Soviet Union have become more aggressive-above all in Lithuania, Latvia, western Ukraine, and Byelorussia."[59]

[53] Victor Zaslavski (December 27, 2019), Католики в Радянському союзі: боротьба за виживання, Радіо Марія.

[54] David Yallop, The Power and the Glory: Inside the Dark Heart of Pope John Paul II's Vatican (Constable & Robinson Ltd, London, 2007), op. cit.

[55] Malachi Martin, The Keys of This Blood: The Struggle for World Dominion Between Pope John Paul II, Mikhail Gorbachev, and the Capitalist West (Simon & Schuster, New York, 1990), ob. cit.

[56] Ibid.

[57] Victor Zaslavski (December 27, 2019), Католики в Радянському союзі: боротьба за виживання, Радіо Марія.

[58] Carl Bernstein and Marco Politi, His Holiness: John Paul II and the History of Our Time (Penguin Books, Nueva York, 1997), p. 262.

[59] Ibid, p. 308.

With the collapse of the Soviet Union, the Russian Orthodox Church reemerged with a vengeance, while the Catholic Church grew to 1,300,000 members, representing one of the smallest religious groupings in the country. Although the majority of its faithful are German, French, and particularly Polish.[60]

There are major differences between the Russian Catholic Church and the nation's Orthodox Church, which is the majority.[61]

It should be noted that the subversive intelligence activities of the Soviet Union against the Vatican, Ukraine, and Poland were prominent until the very fall of communism, as they recognized the power of the Vatican intelligence service.[62]

The Balkan War and the indirect promotion of Catholic interests through U.S. and NATO support

On June 28, 1989, Slobodan Milošević, then president of the Socialist Republic of Serbia, gave a speech before about one million people in Gazimestan, in the municipality of Kosovo Polje, in commemoration of the 600th anniversary of the Battle of Kosovo, which marked the defeat of the Principality of Serbia against the Ottoman Empire. Being a referent of Serbian nationalism since 1987, Milošević exalted in his speech the new Greater Serbia, with ultra-nationalist sentiments[63] that would lead to a great and painful war in the Balkans during the 1990s.

With the disintegration of the USSR in 1991, came the independence of the nations that made up the Socialist Federal Republic of Yugoslavia (SFRY), which was under Josip Broz Tito until he died in 1980, but governed by other leaders since then.[64]

"Tito, a Croatian Communist, had presided over a federation of republics with disparate religions and cultures with consummate skill. He rotated the presidency so that a Croatian followed a Serb or a Slovenian or a member of one of the other federal units in what was a one-party state. No discussion of the solely artificial boundaries that had been created was permitted and Tito observed that the frontiers between the various republics were only 'administrative'."

But after Tito's death, the collective presidency, despite the nationalist aspirations that began to emerge, remained united until the federal elections of 1990. The six republics were: the Federal Republic (FR) of Slovenia; the Federal Republic of Croatia; the Federal Republic of Bosnia and Herzegovina; the Federal Republic of Montenegro; the Federal Republic of Serbia; and the Federal Republic of Macedonia.

History notes that in late 1989, the SFRY Assembly approved amendments to the constitution, replacing the one-party system with a multiparty system.

---

[60] Catholic Radio & Television Network (Producer) (2005), Catholics in Moscow.

[61] Ibid.

[62] Christopher Andrew and Vasili Mitrokhin, The Mitrokhin Archive: The KGB in Europe and the West (Penguin Books, 2015).

[63] Ramón Álvarez (October 22, 2021), Milošević's proclamation that set the Balkans on fire, La Vanguardia.

[64] David Yallop, The Power and the Glory: Inside the Dark Heart of Pope John Paul II's Vatican (Constable & Robinson Ltd, London, 2007), op. cit.; Alfredo Relaño (May 24, 2020), La patada de Boban que entró en la historia, El País. Note: unless otherwise indicated, from here on these are the same sources and others consulted.

At the end of January 1990, at the XIV SKY Congress in Belgrade and after strong verbal confrontations between Slovenian and Serbian delegates concerning the future of the SFRY, the former left the session, followed immediately by the Croatian FR delegation, which brought the issue to the floor of the congress. After these delegations, the delegations of the FR of Bosnia and Herzegovina and the FR of Macedonia also left. Thus, the Alliance of the Communists of Yugoslavia collapsed.

Subsequently, after the multi-party elections held in the Croatian FR on April 22, 1990, the HDZ party won with its political program with a desire for independence and separation from the SFRY. Its new president, elected in May, was Franjo Tudjman, with neighboring Slovenia also emerging with a new government under Milan Kučan. Before the elections in their respective countries, there was an open telephone between the two republics to coordinate their plans for the dissolution of the Yugoslav federation.

Franjo Tudjman acted under the paradigm of the deepest Croatian ultranationalism, recovering the teachings of the Ustashas. There was great euphoria from the Croatian FR, with displays of images of Ustasha war criminals such as Ante Pavelić, Alojzije Stepinac, Vjekoslav Luburić, and others. There were also greetings and Ustashas songs that were frequently heard. This brought back memories of the genocide against Serbs during World War II by the Independent State of Croatia. There was fear by Serb survivors of what might happen, as I was told by a descendant of victims of the Ustasha regime during 1941-45. And indeed, the survivors were fearful of this resurgence.

The ultra-nationalist Croats under Tudjman complained: "We are European Catholics administered by Byzantine Orthodox."

In the spring, Franjo Tudjman and the HDZ took control of the police, the media, the prosecutor's office, and the state administration. At that time, Serbs working in the police were forced to leave. At the Maksimir soccer stadium in Zagreb, there was a conflict between fans of Dinamo Zagreb (Croatian ultranationalism) and Red Star Belgrade (Serbian ultranationalism), where Croatian fans took the opportunity to display anti-Serb propaganda.

Croatian Dinamo had its large ultra group, extremely violent and named Bad Blue Boys (BBB), who supported Tudjman. A Serbian ultra-nationalist group was Delijes, which was also extremely violent, and which completely rejected Tudjman's government. The scenes that followed were fraught with violence.

Now, since May 1990, the situation in FR of Croatia began to worsen, and Serbs greatly feared for their safety and property. Ustasha graffiti, slogans, and posters began to appear regularly, and a large number of Serbs received threats by telephone that they had to move out of their homes and go to SR of Serbia. They also received threatening letters with the signature "HDZ." Also, Croats married to Serbs received threats. And Serbs in Croatia were fired from their jobs, and even their children were mentally and physically abused in their schools. In almost all settlements where Croats were in absolute or relative majority, certain HDZ party members spied on their Serb neighbors.

Once Germany was unified, it would become involved in a key role in the disintegration of Yugoslavia, "aided and abetted by Pope John Paul II and his Secretariat of State."

However, the overwhelming majority of European Union member states believed that Yugoslavia had a future as a single entity. Germany, however, under its Chancellor

Helmut Kohl, was very receptive to the persuasive Stjepan Mesic, who had assumed the rotating national presidency in Croatia in May 1990.

Since 1991, and perhaps even earlier, Germany had been supplying arms to Croatia through Italy, Hungary, and Czechoslovakia. More than a thousand vehicles carrying small arms, as well as anti-aircraft and anti-tank weapons, ammunition, and spare equipment. Croatia and Slovenia declared their independence simultaneously on June 25 of the same year (1991). Both nations received assurances of support from both Germany and the Vatican. Speaking in the Hungarian city of Pecs in August 1991, John Paul II urged the world to "help to legitimise the aspirations of Croatia."

Archbishop Jean Louis Tauran, then a member of the Vatican Secretariat of State, was very active on behalf of Croatia and Slovenia in the second half of 1991, using Vatican diplomatic channels to rally support for the two countries.

On June 26, one day after the Croatian and Slovenian declaration of independence, the Yugoslav army, on orders from Slobodan Milošević, president of Serbia, acted to secure airports and border posts between Slovenia and Serbia, meeting fierce resistance. But there was also resistance between Yugoslav troops and Croatian forces. Dubrovnik was already under siege from the beginning of the same month, and Vukobar was reduced to rubble between August and November of the same year.

However, the Yugoslav government, under Slobodan Milošević, would also carry out a campaign of ethnic cleansing by committing a whole series of heinous crimes against Croats and Muslims for almost a decade, exemplified especially under the Srebrenica massacre.[65] But clearly, Milošević does not represent the entire Serbian people, any more than Tudjman represents the entire Croatian people.

Now, for his part, Tudjman had, since June 1991, activated a policy of ethnic cleansing aimed at eliminating hundreds of thousands of Serbs, Muslims, and Jews in Croatia and Bosnia.[66] Most of the Croatian Catholic Church, the most extreme nationalist force in Croatia, supported Tudjman to the hilt.[67] Indeed, under the Tudjman regime (1990-1999), the Croatian Catholic Church grew even stronger and continued the nationalization project in the post-Tudjman era.[68]

Franciscan priests in Western Herzegovina commemorated the defunct criminal Ustasha regime as martyrs and heroes of the Greater Croatia project restored during the 1990s in the form of Croatian separatism in Herzegovina.[69]

On the other hand, Bosnian Franciscans fought for a unified Bosnia and Herzegovina, and denounced ethnic cleansing and war crimes, with Muslims being the

---

[65] On this entire history, see for example: Misha Glenny, The Fall of Yugoslavia: The Third Balkan War (Penguin Books, Third Revised Edition, New York, 1996); Laura Silber and Allan Little, Yugoslavia: Death of a Nation (Penguin Books, New York, 1997); Peter Maass, Love Thy Neighbor: A Story of War (Vintage Books, Reprint Edition, 1997); Alastair Finlan, The Collapse of Yugoslavia: 1991-99 (Osprey Publishing, 2022); Jan Willem Honig, Norbert Both, Srebrenica: Record of a War Crime (Penguin Books, New York, 1997); David Rohde, Endgame: The Betrayal and Fall of Srebrenica, Europe's Worst Massacre Since World War II (Penguin Books, New York, 2012).

[66] David Yallop, The Power and the Glory: Inside the Dark Heart of Pope John Paul II's Vatican (Constable & Robinson Ltd, London, 2007), op. cit.

[67] Vjekoslav Perica (2015), Power, Corruption and Dissent: V , Corruption and Dissent: Varieties of Contempor arieties of Contemporary Croatian Political Catholicism, Occasional Papers on Religion in Eastern Europe, Volume 35, Issue 4, Article 2, p. 1, 5.

[68] Ibid, p. 7.

[69] Ibid, p. 16.

main victims. They would also condemn the forces that incited the Croat-Muslim war of 1993-4 and the Serbo-Croat collaboration at the expense of Muslims.[70]

However, since April 1992, the Croatian Catholic Church, starting with its top leaders, was against the new Tudjman government's policy of discrimination, leading to hostilities by members of the government against the Church, leading to a meeting with Vatican officials in 1995 over the pope's concerns about the situation in Croatia.[71]

John Paul II, moreover, urged a peaceful resolution of Croatia's issues with the Serbian people.[72]

However, Croatian militant Catholicism would be of greater influence in the life of the nation, including by communists, being that:

"In Tudjman's Croatia, crowds of ex-communists including Tudjman himself, flocked to churches and cathedrals, received sacraments and adopted theological terms as politically correct features of new citizenship and political jargon."[73]

Thus, the Catholic Church became the most powerful institution in the Croatian state.[74]

According to Tudjman, the Croatian Catholic Church was the only organized force that provided consistent opposition to the communist authorities. Tudjman further insisted that in fulfilling this role, the Church was responsible for nurturing Croatian national identity.[75]

"Many within the church itself shared this view of the relationship between church and nation. Friar Ilija Zivkovic, secretary to the Croatian Bishops' Conference and head of the Croatian Catholic radio station, argued that by its very existence the church acted as a voice for the nation and helped to perpetuate the maintenance of Croatian identity, for example by allowing the singing of the Croatian national anthem during church services. Likewise Cardinal Kuharic, head of the Croatian church until his death in 1996, outlined what he believed to be the good of the nation and what the church should try to secure for 'its' people: 'freedom to live and to develop its identity and sovereignty in all areas of life: moral, spiritual, cultural, material, finding its expression in statehood'. Church and nation were thus often seen to be mutually constituent and the Croatian Democratic Union (*Hrvatske Demokratska Zajednica* (HDZ)) government attempted to coopt Catholicism into its conception of national identity. This cooption was welcomed by nationalist elements within the church."[76]

---

[70] Ibid, pp. 16, 17.

[71] Biljana Ribić (2009), Relations Between Church and State in Republic of Croatia, Politics and Religion Journal, Vol. 3 No. 2, p 5; Alex J. Bellamy (2002), The Catholic Church and Croatia's Two Transitions, Religion, State & Society, Vol. 30, No. 1, pp. 52, 53.

[72] Ana Holjevac Tuković, Robert Holjevac (2019), The Role of the Holy See and Pope John Paul II in the International Recognition of the Republic of Croatia, Bogoslovska smotra, Vol. 89, No. 1, p. 64.

[73] Vjekoslav Perica (2015), Power, Corruption and Dissent: V , Corruption and Dissent: Varieties of Contempor arieties of Contemporary Croatian Political Catholicism, Occasional Papers on Religion in Eastern Europe, Volume 35, Issue 4, Article 2, p. 28.

[74] Ibid, p. 32.

[75] Alex J. Bellamy (2002), The Catholic Church and Croatia's Two Transitions, Religion, State & Society, Vol. 30, No. 1, pp. 46, 47.

[76] Ibid, p. 47.

Under the auspices of the European Community (EC), on July 7, 1991, the Brioni Declaration was adopted, which maintained Yugoslavia as a single entity.[77] Thus, Croatia and Slovenia agreed to suspend their decisions to declare their sovereignty and independence for three months. Thus, on September 7, the EC Peace Conference on Yugoslavia began in The Hague. While some were genuinely striving for a peaceful solution, others were busy fanning hopes for independence.

The view of the EC - then with twelve members - to keep Yugoslavia united was shared by many beyond Europe, such as the United States, in order to maintain peace in that region.

However, only Germany and the Vatican maintained their position of independence for the countries that made up Yugoslavia, under the banner of "democracy."

German Chancellor Helmut Kohl was interested in this independence since there were half a million Croatians living in Germany, which ensured the constancy of the anti-Serbian sentiment.

Kohl cherished the hope of being designated the Bismarck of his time, and to assist Croatia and Slovenia in a full and lasting independence.

The Catholic Church helped Kohl and Genscher every step of the way. Bishop Kamphaus of Limburg was dispatched to Croatia in October by the president of the German Bishops' Conference. On his return, he criticized the EC's commitment to a unified Yugoslavia and demanded speedy recognition of Croatia's independence. He said that if the 12 countries that made up the EC upheld his position, "Germany should make a unilateral declaration of recognition." Monsignor Stimphle, another German bishop, organized street demonstrations to demand "military aid for Croatia, the bastion of the liberal democratic order." By then, shipments from Austria and Germany were already being sent to Croatia and Bosnia and, later, evidence emerged of $40 million worth of Vatican bearer bonds provided to the Croatian government for the purchase of arms.[78]

German Foreign Minister Hans-Dietrich Genscher, speaking in the Bundestag in November 1991, declared that Germany demanded from its European Union partners immediate recognition of Slovenia and Croatia and sanctions against the Serbs, or "otherwise, the Community will face a serious crisis."[79] In people of a certain age, with old memories, and in scholars of the history of World War II, that message and his overwhelming desire to be the "protector" of Croatia induced deep unease.

Someone by the name of Stjepan Mesić, who was clandestinely taken to Bonn, Germany, to participate in another series of secret meetings, was informed by Genscher that he was fully committed to the complete independence of both countries, as well as to the inevitable further dissolution of the other parts of Yugoslavia. Dr. Bozo Dimnik, who arranged the meeting, recalls:

---

[77] David Yallop, The Power and the Glory: Inside the Dark Heart of Pope John Paul II's Vatican (Constable & Robinson Ltd, London, 2007), op. cit. Note: unless otherwise indicated, this is the same source.

[78] See also Chris McGreal and Philip Willan (November 19, 1999), Vatican 'secretly armed Croatia', The Guardian.

[79] David Yallop, The Power and the Glory: Inside the Dark Heart of Pope John Paul II's Vatican (Constable & Robinson Ltd, London, 2007), op. cit. Note: unless otherwise indicated, this is the same source.

"'Genscher said "I will help you but as Foreign Minister of Germany and because of the things that happened during the Second World War, I cannot openly support your cause." He was referring to the historic relationship between Croatia and Nazi Germany. He suggested that Mesic should talk to both Andreotti and the Pope, 'Genscher wanted to hide behind the Pope's robes.'"

The following month, the doors were opened to the Italian Prime Minister, Giulio Andreotti, as well as to the Vatican's Cardinal Secretary of State, Angelo Sodano. Sodano assured him that John Paul II was fully informed of the various Croatian demands and that he fully supported them. The pope also agreed to maintain Croatian independence.

Between July and late autumn, intense papal diplomacy narrowed the eleven EC nations to eight against four on the independence of Croatia and Slovenia, as only Germany was in favor from the start.

At the end of 1991, senior representatives of the EC met in Maastricht, where Germany spoke out on the question of Croatian and Slovenian independence. At 10:00 pm, German Foreign Minister Genscher said he would not leave the table until all EC members voted unanimously in favor of the resolution. Apparently, he was prepared to torpedo the entire Maastricht treaty unless the remaining EC members submitted to the German view. By 4:00 am, Genscher, Kohl, Pope John Paul II, and his Secretary of State had prevailed. David Yallop comments:

"That extraordinary turnaround came despite the profound misgivings of the French President Francois Mitterand, the British Prime Minister John Major and his Foreign Secretary Douglas Hurd and a host of other senior players both at the table and further afield, including the United Nations Secretary General, the US President George Bush and his Secretary of State James Baker who had predicted in June that

'If there are unilateral declarations of independence followed by use of force that forecloses possibilities for peaceful break and peaceful negotiations, as required by the Helsinki Accord, it will kick off the damndest civil war that this region has ever seen.'"

The joint declarations, in addition to the use of force to seize border posts by Slovenia and Croatia, led to the great violence that followed between June and December 1991. This should have been sufficient cause for urgent peace negotiations. However, the two illegal acts of independence led to the further inflaming of the degrading and horrific situation that followed in the years to come.

The EC recognized these two republics on January 15 of the same year, but on the condition that both commit themselves to respect human rights and minorities and that they show willingness to resolve border issues peacefully and other disputes to ensure democratic government. But the Germans said they would recognize both countries immediately.

Again, Yallop explains:

"In 1991, echoing Pavelic, the new President Tudjman of Croatia introduced a 'new' constitution that defined Croatia as a national state of Croatian people 'and others' immediately relegating the Serbs, Muslims, Slovenes, Czechs, Italians, Jews and Hungarians and other Croatian-born nationals to a second-class status. On the orders of President Tudjman all the remaining buildings and structures of the Jasenovac concentration camp with many of the artefacts and records inside were destroyed 'to make way', Tudjman explained, 'for a rare bird sanctuary'."

On January 20, 1992, only a week after Croatia and Slovenia were recognized by Germany, the Vatican, and later by the rest of the EC members as independent states, Tudjman told the attendees at a large rally: "We are in a war against the JNA (the Yugoslav Army). Should anything happen, kill them all in the streets, in their homes, throw hand grenades, fire pistols in their bellies, women, children… We will deal with Knin (a Croatian Serbian area) by butchering."

Tudjman's ambitions went much further, for example when in a fit of anger he grabbed Prime Minister Mesić by the throat and shouted, "All I want is Bosnia. Give me that and I will demand no more!"

The slaughter was perpetrated everywhere and in sections of Croatia. As a result, between 1992 and 1995 more than 200,000 people were killed, and more than two million were left homeless.

On October 3, 1998, despite the advice and enormous discontent of the Serbian population and the country's Orthodox Church, John Paul II beatified the war criminal and Cardinal Alojzije Stepinac.

We should also mention the Lora concentration camp in Split, Croatia, where horrendous tortures occurred by the prison police against Serbs, where Ustasha symbols were used and the practice of Catholicism was superimposed on the prisoners. It was in operation from 1992-97.[80] I have had contact with people who know survivors of that camp, who today refuse to talk about what happened for understandable reasons.

As Tudjman's rule neared its end, Tudjman collaborated with the Vatican on the state religion project. There were four treaties between Croatia and the Vatican that were signed in 1998, establishing the Church as a national institution, co-governing of Tudjman, and guardian of the society. One of the great privileges of the Croatian Catholic Church is that it receives annually significant sums of money from all taxpayers, regardless of their (non-) religious affiliation, plus additional payments for the restitution of nationalized properties, instructors of religious schools, parishes, and monasteries.[81]

For his part, Milošević saw the end of his dictatorial regime on October 5, 2000, due to the protests that led to his fall, after the crime and corruption that reigned during his long mandate.[82] For months before his overthrow, the U.S. authorities carried out a campaign for regime change through the National Endowment of Democracy, with the use of newspapers, television, and radio, and the participation of famed investor and businessman George Soros. In this way, they had groups led by young people helped by the National Democratic Institute, who held protest marches and resistance marches

---

[80] Crime of Genocide Against Serbs in the Prison Camp 'Lora' in Split in the Period 1991-1997, Committee for Compiling Data on Crimes Against Humanity and International Law (Belgrade), October, 1998.

[81] Vjekoslav Perica (2015), Power, Corruption and Dissent: V , Corruption and Dissent: Varieties of Contempor arieties of Contemporary Croatian Political Catholicism, Occasional Papers on Religion in Eastern Europe, Volume 35, Issue 4, Article 2, p. 9.

[82] Reuters staff (September 30, 2010), Timeline - Serbia, 20 years since Milosevic came to power, Reuters.

to call for change. They also had a candidate favored and financed by the Washington government.[83]

Years passed, and when Pope John Paul II visited Bosnia-Herzegovina in June 2003, he traveled to Banja Luka (in that place, during World War II there was a massacre of the surrounding villages led by the bishop) to beatify in the monastery in Petrićevac, Ivan Hans Merz, the ideologue of the Ustasha. Amidst the protests of many, someone furious ran to rush at the pope but was prevented from doing so.

After Tudjman's presidency ended, the Catholic Church did everything possible to ensure that the Croatian Democratic Union founded by Tudjman would remain in power. For this reason, during the two terms in power of the center-left coalitions (2000-3 and 2012-15), some church leaders branded the democratically elected government as "traitorous," "unpatriotic" and "against the people."[84]

The Catholic Church did not tolerate the two leftist legislatures, thus leading it to openly support the right-wing opposition, including moves best described as coup attempts. The first occurred in 2000, which was overcome by the energetic President Stjepan Mesić, being quietly assisted by Vatican diplomacy.[85] Such ambiguities on the part of the Vatican, as I know from sources close to Serbian and Vatican authorities, are due to the fact that the Holy See supports governments that respect the Catholic cause, even if they do not entirely agree with the moral and political thinking of the Holy See. These "discordances" have been seen in Pope Francis' papacy and are not new, as we have seen throughout this essay.

When Ivo Sanader - a prominent lay Catholic - was prime minister from 2003-2009, and who was also Tudjman's successor in the HDZ presidency, he received the backing of the Catholic Church. He was subsequently sentenced to ten years in prison for corruption and criminal privatization, but the church never explicitly condemned his crimes.[86]

As early as August 2009, Mesić, complained that he might report Bishop Jurij Jezerinac to the Holy See for interfering in politics by quoting a song by a controversial singer, Mark Thomson Perkovic, for containing in its lyrics the Ustasha movement's greeting, "Ready for the Homeland."[87] During a September meeting between Mesić and the then Cardinal Secretary of State, Tarcisio Bertone, the latter told President Mesić that he agreed that the Croatian Catholic Church should close the chapter that occurred in World War II, and not interfere in Croatian state affairs. [88]

The same happened during the meeting between Mesić and Pope Benedict XVI at the Vatican in November 2009, agreeing that the bishops and the Croatian government should have a constructive dialogue, without the Church meddling in state affairs.[89]

For his part, in April 2011, Croatian General Ante Gotovina, arrested in Spain in December 2005,[90] was sentenced to 24 years in prison, because between August and

---

[83] Branislav Malagurski (Producer) Boris Malagurski (Director). (2014), The Weight of Chains 2. (Malagurski Cinema).

[84] Vjekoslav Perica (2015), Power, Corruption and Dissent: V , Corruption and Dissent: Varieties of Contempor arieties of Contemporary Croatian Political Catholicism, Occasional Papers on Religion in Eastern Europe, Volume 35, Issue 4, Article 2, p. 7.

[85] Ibid.

[86] Ibid, p. 9.

[87] BIRN (August 14, 2008), Croatia President to Report Bishop to Vatican, Balkan Insight.

[88] IKA (September 19, 2008), President Mesić Receives Cardinal Bertone, Informativna katolička agencia.

[89] BIRN (November 13, 2009), Croatian President meets Pope Benedict XVI, Balkan Insight.

November 1995 during Operation Storm, he crushed rebel Serb forces and carried out persecutions, deportation, inhumane acts, murder, looting, and destruction.[91] In addition, forces under Ante Gotovina's command were accused of killing dozens of Serbs and expelling 200,000 from the Krajina region, which is now part of Croatia.[92]

In 2005 Carla del Ponte, the chief prosecutor of the UN war crimes tribunal, said she believed that Catholic monasteries in Croatia were aiding or harboring Croatian war criminal General Ante Gotovina.[93] Del Ponte said she had appealed for help to senior Church officials and Pope Benedict XVI but had received no response.[94] The Croatian Catholic Church also denied del Ponte's claims that Gotovina was sheltering in a Franciscan monastery in Croatia.[95] The UN prosecutor, speaking to the Vatican's foreign minister, Archbishop Giovanni Lajolo, received from him a denial that the Vatican had an intelligence service, but she said "I don't believe that. I think that the Catholic Church has the most advanced intelligence services."[96] And she was right.

However, by an appeal in November 2012, Ante Gotovina was released in what was seen as a political act, being that he is considered a hero in Croatia.[97]

Three years later, in May 2015, a group of war veterans took to the streets of Zagreb, defying the incumbent government, and clashed with the police, later finding refuge in a church. In each coup attempt, religious symbols were displayed, prayers were said in public, and Catholic priests were on hand to help.[98]

Leaders of the Croatian Catholic Church have sporadically expressed concern about the growing poverty in society, but the Church itself has become one of the wealthiest institutions and the main beneficiary of 'criminal privatization'.[99]

Since Tudjman's time, Glas koncila [Voice of the Council], which is the Church's semi-official newspaper, publishes revisionist articles and interviews about the Holocaust and readers' letters to the editor. Sometimes even editorials and columns "entail attacks on Jews, freemasons, communists, homosexuals, Serbs, and antifascist Croats." The Church officially registered and financed in 2015 the association "The Triple Myth of Jasenovac," which is led by a senior Catholic cleric. Arguing that the Jasenovac concentration camp, operated in the period of World War II and run by the Croatian fascist Ustasha regime where hundreds of thousands of Serb, and tens of thousands of Jewish, Roma, and Croatian anti-fascist victims were tortured and

---

[90] Radio Free Europe/Radio Liberty (December 8, 2005), Fugitive Croatian General Gotovina Arrested In Spain, Radio Free Europe/Radio Liberty.

[91] Marlise Simons (April 15, 2011), Croatian Generals Guilty of War Crimes, The New York Times.

[92] BBC (September 20, 2005), War crimes chief accuses Vatican, BBC News.

[93] See e.g. VOA (October 31, 2009), Vatican Needs to Help Find War Crimes Suspect, says UN Prosecutor, VOA News.

[94] VOA (October 31, 2009), Vatican Needs to Help Find War Crimes Suspect, says UN Prosecutor, VOA News.

[95] BBC (September 20, 2005), War crimes chief accuses Vatican, BBC News.

[96] Patrick Moore (September 21, 2005), Croatia: Hague Prosecutor Says Vatican Is Shielding Top War Crimes Fugitive, Radio Free Europe/Radio Liberty.

[97] Julian Borger (November 16, 2012), War crimes convictions of two Croatian generals overturned, The Guardian.

[98] Vjekoslav Perica (2015), Power, Corruption and Dissent: V , Corruption and Dissent: Varieties of Contempor arieties of Contemporary Croatian Political Catholicism, Occasional Papers on Religion in Eastern Europe, Volume 35, Issue 4, Article 2, p. 7.

[99] Ibid, p. 9; citing "Ailing Croatia: A Mighty Mess. Croatia is the EU's Newest Basket Case." The Economist, July 26, 2014.

murdered is "a myth, an anti-Croat conspiracy plotted by Serbs, Jews, and communists," is the mission of that association.[100]

---

[100] Ibid, p. 11.

CHAPTER
6

War on terror: the U.S.-Vatican crusade against Islam

George W. Bush and the extreme Christian right in the U.S.
On May 5, 1903, Archbishop Quigley stated in *The Chicago Daily Tribune*: "When the United States rules the world, the Catholic church will rule the world."[1] That was then the thinking of many sectors of the American clergy since the 19th and early 20th centuries.

The warning of Christian fascism was described by Chris Hedges when he referred to the warnings of Dr. James Luther Adams, professor of ethics at Harvard Divinity School who was in Germany in 1935 and 1936 and experienced Nazism firsthand:

"The warning came at the moment Pat Robertson and other radio and televangelists began speaking about a new political reli· gion that would direct its efforts at taking control of all institutions, including mainstream denominations and the government. Its stated goal was to use the United States to create a global Christian empire. It was hard, at the time, to take such fantastic rhetoric seriously, especially given the buffoonish quality of leaders in the Christian Right who expounded it. But Adams warned us against the blindness caused by intellectual snobbery. The Nazis, he said, were not going to return with swastikas and brown shirts. Their ideological inheritors in America had found a mask for fascism in patriotism and the pages of the Bible."[2]

In early 2000, the U.S. House of Representatives was in need of a new chaplain, selecting three finalists from among 50 candidates proposed by a bipartisan commission - as G. Edward Reid comments. House Speaker Dennis Hastert, as well as Majority Leader Dick Armey, secured the appointment of the Presbyterian Reverend Charles Wright, but according to *Time magazine* of March 6, 2000, in doing so, they passed over the committee's favorite: Catholic priest Timothy O'Brien. The Catholic Church reacted by accusing Hastert of bigotry and prejudice of an anti-Catholic nature; and as a result, according to the Catholic weekly *Our Sunday Visitor* of April 9, it was reported that in the face of such accusations, Republican leaders decided to appoint Catholic priest Daniel Coughlin.[3] Thus, pressure from the American Catholic Church bore fruit in the House of Representatives.

---

[1] Archbishop James Edward Quigley (May 5, 1903), Quigley as an Optimist, The Chicago Daily Tribune, Volume LXIL.-No. 125, p. 1.

[2] Chris Hedges, American Fascists: The Christian Right and the War On America (Free Press, New York, 2006), p. 194.

[3] G. Edward Reid (Fall, 2001), The Nearness of the Second Coming, Adventists Affirm, Vol. 15, No. 3, ob. cit.

In another development, on May 24 of that same year, Congressman Chris Smith introduced legislation to award the Congressional Gold Medal to Pope John Paul II, which passed the House and Senate in early July. On the 27th of the same month, President Bill Clinton signed the measure, and it was reported in January 2001 that more than a dozen members of Congress and Chaplain Daniel Coughlin would present the medal to the pope at the Vatican on the 8th of that month.[4]

It was July 2000, and the House of Representatives voted 416 to 1 to maintain a strong Vatican voice at the United Nations, against some 370 international family planning groups that sought to reduce the Vatican's influence at the body. Congress did not stand idly by as hundreds of organizations rammed the Vatican, as *The Washington Times* reported.[5] Dick Armey, a Texas Republican and House Majority Leader, said after the vote:

"The Vatican is under attack by pro-abortion extremists, and Congress will not let the attack continue unanswered...we will not tolerate this effort to silence the Vatican."[6]

Another Republican, Christopher H. Smith of New Jersey, said, "If anything, the Holy See deserves a more prominent role at the U.N."[7]

Frances Kissling, president of Catholics for a Free Choice, also spoke out:

"The question of the appropriate role for the Roman Catholic Church in the U.N., whether it is called the Holy See or the Vatican, is a legitimate question of the separation of church and state that deserves serious consideration by both the United Nations and the U.S. Congress"[8]

The resurrection of the debate over what is permissible or not, in terms of religious expressions regarding members of the military corps, reappeared with great preeminence in 2000 during the U.S. presidential campaign, with Republican George W. Bush.[9]

Bush Jr. was a highly controversial U.S. president (2001-2008). He was widely criticized for his ultra-right-wing Christian policies, the invasion of Iraq (2003-2011), and other far-reaching issues.

During the presidential primaries, candidates from both parties courted the Catholic vote, although Arizona Senator John McCain accused Governor George W. Bush of Texas, of being anti-Catholic because he gave a speech at Bob Jones University in South Carolina, considered a staunchly anti-Catholic Protestant institution of higher learning. Bush felt very sensitive to the criticism, so he was considering prominent Catholics as running mates, including Governor Frank Keating of Oklahoma, and Governor Tom Ridge of Pennsylvania.[10]

---

[4] Ibid.

[5] (July 12, 2000), House votes 416-1 for strong Vatican voice in U.N., The Washington Times.

[6] Ibid.

[7] Ibid.

[8] Ibid.

[9] James E. Parco, PhD (February, 2013), For God and Country: Religious Fundamentalism in the U.S. Military, Center for Inquiry Office of Public Policy, pp. 2, 3.

[10] The Washington Times (July 12, 2000), House votes 416-1 for strong Vatican voice in U.N., The Washington Times.

As for the group that led him to be elected president in the 2000 election, *Chuch and State* documents that on September 13, 1997, state leaders of the Christian Coalition of America held a closed-door breakfast in Atlanta. The well-known Christian leader Pat Robertson, "offered a detailed "game plan" for delivering the White House to a hand-picked Christian Coalition GOP candidate in the year 2000." [...] "We're not a bunch of ingenues anymore, we're a seasoned group of warriors," he said. "And we have to know what we're dealing with. We can't be swayed just by rhetoric.... I told [new Coalition President] Don Hodel when he joined us, I said, 'My dear friend, I want to hold out to you the possibility of selecting the next president of the United States because I think that's what we have in this organization.' And I believe we can indeed." [...] "According to Robertson, the nation faces the threat of annihilation by God due to legal abortion. The only way to save the country from God's wrath, he added, is for the Christian Coalition to elect a president who will implement the organization's agenda." [...] We just tell these guys, Look, we put you in power in 1994, and we want you to deliver,'" observed Robertson. "'We're tired of temporizing. Don't give us all this stuff about you've got a different agenda. This is your agenda. This is what you're going to do this year. And we're going to hold your feet to the fire while you do it.'" Someone presented at the meeting recorded Robertson's speech and made it public.[11]

Before Bush became president, his former political advisor, Karl Rove, invited Catholic intellectuals to Texas to enlighten Bush on Church teaching.[12]

The media announced that Al Gore, candidate for the Democratic Party, had won the majority of the votes in Florida, a state that would define the elections.[13] However, Fox News announced that Bush won the majority of votes in that state, something that was communicated to the network by John Ellis, who was in charge of the decision table that night at Fox and who was Bush's first cousin. It also helped that Jeb Bush, brother of the Republican candidate, was the governor of Florida.

George W.'s campaign chairwoman was also in charge of the vote count; and her state hired a firm that would remove from the rolls voters who were not likely to vote for him: the black community. George Bush Sr. also enlisted the help of his friends on the Supreme Court, who ruled in Bush's favor. Gore disagreed, but accepted the Supreme Court's decision, despite numerous independent investigations that showed he had won in Florida. Many congressmen complained about it on the day the election results were to be certified, but they were not supported by any senator.

Michael Northcott explains that Bush's victory in the 2000 presidential election was due to the millions of conservative Christians who voted for him as the chosen candidate of the Christian Right, and whose central moral concerns were abortion, family values, and Israel.[14]

---

[11] Rob Boston and Joseph Conn (October 1, 1997), Boss Pat: comparing the Christian Coalition to the Tammany Hall political machine, Pat Robertson shares with top lieutenants his secret 'game plan' for taking the White House and ruling America, Church and State, pp. 4-9.

[12] Malcolm Moore (June 13, 2008), George W Bush meets Pope amid claims he might convert to Catholicism, The Telegraph.

[13] Agnès Mentre, Bob Weinstein, Harvey Weinstein (Producer) Michael Moore (Director) (2004), Fahrenheit 9/11 (With Dog Eat Dog Films, Fellowship Adventure Group). Note: unless otherwise noted, this is the same source.

[14] Michael Northcott, An Angel Directs the Storm: Apocalyptic Religion and American Empire (I.B. Tauris & Co Ltd, New York, 2004), p. 2.

However, the electoral votes of the highly Catholic states of Pennsylvania, Ohio, Michigan, and Illinois cannot be overlooked. The Republican National Committee's Catholic Task Force, formed in 1996, was revitalized in February 1999, one year before the U.S. presidential election. That Catholic committee was chaired by Jim Nicholson, a businessman whom Bush himself later selected as U.S. ambassador to the Vatican. The Task Force planned to make use of an article that appeared in *Crisis Magazine*, written by pollster Steve Wagner, which was based on polls conducted by Robert P. George, the Princeton University political scientist who served on the board of directors of the IRD, the EPPC, the Catholic League for Religious and Civil Rights, and the anti-gay Alliance for Marriage. George became a regular advisor to George Bush on Supreme Court nominations, stem cell research, and the faith-based initiative.[15]

Returning to Nicholson, he was the chairman of the Republican National Committee (1996-2000) who orchestrated the election of Bush.[16] During an interview with *Inside the Vatican*, Nicholson referred to the interests of the Church and the U.S. government when he stated, "The values of this [the Bush] Administration and those of the Vatican line up hand in glove."[17]

Ed Gillespie, former chief operating officer of Bush's Republican National Committee as well as head of Enron, also a far-right Catholic, singled out Robert P. George and others for instructing Bush on how to "speak Catholic."[18] *Crisis Magazine* indicated that "If there really is a vast, right-wing conspiracy, its leaders probably meet in George's basement."[19]

"Priests, bishops, archbishops and cardinals aligned themselves with, and curried friendship with, Task Force members although the Task Force declared itself blatantly partisan and its goal as strictly political. It was what it claimed to be: "A leadership of dedicated lay Catholic Republicans whose mission is to influence the Catholic vote in favor of Republican candidates in 2000."[20]

As Michael Lind, Whitehead's senior fellow at the New America Foundation would say in an article in *The Daily Beast*:

"The battle in Washington is not between liberals and conservatives; it is between the Union and the South. [...] The rest of the country needs to understand [...] Its [of the Republican Party] spiritual ancestors are the old states' rights Southern conservative Democrats [...]."[21]

---

[15] Betty Clermont, The Neo-Catholics: Implementing Christian Nationalism in America (Clarity Press, 2009), ob. cit.

[16] G. Edward Reid, JD, MDiv, MPH (Fall 2005), The Papacy and American Politics, Adventists Affirm, Vol. 19, No. 3, ob. cit.

[17] Ibid., citing Inside the Vatican (Urbi et Orbi Communications, December 2001), pp. 24, 25.

[18] Betty Clermont, The Neo-Catholics: Implementing Christian Nationalism in America (Clarity Press, 2009), ob. cit.

[19] Ibid; citing Max Blumental, quoted by Rev. Andrew J. Weaver, Ph.D., "Neocon Catholics target mainline Protestants" Media Transparency, August 11, 2006:
http://mediatransparency.org/storyprinterfriendly.php?storyID=142

[20] Ibid.; quoting Frances Kissling, "Is God a Republican" Religion News Service: http://www.beliefnet.com/story/21/story_2166.html.

[21] Michael Lind (January 29, 2009), The South Vs. Obama, The Daily Beast.

The reader should know that the Confederates in the South (a historical link Lind makes in his article) were mostly Catholic and that they temporarily enjoyed the support of the Holy See.

The New York Times referred to the importance Bush placed on his Catholic electorate:

"This year [2000], spurred by an unexpectedly contentious Republican primary, the nation is witnessing a 180-degree turn on the historic Kennedy confrontation. This time, it is a worried Protestant candidate from Texas, Gov. George W. Bush, who is now daily seeking out Catholic forums and photo ops, replete with church banners and Roman-collared clerics, to assure one and all his presidency would not be an instrument of a dominant religious group -- evangelical Protestantism."[22]

Several Catholic prelates lined up and showed their support for Bush, and when he visited churches in Philadelphia, Tierney (a knight of the papal order of St. Gregory the Great), listed the names of three million Catholics for a direct political campaign by mail and phone.[23]

By the end of September, Bush met with Cardinal Roger Mahoney of Los Angeles; and in October he had a private meeting with Cardinal Edward Egan, who nine days later issued a pastoral letter urging Catholics to vote for those "who share our commitment to the fundamental rights of the unborn." On October 26, Bush met with the then Bishop of Pittsburgh, Bishop Donald Wuerl... and then finally met with a dozen bishops during the presidential campaign.[24]

Before winning the race for the White House, Bush confessed that he believed he had been divinely chosen to serve his country in some moment of great crisis, when he said, "I feel like God wants me to run for president. I can't explain it, but I sense my country is going to need me. Something is going to happen. And at that time my country will need me."[25]

George W. Bush began serving as president and by then, *Christianity Today* magazine published a *Religion News Service* article on February 5, 2001, indicating that Catholics were still the largest bloc in Congress (since 1964). By then, of the 535 members of the 107th Congress, 150 were Catholic, including 91 Democrats and 59 Republicans. Baptists and Methodists followed, and these in turn were followed by other religious denominations.[26]

On January 29, 2001, Bush established the Office of Faith-Based Initiatives within the White House, which was part of the Executive Office of the President.[27] This initiative aims to strengthen faith- and community-based organizations to expand their

---

[22] Francis X. Clines (March 5, 2000), "The Nation: Cross Purposes; Mixing God and Politics And Getting Burned," New York Times.

[23] Betty Clermont, The Neo-Catholics: Implementing Christian Nationalism in America (Clarity Press, 2009), ob. cit.

[24] Ibid.; citing Miller, supra note 4.

[25] Michael Northcott, An Angel Directs the Storm: Apocalyptic Religion and American Empire (I.B. Tauris & Co Ltd, New York, 2004), p. 3; citing Stephen Mansfield, The Faith of George W. Bush (Lake Mary, FL: Charisma House, 2003), pp. 85 - 6 and 92 - 6.

[26] Religions News Service (Feb. 5, 2001), Catholics Remain Largest Bloc in Congress, Christianity Today.

[27] Michael Northcott, An Angel Directs the Storm: Apocalyptic Religion and American Empire (I.B. Tauris & Co Ltd, New York, 2004), p. 3; citing Stephen Mansfield, The Faith of George W. Bush (Lake Mary, FL: Charisma House, 2003), pp. 85 - 6 and 92 - 6.

capacity to provide federally funded social services, although it cannot be used to support inherently religious activities, such as prayer, religious instruction, and proselytizing. Still, it remains a two-edged sword, which is why organizations such as Americans United for Separation of Church and State and the American Civil Liberties Union claim that the organization violates the Establishment Clause because it uses tax dollars to fund religion.

Deal Hudson, Washington's most influential Catholic, wrote in a November 2003 newsletter to supporters that he continued to lead an informal advisory group of White House Catholics, as well as communicate with White House staff almost daily regarding appointments, policy, and events, whose efforts had helped place faithful and informed Catholics in influential positions.[28] Every Thursday morning, Hudson met with Tim Goeglin (Karl Rove's assistant), to hold a conference discussing Catholic issues such as faith-based initiatives, educational vouchers, judicial nominations, abortion, gay marriage, and stem cell research.[29] In December and January, Hudson attended meetings at the White House, helping to advance the National Republican "Catholic Outreach" Committee.[30]

But another bloc of the Christian right supported the Bush administration, and on September 7-8, 2001, Christian Churches Together in the United States began a meeting of church leaders exploring the need to expand fellowship, unity, and witness among diverse expressions of faith; such as historic Protestant, African-American, Roman Catholic, Pentecostal, Evangelical, and Orthodox churches, to "strengthen their unity in Christ and empower their mission." They held another meeting on April 4-6, 2002 in Chicago to further explore and have a broader participation of other church leaders from different churches. It was there that the vision of the organization was realized.

At a meeting on January 29, 2003, leaders of 46 churches from numerous denominations and parachurch agencies across the country gathered on the campus of Fuller Theological Seminary in Pasadena, California, where they initiated a constitution for the organization, intended to bring together virtually every religious group in the country. The Catholic Church officially joined the ecumenical movement on November 17, 2004.

When Bush was re-elected president that year, Bob Jones III, president of the South Carolina university of the same name founded by his grandfather to foster a "Christ-like" character, said:

"Don't equivocate. Put your agenda on the front burner and let it boil. You owe the liberals nothing."[31]

The Peruvian-Spanish Vaticanist Eric Frattini, whose book The Entity: Five Centuries of Secret Vatican Espionage was given pride of place by CIA revisionists in

---

[28] Betty Clermont, The Neo-Catholics: Implementing Christian Nationalism in America (Clarity Press, 2009), ob. cit.

[29] Ibid.

[30] Ibid.

[31] Karen Tumulty and Matthew Cooper (February 7, 2005), Does Bush Owe the Religious Right?, Time Magazine.

2010,[32] knew that the campaign for Bush during the US election was a goal of the Vatican espionage service, known as "The Entity."[33]

Since 2003, in particular, the United States has come to regard the Vatican as the most important global entity for the progress of the world to come.

Indeed, the United States, under the leadership of George W. Bush, decided to formalize an important alliance with the Vatican as the most significant confederation in the field.

In a cable entitled "Partners for Progress-Working with Vatican Development Agencies" dated January 24, 2003, the U.S. Embassy at the Vatican warned that the United States and the Vatican are in agreement regarding their opposition to liberation theology.[34]

In the summary of the document, the U.S. Embassy acknowledges:

"The Holy See, Catholic dioceses worldwide, affiliated NGO's and Catholic religious orders are significant, if often overlooked, players in international development and humanitarian relief efforts. The Catholic Church is in effect the world's largest international development agency: some four million lay people, sisters, monks, priests and bishops working in various forms of development activity make a contribution worth billions of dollars in hospitals, schools, universities, technical, agricultural and vocational facilities, and social development centers throughout the developing world. This "commitment to Justice" is deeply rooted in the church's social doctrine, which has been expanded and intensified in the post-Vatican II period when the Church first linked world peace to human development. For the Holy See, the inherent and inalienable dignity of the human person forms the core of its development policy; people matter, and their spiritual, social and physical well-being is at the heart of the Holy See's approach to foreign policy."[35]

That diplomatic cable praises the work of orders such as the Jesuits, Franciscans, and Dominicans, and national bishops' conferences around the world that engage in development projects "often in collaboration with UN agencies and international NGOs."

Also, in a section labeled "Sensitive," "Implement the Holy See's development across the globe" is documented under "Partners in Progress - Working with Vatican Development Agencies." This is done through collaboration with various religious orders and semi-official bodies such as Caritas International, the Sant'Egidio Community, and private agencies. It also highlights the partnerships the Holy See has formed with UN agencies and other secular international organizations, as well as national governments to address poverty, underdevelopment, refugee crises, pandemics, and famine. The role of the Pontifical Council for Justice and Peace, which fosters the development of needy regions and promotes social justice internationally, is nuanced and includes social work, international relations, development policy, and

---

[32] Studies in Intelligence, vol. 54, no. 4 (December 2010) - CIA, p. 62.

[33] (October 26, 2004), Murders, arms sales or financing of dictatorships, targets of the Vatican Espionage Service according to a book, Europa Press.

[34] Partners for Progress-Working with Vatican Development Agencies: 03Vatican283_a (January 24, 2003): https://wikileaks.org/plusd/cables/03VATICAN283_a.html Accessed March 5, 2024. Note: unless otherwise indicated, this is the same source.

[35] Ibid.

social development. It also promotes reflection on economic and financial systems, including the impact of globalization. It is documented that the Council also addresses environmental and natural resource issues. It addresses issues related to war, disarmament and arms trafficking, international security, and violence in all its manifestations - including terrorism and xenophobia. It discusses how the Catholic Church and the State can work together in a "balanced" way.

With this background in mind, under the (Bush) administration, in June 2005, the Supreme Court fractured in its struggle to define a constitutional framework for government display of religious symbols, upholding the installation of a six-foot tall monument with the Ten Commandments inscribed on the capitol grounds in Texas, while copies of that inscription on the walls of two Kentucky courthouses were unconstitutional.[36]

The question to be decided was whether any such display violated the First Amendment's prohibition against the "establishment" of an official religion. The Supreme Court was left to face with suspicion and distaste any new case that might seek to advance a modern religious agenda.

Justice Sandra Day O'Connor, who held both cases to be unconstitutional, indicated that the country was correct in upholding religion as:

"a matter for the individual conscience, not for the prosecutor or bureaucrat." She added: "Those who would renegotiate the boundaries between church and state must therefore answer a difficult question: why would we trade a system that has served us so well for one that has served others so poorly"

For his part, Justice Antonin Scalia accused the majority of manifesting hostility against religion, and of deviating from the intentions of the framers of the Constitution by stating that, "Nothing stands behind the court's assertion that governmental affirmation of the society's belief in God is unconstitutional except the court's own say-so."

Scalia notes that the people's willingness to accept his interpretation of the Constitution as final is greater than that of the democratically elected branches.

Among those who accepted the Ten Commandments monument stay were then-Supreme Court Justice William H. Rehnquist, Justice Breyer, Antonin Scalia himself, Anthony M. Kennedy, and Clarence Thomas. Rehnquist stressed that although the Ten Commandments are religious, they have a valuable secular quality that does not violate the Establishment Clause. This, even though Justices John Paul Stevens, Ruth Bader Ginsburg, and Souter and O'Connor were the dissenters in the case.

Justice Stevens indicated that the Ten Commandments are inherently religious and that their display in Texas provided the message that "this state endorses the divine code of the Judeo-Christian God."

Carlton W. Veazey stated in his article, "On the Brink of 'Theocracy,'" in a 2005 edition of Voice of Reason (the fact sheet for Americans on religious liberty about that case), the following:

---

[36] Linda Greenhouse (June 28, 2005), Justices Allow a Commandments Display, Bar Others, The New York Times. Note: unless otherwise noted, it is the same source.

"Progressives who think warnings about "theocracy" are an exaggeration should take a closer look at "Justice Sunday: Filibustering People of Faith," the Christian Right telethon headlined by Senate Majority Leader William Frist. Envision the carefully designed image that the far-right Family Research Council, the main organizer of the April 24 event, beamed into conservative churches across the country: a political rally from a large, comfortable mega-church in Louisville, with a middle-class audience listening with rapt attention to political operatives who self-identify as religious leaders-and at the bottom of the screen, streaming video with the photos, names and phone numbers of targeted U.S. senators. The visual message was clear: the church is dominant over the state and senators should toe the line on eliminating the filibuster and confirming Bush judges or pay the price."[37]

The Ten Commandments Commission (TCC) was formed in 2005.[38] Its main purpose "is to rally public officials, community leaders, international diplomats, and grassroots activists to instill Judeo-Christian values in society." They are made up of some of the largest ministries in the country. The First Annual Ten Commandments Day was held on May 7, 2006, when thousands of churches and synagogues celebrated the Ten Commandments by discussing their importance in society. On that day, a national broadcast was organized by many of the member ministry organizations.

The event was held on the first Sunday of May each year. The TCC and the event also aim to use the Supreme Court's rulings on the removal of the Ten Commandments from public places to reverse that situation. United under a vast number of conservative groups. TCC believes that they cannot be passive bystanders and watch the removal of the principles that made the United States of America great. For, "The Ten Commandments are the heart of all moral code and must be restored to the heart of our society." Thus, they believe the nation must be under God.

"House Resolution 598 was championed by representative Akin (R-MS) and co-signed by 30 more members of congress, in support of the goals of the Ten Commandments Commission as the corner stone of western law. The Resolution is pending a vote in the House. Senate Resolution 453 was carried by senator Lieberman (IND-CN) and Senator Brownback(R-KN), support the Ten Commandments Commission, and proclaims the Ten Commandments Weekend as the first weekend in the month of May of each year."

The petition is dated March 13, 2008.
TCC had on the Advisory & Support Board: "Mrs. Roberta Combs, Christian Coalition, Washington, DC, Dr. James Dobson, Focus on the Family, Rev. Jerry Falwell, Liberty Alliance, Dr. D. James Kennedy, Mr. William Murray, Religious Freedom Coalition, Rev. Pat Robertson, Christian Broadcasting Network, Dr. Rick Scarborough, Vision America, Dr. Fredrick Price, Judge Roy Moore, Pastor Rod

---

[37] Reverend Carlton W. Veazey (2005), On the Brink of 'Theocracy', Voice of Reason, No. 3 [92], p. 8.
[38] Who we are: Ten Commandments Commission A Judeo-Christian Initiative for a Better Tomorrow:http://www.tencommandmentsday.com/index55.html?http%3A//www.tencommandmentsday.com/who_we_are.html; accessed January 18, 2017. Note: unless otherwise noted, this is the same source.

Parsley, Center of Moral Clarity, Pastor Tommy Barnett, The Dream Center." Not to mention the enormous number of members on other committees of the organization.[39]

Of the members quoted above, Rod Parsley is a fanatical Christian who said of Islam, "The fact is that America was founded, in part, with the intention of seeing this false religion destroyed, and I believe September 11, 2001, was a generational call to arms that we can no longer ignore."[40]

Also, a few weeks after Pope Benedict XVI was elected, President George W. Bush and Archbishop Charles Chaput of Colorado addressed the Second National Catholic Prayer Breakfast on May 20, 2005. Both praised Pope Benedict XVI and politicians who adhered to Catholic doctrine, primarily because the pope spoke with affection for the American model of freedom, as Bush put it.[41]

For his part, Chaput pointed out that faith must affect the nation's political decisions and that Catholics must work to prevent religion from being banished from public discourse since the major task of Catholics is the renewal of American public life.[42]

Not for nothing, *The New York Times* stated that the "New Pope Could Influence Political Life in America."[43]

Time Magazine published an article in 2005 underlining that Bush was acting on behalf of the Christian Right.[44]

The U.S. president, in his attempt to "Christianize" the nation, chose the Catholic John Roberts as the new chief justice of the Supreme Court[45] thus supplanting Rehnquist, when he took office on September 29 of the same year (2005).

Bush would choose another conservative Roman Catholic judge to serve on the Supreme Court, namely Samuel Alito. These moves were influenced by conservative Christian Majority Leader Jerry Falwell and others. On April 18, 2007, the Supreme Court voted 5-4 in favor of banning partial-birth abortion in the country.[46]

Consider this, in light of the fact that the Supreme Court would later be composed of 4 Catholics out of 9 justices.[47]

And all this occurred, in a decade when Republicans won a majority in Congress for the first time in 40 years; something credited to half of the congress members by the votes of conservative Christians.[48]

George W. Bush, in his remarks to cardinals, bishops, and Catholic leaders at the White House on March 21, 2001, said of Pope Wojtyla: "The best way to honor Pope

---

[39] Ten Commandments Commission Boards of Members & Supporters:
http://www.tencommandmentsday.com/index55.html?http%3A//www.tencommandmentsday.com/support.html; accessed January 18, 2017.

[40] David Corn (March 12, 2008), McCain's Spiritual Guide: Destroy Islam, Mother Jones.

[41] G. Edward Reid, JD, MDiv, MPH (Fall 2005), The Papacy and American Politics, Adventists Affirm, Vol. 19, No. 3, ob. cit.

[42] Ibid.

[43] Adam Nagourney (April 4, 2005), New Pope Could Influence Political Life in America, The New York Times.

[44] Karen Tumulty and Matthew Cooper (February 7, 2005), Does Bush Owe the Religious Right, Time.

[45] Jody Gottlieb (Director). Jen Christensen (Producer) (2007), God's Warriors. CNN Presents, United States.

[46] Ibid.

[47] G. Edward Reid, JD, MDiv, MPH (Fall 2005), The Papacy and American Politics, Adventists Affirm, Vol. 19, No. 3, ob. cit.

[48] Jody Gottlieb (director). Jen Christensen (producer) (2007), God's Warriors. CNN Presents, United States.

John Paul II, truly one of the great men, is to take his teaching seriously, is to listen to his words and put his words and teachings into action here in America. This is a challenge we must accept."[49]

Bush gave a speech at the dedication of the John Paul II Cultural Center in Washington D.C. on March 22, 2001.[50] He quoted positively the words of Gorbachev when he said that John Paul II was "the highest moral authority on earth."[51] This was also reflected in Bush's own words on the death of the pope:

"Laura and I join people across the Earth in mourning the passing of Pope John Paul II. The Catholic Church has lost its shepherd. The world has lost a champion of human freedom, and a good and faithful servant of God has been called home.

Pope John Paul II left the throne of Saint Peter in the same way he ascended to it, as a witness to the dignity of human life. In his native Poland, that witness launched a democratic revolution that swept Eastern Europe and changed the course of history. Throughout the West, John Paul's witness reminded us of our obligation to build a culture of life in which the strong protect the weak. And during the Pope's final years, his witness was made even more powerful by his daily courage in the face of illness and great suffering.

All Popes belong to the world, but Americans had special reason to love the man from Krakow. In his visits to our country, the Pope spoke of our "providential" Constitution, the self-evident truths about human dignity in our Declaration, and the "blessings of Liberty" that follow from them. "It is these truths," he said, "that have led people all over the world to look to America with hope and respect."

Pope John Paul II was, himself, an inspiration to millions of Americans and to so many more throughout the world. We will always remember the humble, wise, and fearless priest who became one of history's great moral leaders. We're grateful to God for sending such a man, a son of Poland, who became the Bishop of Rome and a hero for the ages."[52]

Many countries of the world expressed their appreciation and praise to John Paul II on the occasion of his death. Kings, queens, prime ministers, and presidents from over 100 countries attended his funeral. Even Prince Charles of Great Britain postponed his wedding to attend the funeral. The U.S. delegation included President George Bush, his wife Laura, former President George H. W. Bush, former President Bill Clinton, and Secretary of State Condoleezza Rice. That delegation was given preferential seating at one wing of Wojtyla's remains, one day before his funeral, and kneeling before the body in prayer (Bush Sr. and Bill Clinton did not do so). Nearly four million people

---

[49] Weekly Compilation of Presdential Documents (Monday, March 26, 2001), Vol. 37, Number 12, p. 483.

[50] (March 28, 2001), President Bush's Address at the Dedication of the John Paul II Cultural Center, Catholic Exchange; Weekly Compilation of Presdential Documents (Monday, March 26, 2001), Vol. 37, Number 12, p. 490.

[51] (March 28, 2001), President Bush's Address at the Dedication of the John Paul II Cultural Center, Catholic Exchange.

[52] John Esterbrook (April 2, 2005), Bush: Pope 'Hero For The Ages, AP, CBS News. See also George W. Bush, Book 1: January 1 to June 30, 2005 (United States Government Printing Office, Washington: 2007), p. 550.

from all over the world attended, making it the largest funeral in history, with an estimated two billion people watching the event on television.[53]

The organizer of the funeral, Bishop Renato Boccardo, noted, "When they all knelt in front of the pope, I thought, those who are leading the world, they are kneeling in front of this poor man [...] He didn't have military forces or money or power, but those who are leading the World, are here recognizing the grandezza (the greatness) of the man."[54]

George Bush has been the U.S. president with the most meetings with popes. He met John Paul II on three occasions: July 23, 2001; May 28, 2002; and June 4, 2004, all at the Vatican.[55] On that last occasion, Bush presented the pope with the Medal of Freedom on behalf of the United States,[56] and where he stated in part:

"Your Holiness, thank you very much for receiving Laura and me and our delegation. I bring greetings from our country, where you are respected, admired, and greatly loved. I also bring a message from my Government that says to you, sir, we will work for human liberty and human dignity, in order to spread peace and compassion, that we appreciate the strong symbol of freedom that you have stood for, and we recognize the power of freedom to change societies and to change the world."[57]

Bush also met with Benedict XVI: on June 9, 2007 (at the Vatican); on April 15 and 16, 2008 in Washington D.C. (where his birthday was celebrated); and on June 13 of the same year, at the Vatican.[58] It should be noted that on the occasion of Pope Benedict's visit to the United States, Bush had never met any other leader at any of the nation's airports: only Pope Benedict XVI.[59] In 2012, the pontiff became one of the ten most admired personalities by Americans.[60]

First Lady Laura Bush paid him a visit on February 9, 2006, at the Vatican.[61]

The religious climate in the United States was at its peak. Bill Moyers, in the one-hour documentary on his PBS news program Moyers on America, highlights a growing holy war within the evangelical community that was hard at work in American politics.[62]

In 2008, Rev. Jerry Falwell founded Faith and Values Coalition, which he described as a "21st century resurrection of the Moral Majority." The coalition would go on to push for pro-life judicial appointments and a federal amendment to ban same-sex marriages, as well as provoke the re-election of another conservative president in the 2008 election. It was not possible in the following two elections, although they pledged to recruit and train millions of Americans in all 50 states to become partners in the task

---

[53] G. Edward Reid, JD, MDiv, MPH (Fall 2005), The Papacy and American Politics, Adventists Affirm, Vol. 19, No. 3, ob. cit.
[54] Ibid.; citing Inside the Vatican (August-September 2005).
[55] Rachel Wellford (March 27, 2014), A history of papal visits by U.S. presidents, PBS.
[56] Records Management, White House Office of Subject Files - TR247-01 (Rome, Italy, 06/04/2004 - 06/05/2004). See letter of July 2, 2004.
[57] (June 4, 2004), Remarks by George W. Bush to John Paul II, ZENIT.
[58] Rachel Wellford (March 27, 2014), A history of papal visits by U.S. presidents, PBS.
[59] (April 14, 2008), Bush To Roll Out Red Carpet For Pope, CBSNEWS/ CBS/AP.
[60] (January 2, 2012), The Pope, among the 10 people most admired by Americans, ABC Spain.
[61] Joel Roberts (Feb. 9, 2006), Laura Bush Meets Pope Benedict, CBS News.
[62] Tom Casciato (Producer) Tom Casciato (Director) (2006), Is God Green. United States (PBS. Moyers on America).

of "bringing this nation back to the moral values of faith and family on which it was founded."[63]

Falwell further stated, "One of our primary commitments is to help make President Bush's second term the most successful in American history," Falwell said. "He will certainly need the consistent prayer and support of the evangelical community as he continues to spearhead the international war on terror and the effort to safeguard America."[64]

In "God Bless America," Vision TV's renowned Canadian documentary, it was reported that the United States wants a president who recognizes God and praises him.[65]

When President Bush met with Pope Benedict XVI at the Vatican in mid-June of that year (2008), it was rumored in Italy that he would follow in Tony Blair's footsteps by converting to Catholicism. *The Telegraph* also reported that George W. Bush repeatedly stated that he was an admirer of Benedict XVI and that he had read some of his theological books. A source close to the Vatican indicated that Bush was the most Catholic-minded president since John F. Kennedy. The U.S. president filled the White House with speechwriters and consultants of the Catholic denomination, and it was said he asked a Catholic priest to bless the West Wing.[66]

As Italian journalist Sandro Magister rightly points out:

"Bush seemed to breathe new life into the dream that had taken shape in the years of Ronald Reagan's presidency and John Paul II's first year with the collapse of the Soviet empire and the peaceful Christian revolution in Eastern Europe: a providential and lasting alliance between the Catholic Church and the United States, founded on shared values such as the defense of human life and the family, and on common geopolitical goals such as human rights, economic freedom and democracy. The U.S. cardinals and the White House enjoyed cordial relations. Bush met twice with the pope in one year. To serve as ambassador to the Holy See, the president appointed Jim Nicholson, a fervent Catholic, a gentleman from Malta, and one of the key organizers of his election victory."[67]

Henry Fairlie, a British journalist, compared in 1967 the American orientation toward the presidency to "Caesaropapism," which is defined as the union of secular and religious authority in the person of a national ruler; which system is associated with Constantine I the Great.[68] Bush was thus considered by millions of American right-wingers and ultra-right-wingers.

Time would pass... and the president would be assisted by the Bin Laden Issue Station, codenamed Alec Station, which was an organization founded by the CIA and

---

[63] Susan Jones (July 7, 2008), Reverend Jerry Falwell Planning an 'Evangelical Revolution', CNS news.
[64] Ibid.
[65] Allan Novak (Director). Cortney Pasternak (Producer) (2009), God Bless America. Vision TV Canada.
[66] Malcolm Moore (June 13, 2008), George W Bush meets Pope amid claims he might convert to Catholicism, The Telegraph.
[67] Sandro Magister (July 29, 2003), With the Pope or with Bush? "Studi Cattolici" Stands with Both, Chiesa news.
[68] Gene Healy, The Cult of the Presidency: America's Dangerous Devotion to Executive Power (Cato Institute, Washington D.C., 2008), p. 282.

FBI to track Bin Laden and his associates in the Al-Qaeda network [from 1996-2005].[69] It was named after the son of its first station chief, CIA's Michael Scheuer: being a devout Catholic and Jesuit-trained, he saw the terrorist threat in apocalyptic terms, as *The New Yorker*'s Jane Mayer noted.[70]

With all this historical framework on the then commander-in-chief of the country, as well as on several organizations, the crusade would take place...

U.S. "crusade" plans against Islam and Vatican support
It was 1999, and Pope John Paul II came under fire for his refusal to apologize for the Crusades of the thirteenth century and beyond.[71] Most of the world would believe he did so on March 12, 2000, on the "Day of Forgiveness" when he apologized to Muslims for the crusades against them; to Jews for Catholic anti-Semitism; to Orthodox Christians for the sacking of Constantinople; to Italians for Vatican associations with the Mafia; and to scientists for the persecution of Galileo. But as an official Catholic source indicated: "it is a misconception that Pope John Paul II apologized for the Crusades. He did not," since in his request for forgiveness he indicated that those enterprises were carried out by "some," but not of the hierarchy of the Catholic Church.[72]

L. Paul Bremer III, a U.S. diplomat as well as "a conservative Catholic convert [...] and was respected by right-wing evangelicals and neoconservatives alike,"[73] expressed 48 hours after the September 11, 2001 attacks, as reported by Scahill citing the Washington Post:

"Our retribution must move beyond the limp-wristed attacks of the past decade, actions that seemed designed to 'signal' our seriousness to the terrorists without inflicting real damage. Naturally, their feebleness demonstrated the opposite. This time the terrorists and their supporters must be crushed. This will mean war with one or more countries. And it will be a long war, not one of the 'Made for TV' variety. As in all wars, there will be civilian casualties. We will win some battles and lose some. More Americans will die. In the end America can and will prevail, as we always do." Bremer concluded, "[W]e must avoid a mindless search for an international 'consensus' for our actions. Today, many nations are expressing support and understanding for America's wounds. Tomorrow, we will know who our true friends are."[74]

After the attacks of September 11, 2001, Timothy A. Norton of the Lord's Day Alliance wrote in a letter dated December of the same year, that the spiritual quest of

---

[69] Peter F. Panzeri Jr, Killing Bin Laden - Operation Neptune Spear 2011 (Osprey Publishing, 2014), p. 18.
[70] Jane Mayer, The Dark Side: The Inside Story of How the War on Terror Turned Into a War on American Ideals (Double Day, 2008), ob. cit.
[71] Thomas F. Madden (November 2, 2001), Crusade propaganda, National Review.
[72] Robert Spencer (March 11, 2006), Modern Aftermath of the Crusades, Zenit.
[73] Jeremy Scahill, Blackwater: The Rise of the World's Most Powerful Mercenary Army (Serpent's Tail, London, 2008), ob. cit.
[74] Ibid, quoting L. Paul Bremer III, "Crush Them; Let Us Wage Total War on Our Foes," op-ed, Wall Street Journal, September 13, 2001.

the people given the tragic events, was the greatest opportunity to make Sunday known as the Lord's Day.[75]

In his inaugural address in response to the September 11, 2001 attacks, Bush recalled America's religious roots and called on Americans to return to the "sacred origins" and, consequently, to the "sacred calling" of their nation.[76] In Nashville, in a speech to Christian broadcasters, Bush asserted that the United States had a God-given mission to bring the divine gift of freedom "to every human being in the world."[77]

On the above, Michael Northcott said:

"For Bush, America is not only divinely chosen to be a place of safety for the persecuted from other lands, but also to be the instrument that God will use to bring liberty and democracy to the nations of the world. Instead of a refuge from the storm, America becomes the storm, threatening to visit its military might, and its unchallenged supremacy as the sole remaining superpower, on those who would resist its influence: the 'enemies of freedom'. From a liberated people America has become in Bush's mind the liberator. Instead of the plot of the Exodus from Israel Bush has adopted the plot of *Rambo* or *Terminator*."[78]

And in his inaugural address, he noted:

"We will build our defenses beyond challenge, lest weakness invite challenge. We will confront weapons of mass destruction, so that a new century is spared new horrors. The enemies of liberty and our country should make no mistake: America remains engaged in the world by history and by choice, shaping a balance of power that favors freedom. We will defend our allies and our interests. We will show purpose without arrogance. We will meet aggression and bad faith with resolve and strength. And to all nations, we will speak for the values that gave our nation birth."[79]

George W. Bush said in his speech that it is "the angel of God who directs the storm."[80] That storm would be directed by the government itself to his own country: Tom Ridge, the head of Homeland Security, a Catholic and a Knight of Columbus (an order of the Catholic Church), said that the threat of terrorism could force government planners to consider using military forces for domestic law enforcement; something sufficiently prohibited by federal law at the time.[81] He called on Congress to thoroughly review the law that prohibits the Army, Navy, Air Force, and Marines from engaging in arrests, raids, seizure of evidence, and other law enforcement-type activities on U.S. soil.[82]

---

[75] A. Norton, Timothy, Timothy A. Norton to Dear Friends of the Lord's Day Alliance. December, 2001.

[76] Michael Northcott, An Angel Directs the Storm: Apocalyptic Religion and American Empire (I.B. Tauris & Co Ltd, New York, 2004), p. 5.

[77] Ibid, pp. 5, 6; quoting Howard Fineman, 'Bush and God,' Newsweek, March 10, 2003.

[78] Ibid., p. 6.

[79] Ibid; quoting Bush, 'Inaugural Address'.

[80] Ibid.; citing Ibid.

[81] Pete Brush (June 20, 2002), Domestic Military Law Under Review, CBS News.

[82] Ibid.

The Patriot Act, which was adopted by Congress and signed by Bush six weeks after 9/11, allowed the search of medical and financial records, computer and telephone conversations, and even books checked out of the library.[83]

A year later, Bush addressed the nation and the military from the desk of the aircraft carrier Lincoln on the day victory was declared after the invasion that cost the lives of 3,000 Iraqi civilians and far more military personnel, as well as less than 150 U.S. and British troops, saying:

"Wherever you go, you carry a message of hope – a message that is ancient and ever new. In the words of the prophet Isaiah, 'To the captives, "come out" and to those in darkness "be free"'."[84]

Before the 21st century, about 40% of Americans describe themselves as evangelical Christians, while a quarter of all believe they are living in the end times.[85] For their part, evangelical Protestants supported the massive Iraq war, accounting for 77% support, versus 36% of African-American Protestants and 44% of American atheists, agnostics, or no religious preference.[86]

The invasion and occupation of Iraq by the United States in 2003 was considered by almost everyone to have no basis in international law and was treated as unjust and immoral.[87]

The CIA founded and trained a new Polish special forces unit called GROM, which was one of the first units to be in Iraq along with the CIA even before the war. A senior former Warsaw intelligence officer was awarded for, "highly sensitive and successful operations in support of Operation Iraqi Freedom, from July 2002 to Dec. 3, 2003" when the war was not supposed to have started until March of that year.[88]

Also involved were 1074 federal government organizations, and about 2000 private companies involved with counterterrorism, homeland security, and intelligence-related programs, at some 17,000 locations throughout the United States, working at the top secret classification level.[89]

Although the U.S. invasion of Iraq was supported by England, Spain, and other nations, political leaders from France, Germany, Russia, and Canada were opposed: they refused to participate in the conflict, in the pacification and reconstruction of the country after the war. John Paul II *opposed* the war, while Anglican Archbishop Rowan Williams' resistance was more genuine than his; but so did the leader of the United Methodist Church, of which then President George W. Bush was a member; as well as

---

[83] Agnès Mentre, Bob Weinstein, Harvey Weinstein (Producer) Michael Moore (Director) (2004), Fahrenheit 9/11 (With Dog Eat Dog Films, Fellowship Adventure Group).

[84] Michael Northcott, An Angel Directs the Storm: Apocalyptic Religion and American Empire (I.B. Tauris & Co Ltd, New York, 2004), p. 7; quoting George W. Bush, 'Victory Speech at the Abraham Lincoln', April, 2003.

[85] Ibid., p. Catherine Keller, Apocalypse Now and Then: A Feminist Guide to the End of the World (Boston: Beacon Press, 1996), p. 8.

[86] Youssef Bassil (November-December, 2012), The 2003 Iraq War: Operations, Causes, and Consequences, Journal of Humanities and Social Science, Volume 4, Issue 5, p. 33.

[87] Michael Northcott, An Angel Directs the Storm: Apocalyptic Religion and American Empire (I.B. Tauris & Co Ltd, New York, 2004), p. 1.

[88] Dana Priest and William Arkin, Top Secret America: The Rise of the New American Security State (Little, Brown and Company, New York, 2011), ob. cit.

[89] Ibid.

the leaders of Lutheranism, most of the Presbyterian churches, as well as most of the world communions such as the Baptists and the Orthodox. Yet millions of American Christians, as was the case with Southern Baptists, fast-growing conservative churches, and suburban mega-churches, did support the war.[90]

Almost everyone knows today, after the tragic events of September 11, 2001, that George Bush sold the public a story that was far from credible; namely, that Saddam Hussein backed Al Qaeda and had weapons of mass destruction.[91] That was all a fabrication by a German whose intelligence source code name was Curveball (his real name was Rafid Ahmed Alwan al-Janabi), who was really an Iraqi living in Germany who peddled the story about Saddam Hussein's biological weapons and influenced the U.S. government, something he admitted to making up when in 2011 *The Guardian* published his confession.[92]

But how did the Catholic Church and the Vatican in the United States intervene in the whole situation?

Richard John Neuhaus, a theologian and Jesuit priest, and political analyst, along with Michael Novak, a theology graduate of the Pontifical Gregorian University in Rome, were two of Bush's various spiritual guides in the White House. Novak traveled to the Vatican before the Iraq war to present the theological justifications for Bush's decision to launch an attack on the Muslim world (Iraq, momentarily). For his part, Richard John Neuhaus needed Avery Dulles, a Jesuit who became a cardinal in 2001, as a collaborator: both were known to have broad anti-Islamic roots.[93]

On the side of the U.S. Conference of Catholic Bishops, there were two varying statements: the first on September 13, as recorded in a letter to President Bush:

"We conclude, based on the facts that are known to us, that a preemptive, unilateral use of force is difficult to justify at this time. We fear that resort to force, under these circumstances, would not meet the strict conditions in Catholic teaching for overriding the strong presumption against the use of military force. Of particular concern are the traditional just war criteria of just cause, right authority, probability of success, proportionality and noncombatant immunity."[94]

This contrasts with the opinions expressed by the Conference of Bishops in addressing the nation's actions under just war criteria based on natural law on September 13, 2002, and January 12, 2007.[95] Archbishop Edwin O'Brien, head of the Archdiocese for the Military Services of the United States, noted that, "It was the opinion of the USCCB that given the complexity of the countless elements and arguments on either side, people of good faith could arrive at differing conclusions as

---

[90] Michael Northcott, An Angel Directs the Storm: Apocalyptic Religion and American Empire (I.B. Tauris & Co Ltd, New York, 2004), p. 1.

[91] Ibid., pp. 1, 2.

[92] Dana Priest and William Arkin, Top Secret America: The Rise of the New American Security State (Little, Brown and Company, New York, 2011), ob. cit.

[93] Abid Ullah Jan, Afghanistan-The Genesis of the Final Crusade (Pragmatic Publishing, Ottawa, Canada, 2006), pp. 42, 43.

[94] Bishop Gregory, Wilton D. Letter to President Bush Regarding Iraq, September 13, 2002. The White House. September 13, 2002.

[95] Edwin F. O'Brien (June, 2007) A message: During this time of continuing conflict, The Catholic Herald.

to the moral justification of our armed interventions."[96] Most of the bishops, according to the *National Catholic Reporter*, "supported Catholic participation in the war to avoid even the appearance of being unpatriotic or not supportive of the troops."[97] George Weigel, the renowned American Catholic neoconservative author, political analyst, and social activist, "was a charter signatory of the Project for the New American Century, which anticipated the need for something like 9/11 that would serve as another Pearl Harbor and galvanize the country behind the neoconservative agenda. He has long understood how important Catholic support is for the multiple wars the project believed would have to be waged to maintain U.S. dominance in the world."[98]

For their part, among the sixty most influential Americans who signed the "letter From America" shortly after the attacks were the famous Catholics Novak, Weigel, Mary Ann Glendon, and others: a letter that sought to justify the war against Afghanistan.[99]

However, Wayne Madsen, an investigative journalist and former National Security Agency intelligence officer, indicated that sources close to the Vatican indicated that Pope John Paul II wished he were younger and in better health to confront the possibility that Bush was the person prophesied in the book of Revelation. The pope also suspected -according to journalists close to the Vatican- that the Bush administration had prior knowledge of the 9/11 attacks.[100]

But James Nicholson [U.S. Ambassador to the Vatican] wrote about a conversation he had with Pope John Paul II just two days after the 9/11 attacks:

"I met the Pope at Castelgandolfo for about twenty minutes.... After we had spoken at length and prayed together, the Pope told me that he believed the events of September 11 were truly an attack,' and that we were justified in taking defensive action..... It was at this meeting that the foundations were laid for the support of the Holy See for our campaign against terrorism. It is extraordinary that the Pope and the Church wished to help us, and likewise worth noticing that this support continues today."[101]

In other words, John Paul II gave his approval and support to the U.S. military intervention in Iraq on the same day that the U.S. Conference of Catholic Bishops seemed to communicate something different.

In a letter dated September 13 - two days after the attacks - the pope wrote to President George W. Bush, in a clear reference to Islamic extremists, that, "Even if the forces of darkness appear to prevail, those who believe in God know that evil and death

---

[96] Art Laffin (December 24, 2004), Bishops called to speak out against Iraq war, National Catholic Reporter.

[97] Mark Scibilia-Carver (Nov. 5, 2013), Bishops' support for wars underpins collection for military archdiocese, National Catholic Reporter.

[98] Ibid.

[99] Abid Ullah Jan, Afghanistan-The Genesis of the Final Crusade (Pragmatic Publishing, Ottawa, Canada, 2006), p. 53.

[100] Wayne Madsen (April 22, 2003), Bush's "Christian" Blood Cult, CounterPunch.

[101] Abid Ullah Jan, Afghanistan-The Genesis of the Final Crusade (Pragmatic Publishing, Ottawa, Canada, 2006), pp. 45, 46.

do not have the final say. Christian hope is based on this truth; at this time our prayerful trust draws strength from it."[102]

Similarly, Cardinal Ruini with senior Vatican figures, told John Bolton, the U.S. special envoy, that the Vatican respects Bush's decision to invade Iraq, and proposed working with the U.S. to bring humanitarian aid to the population on the same day U.S. troops occupied Baghdad.[103]

Likewise, not long after 9/11, the Vatican stepped up its attempts to influence future 'puppets' in Afghanistan, when a papal delegation met with the former king of Afghanistan, Zahir Shah, in late November 2001 at his villa, but without providing details of the meeting.[104] Not for nothing did the Vatican quietly express its support for the war in Afghanistan when the Holy See spokesman, Joaquin Navarro-Valls, told Reuters, although *La Civiltà Cattolica* condemned U.S. interference in the war as a whole.[105]

Not long after the attacks, Bush's ominous talk of a crusade against terrorism became known, but he soon retracted his use of the term when he said that, to Muslim ears, it reminded them of the brutal invasions of the Islamic nations of the medieval Christian crusades.[106]

However, Taliban leader Mullah Omar declared that "President Bush has told the truth that this is a crusade against Islam," although in a 1998 manifesto co-signed by the leaders of Islamist groups in Egypt, Pakistan, and Bangladesh, Osama bin Laden declared war against the "Jews and the Crusaders;" the latter in reference to the United States.[107] And when U.S. troops began attacks in Afghanistan, bin Laden said from a cave in a live speech that Bush was "the leader of the infidels" in a world war against Islam; although he had earlier warned that Bush the "crusader" would lead the infidel forces in Afghanistan "under the banner of the cross."[108]

For its part, the Catholic Church had good relations with the Iraqi government, and when a terrible conflict could break out between Sunni Muslims and Shiites, Saddam favored the former, who represented 32 to 37 percent of the population. The Shiite Muslims were persecuted by the Iraqi regime, suppressing their expansion of their teaching and lifestyle by massacring them, and the Vatican kept silent.[109]

The U.S. Catholic bishops wrote a letter to President George Bush on September 13, 2002, which was signed by the president of the U.S. Conference of Bishops, Wilton D. Gregory, and sent to him through Secretary of State Condoleezza Rice. In this letter, the bishops denounced the seriousness of the threat imposed by Saddam Hussein's regime, and called for an international mobilization that could overturn it Although

[102] (September 13, 2001), Letter to President Bush by Pope John Paul II, Catholic Exchange.
[103] (April 26, 2011), Wikileaks reveals collaboration between the US and the Vatican after the invasion of Iraq, Rádio Renascença.
[104] Abid Ullah Jan, Afghanistan-The Genesis of the Final Crusade (Pragmatic Publishing, Ottawa, Canada, 2006), p. 51.
[105] Sandro Magister (July 29, 2003), With the Pope or with Bush? "Studi Cattolici" Stands with Both, Chiesa news.
[106] Richard T. Cooper (October 16, 2003), General Casts War in Religious Terms, Los Angeles Times.
[107] Thomas F. Madden (November 2, 2001), The abuse of Christianity's holy wars, National Review.
[108] Ibid.
[109] Sandro Magister (November 27, 2002), Saddam Hussein massacres Shiite Muslims, and the Vatican looks away, Chiesa news.

they were skeptical about the use of military force, they did not rule it out completely, when they appealed to the United Nations for review.[110]

By early 2003, President George W. Bush was seeking war against Iraq. John Paul II was quoted in numerous media as being against the armed conflict.[111] Indeed, James Nicholson, U.S. ambassador to the Vatican, tried in January 2002 to influence the Holy See and consequently the pope, to obtain their support for the war; something Nicholson found shortly after the 9/11 attacks, but which John Paul II now refused to consent to;[112] but not totally, as Nicholson rightly put it.[113] On March 29, 2003, Cardinal Pio Laghi was chosen as John Paul II's special envoy for the purpose of "preventing" the Iraq war, noting that the conflict would be a disaster;[114] and warning in turn of the possibility of a new gulf between Islam and Christianity.[115] Lagui, although chosen for this mission because he was a friend of the Bush family, ran into obstacles when the day before the meeting with the U.S. president, he was asked to meet with State Department officials, as the president wanted to know the agenda in advance.[116] Condolezza Rice, the National Security Advisor, consulted Lagui about the reasons. The next day, Rice was a participant in the meeting between the cardinal and President George W. Bush; also General Peter Pace, vice chairman of the Joint Chiefs of Staff; Jim Nicholson, the ambassador to the Vatican; and Archbishop Gabriel Montalvo. After the cardinal handed the letter to the U.S. president, he immediately placed it on the side of the table, without even opening it. Afterward, Bush began to defend the conflict, and told Lagui that he was "convinced it was God's will." Lagui interrupted the president's "sermon," telling him that he had a message from the pope and wanted him to listen to it. The cardinal referred to the many deaths and injuries that would be inflicted on both sides; of a subsequent civil war, and the difficulty for the United States to later emerge from the conflict. He told him rather that with peace nothing would be lost, but with war, there would be great unrest, especially in the Arab world. At the same time, the cardinal said that the most important problem in the Middle East was the Israeli-Palestinian conflict, which should be resolved through peace. Bush told Lagui, "We are not in agreement on Iraq but we are in agreement on other positions important to the Catholic Church and the Holy Father." Lagui nodded but insisted that they not go to war, failing in his enterprise, but Peter Pace bid him farewell by saying, "Your Eminence, don't be afraid. We'll do it quickly and we will do it in the best way."

Not everyone agreed that Pio Lagui was the pope's intermediary because of his past as nuncio of ex-admiral Massera during the dictatorship of Jorge Rafael Videla in Argentina; with whom he played biweekly tennis matches. He was denounced in Italy

---

[110] Sandro Magister (September 18, 2002), Iraq. Anche il papa dà l'ultimatum a Saddam, Chiesa news.

[111] (March 12, 2003), Vatican Strongly Opposes Iraq War, Associated Press.

[112] Sandro Magister (January 27, 2002), Exclusive Interview with Ambassador Nicholson: "The Points of Disagreement between Bush and the Pope," Chiesa news.

[113] Giulio Andreotti (2004), THE USA AND THE HOLY SEE. The Long Road, 30Days in the Church and the World, no. 3.

[114] (March 6, 2003), Vatican to Bush: Iraq War would be 'disaster', CNN; Johanna Neuman (March 6, 2003), Pope's Emissary Meets With Bush, Calls War 'Unjust', Los Angeles Times.

[115] Edwin F. O'Brien (June, 2007) A message: During this time of continuing conflict, The Catholic Herald.

[116] Gerard O'Connell (September 17, 2011), When Bush put John Paul II's letter on the side table without opening it, La Stampa. Note: unless otherwise noted, this is the same source.

in 1997 for complicity with the dictatorship and its systematic plan of disappearance of people.[117]

The Order of Malta echoed an article in *L'Osservatore Romano*, the Vatican's best-known newspaper and run by the Jesuits, about Pio Lagui's visit to President Bush, which more or less veiled, supported military intervention in Iraq with the permission of the United Nations, but warned of the consequences.[118]

According to Phil Lawler, editor of *Catholic World News*, despite the flurry of media reports to the contrary, John Paul II did not issue a moral condemnation of the military action against Iraq.[119]

Lawler points out that the *Associated Press* has quoted the U.S. press as saying that the pope said that there is no legal or moral justification for military action, and therefore it would be an unjust war. But in the weeks leading up to the armed conflict, the Holy See insisted that Iraq must disarm, but without the use of military force and through the authority of the United Nations; while noting that it was a pity that Baghdad did not comply with the measures of the international community, because the use of force was a last resort. The Holy See pointed out that whoever decides that all the peaceful means that international law has placed at our disposal have been exhausted, assumes "a serious responsibility before God, his conscience and history." But the Holy See did not condemn the war at all: bearing in mind that the Catechism of the Catholic Church teaches that political leaders have the ultimate responsibility to judge whether the requirements for a "just war" have been met. Thus, the Italian newspaper *L'Espresso* reported that a group of Catholic pacifists wrote an open letter to John Paul II asking for a simple and unequivocal denunciation of the war, but were left unsatisfied.[120] Nor did Joaquin Navarro-Valls, the Vatican spokesman, who said that the conditions for justifying war are in the contemporary context so rare as to be practically non-existent,[121] satisfy the pacifists. Moreover, in May 2003, Yosef Naville Lamdan, former Israeli ambassador to the Vatican, indicated that the Vatican was watching Islam closely because of the faith of Christians in Muslim countries, the rivalry of the two religions in gaining new adherents in both Africa and Asia, and the growing Muslim presence in Europe.[122] Moreover, on April 27, pope John Paul II prayed the "Regina Coeli," addressing his fellow Poles by saying:

"Blessed Mark of Aviano was also part of our history; as the papal legate, after the victory of John Sobieski over the Turks at Vienna, he carried the following message from the king to the pope: Veni, vidi, Deus Vicit! [I came, I saw, God conquered!]."[123]

---

[117] Caren de Carlos (January 13, 2009), Muere el cardenal Pío Lagui, el nuncio amigo de Massera, ABC España.
[118] (March 7, 2003) Washington: White House talks between papal envoy and president Bush (from the March 7, 2003 edition of the Osservatore Romano), Order of Malta News.
[119] Phil Lawler (March 24, 2003), Has the Pope Condemned the War, Catholic World News; see also Sandro Magister (March 20, 2003), War in the Gulf. What the Pope Really Said, Chiesa news.
[120] Ibid.
[121] Michael Griffin, CSC, Patrick O'Neill (Easter, 2003), The Pope, the President, and how the U.S. Catholics engaged the war effort, The Sign of Peace, Vol. 2. 2, p. 4.
[122] Sandro Magister (May 6, 2003), Strategy Change in the Vatican: The Islamic Party Is Born, Chiesa news.
[123] Sandro Magister (May 12, 2003), Poland's Catholics Depart for Iraq. With the United States and the Pope, Chiesa news.

This is how John Paul II referred to the Polish battle led by King John III Sobieski, with the spiritual support of the Capuchin friar Marco d'Aviano against the Muslim Turks, whom the pope beatified on April 27, 2003. The Italian journalist, Sandro Magister, pointed out that the Polish pope may have dared to express such incorrect words perhaps because Poland is the only major Catholic country in Europe that could hear them without being scandalized; and because it was the third European nation, with Italy and Spain, to align itself with the United States in supporting the war in Iraq. And indeed, the Catholic Church, and Catholics in large part, supported the war. The *Tygodnik Powszechny*, a Polish weekly newspaper printed in Krakow and the voice of very prestigious Catholic intellectuals, always had the support and friendship of John Paul II, who was a writer even before he became pope. During the years of transition from communism to democracy, the main leader of the newspaper was Jerzy Turowicz (1912-1999), a leading exponent of liberal Catholicism and a great friend of Wojtyla. The editor of the newspaper at the time when John Paul II spoke of Marco d'Aviano, was the priest Adam Boniecki, who was also former editor of the Polish edition of *L'Osservatore Romano*; and very close to the pope.[124] On March 30 (a little more than a month after the Pope's words to the Poles), Adam Boniecki published in the newspaper that the Pope had expressed words of sorrow that the United States had not followed UN regulations, but had not condemned the war.[125] For his part, Jesuit priest Stanislaw Musial said in the April 13 edition:

"[É] No one in the world, not even the most unrelenting antipapist or Islamic fundamentalist, will ever say that the Holy Father was not and is not, with his whole being, against this war. [É] If the role of the Holy Father and the church should limit itself to expressing grief without condemnation, Christianity truly would be the 'opiate of the people' in the classic 1800s sense of the phrase. But fortunately this is not the case. [É]"[126]

La Civiltà Cattolica (of the Jesuits in Rome), whose articles are approved by the Cardinal Secretary of State, in its October 18, 2005 edition, published a severe article by Jesuit Giuseppe De Rosa on the condition of Christians in Muslim countries, and alluding to the history of war and conquest of Islam for nearly a thousand years.[127]

Meanwhile, in the United States, the media expressed itself about radical Islamism with an air of war and an extremist spirit, as Abid Ullah Jan rightly pointed out:

"Brimming with confidence after the successful day of 9/11, Bush referred to his pre-planned war as a "crusade," hardly the way to endear himself to Muslims. The American media also tended to answer the question, "Why do they hate us?" by referring to the nature of Islam and 1.2 billion Muslims, rather than discussing the real issues. The so-called main-stream newspapers, such as the *New York Times*, started developing a mindset for religious war with one article after another with such titles as "This is a Religious War: September 11 was Only the Beginning," "Yes, this is About Islam," "The Core of Islamic Rage," "*Jihad* 101," "The Deep Intellectual

---

[124] Ibid.

[125] Cited in Ibid.

[126] Ibid.

[127] Sandro Magister (October 21, 2003), The Church and Islam: La Civiltà Cattolica Breaks the Cease Fire, Chiesa news.

212

Roots of Islamic Terror," "Faith and the Secular State," "Kipling Knew What the United States May Learn Now," "Al-Jazeera: What the Muslim World is Watching," "The Real Cultural Wars," "The Revolt of Islam," "The One True Faith," "Holy Warriors Escalate an Old War on a New Front," and "Feverish Protests Against the West Trace to Grievances Ancient and Modern."[128]

Bush and then British Prime Minister Tony Blair reportedly met at the U.S. president's ranch in Crawford, Texas, to discuss the summit at which the invasion of Iraq had been discussed in principle. When the news came to light, Blair refused to admit or deny the claim.[129]

The Guardian reported on George W. Bush's spiritual agenda on Iraq:

"Mr Bush revealed the extent of his religious fervour when he met a Palestinian delegation during the Israeli-Palestinian summit at the Egpytian resort of Sharm el-Sheikh, four months after the US-led invasion of Iraq in 2003.

"One of the delegates, Nabil Shaath, who was Palestinian foreign minister at the time, said: "President Bush said to all of us: 'I am driven with a mission from God'. God would tell me, 'George go and fight these terrorists in Afghanistan'. And I did. And then God would tell me 'George, go and end the tyranny in Iraq'. And I did."

"Mr Bush went on: "And now, again, I feel God's words coming to me, 'Go get the Palestinians their state and get the Israelis their security, and get peace in the Middle East'. And, by God, I'm gonna do it."[130]

But the White House issued through spokesman Scott McClellan that this claim was "absurd."[131]

Another impressive story was told by journalist and autor James A. Haught, when he related that George Bush telephoned then French President Jacques Chirac in early 2003, telling him: "Gog and Magog are at work in the Middle East. The biblical prophecies are being fulfilled. This confrontation is willed by God, who wants to use this conflict to erase his people's enemies before a New Age begins." Chirac was stunned and unresponsive; and sought advice from Thomas Römer, professor of theology at the University of Lausanne, who explained that in the Old Testament book of Ezekiel, chapters 38 and 39, the wrath of God rises against Gog and Magog, mysterious forces that rise up against Israel, and which also appear in the book of Revelation, and are finally punished by God.[132]

Römer confirmed this story in the Lausanne University magazine (Allez Savior), and the newspapers *Le Matin Dimanche* and *La Liberté* also commented on the news, but in

---

[128] Abid Ullah Jan, Afghanistan-The Genesis of the Final Crusade (Pragmatic Publishing, Ottawa, Canada, 2006), pp. 19, 20.
[129] Ewen MacAskill (October 7, 2005), George Bush: 'God told me to end the tyranny in Iraq', The Guardian.
[130] Ibid.
[131] (Oct. 6, 2005), White House denies Bush God claim, BBC News.
[132] James A. Haught (August/September 2009), A French Revelation, or The Burning Bush, Free Inquiry, Vol. 29, No. 5, p. 20.

a sarcastic tone. In North America, the *Charleston Gazette* in West Virginia and the *Toronto Star* in Canada commented on the news.[133]

Chirac himself confirmed the fact in an extensive interview with French journalist Jean-Claude Maurice, who recounted it in his book Si Vous Répétez, Je Démentirai, published by *Plon*.[134]

All of the above facts, and others, belie Bush and his administration's insistence that this was not a religious war; as well as Bush's praise of Islam as a religion of peace; his widespread invitation of Muslim clerics to the White House for Ramadan meals, as well as his criticism of evangelicals who consider Islam a dangerous faith.[135]

Instead, Bush did not hold back when Donald Rumsfeld, then Secretary of Defense (Pentagon) with the support of other military aides, provided President Bush with secret intelligence reports headed with biblical passages and portrayed with triumphant images of US military personnel and Iraqis in a position of worship, to propel the US president into the same position as the Secretary of Defense, and regardless of warnings that if the communiqués were leaked, Muslims would see the conflict as a crusade against Islam. The cover of one of the intelligence reports, portrays U.S. soldiers praying on their knees, and headed with a text from Isaiah that reads, "Whom shall I send, and who will go for us?/ Here I am Lord, send me!" Another cover, shows images of U.S. military vehicles and troops plodding through desert landscapes, manning a machine gun emplacement, and U.S. soldiers inside what appears to be a luxurious palace belonging to Saddam Hussein, and an image of Saddam speaking before a television camera and quoting 1 Peter 2:5: "It is God's will that by doing good you should silence the ignorant talk of foolish men."[136]

A Muslim member of the Pentagon staff took great offense at this.[137]

Glen Shaffer, a senior general who reported to Rumsfeld, was the one who conceived the documents[138] but was unrepentant even after the report was leaked.[139] Shaffer alleged that upon complaint from several officers, he told them that the practice would continue, as it was appreciated by his superiors, "Mr Rumsfeld and Mr Bush."[140] Rumsfeld indicated in June 2015, however, that George W. Bush's attempts to try to build a democracy in Iraq were misguided, as he did not believe it would work.[141]

The influence of Christian fundamentalists in the Department of Defense is not causal. In 2004, Air Force Major General Pete Sutton appeared in uniform at the Pentagon in the Campus Crusade for Christ Christian Embassy promotional video, which featured many government and senior military officials saying things like, "we're the aroma of Jesus Christ." Not long after appearing in the video, Sutton was assigned to the U.S. European Command in Ankara, Turkey, as head of the Office of

---

[133] Ibid.

[134] Ibid.

[135] Richard T. Cooper (October 16, 2003), General Casts War in Religious Terms, Los Angeles Times.

[136] Daniel Nasaw (May 18, 2009), Iraq war briefings headlined with biblical quotes, reports US magazine, The Guardian.

[137] Ibid.

[138] Ibid.

[139] (May 20, 2009), Retired General Stands by Bible Verse Decision, CBN News.

[140] Paul Thompson (May 20, 2009), Donald Rumsfeld's holy war: How president Bush's Iraq briefings came with quotes from the Bible, Daily Mail.

[141] Amanda Sakuma (June 9, 2015), Donald Rumsfeld: George W. Bush was wrong about Iraq, MSNBC.

Defense Cooperation.[142] The Defense Department considered the matter, and respective action was taken but without serious consequences, as indicated in a 45-page document.[143]

But in another government move, again by the Pentagon, the U.S. media filed a report in 2012 about the practice of a Pentagon training course for military personnel, in which one of the instructors advocated an all-out fight against Islam, including the destruction of Muslim holy sites without concern for civilian casualties.[144] Before that program was suppressed, nearly eight hundred officers received it, something Mikey Weinstein says is not the only case:

"We have all the evidence that there was a statement that said that Islam must be destroyed. And that's what they teach in the Air Force academies. But it was also disseminated among Navy and Army soldiers."[145]

The instructor was suspended, and Leon Panetta himself, then Secretary of Defense, was deeply troubled by some of the material being taught in the course, such as the slide suggesting that the United States was at war with Islam.[146]

But a few years before this incident, the Pentagon had also propagated a video game called "Left Behind: Eternal Forces," which was very popular among the U.S. military.[147] The video game was based on Tim LaHaye and Jerry Jenkins' famous series of stories about a bloody battle of Armageddon, where "born-again" Christians are in conflict against anyone who does not adhere to their particular theology. The game turns players into commanders of a virtual evangelical army, in a post-apocalyptic landscape that curiously resembles New York after the September 11, 2001 attacks; with tanks, helicopters, and a fearsome arsenal of automatic weapons at their disposal, they wage violent war against the United Nations peacekeepers, which according to LaHaye's interpretation, represent the forces of the anti-Christ. Whenever a "Christian" soldier kills a UN soldier, the virtual character exclaims, "Praise the Lord!"[148]

Blumenthal of *The Nation*, comments:

"To win the game, players must kill or convert all the non-believers left behind after the rapture. They also have the option of reversing roles and commanding the forces of the Antichrist."[149]

[142] Chris Rodda (Nov. 18, 2009), Top Ten Ways to Convince the Muslims We're On a Crusade, Hufftington Post.

[143] Department of Defense. Alleged Misconduct by DOD Officials Concerning Christian Embassy. Inspector General Report No. H06L102270308, July 20, 2007.

[144] (May 17, 2012), ¿Cruzados del Siglo XXI? Propaganda de guerra contra el Islam en EE.UU., RT en Español.

[145] Ibid.

[146] David Alexander (June 20, 2012), Military instructor suspended over Islam course, Reuters.

[147] Max Blumenthal (August 8, 2007), Kill Or Convert, Brought To You By the Pentagon, The Nation; (May 17, 2012), ¿Cruzados del Siglo XXI? Propaganda de guerra contra el Islam en EE.UU., RT en Español.

[148] Max Blumenthal (August 8, 2007), Kill Or Convert, Brought To You By the Pentagon, The Nation.

[149] Ibid.

Stephen Baldwin, a famous Hollywood actor and convert to right-wing Christianity after the 9/11 attacks, was the star of Operation Straight Up (OSU), which was an evangelical entertainment company that proselytized active members of the U.S. military.[150] Baldwin has been deemed a Christian by the well-known evangelical program, the 700 Club.[151] OSU was an official arm of the Defense Department's America Supports You program, and planned to mail copies of the controversial video game to soldiers serving in Iraq.[152] OSU also envisioned embarking on a "Military Crusade in Iraq" in the near future.

"We feel the forces of heaven have encouraged us to perform multiple crusades that will sweep through this war torn region," OSU declares on its website about its planned trip to Iraq. "We'll hold the onlyreligious crusade of its size in the dangerous land of Iraq."

The Department of Defense Chaplain's Office that oversaw OSU activities was telephoned to inquire about this but never responded.

Mikey Weinstein, founder of the Military Religious Freedom Foundation, and a former White House advisor to the Reagan Administration and former Air Force judge advocate, noted that "The constitution has been assaulted and brutalized."

He also said:

"Thanks to the influence of extreme Christian fundamentalism, the wall separating church and state is nothing but smoke and debris. And OSU is the IED that exploded the wall separating church and state in the Pentagon and throughout our military." Weinstein continued: "The fact that they would even consider taking their crusade to a Muslim country shows the threat to our national security and to the constitution and everyone that loves it."

OSU promoted an apocalyptic stigma with Christian-evangelical undertones to active American soldiers serving in Muslim-dominated regions of the Middle East.

In its beliefs, OSU contained two passages from the book of Revelation (19:20; 20:10-15), which represent the cornerstone of the end-time theology of the Christian right: "The devil and his angels, the beast and the false prophet, and whosoever is not found written in the Book of Life, shall be consigned to everlasting punishment in the lake which burns with fire and brimstone, which is the second death."

The producers of the video game faced a major controversy after Jonathan Hutson exposed its eliminationist overtones on Talk2Action; so both the Anti-Defamation League, the Conference on American-Islamic Relations, the Christian Alliance for Progress, and others condemned the game and demanded that Walmart pull it from its shelves. Marvin Olasky, the evangelical author and mastermind of "compassionate conservatism," as well as the force behind the Bush Administration's White House Office of Faith-Based and Community Initiatives, denounced the video game,

---

[150] Ibid.

[151] Shannon Woodland and Scott Ross (2006), Stephen Baldwin: The Jesus Freak of Hollywood, The 700 Club.

[152] Max Blumenthal (Aug. 8, 2007), Kill Or Convert, Brought To You By the Pentagon, The Nation. Note: unless otherwise noted, this is the same source.

describing it as akin to "the way homicidal Muslims think." As a result, Left Behind Games fired its senior vice president as well as three board members.

Mikey Weinstein and the Military Religious Freedom Foundation successfully lobbied the Pentagon to stop the delivery of the video game.[153]

Yet OSU, after a hard day of house-to-house canvassing and counterinsurgency against Iraqi insurgents, continued to encourage U.S. troops to play virtual kill-or-convert rounds. OSU's "Freedom Packages" included a copy of evangelical pastor John McDowell's "More Than A Carpenter," billed as "one of the most powerful evangelism tools worldwide," and also in Arabic, to evangelize among Iraqi civilians.[154]

OSU and the Department of Defense cultivated mutual support for years; and on one occasion, Pentagon employees and active duty service members gathered to enjoy breakfast with Spinks and Baldwin (of OSU), followed by an OSU performance where received "spiritual encouragement via a Biblical message." The events were held in the Pentagon Executive Dining Room and the Pentagon Auditorium.[155]

Similarly, the Pentagon assigned the task of tracking down and eliminating Osama Bin Laden, Saddam Hussein, and other high-profile targets to Lieutenant General William G. "Jerry" Boykin, then the new Deputy Assistant Secretary of Defense for Intelligence, as well as an evangelical Christian who saw "the war on terrorism as a clash between Judeo-Christian values and Satan."[156]

In June 2003, he appeared in uniform and polished jump boots before a religious group in Oregon, declaring that radical Islamists hated America "because we're a Christian nation, because our foundation and our roots are Judeo-Christian... and the enemy is a guy named Satan."

He also stated to another audience when referring to the battle against a Muslim warlord in Somalia, that, "I knew my God was bigger than his. I knew that my God was a real God and his was an idol."

"We in the army of God, in the house of God, kingdom of God have been raised for such a time as this," Boykin said last year."

Boykin also said publicly that Muslim radicals who resort to terrorism are not representative of the Islamic faith, and has compared the extremists to "hooded Christians" who terrorize blacks, Jews, and others under the robes of the Ku Klux Klan.

Again in June, this time in Sandy, Oregon, he said of Bush that "He's in the White House because God put him there."

Rarely, if ever, did the military take any government action against officers for overt religious speech, but experts saw such statements as sending the wrong message to the Arab and Islamic world.

---

[153] (May 17, 2012) Crusaders of the 21st Century? War propaganda against Islam in the U.S., RT en Español; Danielle Berrin (September 8, 2007), Chair dancing with the 'Jersey Boys,' Mikey Weinstein blocks prosyletizing Pentagon video game, Jewish Journal.

[154] Max Blumenthal (August 8, 2007), Kill Or Convert, Brought To You By the Pentagon, The Nation.

[155] Ibid.

[156] Richard T. Cooper (Oct. 16, 2003), General Casts War in Religious Terms, Los Angeles Times. Note: unless otherwise noted, this is the same source.

The president of the Institute for Middle East Peace and Development in New York, Stephen P. Cohen, said, "The phrase 'Judeo-Christian' is a big mistake. It's basically the language of Bin Laden and his supporters" He further added:

"They are constantly trying to create the impression that the Jews and Christians are getting together to beat up on Islam.... We have to be very careful that this doesn't become a clash between religions, a clash of civilizations."

George Bush said he did not agree with General Boykin's remarks and that it was not the policy of his administration, although then Secretary of Defense Donald Rumsfeld declined to express any criticism, especially since the Pentagon considered Boykin's remarks a minimal violation, although it did issue a statement indicating that the general wanted to apologize to those who were offended by his remarks.[157]

A former congressional supporter of Boykin, Robin Hayes, told a Rotary Club meeting in his hometown of Concord, North Carolina, in December 2006 that stability in Iraq ultimately depended on, "spreading the message of Jesus Christ, the message of peace on earth, good will towards men. ...Everything depends on everyone learning about the birth of the Savior."[158]

Chris Rodda, MRFF senior research director, revealed in 2009 that many U.S. government representatives made it clear that they consider the United States to be a Christian nation and that the war on terror was a spiritual battle. Thus, for example, Congressman Trent Franz in his remarks on the passage of H. Res. 847, a resolution, "recognizing the importance of Christmas and the Christian faith," stated that "...American men and women in uniform are fighting a battle across the world so that all Americans might continue to freely exercise their faith..."[159]

But among Catholics, there were also voices justifying the Iraqi conflict.

The renowned American Catholic political scientist and social activist, George Weigel, noted the following in *America Magazine*:

"Many American religious leaders and religious intellectuals have found the Bush administration's just war case for the war wanting. I have a different view; I believe that a compelling case can be made for using proportionate and discriminate armed force to disarm Iraq.
[...]
"Just cause is satisfied by recognizing that the present Iraqi regime, armed as it is and as it seeks to be, is an *aggression underway*. The United Nations recognized that in 1991 when it demanded Iraq's disarmament. To disarm Iraq now, by using proportionate and discriminate armed force if necessary, is to support the minimum conditions of world order and to defend the ideal of a law-governed international community. Thus military intervention to disarm Iraq is not pre-emptive war, nor is it preventive war, nor is it aggression.
[...].

---

[157] Douglas Jehl (October 23, 2003), Bush SaysHe Disagrees With General's Remarks on Religion, The New York Times; (October 28, 2003), Bush renews rebuke of Boykin, The Washington Times; (August 19, 2004), US general 'censured' for remarks, BBC News.

[158] Chris Rodda (Nov. 18, 2009), Top Ten Ways to Convince the Muslims We're On a Crusade, Hufftington Post.

[159] Ibid.

"Last resort is also a matter of prudential judgment, not algebraic certitude. I judge that last resort was reached in the first months of 2003 [...]"[160]

This article was published on March 31, 2003, in none other than *America Magazine*, the renowned publication of the Jesuits in the United States. What is ironic about the issue in which this article appeared is that the editors also published another article severely condemning the war in Iraq.[161]

On May 22 of the same year, the United Nations Security Council approved the resolution to give the power to govern Iraq and use its oil resources for the reconstruction of the country, through the United States and the United Kingdom.[162] L. Paul Bremer III, the American diplomat and "conservative Catholic convert [...] and was respected by right-wing evangelicals and neoconservatives alike," already mentioned elsewhere, took over the interim government in Iraq from May 12, 2003, to June 28, 2004. And Bremer acted like a dictator.[163]

After these surprising revelations, let us say that when the end of the Iraq war had been officially announced in other countries (the conflicts continued) on April 4, 2004 - with the Bremer dictatorship in Iraq - John Paul II exclaimed on Easter Day (April 20) to the crowd gathered in the splendorous setting of Bernini's colonnade: "Peace in Iraq! With the support of the international community, may the Iraqis become protagonists of a reconstruction of their country in solidarity!"[164]

Similarly, Pope Wojtyla's speech after meeting with Bush on June 4, 2004, provided the certainty of "a long-term consensus between the world's lone religious and political fronts against Islam. Military might is an effective tool in the hands of a political front."[165]

In that meeting between the U.S. president and the Polish pope, after the latter reiterated to Bush the Vatican's position against the Iraqi conflict, at the end of the interview Bush accepted the pope's recommendations, agreeing with him.[166] This contrasted with the statements made by Ari Fleischer, Bush's spokesman, in March 2003 -more than a year earlier- when he said that the president would not allow himself to be conditioned by the pope and the multiple efforts of Vatican diplomacy to avoid the conflict.[167]

By the same year, headlines appeared such as, "Trying Democracy in Baghdad, with the Vatican's Blessing"; "The Vatican Deploys its Divisions in Iraq - Under the Banner of NATO"; "The Pope Receives Iraqi premier Allawi"; and "Church Encourages Islamic Journey to Democracy"; "The Pope Receives Iraqi premier Allawi"; and

---

[160] George Weigel (March 31, 2003), The Just War Case for the War, America.

[161] The Editors (March 31, 2003), God or Country?, America.

[162] (Aug. 15, 2003), United Nations Mandate for Iraq, DW.

[163] Jeremy Scahill, Dirty Wars: The World Is a Battlefield (Nation Books, New York, 2013), ob. cit.

[164] Carlos Corral Salvador, Gloria Moreno (October, 2004), Hacia la recuperación de la soberanía de Irak y su reconstrucción: Juan Pablo II ante Bush, UNISCI Discussion Papers, p. 1.

[165] Abid Ullah Jan, Afghanistan-The Genesis of the Final Crusade (Pragmatic Publishing, Ottawa, Canada, 2006), p. 40.

[166] Carlos Corral Salvador, Gloria Moreno (October, 2004), Hacia la recuperación de la soberanía de Irak y su reconstrucción: Juan Pablo II ante Bush, UNISCI Discussion Papers, pp. 2, 4.

[167] Ibid., p. 4.

"Church Encourages Islamic Journey to Democracy"; thus revealing a crusade to democratize Islam through the added interference of the Vatican itself.[168]

John Paul II received Allawi, his wife Thana, and a delegation from Baghdad on November 4, 2004, in Rome, giving recognition to the authoritarian government imposed by the United States. The delegation included development minister Mehdi Hahedh; human rights minister Bakhtiar Amin; and the new Iraqi ambassador to the Vatican, Albert Yelda (a Christian). Allawi then met with the Vatican Secretary of State, Cardinal Angelo Sodano, as well as the Vatican's foreign minister, Archbishop Giovanni Lajolo. While the Holy See gave full legitimacy to the new Iraqi government, in the ten-minute meeting with Mehdi Allawi, John Paul II encouraged "the efforts made by the Iraqi people to establish democratic institutions which will be truly representative and committed to defending the rights of all, in complete respect for the [sic] ethnic and religious diversity." Sandro Magister of the daily Chiesa noted, "These words confirm that the Vatican authorities have by now adopted a particular doctrine." That doctrine defends the compatibility between Islam and democracy, and "maintains the duty to assist in the birth and development of democratic institutions in Muslim countries."[169] For that reason, *La Civiltà Cattolica* (of the Jesuits in Rome and supervised and authorized by the Secretary of State) last winter of that year, "wrote that the pretext of transplanting democracy to these countries is "particularly offensive for the Islamic community," and to this is added that, "Today, the Vatican believes that Muslim communities must accommodate occupation forces, so that they may plant democracy there."[170] In other words, support for a compelling interference in the Islamic country. Since then, every proclamation by Vatican authorities on the issue has been in favor of the democratization of Muslim countries.[171]

In the meeting between John Paul II and Mehdi Allawi, the Pope expressed his hope for the "contribution to the growth of democracy" by the Christian community "present in Iraq from apostolic times." In this context, Magister underlined that on October 29 (the month before this meeting), an important meeting was held in Najaf, between the Patriarch of Baghdad of the Chaldean Catholics Manuel III Delly, and the Iraqi Ayatollah Ali al-Sistani, the most authoritative religious leader of the Shiite Muslims, that constitute the majority of the Iraqi population. Al-Sistani was a decisive promoter of the peaceful introduction of democracy in the country. The meeting was a success, as Delly later told Asia News.[172]

"Long before the Vatican's open declaration of supporting the United States occupation of Iraq, on September 20, 2004, Cardinal Ruini spoke to the permanent council of the Italian bishops' conference. Ruini repeated the duty of the Christian West to "oppose organized terror with the greatest energy and determination, without giving the slightest impression of considering their blackmail and their

---

[168] Abid Ullah Jan, Afghanistan-The Genesis of the Final Crusade (Pragmatic Publishing, Ottawa, Canada, 2006), p. 50.

[169] Sandro Magister (November 8, 2004), Trying Democracy in Baghdad, with the Vatican's Blessing, Chiesa news.

[170] Abid Ullah Jan, Afghanistan-The Genesis of the Final Crusade (Pragmatic Publishing, Ottawa, Canada, 2006), p. 51.

[171] Sandro Magister (November 8, 2004), Trying Democracy in Baghdad, with the Vatican's Blessing, Chiesa news.

[172] Ibid.

220

impositions," and at the same time, to transform into "our principal allies" the elements of the Muslim world that desire "liberty and democracy."[173]

The day after the council, the Italian newspaper *Il Foglio* appealed to the Italian government to become a promoter within NATO and the European Union of a massive deployment of Atlantic Alliance troops, "for the time necessary to secure the right of the Iraqis to vote and to select for the first time their parliament, their constitution, and their government."[174] This appeal was signed by Marta Dassù, editor of the journal of the Aspen Institute in Italy, as well as Giuliano Ferrara, editor of *Il Foglio*; Piero Ostellino, former editor of *Corriere della Sera*; and Vittorio E. Parsi, of *Avvenire*, the Catholic bishops' newspaper, something Vatican observers were intrigued by.

The following day (22), the correspondent of the newspaper *La Stampa*, Paolo Mastrolilli, interviewed the Cardinal Secretary of State, Angelo Sodano, who was in New York. Sodano expressed his admiration for the United States and criticized secular and anti-American Europe, as well as the "wearing down" of the UN. He was silent, however, on the theory of preventive war, but called for the UN Charter to recognize the right of military intervention in countries that trample on human rights. It can all be translated, as well as much more information in the present chapter, that the Vatican intended to extend the crusade against the entire Muslim world and any government labeled by them as oppressive, thus serving the interests of Catholicism.

Sodano was elusive of what Cardinal Ruini called the "global threat" of Islamic origin, so he limited himself to speaking of "criminal gangs." He patently defined as a "duty" the support of the international community towards the new Iraqi government under Iyad Allawi, declaring that "The child has been born. It may be illegitimate, but it's here, and it must be reared and educated."

Just three days later (September 26), international politics expert and professor at the Catholic University of Milan, Vittorio E. Parsi, indicated in an editorial in *Avvenire* that Europe and the West have a duty to ensure free elections in Iraq by reinforcing their military presence in the country through "the only body with the necessary resources: NATO." The decision to publish such an editorial on the front page of the bishops' newspaper came from the highest levels of the Vatican.

The Secretary of State, Cardinal Angelo Sodano, called for increased military support to the Allawi government for the emerging Iraqi democracy through a heavy deployment of NATO troops, a further sign of the papal see's support for the upcoming outcome of the conflict.

Regarding the U.S. religious environment under the Bush administration, A.U. Jan wrote that Wes Allison of the Times, "concludes that Evangelicals are dominating the United States policy in the new era and "religious conservatives have the most political power in generations." The slogan, "Let's Take America Back!" was part of the Christian Coalition's campaign. Alan Keyes, a candidate for U.S. Senate in Illinois and founder of Renew America, a conservative political action group that warned

---

[173] Abid Ullah Jan, Afghanistan-The Genesis of the Final Crusade (Pragmatic Publishing, Ottawa, Canada, 2006), p. 51.
[174] See Sandro Magister (September 29, 2004), The Vatican Deploys its Divisions in Iraq - Under the Banner of NATO, Chiesa news. Note: unless otherwise noted, this is the same source.

"American liberty is under internal attack as never before in our history."[175] Vijay Prashad, writing for Frontline, indicated that "American evangelicalism does not represent Christianity, but, nevertheless, represents the Bush administration's agenda."[176]

Organizations, people, and other facts related to the Iraq invasion

The Iraqi nation was filled with missionaries and evangelists, both civilian and militia, who showed little or no respect for military regulations.[177] The Campus Crusade for Christ's (CCC) Military Ministry aims to transform its enlisted students and future officers into "government-paid missionaries for Christ" and is present at all major U.S. military basic training centers, as well as at military service academies and ROTC (Reserve Officers' Training Corps) campuses. Likewise, the vision of the Military Missions Network is "An expanding global network of kingdom-minded movements of evangelism and discipleship reaching the world through the military of the world." The Officers' Christian Fellowship, consisting of some fifteen thousand officers operating at virtually all U.S. military installations worldwide, stated that its mission was to "create a spiritually transformed U.S. military, with Ambassadors for Christ in uniform, empowered by the Holy Spirit" and linked with the CCC.

According to Warrant Officer Rene Llanos of the 101st Flying Division, hundreds of thousands of Bibles stamped with military emblems were distributed in Iraq and Afghanistan, as well as a daily Bible study devotional published and donated by Bible Pathways Ministries to do missionary work among the locals, she told Mission Network News. There were also Bibles bearing official military logos that were produced with Pentagon permission, one of which was designed by Pentagon chaplains.

"Revival Fires Ministries, "at the request of the Chief Chaplains of the Pentagon," has been shipping these Bibles to Iraq, via military airlift, since 2003, and, according to a ministry press release, this "full Bible is designed and authorized by the Chief Chaplains of the Pentagon."

Chris Rodda reports that the man in charge of promoting the Bibles was Navy Chaplain Brian K. Waite (an Anglican Catholic), who before becoming a Navy chaplain, wrote a virulent anti-Muslim book, who considered it a religion that holds Islam responsible for terrorism and compares Islam to Nazism.

In addition, thousands of Bibles bearing official U.S. military emblems in Arabic, Dari, and Pashtu were often distributed in Iraq and Afghanistan with the assistance of U.S. military personnel.

Likewise, "tracts, videos, and audio cassettes have made their way into Iraq and Afghanistan, along with Christian comic books, coloring books, and other materials to evangelize Muslim children."

---

[175] Abid Ullah Jan, Afghanistan-The Genesis of the Final Crusade (Pragmatic Publishing, Ottawa, Canada, 2006), p. 69; citing Wes Allison, Evangelicals Sway Policy in the New Era," Times, October 11, 2004.

[176] Ibid; Vijay Prashad, "Eastward, evangelical soldiers," Frontline, Volume 22, 4th Edition, February 12-25, 2005.

[177] Chris Rodda (Nov. 18, 2009), Top Ten Ways to Convince the Muslims We're On a Crusade, Hufftington Post. Note: unless otherwise noted, this is the same source.

222

Incidentally, the German news program Panorama reported in June 2004 that radical American Christians wanted to convert the whole world to Christianity; and as an example, they did a report on American fundamentalism in Iraq. For example, a building that did not look like a church housed Iraqi Christians during a liturgy, and among them were American missionaries. Tom White, for example, appeared with dyed hair, a false beard, and glasses among the attendees disguised as a tourist; while in an adjoining room, there were a few tons of Christian literature, with thousands of full-color Bibles having been distributed in the Arab country, including Bibles for children and stories such as "The Life of Jesus," and others. The whole activity was promoted by The Voice of the Martyrs organization, but it is the Southern Baptist Convention (which supported the war in Iraq) which had the largest presence in the country, and which by the way had brought Bush to power by its support at the ballot box.[178]

As for some of the most important players in the U.S. military against Iraq, they obtained their training in Catholic institutions. Some of them were General Peter Pace, then Director of the Joint Chiefs of Staff and the first U.S. Marine, who served in that capacity as one of the nation's highest-ranking military officers below the president. A 1992 graduate of Georgetown University's Jesuit flagship Leadership Seminar in Washington, D.C.; as well as the Edmund A. Walsh School of Foreign Service at the same institution.

Another was David Howell Petraeus, also trained at Georgetown University; and former commander of the Multinational Forces in Iraq.

U.S. Secretary of Defense Robert Gates; educated at Georgetown University.

George Tenet, CIA Director from 1996 to 2004; Roman Catholic and Georgetown University educated.

Gen. James Jones, director of the Congressional Independent Commission on Iraqi Security Forces, and trained at Georgetown University.

George W. Casey, Jr., Chief of Staff of the U.S. Army and former Commander of Multinational Forces Iraq, also trained at Georgetown University.

So, the case with the Jesuits is highly relevant here. Jesuit universities in the United States, especially, promote the ROTC (Reserve Officers' Training Corps) program, which is the official training program for commissioned officer training in the U.S. armed forces.

Colman McCarthy, of *In All Things* (a publication described as "a Jesuit social apostolate magazine" and whose motto is "Building a Culture of Peace"), writes, "Why is Roman Catholicism not a religion of peace [...] Why are Jesuit schools so lukewarm when it comes to peace education?" He points out that the Society of Jesus is pro-peace, yet is not emphatic about it. Jesuit pacifist Richard McSorely, noted that Georgetown's ROTC program has a strong emphasis on the institution, but not on peace. McCarthy believes that in the last ten years (1994-2004), he was invited to give lectures on nonviolence at eight of the Society of Jesus' educational institutions, hence of the 28 colleges and universities it owns, 20 of them do not offer peace specialties.[179]

John Dear, who was expelled from the Jesuits by his superiors for his pacifist attitude over the years, says of the Jesuits: "We run 28 universities, all of whom train young people to kill through ROTC. There was a lot of pressure in the Jesuit order to

[178] Anja Reschke (June 24, 2004), Amerikas heilige Krieger - Christliche Missionare im Iraq, Panorama.
[179] Colman McCarthy (Spring, 2004), Cheating Students out of a (Peace) Full Education, In All Things, Vol. 5, No. 1, pp. 8, 9.

stop me, and they stopped me, and I eventually left."[180] Thus, for example, there are two graduates of Boston College (Jesuit's top institution): Lieutenants Richard J. Holahan and John Beary, who in their defense of the program stated that "ROTC espouses Jesuit values to the core."[181]

Brian F. Linnane, a Jesuit priest and the president of Loyola University in Baltimore, Maryland, said in July 2011 that they hold their required ROTC ceremony every May in their graduate memorial chapel. He justified the program by saying that the Roman Catholic tradition has never been one of staunch pacifism. St. Augustine grappled with the problem in the 5th century stating that there are too many bad things in the world and so, Catholics have the obligation to defend the innocent from aggression.

Continues Linnane, the men and women who take their oaths in the ceremony swear to protect the Constitution of the United States.[182]

It seems that the Iraqi conflict would have encouraged the involvement of many Jesuit priests in the U.S. military, since John Dear notes that in recent years (he wrote in 2014), he has seen many Jesuits involved in the military, at Los Alamos National Laboratory, West Point and Abu Ghraib prison in Iraq.[183]

But some Jesuits are regular pacifists, who do not like the ROTC program in Jesuit higher education institutions. These include Richard McSorely, John Dear, and Steve Kelly.[184]

But the Society of Jesus in general, as in the United States, has military interests in spreading Catholicism in other regions. For example, John Dear, who was at Georgetown University in the early 1980s, watched through his window as ROTC cadets waved their rifles, chanted war slogans, and pretended to fight. He then wrote to the institution's Jesuit president asking him to discontinue the program at the university. He related his concern, citing the institution's financial, academic, and public support of the U.S. military system and structures of violence by appealing to the example of Jesus, who never used violence.[185] He called for closing the ROTC program and its related scholarships, as well as the Center for Strategic and International Studies and its research on nuclear weapons and post-nuclear laser warfare at Georgetown. He also called for the return of all financial contributions from the US Department of Defense and the cessation of all future cooperation with the Pentagon.[186]

He then wrote in his letter that although he knew these were difficult decisions to make, he was confident that God would give him the courage to speak and act accordingly and make Georgetown a better institution. Two weeks later, the president's secretary called John Dear and asked him to report immediately to the president's

---

[180] Megan Sweas (March 6, 2014), Fr. John Dear, Dismissed from Jesuits: "It Is So Strange to Be Hated by So Many Church Leaders", Religion Dispatches.

[181] Richard J. Holahan, Lt. John Beary (April 14, 2005), ROTC espouses Jesuit values through and through, The Heights, Vol. LXXXVI, No. 20, p. A7.

[182] Brian F. Linnane, S.J. (July 11, 2011), President's Message: ROTC at a Jesuit University, Loyola Magazine.

[183] John Dear (January 7, 2014), Leaving the Jesuits after 32 years, National Catholic Reporter.

[184] Colman McCarthy (Spring, 2004), Cheating Students out of a (Peace) Full Education, In All Things, Vol. 5, No. 1, pp. 8, 9.

[185] John Dear, SJ, A Persistent Peace: One Man's Struggle for a Nonviolent World (Loyola Press, Chicago, Illinois, 2008), p. 103.

[186] Ibid., p. 104.

office.[187] Dear saw him enter through a side door and burst in, slamming it shut and saying to him:

"How dare you write me a letter like that!" he began. What gives you the right to instruct me about the operations of this university? Do you realize that if we don't have Christians running the Pentagon, there will be even more wars, even worse atrocities? We need Jesuit-educated people running the Pentagon, the military, and our nuclear arsenal.... You're a disgrace to the Society [of Jesus]."[188]

Dear further writes, "The leading Jesuit publication, *America*, features regular ads paid for by the Pentagon to recruit priests to join the military in support of their killing campaigns."[189]

Who would think that some in the Society of Jesus would have such a vested interest in dominating the U.S. military spectrum? Although they have been assumed to be the most progressive wing of the Catholic Church.

In addition, a majority of leaders in the U.S. Catholic Church (and elsewhere) gave more open support to the war on terror. The head of the Archdiocese for the U.S. Military Services until 2008, now Cardinal Edwin Frederick O'Brien, was an avid supporter of the Vietnam War, indicating that that conflict was in accord with the Gospel of Jesus Christ and the Catholic just war theory.[190] Conflict that served the interests of the Holy See in a crusade against Buddhism and later Protestantism to implement the Catholic religion in the Asian nation.[191]

O'Brien also defended the military incursions in Iraq and Afghanistan; and when the former conflict began on the eve of March 19, 2003, he was the most outspoken Catholic hierarch in his support for the war.[192]

The U.S. Jesuit magazine, *America*, noted that early in the war Archbishop O'Brien, in his position as head of the country's Archdiocese for the Military Services, sent a pastoral letter to Catholic chaplains, advising them to calm soldiers' doubts by telling them that their government leaders were privy to more information than was publicly available, and that they could therefore trust their claims about the "justice" of the cause. In contrast, John Michael Botean, the bishop of the Romanian Catholic Diocese in Canton, Ohio, forbade his faithful to participate in the Iraqi conflict on pain of mortal sin.[193]

In March 2003, at the beginning of Operation Iraqi Freedom, Florida Congressman Tom Rooney was feeling unsettled, as he was a member of the US Army JAG Corps stationed at Fort Hood, Texas. He knew (falsely) that Pope John Paul II and the U.S. bishops were opposed to the war, so he sought spiritual guidance from Archbishop O'Brien. Rooney told him, "I would never disrespect my superiors in the Catholic faith, especially on matters of doctrine," Rooney recounted. "Archbishop [Edwin] O'Brien

---

[187] Ibid.

[188] Ibid., pp. 104, 105.

[189] John Dear (January 8, 2008), The Jesuits gather in Rome, National Catholic Reporter.

[190] Emmanuel Charles McCarthy (Jan. 7, 2012), Edwin O'Brien appointed cardinal, in a confusing blow to the core non-violent message of Christianity, Catholic Democrats.

[191] See Avro Manhattan, Vietnam: Why Did We Go? (Chick Publications, CA, 1984).

[192] Emmanuel Charles McCarthy (Jan. 7, 2012), Edwin O'Brien appointed cardinal, in a confusing blow to the core non-violent message of Christianity, Catholic Democrats.

[193] Tom Cornell (November 17, 2008), The Chaplain's Dilemma, America.

reminded me that the Catechism says whenever your country sends you into battle— if history shows that conflict to be unjust — the final judgment will be on the leaders who sent us there."[194]

O'Brien was discouraged when the U.S. media showed the most negative side of the conflict, stating that, "The news only shows cars being blown up," he said. "But the soldiers see hospitals being built and schools opening."[195] All this clearly shows his interpretation of what a democracy is, despite the terrible results of the conflict.

In 2007, he wrote a statement in which he expressed his support for the U.S. military interventions in Iraq in the following words:

"It is also important to note at the outset that to raise serious moral questions about U.S. involvement in Iraq is not to question the moral integrity of our military personnel. Indeed, the Holy Father's remarks to the Fifth International Convention of Military Ordinaries, citing the Second Vatican Council, can certainly be applied to those of our military who serve as 'ministers of the security and freedom of peoples' (Bishop Thomas Wenski, chairman of the U.S. Catholic Conference of Bishops' Committee on International Policy, 2006)."

"The U.S. Conference of Catholic Bishops, in statements on Iraq, has consistently offered pastoral support to the men and women in uniform "who serve bravely, generously, and at grave risk."[196]

Note that O'Brien does not question the moral integrity of the personnel, despite the many abuses that took place by a large number of U.S. military personnel. He also emphasizes that the words of the Pope (then Benedict XVI), pronounced at the Fifth International Convention of Military Ordinaries, citing the Second Vatican Council, would support the military in serving as "ministers of the security and freedom of peoples," and; in that context, Pope Benedict cited at the same Convention the words of John Paul II, which state that:

"This insistent appeal for peace has influenced Western culture, fostering the ideal that the Armed Forces are "an exclusive service for the security and freedom of peoples" (John Paul II, Address, Third International Convention of Military Ordinariates; ORE, 23 March 1994, n. 5, p. 6)." [197]

Thus, O'Brien clearly saw in the words of the Pope himself that the role of the West (United States (2006)), in promoting the idea that the armed forces should be at the service of the defense of the security and freedom of peoples, represented a clear support for the armed conflict in Iraq. Moreover, Pope Benedict XVI made it clear at the convention that the purpose was to implant the Catholic faith, as well as in any armed conflict in which the Church was involved:

---

[194] (February 1, 2009), Winning the war on terror, Legatus.

[195] Regina Linskey (December 14, 2006), Iraq: More deaths, few stories of hope leave many asking wthat's next, Catholic News Service.

[196] Edwin F. O'Brien (June, 2007), A message: During this time of continuing conflict, The Catholic Herald. Note: of a Spanish translation, retranslated back into English.

[197] Address of the Holy Father Benedict XVI to the participants in the Fifth International Congress of Military Ordinaries (Thursday, October 26, 2006).

"From within the military world, the Church will continue to offer her specific service to the formation of consciences, certain that God's Word, liberally scattered and courageously guided by the service of charity and truth, will bear fruit in its own good time.

"Dear and venerable Brothers, to offer people adequate pastoral care and to carry out the evangelizing mission, Military Ordinariates need priests and deacons who are motivated and trained, as well as lay people who can collaborate actively and responsibly with Pastors.

"I therefore join you in praying to the Lord of the Harvest that he will send workers out to this harvest in which you are already working with admirable zeal."[198]

It should be noted that in January 2006, Pope Benedict had concluded in a meeting with Jesuits Joseph Fessio, Christian W. Troll, and Samir Khalid Samir that Islam was incapable of reform, although they disagreed with him and Fessio tried to smooth things over by stating that the pope saw it as very difficult, though not impossible.[199] The previous November, the Vatican had also issued diplomatic objections because of Iran's nuclear weapons and Iran's threat to eliminate the state of Israel and the Vatican, in addition to the ayatollahs' Islamic repression of Christians in that country.[200]

Given all this, it is perhaps understandable that O'Brien stressed especially in 2007 that at no time did the Vatican or the U.S. Conference of Bishops question the motives of the national leadership in the U.S. Executive or Congressional branches about the threat, despite the violence unleashed in Iraq and the death of civilians.[201] Art Laffin of the *National Catholic Reporter* had the opportunity at the time of the Iraq conflict to speak with military chaplains, including Archbishop Edwin O'Brien (now a cardinal). There he asked them to call on all Catholic soldiers to leave Iraq so as not to participate in this "sinful occupation," but his appeal was not well received.[202] Instead, on June 29, 2008, Pope Benedict XVI awarded Archbishop O'Brien the pallium,[203] which is an ornament that popes place on metropolitans and primates as a symbol of jurisdiction granted to them by the Holy See, and thus connected to the papacy itself. Likewise, the pope appointed him as archbishop of Baltimore on July 12, 2007;[204] but then elected him grand master of the Equestrian Order of the Holy Sepulchre of Jerusalem.[205] In addition, and as if that were not enough, Benedict XVI elevated him to cardinal on

---

[198] Ibid.

[199] David P. Goldman (April 30, 2009), Fr. Samir's III Questions on Islam, First Things.

[200] Sandro Magister (November 11, 2005), The Church Breaks its Silence over the Islam of the Ayatollahs, Chiesa news.

[201] Edwin F. O'Brien (June, 2007) A message: During this time of continuing conflict, The Catholic Herald.

[202] Art Laffin (May 19, 2013), A call to repentance on the 10th anniversary of the U.S. invasion of Iraq, National Catholic Reporter.

[203] Carol Glatz (June 30, 2008), Pope gives palliums to archbishops, says church's mission is to unite, Catholic News Service.

[204] (July 12, 2007), Archbishop Edwin F. O'Brien named 15th archbishop of Baltimore, Catholic Review.

[205] Arthur Hirsch (August 30, 2011), Archbishop O'Brien leaving Baltimore for post in Rome, The Baltimore Sun.

January 6, 2012.[206] Not bad for a prelate who strongly supported a rather open war against Islam, and supported by the pontificates of Pope Benedict XVI and John Paul II.

The support of the Vatican and the U.S. bishops was also reflected in many Catholic members of the military.

For example, Jesuit priest Michael C. Barber was group chaplain from January to August 2003 in the Marine Aircraft Group 11, 3rd Marine Air Wing, and on active duty during Operation Iraqi Freedom;[207] serving six thousand soldiers deployed in Iraq.[208] It is worth noting that in 2007, he was elected as Magistral Chaplain of the Order of Malta and, as we shall see, the Sovereign Military Order of Malta (an order of the Catholic Church with its headquarters in the Vatican) supported the conflict under the banner of a crusade against Muslims.[209]

The U.S. Military Academy at West Point, N.Y., sent another Jesuit priest (Timothy Valentine) to the front lines to minister to the border guards of the Long Knife Brigade in Iraq. As a chaplain, Valentine was the only Catholic priest assigned to the 4th Brigade Combat Team, 1st Cavalry Division, to provide spiritual fitness to soldiers at many of the bases and outposts in the Dhi Qar, Maysan, and Muthanna areas. Chaplains held religious services open to troops and civilians of all denominations.[210]

Jesuit John Dear, noted that Tim Valentine ministered not to the tortured, but to the torturers, in Iraq's Abu Ghraib prison.[211]

At the prison, Lynndie England and her boss Charles Graner, as well as Janis Karpinski and Sabrina Harman and others, were part of what *El Clarín* described as, "Worthy of a black archive of sadism, a cascade of new images of torture, including sexual humiliation in Iraqi prisons [...]."[212] We do not know how much Tim Valentine knew, but we do know that Michael E. Cannon, author of the book *Abu Ghraib: Reflections in the Looking Glass*, was the chaplain of the 800th Military Police Brigade while it was assigned to guard Iraqi detainees in that prison, and who deplored what happened there.[213]

Among the many representatives of various denominations, as well as Catholic priests who were against what happened, was Gerard J. McGlone, a Jesuit who serves as a professor of psychiatry at Georgetown University, who even considered the Iraq war was being fought as if it were a crusade against Islam, something that was dangerous.[214]

On hostilities against Islam, former Baghdad mosque imam Taha Azeez, spokesman for the Front for Struggle and Change against the new Iraqi government, was arrested

[206] Joseph Berger (January 6, 2012), Another Step Up for a Bronx Native Who Led the Archdiocese in Baltimore, The New York Times.

[207] http://www.oakdiocese.org/diocese/bishop; accessed September 23, 2015.

[208] Catherine Harmon (May 3, 2013), Fr. Michael Barber, SJ named new bishop of Oakland, Catholic World Report.

[209] http://www.oakdiocese.org/diocese/bishop; accessed September 23, 2015.

[210] (March 24, 2009), West Point Priest in Iraq, America's North Shore Journal.

[211] John Dear (January 8, 2008), The Jesuits gather in Rome, National Catholic Reporter.

[212] Matilde Sanchez (May 31, 2009), Consideraciones sobre la tortura después de Abu Ghraib, en Irak, Clarín; véase el reporte de Ruth Wittwer (28 de abril, 2014), "EE.UU. ha aprendido poco de Abu Ghraib", DW.

[213] (May 11, 2005), Book Discussion on Abu Ghraib: Reflections in the Looking Glass, C-SPAN.

[214] Caryle Murphy (May 29, 2004), Grappling With the Morals On Display in Abu Ghraib, The Washington Post, p. B09.

in 2005 by US soldiers on hitherto unknown charges, and taken to Abu Ghraib prison: he claimed that the horrors of that location were still being repeated even a year after the prison scandal was uncovered.[215]

John Quinn, a Jesuit priest who administered communion and sacraments to firefighters and police officers assisting in the rescue at the Pentagon the day after 9/11, also requested to go to Iraq as a military chaplain.[216]

Likewise, Paul J. Shaughnessy, another Jesuit priest, with a unique 32,000-square-mile congregation in Iraq's Anbar province, served troops of all faiths at numerous outposts as chaplain for Marine Regimental Combat Team 5. He conducted masses at the megabase in Al Asad, which could attract a hundred or more Marines, sailors, soldiers, and others. Dozens of his top military commanders would be targeted for court-martial.[217]

Catholic priest Mark Beren was stationed in Balad, Iraq;[218] and priest John Barkemeyer at the combat base in Ramadi.[219] He did not believe in the war against Iraq but decided to serve the military and still consider the Iraqi troops as his enemies.[220]

Catholic priest, Patrick Van Durme, was a chaplain in Iraq and served on several U.S. military bases in 2010.[221]

Other Catholic priests were Michael Dory and Br. Timothy Vakoc.[222] Also John Barkemeyer and Waldemar Kilian.[223]

Bishop Robert J. Coyle also served in Operation Iraqi Freedom from 2002 to 2003.[224]

Likewise, 1st Lieutenant of the Latvian Forces Raimond Krasinskis, and Polish Army Lieutenant Colonel Wladyslaw Jasica, were Catholic priests serving in Iraq to liberate the country from Saddam Hussein's regime.[225] For his part, Monsignor Philip Hill, who was the chief of staff to the head of the U.S. Army Chaplains Office at the Pentagon,[226] was later chosen as the deputy chief of chaplains serving in Iraq; and lecturing to chaplains of different denominations in the country.[227]

---

[215] Joan Fauz (December 12, 2011), "Las torturas siguieron en Abu Ghraib incluso después del escándalo", Público.

[216] Christopher F. Aguilar (Dec. 22, 2004), Catholic priest joins military to be a chaplain in Iraq, The Florida Times Union.

[217] (October 1, 2008), Observations from Iraq, Iran, Israel, the Arab World and Beyond, Los Angeles Times.

[218] Sergeant Major, Nicholas Conner (September 29, 2007), Top Chaplains visit Camp Liberty, dvids.

[219] Oliver North, American Heroes (B&H Publishing Group, Nashville, Tennessee, 2012), ob. cit.

[220] John Lasker (November, 2009), In the service: Priests in the military, U.S. Catholic.

[221] Sergeant Major, Christina Turnipseed (February 12, 2010), 1st Brigade Combat Team, 1st Armored Division, Catholic priest makes FOB calls, dvids; Mike Latona (May 18, 2010), Priest feels called to serve soldiers in Iraq, Catholic Courier.

[222] Joseph Pronechen (May 30, 2004), In Iraq, Soldiers Find Their Greatest Alliens in Chaplains, National Catholic Register.

[223] Cardinal Francis George (January 30, 2005), If war is hell, why are there military chaplains, The Catholic New World.

[224] http://www.milarch.org/site/c.dwJXKgOUJiIaG/b.8565621/k.9076/Bishop_Coyle.htm: accessed December 29, 2015.

[225] Sergeant Major, Nicholas Conner (September 29, 2007), Top Chaplains visit Camp Liberty, dvids.

[226] Joseph Pronechen (September 11, 2011), Remembering 9/11, National Catholic Reporter; Sergeant Major, Nicholas Conner (September 29, 2007), Top Chaplains visit Camp Liberty, dvids....

[227] Ibid.

Blackwater and military evangelism in Iraq

An element of religious fanaticism on the part of many evangelicals and Catholics was seen in the private American militia then known as Blackwater (now Constellis Holdings, purchased years ago by a group of investors), which was in many ways an extension of the CIA, especially since the early 2000s. It was founded in 1997 by Erik Prince.[228] Prince notes in his book Civilian Warriors, that Paul Behrends, a Navy reserve commander and Catholic, was his inspiration for converting to Catholicism; later indicating that he and his family were proud Catholics.[229] Journalist Jeremy Scahill writes of the religious element of that entity:

"What is particularly scary about Blackwater's role in a war that President Bush labeled a "crusade" is that the company's leading executives are dedicated to a Christian-supremacist agenda. Erik Prince and his family have provided generous funding to the religious right's war against secularism and for expanding the presence of Christianity in the public sphere. Prince is a close friend and benefactor to some of the country's most militant Christian extremists, such as former Watergate conspirator Chuck Colson, who went on to become an adviser to President Bush and a pioneer of "faith-based prisons," and Christian conservative leader Gary Bauer, an original signer of the Project for a New American Century's "Statement of Principles," whom Prince has worked alongside since his youth and who was a close friend of Prince's father. Some Blackwater executives even boast of their membership in the Sovereign Military Order of Malta, a Christian militia formed in the eleventh century, before the first Crusades, with the mission of defending "territories that the Crusaders had conquered from the Moslems." The Order today boasts of being "a sovereign subject of international law, with its own constitution, passports, stamps, and public institutions" and "diplomatic relations with 94 countries." The outsourcing of U.S. military operations in Muslim countries and in secular societies to such neo-crusaders reinforces the greatest fears of many in the Arab world and other opponents of the administration's wars."[230]

The Economist also published in August 2009 that Erik Prince wanted to start a crusade against Muslims.[231]

Blackwater was under investigation that year for its involvement in shooting deaths in Iraq. One witness stated in a sworn affidavit to a Virginia court that Erik Prince "views himself as a Christian crusader tasked with eliminating Muslims and the Islamic faith from the globe."[232] Let's look at the rest of the affidavit:

"To that end, Mr. Prince intentionally deployed to Iraq certain men who shared his vision of Christian supremacy, knowing and wanting these men to take every available opportunity to murder Iraqis. Many of these men used call signs based on the Knights of the Templar, the warriors who fought the Crusades.

---

[228] Eli Lake (March 14, 2013), Exclusive: Court Docs Reveal Blackwater's Secret CIA Past, The Daily Beast.
[229] Erik Prince, Civilian Warriors: The Inside Story of Blackwater and the Unsung Heroes of the War on Terror (Portfolio, 2014), ob. cit.
[230] Jeremy Scahill, Dirty Wars: The World Is a Battlefield (Nation Books, New York, 2013), ob. cit.
[231] The Economist/New York (August 6, 2009), Erik Prince anf the last crusade, The Economist.
[232] Ibid.

Mr. Prince operated his companies in a manner that encouraged and rewarded the destruction of Iraqi life. For example, Mr. Prince's executives would openly speak about going over to Iraq to "lay Hajiis out on cardboard." Going to Iraq to shoot and kill Iraqis was viewed as a sport or game. Mr. Prince's employees openly and consistently used racist and derogatory terms for Iraqis and other Arabs, such as "ragheads" or "hajiis."[233]

Prince's contractors in Iraq wore codes and insignia based on the Knights Templar.[234]

Although Prince viewed with disdain that he was looked upon by some as a Roman Catholic war hoarder.[235] But he also became a major funder of extremist Catholic organizations.[236] Some of them I am aware, do not believe in the separation of Church and State. Scahill adds:

"Erik Prince has been in the thick of this right-wing effort to unite conservative Catholics, evangelicals, and neoconservatives in a common theoconservative holy war—with Blackwater serving as a sort of armed wing of the movement. As Prince himself once envisioned the role of his mercenaries, "Everybody carries guns, just like Jeremiah [it was actually Nehemiah] rebuilding the temple in Israel—a sword in one hand and a trowel in the other."[237]

Relatives of Erik Prince, have been major contributors to the Republican party.[238]

Joseph E. Schmitz, a Blackwater executive and George W. Bush appointee as Pentagon Inspector General served as an ideological soldier for right-wing causes long before assuming that position. That duty is the highest-ranking duty with direct oversight of military contracts, which at the time were Iraq and Afghanistan. He served legally in the Bush administration from 2002 to 2005, a scandal-filled period in that post. After he resigned, both Democrats and Republicans accused him of protecting the same war contractors because he allowed corruption and cronyism to go unchecked. During Schmitz's tenure at the Pentagon, Blackwater went from being - in Scahill's words - "a small private military and law-enforcement training facility to a global mercenary provider with hundreds of millions of dollars in U.S. government contracts."[239]

Before his resignation after the scandals that followed an official investigation, Schmitz indicated that he intended to continue his career working for Erik Prince at

---

[233] Ibid.

[234] Joshua E. Keating (January 19, 2011), Who Are the Knights of Malta - and What Do They Want, Foreign Policy.

[235] Erik Prince, Civilian Warriors: The Inside Story of Blackwater and the Unsung Heroes of the War on Terror (Penguin Group, Hudson Street, New York, 2013), .

[236] Jeremy Scahill, Blackwater: The Rise of the World's Most Powerful Mercenary Army (Serpent's Tail, London, 2008), ob. cit.

[237] Ibid; citing Nathan Hodge, "Blackwater CEO Touts Private Peacekeeping Model," Defense Daily, February 23, 2005.

[238] Corey Flintoff (Sept. 25, 2007), Blackwater's Prince Has GOP,Christian Group Ties, NPR.

[239] Jeremy Scahill, Blackwater: The Rise of the World's Most Powerful Mercenary Army (Serpent's Tail, London, 2008), ob. cit.

Blackwater.[240] But his interest in the company was beyond his dedication to wars and money, as Jeremy Scahill tells us:

"Joseph Schmitz, like Erik Prince and other executives at Blackwater, was a Catholic and a Christian fundamentalist. Some would go so far as to say he was a religious fanatic obsessed with implementing "the rule of law under God." In numerous speeches given during his time as Pentagon Inspector General, Schmitz articulated his vision and understanding of the global war on terror, employing the rhetoric of Christian supremacy. "No American today should ever doubt that we hold ourselves accountable to the rule of law under God. Here lies the fundamental difference between us and the terrorists," Schmitz said in a June 2004 speech, just after returning from trips to Iraq and Afghanistan. "It all comes down to this—we pride ourselves on our strict adherence to the rule of law under God." On his official biography, Schmitz proudly listed his membership in the Sovereign Military Order of Malta, a Christian militia formed in the eleventh century, before the first Crusades, with the mission of defending "territories that the Crusaders had conquered from the Moslems." The Order today boasts of being "a sovereign subject of international law, with its own constitution, passports, stamps, and public institutions" and "diplomatic relations with 94 countries."[241]

It is worth mentioning that some Blackwater tanks had red crosses on a white background, similar to those of the Crusades. One US Army tank had a cannon with the word "Apocalypse" on it, while another had a rosary hanging from it.

About 30 Catholic priests were chaplains in the thick of the war. But the worst came with the conquest of the city of Fallujah.

By March 31 of the same year (2004), insurgents in that city killed four Blackwater contractors.[242]

From April 4 to May 1, 2004, in response to the assassinations, the First Battle of Fallujah, codenamed Operation Vigilant Resolve, was a failed attempt to occupy Fallujah.

Two important facts about the city should be emphasized: under Saddam Hussein, Fallujah had benefited economically across the board and many residents were employed as military and intelligence officers by his administration.[243] Also, Fallujah was one of the most traditional cultural and religious areas.[244] It was known before the last attack, which destroyed much of the city, as "The City of Mosques," with two hundred mosques, sixty of which were subsequently destroyed.

---

[240] Ibid. (Prince wrote a book about Blackwater: Civilian Warriors: The Inside Story of Blackwater and the Unsung Heroes of the War on Terror (Portfolio, 2014); but many of his claims about the events recounted have been disproved by military personnel and the wives of other soldiers.)

[241] Ibid.

[242] Laura Parker (June 11, 2007), What exactly happened that day in Fallujah?, USA Today; Jeffrey Gettleman (March 31, 2004), Enraged Mob in Falluja Kills 4 American Contractors, The New York Times.

[243] "Violent Response: The US Army in Al-Falluja," Human Rights Watch Report (June, 2003), Vol. 15, No 7, p. 3.

[244] Christian Parenti (February 26, 2004), Scenes From a Nasty, Brutish, Long War, The Nation.

During the U.S. military's Operation Vigilant Resolve, officials in Fallujah reported that 600 Iraqis had been killed.[245] Iraqi sources report that more than half were women and children: 160 women and 141 children, in addition to 1250 wounded.[246]

The Second Battle of Fallujah (November 7 to December 23, 2004), called Operation Al-Fajr, or Operation Phantom Fury, which took place with the assistance of British and Iraqi forces, totaled 13,500; with 6500 U.S. Marines and 1500 U.S. troops, and 2500 Navy personnel in support roles.[247]

The armed forces near Fallujah had air and artillery support. It was a bloody battle with 1200 to 1500 or even 2000 insurgents killed (there are no exact figures). A total of 5685 high explosives, 318 precision bombs, 391 rockets and missiles, and 93 machine guns and cannon grenades were used. *AFP's* Patrick Baz, photographed on November 7, 2004, a machine gun barrel from which hung a rosary mounted on a Bradley outside Fallujah belonging to the Americans (the city was attacked that day).[248]

On November 7, Marines of the First Expeditionary Force, 1st Battalion, prayed at a Protestant church service in anticipation of the final offensive.[249]

Among the Catholic priests who acted as chaplains for the U.S. military in Fallujah was Bill Devine, who after the brutal battle of Fallujah, said at a memorial service for his fallen brothers at RCT-7, that "There is nothing more Christian than what we are doing here," referring to the sacrifice of those who had fought against great odds so that "the Iraqi people could enjoy their God-given freedom."[250]

Another priest was Merrell D. Knight Jr. who was the chaplain for the 1st Battalion, No. 505th Parachute Infantry from July 2003 to April 2004, in support of Operation Iraqi Freedom, where he conducted Sunday Masses with another priest for the soldiers.[251] Knight interacted amicably with the imams (the religious leaders of Fallujah) and civilians, speaking to them about faith and how the two religions could coexist peacefully or ecumenically.[252]

Also on hand was Chaplain John Gwudz, who once led an Easter Mass to about 100 Marines in a theater that was once part of Saddam Hussein's palace compound.[253] Gwudz encouraged the soldiers by telling them that in the hardships of war, a deeper appreciation of what God has bestowed can be gained.

---

[245] Robin Gedye (November 12, 2004), US claims 600 rebels killed in Fallujah battle, The Telegraph; (April 14, 2004), Nine Iraqis killed, 38 wounded in Fallujah clashes: hospital, The Daily Star, Lebanon.

[246] (April 14, 2004), Nine Iraqis killed, 38 wounded in Fallujah clashes: hospital, The Daily Star, Lebanon.

[247] Thomas E. Ricks, Fiasco: The American Military Adventure in Iraq (Penguin Group (USA) Inc., 2006), ob. cit.

[248] http://www.theage.com.au/ftimages/2004/11/11/1100021914568.html; accessed July 15, 2015.
http://news.xinhuanet.com/english/2004-11/08/content_2192325.htm; accessed July 15, 2015.
http://www.gettyimages.com/detail/news-photo/rosary-hangs-from-the-barrel-of-a-machinegun-mounted-on-a-news-photo/51693778; accessed July 15, 2015.
See these and others, at http://newzcard.com/event/ggNNo; accessed July 15, 2015.

[249] http://www.gettyimages.com/detail/news-photo/marines-from-the-1st-expeditionary-force-1st-battalion-pray-news-photo/51692881; accessed July 15, 2015.

[250] Oliver North, American Heroes in the Fight Against Radical Islam (B&H Publishing Group, 2008), p. 229.

[251] Laurence Lessard (June 8, 2007), Interview with CH (MAJ) Merrell D. Knight Jr, Operational Leadership Experiences, p. 6.

[252] Joan Frawley Desmond (Dec. 5, 2011), As U.S. Withdraws From Iraq, a Chaplain Completes 2nd Tour, National Catholic Register.

[253] Lourdes Navarro (April 11, 2004), Marines hold Easter services in Fallujah, AP.

Catholic priest Joel Panzer joined the U.S. Army Reserve as a chaplain in 2006 and went on active military duty in 2008 on his second deployment to Iraq at the 25th Infantry Division Headquarters.[254]

Another priest was Ron Moses Camarda, who served with the Marines at Bravo Surgical Company during the Battle of Fallujah.[255] So, too, was Conrad Targonski, who was present on the day of the attack (November 7, 2004) and during the days following.[256]

Some Catholic priests are mentioned after the occupation of Fallujah at the siege, such as John J. Gayton, of the Archdiocese for U.S. Military Services.[257] Michael R. Duesterhaus was there throughout the difficult part of the conflict.[258] He was assigned to Fallujah at the 1st Expeditionary Force Group Headquarters and admitted that he was serving the U.S. Armed Forces in their fight for the cause of freedom.[259]

A few miles from Fallujah, a Catholic chaplain performed two dozen adult confirmations or baptisms over seven months.[260]

Evangelical chaplains also participated in the battle of Fallujah, and one was even directly involved in the hostilities.

Operation Phantom Fury, which ended up conquering the city, was a most horrifying massacre, a great bloodbath.[261] But this "crusade" would later become more acute: in March 2008, Osama Bin Laden threatened the life of Benedict XVI.[262] Bin Laden repeated threats against the pope, whom he accused of "leading a crusade against Islam."[263] In the same month, the Vatican and its security forces decided to reinforce measures for the events planned for Holy Week, because the CIA headquarters in Rome warned the Vatican gendarmerie through John D. Peters, the head of the section, to the inspector general of the gendarmerie, Domenico Giani. Bin Laden's threat was on audio and the CIA believed it was from him. On Friday, December 19, the U.S. Embassy in the Vatican transmitted a telegram classified as "secret" to Condoleezza Rice, the U.S. Secretary of State, and copied to Mike Miller of ATA (Anti-Terrorism Assistance), in order to negotiate with the Vatican to deal with a possible crisis against the small state and with the help of the Regional Security Office and the FBI.[264]

Papal biographer David Gibson commented that after that threat, the United States and the Vatican "formed a bulwark against radical Islamism in the age of terrorism";

---

[254] Ibid., p. 8.

[255] Joseph Pronechen (November 11, 2010), The Heroism of Our Veterans and Their Chaplains, National Catholic Register.

[256] Ricardo Torres (November 12, 2014), Proud to have served, Catholic Herald.

[257] John J. Gayton (July 17, 2007), One Day in the Lufe of a Priest in Iraq, Catholic Mil.

[258] Bill Kirst (Spring 2011), Chaplain to Warriors, Salute, p. 23.

[259] Mary DeTurris Poust (June 25, 2006), A Catholic on the frontlines, Our Sunday Visitor.

[260] Mike Dorning (March 15, 2005), Finding their religion, Chicago Tribune.

[261] RAI News 24 (Producer) (2005), Fallujah: The Hidden Massacre. The United Arab Emirates enlisted Prince's services in 2011 from his new company, Reflex Responses, signing a $529 million contract to form an 800-member battalion of foreign mercenaries to be deployed in case foreign workers lend themselves to labor camp revolts, or in case the UAE is challenged by pro-democracy protests that shake the Arab world. Prince's only rule is "no Muslims." See Jeremy Scahill (May 16, 2011), Erik Prince, You're No Indiana Jones, The Nation; (May 18, 2011), Jeremy Scahill on Blackwater Founder Erik Prince's Private Army of "Christian Crusaders" in the UAE, Democracy Now!

[262] Ian Fisher (March 21, 2008), Vatican Security Worries Over bin Laden Tape, The New York Times.

[263] Malcolm Moore (June 11, 2008), Pope Benedict XVI sets up anti-terrorist squad, The Telegraph.

[264] Eric Frattini, La CIA in Vaticano: Da Giovanni Paolo II a Francesco: come i servizi segreti USA sorvegliano il Papa (Sperling & Kupfer, 2014), ob. cit.

facing a common enemy.[265] For his part, Spanish journalist Eric Frattini found that the conflict in the Middle East and the war in Iraq (due to the destruction of churches), was a target of the Vatican intelligence service known as "The Entity."[266]

Why the threat against the pope? Because Benedict XVI expressed in a speech at the University of Regensburg, Germany (2006), that Islam was an "evil and inhuman" religion. Although his views against Islam have been known since the 1990s.[267]

On November 19, 2007, Pope Benedict appointed Archbishop Timothy P. Broglio as the head of the Archdiocese for the Military Services of the United States.[268] Broglio was formally installed in that capacity on January 25, 2008, at the Basilica of the National Shrine of the Immaculate Conception, located in the District of Columbia.

Benedict XVI also created an anti-terrorist squad to protect him and the Vatican in June 2008 in the face of Al-Qaeda threats against him.[269] Vatican security forces included a bomb squad and a rapid response team, according to Domenico Giani, the 130-man head of the Vatican gendarmerie. The Holy See worked more closely with Interpol to gather threat information, and a deal with Europol, the pan-European police agency, aimed to gain "access to a large data bank of suspects and information on the latest anti-terrorism techniques."[270]

The Swiss guards also received anti-terrorist training: they possessed SIG P75 pistols and Heckler-Koch MP5 machine guns, as well as their traditional halberds.[271]

The leading Catholic-executive peer group *Legatus*, whose members had personal audiences with the Pope, published in 2009 an article entitled, "Winning the war on terror." The article supported condemnation of terrorism against Christians and Westerners, such as the assassination of the Archbishop of Mosul, Faraj Rahho, who was the highest-ranking Chaldean Catholic cleric to be killed in five years of war.[272]

Benedict XVI, the article notes, prayed for peace in the Middle East and the safeguarding of Christians living there. In this context, it notes that for Catholic servicemen and women in Iraq and Afghanistan, the war on terror became a way of living their Catholic faith. Brian Rooney, a military man and devout Catholic (now after that for the conservative Catholic Thomas More Law Center), recalls that he was a daily communicant in Iraq; and that Sunday Mass was full and estranged Catholics renewed their faith.[273] In Rooney's opinion:

"When you look at history," he said, "the Catholic Church has always defended the forces of Western Civilization against the forces of Islam. We have Charles Martel defeating Muslims in 732, the Battle of Lepanto in 1571 and the Battle of Vienna in 1683. In each one of those battles, Western civilization would have been lost if the

[265] The History Channel (Producer) (2011), Secret Access: The Vatican.
[266] (October 26, 2004), Murders, arms sales or financing of dictatorships, targets of the Vatican Espionage Service according to a book, Europa Press.
[267] Jane Kramer (April 2, 2007), The Pope and Islam, The New Yorker.
[268] Malcolm Moore (June 11, 2008), Pope Benedict XVI sets up anti-terrorist squad, The Telegraph.
[269] Ibid.
[270] Ibid.
[271] Ibid.
[272] Sabrina Arena Ferrisi (February 1, 2009), Winning the war on terror, Legatus.
[273] Ibid.

forces of Christendom had not prevailed. Today, America — a largely Christian country — is answering the call."[274]

Tim Valentine, the aforementioned Jesuit priest who served as a chaplain in Iraq, said of the formation of democracy in that country that he believed firmly that the U.S. soldiers did a noble job in Iraq. Valentine observed a military training team composed largely of Catholics who were instrumental in teaching the police, soldiers, and legal officials of the new Iraqi government key concepts of human rights and due process. He said they did a wonderful job influencing a whole culture. Those soldiers and officers -continued the Jesuit-came to church, down the road.[275]

Back at West Point, and serving in the Catholic chapel while teaching, Valentine believed it imperative that the Church maintain a presence in the military by providing spiritual guidance to the people charged with carrying out national policy.[276]

The U.S. military was to withdraw from the country in 2011, but no mention was made of the 150,000 people working in private security companies in Iraq, the country being (in the opinion of Taha Azeez, a former imam at a mosque in Baghdad), a puppet of Washington.[277]

Detention centers

The American Civil Liberties Union, through the Freedom of Information Act, obtained at least nine documents revealing that military chaplains at detention centers in Iraq knew about the harmful treatment of prisoners and reported abuses.[278]

But how much evil would have been avoided by a war labeled as a crusade and supported by many American Protestant and Catholic leaders and the Vatican? Here are some facts of importance before documenting the detention centers for the prisoners.

Many Catholic chaplains were ministering to U.S. soldiers and many other chaplains from other denominations.

There were soldiers with missals, bibles, Catholic service sites, and others who were assisted by the military after conquering specific regions of Iraq.

Because of the nature of the war, the aforementioned David Howell Petraeus, who was trained at Jesuit Georgetown University and was commander of the Multinational

---

[274] Ibid.

[275] Peter Feuerherd (March 21, 2007), Army chaplain sees job as forming 'people of peace', The Long Island Catholic, Vol. 45, No. 52.

[276] Ibid.

[277] Joan Fauz (December 12, 2011), "Torture continued at Abu Ghraib even after the scandal," Público.

[278] Army Detainee Operations Report: DOD Questionnaire of Chaplain/Captain re: Detainee Operations (Mar. 19, 2004) DOD, ACLU-RDI 157; DOD Questionnaire: Questions for Officer/Chaplain on Detainee Treatment and Rules of Engagement (Mar. 22, 2004) DOD; ACLU-RDI 1703; DOD Questionnaire: Questions for Chaplain on Detainee Treatment and Rules of Engagement (Mar. 25, 2004) DOD, ACLU-RDI 1695; Army Detainee Operations Report: DOD Questionnaire of Major/Chaplain re: Detainee Operations (March 26, 2004) DOD; ACLU-RDI 1606; DOD Questionnaire: Questions for Chaplain on Detainee Treatment and Rules of Engagement (March 26, 2004) DOD; ACLU-RDI 1474; Army Detainee Operations Report: DOD Questionnaire of Major/Chaplain re: Detainee Operations (March 29, 2004) DOD; ACLU-RDI 1605; DOD Questionnaire: Questions for Chaplain on Detainee Treatment and Rules of Engagement (March 30, 2004) DOD; ACLU-RDI 1516; Army Detainee Operations Report: DOD Questionnaire of Chaplain re: Detainee Operations (April 7, 2004) DOD; ACLU-RDI 1375; Army Detainee Operations Report: DOD Questionnaire of Chaplain re: Detainee Operations (April 7, 2004) DOD, ACLU-RDI 1363.

Forces of Iraq, was not supported by anti-war liberals, especially those who see evangelical Christianity sliding over the military's wall of church-state separation.[279]

The Military Religious Freedom Foundation, for example, chastised the general for endorsing the book, "Under Orders: A Spiritual Handbook for Military Personnel," which was written by the now ex-Lutheran chaplain William McCoy, who promotes Christianity among the military and denigrates agnostic and atheist soldiers.[280] Petraeus, who was considered one of the "crusaders" of the war against Islam,[281] was a superior of James Steele and James Coffman (involved in dirty wars in Central America in the 1980s), where the former was the civilian advisor to train the Special Police Commandos, which was a para-military group known as the Wolf Brigade in Iraq.[282] He was later indicted by a UN official for torture and murder; as well as death squads.[283] Both Steal and Coffman reported to General Petraeus and Donald Rumsfeld, who, as we have seen, also considered the war a crusade against Islam.[284]

These were clandestine detention operations and torture centers that were organized to extract information from the insurgents.[285] Tortures that were most horrific and chilling included on at least one occasion a 14-year-old boy.[286]

One of the torture rooms had blood all over it, and another witness recalls hearing from one of the rooms, terrible screams of panic and terror of someone shouting, 'Allah, Allah, Allah!,' as he called for help. And all as part of the torture centers that were set up throughout the country.[287] In 2004, Donald Rumsfeld enlisted Colonel James Steele, also a retired special forces veteran and counterinsurgency specialist, to create a Shiite militia to crush the Sunni rebels, backed by millions of U.S. dollars.[288] Steele was in Iraq from 2003 to 2005. Rumsfeld came to value Steele's reports so highly that he passed them on to Bush and Dick Cheney.[289]

A soldier from the 69th Armored Regiment who was deployed to Samarra in 2005 indicated of the torture that, "It was like the Nazis... like the Gestapo basically. They [the commandos] would essentially torture anybody that they had good reason to suspect, knew something, or was part of the insurgency... or supporting it, and people knew about that."[290]

---

[279] Daniel Burke (Nov. 14, 2012), With Petraeus, echoes of that other warrior David, Religion News Service.

[280] Ibid.

[281] Horace Campbell, Global NATO and the Catastrophic Failure in Libya (Monthly Review Press, 2013), p. 234.

[282] Andrew Buncombe, Patrick Cockburn (February 26, 2006), Iraq's death squads: On the brink of civil war, Independent; (October 25, 2010), Wikileaks: Americans handed over captives to Iraq torture squads, The Telegraph; (October 25, 2010), Wikileaks war logs: who are the 'Wolf Brigade'?, The Telegraph.

[283] Ibid.

[284] (March 6, 2013), The Guardian: "US had systematic torture centers in Iraq, DW."

[285] Ibid.

[286] Mona Mahmood, Maggie O'Kane, Chavala Madlena, Teresa Smith (March 6, 2013), Revealed: Pentagon's link to Iraqi torture centres, The Guardian.

[287] Ibid.

[288] James Nye (March 7, 2013), Special Forces 'dirty wars' veteran named as the man sent by General Petraeus to Iraq to set up 'torture' centers, Daily Mail.

[289] Mona Mahmood, Maggie O'Kane, Chavala Madlena, and Teresa Smith (March 6, 2013), Revealed: Pentagon's link to Iraqi torture centres, The Guardian.

[290] Mona Mahmood et al. (March 6, 2013), From El Salvador to Iraq: Washington's man behind brutal police squads, The Guardian.

One of the victims revealed:

"There was no sleep. From the sunset, the torture would start on me and on the other prisoners.

"They wanted confessions. They'd say: 'Confess to what have you done.' When you say: 'I have done nothing. Shall I confess about something I have not done?', they said: 'Yes, this is our way. The Americans told us to bring as many detainees as possible in order to keep them frightened.'"[291]

Neil Smith, a young doctor based in Samarra, recalled what American soldiers said in the mess hall:

"What was pretty widely known in our battalion, definitely in our platoon, was that they were pretty violent with their interrogations. That they would beat people, shock them with electrical shock, stab them, I don't know what else... it sounds like pretty awful things. If you sent a guy there he was going to get tortured and perhaps raped or whatever, humiliated and brutalised by the special commandos in order for them to get whatever information they wanted."[292]

Samarra, regarded as a holy city among Muslims, was desecrated by some U.S. soldiers who vandalized mosques by spray-painting Christian crosses on them. Likewise, the Special Forces interpreter - an Iraqi from Texas - was commissioned to paint a legend in Arabic on the frame of a Bradley tank that read: "Jesus killed Mohammed." Some soldiers turned it into an exclamation accompanied by gunfire to insult Muhammad himself.[293]

Regarding Steele, he won Dick Cheney's admiration for his efforts to fight leftists in Nicaragua and El Salvador;[294] which the Vatican supported through the dirty wars waged in Latin America.[295] *The Guardian/BBC* Arabic asked Petraeus about torture and his relationship with Steele, and received a response from an official close to the general:

"General (Ret) Petraeus's record, which includes instructions to his own soldiers... reflects his clear opposition to any form of torture."

"Colonel (Ret) Steele was one of thousands of advisers to Iraqi units, working in the area of the Iraqi police. There was no set frequency for Colonel Steele's meetings with

[291] Ibid.
[292] Ibid.
[293] Jeff Sharlet (May, 2009), Jesus Killed Mohammed, Harper's Magazine, p. 32.
[294] Mona Mahmood et al. (March 6, 2013), From El Salvador to Iraq: Washington's man behind brutal police squads, The Guardian.
[295] Robert Parry (March 16, 2013), Pope Francis, CIA and 'Death Squads', Consortium News; Carl Bernstein and Marco Politi, His Holiness: John Paul II and the History of Our Time (Penguin Books, Nueva York, 1997), pp. 212-233, 290, 311, 331, 350, 351, 388-396, 494-499; Avro Manhattan, The Vatican Moscow Washington Alliance (Chick Publications, CA, 1982); Gerald Posner, God's Bankers: A History of Money and Power at the Vatican (Simon & Schuster Paperbacks, New York, 2015), pp. 310, 311; Juan Pablo Somiedo García (2014), The Influence of U.S. Geopolitics on Latin American Liberation Theology in the 1960-1990 period, Geopolitics, vol. 5, no. 1, pp. 86-90.

General Petraeus, although General Petraeus did see him on a number of occasions during the establishment and initial deployments of the special police, in which Colonel Steele played a significant role."[296]

However, Peter Maass, reporting for the *New York Times* and who interviewed both individuals, indicated:

"I talked to both of them about each other and it was very clear that they were very close to each other in terms of their command relationship and also in terms of their ideas and ideology of what needed to be done. Everybody knew that he was Petraeus's man. Even Steele defined himself as Petraeus's man."[297]

For its part, *Human Rights Watch* documented in July 2006 allegations of abuse in detention facilities at the Mosul airport in northern Iraq. These abuses were committed in the "Brigade Holding Area" by the 2nd Brigade Combat Team (a unit of the 101st Airborne Division in Mosul) and in a separate detention compound at the airport, used exclusively by the Navy SEALS special team: "Navy SEAL Warfare Squadron 7" also known as Navy SEAL Team 7. They were based at Mosul airport from 2003 to 2004 at the Camp Diamondback and Camp Glory facilities.[298]

Military intelligence officers encouraged interrogators to use increasingly cruel techniques on detainees: painful stress positions; forced exercises; sleep deprivation and the threat of detainees being blindfolded; with military guard dogs, severe exposure to cold and heat; use of loud music (heavy metal) and strobe lights to disorient detainees and keep them awake; beaten with water bottles.[299] Abusive techniques were common there in Mosul and the overall situation was chaotic.[300] Also, prisoners were sometimes seen with bruises; and one young teenager was hit in the jaw, which broke.[301] At least one was kicked and beaten continuously with a stick.[302]

Two of these places in Mosul were called "the disco."[303]

Another method of torture consisted of wrapping the Muslim prisoner's head with adhesive tape for having chanted the Koran; then a soldier dressed as a catholic priest who then pretended to baptize the prisoner.[304]

Forward operating base Diamondback was home to four Army chaplains: one in the battalion, another in the chapel, a third in the combat support hospital, and the fourth stationed in the special forces compound. Different chaplains served in the area,

---

[296] Mona Mahmood et al. (March 6, 2013), From El Salvador to Iraq: Washington's man behind brutal police squads, The Guardian.

[297] Ibid.

[298] (July 22, 2006), Mosul: Camp Diamondback/Camp Glory, Human Rights Watch Report, Volume 18, No. 3(G), p. 38.

[299] Ibid., pp. 38-40, 42.

[300] Ibid., p. 40.

[301] Ibid, p. 42.

[302] Ibid, p. 46.

[303] Ibid; Douglas A. Pryer, The Fight for the High Ground: The U.S. Army and Interrogation During Operation Iraqi Freedom I, May 2003- April 2004 (CGSC Foundation Press; Fort Leavenworth, Kansas, 1st edition, 2009), p. 55.

[304] Christopher H. Pyle, Getting Away with Torture: Secret Government, War Crimes, and the Rule of Law (Potomac Books, Inc., Washington, D.C., 2009), ob. cit.

including John P. Smith II, Jamie Deason, who came to replace Chaplain Michael A. Morehouse (who served in 2005); and James Bailey, who replaced Sgt. Joel Larson.[305]

Jamie Deason conducted four different Protestant services in his chapel at Diamondback; as well as a Catholic mass and a service for Mormons.[306] The above chaplains did not directly serve the detention centers, and whose torture is documented from 2003 to 2004, at least as far as we have documentation.[307] We do not know their knowledge of the tortures in the detention centers before and by then, but the question rests on the spiritual status accorded to the U.S. military area where those tortures took place.

Chaplains Terry Romine, Brad P. Lewis, and David Sivret were three of the chaplains not mentioned above, serving from 2003, 2004, at Mosul airport.[308]

Camp Nama in Baghdad, as well as Forward Operating Base "Tiger" near al Qaim, were other U.S. torture centers.[309]

The "black sites" spreading to the world...

This refutes the assertion by US authorities that cases of torture such as the one reported at Abu Ghraib prison were the misconduct of individual soldiers, but not a widespread practice.[310] Rumsfeld was blamed by the US Senate for the torture at Abu Ghraib and Guantanamo, according to the report presented by Senators Carl Levin (Democrat) and John McCain (Republican).[311]

In addition, a covert action program, code-named Greystone, had hundreds of subcomponents, including post-9/11 detentions, interrogation and rendition programs, and all the required logistics such as planes to transport detainees around the world under false names to secret overseas prisons, where detainees were held in solitary confinement, sometimes for years.[312]

On July 24, 2005, John McCain introduced an amendment to the Department of Defense budget to prohibit military interrogations that use more force than is permitted by the traditional limits in the Army Field Manual, even if ordered by the commander-in-chief.[313] The bill also prohibited U.S. personnel, such as the CIA, from engaging in torture and other cruel, inhuman, and degrading forms of torture of prisoners anywhere on the planet.

But Cheney went to Congress personally to lobby against the ban, meeting three times with McCain himself. Dick Cheney's argument was that it was the only way to

---

[305] Kristin Henderson (April 30, 2006), 'In the Hands of God,' The Washington Post.
[306] Ibid.
[307] (July 22, 2006), Mosul: Camp Diamondback/Camp Glory, Human Rights Watch Report, Volume 18, No. 3(G), p. 38.
[308] (April 21, 2003), ARTEFFACTS; Windows Shattered, but Faith Unbroken, The New York Times; (Winter, 2006), Where the Rubber Meets the Road, Rapport, Vol. 22, No. 1, p. 16; (April 23. 2004), 'I prayed with them', Sun Journal.
[309] (July 22, 2006) I. Task Force 20/121/6-26/145 Camp Nama, Baghdad, pp. 6-25; II. Forward Operating Base "Tiger," near al Qaim, Iraq, pp. 25-38, Human Rights Watch Report, Volume 18, No. 3(G).
[310] (March 6, 2013), The Guardian: "US had systematic torture centers in Iraq, DW."
[311] (December 12, 2008), El Senado de EEUU culpa a Rumsfeld de las torturas en Abu Ghraib y Guantánamo, EFE.
[312] Dana Priest and William Arkin, Top Secret America: The Rise of the New American Security State (Little, Brown and Company, New York, 2011), ob. cit.
[313] Jane Mayer, The Dark Side: The Inside Story of How the War on Terror Turned Into a War on American Ideals (Double Day, 2008), ob. cit. Note: unless otherwise noted, this is the same source.

extract information, in order to prevent the next terrorist attack. But McCain asked for evidence that the system worked, to which Cheney and other advocates of the program shared a handful of cases that even CIA experts admitted much of the information was unreliable. John McCain believed that torture was just an excuse and in the fall, with the assistance of Human Rights First, more than a dozen generals, including former Secretary of State Colin Powell and former chairman of the Joint Chiefs of Staff, signed an angry letter urging Congress to accept John McCain's legislation. Bush threatened on Oct. 5 to exercise his veto power to kill McCain's bill if it passed. And hours later, the Senate overwhelmingly approved the measure by a 90-9 margin, which included 46 of the 55 Republican members.

Dick Cheney continued the feud when, on November 2, he returned to Capitol Hill to prevent a version of the legislation involving the House of Representatives and an exemption for the CIA from such codes of conduct, an action that earned him the nickname "Vice President for Torture" on a Washington Post editorial page. That same day, the same Washington Post published a stunning exposé by journalist Dana Priest, describing a global network of secret-dark prison sites, some of which were located in former Soviet states in Eastern Europe. The White House did not know where to put the thousands of high-profile prisoners they had in custody from all over until a prison camp was opened at the U.S. base at Guantanamo Bay, Cuba, in January 2002; but with subsequent legal problems for its operation. The CIA was seeking complete isolation for the prisoners and total secrecy and control. When looking for where in the world to place the prisoners, another agency said it was to investigate "how to make people disappear."

Other allied countries, including several satellite states hoping to curry favor with the United States for their ambitions to join NATO, also agreed to have ghost prisons. As well documented by journalist Jane Mayer in her book The Dark Side, many credible reports identified Poland and Romania in particular as hosting such prisons outside the protection of the law, although their leaders denied it. However, prisons were also found in Thailand and Afghanistan.[314] A cynical former CIA officer, as reported by Mayer, stated "We told them we'd help them join NATO if they helped us torture people." Classified documents refer to the locations of those prisons as black sites, where at least eight countries participated.[315] What was not known at the time (until 2010), however, is that there were 28 countries that cooperated with the United States in taking over an estimated 50 detention prisons in the "black sites": Algeria, Azerbaijan, Bosnia, Djibouti, Egypt, Ethiopia, Gambia, Israel, Jordan, Kenya, Kosovo, Libya, Lithuania, Mauritania, Morocco, Pakistan, Poland, Qatar, Romania, Saudi Arabia, Syria, Somalia, South Africa, Thailand, United Kingdom, Uzbekistan, Yemen and Zambia. Plus 25 additional prisons operated either by the United States or by the occupied government of Afghanistan on behalf of the United States. And 20 more prisons operated in Iraq. Several countries had suspects imprisoned on behalf of the CIA, and others on behalf of the U.S. military; or both. At least until 2004, detainees came from 21 countries: Algeria, Egypt, India, Iran, Iraq, Israeli-occupied Gaza and the West Bank, Jordan, Lebanon, Libya, Malaysia, Oman, Saudi Arabia, Somalia, Sudan,

---

[314] Dana Priest (November 2, 2005), CIA Holds Terror Suspects in Secret Prisons, The Washington Post.
[315] Jane Mayer, The Dark Side: The Inside Story of How the War on Terror Turned Into a War on American Ideals (Double Day, 2008), ob. cit.

Syria, Sweden, Tunisia, Turkey, Ukraine, the United Kingdom and Yemen. About 100,000 detainees were reported from these countries.[316]

The news sparked an international outcry and the next day, Judge Brinkema issued a modified order to the government to provide any video or tape recordings of the interrogations. But 11 days later, the Bush administration said it did not possess those tapes, something that senior CIA officials knew was a lie. That same month, José Rodríguez Jr, the CIA's chief of clandestine operations, ordered the tapes destroyed. For his part, CIA Director Michael Hayden said the agency's actions were in line with the law, but several former CIA officials said the tapes "definitely would have shocked the conscience of the country-the impact would have been unmanageable."[317] On December 30, Bush signed McCain's Detainee Treatment Act, which was a supplement to the senator's bill that, in short, supplemented it to give government agents and military personnel in civil and criminal actions immunity from using interrogation techniques that were officially authorized and determined to be lawful. Following the passage of the bill, Bush issued a signing statement in which the U.S. president outlined his interpretation of a new law, indicating that the executive branch would interpret the detainee-related provisions of that legislation in a manner consistent with the president's constitutional authority to protect the American people from further attacks. *The Boston Globe* indicated that in that legislation, Bush quietly reserved the right to circumvent the law by virtue of his powers as commander in chief, a senior administration official told the newspaper.[318] Similarly, a new secret White House-commissioned memo from Steven Bradbury at OLC argued that none of the CIA's interrogation techniques were cruel, inhumane, or degrading.[319]

What we will discuss below as part of this story, apart from all the above, is chilling....

David Addington, chief advisor to Vice President Cheney since 2001 and appointed chief of staff in 2005, is a Roman Catholic from a traditional Catholic military family.[320] A graduate of Georgetown University's School of Foreign Service, Addington called attempts to revive the Geneva Conventions against torture an abomination.[321] The Times had reported in December 2005, that since 2002, President Bush in his pursuit of terrorists, secretly authorized the National Security Agency (NSA) to spy on U.S. citizens without first obtaining a warrant from the Foreign Intelligence Surveillance Court, as required by federal law.[322] Michael Hayden was the director of the NSA (1999-2005), a Catholic who believed in proportionality in warfare.[323] Former Secretary of State Colin Powell expressed, "It's Addington" "He doesn't care about the Constitution." The "New Paradigm," as they called it, is that the

---

[316] Sherwood Ross (April 1, 2010), More Than Two-Dozen Countries Complicit In US Torture Program, The Public Record.

[317] Jane Mayer, The Dark Side: The Inside Story of How the War on Terror Turned Into a War on American Ideals (Double Day, 2008), ob. cit.

[318] Charlie Savage (January 4, 2006), Bush could bypass new torture ban, The Boston Globe.

[319] Jane Mayer, The Dark Side: The Inside Story of How the War on Terror Turned Into a War on American Ideals (Double Day, 2008), ob. cit.

[320] Jane Mayer (July 3, 2006), The Hidden Power, The New Yorker.

[321] Jane Mayer, The Dark Side: The Inside Story of How the War on Terror Turned Into a War on American Ideals (Double Day, 2008), ob. cit.

[322] Jane Mayer (July 3, 2006), The Hidden Power, The New Yorker.

[323] Shane Harris, The Watchers: The Rise of America's Surveillance State (The Penguin Pres, New York, 2010), ob. cit.

president has the power to disregard virtually all known legal limits if national security requires it. Jane Mayer wrote, "The Addingtons were a traditional Catholic military family."[324] Addington is driven in his accumulation of ideological influences, by deep convictions of his Catholic faith,[325] and who was trained by the Jesuits; as they admitted.[326]

Labeled as a hardcore neoconservative, he helped author the policy documents justifying torture, as well as the marginal papers to the Geneva Conventions that led to the terrible events at Abu Ghraib.[327] Briefly, the other formulator of those documents was then-Justice Department official Robert Delahunty, a Catholic scholar who believes that politics is largely served by Roman Catholicism in the world.[328] He came into contact with the Society of Jesus while attending one of its high schools...and despite revelations about his involvement in the formation of the torture documents, the University of St. Thomas solicited him to its credit as a professor.[329]

But going back to David Addington, he advanced the argument that suspects can be detained without access to any judicial review, something that is completely unconstitutional.

Marc Thiessen, White House Director of Speechwriting who wrote Bush's speeches, is also a Catholic and defended torture, claiming that Catholic theology permitted it.[330]

When I asked John Kiriakou, former CIA officer and first whistleblower of the black sites, if there was any extremist Christian motivation behind them, given that some Bush administration officials were involved with many Christian personalities in the United States, he indicated that this was indeed the case. And adding:

"In the CIA there are a large number of Christian fundamentalists, but not in the conventional evangelical sense. They are almost entirely fundamentalist Catholics, particularly Opus Dei, and Mormons. See "Stephen Kappes," for example."

Kappes was Deputy Director of CIA Operations in 2004 and Deputy Director of the CIA from 2006-2010. He is a devout Catholic who attends daily Mass at a church where the parish priest is a former State Department security officer. Involved in conversations about St. Augustine or Thomas Aquinas. And was involved at some level in the development of the black sites.[331]

On June 29, 2006, the Supreme Court ruled emphatically that the Bush administration had to comply with the Geneva Convention laws against torture.[332]

---

[324] Jane Mayer (July 3, 2006), The Hidden Power, The New Yorker.

[325] Robert Klein Engler, Reasons to Resist (Alphabeta Press, Omaha, NE, 2014), p. 31.

[326] http://jesuits.webs.com/jesuit-trained; accessed December 30, 2015.

[327] Coleen Rowley (May 25, 2011), Why Many Catholics Are Confused About Torture, The Hufftington Post.

[328] David K. Ryden, Is The Good Book Good Enough: Evangelical Perspectives on Public Policy (Lexington Books, 2011), p. 158.

[329] Dr. Steven H. Miles (Sept. 1, 2009), The Robert Delahunty torture-memo controversy at St. Thomas, MinnPost.

[330] Mark Oppenheimer (26 de febrero, 2010), Defender of Waterboarding Hears From Critics, The New York Times.

[331] Jeff Stein (March 25, 2010), Inside Man, Washingtonian.

[332] Jane Mayer, The Dark Side: The Inside Story of How the War on Terror Turned Into a War on American Ideals (Double Day, 2008), ob. cit. Note: unless otherwise noted, this is the same source.

Addington was outraged, and what he subsequently did shocked several colleagues: he did not comply with the Supreme Court's ruling, but instead made use of legislation to overturn the Court, saying simply that the Geneva Conventions did not give suspected terrorists access to U.S. courts and that the president had the authority to try them in military tribunals.

There was a constitutional crisis that got so bad that Bellinger - the State Department's top lawyer - and Waxman (State Department) threatened to resign. Condolezza Rice intervened in the case, pleading with the president with the words, "Mr. President, you can't reverse the court!" The head of the Office of Public Liaison at the State Department, Karen Hughes, also intervened to stop the president. Bush noted at the end, siding with both, "I accept the decision."

Nevertheless, Cheney and his staff went to work closely with Congress to restore virtually every aspect of the previous executive branch's power over detainees, including the military commissions. Congress ratified most of the White House's wishes. Subsequently, calls within the CIA called for transferring prisoners out of the black sites to Cuba, which Bush announced on September 26 that he had done, thus emptying the black sites, but insisted that the program was one of the most vital in the war on terrorism.

There was a general silence from the U.S. Catholic Church on torture and the Iraq war because of the support its leaders gave to Addington and Delahunty. Thus, polls showed that Catholics, more than the general public and more than Protestants and evangelicals, supported torture in interrogations.[333] Of course, not all Catholics and clergy think alike.

But in 2006, the U.S. Conference of Catholic Bishops issued a document against torture amid scandals permeating Iraqi prisons. It cites John Paul II's encyclical Veritatis Splendor, which considers "physical and mental torture" as "shameful" in a long list of great evils; and considered as such by the Second Vatican Council and as "intrinsically evil." A condemnation that, according to Priest Perry, "was the culmination of teaching against torture by the papal magisterium that increased in severity through the course of the 20th century." Alluding to Pope Benedict XVI, the document cites - for example - his words at an international congress of Catholic prison ministers, stating that: "Means of punishment or correction that either undermine or debase the human dignity of prisoners" must be eschewed by public authorities, he said. Immediately he added the following statement, which incorporates a quote taken from the Compendium of the Social Doctrine of the Church: "The prohibition against torture 'cannot be contravened under any circumstances'" (No. 404)."[334]

The Catholic Bishops' Conference document cites the Abu Ghraib prison scandals as an example.[335]

But other documents sent to government entities by the church also refer to the subject.[336]

---

[333] Coleen Rowley (May 5, 2008), Why Many Catholics Are Confused About Torture, The Hufftington Post.

[334] Torture: Torture is a Moral Issue-A Catholic Study Guide, USCCB.

[335] Ibid.

[336] Bishop John H. Ricard (2004) Letter to Congress on Human Rights and Torture; Bishop John H Ricard (October 4, 2005), Letter to Senate on Prohibition of Torture; (October 23, 2006), Statement: Torture is a Moral Issue; Bishop Thomas G. Wenski (January 30, 2008), Letter to Senate Supporting Expansion of the Ban on Torture; Bishop Francis George (March 5, 2008), Letter to President Bush on Torture. Wenski

In December 2014, the U.S. bishops again condemned Central Intelligence Agency torture as a betrayal of the nation's values.[337] Yet such statements have little validity from the perspective of the facts demonstrated regarding the papacy by virtue of supporting causes that generate power and influence for it. Even when events happen with which they do not agree with what is used to achieve their ends, according to several of them: in other words, an end that justifies the means; even if they do not know what will happen next.

Afghanistan and more...

As a part of the war against radical terrorism, hostilities on Afghan territory began on October 7, 2001, and lasted until December 28, 2014. The U.S. Army defeated the Islamic Emirate of Afghanistan, which was the official name of the Islamist regime that was established by Taliban fundamentalists. On December 17, 2001, the last Taliban Army positions finally fell.

Other later achievements by the U.S. military were:

The destruction of Al-Qaeda camps; the establishment of the new Afghan government; the creation of the New Afghan National Army; the return of more than 5.7 million refugees from Pakistan and Iran; the transfer of the combat role to the Afghan Armed Forces; and the death of Osama bin Laden on May 2, 2011, in Pakistan.

In 2010, U.S. media reported on coded references to New Testament biblical passages inscribed on high-powered rifles laid out for the U.S. military by a Michigan company called Trijicon.[338] Passages such as John 8:12 and 2 Corinthians 4:6 are found. Such coded rifles were supplied to U.S. soldiers in both Iraq and Afghanistan, even though U.S. military rules prohibit proselytizing any religion in both countries; to avoid criticism that the U.S. embarked on a religious crusade in its war against Al-Qaeda forces and Iraqi insurgents. Trijicon's sales and marketing director, Tom Munson, said the inscriptions "have always been there" and that there was nothing wrong or illegal in adding them; he also noted that the protest comes from a non-Christian group. The practice began under the company's founder, Glyn Bindon, a devout Christian from South Africa who died in a plane crash in 2003.

Meanwhile, U.S. Army and Marine Corps spokesmen reported that their services were not aware of the biblical labels. They indicated that officials were discussing what action to take in light of the ABC report.

(Jan. 30, 2008), Letter to Senate Supporting Expansion of the Ban on Torture; Cardinal Francis George (March 5, 2008), Letter to President Bush on Torture; Bishop Thomas G. Wenski (June 25, 2008), Support for Presidential Executive Order Banning Torture; Bishop Howard J. Hubbard (January 9, 2009), Coalition Letter to President-Elect Obama on Torture; Torture is an Intrinsic Evil: Study Guide: A Catholic Study Guide for a One-Session Workshop Facilitator Packet; The problem with torture: Excerpts from Pope Benedict XVI's World Day of Peace Message, 2006; Bishop Thomas G. Wenski (December 17, 2007), Letter to U.S. Senate on Torture; (February 2013), Background on Torture; Bishop Oscar Cantú (June 10, 2015), Letter to the Senate on Amendment Prohibiting the Use of Torture During Interrogations; etc.

[337] Peter Kenny (December 13, 2014), US bishops say CIA torture a betrayal of American values, Ecumenical news.

[338] Joseph Rhee, Mark Schone (Jan. 19, 2010) Marine Corps Concerned About 'Jesus Guns,' Will Meet With Trijicon, ABC News. Note: unless otherwise noted, this is the same source.

Mikey Weinstein noted for his part that, "It allows the Mujahedeen, the Taliban, al Qaeda and the insurrectionists and jihadists to claim they're being shot by Jesus rifles."[339]

Weinstein also noted that members of his group who serve in the military have told him that there are commanders who have referred to the weapons they possess as "spiritually transformed weapons of Jesus Christ."[340]

However, many soldiers expressed deep concern about a "crusader" subculture among other U.S. soldiers. Several cases are found for example in the wearing of T-shirts, badges, bullet liners, rifle sights, as well as tattoos with the term "Kafir" (which translates to infidel in Arabic); and "Infidel". One Navy-SEAL for example, sported a collection of patches that included the words "Infidel strong" and "Hadji Don't Surf;"[341] where Hadji is used as a derogatory term by many people towards Arabs, Muslims, and Middle Eastern people in general.

Another patch contains the image of a crusader ready to eat pork and the words in both English and Arabic read: "Pork Eating Crusader"[342] - in clear mockery of Muslims, who abstain from eating it. This case involved a German soldier belonging to NATO's International Security Assistance Force in Afghanistan.

Browsing the website of Opsgear (one of the companies offering several of the items listed), it is noted that they continued to offer for sale implements such as mugs, coats, t-shirts, and mouse pads with crusader messages. All of the aforementioned items contain the American flag in the background and a crusader soldier with his sword drawn and riding a horse.

Likewise, the J.K. Army company offers military-grade patches for Navy-SEALs that carry the name Crusader Cross patch for Navy-SEALs. But there are other companies with the same propaganda, such as Red Wolf AIRSOFT.

Crye Precision, a company under contract to the Department of Defense for the production of multi-camera camouflage for the U.S. military, is involved in the anti-Muslim/Islamic trade by offering the "Infidel" label on various wearable clothing and accessories.[343]

Similarly, some U.S. fighter planes have undergone changes that were extremely reminiscent of the Crusades of the Middle Ages. For example, in April 2012, the 122nd Fighter Squadron changed its name to the "Crusaders," and F-18 aircraft have white flags with red crosses (like the symbol of the Crusades) painted on their tails.[344]

Several experts suspect that behind these symbols - in a war against Islamic forces - lies the intention to impose Christianity on the region.[345]

---

[339] Crimesider Staff (January 20, 2010), What Would Jesus Shoot? U.S. Guns in Afghanistan and Iraq Bear Biblical Inscriptions Praising Christ, CBS News.

[340] Joseph Rhee, Mark Schone (Jan. 19, 2010) Marine Corps Concerned About 'Jesus Guns,' Will Meet With Trijicon, ABC News. Note: unless otherwise noted, this is the same source.

[341] Jacob Hausner (Nov. 12, 2013), Exclusive: The Crusader Sub-Culture in the US Military, Americans Against Islamophobia.

[342] Ibid.

[343] Ibid.

[344] (May 17, 2012), ¿Cruzados del Siglo XXI? Propaganda de guerra contra el Islam en EE.UU., RT en Español; see also Patrick Donohue (April 14, 2012), 'Crusaders' return: Air station squadron returns to old moniker, The Beaufort Gazette.

[345] (May 17, 2012), ¿Cruzados del Siglo XXI? Propaganda de guerra contra el Islam en EE.UU., RT en Español

"According to Boston University Professor of International Relations and former U.S. Army officer Andrew Basevich, "one of the doctrines assumes that with U.S. power we will be able to determine the fate of a large part of the world. But when are we going to recognize that we are not capable of determining the fate of 1.4 billion Muslims? We have no wisdom and no will and no well-lined purse."[346]

It should be noted that this squadron bore this name until 2008. That is, in the middle of the war in Iraq. But the unit's commander, Lieutenant Colonel William Lieblin, changed it to its former name: the "Werewolves," because according to him "The notion of being a crusader in that part of the world doesn't float."[347]

However, when Wiegel returned to the name "Crusaders" in 2012, he indicated that it was a way for his Marines to enlist in it and make their own history under the same name. And since the squadron was preparing for its seventieth-anniversary celebration, the intention was to return to the original name because for fifty years they were under this name; as an indication of their own heritage. It should be emphasized that the name "Werewolves" was the original name and that in 1958 it was changed to the "Crusaders." Thus, Weigel does not consider the original name to reflect the squadron's heritage... but the "Crusaders" does.[348] It should be stressed that members of the armed forces who contacted Weinstein's group, who are mostly Catholics and moderate Protestants, felt that the decision was blatantly religious and that they were told that, "the enemy gets to have Allah in their fight. We need to get our Lord and Savior back into our fight."[349]

The Military Religious Freedom Foundation intervened to make the squadron reverse its decision on the name "Crusaders;" its logos; etc.; since it violated the separation between Church and State in the American armed forces. His intervention was successful in May of that same year, as reported by Lieutenant Colonel Joseph Plenzler.[350]

Weinstein and his organization had to attend another trial (among many they have known), such as a piece of artwork that adorned the wall of the Wagon Wheel dining hall at Mountain Home Air Force Base in Idaho; it proclaimed the message of Matthew 5:9 - "Blessed are the peacemakers" - as well as the word "Integrity." The image portrayed a U.S. soldier next to a medieval crusader with his sword drawn, and a crusader flag mingled with the U.S. flag behind them. The artwork was removed after contacting the Pentagon.[351]

In Iraq and Afghanistan, General Schwarzkopf allowed Christian troops and chaplains to deploy Christian symbols such as large crosses erected around their military bases in those Muslim lands.[352]

---

[346] Ibid.

[347] Chris Rodda (April 17, 2012), Marines Return to Being "Crusaders," Alternet; Karis Huus (April 18, 2012), Group blasts Marine Corps for reviving 'Crusaders' name and symbols, NBC News.

[348] Ibid.

[349] Karis Huus (April 18, 2012), Group blasts Marine Corps for reviving 'Crusaders' name and symbols, NBC News.

[350] Karis Huus (May 24, 2012), Marine Werewolves transform into Crusaders, and back again, NBC News.

[351] Chris Rodda (May 31, 2013), The Pentagon Most Certainly is Listening to Mikey Weinstein, Huff Post.

[352] Chris Rodda (Nov. 18, 2009), Top Ten Ways to Convince the Muslims We're On a Crusade, Hufftington Post.

Also in Iraq, large murals with Christian motifs were painted on the outside of the T-barriers surrounding the chapel at Warhorse AFB. For example, on one side there was a Catholic cross on a green background and blue sky; and next to it, another painting depicting a soldier praying on his knees with his machine gun in his hands; and on another side a dove representing the Holy Spirit; and next to it, Jesus Christ carrying his cross.[353]

For its part, the barrel of one tank bore the words "New Testament"; while another contained the word "Apocalypse."[354] Afghanistan was a cadre of operations for the "Kill Team," a group of U.S. soldiers who would murder innocent civilians. In early 2010 and after six months of hard work, a group of infantrymen decided it was time to kill a haji (Afghan civilian). According to *Rolling Stone*, Bravo Company descended on the barren plains of Kanhadar not long after the start of the new year, when they would begin the hunt for Afghan civilians regardless of age.[355]

In addition, other U.S. military fundamentalists attempted to convert Afghans to Christianity.[356]

But Afghanistan would nevertheless be controlled by the Taliban.[357]

The war on terror would extend far beyond Iraq and Afghanistan; for it also went into Libya in 2011, by engaging in its civil war.

On January 17, 2011, the New Yorker's renowned American investigative journalist Seymour Hersh, Pulitzer Prize winner for The My Lai massacre, gave a major speech in Doha, Qatar, sponsored by the Center for International and Regional Studies at Georgetown (Jesuit) University.[358] After questioning the existence of democracy because of the foreign policies of former President George W. Bush and current President Barack Obama, he modulated former President Dick Cheney during the war on terror, commenting:

"We're going to change mosques into cathedrals. And when we get hold of all the oil, nobody's going to give a damn." That's the attitude: "We're going to change mosques into cathedrals."

"That's an attitude that pervades, I'm here to say, a large percentage of the Special Operations Command, the Joint Special Operations Command and Stanley McChrystal, the one who got in trouble because of the article in Rolling Stone, and his follow-on, a Navy admiral named McRaven, Bill McRaven — all are members or at least supporters of Knights of Malta. McRaven attended, so I understand, the recent annual convention of the Knights of Malta they had in Cyprus a few months back in November. They're all believers — many of them are members of Opus Dei.

---

[353] Ibid.

[354] Ibid.

[355] Mark Boal (March 27, 2011), The Kill Team: How U.S. Soldiers in Afghanistan Murdered Innocent Civilians, Rolling Stone.

[356] (May 6, 2009), Are US Forces Trying to Convert Afghans to Christianity? Democracy Now 1 of 2, Democracy Now!": https://www.youtube.com/watch?v=sSvnyNDsbBk; accessed December 29, 2015.

[357] Nir Rosen (January 31, 2011), Journey Into Taliban-Controlled Afghanistan, Rolling Stone; (March 25, 2013), The Obama/Bush Foreign Policies: Why Can't America Change? / Seymour Hersh, Center for International and Regional Studies: https://www.youtube.com/watch?v=yYy-WFdRzmo; accessed October 29, 2015.

[358] Blake Hounshell (January 22, 2011), Transcript: "The Obama/Bush Foreign Policies: Why Can't America Change?," Foreign Policy.

They do see what they are doing — and this is not an atypical attitude among some military — it's a crusade, literally. They see themselves as the protectors of the Christians. They're protecting them from the Muslims in the 13th century. And this is their function. They have little insignias, they have coins they pass among each other, which are crusader coins, and they have insignia that reflect that, the whole notion that this is a war, it's culture war.

"Look, Knights of Malta does great stuff. They do a lot of charity work; so does Opus Dei. It's a very extreme, extremely religious, Roman Catholic sect, if you will. But for me, it's always, when I think of them, I always think of the line we used about Werner von Braun. Werner Von Braun was the German rocket scientist who invented the V-2. And after WWII we had a secret program of bringing and sort of de-Nazifying some of the German scientists who were valuable to our own energy, our own missile program. And we brought him here — I think it was called PAPERCLIP, the secret program — and we brought him here to sort of recreate his life. You know, he was this nuclear... he was this scientist, he was a rocket scientist. So there was a wonderful satirist named Tom Lehrer [Mort Sahl -Ed.] — some of you old-timers might remember him, he wrote ditties. And one of his ditties about Werner von Braun was, oh yes, "Werner von Braun, he aimed for the moon but often hit London." With his rockets. So the trouble with some of these religious groups is they may have good things, but right now there is a tremendous, tremendous amount of anti-Muslim feeling in the military community."[359]

Following these revealing statements, *Foreign Policy* magazine criticized them, arguing that, "There's not much evidence to suggest that the Knights of Malta are the secretive cabal of anti-Muslim fundamentalists that Hersh described."[360]

The Washington Post, for its part, indicated that one of the problems with Hersh's claims is that Stanley McChrystal's spokesman, David Bolger, said that the general "is not and never has been" a member of the Knights of Malta and that the link Hersh tried to make was "completely false and without basis in fact."[361] However, we must emphasize that Hersh said in his speech that they "are all members of, or at least supporters of, Knights of Malta." McRaven and JSOC declined to comment.[362]

Interestingly, Jeremy Scahill, then of *The Nation*, wrote in his book *Dirty Wars*:

"McChrystal, he said, "presided over this black world where any actions were justified against Muslims because you were fighting against the Caliphate."[363]

He shared the political conviction that the United States was indeed at war with the Islamic world. Colonel McGregor, McChrystal's roommate at Westpoint, revealed that

---

[359] Ibid.
[360] Joshua E. Keating (January 19, 2011), Who Are the Knights of Malta - and What Do They Want, Foreign Policy.
[361] Paul Farhi (January 21, 2011), New Yorker's Hersh sparks anger, puzzlement with remarks on military 'crusaders,' The Washington Post; Paul Farhi (January 21, 2011), Hersh rebuked on 'crusaders,' The Washington Post; Jeff Schogol (January 21, 2011), McChrystal denies claims of secret military crusade against Islam, Stars and Stripes.
[362] Blake Hounshell (January 21, 2011), Seymour Hersh, the Knights of Malta, and me, Foreign Policy.
[363] Jeremy Scahill, Dirty Wars: The World Is a Battlefield (Nation Books, New York, 2013), ob. cit.

249

after 9/11, McChrystal believed there was a "global" Caliphate (the same one that Donald Rumsfeld, the Pentagon's Secretary of Defense, spoke of).[364]

Pentagon sources, meanwhile, said there is little evidence of a broad fundamentalist conspiracy in the military, although there have been incidents where officers have proselytized their subordinates, and that the military discourages partisan religious promotion.[365] Bill Donohue of the Catholic League noted that Hersh demonized the Knights of Malta.[366]

Hersh indicated at the time, that he did not remember every detail of his speech because it was "a rumination" rather than a scripted talk.[367] He also noted:

"no one said the whole war was waged as a crusade. My point is that some leaders of the Special Forces have an affinity for that notion, the notion that they're in a crusade.

"I'm comfortable with the idea that there is a great deal of fundamentalism in JSOC. It's growing and it's empirical.... There is an incredible strain of Christian fundamentalism, not just Catholic, that's part of the military."[368]

Salon came to Hersh's defense, stating that according to the Knights of Malta's website, they work on the front lines in cases of natural disasters and armed conflict... Likewise, Matthew Phelan, author of the article in *Salon* highlighted a whole range of historical figures and events where men in key intelligence and government positions were Knights of Malta who acted in accordance with their religion and its tenets.[369] A similar defense was made by *The Nation* in 2015, in addition to other aspects that Hersh has been criticized for.[370] To no avail was the Order of Malta's denial of involvement in any activity in Iraq or any other country in the world.[371]

JSOC was led by then Vice President Dick Cheney and former Secretary of Defense Donald Rumsfeld, turning the White House itself into a global capture and assassination machine.[372] Indeed, "Rumsfeld created a JSOC human intelligence collection operation, called the Strategic Support Branch, that mirrored the capabilities of the CIA." JSOC was thus converted into a spy agency as well; in addition to its other military mission tasks.

Before 9/11, JSOC was composed of just over 2,000 troops, and by 2013 numbered 25,000. Since then it has operated more aggressively than ever and most of its operations are classified. Col. Walter Patrick Lang, who spent much of his career in covert operations, indicated to Scahill about JSOC that, "Their real days of glory...

---

[364] Ibid.

[365] Paul Farhi (Jan. 21, 2011), New Yorker's Hersh sparks anger, puzzlement with remarks on military 'crusaders,' The Washington Post; Paul Farhi (Jan. 21, 2011), Hersh rebuked on 'crusaders,' The Washington Post.

[366] Bill Donohue (January 18, 2011), Knights of Malta demonized, Catholic League.

[367] Paul Farhi (Jan. 21, 2011), New Yorker's Hersh sparks anger, puzzlement with remarks on military 'crusaders,' The Washington Post; Paul Farhi (Jan. 21, 2011), Hersh rebuked on 'crusaders,' The Washington Post.

[368] Ibid.

[369] Matthew Phelan (February 28, 2011), Seymour Hersh and the men who want him committed, Salon.

[370] Greg Grandin (May 12, 2015) It's a Conspiracy! How to Discredit Seymour Hersh, The Nation.

[371] (Dec. 14, 2007), Italy: Knights of Malta rejects alleged link to military action, Adnkronos Religion.

[372] Michael B. Kelley (May 10, 2013), US Special Ops Have Become Much, Much Scarier Since 9/11, Business Insider. Note: unless otherwise noted, this is the same source.

really only started after 9/11," Colonel Walter Patrick Lang, who spent much of his career in covert operations, told Scahill. "They didn't do a lot of fighting before that."

According to General Hugh Shelton, Chairman of the Joint Chiefs of Staff under former President Clinton, "They're the ace in the hole."

JSOC was "created in secrecy to perform operations that were kept hidden to virtually all other entities of military and governments."

According to Vincent Cannistraro, a career CIA counterterrorism officer, "It grew and went out of control under the vice president. It kinda went wild." Indeed by 2003, being led by General Stanley McChrystal, it was running the show in Iraq, as well as the Iraqi Special Operations units that became countless death squads. But their presence was also in Afghanistan.

A chilling point in JSOC's reach occurred in early 2004 when Donald Rumsfeld signed the Al Qaeda Network Execute Order, which "streamlined JSOC's ability to conduct operations and hit targets outside of the stated battlefields of Iraq and Afghanistan." Thus, by the middle of that year, the command's operations in Iraq accelerated dramatically to the point where they were "running the covert war buried within the larger war and controlling the intelligence," according to Scahill.

However, the Obama administration has expanded such operations around the world so formidably (from Iran to Bolivia to Yemen) that no administration has matched it, according to a special operations source.[373] By 2010, there were 75 countries.[374] By January 2014, they had expanded to nearly 100 nations, making them about 60% of the inhabited world.[375] Put another way, from the 2000s to 2013, JSOC vastly increased its operations; its number of squadrons; its worldwide presence, and covert operations: which goes hand in hand with the promotion of Christian fundamentalism among the military and academies, such as West Point from 2001 to the present.[376]

A source whose face could not be disclosed to protect him revealed regarding JSOC's ideology that the world is a battlefield and therefore, the Joint Special Operations Command can go wherever it pleases and do whatever it wants to do, to achieve the national security objectives, of whatever administration is in power.[377]

As far as missions were concerned, there were doubts about what their soldiers were asked to do, where, and for what purpose. Many of those missions were of questionable legality.[378] Many of those were not battlefields. They ranged from kinetic operations to capture or assassination; and in some cases detaining people as directed by the U.S. government.[379]

---

[373] Karen DeYoung and Greg Jaffe (June 4, 2010), U.S. 'secret war' expands globally as Special Operations forces take larger role, The Washington Post; Jeremy Scahill (June 4, 2010), Obama's Expanding Covert Wars, The Nation.

[374] Ibid.

[375] Nick Turse (January 7, 2014), Why Are US Special Operations Forces Deployed in Over 100 Countries, The Nation.

[376] James E. Parco, PhD (February, 2013), For God and Country: Religious Fundamentalism in the U.S. Military, Center for Inquiry Office of Public Policy, p. 2. See further documentation on JSOC in the following works: Sean Naylor, Relentless Strike: The Secret History of Joint Special Operations Command (St. Martin's Press, 2015); Jeremy Scahill, Dirty Wars: The World Is a Battlefield (Nation Books, New York, 2013), ob. cit.

[377] Rick Rowley (Director). Jeremy Scahill (Producer) (2013), Dirty Wars. Big Noise Films and Civic Bakery.

[378] Ibid.

[379] Ibid.

Having an internalized interrogation program where torture was practiced: a program without the knowledge of conventional U.S. military forces or even the CIA.[380]

Bagram Air Base in Afghanistan is said to have been a secret prison where prisoners were abused, according to nine witnesses whose stories were documented by the BBC.[381] At that air base, a military chaplain gave Bibles to soldiers encouraging them to evangelize Afghans, an action they tried unsuccessfully to deny having carried out. A distribution of Bibles in Dari and Pashtu languages was also planned. General Roger Brady, an evangelical Christian, ignored the regulations on religion, which do not allow Christian symbology on bases to avoid conflicts on non-majority Christian soil.[382] We knew of at least one Catholic priest, chaplain and captain at that air base.

In March 2015, Catholic priest Paul K. Hurley was elected by the Senate as Major General and Chief of Chaplains of the U.S. Army, supplanting Monsignor Donald Rutherford.[383] His presence in Iraq was significant.

And what was the point of all this conflict? Donald Rumsfeld acknowledged in 2015 that it was a mistake to want to impose democracy in Iraq.[384]

This is how the events of the conflict against Iraq and Afghanistan unfolded. All under the banner of a crusade. As labeled by Bush and with the blessing of many sectors of the Catholic Church and many Protestants. Also, the battle against terrorism, whether Islamic, or secular, or Christian. All when (as Francis Fukuyama rightly wrote) "the United States can affect many countries around the world without their being able to exercise a reciprocal degree of influence on the United States."[385]

But other things were to happen after this conflict, as we will see.

---

[380] Ibid.

[381] Hilary Andersson (April 15, 2010), Afghans 'abused at secret prison' at Bagram airbase, BBC News; see also Matthias Gebauer, John Goetz and Britta Sandberg (September 21, 2009), The Forgotten Guantanamo: Prisoner Abuse Continues at Bagram Prison in Afghanistan, Spiegel International.

[382] James E. Parco, David A. Levy, Attitudes Aren't Free: Thinking Deeply About Diversity in the U.S. Armed Forces (Air University Press, Maxwell Airforce Base, Alabama, 2010), p. 26.

[383] Aneri Pattani (March 30, 2015), Boston priest named US Army chief of chaplains, The Boston Globe.

[384] Melanie Phillips (June 6, 2015), Bush was wrong on Iraq, says Rumsfeld, The Sunday Times; (June 8, 2015), Donald Rumsfeld: "Fue un error quere imponer la demcoracia en Iraq," RT.

[385] Francis Fukuyama, America at the Crossroads: Democracy, Power, and the Neoconservative Legacy (Yale University Press, 2006), p. 156.

CHAPTER

7

Attempts to establish a theocracy, the spies, and more "black sites"

Attempt to establish martial law

On September 26, 2006, President George Bush urged the U.S. Congress to consider revising federal laws to allow the U.S. military to restore public order and enforce laws in the event of a natural disaster, terrorist attack or incident, or other condition. Subsequently, the changes were included in the John Warner National Defense Authorization Act for Fiscal Year 2007, or H.R. 5122, which was signed into law on October 16, 2007.

Said Act authorized FY2007 appropriations for military activities of the Department of Defense, for military construction; and for defense activities of the Department of Energy, to prescribe personal military forces for said year, as well as other purposes.

Section 1076, in section 333 of title 10, United States Code reads in large part and under the heading "Use of the Armed Forces in Major Public Emergencies." It stated that the President of the United States could employ the armed forces, including the National Guard in Federal service to restore public order and enforce the laws of the Nation as a result of natural disasters, epidemics, or other serious public health emergencies, terrorist attack or incident; or other condition in any State or possession of the country. The President could suppress in the aforementioned possessions any insurrection, domestic violence, unlawful variant, or conspiracy.[1]

And then the exorbitant amounts allocated to the military forces:

"(1) For the Army, $10,876,609,000.
(2) For the Navy, $17,383,857,000.
(3) For the Air Force, $24,235,951,000.
(4) For Defense-wide activities, $21,111,559,000, of which $181,520,000 is authorized for the Director of Operational Test and Evaluation."[2]

All the demands of George W. Bush's administration could only influence a policy not only foreign - as we have seen - but also domestic, affecting the nation's democracy and creating a breach in the separation between Church and State. Many of his government's regulations are not necessarily inspired by a religious zeal to tear down that wall, but together with all the ultra-right-wing so-called Christian actions, they serve as an instrument to create a form of authoritarianism and also persecution against men and women of faith.

---

[1] [H. R. 5122] Public Law 109-364-OCT. 17, 2006.
[2] Ibid.

Although that law did not last long, as the National Defense Authorization Act for Fiscal Year 2008 [H.R. 4986], uprooted much of the language contained in section 1076, to limit the powers of the President of the United States, something that was considered salutary.

The Washington Post reported in December of that year that the U.S. military expected to have 20,000 uniformed troops inside the United States by 2011 to help state and local officials respond in the event of a nuclear terrorist attack or other national catastrophe, according to Pentagon officials. Some critics within the military itself, and among civil liberties and libertarian groups, worried that such measures threatened to strain the military and even undermine the Posse Comitatus Act (a law restricting the military's role in enforcing domestic laws at home).[3]

But during the Barack Obama administration, *The Washington Post* revealed in 2010 that the CIA and JSOC had placed U.S. citizens on a list to be killed or captured.[4] That list was confirmed by Admiral Dennis C. Blair, then Director of National Intelligence, before the House Select Committee on Intelligence on February 3, 2010, stating:

"[...] a decision to use lethal force against a U.S. citizen must get special permission" before the targeting of a United States citizen can be granted and that "being a U.S. citizen will not spare an American from getting assassinated by military or intelligence operatives overseas if the individual is working with terrorists and planning to attack fellow Americans."[5]

The Nation reported in November 2009 that private security contractor Blackwater Worldwide (later Xe Services, later Academy, and finally Constellis Holdings) was intimately involved with the CIA- and JSOC-directed assassination programs on Pakistani soil.[6]

As early as 2009, Obama stated as his administration's policy that, "There may be a number of people who cannot be prosecuted for past crimes, in some cases because evidence may be tainted, but who nonetheless pose a threat to the security of the United States." *NBC*'s Rachel Madow, rightly pointed out in her critique of that statement that, "We're not prosecuting them for past crimes, but we need to keep them in prison because of our expectation of their future crimes."[7]

For his part, Democrat Dennis Kucinich had sent several letters to the Obama administration asking several questions about the potential unconstitutionality of the rule and possible violations of international law but did not get a response.[8] Kucinich considered the rule to be extra-constitutional and extra-judicial because it "vitiates the presumption of innocence and the government then becomes the investigator, policeman, prosecutor, judge, jury, executioner all in one." He wondered how we know

---

[3] Spencer S. Hsu and Ann Scott Tyson (December 1, 2008), Pentagon to Detail Troops to Bolster Domestic Security, The Washington Post.
[4] Dana Priest (Jan. 27, 2010), U.S. military teams, intelligence deeply involved in aiding Yemen on strikes, The Washington Post.
[5] H.R.6010 — 111th Congress (2009-2010).
[6] Jeremy Scahill (November 23, 2009), The Secret US War in Pakistan, The Nation.
[7] (May 26, 2009), 'The Rachel Maddow Show' for Thursday, May 21, NBC News.
[8] Jeremy Scahill, Dirty Wars: The World Is a Battlefield (Nation Books, New York, 2013), ob. cit. Note: unless otherwise indicated, this is the same source.

why certain people are killed and who makes that decision. He added... "It's like a God-like power." He then told journalist Jeremy Scahill:

"We are acting out of fear. We've forgotten who we are," he told me. "We're knocking out pillars of our democratic traditions here. The right to a trial? Gone. The right to be able to confront those who are accusing you? Gone. The right to be free from cruel and unusual punishment? Gone. All of these anchors are being pulled away." He added, "Don't think for a moment that we can do these kinds of things without it having a direct effect here at home. You can't have one America abroad and another one at home. It's all the same. The erosion of integrity, the erosion of democratic values, the erosion of a benevolent intent all augurs a nation in which the basic rights of our own people can no longer be secured. They are up for the auction of the assassin."

On July 30, 2010, Kucinich introduced H.R. 6010, a bill "to prohibit the extrajudicial killing of United States citizens." However, only six members of the House of Representatives signed that bill; and without the support of a single senator, so it died immediately.

Senator Ron Wayden told Jeremy Scahill on camera that if the American people knew that what they thought a law said, was interpreted very distinctly in secret by the government, they would be exceptionally surprised.[9]

Again, Kucinich introduced the bill this time as H.R. 6357 on August 3, 2012, but it was again defeated.

In his May 2013 speech on counterterrorism, Obama sought to justify "just war" by invoking centuries-old thinking on the matter,[10] beginning with St. Augustine.

Regarding the aforementioned war, he justified the killing of four U.S. citizens with drones in Yemen and Pakistan in 2011.[11]

And when on September 30 of the same year a drone killed U.S. cleric Anwar Al-Awlaki (along with American Samir Khan), of Yemeni descent but born in the United States, it was a decision Barack Obama told his colleagues was "an easy one."[12] Al-Awlaki's son, just 16, Abdulrahman al-Awlaki, also a U.S. citizen, and his Yemeni cousin, 17, were killed by another drone a month after Anwar.[13]

Barack Obama made John Brennan, director of the CIA (elected in 2013), his moral consultant on targets to kill; "a priest whose blessing has become indispensable to Mr. Obama, echoing the president's attempt to apply the "just war" theories of Christian philosophers to a brutal modern conflict."[14] Indeed, the "just war" theory invoked by Obama primarily from medieval Catholicism comes from John Brennan, who is a

[9] Rick Rowley (Director). Jeremy Scahill (Producer) (2013), Dirty Wars. Big Noise Films and Civic Bakery.
[10] Joe Boyle (May 24, 2013), Just war: From Augustine to Obama, BBC News.
[11] Mark Mardell (May 24, 2013), Barack Obama defends 'just war' using drones, BBC News.
[12] Jo Becker and Scott Shane (May 29, 2012), Secret 'Kill List' Proves a Test of Obama's Principles and Will, The New York Times.
[13] Peter Finn and Greg Miller (October 17, 2011), Anwar al-Awlaki's family speaks out against his, son's deaths, The Washington Post.
[14] Jo Becker and Scott Shane (May 29, 2012), Secret 'Kill List' Proves a Test of Obama's Principles and Will, The New York Times.

Roman Catholic and who was educated by the Jesuits at Fordham University.[15] He played a leading role in the Obama administration in reaching out to Muslims, especially naturalized Americans, advocating to stop the use of offensive terms toward Muslims.[16]

Fordham University was rebuked in 2012 when the board of trustees chose Brennan to deliver the commencement address and to award him an honorary degree. The refusal was due to public revelations that the CIA, with Brennan's support, endorsed interrogation torture (in 2012, Brennan was assistant to the president for national security and counterterrorism). Many university faculty members, as well as students, disagreed about the awards and petitioned the few faculty members who granted them to remove the honorary degree awarded to the future CIA director (January 2013).[17] Jesuit priest and Fordham president Joseph McShane refused to revoke the degree.[18]

Former CIA intelligence analyst as well as military analyst for 30 years, Ray McGovern, writes of Brennan's "open identification with torture, secret prisons and other abuses of national and international law."[19] And he notes that "Brennan is widely known for his advocacy of kidnapping-for-torture (also known as 'extraordinary renditions') and assassination of 'militants' (including U.S. citizens) with 'Hellfire' missiles fired by 'Predator' and 'Reaper' drones."[20]

In October 2015, Brennan's email was hacked and documents were uploaded to the Wikileaks website.[21] One of them, dated May 7, 2008, from the Select Committee on Intelligence and written by Vice Chairman Christopher S. Bond, addresses his colleagues to propose a solution for Congress to accept legislation that would allow means of interrogation that do not conflict with the rejected. We read in part:

"(1) to forbid the use of harsh interrogation techniques that may run afoul of the Geneva Conventions; and (2) to give our intelligence agencies the tools and flexibility they need to conduct full and timely interrogations of terrorists and other detainees.

"Rather than authorizing intelligence agencies to use only those techniques that are *allowed* under the AFM [Army Field Manual], I believe the more prudent approach is to preclude the use of specific techniques that are *prohibited* under the AFM. In this way, the Congress can state clearly that certain harsh interrogation techniques will not be permissible. At the same time, this approach allows the possibility that new techniques that are not explicitly authorized in the AFM, but nevertheless comply with the law, may be developed in the future."[22]

---

[15] Jamie Mason (April 1, 2015), Honorary degree violated Jesuit mission, some Fordham University faculty members say, National Catholic Reporter.

[16] Patrick Goodenough (January 9, 2013), Islam 'Helped to Shape' CIA Nominee John Brennan's World View, CNS news.

[17] Jamie Manson (April 1, 2015), Honorary degree violated Jesuit mission, some Fordham University faculty members say, National Catholic Reporter.

[18] Jamie Manson (May 20, 2015), Fordham University's president rejects call to revoke honorary degree, National Catholic Reporter.

[19] William Alberts (June 19, 2012), Christians and the Kill List, CounterPunch Magazine.

[20] Ibid.

[21] Tal Kopan (Oct. 27, 2015), CIA Director John Brennan 'outraged' by hack of his emails, CNN.

[22] https://wikileaks.org/cia-emails/Torture/Torture.pdf; accessed December 31, 2015.

A draft of such a bill was found in Brennan's mail.[23]

Nevertheless, on July 13, 2016, Brennan expressed that if the president of the United States gave an order to the CIA to execute torture on prisoners, it was absolutely the director's responsibility to do so or not in good conscience, but if he were asked to do so, they should look for another director.[24]

Sarah Childress of *PBS*'s *Frontline* program provided six reasons why "black sites" could still exist under the Obama administration: 1. The executive order signed by Barack Obama banning the practice of torture could easily be repealed by the next administration secretly, without a formal announcement.[25] 2. The government has not reissued the Army Field Manual to delete Appendix M (introduced by the Bush administration in 2006), which authorizes the isolation of detainees to prevent them from gathering information from others or learning new cross-examination techniques: a tactic that can inflict physical and mental stress, and that technically could allow them to be interrogated for forty hours straight with only four-hour rest periods at each end. In addition, the document's appendix, while prohibiting sensory deprivation, permits the use of goggles, blindfolds, and handcuffs to "generate a perception of separation" for up to twelve hours or more if security requires it. Interrogations with the use of torture began, as far as there is evidence, during the Clinton administration; or in other words, after the 1993 World Trade Center bombings, after which the government sent suspects abroad, not for trial, but for interrogation through the use of torture. 4. For all of the above, it is difficult to know whether the Obama administration has been accountable, as he fought in civil and criminal cases to prevent the CIA from disclosing any information about the treatment of detainees, encouraging them not to share what they know.

The Obama administration also focused on prosecuting government employees who leaked classified information under the Espionage Act, doing so more than previous administrations. Although President Obama pledged to close the Guantanamo detention facility before he was elected president in 2008, the prison remained open. As of the time of the report - 2013 - there were 166 detainees; 86 that were approved for release, and 46 whom the Obama administration decided to hold indefinitely without charge or trial. More than half of the detainees were on hunger strike, and some were being restrained and tube-fed so as not to allow them to starve to death, the Pentagon said. By 2009, Obama established military commissions for some detainees, but the processes have been tense, as defense lawyers for the detainees worried that communications with their clients are being monitored and that their documents have been reviewed and subjected to a data breach in the Pentagon's computer system. The United States has so far ignored the 9/11 Commission's recommendation to develop a common course for the treatment and detention of terrorism suspects.[26]

Since the murder of 16-year-old Abdulrahman al-Awlaki in Yemen, President Obama's pro-presidential lawyers (Eric Holder and John Brennan) have explicitly

---

[23] https://wikileaks.org/cia-emails/Torture-Ways/Torture-Ways.pdf; accessed December 31, 2015.

[24] Alex Emmons (July 13, 2016), CIA Director Says Next President Could Order Agency to Torture and It Might Comply, The Intercept.

[25] Sarah Childress (April 22, 2013), Six Reasons the "Dark Side" Still Exists Under Obama, Frontline Enterprise. Note: unless otherwise noted, this is the same source.

[26] Ibid. See also in detail, The Report of The Constitution Project's Task Force on Detainee Treatment (The Constitution Project, Washington, D.C., 2013).

argued that he is and should be vested with the most extreme power he could have.[27] No president has ever had the legal authority to kill U.S. citizens.[28] That entire process was carried out solely within the Executive Branch. In other words, with no controls or oversight of any kind; with zero transparency and accountability, where everything was intended to be kept in the utmost secrecy.[29] *The Guardian* reports:

"What has made these actions all the more radical is the absolute secrecy with which Obama has draped all of this. Not only is the entire process carried out solely within the Executive branch - with no checks or oversight of any kind - but there is zero transparency and zero accountability. The president's underlings compile their proposed lists of who should be executed, and the president - at a charming weekly event dubbed by White House aides as "Terror Tuesday" - then chooses from "baseball cards" and decrees in total secrecy who should die. The power of accuser, prosecutor, judge, jury, and executioner are all consolidated in this one man, and those powers are exercised in the dark.

"In fact, The Most Transparent Administration Ever™ has been so fixated on secrecy that they have refused even to disclose the legal memoranda prepared by Obama lawyers setting forth their legal rationale for why the president has this power."[30]

The Justice Department had submitted a 16-page justification document to President Obama to target for assassination of U.S. citizens who constituted a danger to national security in the fight against terrorism.[31] However, the degree of power granted to the president was not justified.

There was another attempt; but this time from the White House when it released a 50-page legal justification given to the Senate Committee on Intelligence in an attempt to relieve pressure on John Brennan in 2013.[32]

Eric Holder argued in March before the Senate Judiciary Committee that the use of lethal military force against a U.S. citizen in his country would be legal and justified in "extraordinary circumstances" compared to 9/11:[33]

"The president could conceivably have no choice but to authorize the military to use such force if necessary to protect the homeland."[34]

David Barron and Martin S. Lederman, meanwhile, were involved with the 7-page memo to give Obama legal permission to carry out extrajudicial killings.[35] Lederman

---

[27] Ibid.

[28] Scott Shane (April 6, 2010), U.S. Approves Targeted Killing of American Cleric, The New York Times.

[29] Glenn Greenwald (February 5, 2013), Chilling legal memo from Obama DOJ justifies assassination of US citizens, The Guardian.

[30] Ibid.

[31] Charlie Savage (Oct. 8, 2011), Secret U.S. Memo Made Legal Case to Kill A Citizen, The New York Times; http://msnbcmedia.msn.com/i/msnbc/sections/news/020413_DOJ_White_Paper.pdf; accessed Dec. 31, 2013.

[32] Steve Holland and Susan Heavey (February 5, 2013), Memo justifies drone kills even with patchy intelligence, Reuters.

[33] Jon Swaine (March 6, 2013), Barack Obama 'has authority to use drone strikes to kill Americans on US soil', The Telegraph.

[34] Ibid.

was then and remains an associate professor of law at the Jesuit-owned Georgetown University Law Center. Despite his involvement in the memo. This led to suspicions that martial law would be installed in the nation.

And although USNORTHCOM (the US division of JSOC), attempted to deny the threat of martial law in the United States through its forces, because a US Army unit was training for domestic operations under its control in October 2008, they indicated that the force "may be called upon to help with civil unrest and crowd control."[36] There have already been cases of recent militarized police forces in parts of the United States: for example, after a police officer shot and killed unarmed black teenager Michael Brown, large protests in Ferguson, Missouri, erupted and clashed with police. Democrat John Lewis said on August 14 of that year that Obama should declare martial law to protect the outraged.[37] The police used extreme military tactics and equipment.[38]

U.S. spying system on civilians and terrorists

Let's detail some more about the spying system that the government began to manage through the NSA and other government agencies: the US division of JSOC, or USNORTHCOM -United States Northern Command-, which was established on October 1, 2002: the national map that NorthCom holds to monitor the nation of terrorists and US citizens and any other individual, contained as of 2011, about 11 million records of people (almost twice as many as three years before); 44.000 government entities identified and mapped; 116,000 emergency services and 182,000 public health facilities.[39] Thirty-two new datasets were included for military recruiting stations, a good number of which were the target of protests and even attacks. Seventeen thousand "national symbols" were added; as well as 315,000 "public places" and a hodgepodge under the category "other," which included "places of worship." The Pentagon softened the official jargon to make the mission sound less offensive. After Sept. 11, 2001, several military planners replaced the phrase, "Military Support to Civil Authorities" with "Defense Support of Civil Authorities" (DSCA), a less martial wording in an ever more militarized America. Similarly, in its voluminous January 2011 *Handbook* laying out planning factors to be used by local military forces operating in the United States, sternly mandating that they "*do not use the terms* 'Intelligence, Surveillance and Reconnaissance (ISR)' or 'Intelligence Preparation of the Battlefield (IPB).' The appropriate terminology in a DSCA [Defense Security Cooperation Agency] environment is *Incident Awareness and Assessment*." As the writers of Top Secret America point out, there is abundant evidence of what goes on in

---

[35] Conor Friedersdorf (Aug. 18, 2014), 7 Pages That Gave President Obama Cover to Kill Americans, The Atlantic.

[36] (Oct. 7, 2008), Is Posse Comitatus Dead? US Troops on US Streets, Democracy Now.

[37] Pema Levy (Aug. 14, 2014), Rep. John Lewis, Civil Rights Icon, Calls for 'Martial Law' in Ferguson, Mo., Newsweek.

[38] Marisol Bello andYamiche Alcindor (Aug. 19, 2014), Police in Ferguson ignite debate about military tactics, USA Today; Thomas Gibbons-Neff (Aug. 14, 2014), Military veterans see deeply flawed police respólice in Ferguson, The Washington Post; (Aug. 14, 2014), McCaskill: Police 'Militarization' Escalated Unrest In Ferguson, NBC News; Sen. Rand Paul (Aug. 14, 2014), Rand Paul: We Must Demilitarize the Police, Time Magazine; Steve Holland and Andrea Shalal (Aug. 23, 2014), Obama orders review of police use of military hardware, Reuters.

[39] Dana Priest and William Arkin, Top Secret America: The Rise of the New American Security State (Little, Brown and Company, New York, 2011), ob. cit. Note: unless otherwise noted, this is the same source.

communities and local police stations across the country, where the intent is sometimes less than fair in offering support and comfort to distressed citizen. Thus, USNORTHCOM has carefully cataloged places of religious worship on The Map as part of its emergency management missions; and since the events of 9/11, many have developed faith-based cooperative initiatives where police work with religious communities to prepare for a hostile event such as an act of violence or vandalism. Dana Priest and William Arkin pointed out:

"In 2008, the National Geospatial-Intelligence Agency decided to purchase its own information on places of worship. It went to a small company, Ionic Enterprise (since bought and gone out of business), that was already tracking the data for commercial vendors and numerous state governments. The government asked for the data to be delivered in four subgroups—Catholic churches, Protestant churches, mosques, and synagogues—with quarterly updates, according to the mapping contract."

Some state officials were confused by the priority the federal government placed on religious institutions, but as a young USNORTHCOM intelligence officer explained, "It isn't only response that's important," adding, "Our responsibility is also to look at the threat." When asked if religious institutions posed a threat, she did not respond... But strangely, only churches with congregations larger than 750 people were tracked, as well as all synagogues and mosques.

A 161-page document under the title, June 2010 DHS *Geospatial Concept of Operations*, contains "the authority data matrix" for map users, where there are two subcategories: "houses of worship" and "mosques;" and in USNORTHCOM intelligence egg, and in Room 111 where the Top Secret version of The Map is kept, the Integrated Common Operating Picture contains "Muslims in America" is one of the categories of information collected and mapped, 24/7."

"In the top secret version of the nation's geography, the government tracks all threats picked up by U.S. intelligence and law enforcement in the past forty-eight hours. NorthCom analysts and interagency liaison officers from the CIA, the NSA, the FBI, and other intelligence agencies can access the raw intelligence—the actual reports from local authorities, in many cases—and can interact with colleagues across the nation via specialized chat rooms for those following gangs, drugs, human smuggling, or reports and even suspicions about people and places on the map just possibly linked to terrorism. As the young intelligence officer in the top secret egg proudly summed up: "It's all here.""

Although we do not go into details, it is worth noting that each division has its own dedicated chaplain's office for natural disasters, where the armed forces of each division take part in the solution. They range from Baptists, Pentecostals, Catholics, and many others.

By then, the Obama administration expanded the elite military unit's powers to hunt down foreign fighters around the world through JSOC.[40]

---

[40] Thomas Gibbons-Neff and Dan Lamothe (November 25, 2016), Obama administration expands elite military unit's powers to hunt foreign fighters globally, The Washington Post.

CHAPTER
8

"My name is Jorge Bergoglio"

From Bergoglio to Francis, Pontiff of the Roman Catholic Church
a. His role during the Argentine dictatorship

On July 31, 1973, the Provincial Superior of the Society of Jesus in Argentina, Ricardo O'Farrell, was succeeded by the Master of Novices and Rector of the Colegio Máximo de San Miguel (San Miguel Maximo College), Jorge Mario Bergoglio. At only 36 years of age, only seven years as a priest, and only three months after making perpetual profession, his appointment was unusual: in an order that demands long years of formation, as well as severe discipline and obedience for its members to be elected to such positions.[1]

But not only that. Bergoglio was also a militant in the Peronist organization Guardia de Hierro (Iron Guard), which formed (together with Frente Estudiantil Nacional (National Student Front)) the main youth nucleus that opposed the groups led by Montoneros, the Organización Única del Trasvasamiento Generacional (Unique Organization of Generational Transfer). It was made up of Catholic, atheist, socialist, Marxist, and spiritualist members.[2] As documented by Argentine journalist Horacio Verbitsky:

"[...] the name Iron Guard was a tribute to the eponymous paramilitary and anti-Semitic organization founded by the Romanian Catholic leader Corneliu Codreanu from his Legion of the Archangel Michael."[3]

The slogan of the organization was "Loving Perón," an activity to which Jorge Mario Bergoglio and others dedicated themselves from the inside.[4]

Bergoglio belonged to "the old generation" - in Olga Wornat's words - of Jesuit thought.[5]

The same writer, collecting the testimonies of two priests regarding Jorge Mario Bergoglio, comments:

"Members of the Society of Jesus and some of his colleagues in the Episcopate have opposing opinions. The prestigious Uruguayan Jesuit Luis Perico Pérez Aguirre, founder of the Peace and Justice Service in the neighboring country and advisor to the UN, who recently died in an accident, spoke at length with me in April 2000, while he

---

[1] Horacio Verbitsky, Vigilia de armas (Tomo III). Del Cordobazo de 1969 al 23 de marzo de 1976: Historia política de la iglesia católica (Random House Mondadori S.A., Buenos Aires, 2013), ob. cit.
[2] Ibid.
[3] Ibid.
[4] Ibid.
[5] Olga Wornat, Nuestra Santa Madre: Historia pública y privada de la Iglesia Católica Argentina (Ediciones B Argentina S.A., Buenos Aires, 2002), ob. cit.

was hospitalized in Montevideo. "I do not have good memories of Jorge (Bergoglio). The Society of Jesus in Buenos Aires, the Colegio Máximo, was a luxury in Latin America and it collapsed when he was Provincial and because of his management. From here we always sent seminarians to be formed there, but after him, we did not send anyone else. The Society in Argentina changed from progressive to conservative and retrograde. I have nothing to do with Bergoglio, nor with his way of seeing the world and in particular the Church, nor with his way of acting during the dictatorship, but I don't want to talk. We met many years ago and there are very unpleasant situations that I prefer to forget." An emblematic and verbose Bishop of the province of Buenos Aires, confessed to this journalist: "I do not speak to Bergoglio since I learned about the horrors that the Jesuits told me about him. He was Massera's friend, he ate with him. He is very dangerous."[6]

Massera, Emilio Eduardo, was a well-known Argentine military officer, and genocide during the dictatorship.

The Chancellery of Argentina keeps in its archives a document from an information service specialized in the monitoring of ecclesiastical issues and actors, where it is stated that Bergoglio himself intended to cleanse the Society of Jesus of "left-handed Jesuits."[7] He expanded this phrase to members of his society in his preaching, because for him it was necessary for the Jesuits to avoid "abstract ideologies that do not coincide with reality" and that they should react with "[...] a healthy allergy every time they try to recognize Argentina through theories that have not arisen from our national reality and especially in the recognition of the sense of religious reserve that the faithful people have."[8] For that, they should be inspired by the criteria of Ignatius of Loyola, founder of the Society of Jesus when he said that, "Unity is superior to conflict, the whole is superior to the part, time is superior to space, reality is superior to the idea."[9]

The Society of Jesus, led by Bergoglio, then took on the struggle against liberation theology as its axis.[10]

Miguel Ignacio Mom Debussy, who was a Jesuit and close to him, says that Bergoglio was absolutely opposed to liberation theology; very extremist in his right-wing position.[11]

Bergoglio's cleansing of "left-handed Jesuits" began in Barrio Belén in the slum of Bajo Flores, where they carried out promotional tasks in a community work: with the Hungarian Jesuit exiled from a noble family, Francisco Jalics, as well as another Jesuit (a theologian named Orlando Yorio), who created it, and some other jesuits. They were members of the pastoral team of villas of the Archdiocese of Buenos Aires. Several

---

[6] Ibid.

[7] Culto, caja 9, bibliorato 2b, Arzobispado de Buenos Aires, documento 9; and referenced in Horacio Verbitsky, Vigilia de armas (Tomo III). Del Cordobazo de 1969 al 23 de marzo de 1976: Historia política de la iglesia católica (Random House Mondadori S.A., Buenos Aires, 2013), ob. cit.

[8] Horacio Verbitsky, Vigilia de armas (Tomo III). Del Cordobazo de 1969 al 23 de marzo de 1976: Historia política de la iglesia católica (Random House Mondadori S.A., Buenos Aires, 2013), ob. cit.

[9] Ibid.

[10] Horacio Verbitsky, La mano izquierda de Dios (Volume IV). La última dictadura (1976-1983): Historia política de la iglesia católica (Random House Mondadori, S.A., Buenos Aires, 2012), ob. cit.

[11] Annalisa Melandri (April 6, 2013), "Bergoglio? È Papa grazie alla sua sete di potere," Linkiesta.

collaborators in the villa were kidnapped by the dictatorship of the last years (1976-1983). They were seen as ideologues and therefore more dangerous than anyone else.[12]

In a twenty-seven page letter from the Argentine Jesuit priest Orlando Yorio, dated November 24, 1977 to Father Moura, we read that Bergoglio told him that there were serious accusations against him.[13]

During a two-day meeting in 1974, Yorio and Jalics told Bergoglio that they were willing to go wherever he wanted, to which the provincial insisted them especially if they were willing to dissolve the community where they worked. Bergoglio further indicated to them that he had nothing against them, but that he needed Father Rastellini to be sent elsewhere and that the other three jesuits would continue the same experience, but that they should change dioceses and deal with the bishop of Avellaneda to settle there.[14]

Again, in 1975, Bergoglio held a series of talks with Jalics, Rastellini, and later with Yorio about very serious accusations against Yorio; who said Yorio he had a clear conscience.[15] In another meeting, Bergoglio told them that he had many pressures on him against the community coming from Rome and other sectors of the Argentinean church.[16]

It was then that Bergoglio made them aware of the letter of the Jesuit General Pedro Arrupe about the "praying community" (it was August/September 1975).[17] Yorio learned that the previous provincial wanted to remove him from the Colegio Maximo because he said Yorio was doing too much harm: it was rumored that Yorio and Jalics were involved in the guerrilla.[18]

In the same year, Cardinal Juan Carlos Aramburu, Archbishop of Buenos Aires and Primate of Argentina, took away their license to say Mass and they were expelled from the Jesuits because, according to Bishop Zazpe, Bergoglio accused them.[19]

Since Bergoglio did nothing to testify to their innocence before the Company and the Armed Forces, Yorio and Jalics began to suspect his honesty.[20]

Not being Jesuits, Bergoglio recommended Yorio and Jalics to see the bishop of Morón, Miguel Raspanti, in whose diocese they could save their priesthood and life.[21] The Jesuit provincial hastened to send a favorable report so that they could be accepted, but Yorio and Jalics learned from the vicar and some priests of the diocese that Bergoglio's letter to Raspanti contained accusations "sufficient for us to no longer be

---

[12] Horacio Verbitsky, La mano izquierda de Dios (Volume IV). La última dictadura (1976-1983): Historia política de la iglesia católica (Random House Mondadori, S.A., Buenos Aires, 2012), ob. cit.
[13] Ibid.
[14] Ibid., p. 7.
[15] Ibid., pp. 11, 12.
[16] Ibid., p. 12.
[17] Ibid.
[18] Ibid, pp. 12, 15.
[19] Horacio Verbitsky, La mano izquierda de Dios (Volume IV). La última dictadura (1976-1983): Historia política de la iglesia católica (Random House Mondadori, S.A., Buenos Aires, 2012), ob. cit. Ibid. Jalics was confirmed in the Cult, box 9, bibliorato 2a, Archbishopric of Buenos Aires II, document 10, Passport of Fr. Jalics; Orlando Yorio, letter to the assistant general of the Society of Jesus, Father Moura, November 24, 1977. Copy provided by Yorio's brothers and nephews to Verbitsky, and referenced in Ibid.
[20] Horacio Verbitsky (April 11, 2010), "Mentiras y calumnias," Página 12.
[21] Horacio Verbitsky, La mano izquierda de Dios (Volume IV). La última dictadura (1976-1983): Historia política de la iglesia católica (Random House Mondadori, S.A., Buenos Aires, 2012), ob. cit.

able to exercise the priesthood."[22] It came out, because a theology student at Collegio Maximo, Marina Rubinom, found Monsignor Raspanti alone in the entrance hall, his face haggard and pale. Raspanti told her that "With the bad references that Bergoglio had sent him, he could not receive them in the diocese."[23]

In mid-2000, shortly before Yorio's death, he told Olga Wornat:

"Bergoglio never warned us of the danger we were in. On the contrary, I am sure that he gave the list with our names to the sailors. At the Máximo School, some versions said that I was a montonero leader and that I was with women. Francisco Jálics was the first to point out the danger several times, and he warned the Jesuits in writing what the Society was exposing me to, pointing out Bergoglio's responsibility. Some Jesuits warned me that Bergoglio himself was the one who was spreading them. And in those days, that was a sure passport to death and expulsion. One day, I spoke to him personally and asked him why he was doing it. But with the utmost coldness, he denied me everything [...]"[24]

The Jesuits confirmed for themselves that the rumors against them in sectors of the church were unfounded, and that Bergoglio gave a negative report on them.[25] Yorio and Jálics blamed Bergoglio for that - it was 1976 - but he changed the subject saying that there were complaints from the bishops against Jalics.[26]

In February, Bergoglio read them a letter from the Jesuit general, Pedro Arrupe, in which Bergoglio was instructed to dissolve the community within 15 days, sending Jalics to the United States and Yorio to another house in the Province.[27]

The Navy interpreted the withdrawal of Yorio's and Jalics' licenses, added to the "critical manifestations of their Jesuit provincial, Jorge Bergoglio, as an authorization to proceed" with their arrest, which occurred on May 23, 1976.[28]

A hooded man told the catechists early the next morning that, "I am the Executioner. Don't set foot in the village again or you will appear in a ditch" -after he interrogated them about Yorio and Jalics and being abandoned on a highway-. [29]

Yorio and Jalics were held in custody for five months, where they were interrogated and tortured.[30]

"Fortunato Mallimaci recalls a dialogue with Orlando about the interrogations he endured when he was kidnapped along with Francisco Jalics by a Navy task force. One day, Yorio told him:

---

[22] Ibid.

[23] Horacio Verbitsky (April 18, 2010), Recordando con ira, Página 12.

[24] Olga Wornat, Nuestra Santa Madre: Historia pública y privada de la Iglesia Católica Argentina (Ediciones B Argentina S.A., Buenos Aires, 2002), ob. cit.

[25] Letter from Father Orlando Yorio to the Assistant General of the Society of Jesus, Father Moura, dated Rome, November 24, 1977, pp. 16, 17.

[26] Ibid, p. 17.

[27] Ibid, p. 18.

[28] Horacio Verbitsky, La mano izquierda de Dios (Volume IV). La última dictadura (1976-1983): Historia política de la iglesia católica (Random House Mondadori, S.A., Buenos Aires, 2012), ob. cit.

[29] Ibid.

[30] Ibid.

"I'm going to take you to where they tortured me. They questioned me about things that only my superior knew. Do you realize that my superior, who I trusted and told him everything, then takes him... and when they torture me, it's the same questions...?"[31]

They were released on October 24, 1976, when they were drugged and taken by helicopter to a marshland in Cañuelas, where they woke up surrounded by grasslands.[32]

Verbitski found in the archives of the Foreign Ministry a document that states that Bergoglio had informed the military government that Yorio was "suspected of contact with guerrillas" and that Jalics had conflicts of obedience due to his "dissolute activity in women's religious congregations."[33]

Bergoglio claims to have warned Jalics and Yorio of the danger and that he interceded for them before Massera and Videla, when as a result of the disobedience of both Jesuits, they were kidnapped.[34] But there is a document in which the Provincial affirmed that Yorio said the opposite.[35]

Yorio and Jalics assured that they were freed through the efforts of Emilio Mignone, the priest Gavina and the Vatican, through Cardinal Pironio; but Bergoglio's friends say that the same provincial met with Videla and Massera on several occasions to demand the freedom of both Jesuits until he succeeded.[36] But it was a lie.

Wolnat tells us something very interesting in her book *Nuestra Santa Madre* (*Our Holy Mother*):

"Bergoglio has all the documentation of this case. The proofs that Yorio and Jálics had left the Society of Jesus of their own free will and that they had formed another order. There are the documents with their signatures before a notary public," says a priest close to the cardinal, who follows him everywhere. "When I asked to see those documents, there was always an excuse appropriate to the case: that they were there, but that they were not available at that moment, that one day they would call me to see them, that another day it could be. Or whatever. But there was always something that prevented it."

A Jesuit religious says that those documents with the signatures of Yorio and Jálics - if they are there - were "forged." And that it was very strange that Bergoglio was concerned about the kidnapped Jesuits only five months later."[37]

In a document of an intelligence service found in the Chancellery and called "expropiación Nueva argentino jesuita" ("expropriation New Argentine Jesuit"), it is

[31] Horacio Verbitsky (August 16, 2020), Gritarán las piedras, El Cohete a la Luna.

[32] Letter from the priest Orlando Yorio to the Assistant General of the Society of Jesus, Father Moura, dated from Rome, November 24, 1977, p. 24; Horacio Verbitsky, La mano izquierda de Dios (Volume IV). La última dictadura (1976-1983): Historia política de la iglesia católica (Random House Mondadori, S.A., Buenos Aires, 2012), ob. cit.

[33] Horacio Verbitsky, La mano izquierda de Dios (Volume IV). La última dictadura (1976-1983): Historia política de la iglesia católica (Random House Mondadori, S.A., Buenos Aires, 2012), ob. cit.

[34] Alicia Oliveira, interview with the author, March 3, 1998; Jorge Mario Bergoglio, interview with the author at the Archbishopric of Buenos Aires, May 7, 1999; quoted in Ibid.

[35] Culto, caja 9, bibliorato 2a, Arzobispado de Buenos Aires II, documento 10, Pasaporte del P. Jalics; as cited in Ibid.

[36] Ibid.

[37] Olga Wornat, Nuestra Santa Madre: Historia pública y privada de la Iglesia Católica Argentina (Ediciones B Argentina S.A., Buenos Aires, 2002), ob. cit.

stated that despite the good will of Father Bergoglio, the company (referring to the Jesuits) in Argentina has not been cleaned.[38] The text literally states that, "Despite the good will of Father Bergoglio, the Argentine Society of Jesus has not cleaned up its interior."[39]

A folder with documents in the archive of the Ministry of Foreign Affairs, whose location in the archive was certified by a notary public and whose director was Carlos Dellepiane, who kept them in the safe to prevent their theft and destruction, is decisive.[40] It is revealed that Bergoglio did what he said: to help the Jesuits.[41] But at the same time, there is a letter of request dated December 4, 1979, where Bergoglio asks the National Director of Worship to renew Jalics' Argentine passport from Argentina, who is in Germany, without the need to make such a costly trip.[42] In another document, entitled "PADRE FRANCISCO JALICS" ("FATHER FRANCISCO JALICS"), the reasons why it is not recommended to accede to the request are exposed, where it is said:

"- Dissolving activity in women's religious congregations (Conflicts of obediences).
"- Detained at the Escuela de Mecánica de la Armada (Navy Mechanics School) 24/5/76
   XI/76 (6 months) accused with Father Yorio
   Suspected guerrilla contact

"They lived in a small community that the Jesuit Superior dissolved in February 1976 and they refused to obey and asked to leave the Society on 3/19, they received 2 expulsion, Father JALICS did not because he has solemn vows.
No Bishop of Greater Buenos Aires wanted to receive him.
"NB: this information was provided to Mr. ORCOYEN by Father BERGOGLIO himself, signatory of the note, with a special recommendation that what he is requesting should not be granted."[43]

In another letter, this time dated December 20 of the same year, the General Directorate of Information and the National Director of Worship, Orcoyen, with Minister Héctor Villanueva wrote "that what he is requesting should not be granted."[44]

In 2005, Verbitsky published several of his findings in Página/12, which became the main plank in preventing Bergoglio from being elected pope at that year's conclave to succeed Pope Wojtyla. A dossier was sent to a large number of cardinals at the head of the conclave (the documents did not cause his non-election, as will be seen in due course).[45]

---

[38] Rosario Ayerdi (March 15, 2013), Verbitsky redobla la apuesta contra el Papa, Perfil.
[39] Sandro Magister (September 27, 2013), El jesuita humilló a los generales, Chiesa.
[40] Horacio Verbitsky (March 17, 2013), Cambio de Piel, Página 12.
[41] (March 18, 2013), La "duplicidad" de Jorge Bergoglio, BBC Mundo.
[42] Horacio Verbitsky, El Silencio: de Paulo VI a Bergoglio: las relaciones secretas de la Iglesia con la ESMA (Editorial Sudamericana, 2005), p. 110.
[43] Ibid., p. 111; see also Horacio Verbitsky (March 17, 2013), Cambio de Piel, Página 12.
[44] See this and the other documents likewise at: (March 12, 2016), Horacio Verbitsky on election of Pope Bergoglio, Millstream Films and Media: https://www.youtube.com/watch?v=UppRmyjqm7g; accessed March 29, 2016.
[45] Paul Valley, Pope Francis: Untying the Knots (Bloomsbury Publishing Plc, 2013), ob. cit.

Ignacio Covarrubias, journalist and former disciple of Jalics, telephoned him and received as a reply that he had been imprisoned for five months for a false accusation and preferred "not to stir up these things of the past." He refused to give an opinion on Bergoglio's role: "Neither for nor against" - he said.[46]

Jalics sent an email to Graciela, Orlando Yorio's sister, in April 2010, in which he said that "Justice was not done to Orlando, nor to Jesus Christ, and two thousand years have passed." He was convinced that "only forgiveness can help and give peace." For that reason, Jalics had accepted Jorge Bergoglio's invitation to meet in Buenos Aires, but he suspected that Bergoglio was doing it "to be able to say that nothing happened with me."[47]

After Bergoglio was elected pope, Jalics stated contrastingly that "Neither Orlando Yorio nor I were denounced by Father Bergoglio."[48] Apparently this was due to his anti-leftist attitude, which would have led to both Jesuits being kidnapped and tortured, but not denounced by the provincial.

The revocation of Jalics, who lived in a Jesuit residence in Bavaria, was due to the fact that the Society of Jesus ordered him to retract his accusations.[49]

After his election as pope, the then Vatican spokesman, Jesuit Federico Lombardi, said that the claims about Bergoglio's role during the dictatorship were accusations made by "an anti-clerical left to attack the Church, which must be decisively rejected."[50] The Argentine newspaper *La Nación* pointed out in an article that Francisco Jalics was reconciled with the pope.[51] But the newspaper transcribed the words of the priest, who said:

"I am reconciled with those events and for me that episode is closed [...] After our release, I left Argentina [...] It was only years later that we had the possibility of talking about those events with Father Bergoglio, who in the meantime had been appointed Archbishop of Buenos Aires. After that meeting, we celebrated a public Mass together and solemnly embraced each other again. I wish Pope Francis God's rich blessing on his office."[52]

Carmelo Giaquinta, an Argentine theologian, said that these words of reconciliation allude to "forgiving one's neighbor from the heart for the offenses received."[53]

Shortly after Bergoglio's election to the papacy, Jalics said that in the late 1990s and after numerous conversations, it became clear to him that his suspicion was unfounded.[54]

Francis received Jalics at the Vatican on October 5, 2013.[55]

---

[46] Interviews of Jalics with Covarrubias and of Covarrubias with the author, both on April 16, 2005; quoted in Ibid.

[47] Horacio Verbitsky (March 16, 2014), La retractación, Página 12.

[48] (March 20, 2013), Sacerdote secuestrado por dictadura: "El Padre Bergoglio no nos denunció", Aciprensa.

[49] Horacio Verbitsky (February 14, 2021), Bergoglio tiene la última palabra, El Cohete a la Luna.

[50] Elisabetta Piqué (March 16, 2013), Denunció el Vaticano una campaña de "calumnias" contra el Papa, La Nación.

[51] Ibid.

[52] Ibid.

[53] (October 9, 2013), El Papa recibe al Padre Jalics que fue secuestrado por la dictadura en Argentina, Aciprensa.

[54] (March 20, 2013), Jalics: "Bergoglio no denunció a Orlando Yorio ni a mí", El Observador.

Because of this, from the beginning of 2013 until the end of January of the following year, Graciela Yorio (Orlando's sister) sent letters to Jalics kindly asking him for concrete data favorable to Bergoglio, since they only had what Orlando had written to the Society of Jesus and the opinions of Jalics himself, but he wrote to her to "have some patience" because "now I have too many things. I will write to you."[56] Both Graciela, on December 1, 2013, and Horacio Verbitsky in March 2014, wrote to Jalics but got no response.[57]

In 1994 in his book, Ejercicios de Meditación (Meditation Exercises), as documented by Página 12:

"Jalics does not deny the facts, which he narrated in his 1994 book Ejercicios de meditación: "Many people who held extreme right-wing political convictions took a dim view of our presence in the slums. They interpreted the fact that we were living there as support for the guerrillas and wanted to denounce us as terrorists. We knew where the wind was blowing and who was responsible for these slanders. So I went to talk to the person in question and explained that he was playing with our lives. The man promised me that he would let the military know that we were not terrorists. From subsequent statements by an officer and thirty documents that I was later able to access we were able to prove beyond a shadow of a doubt that this man had not kept his promise but, on the contrary, had filed a false complaint with the military." In another part of the book he adds that this person made "the slander credible by using his authority" and "testified before the officers who kidnapped us that we had worked at the scene of the terrorist action. Shortly before, I had told him that he was playing with our lives. He must have been aware that he was sending us to certain death with his statements."[58]

That person was Jorge Mario Bergoglio, and it is striking that Jalics claimed to have had access to thirty evidentiary documents. Moreover, Jalics confirmed to Verbitsky by telephone that it was Bergoglio.[59]

Before her death, Graciela Yorio left two letters signed by Jalics to her son Mariano, but not dated. As one of them states that she was about to turn 87 years old, it indicates that the letters are from 2014.[60] In one of the letters, Jalics seems to express concern that the letters will become public, stating, "I trust that nothing of this letter becomes public, not even the fact that I wrote to you. That would put me in a very unpleasant situation."[61] Jalics referred to Yorio's case and his own:

"I don't think the military did anything truly grossly unfair to him or to me when they followed the information they had had.
"I can't say the same for the Church or the Society [of Jesus]."[62]

---

[55] (October 9, 2013), El Papa recibe al Padre Jalics que fue secuestrado por la dictadura en Argentina, Aciprensa.

[56] Horacio Verbitsky (March 16, 2014), La retractación, Página 12; Horacio Verbitsky (February 14, 2021), Bergoglio tiene la última palabra, El Cohete a la Luna.

[57] Horacio Verbitsky (February 14, 2021), Bergoglio tiene la última palabra, El Cohete a la Luna.

[58] Horacio Verbitsky (March 17, 2013), Cambio de Piel, Página 12.

[59] Horacio Verbitsky (February 14, 2021), Bergoglio tiene la última palabra, El Cohete a la Luna.

[60] Ibid.

[61] Ibid; Jalics S.J., Franz. Letter to Graciela Yorio. Undated.

[62] Ibid.

In other words, Jalics maintained that "the information that the military had had" was the reason for his arrest. And that it was the Church and the Society of Jesus that did "anything truly grossly unfair" to both of them. Jorge Mario Bergoglio was the one accused and proved to be the one who disseminated the false reports against them.

Rodolfo Yorio tells about Bergoglio:

"I know people he helped. That speaks of his two faces and his closeness to military power. He handled ambiguity with mastery. If they were killed he got rid of them, if they were saved he had saved them. That is why there are people who consider him a saint and others who are terrified of him."[63]

b. The military chaplains of the Society of Jesus endorsed by Bergoglio and a history of torture and kidnapping

Ariel Lede and Lucas Bilbao documented that during his time as provincial (1973-1979), Bergoglio authorized at least seven chaplains, four of whom served in Army units in charge of the CCD/Centro Clandestino de Detención (CDC/Clandestine Detention Center):[64]

"Jorge Mario Hardoy was chaplain of the Communications Battalion 141 of Córdoba. José Andrés Agüero assisted from December 1975 until the end of the dictatorship the chiefs of Artillery Group 7 of Resistence, in command of military area 233 and of at least two CDC, one of them housed in the same unit. Martín González was chaplain of the Warrant Officers School for Combat Support in Campo de Mayo, between 1971 and 1977, where he was accused of participating in torture and interrogation sessions. And César Benzi was chaplain at the Artillery School of Campo de Mayo, unit in charge of military area 450 and at least one CDC."[65]

Roberto Scordato, a founder of the secular Fraternity of Fraternidad seglar de los Hermanitos del Evangelio Charles de Foucald (Little Brothers of the Gospel Charles de Foucald), tells that between the end of October and the beginning of November 1976, he met in Rome with Cardinal Eduardo Pironio, who was prefect of the Vatican Congregation for Religious, and to whom he communicated the name and surname of a Jesuit from the community of San Miguel who participated in the torture sessions in Campo de Mayo with the role of "spiritually softening" the detainees. He asked Eduardo Pironio to transmit the information to Pedro Arrupe, general of the Society of Jesus, but he did not know what happened. About this, Patrick Rice, superior of the Little Brothers of the Gospel and who was kidnapped and tortured that year, said that it was impossible for such misfortunes to happen without the approval of the father provincial, Jorge Mario Bergoglio.[66]

Miguel Ignacio Mom Debussy, a former Jesuit of whom Bergoglio was his ordination godfather on December 3, 1984, points out that the use of weapons was habitual in the Jesuit premises: Bergoglio sent them to stand guard at night with 22

---

[63] Horacio Verbitsky (April 11, 2010), "Una persona ávida de poder," Página 12.
[64] Lucas Bilbao, Ariel Lede, Profeta del genocidio: El Vicariato castrense y los diarios del obispo Bonamín en la última dictadura (Penguin Random House Grupo Editorial Sudamericana, 2016), ob. cit.
[65] Ibid.
[66] Horacio Verbitsky (April 18, 2010), Recordando con ira, Página 12.

carbines and lead bullets.[67] When the swimming pool at the back of the Colegio Máximo was recovered and there was an attempt to swim in it by the people of the surrounding neighborhood, they were watched. Riquelme tried it and told that the Jesuit brother Rivisic shot him with the 22 for getting into the pool, passing close to his leg. Rivisic told him that next time he would hit him.

Mom Debussy and Riquelme, separately recall that the Observatory was cleansed of leftists by the Navy; and that in 1975 a Congress controlled by SIDE and the Navy was held. Debussy recalls:

"Bergoglio used to invite officers from Campo de Mayo, who came in uniform, to the Colegio Máximo. Once several came with combat clothes and some round grenades hanging. He received them in the old dining room on the third floor, which Bergoglio himself later closed. We were having dinner and they arrived with a chaplain."

Both Podestá and Ríos recall that in the neighborhood there are stories of bodies buried adjacent to the Colegio Máximo and its old cemetery.

Mom Debussy wrote in his handwritten letter requesting the pope to dispense him from priestly celibacy and the Society of Jesus from his vows of poverty, chastity, and obedience in February 1989, containing explicit remarks about Bergoglio:

"Jorge Mario Bergoglio depersonalized me, prevented me from maturing and ended what little autonomy I had left." Mom Debussy writes that he endured "oppression, falsehood and contempt." Her entry into the Society and his ordination to the priesthood were mistakes influenced by "my lack of freedom and the 'paternal' oppression and 'brainwashing' brought about with the consent of my weakness, confusion and fear of loneliness and contempt for Fr. Bergoglio," whom "I consider a madman at best and a bad person in many others."[68]

Argentine journalist Horacio Verbitsky overtly quotes Mom Debussy:

"Bergoglio is a sociopath who did not hesitate to psychologically subdue as many Jesuits as he could, starting with the novices and scholastics (among whom was me). He succeeded, in general. Several of the victims ended up resigning from the Society. I am also aware that he acted unscrupulously against other Jesuits (from Centro de Investigaciones y Acción Social, CIAS [Center for Research and Social Action, CIAS in Spanish]) and lay people close to the Society, especially at the Universidad del Salvador [University of Salvador]."[69]

Continued:

"When Ubaldo Calabresi succeeded Laghi as nuncio in 1981, Bergoglio took him to the Máximo and invited him to celebrate Mass in Latin. "No one understood anything," says Mom Debussy. When his colleague Jorge Seibold was appointed Rector of Philosophy at the San Miguel branch of the Universidad del Salvador,

---

[67] Horacio Verbitsky (May 2, 2010), "La patota salió del Colegio Máximo," Página 12. Note: unless otherwise indicated, this is the same source.

[68] Horacio Verbitsky (May 2, 2010), Fama, dinero y poder, Página 12.

[69] Ibid.

Bergoglio made him kneel in the chapel of the Maximo and say the oath against modernism that Pius X established in 1910 and which was in complete disuse. (The content of that oath is very similar to Cardinal Antonio Caggiano's questioning of the Movement of Priests for the Third World.) "Bergoglio boasted of having forced him to that oath, and one of his bedside books was The Prince."[70]

c. Jorge Mario Bergoglio and Commander Emilio Eduardo Massera
During the trips between San Miguel and the City of Buenos Aires in which Mom Debussy was his chauffeur, Bergoglio spoke to him sympathetically about the political project of the head of the Navy Emilio Massera, telling him that he had met him several times.[71]

"He told me that he wanted to protect the novices and students [...] They were in negotiations with him because he wanted the Navy to buy the Cosmic Physics Observatory, adjacent to Colegio Máximo." No agreement was reached and in December 1977 the Air Force bought it. Several people who worked there "were kidnapped and when they regained their freedom, they were fired by Bergoglio," says Riquelme. "There are those who say that he protected them, because he paid their last salary."[72]

In 1977, after establishing important political contacts and removing obstacles for the purchase of war material through Licio Gelli, the Italian financier and Venerable Master of the Masonic lodge Propaganda Due (P2) involved in banking scandals involving the Vatican, Massera met in an audience with Pope Paul VI, on October 26, 1977.[73] Paul VI was pleasantly impressed by Admiral Massera's personality and was satisfied with the conversation held.[74] The Pope wished peace and prosperity to the Argentine nation. Less than a month after the papal audience, the Universidad del Salvador (Argentina's Jesuit university), appointed Massera honorary professor, who spoke "on some classic themes of Catholic integrism: promiscuous love, drugs and the "foreseeable derivation" of that "sensory escalation" in "the shuddering of the terrorist faith."[75]

"He reviewed the three volumes of Das Kapital, which he named in German, in which Marx questioned the inviolable character of private property; Freud's aggression to the "sacred space of the private sphere" in The Interpretation of Dreams, and the Theory of Relativity with which Einstein put in crisis the "static and inert condition of matter." His audience did not need him to say that Marx, Freud and Einstein were Jews."[76]

---

[70] Ibid.
[71] Horacio Verbitsky (May 2, 2010), "La patota salió del Colegio Máximo," Página 12.
[72] Ibid.
[73] Horacio Verbitsky, La mano izquierda de Dios (Volume IV). La última dictadura (1976-1983): Historia política de la iglesia católica (Random House Mondadori, S.A., Buenos Aires, 2012), ob. cit.
[74] Secret Memo 522/79 from Ambassador Rubén M. Blanco to Undersecretary Commodore Carlos Cavandoli, August 28, 1979, Culto, box 9, bibliorato 2c, Archbishopric of Buenos Aires, document 1, murder of the Pallottine Fathers; quoted in Ibid.
[75] Horacio Verbitsky, La mano izquierda de Dios (Volume IV). La última dictadura (1976-1983): Historia política de la iglesia católica (Random House Mondadori, S.A., Buenos Aires, 2012), ob. cit.
[76] Ibid.

The Jesuit Superior General who granted this distinction to Massera was Jorge Mario Bergoglio. It happened in 1975, when the university was transferred by the same Jesuit provincial to a civil foundation, keeping only the faculties of Theology and Philosophy in San Miguel. This foundation was managed by Guardia de Hierro, to which Bergoglio belonged and which in 1976 came under the protection of Massera. Bergoglio made this move as part of his battle against the "left-handed Jesuits" from whom he was trying to cleanse the Society of Jesus.[77] Francisco Cacho Piñón - the university rector - apparently took advantage of the contact between Guardia de Hierro and Massera to obtain protection from the general for the university and its staff, even though he and Bergoglio were against his ideas.[78]

Then Massera was invited to speak at the Jesuit Georgetown University in Washington D.C., where Irish priest Patrick Rice, who left Argentina after being kidnapped and beaten, interrupted the conference demanding explanations for the crimes of the dictatorship. According to the priest, the U.S. provincial would not have invited Massera without Bergoglio's approval or request.[79]

Religious people who knew Bergoglio say that like most of the Argentine establishment, he thought liberation theology was too political. Some in the church hierarchy considered him divisive and autocratic in his 15 years leading the Jesuits.[80] And some in the Society considered him an arch-conservative.[81]

d. A renewed Bergoglio - from conservatism to liberation theology, freemasonry and mysticism

Andrés Swinnen, a Dutchman, succeeded Bergoglio as provincial of the Society of Jesus in Argentina in December 1979.[82] In 1980, Bergoglio was elected rector of the Colegio Máximo de San Miguel. The criticisms of the Jesuits of the CIAS (leftists) towards Bergoglio were accepted without question in Rome and throughout Latin America. Argentina had been an exception regarding the leadership of the Society of Jesus and was a problem for the Jesuits. Austen Ivereigh points out that "the prejudices" of the advisors of the new Jesuit general, the Dutch Peter Hans Kolvenbach, were obvious when they visited the Colegio Máximo in the 1980s.

Kolvenbach supported the CIAS and when Swinnen's term was coming to an end, Father General intervened in the Argentine province to impose a new north. Then at Borgo Santo Spirito in Rome, the Jesuit general elected Zorzín as the new provincial. Kolvenbach appointed as his associate or assistant, Ignacio García-Mata, director of CIAS and one of Bergoglio's staunchest critics.

There was a policy of cleansing the Bergoglian Jesuits. There were no more of them and the lay people faithful to Bergoglio's project were dismissed. In order to make room for the new provincial regime, Bergoglio agreed with Victor Zorzín in May 1986 to take a sabbatical leave in Germany at the Jesuit Faculty of Theology near Frankfurt,

---

[77] Ibid.

[78] Austen Ivereigh, The Great Reformer: Francis and the Making of a Radical Pope (Henry Holt and Co., New York, 2014), ob. cit.

[79] Horacio Verbitsky (March 17, 2013), Cambio de Piel, Página 12.

[80] Jim Yardley and Simon Romero (May 23, 2015), Pope's Focus on Poor Revives Scorned Theology, The New York Times.

[81] Jim Yardley (September 18, 2015), A Humble Pope, Challenging the World, The New York Times.

[82] Austen Ivereigh, The Great Reformer (Ediciones B, S.A., 2015), ob. cit. Note: unless otherwise noted, this is the same source.

Sankt Georgen, to obtain a doctorate in Romano Guardini, one of the most influential German priest-philosophers of the Second Vatican Council and who, strangely enough, had fascinated Bergoglio since he was a novice. Guardini influenced Catholic-American luminaries in the 1950s, such as the monk-poet Thomas Merton (whom, already as pope, Bergoglio would mention in September 2015 in the U.S. Congress). Guardini influenced, among others, German Catholic theologians such as Hans Urs Von Balthasar, Karl Rahner and Walter Kasper, from the progressive wing of the church. Bergoglio's specific interest was Guardini's text Der Gegensatz ("Contrast," 1925), which was a critique of Hegelian and Marxist dialectics that Bergoglio believed could be useful in conceptualizing the dynamics of disagreement. Guardini drew on the work of the 19th century Tübingen theologian Johann Adam Möhler, who brought out that contrasting points in the Church are useful, as long as they do not create disunity, and thus no real ecclesial reform; something already examined by Bergoglio when reading Yves Congar. Bergoglio, therefore, would make a kind of mixture of modernism and conservatism that would mark him forever... something that as a cardinal he would promote as a "culture of encounter."

However, in insubordination to his superiors, he returned to Argentina three months later. Surprised by this report, Victor Zorzín assigned Bergoglio a room at the Colegio del Salvador in the heart of Buenos Aires. There, he taught some material while continuing his doctoral research.

He taught pastoral theology at the Colegio Máximo. But his return to Argentina reignited the old debates of how to be a proper Jesuit.[83] Bergoglio's circle clashed with the new Jesuit superiors and Bergoglio did little to stop it. In 1990, his superiors thought enough was enough and sent him to Cordoba 500 miles away. He took up residence in room number 5 of the Jesuit residence, where his official mission was to hear confessions. Some confessors avoided him. He helped with household chores, preparing meals, folding laundry, and changing the sheets of old and sick Jesuits. Occasionally he gave Mass and, according to his own account as pope, returned to study to see if he could advance in his doctoral thesis, but he was unable to finish it: nevertheless, this study helped him a lot to face what happened later.[84]

He read and prayed, thought and wrote, reflecting on his childhood, and the problems that plagued religious communities, and set himself the task of reading a five-volume history of the popes. He was angry at being sidelined and accused Argentina's Jesuit leaders of uprooting the Society from its traditional missions.[85] Bergoglio spent two years there (1990-1992) in what he called "inner purification," something he called an experience that had more to do with his inner life.[86] Already as pope, in 2013, he confessed to the Jesuit Antonio Spadaro that being provincial of the Society of Jesus in Argentina, he was very young -barely 36 years old- and that he was never ultraconservative but very authoritarian -deciding for himself-.[87] There he wrote "Silencio y Palabra" ("Silence and Word"), on how to resolve conflicts... based on his

---

[83] Daniel Burke (September, 2015), The Pope's Dark Night of the Soul, CNN. Note: unless otherwise noted, this is the same source.
[84] Sandro Magister (December 17, 2014), Padre Jorge e i suoi confratelli. Perché vollero liberarsi di lui, l'Espresso.
[85] Daniel Burke (September, 2015), The Pope's Dark Night of the Soul, CNN.
[86] Sandro Magister (December 17, 2014), Padre Jorge e i suoi confratelli. Perché vollero liberarsi di lui, l'Espresso.
[87] Antonio Spadaro, S.J. (September 30, 2013), A Big Heart Open to God, America.

experience, as well as El Exilio de Toda Carne ("The Exile of All Flesh") which begins with notes of a spiritual retreat he conducted in 1990 as a foreshadowing of his next exile to Cordoba. Priest Angel Rossi, Bergoglio's spiritual son, said that Cordoba changed Bergoglio for the better.[88] He described him in positive terms:

"He is humble but confident, a disciplined rule-breaker. He is quiet but freely speaks his mind. He is deeply spiritual, but crafty -- a cross between a desert saint and a shrewd politician. He is a man of power and action, who spends a great deal of time in prayer and contemplation."[89]

Such a description, which many Jesuits would recognize in themselves, is something Rossi described as "Contradiction is part of who we are."[90]

Rossi also expressed that "many things that he [Bergoglio] is living through today got their start here in Cordoba." He also explained that the one who left "is not a different Bergoglio. [...] It is a fully blossomed Bergoglio, one who has amplified his reach and found his mission."[91]

However additional episodes in his life pushed him to new horizons.

Cardinal Giuseppe Siri had expressed in February 1988 to two journalists of *30 Giorni*, the fear that Freemasonry could manipulate the conclaves and, therefore, elect its own pope.[92]

With this in mind, Ricardo González, a Peruvian researcher and writer, as well as the late Argentine journalist Roberto Villamil, wrote, "According to our investigations, and according to information provided by high members of Argentine Freemasonry -whose names, for reasons that the reader will understand, we cannot divulge-, Jorge Mario Bergoglio would have been for many years a Freemason..."[93] They further added: "Master Mason, to be exact, and formed in the so-called "covert lodges," not the "public" ones."[94]

Also on the Argentine program *La Mirada - by Roberto García* - on Channel 26, the Argentine writer and politician, Juan Bautista "Tata" Yofre, who was Secretary of State Intelligence (1989-1990) and ambassador during the government of Carlos Menem, referred to the telephone calls about the negotiations with Iran. He is referring to the investigations of the special prosecutor Alberto Nisman into a terrorist attack on Argentine soil. One of the tapped calls was between Yussuf Khalil and Abdul Karim Paz. The calls were published by the Argentine newspaper *La Nación*, but the recording in question later disappeared... Yussuf told Karim that he had had a meeting with the head of the Vatican intelligence services in Argentina, whom Yofre knows

---

[88] Daniel Burke (September, 2015), The Pope's Dark Night of the Soul, CNN.

[89] Ibid.

[90] Ibid.

[91] Ibid.

[92] Carlo Alberto Agnoli, La Massoneria alla conquista della Chiesa (E.I.L.E. S, 1996), p. 39; cf. Il Sabato, March 30, 1981, in the context of the article "L'Ombra della Loggia" on page 25 entitled "Ci sono eccome eccome...Un dialogo con Siri."

[93] Ricardo González, Roberto Villamil, El Enigma del Hombre Gris: Las profecías de Parravicini, Francisco y los secretos del Vaticano (ECIS Publicaciones, First Edition, Buenos Aires, June 2014), p. 172.

[94] Ibid, p. 176.

personally.[95] We know that he is/was Héctor Luis Yrimia, a former judge and prosecutor, an expert in intelligence operations, who would introduce Yussuf to the head of the Vatican Entity (Vatican Intelligence agency, as the reader may recall).[96]

The intelligence chief told Yussuf that he was a Freemason; so was Pope Francis.[97]

We have verified the recording of this call and Yofre's account of the pope's status as a Freemason.[98] Not only that but in the recording of the intercepted call, it is revealed that the Vatican intelligence services, starting from its very director, would be very involved with Freemasonry.[99]

Reliable sources have also provided us with confirmation of Bergoglio's membership in Freemasonry, and indeed, in a covert lodge.

In 2013, Ángel Jorge Clavero, then Grand Master of the Grand Lodge of Argentina, told the newspaper *Época* that although there is not a fluid relationship between Freemasonry and the Catholic Church, the Jesuits are the closest, bridging distances and differences. He pointed out that, "There have even been Jesuits who, with the permission of their priors or provincials, have belonged to Freemasonry."[100]

Two years after his exile, in June 1992, Bergoglio was appointed auxiliary bishop of Buenos Aires.[101] It is said among some Argentine traditionalist Catholic circles, that before assuming that position, he disappeared for a while from circulation and was initiated into Freemasonry, being later elected as auxiliary bishop.[102]

Bergoglio underwent a profound conversion in Cordoba that also led him to such circles, and, upon becoming bishop the old Bergoglio disappeared and he adopted a new model of leadership that involved "listening, participation and collegiality."[103]

He served in that position from 1992 until 1997, when he was elected archbishop until 2013, when he was elected pope. As archbishop, he was deeply loved by ordinary people for his special concern for the marginalized. He manifested a personal concern for the poorest of the poor, wherever they were, and performing Masses in a square or near a garbage dump. He preferred to travel by bus or subway. His residence was a

---

[95] (December 2, 2017), La Mirada de Roberto Garcia | Full Program | Monday, November 27, 2017, La Mirada de Roberto Garcia: https://www.youtube.com/watch?v=z6EdvEeIzWI; accessed February 1, 2023.

[96] Auto desestimando la denuncia hecha por el Fiscal Nisman por encubrimiento del atentado a la AMIA, Buenos Aires, February 26, 2015.

[97] (December 2, 2017), La Mirada de Roberto Garcia | Full Program | Monday, November 27, 2017, La Mirada de Roberto Garcia: https://www.youtube.com/watch?v=z6EdvEeIzWI; accessed February 1, 2023.

[98] https://especialess3.lanacion.com.ar/audios_nisman/IN-12177-20140119-003044.mp3 Accessed September 14, 2023. See context if needed in previous call:
https://especialess3.lanacion.com.ar/audios_nisman/B-1009-2014-01-19-002737-2.mp3 Accessed September 14, 2023. Links referenced here:
https://docs.google.com/spreadsheets/d/1zjeTlIk_MaStFy5L779kAvvvPTjZJOrv_slYhAJhtcA/edit#gid=0 (Both under the same date: January 19, 2014) Accessed September 14, 2023.

[99] (December 2, 2017), La Mirada de Roberto Garcia | Full Program | Monday, November 27, 2017, La Mirada de Roberto Garcia: https://www.youtube.com/watch?v=z6EdvEeIzWI; accessed February 1, 2023.

[100] Redacción Época (March 31, 2013), Clavero: "La masonería lo que quiere es enseñar a pensar, ese es el fin último," Diario Época.

[101] Daniel Burke (September, 2015), The Pope's Dark Night of the Soul, CNN.

[102] OnePeterFive (April 7, 2017), Why do the Freemasons Love Pope Francis, One Peter Five.

[103] Thomas P. Rausch, SJ & Richard R. Gaillardetz (eds.), Go into the Streets!: The Welcoming Church of Pope Francis (Paulist Press, New York, 2016), ob. cit.

small apartment shared with two priests and he often cooked for himself. He also revealed a love for the clergy, but also a persistent antipathy for clericalism.[104]

In 1998, he was named archbishop of the same city, or, the most powerful Catholic in Argentina. All this he learned from his exile, as he expressed to a politician who was forced to resign by saying, "You must live your exile. And when you return you will be more compassionate, more kind, and you will want to serve your people better." Bergoglio wanted to make sure he did not make the same mistakes and consulted his bishop and assistant priests (a tradition he carried into his papacy).[105]

He was uncomfortable for the governments of Carlos Menem in the 90's in Argentina and the Kirchner's until he reached the papacy.[106]

e. Ambiguities and cover-ups in the 21st century

Estela de la Cuadra, daughter of the first president of las Abuelas de Plaza de Mayo (the Grandmothers of Plaza de Mayo), recalled in 2011 that Bergoglio had testified as a witness on the ESMA case before the lawyer Myriam Bregman (within the framework of the investigation into the kidnapping of priests Orlando Yorio and Francisco Jalics), that he had known about the theft of babies during the Argentine dictatorship for ten years.[107] However, the truth is that Bergoglio had known about this sinister for 34 years.[108] The Argentine newspaper *Página 12* reported:

"Licha de la Cuadra" was Alicia Zubasnabar de la Cuadra, the first president of Abuelas de Plaza de Mayo. Yesterday, for almost four hours, the Federal Oral Tribunal 6 heard the testimony of one of her daughters, who arrived at the hearing with a huge suitcase. Inside the suitcase, Estela de la Cuadra had papers that one by one she took out during the whole story, papers with which the Grandmothers documented the desperate search for their grandchildren with originals of the petitions, the letters to the Supreme Court of Justice of the Nation, to the then Archbishop Raul Primatesta and to the now Cardinal Jorge Bergoglio. Estela, who is still looking for Ana, her sister's daughter, asked the Court again what she asks in each of the trials: "How is it that Bergoglio says that only ten years ago he knew about the theft of babies?" And she asked several times: "Why don't you summon him? Is it not important that he declare what happened with Ana de la Cuadra?" Prosecutor Martín Niklison took up the message at the end of the hearing and, accompanied by the lawsuits of las Abuelas de Plaza de Mayo and María Isabel Chorobick de Mariani, asked the Court for the same summons."[109]

Bergoglio chose to speak in writing, "hiding from society's gaze, to avoid going to a public audience."[110]

---

[104] Michael L. Budde (editor), New World Pope: Pope Francis and the Future of the Pope (Cascade Books, Eugene, Oregon, 2017), p. 46.

[105] Daniel Burke (September, 2015), The Pope's Dark Night of the Soul, CNN.

[106] Hugo Alconada Mon (March 17, 2013), "Soy Bergoglio, cura": vida íntima y obra del Papa que llegó del fin del mundo, La Nación.

[107] Alejandra Dandan (May 3, 2011), "¿Por qué no citan a Bergoglio?," Página 12.

[108] Ibid.

[109] Ibid.

[110] Carlos Pisoni (June 6, 2011), Bergoglio en su laberinto, Página 12.

In another case, El Silencio Island was owned by the Archbishopric of Buenos Aires, but during the dictatorship, the priest Emilio Grasselli sold it to the ESMA task force, which was bought with a false document in the name of its prisoners. There, the Navy hid 60 detainees-disappeared so that the Inter-American Commission on Human Rights would not find them. Jorge Mario Bergoglio supplied the journalist Horacio Verbitsky with the precise data to find the file where the property titles were found, and where Antonio Arbelaiz, the Curia's administrator, was listed as the owner. In spite of the note written in Bergoglio's handwriting, he said in one of his judicial testimonies that he had never heard of the island "El Silencio."[111]

Another case is the Fraternidad de Agrupaciones Santo Tomás de Aquino (FASTA/in English, Fraternity of St. Thomas Aquinas Associations), which is a right-wing nationalist fraternity founded by the Dominican priest Aníbal Fosbery,[112] who headed a clandestine mission in the 1970s together with López Rega to buy weapons from the Libyan dictator Muammar Gaddafi for the Falklands War.[113] Fosbery and FASTA supported the military dictatorship in Argentina by sowing terror and, by early April 2003, he inaugurated a FASTA headquarters in Bariloche. There, Fosbery defended a Nazi officer who escaped to Argentina for the massacre of 335 Italian civilians in 1944, with the following words: "Allow me to personally express on behalf of FASTA our memory and gratitude to the then president of the German-Argentine Association in Bariloche, Mr. Erich Priebke."[114]

Fosbery and Jorge Mario Bergoglio have been good acquaintances since their youth.[115] Bergoglio supports FASTA and participated in several of its activities. FASTA uses fully aroused youths as soldiers to provoke riots at events they consider inappropriate, inciting violence and using minors for criminal acts.[116] FASTA has supported groups resisting the advancement of trials for the dictatorship's crimes.[117]

On December 6, 2009, Bergoglio, as Archbishop of Buenos Aires and Primate of Argentina, conferred the sacrament of Holy Orders on two FASTA militia deacons.[118] He told them: "you have to teach in the name of Christ, announcing to all men the Word of God that you have received [...] keep the faith of the Church, and never negotiate it for any ideology."[119]

On June 17, 2012, Bergoglio presided at the Metropolitan Cathedral of Buenos Aires at the Mass of Thanksgiving for the 50th anniversary of the founding of FASTA.[120] The ceremony was concelebrated with the priest Aníbal Fosbery, who at the beginning of the ceremony addressed a few words to Cardinal Bergoglio:

---

[111] Horacio Verbitsky (March 17, 2013), Cambio de Piel, Página 12.
[112] Franco Mizrahi (July 16, 2010), Paga Dios, El Argentino.
[113] (April 15, 2003), La reivindicación de un nazi, Página 12.
[114] Franco Mizrahi (July 16, 2010), Paga Dios, El Argentino.
[115] (May 16, 2013), Francisco recibió al Padre Fosbery, Sitio Noticias Universidad FASTA.
[116] Edgar González Ruiz (April 15, 2013), Bergoglio: a pontiff of the Argentine ultra-right, Voltaire Network.
[117] Horacio Verbitsky (October 1, 2006), Los único que FASTAba, Página 12.
[118] (December 14, 2009), Golden Jubilee of Fr. Fosbery and priestly ordinations of Fasta, Datum.
[119] Ibid.
[120] (June 25, 2012), Cardinal Bergoglio presided at the Mass for the 50th anniversary of FASTA, Agencia Informativa Católica Argentina.

"Your Most Reverend Eminence, neither you nor I dreamed, when we walked together, young teenagers, the parish of Flores, that a day like today would happen: you, Archbishop of Buenos Aires, receiving these dear children of FASTA who come to thank God for these fifty years of foundation. And allow me then, dear Cardinal, to thank you in the name of all FASTA, for your paternal benevolence towards us, always."[121]

For his part, Bergoglio said in part that, "To be a militiaman - a term with which the members of FASTA identify themselves - speaks of commitment, of work, of giving oneself to the Gospel, and that it is, in short, military in holiness." He exhorted the members of the institution to "continue serving the Church, in holiness, being militiamen in their own demands, in daily sacrifice, with 'the psychology of the exile' who are 'secure in the anchor, which they already have nailed in the other homeland' [...] "Look at that homeland, work for this one, but there. They are exiles who are on the way."[122]

FASTA took an active part in the campaigns led by Bergoglio against the decriminalization of abortion and against the recognition of same-sex marriages.[123]

When Bergoglio was elected pope, Fosbery wrote a reflection:

"Jorge Mario Bergoglio, auxiliary bishop of the unforgettable Cardinal [Antonio] Quarracino. You blessed my apostolic dreams and blessed the sending of our FASTA laity, then the priests, and now the 'catherinas' (consecrated laywomen). Transformed by the grace of the Holy Spirit into Pope Francis, he continues to listen to us, to accompany us, and to send us."[124]

On May 15, 2013, Pope Francis received Friar Aníbal Fosbery in a private audience and with a warm embrace, where they discussed the current affairs of the Church and FASTA University. The Pope gave his blessing to the work and asked them to continue working in the apostolic task at the service of the Church. Francis was pleased to learn of the growth and expansion in Africa and of the dialogue with ecclesial referents from other countries.[125]

When Mom Debussy was asked why Bergoglio is considered a progressive by one side and by others as a conservative, he said that Bergoglio is a very politically savvy person and that he is very intelligent: "He is very capable of moving between two waters and making everyone feel close to him."[126]

[121] Ibid.
[122] Ibid.
[123] Edgar González Ruiz (April 15, 2013), Bergoglio: a pontiff of the Argentine ultra-right, Voltaire Network.
[124] (March 15, 2013), Instituciones y movimientos eclesiales saludaron la elección de Francisco, Agencia Informativa Católica Argentina.
[125] (May 16, 2013), Francisco recibió al Padre Fosbery, Sitio Noticias Universidad FASTA.
[126] Annalisa Melandri (April 6, 2013), "Bergoglio? È Papa grazie alla sua sete di potere," Linkiesta.

CHAPTER
9

The resurgence of the papacy: a pope from the end of the world

Still in the 21st century: among Freemasons, "contactees" and "prophecies"
With the arrival of Bishop Jorge Bergoglio to the Archbishopric of Argentina on February 28, 1998, the Masons had many positive expectations. Especially in the group of the Commission of Culture, whose visible face was Luis J. Vincent de Urquiza, as well as other well-known Masons.[1] Thus, on August 26 in a prominent Argentinean newspaper, *La Nación* (founded by the Freemason Bartolomé Mitre), appeared in an article entitled "Un inusual encuentro entre jesuitas y masones" ("An unusual meeting between Jesuits and Masons"), reporting that the French Jesuit priest Jean-Ives Calvez would speak that day at the headquarters of the Grand Lodge of Argentina, "after centuries of sharp confrontations."[2] It should be noted that in 1943, Calvez began his studies in France to become a Jesuit priest. On July 31, 1957, he was ordained priest and was Provincial of the Society of Jesus in France from 1967 to 1971. He also served as assistant to the general of the Jesuit order, Pedro Arrupe, from 1971 to 1983.[3] During one of his seasons as a Jesuit, Joseph Berteloot was provincial of the Society of Jesus, who, as we recall in a chapter of this essay, was the protagonist of the plot of the Jesuits to take over the French Freemasonry and thus undermine its influence in the affairs of the democracies, using it. And indeed, we have corroborated in a separate note, that Calvez was aware of this plot on the part of the Society. But not all Masons have since the times of Berteloot and earlier, a secret hostility against Freemasonry, as I have had the opportunity to corroborate. What is certain, and what we have also verified by talking with important people in the Society of Jesus, is that the Jesuits believe it is necessary for the Catholic Church to play a leading role in the formation of consciences and policies that adhere to their great political, moral and spiritual ideal.

Calvez visited Argentina every year for summer classes.

Regarding the conference that Calvez would give at the Grand Lodge of Argentina, Luis J. Vincent de Urquiza expressed that: "this meeting between Jesuits and Masons shows the new attitude of the Catholic Church in today's world, which will become, we have no doubt, a gesture of great symbolic value."[4]

The Argentine Jesuit Ignacio Pérez del Viso, sent a letter to the readers of *La Nación*, highlighting the confrontations between Freemasonry and the Church,

---

[1] Eduardo R. Callaey (March 24, 2013), Los jesuitas y el diálogo entre Masonería e Iglesia en Argentina, Eduardo Callaey.
[2] Ibid; Jorge Rouillon (August 26, 1998), Un inusual encuentro de jesuitas y masones, La Nación.
[3] Nelson-Gustavo Specchia (Fall 2009), In Memoriam Jean-Yves Calvez, Studia Politicæ, No. 17, p. 131.
[4] Jorge Rouillon (August 26, 1998), Un inusual encuentro de jesuitas y masones, La Nación.

concluding that, "Those whom the past has confronted, the future can summon us to the defense of human dignity."[5]

The successful conference was also attended by a good number of people of known Catholic militancy; for example, Victor Luis Funes, president of the Academia de la Plata historically linked to the Society of Jesus; as well as the priest Daniel Zaffaroni, who attended with the permission of his bishop, Jorge Bergoglio. The Jesuit priest Ignacio Pérez del Viso was also present, to name a few.[6] The negative reaction of the conservative Catholic sector was not long in coming, and with the response of a Jesuit:

"On August 13, Horacio Walter Bauer, a member of the Editorial Board of the magazine L'Arche - a Catholic connoisseur of the conservative wing of the Church - seemed to lead the counter-offensive with a devastating letter published in La Nación. This missive, which put an end to any possibility of dialogue between Freemasonry and the Church, would be answered, surprisingly, by a Jesuit, Father Ignacio Pérez del Viso, who made an extensive review of the relations between Freemasonry and the Church and ended with the hope that "Those whom the past has confronted, the future can summon us to the defense of human dignity."[7]

Ricardo González, as well as Roberto Villamil, wrote about "the cracking of the ice": "From there -our sources assured us– the rapprochement between Argentine Jesuits and Freemasons -and their common interest in the Vatican– has grown and reached its climax with the election of Bergoglio as Pope...."[8]

In June 1999, Dr. Jorge Vallejos assumed the Grand Mastership of the Grand Lodge of Argentina.[9] Shortly after his assumption, a document entitled "Masonería e Iglesia, Una Propuesta de Trabajo" ("Masonry and Church, A Working Proposal") was discussed, producing remarkable results in the following six years. A few months later, Monsignor Karlic, President of the Argentine Episcopate, officially received a delegation of the Grand Lodge of Argentina, led by its Grand Master. The newspaper *Clarín* echoed this dialogue in April 2000, in an article entitled "Encuentro sin precedentes entre la Iglesia y los masones" ("Unprecedented meeting between the Church and the Masons"). Ties were forged between some members of the Catholic Church and the Freemasons. Many ecclesiastics were more than willing to advance this dialogue, which took place in absolutely private meetings. The Jesuits, but not only the Jesuits, continued to be a reference in this exchange.

As was to be expected, there were reactions from Catholic nationalism against Karlic for this dialogue.

In 2007, tensions over the rapprochement between Freemasonry and the Catholic Church worsened within the Grand Lodge of Argentina, and a growing advance of the most radical sectors was perceived, leading to a confrontation with the Catholic Church. However, the then Grand Master Sergio Nunes, held a private meeting with

---

[5] Ibid.
[6] Eduardo R. Callaey (March 24, 2013), Los jesuitas y el diálogo entre Masonería e Iglesia en Argentina, Eduardo Callaey.
[7] Ibid.
[8] Ricardo González, Roberto Villamil, El Enigma del Hombre Gris: Las profecías de Parravicini, Francisco y los secretos del Vaticano (ECIS Publicaciones, First Edition, Buenos Aires, June 2014), p. 172.
[9] Eduardo R. Callaey (March 24, 2013), Los jesuitas y el diálogo entre Masonería e Iglesia en Argentina, Eduardo Callaey. Note: unless otherwise noted, this is the same source.

Cardinal Bergoglio, "of which no further details were revealed," says historian and Mason, Eduardo Roberto Callaey.

In that year or in 2008, Jorge Bergoglio visited the "puppeteer" or former Grand Master of Propaganda Due or Lodge P2, at his mansion in Villa Wanda, in Italy. Bergoglio met Gelli in 73, when Gelli was Argentine Minister Plenipotentiary and a great friend of Perón.[10] It is also curious that Massera, with whom Bergoglio had a positive relationship, usually stayed with his wife at Villa Wanda when they traveled to Italy.[11]

An additional aspect of Bergoglio is his interest in the UFO phenomenon, the "extraterrestrial," contactism, and the *prophetic* future of the Roman Catholic Church. He attended with political personalities, artists, and writers, among others, to gatherings with the Argentinean ufologist Pedro Romaniuk to talk about the UFO phenomenon, extraterrestrial life, and the prophecies of the Argentinean artist Benjamin Solari Parravicini, who died in 1974.[12] Romaniuk, who was a personal friend of Bergoglio, was a disciple of Parravicini, who claimed to have been contacted by extraterrestrials and to have received prophetic messages from them.[13] I consulted several solid Argentine sources who know firsthand that such encounters occurred.

Bergoglio listened attentively and thoughtfully to Romaniuk and the others present, and on one occasion said: "Something important will happen with these prophecies that will be fulfilled in Argentina." Romaniuk "was explaining to the future Pope the prophecies of Parravicini that referred to the collapse and subsequent renewal of the Church," but Bergoglio was especially interested in the psychographs that mention that "the Church must go out into the streets."

Parravicini referred to the arrival of the enigmatic "Gray Man," who would be a key character or a collective of people, or a movement that would emerge in Argentina during a crisis that would have repercussions in the world.[14]

It would be a new paradigm, a new man, who does not choose between black and white, between left and right.[15]

But this little-known aspect of Pope Francis will be discussed in much greater detail in the final chapter of this book.

But to better understand Bergoglio, we must refer to some past events, although not all of them are related to his actions.

---

[10] (September 7, 2014), Odo Gelli far festa - la vita del Gran Maestro diventa un film "con Ryan Gosling e Ornella Muti," parola della 'venerabile' Michela Scolari, unica depositaria delle sue memorie: "Berlusconi cacciato dalla P2 per Coca e Mignotte. Papa Francesco è venuto qui 6-7 anni fa," Dagospia.

[11] Carlos Manfroni, Montoneros. Soldados de Massera: La verdad sobre la contraofensiva montonera y la logia que diseñó los 70 (Sudamericana, 2012), ob. cit.

[12] Yohanan Diaz Vargas (May 2018), Francisco, el Papa ocultista, Año/Cero, Year XXIX Issue 05-334, pp. 24, 25.

[13] Ibid, p. 25. Note: unless otherwise indicated, from here on it is the same page.

[14] Ricardo González, Roberto Villamil, El Enigma del Hombre Gris: Las profecías de Parravicini, Francisco y los secretos del Vaticano (ECIS Publicaciones, First Edition, Buenos Aires, June 2014), p. 152.

[15] (August 11, 2021), Las profecías de Benjamín Solari Parravicini se "actualizan" en pandemia, Clarín.

Malachi Martin, and Lucifer at the Vatican

Undoubtedly, the Second Vatican Ecumenical Council and other influences explain the election of Jorge Mario Bergoglio to the papacy. However, we have left for this section and the next, a story that helps us to understand much better how we got here.

On the night of June 29, 1963, says Jesuit priest Malachi Martin, a group of high-ranking Masonic clerics and senior laymen held in the Pauline Chapel located near the Vatican's Apostolic Palace, an enthronement ceremony of Lucifer, in order to use the Catholic Church as a vehicle for the "New Age" of man. It is said that all the elements of the enthronement were used, but other rubrics could not go unnoticed, so the ceremony would be held in parallel in a transmitting chapel in South Carolina, in the United States.[16]

Participants in both places were to direct all elements of the ceremony to the Roman chapel.[17] The transmitting chapel in South Carolina, led by Bishop John J. Russell, would have had as its victim an eleven-year-old girl.[18] The ceremony would have been held in parallel by telephone, where the priest Joseph Bernardin was Bishop Russell's assistant in South Carolina.[19]

Regarding the Catholic Church, Bishop John Russell preferred "to make that organization into something truly useful, to homogenize and assimilate it into a grand worldwide order of human affairs. To confine it to broad humanist—and only humanist—goals," wrote Martin.[20]

Russell had as participants at the ceremony in South Carolina, "men and women who had made their mark in corporate, government and social life."[21]

Although Malachi Martin confirmed that these events were real, including the ceremony in the targeting chapel[22] and that it occurred in 1963,[23] it is a fact that the sexual abuse of the child - "Agnes," to protect her identity - occurred in the fall of 1957 in Greenville, South Carolina; in the Diocese of Charleston. When the now-adult "Agnes" visited Bishop John Russell in a nursing home, he told her he would testify against Bernardin; but that did not happen.[24]

Malachi Martin, who helped her get her information to the Vatican[25] documented the fact.

Agnes had testified to her story over the previous twelve years "in sworn deposition, in accounts to investigators, in affidavits in support of the cases of others, in direct statements to Bernardin, in telephone calls and letters to Church officials, and in

---

[16] Malachi Martin, Windswept House: A Vatican Novel (Broadway Books, New York, 1996), p. 7-20.
[17] Ibid, p. 8.
[18] Ibid, p. 12 et seq.; WHO'S WHO IN "WINDSWEPT HOUSE": A KEY TO THE CHARACTERS IN FR. MALACHI MARTIN'S "WINDSWEPT HOUSE," TRADITIO Traditional Roman Catholic Network. Last Revision: 7/22/18.
[19] Ibid, p. 8 et. seq.
[20] Malachi Martin, Windswept House: A Vatican Novel (Broadway Books, New York, 1996), p. 9.
[21] Ibid.
[22] John F. McManus (June 9, 1997), The Catholic Church in Crisis, The New America.
[23] Father Brian W. Harrison, O.S. (May 3, 2021), The 1963 Vatican Enthronement of Lucifer: A 'Windswept House' Update, The Remnant.
[24] Stephen Brady (Spring/Summer 2000), The beginning of The End of The Bernardin Legacy, Ad Majorem Dei Gloriam, p. 12.
[25] Ibid.

correspondence with Vatican officials."[26] Such documentation was leaked from the Archdiocese of Chicago, as can be corroborated.[27]

For his part, an Augustinian priest who was in the Vatican during the last stage of Pope Pius XII's pontificate, also said that this ritual took place in the Pauline Chapel.[28]

An important source connected to the Vatican's intelligence services or The Entity, and who served as an assistant in organizing documentation for an intensive investigation inside the Vatican since the time of Paul VI, in response to my question as to whether the above-mentioned by Malachi Martin occurred, told me, "There was a desecration in the Vatican in the 1960s, that's true." But to my astonishment, when I asked him if it was a Masonic ceremony, he said, "It seems so. It seems so. There is no concrete proof. I repeat: it seems so, but it is by no means certain." I was told that there was a Masonic connection to the ritual.

Additional testimony comes from Chad Alec Ripperger, an American Catholic priest, theologian, philosopher, and exorcist, well known for his lectures throughout the United States. He said in October 2023, that there have been other sources confirming that this ritual occurred. About the ritual in South Carolina, he pointed out that the bishop of Charleston, investigated and discovered in the archives that it was true, so he reconsecrated the church. In addition, he indicated that in fact from exorcist sources that are now deceased, several knew that something happened in the early 60's about an enthronement of Lucifer in the Vatican.[29]

It is worth noting that a high exponent of the Society of Jesus, the Jesuit theologian R. T., said during an interview with Galeazzi and Pinotti that no Masonic obedience is equal to another in its beliefs, since, if true, "some explicitly practice Satanism, others venerate extraterrestrials..., others are fervent believers of Christianity."[30]

Satanism in the Vatican and inside the U.S. Catholic Church under Cardinal Bernardin

Yet, as Gordon Thomas and Max Morgan-Witts reported on the time of Paul VI:

"The Apostolic Penitentiary handles complex problems of conscience: Can a priest kill to protect himself? Should he, as some are doing in Latin America, bear arms? It also advises on the penalties a pope may impose for such a dire crime as a priest saying a black mass. Every year there are a number of such cases; they frighten Paul more than

[26] Ibid.

[27] Sidlowski, Steve. Letter to "Agnes. Archdiocese of Chicago. April 14, 1993; ___. Letter to Rev. Cacciavillan. ___. June 18, 1993; Msgr. L. Sandri. Letter to "Agnes." Vatican Secretary of State. September 4, 1993; "Agnes." Letter to Cardinal Gantin. Prefect, Congregation for Bishops. Piazza Pio XII, Rome, Italy. Unpublished date; "Agnes." Letter to Cacciavillan, Agostino. Apostolic Pronunciature. Apostolic Nunciature, United States of America, Washington. April 3, 1995; "Agnes." Letter to Sidlowski, Steve. Chicago, Illinois. Unpublished date; Sister Mary Brian Costello, R. S. M. Chief of Staff. Letter to Mr. Stephen Brady, "Agnes?." Archdiocese of Chicago. June 24, 1996.

[28] Fr. John Zuhlsdorf (August 14, 2019), A Black Mass in the Vatican at the time of Vatican II? Fr. Z's Blog.

[29] (Oct. 19, 2022), Interview with a Real Exorcist Father Chad Ripperger on Diabolic Influence: Dr Marshall Podcast: https://www.youtube.com/watch?v=GMUjC8YRB5I 13:34-20:07 Accessed Feb. 4, 2024.

[30] Giacomo Galeazzi, Ferruccio Pinotti, Vaticano Massone: Logge, denaro e poteri occulti: il lato segreto della Chiesa di papa Francesco (Piemme, 2014), ob. cit.

anything else. He regards them as proof the devil is alive and well and hiding inside the Church."[31]

Such rituals would then be reported from the late 1950s onwards. In fact, after some interactions I had with someone who knew and was friends with Malachi Martin for a decade, he was able to confirm to me that the apparent enthronement of Lucifer in the Vatican would have occurred in the late 1950s or 1960s.

Charles Murr, a Catholic priest and doctor of philosophy, knew Paul VI and worked in the Vatican during part of his and John Paul II's papacy. He wrote that he learned firsthand of the investigation of Freemasonry in the Vatican commissioned by then Bishop Édouard Gagnon.[32] He told me that according to some accounts, he heard firsthand at the Vatican, that there was a sacrilegious mass celebrated inside the Vatican in the early 1970s by an Italian Freemason bishop. But the room where the desecration took place, would have been exorcised. We have been able to have testimonial information that the alleged enthronement of Lucifer took place due to other sources.

For his part, David Yallop, the renowned British journalist now deceased, indicated that Masonic intrigue continued in the Vatican; as well as: "the mafia of Bologna, the axis of Venice, the clans of Romana and Pacienza. There is the Emilian mafia." There also emerged from various schools their own Vatican "lodges." But he adds: "There is even evidence that Satanism is good and healthy in the Vatican. Each new member of the curia is delicately lobbied by various emissaries. And he had better think it through. No membership decision has a retraction clause. This is for life.[33]

In fact, referring to Archbishop Paul Marcinkus and the Vatican, the former mafia member of Cosa Nostra in Italy, Vincenzo Calcara, who is now collaborating with the Italian justice system, indicated that satanic and Masonic rites involving sexual orgies took place behind the Vatican walls.[34] This may have had something to do with the case of Emanuela Orlandi, the daughter of a Vatican City employee who mysteriously disappeared on June 22, 1983.

Yallop adds, thus:

"Homosexuality, if not rife within the Vatican, is constantly evident, and is a frequent factor in career advancement. Young attractive priests, invariably referred to as *Madonni*, use their charms to accelerate their promotion. Certain bishops have found the need to work late in a locked room with only a *Madonno* to assist them. Satanic masses have happened regularly with hooded semi-naked participants and porn videos have been shown to very carefully selected audiences. I was introduced through one source to an elegant Roman whose main source of income was arranging 'safe apartments' for Vatican assignations both heterosexual and homosexual. His clientele

---

[31] Gordon Thomas & Max Morgan-Witts, Pontiff: The Vatican, the KGB, and the Year of the Three Popes (Open Road Integrated Media, New York, 2014), ob. cit.
[32] Charles Theodore Murr, Murder in the 33rd Degree: The Gagnon Investigation into Vatican Freemasonry (Independent Publication, Charles T. Murr, 2022).
[33] David Yallop, The Power and the Glory: Inside the Dark Heart of Pope John Paul II's Vatican (Constable & Robinson Ltd, London, 2007), op. cit.
[34] Redazione (June 15, 2014), Esclusiva, L'ultima rivelazione di Calcara: "Dietro Papa Francesco c'è un potente Cardinale," In Libertà; (July 28, 2014), Pentito Calcara rivela particolari su norte Papa Luciani, News Cattoliche.

includes two homosexual cardinals, a German priest who has frequent assignations with his 'wife' and until recently an American bishop who had conducted an affair with a former beauty queen over many years. He also supplies child pornography videos to 'a number' of Vatican residents."[35]

The late Monsignor Luigi Marinelli, then retired and a member of the Congregation for Oriental Churches, also wrote that in the Roman sanctuary della Madonna del Divino Amore, a point of successive organized and individual pilgrimages, late in the afternoon and mixed among the others, a very upset and disturbed penitent approached the confessional, saying that for ten years he had belonged to a satanic sect in which he played an important role and that he had dragged many into it. He convinced them to attend black masses and other satanic rites. But one day, he was the guest at a black mass in the Vatican itself. But he could not recognize the others because they were all hooded and covered from head to toe, and their voices were deep.[36]

Also, during a speech in Rome on November 22, 1996, on the occasion of Fatima 2000, Archbishop Emmanuel Milingo, then secretary of the Holy See on immigrants, said that among the curial bureaucrats in the Vatican, there were Satan worshippers.[37]

The Vatican exorcist, priest Gabriele Amorth (who died in 2016), stated on several occasions that in the Vatican there are members of satanic sects, such as priests, monsignors, and even cardinals; something that Benedict XVI himself knew.[38]

Malachi Martin speaks extensively about Joseph Bernardin as the cardinal of "Centurycity" -Archdiocese of Chicago-, where those satanic rituals sodomizing children were carried out by priests.[39] He points out, as he described in his novel based on historical facts, Windswept House, what John Paul II knew about it:

"Suddenly it became unarguable that now, during this papacy, the Roman Catholic organization carried a permanent presence of clerics who worshiped Satan and liked it; of bishops and priests who sodomized boys and each other; of nuns who performed the "Black Rites" of Wicca, and who lived in lesbian relationships within as well as outside of convent life. Suddenly it became clear that during this papacy the Roman Catholic Church organization had become a place where every day, including Sundays and Holy Days, acts of heresy and blasphemy and outrage and indifference were committed and permitted at holy Altars by men who had been called to be priests. Sacrilegious actions and rites were not only performed at Christ's Altars, but had the connivance or at least the tacit permission of certain Cardinals, archbishops and

[35] David Yallop, The Power and the Glory: Inside the Dark Heart of Pope John Paul II's Vatican (Constable & Robinson Ltd, London, 2007), op. cit.

[36] Los Milenarios, El Vaticano Contra Dios (Ediciones B, S.A., Barcelona, Spain, 1999), ob. cit.

[37] Archbishop Emmanuel Milingo (Winter 1997), The Three Dimensions of Evil, The Fatima Crusader, Issue 54, pp. 11, 12.

[38] Stefano Maria Paci (2001), Il fumo di Satana nella casa del Signore, 30Giorni; CBN. Is The Devil Gaining a Foothold in Rome [Video Archive] (2008). Retrieved from http://www1.cbn.com/content/devil-gaining-foothold-rome; Marco Ansaldo (March 10, 2010), Il Diavolo abita anche in Vaticano, La Repubblica, p. 1; Interview by Vittorio Zincone with Gabriele Amorth (June 7, 2010): http://vittoriozincone.it/2010/06/17/gabriele-amorth-sette-giugno-2010/; accessed April 8, 2010; Alessandro Capriccioli (October 29, 2012), Qualcuno fermi padre Amorth, L'Espresso; William Friedkin (December, 2016), The Devil and Father Amorth: Witnessing "the Vatican Exorcist" at Work, Vanity Fair.

[39] Malachi Martin, Windswept House: A Vatican Novel (Broadway Books, New York, 1996), p. 242 et. seq.

bishops. Suddenly shock set in at the actual lists of prelates and priests who were involved. In total number, they were a minority—anything from one to ten percent of Church personnel. But of that minority, many occupied astoundingly high positions of rank and authority in chanceries, seminaries and universities.

Appalling though it was, however, even this picture wasn't the whole cause of His Holiness' crisis. The facts that brought the Pope to a new condition of suffering were mainly two: The systematic organizational links—the network, in other words—that had been established between certain clerical homosexual groups and Satanist covens. And the inordinate power and influence of that network."[40]

When Joseph Bernardin - already mentioned in the satanic event mentioned by Malachi Martin - was in Charleston, it is known that the diocese was recognized as a seat of progressivism from the days of Bishop John England.[41]

Several priests who were Bernardin's associates before his time in Chicago revealed that they had "partied" together with Bernardin, and they spoke about his visits to socialize with seminarians at Josephinum.[42] His close friend in his South Carolina days, Monsignor Frederick Hopwood, had been accused of molesting hundreds of boys since the early 1950s; when he and Bernardin shared a residence at the Cathedral of St. John the Baptist in Charleston, where some of the abuse occurred. One of Hopwood's victims, Marion Lafong, stresses that Bernardin, Hopwood, and other priests were colleagues. In addition, she said that in negotiations with lawyers for the Chicago archdiocese to reach a settlement without trial, Bernardin's name came up a number of times, along with allegations that Hopwood presided over satanic animal rituals in the woods where some of his victims were abused.[43]

Bernardin quickly gained power. While his Charleston friends continued to sodomize children, he used his influence beginning in 1968 as Secretary General of the U.S. Catholic Conference to select bishops who would approve and promote homosexuality as an acceptable lifestyle and tolerate the sexual abuse of children by priests.[44]

Bernardin was archbishop of Cincinnati from 1972 to 1982, as well as archbishop of Chicago from 1982 to 1996, when he died. Bernardin was accused of having abused minors, as was the case of Steve Cook, who accused him,[45] and whose case is a mystery. When Bernardin was in Chicago, there was a secret clerical club known as the "Boys Club," which included not only homosexual assignations but also ritualistic and occult cults, as well as sexual abuse of young boys.[46]

Two investigators, Bill Callaghan and Hank Adema, confirmed the existence of this clerical pedophile ring operating out of the Archdiocese of Chicago.[47]

---

[40] Ibid, pp. 492, 493.

[41] Randy Engel, The Rite of Sodomy - Homosexuality and the Roman Catholic Church (New Engel Publishing, 2006), ob. cit.

[42] Ibid.

[43] Paul Likoudis, Amchurch Comes Out: The U.S. Bishops, Pedophile Scandals and the Homosexual Agenda (Roman Catholic Faithful Inc., 2002), ob. cit.

[44] Ibid.

[45] Randy Engel, The Rite of Sodomy (New Engel Publishing, Export, Pennsylvania, 2012), Volume IV, pp. 889-917.

[46] Ibid, p. 904.

[47] Ibid.

Frank Pellegrini, organist and choir director at All Saints - St. Anthony of Padua Roman Catholic Church on the south side of Chicago, had (his girlfriend said), a relationship with a Chicago priest who was part of the club. Pellegrini contemplated meeting with Foreign Ministry officials to discuss the matter, but it was not known if it happened. Shortly thereafter, on May 30, 1984, Pellegrini was found brutally murdered in his apartment.

Similarly, in the 1980s, a small group of prelates abused young candidates for the priesthood at Immaculate Heart of Mary Seminary in Winona, Minnesota. The bishops involved in the affair were Joseph Bernardin, John Roach, Robert Brom, and an unknown fourth bishop. One of the seminarians indicated that some of the activities at the seminary were connected with occult and satanic rituals.[48]

The renowned Catholic priest, sociologist, journalist, and novelist Andrew Greeley, wrote in his memoirs that there is a scattered national network of pedophile priests; but the problem is especially acute in the Archdiocese of Chicago, where Bernardin inherited the problem without confronting it with any particular vigor.[49] The network of such priests was so brazen there that it seemed to flaunt its power and influence and the importance of retribution.[50]

Greeley wrote in 1999 on the Chicago network: "They are a dangerous group. There is reason to believe that they are responsible for at least one murder and may perhaps have been involved in the murder of the murderer. Am I afraid of them? Not particularly. They know that I have in safekeeping information which would implicate them. I am more of a threat to them dead than alive."[51]

James Hitchcock wrote of Bernardin's legacy as Archbishop of Chicago, "He [Bernardin] consistently used his influence to promote liberal causes, even attacks on Church teachings and traditions." [...] "...he consistently used his power to build a network of allies within both the hierarchy and the bureaucracy, a network which in effect has controlled the direction of the 'American Church'.'"[52]

Bernardin received the presidential award from U.S. President Bill Clinton and was honored posthumously by the Masons.[53] Interestingly, John Cody, Archbishop of Chicago from 1965-1982, was a Masonic sympathizer.[54]

Dozens of schools and parishes were closed, and progressive sex education was commonplace. There were also an alarming number of cases of sexual abuse coming to light.[55]

Bernardin was a supporter of the gay community.[56] And indeed, the *Washington Blade*, a famous LGBT newspaper, reported in November 1997, that Cardinal Joseph

---

[48] Randy Engel, The Rite of Sodomy - Homosexuality and the Roman Catholic Church (New Engel Publishing, 2006), ob. cit.

[49] Andrew Greeley, Confessions of a Parish Priest: An Autobiography (Pocket Books, New York, 1987), p. 130.

[50] Ibid.

[51] Andrew M. Greeley, Furthermore! Memories of a Parish Priest (Forge Book, Tom Doherty Associates Book, New York, 1999), p. 80, note 47.

[52] Stephen Brady (Spring/Summer 2000), The beginning of The End of The Bernardin Legacy, Ad Majorem Dei Gloriam, p. 9.

[53] Ibid.

[54] Giacomo Galeazzi, Ferruccio Pinotti, Vaticano Massone: Logge, denaro e poteri occulti: il lato segreto della Chiesa di papa Francesco (Piemme, 2014), ob. cit.

[55] Stephen Brady (Spring/Summer 2000), The beginning of The End of The Bernardin Legacy, Ad Majorem Dei Gloriam, p. 9.

Bernardin arranged for the Windy City Gay Chorus to sing at his wake at Holy Name Cathedral.[57]

As Stephen Brady of *Roman Catholic Faithful* aptly put it, "The Bernardin legacy is the current condition of the Catholic Church in America."[58] Kevin Mannara wrote in similar terms, that American Catholicism today is a reflection of the late Joseph Bernardin's mandate and American culture.[59]

In late January 2014, the British newspaper, *The Guardian*, reported that the Archdiocese of Chicago released documents detailing a cover-up of child sexual abuse. There had been decades of evasion and failed actions by church officials; revealing six thousand documents chronicling the abuse of children by Roman Catholic priests in the Chicago archdiocese. The allegations were kept secret as the accused were moved from one parish to another. It describes how church leaders, including Cardinals John Cody and Joseph Bernardin, approved the reassignments of the abusers.[60] In November of the same year, fifteen thousand pages of abuse committed by thirty-six priests beginning in 1952 were released.[61]

Malachi Martin and *The Last Pope*

Paul Likoudis of *The Wanderer* newspaper interviewed in June 2007 the controversial Irish-born author, Jesuit Malachi Martin, about his latest book (novel), entitled Windswept House.[62]

Martin was asked, "How much of Windswept House is true?" And he replied that about 85% of the characters are real, and 85% of the events depicted in the book are also real; except for those that are obviously mythical, such as the end of the Slavic pope's stay in Poland.[63] The book especially portrays the plans of high-ranking clerics such as cardinals, archbishops, and prelates of the Roman Curia who meet with secular internationalists and Freemasons to force the pope to abdicate in order to elect a successor who will transform the orthodox faith of world Catholicism and establish a new order in the world. In fact, the enthronement of Lucifer in the Vatican and the Satanism among clerics and nuns that we have documented first became known through that book.

Attempts have been made to identify the characters and their names with their actual personalities.[64] And although many names seem plausible, it results in speculation. But in the interview with Malachi Martin, he identified the Slavic pope of Poland as Pope

---

[56] Laurie Goering (May 10, 1987), Bernardin's Speech Leaves Gay Catholics Pleased, Encouraged, Chicago Tribune; Jeffrey Felshman (August 29, 1996) How to Win Enemies and Influence People, Chicago Reader.

[57] Stephen Brady (Spring/Summer 2000), The beginning of The End of The Bernardin Legacy, Ad Majorem Dei Gloriam, p. 9.

[58] Ibid, p. 10.

[59] Kevin J. V. Mannara, CSB (March, 2016), Bernardin and Bergoglio: What the Cardinal's Legacy Offers to a Church Led by Pope Francis, NTR, volume 28, number 2, pp. 38, 39.

[60] Karen McVeigh (January 21, 2014), Chicago Catholic archdiocese releases documents detailing cover-up of abuse, The Guardian.

[61] Mark Guarino (Nov. 6, 2014), Chicago Catholic archdiocese releases new sexual abuse files on 36 priests, The Guardian.

[62] Cited in: (June 8, 1997), Interview from The Wanderer, RFC.

[63] Ibid.

[64] (July 11, 2007) A Key to the Characters in Fr. Malachi Martin's "Windswept House," Traditio.

John Paul II. Cardinal Secretary of State Maestroianni with Cardinal Agostino Casaroli, who served in office from 1979 to 1990. And as we saw, he was a Freemason.

Martin commented that a plot meeting held in Strasbourg, France, did not occur. But it reveals the attempts from within to elect a new pontiff who would modify Catholic orthodoxy and lead the Catholic Church to be the leader of a new world order.[65]

He wrote that Maestroianni (Cardinal Secretary of State Agostino Casaroli), gave a brief speech in the gigantic Palais de l'Europe, in Strasbourg, where the European Parliament was meeting. He would have given a brief speech where he pointed out that the Europe they are building constituted the future hope of many millions; transmitting almost the same words that the Slavic pope (John Paul II) transmitted only three days later.[66] However, Pope John Paul II's only visit to the European Parliament in Strasbourg was on October 11, 1988, and Casaroli's words in Martin's book are very similar.[67] Also in 1988, Casaroli was the Cardinal Secretary of State, but he never gave a speech in the European Parliament. Moreover, as Martin said, the meeting that described the conspirators is fictitious but reflects the importance of what was being instituted from within the Vatican itself.

The pope had asked the European Parliament to open up to the countries of the East,[68] which would be part of the plan between Reagan's United States and Pope John Paul II to bring down communism.

It is also known that Agostino Casaroli - not willingly - together with John Paul II, were the main driving forces in the Vatican that pushed a driving force behind the democratic changes in the large bloc of Eastern countries dominated by the Soviet Union in the late 1980s.[69] Thus, he was known as the great architect of Vatican Ostpolitik.[70] In this way, Martin places the conspiratorial meeting towards the end of the 1980s, when the USSR would fall in 1991, and thus to a US-Vatican alliance that would shape a different world order.

Among those attending the fictitious meeting (Russians, ministers of the Anglican Church, etc.) we mention concisely for the sake of relevance, there was as one of the main protagonists an American named "Benthoek" (there is also Gibson Appleyard, of the American intelligence), who declared in the fictitious secret meeting of Strasbourg that: "Above all, that Church is a sine qua non [indispensable] for the advent of a New World Order in human affairs."[71] That was their fundamental conclusion and one on which they all agreed. Also, at the meeting, the one who took the most important part in all the planning was the Jesuit general, Michael Coutinho, who, as we move to the late 1980s, would be the Dutchman Peter Hans Kolvenbach. Especially since it is mentioned that his predecessor was Pedro Arrupe,[72] as he really was. But at the same time, we know very well from various sources that Martin was referring to the late progressive Jesuit, Carlo Maria Martini.

---

[65] Cited in: (June 8, 1997), Interview from The Wanderer, RFC.

[66] Malachi Martin, Windswept House: A Vatican Novel (Broadway Books, New York, 1996), p.

[67] Visita al Parlamento Europeo en el Palacio de Europa (Strasbourg, Tuesday, October 11, 1988, Libreria Editrice Vaticana, 1988), pp. 1, 3.

[68] Ibid.

[69] Alessandra Stanley (June 10, 1998), Agostino Cardinal Casaroli, 83, Dies; Led Vatican to Detente, The New York Times.

[70] (Dec. 10, 2013), Casaroli and Wyszynski: Facts and falsehoods revealed, Vatican Insder.

[71] Malachi Martin, Windswept House: A Vatican Novel (Broadway Books, New York, 1996), p. 4.

[72] Ibid, p. 94.

Malachi Martin wrote that the Jesuit general spoke of the need for a radical change from the highest levels of the Holy See; a different form of organization. The Jesuit general recalled how in 1981, the Slav pope (John Paul II), had dismissed Pedro Arrupe and disciplined the Society of Jesus with a very heavy hand for its adventures with liberation theology in Latin America. The novel describes Father General silently throwing his anger at the pope: "We will not forget this needless humiliation!" -read on his face. He advocated a radically changed Catholic Church for the defense of the poor; under the thinking of the Society of Jesus itself.[73]

"Every man present was fixed by the passion in Michael Coutinho's eyes as he made plain the present position his global Order had adopted. "We in our Society are completely at peace in our consciences. We are bound by our vows to Christ. And we are bound to serve the Vicar of Peter, the Bishop of Rome. Insofar as vve can see he conforms to the manifest will of Christ, as that will is shown to us in the human events of our day, we are bound to serve him. That is all I have to say."

[...] the Jesuit had changed his allegiance. He served the Pope now not as the Vicar of Christ, the Creator; but as the Vicar of Peter, the creature. The regulator for his policies was not some transcendent goal formulated in the sixteenth century by a long-dead St. Ignatius of Loyola, but the clear lineaments of political and social evolution at the end of the twentieth century."[74]

Today, Pope Francis also calls himself the Bishop of Rome.

Another of those present at the meeting, Cardinal Noah Palombo, suggested that the point made by the Jesuit General, namely the radical change needed in Roman Catholicism, be placed on the table. Cardinal "Leo Pensabene" expressed that some within the Curia would support (and in summary of his words) and that the thinking of the Second Vatican Council since 1965 on such reforms in the liturgical and ideological part should be invoked, to influence the personal, social, and political; something that had been very successful in third world countries: such as the Latin American region. It was so much so that many bishops spoke in place of the Holy See in that paradigm or under less centralism.[75]

In fact, from the beginning of his papacy, Francis met with an advisory council of cardinals at the Vatican. And through the various annual synods of bishops, especially with the Synod of Synodality held in October 2023, which favored a synodal church: or communion, participation, and mission.

Now, "Pensabene" indicated that, "As soon as possible, we need to have a papacy that conforms to the new reality. A papacy that conforms to the concrete, de facto situation. In fact, a papacy that accepts that situation as de jure." Thus, it was concluded that if thar resolution was approved and the Strasbourg alliance was successful, the Slavic pope would adjust to the conditions described, or else he would have to abdicate the papal office.[76]

After a 15-minute recess, the delegate from the Anglican Church, Rev. Tartley, reminded those present, that "her Majesty the Queen had pointed out to him the need of

---

[73] Ibid, pp. 106, 107.
[74] Ibid.
[75] Ibid, pp. 107, 108.
[76] Ibid, p. 109.

"a universal teacher" in our present world. Someone who would be described as universal because he would be accepted by all as having the wisdom "to cater to everyone's needs, but not to move exclusively."[77] It describes, no doubt, Bergoglio's future papacy. "Tartley:"

"There could, he explained by example, be no real collaboration between "the Holy See and the vast majority of Christians" until Rome abandoned its obstinate views on such basic questions as divorce, abortion, contraception, homosexuality, the ordination of women, marriage for priests, and fetal engineering."[78]

It is as if "he" was describing first hand the current Pope Francis, where many of those aspects have been greatly minimized.

"Tartley" further indicated that such a step was possible only through a change in pontifical administration, on which all agreed.[79]

Cardinal "Palombo" points out:

"The situation is clear," Palombo began. "And my second recommendation is accordingly very simple. The basic reason for the consensus that has just been demonstrated among us is the pressure—the force—of human events. Events outside the operational scope of the churchmen here tonight. I speak of the rush of men and women the world over toward a new unity. Toward a new arrangement among the nations, and among all people of our modern society."[80]

The general of the Society of Jesus agreed, among other things, that in South America millions of men and women embraced their successful financial, economic and political liberation.[81]

"Palombo" then expressed:

"Acid-faced and intent, Palombo turned now toward each of his fellow Cardinals. "We have heard tonight from my venerable brother Cardinal Pensabene, for example, that the Catholic mind has now been disaffected from its recent slavery to the papalisr motive. That mind has also been disaffected from the whole confused *mixtum-gatherum* of mental habits that once conformed Catholics to a model of human behavior that is refused and rejected by the vast majority of men and women today. Thanks to the use of advanced psychological techniques employed by Marriage Enjoinder, Origins and RENEW—to name just a few of the processes formulated to further our agenda— even the vast majority of Catholics today reject those old models of behavior.

"More to the point, those very processes have moved Catholics themselves—again, 1 speak of men and women in their millions—to the acceptance of everything we in this room envision for the New World Order. No longer do Catholics suffer under the conviction that they belong to some special group. Or that they have exclusive possession of the moral and religious values by which men and women must live in

---

[77] Ibid, p. 114.
[78] Ibid.
[79] Ibid, p. 115.
[80] Ibid, p. 116.
[81] Ibid.

order to—to be..." Just this once, Noah Palombo stumbled over his words. "To be—as they used to say—to be saved."

[...] "Right now, through the Roman center—through every diocese and parish; through every seminary and university and school that is called Catholic— there runs a new and different current. Throughout the Church, there is born a new type of Catholic. Now, Catholics are disposed and ripe to be assimilated to the general type of men and women. Now, Catholics desire what we ourselves desire. Now, Catholics are ready to inhabit and give life to the New World Order that we, here in this room, intend to make a reality."[82]

During another meeting with other participants and some of the Strasbourg participants held in New York, an expert in comparative religions from Yale, "Dr. Ralph Channing," spoke of the progressive spirit of man, which means progress in religion, as a religious phase or "The final stage" of the creation of a religion for a unique world without nationalisms, particularisms and culturalisms of the past; where there would be a mechanism to remodel the religious phase to a new world order. A document was also read at the meeting. At the end it was concluded that it was necessary to wait for the death of the Slavic pope -John Paul II- to choose a new pope to be chosed by those in cahoots. A pope who would embrace all religions and place less emphasis on "such basic questions as divorce, abortion, contraception, homosexuality, the ordination of women, marriage for priests, and fetal engineering" - as we have seen.[83] The plan to reform the Catholic Church from the papacy - let us remember - is proposed in Malachi Martin's novel by the general of the Jesuits so that it would keep a mentality similar to that of the Society of Jesus. As we will see shortly, such was the effort that was planned from the late 1970s until the conclave of March 2013, when Cardinal Jorge Bergoglio, a Jesuit, was elected Pope Francis.

Martin wrote of the aforementioned 'meeting' that it was stated: "the candidate to replace the present holder of the office will be someone acquainted with our aims, acquiescent in them at the very least and even fully disposed to collaborate in achieving those aims."[84]

About making the pope resign it was *stated:*

"There remains, then, the Chosen Alternative. The Categoric Choice by which we will achieve our goal is resignation. Briefly stated, the present holder of the office will be induced to resign from that office—and without prejudice.

"A voluntary papal resignation, at this crux of divisiveness and disunity among the ordinary RC lairy and between churchmen themselves, would be a powerful signal; nothing less than an admission of defeat for important elements who stand against us. It would be a declaration to the remaining defenders of the old order of things that the past is irretrievable. Indeed, the climate is such that there is already a certain sympathy among the old order for our Chosen Alternative."[85]

---

[82] Ibid, pp. 116, 117.
[83] Ibid, pp. 123 et seq. 127-130, p. 114.
[84] Ibid, p. 130.
[85] Ibid, p. 131.

The Vatican Secretary of State "Maestroianni"/or Cardinal Agostino Casaroli, who arrived at the meeting later, told Dr. Channing that they were looking for a substitute pope for the current pontiff; who had to eliminate centralism and give greater collegiality to the bishops of the world to sustain a common criterion of the same; and that the new pope should not consider himself the vicar of Christ, but of Peter.[86] In other words, by not flaunting such a centralist authority because of his own ideology, "but rather a more benevolent and humble one." The novel echoes the term collegiality on different occasions, as will be seen in the next section.

Later in the book, the general of the Society of Jesus, Michael Coutinho, is placed in a position where he is elected archbishop of Genoa, which always carries the cardinal's biretta. And from there he is promoted to the Sacred College of Cardinals, where he could participate in the conclave that would replace the pope.[87] Much of that happened in real life with Cardinal Carlo Maria Martini (now deceased), and it reflects an image of a Vatican led by a progressive Jesuit priest.

During a dinner with a journalist, "Maestroianni" notes that the Jesuit was someone to watch (as a candidate for the papacy) because he was:

"A man willing to envisage changes and adaptations of Church disciplinary law regarding contraception, for example, as well as abortion and fetal research. As a man not unfriendly, either, to changes in the Church's position on homosexuality, married priests and the ordination of women. In sum, as a man of the future."[88]

The U.S. bishops seemed that were aligning themselves under the criteria of the preferred candidate. From the Strasbourg group, they were moving to promote the candidacy of the Jesuit who would lead the Church into the third millennium.[89]

The candidate, according to reports of both meetings in the fictional-fact novel, had to look for his greatest ally in the European Community and the United States.
And indeed, in U.S. government circles they wanted a more universalist pope.

The last pages of the novel conclude with the expectation of the Slavic pope's resignation, which is about to become public...[90]

About a week before he died - on July 27, 1999 - Jesuit Malachi Martin informed Father Fiore that he was preparing an essay on the power of the Vatican as we were approaching the third millennium, entitled "Primacy: How the Institutional Roman Catholic Church Became a Creature of the New World Order," which he apparently failed to finish.[91]

One of the great Vaticanists of the last century, Baron Avro Manhattan, had expressed in 1982 that "Popes are a reflection of the age in which they reign." Thus, exposed to extreme left-wing ideologies in the last quarter century, the election of a Marxist pope could be expected; added to the radical innovations of the Second Vatican Council and amplified by its post-Vatican Council policies. Avro Manhattan stated that we might not see a Marxist pope 'tomorrow', but that one would come in the

---

[86] Ibid, p. 137.
[87] Ibid, pp. 427, 428.
[88] Ibid, p. 428.
[89] Ibid, p. 408, 409, 476.
[90] Ibid, p. 635-646.
[91] Jon Dougherty (August 2, 1999), Malachi Martin: Dispelling the myths, WorldNetDaily.

not too distant future: before the close of this century.[92] Which did not happen then, but would come later with a pope not entirely Marxist, but with a strong ideology that unites him to a socialist ideology.

Such a papacy would be in a world dominated by such ideas, something that will lead the West (the United States, specifically) to overthrow the current world order in order to establish a new one.[93]

Towards a new papal election: the candidacy of Jorge Bergoglio and the Sankt Gallen group

At the beginning of the papacy of the Polish Pope John Paul II, Pedro Arrupe, of whom the Jesuit Malachi Martin wrote, was General of the Society of Jesus:

"There were continual streams of complaints arriving at the papal office, all detailing the unorthodox opinions being taught by Jesuits in Europe and the United States. There were, in addition, revelations that certain circles of the international section of the Masonic Lodge in Europe and Latin America were actively organizing opposition to the Pontiff in Poland; that Vatican prelates-some twenty in all-were formal members of the Italian Lodge; and that once again Arrupe's Jesuits seemed involved with the Lodge circles opposed to the Pontiff."[94]

Likewise, at the end of 1980, during a visit to the Catholic historian Roberto de Mattei, who at the time lived in Via della Lungara, next to the Porta Septimiana and close to the Vatican, the priest Mario Marini, deeply concerned about the Church, "asked for my help in making known the existence of a real "Mafia" that controlled power under the pontificate of John Paul II."[95] He recounted that when Pope Paul VI died on August 6, 1978, two powerful regional groups or clans were vying for power in the Vatican: the Lombard-Piemontese "Family" and the Romagnola "family." The first clan, the Lombard Piedmontese "family," revolved around Monsignor Pasquale Macchi, Paul VI's private secretary. We have already seen in another chapter that Macchi was a Freemason, with powerful connections and and was largely responsible for the reconstruction of the "new church." Macchi included the future Cardinals Giovanni Coppa, advisor to the Secretariat of State; Monsignor Francesco Marchisano, another important Mason and conspirator, Undersecretary of Catholic Education; Monsignor Luigi Maverna, Secretary of the Italian Episcopal Conference; and Monsignor Virgilio Noé, Pontifical Master of Ceremonies.

The second family, the Romagnola, was made up of four companions from the regional seminary of Bologna; namely, the future cardinals Monsignor Achille Silvestrini, Monsignor Pio Laghi (both Masons, as we saw[96] - and Lagui would be apostolic nuncio in Argentina), Monsignor Dino Monduzzi, prefect of the pontifical

---

[92] Avro Manhattan, The Vatican Moscow Washington Alliance (Chick Publications, CA, 1982), pp. 271, 272.

[93] Ibid.

[94] Malachi Martin, The Jesuits: The Society of Jesus and the Betrayal of the Roman Catholic Church (Simon & Schuster Paperbacks, New York, 1987), p. 76.

[95] Roberto de Mattei (Nov. 19, 2021), A Mafia in the City of Popes, Roberto de Mattei/Advance Faith. Note: unless otherwise noted, this is the same source.

[96] Discípulos de la Verdad, Mentiras y crímenes en el Vaticano: la verdad sobre el triple asesinato en las dependencias de la Guardia Suiza (Ediciones B, 200), p. 67.

house; and Monsignor Franco Gualdrini, rector of the Capranica College.[97] The spiritual director of this quartet was Monsignor Salvatore Baldassari, who has ultra-progressive ideas.

After the death of Paul VI, both families sealed a *pact of steel* to control the Vatican. The architect of this agreement was Monsignor Monduzzi, but the one in charge was Monsignor Achille Silvestrini, who had succeeded Agostino Casaroli as secretary of the Council for Public Affairs of the Church.

"Every morning at nine o'clock," Don Marini explained, the political group that runs the Vatican, composed of these characters, meets and prepares its reports for the Pope. But the real decisions have already been taken by an occult 'directorate' that effectively controls all the information, kept in inaccessible archives and appropriately filtered in order to guide the choices and propose appointments under apparently obvious pretexts."

In fact, this board of directors was headed by Monsignor Achille Silvestrini.

Unlike the central ideology that governed both *families*, John Paul II chose to rule monarchically, due to the divisions that occurred in the Church. The conclusions of the synods were controlled by the Curia, and the Church only had a "Magisterium" or doctrinal authority closed in that circle, taking influence away from the Episcopal Councils of the world.[98] And the Lombard-Piemontese and Romagnolo "families" were not happy with Wojtyla's papacy.

In fact, in 1992, the Prefect of the Sacred Congregation for the Doctrine of the Faith, Joseph Ratzinger, adopted a position that several critics considered as a return to the times before the Second Vatican Council.[99] Ratzinger defended that the universal Church is "ontologically prior" to the local Church.[100]

Indeed, the 1990s witnessed a growing sense among bishops visiting Rome that the Vatican leadership did not take them into account; or in other words, that it regarded them as mere delegates of the Curia. It was this growing concern for centrality that prompted the Sankt Gallen meetings.[101] A group that was founded in 1995 and, according to the authorized biographers of Cardinal Danneels (a member of the group), Sankt Gallen group members met annually to discuss the situation of the Church; the 'primacy of the pope'; 'collegiality' and the succession of Pope John Paul II.[102] It was Sankt Gallen bishop, or Ivo Fürer, who in the late 1990s began to organize these private meetings at his residence of European cardinals and archbishops which, in

---

[97] Roberto de Mattei (Nov. 19, 2021), A Mafia in the City of Popes, Roberto de Mattei/Advance Faith. Note: unless otherwise noted, this is the same source.

[98] Austen Ivereigh, The Great Reformer: Francis and the Making of a Radical Pope (Henry Holt and Co., New York, 2014), ob. cit.

[99] Ibid.

[100] Congregation for the Doctrine of the Faith, "Letter to the Bishops of the Catholic Church on Some Aspects of the Church Understood as Communion" (May 28, 1992) at www.vatican.va; quoted in Ibid.

[101] Austen Ivereigh, The Great Reformer: Francis and the Making of a Radical Pope (Henry Holt and Co., New York, 2014), ob. cit.

[102] Edward Pentin (Sept. 26, 2015), Cardinal Danneels' Biographers Retract Comments on St. Gallen Group, National Catholic Reporter.

themselves - writes Austen Ivereigh - "which in themselves were expressions of collegiality."[103]

The *Courrier de Rome* reported in December 1992 that, "It is now absolutely certain that, for certain persons, preparations for the next Conclave have already been under way for quite a while; and have now taken on a sense of urgency since Pope John Paul II's hospitalisation, last summer, at the Gemelli Polyclinic."[104] The article further reports:

"On several occasions, independent journals have revealed that in the very heart of the Vatican, there presently exists a secret power group - in the form of a true organization, made up of the press, information services as well as minions strategically placed in the internal structure of the Church (Apostolic Nunciatures, Offices of the Holy See, different Commissions, in dioceses, Episcopal Universities and Conferences, etc.), or having connections with other power groups outside the Church."[105]

On the occasion of the October 1992 Synod, Cardinal Achille Silvestrini, also a member of the Sankt Gallen Group, declared in a secret meeting about the next pope: "In the future, who knows, it could very well be a Latin American or even an African who emerges."[106]

The first to comment on the Sankt Gallen group and its purpose was Austen Ivereigh, who is a British-Catholic journalist, writer, and deputy editor of *The Tablet*. He was also director of public relations for Cardinal Cormac Murphy-O'Connor and founder and coordinator of Catholic Voices. He is also a contributor to *Our Sunday Visitor* and *The Guardian*. A scholar of Argentine history on which he based his doctorate at Oxford University.[107] Ivereigh wrote verbatim in his celebrated biography of Pope Francis, *The Great Reformer*:

"The story of how Jorge Mario Bergoglio came to be a contender in the conclave of 2005 and to be elected pope in 2013 begins a long way from Argentina, in a pretty, snowclad town in northeastern Switzerland. With its location in the precise center of Europe and its multilingual population of seventy-five thousand, St. Gallen [Sankt Gallen] is well placed to headquarter the Council of the Bishops' Conferences of Europe."[108]

The Jesuit Carlo Maria Martini - Sankt Gallen group - was the dominant figure who until 2002 was archbishop of Milan. But Godfried Danneels, a powerful cardinal, was

[103] Austen Ivereigh, The Great Reformer: Francis and the Making of a Radical Pope (Henry Holt and Co., New York, 2014), ob. cit.

[104] si si no no (April 1993), Secret Vatican Power Group Preparing Next Conclave, si si no no, No. 1. Translated from Courrier de Rome, December 1992.

[105] Ibid; citing cf. *Impact Suisse* February/March/April 1981; cf. *Il Settimanale* May 5, 1981; cf. *si si no no* November 15,1985 and May 31,1987.

[106] si si no no (October 1995), The Next Conclave: Vatican Politics in View of the Next Conclave, si si no no, No. 13. Translated from *Courrier de Rome*, March 1995.

[107] Redacción (Dec. 1, 2014), Redacción (1 de diciembre, 2014), Aclaración del padre Lombardi sobre el libro de Austen Ivereigh, Zenit.

[108] Austen Ivereigh, The Great Reformer: Francis and the Making of a Radical Pope (Henry Holt and Co., New York, 2014), ob. cit. Note: unless otherwise noted, this is the same source.

also a significant voice at the meetings. Such meetings, which lasted two days around the discussion table, usually included six or seven other prelates from central or northern Europe. Three archbishops named cardinals in 2001 (at the same time as Bergoglio) joined the same year. Yet another was Germany's Walter Kasper, the bishop of Rottenburg-Stuttgart, who in 1999 was appointed president of the Vatican department in charge of Christian-Jewish relations.

The other two cardinals were presiding bishops' conferences from Germany and England and Wales: Karl Lehmann, Bishop of Mainz, and Cormac Murphy-O'Connor of Westminster, England. There were also sporadic participants from France and the Central European region, but the aforementioned were the core of the Sankt Gallen group.

Martini and Danneels were occasionally described by journalists as liberals or progressives, but Ivereigh says they were more like reformists (riformisti).

On the other hand, the conservatives, or rigoristi, dominated the Curia of John Paul II. They wanted the doctrine of the Catholic Church to be above all clear and forceful; but the riformisti wanted it to be credible in a pluralistic society.

But back to the Sankt Gallen group, several of them were actually progressive. Godfried Danneels, for example, in 1990 advised the king of Belgium to sign a pro-abortion law, and refused to ban "educational" pornographic materials to be used in Belgian Catholic schools. He congratulated the Belgian government for passing legislation in favor of same-sex marriages, although distinguishing it from Catholic marriage.[109]

Now retired, in June 2013 he said that laws that would allow Belgian states to marry same-sex couples was a positive development.[110] And in September 2015, he congratulated the Belgian government for legalizing same-sex marriage.[111]

He was harshly criticized by some circles because in 2008 he admitted to wearing the white ritual garb of Freemasonry in order to give a speech at the Masonic Temple in Belgium.[112]

Danneels wrote in 1991 in his book Words of Life, Volume 1, writing about the cause of sadness in society and using St. Francis of Assisi as an example:

"May God send us, too, a Francis who is able to recognize the cause: a man or woman who sees the evil afflicting the age and is able to cure it. [...]

Where the poor are evangelized, there God reigns. Francis addressed himself to all, but especially to poor farmers, country-folk, beggars, and vagrants, the marginalized people in the towns, all the people to whom no one speaks of God's kingdom. And they listened him; the poor understood their fellow poor man. What of us? Who are the poor of our day to whom the Father reveals his secrets? They include the crowds who never enter our churches, the Third and Fourth World, then all the people who

[109] Edward Pentin (Nov. 5, 2015), Still Controversial: Cardinal Daneels and the Conclave of 2005, National Catholic Register.
[110] Hilary White (June 5, 2013), Gay 'marriage' a 'positive development': retired Belgian Cardinal Danneels, LifeSiteNews.
[111] Jeanne Smits (September 23, 2013), Cardinal Danneels congratulated Belgian gvmt for legalizing gay 'marriage': new book, LifeSiteNews.
[112] Michael Hichborn (October 6, 2015), "Satan Must Reign in the Vatican.The Pope Will Be His Slave.," Lepanto Institute.

are so battered and bruised, the captives, the foreigners. And all those who adore the Moloch of consumption, for they are unhappy. [...]

Like St. Francis, we are witnessing the birth of a new world. One century is dying, another is making its presence felt in the pangs of birth. Do we not need another Francis who knows his age and knows how to heal it?"[113]

The *Courrier de Rome* also reported on Pio Laghi (member of the Sankt Gallen group):

"After almost 10 years as Nuncio in the United States, Pio Laghi began to visit Rome in order to start his electoral campaign. He went around saying that, henceforth, he would be ready to take on important posts within the Roman Curia. He was supported by the Vaticanists of the "Casarolian" press and those of Belleri. But things did not turn out as expected. Casaroli's post, which he hoped to obtain, went up in smoke and today, he is, against his wishes, Prefect for Seminaries."[114]

The same publication stresses that "It was Vittorio Messori who sounded the alarm:"

"They are organizing opposition to the Pope. I am speaking of clerical opposition, internal opposition coming from the "catho-progressives." Their goal is unmistakably clear: It is to force John Paul II to resign, or at least to discredit him as a sick old man whose only ambition is to cling to power as long as possible, simply refusing to let go the reins of government and thus proving harmful to the Church (La Voce, November 1, 1994)."

[...] "Zizola also alludes to other mysterious clandestine encounters of central-European cardinals who met in Paris to discuss this very same subject (*Il Conclave*, p.372)."[115]

For more than ten years, many people expected the Jesuit Carlo M. Martini – again, Sankt Gallen group member- to conceive the Catholic Church to be in the seas of postmodernity - guiding it.[116] Thus, for example, in 1993, the London *Sunday Times* magazine hinted that he could be the next pope. The press was fascinated, and the *Independent* in 1994 saw the possibility of Martini being a great pope. *The Observer* also published in 1994: "Churches unite in their taste for Martini."[117] Cormac Murphy-O'Connor wrote that, "If there had been a conclave a decade earlier [than the 2005 conclave], Martini might, I think, have been elected pope."[118] But just as John Paul II developed Parkinson's in 1990, so did Martini in the middle of that decade.[119]

---

[113] Cardinal Godfried Danneels, Words of Life (Sheed & Ward, Kansas City, MO, 1991), Volume 1, pp. 11, 18, 23.

[114] E. M. (March, 1995), Papabili?, Courrier de Rome.

[115] Ibid.

[116] Julia Meloni, The St. Gallen Mafia: Exposing the Secret Reformist Group Within the Church (TAN Books, Gastonia, North Carolina, 2021), ob. cit.

[117] Ibid; quoting John Cornwell, "The Next Pope?" Sunday Times Magazine, April 25, 1993.

[118] Ibid; quoting Cormac Murphy-O'Connor, An English Spring: Memoirs (London: Bloomsbury, 2015), 148, NOOK.

[119] Ibid; citing Andrea Tornielli, *Carlo Maria Martini: El Profeta del Diálogo* (Santander: Sal Terrae, 2013), loc. 2145 of 2606, Kindle.

Martini supported same-sex marriages, questioned the church's position on the divorced, and was in favor of deaconesses in the church.[120]

He also questioned the church's position on not allowing the use of condoms, and he supported their use in certain cases to prevent AIDS and viewed the legalization of abortion as a positive development but in limited cases. He supported the idea of euthanasia and questioned priestly celibacy. In fact, two weeks before he died in 2012 and after saying that the church was 200 years behind the times,[121] said:

"Our culture has aged, our churches are big and empty and the church bureaucracy rises up, our rituals and our cassocks are pompous," the Cardinal said. "The Church must admit its mistakes and begin a radical change, starting from the Pope and the bishops. The paedophilia scandals oblige us to take a journey of transformation."[122]

Martini was also highly respected, for example, by the Masonic obedience of the Grand Orient of Italy[123] and others.

Although not all the bishops in the Sankt Gallen group shared the same sympathies as Danneels and Martini, there was a certain progressive tendency towards what the Church believes and does.

Another bishop *of* Sankt Gallen, was the Austrian Cardinal and Archbishop of Vienna, Christoph Schönborn, who in May 2014 made postmodernist masses, and supports the homosexual lifestyle.[124] Also on December 1, 2017, he celebrated in the Vienna Cathedral the memorial service for the victims of AIDS, where they had several artists. Schönborn and Gery Keszler were the organizers. Keszler made a career as the openly homosexual founder of the Life Ball of Vienna.[125] But Schönborn organized similar events on Dec. 4, 2018, and Nov. 30, 2019, claiming that God does not want anyone to be excluded. There was dancing, secular singing and at one of the events, performers dressed as demons, and promoting acceptance of the homosexual lifestyle.[126]

It is noteworthy that the father of the Cardinal of Vienna, Hugo-Damian Graf Schönborn, was a Freemason. During the Masonic commemoration of his death, the Cardinal expressed himself about his father by saying: "Now my father has gone to the Eternal Grand Orient," as described by the Masons, and by the testimony of the politician Ewald Stadler in his relations with the Masons. But the direct source was Nikolaus Schwärzler, Grand Master of Innsbruck.[127]

---

[120] Michael Day (Sept. 3, 2012), Cardinal Carlo Maria Martini, his final interview, and a damning critique that has rocked the Catholic Church, Independent.

[121] Ibid.

[122] Ibid.

[123] (August 31, 2012), Martini: Raffi (GOI), addio a un uomo di dialogo, grande espressione della Chiesa-Parola, Grande Oriente d'Italia: https://www.grandeoriente.it/martini-raffi-goi-addio-a-un-uomo-di-dialogo-grande-espressione-della-chiesa-parola/ Accessed November 13, 2023.

[124] Christa Pongratz-Lippitt (May 22, 2014), Cardinal praises Eurovision-winning transvestite, The Tablet; Maike Hickson (Dec. 4, 2018), Charity concert at Cdl. Schönborn's cathedral features shirtless actor dancing on Communion rail, LifeSiteNews.

[125] Roy Knoops (Dec. 4, 2017), Austria: Conchita in special mass for World Aids Day 2017, Desctoday.

[126] Maike Hickson (Dec. 4, 2018), Charity concert at Cdl. Schönborn's cathedral features shirtless actor dancing on Communion rail, LifeSiteNews.

[127] Logen (October 24, 2013), Ist Kardinal Schönborn gar ein Schürzenjäger, Katholische Nachrichten.

Stadler also said that he found the former editor-in-chief of the *Wiener Kirchenzeitung* (Vienna Church Newspaper), Walter Ramig, and the former tax advisor of the Archdiocese of Vienna, Josef Böck, on a list of Masonic lodges. Both had become Freemasons at the express wish of the late Cardinal König.[128]

It is known that the Austrian Jesuits and Freemasons have good relations and joint purposes.[129]

The Sankt Gallen group felt that the lack of collegiality in the Catholic Church hindered the task of evangelization and the search for ecumenical unity. Although in 1995 John Paul II offered the other churches to help him find new ways of exercising his primacy, it was difficult to take the offer seriously when there was a growing centralism, and little progress was made in this regard.[130]

Joseph Bernardin, mentioned by Malachi Martin, was the last great American Catholic leader of the Second Vatican Council era.[131] *The New York Times Magazine* reported on an interview with Bernardin about John Paul II's successor:

"Q: What are the issues you think the next Pope will have to face?

A: Two come to mind. The first is what should be the relationship between the center and the periphery. The Second Vatican Council highlighted the notion of collegiality. And strictly speaking, that refers to the relationship between the Pope and the bishops. We need the Pope. He is the symbol and also the human instrument of unity. But the bishops have a responsibility for the well being of their dioceses.
[...]
The other issue has to do with the notion of subsidiarity; that you shouldn't insist that a higher level do something that can be done or should be done at the lower level. Sometimes we don't give enough freedom to people at a lower level."[132]

During the 1980s and 1990s, Cardinal Carlo Maria Martini, Cardinal Joseph Bernardin of Chicago, and Cardinal Basil Hume, Archbishop of Westminster, worked intimately together and were considered among the leading pastoral prelates of the Catholic Church.[133]

The Italian Vaticanist Sandro Magister, points out that to understand Pope Francis, he must be considered in the light of the line of Cardinals Carlo Maria Martini of Milan and Joseph Bernardin of Chicago, because of his approach to the world. There was talk,

---

[128] Ibid.

[129] Ibid.

[130] Austen Ivereigh, The Great Reformer: Francis and the Making of a Radical Pope (Henry Holt and Co., New York, 2014), ob. cit.

[131] The New York Times Magazine (December 1, 1996), Death as a Friend, The New York Times Magazine.

[132] Ibid.

[133] Thomas C. Fox (Sept. 2, 2013), Francis hails late Cardinal Carlo Martini, National Catholic Reporter. Martini was part of the Sankt Gallen Group, which would conspire to bring Bergoglio to papal power; and Archbishop Basil Hume who died in 1999, was heir to the group's English representative (Cormac Murphy-O'Connor): see Henry Sire, The Dictator Pope: The Inside Story of the Francis Papacy (Regnery Publishing, Washington D.C., 2018), ob. cit. See also Marco Tosatti (September 24, 2015), Francesco: elezione preparata da anni, La Stampa.

for example, of the pope's (Francis) words about talking less about abortion, gay marriage, and contraception.[134]

When the Sankt Gallen Group began meeting in the late 1990s, John Paul II's health was beginning its rapid decline.[135] And Cardinal Martini expressed at the synod on Europe that another assembly of bishops from around the world needed to be convened to implement the collegiality proclaimed by the Second Vatican Council, but now hindered by the Vatican Curia. The organ of the Curia organizing the synod, suppressed the publication of the speech; and the press only found out about it through leaks.

Another voice of the Sankt Gallen group that outlined his manifest opinion was Walter Kasper, who disputed amicably with Cardinal Ratzinger on the issue of the primacy of the universal and local Churches. In his widely circulated article in December 2000, Kasper questioned Ratzinger's 1992 document, stating that its formulation was "really problematic when the one universal Church is identified with the Roman Church, and de facto with the Pope and the Roman Curia," which he described as "an attempt to restore Roman centralism." Kasper argued that collegiality was vital to the solution of pastoral issues, such as the total exclusion of remarried divorcees from the sacraments and making Catholicism's quest for Christian unity more credible. He advocated a "reconciled diversity;" a phrase adopted by Jorge Mario Bergoglio in Buenos Aires when addressing relations with other Christians and faiths.

Now, when Bergoglio was appointed Archbishop of Buenos Aires on February 28, 1998, Yorio's sister sent an email to Horacio Verbitsky that read:

"I can't believe it. I'm so distraught and so angry that I don't know what to do. He got what he wanted. I'm seeing Orlando in the dining room at home, already a few years ago, saying 'he wants to be pope'. He is the right person to cover up the rottenness. He is the expert in covering up.[136]

During Pope Wojtyla's winter years (1999-2005), the Sankt Gallen group was concerned about the deterioration in the Vatican a weakened pontiff was unable to prevent.[137] Thus, around 2000, the group became regularly obsessed with the issues of homosexuality, communion for the divorced and civilly remarried, and the succession of John Paul II.[138] Under Secretary of State Angelo Sodano, the Curia became haughty and intransigent, and at times its rulings were linked to cases of corruption, such as the case of Father Marcial Maciel, founder of the Mexican order of the Legionaries of Christ, for his pederasty and drug addiction.[139]

The Sankt Gallen group criticized the synod as cumbersome and unproductive because of its centralism. That excessive centralism bothered them, especially when the

---

[134] Russell Shaw (October 17, 2013), Martini, Bernardin, and Pope Francis, The Catholic World Report.

[135] Austen Ivereigh, The Great Reformer: Francis and the Making of a Radical Pope (Henry Holt and Co., New York, 2014), ob. cit. Note: unless otherwise noted, this is the same source.

[136] Horacio Verbitsky (October 6, 2013), La revelación, Página 12.

[137] Austen Ivereigh, The Great Reformer: Francis and the Making of a Radical Pope (Henry Holt and Co., New York, 2014), ob. cit.

[138] Julia Meloni, The St. Gallen Mafia: Exposing the Secret Reformist Group Within the Church (TAN Books, Gastonia, North Carolina, 2021), ob. cit.

[139] Austen Ivereigh, The Great Reformer: Francis and the Making of a Radical Pope (Henry Holt and Co., New York, 2014), ob. cit. Note: unless otherwise noted, this is the same source.

Vatican played deaf, isolated and defensive in the face of the emerging clergy sexual abuse crisis.

Thus, the Sankt Gallen group believed that a profound reform of ecclesial governance was lacking, a concern shared by others, especially among the Latin American archbishops. At that time, new pastoral leaders from that region, who were members of a different generation, were about to be appointed cardinals. Among these was the Archbishop of Buenos Aires, Jorge Mario Bergoglio, who was influenced by the leader of the Sankt Gallen nucleus, Jesuit Cardinal Carlo Maria Martini. But he also had many reasons of his own to identify with the turmoil of the Sankt Gallen members.

On February 21, 2001, John Paul II created 135 new cardinals who would be the new electors for the next conclave (2005), where Ratzinger would be elected, taking the name Benedict XVI. The cardinals gathered on that day knew that their most solemn responsibility would be to elect John Paul II's successor. This was the most global college of cardinals in history: sixty-five Europeans (twenty-four of them Italians) still made up the largest continental group, but for the first time they were surpassed by non-Europeans, since Latin America had twenty-seven cardinals, while North America, Africa and Asia had thirteen per continent and Oceania had four.

It was clear from the boisterous crowd in St. Peter's Square that the time had come for Latin America.

"Yet there were few Argentines among them, because Bergoglio had stopped a campaign to raise funds for pilgrims to travel to Rome, telling its organizers to distribute what they had raised to the poor. During the consistory he opted for austerity and a low profile. Where others were put up in their colleges or hosted by relatives in large hotels, he stayed, as he always did in Rome, in a simple priests' guesthouse at no. 70 Via della Scrofa, not far from the Piazza Navona, where he prayed at 4:30 a.m. before saying Mass in the chapel. Where others were driven to the Vatican by priest secretaries, he walked alone each morning over the Tiber; where others had ordered their scarlet vestments from Gamarelli, Rome's ecclesiastical tailor, Bergoglio's wore Quarracino's hand-me-downs, taken in by the nuns; and where others—not least the energetic, communicative Cardinal Rodríguez Maradiaga, a pilot and piano player— held press conferences and parties, Bergoglio put on his customary cloak of invisibility."[140]

On May 21, 2001, John Paul II opened an extraordinary meeting with cardinals from around the world to discuss the challenges of the Church of the future.[141] One of the themes of the consistory was how to increase communion or the bonds of unity in the Church.[142] Brazilian Cardinal Aloisio Lorscheider, "bluntly accused the Curia of holding the Pontiff "prisoner." Close to liberation theology, he wanted to ask the pope for less centralization and more collegiality, one of the topics on the vast agenda under discussion. In fact Bergoglio was among those present.[143]

---

[140] Ibid.

[141] (May 22, 2001), En el Vaticano se oyen voces de transición, La Nación.

[142] Austen Ivereigh, The Great Reformer: Francis and the Making of a Radical Pope (Henry Holt and Co., New York, 2014), ob. cit.

[143] (May 22, 2001), En el Vaticano se oyen voces de transición, La Nación.

The cardinals of the Sankt Gallen group firmly believed that communion should be forged and expressed through greater and more effective collegiality.[144]

One of its members, Karl Lehmann, "declared that the national bishops' conferences should play a greater role in Church decision-making. Danneels, for his part, anticipated to journalists that "the theme of collegiality will be without doubt one of the major challenges for the third millennium." Cardinal Rodriguez Maradiaga agreed on behalf of the Latin Americans saying that, "All of us are convinced it is necessary to increase collegiality." According to leaks from journalists, Carlo Maria Martini, Godfried Danneels, Karl Lehman and Murphy O'Connor (all from the Sankt Gallen core), made similar calls during the consistory but the issue was barely addressed. The Vatican Secretariat of State had twenty-one points drawn from the pope's recent encyclical to be addressed in that consistory. The Curia counterattacked.[145]

Bergoglio listened to and became closer to several cardinal confreres.[146] He reconnected with Martini, whom he had known since they both participated as provincials in the 1974 General Congregation, and whom Bergoglio frequently quoted. Martini introduced Bergoglio to the cardinals of Sankt Gallen in 2001, which began a series of relationships that developed during Bergoglio's fleeting visits to Rome over the next few years.

A few months later, in June, Belgian Cardinal Jan Schotte, the Curia member in charge of the synod, insisted that there was no authentic collegiality "there was no true collegiality outside an ecumenical council such as Vatican II, only "expressions" of it; this was the standard curial defense of the status quo." The bishops did not overlook the missive.

But in October of the same year, Bergoglio returned to Rome as vice president of the synod of bishops, whose role was to assist the rapporteur (*relator*) - Cardinal Edward Egan of New York, who arrived at the Vatican devastated by the events of Sept. 11 of that year. Ironically, the role of the bishop was discussed, naturally raising the issue of relations between the episcopate and the Vatican. However, collegiality was mentioned only twice throughout the common working document.

Bergoglio gave his brief speech as a lyrical meditation on the distinction of a bishop who oversees and watches over his people, and on the other hand, one who keeps watch over them:

"*Overseeing* refers more to a concern for doctrine and habits, whereas *keeping watch* is more about making sure that there be salt and light in people's hearts. Watching over speaks of being alert to imminent danger; *keeping watch*, on the other hand, speaks of patiently bearing the processes through which the Lord carries out the salvation of his people. To *watch over* it is enough to be awake, sharp, quick. To *keep watch* you need also to be meek, patient, and constant in proven charity. *Overseeing* and *watching over* suggest a certain degree of necessary control. *Keeping watch*, on the other hand,

---

[144] Austen Ivereigh, The Great Reformer: Francis and the Making of a Radical Pope (Henry Holt and Co., New York, 2014), ob. cit.

[145] Ibid.; citing in the latter Robert Mickens (May 26, 2001), "Extraordinary Rome Meeting Brings Ordinary Results," The Tablet; Robert Mickens (June 2, 2001), "Cardinals Press for More Sharing in Church Government," The Tablet.

[146] Austen Ivereigh, The Great Reformer: Francis and the Making of a Radical Pope (Henry Holt and Co., New York, 2014), ob. cit. Note: unless otherwise noted, this is the same source.

suggests hope, the hope of the merciful Father who keeps watch over the processes in the hearts of his children."

The above brings to mind the reason for Bergoglio's campaign for the papacy in 2010, with his book *The Jesuit*, as we will mention in due course.

Returning to the October synodal -Ivereigh describes:

"Inside the hall, Bergoglio received high praise for the way he reflected bishops' concerns without causing disunity. "What people admired him for was how he rescued the best of the synod debate despite the limitations of the structure and method," recalls Bergoglio's long-standing friend in Rome, Professor Guzmán Carriquiry."[147]

That synod marked the projection of Jorge Mario Bergoglio to the universal church, only a few months after he was introduced to the Sankt Gallen group.

Federico Wals, Bergoglio's press officer since 2007, said that for Bergoglio, Rome represented "the heart of everything that he believed the Church should not be: luxury, ostentation, hypocrisy, bureaucracy—everything that was 'self-referential.' He hated going." But despite everything, many people remembered him, such as Vaticanist Sandro Magister who wrote from the synod:

"[...] the thought of having him return to Rome as the successor of Peter has begun to spread with growing intensity. The Latin-American cardinals are increasingly focused upon him, as is Cardinal Joseph Ratzinger. The only key figure among the Curia who hesitates when he hears his name is Secretary of State Cardinal Angelo Sodano—the very man known for supporting the idea of a Latin-American pope."[148]

For the Sankt Gallen "mafia" - so named by Danneels - at their January 2002 meeting, Jorge Bergoglio was a topic of conversation. At the time, he received criticism from Rome for not opposing a law on civil unions between same-sex couples in Buenos Aires; something the archbishop considered purely civic and legal, not affecting marriage.[149]

The Congregation for the Doctrine of the Faith, headed by Joseph Ratzinger, expressed in 2003 that the bishops "clearly and categorically" oppose the legal recognition of any type of same-sex union.

The editor of the Catholic magazine *Inside the Vatican*, Robert Moynihan, had a conversation with Cardinal Joseph Ratzinger in his apartment, not far from St. Anne's Gate, just a few years before becoming pope. The two talked about a theological conflict Ratzinger had with Cardinal Walter Kasper, which was then much in the media. Moynihan asked Ratzinger where the danger to the authentic Catholic faith lay, to which the cardinal, looking the journalist straight in the eye and after a pause, as if reflecting, said: "It is Freemasonry."[150]

---

[147] Austen Ivereigh, The Great Reformer (Ediciones B, S.A., 2015), ob. cit. Note: unless otherwise noted, this is the same source.

[148] Ibid.; quoting Sandro Magister, L'Espresso, no. 49 (November 28–December 5, 2002), translation "Jorge Mario Bergoglio, Profession: Servant of the Servants of God" at www.chiesa.espresso.repubblica.it.

[149] Quoting Ivereigh, The Great Reformer, ob. cit.

[150] Robert Moynihan (Thursday, April 23, 2020), Letter #8: The Long Hand, Inside the Vatican.

In fact, when Ratzinger became pope, the then prefect of the Congregation for Divine Worship at the Vatican, Cardinal Antonio Cañizares Llovera, whom Pope Benedict XVI would consider with favor, told Cañizares in a meeting that he had three great fears: the secularization of the Catholic Church, the peaceful invasion of Europe by Islam, and the increasing control "of freemasonry on the cultural level and of the centers of power of the European Union."[151]

A German Freemason named Axel Pohlmann, complained in the winter of 2004-2005 in the British Masonic magazine *Freemasonry Today*, saying that when John Paul II died and Ratzinger was no longer in charge at the Vatican, Freemasons would do everything possible to convince the Catholic Church to remove all condemnation against Freemasonry.[152] Antonio Socci, a well-known Italian journalist, wrote:

"Globalization," Diana Johnstone explains, "means the Americanization of the entire world. Our interests and values must predominate everywhere."
[...]
The new type of capitalism that made inroads in the 1990s even presented itself as "the end of history" (a term coined by Francis Fukuyama), a pretentious Hegelian-flavored formulation that wanted to declare "the end" of history, as if the new global order, which was really the Americanization of the planet, contained the meaning and fulfillment of human history.
In 1998 the book *Project for the New American Century* was published, which in essence laid out the plan for a unipolar imperialism to be imposed on the planet. It was a project that drew in both neocons and liberals in varying shades (both John McCain and Hillary Clinton, to be clear), who then later found themselves united together in opposition to the barbarian Trump, guilty of contesting this globalization and this insane ideological utopia."[153]

The Italian newspaper *La Stampa*, for its part, describes:

"Martini was well aware that after John Paul II's long illness, the Church could not afford to have another ill Pope. In 2005 the effects of the Parkinson's disease which Martini was suffering from became apparent; hence he could not really present himself as a candidate for the papacy."[154]

Cardinal Achille Silvestrini acted as the "mastermind" of the agitators, replacing Martini in the Sankt Gallen group after Martini retired in Jerusalem following a diagnosis of Parkinson's disease in 2002.[155] According to an anonymous Latin

---

[151] Robert Moynihan (2011), Letter #23: The Shadow over Europe: What Pope Benedict Fears, Inside the Vatican.
[152] Axel Pohlmann (Winter 2005), Not a Crime, But a Sin?, Freemasonry today, Issue 31, ob cit.
[153] Antonio Socci, The Secret of Benedict XVI: Is He Still the Pope? (Angelico Press, Monitor Street Brooklyn, NY, 2018), ob. cit.; citing Diana Johnstone, Hillary Clinton. Regina of Chaos, p. 44.
[154] La Stampa (September 1, 2012), "Parkinson's prevented Martini from entering conclave as potential papal candidate," La Stampa.
[155] Julia Meloni, The St. Gallen Mafia: Exposing the Secret Reformist Group Within the Church (TAN Books, Gastonia, North Carolina, 2021), ob. cit; citing Mettepenningen and Schelkens, Godfried Danneels, 456.

American cardinal who knew Silvestrini, the Italian was a "formidable maneuverer."[156] And indeed, Achille Silvestrini, who for decades had been close to John Paul II, had given the group first-hand information about the pope's deteriorating health.[157] Silvestrini was one of the last to see John Paul II alive, on April 2, 2005. Only three days after his death, Silvestrini invited Martini and the Sankt Gallen group to Villa Nazareth to discuss their anti-Ratzinger plot.[158]

Once there, after considering several candidates, they thought of the Cardinal Primate of Argentina, Jorge Mario Bergoglio, whom Murphy O'Connor had befriended in 2001 in Rome.[159] O'Connor advised the rest of the group, but Silvestrini tried to convince Martini, who refused to endorse him because he knew from Pedro Arrupe, former Jesuit general, that Bergoglio was more conservative and was against several of Arrupe's positions.[160]

After the death of John Paul II, serious discussions took place during the nights about who could be his successor, when the cardinals organized discreet meetings in their respective colleges or, in the case of the curiali, in their Roman apartments.[161]

Already in the days leading up to the conclave, the cardinals of Sankt Gallen sent a postcard to their founder, Bishop Ivo Fürer, with the message, "We are here in the spirit of Sankt Gallen."[162]

Cardinal Cormac Murphy-O'Connor hosted a dinner for the group and their guests at the English College in Rome.[163] The German journalist and writer, Paul Badde, reported Cardinal Joachim Meisner's strong resistance to the group's campaign, since it contravened the rules of the conclave. They met at Villa Nazareth at the invitation of Cardinal Silvestrini, who was an ardent opponent of Ratzinger and was trying to make either Martini or Bergoglio the next pope - it was April 16, 2005.[164]

Most of the cardinals, especially those from Asia and Africa, were unaware of these meetings and depended on the general congregations for their knowledge.[165]

But the riformisti did not have a clear candidate, since Martini was in his eighties and suffered from Parkinson's; he also walked with a cane and had excluded himself.

The Curia chose Ratzinger as their candidate and promoted him among the English, German, Spanish, and Portuguese-speaking cardinals.

Anonymously, a Brazilian cardinal told *O Globo* that year that shortly after the two Latin American curials (Alfonso López Trujillo and Jorge Medina Estévez) lowered

---

[156] Ibid; quoting Nicolas Diat, L'Homme Qui Ne Voulait Pas Être Pape: Histoire Secrète d'un Règne (Paris: Albin Michel, 2014), 97.

[157] Ibid; citing Mettepenningen and Schelkens, Godfried Danneels, 456.

[158] Ibid.

[159] Ibid.

[160] Ibid; citing Diat, L'Homme, 97-98.

[161] Austen Ivereigh, The Great Reformer: Francis and the Making of a Radical Pope (Henry Holt and Co., New York, 2014), ob. cit.

[162] Edward Pentin (September 26, 2015), Cardinal Danneels' Biographers Retract Comments on Sankt Gallen Group, National Catholic Register.

[163] Austen Ivereigh, The Great Reformer: Francis and the Making of a Radical Pope (Henry Holt and Co., New York, 2014), ob. cit.

[164] Edward Pentin (Nov. 5, 2015), Still Controversial: Cardinal Danneels and the Conclave of 2005, National Catholic Register.

[165] Austen Ivereigh, The Great Reformer: Francis and the Making of a Radical Pope (Henry Holt and Co., New York, 2014), ob. cit. Note: unless otherwise noted, this is the same source.

their luggage, they were invited to attend meetings and dinners, where they made it clear that they consulted Ratzinger and that he gave the green light to the campaign.

Just before the conclave, Italian newspapers claimed that Ratzinger might have forty votes. Although there was a long list of potential papabili, the main speculation was that the next pope would be Latin American, and among these was Bergoglio as the frontrunner.

Jorge Bergoglio refused all invitations to dinners, did not grant interviews, and remained discreetly - as he used to do - in Via della Scrofa, where he preferred to dine with friends in Rome rather than with other cardinals.

Just three days after the conclave, a human rights lawyer filed a complaint in court accusing Bergoglio of being an accomplice in the kidnapping of Jesuits Yorio and Jalics. Bergoglio brought with him Father Guillermo Marcó, who, responding to questions from the press, called the claim an "old calumny;" which did not have any legal trajectory. Although it generated news in the media as well as the impression that on the eve of the voting, should he become pope, Bergoglio's past would be questioned. The complaint was based on El silencio, the book by Horacio Verbitsky, whose denunciations were sent in anonymous envelopes and to the e-mail accounts of the Spanish-speaking cardinals who were in Rome in the days prior to the conclave. It was even suspected that it was a move of Cristina F. Kirchner's government.

On April 19, Cardinal Joseph Ratzinger was elected as successor to the papacy, taking the name Benedict XVI. Although the reports against Bergoglio did not make a dent in his appointment.

Austen Ivereigh indicates that despite the vow of confidentiality of the cardinal electors, the anonymous diary of one of them reflected in detail what happened. The account in the Italian newspaper *Limes* was not denied, and most Vaticanists believe it to be true because of the graphic nature of the account.

On the first ballot on April 17, Cardinal Joseph Ratzinger received 47 votes, followed by Bergoglio with 10 and Martini with 9.[166] Other cardinals received fewer votes. Support for Bergoglio showed that more than half of the eighteen resident cardinals voted for him and the remaining majority for Rodriguez and Hummes. The riformisti, especially from the Sankt Gallen group, deduced that if Bergoglio - a Latin American and Jesuit pastoral archbishop - and one who shared the reformers' concerns about collegiality, was added the votes of Martini, Rodriguez and Hummes to his, there could be a two-way race.

Back in Santa Marta for the second round of voting, Karl Lehmann and Godfried Danneels of *Sankt Gallen* were the leaders of a significant group of U.S., European, and Latin American cardinals, and a couple of cardinals from the Curia, who could swing the vote. The riformisti sought to increase support for Bergoglio to at least 39 votes. If so, Ratzinger would fall short of the two-thirds majority needed, or seventy-seven votes. In that case, other voters would decide for Bergoglio or, if the college remained divided, a third candidate would emerge. On the morning of April 18, there were two scrutinies: in the first one Ratzinger obtained 65 votes, and Bergoglio got 35. Those of Martini, Rodriguez and Hummes favored Bergoglio. On the second ballot, Ratzinger got 72 votes: five short of the two-thirds majority needed. Bergoglio obtained 40. When both groups returned to Santa Marta in a state of exaltation,

---

[166] Lucio Brunelli (August 31, 2009), Così eleggemmo papa Ratzinger, Limes. Note: unless otherwise indicated, this is the same source.

Bergoglio deactivated the operation. During the time of the dinner, he begged the remaining cardinals, almost with tears in his eyes, to vote for Ratzinger. The Jesuit Silvano Fausti, who was Carlo Maria Martini's confessor, says that Martini obtained a number of votes that were given to Ratzinger in order to avoid a confrontation of sides that would be rejected, encouraging him to opt for a preferred candidate of the unreformable Roman Curia. Bergoglio thought the same. Carlo Maria Martini went to Ratzinger in the afternoon and told him: "you accept, you have been in the Curia for 30 years and you are intelligent and honest: if you manage to reform the Curia great, if not, you step down."[167]

In the afternoon, Bergoglio's support dropped to 26 votes and Ratzinger was elected with 84. Bergoglio went to cast his vote with a gesture of suffering and raising his eyes towards Michelangelo's Last Judgment, as if imploring: "don't do this to me." One commentator judges that Bergoglio was angry because he felt used by the progressive group, which would have misunderstood him; since he himself was part of the pro-Ratzinger coalition (but not associated with any group); and he was scandalized by the exercise done in his name, since he did not want to see a church divided into two camps. The cardinals of Sankt Gallen made the mistake of not inquiring whether Bergoglio was open to the papacy.[168] But as Austen Ivereigh points out, when Cardinal Francesco Marchisano (Mason), archpriest of St. Peter's, asked him after the conclave what name he would have taken had he been elected, he said without hesitation, "I would have taken the name, John, after il papa buono [the 'good pope,' John XXIII] and I would have been totally inspired by him." But that answer does not reveal an insecure or frightened man.[169] Latin America was not ready for a pope from its continent, since the Catholic Church went from being a "source Church" that eventually infused vigor into the Universal Church, whose process was reversed in the 1980s and 1990s, so any Latin pope would have been seen only as a reflection of the European Church in his country. Methol Ferré so concluded, while believing that a transitional European pope was needed and that Ratzinger was the right one, which Bergoglio also believed.[170]

Ratzinger's election would not please Western and progressive democracies. Antonio Socci, an Italian Catholic journalist, in "The Secret of Benedict XVI," talks about the unprecedented crisis suffered by the Roman Catholic Church, which would have been influenced behind the scenes by U.S. agents to democratize it and make it more in line with the liberal values of the Democratic Party.[171]

"The drama, which is much more vast and profound, is centered on the crisis of credibility of the papacy of Jorge Mario Bergoglio, source of immense confusion among the faithful, and around the looming risk of deviations from Catholic doctrine that could lead Christianity into apostasy and schism."

---

[167] (July 18, 2015), Martini: Benedict XVI's resignation and the 2005 Conclave, Vatican Insider.
[168] Austen Ivereigh, The Great Reformer: Francis and the Making of a Radical Pope (Henry Holt and Co., New York, 2014), ob. cit.
[169] Ibid; quoting from Diario di un papista (Segno, Tavagnacco, 2013).
[170] Ibid.
[171] Antonio Socci, The Secret of Benedict XVI: Is He Still the Pope? (Angelico Press, Monitor Street Brooklyn, NY, 2018), ob. cit. Note: unless otherwise noted, this is the same source.

For Socci, Benedict XVI would have been the last bastion opposed to the globalization of consciences, when the Catholic Church had not succumbed to the spirit of the world since the French Revolution and with superlaicist and anti-Catholic attacks. The secularist ideology coming from the presidency of Bill Clinton, then with the presidency of Barack Obama/Hillary Clinton, would have been imposed on a planetary scale, as being politically correct.

Socci continues, that the pontificate of Benedict XVI was an obstacle and the Catholic Church found itself defenseless and without alliances.

Barack Obama promoted the defense of homosexual marriages, abortion, stem cell research. Even the U.S. bishops' conference itself did not agree with the Obama administration on health care reform or on the so-called liberal agenda.

Benedict XVI, shortly after his election, had said: "Pray for me, that I may not flee for fear of the wolves." The American hegemony to achieve a unipolar world would seek to subdue everyone, including Russia, which knows that without Christianity the nation and the world are threatened. Hence, the ever stronger implosion of the US Democratic party against Putin's Russia, who does not support the liberal agenda of that party and which has permeated Europe to a large extent (that is not to say that Putin does not have imperialistic ambitions and corruption).

"During the years of his pontificate, Benedict XVI was subjected to systematic and continuous attacks, and he found himself in a position of obvious isolation that grew ever more intense, until it reached the point that he did not have any real power within the Curia. Finally, the Vatileaks affair revealed that the situation even within his personal residence was truly unheard-of and astonishing.

What especially made a stir was the dissent of bishops and cardinals that was constantly amplified by the media. A prime example was the case of Cardinal Carlo Maria Martini, who became ever more prominent because his statements were read and presented as being directly opposed to the pontificate of Benedict XVI."

Because of this, Jorge Mario Bergoglio would have been the perfect candidate to give continuity through the papacy, if not all but a major part, to the liberal agenda of American democracy under the Democratic Party, which is in line with the European ideals that are the majority in those countries.

Other negative reactions to Ratzinger's election to the papacy were yet to emerge. Piero Laporta is a retired brigadier general who worked for the Joint Chiefs of Staff of the Italian Armed Forces. He mentioned a few days after Benedict XVI's death in December 2022, of a vast Roman circle, active to this day, and a prominent U.S. government emissary with his hands in Italian finance and politics; and who is a figure in the upper echelons of the NSA or U.S. National Security Agency. A few weeks after the beginning of Benedict XVI's pontificate, this agent boasted that the new pope would soon be forced to resign. And the Roman circle was alarmed by Ratzinger's election to the papacy.[172]

---

[172] Piero Laporta (January 3, 2023), Santegidio "coccodrilla" S.S. Benedetto XVI, Incredibile, OltreLaNotizia-Piero Laporta: https://pierolaporta.it/santegidio-coccodrilla-s-s-benedetto-xvi-incredibile/; accessed June 29, 2023.

On the very night of Ratzinger's election to the papacy, a Latin American cardinal bumped into Silvestrini near St. Peter's, noting him as a "defeated man."[173] For Silvestrini, Ratzinger's papacy would be only transitional, and so the cardinal declared "a form of war."[174]

Thus, a few months after Benedict's election, a mysterious conclave diary appeared that read like an early assault on Benedict XVI's pontificate, and like a campaign material for Bergoglio's upcoming papal career.[175] According to high-ranking prelates, the author of the diary was Silvestrini himself.[176]

Also in 2007, the memoirs of a retired cardinal entitled *Confession d'un Cardinal*, whose author identified himself as a good friend of Martini and Kasper, was made known.[177] In it, the author referred to the reasons why he did not vote for Ratzinger: his age and his anti-modernism; but he also pointed out that he believed that his papacy was a transitional one and that Bergoglio should therefore be taken into account (the cardinal of such memoirs was said to be Silvestrini).[178]

The mysterious cardinal indicated that time is "our first master," arriving on time either by "chance" or by "calculation," taking control of his own destiny.[179] He indicated that sometime in 2005 (when Ratzinger was elected), he announced an "appointment with history" that the Church needed to keep.[180] The Church had to be "global" and "work with institutions to fight merciless market logic, had to bring "tenderness" to the world in this specific, fleeting window of time."[181]

Also in his book *L'Espérance du Cardinal*, the Cardinal spoke of St. Francis of Assisi, nature, and the universal dream of fraternity.[182] He also indicated that on a flight of reverie, after attending the interreligious meeting in Assisi in 1986, he stayed to read Francis of St. Bonaventure's *vita*, walking "the streets of Assisi-praying, admiring nature, and searching for Francis, bearer of God's tenderness."[183] In fact, the papal encyclical of the future Pope Francis, Laudato Si, would mark many of the points of the mysterious cardinal, as well as of Martini: peace, fraternity, justice, and care for creation.[184]

The cardinal wrote in his book *Confession d'un Cardinal*, that in 2005 he spoke of considering Cardinal Bergoglio in case Benedict's pontificate did not last that long.[185]

According to the cardinal, Benedict XVI's successor would carry out his projects (succesor's and the group's -Sankt Gallen) in regional councils, and that the election of

---

[173] Julia Meloni, The St. Gallen Mafia: Exposing the Secret Reformist Group Within the Church (TAN Books, Gastonia, North Carolina, 2021), ob. cit.

[174] Ibid; citing Nicolas Diat, L'Homme Qui Ne Voulait Pas Être Pape: Histoire Secrète d'un Règne (Paris: Albin Michel, 2014), 98.

[175] Ibid.

[176] Ibid; citing Diat, L'Homme, 99-100.

[177] Ibid; citing Olivier Le Gendre, Confession d'un Cardinal (Paris: JC Lattès, 2007), NOOK.

[178] Ibid; quoting Le Gendre, Confession d'un Cardinal, 65, 121.

[179] Ibid; citing Olivier Le Gendre, Confession d'un Cardinal (Paris: JC Lattès, 2007), 67, NOOK.

[180] Ibid.

[181] Ibid; citing Le Gendre, Confession d'un Cardinal, 297-300.

[182] Ibid.

[183] Ibid; citing Olivier Le Gendre, L'Espérance du Cardinal (Paris: JC Lattès, 2011), 141-146, NOOK.

[184] Ibid.

[185] Ibid; quoting Le Gendre, Confession d'un Cardinal, 2121.

the next pope would be determined by the personality of the man and the time of the conclave.[186]

Martini changed his position and defended Bergoglio out loud and in writing.[187]

Jorge Bergoglio rose even higher within the Church, as when he was elected president of the Argentine Episcopal Conference in November. Already in 2006, the Argentinean cardinal was getting bolder and bolder.

In 2010, while in Germany "the failed papacy of Benedict XVI" was being watched over by a critical article in the most important magazine of the country (*Der Spiegel*), in which it was said that many voices were calling for his resignation, in Argentina, the newspaper *Página 12* wrote that Bergoglio was trying to clean his image while waiting for an eventual new conclave in case of a sudden resignation of Pope Benedict. That year, Jorge Bergoglio made public his biographical work *El Jesuita*, where an angelic version of his person was promoted.[188] The work was presented in a press conference that had all the paraphernalia of a political launching: with music beforehand, an audiovisual, etc.[189] *Página 12* reported that Jorge Mario Bergoglio continued his campaign as a candidate to succeed Benedict XVI with the presentation of his book *El Jesuita*, at the OSDE auditorium. During the presentation, a video was shown stating that Bergoglio was the most voted candidate after Joseph Ratzinger in the 2005 conclave. It was "exciting to see the figure of a candidate for sainthood," said Juan Carr.[190]

Sergio Rubin, co-author of the book and unofficial spokesman for Bergoglio, was also a former spokesman for Cardinal Raul Primatesta, as well as a defender of the Argentine dictatorship through the Catholic magazine *Esquiú*. During the book event, Rubin divulged Bergoglio's views on the future of the Catholic Church in the next fifty years, which looked a lot like an election platform.[191]

In addition, Bergoglio was the first Catholic hierarch to visit the headquarters of the Jewish organizations DAIA and AMIA in his so-called 'electoral effort'. There he met with the directors of both organizations and with the Chief Rabbi of Argentina, Salomon Benhamu Anidjar, also a collaborator of the dictatorial repression since 1976.[192]

---

[186] Ibid; quoting Le Gendre, Confession d'un Cardinal, 210.
[187] Ibid; citing Scalfari, "Quel Rivoluzionario"; Carlo Maria Martini, Qualcosa di Cosi Personale: Meditazioni sulla Preguiera (Milan: Mondadori, 2009), 131.
[188] Horacio Verbitsky (April 11, 2010), Operación cónclave, Página 12.
[189] (March 12, 2016), Horacio Verbitsky on election of Pope Bergoglio, Millstream Films and Media: https://www.youtube.com/watch?v=UppRmyjqm7g; accessed May 26, 2016.
[190] Horacio Verbitsky (June 13, 2010), El candidato, Página 12.
[191] Ibid.
[192] Horacio Verbitsky (June 13, 2010), El candidato, Página 12.

Road to abdication, part one

All of the above was accompanied by some events that took place at the end of 2011 concerning Pope Benedict XVI.[193] On November 11, the Pope's Secretariat received a letter from Adolfo Nicolás Pachón, the then Superior General of the Society of Jesus:

"Holy Father:

I have had the honor and privilege of meeting and speaking with Mr. Huber and Mrs. Aldegon de Brenninkmeijer, long-time benefactors of the Church and the Society of Jesus.

What impresses me most when I talk to them is their sincere and deep love for the Church and the Holy Father, and also their commitment to do something that can influence what they see as a serious crisis in the Church.

They asked me for a guarantee that this letter, written from the heart, will reach the hands of Your Holiness, without intermediaries. For this reason I have asked Father Lombardi [spokesman for the Holy See and a member of the Society of Jesus] to act as messenger. I humbly ask forgiveness if this is not the appropriate way.

I share the concerns of Mr. and Mrs. Brenninkmeijer and I am impressed that these lay faithful take so seriously their responsibility to do something for the Church. I am also very encouraged to see and hear that they have attitudes and orientations totally in harmony with the indications contained in the rules received by our founder St. Ignatius as their regulator for sentire cum Ecclesia.

As you know, the Society of Jesus continues to be totally at the service of the Holy Father and the Church."[194]

More letters arrived at the Vatican to denounce the nepotism and corruption that prevailed.[195]

A couple of months later - it was January 2012 - the Pope received another letter regarding the Vatican crisis. *Il Fatto Quotidiano* made public on February 10, an anonymous letter written in German with the caption, "strictly confidential for the Holy Father" and dated December 30, 2011. It was addressed to Pope Benedict XVI[196] and was delivered in early January 2012.[197] The letter warned of a plot to kill Pope Benedict XVI, and that the attack would occur within the next twelve months, that is, in December.

The elderly Colombian cardinal, Dario Castrillon Hoyos, delivered the letter to the Pope and the then Secretary of State, Cardinal Tarcisio Bertone. The Italian newspaper reported that the document reveals that the Italian Cardinal Paolo Romeo, during a trip to China, "very sure of himself, prophesied the death of Pope Benedict XVI in the next 12 months."

"The Cardinal's statements were exposed by a person probably informed of a serious criminal plot, with such certainty and firmness, that his interlocutors in China have thought, with horror, that an attempt on the Holy Father's life is being planned."

---

[193] Ibid.

[194] Eric Frattini, Los cuervos del Vaticano. Benedicto XVI en la encrucijada (Espasa, 2012), ob. cit.

[195] Ibid.

[196] Ibid.

[197] Elisabetta Piqué (February 10, 2012), Una carta anónima advierte que el Papa morirá en 12 meses por un complot, La Nacion. Note: unless otherwise noted, this is the same source.

The text denounces "palatial and poisonous internal affairs within the Vatican." It revealed that the relationship between Pope Benedict and his Secretary of State, Cardinal Bertone, would be very conflictive. Cardinal Romeo added that Pope Benedict XVI would hate Tarcisio Bertone, and would willingly replace him with another cardinal.

The missive assures that the pope was already preparing his succession, in which the Italian Cardinal Angelo Scola, then Archbishop of Milan and Patriarch of Venice, appeared as the number one candidate for his replacement, "because he is closer to his personality." That means the pope was preparing his resignation around December 2011-January 2012. Part of the text of the letter reads:

"Secretly, the pope is working on his succession and has already chosen Cardinal Scola as a suitable candidate, being closer to his own personality. Slowly, but surely, he is preparing and forming him to become pope. At the initiative of Benedict XVI, Scola had been sent from Venice to Milan to prepare himself calmly to become pope. Cardinal Romeo has further surprised his interlocutors in China by adding further indiscretions."[198]

However, Cardinal Romeo considered the attribution of the letter as baseless, adding, "It appears so out of touch with reality that it should not be taken into consideration." But he admitted to having made a five-day private trip to China.[199] But the cardinal's denial is aimed more at quelling a media scandal that could arise over a real threat to Pope Benedict.

The one who delivered the letter to the pope was Cardinal Dario Castrillon, who confessed that he once received a letter written in Chinese, warning about a plot to end the pope's life. When he gave the document to the pope, they both decided to keep the matter secret. He then pointed out a revealing aspect: as described in the leaked information, months later the pope resigned.[200]

The struggle between Pope Benedict and Cardinal Tarcisio Bertone was aired the year that the letter was leaked. Added to the many other major scandals that engulfed the Vatican in what became known as the Vatileaks. An insider gave the press a trove of documents that revealed death threats, gay smear campaigns, tax scandals...; in a scenario of nepotism and corruption that poured into front-page news in many newspapers around the world.[201] Most of the documents were published by the Italian journalist Gianluigi Nuzzi, during a series of television programs, and in his book, *Ratzinger was afraid: The secret documents the money and the scandals that overwhelmed the Pope*. Another work is that of the Peruvian-Spanish journalist Eric Frattini, entitled *Los cuervos del Vaticano (The Vatican Crows)*.

When Benedict XVI was serious about resigning, on January 7, 2012, Carlo Maria Martini spoke about the future of the Church to a confidante, Renata Patti:

---

[198] Eric Frattini, Los cuervos del Vaticano. Benedicto XVI en la encrucijada (Espasa, 2012), ob. cit.

[199] Elisabetta Piqué (February 10, 2012), Una carta anónima advierte que el Papa morirá en 12 meses por un complot, La Nacion.

[200] (February 9, 2015), How he saved Benedict XVI's life, and more confessions of the Colombian who could have been Pope, Pulzo.

[201] Michael Day (May 28, 2012), Vatileaks: Hunt i son to find Vatican moles, Independent.

"Patti: "But then, Your Eminence, is it really necessary to weep for our Church..."

"Martini: "No. This will pass, it will pass!"

"Patti: "Will it pass?" And Benedict XVI?"

"Martini: "He too will pass. I saw him in April [2011]. I have seen an old and tired man. I hope he will resign soon. So we will end up with the Secretary of State and the Secretariat of State."

"Patti: "And then, Eminence?"
Martini: "Then there will be a conclave that will choose. Maybe [Angelo] Scola."[202]

During a conversation on March 12, referring to the Focolare movement, Martini told Renata Patti that "in April we will go with some bishops to Switzerland." Sandro Magister recounts that this trip took place.[203]

The pope's closest collaborators admitted that Benedict XVI ultimately made the decision to resign after his visit to Mexico and Cuba in March 2012.[204]

Road to abdication, part two
First of all, when Benedict XVI was about four years into his pontificate, in 2009 he was already tired of the infighting within the Vatican, and wrote a letter to the bishops admonishing them that, "If you bite and devour one another, you will end up destroying each other."[205]

"The leak of documents that provoked the outbreak of the Vatileaks case brought to light the evidence that the Vatican had become a veritable battlefield between factions of the curia and Tarcisio Bertone was the one who came off worst. In almost all of them, the number two of the Vatican State appeared as a real conspirator, ambitious, manipulative, and an enemy of transparency. The same newspaper even stated that Benedict XVI had already told Cardinals Camillo Ruini, Marc Ouellet, Jean-Louis Tauran, George Pell, and Jozef Tomko, known in the Vatican as the "five wise men," that Bertone would not continue in his post "of his own free will" and that he would ask the Holy Father for permission to retire since he had reached the retirement age limit for religious three years ago, which is seventy-five years old."

It was in 2011, that Ettore Gotti Tedeschi, the director of the IOR or Vatican Bank, did not agree to the acquisition of the San Raffaele hospital with IOR money after reviewing the hospital's accounts in the red. The hospital was placed in the same line of Cardinals Attilio Nicora and Dionigi Tettamanzi, and even Pope Benedict did not agree, since in it and in buildings attached to the university, teachings and medical research practices contrary to Catholic doctrine were being imparted. Nevertheless,

---

[202] Sandro Magister (November 8, 2018), Jesuitas contra Focolares. La beatificación de Chiara Lubich en suspenso, L'Espresso.
[203] Ibid.
[204] (July 18, 2015), Martini: Benedict XVI's resignation and the 2005 Conclave, Vatican Insider.
[205] Eric Frattini, Los cuervos del Vaticano. Benedicto XVI en la encrucijada (Espasa, 2012), ob. cit. Note: unless otherwise indicated, this is the same source.

Bertone wanted to devise a strategy to acquire it, as well as the Gemelli clinic. But Angelo Sodano, the powerful captain of the diplomats/cardinal curia from the 'Pontificia Ecclesiastica Academia' or diplomatic school of the Holy See, as well as a player in John Paul II's old guard, opposed him with great force. That time is known as the period of the church of the "Bertonians" and the "diplomats." Vatican spokesman Federico Lombardi said that "leaks of "reserved" Vatican documents to the Italian media clearly showed harsh clashes between curial departments, power struggles between "Bertonians" and "diplomats" within the Secretariat of State, corruption in the IOR, waste and squandering in sections of the Governorate, attempts to assassinate the pope, etc." The IOR had accounts on record from criminal groups such as the Mafia or the Cosa Nostra, and Ettore Gotti Tedeschi feared for his life if these reports were given to justice.

Faced with these facts, Federico Lombardi came to the defense of the IOR and those who ran it to clean up the Vatican's image.

Similarly, in June 2011, the name of Luigi Bisignani, grand master of Italy's powerful Propaganda 4 or P4 Masonic lodge, came to light; and whom investigators from the Naples Prosecutor's Office linked to major figures in politics, industry, and religion. Bisignani was someone of whom the Italian newspaper *La Republica* wondered, "Is this the man who controls Italy?" Indeed, Bisignani had a powerful and extensive network to condition the strings of power in Italy. A document circulating in the Vatican states:

"No one can deny that in the Vatican, for too long, there have been shady dealings and cases of corruption that no one has had the courage to denounce except for the former Secretary General of the Interior, Carlo Maria Viganò, who has been inexplicably transferred to Washington. The fact that the curia is both victim and aggressor of the Vatican P4 business is no mystery to anyone. What is even more serious is the fact that those who have been caught in flagrante delicto continue to act quietly and protected by the higher echelons and even transferred to other departments with a large amount of money in movements such as the Vatican Museums or the contracting section of the Governorate."

Marco Simeon, a man close to Opus Dei and Bertone's protégé, was a mysterious executive on the rise within the IOR or Vatican Bank, involved in the organization's encrypted accounts, and in 2009, he was named the new director of Institutional and International Relations of the RAI.

The P4 used it; and the former director of the IOR, Ettore Gotti Tedeschi, declared to investigators that he was the victim of a Masonic conspiracy and gave several names, among which he revealed that of Marco Simeon. When *Il Fatto Quotidiano* asked Simeon if he belonged to Freemasonry, he answered "No, although I can only say that Freemasonry is a fundamental element of power in Italy."

Concerning the whistleblower who leaked the documents, the agents of the Information Services of the Vatican Gendarmerie, as well as the Entity (the Vatican intelligence service), set out to uncover the mole who leaked the information to the Italian media. Thus, on Tuesday, April 24, 2012, Pope Benedict XVI ordered the creation of a Cardinal Commission of Inquiry which was chaired by the Spanish Cardinal and member of Opus Dei, Julian Herranz. Finally, on May 23, the mole was arrested: it was the papal butler Paolo Gabriele. Agents of the Entity placed on

Benedict XVI's desk a false document in a folder stamped, "Under Pontifical Secrecy"; and Paolo Gabriele took the bait.

Among the thousands of pages of documents seized on May 25, 2012, in the house of the papal butler Paolo Gabriele, "many referred to Freemasonry and the secret services"; as declared in the courtroom on October 2 of that year by agents of the gendarmerie who carried out the raid. Among the various documents seized, there were also files of the Masonic lodges P3 and P4.[206]

In one of the many interrogations in the late spring of 2012, an Italian layman and employee of the Secretariat of State, framed his participation almost in tears in the leak of documents, when he said: "I put myself at the service of a Masonic lodge that operates within the Vatican and also includes cardinals. The purpose of our action, carried out with the conviction of doing good to the Church, is to put an end to the current situation of anarchy that puts Christianity at risk."[207] The immediate objective was to strike at Cardinal Tarcisio Bertone "in order to obtain his replacement."

All of the above is indicative of Freemasons using the Catholic Church for lucrative purposes, while other Freemasonry infiltrating the Vatican would seek to clean up internal corruption.

Furthermore, the Grand Master of Catania, in Italy, Vincenzo Di Benedetto, head of the Grand Lodge Serenissima of Piazza del Gesù, said to the question, "Various sources indicate the existence of Masonic lodges also in the Vatican; do you think it is possible?," he answered without hesitation: "Absolutely yes, regardless of the denomination used."

Among the network of confidants of Benedict XVI's former butler were influential cardinals: "such as the papal vicar of Vatican City Monsignor Angelo Comastri and the former Camerlengo deputy Paolo Sardi, pointed out as belonging to an internal Masonic lodge; bishops such as Francesco Cavina (who was in the Secretariat of State), and people in the past very close to Pope Ratzinger, such as former secretary Ingrid Stampa."

It should be noted that Cardinal Angelo Comastri was appointed by Pope Francis - who read the documents - already in his positions as Archpriest of St. Peter's Basilica, as Vicar General of His Holiness for Vatican City and President of the Fabric of St. Peter's - until his resignation in February 2021.

In office, he was one of the cardinals closest to Pope Francis.

Paolo Gabriele was profusely interested in Freemasonry and knew everything about the exploits of Luigi Bisignani [Italy's most powerful P2 Freemason], the huge Enimont bribe, and even the P4 lodge scandal. He had accumulated a wealth of information on international Freemasonry, and an impressive number of secret agent information manuals. There were also numerous dossiers on individual congregations, church movements, and religious organizations fighting the clandestine war outside and inside the Leonine Walls. But:

---

[206] Giacomo Galeazzi, Ferruccio Pinotti, Vaticano Massone: Logge, denaro e poteri occulti: il lato segreto della Chiesa di papa Francesco (Piemme, 2014), ob. cit.; citing Francesco Bonazzi, "Il Secolo XIX," May 30, 2012.

[207] Ibid. Note: unless otherwise noted, this is the same source.

"[...] what most surprised the Vatican gendarmerie, led by Commander Domenico Giani - former agent of the Italian secret services and close collaborator of super spies like Pollari and Mancini - were the folders of the investigation of the Naples prosecutor's office on the alleged P4 of Luigi Bisignani."

Gabriele had studied all the records of the last investigations, pointing out the Vatican links and who could be the cardinals related to Bisignani. Many documents on Masonic lodges and the various Masonic obediences were found.

By June 2012, Benedict XVI began to replace bishops and cardinals close to Bertone; and he was thinking more strongly about resigning, as he could no longer bear the burden of fighting the internal intrigues and corruption prevailing in the Vatican.[208] He had confessed in 2010 to the writer and Vaticanist Peter Seewald that he might resign if he realized that he was no longer physically, psychologically, or spiritually capable of holding the office.[209] Luigi Bettazi, the bishop emeritus of Ivrea, Italy, stated that "the Vatileaks scandals could be a strategy to prepare for the eventuality of resignation." Benedict XVI was preparing a better Vatican leadership by looking for replacements before his more decisively planned resignation, in fact, to begin in June.

In the same year, Cardinal Walter Kasper of *Sankt Gallen*, spoke of the "southerly wind" rising in the Church, something that was interpreted as foreshadowing Jorge Bergoglio.[210]

Something remarkable happened in that month of June, when the pope considered his succession more strongly. The Jesuit Cardinal of *Sankt Gallen*, Carlo Maria Martini, had his last conversation with Pope Benedict XVI (Martini died on August 31 of that year) on the occasion of the World Meeting of Families. Martini was seriously ill with Parkinson's disease and met with the pope at the archbishop's residence in the early afternoon. Silvano Fausti, a Jesuit priest and Martini's confessor, recounts that before he died, Martini told him the facts. Despite their differences, Martini and Pope Benedict were fond of each other. Martini told the pope that the time had come to resign from the papacy because the Roman Curia seemed unreformable, telling him that "The Curia is not going to change; you have no choice but to leave [...] The time [for resignation] is now; nothing can be done here anymore." Let's remember that Martini told Ratzinger before the last vote in the conclave of 2005, to accept the position so as not to create compromises and an undesirable candidate emerging from the Curia, and that if he succeeded in reforming the Curia, fine, and if not, to resign.[211]

During their conversation in June, Martini suggested to the pope that he reconcile with Danneels, which happened in September.[212]

[208] Eric Frattini, Los cuervos del Vaticano. Benedicto XVI en la encrucijada (Espasa, 2012), ob. cit.

[209] Peter Seewald, Benedict XVI. Light of the World: The Pope, the Church and the Signs of the Times (Ignatius Press, New York, 2010), ob. cit.

[210] Julia Meloni, The St. Gallen Mafia: Exposing the Secret Reformist Group Within the Church (TAN Books, Gastonia, North Carolina, 2021), ob. cit.; citing Antonio Spadaro and Carlo Maria Maria Galli, For a Missionary Reform of the Church: The La Civiltà Cattolica Seminar (Mahwah, NJ: Paulist Press, 2017), loc. 882 of 13161, Kindle. See also Walter Kasper, Chiesa Cattolica: Essenza, Realtà, Missione (Brescia: Queriniana, 2012), 46.

[211] Ibid.

[212] Edward Pentin (Sept. 26, 2015), Cardinal Danneels' Biographers Retract Comments on St. Gallen Group, National Catholic Register.

A month after the conversation between Pope Benedict and Cardinal Martini, a rumor spread in the Vatican that the pope was planning to resign.[213] Peter Sewald interviewed the pope and asked him what more could be expected from his papacy:

"From me? Not much," said Benedict. "I am an old man and the strength stops. I think what I have done is enough." Asked then if he would abdicate, Benedict said, "That depends on how much my physical strength will be necessary for me."[214]

Martini passed away that same month. Gustavo Raffi, Grand Master of the Grand Orient of Italy (GOI) expressed his thoughts on Martini's death:

"A man of dialogue and deep culture, who knew how to speak to the youth and was always open to face changes. He had a strong spirituality, he was a great expression of the Church-Word, that is, of that 'kerygma' that goes beyond all structure and convention."
[...]
He believed in ecumenism and dialogue with civil society and other religions, beginning with Judaism. [...] His great humanity and the example of his reflections addressing the great issues of human life will be missed by believers and non-believers alike."[215]

Georg Gänswein, bishop and Prefect of the Pontifical Household and personal secretary to the pope, said he learned of Benedict XVI's resignation seven months before making it public, taking us to mid-June 2012,[216] precisely when Martini spoke with the pope.

Likewise, the *Catholic Herald* echoed Bertone's words, when the cardinal said he learned of Pope Benedict's resignation seven months before being published (again in June). Bertone recounts that he asked Benedict XVI: "Holy Father, you must bestow upon us the third volume on Jesus of Nazareth and the encyclical of faith, before you sign things over to Pope Francis."[217]

Faced with that statement, one wonders if that was an indiscretion by the cardinal, or if it was a way of telling a newspaper that he was referring to Pope Benedict's successor by name, since at the time of the interview, because everyone knew the new pontiff. But the *Catholic Herald* did not discuss that detail and it seems to us that no other media; but what is certain is that it arouses suspicions.

Cormac Murphy O'Connor of the Sankt Gallen Group said after the resignation that the new pope should not condemn contraception.[218]

---

[213] Julia Meloni, The St. Gallen Mafia: Exposing the Secret Reformist Group Within the Church (TAN Books, Gastonia, North Carolina, 2021), ob. cit.

[214] Ibid; quoting Edward Pentin, "The Pope Benedict's Decision: Truth vs. Conjecture," Edward Pentin (blog), February 19, 2013, https://edwardpentin.co.uk/477/.

[215] Gustavo Raffi (August 31, 2012), Martini: Raffi (GOI), addio a un uomo di dialogo, grande espressione della Chiesa-Parola, Grande Oriente d'Italia.

[216] Vatican Insider (July 18, 2015), Martini: Benedict XVI's resignation and the 2005 Conclave, Vatican Insider.

[217] Staff Reporter (Feb. 19, 2015), Cardinal Bertone: I knew of Benedcit's plan to resign seven months in advance, Catholic Herald.

[218] John-Paul Ford Rojas (February 12, 2013), New pope should not condemn contraception, says cardinal, The Telegraph.

Cardinal O'Connor was credited with the words, "there is going to be another conservative Pope – perhaps the last before a great explosion in the Church." However, he denied the claim.[219] The person who said it was Diarmaid MacCulloch, professor of history at Oxford University.[220] But those words set a familiar precedent: that a revolutionary pope was needed and would be elected.

On February 11, 2013, Pope Benedict announced his resignation as pontiff of the Roman Catholic Church. When Jorge Bergoglio heard the news, he praised the decision as a "revolutionary act" that had been carefully considered in the presence of God.[221]

A few days later, Benedict XVI appointed Erns von Freyberg - a devout Catholic and knight of Malta - as president of the IOR.[222] Freyberg is a billionaire industrialist, then chairman of the Blohm+Voss Group, a shipbuilder that also makes battleships.[223] The pope was preparing a series of changes in the Catholic Church before the next conclave that would elect his successor.

"Operation Conclave," as Horacio Verbitsky called it, would gain more strength because Bergoglio was trying to become pope to clean his image and because of his ambition for power and the supposed fulfillment of some prophecies in which he believed, which will be discussed in a chapter of this book.

When the voting cardinals arrived at the Vatican, they would hold the general congregations arranged before the conclave behind closed doors.[224] And although the Sankt Gallen Group had not met since 2006, it helped to form a network that had been paving the way to favor its candidate for several years.[225]

The malfunctioning of the Vatican due to corruption was a recurring theme in the speeches. Three of the cardinals chosen by Benedict to probe the level of decay were ready to transmit to their fellow voters the confidential 300-page report that would be on the next pope's desk. The U.S. cardinals were key players in those deliberations and in the conclave itself.[226]

These cardinals expressed a special interest in addressing the issue of the malfunctioning of the Vatican, since during the previous months they were able to access very complete information.[227] The American and German churches are the main financiers of the Vatican and they wanted the next pope to do an effective cleaning, as the Cardinal of New York, Timothy Dolan, said: "We knew that the world awaited the election of a pontiff who might usher in some significant reforms that begged for

[219] Gerard O'Connell (February 20, 2013), Cardinal Murphy O'Connor: We need a strong Pope to govern the Church, Vatican Insider.

[220] John Bingham and Nick Squires (February 12, 2013), Pope Benedict XVI's replacement will be 'ideological clone', The Telegraph.

[221] Austen Ivereigh, The Great Reformer: Francis and the Making of a Radical Pope (Henry Holt and Co., New York, 2014), ob. cit.

[222] José Ospina (February 16, 2013) Ernst von Freyberg is the German who will chair the Vatican Bank, DW.

[223] Emiliano Fittipaldi, Avaricia (Ediciones Akal, S. A., 2015), ob. cit.

[224] Austen Ivereigh, The Great Reformer: Francis and the Making of a Radical Pope (Henry Holt and Co., New York, 2014), ob. cit.

[225] Edward Pentin (September 26, 2015), Cardinal Danneels' Biographers Retract Comments on Sankt Gallen Group, Nationa Catholic Register.

[226] Austen Ivereigh, The Great Reformer: Francis and the Making of a Radical Pope (Henry Holt and Co., New York, 2014), ob. cit.

[227] Ibid.

implementation within the Church."[228] "What was needed," writes Ivereigh, "was wholesale culture change-a new ethos of service to the pope's mission."[229]

"There was much talk of reform of governance—the need for a pope who was accessible, informed, and free to act— and for fluid contact between Rome and the local Church. Collegiality had been "a constant theme in these discussions," Father Lombardi told journalists on March 9. "We were all pretty certain that there would be dramatic changes and a new way of looking at the Curia, with more collegiality," recalls the archbishop of Boston, Cardinal Seán O'Malley."[230]

During these meetings, one cardinal suggested that the task of governing the universal Church was too arduous for one, and proposed a cardinal's council of advisors from outside Rome to assist the new pope. One of the most eloquent was Cardinal Francesco Coccopalmerio; a Vatican lawyer of canon law who was auxiliary bishop to the late Cardinal Martini in Milan.[231]

Supporters of Tarcisio Bertone and Sodano's side, as well as numerous Italian diocesan leaderships, were unanimous in not wanting Angelo Scola to be the new pontiff (Benedict XVI's favorite). There were plots to vote for an outsider who would be malleable and maintain the status quo, but it failed when it was revealed to the press before the general congregations.[232]

Cormac Murphy O'Connor of *Sankt Gallen* mobilized. The English-speaking cardinals from developing countries as well as from the British Commonwealth met at the British embassy to the Holy See placed at the disposal of the English diplomat Nigel Baker, which was precisely the ambassador's residence: Palazzo Pallavicini. What for? To discuss the next succession to the papal throne.[233]

For Tim Fisher, Australian ambassador to the Holy See and his nation's deputy prime minister:

"The British influence on the conclave was against all the odds, yet it happened. That was down to one of the most capable cardinals I've ever met – Cormac Murphy-O'Connor – playing the most powerful non- voting role in the choosing of a pope I've ever known.""[234]

Nigel Baker, writing in *L'Osservatore Romano* in December 2014 about the usefulness of the Holy See in a world of soft power, or in other words, the ability to influence the actions or interests of other actors through cultural and ideological means, said:

---

[228] Dolan, Praying in Rome: Reflections on the Conclave and Electing Pope Francis, quoted in Ibid.

[229] Austen Ivereigh, The Great Reformer: Francis and the Making of a Radical Pope (Henry Holt and Co., New York, 2014), ob. cit.

[230] Cardinal O'Malley interview with Father Thomas Rosica, Salt & Light TV, October 4, 2013, quoted in Ibid.

[231] Austen Ivereigh, The Great Reformer: Francis and the Making of a Radical Pope (Henry Holt and Co., New York, 2014), ob. cit.

[232] Ibid.

[233] Catherine Pepinster, The Keys and the Kingdom: The British and the Papacy from John Paul II to Francis (Bloomsbury T&T Clark, 2017), p. 69.

[234] Ibid, p. 73.

"We have an embassy to the Holy See because of the extent of the Holy See soft power network, the infl uence of the pope, and the global reach and perspective of papal diplomacy focused on preserving and achieving peace, on the protection of the planet, and on bringing people out of poverty."[235]

Murphy O'Connor was too old to participate in the conclave, but Walter Kasper, Godfried Danneels and Karl Lehmann were eligible to be electors. According to the rules of the conclave, Bergoglio was not asked if he wanted to be a candidate. However, they believed that the current crisis in the Church would make it too difficult for him to refuse election should it occur. But O'Connor warned him to be careful, as it was now his turn, receiving an "I understand" in response. "The Mafia" of Sankt Gallen went around the cardinals' dinners to promote Bergoglio, arguing that his age (76), was no longer an obstacle to considering an eventual resignation by the new pontiff. They wanted to secure 25 votes from the beginning in the first round.[236]

Geert De Kerpel, spokesman for the Archdiocese of Mechelen-Brussels, had said in a telephone interview with *The New York Times* in March 2019, that Danneels, "Years before the last conclave, he told me that the church needed a Francis as head of the church."[237]

During a press conference shortly before the conclave, Danneels outlined the profile of the ideal pope: someone who would seek decentralization, synodality, a "crown council," and perhaps a Vatican III: "We need a Francis," the Belgian cardinal said.[238]

Now, the cardinals from North America -the United States and Canada- were the most numerous after the Europeans and Latin Americans, which was fundamental, together with other groups from different countries, to achieve victory.[239] Then, since March 5, the cardinals considered Bergoglio at a dinner in the Red Room of the North American Pontifical College (NAC) attended by, among others, Cormac Murphy O'Connor who, although he could not vote because of his age, took part in these pre-conclave discussions. Most Vaticanists continued to believe that there was no organized effort prior to the conclave to make Bergoglio's election possible. The U.S. cardinals, at one point, felt they were being boycotted by the Italians for their unequal line on the next candidate.

On the morning of March 7, Bergoglio addressed the General Congregation giving a powerful speech of only three and a half minutes, where he portrayed the moment in which the Church found herself and offered the diagnosis and remedy. He spoke of the task of evangelization as the raison d'être of the Church, which should shed light on the possible changes and reforms to be made to save souls. About the next pope, he expressed:

---

[235] Ibid, p. 62; citing Baker, Nigel (2014), *L'Oservatore Romano*.

[236] Austen Ivereigh, The Great Reformer: Francis and the Making of a Radical Pope (Henry Holt and Co., New York, 2014), ob. cit.

[237] Gaia Pianigiani (March 24, 2019), Godfried Danneels, Liberal Cardinal Tainted by Sex Scandal, Dies at 85, The New York Times.

[238] Julia Meloni, The St. Gallen Mafia: Exposing the Secret Reformist Group Within the Church (TAN Books, Gastonia, North Carolina, 2021), ob. cit.; citing Pentin, "Cardinal Danneels' Biographers Retract Comments."

[239] Austen Ivereigh, The Great Reformer: Francis and the Making of a Radical Pope (Henry Holt and Co., New York, 2014), ob. cit. Note: unless otherwise noted, this is the same source.

"[...] he should be a man who, through the contemplation of Jesus Christ, from the adoration of Jesus Christ, helps the Church to go out from itself toward the existential peripheries, and helps her to be the fruitful mother who lives from "the sweet and comforting joy of evangelizing."

After his speech, there was a "strident" silence and Cardinal Schönborn - from *Sankt Gallen* - turning to the person next to him, said: "That's what we need." While Cardinal Ortega described the intervention as "magisterial, illuminating, commited, and true." Bergoglio's words convinced Cardinal George, who told Murphy-O'Connor that he now knew what they meant when they spoke of the Argentine cardinal. That evening, the cardinals decided to begin the conclave the following Tuesday - March 12. After leaving the synod hall, Cardinal George, with a beaming expression, told reporters, "We're ready!"

After the pre-conclave Mass leading up to the March 13 vote, Bergoglio and Angelo Scola were the main contenders.

But the day before, the media reported that the anti-mafia police raided Scola's diocese for possible corruption links due to his previous links to the Communion and Liberation association; and from this to the Calabrian mafia.[240] It is suspicious that this news was leaked to the press the day before the final vote.

Later at lunch in Santa Marta, Bergoglio was tense; and Cardinal O'Malley said he saw him somber and barely eating; very overwhelmed by what was going on.[241] There are those who claimed that Scola asked his supporters to vote for Bergoglio. In the afternoon vote, the Argentine cardinal was already serene and calm.[242]

Washington Cardinal Donald Wuerl, played a key role in uniting Americans in favor of Bergoglio, who were followed by European bishops.[243]

ABC of Spain reported:

"Bergoglio's name was circulating very low on the lists and he has turned out to be the **hidden candidate** of the reformist camp.

"This sector, which wants cleanliness and reforms, would be made up of the survivors of the old **progressive nucleus** formed around Martini, with Kasper and Danneels, the foreigners who wanted a non-European Pope, the entire American and Latin American "lobby," which has moved compactly, and **weighty figures** who drag consensus such as the Austrian Schönborn and the French Vingt-Trois. In other words, those loyal to Ratzinger's line of cleanliness and rigor have also joined in."[244]

[240] John Hooper and Lizzy Davies (March 12, 2013), Papal conclave: anti-mafia pólice raid offices in diocese of frontrunner, The Guardian.
[241] Austen Ivereigh, The Great Reformer: Francis and the Making of a Radical Pope (Henry Holt and Co., New York, 2014), ob. cit.
[242] Ibid.
[243] David Gibson (March 15, 2013), The story behind Pope Francis' election, Religion News Service.
[244] (March 15, 2013), ¿Por qué los cardenales no eligieron a Scola?, ABC.

When the vote tellers pronounced the phrase "Eminentissimo Bergoglio" for the seventh time, there was a collective sigh and the cardinals stood up and applauded; apparently all with moistened eyes.[245]

Brazilian Cardinal Claudio Hummes told him: "Don't forget the poor." Bergoglio said that this led him to choose the name "Francis," after "Francis of Assisi, the man of poverty, the man of peace, the man who loves and cares for creation." Who repaired the Church. When asked if he accepted the choice, he expressed his traditional acceptance and also added: "even though I am a great sinner." Cardinal Cormac Murphy O'Connor, Bergoglio's mysterious promoter, was outside when the white smoke announced the election of the new pope. He told an emissary of Austen Ivereigh that "as it had been a short conclave, the new pope could well be Jorge Mario Bergoglio."[246]

O'Connor attended a meeting with all the cardinals on March 15 (two days after Bergoglio's election); and Francis greeted him warmly by saying something like, "It's your fault. What have you done to me?"[247]

Already as pope, a year after Cardinal Martini's death, Francis said during a meeting with Italian Jesuits that Martini was "a father for the whole Church," and that remembering him "is an act of justice."[248] Sandro Magister, an Italian Vaticanist, quoted in an article titled, "Martini Pope. The Dream Come True," Marco Garzonio, the leading Martini expert, in writing of the new pope that, "as bishop of Rome, and therefore without claims of hegemony and proselytism ("a solemn foolishness," Bergoglio says), he is clearing the way for the ecumenism and interreligious dialogue on which Martini centered his episcopate, garnering more than one official reproach for his lack of attention to proselytism."[249]

Garzonio stated:

"Martini believed in and never gave up on the "dream," which Bergoglio is now trying to get onto its feet so that it can be turned into reality."[250]

Martini said shortly before his death that the leader of the Catholic Church should surround himself with twelve bishops and cardinals if he wanted the boat of Peter not to be submerged by internal waves and by a society that no longer believes in it. He stated that it was two hundred years behind on issues such as family, youth, the role of women (the latter being a topic Pope Francis promised to discuss more).[251]

When Austen Ivereigh's book was published and the accounts of the Sankt Gallen Group became notorious, the Holy See replied through the director of the Press Office, Federico Lombardi, stating that the four cardinals in the group expressly denied the description of the facts. They also wanted the public to know that they were surprised

[245] Austen Ivereigh, The Great Reformer: Francis and the Making of a Radical Pope (Henry Holt and Co., New York, 2014), ob. cit.
[246] Ibid.
[247] Miguel Cullen (Sept. 12, 2013), Pope sent greetings to the Queen straight after his election, says cardinal, Catholic Herald.
[248] Carol Glatz (Sept. 2, 2013), Pope Francis hails Cardinal Martini as 'a father for the whole Church', Catholic Herald.
[249] Sandro Magister (October 15, 2013), Martini Pope. The Dream Come True, Chiesa.
[250] Ibid.
[251] Ibid.

and disappointed.[252] Additionally, Cardinal Cormac Murphy O'Connor's press secretary reported that the prelate wanted to dispel any misunderstanding about the journalist's book, stating that they never approached Bergoglio before the conclave to promote his candidacy.[253] There were others who dismissed Ivereigh's account as a scandal. However, Cardinal Godfried Danneels revealed during the launch of his biography that he belonged to a secret club of cardinals opposed to Pope Benedict XVI, which he called "the mafia" and which went by the name of the Sankt Gallen group.[254] He also said that as a group they intended to seek a drastic reform in the Church by modernizing it, and about having Bergoglio to lead it.[255] Moreover, the authors of Danneels' authorized biography reported that the Sankt Gallen club was a lobby of reformist prelates who groomed Bergoglio to be pope; but to the surprise of the public and the authorities, they retracted that claim.[256] But Danneels had already declared.

In addition, Swiss bishops from the Diocese of Sankt Gallen and the group's founder, Ivo Fürer, acknowledged the existence of the club and their discussions about the profile of the new pope after the death of John Paul II. They added that Bergoglio was a favorite of the group's members.[257]

Towards the end of May 2016, Archbishop Georg Gänswein, Prefect of the Pontifical Household in the Vatican, speaking about the dramatic conclave of 2005, referred to the Sankt Gallen Group as the nucleus that had its candidate; but he also mentioned the Salt of the Earth Party, made up of Cardinals López Trujillo, Ruini, Herranz, Ruoco Varela or Medina, opponents of the former.[258]

Today, as David Gibson, a renowned Vaticanist, comments, looking at Pope Francis as the revival of Joseph Bernardin:

"[...] many say the pope's remarks repeatedly evoke Bernardin's signature teachings on the "consistent ethic of life" – the view that church doctrine champions the poor and vulnerable from womb to tomb – and on finding "common ground" to heal divisions in the church."[259]

[252] Editor (Dec. 1, 2014), Father Lombardi's clarification of Austen Ivereigh's book, Zenit.

[253] (Nov. 25, 2014), Letters: Boris should tale a leaf out of Amsterdam's book, The Telegraph-Papal plot.

[254] Phil Lawler (September 28, 2015), A conspiracy to elect Pope Francis? Don't believe it, Catholic Culture.

[255] Edward Pentin (September 24, 2015), Cardinal Danneels Admits to Being Part of 'Mafia' Club Opposed to Benedcit XVI, National Catholic Register; see also original news story with Danneels' statements on video: (September 23, 2015), Danneels: "Zat in soort maffiaclub," VTM NIEUWS.

[256] Edward Pentin (Sept. 26, 2015), Cardinal Danneels' Biographers Retract Comments on St. Gallen Group, National Catholic Register.

[257] (September 29, 2015), Sensationsmeldung?, Bistum St.Gallen Aktuelles; Kommunikationsstelle Bistum Sankt Gallen Sabine Rüthemann, Bistum Sankt Gallen; See also in (September 30, 2015), Papst-Wahl aus Sankt Gallen gesteuert, 20Minuten.

[258] Edward Pentin (May 23, 2016), Archbishop Gänswein: Benedict XVI Sees Resignation as Expanding Petrine Ministry, National Catholic Register; Diane Montagna (May 30, 2016), Complete English Text: Archbishop Georg Gänswein's 'Expanded Petrine Office' Speech, Aleteia.

[259] David Gibson (Oct. 24, 2013), Pope Francis breathes new life into Cardinal Bernardin's contested legacy, Religion News Service.

For his part, Joseph Fiorenza, retired Archbishop of Galveston-Houston and former president of the U.S. Conference of Catholic Bishops: "I certainly think that if Cardinal Bernardin were alive he would be very pleased with what Pope Francis is saying and doing." Several bishops, Church officials and observers have agreed.[260]

Giacomo Galeazzi and Ferruccio Pinotti of *La Stampa* and *Corriere della Sera*, respectively, indicated:

"The election of a Jesuit, Father Jorge Mario Bergoglio, to the throne of Peter represents a momentous event.

The victory in the conclave of the first Jesuit pope in history came after a gigantic clash of power, the proportions of which are still not understood. The pendulum of history has swung, making a very big turn, which changes the balance of the oldest institution in the world. [...] everything seems to change, bringing a new air to the dark rooms of the curia but also to the worldwide Catholic community and in the wider theater of geopolitics, of which the Vatican is a very important actor."[261]

They also add:

"What forces overturned the apparently written result of a conclave that seemed to assign the papacy to figures far removed from Bergoglio's and even antagonistic, as in the case of Cardinal Angelo Scola, exponent of Communion and Liberation?

Public opinion has begun to perceive that behind the unprecedented internal conflict there is much more: a struggle between factions disputing the very future of the Church of Rome. One senses the presence of a dark design, of a much higher "level" of comparison: and there are many knots to untie to understand what is going on."[262]

That was the election of Jorge Bergoglio to the papacy. The pope who came to try to transform or revolutionize the thinking of the world and the church, and to try to unite humanity for the common good.

An agenda driven under the mastery of ambiguity: Background

Adolfo Pérez Esquivel, winner of the Nobel Peace Prize, said in 2005 that many Argentine bishops had a double discourse and, when he was consulted about Bergoglio's performance, he answered without hesitation that "Bergoglio's attitude is part of all these policies of thinking that all those who worked socially with the poorest and neediest sectors were communists, subversives, terrorists." And when the journalists asked him for his opinion on a possible election of Bergoglio to the papacy in the conclave that was approaching in April, Pérez Esquivel answered clearly: "A pope has to have very clear, very concrete definitions. Bergoglio is an intelligent man, he is a capable man, but he is an ambiguous person. I hope that the Holy Spirit will be awake that day, and will not make a mistake." However, after Bergoglio's election to the papacy in March 2013, Pérez Esquivel changed his mind and said that other bishops

---

[260] Ibid.
[261] Giacomo Galeazzi, Ferruccio Pinotti, Vaticano Massone: Logge, denaro e poteri occulti: il lato segreto della Chiesa di papa Francesco (Piemme, 2014), ob. cit.
[262] Ibid.

collaborated with the dictatorship, but not Bergoglio. That at most, he was not too energetic in his defense of human rights.[263]

On March 21, 2013, Esquivel met with Francis at the invitation of the pope himself, and the two discussed human rights.[264] After the meeting, Esquivel told journalists that the pope was not an accomplice of the dictatorship and that he carried out silent diplomacy.[265] He also added: "I think Verbitsky makes many mistakes with accusations of that kind."[266]

Much of Argentine journalist Horacio Verbitsky's research on Bergoglio was disbelieved, due to Gabriel Levinas' book about the journalist, where it is revealed with documents and testimonies Verbitsky's alleged collaboration during the dictatorship by writing paid speeches for a sector of the Argentine regime.[267]

But let's look at the facts: when Bergoglio went to testify before an Argentine court, he said that he did not know about the theft of babies during the nation's dictatorship, although he had told the De la Cuadra family in 1977 that he did know about the case when he refused to return the family's baby. Furthermore, there is also a letter in Bergoglio's own handwriting from that time, as a witness against him that he indeed knew.[268]

Similarly, there is the case of the island "El Silencio," which was the resting place of the Archbishopric of Buenos Aires and owned by the Catholic Church. Because in 1979 the Inter-American Commission on Human Rights was to visit the country, the Navy Mechanics School Task Force needed a place to hide sixty prisoners to prevent the commission from finding them. After selling the property to Monsignor Emilio Grasselli, secretary general of the Military Vicariate, he in turn transferred it that same year to the ESMA Task Force, where they hid the prisoners.[269]

Bergoglio indicated in 1999 in his own handwriting to Verbitsky, in which court was the file on the sale of "El Silencio." However, in one of his court testimonies, Bergoglio said that he never heard of the island "El Silencio."[270]

A brother of the late Jesuit Orlando Yorio, Rodolfo, told the German magazine *Spiegel*: "I know people he helped. That is what reveals his two faces and his proximity to military power. He was a master of ambiguity. When the army killed someone, Bergoglio got rid of him, when someone was saved, he was the one who had saved them. That is why there are people who see him as a saint and others who fear him."[271]

Back in 2013, Bergoglio/Pope Francis told journalists, "If someone is gay and he searches for the Lord and has good will, who am I to judge?"[272] That statement

---

[263] Horacio Verbitsky (March 24, 2013), Se equivocó la paloma, Página 12.

[264] (March 21, 2013), De qué hablaron el Papa Francisco y Péres Esquivel, La Gaceta.

[265] (March 21, 2013), Premio Nobel argentino tras reunión con Papa Francisco: "El no fue cómplice de la dictadura", Mundo.

[266] Horacio Verbitsky (March 24, 2013), Se equivocó la paloma, Página 12.

[267] Gabriel Levinas, Doble agente: La biografía inesperada de Horacio Verbitsky (Editorial Sudamericana, 2015).

[268] Giacomo Galeazzi, Ferruccio Pinotti, Vaticano Massone: Logge, denaro e poteri occulti: il lato segreto della Chiesa di papa Francesco (Piemme, 2014), ob. cit.; Daniel Satur (September 20, 2014), EXCLUSIVO. La carta que oculta Bergoglio, La Izquierda Diario.

[269] Horacio Verbitsky (December 1, 2013), El primer caso, Página 12.

[270] Ibid.

[271] Horacio Verbitsky (March 24, 2013), Papamanía, Página 12.

[272] Rachel Donadio (July 29, 2013), On Gay Priests, Pope Francis Asks, 'Who Am I to Judge?', The New York Times.

generated massive support for him on the one hand; and strong criticism on the other. However, in January 2016, the pope explained to Italian journalist Andrea Tornielli that, "I was paraphrasing by heart the Catechism of the Catholic Church where it says that these people should be treated with delicacy and not be marginalized."[273] But the pope did not explain why the phrase alludes to a gay priest seeking God, and who possesses good will and should not be judged. Such ambiguity is also notable when he said in January 2023, that being homosexual is not a crime, but a sin. But later he clarified that what he meant was that any relationship outside marriage is a sin and not necessarily being homosexual.[274] But in Argentina he declared war against equal marriage.[275]

Professor Leonardo Lugaresi, commenting on a letter that Cardinal Gerhard Ludwig Müller sent to his brother Dominik Duka, said that it indicates "the way to escape the deliberate and systematic ambiguities of Francis on some points of doctrine that he, the Pope, insists on declaring unchanged...but at the same time he treats them as if they were in a fluid, liquid state."[276] In fact, it seems to many that a peculiar defect in Francis' teaching is its ambiguity.[277] Lugaresi writes:

"To state that the Pope's teaching is often ambiguous is not to be hostile or disrespectful to him: I would say that it is, more than anything else, the observation of an obvious fact. As you yourself, Magister, recalled in presenting Müller's letter, there are countless cases today in which the Pope has made statements that are equivocal (in the sense that they lend themselves to opposing interpretations) and/or contradictory to one another because they diverge from one another. Different from one another, and every time he was asked to specify the meaning univocally, he avoided answering or did so, often indirectly, in an equally ambiguous and elusive manner."[278]

Lugaresi stresses that Francis has appealed on several occasions to the axiom that "reality is superior to the idea," to the point that "it crushes the principle of non-contradiction and the consequent affirmation that one cannot affirm an idea and at the same time also its opposite."[279]

Bergoglio's personal strategy is synthesized in the recommendation "think clearly, but speak obscurely," as commented by Argentine journalist Ignacio Zuleta:

"In this, he seems like a textbook Jesuit. As in 2013, when he recommended to Monsignor Bruno Forti, secretary of the Synod on the Family: "If we talk about giving communion to the divorced and remarried, you don't know what a mess we are making. So, no direct talk, just make the premises explicit, then I will be the one to draw the conclusions." "Typical of a Jesuit," Forte joked about this example of liquid

---

[273] Joshua J. McElwee (Jan. 10, 2016), Francis explains 'who am I to judge?', National Catholic Reporter.
[274] Nicole Winfield (Jan. 28, 2023), Pope clarifies homosexuality and sin comments in note, Associated Press.
[275] Maciek Wisniewski (April 7, 2013), El Papa de todas las ambigüedades, La Jornada.
[276] ACN (Oct. 20, 2023), El cardenal Müller enseña cómo remediar las ambigüedades de Francisco, Agencia Católica de Noticias.
[277] Ibid.
[278] Ibid.
[279] Ibid.

magisterium when he recounted it at a round table on the apostolic exhortation *Amoris Laetitia.*"[280]

Zuleta goes on to explain how Bergoglio envisions global unity:

"The appeal of the polyhedron is to imagine reality as a whole where the elements are not defined by opposition, as formulated by structuralism, but by complementation. Each facet of the polyhedron coexists with the others and contributes to the understanding of the whole. [...]

This is how one of Bergoglio's finest hermeneuticists explains it: "Bergoglio advances towards a superior synthesis that does not erase tensions, but understands them, vivifies them, makes them fruitful and opens them to the future. For, as I have already said, for him the model is not the sphere, which is not superior to the parts, where each point is equidistant from the center and there are no differences between one and the other. The model is the polyhedron, which reflects the confluences of all the parts that in it preserve their originality".[281]

Likewise, the renowned Argentine sociologist, literary critic, and philosopher, Juan José Sebreli, indicates that Bergoglio has always tried to bring religion closer to politics; and that he is a conservative populist, but that the left, which is delighted with him, is not capable of seeing anything; and that his position with religion and with the pope is merely tactical: "religion as an agglutinator of the masses."[282]

Millstream Media and Films broadcast on March 12, 2016, the words of Horacio Verbitsky, a journalist at the time of the newspaper *Página 12:*

"And Jorge Bergoglio is a man who adds to the... to the popular sense and charisma of Giovanni Paolo Secondo [John Paul II], the intellectual subtlety of... Ratzinger. But he is very skillful because he is a great politician. A great politician. And that Church in crisis needs a great politician to lead it, to rescue it... from the disaster from which it was heading. And that is why they have chosen a great politician. He has that... he has that sympathy of the porteño, he is an awake porteño, quick, he makes jokes, he is nice, he laughs. He is not at all solemn, not at all formal. He's... he's going to get everybody into his pocket, this man. I have no doubt about that."[283]

Action

In 2013, Pope Francis criticized the Catholic Church for obsessing over the issues of abortion and gay marriage.[284]

Likewise, when he convened the Synod on the Family in October 2015, it was striking that he did not invite André-Joseph Léonard, the primate of Belgium who replaced Godfried Danneels by mandate of Benedict XVI in 2010 so that there would not be another liberal in Danneels' place. Instead, Pope Francis chose Danneels, which

---

[280] Ignacio Zuleta, El Papa peronista: Historia secreta de cómo Francisco opera en el día a día a día de la política argentina (Ariel Argentina, 2019), ob. cit.
[281] Ibid.
[282] Ricardo Dudda (July 2018), Entrevista con Juan José Sebreli: "El papa Francisco es un populista de derechas," Letras Libres, Number 202, pp. 32, 33.
[283] (March 12, 2016), Horacio Verbitsky on election of Pope Bergoglio, Millstream Films and Media: https://www.youtube.com/watch?v=UppRmyjqm7g; accessed May 26, 2016.
[284] Pablo Ordaz (September 19, 2013), El Papa: "Jamás he sido de derechas", El País.

he also did the previous year. Note, that by 2013, although Léonard could have received the cardinal's biretta after Danneels turned eighty, the pope passed him over during the consistories of 2014 and 2015.[285]

Danneels appeared second on the 2015 consistory guest list.[286]

Some media noted that many of the guests were controversial for their ideas about family according to Catholic doctrine.[287] With ideas such as allowing communion to the divorced; contraception; allowing abortion; and defending homosexual relationships at various levels. The list contained twelve cardinals: Walter Kasper; Godfried Danneels; Christoph Schönborn (these three from the Sankt Gallen group); Timothy Dolan; Donald Wuerl; Dionigi Tettamanzi; Angelo Sodano; Oscar Andrés Rodríguez Maradiaga; Lluís Martínez Sistach; Raymundo Damasceno Assis; Luis Antonio Tagle; and John Dew. There were two archbishops -Blase Cupich and Bruno Forte-. And the Jesuit priest Antonio Spadaro; director of *La Civiltà Cattolica*.[288]

In late August of the same year, TFP Student Action collected half a million signatures from around the world urging the pope to reinforce the Church's teaching on marriage at the synod.[289]

La Voz de la familia expressed its opinion:

"The time has come for all Catholics, at every level of the Church, to recognize the full gravity of the crisis that now engulfs us," the group said. "Each and every one of us, clergy or lay, has the right and the duty to defend Catholic doctrine and practice from attacks by members of the hierarchy."[290]

In contrast to the long list of progressives summoned to the Vatican, only three were conservatives: Cardinals Wilfrid Napier, Elio Sgreccia, and Carlo Cafarra.[291] Faced with that list, another collision like the one that occurred in 2014 was predicted. U.S. Cardinal Raymond Burke, champion of the conservative wing of the synod, was no longer on the 2015 list.[292] Moreover, the month after the 2014 synod, the pope removed him from his position as director of the Supreme Tribunal of the Apostolic Signatura and appointed him patron of the Order of the Knights of Malta.[293]

Many feared a schism if radical changes were made to the Church's doctrine on marriage.[294] But nothing could be changed at both synods.

---

[285] Fr Raymond de Souza (January 21, 2016), "Is Francis really against Benedict?," Catholic Herald.

[286] Damian Thompson (Oct. 8, 2015), Three things you need to know about Pope Francis and the cardinal disgraced in a sex abuse scandal, The Spectator.

[287] Ibid.

[288] Pete Baklinski (Sept. 15, 2015), Family leaders alarmed at Pope Francis' personal invitations for Synod, LifeSiteNews.

[289] Staff Reporter (Aug. 25, 2015), Half a million people sign petition urging Francis to reinforce Church teaching on marriage at synod, Catholic Herald.

[290] Pete Baklinski (Sept. 15, 2015), Family leaders alarmed at Pope Francis' personal invitations for Synod, LifeSiteNews.

[291] Ibid.

[292] Inés San Martín (September 15, 2015), List of participants augurs another rollicking synod on the family, Crux.

[293] Inés San Martín (November 8, 2014), Pope makes it official: US Cardinal Raymond Burke is demoted, Crux.

[294] Pete Baklinski (Sept. 15, 2015), Family leaders alarmed at Pope Francis' personal invitations for Synod, LifeSiteNews.

As Julia Meloni documented, "Francis soon invited Danneels to be a special papal delegate to the 2014 and 2015 family synods. Danneels's name was listed as second in importance on the Vatican's official list of Francis's personal appointees."[295] She added, "According to journalist Damian Thompson, a senior Vatican source once told him that Francis invited Danneels to the synods "as a thank-you for the votes he helped deliver" for Francis's election."[296]

Frédéric Martel, himself homosexual and left-leaning, in his well-documented book *In the Closet of the Vatican: Power, Homosexuality, Hypocrisy*, reveals how Pope Francis launched his secret plan to steer the church toward acceptance of remarriage and homosexuality during the two Synods on the Family. A crucial role in the synods was played by Cardinal Walter Kasper, one of the "most open and gay-friendly cardinals." Cardinal Lorenzo Baldisseri said of the synods, "Our line was essentially Kasper's."[297]

With Kasper's help, Pope Francis invited Dominican theologian Adriano Oliva to write a book titled *Amours* that quoted St. Thomas Aquinas in an attempt to approve homosexual relationships; and then the book was distributed to participants of the second synod on the family in 2015. Baldisseri said, "The pope wanted to open doors and windows." The debate was to take place "in the episcopal conferences, in the dioceses, among the faithful."[298]

Martel wrote that "Walter Kasper announced publicly, even before the Synod, that 'homosexual unions, if they are lived in a stable and responsible manner, are respectable'."[299]

In addition, one of the secretaries in charge of writing a draft of Pope Francis' *Amoris Laetitia* was a "homosexual activist."[300]

Francis' participation was evident because he went to the synods every week and personally presided over the sessions where the proposals were discussed, Baldisseri commented.[301]

The controversial paragraph in the draft document on the positive aspects of homosexual relationships, which did not receive sufficient support from the group of Synod fathers, was deliberately added by Pope Francis' team. The Vatican was willing to recognize what it considered the "qualities" of young people living together, remarried divorcees, and homosexual civil unions. The main thing about Pope Francis' agenda and revolution.[302]

---

[295] Julia Meloni, The St. Gallen Mafia: Exposing the Secret Reformist Group Within the Church (TAN Books, Gastonia, North Carolina, 2021), ob. cit.

[296] Ibid; quoting Damian Thompson, "Three Things You Need to Know about Pope Francis and the Cardinal Disgraced in a Sex Abuse Scandal," The Spectator, October 8, 2015, https://www.spectator.co.uk/article/three-things-you-need-to-know-about-pope-francis-and-the-cardinal-disgraced-in-a-sex-abuse-scandal. See also Damian Thompson (@holysmoke), "For me, alarm bells went off when Danneels attended the Synod in the Family. I asked a cardinal why Francis invited him - 'To thank him for votes'..." Twitter, Aug. 20, 2018, 7:29 a.m., https://twitter.com/holysmoke/status/1031518513658294272.

[297] Frédéric Martel, In the Closet of the Vatican: Power, Homosexuality, Hypocrisy (Bloomsbury Continuum, London, 2019), p. 89.

[298] Ibid, pp. 103, 104, 89.

[299] Ibid.

[300] Ibid, pp. 89, 90.

[301] Ibid, p. 90.

[302] Ibid, pp. 90, 91.

The pope had been upset at being blocked by conservative cardinals in the curia in rejecting his major proposals at the 2014 synod. Cardinals Raymond Burke, Gerhard Müller, and Carlo Caffara wrote a book entitled *Remaining in the Truth of Christ: Marriage and Communion in the Catholic Church.*[303]

"The five cardinal authors of the book are Gerhard Müller, Prefect of the Congregation for the Doctrine of the Faith; Raymond Leo Burke, Prefect of the Supreme Tribunal of the Apostolic Signatura; Walter Brandmüller, President Emeritus of the Pontifical Committee for Historical Sciences; Carlo Caffarra, Archbishop of Bologna and one of the theologians closest to St. John Paul II on questions of morality and the family; and Velasio De Paolis, President Emeritus of the Prefecture for the Economic Affairs of the Holy See."[304]

Four professors and theologians also contributed to the book: Robert Dodaro (OSA), editor John Rist, Jesuit Paul Mankowski, and Archbishop Cyril Vasil.[305]

The pope prepared an offensive using three techniques simultaneously and at extraordinary speed for that 2014 synod, but it did not work. Martel wrote that it was like a war machine that used nuncios, allies, friendly cardinals, and in every country he could.[306]

For his part, at the 2015 synod, Sandro Magister commented in *Chiesa*, that on October 5 - at the beginning of the 2015 synod - Cardinal George Pell delivered a letter to the pope on behalf of himself and twelve other cardinals who signed it, communicating his serious concerns and those of other synod fathers about the assembly's proceedings which, in his view, was "designed to facilitate predetermined results on important disputed questions;" and about the "Instrumentum laboris," which was seen as inadequate as a "guiding text or the foundation of a final document." One of the signatories was Cardinal Timothy Dolan of New York, who, while considered liberal on homosexual unions, was not liberal on their marital and other status. What Pope Francis rejected were calls for a lack of genuine openness and collegiality.[307]

He said in his closing speech that, "the challenge before us is always the same: to proclaim the Gospel to the people of today, defending the family from all ideological and individualistic attacks."[308]

Also, eleven cardinals joined forces to prevent reforms to the church's position in the book entitled, *Eleven Cardinals Speak on Marriage and the Family: Essays from a Pastoral Viewpoint.*[309] About the participants:

---

[303] ACI Prensa (September 14, 2014), publican libro en defensa de la doctrina de la Iglesia sobre el matrimonio, ACI Prensa.

[304] Ibid.

[305] Ibid.

[306] Frédéric Martel, In the Closet of the Vatican: Power, Homosexuality, Hypocrisy (Bloomsbury Continuum, London, 2019), pp. 88, 89.

[307] Sandro Magister (Oct. 12, 2015), Thirteen Cardinals Have Written to the Pope. Here's the Letter, Chiesa.

[308] Alvaro de Juana (October 24, 2015), El Papa a Sínodo: Anunciemos el Evangelio y defendamos la familia ante ataques ideológicos, ACI Prensa.

[309] Andrea Gagliarducci (August 24, 2015), Sínodo: Once cardenales unen fuerzas para defender matrimonio y familia en nuevo libro, ACI Prensa.

"The eleven cardinals participating in this project are: **Carlo Caffarra**, Archbishop of Bologna (Italy); **Baselios Clemis**, President of the Catholic Bishops' Conference of India; **Joseph Cordes**, President Emeritus of the Pontifical Council Cor Unum; **Dominik Duka**, Archbishop of Prague (Czech Republic); **Willem Jacobus Eijk**, Archbishop of Utrectht (Netherlands); **Joachim Meisner**, Archbishop Emeritus of Cologne (Germany), **John Onaiyekan**, Archbishop of Abuja (Nigeria); **Antonio María Rouco Varela**, Archbishop Emeritus of Madrid (Spain); **Camillo Ruini**, Vicar Emeritus of the Diocese of Rome and former President of the Italian Episcopal Conference; **Robert Sarah**, Prefect of the Congregation for Divine Worship and the Discipline of the Sacraments; and **Jorge Urosa Savino**, Archbishop of Caracas (Venezuela)."[310]

The month after the Synod, Francis appointed Jozef De Kesel, the new archbishop of the principal see of Mechelen-Brussels. De Kesel is a well-known progressive archbishop and a protégé of Danneels, who would have insisted on his election.[311]

In late October, Cardinal Secretary of State Pietro Parolin announced that the pope would produce a document on the family.[312]

The post-synodal apostolic exhortation was entitled –as mentioned- Amoris Laetitia; and was published on April 8, 2016.

It was very well received by most Catholics.[313] But other Church circles rejected some ideas that seemed liberal on family and other issues.[314] There was a guide to reading the document,[315] and those who supported the content of the document came to its defense.[316]

Richard A. Spinello of *Crisis Magazine*, aptly wrote, "*Amoris Laetitia* is an ambiguous document, so it is sometimes difficult to discern what Pope Francis is really trying to accomplish."[317]

This is indeed the case. An ambiguity that was born long before his pontificate, in order to embrace everyone as much as possible.

---

[310] Ibid.

[311] Jeanne Smits (Nov. 6, 2015), Pope appoints well-known 'progressive' protégé of Cardinal Danneels to major see of Brusels, LifeSiteNews.

[312] Alvaro de Juana (October 29, 2015), Secretario de Estado Vaticano: Papa Francisco hará un documento sobre la familia, ACI Prensa.

[313] Andrea Tornielli (June 13, 2016), Fernández: "El pueblo de Dios ha recibido bien 'Amoris laetitia'," Vatican Insider.

[314] (April 8, 2016), Catholics cannot accept elements of Apostolic Exhortation that threaten faith and family, Voice of the Family; Crux Staff (April 11, 2016), Two views on what 'Amoris Laetitia' really means, Crux; Fr. Brian W. Harrison, O.S. (April 13, 2016), Priest: Pope Francis' pastoral revolution goes against 2,000 years of tradition, LifeSiteNews; Edward Pentin (April 18, 2016), EWTN's 'World Over' Panel Highlights Concerns Over 'Amoris Laetitia', National Catholic Register; E. Christian Brugger (April 22, 2016), Five Serious Problems with Chapter 8 of Amoris Laetitia, The Catholic World Report.

[315] (April 8, 2016), 9 keys to reading the Pope's exhortation Amoris Laetitia on love in the family, ACI Prensa.

[316] James Martin S.J. (April 13, 2016), What Some Critics of 'Amoris Laetitia' Are Missing, America; Néstor Martínez (April 19, 2016), Lo que no dice "Amoris Lactitia", cap. VIII, pero parece decir, InfoCatólica.

[317] Richard A. Spinello (May 10, 2016), Does Amoris Laetitia Retreat from Absolute Moral Norms, Crisis Magazine.

Cardinal Raymond Leo Burke indicated that the exhortation is a revolution in the Church's teaching since it is not magisterial by definition, and therefore has no authority to change its teaching or practice.[318]

Although the apostolic exhortation pronounces itself against same-sex marriages,[319] explains in turn:

"We need to acknowledge the great variety of family situations that can offer a certain stability, but de facto or same-sex unions, for example, may not simply be equated with marriage."[320]

In other words, although homosexual unions cannot be equated to the marriage bond, such unions, which are described as "the great variety of family situations," "can offer a certain stability." This is the same position that Pope Francis took in Argentina on homosexual unions: it sanctions them but not in a marriage bond.

On his return from his trip to Lesbos in mid-April 2016, someone asked the pope a question, where we reproduce the query and the answer:

"Question: After the questions on immigration, one on the apostolic exhortation Amoris Laetitia: some say that nothing has changed with regard to the rules on access to the sacraments for the divorced and civilly remarried, and that the law, pastoral praxis and obviously the doctrine remain the same; then there are those who say that much has changed and that there are many new openings and possibilities. Are there new concrete possibilities that did not exist before the publication of the exhortation, or not?

"Pope Francis: "I could say 'yes', but it would be too brief an answer. I recommend to you to read the presentation by Cardinal Schönborn, who is a great theologian. He is a member of the Congregation for the Doctrine of the Faith and he knows the doctrine of the Church well. In that presentation your question will be answered"."[321]

Schönborn quotes the Pope's words in stressing that, "It is about integrating everyone," since everyone needs mercy. It is about a love that excludes no one; where "the various situations of life have been simply accepted, without judging or condemning them immediately." As for the divorced and others, such as gays - according to the exhortation - Schönborn writes that there is "profound respect before each person who is never, in the first place, a "problematic case," a "category," but an unmistakable human being, with his history and his journey with and towards God."[322] After quoting Romans 11:32 under a contemporary interpretation with the intention to include every human being, he wrote:

---

[318] John Jalsevac (April 11, 2016), Cardinal Burke's puzzling response to the pope's exhortation... makes perfect sense, LifeSiteNews.

[319] Pope Francis, Amoris Laetitia: Post-Synodal Apostolic Exhortation on Love in the Family (Vatican Press, March 2016), p. 41.

[320] Ibid., pp. 41, 42.

[321] (April 18, 2016), Conversation with the Pope on return flight from Lesbos, Sala Stampa Della Santa Sede, p. 3.

[322] (April 8, 2016), Conferenza Stampa per la presentazione dell'Esortazione Apostolica post-sinodale del Santo Padre Francesco "Amoris laetitia," sull'amore nella famiglia, BO241.

"Obviously, this continuous principle of "inclusion" worries some. Does it not speak here in favor of relativism? Does it not turn the much-evoked mercy into permissiveness? Is there no more clarity about the limits that must not be exceeded, about situations that are objectively defined as irregular, as sinful? Does this exhortation not favor a certain laxity, an "anything goes"? Is not Jesus' own mercy, on the other hand, often a severe, demanding mercy?

"To clarify this Pope Francis leaves no doubt about his intentions and our task:

"Christians cannot renounce proposing marriage in order not to contradict current sensibilities, to be fashionable, or out of feelings of inferiority in the face of moral and human disaster. We would be depriving the world of the values that we can and should contribute. It is true that it does not make sense to remain in a rhetorical denunciation of current evils as if that could change anything. Nor is it useful to try to impose norms by force of authority. It is up to us to make a more responsible and generous effort, which consists in presenting the reasons and motivations for opting for marriage and the family so that people will be better disposed to respond to the grace that God offers them" (AL 35).[323]

In other words, although same-sex unions are not accepted, or communion to the divorced in different cases, all are included simply because we are on the same path to repentance for "the Lord".

It is simply an idea to admit everyone, "without" changing the dogmas of the Church. CNN said that what the pope is saying to the Church is, "be more accepting of gays and lesbians, divorced Catholics and other people living in what the church considers "irregular" situations."[324]

In May 2016, Pope Francis said he would propose a commission to study women's access to the diaconate, which would supposedly allow them to perform baptisms, marriages or administer the anointing of the sick and proclaim the Gospel; and preach and hold positions of responsibility in clerical structures.[325]

At the end of 2013, the Pope commented during an interview with *La Civiltà Cattolica* that, "The Virgin Mary was more important than the Apostles, the bishops, the deacons, and the priests. **Women, in the Church, are more important than bishops and priests; the how is what we must try to explain better**."[326]

When returning from his trip to Armenia in June, the pope told journalists that Christians should apologize to gays for having been offended and exploited by the church; this is supported by the Catechism: that they should not be discriminated against and should be respected and accompanied pastorally.[327]

---

[323] Ibid.

[324] Richard Allen Greene (April 8, 2016), Pope to church: Be more accepting of divorced Catholics, gays and lesbians, CNN.

[325] (May 12, 2016), El Papa Francisco propondrá una comisión para estudiar el acceso de las mujeres al diaconado, ABC España.

[326] Ibid. Note: bold is from the original.

[327] Delia Gallagher and Daniel Burke (June 27, 2016), Pope says Christians should apologize to gay people, CNN.

But while in Poland in late July, he lamented to the bishops that children are being taught in school that they can change their gender. He said it is an ideological colonization backed by very influential countries, adding that this is the age of sin.[328]

When he visited Georgia Sept. 30-Oct. 2, he said the world today is at war with marriage; and he urged couples to fight modern threats to the sacrament, such as gender ideology.[329]

In October, he appointed new cardinals of progressive tendencies.[330]

But in November, in an ambiguous statement, he said that women will never enter the priesthood.[331]

However, on November 18, while returning from his visit to Azerbaijan, he told the *Avvenire* newspaper regarding the critics of Amoris Laetitia (Brandmüller, Burke, Cafarra, Meisner, etc.) who threatened to request a formal act of correction of a serious error,[332] that they suffer from "a certain legalism, which can be ideological." He added, "Some- think about the responses to *Amoris Laetitia*- continue to not understand."[333]

But the U.S. Cardinal Raymond Burke, who leads the plot against the Pope and is an open supporter of Donald Trump, induced the forced suspension by the Pope of the previous two days of meetings with the members of the College of Cardinals arriving in Rome for the Consistory of Cardinals, which ended on November 17. This rebellion was aggravated by the most conservative sectors of the Catholic Church, and it was said that there would surely be new episodes of aggression against Pope Francis with serious repercussions.[334]

The aim is to create a climate of permanent instability around the pope - to isolate him - to increase the idea both inside and outside the Church that the pope is in error and heresy.[335] That is why three new U.S. cardinals condemned the polarization and division in the Church itself.[336]

Cardinal Raymond Burke gave Francis an ultimatum, indicating that if he did not respond to the five "dubia" on the exhortation "Amoris Laetitia," he would proceed

[328] Associated Press (Aug. 2, 2016), Pope complains schools are telling children they can choose their gender, The Guardian.

[329] Elise Harris (Oct. 1, 2016), Pope in Georgia blasts gender theory as the 'great enemy' of marriage, CNA/EWTN News.

[330] Staff Reporter (Oct. 10, 2016), Women priests, politics and Communion: what the Pope's new cardinals believe, Catholic Herald.

[331] Stephanie Kirchgaessner (November 1, 2016), Pope Francis says women will never be Roman Catholic priests, The Guardian.

[332] Valeria Perasso (Nov. 15, 2016), Los cardenales rebeldes del Vaticano que acusan al papa Francisco de hereje, BBC; Joshua J. McElwee (July 22, 2016), Signers of document critiquing 'Amoris Laetitia' revealed, National Catholic Register; Edward Pentin (Nov. 15, 2016), Cardinal Burke on Amoris Laetitia Dubia: 'Tremendous Division' Warrants Action, National Catholic Register.

[333] Inés San Martín (Nov. 18, 2016), Pope fires back at his critics over 'Amoris' and discusses ecumenism, Crux Catholic Media.

[334] Julio Algañaraz (November 18, 2016), El cardenal que elogia a Trump y lidera la conspiración contra el Papa, Clarín.

[335] Ibid.

[336] Michael O'Loughlin (Nov. 20, 2016), New U.S. Cardinals Condemn Polarization and Division inside the Church, America.

with a "formal correction" to the pope after the Christmas holidays.[337] However, most U.S. bishops are more positive about Amoris Laetitia.[338]

Francis also faces the confusion caused by "Misericordia et Misera," for granting pardon to women who have had abortions.[339]

Monsignor Fisichella, the president of the Pontifical Council for the New Evangelization, said during his presentation of Pope Francis' apostolic letter, Misericordia et Misera, that canon law on abortion would change; guaranteeing absolution of that sin by the bishop in some instances.[340]

But Francis would have problems with others, and in this case with the Sovereign Order of Malta. On December 22, Francis appointed a five-member commission to investigate the expulsion of Albrecht von Boeselager over an alleged condom scandal, and others.[341] The *Associated Press* reported two days later that the Order of Malta indicated that the replacement of its chancellor was an "act of internal governmental administration of the Sovereign Order of Malta and consequently falls solely within its competence."[342]

In early January 2017, the Grand Master of the Order of Malta, Matthew Festing, pledged allegiance to Pope Francis amid the investigation.[343]

However, in that month, the Order communicated that they would not collaborate at all with the commission, which they described as "legally 'irrelevant.'"[344]

The Spanish newspaper *El Confidencial* summarizes the polemical tendency of Pope Francis in these words:

"A Pope who attracts the **sympathies of Pablo Iglesias** and **Michael Moore**, who finds the speech of former Uruguayan president and ex-guerrilla **Francisco Mújica inspiring**, who is **flattered daily** by atheist intellectuals, who admits "never having been a right-winger" and adds that "it is the communists who **think like Christians**." A Pope who opens the door of the Church to **divorcees and homosexuals**, who receives **in audience** transsexuals and prostitutes, and who allows any parish priest to absolve anyone who aborts. A "pro-green Pope," some people in Spain caricature him. A "**Peronist Pope**," they respond in Argentina."[345]

Roberto de Mattei, director of the magazine *Raíces Cristianas*, who was expelled from Vatican Radio in 2014 for making public his displeasure with Pope Francis from

[337] Andrea Tornielli (Dec. 21, 2016), "Amoris Laetitia": Burke's ultimatum to Francis, Vatican Insider.
[338] Catholic News Service (Sept. 28, 2016), Amoris Laetitia will inspire new 'comprehensive plan for marriage and family life,' say US bishops, Catholic Herald.
[339] Ed Condon (Nov. 22, 2016), The Pope's abortion comments have provoked confusion. The Curia could have avoided this, The Catholic Herald.
[340] Iacopo Scaramuzzi (Nov. 21, 2016), Canon law on abortion is going to change, says Fisichella, Vatican Insider.
[341] Nicole Winfield (Dec. 22, 2016), Pope investigates departure of Order of Malta hierarch, 20 Minutes.
[342] Nicole Winfield (Dec. 24, 2016), Knights of Malta to pope: Stay out of our internal affairs, Associated Press.
[343] Staff Reporter (Jan. 2, 2017), Order of Malta leader professes loyalty to Pope Francis amid Vatican investigation, Catholic Herald.
[344] Associated Press (Jan. 11, 2017), Knights of Malta refuse to assist 'irrelevant' Vatican investigation, Catholic Herald.
[345] Ángel Villarino (December 4, 2016), Católicos contra el Papa: "Lo que hace Bergoglio es muy preocupante," El Confidencial.

the beginning, has pointed out that, "I believe that since the time of the Council, there has not been a Pope who has had such a wide level of criticism."[346] He has also expressed:

"We are in a situation where bishops attack bishops, priests attack priests. Bergoglio even **calls into question the 10 commandments**. We cannot admit this because if morality tolerates exceptions, it collapses. The moral law is either absolute or it is not, especially on such serious matters as abortion, euthanasia, etc. We are living in very confusing times in the Church and there is going to be an explosion in Christianity. In Rome, the atmosphere is more intense than in Spain and the boiling is very evident. It is a question of time. I don't think we should declare ourselves in disobedience, but if we want to avoid a religious civil war, we must fraternally correct the Pope."[347]

Criticism is coming not only from Spain but also from other parts of the world.[348]

With news such as the following: Bishop John E. Stowe of Lexington, Kentucky, longs for the U.S. Conference of Catholic Bishops to take seriously the priorities of Pope Francis; such as those outlined in Laudato Si, Amoris Laetitia, and Fratelli Tutti.[349]

Cardinal Robert W. McElroy of San Diego supports the inclusion of the LGBT community, women, and others in the Catholic Church. He indicated that the question of women's ordination to the priesthood would be one of the issues confronting the 2023 and 2024 synods.[350]

A very decisive step taken by Francis was when, on December 18, 2023, he approved through the Dicastery for the Doctrine of the Faith, the permission for priests to bless same-sex relationships, even if it does not include marriage.[351] Although he had already said in October that the Church still considered homosexual relationships "objectively sinful," so it would not recognize marriage between them.[352]

On the Independent State of Croatia

In February 2015, Ms. Dragana Tomasevic, the director of the Jasenovac and Holocaust Memorial Foundation, an important UK-registered charity, together with Professor Srboljub Zivanovic, President of The International Commission for the Truth on Jasenovac, sent letters to Pope Francis.[353]

---

[346] Ibid.

[347] Ibid.

[348] Ibid.

[349] Kevin Clarke (Nov. 22, 2022), Interview: Bishop Stowe wants the USCCB to take Pope Francis' priorities seriously, America Magazine.

[350] Robert W. McElroy (January 24, 2023), Cardinal McElroy on 'radical inclusion' for L.G.B.T. people, women and others in the Catholic Church, America Magazine.

[351] Jason Horowitz (Dec. 18, 2023), Francis allows priests to bless same-sex relationships, The New York Times.

[352] Christy Cooney (Oct. 3, 2023), Bendecidas quizás, pero aún pecaminosas: la declaración del Papa sobre la postura de la Iglesia respecto a las parejas del mismo sexo, BBC News.

[353] Tomasevic, Dragana, Director of the Jasenovac and Holocaust Memorial Foundation. Letter to Francis, Pope, His Holiness. February 26, 2015; Zivanovic, Prof Srboljub, President of The International Commission for the Truth on Jasenovac. Letter to Pope Francis 1°, His Holiness. February 26, 2015.

The letters briefly point to the tragic events in Croatia during World War II that we have already referred to in this book. As we saw, under the leadership of Ante Pavelić and the complicity of the Croatian Catholic Church, hundreds of thousands of Serbs, along with tens of thousands of Jews and Gypsies, died under the most gruesome massacres. Among those responsible mentioned in the letters are Ante Pavelić, priest Miroslav Filipović-Majstorović, and the Primate of Zagreb, Archbishop Alojzije Stepinac.

Zivanovic wrote to Francis that it would be good if he could visit Jasenovac and Donja Gradina. That he could promote "an operation of justice and forgiveness between Catholics and Orthodox in the Balkans."[354]

Dragana Tomasevic further wrote to him that she has a dream that a Memorial Center with a library, research facilities, a church, a synagogue, and a place of Gypsy worship could be erected. "A real protection to prevent the river Sava from flooding the mass graves and from digging its banks, swallowing skeletons," Tomasevic wrote.[355]

The construction of that center is to bring Catholics and Orthodox a little closer together and, therefore, under a vision of reconciliation, and forgiveness, but not to forget the 110,000 innocent children killed there.[356]

Pope Francis did not respond to the senders. But in January 2016, he opened a Catholic-Orthodox commission to investigate Stepinac's case, which ultimately disagreed on its conclusions upon completion of its task in 2017.

For Francis, who was considering Stepinac's canonization, he is a saint.

Mrs. Tomasevic told me that she sees the possibility of such a commission being formed by Francis as a consequence of the letters already mentioned.

Superstar pope

Politico Magazine on September 4, 2014, named Pope Francis as the number 6 leader on its "The Politico 50" list and listed him as "Washington's Favorite Populist."[357]

Also in December 2013, while Obama was drafting a major speech, he sent it back to his writer, requesting the inclusion of a quote from Pope Francis related to the economy.[358]

Eric Frattini reminds us:

"In December 2013, major international newspapers and magazines were naming Francis "Person of the Year." Forbes magazine and other bibles of capitalism included him among the most influential people on the planet."[359]

---

[354] Zivanovic, Prof Srboljub, President of The International Commission for the Truth on Jasenovac. Letter to Pope Francis 1°, His Holiness. February 26, 2015, p. 4.

[355] Tomasevic, Dragana, Director of the Jasenovac and Holocaust Memorial Foundation. Letter to Francis, Pope, His Holiness. February 26, 2015, p. 2.

[356] Ibid.

[357] Michael O'Loughlin (September 4, 2014), Pope Francis ranked among Washington's political elite, Crux Catholic Media.

[358] Ibid.

[359] Eric Frattini, El Libro Negro del Vaticano: Las oscuras relaciones entre la CIA y la Santa Sede (Espasa, Barcelona, 2016), ob. cit.

338

On December 11, 2014, the Pew Research Center released a statistical report communicating that the pope's image was positive in most parts of the world.[360]

Another report on March 13, 2015, explained that his popularity extended beyond Catholics in the United States.[361] Quinnipiac University, released a poll on September 3 of that year, indicating that 66% of Americans had a favorable or very favorable opinion of the pope.[362] His impending visit to the United States further boosted his popularity among Americans, according to a September 17 report.[363] *The New York Times* reported on September 23 that month that when the pope speaks, millions listen to him-whether Muslim or Baptist, Hindu or atheist.[364] Four days later, *Business Insider* reported that the pope was very popular because: 1. He is the people's pope. 2. He accepts people that the Church has silenced. 3. He goes to people who want to communicate with him and from any social stratum. He is reconciling science with the Catholic Church. 5. He loves soccer. 6. He is aware of his power, which he uses to ameliorate tense political situations and ongoing conflicts. 7. He does not shy away from selfies.[365]

The pope's Jesuit ideals have been clear during his tenure as the new bishop of Rome.[366] His personality has attracted American and other celebrities (due to the aforementioned inclusion, and others): Kerry Washington, Mark Wahlberg, Jim Gaffigan, Russell Crowe, Chris Rock, Susan Sarandon, Martin Sheen, Jane Fonda, Maria Shriver, Oprah Winfrey,[367] Angelina Jolie, Lionel Messi, Joseph Fiennes, Eva Longoria, Tim Cook, Leonardo DiCaprio,[368] Josh Duhamel, Leah Remini, Bill Maher (atheist), Nicole Polizzi, Jennifer Hudson, Gloria Stefan, Harry Connick Jr,[369] Larry King, Jim Carey, Elton John, Patti Smith, Jon Stewart, Jimmy Kimmel,[370] Maria Shriver,[371] George Clooney, Richard Gere, Salma Hayek,[372] Ruppert Murdoch, Viggo Mortensen, Diego Maradona,[373] Madonna, Teresa Giudice, Matt Lauer, Savannah Guthrie, Sandra Lee.[374] He is also famous among Internet celebrities.[375]

---

[360] (Dec. 11, 2014), Pope Francis' Image Positive in Much of World, PewResearchCenter.

[361] David Masci (March 13, 2015), Pope Francis' popularity extends beyond Catholics, Pew Research Center.

[362] Tanya Basu (September 3, 2015), Here's What America Thinks of Pope Francis, Time Magazine.

[363] Rachel Zoll (Sept. 17, 2015), Popular Pope Francis Has Revived, Ruffled U.S. Catholic Church, NBC New York; see also Michael S. Rosenwald, Michelle Boorstein and Scott Clement (Sept. 20, 2015), Poll: Americans widely admire Pope Francis, but his chuch less so, The Washington Post.

[364] Vivian Yee (September 23, 2015), Pope Francis' Popularity Bridges Great Divides, The New York Times.

[365] Barbara Tash (September 27, 2015), 7 reasons why the pope is so popular, Business Insider.

[366] Luis Badilla (Oct. 10, 2015), Francisco, "jesuita y latinoamericano"… está bien, pero…, Vatican Insider.

[367] THR Staff (Sept. 26, 2015), Celebrities Who Support Pope Francis, The Hollywood Reporter.

[368] Paul Asay (March 21, 2016), A-list celebrities line up to meet the Pope, For Her.

[369] Mike Vulpo (September 22, 2015), Pope Francis Comes to America: Oprah Winfrey, Angelina Jolie and More Fans of the Religious Leader, ENews.

[370] (September 25, 2015), Pope Francis' biggest celebrity fans, NY Daily News.

[371] Shilpa Bansal (December 17, 2015), Pope Francis 79th birthday: What celebrity fans have to say about His Holiness, International Business Times-India.

[372] Thomas D. Williams, Ph. D. (May 30, 2016), Pope Awards Medals to Celebrities George Clooney, Richard Gere, Salma Hayek, Breitbart.

[373] Madeleine Teahan (June 11, 2014), Meet the Pope's unlikely celebrity fans, Catholic Herald.

[374] Kathy Ehrich Dowd (September 25, 2015), Madonna! Kerry Washington! Donald Trump?! Celebs Go Ga-Ga for Pope Francis in N.Y.C., People Magazine.

In terms of faith, he has won admirers from Methodism, Mormonism, atheism, and agnosticism.[376]

In May 2013, he said that atheists are good if they do good.[377]

"Representatives of atheist organizations noted that Pope Francis made a historic approach that will help break down very old barriers after the Pontiff said that God redeems non-believers."[378]

The following were the pope's words:

"The Lord redeemed all of us, all of us, with the Blood of Christ; all of us, not just Catholics. All of us," the Pope said at morning Mass last Wednesday.

"'Father, what about the atheists?' Even the atheists - all of them!" he said.
"Francis continued, "We must come together in doing good. 'But I do not believe, Father, I am an atheist!' But do good: we will gather there."[379]

The Vatican later explained that Francis was referring to the fact that Christ also died for atheists and that they can be saved if they repent.[380] Nevertheless, the seed was sown.

The *Times* magazine chose him as Man of the Year in 2013.[381]

The Pope has received atheists and agnostics at the Vatican, who feel very comfortable with him.[382]

He has been able to take advantage of the Internet and social networks to communicate his message more broadly.

For example, on January 15, 2016, Eric Schmidt, executive chairman of Google's parent company Alphabet, held a private meeting with Pope Francis. The two discussed a common project as they greeted each other.[383] Schmidt was accompanied by Tim Cook, Apple's executive chairman.[384]

Also, on February 26, Francis held a meeting with Instagram CEO Kevin Systrom. The two discussed the power of images.[385]

On August 29, the pope met with Facebook CEO Mark Zuckerberg. Zuckerberg told the pope he hoped to help spread his message of mercy and tenderness. The two talked about "how communications technology can be used to alleviate poverty, encourage a culture of encounter, and help deliver a message of hope, especially to the most

---

[375] Rosie Scammell, Religion News Service (May 30, 2016), Pope Francis ells Internet celebrities to take 'path of optimism and hope', The Catholic Register.
[376] Jessica Ravitz (Sept. 15, 2015), The Pope: Not just for Catholics anymore, CNN.
[377] (May 22, 2013), Los ateos son buenos si hacen el bien, dice el Papa Francisco, Reuters.
[378] Dan Merica (May 26, 2013), papa Francisco 'abre las puertas del cielo' para los ateos, Expansión.
[379] Ibid.
[380] Ibid.
[381] Lizzi Davis (December 11, 2013), Pope Francis is Time Magazine Person of the Year, The Guardian.
[382] Juan Arias (May 14, 2015), Does Francis sympathize with Christian atheism, El País.
[383] James Eng (Jan. 15, 2016), Google's Eric Schmidt Meets With Pope Francis at the Vatican, NBC News.
[384] Bill Murphy Jr. (Jan. 26, 2016), Wait, Why are Apple and Google Execs Meeting With the Pope, Inc.
[385] Olivier Laurent (February 26, 2016), Pope Francis Met With Instagram CEO to Discuss Power of Images, Time Magazine.

disadvantaged people."[386] The pope now has millions of followers on his Facebook and Twitter accounts.

"The Francis effect," as he is known around the world, is due to the legend he is creating for his "honesty and simplicity," such as: carrying his own suitcase, refusing to live in the papal palace; and preferring to live in a simple hostel.[387] Not wearing the red shoes and wearing his own black ones. By telephoning personally, skipping protocol on several occasions. He wants "a poor Church, for the poor." "It's not the institution that counts, it's the mission." He is a Jesuit pope, determined to win the game of the Church's mission.

He has criticized excessive capitalism, where the employee is seen as a mere tool to create income; criticizing the "slave labor" of a global economic order that worships "an idol called money." An "unbridled capitalism" with an attitude of throwing away everything from unwanted food to unwanted old people.

Sarah Palin said he was a "kind of liberal." His campaign against corruption could put him in the eye of the Italian mafia.

But as the Jesuit Malachi Martin wrote about the successor to the "Slavic pope" - fulfilling himself in Benedict XVI:

"For the true role of the Church, Maestroianni now understood, was as one player in a vaster evolution—a vaster Process—than the Slavic Pope seemed able to encompass. A vast Process, and a very natural one, that recognized the fact that all the woes of the human family were caused in the first place not by some primitive notion called Original Sin, but by poverty and want and ineducation. A Process that would at last clear humanity of those troubles, and so would ultimately harmonize the spirit of man, God and the cosmos. When the Process was fully accomplished in the new political order of mankind, then would the Church be one with the world. For only then would the Church take its proud and rightful place as part of the human heritage. As a stabilizing factor in the New World Order. As a true and bright mirror of the untroubled mind of God.

[…]

On the other hand, once Maestroianni had himself reached the maximum of his power as Vatican Secretary of State, he had used the entire administrative machinery of the Roman Church's organization to forge its greater alignment with the Process. Nothing went out trom the papal desk that did not pass through the Cardinal Secretary's office."[388]

---

[386] Junno Arocho Esteves (Aug. 29, 2016), Pope meets with Facebook founder Mark Zuckerberg, Catholics News Service.

[387] Jonathan Freedland (November 15, 2013), Why even atheists shpould be praying for Pope Francis, The Guardian. Note: unless otherwise noted, this is the same source.

[388] Malachi Martin, Windswept House: A Vatican Novel (Broadway Books, New York, 1996), pp. 77, 78.

CHAPTER

10

Pope Francis and Freemasonry

A Mason pope, very well received by freemasons

As we saw in a previous chapter, Giacomo Galeazzi and Ferruccio Pinotti, Italian journalists, reported that various sources have suggested and affirmed that behind the revolutionary events in the Vatican since the resignation of Pope Benedict XVI, there is the hand of the lodges. Moreover, in the corridors of the Sacred Apostolic Palaces, it was rumored that the election of the new pontiff was the work of the Freemasons.[1]

The journalists also expressed that after a closing pontificate like that of Ratzinger, it is probable that many of the affiliates hoped to revive the old sympathy between the Society of Jesus and the Masons thanks to the Jesuit Jorge Mario Bergoglio.[2] This can also be said of other sectors of the Church in general.

Fabio Venzi, the Grand Master of the Regular Grand Lodge of Italy, said that within his Masonic obedience, the only one recognized by the Grand Lodge of England, there are many Catholic priests. Venzi has been opening a front of dialogue with exponents of the Vatican. And he admits that "relations between the Church and Freemasonry remain unchanged. Formally there is no great openness on the part of the Church. However, it should be noted that we have several Catholic priests within us."[3]

During an interview with the Italian journalist Ferruccio Pinotti, the former Grand Master of the Grand Orient of Italy, Giuliano di Bernardo, said of the rapprochement between the Jesuits and the Masons:

"The mention of the role of the Jesuits allows me a small digression: are there really "approximations" between the Jesuits and Freemasonry? Any concordance?

Di Bernardo lights up: "There are always concordances, from above. At a certain level, there have always been, in secret. When we speak of this secret thread, we speak of a subtle, profound dialogue that exists between people of quality. It is these convergences that avoid - in case of crisis or conflict - the greatest damage, irreparable situations. It is clear that, at the base of the pyramid, there are the priest and the mason who behave like Don Camillo and Peppone. But the summits, being enlightened summits, always touch each other."[4]

For his part, from Argentina -the homeland of Pope Francis-, the then Grand Master of Argentine Freemasonry, Nicolás Orlando Breglia, said in July 2017 in an interview with Ignacio Villanueva's "Ayer y Hoy":

---

[1] Giacomo Galeazzi, Ferruccio Pinotti, Vaticano Massone: Logge, denaro e poteri occulti: il lato segreto della Chiesa di papa Francesco (Piemme, 2014), ob. cit.
[2] Ibid.
[3] Ibid.
[4] Ferruccio Pinotti, Fratelli d'Italia (BUR Biblioteca Univerzale Rizzoli, 2007), ob. cit.

"Here there is a sector of the Church where there is a great tolerance for Freemasonry, which is the Jesuits. And why do the Jesuits have a greater...? Because the Jesuits were born at the same time that modern Freemasonry was born. And they are influenced by the Enlightenment and rationalism.

It is the most rational part of the Church."[5]

Asked how he defined the Church at that time with Pope Francis, Breglia responded:

"There has been an exponential change [...] Very good. The Pope has assumed, when he assumes, he says: "I am republican, secular, democratic, and anticlerical." These are the ideas that Freemasonry has supported for three hundred years. And if he assumes our ideas, we cannot be anything less than in favor of him. What we will guard is that they are fulfilled.

[...] He is anticlerical because he is against the use of faith to hold public office. That we also agree with. There has been a great renewal within the Church and it is adopting frankly progressive positions."[6]

He also added:

"[...] the lodge where I have been, there have been Catholic priests. What happens is that, since there is a very conservative and refractory sector of Freemasonry, when one enters a priest to the lodge, one has to do it with changed names."[7]

Angel Jorge Clavero, Grand Master of the Grand Lodge of Argentina of Free and Accepted Masons years ago, before Breglia, said in response to a query during an interview for *Época*, published at the end of March 2013:

"Is it important to you that the new Pope Francis belongs to the Jesuit order, an order that in its time was once a thinned-out one, and that for the first time, someone from the Jesuits has become pope?

"We await this with expectation because it is the first time that there is a Pope who belongs to the Jesuit Order, whose members are so learned, and we hope that they will modernize the Church a little, that is the expectation that everyone has.
Even though there is not a fluid relationship, those who are closer to an orientation like the one we have, within the clergy, are the Jesuits; they are the ones who are closer to Freemasonry, of course, saving the distances or the differences.
There have even been Jesuits who, with the permission of their priors or provincials, have belonged to Freemasonry. On the other hand, with 2000 years, the Church has become a bit bureaucratic, maybe there are new airs with this Pope. But we do not know how the Church works internally. Therefore we cannot give a certain opinion, we can see it from our point of view."[8]

---

[5] (July 7, 2017), Ayer y Hoy, Confirmando Entrevistas: https://www.youtube.com/watch?v=ggf2AI4y0dg; accessed April 19, 2023.
[6] Ibid.
[7] Ibid.
[8] Época Newspaper (March 31, 2013), Clavero: "La masonería lo que quiere es enseñar a pensar, ese es el fin último," Época Newspaper.

Angel Clavero, the Grand Master of the main Masonic lodge in Argentina, expressed his satisfaction:

"We welcome the election of an Argentine citizen to the papacy with great joy. There are those who think that Freemasonry is against the Church and in no way it is so; that is part of the myths of the collective unconscious."[9]

The official statement of the Masonic entity also reads:

"[...] the Grand Lodge of Argentina of Free and Accepted Masons, an institution rooted in our country since 1857, welcomes the appointment of the compatriot Cardinal Jorge Bergoglio as Pope Francis."

"A man of austere life and devoted to his devotions, the appointment of the new pontiff of the Catholic Church is a high recognition for the Argentine Nation."[10]

The Grand Master of the Regular Grand Lodge of Italy, Fabio Venzi, said:

"In 1972 Cardinal Franjo Seper, Ratzinger's predecessor in the congregation for the doctrine of the faith, tried to open up a little to the Masons by broadly interpreting the canonical code. The bishops' conference of South America - in South America, there is a large Masonic presence, perhaps the largest in the world - wrote to Cardinal Seper, who headed the congregation for the doctrine of the faith, to find out what to do. There was a practical problem: how should we behave with South American Catholics who are also Masons? Should we excommunicate them or not? It was a question that troubled half a million people, both Catholics and Freemasons. Seper invented a trick: all those Freemasons who are part of Freemasonries that conspire against the Church should be condemned. It was an important step, an intelligent opening."[11]

Before Jorge Mario Bergoglio was elected pope, *Il Giornale* reported that a long, detailed, and forceful speech delivered by a cardinal at the general congregations preceding the conclave astonished those present. This cardinal said that the question of Freemasonry had to be seriously confronted and possible infiltrators in the Vatican had to be found. He said, "The matter of Freemasons in the Vatican is getting too big." He indicated that this should be one of the first points to be addressed by the new pontiff.[12]

But Bergoglio would fight against anti-clerical Freemasonry. Take into account that the congratulations to Bergoglio by Freemasons from all over the world were overwhelming.

Next, let us now look at several messages of congratulations and support for Jorge Bergoglio after he was elected pope.

---

[9] Popular (April 18, 2013), Los masones también celebraron al Papa Francisco, Popular.
[10] Ibid.
[11] Giacomo Galeazzi, Ferruccio Pinotti, Vaticano Massone: Logge, denaro e poteri occulti: il lato segreto della Chiesa di papa Francesco (Piemme, 2014), ob. cit.
[12] Fabio Marchese Ragona (May 12, 2013), Quel patto con la massoneria è il nuovo mistero vaticano, il Giornale.

Freemason Nicola Spinello, Grand Master Vice Vicar of the Communion of Piazza del Gesù, said on March 20, 2013, to the question:

"What is the relationship between Jesuits and Freemasonry? I believe that Jesuits and Freemasonry have always had a great mutual speculative interest..."[13]

And added to the question: "The pope is Argentinean, and in Argentina, there is a great Masonic tradition; he was archbishop of Buenos Aires. Do you think he may have had relations with Freemasonry?"

Spinelli replied: "I would be amazed at the exact opposite: if he hadn't had them. The Masonic tradition in Argentina is very powerful..."[14]

Finally, Spinelli indicated: "I believe that this pope is the realization of a design that has been wanted to be adopted for a long time...."[15]

Also, after Bergoglio's election, the Grand Master of the GOI (Grand Orient of Italy), Gustavo Raffi, wrote:

"With Pope Francis, nothing will ever be the same again. A clear choice of fraternity for a Church in dialogue, uncontaminated by the logic and temptations of temporal power. [...]
We hope that the pontificate of Francis, the pope who 'comes from the end of the world,' can mark the return of the Church-Word with respect to the Church-institution, promoting an open dialogue with the contemporary world, with believers and non-believers, according to the springtime of the Second Vatican Council."[16]

On the 15th, the website of the Virtual Grand Lodge of Italy (*GLVDI*) published a statement originally from the 13th, by Grand Master Luciano Nistri regarding the election of Bergoglio:

"The Catholic Church has chosen as Pope the Jesuit Jorge Mario Bergoglio who assumed the name of Francis. A clear-cut choice, away from the logic of the Roman Curia and of the temporal power. From the first moment on, Pope Francis, a man who comes "nearly from the end of the world," rejecting the ermine robe and gold cross and replacing it with an iron cross, made his first tangible act. In his first words of greeting he fostered a desire for dialogue with the world and with mankind, nurturing the vivid hope for laymen and nonbelievers that change is underway. Maybe this is really what the world expects and what it expected. A new Church that knows how to reconnect love with truth in a confrontation among institutions not entrenched in the defense of their own power. It is that same hope for which the world — and especially Latin America, where the Masons Simon Bolivar, Salvador Allende and the same Giuseppe Garibaldi [especially while in Brazil] among the many who have given liberty to those peoples — has always longed for.

---

[13] Ibid.

[14] Ibid.

[15] Ibid.

[16] Gustavo Raffi (March 14, 2013), Il Gran Maestro Raffi: "Con Papa Francesco nulla sarà più come prima. Chiara la scelta di fraternità per una Chiesa del dialogo, non contaminata dalle logiche e dalle tentazioni del potere temporale," Grande Oriente d'Italia.

"A message that Freemasonry itself perceives a sharp break with the past and one which is turned now to listening to the poor, the marginalized and the weakest. To the new Pontiff we send our best wishes for his good work for years to come. Luciano Nistri, Grand Master GLVDI."[17]

The Masonic site *Fenix News*, directed by Peruvian Mason Mario Rolleri 33° (Luis Heysen Inchaustegui Lodge, Lima, Peru), made public on the 15th a communiqué from the Grand Lodge of Lebanon. Rami Haddad, Grand Master, as well as the Sovereign Grand Commander Jamil Saade, congratulated Argentina and the Women's Grand Lodge of Argentina for the election of Bergoglio.[18]

Also, in April, the Canadian Masonic Bulletin, *The Watermark*, noted that despite the new pope's conservatism, they were confident that he would be willing to build a better relationship between Catholicism and Freemasonry.[19]

Gustavo Raffi, Grand Master of the GOI, on the occasion of the death of his friend Cardinal Tonini on July 28, 2013, referred regarding the pope:

"A great soul has left us. I mourn the friend, the man of dialogue even with the Masons, the master of the social gospel" [...].
Humanity is poorer today," Raffi continued, "and so is the Catholic Church. But that of Pope Francis is a Church that promises to be respectful of otherness and to share the idea that the secular State favors peace and the coexistence of different religions." Ersilio Tonini has passed the baton. We will always remember him [...] for having reminded us of the taste of life and for having taught us that it is good to love each other."[20]

Sergio Héctor Nunes, who was then Grand Master of the Grand Lodge of Argentina, said that the relationship between Freemasonry and the Catholic Church in the country is one of "coexistence." He said that Freemasons can profess the faith of their choice and affirmed that they share Bergoglio's position "on poverty, social asymmetries and the need to achieve equal opportunities for human beings."[21]

In the same month, the Master of the Lodge "Luz do Planalto" of Brazil, Derildo Martins Da Costa, also supported the image and actions of Pope Francis, of respect for humanity regardless of belief. [22]

---

[17] OnePeterFive (April 7, 2017), Why do the Freemasons Love Pope Francis?," OnePeterFive; citing GLVDI Notiziario - Notiziario Massonico Gran Loggia Virtuale d'Italia, R.S.A.A. Massoneria Italiana, Comunicato Post n° 159 published on 15 March 2013, http://blog.libero.it/GLVDI/11982726.html

[18] Ibid; quoting "United Grand Lodge of Lebanon greets the Grand Women's Lodge of Argentina on the election of the new Pope Francis," http://www.fenixnews.com/2013/03/15/gran-logia-unida-del-libano-saluda-a-la-gran-logia-femenina-de-argentina-por-eleccion-de-nuevo-papa-francisco/.

[19] Ibid; quoting "A New Pope - A New Relationship With the Roman Catholic Church?" in The Watermark - Canada's online Masonic Philatelic Newsletter, Vol. 3 - Issue 4 - April 2013, p. 3: http://bytown.ottawamasons.ca/Watermark%20April%202013.pdf

[20] Gustavo Raffi (July 28, 2013), Scomparsa card. Tonini: Gran Maestro Raffi, piango l'amico e l'uomo del dialogo con tutti, Grande Oriente d'Italia.

[21] Armando Maronese (August 10, 2013), Renacen con vigor las logias masónicas - Presidentes argentinos, Redacción digital.

[22] August 2013, of the Grande Oriente do Brasil, Stato dello "Espirito Santo" (GOB-ES); cited in OnePeterFive (April 7, 2017), Why do the Freemasons Love Pope Francis?," OnePeterFive.

The conservative site *OnePeterFive*, documented:

"In the issue 1-2 /2013 (on pages 65-66) of the magazine *L'Acacia* of the *Italian Grand Lodge* for the *Symbolic Rite*, the chief editor Moreno Neri hopes that Pope Francis, a Jesuit, can really reform the Church ("no one else but a Jesuit might be suitable to take up the challenge of the changes that await the Church"), and commends Cardinal Martini. The Mason Neri hopes that the Church is no longer a "closed and dusty system."[23]

Likewise, the Grand Master of the Grand Lodge of Italy, Gian Franco Pilloni, wrote an open letter to Pope Francis on September 9:

"Extremely moved and with great joy, I address Your Holiness to make a humble request to put an end to the divisions in the relationship between the Catholic Church and Freemasonry, in the hope that, finally, a just peace may reign between the two organizations, putting an end to the differences that still today raise a wall between our relationship."[24]

In a two-page letter, Pilloni wrote -we quote in extenso-, without the letterhead:

"The Grand Master

"To: Your Holiness
The Holy Father
FRANCISCO
Its Headquarters,
Rome

"It is with extreme emotion and infinite joy that I address Your Holiness to humbly ask you to strive to put an end to the divisions that exist in the relations between the Catholic Church and Freemasonry, in the hope that at last just serenity will reign between the two components, putting an end to the differences that still today raise a wall between the relations.

Holiness, allow me to tell you that we are not a component opposed to the Catholic Church that you worthily represent, quite the contrary. Our paths run parallel; in fact, we think like you in all the problems that afflict contemporary society, like you, we fight for a World of Peace and respect for the Human Being without distinction and absolute respect for all religions.

Your Holiness, the position that the Church has maintained and maintains, penalizes the Freemason Brethren of the Catholic Creed, forcing them to profess their faith outside the Church and making them feel almost like intruders or unwanted faithful. Your Holiness, I appeal to You, Man of extraordinary human qualities, to put an end to this injustice that for centuries has penalized millions of Freemasons scattered throughout the world, I remind You that Freemasons take an oath on the

---

[23] OnePeterFive (April 7, 2017), Why do the Freemasons Love Pope Francis, OnePeterFive.
[24] Gian Franco Pilloni (September 9, 2013), Il Serenissimo Gran Maestro della Gran Loggia d'Italia umsoi Gian Franco Pilloni, scrive una lettera a Papa Francesco, Notiziario Massonico Internazionale.

Holy Bible and in our Temples we work for the elevation of the spirit and the betterment of the individual.

Personally, I consider myself a good Christian, maintaining an excellent relationship with the Christian community of the village where I was born (Jerzu Prov. OG) and with the Diocese of Ogliastra itself, helping according to my possibilities, but from my heart, the Holy Catholic Church, the only eternal salvation.

I believe in the good of "Creation" through the way, the truth, and the life taught by Jesus in the Gospels, for this concept is so great, that if it were put into practice it would be the pearl of creation; I have tried with human fraternity to build an "OPUS CARITATIS" supported above all by Christian teaching; given the role I have the honor to play, many are the people I have met in the world with similar Christian prerogatives and true values of subsidiarity with objectives for the world social good, global peace, charity, (these noble and mysterious concepts, are not realized because they lack an initial charitable spark) after deep studies, working tables, I have found in this strong box closed by the world and kept deliberately well closed called "MASSONERIA."

The Grand Lodge of Italy u. m.s.o.i. (founded by Armando Corona) Recognized by the American Grand Lodges of which I am a member, as Grand Master I would like it to be a golden key to open a glimpse of true tangible collaboration with the Holy Roman Catholic Apostolic Church.

I ask Your Holiness for an effort to completely eliminate the outdated intolerance towards us, publicly, accepting me, as a result of my supplication, to You; to transform our "Temples" into Temples of Peace, places of encounters, places of testimony, of the highest and loftiest feelings of solidarity and human brotherhood and admirable example of exceptional abnegation to You; civic, religious, spiritual and cultural virtues chosen and tested, brought with the Roman Catholic Apostolic Faith (through our Baptism) by all of us.

I hope to hear from you, it would be for me a great honor and an infinite emotion to meet you and talk to you in person about the subject expressed here, consider me at your entire disposal for any eventuality.

"Magistral Headquarters of Cagliari, September 09, 2013."[25]

Again, GOI Grand Master Gustavo Raffi, during the celebrations of the Masonic obedience on the occasion of the recurrence of September 20 and the Fall Equinox, stated:

"Pope Francis launches messages of humanity that are in tune with what we have been saying for years. He also invites people to come out of the catacombs and not to withdraw but to witness among the different peoples to one's own values [sic], in speaking to society. The reflections should not be limited to today but should build the future. This is a living Masonry, talking to people [in a dialogue]."[26]

---

[25] Pilloni, Gian Franco, Grand Master, Grand Lodge of Italy. Letter to His Holiness, The Holy Father Francis. September 9, 2013.

[26] OnePeterFive (April 7, 2017), Why do the Freemasons Love Pope Francis, OnePeterFive; citing Erasmo notizie, Bollettino d'informazione del Grande Oriente d'Italia, Year XIV, Issue 17-18, 31 October 2013, p. 6.

Also, on an unspecified date but always in 2013, on the website of the *Southern Leyte Times* magazine, Mason Antonio M. Reyes wrote that the great Philippine national heroes are Freemasons and, contrary to the Catholic Church's official condemnation of Freemasonry, that he believed that with Pope Francis the situation would change; because even for the Pope, as well as for Freemasons, all religions and brotherhood associations of believers in God should not be condemned.[27]

Come 2014, on the occasion of the meeting of the Grand Lodge of Free and Accepted Masons of Florida, USA, Gilbert Weisman, the Grand Orator of the Grand Lodge, apart from quoting Mason Albert Pike, also mentioned some words from a homily of Pope Francis on January 1 of that year:

"As Pope Francis pointed out in his New Year's Day Service on January 1, 2014: 'We are all children of one Heavenly Father, we belong to the same Human Family, and we share a common destiny. This brings a responsibility for each to work, so that the world becomes a Community of Brothers who respect each other, accept each other in one's diversity, and take care of one another.' He could just as well be speaking to a body of Freemasons."[28]

Pierre-Alexandre Joye, a Freemason who wrote in the Swiss Masonic magazine *Alpina* in March 2014, pointed out that the Catholic Church and Freemasonry were based on different traditions, but with Pope Francis, the South American Jesuit, the Masonic-Catholic dialogue could be relaunched. He pointed out that the spiritual forces should not be divided, but united for social justice, human rights, and freedom. In short, he pointed out that the Catholic Church and Freemasonry should aspire to what unites them.[29]

Gustavo Raffi, in his last speech as Grand Master of the Grand Orient of Italy in April 2014, expressed:

"We observe with care and respect as this Pope is accelerating the timing of an epochal change within the horizon of structures traditionally reluctant to welcome the innovative ferment. And the reflections of his influence echo far beyond the borders of the sacristy. But it's also up to us. It's up to us to make the crossing of this liquid reality happen."[30]

Stefano Bisi became in 2014 the new Grand Master of the GOI, and said that Pope Francis was very open to novelties and his openness with the world, which created him hope for rapprochement.[31]

Also on August 25 of that year, the Freemason Barbosa Nunes, published for the Grand Orient of Brazil (GOB):

---

[27] Ibid; quoting http://www.southernleytetimes.com/No_way_to_treat_our_heroes.html

[28] OnePeterFive (April 28, 2017), Why do the Freemasons Love Pope Francis? Part II, OnePeterFive, note 26; citing http://grandlodgefl.com/archive_2014/grand_oration_2014.html.

[29] OnePeterFive (April 28, 2017), Why do the Freemasons Love Pope Francis? Part II, OnePeterFive.

[30] OnePeterFive (April 28, 2017), Why do the Freemasons Love Pope Francis? Part II, OnePeterFive; quoting Raffi, il "mondo liquido" e la missione della massoneria, in Erasmo notizie, bollettino del Grande Oriente d'Italia, year XV, number 7-8, 30 April 2014, Rome, p. 6.

[31] Ignazio Ingrao (April 3, 2014), "Farò come Papa Francesco: la promessa del nuovo Gran Maestro della Massoneria, Panorama.

"Jorge Mario Bergoglio, "Pope Francis," formerly titled for his social performance as "Cardinal of the Argentinean poor." He continues after assuming the highest representation of the Catholic Church and as head of state. He has not stopped, he is taking sure steps to build a new church. New style in the Vatican, an image of a personality who knows and faces the challenges ahead."[32]

For his part, on April 11, 2015, during a GOI celebration in Rimini, Mason Claudio Bonvecchio presented his book *L'ora del dialogo. Il Papa, la Chiesa, la Libera Muratoria - intervista di Sabatino Alfonso Annecchiarico* [The Hour of Dialogue. The Pope, the Church, Free Masonry - interview by Sabatino Alfonso Annecchiarico].[33] A synopsis of the work, which echoes the pope's message, tells us:

"Faith, reason, humanism, spirituality, pairs of concepts, values – they have diverged in the history of the Christian Church and secular culture. Especially now, with Pope Francis' impulse, the time of this misunderstanding seems to have ended. The Church of the people's pope returns to talking about feelings, but also about the rational confrontation with society and history. This book builds a bridge for the most delicate, but most profitable, confrontation. It is a possible document for a new alliance that has man as its object [a "cult of man"]. An initiative of a dialogue without discount on the side of a free, mature rationalism of the Masonic culture, but without foreclosure."[34]

Referring to Pope Francis' address to the U.S. Congress, Senior Director of St. John's Lodge No. 9 F. & A.M. of Seattle, U.S.A., Mason John Murray, wrote for the lodge's magazine in the October 2015 issue:

"I found the address to the joint session of Congress by Pope Francis very Masonic in nature. He spoke from a universal truth and understanding of God's love for the earth and humanity. His message was nonpartisan and nonsectarian. Pope Francis understands that, if we destroy mother earth, we destroy ourselves. He spoke directly to the leaders of the world about the interconnectedness of all life. He pleaded with us to foster and promote the common good of all mankind. Seems like a Masonic message to me."[35]

In mid-February 2016, Italian Cardinal Gianfranco Ravasi, President of the Pontifical Council for Culture, wrote in *Il Sole 24 Ore* a message entitled *Cari fratelli massoni* - "Dear Brother Masons"-, in which he called for a dialogue between the Catholic Church and that institution on common values, such as the sense of community, charity, the fight against materialism and the defense of human dignity.[36]

---

[32] Barbosa Nunes (August 25, 2014) A VERDADE NO PAPA FRANCISCO - Artigo de Barbosa Nunes para o Diário da Manhã, Grande Oriente do Brasil: https://www.gob.org.br/a-verdade-no-papa-francisco-artigo-de-barbosa-nunes-para-o-diario-da-manha/; accessed April 19, 2014.

[33] OnePeterFive (April 28, 2017), Why do the Freemasons Love Pope Francis? Part II, OnePeterFive, note 26; quoting http://www.agenparl.com/gran-loggia-2015-servizio-biblioteca-gli-appuntamenti/

[34] Ibid.

[35] OnePeterFive (May 11, 2017), Why do the Freemasons Love Pope Francis? Part III, OnePeterFive; citing http://seattlemasons.com/2015/1510_trstbd.pdf, p. 4.

[36] Gianfranco Ravasi (February 14, 2016), *Cari fratelli massoni, Il Sole 24 Ore, domenica*, p. 29.

He called for overcoming the attitudes of Catholic fundamentalist environments, asking "to go beyond hostility, insults and reciprocal prejudices."[37]

Days later, Stefano Bisi, the Grand Master of the GOI, wrote to the editor-in-chief of the magazine, where we quote the most significant excerpts, and where he mentions the pope:

"I have carefully read and appreciated the article that Cardinal Gianfranco Ravasi wrote in his authoritative periodical in the valuable cultural insert "Domenica" of February 14." [...]
I was pleased to know that, without prejudice and with the broad cultural vision that distinguishes him, he spoke of Freemasonry and, beyond the official and written positions of the Church, widely known, he recognized, without preconceived ideas, that between both realities there are also common values that unite, without ipso facto annulling those that are different visions and marked if not clear differences.
[...]
Universal Free Masonry is by its very nature neither a Religion nor a substitute for it, it has no dogmatic positions, and it does not propose salvific ways of the soul, but to be admitted it only asks the person to believe in a Supreme Being. We simply call him, without giving him specific attributes as in the Christian religion, the Great Architect of the Universe.
[...] to try to open a constructive dialogue in new and peaceful environments and full respect for different identities.
The Grand Orient of Italy has been trying for a long time to break down walls that now have no reason to exist. In my first celebration on September 20, I said that "my great dream was that one day a Pope and a Grand Master could attend together the anniversary of Porta Pia, putting an end to the secular dispute.
Freemasonry is not an enemy of the Church, of any Church, and has always been the House of Dialogue and Tolerance. It is not opposed to any religion and leaves its brethren the freedom to follow their faith. But times are changing and Humanity is threatened by great dangers: such as fundamentalist terrorism, the decline of values, and unbridled globalization. The greatness of secular, spiritual, and religious institutions, to which Man adheres in search of personal paths of improvement and elevation, lies in knowing how to face the delicate challenges by participating and sharing the needs and problems that arise. And it also lies in having the courage to go beyond "hostilities, outrages, prejudices, mutualisms," as in the case of the Church and Freemasonry."[38]

The Spanish Grand Lodge also declared itself in favor of Ravasi's brief, eagerly awaiting a dialogue.[39]

---

[37] Ibid.

[38] Stefano Bisi (February 21, 2016), Chiesa e Massoneria. Articolo "Cari fratelli massoni" del Cardinale Ravasi. Risponde il Gran Maestro, Grande Oriente d'Italia.

[39] VN (April 8, 2016), "La mitad de los masones españoles son católicos," Vida Nueva Digital: https://www.vidanuevadigital.com/2016/04/08/la-mitad-de-los-masones-espanoles-son-catolicos-gianfranco-ravasi-gran-logia-de-espana/; accessed April 18, 2023.

Catholic Church and Freemasonry during Francis' papacy

A Jesuit, the bishop of the Diocese of Lomas de Zamora, Jorge Rubén Lugones, and close to Pope Francis, sent his congratulations to the Masonic Lodge Giuseppe Mazzini No. 118 on its 126th anniversary. The letter, dated September 11, 2018, reads in part:

"May this celebration encourage you to continue to work and develop your ideals of love, service to humanity, and universal brotherhood, to forge a nation *"whose identity is a passion for truth and commitment to the common good."*

On the same day, the lodge released that letter stating: "Today we received this greeting from the Diocese of Lomas de Zamora. We publicly thank you for your reverence and reaffirm our commitment to work together for greater freedom, equality, and fraternity, leaving aside anachronistic differences."

Likewise in Italy, there was a meeting in Baccaresca on October 19, 2018, entitled "Church and Freemasonry: a possible dialogue?" It was attended by representatives of the GOI, the Catholic Church and the mayors Fossato di Vico and Gualdo Tadino, Monia Ferracchiato and Massimiliano Presciutti, and the vice president of the provincial ACLI Marta Ginettelli. It was inaugurated by the president of the ACLI club Sante Pirrami. At the meeting, the possibility of a rapprochement between the two institutions was considered very positive.[40]

In conjunction, Michael Heinrich Weninger is an Austrian Catholic priest and a member of the Vatican's Pontifical Council for Interreligious Dialogue. He is also a Freemason and chaplain of three Austrian lodges.[41] The *Infovaticana* website reports on the news:

"In October 2014, the website of the "East Lancashire Provincial Grand Lodge of Mark Master Masons" (English "Mark" Masonry, or "Mark Masonry," was formed by Master Masons of the "United Grand Lodge of England" - UGLE) reports that a few days earlier, in the presence of an English Masonic delegation, three Venerable Installation of Masters ceremonies were held in Austria of two Lodges of Mark Master Masons ("St. Margaret's Lodge of MMMs" and "New Quarries Lodge of MMMs ") And a" Royal Ark Mariner "Lodge ("New Shores Lodge of RAMs"). Margaret's Lodge of MMMs" and "New Quarries Lodge of MMMs") and a "Royal Ark Mariner" Lodge ("New Shores Lodge of RAMs"). Those three Austrian Lodges with English names are related to English Freemasonry and use rituals in the English language. In each of those three Lodges, "Brother" Rev. Michael Weninger ("Bro. Rev. Michael Weninger") was installed as Chaplain for the year 2014-2015, who also celebrated a commemoration Mass for the anniversary of the consecration of "New Quarries Lodge" and for the consecration of "St. Margaret's Lodge." There were 500 Masons of all faiths at the Mass. The Masonic website adds that "Bro. Rev. Michael" ("Brother "= Brother = Brother = Brother, i.e., Mason) is well qualified for the

---

[40] Editorial Staff Gualdo News (October 23, 2018), E' possibile un dialogo tra Chiesa e Massoneria? Se ne è parlato a Baccaresca, Gualdo News.
[41] Cameron Doody (Feb. 15, 2020), Catholic Freemasons "certainly not" excommunicated, says Austrian member of Vatican interfaith dialogue body, Novena News.

position of Lodge Chaplain since he lives in the Vatican as a member of the Pontifical Council for Interreligious Dialogue."[42]

Michael Weninger's doctoral thesis on the compatibility between the Catholic Church and Freemasonry was well received by the Pontifical Gregorian University in Rome in 2019. And in 2020, the same was published in book format under the title Loge und Altar (Lodge and Altar).[43] He presented his work in Vienna with the then Grand Master of the Grand Lodge of Austria, George Semler, who is also a Catholic.[44]

Weninger noted that copies of his book were distributed to both Pope Francis and various cardinals, including Cardinal Christoph Schönborn of Vienna. All received it "with benevolence, without exception."

The book argues that a Catholic can be a member of a regular Grand Lodge recognized in Britain and that it requires a belief in God. Whereas anti-clerical lodges such as the Grand Orient of France and the Grand Orient of Italy, are a problem in that respect.

Until 2021 at least, we learned for contacts with the Grand Lodge of Austria, that beyond that, relations remained open and positive.

Pope Francis' ambiguities about his attitude towards Freemasonry

Incidentally, the above would explain why in 2013 Pope Francis removed a French Catholic priest from office and stripped him of his public ministry for refusing to renounce Freemasonry.[45] Pascal Vesin has belonged since 2001 to the Grand Orient of France.[46] But Vesin was also in favor of priests marrying and did not support the Catholic manifestations in Paris against homosexual marriages.[47]

It could also explain that in 2017, Francis personally told Lebanon's Prime Minister Saad Hariri that he did not accept the appointment of diplomat Johnny Ibrahim as ambassador to the Holy See because of his membership in Freemasonry, having been linked to a French Masonic lodge. Apparently, the pope respects the official position of the Church, that membership in Freemasonry is irreconcilable with Catholicism, and that the pope is "deeply hostile" to Freemasonry.[48] However, such a statement was written by Sandro Magister in L'Espresso, who referred to the pope's statement of a Masonic lobby and anti-Catholic Freemasonry, of which he is intolerant and claimed that they infiltrated the Order of Malta, asking Cardinal Raymond Burke to cleanse the order of them.[49]

---

[42] Specola (Feb. 27, 2020), El viaje a China del Papa Francisco puede esperar, el masón Padre Weninger en el Vaticano, rogativas por la peste, Infovaticana.

[43] Robert Moynihan (August 1, 2020), New Openings to Make Masonic Membership Permissible?," Inside the Vatican.

[44] Ibid.

[45] Ibid.

[46] Redacción ACI Prensa/EWTN Noticias (May 27, 2013), Obispo retira a sacerdote que no quiso abandonar masonería en Francia, ACI Prensa.

[47] El Plural (May 27, 2013), La Gran Logia de España lamenta el cese de un sacerdote francés por su pertenencia a la masonería, El Plural.

[48] Julio Algañaraz (October 24, 2017), El Papa rechazó por masón al nuevo embajador designado por el Líbano, Clarín.

[49] Infobae (October 24, 2017), La masonería, la "bestia negra" del papa Francisco: el conflicto detrás de su rechazo al embajador libanés, Infobae; Infovaticana; Infovaticana (May 4, 2017), El Papa tiene claro que la masonería es una grave problema a combatir, Infovaticana.

But as we shall see, the Grand Orient of Italy (GOI) has made a rapprochement with the Vatican. It is part of the ambiguities of Pope Francis' papacy.

On the other hand, following the consultation of a Filipino bishop about the presence of many Catholic Masons in his country; and after an audience with Pope Francis on November 13, 2023, Cardinal Víctor Manuel Fernández, Prefect for the Dicastery for the Doctrine of the Faith, drafted and signed a document to which Pope Francis himself added his signature, recalling that "the active membership of the faithful in Freemasonry is forbidden, due to the incompatibility between Catholic doctrine and Freemasonry."[50]

We read in the heading of the letter "Dicasterium pro Doctrina Fidei" or Dicastery for the Doctrine of the Faith, which is charged with assisting the pope and bishops in proclaiming Catholic teaching throughout the world while promoting and safeguarding the integrity of Catholic doctrine. Why such ambiguity?

Charles Murr, the Catholic priest who helped organize Archbishop Édouard Gagnon's information about Freemasonry in the Vatican decades ago, told Catholic journalist Robert Moynihan that he does not believe in the seriousness of the Vatican statement, since under the present papacy the Vatican has said things that have changed in as little as a month. So over time, Murr points out, the statement could be reversed or related contradictory actions could occur.[51]

However, Murr believes that the Vatican's statement could be due to confidential information he received: that his book has been read in the Vatican and perhaps this has motivated the statement.[52] Another motivation could be that after Fernández was elected to the dicastery by Pope Francis in July, he received a lot of criticism from conservative sectors in Argentina and Catholic personalities in other parts of the world, accusing him of being a progressive.[53] Another criticism was that he was a Freemason, which he decisively denied.[54]

But on February 16, 2024, an important meeting behind closed doors entitled "The Catholic Church and Freemasonry," was held in the Diocese of Milan. It was attended by the Grand Masters of the Italian Masonic lodges: Stefano Bissi for the Grand Orient of Italy, Luciano Romoli for the Grand Lodge of Italy of Ancient Free and Accepted Masons, and Fabio Venzi (connected from Rome) for the Regular Grand Lodge of Italy, with senior leaders of the Catholic Church. Church participants were Cardinal Francesco Coccopalmerio, President Emeritus of the Pontifical Council for Legislative Texts, the Franciscan theologian Zbigniew Suchecki, and, above all, Bishop Antonio

---

[50] The Catholic Herald (Nov. 17, 2023), Vatican upholds ban on Catholics becoming Freemasons, Catholic Herald; G. de A. (Nov. 15, 2023), El Papa y el cardenal Fernández corroboran la «incompatibilidad» entre el catolicismo y la masonería, Religión en Libertad; L'Osservatore Romano (Nov. 17, 2023), La fe católica es irreconciliable con la masonerìa, L'Osservatore Romano; Cortes, Msgr. Julito. (Nov. 13, 2023). [Foglio di Udienza con il Santo Padre. Richiesta di Sua Ecc.za Mons. Julito Cortes, Vescovo di Dumaguete (Filippine) circa il "best pastoral approach" riguardo all'adesione alla massoneria da parte di fedeli cattolici].
[51] (Nov. 15, 2023), Bishop Strickland's Rosary, Urbi et Orbi Communications: https://www.youtube.com/watch?v=uSU76Ultwgs; accessed Nov. 27, 2023. 26:18-29:45.
[52] Ibid.
[53] Almudena Calatrava and Natacha Pisarenko (July 16, 2023), La controvertida llegada al Vaticano de un arzobispo argentino que hace 30 años escribió sobre besar, Associated Press.
[54] Elise Ann Allen (July 7, 2023), Pope's new doctrine watchdog assures: 'I'm not a Soros spy', Crux Catholic Media, Inc.

Staglianò, President of the Pontifical Academy of Theology and the real protagonist of the evening.[55]

The Archbishop of the Diocese of Milan, Mario Delpini, welcomed the guests and explained the reasons for the initiative.[56]

Cardinal Francesco Coccopalmerio said: "From what I have been able to understand, but I am not a great expert on this subject, I believe that there is an evolution in mutual understanding. Fifty years ago there was less knowledge but things have advanced and I hope that these meetings do not stay here. I wonder if we could not think of a permanent table, even at the authority level, to discuss things better."[57]

Stefano Bisi, Grand Master of the Grand Orient of Italy, said: "My wish - which is also a hope - is that one day a Pope and a Grand Master can meet and walk a stretch of the road together, in the light of the sun. I would say in the light of the Great Architect of the universe."[58]

For his part, the president of the Pontifical Academy of Theology, Bishop Antonio Staglianò, dismissed Church doctrine as a barrier to encounter and dialogue with Freemasonry, emphasizing instead the manifestation of Jesus Christ as "God who is love, only and always love" to bring about rapprochement. He criticized the document of the Dicastery for the Doctrine of the Faith of November 2023, which reiterates the prohibition for Catholics to belong to Freemasonry.[59]

However, days after the meeting, Staglianò, who is also the pope's theological advisor, closed the door to Freemasonry by highlighting the reasons for the profound incompatibility between it and Catholic doctrine. He reiterated the November 2023 prohibition document, and added: "Within Freemasonry, plots of occult power are developed that are in contradiction with Christian action," Staglianò told Vatican Media. "In short, when we speak of irreconcilability, we are referring to profound contradictions."[60]

However, it seems that the contradictions of this papacy concerning Freemasonry, especially fall within its continued ambiguity, something that we have already discussed in the previous chapter, in order to unite everyone; especially about Freemasonry.

---

[55] Franca Giansoldati (17 de febrero, 2024), Chiesa-Massoneria: un cardinale per la prima volta propone un tavolo permanente per dialogare con il Grande Oriente, Il Messagero; Riccardo Cascioli (19 de febrero, 2024), La Massoneria vuole il "mea culpa", la Chiesa inizia con l'esame di coscienza, La Nuova Bussola Quotidiana.

[56] Riccardo Cascioli (19 de febrero, 2024), La Massoneria vuole il "mea culpa", la Chiesa inizia con l'esame di coscienza, La Nuova Bussola Quotidiana.

[57] Franca Giansoldati (17 de febrero, 2024), Chiesa-Massoneria: un cardinale per la prima volta propone un tavolo permanente per dialogare con il Grande Oriente, Il Messagero.

[58] Riccardo Cascioli (19 de febrero, 2024), La Massoneria vuole il "mea culpa", la Chiesa inizia con l'esame di coscienza, La Nuova Bussola Quotidiana.

[59] Franca Giansoldati (17 de febrero, 2024), Chiesa-Massoneria: un cardinale per la prima volta propone un tavolo permanente per dialogare con il Grande Oriente, Il Messagero; Riccardo Cascioli (19 de febrero, 2024), La Massoneria vuole il "mea culpa", la Chiesa inizia con l'esame di coscienza, La Nuova Bussola Quotidiana.

[60] Crux Staff (26 de febrero, 2024), After apparent opening, Pope's theological advisor closes door anew to Masonry, Crux Catholic Media.

CHAPTER

11

The new "Holy Alliance"

New U.S.-Vatican alliance: influences and the alliance between Obama and Pope Francis

The strength of Roman Catholicism in the United States is undeniable. Let's look at one example before we begin to substantiate the new "Holy Alliance" that took place some years ago. Nancy Pelosi, a Catholic and then the House Democratic Minority Leader, told NBC in August 2008 that the question of abortion had never been clearly defined by the Church for centuries and therefore women should have the right to choose.[1] A firestorm of criticism arose from U.S. Catholic authorities responding to the contrary.[2]

When Pelosi visited Pope Benedict XVI at the Vatican in February of the same year, he strongly reprimanded her on the issue.[3]

The U.S. federal government for decades included health-related legislative variations of the Hyde Amendment, prohibiting the use of taxpayer dollars for abortion services. Pelosi, opposed by 40 pro-life deserters, sought more compromising language to be included in the final version of the bill. But pro-life lawmakers, backed by the U.S. Conference of Catholic Bishops, insisted on an amendment that would deny abortion services to any participant in the exchange whose premiums would be subsidized by taxpayers.[4] Thus, any woman seeking abortion coverage would not find it in the new health coverage.[5] As a result, Pelosi agreed to make an anti-abortion amendment, which was very unpopular with liberal Democrats and others.[6] But in subsequent years, she would have other collisions with the country's Catholic authorities.[7]

---

[1] Ed Morrissey (August 26, 2008), Catholic House Republicans respond to Pelosi's abortion lies, Hot Air; Ed Stoddard (August 27, 2008), Pelosi's abortion comments provoke Catholic criticism, Reuters; CE Webmaster (August 30, 2008), Bishops Respond to House Speaker Pelosi's Misrepresentation of Church Teaching Against Abortion, Catholic Exchange; Valerie Schmalz (September 28, 2008), Return of the 'Communion Wars' Bishops continue to struggle over dilemma of pro-choice Catholic politicians, Our Sunday Visitor.

[2] Ibid; Jacqueline L. Slamon (Aug. 27, 2008), Archbishop Disputes Pelosi's Statements, The Washington Post; Phil Brennan (Sept. 7, 2008), Bishop Summons Pelosi, Newsmax.

[3] (Feb. 18, 2009), Pope Benedict strongly rebukes Pelosi over abortion, Catholic News Agency.

[4] Ronald M. Peters, Jr, Cindy Simon Rosenthal, Speaker Nancy Pelosi and the New American Politics (Oxford University Press, Inc., 2010), p. 186.

[5] Stephen T. Dennis and Jennifer Bendery, "House OK's Stupak Anti-Abortion Amendment," Roll Call, November 7, 2009; quoted in Ibid.

[6] Ronald M. Peters, Jr, Cindy Simon Rosenthal, Speaker Nancy Pelosi and the New American Politics (Oxford University Press, Inc., 2010), p. 186.

[7] Edwin Mora (Dec. 1, 2011), Pelosi Dismisses Catholic Bishops as 'Lobbyists'-For Opposing Obamacare Reg Forcing Catholics to Act Against Faith, CNS News; Christine Dhanago (Feb. 6, 2012), Pelosi: 'I am going to stick with fellow Catholics' in supporting Obama birth control mandate, LifeSiteNews; Lauretta

What would come next? On July 10, 2009, Barack Obama visited Pope Benedict XVI at the Vatican. The two leaders of state spoke for forty minutes about bioethics, the question of immigration, peace in the Middle East, development aid for Africa and Latin America and the problem of drug trafficking.[8]

The journalist-writer and Vaticanologist Eric Frattini, wrote in his work *El Libro Negro del Vaticano* (*The Vatican Black Book*), in chapter 38 entitled "United States: Obama-Benedict XVI, the New World Order that could not be," that when Barack Obama visited the Vatican to meet with the Pope in July 2009, his arrival was sold by the Vatican Secretariat of State as the beginning of a new world order; as a kind of consolidated axis between Reagan and John Paul II.[9] However, because Obama's politics were not the same as Reagan's, and Pope Ratzinger did not have precisely all the same objectives as his predecessor, it could not be realized.

The report of the U.S. Embassy to the Vatican sent to the Secretary of State in Washington on June 26 of the same year, and which was to be declassified until June 26, 2019, pointed out the points under discussion, among which are common objectives to achieve global peace, justice, development.... interfaith understanding, Iraq, immigration... and other sensitive ones such as bioethics... In most of the subjects they reached common agreements, but on issues such as bioethics and given the Vatican's rejection of Caroline Kennedy's appointment as the new Vatican Ambassador for her support of abortion, a dent was created; causing Obama's desired alliance with the Vatican to fade. The title of the telegram was, "Holy See: Scenesetter for President's July 10 visit."

Among the issues discussed by the two heads of state were the financial crisis, interreligious dialogue, and the environment. Thus, point 1 of the document states in part:

"Your meeting with Pope Benedict XVI will be an opportunity to discuss our shared commitments to overarching goals such as peace, justice, development, human dignity, and inter-faith understanding. From the Vatican's perspective, it will also provide a forum to discuss sensitive bioethical issues in a mutually respectful way. In your meeting with him, or possibly with other Vatican officials on the margins, you may cover other topics of special interest, such as the Middle East, Iraq, immigration, and the environment. Your discussions at the Holy See will help deepen our mutual collaboration on issues around the world. End Summary."

In points 2 and 3, U.S. analysts point out that the presence of religious in every country in the world and the 177 countries with which the Vatican had diplomatic relations at the moment, second only to the United States with 188 nations, make the Vatican one of the best-informed states in the world.

Despite not agreeing on everything and not achieving a more consolidated alliance, the Vatican, through its Secretary of State Tarcisio Bertone, assured that they wanted a

Brown (Jan. 26, 2015), SF Archbishop on Pelosi: No Catholic Can Dissent from Church Teaching on Abortion, CNS News.
[8] Redacción (July 10, 2009), Primer encuentro entre Obama y el Pope, BBC Mundo.
[9] Eric Frattini, El Libro Negro del Vaticano: Las oscuras relaciones entre la CIA y la Santa Sede (Espasa, Barcelona, 2016), ob. cit. Note: unless otherwise noted, this is the same source.

constructive dialogue with the President of the United States on issues such as peace in the Middle East, the environment and dialogue with the Muslim world.

Benedict XVI gave support to the United States, to Obama, and his foreign policy by stating after the meeting between the two, that he:

"prayed for a world authority to govern us all" and stressing that "there is an urgent need for a true world political authority whose task is to manage the world economy, revive the economies affected by the crisis, prevent any deterioration of the present crisis and the further imbalances that could result. This 'world authority' should achieve timely comprehensive disarmament, food security, and peace."

The Holy See would do its part, but without identifying too closely with the Obama administration on various issues. For example, on October 24, 2011, *Rome Reports* reported that "The Vatican proposes a world government to stabilize the financial system." A document entitled, "Towards Reforming Financial and Monetary Systems in the Context of Global Public Authority with universal competence" which corresponds to a Note of the Pontifical Council for Justice and Peace - although not a text of the papal magisterium - says a lot about the Vatican's thinking in this regard: "It proposes a world political authority, which would set the rules of the game and force respect for them." This document denounced that the leadership of the G7 or G20 is informal and that it excludes a good part of the nations.[10] Italian economist Leonardo Becchetti explained the proposal:

"Protecting some global public goods requires rapid responses and global coordination between states. For example, issues such as pollution or the stability of the financial system to deal with the crisis. More coordination between countries, speed of response, and representativeness are needed."[11]

The Vatican's proposal involved the establishment of a World Central Bank to regulate currency exchange, a World Bank Recapitalization Fund, different rules for commercial and investment banking, as well as a tax on financial transactions.[12]

Becchetti explained:

"This crisis is the result of financial causes that have weakened the States, and now weak States are putting the banks in trouble. It is therefore normal to ask finance to pay so that the weakest and the welfare state do not have to pay for the crisis. The Church is in the front line and endorses this proposal of civil society, which is already supported by some states and the President of the European Commission."[13]

The document refers to Pope John XXIII's "prophetic" encyclical letter Pacem in terris (1963), in which he warned that the world was moving towards ever greater unification. He foresaw the creation of a "World Public Authority" that would correspond to global political organization and the objective demands of the common

---

[10] (Oct. 24, 2011), Vatican proposes world government to stabilize financial system, Rome Reports.
[11] Ibid.
[12] Ibid.
[13] Ibid.

good. Becchetti further expressed that, "Benedict XVI himself, in the furrow traced by Pacem in terris, has expressed the need to constitute a world political Authority."[14] The 2011 document continues:

"Think, for example, of peace and security; disarmament and arms control; promotion and protection of fundamental human rights; management of the economy and development policies; management of migratory flows and food security; and protection of the environment. In all these areas, the growing interdependence between States and regions of the world becomes more and more obvious as well as the need for answers that are not just sectorial and isolated, but systematic and integrated, rich in solidarity and subsidiarity and geared to the universal common good.
[...]
"A supranational Authority in this arena should have a realistic structure and be set up gradually. It should be favourable to the existence of efficient and effective monetary and financial systems; that is, free and stable markets overseen by a suitable legal framework, well-functioning in support of sustainable development and social progress of all, and inspired by the values of charity and truth(15). It is a matter of an Authority with a global reach that cannot be imposed by force, coercion or violence, but should be the outcome of a free and shared agreement and a reflection of the permanent and historic needs of the world common good. [...].
"The establishment of a world political Authority should be preceded by a preliminary phase of consultation from which a *legitimated* institution will emerge that is in a position to be an effective guide and, at the same time, can allow each country to express and pursue its own particular good. The exercise of this Authority at the service of the good of each and every one will necessarily be *super partes* or impartial: that is, above any partial vision or particular good, with a view to achieving the common good. Its decisions should not be the result of the more developed countries' superior power over weaker countries. Instead, they should be made in the interest of all, not only to the advantage of some groups, whether they are formed by private lobbies or national governments."[15]

A note highlights the fact that countries should not sell their sovereignty to the Authority, even though it has fixed rules to be respected.[16]

The document also highlights: "In a world on its way to rapid globalization, orientation towards a world Authority becomes the only horizon compatible with the new realities of our time and the needs of humankind."[17]

In the year 2013, we had a new pope at the head of the world's 1.2 billion Catholics-pope Francis. Numerous state leaders sent their congratulatory messages. For the purposes of this chapter, in what we will see, it is worth highlighting the words of political leaders in Washington and on behalf of the United Nations.

In this context and on behalf of the American people, Obama and his wife Michelle offered their warmest wishes to Pope Francis at the beginning of his papacy as a

---

[14] Towards Reforming Financial and Monetary Systems in the Context of Global Public Authority with universal competence, Pontifical Council for Justice and Peace (Vatican City, 2011).
[15] Ibid.
[16] Ibid.
[17] Ibid.

champion of the poor and the most vulnerable, carrying the message of love and compassion that has inspired the world for more than two thousand years, seeing in others the face of God. Obama said that as the first pope of the Americas, his election also speaks to the strength and vitality of a region that is increasingly emerging in the world. He said that just as he appreciated his work with Pope Benedict XVI, "I look forward to working with His Holiness to advance peace, security, and dignity for our fellow human beings, regardless of their faith."[18]

The U.S. Secretary of State John Kerry wrote:

"Teresa and I will keep the Holy Father in our prayers as he begins a new era for our Church. On this momentous day, the United States renews our commitment to working closely with the Holy See to advance our shared belief in peace and humanity. We offer the Holy Father our warmest wishes of success in advancing peace, freedom, and human dignity throughout the world."[19]

Joe Biden, a Catholic and then vice president of the country:

"The Catholic Church plays an essential role in my life and the lives of more than a billion people in America and around the world, not just in matters of our faith, but in pursuit of peace and human dignity for all faiths. I look forward to our work together in the coming years on many important issues."[20]

For his part, then-House Speaker John Boehner, also a Catholic:

"For me, it is truly inspiring that our new pope has taken the name of Francis, the saint who lived a simple life of humility and charity, setting an example for how to make God's love visible to all, especially those in despair or pain."[21]

The pope's harsh criticism of excessive capitalism has earned him labels as a socialist, although in reality, he seeks a moral capitalism towards the entire human race[22] under socialist principles, thus bringing him close to the heart of Washington - especially the Democratic party.

He has stated that capitalism is a much bigger problem than overpopulation, criticizing market systems and the behavior of a consumerist society.[23]

By the end of June 2014, he said that the communists had stolen the flag from the Christians - poverty; so they were doing well.[24]

He noted in late 2013 that he had met good Marxists, but also explained that "Marxist ideology is wrong."[25]

---

[18] The White House, Office of the Press Secretary (March 13, 2013). Statement from the President on His Holiness Pope Francis [Press Release]. Retrieved from https://www.whitehouse.gov/the-press-office/2013/03/13/statement-president-his-holiness-pope-francis; June 23, 2016.
[19] Caleb K. Bell (March 13, 2013), Reactions to Pope Francis' election, Religion News Service.
[20] Ibid.
[21] Ibid.
[22] Cristina Odone (December 22, 2013), Is the Pope a Socialist, Newsweek.
[23] Zoë Schlanger (June 18, 2015), Pope Francis on Twitter: The Earth Looks Like 'an Immense Pile of Filth,' and It's Capitalism's Fault, Newsweek.
[24] Philip Pullella (June 29, 2014), Pope says communists are closet Christians, Reuters.

However, in September, he also declared that "I have never been right-wing."[26] Part of his well-known ambiguity.

The Pope's reputation as a Marxist has grown in the United States. The most conservative sectors have been the most critical, even though Francis has said he is not a Marxist. The BBC comments that the pope has said that "his views on the redistribution of wealth, the injustices of the capitalist system, and the need to help the poorest come from the Gospels."[27]

But this was not the case with John Paul II and Benedict XVI, who addressed themselves more to the morals and doctrine of the Church.[28]

The Italian newspaper *La Stampa*, published in February 2019, that Francis "lifted all canonical censures that weighed on the Nicaraguan priest, poet and social activist, icon of liberation theology" to the Jesuit Ernesto Cardenal. After almost 35 years of his separation from the priesthood, which was imposed on him by John Paul II.[29]

Now, Bergoglio's papacy seeks to embrace all political, social, and spiritual realities to achieve global peace, as expressed by the newly elected Vatican Cardinal Secretary of State, Pietro Parolin, on September 23, 2013, in Venezuela:

"I believe that today, obviously, the fundamental Berlin wall is to achieve peace amid the diversity we have in a multipolar world. There are no longer blocs as there used to be. This is a common geopolitical analysis. There are different powers. Different powers have emerged, with all the problems they entail. Because we thought in our desires for peace and happiness, that the fall of the traditional walls: the Berlin wall, the wall of the bloc between communist countries and the West, was going to bring peace and happiness to the world. And it didn't. The whole problem of terrorism was unleashed.

"So, I believe that the wall that must be broken down is how to get all these different realities to agree and work together for the good of all. To put together the differences so that they are not divisions, but become collaborations for the benefit of all humanity.

[...]

"If there is no common ground that can be trodden; that is, if there is no objective truth in which we all recognize ourselves, it will be much more difficult to seek common ground. This common ground is the dignity of the human person in all its dimensions, where the transcendent dimension is not excluded; it is not only the personal, social, political, and economic dimension, but also the transcendent dimension, by which it is recognized that man is made in the image and likeness of God, and that God is his source."[30]

---

[25] Lizzy Davies (15 de diciembre, 2013), Pope says he is not a Marxist, but defends criticism of capitalism, The Guardian.

[26] Pablo Ordaz (September 19, 2013), El Papa: "Jamás he sido de derechas," El País.

[27] Editor (September 22, 2015), La fama de "marxista" que persigue al papa Francisco en EE.UU., BBC Mundo.

[28] Ibid.

[29] Andrés Beltramo Álvarez (February 19, 2019), Una misa para Ernesto Cardenal, emblema de la liberación, La Stampa.

[30] Archbishop Pietro Parolin (Sept. 9, 2013), Mons. Parolin: Razón de ser de la diplomacia del Vaticano es buscar la paz, ACI/EWTN Noticias.

He then referred to the use of the instruments of Vatican diplomacy "to achieve the great objectives for the good of humanity," in which the Church will have a more prominent role.[31] This is exactly what the Jesuit Malachi Martin warned for the new pope to be elected in his novel Windswept House.

Author and journalist Eric Frattini wrote that in just two years of papacy (2013-2015), "by his own weight and by the weight of his diplomacy, Francis has earned the nickname "pope of the world."[32]

By October 2013, Cardinal Timothy Dolan, then president of the United States Conference of Catholic Bishops, and Vice President Archbishop Joseph Kurtz, took a small delegation of USCCB leadership to Rome as part of their annual visits to the Vatican to exchange information with the prefects of the various Pontifical Congregations on developments in the U.S. Church and other churches around the world.[33]

Of his half-hour with the pope, Cardinal Dolan said, "we conveyed to him the love and the admiration and the esteem and gratitude of the Catholic people of the United States, and indeed of the people of the United States and especially the bishops. We had spoken about a beautiful new sense of freshness and creativity within the Church that's thanks to his providential leadership."[34]

Francis was curious and interested in the issues the bishops' conference was working on. They told him about immigration and he asked them about their Catholic schools, about vocations, and about the Latino population. Dolan said that as he walked the streets of New York, he noticed that the pope has received universal acclaim: Catholics, Catholics away from Catholicism, people who do not belong to any religion, or religions that are not Catholic. Dolan further reported that "they loved Pope Benedict too and they loved Pope John Paul II. But there seems to be almost like a fresh romance with Pope Francis."[35]

That same month, the U.S. federal government executed a government shutdown because Republicans were unhappy with the Affordable Care Act, or Patient Protection and Affordable Care Act, which reformed the U.S. healthcare system but allowed abortion into the program. A week before the government shutdown and in an effort to force President Obama to enact many of the USCCB's preferred policies, the USCCB, led by Cardinal Dolan, wrote to members of Congress requesting a government shutdown and, potentially that the nation be forced to default. In a letter signed by Cardinal Sean O'Malley of Boston and Archbishop William Lori of Baltimore, they addressed lawmakers saying, "We have already urged you to enact the **Health Care Conscience Rights Act** (H.R. 940/S. 1204). As Congress considers a Continuing Resolution and debt ceiling bill in the days to come, we reaffirm **the vital importance of incorporating the policy of this bill into such "must-pass" legislation.**" Several members of Congress asked that the same request from the bishops be taken into consideration in the debt ceiling debates as a condition for proceeding. This

---

[31] Ibid.
[32] Eric Frattini, El Libro Negro del Vaticano: Las oscuras relaciones entre la CIA y la Santa Sede (Espasa, Barcelona, 2016), ob. cit.
[33] (Oct. 9, 2013), Cardinal Dolan on meeting with Pope Francis, U.S. reaction to new Pope, Vatican Radio.
[34] Ibid.
[35] Ibid.

additionally forced a government shutdown.[36] Criticism from some Catholic circles upset that the USCCB was accused of the above was not long in coming... but could not be answered directly.[37] There were some fears of economic collapse until an agreement was reached (not favorable to Catholics) that ended the government shutdown.

Months later, in mid-January 2014, it was announced that Obama would visit the Vatican to meet with Pope Francis; where diplomacies were working to anticipate such a visit "in view of a partnership based on social issues."[38]

Before continuing with the topic of Obama's visit to Pope Francis, let's look at some of the cultural aspects that united the two leaders, even on the part of the Catholic Church itself.

The aforementioned Joseph Bernardin was admired by Barack Obama when he was then a young Chicago organizer.[39]

George Neumayr wrote in 2012, that, "Barack Obama rose to power not in spite of the Catholic Church but in part because of it." During Joseph Bernardin's era as archbishop of the Archdiocese of Chicago, the archdiocese helped fund Obama's radicalism in the 1980s. He began his work as a community organizer in the rectory rooms of Holy Rosary Parish on Chicago's South Side.[40] Obama, then 25, trained an engrossed group of Roman Catholics in a meeting room under Chicago's Holy Name Cathedral in 1987 to lobby fellow delegates at a national congress in Washington on issues such as empowering lay leaders and attracting more believers. Obama had a desk at a South Side parish and was cultivated in the social justice wing of the Church, "which played a powerful role in his political formation." One plan that succeeded.[41] The Developing Communities Project, which was the group Obama worked for, received tens of thousands of dollars for the CCHD, or Catholic Campaign for Human Development.[42] CCHD has at its very core a philosophy of left-wing revolutionary ideas. The institute has been criticized for funding organizations that promote homosexuality, abortion, prostitution, and socialism.[43]

Neumayr wrote:

"Bernardin was not only a socialist in his economic views but also a gay-friendly bishop supportive of the Democrats' moral drift. Bernardin was so gay-friendly in fact that he requested that the "Windy City Gay Chorus" perform at his funeral. Needless to say, he personified Obama's conception of a "good" bishop."[44]

---

[36] Adele M. Stan (Oct. 7, 2013), At Any Cost: How Catholic Bishops Pushed for a Shutdown—and Even a Default—Over Birth Control, Rewire News Group; https://www.usccb.org/issues-and-action/religious-liberty/conscience-protection/upload/omalley-lori-letter-to-house-2013-09-26.pdf accessed March 20, 2024.

[37] (November, 2013), UNFAIR CRITICS RIP USCCB, Catholic League For Religious and Civil Rights.

[38] Paolo Mastrolilli (January 15, 2014), Obama y Francisco. «El encuentro puede ser en marzo», La Stampa.

[39] David Gibson (Oct. 24, 2013), Pope Francis breathes new life into Cardinal Bernardin's contested legacy, Religion News Service.

[40] George Neumayr (September 11, 2012), Catholic Left Created Obama, RealClear Religion.

[41] Jason Horowitz (March 22, 2014), The Catholic Roots of Obama's Activism, The New York Times.

[42] George Neumayr (September 11, 2012), Catholic Left Created Obama, RealClear Religion.

[43] Michael Hichborn (Nov. 18, 2015), The Marxist Core of the Catholic Campaign for Human Development, Lepanto Institute.

[44] George Neumayr (September 11, 2012), Catholic Left Created Obama, RealClear Religion.

Likewise:

"So cozy was the relationship between Obama and Cardinal Bernardin that when Obama went out to Los Angeles for a 1986 training session organized by Saul Alinsky's Industrial Areas Foundation he had the archdiocese pay for his plane fare. The conference was held at a Catholic college in Southern California, Mount St. Mary's, which to this day holds events for the Industrial Areas Foundation."[45]

Obama "[…] fit seamlessly into a 1980s Catholic cityscape forged by the spirit of Vatican II, the influence of liberation theology and the progressivism of Cardinal Joseph L. Bernardin, the archbishop of Chicago, who called for a "consistent ethic of life" that wove life and social justice into a "seamless garment."[46]

In May 2009, Obama told graduates at the Catholic University of Notre Dame that Cardinal Bernardin had touched his mind and heart.[47]

What about the Jesuits and Obama?

While liberals in 2008 accused the bishops of having made an unholy alliance with the Republican party, Catholic liberals played an important role in Obama's presidential campaign, claiming that abortion was not really important. The Democratic platform spoke vaguely of reducing abortions,[48] but it didn't.

The Democratic Party consulted Jesuit priest Thomas Reese, then the media's favorite secular commentator, on how to appeal to Catholic voters.[49] Once Obama was elected president, Reese dismissed abortion as unimportant, and the pro-life movement as "a small group of people for whom there is only one issue, and they will make noise."[50]

In the 2008 presidential campaign, Catholics in Alliance for the Common Good (funded by George Soros); and Catholics United were formed for the sole purpose of encouraging Catholics to vote for Obama, something they claimed was dictated by Catholic doctrine.[51]

Raymond Schroth, a Jesuit priest, passed on to the *Reporter* any information against John McCain (Republican candidate) that could be used by the liberal media.[52]

But Douglas W. Kmiec, a former official in the Reagan administration who had written in 1995 that religious conservatives should surrender the public sphere to secularists, announced that Obama emerged as the natural candidate for Catholic support and raised the extraordinary prospect of "Reaganites for Obama."[53]

Let's take a look at what happened when President Obama visited Pope Francis at the Vatican. With all this in mind, about Obama's visit to Francis, the Italian newspaper *La Stampa* reported:

---

[45] Ibid.
[46] Jason Horowitz (March 22, 2014), The Catholic Roots of Obama's Activism, The New York Times.
[47] Ibid.
[48] James Hitchcock, Abortion, Religious Freedom, and Catholic Politics (Routledge, Taylos & Francis Group, New York, 2016), p. 15.
[49] Ibid, p. 16; citing Reporter, August 8, 2008.
[50] Ibid; citing Reporter, May 15, 2009.
[51] Ibid; citing CWR, November, 2010.
[52] Ibid.
[53] Ibid.

"Kerry, who as the first Catholic Secretary of State since the time of Edmund Muskie intends to take care of relations with the Vatican, explained what are the areas of common interest: Syria, peace negotiations in the Middle East, Sudan, and Africa in general, respect for religion and human rights in Cuba, the issue of extreme poverty at the global level. On this last point, in particular, the United States hopes to be able to collaborate more with the Holy See, so the meeting between Francis and Obama could seal a new alliance."[54]

Obama made his visit on March 27, 2014. By then, the president only had the support of half of the U.S. population, in comparison with Francis who had the world leadership (85% in his favor), which suited the president to visit him, as Professor Rafael Domingo Oslé pointed out to CNN in Spanish.[55]

The U.S. president, who inherited from his father Frank Marshall Davis some Marxist positions, appreciated this ideology during his youth. Obama's mentor at Harvard University was the Brazilian socialist Roberto Mangabeira Unger;[56] an influence that led him to declare that the free market did not work and never had.[57]

ABC España reported on the prelude prepared by Barack Obama the day before his visit:

"Obama contributed to preparing a climate of harmony by declaring the day before to "Corriere della Sera" that he was coming to Rome "to listen" to the Pope because "his thought is extremely valuable for understanding how we can overcome the challenge of extreme poverty and reduce inequality in the distribution of income. By making demands on us in matters of social justice, he alerts us to the danger of becoming accustomed to extreme inequalities."

"The president acknowledged that "the Pope challenges us. He implores us to remember the people, families, and the poor. He invites us to reflect on the dignity of the human person."[58]

Despite his differences with the pope, Obama said that "his is a voice that the world must listen to [...] With a single sentence, he manages to focus the attention of the planet on some urgent issue."[59]

[54] Paolo Mastrolilli (January 15, 2014), Obama y Francisco. «El encuentro puede ser en marzo», La Stampa.

[55] (March 27, 2014), ¿Por qué es importante la visita de Obama al Papa Francisco?, CNN en español: https://www.youtube.com/watch?v=EIpxb8N9lf8; accessed July 17, 2015.

[56] Stanley Kurtz, Radical-in-Chief: Barack Obama and the Untold Story of American Socialism (Threshold Editions, New York, 2010), pp. 88-92; Dinesh D'Souza, Obama's America: Unmaking the American Dream (Threshold Editions, New York, 2012), pp. 50, 68, 69, 77, 133; Paul Kengor, The communist: Frank Marshall Davis: the untold story of Barack Obama's mentor (Threshold Editions/Mercury Ink, New York, 2012), ob. cit; Robert Chandler, Shadow World: Resurgent Russia, The Global New Left, and Radical Islam (Regnery Publishing, Inc., 2008), pp. 220, 281, 334, 344-358; Mark Hendrickson (July 26, 2012), President Obama's Marxist-Leninist Economics: Fact And Fiction, Forbes.

[57] Craig Covello (December 9, 2011), Obama Declares Free Market Doesn't Work, Western Journalism; Harry Binswanger (December 31, 2013), Obama To Americans: You Don't Deserve To Be Free, Forbes.

[58] Juan Vicente Boo (28 de marzo, 2014), Obama, al Papa Francisco: «Es maravilloso poder conocerle», ABC España. [Tr] Note: translated in turn from Spanish into English.

[59] Massimo Gaggi (March 28, 2014), Barack Obama: "El Papa logra que la gente se ponga a pensar y a rever hábitos," La Nación Argentina. Note: translated in turn from Spanish into English.

From the beginning, the meeting between the two had a very cordial tone. Pope Francis received him in the anteroom, greeting him: "Welcome!," while Obama responded emotionally, saying: "Thank you very much. It is wonderful to meet you. It's a great honor. I am a great admirer. Thank you so much for having me."[60]

Obama addressed (officially, as will be seen) with Pope Francis, for 52 minutes,[61] issues such as legislative reform to solve the problem of the eleven million illegal immigrants in the United States; measures to address the aftermath of inequality caused by the long economic crisis; as well as the problems with the Middle East, Ukraine, and China. They also discussed "the exercise of the rights to religious freedom, to life and conscientious objection"; as well as the common effort to eliminate human trafficking in the world.[62]

The newspaper *La Stampa*, in its article entitled, "Esa «rara» alianza entre el Vaticano y Obama" ("That "rare" alliance between the Vatican and Obama"), published the background of the meeting between Obama and the Pope on the agreements reached.[63] The documents classified as "sensitive" and "confidential," reinforced the alliance that the United States and the Vatican have been building. This would be consolidated in Washington when the Pope visited the country on September 22 and met with Obama on the 23rd at the White House.

One of the texts of the meeting and the State Department for the preparation of the meeting between the U.S. president and Pope Francis at the Vatican points out:

"Pope Francis' diplomatic legacy is still under construction, but the 'pastoral conversion' that is the hallmark of his Pontificate is taking on important forms. The Pontiff's presence on the global stage means that his pastoral actions will have broad political implications."

From the reports "there emerges an absolute harmony with the objectives of Francis." Specific points of interest and possible collaboration were the fight against hunger and poverty, the environment, the war in Syria, the peace negotiations between Israel and Palestine, Cuba, and human trafficking.

On the fight against poverty and economic inequality, the document notes:

"Since his election in March 2013, Pope Francis has attracted the world's attention with his unique style of leadership, his evident humanity and empathy, and his devotion to the poor. While reinforcing traditional Church teachings, he has made it clear that attention to hot-button social issues, such as abortion or gay marriage, should not obscure other pastoral concerns, including care for the poor, the sick, and the needy."

---

[60] Juan Vicente Boo (28 de marzo, 2014), Obama, al Papa Francisco: «Es maravilloso poder conocerle», ABC España. Note: translated in turn from Spanish into English.

[61] Stephan Faris (March 27, 2014), Inside Obama's Meeting With Pope Francis, Time.

[62] Juan Vicente Boo (28 de marzo, 2014), Obama, al Papa Francisco: «Es maravilloso poder conocerle», ABC España. Note: translated in turn from Spanish into English.

[63] Paolo Mastrolilli (14 de septiembre, 2015), Esa «rara» alianza entre el Vaticano y Obama, Vatican Insider. Note: translated in turn from Spanish into English. Note: unless otherwise noted, this is the same source.

Such concerns, shared by the White House, find common ground in the struggle for economic reform, recalling the exhortation of 'Evangelii gaudium' when it calls for, "the elimination of the structural causes of poverty, and denounces a financial system that governs, rather than serves." Obama's advisors stressed that "some observers have seen this document as a challenge to the excesses of capitalism," while dismissing accusations of Marxism by pointing out that, "The Pope's views on economics are rooted in millennia of Catholic doctrine. Human welfare is determined by moral choices, and the Church must always focus on the defense of the poor."

The document further states that Pope Francis' emphasis on human dignity "is a common Catholic vernacular, but Francis deals with it in surprising ways. He sets a personal example. It follows the tradition from the "Compendium of Social Doctrine" published by John Paul II in 2004 to "The Church in the Modern World" of 1966.

The White House stressed that the Vatican considers environmental protection a "moral obligation;" and has high hopes for the new encyclical (which would be Laudato Si):

"For the Holy See, the environment and economic policy concerns are strongly linked, and Pope Francis' forthcoming apostolic exhortation will draw attention to this connection. The Vatican publicly acknowledged the serious and potentially irreversible effects of global warming."

This is the precise alliance that Obama wished to have, on the occasion of his visit to Benedict XVI in July 2009, but which failed for the most part.

On the problem in Syria, Obama and Francis agreed on helping the people to save them from extremism. And on the Middle East, they agreed on support for "direct negotiations and the resolution of the conflict within the framework of two sovereign states. Pope Francis has spoken out on several occasions in support of U.S. efforts to restart the talks." These were led for months with great determination by the U.S. Secretary of State, John Kerry. On Cuba, the document anticipates the Vatican's mediation by stating:

"We respect the Vatican's view on U.S. economic sanctions toward Cuba, but we note that, despite these sanctions, the United States is one of the island's major trading partners. Every year, we are the first or second largest source of food imports to Cuba.

"More than the embargo, the roots of Cuba's difficulties lie in the policies and actions of its government. Until it limits economic freedom, fearing that it will damage its monopoly on political power, the country will have problems. Positive actions by the government in these areas will inevitably produce closer interaction with the United States, including increased levels of trade and travel."

They also agreed on the fight against human trafficking as a "modern form of slavery" that exploded with the phenomenon of migration, initiatives against hunger, and against the persecution of religious minorities:

"Francis has demonstrated the ability to draw the attention of Catholics and not only on the global stage. In conflict situations, he will continue to be a voice for reconciliation. Concern for the persecution of Christians will push the Church toward pragmatic policies. Where religious freedom is restricted, as in China, Francis will seek pastoral opportunities to reach out to the faithful without confrontation."

Pope Francis has been called the Obama of the Catholic Church for a reason.[64]

Simone Campbell of the *National Catholic Reporter* made special reference to the discussion between the two leaders on the moral economic crisis with growing income inequality.[65]

Indeed, Francis "has deplored "unfair economic structures that create huge inequalities;" while Obama called inequality "the defining issue of our time.""[66]

Under such considerations, Campbell also expresses the Pope's call to the faithful "to fight for social benefits, a dignified retirement, holidays, rest, and freedom for trade unions. All of these issues create social justice."[67]

Thus, it should be noted that in 2008, when Obama was still a candidate for the U.S. presidency, he called for freeing people from "juggling work and parenting." Paul Edenfield indicated at the time that the candidates' concern came at a time when job demands were occurring as businesses tried to stay open most of the day and for seven days a week, alluding to the need for the traditional Sunday rest (a Catholic teaching and tradition).[68]

Consider that since 2007, excessive global food price increases have provoked unprecedented protests and riots around the globe.[69] And despite some adjustments to lower prices in 2015,[70] there were risk reports in February that the global price hike would provoke more upheavals.[71] Thus, at the end of June 2016, a contractor for the FEMA organization in the United States was again predicting social unrest triggered by 395% spikes in food prices.[72] With revolutionary and even hostile movements all over the United States, such as Occupy Wall Street, it is no wonder that Robert David Steele, former Marine and CIA officer, as well as co-founder of the US Marine Corps

---

[64] Adam Shaw (Dec. 4, 2013), Pope Francis is the Catholic Church's Obama - God help us, Fox News.

[65] Simone Campbell (June 18, 2014), What Francis would say to Obama: Let workers unionize, National Catholic Reporter.

[66] Ibid.

[67] Ibid. Boldface is mine.

[68] Paul Edenfield (April 7, 2008), The New Blue Laws: They're about giving workers a break, not forcing church attendance, Slate.

[69] (April 14, 2008), Riots, instability spread as food prices skyrocket, CNN; David Derbyshire (January 24, 2011), Food prices to rocket by 50% as global hunger epidemic causes riots and famines, Daily Mail; Sandrine Rastello (February 15, 2011), Food Surge Is Exacerbating Poverty, World Bank Says, Bloomberg; (August 15, 2011), The Cause Of Riots And The Price Of Food, MIT Technology Review; (August 30, 2012), Food prices jump will hit poor, World Bank warns, BBC News; Nafeez Mosaddeq Ahmed (March 6, 2013), Why food riots are likely to become the new normal, The Guardian; Joshua Keating (April 8, 2014), A Revolution Marches on Its Stomach, Slate; Food Price Watch (May 24), Year 5, Issue 17. Frederick Reese (June 5, 2014), World Bank Report Warns Of Increased Rioting As Food Prices Rise, MintPress News.

[70] (April 2, 2015), El índice de precios de los alimentos de la FAO baja de nuevo en marzo, lastrado por la fuerte caída del azúcar, FAO Noticias; (September 10, 2015), El índice de precios de los alimentos registra su mayor caída mensual desde 2008, FAO Noticias.

[71] Cullen S. Hendrix and Stephan M. Haggard (February 22, 2015), Where and why food prices lead to social upheaval, The Washington Post.

[72] Nafeez Ahmed (June 26, 2016), FEMA Contractor Predicts 'Social Unrest' Caused by 395% Food Price Spikes, Motherboard.

intelligence activity, predicted in June 2014, that open revolution is coming and that it will defeat the 1% (the rich).[73]

But at the end of the meeting between the leader of the Catholic Church and the head of state of the United States, Pope Francis gave Barack Obama a copy of the apostolic exhortation Evangelii Gaudium (The Joy of the Gospel), which outlines the renewal program of his pontificate, as well as a medallion to remind the U.S. president of his responsibility to promote peace. Obama thanked him for the book and confided: "You know, I'll probably read it when I'm in the Oval Office and I'm deeply frustrated. I'm sure it will give me strength and calm me down."[74]

Regarding the effective relations between the United States and the Vatican, Ben Wolfgang of The Washington Times referred to this alliance in December:

"President Obama increasingly is finding a key policy ally in the Vatican, with Pope Francis standing virtually shoulder to shoulder with the White House on income inequality and a historic diplomatic reboot with communist Cuba. The pontiff next year also appears poised to offer greater support to the president on climate change initiatives and reportedly wants to be a leading voice at a U.N. global warming summit next year, where the American president will make perhaps his greatest pitch to date for more dramatic action on the environment.

"For Mr. Obama and fellow Democrats, aligning with Francis offers clear benefits in the short term, as they are able to highlight agreement on controversial issues with one of the most respected figures on the planet."[75]

Indeed, Pope Francis helped mediate between the United States and Cuba to reestablish diplomatic relations between the two countries.[76]

Francis favors policies of greater wealth distribution, just like the Democrats' policies on Americans struggling to get ahead.[77]

Obama, for his part, in a speech in Seattle on the evening of July 22, 2014, during a Democratic National Committee fundraiser, expressing himself about various conflicts in Europe and the Middle East, noted:

"[...] part of people's concern is just the sense that around the world the old order isn't holding and we're not quite yet to where we need to be in terms of a new order that's based on a different set of principles, that's based on a sense of common humanity, that's based on economies that work for all people."[78]

---

[73] Nafeez Ahmed (June 19, 2014), The open source revolution is coming and it will conquer the 1% - ex CIA spy, The Guardian.

[74] Juan Vicente Boo (March 28, 2014), Obama, al Papa Francisco: «Es maravilloso poder conocerle», ABC España. Note: translated in turn from Spanish into English.

[75] Ben Wolfgang (Dec. 30, 2014), President Obama sees Pope Francis as political ally, The Washington Times.

[76] Barbie Latza Nadeau (Dec. 17, 2014), The Pope's Diplomatic Miracle: Ending the U.S.-Cuba Cold War, The Daily Beast.

[77] Ibid.

[78] Briefing Room (July 22, 2014), Remarks by the President at a DNC Event -- Seattle, WA, The White House Office of the Press Secretary: https://obamawhitehouse.archives.gov/the-press-office/2014/07/22/remarks-president-dnc-event-seattle-wa; accessed November 28, 2023.

Pope Francis' address to the European Parliament (brief account)

The pope would attempt another important rapprochement. On November 25 of the same year, he traveled to Strasbourg, France, to address the European Parliament.[79]

It would be the second time that the Parliament would receive a pontiff of the Catholic Church after 26 years, when Pope John Paul II gave his historic speech in October 1998.[80]

Regarding Francis' visit to the Parliament, *El Mundo* reported on the European authorities who would receive the Pope:

"The main European authorities will be there to welcome Bergoglio. The President of the Commission, **Jean-Claude Juncker**, together with his College of Commissioners. The President of the European Parliament, **Martin Schultz**. The President of the European Council, **Herman Van Rompuy**, in one of his last acts; the President-in-turn of the Council, the Italian **Matteo Renzi**. The Secretary General of the Council, the Norwegian **Thorbjørn Jagland**. Belgian Prime Minister **Charles Michel**, the current President of the Council, as well as the Presidents of the Parliamentary Assembly, **Anne Brasseur**, and of the European Court of Human Rights, **Dean Spielmann**."[81]

But the Plural Left, which considered the event as a clear violation of the necessary and strict separation between religion and public institutions, as well as a serious offense to the secularity of millions of European citizens, sent a letter of protest to Schultz.[82] Martin Schultz, president of the organization, corresponds to the socialist-democratic ideology, which would attract him to certain tendencies of the pope.

Consider also that the Conservatives won the European Parliament elections in May 2014,[83] with Jean-Claude Junker, a Catholic and President of the European Commission.[84]

During his speech, Francis highlighted the predominant unity of European nations, but that the world was less Eurocentric because it is more interconnected and global.[85] He called for a return to the ability to work together to overcome divisions by fostering peace and harmony among all the peoples of the continent. Valuing human dignity, discarding treating people as if they were objects.[86] Said the pope:

"In the end, what kind of dignity is there without the possibility of freely expressing one's thought or professing one's religious faith? What dignity can there be without a clear juridical framework which limits the rule of force and enables the rule of law to prevail over the power of tyranny? What dignity can men and women ever enjoy if they are subjected to all types of discrimination? What dignity can a person ever hope

---

[79] Pablo R. Suanzes (November 25, 2014), El Papa Francisco visita el Parlamento Europeo, El Mundo.
[80] Ibid.
[81] Ibid.
[82] Ibid.
[83] (May 25, 2014), Victory for conservatives across Europe in EU elections, DW.
[84] (July 15, 2014), El Parlamento Europeo elige a Jean-Claude Juncker presidente de la Comisión, Notas de Prensa-Parlamento Europeo.
[85] Visit of His Holiness Pope Francis to the European Parliament and the Council of Europe (Strasbourg, November 25, 2014), Library Editrice Vaticana, p. 1.
[86] Ibid, p. 2.

to find when he or she lacks food and the bare essentials for survival and, worse yet, when they lack the work which confers dignity?"[87]

He referred to the individualism that emerges from the human person in the social context of others, to achieve the common good.[88]

He criticized the distant institutions that do not consider the sensibility of each people, and that Europe is getting tired of them. He reproached the "throwaway culture" and "uncontrolled consumerism" that does not value human life -such as abortion-: a criticism of the great European secularism. He stated that Europe cannot move forward without God and that its future depends on it. He warned that this contribution does not threaten the secularity of the States and the independence of the Union's institutions, "but rather an enrichment."[89] He also explained:

"I wish, then, to reiterate the readiness of the Holy See and the Catholic Church, through the Commission of the Bishops' Conferences of Europe (COMECE), to engage in meaningful, open and transparent dialogue with the institutions of the European Union. I am likewise convinced that a Europe which is capable of appreciating its religious roots and of grasping their fruitfulness and potential, will be all the more immune to the many forms of extremism spreading in the world today, not least as a result of the great vacuum of ideals which we are currently witnessing in the West, since "it is precisely man's forgetfulness of God, and his failure to give him glory, which gives rise to violence."[90]

Later, he explained that unity in diversity was important. Keeping democracy alive in Europe requires avoiding so many "globalizing tendencies" of diluting reality: angelic purisms, dictatorships of relativism, ahistorical fundamentalisms, ethicisms without goodness, intellectualisms without wisdom. He spoke about the waste of tons of food, the care of the environment, and the migration issue.[91]

He pointed out that two thousand years of history united Europe and Christianity, an identity that was worth safeguarding to obtain peace.[92]

He concluded:

"An anonymous second-century author wrote that "Christians are to the world what the soul is to the body". The function of the soul is to support the body, to be its conscience and its historical memory. A two-thousand-year-old history links Europe and Christianity. It is a history not free of conflicts and errors, and sins, but one constantly driven by the desire to work for the good of all. [...]

"Dear Members of the European Parliament, the time has come to work together in building a Europe which revolves not around the economy, but around the sacredness of the human person, around inalienable values. In building a Europe which

---

[87] Ibid.
[88] Ibid, p. 3.
[89] Ibid, p. 4.
[90] Ibid, p. 5.
[91] Ibid., pp. 5, 6.
[92] Ibid., pp. 7, 8.

courageously embraces its past and confidently looks to its future in order fully to experience the hope of its present. [...]

"Thank you!"[93]

This much-applauded speech was echoed by several media outlets.[94]

Accelerated ecumenism

Francis has been the pontiff who has reached out to different Christians of other denominations in a dizzying way. We will mention some extremely significant ecumenical encounters during his papacy, before talking about his visit to the United States and what it would mean.

By March 2013, he was visited by leaders of different religions: various Christian denominations, Jews, Muslims, and other religions.[95]

He was visited by Dr. Nikolaus Schneider, president of the Council of the Evangelical Church in Germany in April of the same year.[96] He met with a delegation that included Joel Osteen, a Mormon senator, and other North American leaders in June 2014.[97]

Kenneth Copeland, a well-known charismatic minister of the prosperity movement, ceded the platform to Anglican Tony Palmer at his church in Fort Worth, Texas in February of that year. There, he said, Luther's protest was over. Fifty-three thousand new denominations had been formed. But that "diversity is divine. It's division that's diabolic."[98] He expressed that the glory of God's presence is what matters and not the doctrines of the denominations.

Afterward, a video was projected with a message from Francis to the Copeland Church: "Excuse me, because I speak in Italian [...] But I will not speak in Italian, nor in English, but with my heart. It is a simpler, more authentic language, and this language of the heart has a special language and grammar. A simple grammar."[99]

He continued in part:

"Two rules: love God above all else and love the other, because he is your brother and sister. With these two rules we can move forward [...].

I feel nostalgic that this separation will come to an end and that it will give us communion. I am nostalgic for that embrace. That the Holy Scripture speaks of when Joseph's brothers began to starve; they went to Egypt [...] they found their brother [...] We must find each other as brothers. We must weep together as Joseph did.

---

[93] Ibid.

[94] Bernd Riegert (November 25, 2014), El Papa ante el Parlamento Europeo: "Un mensaje de esperanza y aliento," DW.

[95] Jim Yardley (March 20, 2013), Pope Meets Other Religious Leaders, Pledging Respect, The New York Times.

[96] Cindy Wooden (April 9, 2013), Evangelical pastor meets Pope Francis in Rome, Catholic Herald.

[97] Nicola Menzie (June 7, 2014), Pastor Joel Osteen, Mormon Senator, Other US Leaders Meet With Pope Francis in Rome (VIDEO), The Christian Post.

[98] (Feb. 28, 2014), Bishop Tony Palmer and Pope Francis - The Miracle of Unity has Begun: KCM Minister's Conference 2014, Tony Palmer: https://www.youtube.com/watch?v=YrS4IDTLavQ; accessed July 11, 2016.

[99] Ibid.

These tears will unite us. The tears of love. [...] the miracle of unity has begun [...] He will complete this miracle of unity."[100]

In July, Kenneth Copeland, James Robison, and Tony Palmer met with the pope at the Vatican for an ecumenical meeting.[101]

Also, at the end of July, Francis visited the Evangelical Church of Reconciliation in the southern Italian city of Caserta, where he spoke to 350 Pentecostals and asked forgiveness for the Catholic persecution of Pentecostals during Italian fascism.[102]

The following month, during his visit to South Korea, Pope Francis met with religious leaders at the Myeong-dong Cathedral in Seoul.[103]

He also received a delegation from the World Evangelical Alliance in November.[104] A few days later, Rick Warren during a conference on the family at the Vatican.[105]

Similarly, the pope visited the Evangelical Waldensian Church in Turin in June of the following year and asked forgiveness for how the Catholic Church had treated them in the past.[106]

He explained that Christ wants Christians united in "one body"[107] and that it is a "scandal" the division among them;[108] as well as other phrases.

At the end of May, he referred to the ecumenism of blood due to the persecutions of the Islamic State against Christians in the Middle East.[109] He indicated that it was time for Christians to unite in one body and that, "disunity is the work of the father of lies, the father of discord, who always seeks to divide brothers."[110] The pope had already referred to this in a less obvious tone in January.[111]

On May 23, 2016, Francis and the Grand Imam of Cairo, Ahmed al-Tayeb, embraced in a historic meeting at the Vatican, marking the culmination of a significant improvement in relations between the two religions.[112]

Religion News Service also announced on August 15 that the largest Lutheran denomination in the United States approved a statement acknowledging that, "there are no longer church-dividing issues" on many points with Catholicism.[113]

---

[100] Ibid.

[101] Sarah Pulliam Bailey (July 10, 2014), Pope Francis Meets With Kenneth Copeland, James Robison-High Fives Ensue, Charisma News.

[102] Nicole Winfield (July 28, 2014), Papal first: Francis visits Pentecostal church, Associated Press.

[103] Jung Yeon-je, Pool (Aug. 17, 2014), Pope Francis meets with South Korea's religious leaders at Myeong-dong Cathedral in Seoul, South Korea, on Monday, Aug. 18, 2014, Associated Press.

[104] Mark Woods (Nov. 6, 2014), 'New era' hailed in Evangelical-Roman Catholic relationships, Christian Today.

[105] Erika I. Ritchie (Nov. 17, 2014), Pastor Rick Warren speaks at Vatican conference on family, marriage, The Orange County Register.

[106] Domenico Agasso Jr. (June 22, 2015), Francis to Waldensians: "Forgive us for how we have treated you," Vatican Insider-La Stampa.

[107] Alvaro de Juana (Jan. 25, 2015), Papa Francisco: Jesús quiere a los cristianos unidos como "un solo cuerpo", ACI/EWTN Noticias.

[108] Alvaro de Juana (June 25, 2015), Papa Francisco asegura que es un "escándalo" la división entre los cristianos, ACI/EWTN Noticias.

[109] Alvaro de Juana (May 24, 2015), Hoy vivimos "ecumenismo de la sangre", dice el Papa sobre persecución contra cristianos, ACI Prensa.

[110] Ibid.

[111] (Jan. 26, 2015), Ecumenismo de la sangre, L'Osservatore Romano.

[112] (May 23, 2016), Pope and top imam embrace in historic Vatican meeting, AFP.

In a similar context, the Pope received about a thousand pilgrims at the Vatican, many of them German Lutherans, as part of the ecumenical preparations for the celebration of the 500th anniversary of the beginning of the Lutheran Reformation. The Pope encouraged those present to seek unity through charity, noting that by serving those most in need, unity is already experienced, because, "it is the mercy of God that unites us." He also referred to "how Catholics and Lutherans are part of the same body of Christ."[114]

The 500th anniversary of the Lutheran Reformation in Lund, Sweden, was marked by the participation of Pope Francis, where after the historic ecumenical celebration, the pope and the general secretary of the world's Lutheran churches agreed to work together for a shared Eucharist.[115]

On September 9, Francis met with a group of Pentecostal pastors, where he told them that unity is achieved by patiently walking together.[116]

On September 20, there was a large gathering of 500 religious leaders from all over the world in Assisi; from the Islamic, Orthodox, Anglican, Jewish, and Buddhist religions.[117]

Taking all this into account, the Deputy Grand Imam of the Egyptian Islamic University of Al-Azhar, Abbas Shuman, as well as delegate for interfaith dialogue, revealed the intention to organize a world interfaith conference on peace with the Vatican.[118] And all with the intention of working to convince politicians and world decision-makers to adhere to a serious dialogue; abandoning all violent methods of resolving crises and problems.[119]

Also on November 3, the Pope received 200 members of the Christian, Jewish, Muslim, Buddhist, Hindu, and other religions involved in charity and mercy. The audience was held in the context of the Jubilee Year. He appealed to them for mercy and peace in times of war and general disorientation.[120]

Pope Francis' visit to the U.S. Congress

But it was in the framework of the ecumenical meetings of 2013-15, that Francis would make a historic visit to the United States from September 22-27, 2015 (previously visiting Cuba).

Archbishop Bernardito Auza, permanent observer of the Holy See to the UN and the OAS (Organization of American States) in Washington, was a member of the committee for the Pope's visit and revealed details of the proposed schedule, which would include a visit to the White House on the 23rd.[121] There he would meet with

---

[113] Emily McFarlan Miller (Aug. 15, 2016), US Lutherans approve document recognizing agreement with Catholic Church, Religion News Service.

[114] (Oct. 13, 2016), Pope Francis to Lutheran pilgrims: seek unity through charity, Vatican Radio.

[115] Austen Ivereigh (October 31, 2016), Catholic and Lutheran Churches pledge to work for shared Eucharist, Crux.

[116] (Sept. 9, 2016), Pope holds private encounter with Pentecostal pastors, Vatican Radio.

[117] Ary Waldir Ramos Diaz (September 20, 2016), Papa Francisco a los líderes religiosos del mundo en Asís, Aleteia.

[118] Editor (Sept. 21, 2016), Al-Azhar planea un cumbre interreligiosa de paz con el Vaticano, Zenit.

[119] Ibid.

[120] Ary Waldir Ramos Diaz (November 3, 2016), Papa Francisco: No hay tecnología que sacie la sed de misericordia, Aleteia.

[121] Alan Holdren and Elise Harris (Jan. 18, 2015), Exclusive: Details of the proposal for Pope Francis' US visit revealed, Catholic News Agency.

Obama to discuss poverty, climate change, and the conflict in the Middle East.[122] Consider that Obama believed that Francis is "a transformational leader, not just within the Catholic Church, but globally."[123]

Francis would also celebrate an open-air Mass at Catholic University in D.C.[124] For that same day -23, he would canonize Fray Junipero Serra, an 18th century Majorcan Franciscan friar from Majorca, founder of several missions in California;[125] and commissary of the Holy Office in Mexico, a title granted by the Inquisition in 1752 for all of New Spain and adjacent islands.[126]

Francis would address the U.S. Congress on the 24th.[127] He would be the first pope to address the U.S. Congress, something that would undoubtedly be historic and very significant.

On the 25th, the pope would give his long-awaited address to the United Nations[128] and hold an interfaith meeting. On that day, he was expected to visit Ground Zero in New York, where the September 11, 2001 attacks occurred.[129]

He would also celebrate an open-air Mass in Philadelphia around the events of the World Meeting of Families,[130] which would take place on the 26th and 27th.[131]

His words on the family, human dignity in general, and its relation to Sunday rest should be emphasized:

"Together with a culture of work, there must be a culture of leisure as gratification. To put it another way: people who work must take the time to relax, to be with their families, to enjoy themselves, read, listen to music, play a sport. But this is being destroyed, in large part, by the elimination of the Sabbath rest day. More and more people work on Sundays as a consequence of the competitiveness imposed by a consumer society." In such cases, he concludes, "work ends up dehumanizing people."[132]

And again, this time in July 2014, he referred to the negative impact on families and friends of abandoning Sunday rest[133] and related it to respect for God's creation.[134]

---

[122] Sarah Pulliam Bailey (April 28. 2015), Pope Francis will visit DC Sept. 22-25. Obama hints at what he expects to speak with Pope Francis, The Washington Post.

[123] (Apr. 27, 2015), WSJ Interview Transcript: President Obama on TPP, China, Japan, Pope Francis, Cuba, Wall Street Journal.

[124] Sarah Pulliam Bailey (April 28. 2015), Pope Francis will visit DC Sept. 22-25. Obama hints at what he expects to speak with Pope Francis, The Washington Post.

[125] (April 20, 2015), Papa Grancisco canonizará a Fray Junípero Serra en Washington D.C., ACI/EWTN Noticias.

[126] Gaspar de Portola, Crónicas del descubrimiento de la Alta California, 1769 (Ediciones de la Universidad de Barcelona, 1984), p. 285.

[127] Ibid.

[128] Ibid.

[129] Alan Holdren and Elise Harris (Jan. 18, 2015), Exclusive: Details of the proposal for Pope Francis' US visit revealed, Catholic News Agency.

[130] Sarah Pulliam Bailey (April 28. 2015), Pope Francis will visit DC Sept. 22-25. Obama hints at what he expects to speak with Pope Francis, The Washington Post.

[131] Alan Holdren and Elise Harris (Jan. 18, 2015), Exclusive: Details of the proposal for Pope Francis' US visit revealed, Catholic News Agency.

[132] Mark Oppenheimer (April 26, 2013), Pope Francis Has a Few Words in Support of Leisure, The New York Times.

[133] (July 5, 2014), Pope: No-work Sundays good, not just for faithful, AP.

A top Vatican adviser, Jeffrey Sachs, a writer on sustainable economics,[135] said that when the pope visits the nation in September, he would directly challenge the "American idea" of God-given rights in the Declaration of Independence.[136]

Sachs wrote in *America*, the American Jesuit publication, that the United States is "a society in thrall" to the idea of the inalienable rights to life, liberty, and the pursuit of happiness; and that the "urgent core of Francis' message" will be to challenge "this American idea by proclaiming that the path to happiness lies not solely or mainly through the defense of rights but through the exercise of virtues, most notably justice and charity."[137] These comments constitute a frontal assault on the American ideal of liberty and national sovereignty.[138]

Sachs expected the Vatican to engage in a global campaign to increase the power of global or foreign (dominated) organizations and movements.[139]

Global government, according to him, must make us live according to international development standards. Global organizations such as the UN must dictate the course of nations, and individual rights "must be sacrificed for the greater good."[140]

In this regard, the *National Catholic Reporter* indicated that the pope would recommend to Obama that workers unionize, as the pope deplores "unjust economic structures that generate enormous inequalities"; and Obama has called inequality "the defining issue of our time."[141] In allusion to this, the economic structure would change for everyone, as Francis called on the faithful "to fight for social benefits, a dignified retirement, holidays, rest, and freedom for unions. All these issues create social justice.[142]

Pope Francis would address the UN on climate change, hoping to make a big impact.

Being a global and influential pope, it was not for nothing that *Time* Magazine published a long article on September 17 of that year entitled, "Pope Francis and the New Roman Empire." The article noted his role from Cuba to climate change, that Pope Francis "has revitalized the Vatican's role in global diplomacy." And that his

---

[134] (July 7, 2014), Pope travels to Molise, speaks on respect for creation, Sunday rest, Catholic World News.

[135] Jeffrey D. Sachs, The End of Poverty: Economic Possibilities for Our Time (The Penguin Press, New York, 2005); Jeffrey D. Sachs, Common Wealth: Economics for a Crowded Planet (Penguin Books, New York, 2009); Jeffrey D. Sachs, The Price of Civilization: Reawekening American Virtue and Prosperity (Random House, New York, 2011); Jeffrey D. Sachs, The Age of Sustainable Development (Columbia University Press, 2015); Jeffrey D. Sachs, Building the New American Economy: Smart, Fair, & Sustainable (Columbia University Press, New York, 2017); Jeffrey D. Sachs, The Age of Sustainable Development (Columbia University Press, 2015). Sachs, The Age of Sustainable Development (Columbia University Press, 2015); Jeffrey D. Sachs, Building the New American Economy: Smart, Fair, & Sustainable (Columbia University Press, New York, 2017); Jeffrey D. Sachs, A New Foreign Policy: Beyond American Exceptionalism (Columbia University Press, New York, 2018); Jeffrey Sachs (December 5, 2019), Getting to a Carbon-Free Economy, The American Prospect.

[136] Cliff Kincaid (May 19, 2015), Vatican Adviser Says America's Founding Document Is Outmoded, Reveals Global Game Plan, Western Journalism.

[137] Jeffrey D. Sachs (May 6, 2015), A Call to Virtue: Living the Gospel in the land of liberty, America Magazine.

[138] Cliff Kincaid (May 19, 2015), Vatican Adviser Says America's Founding Document Is Outmoded, Reveals Global Game Plan, Western Journalism.

[139] Ibid.

[140] Ibid.

[141] Simone Campbell (June 18, 2014), What Francis would say to Obama: Let workers unionize, National Catholic Reporter.

[142] Ibid.

activist agenda was brought to the United States. His trips to countries in the Global South such as Sri Lanka, the Philippines, Bolivia, and Brazil are mentioned. Mention is made of his mediation to avoid military intervention in Syria, the dialogue in Iraq, his encyclical on climate change, his approaches to China, to the Dalai Lama, and his historic visit to the United States: the White House, Congress, the UN, etc.[143]

After he visited Cuba to strengthen ties between the United States and the Latin American country, Pope Francis arrived on September 22 at Andrews Air Force Base, where he was received by an entourage, including President Barack Obama. On the 23rd, he met with the U.S. president in the White House gardens, offering a speech attended by thousands and thousands of people (10 thousand),[144] and many others greeted the "Pope of the people" -as they call him in the United States- on his way to his destination, who were waiting for him in the early hours of the morning.[145]

Obama delivered a welcoming speech in which he praised Francis for giving a moral and religious connotation to efforts to combat global warming.[146]

"He reminds us that we have a sacred obligation to our planet, God's magnificent gift to us. We support his call to world leaders (...) to join together to preserve our precious planet for future generations."[147]

Francis, for his part, addressing President Obama, told him that "together with their fellow citizens, American Catholics are committed to building a society which is truly tolerant and inclusive, to safeguarding the rights of individuals and communities, and to rejecting every form of unjust discrimination."[148]

Then, about the deterioration of religious freedom suffered by Catholics and other denominations due to the practice of compulsory abortion in their medical institutions, he pointed out:

"With countless other people of good will, they are likewise concerned that efforts to build a just and wisely ordered society respect their deepest concerns and their right to religious liberty. That freedom remains one of America's most precious possessions. And, as my brothers, the United States Bishops, have reminded us, all are called to be vigilant, precisely as good citizens, to preserve and defend that freedom from everything that would threaten or compromise it."[149]

He then praised the government's concern for an initiative to reduce air pollution, stating that climate change is an issue that can no longer be left for a future generation and that in that respect, "we are living at a critical moment of history."[150]

---

[143] Elizabeth Dias (September 17, 2015), Pope Francis and the New Roman Empire, Times Magazine.

[144] (September 23, 2015), Papa Francisco se reúne con Barack Obama en la Casa Blanca, La Nación Costa Rica.

[145] Paula Lugones (September 23, 2015), Miles de personas rodean la Casa Blanca para ver al "Papa de la gente", Clarín.

[146] (September 23, 2015), Papa Francisco se reúne con Barack Obama en la Casa Blanca, La Nación Costa Rica.

[147] Ibid.

[148] Kirsten Andersen (September 24, 2015), Pope to Congress: Love People Like It's Your Job, Because It Is, Aleteia

[149] Ibid.

[150] Ibid.

They then met privately in the Oval Office, where they discussed the Syrian refugee crisis, climate change, poverty, and religious freedom.[151]

On September 24, the Pope went to Capitol Hill where he gave his address to the U.S. Congress. He was accompanied by legislators of all tendencies and religious confessions, committed to pause in the discussions and dysfunction that characterize them, to listen to what the pontiff of the most influential church in the world had to say.[152]

But also in attendance were Supreme Court Justices (some Catholics among them), Cabinet secretaries, and other guests. Early in the morning, "people began to arrive amidst security measures and a police presence similar to that surrounding an annual swearing-in or speech of the president."[153]

"Lawmakers from both parties have sought political mileage from Pope Francis' positions. Democrats are thrilled with his support for reforming immigration laws, as well as fighting climate change and income disparity."[154]

The main points of his speech were that they, the legislators, as the face of their people, are called to defend and preserve the dignity of their compatriots in the tireless and demanding pursuit of the common good, as it is the primary goal of all politics.[155] Indeed, the pope "has deplored "unfair economic structures that create huge inequalities;" while Obama called inequality "the defining issue of our time."[156] Simone Campbell described the pope's call "to fight for social benefits, a dignified retirement, holidays, rest, and freedom for trade unions. All of these issues create social justice."[157]

Pope Francis linked that responsibility with the legislature of Moses, which must lead to God:

"Yours is a work which makes me reflect in two ways on the figure of Moses. On the one hand, the patriarch and lawgiver of the people of Israel symbolizes the need of peoples to keep alive their sense of unity by means of just legislation. On the other, the figure of Moses leads us directly to God and thus to the transcendent dignity of the human being."[158]

He mentioned men and women in U.S. history who forged a better future for their country. He alluded to Abraham Lincoln, Martin Luther King, Dorothy Day, and Thomas Merton. Dorothy Day was a Catholic who had the patronage of Christian trade

---

[151] Feed Lucas (Sept. 23, 2015), Obama, Pope Exchange Gifts, Talk Refugee Crisis and Religious Freedom in Oval Office Meeting, The Blaze.

[152] La Prensa (September 24, 2015), Francisco, el primer papa en el Congreso de Estados Unidos, La Prensa Panamá.

[153] Ibid.

[154] Ibid.

[155] Kirsten Andersen (September 24, 2015), Pope to Congress: Love People Like It's Your Job, Because It Is, Aleteia.

[156] Simone Campbell (June 18, 2014), What Francis would say to Obama: Let workers unionize, National Catholic Reporter.

[157] Ibid.

[158] Kirsten Andersen (September 24, 2015), Pope to Congress: Love People Like It's Your Job, Because It Is, Aleteia. Note: unless otherwise noted, this is the same source.

unionists, but she was also a consummate communist. Thomas Merton was a Trappist monk also attracted to communist ideas.

About Abraham Lincoln, being the best-known president of the United States, Francis referred to him as the guardian of freedom, someone who worked tirelessly so that, "this nation, under God, [might] have a new rebirth of freedom."

When referring to ideological extremism:

"This means that we must be especially attentive to every type of fundamentalism, whether religious or of any other kind. A delicate balance is required to combat violence perpetrated in the name of a religion, an ideology or an economic system, while also safeguarding religious freedom, intellectual freedom and individual freedoms."

Later he said:

"In this land, the various religious denominations have greatly contributed to building and strengthening society. It is important that today, as in the past, the voice of faith continue to be heard, for it is a voice of fraternity and love, which tries to bring out the best in each person and in each society. Such cooperation is a powerful resource in the battle to eliminate new global forms of slavery, born of grave injustices which can be overcome only through new policies and new forms of social consensus."

In other words, for Pope Francis, these new forms of global slavery are "forced labor, prostitution, organ trafficking" and others.[159] On forced labor, *The New York Times*, reporting on Francis' book "Pope Francis: His Life in His Own Words," indicated that more and more people work on Sundays as a consequence of the competitiveness imposed by a consumerist society, which ends up dehumanizing people.[160] The *Associated Press* reported that Francis regretted the abandonment of the traditional "Christian" practice of not working on Sundays, since it had a negative impact on families and friendships; and that opening stores and other businesses on that day as a way to create jobs was not beneficial to society. He expressed that the priority should be "not economic but human." That the emphasis should rest on family and friendships; and not on commercial relationships. "Maybe it's time to ask ourselves if working on Sundays is true freedom" - the pope said.[161] During an interview in July 2014 with the Argentine newspaper *Clarín*, he offered 10 "tips" to be happy, among which was to "Share Sundays with the family."[162] Months later, in 2015, Pope Francis referred to the right to work and rest, particularly the *biblical* weekly rest.[163] The pope was more precise when on August 12 of the same year, he said, "we must never be

---

[159] Sergio Mora (Dec. 2, 2014), Líderes religiosos firmaron con el papa contra la trata de personas, Zenit.

[160] Mark Oppenheimer (April 26, 2013), Pope Francis Has a Few Words in Support of Leisure, The New York Times.

[161] AP (July 5, 2014), Pope: No-work Sundays good, not just for faithful, Associated Press.

[162] (July 28, 2014), En palabras de Francisco: el Papa exlica sus 10 "tips" para ser feliz, Clarín.

[163] Ann Scneible (Nov. 7, 2015), If you have the right to work, you have the right to rest, Pope says, CNA/EWTN News.

slaves to work but rather its master."[164] He expressed it - though not only - but especially about Sunday rest.[165]

Returning to the speech, the pope invoked the Declaration of Independence [this is in the original, but not read in Congress]:

"We hold these truths to be self-evident: that all men are created equal, that they are endowed by their Creator with certain inalienable rights, among which are life, liberty and the pursuit of happiness."[166]

With this in mind, for the pope, modern forms of slavery must be addressed by lawmakers, by granting those inalienable rights that God endowed and that are within the framework of "life, liberty and the pursuit of happiness." For this reason, he almost immediately stated: "If politics must truly be at the service of the human person, it follows that it cannot be a slave to the economy and finance."
"I am happy that America continues to be, for many, a land of "dreams"." - the pope said, drawing applause from lawmakers.

He referred to the creation of redistribution of wealth, the correct use of natural resources, the common good in the creation of jobs, and the issue of climate change: issues that must be fought for.

He spoke about the service of dialogue and peace to minimize and, in the long term, end all wars in the world, as well as to stop arms trafficking.[167]

Pope Francis concluded his speech by saying:

"In these remarks I have sought to present some of the richness of your cultural heritage, of the spirit of the American people. It is my desire that this spirit continue to develop and grow, so that as many young people as possible can inherit and dwell in a land which has inspired so many people to dream. (*applause*)

"God bless America! (*standing ovation, loud cheering*)"

His speech was the subject of great admiration by many media all over the world.[168]

Luis Rosales of *Infobae* wrote an article entitled, "EEUU de rodillas ante Francisco" ("USA on its knees before Francis").[169]

Howard Fineman, in the September 24 *Huffington Post* article, entitled, "Pope Francis Wants To Be President Of The World," indicated that Francis demonstrated his

---

[164] (Aug. 12, 2015), Pope Francis: Audience reflection on celebration, work and prayer, Vatican Radio.

[165] Ibid; see also Peter Kenny (Aug. 13, 2015), Pope Francis says Sundays are a gift from God not to be shunned, Ecumenical News.

[166] Kirsten Andersen (September 24, 2015), Pope to Congress: Love People Like It's Your Job, Because It Is, Aleteia., 2015), Pope to Congress: Love People Like It's Your Job, Because It Is, Aleteia. Note: unless otherwise noted, this is the same source. Note: unless otherwise noted, this is the same source.

[167] Ibid.

[168] Rory Carroll (Sept. 24, 2015), Pope Francis electrifies Congress with speech laying out bold vision for US, The Guardian; Domenico Montanaro (Sept. 24, 2015), The 10 Most Political Moments In Pope Francis' Address To Congress, NPR; Stephen Collinson and Daniel Burke (Sept. 24, 2015), Pope delivers political message on immigration, tolerance to Congress, CNN.

[169] Luis Rosales (Oct. 5, 2017), EEUU de rodillas ante Francisco, Infobae.

desire for the presidency "in a massive legislative building" (Congress) by moving his campaign by taking his public, secular and political discourse around the world.[170]

Fineman indicated that the pope knows the demographic areas: in Latin America, Africa, and elsewhere, where the Catholic Church is in competition with Islam and evangelical Protestantism; and that he wants to win the battle. Washington, for him, was another stop on his campaign.[171]

Pope Francis and the UN Agenda
a. Brief History of the Climate Change Agenda
Mikhail Gorbachev said in his speech at the Opening of the Fourth International Global Forum of Spiritual and Parliamentary Leaders held on April 20, 1993 in Kyoto, Japan:

"The emerging 'environmentalisation' of our civilization and the need for vigorous action in the interest of the entire global community will inevitably have multiple political consequences. Perhaps the most important one of them will be a gradual change in the status of the United Nations. Inevitably, it must asume some aspects of a world government. Indeed, such a process has already begun. One day, however, the entire structure of the organization will have to be reconsidered."[172]

For Gorbachev, it was a race against time to save the planet and for the renewal of civilization.[173]

In 1995, together with New Age theologian and idealist James Garrison, he created the State of World Forum, intending to establish a global network of leaders dedicated to a more sustainable global civilization.[174]

Before the first Forum to be held that year, Garrison stated in an interview with *San Francisco Weekly* magazine that the first Forum would address issues such as nuclear weapons proliferation and environmental decay. When asked what would follow, he said, "Over the next 20 to 30 years, we are going to end up with world government," he says. "It's inevitable."[175]

The Forum now has partners from around the world who meet annually to develop a search for solutions to critical global challenges. It also had about 20 co-chairs, including some moderates. But it has been strongly left-leaning, which included Ruud Lubbers, Rigoberta Menchu Tum, Ted Turner, Maurice Strong, and others.

At the 1995 World State Forum held in San Francisco from September 27 to October 1, unity in diversity-rich and poor; cultural differences and selected religious beliefs-with full conformity of all to a new international law was discussed.[176] Throughout the

---

[170]. Howard Fineman (September 24, 2015), Pope Francis Wants To Be President Of The World, The Hufftington Post.

[171] Ibid.

[172] Mikhail Gorbachev and Green Cross International, Mikhail Gorbachev: Prophet of Change: From the Cold War to a Sustainable World (Clairview Books, 2011), p. 78.

[173] Ibid.

[174] Robert Chandler, Shadow World: Resurgent Russia, The Global New Left, and Radical Islam (Regnery Publishing, Inc., 2008), p. 518.

[175] George Cothran (May 31-June 6, 1995), One World, Under Gorby, San Francisco Weekly, Vol. 14, No. 16, ob. cit.

[176] Samantha Smith, "Gorbachev Forum Highlights World Government," Hope for the World Update, (Noblesville, IN: Hope for the World, Fall 1995), p. 2.; quoted in Gary H. Kah, The New World Religion:

conference, the words "New World Order," "World Government," "Global Governance" and "Global Government" were heard. Zbigniew Brzezinski (Jimmy Carter's National Security Advisor), said that World Government is a process... and the precondition for genuine globalization is progressive regionalization.[177]

Author and journalist Samantha Smith criticized the presence of a group of New Age elitists, such as Shirley MacLaine, Dennis Weaver, John Denver, John Naisbitt, Carl Sagan, Ted Turner, Jane Fonda, Barbara Marx Hubbard, Maurice Strong, Robert Muller, Dr. Deepak Chopra, Matthew Fox, Alan Jones, Michael Murphy, and James Garrison.[178]

The argument of the spiritual was woven throughout the conference, and one of the sessions was entitled, "The Global Crisis of Spirit and the Search for Meaning." Attendees were told that they had a god void in their hearts that needed to be filled. Eagerly, the religious panelists offered several different *gods* and Eastern philosophies from which they could choose. Spiritual leaders invited to the Forum: Isabel Allende- the author of The House of the Spirits; Richard Baker, Abbott of the Crestone Mountain Zen Center; Akio Matsumura, founder of the Global Forum of Spiritual and Parliamentary Leaders, as well as Sonia Gandhi, the founder of the Rajiv Gandhi Foundation (who co-sponsored the event). To name but a few.[179]

Gorbachev chose Thich Nhat Hanh, a renowned Vietnamese monk to lead a special half-day meditation during the Forum.[180]

The Los Angeles Times conducted an interview with Gorbachev that was published on May 13, 1997, stating, "In this new synthesis, we need democratic, Christian and Buddhist values as well, which affirm such moral principles as social responsibility and the sense of oneness with nature and each other. The future should be built with these moral building blocks that are centuries old."[181] He warned that a new international legal code on the environment rooted in the Earth Charter was needed; "a covenant similar to the United Nations Declaration of Human Rights. .... My hope is that this charter will be a kind of Ten Commandments, a "Sermon on the Mount", that provides a guide for human behavior toward the environment in the next century and beyond."[182]

The Earth Charter calls to: "Eliminate discrimination in all its forms, such as that based on race, color, sex, sexual orientation, religion, language, and national, ethnic or social origin."[183]

The Spiritual Roots of Global Government (Hope International Publishing, Inc. Indiana, U.S.A., 1998), p. 140.

[177] Ibid.

[178] Ibid, p. 141.

[179] Ibid.

[180] Ibid.

[181] Mikhail Gorbachev, "Environment: Act Globally, Not Nationally," Interview with The Los Angeles Times, (Thursday, May 8, 1997). Green Cross International (web page http://www.gci.ch/GreenCrossFamily/gorby/newspeeches/interviews/laTimes.html [Accessed March 20, 1998]); cited in Gary H. Kah, The New World Religion: The Spiritual Roots of Global Government (Hope International Publishing), ob. cit.

[182] Green Cross International, "Interview-Environment: 'Act Globally, not Nationally,'" Los Angeles Times, May 8, 1997, http://www.greencrossinternational.net/GreenCrossFamily/gorby/newspeeches/interviews/laTimes.htmlIm preso on 09/05/03; quoted in Lee Penn, False Dawn: The United Religions Initiative, Globalism, and the Quest for a One-World Religion (Sophia Perennis, Hillsdale NY, 2004), p. 380.

[183] https://earthcharter.org/wp-content/uploads/2020/03/echarter_english.pdf?x68263; accessed March 22, 2024.

In this regard, the aspects of the elimination of discrimination based on "sexual orientation" and "religion" are significant. These are advocated today - in addition to the rest - by the United Nations and Pope Francis. Likewise, liberation theologian Leonardo Boff, who is also a member of the Earth Charter Initiative, highlighted the affinities between the Earth Charter and Pope Francis' encyclical on climate: "Laudato Si."[184] Pope Francis in his encyclical endorses the Earth Charter:

"The Earth Charter asked us to leave behind a period of self-destruction and make a new start, but we have not as yet developed a universal awareness needed to achieve this. Here, I would echo that courageous challenge: "As never before in history, common destiny beckons us to seek a new beginning… Let ours be a time remembered for the awakening of a new reverence for life, the firm resolve to achieve sustainability, the quickening of the struggle for justice and peace, and the joyful celebration of life".[185]

When he was Archbishop of Buenos Aires, Jorge Mario Bergoglio (now Pope Francis) met in May 2007 with religious leaders of Argentina at the Metropolitan Cathedral of Buenos Aires, and with Episcopal Bishop William Swing, founder in 2000 of the United Religions Initiative (URI), headquartered at the United Nations in New York.[186] This organization brings together countless religions from all over the world, including New Agers. It is widely spread globally. The late Swing was a strong believer in the LGBT-inclusive community and he ordained gay parishioners in his church.[187]

Luis Dolan, an Argentine Catholic priest, was its coordinator in Latin America. He declared in 1997 that the United Nations is like a cathedral where one can worship as one wishes.[188] He also said that for the creation of "the future world order," the "Church of the future needs to come across primarily as a community of believers, rather than as an institution with a hierarchical structure." And he opposed the "belligerent attitude" of the Vatican at UN conferences,[189] a scheme that Pope Francis has almost completely changed.

Dolan drew attention to the UN's conscious attitude to global governance calling for a new vision; which will not work unless it is presented as a religious ideal.[190] And he referred to a syncretism that must be adapted to the world of the future.[191]

---

[184] Leonardo Boff (July 27, 2015), Leonardo Boff: Affinities between the Encyclical "Laudato Si" and the "Earth Charter," Earth Charter Initiative News.

[185] Pope Francis, Encyclical Letter Laudato si' of the Holy Father Francis on care for our common home (Vatican Press, May 24, 2015), p. 160; citing *Earth Charter*, The Hague (29 June 2000).

[186] Maria Eugenia (March 13, 2014), One year back…reflections on Pope Francis, URI News Desk.

[187] Sonia Arrison, 100 Plus: How the Coming Age of Longevity Will Change Everything, From Careers and Relationships to Family and Faith (Basic Books, 2011), ob. cit.

[188] Fr. Luis Dolan, "Development and Spirituality: Personal Reflections of a Catholic," (Global Education Associates), http://www.globaleduc.org/dolan.htm, printed 5/14/99; quoted in Lee Penn, False Dawn: The United Religions Initiative, Globalism, and the Quest for a One-World Religion (Sophia Perennis, Hillsdale NY, 2004), p. 167.

[189] Ibid.; quoted in Ibid.

[190] Lee Penn (Fall/Winter 1999), The United Religions Initiative: Globalist and new age Plans (part 2 of 3), SCP Journal, Vol. 23; ob. cit.; cited in Catholic Culture: https://www.catholicculture.org/culture/library/view.cfm?recnum=2924; accessed July 1, 2016.

b. The UN surrenders to the Catholic Church

Ban Ki-moon, then UN Secretary-General, addressed Cardinal Jorge Mario Bergoglio on his election to the papacy in the following terms:

"I offer my heartfelt congratulations to Cardinal Jorge Mario Bergoglio of Buenos Aires, Argentina, who has taken the name Pope Francis on his assumption of the papacy, and to all Catholics across the world on this momentous occasion.

"I look forward to continuing cooperation between the United Nations and the Holy See, under the wise leadership of His Holiness Pope Francis.

"We share many common goals – from the promotion of peace, social justice and human rights, to the eradication of poverty and hunger – all core elements of sustainable development.

"We also share the conviction that we can only resolve the interconnected challenges of today's world through dialogue. I am certain that His Holiness will continue to build on the legacy of his predecessor, Pope Benedict XVI, in the promotion of inter-faith dialogue which is at the heart of the Alliance of Civilizations initiative."[192]

The Alliance of Civilizations is a United Nations organization established in 2005, which advocates an alliance between the West and the Arab-Muslim world, intending to combat international terrorism in a non-military way.

However, their development was expanded by indicating that they work for a more peaceful world with more social inclusion by building mutual respect among peoples of different cultural and religious identities, highlighting the willingness of the majority of the world to reject extremism and embrace diversity.

UNAOC (United Nations Alliance of Civilizations) assists in the reduction of hostility and promotes harmony among nations. Ban Ki-moon described it as a soft power tool to bridge differences and promote understanding between countries or identity groups. All to prevent conflict and promote social cohesion.

Nassir Abdulaziz Al-Nasser, UNAOC High Representative, said on March 13, 2013 - when Bergoglio was elected pope - that through cooperation between the UNAOC and the Vatican, both can advance the cause of peace and build bridges of understanding and dialogue instead of hatred and division.[193] Nasser said just weeks into the Pope's one-year pontificate, that Francis has addressed the difficult issues of poverty and development, publicly condemning an "economy of exclusion." He added "Though the pope is a religious figure, his influence extends beyond that of his own faith. This further enforces the reality that religion is profoundly intertwined with

---

[191] Luis Dolan, "Development and Spirituality: Personal Reflections of a Catholic," Internet document (Global Education Associates), http://www.globaleduc.org/dolan.htm, pp. 9-11; quoted in Ibid.

[192] Ban-Ki Moon (March 13, 2013), Statement by the Secretary-General on the election of Pope Francis, United Nations: https://www.un.org/sg/en/content/sg/statement/2013-03-13/statement-the-secretary-general-the-election-of-pope-francis Accessed March 22, 2024.

[193] (March 13, 2013), UN officials congratulate Pope Francis on assuming leadership of Catholic Church, UN News Centre.

economic and social progress."[194] The United Nations affirms that the promotion of interfaith dialogue as a major driver of its agenda is intertwined with the role of economic and social progress, and whose influence extends beyond his faith. The United Nations is thus tacitly uniting the cooperation of Church and State in social and economic matters; and thus contesting the policy of the member nations of the globe.

Likewise, the UN and the Vatican agreed on the issue of the family in world society, as well as support for migration.[195]

The UN has been fully in favor of gay, lesbian, bisexual, and transgender rights since 2012.[196]

The economy, social inequality, inclusion of all religions, and respect for the LGBT community are on the same agenda as Pope Francis.

Another point of agreement, as we will consider later, is global warming.

The aforementioned UNAOC High Representative, Al-Nasser, had an audience in the Vatican with Francis at the end of March 2014. The two discussed several topics related to the condition of world stability, such as conflicts of cultural and religious dimension. They addressed issues related to interfaith dialogue, intercultural understanding, and peaceful mediation, as well as the work of the Alliance of Civilizations in these areas.[197]

The latest developments in the Middle East were also discussed, especially the situation in Syria, the Palestinian question, the crisis in Ukraine, and other global humanitarian issues.[198]

Eight days after his election, Pope Francis - who owes his name to St. Francis of Assisi -[199] again called attention to the need to protect nature, Reuters quoted him as saying:

---

[194] (Feb. 12, 2014), Remarks By H.E. Mr. Nassir Abdulaziz Al-Nasser United Nations High Representative For the Alliance of Civilizations At "World Interfaith Harmony: Vital for Peace and Development," UNAOC Press Room; (Apr. 15, 2013), Ban Ki-moon: Struggle for LGBT right one of the great, neglected human rights challenges of our time, United Nations. https://www.youtube.com/watch?v=7uaHZWCgGss; accessed June 23, 2016; Opening Remarks by UN High Commissioner for Human Rights Navi Pillay at the Free & Equal Campaign Press Launch, United Nations Huma Rights Office of the High Commissioner, Ciudad del Cabo, July 26, 2013; (June 27, 2015), La ONU ve el reconocimiento del matrimonio homosexual en EEUU como "un paso enorme", europa press; Poner fin a la violencia y a la discriminación contra las personas lesbianas, gais, bisexuales, trans e intersex, ACNUDH, September 27, 2015; Secretary-General's remarks at the High Level LGBT Core Group Event "Leaving No-One Behind: Equality & Inclusion in the Post-2015 Development Agenda," United Nations, New York, September 29, 2015; Karthikeyan Hemalatha (September 30, 2015), Ban ki-Moon pushes for equal rights for the LGBT community, The Times of India; (February 7, 2016), La ONU crea sellos para reivindicar la homosexualidad y los 'derechos LGBT', Actuall; "Pathologization - Being lesbian, gay, bisexual and/or trans is not an illness" For International Day against Homophobia, Transphobia and Biphobia, United Nations Human Rights Office of the High Commissioner, May 17, 2016; (June 23, 2016), ONU pide a los Estados redoblar esfuerzos para defender a personas LGBTI detenidas, Centro de Noticias ONU.

[195] (December 2, 2014) Remarks By the High Representative of the United Nations Alliance of Civilizations Nassir Abdulaziz Al-Nasser At The World Family Summit+10 "Families in Balance: Building the Future We Want," UNAOC Press Room.

[196] Born Free and Equal: Sexual Orientation and Gender Identity in International Human Rights Law (Office of the High Commissioner, New York and Genoa, 2012).

[197] (March 28, 2014), The High Representative for the Alliance of Civilizations has audience with His Holiness Pope Francis, UNAOC News.

[198] Ibid.

[199] Elisabetta Piqué (March 17, 2013), "¡Cómo quisiera ver una Iglesia pobre para los pobres!, dijo el Papa", La Nación.

"Here too, it helps me to think of the name of (Saint)Francis, who teaches us profound respect for the whole of creation and the protection of our environment, which all too often, instead of using for the good, we exploit greedily, to one another's detriment."[200]

Less than a month after his election (April 9, 2013), Francis received Ban Ki-moon at the Vatican, who greeted the Pope very cordially and defined him as "the spiritual leader of the world," and indicated that "the UN and the Vatican share many ideas and objectives." The two exchanged views on "situations of conflict and humanitarian emergency," such as the war in Syria and the tensions between the two Koreas. They addressed the issue of refugees and migrants, as well as the problem of human trafficking - especially of women. Francis recalled, "the contribution of the Church in favor of the integral dignity of the person and the promotion of a culture of encounter that contributes to the institutional aims of the UN."[201] Ban Ki-moon opined that interreligious dialogue can delineate a path towards a deeper appreciation of shared values; and that it can lead to inclusiveness and tolerance. The UN Secretary considered it very significant and from the Pope himself, as such unity of the churches can lead to maximum social, cultural, and political tolerance among all countries, creating peace and security.[202] At the same time, the Vatican explained about the meeting that, "the Holy See wishes to express its appreciation for the central role of the UN in the preservation of peace in the world, in the promotion of the common good and the defense of the fundamental rights of man."[203]

Ban Ki-moon extended an invitation to Francis to visit the United Nations in New York.[204]

Pope Francis announced in April 2014 that he would prepare an encyclical on climate change,[205] receiving the support of the United Nations.[206] The gestation of the document, which had been announced months earlier by the Vatican on January 24, 2014, deals with "man's relationship with nature."[207]

On May 9, 2014, Francis again received Ban Ki-moon at the Vatican, who praised the pope's commitment to eradicating poverty and promoting sustainable development.[208]

Ban said during the hearing, "I count on the Catholic Church, under your leadership, to continue to work closely with the United Nations to promote a life of dignity for all." He stressed that the world faces numerous challenges, such as increasing inequality, injustice, and intolerance between people and faiths, which aggravates global security. He referred to the horrific fighting between Christians and Muslims in the Central

[200] Philip Pullella (March 22, 2013), Pope urges dialogue with Islam, more help for the poor, Reuters.

[201] Javier Martínez-Brocal (April 10, 2013), Ban Ki-moon, en su encuentro con el Papa: «Usted es el líder espiritual del mundo», ABC España.

[202] Reporter (April 9, 2013), Ban Ki-moon praises Pope Francis after meeting, Catholic Herald.

[203] Javier Martínez-Brocal (April 10, 2013), Ban Ki-moon, en su encuentro con el Papa: «Usted es el líder espiritual del mundo», ABC España.

[204] Reporter (April 9, 2013), Ban Ki-moon praises Pope Francis after meeting, Catholic Herald.

[205] Juan Vicente Boo (April 12, 2014), El Papa Francisco prepara una encíclica sobre la protección a la naturaleza, ABC.

[206] Sophie Yeo (May 8, 2014), UN to back Pope Francis statement on 'human ecology', RTCC.

[207] Philip Pullella (Jan. 25, 2014), Pope preparing major statement on ecology, Vatican says, Reuters.

[208] (May 9, 2014), UN counts on Catholic Church to help promote dignity for all, Ban tells Pope Francis, UN News Centre.

African Republic, the crisis in Sudan, the Syrian conflict, tensions in Ukraine, and the growing impacts of climate around the world. He called for addressing these realities based on principles such as calm, compassion, cooperation, and courage, which characterize Francis' pontificate and have been an inspiration to people in all regions.[209]

The Pope thanked the UN for its efforts for world peace; for respect for human dignity; for the protection of the poorest and weakest people; and for social and economic development. He further emphasized, that "In the case of global political and economic organization, much more needs to be achieved, since an important part of humanity does not share in the benefits of progress and is relegated to the status of second-class citizens."[210]

The Pope called for a future development agenda to be ambitious and courageous, and to effectively address the structural causes of poverty and hunger:

"Specifically, this involves challenging all forms of injustices and resisting the economy of exclusion, the throwaway culture and the culture of death which nowadays sadly risk becoming passively accepted."[211]

Finally, Francis invited the United Nations to promote a global ethical mobilization that extends beyond differences of creed and political opinion; while spreading a common ideal of fraternity and solidarity, especially with the poorest and most excluded. Encouraging the "legitimate redistribution" of wealth.[212]

Ban Ki-moon invited the pope to address the United Nations convention to give a speech on climate change and others on September 25, 2015.[213]

Through such meetings, a clear and deep cooperation between the two institutions can be seen.

The RTCC (Responding to Climate Change Limited) indicated that the United Nations could increase pressure on the Vatican to communicate concrete action on climate change as other countries work to contribute to a "UN climate change treaty."[214] Such action would be critical to the environmental protection of the entire planet. Such a treaty would be signed in Paris at the end of 2015.[215]

At the 69th Session of the United Nations General Assembly on September 29, 2014, Cardinal Pietro Parolin, Vatican Secretary of State, gave an address giving Pope Francis' greetings in the hope that they would work for a more united and fraternal world by identifying ways to resolve the problems that beset all of humanity. He referred to Francis' suffering over the situation in Iraq and the persecution of Christian minorities. He referred to Syria, to the indifference and death of values in the most affluent societies; and called for a juridical solution to put an end to all these problems.

---

[209] Ibid.

[210] Philip Pullella (May 9, 2014), U.N. should encourage redistribution of wealth, pope says, Chicago Tribune.

[211] Dan Kedmey (May 9, 2014), Pope Francis to World: Redistribute The Wealth, Time Magazine.

[212] Philip Pullella (May 9, 2014), U.N. should encourage redistribution of wealth, pope says, Chicago Tribune.

[213] Ban Ki-moon (September 26, 2015), Ban Ki-moon: escuchen el llamado del papa Francisco para proteger el planeta, CNN en Español.

[214] Sophie Yeo (May 8, 2014), UN to back Pope Francis statement on 'human ecology', RTCC.

[215] Ibid.

He called extensively for the prevention of armed conflicts around the world and the resolution of conflicts in areas that would be affected: such as Europe, Africa, and Asia. He referred to the importance of sustainable development and called for challenging all forms of injustice and resisting the economy of exclusion; the throwaway culture and the culture of death. At the same time, Parolin expressed that the Vatican welcomed the 17 "Sustainable Development Goals" (Agenda 2030 for sustainable development).[216]

At the same time, Pope Francis declared that his mission in 2015 was about climate change through a series of speeches, appearances at conferences, and by calling on Catholics around the world until it led, according to Bishop Marcelo Orondo - Chancellor of the Pontifical Academy of Sciences - to a direct influence of the pontiff on the climate conference to be held in Paris the same year to "determine the planet's future."[217]

On April 23, *Vatican Insider* reported that Ban Ki-moon would visit the pope again - for the third time - because of his environmental encyclical.[218] But he would also do so because of the pope's spiritual and moral leadership. His visit, the Jesuit magazine *America* reported, was part of a larger effort to get countries to negotiate accurate Sustainable Development Goals in New York in September, and to reach a legally binding and universal agreement on climate change at the Paris meeting in December.[219]

In other words, the Vatican would be a spearhead to reinforce one and the other meeting determinants of the future of the world.

During the private audience, Ban Ki-moon expressed his gratitude to the Pope for accepting his invitation to address the United Nations on September 25 of that year, indicating that he was looking forward to his speech, as well as the encyclical on climate change. She also emphasized the UN's commitment to the issues of the environment, migrants, and tragic humanitarian situations in conflict-ridden areas of the world.[220]

After the audience, Ban addressed the international symposium on the moral dimensions of climate change, which was organized by the Pontifical Academy of Sciences, together with the Pontifical Academy of Social Sciences, as well as the Sustainable Development Solutions Network and Religions for Peace, entitled "Protect the Earth, Dignify Humanity: The Moral Dimensions of Climate Change and Sustainable Development." It brought together more than 100 experts, including Nobel laureates, from the worlds of science, politics, business, and academia, as well as religious leaders, to support a global consensus on the urgency of curbing climate change and promoting sustainable development.[221]

---

[216] Pietro Parolin (September 30, 2014), Cardinal Parolin's Address to 69th Session of UN General Assembly, Vatican Insider.
[217] Adam Withnall (December 28, 2014), Pope Francis to issue climate change call to arms for world's Catholics in measures that will anger Vatican conservatives, The Independent.
[218] (April 23, 2015), Ban Ki Moon visits the Pope for the encyclical on the environment, Vatican Insider.
[219] Carol Glatz (April 28, 2015), UN's Ban Ki-moon Seeks Assist From Pope Francis on Eco-Sustainability, America.
[220] Junno Arocho Esteves (April 28, 2015), UN Secretary General Ban Ki-moon Meets Privately With Pope Francis, Zenit.
[221] Carol Glatz (April 28, 2015), UN's Ban Ki-moon Seeks Assist From Pope Francis on Eco-Sustainability, America.

Focusing on including leaders of different religions was a key point, since its impact on people's health, security, food supply, and future makes it, according to Ban, "a moral issue. It is an issue of social justice, human rights and fundamental ethics."[222] He added, "Eradicating extreme poverty, ending social exclusion of the weak and marginalized, and protecting the environment are values that are fully consistent with the teachings of the great religions."[223]

Ban said that promoting sustainable development and mitigating climate change will require more than just global policies and agreements: it will also require a strong and unified stance from the world's religions.[224] *DW* reported in 2013 that people are unaware of the Church's influence on climate issues.[225] Transformation of thinking is required to change economies, and the world's religions can provide valuable leadership in that field.[226]

The issue that requires unity of purpose among governments, private companies, civil society, and faith groups, said Ban, is climate change.[227]

Following are a few words from Bishop Orondo on the subject:

"Our academics supported the pope's initiative to influence crucial decisions next year [2015...] The idea is to convene a meeting with leaders of major religions to raise awareness among all people about the state of our climate and the tragedy of social exclusion."[228]

"[...] bring to a higher level **the debate on the moral dimensions of environmental protection** before the first papal encyclical and allow to **consolidate a global interfaith movement to benefit sustainable development** to combat climate change in 2015 and beyond."[229]

Prior to that event, Francis' main role in influencing the late 2015 meeting in Paris would be to meet with leaders of other religious communities and politicians at the United Nations General Assembly on September 25, when other nations would sign on to new anti-poverty and environmental goals. He would then give his speech at the United Nations on sustainable development.[230]

In fact, in September of the previous year, Francis sent a message to the leaders of Christian churches, ecclesiastical communities, and leaders of world religions participating in the International Meeting for Peace in Antwerp, Belgium, a message

---

[222] Ibid.

[223] Ibid.

[224] Ibid.

[225] Interview: Gianna Grün / ss (February 4, 2013), 'People are unaware of the church's influence on climate issues', DW.

[226] Carol Glatz (April 28, 2015), UN's Ban Ki-moon Seeks Assist From Pope Francis on Eco-Sustainability, America.

[227] Ibid.

[228] John Vidal (December 27, 2014), Pope Francis's edict on climate change will anger deniers and US churches, The Guardian.

[229] Ary Waldir Ramos Díaz (April 28, 2015), Ban Ki-moon: La encíclica sobre ecología del Papa Francisco sale en junio, Aleteia. Bold is part of the original article.

[230] Ibid; Philip Pullella (April 28, 2015), Vaticanosuma fuerzas con la ONU frente a escépticos por cambio climático, Reuters.

that *Aleteia* entitled "Pope Francis to religious leaders: it is time for peace to come to the world."[231]

It was in this context that, on December 2, the Pope brought together religious leaders from around the world to combat slavery in a session at the Vatican. The leaders of the different religions gathered were Muslims, Jews, Orthodox Christians, Anglicans, Hindus and Buddhists.[232]

Pope Francis made a significant act by condemning with them, "the terrible scourge of modern slavery in all its forms"; and they signed a document for its eradication by the year 2020.[233]

Such forms of modern slavery, we saw, are "forced labor, prostitution, organ trafficking" and others.[234] *The New York Times* reported in April 2013 on the Pope's book, "Pope Francis: His Life in His Own Words" pointing out that more and more people work on Sundays as a consequence of the competitiveness imposed by a consumerist society, which ends up "dehumanizing people."[235] Likewise, in July 2014, when speaking about Sunday rest, he said that "Maybe it's time to ask ourselves if working on Sundays is true freedom."[236] Thus, in August 2015 he said that "we must never be slaves to work but rather its master."[237] He stated this - though not only - but especially about Sunday rest.[238]

Likewise, the head of the Roman Catholic Church argued for a new, radically different financial and economic system to avoid human inequality and ecological devastation. Thus, at a meeting of Latin American and Asian landless peasants held in October 2014, he expressed that, "It is no longer man who commands, but money. Cash commands."[239]

In an address on April 18, 2015, at the Plenary Session of the Pontifical Academy of Social Sciences, he referred to the slavery of labor.[240]

Nine days later - on April 27 - Timothy E. Wirth, the vice president of the United Nations Foundation, said he had never seen a pope do anything like this. Adding that, "No individual has as much global influence as he does. What he is doing will resonate with the government of every country that has a leading Catholic constituency."[241]

---

[231] Ary Waldir Ramos Diaz (September 8, 2014), El Papa Francisco a los líderes religiosos: es la hora de que llegue la paz al mundo, Aleteia.

[232] Elisabetta Piqué (December 2, 2014), Junto al papa Francisco, líderes de diversas religiones firman una declaración para erradicar la trata, La Nación.

[233] Ibid.

[234] Sergio Mora (Dec. 2, 2014), Líderes religiosos firmaron con el papa contra la trata de personas, Zenit.

[235] Mark Oppenheimer (April 26, 2013), Pope Francis Has a Few Words in Support of Leisure, The New York Times.

[236] (July 5, 2014), Pope: No-work Sundays good, not just for faithful, Associated Press.

[237] (Aug. 12, 2015), Pope Francis: Audience reflection on celebration, work and prayer, Vatican Radio.

[238] Ibid; see also Peter Kenny (Aug. 13, 2015), Pope Francis says Sundays are a gift from God not to be shunned, Ecumenical News.

[239] John Vidal (December 27, 2014), Pope Francis's edict on climate change will anger deniers and US churches, The Guardian.

[240] Address to participants in the Plenary Session of the Pontifical Academy of Social Sciences (Dicastero per la Comunicazione - Libreria Editrice Vaticana, 18 April 2015), p. 1.

[241] Coral Davenport and Laurie Goodstein (April 27, 2015), Pope Francis Steps Up Campaign on Climate Change, to Conservatives' Alarm, The New York Times.

After meeting with the pope on April 28, Ban Ki-moon told a group of religious, political, and scientific leaders at the Vatican that the conversation was "wide-ranging and fruitful."[242] *ABC* in Spain added:

"Speaking at the international seminar on climate change and sustainable development organized by the Pontifical Academy of Sciences, the UN official said, "Pope Francis has been one of the most passionate **moral authorities** on these issues, and I applaud his leadership."

"Climate change is the defining issue of our time," said Ban Ki-moon. It is taking place now and human activities are the main cause. **Science and religion** are not at odds on this issue. In fact, they are fully **aligned.**

"[...] **Ban Ki-moon** assured that "I look forward with great interest to Pope Francis' upcoming encyclical" as well as his speech at **the United Nations Special Summit** on Sustainable Development next September in New York."[243]

Months ago, in January, the head of the U.S. Environmental Protection Agency (EPA), Gina McCarthy, visited Pope Francis at the Vatican to inform him that Barack Obama shared her views.[244]

Laudato Si became known in June 2015, indicating in the context of Sunday rest, considering the slavery of work:

"Rest opens our eyes to the larger picture and gives us renewed sensitivity to the rights of others. And so the day of rest, centred on the Eucharist, sheds it light on the whole week, and motivates us to greater concern for nature and the poor."[245]

It reminds us of the "Text of Cardinal George's address to Pope Benedict" dated April 16, 2008, on the occasion of the pontiff's visit to the United States, which reads in part:

"The episcopal conference has recently identified the strengthening of marriage and of family life as one of five priorities for our common attention in the next several years. The other four are protecting the life and dignity of the human person at every stage of life's journey; handing on the faith in the context of sacramental practice and the observance of Sunday worship; fostering vocations to ordained priesthood and consecrated life; and profiting from the cultural diversity of the church here, especially from the gifts of Hispanic Catholics."[246]

---

[242] Juan Vicente Boo (April 28, 2015), Ban Ki-moon aplaude el liderazgo del Papa Francisco en la lucha contra el cambio climático, ABC.
[243] Ibid. Bold is part of the original article.
[244] Ibid.
[245] Pope Francis, Encyclical Letter Laudato si' of the Holy Father Francis on care for our common home (Vatican Press, May 24, 2015), p. 173.
[246] (April 16, 2008), Text of Cardinal George's remarks to Pope Benedict, Catholic Review.

The British newspaper *The Guardian* reported in this context that global warming could be significantly mitigated by declaring Sunday a fossil fuel-free or low-carbon day. Or at least an energy-saving day. He points out that not so long ago, Sunday was a day of rest and spiritual renewal for families to get together, but it has been replaced by a day of shopping, flying, and driving. And that in the context of excessive carbon dioxide emissions into the atmosphere bringing catastrophic convulsions, "we can and should restore Sunday to a day for Gaia, a day for the Earth."[247] Sunday rest is a Vatican encouragement to combat global warming.

In mid-June 2015, the pope declared that "Doomsday predictions can no longer be met with irony or disdain," and that a "bold cultural revolution" could save humanity from self-destruction.[248]

On the same day, the British newspaper *The Independent* reported that through the papal encyclical Laudato Si, Francis called for "a new system of global government to tackle climate change."[249] Two weeks later, *The Hufftington Post* reported that in his encyclical, Pope Francis called for a "new global institution to protect the commons, tackle climate and poverty."[250]

The Vatican hosted, on July 21, 2015, more than sixty mayors from around the world who pledged to fight global warming and to help the poor in the face of its effects at a conference that was organized by the Holy See. It lasted two days and also focused on the fight against modern forms of slavery.[251]

The conference brought mayors together to mobilize a base for action and keep the pressure on world leaders for concrete action; ahead of the world summit on climate change scheduled for that December.

The final declaration was signed by the mayors, and defined human-induced climate change as a "scientific reality" and that controlling it is a "moral imperative for humanity." Jerry Brown, the governor of California, said, "We need a moral dimension to the climate change debate, and Pope Francis is providing that."[252]

The following day, on July 22, a smaller symposium was held at the Casina of Pius IV - at the Vatican. It was co-organized by the United Nations and had the theme, "Sustainable Cities: Empowering People, Enabling Prosperity and Protecting the Planet."[253]

It has been admitted that "The Church is ahead of the UN in caring for the Earth." Marcelo Sánchez Sorondo, the prefect of the Pontifical Academy of Social Sciences (PACS), expressed that The Vatican Academy of Sciences, "has been the first institution to address the problem of climate change..."[254] He also added:

---

[247] Satish Kumar (September 7, 2009), Slow Sunday: The simple solution to global warming, The Guardian.

[248] Daniel Burke (June 19, 2015), Pope Francis: 'Revolution' needed to combat climate change, CNN.

[249] Tom Bawden (June 18, 2015), Pope Francis calls for a new system of global government to tackle climate change, The Independent.

[250] Mike Sandler (July 2, 2015) The Pope Calls for New Global Institution to Protect the Commons, Tackle Climate and Poverty, The Hufftington Post.

[251] Gaia Pianigiani (July 21, 2015), At Vatican, Mayors Pledge Climate Change Fight, The New York Times.

[252] Ibid.

[253] (July 22, 2015), In the Vatican, mayors launch alliance ahead of Pope's visit to UN, Vatican Insider.

[254] Ary Waldir Ramos Diaz (July 15, 2015), "La Iglesia va por delante de la ONU en el cuidado de la Tierra," Aleteia.

"Therefore, when they tell us that we (the Church) are following what the United Nations says, it is the opposite. **It is the UN that is following the ideas initiated at the Academy of Sciences 25 years ago**."[255]

On September 1 of that year, the pope called on the rich and powerful to protect the planet, declaring that day the "World Day of Prayer for the Care of Creation."[256]

On the morning of September 16, the Pope received the European Union's environment ministers at the Vatican and told them that the ecological debt must be paid off.[257]

Likewise, when he visited the United Nations headquarters in New York on September 25, Ban Ki-moon told him after welcoming him at the entrance of the Secretariat building: "Whatever our faith, we are inspired by your humanity and humility and your call to all to take action on social justice, climate change and ensuring a life of dignity for all."[258]

Ban Ki-moon welcomed him to the General Assembly:

"Your visit coincides with the adoption of the 2030 Agenda for Sustainable Development. And it is no coincidence. You have often spoken of a holistic ecology, one that includes the environment, economic growth, social justice, and the well-being of humanity."[259]

No pope had ever addressed such a large group of world leaders gathered for the occasion. He delivered his message before the World Summit on Sustainable Development, and it was the first high-level meeting of the body at which a pope spoke. For that reason, Ban Ki-moon told him, "Your Holiness, thank you for making history."[260]

Ban stressed that the pope has called on people around the world to work for the realization of the SDGs, and invited all UN delegates to heed the pope's call to save the planet.[261]

During his speech to the Assembly, Francis referred to exclusion and poverty, to the care of creation -introducing the Creator-, to the rejection of war and the arms trade. He criticized the persecution of Christians; he referred to the need for families to have the minimum material and spiritual support from governments; he mentioned the fight against drug trafficking, as well as respect for life in all its dimensions. He placed special emphasis on the necessary achievements of the 2030 Agenda and encouraged its ratification next December in Paris.[262]

---

[255] Ibid. Note: Bold is part of the original.
[256] AFP (September 1, 2015), Pope Francis calls on wealthy and powerful to protect Earth, AFP.
[257] (Sept. 16, 2016), El Papa a los ministros de Medio Ambiente de la UE: Hay que saldar la deuda ecológica, Vis.
[258] (September 25, 2015), La ONU recibe al Papa Francisco, Centro de Noticias ONU.
[259] Ibid.
[260] EFE (September 25, 2015), Ban Ki-moon califica al papa como una "resonante voz de la conciencia", Agencia EFE.
[261] Ban Ki-moon (September 26, 2015), Ban Ki-moon: escuchen el llamado del papa Francisco para proteger al planeta, CNN en español.
[262] Apostolic Journey of the Holy Father to Cuba, to the United States of America and Visit to the United Nations Headquarters (Dicastero per la Comunicazione - Libreria Editrice Vaticana, September 19-28, 2015).

The speech was profusely applauded and considerably boosted the climate negotiations in Paris.

The *Financial Times* noted that the pope left little doubt that he believed the current system was biased in favor of the rich countries and to the detriment of the poor, advocating a more effective distribution of global power.[263]

The Global Interfaith WASH Alliance, comprised of Baha'i, Buddhist, Christian, Hindu, Islamic, Muslim, Jain, Jewish, and Sikh religious traditions, co-hosted a program with the United Nations, the World Bank, and many other faith-based organizations, where they came together in September to support the Sustainable Development Goals developed in the 2030 Agenda.[264]

The Paris Agreements on COP21 and some of their ratifications
It was on February 3, 2015, that Christiana Figueres, the United Nations senior climate officer, said during a press conference in Brussels:

"This is the first time in the history of mankind that we are setting ourselves the task of intentionally, within a defined period of time to change the economic development model that has been reigning for at least 150 years, since the industrial revolution. That will not happen overnight and it will not happen at a single conference on climate change, be it COP 15, 21, 40 - you choose the number. It just does not occur like that. It is a process, because of the depth of the transformation."[265]

Likewise, David Attenborough, one of the best-known natural scientists on TV, once said, "Instead of controlling the environment for the benefit of the population, perhaps it's time we control the population to allow the survival of the environment."[266]

Within the framework of the United Nations negotiations in Bonn, Christiana Figueres expressed that the imminent message of Pope Francis on the environment could be an element of change in the efforts to achieve an agreement to limit global warming. And that no pope before him had committed himself as he has done.[267] Days before the start of the summit in Paris, Pope Francis said a failure at the COP21 meeting would be catastrophic.[268]

At the time, Rodney L. Petersen, a scholar of history, ethics, and religious conflict, and director of the Lord's Day Alliance, an organization that promotes Sunday rest for families, individuals, and others in religious and secular settings for the good of American society, was one of the religious leaders in American higher education who signed an Open Letter to the United Nations Climate Change Convention in Paris to

---

[263] Shawn Donnan and James Politi (September 25, 2015), Pope Francis calls for end to 'boundless thirst for power', Financial Times.
[264] Interfaith WASH Alliance (September 25, 2015), Moral and Spiritual Imperative to End Extreme Poverty, URI News Desk.
[265] (February 3, 2015), Figueres: First time the world economy is transformed intentionally, United Nations Regional Information Centre for Western Europe.
[266] Kenny Gordon, The Wisdom of David Attenborough: Thoughts of a National Treasure (Create Space Independent Publishing Platform, 2014), p. ob. cit.
[267] Ed King (November 6, 2015), Papal encyclical to have "major impact" says top UN climate official, Climate change news.
[268] Inés San Martín (December 14, 2015), Pope Francis praises 'historic' Paris climate change agreement, The Crux.

encourage participants there to reach agreements to mitigate global warming.[269] The same letter was published on December 4: just seven days before the end of the Conference.

In the spring edition of the *Sunday magazine* of that year, belonging to the Lord's Day Alliance, three sections were published: "Orthodoxy: Sunday as a Mark of Christian Unity," "Sunday as a Mark of Christian Unity and a Call to Holiness" and "Sunday as a Mark of Christian Unity and a Call to Holiness."[270] "Sunday as a Mark of Christian Unity and a Call to Holiness."[271] And "Reflections on Pope Francis' Initiatives and Sunday Observance."[272] Increasingly, the issue of Sunday rest is gaining significant importance in the whole framework.

Similarly, some 800,000 Catholics from around the world united their voices behind the pope's call for urgent action on climate through the Catholic Climate Petition, whose signatures were presented to Christiana Figueres, the UN's executive secretary on climate, on Nov. 28. The delivery of that petition was part of an interfaith event that galvanized the unity of groups such as OurVoices, ACT Alliance, GreenFaith and CIDSE, which is said to have gathered 1.7 million signatures from religious people around the world concerned about climate change.[273] As a follow-up, a Catholic movement collectively collected 1,837,973 signatures presented on December 10 to French President Francois Hollande, just two days after the decisive summit ended, where they met with him at the Elysee Palace.[274] Hollande thanked the group at the ceremony:

"We must protect the planet... Through the petitions, through the walks and pilgrimages, you have committed to defend life [...] It is necessary that all citizens engage and mobilise, like you have done. Your example has paved the way, through all the walks and pilgrimages, together with these petitions."[275]

Leonardo Steiner, auxiliary bishop in Brasilia and spokesman for the Catholic Climate Petition, as well as the secretary general of the Brazilian Catholic Bishops' Conference, spoke on behalf of the Catholic community:

---

[269] (December 4, 2015). An Open Letter to the Paris UN Climate Convention from Religious Leaders in U.S. Higher Education [open letter]. Northeastern University-Center for Spirituality, Dialogue, and Service. Retrieved from http://www.northeastern.edu/spirituallife/an-open-letter-to-the-2015-united-nations-framework-convention-on-climate-change/; December 15, 2016.

[270] Rev. Dr. Demetrios E. Tonias (Spring, 2015), Orthodoxy: Sunday as a Mark of Christian Unity, Sunday magazine, pp. 6, 7.

[271] Scott Brill (Spring, 2015), Sunday as a Mark of Christian Unity and a Call to Holiness, Sunday magazine, pp. 8, 9.

[272] Rev. Dr. Donald B. Conroy, S.T.L., Ph.D (Spring, 2015), Reflections on Pope Francis' Initiatives and Sunday Observance, Sunday magazine, pp. 10, 11.

[273] Christina Leano (Nov. 28, 2015), OVER 3/4 MILLION CATHOLICS UNITE BEHIND POPE'S CALL FOR CLIMATE ACTION; TO JOIN CLIMATE MARCH IN RECORD NUMBERS, Global Catholic Climate Movement.

[274] Ellen Teague (Dec. 26, 2015), Truly a grass roots Catholic movement, Sunday Examiner.

[275] Ibid.

396

"As people of faith, we are extremely pleased to meet you today to deliver these petition signatures and demand climate justice. We are extremely concerned about the climate crisis. But we know that all is not lost."[276]

Yeb Saño, a former Philippine climate negotiator, was also present. He had led a People's Pilgrimage from the Vatican to Paris, and as a climate ambassador for OurVoices, he has been an active member of the Catholic Climate Campaign promoting the signature petition in the Philippines.[277]

On November 30, leaders gathered in Paris for the crucial United Nations summit on climate change to negotiate a treaty to limit global warming to 2C to avoid catastrophic consequences.[278] Laurent Fabius, French prime minister and president of COP21, said "The eyes of the world are upon us." Chinese President Xi Jinping, too, weighed in by saying, "Tackling climate change is a shared mission for mankind. All eyes are now on Paris." Barack Obama said: "Let there be no doubt. The next generation is watching what we do." Francois Hollande, the French president, said, "Here in Paris we will decide on the very future of the planet."

Figueres added, "Never before has a responsibility so great been in the hands of so few."

The then Prince Charles expressed:

"The whole of nature cries out at our mistreatment of her," he lamented. "If the planet were a patient, we would have treated her long ago. You, ladies and gentlemen, have the power to put her on life support, and you must surely start the emergency procedures without further procrastination!"

COMECE, which is the Commission of the Bishops' Conferences of the European Union, and which had met in October in its plenary assembly agenda in Paris, had climate change as its main theme. Catholic priest and professor at the University of Malta, Emmanuel Agius, reports that among the proposals discussed to alleviate the effects of global warming, was the rediscovery of the "rhythm of time the alternation between work and rest with Sunday as the commonly shared weekly day of rest."[279]

Christiana Figueres believes that the window for action is closing rapidly, and the time to act is now.[280] Christiana stated in early April 2016:

"If we continue with the process of destruction of the planet that we have had over the last hundred years, the planet will change, but it will continue in a completely different way than the one we have now. What we are here trying to save is the economic, environmental, productive, and human stability to which we human beings have reached and to try to give a certain stability and a certain... certain possibility of prosperity to the next generations."[281]

---

[276] Ibid.
[277] Ibid.
[278] Emma E. Howard (December 1, 2015), COP21: the best metaphors from the Paris climate talks, The Guardian. Note: unless otherwise noted, this is the same source.
[279] Emmanuel Agius (December 2, 2015), Our common home, Times of Malta.
[280] Michelle Soto M. (April 4, 2016), Christiana Figueres: 'Se nos está cerrando la ventana de acción rápidamente' La Nación Costa Rica.
[281] Ibid.

By the end of April, 175 countries signed the Paris Agreement at UN headquarters, just one step away from the agreement becoming international law. All agree it is an agreement to save the planet. But some wondered if it would work.[282]

That year, the candidates for the next UN Secretary-General were being debated. Of the 12 candidates for UN Secretary-General, 8 were socialists, as we checked. The comprehensive list: Christiana Figueres, Irina Bokova (yes), António Guterres (yes), Danilo Türk (yes), Helen Clark (yes), Igor Lukšić (yes), Miroslav Lajčák (yes), Natalia Gherman, Srgjan Kerim, Susana Malcorra, Vesna Pusic (yes), Vuk Jeremić (yes). [283]

Finally, on October 13, 2016, António Manuel de Oliveira Guterres, a Catholic, was elected as the new secretary-general.[284]

Sunday rest decrees in the world

After Joseph Ratzinger was elected to the papacy on April 19, 2005, he generated a series of statements on the importance of Sunday rest. In May of that year, Benedict XVI would make his first visit outside the province of Rome, in Italy. At that time, he made known the message left by the martyrs of Abitene: "Without Sunday we cannot live," referring to Sunday rest and the Eucharist celebrated on that day.[285] On the 29th of that month, he spoke at length about Sunday as the Lord's day during his homily in Bari.[286] In Vienna Cathedral on September 9, 2007, Benedict said in his homily "Without the gift of the Lord, without the Lord's Day, we cannot live."[287]

In October 2008, in Chile, a mandatory Sunday rest bill was put on the table, which generated a lot of controversy.[288]

In Croatia, stores were closed on Sundays as of January 1, 2009. All this in concession with the Catholic Church.[289]

Pope Benedict XVI took stock of the relations between the Holy See and France in January 2009, because of the dispute over Sunday rest that brought dissatisfaction of the parliament with the French Catholic clergy.

Europe was engaged in the initiatives and process of a European Union-wide Sunday legislation, which was strongly supported by the Secretariat of the Commission of the Bishops' Conferences of the European Union (COMECE), together with the Protestant Churches and the Anglican Church, and whose initiative came from five members of the European Parliament.[290]

ZENIT reported that "In order for the declaration to be accepted, it must be signed by the majority of the members of the European Parliament, that is 394 members, before May 7, 2009."[291]

---

[282] William Yardley and Vera Haller (April 22, 2016), At U.N., 175 nations sign landmark accord on global warming. 'We are in a race against time', Los Angeles Times.

[283] (July 8, 2016), Quiénes son los doce candidatos para la Secretaría General de la ONU, Infobae.

[284] (Oct. 13, 2016), UN appoints A. Guterres new Secretary General: VR interview, Vatican Radio.

[285] Editor's note (May 10, 2005), El Papa relanzará en Bari el mensaje de los mártires de Abitene, Zenit.

[286] Homily of His Holiness Benedict XVI (Dicastero per la Comunicazione - Libreria Editrice Vaticana, May 29, 2005).

[287] Editorial Staff (Sept. 9, 2007), «Sin el Día del Señor no podemos vivir»: Homilía del Papa en la catedral de Viena, Zenit.

[288] (July 30, 2008), El descanso dominical humaniza nuestra convivencia, Prensa CECh.

[289] Thaddeus M. Baklinski (July 16, 2008), Croatia Bans Sunday Shopping and Encourages Citizens to Devote Time To Family and Mass, LifeSiteNews.

[290] Redacción (February 25, 2009), Movimiento para recuperar el domingo como día de descanso, Zenit.

[291] Ibid.

Already in 2011, Christians and European trade unions joined forces to defend Sunday rest.

European religious minorities, such as Muslims, Jews, and Seventh-day Adventists, were concerned that this might infringe on the free expression of religious beliefs of those who observe other days of rest.[292]

In June of that year, COMECE, together with the European Sunday Alliance, held the Expert Conference on Sunday Protection on June 20. The European Sunday Alliance is a network of Sunday alliances, trade unions, civil society organizations, and religious communities committed to raising awareness of the value of Sunday rest.[293]

InfoCatólica reported on the matter:

"On June 20, the European Alliance for Sunday will be launched in Brussels. For the first time, trade unions and churches in Europe are on the same line."[294]

This was assured by the Commission of the Bishops' Conferences of the European Union (COMECE), which warns that the reasons for such an alliance are both religious and social-political.[295]

Similarly, on July 12, 2012, Monsignor Gianni Ambrosio (Italy), Vice-President of COMECE, emphasized the need for Europe and its Member States to preserve Sunday as a common weekly day of rest:

"Especially for the family, for the spiritual life of its members and for human relations, both inside the family and with relatives and friends, the common Sunday rest is of fundamental importance."[296]

He also recalled that the churches, in alliance with the largest trade unions and civil society organizations, joined forces to protect Sunday-free labor in the European Union and the legislation of the Member States.[297]

It was reported on July 28:

"As part of the series of regular encounters between Churches and an incoming EU Presidency, a delegation of Polish and European Church representatives was received by the Polish Minister of Foreign Affairs Radosław Sikorski on 28 July 2011 in Warsaw. They had an exchange of views concerning a series of topics related to the political agenda of the Polish Presidency."[298]

---

[292] ANN Staff (Feb. 11, 2014), In Europe, Adventists call on Sunday Alliance not to discriminate, Adventist News Network.

[293] Alessandro Di Maio (June 20, 2011), Invitation Sunday protection Conference, COMECE Press Conference.

[294] (May 6, 2011), Cristianos y sindicatos europeos se unen para defender el descanso dominical, InfoCatólica.

[295] Ibid.

[296] Alessandro Di Maio (Brussels, July 12, 2012), Intergenerational Solidarity deserves full support by the EU and Member States in order to overcome the economic and demographic crises, COMECE Press Releases.

[297] Ibid.

[298] Alessandro Di Maio (August 1, 2011), Reconciliation, demographic change and famine in Africa on the agenda of the meeting of Churches with the Polish EU Presidency, COMECE Press Releases.

It is emphasized in the report that in the context of social rights, the issue of Sundays off work to enjoy family time and social cohesion in Europe was discussed.[299]

In June 2012, Pope Benedict XVI said that Sundays should be a day of rest dedicated to God and the family.[300]

In addition on March 1, 2013, the European Sunday Alliance with its affiliates, carried out several activities in Europe to ask politicians to stop Sunday work.[301]

In March 2015, the International Free Sunday Day was celebrated. The Free Sunday Alliance in Austria attended with many groups for the European Commission's consultation process for the European Working Time Directive, to promote free Sundays in the European Union.[302]

The European Sunday Alliance also organized a conference on "Work-Life-Balance 4.0-Challenges in a time of digitalization" on November 15, 2016, at the European Parliament.[303]

Among the countries that from 2014 to 2015 considered Sunday rest were Hungary, Poland, France, Greece, Chile, Cyprus, Uruguay, and Israel.[304]

Some regions of Argentina, with the full support of Pope Francis, passed Sunday rest laws in 2014.[305]

Israel pushed in August 2016 to make Sunday an added day of rest.[306]

In early September, half a million signatures were collected in support of a bill in Poland limiting trade on Sundays.[307]

Likewise in the United States, in 2013, at the annual National Back To Church Sunday event, which is an interfaith movement that promotes returning to churches on Sunday, set the record of 3 million people attending.[308]

Catholic World News reported in November 2016, of European bishops endorsing the European Pillar of Social Rights, which is a document on labor, education, and

---

[299] Ibid.

[300] Carol Glatz (June 6, 2012), Sundays must be a day of rest dedicated to God, family, pope says, Catholic News Service.

[301] European Sunday Alliance (March 1, 2013), STOP SUNDAY WORK NOW! [Press release]. Retrieved from http://www.europeansundayalliance.eu/site/home/article/k201.html; December 18, 2016.

[302] (March 2, 2015), PA: EU-Konsultation: Sonntag als wöchentlichen Ruhetag verankern [European Union Consultation: Sunday as a weekly day of rest], Allianz für den freier Sonntag.

[303] Frank-Dieter Fischbach (July 21, 2016), Save the Date, European Sunday Alliance Breaking News.

[304] (December 17, 2014), Hungarian parliament passes Sunday shopping ban, IntelliNews; (January 13, 2015), Za tydzień podpisanie ekumenicznego listu Kościołów o świętowaniu niedzieli [In a week the signing of the charter of the Sunday celebration churches], niedziela; Robert Zaretsky (January 25, 2015), France's Sunday Pirouettes, The New York Times; Nicolaus Koutsokostas (April 5, 2015), Protest march in Athens against Sunday trade - Greece, Demotix; (March 31, 2015), Chile enacts law to guarantee workers Sundays off trade, ICN; (April 29, 2015), Obispos uruguayos: porteger los derechos de los trabajadores, Radio Vaticana; (May 8, 2015), Cyprus parliament restricts Sunday shopping, Famagusta Gazzette; Ido Ben-Porat (September 9, 2015), New Bill to Make Sunday a Day off in Israel, Arutz Sheva-Israel National News.

[305] (April 5, 2014), El Centro de Comercio e Industria se adhiere al domingo laborable, Nuevo Diario.

[306] John Reed (August 10, 2016), Israelis push to make Sunday an extra day to rest and play, Financial Times.

[307] (September 5, 2016), More than half a million signatures in support of Polish draft law on limitation of commerce on Sundays, Uni Europa.

[308] Stoyan Zaimov (September 20, 2013), 3 Million People Came 'Back to Church' on Sunday; Sets New Record, The Christian Post.

other social issues, making it known that COMECE called for the recognition of Sunday rest.[309]

Also, in early May 2017, I spoke with an important representative of COMECE who enthusiastically told me about the purposes they had in introducing since the year 2008 the Sunday rest project in the European Parliament. He told me that as part of COMECE's efforts, some bishops spoke with UK parliamentarians to influence a Sunday rest project in April of that year. Discussions in the European Parliament and its countries have focused especially on Sunday rest for the family, but particularly on improving the economy. The bishops, who influence the European Parliament through two representatives, my source said, are extremely interested in presenting the project as a way to alleviate climate change, since through Sunday rest the production of CO_2 drops considerably because the overproduction of factories would stop on that day, among other related issues.

A little over a month before this conversation, that is, at the end of March, a large number of representatives of the European Union visited Pope Francis, accepting the role of the Vatican and the Catholic Church in saving Europe from the present path it is on, by restoring the "Christian" pillars on which it was founded.[310] My source told me that in October there would be a meeting in Rome led by the Vatican with the cooperation of COMECE; it would be attended by Pope Francis, other religious representatives, and European leaders to offer their help to solve the identity crisis. At the meeting, my source told me, the final manifestations and guidelines for Europe to legislate a Sunday law would be given. I do not know if and how much the issue was finally addressed.

Days later, COMECE and other agencies announced preparations for such a meeting: Rethinking Europe. The COMECE Standing Committee met with the Pope at Santa Marta - in the Vatican - on May 16 of that year in preparation for that dialogue.[311] But no media reported on Sunday's topic. At the meeting, which took place from October 27-29,[312] the pope addressed those present, stressing the importance of Europe's return to its Christian roots.[313]

On the other hand, at the beginning of May, I spoke with a person in charge of environmental justice and climate change at the United States Conference of Catholic Bishops (USCCB). He told me that there is great interest in promoting Sunday rest as a way to help reduce the production of CO_2 into the atmosphere, but that in the United States, this issue is more difficult than in Europe because the continent has a more Catholic tradition than the United States.

---

[309] (Nov. 23, 2016), EU bishops back Pillar of Social Rights, call for recognition of Sunday rest, Catholic World News.

[310] James Kanter and Gaia Pianigiani (March 24, 2017), On Eve of E.U. Anniversary, Pope Warns of Bloc's Fragility, The New York Times; Gerard O'Connell (March 24, 2017), Pope Francis sees hope for European Union, urges leaders to return to roots, America Magazine.

[311] Alessandro Di Maio (May 17, 2017), "Rethinking Europe" Dialogue: COMECE met with Pope Francis, COMECE Press; (May 17, 2017), COMECE to hold congress on Rethinking Europe, Vatican Radio; M. Chiara Biagioni (May 17, 2017), Comece. Card. Marx: "There is no going back. Europe has to move forward, and it must do so as one," AgenSir; (May 16, 2017), +++ Comece: EU Bishops with Pope Francis today. In October, a meeting in Rome about "Re-thinking Europe" with the Holy Father +++, AgenSir.

[312] Alessandro Di Maio (June 10, 2017), (Re)thinking Europe, COMECE Press.

[313] (Oct. 28, 2017), Pope on Christians' contribution to the future of Europe, Vatican Radio.

Events related to the evolution of global solutions to peace and prosperity
Pope Francis, during his speech on the occasion of the distinction awarded to him by the European Parliament of the Carlo Magno Prize on May 6, 2016, expressed in part:

"I offer you a cordial welcome and I thank you for your presence. I am particularly grateful to Messrs Marcel Philipp, Jürgen Linden, Martin Schulz, Jean-Claude Juncker, and Donald Tusk for their kind words. [...]."
If we want a dignified future, a future of peace for our societies, we will only be able to achieve it by working for genuine inclusion, "an inclusion which provides worthy, free, creative, participatory and solidary work". This passage (from a liquid economy to a social economy) will not only offer new prospects and concrete opportunities for integration and inclusion, but will make us once more capable of envisaging that humanism of which Europe has been the *cradle and wellspring.*

"To the rebirth of a Europe weary, yet still rich in energies and possibilities, the Church can and must play her part. Her task is one with her mission: the proclamation of the Gospel, which today more than ever finds expression in going forth to bind the wounds of humanity with the powerful yet simple presence of Jesus, and his mercy that consoles and encourages. God desires to dwell in our midst, but he can only do so through men and women who, like the great evangelizers of this continent, have been touched by him and live for the Gospel, seeking nothing else. Only a Church rich in witnesses will be able to bring back the pure water of the Gospel to the roots of Europe. In this enterprise, the path of Christians towards full unity is a great sign of the times and a response to the Lord's prayer "that they may all be one" (*Jn* 17:21)."[314]

It speaks of a type of semi-socialist system, with the ecclesiastical ideology influencing the civil powers, although not necessarily a political-religious domination.
On December 2-3, the Fortune-Time Global Forum 2016 was held at the Vatican.[315] Time Inc. sponsored it, and it was billed as an unprecedented gathering[316] that brought together 500 executives, scholars, workers, church leaders, and philanthropists. It was intended to address the need for a global economic system that encourages growth and spreads its benefits more widely.[317] *Fortune* announced it as follows:

"Inspired by the Pope's call for more and better jobs, broader prosperity and lasting ways to lift the poor, the theme of the 2016 Global Forum is "The 21st Century Challenge: Forging a New Social Compact." The event will be a solutions-based conversation aimed at encouraging transformative actions by the private sector to help create a more inclusive and humane economy and aid in eradicating poverty and the refugee problem around the world."[318]

---

[314] Conferral of the Charlemagne Prize (May 6, 2016) | Francis (Libreria Editrice Vaticana, Friday, May 6, 2016), pp. 5, 6.
[315] Nancy Gibbs (Dec. 3, 2016), Read TIME and Fortune's Global Forum Report on Ending Poverty, Time Magazine.
[316] Fortune Editors (November 17, 2016), Fortune-Time Global Forum 2016 to Take Place in the Vatican, Fortune Magazine.
[317] Nancy Gibbs (Dec. 3, 2016), Read TIME and Fortune's Global Forum Report on Ending Poverty, Time Magazine.
[318] Fortune Editors (November 17, 2016), Fortune-Time Global Forum 2016 to Take Place in the Vatican, Fortune Magazine.

Forum committee members include executives from Dow Chemical, IBM, Johnson & Johnson, Monsanto, McKinsey, PepsiCo, Siemens, Virgin Group, and WPP, as well as leaders of non-profit organizations including the Rockefeller, Ford, and Mo Ibrahim foundations.[319]

On the first day of the forum, Cardinal Peter Turkson said that executives could be partners with God in bringing resources to humanity.[320]

One of the solutions in the report that was delivered is aimed at improving poverty conditions in regions where climate change has an excessive impact; recommending, for example, to support the Paris agreements.[321]

Eric Frattini, in his book, *El Libro Negro del Vaticano* (*The Black Book of the Vatican*) indicated: "[...] it is possible to think that in the next few years we may see how the motto, which is said to have read the inscription on the crown of Emperor Diocletian (244-311), Roma Caput Mundi (Rome Head of the World) becomes seventeen centuries later, and thanks to a pope who arrived from the end of the world, Vatican Caput Mundi, at least from the political and diplomatic point of view. We shall see..."[322]

Malachi Martin, the late Irish Jesuit, said in an interview with Lee Penn in 1990 that the Vatican believed that both systems - communism and capitalism - would collapse and that a new world order would emerge from the chaos created.[323]

But it was in 2012, during a closed meeting in which I participated, that an important Jesuit Father gave me his solemn conviction, that Francis' role was "prophetic," since he knows where we are going. That when the chaos to which humanity is heading comes, they will turn to him because of his role as shepherd, and that out of disorder a new order will emerge.

In another meeting I had with another Jesuit Father in 2016, he said that the Society of Jesus and the Catholic Church were hoping that the next U.S. president could work side by side with the pope to bring the 2030 Agenda to its conclusion, and then this will be a better world in a few years.

---

[319] Ibid.

[320] Nina Easton (December 2, 2016), How CEO's Can Be 'Partners With God', Fortune Magazine.

[321] Fortune + Time Global Forum Working Group Solutions (Rome, Italy, December 3, 2016), p. 7.

[322] Eric Frattini, El Libro Negro del Vaticano: Las oscuras relaciones entre la CIA y la Santa Sede (Espasa, Barcelona, 2016), ob. cit.

[323] Lee Penn, The Religious Face of the New World Order: From the Vatican to the White House to the United Religions Initiative (America's Survival, Inc., 2010), p. 10.

CHAPTER

12

The Pope and H. Clinton. Trump and the resurgence of Christian fascism

Context – "Catholic Spring"

In February 2012 Sandy Newman, president of Voices for Progress, sent an email to John Podesta, then Hillary Clinton's campaign manager and who served in the White House under both the Bill Clinton and Obama administrations:[1]

"This whole controversy with the bishops opposing contraceptive coverage, even though 98 percent of Catholic women, and their conjugal partners, have used contraception, has me thinking. ... There needs to be a Catholic Spring, in which Catholics themselves demand the end of a Middle Ages dictatorship and the beginning of a little democracy and respect for gender equality in the Catholic church. Is contraceptive coverage an issue around which that could happen? The Bishops will undoubtedly continue the fight. Does the Catholic Hospital Association support of the Administration's new policy, together with "the 98%" create an opportunity?"[2]

He further said, "I have not thought at all about how one would "plant the seeds of the revolution," or who would plant them."[3] Podesta responded in an email, that they created Catholics in Alliance for the Common Good "to organize for a moment like this," but that he currently lacked the leadership to do so (as did Catholics United). He added that "Like most Spring movements, I think this one will have to be bottom up," and that he would discuss it with Tara and Kathleen Kennedy Townsend [a leading Catholic Democratic lawyer].[4]

Newman suggested to Podesta to start with a few organizers who would provoke one or two high-profile Occupy Wall Street-like demonstrations that would be the spark. He referred to contacts who could advise on such a plan.[5]

Crisis Magazine, a conservative Catholic magazine, echoed these emails through an article by priest George W. Rutler, who labeled the plan as the "cynical attempts by political strategist to subvert and suborn the institution, stripping her of supernatural credentials to become a tool of the State"[6]

---

[1] Newman, Sandy. "Re: opening for Catholic Spring? just musing..." Message to Podesta, John. February 10, 2012. E-mail. Retrieved from Wikileaks.

[2] Ibid.

[3] Ibid.

[4] Podesta, John. "Re: opening for Catholic Spring? just musing..." Message to Newman, Sandy, John. February 11, 2012. E-mail. Retrieved from Wikileaks.

[5] Newman, Sandy. "Re: opening for Catholic Spring? just musing...." Message to Podesta, John. February 11, 2012. E-mail. Retrieved from Wikileaks.

[6] Father George W. Rutler (October 17, 2016), Two Newmans and Two Catholic Springs, Crisis Magazine.

For her part, speaking to the 2015 Women in the World Summit, Hillary Clinton, then a U.S. presidential candidate, said that "deep-seated cultural codes, religious beliefs, and structural biases have to be changed." She said this in the context of "reproductive health care" in the United States and far-flung countries. She was referring to abortion rights and contraception.[7]

George Soros, the Vatican, and the U.S. Catholic Church endorsing Hillary Clinton for president in 2016

Brent Budowsky, a political opinion writer and blogger, wrote to John Podesta in February 2015, recommending that Clinton seek to build a special relationship with Pope Francis:

"Historically magical things can happen when the right president builds a special relationship with the right pope. [...] HRC [Hillary Rodham Clinton] could build such as relationship with Pope Francis, and I would be very confident Pope Francis would reciprocate. [...]I would consider the thought of building a special relationship between HRC and Pope Francis near the top of the list of ideas with value. And I would add that Secretary Kerry, who I consider one of the great men of our times, is very attuned to this way of thinking."[8]

During her October 2016 speech at the Al Smith Dinner, Clinton scorned archaic conspiracy theories about a plot by the pope to rule the United States. And she said, "you certainly don't need to be Catholic to be inspired by the humility and heart of the Holy Father, Pope Francis. Or to embrace his message."[9]

Of the wealthy donors to Hillary Clinton's presidential campaign, there were George Soros and Herbert Sandler.[10] In fact, Sergio Knaebel of the Sandler Foundation sent foundation owner Herbert Sandler a June 2015 email from Scott Reed, CEO of PICO about the agency's representatives' visit to the Vatican.[11]

Before looking at its contents, let's say that PICO National Network or Pacific Institute for Community Organization was founded in 1972 by Jesuit priest John Baumann; who worked in the late 1960s with community organizing projects in Chicago, where he became familiar with ideas of Saul Alinsky,[12] an American

---

[7] Kirsten Powers (April 28, 2015), Powers: Saint Hillary seeks to save Christians from Christianity, USA Today.

[8] Budowsky, Brent. "Re: Clinton Foundation etc." Message to Podesta, John. 19 Feb. 2015. E-mail. Retrieved from Wikileaks: https://wikileaks.org/podesta-emails/emailid/59010; Accessed on December 1, 2016.

[9] Hillary Clinton (Oct. 21, 2016), Read the Transcript of Hillary Clinton's Speech at the Al Smith Dinner, Time Magazine.

[10] Matea Gold and Anu Narayanswamy (Oct. 24, 2016), How mega-donors helped raise $1 billion for Hillary Clinton, The Washington Post; Ivona Iacob (May 27, 2016), The Top Donors Backing Hillary Clinton's Super PAC, Forbes. See contacts between Herbert Sandler in support of Hillary Clinton's campaign through his campaign manager, John Podesta: Katie Reilly (Oct. 14, 2016), 5 Business Bigwigs With Cameos in the Hillary Clinton Email Leaks, Fortune; Kenneth P. Vogel and Danny Vinik (Nov. 1, 2016), Podesta paid $7,000 a month by top donor, Politico.

[11] Reed, Scott "Re: PICO: Vatican Visit." Message to Knaebel, Sergio. 22 June 2015. E-mail. Retrieved from Wikileaks: https://wikileaks.org/podesta-emails/emailid/20368; November 27, 2016.

[12] Richard L. Wood, Faith in Action: Religion, Race, and Democratic Organizing in America (The University of Chicago Press, 2002), pp. 95, 97, 163.

sociologist admired by Clinton, and who was greatly associated with the mafia and the Catholic Church in Chicago, for social purposes.

PICO includes "the social Christianity of the historic black churches, the Social gospel and Christian realist perspectives in liberal and moderate Protestantism, the strongly evangelical but socially responsible orientation of the Church of God in Christ, and the intellectual resources, working-class commitments, and Hispanic cultural ties of Roman Catholicism."[13]

During an interview at a conference at Holy Names University in 2014, Baumann said that the father of modern community organizing, "Saul Alinsky was one of the people who delivered a workshop for us, and he was a fascinating person. The way he could describe the importance of how to make democracy work in our communities and the importance of bringing people together was remarkable."[14]

With this in mind, Scott Reed, PICO's CEO, reported in the email that the agency sent a delegation of 15 clergy (African-American pastors and one Catholic priest), leaders, and staff to the Vatican in the second week of June 2015.[15]

The three-day visit included meetings with senior Vatican officials. They met with three of the principal authors of the climate encyclical, as well as the Under Secretary of State in charge of drafting Pope Francis' remarks when he spoke to the U.S. Congress and the United Nations.

They also met with Cardinal Peter Turkson, one of the Pope's close advisors and overseer of Justice and Peace, as well as Archbishop Sánchez Sorondo, who heads the Pontifical Academy of Social Sciences.

The pope honored them with a personal greeting, but did not have time to be with them to discuss substantive matters, because, "For some reason, his meeting with Mr. Putin last Wednesday trumped our visit!"

The visitors expressed that Pope Francis is a world leader of historic importance and that his message regarding exclusion, alarm over growing inequality, and concern over global indifference is an important message for the United States to hear and be encouraged by during the Pope's visit.

From the Vatican, they were told that they intended to amplify the Pope's comments to have, "a more profound moral dialogue about policy choices through the election cycle of 2016."

"In our meetings with relevant officials, we strongly recommended that the Pope emphasize – in words and deeds – the need to confront racism and racial hierarchy in the US.

"Conversations that were originally scheduled for thirty minutes stretched into two hour dialogues. As in our breakfast conversation with Cardinal Rodríguez, senior Vatican officials shared profound insights demonstrating an awareness of the moral, economic and political climate in America. [...] .

---

[13] Ibid., p. 294.
[14] Stephanie Block (Oct. 26, 2016), WikiLeaks: Interfaith-leftist organization seeks Vatican influence in US politics, Spero News.
[15] Reed, Scott. "Re: PICO: Vatican Visit." Message to Knaebel, Sergio. 22 June 2015. E-mail. Retrieved from Wikileaks: https://wikileaks.org/podesta-emails/emailid/20368; Accessed on November 27, 2016. Note: unless otherwise noted, this is the same source.

"At the end of the day, our visit affirmed an overall strategy: Pope Francis, as a leader of global stature, will challenge the "idolatry of the marketplace" in the U.S. and offer a clarion call to change the policies that promote exclusion and indifference to those most marginalized. We believe that this generational moment can launch extraordinary organizing that promotes moral choices and helps establish a moral compass. We believe that the papal visit, and the work we are collectively doing around it, can help many in our country move beyond the stale ideological conflicts that dominate our policy debates and embrace new opportunities to advance the common good."

George Soros, the other donor to Hillary Clinton's campaign for the White House, was complicit with the U.S. Catholic Church in trying to bring the Democratic candidate to power. Soros donated $650,000 to influence the pope's visit to the United States in September 2015 to shift national paradigms and priorities in the run-up to the 2016 presidential campaign.[16] One report indicates that among the successful accomplishments of the grant was "Buy-in of individual bishops to more publicly voice support of economic and racial justice messages in order to begin to create a critical mass of bishops who are aligned with the Pope." The money was given to PICO and Faith in Public Life (FPL). The latter is a progressive group that works in the media to promote support for left-wing 'social justice' causes. The Soros report echoes the support they would give to PICO on their visit to the Vatican for the purposes already discussed.

George Soros' group was pleased with the results of the campaign, witnessing statements by bishops against presidential candidates who used fear, probably referring to the Republican party lineup and perhaps specifically to Donald Trump.

"The impact of this work and the relationships it has fostered can be seen in the broad range of religious leaders hitting pointedly back at presidential candidates for their use of fearmongering."

The money donated by Soros was effective in countering anti-gay rhetoric in the media. It was directly targeted at the "pro-family" agenda, redirecting it toward the defense of marriage to income equality; which included conducting a poll to show that Catholic voters were sensitive to the pope's focus on income inequality.

On Soros, attorney Elizabeth Yore, who served on the Heartland Institute delegation and who traveled to the Vatican in April 2015 to urge the pope to re-examine his reliance on U.N. population control proponents who promote climate change, said that "Catholics serve as a huge and influential voting block in the U.S. election," she said. Soros, she said, is "using the head of the Catholic Church to influence this key voting block," with the "bully pulpit of the papacy" to ensure that Hillary Clinton would win the presidency.

---

[16] John-Henry Westen (Aug. 23, 2016), BREAKING: Leaked e-mails show George Soros paid $650K to influence bishops during Pope's US visit, LifeSiteNews. Note: unless otherwise noted, this is the same source.

According to Yore, Soros also influenced the pope that same year on the climate change agenda. One of the pope's advisors on the issue, Jeffry Sachs, had had George Soros as an ally in the past for other causes.[17]

The high hierarchy of the U.S. Catholic Church kept silent about Hillary Clinton's radical positions in contrast to Catholic doctrine. Perhaps, because during the Obama administration (pro-Hillary Clinton), the most anti-Catholic in U.S. history, the Catholic bishops enjoyed enormous economic benefits from the administration. Both the USCCB, Catholic Charities, and the CRS and International Catholic Migration Commission, were the beneficiaries of a total of $202,247,624 million. However, the bishops received an additional $17,715,636 million.[18] Likewise, the Catholic order of the Knights of Columbus made a video that was highlighted on the Catholic bishops' web page of the country, where it positively highlighted Hillary Clinton.[19]

Budowsky sent another email to John Podesta, indicating that Hillary Clinton should get ahead of the progressive curve before the pope's arrival in September of that year. In support, he wrote a column for the *Observer* titled "Bernie Sanders, Hillary Clinton, and Pope Francis."[20]

Clinton's vice presidential nominee was Tim Kaine, raised in a middle-class Irish Catholic family; and was a student at Rockhurst High School, a Jesuit academy in Kansas City, Missouri.[21]

While Kaine spent months in Latin America, from 1980 to 1981, the Cold War was at its height. He was in Honduras, where he embraced the liberation theology he learned from the Jesuits.[22]

Kaine saw a parallel between his mentors and Pope Francis, of whom he said, "I really feel I know him."[23] *The Washington Post* described Kaine as a "Pope Francis Catholic," and he is cast in the same mold as the pope.[24]

With three days to go before the elections, Pope Francis said during a speech at the Vatican to an audience with representatives of popular movements that they should not indulge in the politics of fear by building walls, but by building bridges. He said that fear weakens and destabilizes us, destroying our psychological and spiritual defenses and that it numbs us to the suffering of others, making us cruel in the end.[25] He was certainly critical of Trump and supportive of Clinton.

---

[17] Nina Munk (June 5, 2007), Jeffrey Sach's $200 Billion Dream, Vanity Fair.

[18] Elizabeth Yore (Sept. 6, 2016), The Money Trail: Why Catholic Bishops Are Silent on Hillary, The Remnant.

[19] Michael Sean Winters (June 14, 2016), Questions for the USCCB, National Catholic Reporter.

[20] Budowsky, Brent. "Re: Column: Bernie Sanders, Hillary Clinton, and Poep Francis | | Observer----." Message to Podesta, John. July 16, 2015. E-mail. Retrieved from Wikileaks: https://wikileaks.org/podesta-emails/emailid/36196; Accessed on December 1, 2016.

[21] Jason Horowitz (September 2, 2016), In Honduras, a Spiritual and Political Awakening for Tim Kaine, The New York Times.

[22] Jeremy Scahill (Oct. 4, 2016), Tim Kaine, John Negroponte, and the Priest Who Was Thrown From a Helicopter, The Intercept.

[23] Jason Horowitz (September 2, 2016), In Honduras, a Spiritual and Political Awakening for Tim Kaine, The New York Times.

[24] Michelle Boorstein and Julie Zauzmer (July 22, 2016), 'A Pope Francis Catholic: Now that Tim Kaine is Clinton's VP pick, will his faith matter?," The Washington Post.

[25] Michael O'Loughlin (Nov. 6, 2016), Days Before U.S. Election, Pope Francis Warns Against Politics of Fear, America.

Insights and other early facts about the 2016 presidential election and its aftermath

Donald Trump fomented distrust and anger against the government from the beginning of his campaign, attacking Washington leaders with offensive phrases.[26] His message was the same everywhere, that people were tired of being lied to by Washington, angering many and emboldening them.

His GOP rivals hit back, claiming that Trump was a threat to the Republican establishment. Lindsey Graham said, "[I'm] Disgusted. I want to talk to the Trump supporters for a minute. I don't know who you are, and I don't know what you like about this. [...] He's a race-baiting, xenophobic, religious bigot. He doesn't represent my party. He doesn't represents the values that the men and women who wear the uniform are fighting for."

Marco Rubio, Republican pre-candidate for the 2016 presidential race: "Guys, we have a con artist as the front-runner in the Republican Party. A guy who has made a career out of telling people lies. [...]"

Ted Cruz, another pre-candidate for president said, "This man is a pathological liar. He lies practically every word that comes out of his mouth."

But Trump viciously attacked all his opponents in the debates as pre-candidates for the presidency. He began to have more and more support from the extremely reactionary elements of society.

A former Trump political advisor, Roger Stone, noted that among Trump's supporters was a not very large and loud group of white supremacists, Ku Klux Klan members, and neo-Nazis that were very loud.

At several of his rallies, Trump instigated violence against opponents. For example on one occasion: "There's a guy. Totally disruptive, throwing punches. I love the old days. You know what they used to do to guys like that when they were in a place like this? They'd be carried out on a stretcher, folks. I'd like to punch him in the face, I'll tell you. Ah, it's true." He said of someone at another one of his rallies, "Knock the crap out of him, would you? Just knock the hell out of him. I promise you I will pay for the legal fees. I promise, I promise."

Before Trump won the Republican nomination, Senator Ted Cruz defeated him in the first race for the nomination by winning the majority of votes in Iowa.[27] Some of Trump's Twitter messages, "Ted Cruz didn't win Iowa, he stole it." And also that, "The state of Iowa should disqualify Ted Cruz from the most recent election on the basis that he cheated—a total fraud."

He then went on to insult, by humiliating Ted's wife, Heidy Cruz. Trump then suggested that Ted's father, Rafael Cruz, was involved in the assassination of John F. Kennedy because he was with Lee Harvey Oswald before the assassination.

---

[26] Michael Kirk (Writer), Mike Wiser (Writer), & Michael Kirk (Director) (2021, January 26). Trump's American Carnage (Season 39, Episode 11) [TV Series Episode]. Raney Aronson, David Fanning (Executive Producers), *Frontline*. Public Broadcasting Service (PBS). Note: unless otherwise noted, this is the same source.

[27] Michael Kirk (Writer), Michael Kirk (Writer), & Mike Wiser (Director) (2022, September 6). Lies, Politics and Democracy (Season 41, Episode 1) [TV Series Episode]. Raney Aronson, David Fanning (Executive Producers), *Frontline*. Public Broadcasting Service (PBS). Note: unless otherwise noted, this is the same source.

We quote in part Cruz's response to the press:

"This man is a pathological liar. He doesn't know the difference between truth and lies. [...] his response is to accuse everybody else of lying.
"He accuses everybody on that debate stage of lying. [...] The man cannot tell the truth, but he combines it with being a narcissist, a narcissist at a level I don't think this country's ever seen.   [...]
Whatever lie he's telling, at that minute, he believes it. [...] The man is utterly amoral. Morality does not exist for him. It's why he went after Heidi directly and smeared my wife, attacked her.
[...]
Today's voting day here in Indiana. [...] I ask the people of Indiana, think about the next five years if this man were to become president."[28]

Cruz continued:

"Think about the next five years, the boasting, the pathological lying [...] Think about your kids coming back and emulating this.

"For people in Indiana who long for a day when we were nice to each other, when we treated people with respect, when we didn't engage in sleaze and lies [...].
"I want everyone to think about your teenage kids. The president of the United States talks about how great it is to commit adultery, and how proud he is, describes his battles with venereal disease as his own personal Vietnam. That's a quote, by the way, on the Howard Stern show.
[...]
I will tell you, as the father of two young girls, the idea of our daughters coming home and repeating any word that man says horrifies me."[29]

Due to the voting results, Cruz announced that he was suspending the campaign.[30] When the Republican convention was to be held where Trump would be officially nominated as their candidate, Ted Cruz was the only reluctant one. His advisors told him, "Ted, not only did this man humiliate you and your family, but this man is undemocratic. This man is anti-constitutional. This man is downright un-American, the way that he talks about things. And you want to be on the right side of history here. This isn't just about 2016 or 2020. In the long run, you will be proven right by standing firm in your convictions and your fidelity to the Constitution and to the principles that you believe in."

Days later, once he had made his decision, the reason Cruz gave his advisors for not endorsing Trump was, "History isn't kind to the man who holds Mussolini's jacket."

---

[28] CNN Newsroom (May 3, 2016), Cruz Rants Against Trump; Indiana Votes. Aired 3-3:30p ET, CNN NEWSROOM/Transcripts.
[29] Ibid.
[30] Michael Kirk (Writer), Michael Kirk (Writer), & Mike Wiser (Director) (2022, September 6). Lies, Politics and Democracy (Season 41, Episode 1) [TV Series Episode]. Raney Aronson, David Fanning (Executive Producers), *Frontline*. Public Broadcasting Service (PBS). Note: unless otherwise noted, this is the same source.

Cruz was booed in his convention speech, but the reality was that when Trump won the Republican nomination, the party leaders he ridiculed and attacked lined up behind him.[31]

Meeting with his advisors that night, there was a feeling that Cruz's political career was going to end, so he ultimately decided to endorse his rival.[32]

Trump's victory spurred applause and fears around the world.[33]

Thousands of people demonstrated in New York, Philadelphia, Seattle, Chicago, Oakland, Washington, and Boston following the New York tycoon's victory. [34]

According to the Pew Research Center, evangelicals and white Catholics voted for Trump in higher proportions than they did for the last two Republican nominees, John McCain and Mitt Romney. But Hispanic Catholics voted in higher proportions for Hillary Clinton.[35]

As *The New York Times* reported:

"Mr. Trump was not the first choice of most evangelicals or Catholics. But he gradually won their trust, speaking at Liberty University in Virginia, the largest Christian college in the country, doing nine interviews with Pat Robertson's Christian Broadcasting Network and building relationships with Pentecostal preachers. In June, he met with nearly one thousand evangelical and Catholic leaders from around the country in a hotel ballroom in New York. In October, he sent a letter to the Catholic Leadership Conference in Denver, promising, "I will fight for you."[36]

Attempts to install a right-wing catholic-protestant theocracy
In mid-January 2016, while giving a speech at Liberty University (a Christian higher institution) in Lynchburg, Virginia, Trump said, "We're going to protect Christianity. I can say that, I don't have to be politically correct. We're going to protect it."[37]

To attract Christian voters, not everything was rosy for Donald Trump. For example, during his return trip to Rome from his visit to Mexico, Pope Francis was asked what he thought about Donald Trump's plan to deport eleven million immigrants from the United States, as well as his plan to build a wall on the border with Mexico to prevent the passage of illegal immigrants. The pope responded, "A person who thinks only about building walls, wherever they may be, and not building bridges, is not Christian." The response was not long in coming, as shortly after, Trump said that he liked the pope, but since ISIS was targeting the Vatican, if they attacked the pope, he would have

---

[31] Michael Kirk (Writer), Mike Wiser (Writer), & Michael Kirk (Director) (2021, January 26). Trump's American Carnage (Season 39, Episode 11) [TV Series Episode]. Raney Aronson, David Fanning (Executive Producers), *Frontline*. Public Broadcasting Service (PBS).

[32] Michael Kirk (Writer), Michael Kirk (Writer), & Mike Wiser (Director) (2022, September 6). Lies, Politics and Democracy (Season 41, Episode 1) [TV Series Episode]. Raney Aronson, David Fanning (Executive Producers), *Frontline*. Public Broadcasting Service (PBS).

[33] Tribune news services (Nov. 9, 2016), Donald Trump's win prompts cheers, fears around the world, Chicago Tribune.

[34] Sandro Pozzi (November 12, 2016), Protestas en varias ciudades de EE UU tras la victoria de Donald Trump, El País.

[35] Laurie Goldstein (Nov. 11, 2016), Religious Right Believes Donald Trump Will Deliver on His Promises, The New York Times.

[36] Ibid.

[37] Melanie Hunter (Jan. 19, 2016), Donald Trump: 'We're Going to Protect Christianity,' CNS News.

wished and prayed that Donald Trump would be elected president.[38] He called Francis' comments unbelievable and a disgrace.[39]

The next day, the head of the Vatican press office, Federico Lombardi, said the pope's comments were not personal, nor were they intended to influence the U.S. presidential election. Trump responded Thursday night to *CNN*, that he did not believe this was a fight, and that, "I think he said something much softer than was originally reported by the media."[40] It seemed that Trump knew that it was not in his best interest to lose the potential of the U.S. Catholic vote.

In fact, in early February 2016, Trump said on *CBN*'s "The Brody File," "I want to give power back to the church." He was referring to the Johnson Amendment, in which the U.S. tax code was altered so that tax-exempt organizations, such as churches, would not be allowed to endorse or oppose political candidates.[41] Ttump's promise was part of what *Time* magazine headlined in an article, "Donald Trump Vowed to Close the Gap Between Church and State."[42] Trump's words were:

"I said, 'I'm going to take this into my own hands and I'm going to figure a way that we can get you back your freedom of speech,'" Trump told the evangelical pastors. "It will be so great for the evangelicals, for the pastors, for the ministers, for the priests, for America."[43]

Georgetown Jesuit University echoed Donald Trump's June 10 remarks on religious freedom, quoting them verbatim:

"Religious freedom, the right of people of faith to freely practice their faith. So important. [...]Keeping people of faith safe from threats like radical Islam, whether protecting them here or standing by Israel, all of us need to confront together the threat of radical Islam. [...]We will protect the right of churches to speak their minds on political matters, free from intimidation. [...] [Hillary Clinton] She'll restrict religious freedom with government mandates. She'll push for federal funding of abortion on demand up until the moment of birth, which is where she is, as you know. [...] We will restore faith to its proper mantle in our society."[44]

---

[38] Jim Yardley (Feb. 18, 2016), Pope Francis Suggests Donald Trump Is 'Not Christian,' The New York Times.

[39] Patrick Healy (Feb. 18, 2016), Donald Trump Fires Back at Sharp Rebuke by Pope Francis, The New York Times.

[40] Cooper Allen (Feb. 19, 2016), Vatican: Pope's comments on Trump not 'personal attack', USA Today.

[41] David Brody (Feb. 18, 2016), Exclusive: Donald Trump Tells Brody File: "I want to give power back to the church," CBN News.

[42] Jeff Nesbit (August 15, 2016), Donald Trump Vowed to Close the Gap Between Church and State, Time Magazine.

[43] Ibid.

[44] (June 10, 2016), Donald Trump on Religious Freedom Issues at the Faith and Freedom Coalition, Berkley Center for Religion, Peace, and World Affairs-Georgetown University: https://berkleycenter.georgetown.edu/quotes/donald-trump-on-religious-freedom-issues-at-the-faith-and-freedom-coalition; accessed November 21, 2016.

Note the emphasis. When he said, "We will restore faith to its proper mantle in our society," he also added, "That's what we have to do, and we have to do that soon. We will respect and defend Christian Americans."[45]

At the end of June of that year, Trump met with hundreds of evangelical leaders in New York. Dr. James Dobson, a renowned Christian psychologist and founder of Focus on the Family, said that Trump's "conversion" to Christianity has been recent and that he supports him.[46]

Frank Amedia, Donald Trump's "Christian policy" coordinator, said God told him last year (2015) that Trump could win the Republican nomination, and help prepare the way for the second coming of Christ. Likewise, Tony Perkins of the Family Research Council said Trump was moving in the direction of returning the U.S. to its own interests in a way that would again honor God to bless it again. Others also said that God gave Trump the anointing to get the mantle of government. Others, the mantle of Elijah; and some more, the anointing of King Cyrus.[47]

Right-wing Christianity worked hard to make Trump the next president of the country, forgiving him for his personal transgressions; as he stoked their fears that a Clinton administration would take away their religious freedoms. That he would take their tax dollars to fund late-term abortions both at home and abroad; and that she would expand gay and transgender rights. Trump said he was the only hope to protect them from a changing culture by telling them that, "This is your last chance."[48]

The Nation published an article by J. Nichols entitled: "Donald Trump Will Lead a Theocratic Party Into the Election."[49] Nichols reported that the Republican National Convention in July approved what right-wing delegates described as, "the most conservative platform in modern history," where religion and politics were mixed:

"The 2016 GOP platform drafters have done their best to break down America's wall of separation—and their own party's regard for pluralism—with a document that is a good deal more aggressive in its language and its proposals than past platforms. [...] But this platform is more ambitious in its embrace of the themes, programs, projects and policies of the right-wing evangelical Christians who have become a powerful force in the modern GOP. The first paragraph of its section on "A Rebirth of Constitutional Government" mentions God a half dozen times and avers that "man-made law must be consistent with God-given, natural rights; and that if God-given, natural, inalienable rights come in conflict with government, court, or human-granted rights, God-given, natural, inalienable rights always prevail; that there is a moral law recognized as 'the Laws of Nature and of Nature's God'..."

---

[45] Melanie Hunter (June 10, 2016), Trump: 'We Will Restore Faith to Its Proper Mantle in Our Society,' CNS News.

[46] Kristen East (June 25, 2016), James Dobson: Trump recently accepted 'a relationship with Christ', Politico.

[47] Peter Montgomery (Aug. 17, 2016), 'God's Guy': 25 Religious Right Justifications For Supporting Donald Trump, Right Wing Watch.

[48] Laurie Goldstein (Nov. 11, 2016), Religious Right Believes Donald Trump Will Deliver on His Promises, The New York Times.

[49] John Nichols (July 19, 2016), Donald Trump Will Lead a Theocratic Party Into the Election, The Nation. Note: unless otherwise noted, this is the same source.

The document also proposed that a Republican president would establish a litmus test for the appointment of jurists who recognize, "the inalienable right to life and the laws of nature and nature's God, as did the late Justice Antonin Scalia."

In the education section, we read, "A good understanding of the Bible being indispensable for the development of an educated citizenry, we encourage state legislatures to offer the Bible in a literature curriculum as an elective in America's high schools." Given their attempts to eliminate gay rights, transgender rights, etc., the Human Rights Campaign expressed, "Unfortunately, we know we can only expect more of the same so long as Donald Trump and Mike Pence are leading the Republican Party backwards into the dark ages."

And Trump sought further support to garner the Catholic vote. For example, in early September he gave a video message praising Mother Teresa.[50]

He said in a Sept. 9 speech at the Values Voter Summit, earning him shouts and applause of support:

"We are all equal, and we all come from the same Creator. If we remember that simple fact, then our future is truly limitless. There is nothing we as Americans can't do.
There's a biblical verse that I have often read, and I want to repeat it again because I think it is so important to what we're trying to achieve right now for our country. It's from 1 John, Chapter 4: "No one has ever seen God; but if we love one another, God lives in us, and His love is made complete in us." So true. So true.
Imagine what our country could accomplish if we started working together as one people under one God, saluting one flag."[51]

In Wisconsin later that month, he said in similar terms:

"I will fight for every neglected part of this nation – and I will fight to bring us all together as Americans.

"Imagine what our country could accomplish if we started working together as One People, under One God, saluting One American Flag."[52]

Also at a rally on October 3 in Pueblo, Colorado:

"We are going to finally rebuild America. We are going to revitalize America. We are going to unite America. We are going to come together as a people. Imagine what our country can accomplish, if we start working together as one people, under one God, saluting one American flag."[53]

---

[50] Staff Reporter (Sept. 5, 2016), Donald Trump releases video praising 'humble and pious' Mother Teresa, Catholic Herald.
[51] Politico Staff (Sep. 9, 2016), Full text: Trump Values Voter Summit remarks, Politico.
[52] Donald J. Trump (September 28, 2016), Follow The Money / Donald J. Trump for President: https://www.donaldjtrump.com/press-releases/follow-the-money1; accessed November 21, 2016.
[53] (Oct. 3, 2016), Presidential Candidate Donald Trump Rally in Pueblo, Colorado, C-SPAN.

There was an explosion of shouts and applause: "USA! USA! USA! USA!...."[54] Many externalized that Trump had become exclusionary about religious faith by supporting only Christianity.[55]

The Jesuit magazine, *America*, rightly pointed out that Trump depended on the Catholic vote, particularly the white vote, to win the White House.[56]

Thus, by September he appointed 34 Catholic advisors to his campaign to help him understand the minds of American Catholics.[57] The future president's campaign announced, "Today, the Donald J. Trump campaign announced a new group convened to provide advisory support to Mr. Trump on those issues and policies important to Catholics and other people of faith in America."[58] But in June, he had also chosen an advisory council of 26 leading evangelicals; such as Michele Bachmann, Kenneth and Gloria Copeland, James Dobson, Jerry Falwell Jr, and Ralph Reed, among others.[59]

Trump contacted other faithful Catholics interested in public policy, pledging to maintain this communication from his desk in the Oval Office if elected president.[60] His low popularity among Catholics led him to make this decision.[61]

The points of religious anxiety, especially from Catholicism were: religious freedom, pro-life ideology, judicial nominations, education, health care, jobs and taxes, safety, and security.[62] Let's look at some of these issues:

"Religious Liberty

"Religious liberty is enshrined in the First Amendment to the Constitution. It is our first liberty and provides the most important protection in that it protects our right of conscience. Activist judges and executive orders issued by Presidents who have no regard for the Constitution have put these protections in jeopardy. If I am elected president and Congress passes the First Amendment Defense Act, I will sign it to protect the deeply held religious beliefs of Catholics and the beliefs of Americans of all faiths. The Little Sisters of the Poor, or any religious order for that matter, will

---

[54] Ibid.

[55] Sarah McCammon (Sept. 18, 2016), What Does Trump's Promise Of A Nation 'Under One God' Really Mean, NPR.

[56] Robert David Sullivan (September 12, 2016), A Trump win depends on white Catholics, America Magazine.

[57] Kathy Schiffer (Sept. 22, 2016), Donald Trump Names 34 Members to Council of Catholic Advisers, National Catholic Register.

[58] (Sept. 22, 2016), TRUMP CAMPAIGN ANNOUNCES CATHOLIC ADVISORY GROUP, Donald J. Trump: https://www.donaldjtrump.com/press-releases/trump-campaign-announces-catholic-advisory-group; accessed Nov. 17, 2016.

[59] Nick Gass (June 21, 2016), Trump's evangelical advisory board features Bachmann, Falwell, Politico Magazine.

[60] Kathy Schiffer (Sept. 22, 2016), Donald Trump Names 34 Members to Council of Catholic Advisers, National Catholic Register.

[61] Michael O'Loughlin (Sept. 23, 2016), Head of Trump's Catholic Advisory Group: It's All About the Judges, America.

[62] Kathy Schiffer (Sept. 22, 2016), Donald Trump Names 34 Members to Council of Catholic Advisers, National Catholic Register.

always have their religious liberty protected on my watch and will not have to face bullying from the government because of their religious beliefs."[63]

How would Trump defend the freedom of conscience of the Catholic Church and other faiths? Let us cite two examples:

"Pro-Life

"I am and will remain pro-life. Public funding of abortion providers is an insult to people of faith at the least, and is an affront to good government and governance, at best. I will work to support the dignity of human life from conception to natural, dignified death."[64]

"Judicial Nominations

"Judicial nominations, particularly appointments to the United States Supreme Court, are one of the most critical issues of this election. I will appoint Justices to the Supreme Court like the late and beloved great Catholic thinker and jurist, Justice Antonin Scalia, who will strictly interpret the Constitution and not legislate from the bench."[65]

In a letter dated October 5, 2016, to the president of the Catholic Leadership Conference, Trump noted:

"First, I would like to send my warm greetings to the Denver Archbishop Samuel Aquila. In discussions with my Catholic Advisory Group, it is clear Archbishop Aqulia's leadership in the Denver Archdiocese has been exemplary, as was the leadership of his predecessor, Archbishop Charles Chaput.

"Second, should I be elected President, I look forward to working with these two respected leaders of the Catholic Church in America, their brother bishops, and Congress, on issues of critical importance to the Catholic Church and Catholics.

"Catholics in the United States of America are a rich part of our nation's history. The United States was, and is, strengthened through Catholic men, women, priests and religious Sisters, ministering to people, marching in the Civil Rights movement, educating millions of children in Catholic schools, creating respected health care institutions, and in their founding and helping the ongoing growth of the pro-life cause.

---

[63] Donald J. Trump (September 22, 2016) Issues of Importance to Catholics, Donald J. Trump: https://www.donaldjtrump.com/press-releases/issues-of-importance-to-catholics; accessed November 17, 2016.
[64] Ibid.
[65] Ibid.

"I have a message for Catholics: I will be there for you. I will stand with you. I will fight for you."[66]

The Catholic network *EWTN* aired a video on the eve of the election where Donald Trump appeared recalling the Obama administration's hostility towards the Catholic Church, which he promised to reverse:

"Catholics are an important part of the American story. America has been strengthened by hard-working Catholics. From New York to California, the Catholic story is truly unique and it's a great story. From marching for civil rights to educating millions of children, serving the poor and helping to define the pro-life movement, Clergy and and lay Catholics across the country have made countless contributions to the America's success and America's success story. Washington politicians have been hostile to the Church, they have been hostile to Catholics, they have been hostile to members of Catholicism. My administration will stand side by side with the with American Catholics to promote the values that we all share as Christians and Americans. God bless you. God bless the United States of America. We will make America great again."[67]

That occurred just when more Republicans in the House identified themselves as Catholic, even more than Democrats.[68]

In that month of the presidential elections, Pope Francis pointed to the terrorism of slander or defamation, referring especially to the Italian press, accused of populism and of feeding bad feelings among different social groups. He also pointed out that every human being can become a terrorist by the mere fact of using abusive language.[69] He indicated that he was referring to a deceptive and hidden form of terrorism that uses words like bombs that explode and wreak havoc on human lives. He said it is a kind of criminality, its root being original sin. It is a way of creating space for oneself by destroying others.[70]

During an interview that month with Eugenio Scalfari of the Italian daily *La Repubblica*, the pope declined to offer any comment on Donald Trump, but said he was concerned about how the policies of politicians can affect the lives of the poor.[71]

In those days, the pope also decried "the "epidemic of animosity" against immigrants, other faiths."[72]

---

[66] Donald J. Trump to Gail Buckely, president of the Catholic Leadership Conference, Oct. 5, 2016, http://www.catholicnewsagency.com/pdf/DJT_catholic_leadership_conference_letter.pdf; accessed Nov. 24, 2016.

[67] (Nov. 9, 2016), Message to Catholics from Donald Trump, fx2py: https://www.youtube.com/watch?v=AgOosN1dlXE Accessed March 26, 2024.

[68] Aleksandra Sandstrom (Jan. 22, 2015), House Catholics are trending Republican, Fact Tank; Michael O'Loughlin (Jan. 5, 2015), Nearly one-third of the incoming Congress is Catholic, Crux; Elizabeth King (Sept. 23, 2015), How Many U.S. Politicians Are Catholic? The Pope Won't Feel Alone When He Addresses Congress For The First Time, Bustle; Claire Zillman (September 24, 2015), Pope Francis addresses a Congress that's 30% Catholic, Fortune Magazine.

[69] (Oct. 28, 2016), Pope Francis in a unique conversation, Dagens Nyheter.

[70] Ibid.

[71] Staff Reporter (Nov. 11, 2016), 'I don't judge politicians': Pope Francis skirts Trump question, Catholic Herald.

He also warned against the "virus of polarization" and hostility that denigrates people of different nationalities, races, or beliefs.[73] However on the day Trump won the presidency, he called for dialogue and mutual acceptance.[74]

All this is because although Trump favored American Catholicism, he did so in a polarized way, one against the other, while Pope Francis sought mutual understanding, respect, and unity amid a diversity of ideas and thoughts. Therefore, he favored Hillary Clinton more, willing to build bridges that the pope desired.

Now, the chaos was beginning, because after Trump was elected president, it was reported in November that firings and discord were putting Trump's transition team in disarray.[75] There were fears of a huge lack of experience in cabinet selection for the White House, which Trump denied.[76]

On the Supreme Court's decision on same-sex marriage, Trump said he was "fine with that," but promised to appoint a justice opposed to abortion rights and to help overturn the 1973 decision in Roe v. Wade, returning the issue to the states.[77]

On the day of his victory, the U.S. bishops congratulated Trump and offered their collaboration in: 1. Listening to the American people. 2. Protecting human life from conception to its natural end. 3. Humanitarian welcome to migrants and refugees. 4. Protection of persecuted Christians in the East. 5. Defending the family and religious freedom in the United States.[78]

The New York Times reported that on November 10, Archbishop José H. Gómez convened an interfaith prayer service at the Roman Catholic Cathedral in Los Angeles, where he referred to Trump's plan for the deportation of immigrants so that this does not happen.[79] On Nov. 15, the archbishop was elected at the bishops' meeting in Baltimore as the vice president of the U.S. Conference of Catholic Bishops, and Cardinal Daniel N. DiNardo, archbishop of Galveston-Houston, as the president. Thus, they launched into a challenge to Donald Trump not to carry out his plan to deport illegal immigrants. Even at the opening of the meeting, they approved a strongly worded letter to Trump extending their congratulations but also noted that the church was committed to refugee resettlement and keeping families intact.[80]

But the bishops found common cause on many other priorities with Trump, such as ending or limiting abortion, reversing the contraceptive mandate in the Affordable Care

---

[72] Philip Pullella (Nov. 19, 2016), Pope decries 'epidemic of animosity' against immigrants and other faiths, Reuters.

[73] (Nov. 19, 2016), Pope Francis warns against "virus of polarization" over race, faith, CBS/AP.

[74] Tara John (Nov. 9, 2016), Pope Francis Calls for 'Dialogue, Mutual Acceptance' After Trump Victory, Time Magazine.

[75] Julie Hirschfeld Davis, Mark Mazzetti and Maggie Haberman (Nov. 15, 2016), Firings and Discord Put Trump Transition Team in a State of Disarray, The New York Times.

[76] Louis Nelson (Nov. 16, 2016), Trump shoots down reports that his transition is in disarray, Politico; Shane Goldmacher, Alex Isenstadt and Nancy Cook (Nov. 16, 2016), Trump lashes out at accusations of transition chaos, Politico; Shane Goldmacher and Andrew Restuccia (Nov. 17, 2016), Trump calm chaos, Politico.

[77] Julie Hirschfeld Davis (Nov. 13, 2016), Donald Trump Appears to Soften Stance on Immigration, but Not on Abortion, The New York Times.

[78] (Nov. 9, 2016), Los obispos de EEUU felicitan a Trump: la Iglesia ayudará a los políticos en estas 5 prioridades, Religión en Libertad.

[79] Laurie Goodstein (Nov. 15, 2016), Catholic Bishops Challenge Donald Trump on Immigration, The New York Times.

[80] Julie Hirschfeld Davis (Nov. 13, 2016), Donald Trump Appears to Soften Stance on Immigration, but Not on Abortion, The New York Times.

Act, and creating exemptions for individuals and religious institutions that oppose same-sex marriage.[81] The bishops expressed concern but at the same time cautious optimism about the new administration.[82]

Francis Rooney, a former U.S. ambassador to the Vatican, as well as one of Trump's Catholic advisors, told *Crux* that Catholics would do well to be thankful that Trump was the president-elect and not Hillary Clinton, because of the reverse government to the Catholic ideal held by Obama and the Democratic nominee. He revealed that the first thing Trump would do was to nominate a Supreme Court justice who would carry on the legacy of Scalia, who was pro-life. He further stated that Trump would make a change in the numerous appellate and district court judges; and without denying the election of two or three conservative judges to the U.S. Supreme Court.

He would eliminate the Hyde Amendment permanently, to prohibit the practice of abortion with federal funds, except in cases where the life of the mother must be saved or, for incest or rape. The passage of the First Amendment Defense Act protects the activities of religious organizations and religious objectors to Obamacare, which was to be dismantled. It was also planned to defund Planned Parenthood, as well as have a balanced economy that works for all citizens, with equitable globalization. When Rooney was told of Pope Francis' words about a globalized marketplace and the use of technology as a win-win for all, he agreed, mentioning that Trump may cancel Obama's Executive Orders and that there would be a replacement for the Affordable Care Act.[83]

Days after his victory, the Christian Right was confident that Donald Trump would deliver on his promises, which included a conservative Supreme Court justice; defunding Planned Parenthood, protecting businesses that refused to provide services for gay weddings, and rescinding the mandate in the Affordable Care Act requiring insurance coverage for birth control.[84]

The Republicans became the party of the American Christian right that won the largest majority in decades in November 2014, ending Democratic control of the Senate.[85] Donald Trump provided Republicans with what they have been seeking for a decade: "unified control of the government and a chance to pursue a conservative agenda, transforming them from the "party of no" into a party that can enact significant legislation."[86] Democrats were reeling and sighted a possible black horizon in the Senate in 2018.[87] Congressman Tim Ryan of Ohio, who was challenging Nancy Pelosi for the party's top Democratic position, said, "I'm pulling the fire alarm right now is what I'm doing in the Democratic Party [...] I believe we're in denial of what's happened. I'm pulling the fire alarm because the house is burning down. We better get our act together or we will cease being a national party, we're going to be a regional

---

[81] Ibid.

[82] Michael O'Loughlin (Nov. 15, 2016), U.S. Bishops Express Concern and Cautious Optimism about Relations with the Trump Administration, America.

[83] Francis Rooney (Nov. 17, 2016), Why Catholics should be grateful for Trump's victory, Crux.

[84] Laurie Goldstein (Nov. 11, 2016), Religious Right Believes Donald Trump Will Deliver on His Promises, The New York Times.

[85] Kristina Peterson (Nov. 5, 2014), House Republicans Achieve Largest Majority in Decades, The Wall Street Journal.

[86] Jennifer Steinhauer (Nov. 9, 2016), Republicans in Congress Plan Swift Action on Agenda With Donald Trump, The New York Times.

[87] Burgess Everett (Nov. 17, 2016), Reeling Democrats confront brutal 2018 Senate map, Politico.

party that fails to get into the majority and fails to do things on behalf of those working class people that were the backbone of the Democratic Party for so long."[88] All in all, when a reporter asked Obama if he was worried that he would be the last Democratic president, he said no, and not even temporarily.[89]

Now let's take a closer look at Trump's cabinet.

The election of Mike Pence as vice president of the country was described by Jeremy Scahill as "a tremendous coup for the radical religious right." He was going to be a powerful hand for Trump, of whom prominent right-wing Christian activist David Barton and president of Wall Builders (an organization dedicated to getting the U.S. government to impose "Christian values" on the nation), expresses that he is God's chosen one.[90] Scahill points out, in unconventional language:

"Trump is a Trojan horse for a cabal of vicious zealots who have long craved an extremist Christian theocracy, and Pence is one of its most prized warriors. With Republican control of the House and Senate and the prospect of dramatically and decisively tilting the balance of the Supreme Court to the far right, the incoming administration will have a real shot at bringing the fire and brimstone of the second coming to Washington."[91]

Jeff Sharlet, scholar and author of two books on the radical religious right, wrote:

"The enemy, to them, is secularism. They want a God-led government. That's the only legitimate government," contends Jeff Sharlet, author of two books on the radical religious right, including "The Family: The Secret Fundamentalism at the Heart of American Power." "So when they speak of business, they're speaking not of something separate from God, but they're speaking of what, in Mike Pence's circles, would be called biblical capitalism, the idea that this economic system is God-ordained."[92]

Pence has a long history of excellent relations with sectors of the U.S. Catholic Church for proposing legislation in Congress that would benefit some of their thinking.[93]

Scahill points out that Mike Pence combines the most horrific aspects of Dick Cheney's worldview with a belief that Tim LaHaye's "Left Behind" fiction novels are not fiction; but an omniscient crystal ball. He had supported the Patriot Act to make it permanent;[94] which is a law brought into vogue to carry out a domestic surveillance state within the United States to track and catch potential terrorists after September 11, 2001. A law that threatens basic liberties of citizens, such as the violation of obtaining

---

[88] Pamela Engel (Nov. 21, 2016), PELOSI CHALLENGER: I'm 'pulling the fire alarm' because 'house is burning down' and we might 'cease being a national party', Business Insider.

[89] Mark Abadi (Nov. 20, 2016), A reporter asked Obama if he was worried he'd be the last Democratic president, Business Insider.

[90] Jeremy Scahill (Nov. 15, 2016), Mike Pence Will Be the Most Powerful Christian Supremacist in U.S., The Intercept.

[91] Ibid.

[92] Ibid.

[93] Michael O'Loughlin (July 15, 2016), Mike Pence's Relationship with the Catholic Church is... Complicated, America.

[94] Jeremy Scahill (Nov. 15, 2016), Mike Pence Will Be the Most Powerful Christian Supremacist in U.S., The Intercept.

their private information. Title 1 of the law contained the prayer of Cardinal Theodore McCarrick, the Archbishop of Washington at a mass on September 12, 2001, for the nation and the victims of the fateful terrorist attacks.

Pence also believed that federal law enforcement agencies should not obtain a FISA (Foreign Intelligence Surveillance Act) warrant to conduct domestic surveillance, and voted against requiring any court order for wiretaps. He supported giving retroactive immunity to telecommunications companies involved in warrantless surveillance.[95] He also did not agree to congressional oversight of CIA interrogations, which Trump believed should include "waterboarding" and other torture, as well as a lot worse than waterboarding. Trump added: "If it doesn't work, they deserve it anyway, for what they're doing. It works."[96] A 2014 poll in the United States, showed that the nation's evangelical Christians were more supportive of torture than those who are not religious.[97]

But let's add that Pence viewed non-coercive interrogation strategies as weak.[98] He was also against whistleblower protections, which prohibit retaliation against whistleblowers for reporting crimes or wrongdoing. He wants the resumption of the practice of detaining new prisoners at Guantanamo Bay, or filling it up; as Trump put it. He also supports the expanded use of the military tribunal. And he supported - and perhaps still supports - a military strike against Iran. He supports militarized use of the war on drugs, including increased militarized patrols in the United States. He opposed the imposition of restrictions on no-bid contracting, which would explain his close relationship with Erik Prince, that far-right Catholic founder of Blackwater, the military crusaders who fought Muslims in Iraq.

But Pence and Prince's relationship also served to advance conservative agendas in government for implementation at home. Prince has long given money to Pence's political campaigns; and toward the end of the presidential election, he contributed $100K to the Trump/Pence PAC Make America Number 1; and Elsa Prince (Erik Prince's mother) donated $50K. Pence has said that he is a born-again Catholic evangelical. One who has strong friendly ties to Christian fundamentalist Charles Colson, who joined with Jesuit priest Richard Neuhaus and others in creating the 1994 document "Evangelicals and Catholics Together: The Christian Mission in the Third Millennium," aimed at uniting church and state in the United States. As Scahill says, "They will now have the opportunity to build the temple they have long desired."

Trump chose Reince Priebus as Chief of Staff, and Stephen Bannon as senior advisor and White House chief strategist. Priebus was the chairman of the Republican National Committee and because of his friendship with House Speaker Paul Ryan, could help secure early legislative victories.[99] By electing Priebus to the post, Trump pleased the

[95] Ibid.

[96] Jenna Johnson (Nov. 23, 2015), Donald Trump on waterboarding: 'If it doesn't work, they deserve it anyway.', The Washington Post.

[97] Heather Digby Parton (June 30, 2016), Trump, torture and religion: Why the Christian Right has flocked to the GOP nominee, Salon.

[98] Jeremy Scahill (Nov. 15, 2016), Mike Pence Will Be the Most Powerful Christian Supremacist in U.S., The Intercept. Note: unless otherwise noted, this is the same source.

[99] Michael D. Shear, Maggie Haberman and Alan Rappeport (Nov. 13, 2016), Donald Trump Picks Reince Priebus as Chief of Staff and Stephen Bannon as Strategist, The New York Times.

Republican establishment.[100] Priebus is a Greek Orthodox Christian,[101] but dislikes the term tolerance on issues outside the conservative policies of the Republican party, and believes that "there's only one sovereign God."[102]

Let's see Stephen Bannon, who is a Catholic and headed the controversial news outlet *Breitbart*, described by Hillary Clinton as the "number one enemy of the Democratic Party."[103] Bannon is considered a white nationalist.[104]

His ex-wife went so far as to accuse him of making anti-Semitic remarks.[105] He says moderate Muslims are increasingly moving toward extremists.[106]

Breitbart tried to clean up its image, publishing an article defending Bannon as a friend of the Jews and defender of Israel.[107]

Similarly, Julia Jones, Bannon's Hollywood screenwriting partner for nearly two decades, said she never met the racist Steve that the media reported. She never heard him telling racist jokes and that his best friend was an African-American who went to college with him; and she never saw a hint of racism from him.[108] Newt Gingrich also defended Bannon, saying he couldn't be anti-Semitic because he worked in finance and Hollywood.[109]

On his side, Trump had Jews and practitioners of Judaism, such as his daughter Ivanka Trump, Jason Greenblatt, Boris Epshteyn, Steve Mnuchin,[110] and his son-in-law Jared Kushner.

Returning to Bannon, although Ben Shapiro, formerly of *Breitbart*, said that Bannon is not a racist or anti-Semite; others point out that under Bannon, the outlet captured the attention of white supremacists, anti-Semites, and so-called "Internet trolls."[111] Which we have been able to verify extensively.

Some think Bannon is a threat to global security because of the hatred he promotes.[112]

---

[100] Katie Zezima (Nov. 14, 2016), Wink to Republican establishment in first appointment to her administration, The Nation.

[101] Michael Gryboski (Nov. 14, 2016), Who is Reince Priebus? 5 Things You Should Know, Christian Post.

[102] Daniel Schultz (July 24, 2013), GOP Chair Reince Priebus: "There's only one sovereign God," Religion Dispatches.

[103] Ediziones (Nov. 15, 2016), Así es Breitbart, el polemic medio que dirigía Stephen Bannon, último fichaje de Trump, Europa Press.

[104] Ellen Killoran (Nov. 14, 2016), Steve Bannon And Breitbart News: Why Everyone But The Alt-Right Fears Trump's Top Adviser Pick, Forbes.

[105] Elizabeth Chuck, Ali Vitali, Andrew Blankstein and Katie Wall (Aug. 27, 2016), Trump Campaign CEO Steve Bannon Accused of Anti-Semitic Remarks by Ex-Wife, NBC News.

[106] Raheem Kassam (March 22, 2016), DATA: Young Muslims in the West Are a Ticking Time Bomb, Increasingly Sympathising with Radicals, Terror, Breitbart.

[107] Joel B. Pollak (Nov. 14, 2016), Steve Bannon: Friend of the Jewish People, Defender of Israel, Breitbart.

[108] Ian Tuttle (Nov. 14, 2016), Steve Bannon Is Not a Nazi-But Let's Be Honest about What He Represents, National Review.

[109] Willa Frej (Nov. 14, 2016), Newt Gingrich: Steve Bannon Can't Be Anti-Semitic Because He Worked In Finance And Hollywood, The Hufftington Post.

[110] Josefin Dolsten (Nov. 14, 2016), Meet the Jews in Donald Trump's inner circle, Jewish Journal.

[111] Ian Tuttle (Nov. 14, 2016), Steve Bannon Is Not a Nazi-But Let's Be Honest about What He Represents, National Review.

[112] Mick Krever (Nov. 14, 2016), Steve Bannon a 'threat to global security,' says civil rights attorney, CNN.

On the other hand, in an interview that Robert P. George, a Princeton law professor conducted with Bannon in March 2016, he said that Paul D. Ryan was "rubbing his social-justice Catholicism in my nose every second."[113]

Regarding the Catholic Church's immigration policy, he said, "I understand why Catholics want as many Hispanics in this country as possible because the church is dying in this country, right, if it was not for the Hispanics." The executive director of the Franciscan Action Network urged the Trump campaign to change its tune and said that "Pope Francis has called on us to build bridges and not walls," regarding Trump's immigration policies. He further said, "In the past, Donald Trump has attacked the Pope, and now his campaign is going after the Church itself […] Enough is enough." All in all, Bannon is a proud Catholic who in the summer of 2014 gave a lecture to the Vatican on the Catholic response to poverty.[114] This was done via Skype, where he expressed that there is a "global tea party movement" and praised European far-right parties such as UKIP in Great Britain and the National Front in France.[115] He said that the West (referring particularly to the United States), was facing a "crisis of capitalism" after losing its "Judeo-Christian foundation"; and cursed Washington's "crony capitalists" for failing to prosecute banker executives for the financial crisis. Bannon missed pre-1914 (World War I) globalized Europe, when the High Church of England, the Catholic Church, and the Christian faith were predominant on the continent. Furthermore, Bannon points out that it was American capitalism, which defeated the Nazis in WW2, that generated tremendous wealth. The wealth that was actually distributed among the middle class, to people who came from truly working-class backgrounds, and that created the so-called Pax Americana (American Peace) for many decades.

But Bannon expressed that since the fall of the Soviet Union, the United States has gone off track and that in the 21st century, there is a crisis of the Church, of faith, of the West, of capitalism. The solution - according to Bannon - is to unite against the very brutal and bloody conflict that was in its initial stages (ISIS), creating within the militant church a body to defend their beliefs in the face of the barbarity that threatens them and that they have to defend from falling from the legacy received from the last 2000 to 2500 years. In other words, the United States and Europe united against the political-economic-warlike evils that threatened to destroy Catholicism and the rest of Christianity.

For that reason, Bannon hoped to confront the kind of capitalism that is eliminating the underlying spiritual and moral foundations of Christianity and Judeo-Christian belief. He advocated, therefore, a return to an economy based on the principles of Catholicism and general Christianity to save the United States and Europe. Thus, he criticizes Russian and Chinese capitalism and also defends Pope Francis' criticism of unbridled capitalism. He also believes that Christian beliefs should influence the highest levels of government.

These statements were made during his presentation and during the 50-minute question-and-answer session that followed, which was sponsored by the Human

---

[113] Jonathan Swan (Aug. 25, 2016), Group condemns Trump campaign CEO for 'anti-Catholic' remarks, The Hill.
[114] Ibid.
[115] J. Lester Feder (Nov. 16, 2016), This Is How Steve Bannon Sees The Entire World, BuzzFeed. Note: unless otherwise noted, this is the same source.

Dignity Institute. A group founded by Benjamin Harnwell, a long-time aide to conservative Member of the European Parliament, Nirj Deva, to promote a Christian voice in European politics. The group had ties to some of the most conservative factions within the Catholic Church, such as U.S. Cardinal Raymond Burke, characterized by leading the opposition against Pope Francis.

Likewise, Bannon was zealous for his daughters to attend a Catholic school.[116]

Let's now look at Kellyanne Conway, who was Trump's campaign manager and a Roman Catholic, political science graduate from Trinity College in Washington D.C. (now university, a Catholic institution), along with Stephen Bannon. But both also have in common, that they are members of the Council for National Policy or CNP (Council for National Policy),[117] which is a secret club founded in 1981 by Tim LaHaye, a well-known evangelical minister now deceased, who created it as a forum for conservative Christians to strategize on how to turn the country to the right.[118] In addition, Conway was listed in 2014 as a member of the Council's Executive Committee.[119] Among its hundreds of members was also James Dobson of Focus on the Family. Also, there was the now-deceased Jerry Falwell Sr. of Liberty University.[120] Other members are/were Pat Robertson, Ralph Reed, and Edgar and Elsa Prince - parents of Erik Prince - the founder of Blackwater: Christian supremacists who spread the "faith" in Iraq.[121] The Council has included members of Christian Reconstructionism, a movement that advocates the execution of adultery, blasphemy, homosexuality, and witchcraft;[122] and in short, defends the application of the Ten Commandments today.[123]

The NPC was influential on the eve of the 1999 presidential primaries in support of George W. Bush. [124]

With this in mind, see what Bannon said in 2016:

"I'm a Leninist [...] Lenin wanted to destroy the state, and that's my goal too. I want to bring everything down, and destroy all of today's establishment."[125]

---

[116] Associated Press (Aug. 27, 2016), Ex-wife accused Trump campaign CEO Bannon of anti-Semitic statements, Fox News.

[117] Troutfishing (Aug. 18, 2016), Theocratic Right Now Runs Trump Campaign - Bannon and Conway are in the CNP !, Daily Kos; Mark Potok (Aug. 31, 2016), Revealed: Conway, Bannon Members of Secretive Group, SPLC.

[118] David D. Kirkpatrick (February 25, 2007), Christian Right Labors to Find '08 Candidate, The New York Times.

[119] Troutfishing (Aug. 18, 2016), Theocratic Right Now Runs Trump Campaign - Bannon and Conway are in the CNP !, Daily Kos; Mark Potok (Aug. 31, 2016), Revealed: Conway, Bannon Members of Secretive Group, SPLC.

[120] David D. Kirkpatrick (February 25, 2007), Christian Right Labors to Find '08 Candidate, The New York Times.

[121] Jeremy Scahill, Blackwater: The Rise of the World's Most Powerful Mercenary Army (Serpent's Tail, London, 2008), ob. cit.

[122] Troutfishing (Aug. 18, 2016), Theocratic Right Now Runs Trump Campaign - Bannon and Conway are in the CNP !, Daily Kos.

[123] Frederick Clarkson (March/June 1994), Christian Reconstructionism, The Public Eye Magazine, Vol. 8, No. 1.

[124] David D. Kirkpatrick (February 25, 2007), Christian Right Labors to Find '08 Candidate, The New York Times.

[125] Ronald Radosh (Aug. 21, 2016), Steve Bannon, Trump's Top Guy, Told Me He Was 'A Leninist' Who Wants To 'Destroy the State,' The Daily Beast.

Of Bannon's membership in the alt-right and the trend itself, Trump told *The New York Times* in November 2016 that he did not want to excite that group and that he disowned it.[126] About Bannon, he said that he has known him for a long time and that if he had known he was a racist or an alt-right, among others, he would not have even thought of hiring him.[127] However, *Breitbart* published an article on March 29 where it defended the alt-right using two images: the first shows the frog (symbol of the movement) hooded during a scary night telling the wounded and frightened Republican elephant to go to its grave.[128] The other image, in essence, shows Donald Trump as one of the movement's frogs driving a train that will not stop; which reads "Trump 2016."[129] Although Milo Yiannopoulos of the alt-right has said that the Ku Klux Klan and neo-Nazis are merely the far right of the alt-right.[130] Nevertheless, the alt-right is being nationalist supremacist in several respects. Bannon has been labeled "the most dangerous political operative in America."[131]

After several controversies, Bannon was fired from his position in August 2017.[132]

Regarding the slogan "Make America Great Again," *The Guardian* expressed this transformation in these terms:

"The neoliberal era in the United States ended with a neofascist bang. The political triumph of Donald Trump shattered the establishments in the Democratic and Republican parties – both wedded to the rule of Big Money and to the reign of meretricious politicians."[133]

A new world order that many feared, as *Politico* noted.[134]

Trump also chose Jeff Sessions as the new attorney general. Sessions is a Methodist and has a history of racist controversy.[135] Rob Boston, of Americans United for Separation of Church and State, wrote on the organization's blog "Jeff Sessions Is No Fan Of Separation Of Church And State." He believes that government officials should be very religious and that the government should base its decisions on a biblical worldview. He also believes that Supreme Court justices should take religious tests to see if they can perform their role well.[136]

---

[126] The New York Times (Nov. 23, 2016), Donald Trump's New York Times Interview: Full Transcript, The New York Times.

[127] Ibid.

[128] Allum Bokhari and Milo Yiannopoulos (March 29, 2016), An Establishment Conservative's Guide To The Alt-Right, Breitbart.

[129] Ibid.

[130] Dan Susman and Adam Sich (Nov. 15, 2016), Stephen Bannon and the alt-right in the White House - video explainer, The Guardian.

[131] Joshua Green (October 8, 2015), This Man Is The Most Dangerous Political Operative in America , Bloomberg....

[132] Jeremy Diamond, Kaitlan Collins and Elizabeth Landers (Aug. 19, 2017), Trump's chief strategist Steve Bannon fired, CNN.

[133] Cornel West (Nov. 17, 2016), Goodbye, American neoliberalism. A new era is here, The Guardian.

[134] Nahal Toosi (Nov. 17, 2016), Trump's new world order, Politico.

[135] Amanda Mars (Nov. 19, 2016), Trump elige a tres ultraconservadores para dirigir Justicia, la CIA y seguridad nacional, El País.

[136] Rob Boston (Nov. 21, 2016), Jeff Sessions Is No Fan Of Separation Of Church And State, Wall Of Separation The official blog of Americans United for Separation of Church and State: https://www.au.org/blogs/wall-of-separation/jeff-sessions-is-no-fan-of-separation-of-church-and-state; accessed Jan. 18, 2018.

Trump chose General Michael Flynn as National Security Advisor.[137] Flynn is a Roman Catholic[138] with deep anti-Islamic roots.[139]

He was in Iraq during the George W. Bush-era invasion of the country as part of the Joint Special Operations Command (JSOC). Flynn conducted himself in Iraq in such a way that the "operations take over the intelligence," hitting the homes of Iraqi civilians and scaring their residents.[140]

Flynn was subsequently promoted to chief of intelligence for the entire NATO force in Afghanistan, where he had a growing conviction that the Christian West was engaged in a battle for civilization against Islam. Private Jack Murphy, who was under Flynn's command, recounted, "Our platoon got together. The chaplain got up and gave his little speech and told us that we were fighting a religious war and make no mistake, men, this a religious war."

Flynn was director of the Defense Intelligence Agency (DIA) from 2012 to 2014, being forced to resign. He left the military and allied himself with Donald Trump in the 2016 presidential campaign against Hillary Clinton.

During an interview with *The Washington Post*'s Dana Priest, which was published on August 15, 2016, Flynn contrasted the radicalized Islamic religious component with Christianity in the United States as if the latter is superior.[141] He said he has been fighting Islam for the past decade, and that Islam is a metastasized cancer that has spread.[142]

Michael Flynn, along with General Stanley McChrystal, transformed Joint Special Operation Command (JSOC), "into history's most lethal terrorist hunting network."[143] Its black operations laid the groundwork for Obama's counterterrorism strategy in Yemen, Somalia, Afghanistan, and others, as Scahill notes.

We said in another chapter that JSOC had a Christian supremacist component, especially Catholic, subtracted from the Knights of Malta and Opus Dei; waging a crusade against Islam. These were black operations of assassination.

We also saw that JSOC used torture in secret or dark CIA prisons against Muslim prisoners to extract information from them. In this context, Flynn, like Donald Trump, gave support to waterboarding;[144] which is a method of torture that consists of covering the face (covering the mouth and nose) of the accused with a cloth soaked in water so that they experience the sensation of drowning. It is used for the very purpose of

[137] Amanda Mars (Nov. 19, 2016), Trump elige a tres ultraconservadores para dirigir Justicia, la CIA y seguridad nacional, El País.

[138] Bryan Bender and Shane Goldmacher (July 8, 2016), Trump's favorite general, Politico.

[139] Editor (Nov. 18, 2016), Quién es Michael Flynn, el general señalado de "islamofobia" que puede ser Consejero de Seguridad de Trump, BBC; The Editorial Board (Nov. 18, 2016), Michael Flynn: An Alarming Pick for National Security Adviser, The New York Times; Daniel S. Levine (Nov. 18, 2016), Michael Flynn & Islam: 5 Fast Facts You Need to Know, Heavy; Joan Faus (Nov. 18, 2016), Michael Flynn, el general islamófobo y afín a Rusia de Donald Trump, El País.

[140] Richard Rowley (Writer), & Richard Rowley (Director) (2022, October 18). Michael Flynn's Holy War (Season 41, Episode 2) [TV Series Episode]. Raney Aronson, David Fanning (Executive Producers), *Frontline*. Public Broadcasting Service (PBS). Note: unless otherwise noted, this is the same source.

[141] Dana Priest (Aug. 15, 2016), Trump adviser Michael T. Flynn on his dinner with Putin and why Russia Today is just like CNN, The Washington Post.

[142] (Jan. 13, 2016), Transcript: Michael Flynn on ISIL, Aljazeera.

[143] James Kitfield (October 16, 2016), How Mike Flynn Became America's Angriest General, Politico Magazine.

[144] Daniel Marans (May 19, 2016), Trump-Advising General Defends Muslim Ban, The Huffington Post.

extracting information; and can cause extreme pain, dry drowning, lung damage, brain damage, broken bones in the struggle against drowning, lasting psychological damage, and death.

But Flynn considered the harsh techniques used by JSOC counterproductive and said he would not want to return to "enhanced techniques" since he helped rewrite the interrogation manual. However, he believes that if the nation is in grave terrorist danger involving weapons of mass destruction, he would enhance interrogation techniques with prisoners in custody who may have information to prevent it.[145] Michael Flynn, "insists that his views are not the extension of personal religious convictions and that he does not view the conflict he describes as a fundamentally religious one."[146] He took the words of Pope Francis - a man of peace; he says, that he even recognizes that there is a world war fought by parties.[147] But many know that Trump and Flynn believe they are in a war against Islam and that it is therefore a religious war.[148] A war that must, according to Flynn, begin with detecting extremist Muslims inside the United States.[149]

One of Trump's campaign advisors, Joseph Schmitz, accused of anti-Semitism,[150] was a member of Blackwater and a Christian supremacist of the Knights of Malta.

Trump's other choice to head Justice, was Mike Pompeo, as CIA director.[151]

Pompeo is a Presbyterian, and he invited Bishop Carl A. Kemme of the Diocese of Wichita in mid-September 2015 to be his escort during Pope Francis' address to Congress, saying, "It is my distinct honor to have Bishop Kemme accompany me to the Holy Father's historic address to Congress," Congressman Pompeo said. "In a time when our country is riddled with uncertainty, Pope Francis' message of compassion and humility is certain to touch the hearts of people everywhere."[152] Pompeo has portrayed the war on terror at some religious events as a battle waged against Islam that fights against Christianity.[153]

He has made no secret of his desire to see Edward Snowden dead, and he is or was also an outspoken advocate of the torture used by the CIA.[154]

Regarding other appointments, Trump also nominated billionaire Betsy DeVos as Secretary of Education.[155] She is the sister of Blackwater founder Erik Prince.[156] Her

---

[145] Ibid.

[146] Ryan Devereaux (July 23, 2016), An Interview With Michael T. Flynn, the Ex-Pentagon Spy, The Intercept.

[147] Lieutenant General Michael T. Flynn and Michael Ledeen, The Field of Fight: How We Can Win the Global War Against Radical Islam and Its Allies (St. Martin's Press, New York, 2016), ob. cit.

[148] Richard Wolffe (November 19, 2016), Michael Flynn will be a disaster as national security adviser, The Guardian.

[149] Pamela Engel (Nov. 19, 2016), Trump's new national security adviser outlines his controversial plan to defeat terrorism, Business Insider.

[150] Eric Cortellesa (Aug. 19, 2016), Trump adviser allegedly bragged about firing Jews from Pentagon Jobs, The Times of Israel.

[151] Amanda Mars (Nov. 19, 2016), Trump elige a tres ultraconservadores para dirigir Justicia, la CIA y seguridad nacional, El País.

[152] http://pompeo.house.gov/news/documentsingle.aspx?DocumentID=398626; retrieved November 20, 2016.

[153] Lee Fang (Nov. 23, 2016), Trump CIA Pick Mike Pompeo Depicted War on Terror as Islamic Battle Against Christianity, The Intercept.

[154] Alex Emmons, Naomi LaChance (Nov. 18, 2016), Obama Refuses to Pardon Edward Snowden. Trump's New CIA Pick Wants Him Dead, The Intercept.

[155] Chase Peterson-Withorn (Nov. 23, 2016), Trump Picks Betsy DeVos, Daughter-In-Law Of Billionaire Amway Cofounder, For Education Secretary, Forbes.

husband is billionaire Dick DeVos, whose father, Richard DeVos, according to journalist Jane Mayer, donated many thousands of dollars during the Reagan era to fund conservative agendas in Washington D.C.[157] They were the biggest bankers of the 1994 Republican Revolution.[158] In addition, they may have raised a lot of money to contribute to President George W. Bush.[159] They have also poured or invested more than $200 million into key institutions of the Christian Right and the conservative movement.[160]

Betsy DeVos is a Roman Catholic and sent her daughters to private Christian schools.[161] She is an enemy of public schools and a supporter of private and religious school vouchers.[162]

Other nominations from the Trump team, were retired Lt. Gen. Keith Kellogg; former Ohio Secretary of State Ken Blackwell, David R. Malpass, and former Attorney General Edwin Meese.[163] Kellogg is reportedly a Catholic; and a notable alumnus of Santa Clara Jesuit University. He was involved in the failed post-war reconstruction of Iraq.[164] As the reader will recall, the U.S. interim government was led by the ultra-right-wing Catholic Paul Bremer.

From 2005 to 2009, Kellogg was a senior executive with CACI International, one of the companies that supplied interrogators who abused and tortured Iraqi prisoners at Abu Ghraib military prison;[165] which was also part of the Christian supremacist crusade carried out by the George Bush Jr. administration.

For his part, Walid Phares, who had been chosen by Trump as an expert advisor on terrorism, counter-terrorism, and Middle East affairs, has a similar if in part rawer story. He is a Lebanese-born Maronite Christian who was a leading ideologue in an armed Christian faction against Muslims during the severe and bloody Lebanese sectarian conflict of the 1980s. In this, they carried out horrific massacres against Islamists.[166]

Ken Blackwell, meanwhile, is a Methodist Christian supremacist and a senior fellow at the Family Research Council, which is a Christian right-wing body.[167] He was

---

[156] Ben Van Heuvelen (October 2, 2007), The Bush administration's ties to Blackwater, Salon.

[157] Jane Mayer, Dark Money: The Hidden History of the Billionaires Behind the Rise of the Radical Right (Double Day, New York, 2016), ob. cit.

[158] (Oct. 3, 2007), Mr. Prince Goes to Washington: Blackwater Founder Testifies Before Congress, Democracy NOW!

[159] Jeremy Scahill, Blackwater: The Rise of the World's Most Powerful Mercenary Army (Serpent's Tail, London, 2008), ob. cit.

[160] Benjy Hansen-Bundy and Andy Kroll (Jan. 21, 2014), The Family That Gives Together, Mother Jones.

[161] Kelsey Harkness (Nov. 23, 2016), Meet Betsy DeVos, Trump's Pick for Education Secretary, The Daily Signal.

[162] Deirdre Fulton (Nov. 23, 2016), Trump Nominates 'True Enemy' of Public Schools for Education Secretary, CommonDreams.

[163] Brian Naylor, Barbara Sprunt (Nov. 16, 2016), From Lobbyists To Loyalists, See Who's On Donald Trump's Transition Team, NPR News.

[164] Shane Harris (March 21, 2016), Donald Trump's New Foreign Policy Advisers Are as Rotten as His Steaks, The Daily Beast.

[165] Tim Sorrock (Nov. 18, 2016), One of Trump's Top Military Advisers Played a Key Role in the Disastrous Iraq Occupation, The Nation.

[166] Adam Serwer (Oct. 27, 2011), Top Romney Adviser Tied to Militia That Massacred, Mother Jones.

[167] Gary Scott Smith, Religion in the Oval Office: The Religious Lives of American Presidents (Oxford University Press, 2015), ob. cit.

chosen by Trump for domestic issues; and envisions an America governed by Christian principles.[168]

Another on the list, David R. Malpass, is a Roman Catholic and a graduate of international economics from Georgetown University.

Edwin Meese, for his part, has defended Christian principles as a principle of government; and expressed himself in this regard, in a speech before the Knights of Columbus.[169]

Governor Nikki Haley was chosen as ambassador to the UN;[170] with nothing strictly controversial in her background.

Trump chose Katharine Gorka as head of the Department of Homeland Security.[171] Gorka is a fervent Roman Catholic involved in influencing even government;[172] and is a staunch anti-Muslim.[173] She was a regular contributor of articles to *Breitbart*. Her husband, Sebastian Gorka, *Breitbart*'s national security editor-in-chief, another fervent Catholic, discussed on November 4, 2016, along with former Blackwater director Erik Prince during a radio show, the battle to liberate Mosul from the Islamic State.[174]

Trump announced on December 1, 2016, that retired General James Mattis would be the country's Secretary of Defense (Pentagon). Mattis does not look favorably on Russian foreign policy; he is against torture and the Iran nuclear deal.[175] He also believes strongly in strengthening NATO. Known as a "mad dog,"[176] Mattis was a protagonist in the battle of Fallujah during the invasion of Iraq; something we saw in another chapter that was performed under the banner of a Catholic-Protestant crusade against "the city of mosques." Mattis said days before the invasion, "We expect to be the best friends to Iraqis who are trying to put their country back together [...] For those who want to fight, for the foreign fighters and former regime people, they'll regret it. We're going to handle them very roughly.... If they want to fight, we will fight." Less than a year later, referring to his time in Iraq and Afghanistan, he said at a public event, "Actually it's quite fun to fight them, you know. It's a hell of a hoot," adding, "It's fun to shoot some people. I'll be right up there with you. I like brawling."[177]

The same month, Donald Trump chose Ben Carson, a Seventh-day Adventist, as secretary of Housing and Urban Development.[178] He supports Trump as of this writing. He defends him, it seems, almost unconditionally.

---

[168] Miranda Blue (Nov. 10, 2016), Religious Right Activist Ken Blackwell Leading Domestic Policy For Trump's Transition Team, Right Wing Watch.

[169] Lee Edwards (Oct. 4, 2016), How This Man Pushed Courts to Respect the Founders' Constitution, The Daily Signal.

[170] Melissa Quinn (Nov. 23, 2016), What You Need to Know About Gov. Nikki Haley, Trump's Pick for UN Ambassador, The Daily Signal.

[171] Alex Emmons, Lee Fang (Nov. 30, 2016), Anti-Muslim Activist Katharine Gorka Named to Homeland Security Transition Team, The Intercept.

[172] https://www.barbaracomstockforcongress.com/catholics-for-comstock/; accessed November 30, 2016.

[173] Alex Emmons, Lee Fang (Nov. 30, 2016), Anti-Muslim Activist Katharine Gorka Named to Homeland Security Transition Team, The Intercept.

[174] Breitbart News (Nov. 3, 2016), Breitbart News Daily: Closing Arguments, Breitbart.

[175] Ibid.

[176] Michael R. Gordon and Eric Schmitt (Dec. 1, 2016), James Mattis, Outspoken Ex-Marine, Is Trump's Choice as Defense Secretary, The New York Times.

[177] Jeremy Scahill, Blackwater: The Rise of the World's Most Powerful Mercenary Army (Serpent's Tail, London, 2008), ob. cit.

[178] Michael D. Shear (Dec. 5, 2016), Carson Is New Sign Trump Plans to Govern From the Right, The New York Times.

Trump chose Rex Tillerson as Secretary of State. Tillerson was the head of the oil company Exxon Mobile and had strong business ties with Russia and its president, Vladimir Putin.[179] Tillerson is a Christian.[180] Both he and his wife Renda donated $5,000 to $6,000 to the National Association of Congregational Christian Churches in 2012.[181] But he is not bigoted, as Trump is.

Donald Trump chose Republican Ryan Zinke as secretary of the Department of the Interior.[182] Zinke is a former Navy SEAL, obsessed with national security and it appears that part of his vision is to keep America as white as possible. He has accepted money from the terrifying white supremacist Earl Holt of the Council of Conservative Citizens.[183] Whose racist writings influenced Dylann Roof, who perpetrated the massacre of nine African Americans at the Emanuel African Methodist Episcopal Church in Charleston, South Carolina.[184] Zinke also supports legislation to make English the official language of the country; and has aligned himself with anti-immigrant groups identified as hate groups by the Southern Poverty Law Center.[185]

Likewise, allies of the billionaire Koch brothers helped launch the Trump administration when they initially refused to support him. His transition and administration team was greatly filled with donors and advocacy groups built by the Kochs, who have sought to shape American politics under their libertarian image.[186] The Kochs funded many opposition campaigns against many of the Obama administration's policies, and have had direct links to the Tea Party.[187] They had already set a budget of $889 million for the 2016 presidential campaign.[188] And despite the Republican campaign not meeting their expectations in early 2016, Charles Koch would donate $900 million to it.[189] The Kochs, as Jane Mayer well documents, were among the leading billionaires who were and have been behind the rise of the radical right, including the nation's branches of Christian fundamentalism to influence policy.[190]

---

[179] Mariana Rambaldi (Dec. 10, 2016), Trump elige a Rex Tillerson, director de la petrolera Exxon Mobil con fuertes lazos con Rusia, como secretario de Estado, Univisión Noticias.

[180] Steve Coll, Private Empire: ExxonMobile and American Power (Penguin Books, New York, 2013), ob. cit.

[181] (September, 2013), Honor Roll of Distinguished Individual Donors, The Congregationalist Magazine of the Congregational Way, Vol. 165/No. 3, p. 7.

[182] Juliet Eilperin (Dec. 13, 2016), Trump taps Montana congressman Ryan Zinke as interior secretary, The Washington Post.

[183] Janet Allon (Dec. 18, 2016), 5 Trump Abominations This Week, Alternet.

[184] Josh Sanburn (June 22, 2015), Inside the White Supremacist Group that Influenced Charleston Shooting Suspect, Time Magazine.

[185] Janet Allon (Dec. 18, 2016), 5 Trump Abominations This Week, Alternet.

[186] Kenneth P. Vogel and Eliana Johnson (Nov. 28, 2016), Trump's Koch administration, Politico Magazine.

[187] Jane Mayer (August 30, 2010), The Koch Brothers' Covert Operations, The New Yorker.

[188] Amanda Holpuch (January 26, 2015), Koch brothers set $889m budget for 2016 presidential election, The Guardian.

[189] Ellen Brait (Jan. 8, 2016), Charles Koch is 'disappointed' in 2016 Republicans - but will still give $900m, The Guardian.

[190] Jane Mayer, Dark Money: The Hidden History of the Billionaires Behind the Rise of the Radical Right (Double Day, 2016), ob. cit.

Democrats and Republicans, who in the past have been sensitive about civil liberties, instead of showing concern and even opposition about such nominations, have decided to give them a chance.[191]

Gregg Popovich, the coach of the San Antonio Spurs basketball team, said, "My big fear is - we are Rome."[192]

But how to understand General Michael Flynn's rapprochement with Russia? During an interview with Dana Priest of the Washington Post, he said that when he was in the Russian intelligence headquarters a short time ago, it was because the Defense Intelligence Agency (DIA) has offices in 142 countries, and he was visiting one of its attachments, in Russia. The relations are convenient because they were dealing with the Russian government on the issue of Iran's nuclear weapons. When asked if he saw the Russian relationship as potentially good for the United States, he replied, "No. No. I saw the relation with Russia as necessary to the U.S., for the interests of the U.S." One mutual interest is defeating ISIS.[193] That is why Flynn identified in his book published in 2016 that North Korea, China, Russia, Iran, Syria, Cuba, Bolivia, Venezuela, and Nicaragua as countries that hate the West; particularly the United States and Israel. He says Putin and the Russian government see the United States as their worst enemy and that is negative.[194] Stephen Bannon criticized the Russian economy under Putin and said that he and his cronies are an imperialist power that wants to expand.[195] Also, Trump himself said in an interview in late March 2016, "I'm not saying Russia is not a threat. But we have other threats."[196]

Regarding Trump's inauguration to the presidency, while a large number of celebrities did not participate in the inauguration on January 20, 2017, a large number of religious leaders took part in the ceremony, reading from the Bible and offering prayers for the work of his administration. Thus, a rabbi, a cardinal, and a diverse group of Protestant preachers (six religious leaders in all) would participate. More than in any previous president. Each would have 60 to 90 seconds to offer a reading or lead a prayer, which would be a record for inaugurations. The names of the participants were: Cardinal Timothy Dolan of New York; Rev. Samuel Rodríguez, president of the National Hispanic Christian Leadership Conference; Pastor Paula White, a televangelist from Florida; Rabbi Marvin Hier, founder and dean of the Simon Wiesenthal Center; the Rev. Franklin Graham, president and chief executive officer of Samaritan's Purse and the Billy Graham Evangelistic Association (believes Trump was chosen by God to return the country to Christian principles); Bishop Wayne T. Jackson, who heads Great Faith Ministries International and the Impact Television Network.[197]

---

[191] Zaid Jilani (Nov. 21, 2016), Congress Show How Not to Respond to Donald Trump's Terrible Nominess, The Intercept.

[192] Jeremy Gottlieb (Nov. 11, 2016), Spurs Coach Gregg Popovich discusses Donald Trump's election: 'My big fear is - we are Rome.', The Washington Post.

[193] Dana Priest (Aug. 15, 2016), Trump adviser Michael T. Flynn on his dinner with Putin and why Russia Today is just like CNN, The Washington Post.

[194] Lieutenant General (Ret.) Michael T. Flynn and Michael Ledeen, The Field of Fight: How We Can Win the Global War Against Radical Islam and Its Allies (St. Martin's Press, New York, 2016), ob. cit.

[195] J. Lester Feder (Nov. 16, 2016), This Is How Steve Bannon Sees The Entire World, BuzzFeed.

[196] Tim Hains (March 27, 2016), Trump: NATO Is Obsolete And Expensive, "Doesn't Have The Right Countries In It For Terrorism," RealClearPolitics.

[197] Liam Stack (Jan. 18, 2017), The Religious Leaders Taking Part in Trump's Inaugural Ceremony, The New York Times.

In his January 9, 2017 address to the diplomatic corps accredited to the Holy See, Pope Francis expressed his "firm conviction that every expression of religion is called to promote peace."[198] With his wish for the coming year "that our countries and their peoples may find increased opportunities to work together in building true peace."[199] And further, that:

"For its part, the Holy See, and the Secretariat of State in particular, will always be ready to cooperate with those committed to ending current conflicts and to offer support and hope to all who suffer."[200]

He thus sends a message of appeasement to the new U.S. administration.

Regarding the Paris agreements on climate change, Trump had already expressed to *The New York Times* on November 22, 2016, that he was watching it very carefully and that he had an open mind. He also admitted to believing that human beings have something to do with global warming.[201]

During an interview on December 11, he said that no one really knows if climate change is real; but that he had an open mind on the subject. He said he was studying whether the U.S. should withdraw from its commitment to limit environmental output, agreed to at the Paris summit in 2015.[202]

Five days after that interview, a public petition sought thousands of Catholics to urge Donald Trump "to take swift and meaningful action" as president on climate change. The petition, drafted by the Catholic Climate Covenant, called on Trump to uphold the Paris accords and other climate change issues.[203]

But on August 4, 2017, already as president, Donald Trump officially announced that the United States would withdraw from the Paris accords, as it would cost the nation trillions of dollars, destroy jobs, and hamper the oil, gas, coal, and manufacturing industries. But he indicated that he was open to seeking an agreement on it but in a more balanced way that would not threaten the country's interests. However, under the Paris agreements, he could not withdraw from it until Nov. 4, 2020, unless someone else was elected president then and wanted to keep it.[204]

Returning to the religious issue, months later, Donald Trump signed the Executive Order of freedom, allowing the various religious denominations to exert greater influence on political activities without being censored, giving them questionable power.[205]

---

[198] Address of his Holiness Pope Francis to the Members of the Diplomatic Corps accredited to the Holy See for the traditional exchange of New Year Greetings (Dicastero per la Comunicazione - Libreria Editrice Vaticana, Sala Regia, Monday, January 8, 2017), p. 2.

[199] Ibid, p. 9.

[200] Ibid.

[201] The New York Times (Nov. 23, 2016), Donald Trump's New York Times Interview: Full Transcript, The New York Times.

[202] Caroline Kenny (Dec. 12, 2016), Trump: 'Nobody really knows' if climate change is real, CNN.

[203] Brian Roewe (Dec. 16, 2016), Catholics petition Trump to uphold climate actions, National Catholic Reporter.

[204] Valerie Volcovici (Aug. 4, 2017), U.S. submits formal notice of withdrawal from Paris climate pact, Reuters.

[205] John Wagner and Sarah Pulliam Bailey (May 4, 2017), Trump signs order seeking to allow churches to engage in more political activity, The Washington Post.

Later that month, Trump visited Pope Francis at the Vatican, holding a half-hour private audience. They shared a commitment to life, freedom of worship, and conscience; and expressed the hope to collaborate in service to the people in the fields of health, education, and assistance to migrants. They discussed the promotion of peace through political negotiations and interfaith dialogue; as well as the need to protect Christian communities in the Middle East.[206]

But on July 14, 2017, the Italian Jesuit magazine *La Civiltà Cattólica*, published an article written by its editor, Jesuit priest Antonio Spadaro, and by Marcelo Figueroa, a Presbyterian pastor who is the editor-in-chief of the Argentine edition of *L'Osservatore Romano*. Note that *La Civiltà Cattólica* is reviewed and approved by the Pope himself.

The article was entitled "Evangelical Fundamentalism and Catholic Integralism: A surprising ecumenism." It criticizes American Protestant ultra-conservatism in different terms, which concentrates on the axis of good and evil, discarding one from the other. A union with fundamentalist Catholics who want to impose the kingdom of God on earth, and that the new role of Constantine in the United States has been inherited by Donald Trump. Under an ecumenism of hatred, where other religious communities are not accepted and respected. Thus, this overreach of the church to influence its interests in the state is not positive; and it is very contrary to the role of Francis worldwide.[207]

It can be noted that the papacy of Francis is against religious intolerance leading to a totalitarianism of theocratic character, so the pope's vision of a dominant religious influence in the political-religious spectrum is against his distinctive vision of a social-religious policy that respects both types of thought and that unite them, although without forming a synthesis of thought.

Now, in addition to everything documented, things seemed to be changing in the foreign sphere. Right-wing policies of intolerance in Europe were led by Marine Le Pen in France and Geert Wilders in the Netherlands, but there were also echoes of intolerance in the Brexit campaign, from the rhetoric of Viktor Orban in Hungary and Jaroslaw Kaczynski in Poland; as well as from far-right parties in Germany and Greece.[208]

The Trump administration's relationship with NATO was little more than barely sustainable.

Lurking danger

When Donald Trump was heading to Capitol Hill for his inauguration as president in January 2017, there were protests with anti-fascist, anti-Nazi, and other signs, and that soon turned to violence.[209] But it was only the beginning, showing himself to be extremely authoritarian.

In his first week as the nation's president, he signed an executive order that sought to prevent the entry of terrorists by blocking the entry of travelers from seven Islamic countries.[210] It generated great controversy, as it dealt with Islam.

---

[206] (May 24, 2017), Trump 'determined to pursue peace' after Pope meeting, BBC.

[207] Antonio Spadaro S. I. - Marcelo Figueroa (July 14, 2017), Evangelical Fundamentalism and Catholic Integralism: A surprising ecumenism, La Civiltà Cattolica.

[208] Kenneth Roth (January 2, 2017), We Are on the Verge of Darkness, Foreign Policy.

[209] Michael Kirk (Writer), Mike Wiser (Writer), & Michael Kirk (Director) (2021, January 26). Trump's American Carnage (Season 39, Episode 11) [TV Series Episode]. Raney Aronson, David Fanning (Executive Producers), *Frontline*. Public Broadcasting Service (PBS).

[210] Ibid.

When Congress could not get the votes needed to repeal Obamacare, since John McCain voted against it, Trump attacked Congress, and its Republican senators, especially Mitch McConnell. But he also demanded that McConnell get to work to make a success of many of his plans as president of the country.[211] Trump believed his success was under threat.

The first three years of his term were marked by numerous conflicts within the White House because of the way he governed. He showed himself to be grossly unaware of the laws of the land, wanting to advance despite them and being dictatorial in his dealings with senior officials in his administration. The most basic laws of government were ignored out of mere ignorance or consciously overlooked. He largely disregarded regulations of various government departments, including military law.[212]

A Very Stable Genius and *Fear: Trump in the White House*, profusely and honestly justify the electrifying story of Trump's presidency and the 'dictatorial' dangers under his rule.[213]

Senior White House officials organized to steal draft executive orders from President Trump's Oval Office so that he would not create regulations that would jeopardize crucial intelligence operations.[214] Renowned journalist Bob Woodward concludes, after extensive detail through "hundreds of hours of interviews with firsthand participants and witnesses, meeting notes, personal diaries, files and government or personal documents," that Trump's "was no less than an administrative coup d'état", "a nervous breakdown of the executive power of the most powerful country in the world."

Because of his America First policy, disregarding every or almost every consequence of his decisions, Trump wanted to terminate the Free Trade Agreement between the United States and South Korea (Korus), because the trade deficit was 18 million dollars a year in that country, and 3500 million dollars a year were spent to maintain US troops in the area. One day, Gary Cohn, former president of Goldman Sachs and economic advisor in the White House, saw a document on the Resolute desk in the Oval Office, containing in its message the intention of withdrawing the United States from the Korus. Trump had not seen it and, therefore, it was not signed. Cohn carefully removed it so that Trump would not sign it, since such a decision would remove U.S. military and intelligence assets from South Korea, indispensable to defend against North Korea. The Special Access Programs (SAPs) "provided sophisticated Top Secret, codeword intelligence and military capabilities. North Korean ICBM missiles now had the capability to carry a nuclear weapon, perhaps to the American homeland;" which would take thirty-eight minutes to reach Los Angeles. The SAPs could detect ICBM missile launches from North Korea in seven seconds. From Alaska, it would take fifteen minutes. In the seven-second range, the U.S. military would have time to shoot down that missile.

But Trump was never interested in the consequences of withdrawing from the Korus. For a while, various White House officials managed to divert Trump's interest. But when one day he made up his mind, they made an emergency phone call to James

---

[211] Ibid.

[212] Philip Rucker, Carol Leonnig, A Very Stable Genius: Donald J. Trump's Testing of America (Penguin Press, New York, 2020), ob. cit.

[213] Ibid; Bob Woodward, Fear: Trump in the White House (Simon & Schuster, New York, 2019).

[214] Bob Woodward, Fear: Trump in the White House (Simon & Schuster, New York, 2019), ob. cit. Note: unless otherwise noted, this is the same source.

Mattis, then Secretary of Defense, who explained to Trump the danger of withdrawing from such an agreement. Trump accepted it momentarily. But at the time, exasperated and alarmed, Mattis said the president had the understanding of a fifth- or sixth-grader.

On March 21, 2018, and after listening to pundits on Fox News, Donald Trump threatened to veto a $1.3 billion spending budget, or the "omnibus," as it is known in Washington.[215] That veto could cripple the government, so Paul Ryan, then speaker of the House of Representatives, headed to the White House. When Trump met with him, he immediately started complaining, saying he didn't care about the ómnibus- as documented by Woodward:

> "This is a terrible deal! Who signed off on this [...]? [...] No one answered.
> [...]
> "The wall! It's not in here!"
> "You have to sign this, we just passed it," Ryan said. "I mean, we discussed this already. This is the military. This is the rebuild. This is veterans."
> When Trump again complained about only getting $1.6 billion for the border wall in the omnibus, Burks said the number in the bill was the number the president had asked for in his own budget.
> "Who [...] approved that? Trump asked.
> No one spoke.
> An hour in, Ryan asked, "Are you going to sign this bill or not?"
> "Yeah. Fine. I'll sign it," Trump said.
> As Ryan and Burks left, they huddled with Marc Short, a Pence adviser for decades who had agreed to serve as Trump's legislative director.
> "What the hell was that?" Ryan asked.
> "It's like this every day around here," Short said.
> "Oh my God. Jesus," Ryan said.

Two days later, when it came time to sign the bill into law, Trump again wavered, as he heard on Fox News that morning from another pundit, Pete Hegseth, that it was "the epitome of a "swamp budget." Likewise, Steve Doocy, one of the co-hosts of *Fox & Friends*, lamented that there was "no wall" in the legislation; whereupon Trump tweeted that he was "considering a veto." Failure to sign the bill at midnight would paralyze the government.

In a frustrated phone conversation, Ryan told Defense Secretary Jim Mattis that if he was standing in front of Trump, he would sign it. Mattis spent several hours with Vice President Pence and Marc Short, urging Trump to sign the bill, who eventually agreed.

As Trump displayed a capricious mandate, Charlottesville, Virginia, witnessed an overnight march of white supremacists heading to the University of Virginia and chanting, "Jews will not replace us!" Many of them were marching in Trump's name.[216]

Anti-fascist demonstrators wanted to tear down a statue of Robert E. Lee, a Confederate general from the American Civil War, the other day. There were extremely

---

[215] Bob Woodward, Robert Costa, Peril (Simon & Schuster, New York, 2023), ob. cit. Note: unless otherwise indicated, this is the same source.

[216] Michael Kirk (Writer), Mike Wiser (Writer), & Michael Kirk (Director) (2021, January 26). Trump's American Carnage (Season 39, Episode 11) [TV Series Episode]. Raney Aronson, David Fanning (Executive Producers), *Frontline*. Public Broadcasting Service (PBS).

violent demonstrations, with baseball bats, punches, kicks, and gas, between white supremacists and counter-demonstrators. A neo-Nazi took his car and drove into several of them and ran them over, injuring and killing 32-year-old Heather Heyer.[217]

Trump consulted with his staff about what happened, and read to the press the following words:

"We're closely following the terrible events unfolding in Charlottesville, Virginia. [...] We condemn in the strongest possible terms this egregious display of hatred, bigotry and violence- on many sides, on many sides [words added by Trump]."[218]

That was not a resolute condemnation of neo-Nazis or white supremacists. And we are not trying to be biased: on another occasion, from New York, Trump's message to the press, we transcribed it in a more extensive context than is usually presented:

"**TRUMP:** Okay, what about the alt-left that came charging at [indiscernible] – excuse me – what about the alt-left that came charging at the, as you say, the alt right? Do they have any semblance of guilt?
"What about this? What about the fact that they came charging – they came charging with clubs in their hands swinging clubs? Do they have any problem? I think they do. [...]
I will tell you something. I watched those very closely, much more closely than you people watched it. And you had, you had a group on one side that was bad. And you had a group on the other side that was also very violent. And nobody wants to say that, but I'll say it right now. You had a group – you had a group on the other side that came charging in without a permit, and they were very, very violent. [...]

"**REPORTER:** Mr. President, are you putting what you're calling the alt-left and white supremacists on the same moral plane?

"**TRUMP:** I am not putting anybody on a moral plane, what I'm saying is this: you had a group on one side and a group on the other, and they came at each other with clubs and it was vicious and horrible and it was a horrible thing to watch, but there is another side. There was a group on this side, you can call them the left. You've just called them the left, that came violently attacking the other group. So you can say what you want, but that's the way it is.

"**REPORTER:** You said there was hatred and violence on both sides?

"**TRUMP:** I do think there is blame – yes, I think there is blame on both sides. You look at, you look at both sides. I think there's blame on both sides, and I have no doubt about it, and you don't have any doubt about it either. And, and, and, and if you reported it accurately, you would say.

---

[217] Ibid.
[218] Michael Kirk (Writer), Mike Wiser (Writer), & Michael Kirk (Director) (2018, April 10). Trump's Takeover (Season 36, Episode 6) [TV Series Episode]. Raney Aronson, David Fanning (Executive Producers), *Frontline*. Public Broadcasting Service (PBS)

"**REPORTER:** The neo-Nazis started this thing. They showed up in Charlottesville.

"**TRUMP:** Excuse me, they didn't put themselves down as neo-Nazis, and you had some very bad people in that group. But you also had people that were very fine people on both sides.
[...] the neo-Nazis and the white nationalists, because they should be condemned totally – but you had many people in that group other than neo-Nazis and white nationalists, okay? And the press has treated them absolutely unfairly. Now, in the other group also, you had some fine people, but you also had troublemakers and you see them come with the black outfits and with the helmets and with the baseball bats – you had a lot of bad people in the other group too."[219]

It begs the question if, in the group of neo-Nazis and white supremacists, there were elements who disagreed with their ideologies. Where did Trump get information from?

When he pointed out that there was violence on both sides confronting each other, but that there were good people on both sides as well, not associated with extremism whether right or left, it is an attempt to remedy his image. He was looking for "balance" but without any evidence, so as not to upset his neo-Nazi and white supremacist supporters, as we'll see. One of the worst aspects is that he gave "moral equivalency to those who stand against hate and the haters—safe harbor for white supremacists and Nazis who were willing to come out in the open."[220]

Trump was not vocal enough to condemn neo-Nazis or white supremacists as he should have been. Moreover, on August 15, 2017, while hiking with his family in Colorado, Paul Ryan, then Speaker of the House of Representatives, received a phone call from an advisor who told him that Trump was harping on the "both sides" argument, and the media was asking him to comment. He sighed, and standing alone on a mountainside, dictated a curt statement that was later tweeted.[221] A while later, Ryan received a phone call from Trump:

"You're not in the foxhole with me!" Trump screamed.
Ryan yelled back. "Are you finished? May I have some time to speak now?"
"You're the president of the United States. You have a moral leadership obligation to get this right and not declare there is a moral equivalency here."
"These people love me. These are my people," Trump shot back. "I can't backstab the people who support me."
There were white supremacists and Nazis in Charlottesville, Ryan said.
"Well, yeah, there's some bad people," Trump said. "I get that. I'm not for that. I'm against all that. But there's some of those people who are for me. Some of them are good people."[222]

Senators who were very clear, such as, for example, Senate Minority Leader Mitch McConnel, said: "There are no good neo-Nazis."[223] Jerry Moran: "White supremacy,

---

[219] Politico Staff (May 15, 2017), Full text: Trump's comments on white supremacists, 'alt-left' in Charlottesville, Politico.
[220] Bob Woodward, Robert Costa, Peril (Simon & Schuster, New York, 2023), ob. cit.
[221] Ibid.
[222] Ibid.

bigotry and racism have absolutely no place in our society, and no one, especially POTUS, should ever tolerate it."[224]

Marco Rubio: "Mr. President, you can't allow #WhiteSupremacists to share only part of blame." John McCain: "There's no moral equivalency between racists and Americans standing up to defy hate and bigotry."

There was a huge explosion of similar messages from senators upset about Trump's bias.

Jeff Flake, Republican senator and representative from Arizona from 2013-19: "I reacted in a way that most of my colleagues did, as well, that this was not where a president should be.

This was a layup. This was easy. If there's white supremacy in any form, you condemn it. I mean, that's the easy thing to do, and he didn't." Although Vice President Pence clearly condemned neo-Nazism and white supremacy, and behind closed doors was horrified, he defended Trump in the media by saying that those responsible for the horrific events should rather be condemned. This is because he did not dare to go against the biased position of the president -according to Olivia Troye, former Pence advisor.

By early 2018, Paul Ryan could take it no more, and on April 11 he said he would not run for re-election, something that stunned the political press world because he could go much further if he stayed. When he met with Senate Majority Leader Mitch McConnell of Kentucky, with whom he had worked together to handle Trump, he told Ryan: "You're a very talented guy. McConnell said. "We had a first-rate relationship." [...]

"I hate to see you abandon the playing field," McConnell said."[225]

So, how would he handle Donald Trump?

Many top aides repeatedly felt discomfiture at the actions of Trump, who daily unsettled and belittled senior staff members.[226] Several of them he treated as stupid and traitors.

John F. Kelly, who would become White House chief of staff, had told Trump privately about the disarray and chaos in which the White House was plunged. But when he, too, noticed Trump's complete rejection of the advice of his advisers and that they knew more than he did, Kelly said in part, "It's pointless to try to convince him of anything. He's gone of the rails. We're in crazytown."

"I don't even know why any of us are here. This is the worst job I've ever had."

The president was making announcements without the approval of other officials, distressingly compromising them.

One of Trump's top officials said he was incapable of empathy or pity for anyone. Practically, anyone who disagreed with him was a traitor. He undermined anyone's

---

[223] Michael Kirk (Writer), Mike Wiser (Writer), & Michael Kirk (Director) (2018, April 10). Trump's Takeover (Season 36, Episode 6) [TV Series Episode]. Raney Aronson, David Fanning (Executive Producers), *Frontline*. Public Broadcasting Service (PBS)

[224] Michael Kirk (Writer), Mike Wiser (Writer), & Michael Kirk (Director) (2021, January 26). Trump's American Carnage (Season 39, Episode 11) [TV Series Episode]. Raney Aronson, David Fanning (Executive Producers), *Frontline*. Public Broadcasting Service (PBS). Note: unless otherwise noted, this is the same source.

[225] Bob Woodward, Robert Costa, Peril (Simon & Schuster, New York, 2023), ob. cit.

[226] Bob Woodward, Fear: Trump in the White House (Simon & Schuster, New York, 2019), ob. cit.

opinion. Everyone was put off because he ignored reason, logic, and sound arguments; because his "America First" slogan turned him into a sentiment that shuts down rationality. And it annoyed him when he was advised to be humble and to apologize even for the most terrible offenses.

In fact, the way he endangered the country not only from external aggressors but from internal chaos, is chilling.[227]

Trump, displeased with the Republican party base, had many critics. Republican Congressman Mark Sanford, who was critical of Trump's authoritarianism, was vilified by him. But Sanford, who was a member of the Freedom Caucus, believed they would support him.[228] He recounts:

"At that time, Justin Amash—I'll never forget this—stood before the Freedom Caucus and said, "Look, if Trump will come after Sanford like he did, then ultimately he'll come after any one of us." And everybody is looking at their feet, looking away, looking at their toes. And these are the folks that you thought were your friends, and you're going, "Oh, my goodness, where am I?" It's mind-blowing."[229]

Mark Sanford lost his primary.[230]

Jeff Flake, spoke out especially against Trump's personality, such as when the president disparaged John McCain as a war hero because he had been taken prisoner. Flake was very critical of Trump, something the president resented and told Flake so. Trump would prove to be resentful and had little or no tolerance for his critics, who saw him as someone who wanted to be a king and not the president.[231]

Instead of showing remorse for his actions, the president railed against his critics, especially Republicans. Rallying his base against Jeff Flake, who was a senator from Arizona, he told a rally in Phoenix: "Well, I'm thrilled to be back in Phoenix, in the great state of Arizona."

"They all said, "Please, Mr. President, don't mention any names." So I won't. I won't!"

"And nobody wants me to talk about your senator, who's weak on borders, weak on crime, so I won't talk about him! No, I will not mention any names." [232]

Without the support of Arizona's majority, Trump ended Flake's political career.[233]

---

[227] Other books: Michael Wolff, Fire and Fury (Vintage, 2018); Michael Wolff, Siege (Vintage, 2019); Chris Hedges, Empire of Illusion: The End of Literacy and the Triumph of Spectacle (Bold Type Books, New York, 2009); Peter Baker, Susan Glasser, The Divider: Trump in the White House, 2017-2021 (Doubleday, 2022); Michael S. Schmidt, Donald Trump v. The United States: Inside the Struggle to Stop a President (Randon House Trade Paperbacks, 2023); Fiona Hill, There Is Nothing For You Here: Finding Opportunity in the Twenty-First Century (Mariner Books, 2021); Ruth Ben-Ghiat, Strongmen: Mussolini to the Present (W. W. Norton & Company, 2021).

[228] Michael Kirk (Writer), Michael Kirk (Writer), & Mike Wiser (Director) (2022, September 6). Lies, Politics and Democracy (Season 41, Episode 1) [TV Series Episode]. Raney Aronson, David Fanning (Executive Producers), Frontline. Public Broadcasting Service (PBS).

[229] Ibid.

[230] Ibid.

[231] Michael Kirk (Writer), Mike Wiser (Writer), & Michael Kirk (Director) (2018, April 10). Trump's Takeover (Season 36, Episode 6) [TV Series Episode]. Raney Aronson, David Fanning (Executive Producers), Frontline. Public Broadcasting Service (PBS)

[232] Michael Kirk (Writer), Mike Wiser (Writer), & Michael Kirk (Director) (2021, January 26). Trump's American Carnage (Season 39, Episode 11) [TV Series Episode]. Raney Aronson, David Fanning (Executive Producers), Frontline. Public Broadcasting Service (PBS).

Before leaving, Flake said on the Senate floor, "I rise today with no small measure of regret. I regret the state of our disunity. [...] But anger and resentment are not a governing philosophy. The impulse to scapegoat and belittle threatens to turn us into a fearful, backward-looking people. In the case of the Republican Party, those things also threaten to turn us into a fearful, backward-looking minority party." Few heard it or gave it any thought."[234]

Trump's actions prevented many Republican senators from criticizing him when they disagreed with him, so Trump had enormous power over the Republican party base.[235] Several refrained from seeking future re-election as senators. Dozens of them saw their careers ruined by the president.

While the Republican party capitulated to the president, he continued to hold rallies, where he further emboldened the most dangerous elements of the American right. Particularly by demonizing immigrants, whom he seemed to want to stop at almost any cost. He separated young children from undocumented families who were caught by border guards. Children suffered terribly because they were unable to see their parents for months.

Some armed civilians also took matters into their own hands and went to "protect" the border.

A few years later, Trump would say in the Oval Office at a meeting, "We're not going to ban Confederate flags. It's Southern pride and heritage." Being that "Meadows said that the Confederate flags could not be banned. It was a freedom of speech issue, and the Pentagon lawyers agreed with him." All, even though the Chief of Staff Mark Milley made simple and compelling arguments for removing all Confederate paraphernalia from the South.[236]

During one of the dozens of protests that occurred across the United States in 2020 over the murder of George Floyd, one in particular proved tragic. But let's contextualize: Derek Chauvin, a Minneapolis police officer, was caught on video when, for 7 minutes and 46 seconds, he squeezed George Floyd's neck with his knee until he died, in what amounted to a racially motivated crime.[237]

The protests, which began at the end of May, included more than 140 cities. Some of them resulted in violent clashes with police and looting. Including arson. Trump had told Bob Woodward in an interview, "These are arsonists, they're thugs, they're anarchists and they're bad people. Very dangerous people.

"These are very well-organized. Antifa's leading it."[238] Likewise, the president had tweeted, "These thugs are dishonoring the memory of George Floyd, and I won't let that happen. Any difficulty and we will assume control, but when the looting starts, the

[233] Ibid.
[234] Michael Kirk (Writer), Mike Wiser (Writer), & Michael Kirk (Director) (2018, April 10). Trump's Takeover (Season 36, Episode 6) [TV Series Episode]. Raney Aronson, David Fanning (Executive Producers), *Frontline*. Public Broadcasting Service (PBS)
[235] Michael Kirk (Writer), Mike Wiser (Writer), & Michael Kirk (Director) (2021, January 26). Trump's American Carnage (Season 39, Episode 11) [TV Series Episode]. Raney Aronson, David Fanning (Executive Producers), *Frontline*. Public Broadcasting Service (PBS). Note: unless otherwise noted, this is the same source.
[236] Bob Woodward, Robert Costa, Peril (Simon & Schuster, New York, 2023), ob. cit.
[237] Ibid.
[238] Ibid.

shooting starts. Thank you!"[239] Days after that troubling comment, things would get worse.

But first of all, General Milley, Chairman of the Joint Chiefs of Staff, "had his staff prepare a daily, classified SECRET report, "Domestic Unrest National Overview." The report tracked the latest violence in American cities with a population over 100,000 people."[240]

The general went over the report with Trump in the Oval Office less than a week after Floyd's murder.[241]

Then, White House speechwriting director Stephen Miller, 34, as well as one of the president's most conservative senior advisers and who had advocated the use of drones in 2018 to blow up boatloads of helpless migrants,[242] said:

"Mr. President," Miller said, piping up from one of the Oval Office couches, "they are burning America down. Antifa, Black Lives Matter, they're burning it down. You have an insurrection on your hands. Barbarians are at the gate."[243]

Milley told Miller to shut his mouth, then told Trump that "they are not burning it down." Citing data from the secret daily report, he said, "Mr. President, there are about 276 cities in America with over 100,000 people. There were two cities in the last 24 hours that had major protests [...] While images of burning and violence had been on television, many of the protests were peaceful—about 93 percent of them, according to a later nonpartisan report." He also added that the situation was not even close to being threatening. After giving him many more facts and several historical comparisons as to why he shouldn't fear worse, Milley communicated regularly with William Barr in recent weeks, asking him to press in Oval Office meetings to keep something worse from happening. He especially feared for Miller's influence over the president. Knowing that Trump was very unstable and capricious.

Milley said the protesters had to be watched so that everything was in order.

On the night of May 31, a fire broke out in the nursery in the basement of the historic St. John's Episcopal Church, just three hundred yards from the White House and often referred to as the Church of the Presidents.

The Secret Service even had to take Trump at one point to the underground bunker.

"Boarded up and charred, the church and the sprawling scene outside brought the racial unrest convulsing the country to Trump's front door."

The next morning, Trump was furious and agitated and summoned senior officials to a meeting. "We look weak," said Trump, furious. "We don't look strong." After asking

[239] Michael Kirk (Writer), Michael Kirk (Writer), & Mike Wiser (Director) (2022, September 6). Lies, Politics and Democracy (Season 41, Episode 1) [TV Series Episode]. Raney Aronson, David Fanning (Executive Producers), *Frontline*. Public Broadcasting Service (PBS).
[240] Bob Woodward, Robert Costa, Peril (Simon & Schuster, New York, 2023), ob. cit.
[241] Ibid.
[242] Miles Taylor, Blowback: A Warning to Save Democracy from the Next Trump (Atria Books, New York, 2023), ob. cit.
[243] Bob Woodward, Robert Costa, Peril (Simon & Schuster, New York, 2023), ob. cit. Note: unless otherwise indicated, this is the same source.

about the Insurrection Act of 1807 "which gave the president the authority to use active-duty troops domestically by simply declaring an insurrection."

The very experienced defense secretary, Mark Esper, who knew that Trump's "we" meant "he," said, "Mr. President, there is no need to call up the Insurrection Act," said Esper, and adding that "The National Guard is on the ground and more suited."

Barr said that an additional police response could be provided, which was the traditional way of handling national protests that gave rise to danger. Barr had FBI and U.S. Attorney data collected by prosecutors on everything happening in the cities, and he spoke almost every day with General Milley. Barr said that no further response was needed because of the evidence laid out.

But Trump, adamant, said he wanted the 82nd Airborne Division, which was the elite military response to the crisis, and it was lethal. Trump wanted it in Washington before sundown. But Esper told the president that such a division had no training in dealing with crowds or civil unrest. But Trump was getting more and more obstinate, and Esper was concerned, so he suggested that they alert the troops and start moving them north, but not yet in the city, and that they could call in the National Guard in time, and if they couldn't and things got out of control, they could rely on both forces. Milley agreed with the approach, as neither he nor Esper wanted a bloody confrontation in the streets and unpredictable.

Trump, arms folded, was *crescendoing* in anger... But at that moment, an official who rushed in told him that the governors were on the phone in conference. Already in the crisis room, he said belligerently that they should crack down on the protesters. "You have to dominate," Trump told them, almost issuing a command. "If you don't dominate, you're wasting your time. They're going to run over you. You're going to look like a bunch of jerks. You have to dominate, and you have to arrest people, and you have to try people and they have to go to jail for long periods of time."

It was agreed.

Milley left the White House and went to visit the FBI command post that was following the demonstrations. Meanwhile, Esper got the head of the National Guard to take a few guardsmen to the cities, and also at least ten states sent their units.

Esper headed to the FBI command center to meet with Milley. He wanted to visit the guards on the streets, thank them, and see what was going on. However, on the way to the FBI, Esper received a call, where he was told: "The president wants you at the White House."

When they arrived at the West Wing, Esper asked where the meeting was, but was told there was no meeting. Esper was surprised.

At 18:30, near the White House in Washington DC, law enforcement officers, some with military vehicles, were dispatched by order of Donald Trump without any provocation from the protesters, throwing a type of chemical gas that burned. There were also beatings by police officers, while people ran and screamed.[244]

Woodward and Costa tell us that at 18:48, Trump said in the White House Rose Garden:

---

[244] Michael Kirk (Writer), Mike Wiser (Writer), & Michael Kirk (Director) (2021, January 26). Trump's American Carnage (Season 39, Episode 11) [TV Series Episode]. Raney Aronson, David Fanning (Executive Producers), *Frontline*. Public Broadcasting Service (PBS).

"I will fight to protect you. I am your president of law and order and an ally of all peaceful protesters," he said, pledging to control the "riots and lawlessness that has spread throughout our country.

"If a city or state refuses to take the actions that are necessary to defend the life and property of their residents," he said, "then I will deploy the United States military and quickly solve the problem for them.

"As we speak, I am dispatching thousands and thousands of heavily armed soldiers, military personnel and law enforcement officers to stop the rioting, looting, vandalism, assaults and the wanton destruction of property."[245]

Surprised by what happened, when Esper and Milley were told that they should head through Lafayette Square because Trump wanted to go through the park and see St. John's Church with the cabinet members, they both felt bamboozled...all the more so when they saw a crowd of reporters with TV and still cameras. Milley left in a huff. He became convinced that the president had used him and politicized the military.[246]

Being that Trump wanted to usurp control of the military, the next day, Milley issued a memo to the heads of all military services and combatant commands, saying that all would remain true to the idea of what the United States is, under respect and freedom of every race and creed, and that the National Guard would be operating under the authorities of state governors.

By June 3, Esper was left very nervous as protests continued in Washington. Trump still wanted 10,000 active duty troops deployed in the city.

Knowing that he had to act in time, Esper stated publicly and unequivocally before the Pentagon press corps, with Milley's support, that there was no reason to invoke the Insurrection Act.

After a few minutes, Mark Meadows, the White House chief of staff, telephoned Esper, saying, "The president is really pissed," Mark Meadows, the White House chief of staff, said within minutes to Esper. "And really mad. He is going to rip your face off." Esper and Milley were due to attend a meeting at the White House.

When they arrived, almost everyone was with their heads down in the Oval Office.

"What did you do?" Trump yelled. "Why did you do that?"

"Mr. President, I told you," Esper said. "What I said before is I do not believe that this situation calls for invocation of the Insurrection Act. I think it would be terrible for the country and terrible for the military."

"You took away my authority!" Trump screamed.

[...]

"Who do you think you are?" Trump screamed at Esper. "You took away my authorities. You're not the president! I'm the god damn president."

Milley, sitting silently next to Esper, watched Trump carefully. He believed the escalation and rage he was witnessing firsthand was disturbing, another face-off that reminded him of *Full Metal Jacket*.

An avalanche of invective kept coming. When the president had fully vented to Esper, he turned to the others sitting in the Oval Office."

---

[245] Bob Woodward, Robert Costa, Peril (Simon & Schuster, New York, 2023), ob. cit.
[246] Ibid.

The president also vociferated to remove coronavirus restrictions in all states.[247] He had told a rally that they should get Michigan Governor Gretchen Whitmer, as a crowd chanted, "Lock her up!", and he responded, "Lock 'em all up." Precisely two weeks after the president tweeted in April 2020, "[...] that woman in Michigan [...] LIBERATE MICHIGAN!," a plot by extremists and supporters of the president to kidnap her and overthrow that state's government was detected.

Across the country, extremist protesters acted violently in several places. But the Republican Party came to the president's defense.

When Trump lost the presidential election in November of that year to Biden, he made a series of false claims alleging voter fraud and many Republicans came out in support of him. And many, many of his supporters among the public also protested that it was a rigged election.

Gabriel Sterling, a Republican election official in the state of Georgia, a state where fraud was allegedly committed according to Trump, told reporters in response to Trump and Mitch McConnell's provocations: "It has all gone too far! [...] Someone's going to get hurt. Someone's going to get shot. Someone's going to get killed. And it's not right. [...] Mr. President, you have not condemned these actions or this language. Senators, you have not condemned this language or these actions. This has to stop."

Despite all the help Trump asked for to reverse the election results from officials, he was denied.

But as journalist Vicens Lozano wrote, Trump "endorsed, helped, protected and projected all the movements of the international extreme right. From the Brazil of former president Jair Bolsonaro to the France of Marine Le Pen, passing through the Hungary of Viktor Orbán, the Italy of Matteo Salvini and Georgia Meloni or the Spain of Vox."[248]

[247] Michael Kirk (Writer), Mike Wiser (Writer), & Michael Kirk (Director) (2021, January 26). Trump's American Carnage (Season 39, Episode 11) [TV Series Episode]. Raney Aronson, David Fanning (Executive Producers), *Frontline*. Public Broadcasting Service (PBS). Note: unless otherwise noted, this is the same source.
[248] Vicens Lozano, Vaticangate: El complot ultra contra el papa Francisco y la manipulación del próximo conclave (Roca Editorial, 2023), ob. cit.

CHAPTER

13

Biden and Francis, the Pandemic and the opportunity for The Great Reset

Biden's strongly Catholic administration and its relationship with the Holy See
National Public Radio reported in September 2020 that Joe Biden draws on his faith for inspiration and comfort to others. His speeches "are woven with references to God, biblical language or the pope." He often carries a rosary in his pocket and attends Mass every Sunday. The president is known as a person of deeply devout faith, "and his campaign sees electoral implications in that." The article is quoted as saying, "Some Democrats would go so far as to say that Biden is running perhaps the most overtly devout Democratic presidential campaign since Jimmy Carter in 1976." And further, "Allies say Biden's faith informs his values and, in turn, his values shape his politics." According to Coons, the president's positions on a diversity of social and environmental issues can be traced to "a deeply rooted sense of fairness that he learned from his parents and the nuns and priests who educated him and helped raise him."[1]

However, this is not an ideology to necessarily unite Church and State. It is not to establish a theocracy in the United States. Biden and the Democratic party see the values of faith as having divine principles to help humanity, but not to install religious dogmas for the government to uphold. It differs significantly from the Republican party. As *NPR* highlights, "Friends and staffers say Biden focuses on faith, rather than religious doctrine; he prays with voters, rather than proselytizes."[2]

Yet, as John L. Allen Jr. wrote days before Biden's inauguration, that if he wants to heal America, he will need his Church.[3] It was said that the president's Catholic roots could help him unify the nation.[4]

Leo O'Donovan, a Jesuit priest and decades-long friend of Biden, as well as former president of Georgetown Jesuit University, delivered the invocation at Biden's inauguration.[5]

The U.S. Conference of Catholic Bishops, through its president, Archbishop José Gómez, sent a communiqué to Biden dated January 20, 2021, showing his support for the president to work together on common agreements.[6] All in all, the communiqué reads:

---

[1] Asma Khalid (Sept. 20, 2020), How Joe Biden's Faith Shapes His Politics, NPR.
[2] Ibid.
[3] John L. Allen Jr. (Jan. 7, 2021), If Biden is to heal America, he'll need his Church, Crux Catholic Media, Inc.
[4] Mark Markuly (Jan. 29, 2021), Biden's Catholic roots may help him unify the nation, The Seattle Times.
[5] Kevin Christopher Robles (January 19, 2021), Who is Father Leo O'Donovan, the Jesuit priest delivering the invocation at Biden's inauguration?," America Magazine.
[6] Archbishop José Gómez (Jan. 20, 2021), USCCB President's Statement on the Inauguration of Joseph R. Biden, Jr., as 46th President of the United States of America, USCCB.

"At the same time, as pastors, the nation's bishops are given the duty of proclaiming the Gospel in all its truth and power, in season and out of season, even when that teaching is inconvenient or when the Gospel's truths run contrary to the directions of the wider society and culture. So, I must point out that our new President has pledged to pursue certain policies that would advance moral evils and threaten human life and dignity, most seriously in the areas of abortion, contraception, marriage, and gender. Of deep concern is the liberty of the Church and the freedom of believers to live according to their consciences."[7]

Cardinal Blase Cupich, Archbishop of Chicago and a key U.S. ally of Pope Francis criticized the Bishops' Conference communiqué, which was reportedly drafted without the participation of the conference's administrative committee.

Both Cupich and Pope Francis sent their congratulations to Biden at his inauguration and without referring to any doctrinal differences. A senior Vatican official called Gómez's words unfortunate and potentially divisive in the U.S. church.[8] The Bishops' Conference delayed the statement after Vatican Secretariat of State officials intervened before its release.[9]

The *National Catholic Reporter* echoed Joe Biden's very Catholic cabinet. With more than a third of its members, Steven Millies, director of the Catholic Theological Union in Chicago, wrote, "There never has been a more Catholic administration in U.S. history."[10] *NPR* reported:

"Joe Biden is not the only Catholic to hold the reins of power right now - Speaker Nancy Pelosi, six Supreme Court justices, some eight of Biden's Cabinet picks and nearly a third of the lawmakers on Capitol Hill. It is a sea change in the political representation of a faith that not so long ago was viewed with suspicion in the United States."[11]

Although Biden said he does not proselytize, he also said his administration will take people of faith seriously.[12]

Next, a U.S. government document entitled Integrated Country Strategy: Vatican, dated April 22, 2022, quoted in extenso:

"The U.S. Embassy to the Holy See (Embassy Vatican) advances U.S. foreign policy through partnership with one of the world's greatest soft powers: the Catholic Church. We are a global engagement post, leveraging the impact and network of the Vatican to promote our common priorities in every region of the world. Embassy Vatican advances U.S. national security goals of defending and advancing religious freedom, safeguarding religious minorities from persecution, and combatting human trafficking.

---

[7] Ibid.

[8] Michael J. O'Loughlin (January 20, 2021), In rare rebuke, Cardinal Cupich criticizes USCCB president's letter to President Biden, America Magazine.

[9] The Pillar (Jan. 20, 2021), Updated: Vatican intervened to spike US bishops' Biden statement release, The Pillar.

[10] Christopher White (Jan. 19, 2021), Joe Biden's very Catholic Cabinet, National Catholic Reporter.

[11] NPR (Jan. 24, 2021), U.S. Government Sees Wave Of Catholic Leaders, NPR.

[12] Christopher White (Jan. 19, 2021), Joe Biden's very Catholic Cabinet, National Catholic Reporter.

"Embassy Vatican's priorities include: (1) **Defending** human rights globally by combatting human trafficking, promoting religious freedom, and advocating for women, peace, and security; (2) **Advocating** for peaceful resolution of conflict and conflict prevention, including supporting mediation efforts by the Vatican and affiliated NGOs and promoting increased access to food, water, and advances in science and health; and (3) **Increasing** awareness of U.S. foreign policy goals and countering disinformation, including from Russia and China, among Holy See officials and the broader Catholic community.

[...]

"In recent years Embassy Vatican has become an inter-agency post. Primary staff are the Ambassador, seven U.S. Direct Hires, two eligible Family Members, and nine local employed staff. Personnel from DHS, FBI, DEA, DoD, and DOJ also engage in our bilateral relationship."[13]

The document also notes that the U.S. embassy at the Vatican intends to strengthen ties with the Holy See on mutual issues "including religious freedom, persecution of religious minorities, conflict mediation, health care, refugees, migration, and human trafficking." And they will use "inter-agency collaboration and the Vatican's global network to advance U.S. policy goals and public diplomacy efforts."[14]

But page 8 of the document is extremely interesting:

"Embassy Vatican can use the worldwide presence of the Catholic Church to serve as a global engagement post – promoting U.S. priorities in all regions of the world through information sharing and policy coordination with the Vatican and affiliated organizations. With a global constituency of over one billion Catholics spread across the globe, the reach of the Catholic Church is unparalleled. By cultivating relationships with the Vatican MFA, members of religious orders and Church-affiliated organizations, Post can provide timely and critical information to Washington policymakers. Cooperation with the Vatican and affiliated organizations on conflict mediation can help advance peace and democracy in countries in Africa, the Middle East, Asia, and Latin America. Post can also work with our Vatican partners to ensure that USG interests are represented in Vatican conferences and fora that help set the policy agenda on the latest developments in science, healthcare, technology, and economics."[15]

President Biden's Background and Relationship with Pope Francis

The renowned American journalist Michael Shellenberger published the bestseller Apocalypse Never: Why Environmental Alarmism Hurts Us All.[16] First, Shellenberger had decades of experience fighting for a greener planet and participated in numerous United Nations Climate Change Conferences. It is known that through his activism he accomplished his work, including working with the Obama administration to promote

---

[13] Integrated Country Strategy: Vatican (April 22, 2022), p. 1.

[14] Ibid, p. 2.

[15] Ibid, p. 8.

[16] Michael Shellenberger, Apocalypse Never: Why Environmental Alarmism Hurts Us All (HarperCollins Publishers, 2020).

renewable energy and reduce emissions.[17] He went on to lead a successful idea of scientists and climate activists to keep nuclear power plants running and avoid emissions spikes.[18] But in 2019, faced with an increase in alarmist messages from individuals and representative movements, he was made to reflect on the consequences of those messages, which were unrealistic and championed other causes. So Shellenberger wanted to separate fact from fiction and noted that most developed countries have been reducing carbon dioxide emissions for more than a decade after peaking. He had access to the IPCC and UN FAO reports.

"In fact, both rich and poor societies have become far less vulnerable to extreme weather events in recent decades. In 2019, the journal *Global Environmental Change* published a major study that found death rates and economic damage dropped by 80 to 90 percent during the last four decades, from the 1980s to the present."

Shellenberger saw that behind the rise of apocalyptic environmentalism, there are powerful financial desires, a desire for status and power, and a desire for transcendence among seemingly secular people.

He saw that nuclear energy should not be condemned, but that it is the best type of technology to help alleviate the consequences of climate change, and that such technologies should be located at strategic points for that contribution.

Shellenberger said: "I decided to write Apocalypse Never after getting fed up with the exaggeration, alarmism, and extremism that are the enemy of a positive, humanistic, and rational environmentalism."

Biden convened a virtual Climate Summit to be held in April 2021; which brought together Putin, Xi Jinping, and Pope Francis; with 40 other world leaders. Dozens of those leaders outlined carbon reduction plans.[19] For Internet Earth Day Live and the Biden Summit, the pope said the planet was "at the brink" and that humanity must avoid "the path of self destruction."[20]

"When the destruction of nature is sparked, it is difficult to stop. But we are still in time and we will be more resilient if we work together instead of alone [...]You do not exit from the crisis the same, we will either exit better or worse. That is the challenge, and if we don't exit better, we will take the path of self-destruction."[21]

When Biden visited the Pope at the Vatican -on October 29, 2021- they discussed climate change, the COVID-19 pandemic, and poverty. The audience with the pope lasted 75 minutes. Biden thanked the pope, in the words of the president, for "his advocacy for the world's poor and those suffering from hunger, conflict, and persecution." He also praised Francis' leadership in fighting the climate crisis and for his advocacy to ensure that the pandemic ends for humanity through the sharing of

---

[17] Paula Corroto (March 29, 2021), El activista climático al que odian los activistas: "El alarmismo es una religión antihumana", El Confidencial.
[18] Michael Shellenberger, Apocalypse Never: Why Environmental Alarmism Hurts Us All (HarperCollins Publishers, 2020). Note: unless otherwise noted, this is the same source.
[19] Jennifer A Dlouhy and Jennifer Epstein (April 21, 2021), Putin, Xi, Pope Join 40 Leaders at Biden's Climate Summit, Bloomberg.
[20] Philip Pullella (April 22, 2021), In Earth Day message, pope warns that planet is "at the brink," Reuters.
[21] Ibid.

vaccines and an equitable global economic recovery.[22] Biden told Pope Francis that he is "the most significant warrior for peace I've ever met."[23] Both have been called the two most powerful Catholics in the world.[24] And even though Francis differs from Biden on positions such as abortion and that the U.S. bishops saw that no pro-abortion politician could receive communion,[25] the U.S. leader said the pope was happy that he was a good Catholic, and that he should continue to receive communion.[26]

Since Francis has brought the Vatican into line with the most modern times, it is not strange that a representative of that state should be involved for the first time in one of the meetings of the Bilderberg Club. We read about it from a French political author:

"The most recent meeting took place over three days, June 7-10, 2018, at an undisclosed location in Turin. The guest of honor was Cardinal Pietro Parolin, Vatican Secretary of State. Among the "working topics," a special place was reserved for the thorny issues of "populism" and "migrants." Cardinal Parolin himself had the honor of representing Pope Francis in Marrakech on December 10, 2018, where he signed the UN migration pact on behalf of the universal Church. One day I asked François Fillon why he had received the Bilderberg Group in Matignon. He answered me, "Because we have no choice: it is the people who govern us!" A little later, in January 2017, he complained that he had been sidelined: "The Bilderberg, despite my friend Castries, preferred Macron, who fits the globalist profile better."[27]

For his part, Paul Elie, a scholar of Catholicism at Georgetown Jesuit University, said of the similarities between Biden and Francis:

"Their informality, the fact that they were elected late in life, the fact that they seem to take issues as they come, listening, discerning and then acting," he says. "And both of them, I think, have surprised their people by turning out to be more progressive than was expected."[28]

America, the U.S. Jesuit magazine, noted that on December 13, 2022, Joe Biden granted legal protection to same-sex married couples in all 50 states; where even if the Supreme Court were to allow states to ban same-sex marriage, those states would have to recognize such marriages legally performed in other states. Significantly, the bill had

---

[22] DW (Oct. 29, 2021), Joe Biden's meeting with Pope Francis goes into overtime, Deutsche Welle.

[23] Christopher White (Oct. 29, 2021), Biden praises Pope Francis at Vatican as 'most significant warrior for peace', National Catholic Reporter.

[24] Maegan Vazquez and Kevin Liptak (Oct. 29, 2021), 'God love ya': Warm relationship between the world's most powerful Catholics on display as Biden and Pope Francis meet, CNN.

[25] Sylvia Poggioli (March 1, 2021), In Pope Francis, Biden Has A Potential Ally - Who Shares The Same Catholic Detractors, NPR.

[26] Michael Collins and Maureen Groppe (Oct. 29, 2021), Biden says Pope Francis OK'd him receiving communion, calling him a 'good Catholic' amid abortion debate, USA Today.

[27] Philippe de Villiers, J'ai tiré sur le fil du mensonge et tout est venu (Fayard, Paris, 2019), ob. cit.; citing Éric Roussel, *Jean Monnet*, *op. cit.*

[28] Sylvia Poggioli (March 1, 2021), In Pope Francis, Biden Has A Potential Ally - Who Shares The Same Catholic Detractors, NPR.

bipartisan support: no Democrats opposed it, but 12 Republicans in the Senate and 39 in the House opposed their party's majority.[29]

While much more can be said, let's just add that Biden has moved dramatically away from his promises to defend human rights and denounce human rights violations; both at home and abroad. And *Human Rights Watch* criticized Biden for his weak defense of democracy. [30]

He continued to sell arms to Egypt, Saudi Arabia, the United Arab Emirates, and Israel, despite persistent repression in those nations. Although the U.S. State Department has issued occasional protests about the repression occurring in some countries, and the Biden administration introduced sanctions against some responsible officials, the president seemed to lose his voice on the issue.[31] In addition, Biden has been on very friendly terms with India's Prime Minister Narendra Modin and invited him to a dinner at the White House, despite his continued repressive human rights violations in the Asian country. Even though he took positions on China, Iran, and Russia.[32] It is also very disturbing that both Democrats and Republicans accepted and applauded (with exceptions), Narendra Modin when he gave his speech to the US Congress in June 2023.[33]

COVID-19

It is unfortunate that numerous highly unique and bordering on paranoid conspiracy theories have been floating around the Internet about COVID-19, including vaccines to combat the SARS-CoV-2 virus. Such theories are mostly held by citizens on the far-right side and, among them, supporters of Christian nationalism do not escape.[34] Some invoked Pope Benedict and have greatly opposed Pope Francis for his support of restrictive measures.[35] Of course, we do not subscribe at all to conspiracy theories; as there are even those against Pope Francis and his support for preventive measures to combat the virus.

However, there is a danger of associating those of us who have had a rational and purely scientific concern about certain vaccines to combat the virus, as conspiracy theorists and associated with the same grouping already indicated. This is not the case.

---

[29] Robert David Sullivan (December 15, 2022), There is no going back on gay marriage after the Respect for Marriage Act, America Magazine.

[30] Reuters (Jan. 13, 2022), Human Rights Watch criticizes Biden, others for weak defense of democracy, Reuters.

[31] Ibid.

[32] Matthew Duss (June 19, 2023), What the Hell Happened to Biden's Human Rights Agenda, The New Republic.

[33] Tori Otten (June 22, 2023), "Embarrassing Spectacle": Progressive Dems Boycott Modi's Congress Speech, The New Republic.

[34] Exline JJ, Pait KC, Wilt JA, Schutt WA. Demonic and Divine Attributions around COVID-19 Vaccines: Links with Vaccine Attitudes and Behaviors, QAnon and Conspiracy Beliefs, Anger, Spiritual Struggles, Religious and Political Variables, and Supernatural and Apocalyptic Beliefs. Religions. 2022; 13(6):519; Whitehead, A. L., & Perry, S. L. (2020). How Culture Wars Delay Herd Immunity: Christian Nationalism and Anti-vaccine Attitudes. Socius, 6; Corcoran KE, Scheitle CP, DiGregorio BD. Christian nationalism and COVID-19 vaccine hesitancy and uptake. Vaccine. 2021 Oct 29;39(45):6614-6621; Drew, Nicole, "Vaccine Hesitancy, the COVID 19 Pandemic, and Christian Fundamentalism" (2021). Student Scholar Symposium Abstracts and Posters. 435; Williams JTB, Rice JD, O'Leary ST. Associations between religion, religiosity, and parental vaccine hesitancy. Vaccine X. 2021 Oct 28;9:100121.

[35] Crux staff (Sept. 7, 2020), COVID deniers invoke Pope Benedict, burn image of Francis at Rome rally, Crux Catholic Media, Inc.

Sometimes the truth can become intermingled with paranoia for certain individuals. And that has happened with history, where authentic historical rigor has been associated with conspiracy theories for a long, long time -decades-. And that is not to discount the reality of World War II and other major historical events.

Our concern lies in the fact that, since numerous high-quality scientific studies tell us of several very worrying side effects for human health from these vaccines, the acceptance of these vaccines has been reached, particularly by the recommendations of the CDC and the US government; even by Pope Francis, the Vatican, the European Union, and practically the rest of the world. With this, we are not saying that measures should not be taken, but they should not provoke something that may even be worse. But this is a subject that we do not deal with in detail here for lack of space.

About side effects, studies, of which there are many to date on the serious and in many cases even devastating side effects due to SARS-CoV-2 vaccines, have been published in prestigious peer-reviewed journals and from different countries. We emphasize that the side effects have occurred with the viral vector and mRNA vaccines: Johnson & Johnson on the one hand, and Pfizer and Moderna on the other, respectively. We do not know about the others.

Among the various side effects, thrombosis with thrombocytopenia syndrome occurs, which is characterized as a single or multiple blood clotting process within the veins, as well as in the arteries, with a predilection for affecting unusual locations, such as the splanchnic territory (intestine, pancreas, and liver) or cerebral venous sinuses.[36] Studies have ranged from the hypothesis to the very confirmation of the disease following the SARS-CoV-2 vaccines. [37]

---

[36] D. García-Azorín, E. Lázaro, D. Ezpeleta, R. Lecumberri, R. de la Cámara, M. Castellanos, C. Iñiguez Martínez, L. Quiroga-González, G. Elizondo Rivas, A. Sancho-López, P. Rayón Iglesias, E. Segovia, C. Mejías, D. Montero Corominas, Thrombosis syndrome with thrombocytopenia associated with adenovirus vaccines against COVID-19: Epidemiology and clinical presentation of the Spanish series, Neurology, 2022, ISSN 0213-4853.

[37] Lee EJ, Cines DB, Gernsheimer T, Kessler C, Michel M, Tarantino MD, Semple JW, Arnold DM, Godeau B, Lambert MP, Bussel JB. Thrombocytopenia following Pfizer and Moderna SARS-CoV-2 vaccination. Am J Hematol. 2021 May 1;96(5):534-537; Greinacher A, Thiele T, Warkentin TE, Weisser K, Kyrle PA, Eichinger S. Thrombotic Thrombocytopenia after ChAdOx1 nCov-19 Vaccination. N Engl J Med. 2021 Jun 3;384(22):2092-2101; Sharifian-Dorche M, Bahmanyar M, Sharifian-Dorche A, Mohammadi P, Nomovi M, Mowla A. Vaccine-induced immune thrombotic thrombocytopenia and cerebral venous sinus thrombosis post COVID-19 vaccination; a systematic review. J Neurol Sci. 2021 Sep 15;428:117607; Iba, Toshiaki MD[1] ; Levy, Jerrold H. MD[2] ; Warkentin, Theodore E. MD[3] . Recognizing Vaccine-Induced Immune Thrombotic Thrombocytopenia. Critical Care Medicine 50(1):p e80-e86, January 2022; Aleem A, Nadeem AJ. Coronavirus (COVID-19) Vaccine-Induced Immune Thrombotic Thrombocytopenia (VITT). 2022 Oct 3. In: StatPearls [Internet]. Treasure Island (FL): StatPearls Publishing; 2023 Jan-. PMID: 34033367; Tsilingiris D, Vallianou NG, Karampela I, Dalamaga M. Vaccine induced thrombotic thrombocytopenia: The shady chapter of a success story. Metabol Open. 2021 Sep;11:100101; Rizk JG, Gupta A, Sardar P, Henry BM, Lewin JC, Lippi G, Lavie CJ. Clinical Characteristics and Pharmacological Management of COVID-19 Vaccine-Induced Immune Thrombotic Thrombocytopenia With Cerebral Venous Sinus Thrombosis: A Review. JAMA Cardiol. 2021 Dec 1;6(12):1451-1460; Pavord S, Scully M, Hunt BJ, Lester W, Bagot C, Craven B, Rampotas A, Ambler G, Makris M. Clinical Features of Vaccine-Induced Immune Thrombocytopenia and Thrombosis. N Engl J Med. 2021 Oct 28;385(18):1680-1689; Novak N, Tordesillas L, Cabanillas B. Adverse rare events to vaccines for COVID-19: From hypersensitivity reactions to thrombosis and thrombocytopenia. Int Rev Immunol. 2022;41(4):438-447; Weiner, M., Rodriguez-Vigouroux, R., Masouridi-Levrat, S. *et al.* Very severe immune thrombocytopenia following SARS-CoV-2 vaccination requiring splenectomy: a case report. *Thrombosis J* 20, 45 (2022); Greinacher A, Langer F, Makris M, Pai M, Pavord S, Tran H, Warkentin TE. Vaccine-induced immune thrombotic thrombocytopenia (VITT): Update on diagnosis and

Another side effect is myocarditis, which is characterized by inflammation of the heart muscle, which can reduce the heart's ability to pump blood. Cases ranging from mild to very severe have appeared. Again, this all started from mild to much more severe concerns, as the same studies have shown.[38]

management considering different resources. J Thromb Haemost. 2022 Jan;20(1):149-156; Cines DB, Greinacher A. Vaccine-induced immune thrombotic thrombocytopenia. Blood. 2023 Apr 6;141(14):1659-1665; Marietta M, Coluccio V, Luppi M. Potential mechanisms of vaccine-induced thrombosis. Eur J Intern Med. 2022 Nov;105:1-7; Lee AYY, Al Moosawi M, Peterson EA, McCracken RK, Wong SKW, Nicolson H, Chan V, Smith T, Wong MP, Lee LJ, Griffiths C, Rahal B, Parkin S, Afra K, Ambler K, Chen LYC, Field TS, Lindsay HC, Lavoie M, Li C, Migneault D, Naus M, Piszczek J, Rahmani P, Sreenivasan G, Wan T, Yee A, Zypchen L, Sweet D. Clinical care pathway for the evaluation of patients with suspected VITT after ChAdOx1 nCoV-19 vaccination. Blood Adv. 2022 Jun 14;6(11):3315-3320; Lee CSM, Liang HPH, Connor DE, Dey A, Tohidi-Esfahani I, Campbell H, Whittaker S, Capraro D, Favaloro EJ, Donikian D, Kondo M, Hicks SM, Choi PY, Gardiner EE, Clarke LJ, Tran H, Passam FH, Brighton TA, Chen VM. A novel flow cytometry procoagulant assay for diagnosis of vaccine-induced immune thrombotic thrombocytopenia. Blood Adv. 2022 Jun 14;6(11):3494-3506. Baker AT, Boyd RJ, Sarkar D, Teijeira-Crespo A, Chan CK, Bates E, Waraich K, Vant J, Wilson E, Truong CD, Lipka-Lloyd M, Fromme P, Vermaas J, Williams D, Machiesky L, Heurich M, Nagalo BM, Coughlan L, Umlauf S, Chiu PL, Rizkallah PJ, Cohen TS, Parker AL, Singharoy A, Borad MJ. ChAdOx1 interacts with CAR and PF4 with implications for thrombosis with thrombocytopenia syndrome. Sci Adv. 2021 Dec 3;7(49):eabl8213; Huynh, A., Kelton, J.G., Arnold, D.M. *et al.* Antibody epitopes in vaccine-induced immune thrombotic thrombocytopaenia. *Nature* 596, 565-569 (2021); Kowarz E, Krutzke L, Külp M, Streb P, Larghero P, Reis J, Bracharz S, Engler T, Kochanek S, Marschalek R. Vaccine-induced COVID-19 mimicry syndrome. Elife. 2022 Jan 27;11:e74974; Pishko AM, Cuker A. Thrombosis After Vaccination With Messenger RNA-1273: Is This Vaccine-Induced Thrombosis and Thrombocytopenia or Thrombosis With Thrombocytopenia Syndrome? Ann Intern Med. 2021 Oct;174(10):1468-1469; King ER, Towner E. A Case of Immune Thrombocytopenia After BNT162b2 mRNA COVID-19 Vaccination. Am J Case Rep. 2021 Jul 21;22:e931478; Huynh A, Kelton JG, Arnold DM, Daka M, Nazy I. Antibody epitopes in vaccine-induced immune thrombotic thrombocytopaenia. Nature. 2021 Aug;596(7873):565-569; Prasad S, Jariwal R, Adebayo M, Jaka S, Petersen G, Cobos E. Immune Thrombocytopenia following COVID-19 Vaccine. Case Rep Hematol. 2022 Jun 25;2022:6013321; Islam A, Bashir MS, Joyce K, Rashid H, Laher I, Elshazly S. An Update on COVID-19 Vaccine Induced Thrombotic Thrombocytopenia Syndrome and Some Management Recommendations. Molecules. 2021 Aug 18;26(16):5004.; Gómez Roldós A, González-Sánchez M, Vales-Montero M, Vázquez-Alen P, Fernández-Bullido Y, Iglesias-Mohedano AM, Díaz-Otero F, García-Pastor A, Gil-Núñez A. Fatal intracerebral haemorrhage associated with thrombosis with thrombocytopenia syndrome after ChAdOx1-S vaccine. Rev Neurol. 2022 Oct 1;75(7):199-202. English, Spanish.

[38] Bozkurt B, Kamat I, Hotez PJ. Myocarditis With COVID-19 mRNA Vaccines. Circulation. 2021 Aug 10;144(6):471-484; Oster ME, Shay DK, Su JR, Gee J, Creech CB, Broder KR, Edwards K, Soslow JH, Dendy JM, Schlaudecker E, Lang SM, Barnett ED, Ruberg FL, Smith MJ, Campbell MJ, Lopes RD, Sperling LS, Baumblatt JA, Thompson DL, Marquez PL, Strid P, Woo J, Pugsley R, Reagan-Steiner S, DeStefano F, Shimabukuro TT. Myocarditis Cases Reported After mRNA-Based COVID-19 Vaccination in the US From December 2020 to August 2021. JAMA. 2022 Jan 25;327(4):331-340; Power JR, Keyt LK, Adler ED. Myocarditis following COVID-19 vaccination: incidence, mechanisms, and clinical considerations. Expert Rev Cardiovasc Ther. 2022 Apr;20(4):241-251; Lane S, Yeomans A, Shakir S. Reports of myocarditis and pericarditis following mRNA COVID-19 vaccination: a systematic review of spontaneously reported data from the UK, Europe and the USA and of the scientific literature. BMJ Open. 2022 May 25;12(5):e059223; Esposito S, Caminiti C, Giordano R, Argentiero A, Ramundo G, Principi N. Myocarditis Following COVID-19 Vaccine Use: Can It Play a Role for Conditioning Immunization Schedules? Front Immunol. 2022 Jun 27;13:915580; Lane S, Yeomans A, Shakir S. Systematic review of spontaneous reports of myocarditis and pericarditis in transplant recipients and immunocompromised patients following COVID-19 mRNA vaccination. BMJ Open. 2022 Jul 1;12(7):e060425; Massari M, Spila Alegiani S, Morciano C, Spuri M, Marchione P, Felicetti P, Belleudi V, Poggi FR, Lazzeretti M, Ercolanoni M, Clagnan E, Bovo E, Trifirò G, Moretti U, Monaco G, Leoni O, Da Cas R, Petronzelli F, Tartaglia L, Mores N, Zanoni G, Rossi P, Samez S, Zappetti C, Marra AR, Menniti Ippolito F; TheShinISS-Vax|COVID Surveillance Group. Postmarketing active surveillance of myocarditis and

These vaccines have also been the cause of neurological complications, such as cerebral thrombosis; already considered in the first condition but with many confirmatory studies that, likewise, went from minor to an extremely worrisome confirmation.[39] To be more specific, cerebral thrombosis is caused by the loss of oxygen to a region of the brain due to the obstruction of a thrombus or clot in the artery that irrigates it. This can be devastating.

Ischemic cerebrovascular disease and intracerebral hemorrhage have also been reported.[40]

pericarditis following vaccination with COVID-19 mRNA vaccines in persons aged 12 to 39 years in Italy: A multi-database, self-controlled case series study. PLoS Med. 2022 Jul 28;19(7):e1004056; Pillay J, Gaudet L, Wingert A, Bialy L, Mackie AS, Paterson DI, Hartling L. Incidence, risk factors, natural history, and hypothesised mechanisms of myocarditis and pericarditis following covid-19 vaccination: living evidence syntheses and review. BMJ. 2022 Jul 13;378:e069445; Dionne A, Sperotto F, Chamberlain S, et al. Association of Myocarditis With BNT162b2 Messenger RNA COVID-19 Vaccine in a Case Series of Children. *JAMA Cardiol.* 2021;6(12):1446-1450; Marschner CA, Shaw KE, Tijmes FS, Fronza M, Khullar S, Seidman MA, Thavendiranathan P, Udell JA, Wald RM, Hanneman K. Myocarditis Following COVID-19 Vaccination. Cardiol Clin. 2022 Aug;40(3):375-388; Rout A, Suri S, Vorla M, Kalra DK. Myocarditis associated with COVID-19 and its vaccines - a systematic review. Prog Cardiovasc Dis. 2022 Sep-Oct;74:111-121; Heidecker B, Dagan N, Balicer R, Eriksson U, Rosano G, Coats A, Tschöpe C, Kelle S, Poland GA, Frustaci A, Klingel K, Martin P, Hare JM, Cooper LT, Pantazis A, Imazio M, Prasad S, Lüscher TF. Myocarditis following COVID-19 vaccine: incidence, presentation, diagnosis, pathophysiology, therapy, and outcomes put into perspective. A clinical consensus document supported by the Heart Failure Association of the European Society of Cardiology (ESC) and the ESC Working Group on Myocardial and Pericardial Diseases. Eur J Heart Fail. 2022 Nov; 24(11):2000-2018; Naveed Z, Li J, Wilton J, Spencer M, Naus M, Velasquez Garcia HA, Kwong JC, Rose C, Otterstatter M, Janjua NZ; Canadian Immunization Research Network (CIRN) Provincial Collaborative Network (PCN) Investigators. Comparative Risk of Myocarditis/Pericarditis Following Second Doses of BNT162b2 and mRNA-1273 Coronavirus Vaccines. J Am Coll Cardiol. 2022 Nov 15;80(20):1900-1908.

[39] Esba LCA, Al Jeraisy M. Reported adverse effects following COVID-19 vaccination at a tertiary care hospital, focus on cerebral venous sinus thrombosis (CVST). Expert Rev Vaccines. 2021 Aug;20(8):1037-1042; Fadul A, Abdalla E, Abdelmahmuod E, Abdulgayoom M, Ali E, Al-Warqi A, Al-Yahary H. COVID-19 Vaccine-Induced Cerebral Sinus Thrombosis: Coincidence vs. Cause? Cureus. 2022 Jun 29;14(6):e26436; de Gregorio C, Colarusso L, Calcaterra G, Bassareo PP, Ieni A, Mazzeo AT, Ferrazzo G, Noto A, Koniari I, Mehta JL, Kounis NG. Cerebral Venous Sinus Thrombosis following COVID-19 Vaccination: Analysis of 552 Worldwide Cases. Vaccines (Basel). 2022 Feb 3;10(2):232; Garg RK, Paliwal VK. Spectrum of neurological complications following COVID-19 vaccination. Neurol Sci. 2022 Jan;43(1):3-40; Chen F, Cao P, Liu H, Cai D. The Impact of COVID-19 and Vaccine on the Human Nervous System. Neuroendocrinology. 2022;112(11):1046-1057; Frontera JA, Tamborska AA, Doheim MF, Garcia-Azorin D, Gezegen H, Guekht A, Yusof Khan AHK, Santacatterina M, Sejvar J, Thakur KT, Westenberg E, Winkler AS, Beghi E; contributors from the Global COVID-19 Neuro Research Coalition. Neurological Events Reported after COVID-19 Vaccines: An Analysis of VAERS. Ann Neurol. 2022 Mar 2;91(6):756-71; Haj Mohamad Ebrahim Ketabforoush A, Molaverdi G, Nirouei M, Abbasi Khoshsirat N. Cerebral venous sinus thrombosis following intracerebral hemorrhage after COVID-19 AstraZeneca vaccination: A case report. Clin Case Rep. 2022 Nov 15;10(11):e6505; Mohamed Elfil, Mohammad Aladawi, Dmitry Balian, Ismail Fahad, Daniel J Zhou, Brian Villafuerte-Trisolini, Thomas Scott Diesing, Cerebral venous sinus thrombosis after COVID-19 vaccination: a case report and literature review, *Oxford Medical Case Reports*, Volume 2023, Issue 1, January 2023, omac154; Frommeyer TC, Wu T, Gilbert MM, Brittain GV, Fuqua SP. Cerebral Venous Sinus Thrombosis Following an mRNA COVID-19 Vaccination and Recent Oral Contraceptive Use. *Life.* 2023; 13(2):464; Chen W-P, Chen M-H, Shang S-T, Kao Y-H, Wu K-A, Chiang W-F, Chan J-S, Shyu H-Y, Hsiao P-J. Investigation of Neurological Complications after COVID-19 Vaccination: Report of the Clinical Scenarios and Review of the Literature. *Vaccines.* 2023; 11(2):425; Chatterjee A, Chakravarty A. Neurological Complications Following COVID-19 Vaccination. Curr Neurol Neurosci Rep. 2023 Jan;23(1):1-14.

[40] Hosseini R, Askari N. A review of neurological side effects of COVID-19 vaccination. Eur J Med Res. 2023 Feb 25;28(1):102.

Analyses of the mechanism that triggers these conditions have also been published.[41]

The number of lives affected by these vaccines, including death, has not been determined. And VAERS reports (administered by the CDC and FDA) that number in the tens of thousands, but are based on unverified reports from the public at large, are not necessarily entirely reliable.[42] All in all, we must ask why then they have such data, if not formally track cases for use and take action on what has happened with the vaccine. Since VAERS reports are based on unconfirmed data, an investigation should be done, because if true, it is a very worrisome number. If not, how about a few thousand, or a few hundred? It is still very worrisome. Moreover, several of the studies we have cited consider many cases, even if they are not counted in the thousands. What about the unreported cases?

Some of the articles referenced above, stress that the veracity of the cases reported in VAERS be investigated. Since science, the real science, has verified these serious side effects and the numbers reported to VAERS are alarming, what are they waiting for?

The CDC published Dr. Tom Shimabukuro's presentation in 2021 on vaccine safety and the high and rising rate of myocarditis and pericarditis, clarifying that it was not necessarily the position of the CDC or the FDA.[43] Beyond that, not much progress has been made.

Although it is true that populations at risk for SARS-CoV-2 vaccines have been detected, being that several of the mechanisms that produce the mentioned and other side effects are known, and therefore warnings and advice can be given to those who present the risk conditions that can lead to serious side effects, it is also true that most of the medical personnel who administer these vaccines do so indiscriminately. Whether some are guilty of negligence or not, others are not.

But it is also true that each of the causes why some people experience side effects from these vaccines is unknown. Is there any causality between the vaccines and some who suffer from the same conditions even though they do not present the risk patterns of the groups that have been verified in the studies? This is another major concern, so how can it be recommended?

---

[41] de Gregorio C, Calcaterra G, Kounis NG, Bassareo PP, Mehta JL. Cerebral venous thrombosis after COVID-19 vaccines: Do we know the mechanism? Lancet Reg Health Eur. 2022 May;16:100387.

[42] Beatrice Dupuy (May 7, 2021), EXPLAINER: How activists target CDC vaccine tracking system, The Associated Press; Angelo Fichera and Beatrice Dupuy (Jan. 12, 2022), One year into COVID shots, misleading VAERS claims persist, The Associated Press; The Associated Press (Sept. 23, 2022), Posts continue to misrepresent VAERS COVID-19 vaccine data, The Associated Press; Melissa Goldin (Jan. 11, 2023), Posts mischaracterize CDC data on COVID-19 vaccine deaths, The Associated Press.

[43] COVID-19 Vaccine safety updates. Advisory Committee on Immunization Practices (ACIP) June 23, 2021. Tom Shimabukuro, MD, MPH, MBA. Vaccine Safety Team CDC COVID-19 Vaccine Task Force: https://www.cdc.gov/vaccines/acip/meetings/downloads/slides-2021-06/03-COVID-Shimabukuro-508.pdf, CDC Emails, Chat Messages on Post-Vaccination Myocarditis. Contributed by Zack Stieber (Epoch Times): https://www.documentcloud.org/documents/23656227-cdc-emails-chat-messages-on-post-vaccination-myocarditis; accessed July 2, 2023.

Much has been said, that the benefits of vaccines outweigh the risks... but until that risk becomes a reality.[44]

What in addition to the aforementioned need to vaccinate children, which is not the most advisable thing to do anyway given what has been said so far? A team of researchers from Johns Hopkins School of Medicine, analyzed summer 2021 approximately 48,000 children under 18 diagnosed with Covid in health insurance data from April to August 2020, finding a zero mortality rate among children without a pre-existing medical condition such as leukemia. Marty Makary, MD, the lead investigator, accused the CDC of basing its advocacy for vaccinating children on weak data. The CDC, Makary points out, based its decision on 335 children under the age of 18 who died with a Covid diagnosis code in their record. But the CDC, with 21,000 employees, "has not investigated each death to find out whether Covid caused it and whether it was a pre-existing medical condition." Incredibly, the CDC's Advisory Committee on Immunization Practices decided in May that the benefits of two-dose vaccination outweigh the risks for all children aged 12-15 years.[45]

Dr. Marty Makary wrote on his Twitter account on February 20, 2023:

"The White House litmus test was ignore natural immunity and support an indiscriminate vax & boost all Americans policy, regardless of age [or data]. Dr. Jha said the science to support the bivalent vax was "Crystal Clear" and lobbied medical association leaders to sign letters of support for a 'bivalent for all' rec with zero randomized trial data. FDA advisor Dr. Paul Offit bravely pushed back in the NEJM &said this is anti-science. In the end, 85% of Americans said no thank you to the bivalent booster."

Similarly, the robust number of scientific studies published in highly reputable scientific journals, which tell us about and demonstrate the enormous benefits of natural immunity, whether equal to or even far greater, as evidenced, than vaccination itself, has been systematically ignored.[46] Unlike a study funded by the Bill & Melinda

---

[44] See for example: Schneider J, Sottmann L, Greinacher A, Hagen M, Kasper HU, Kuhnen C, Schlepper S, Schmidt S, Schulz R, Thiele T, Thomas C, Schmeling A. Postmortem investigation of fatalities following vaccination with COVID-19 vaccines. Int J Legal Med. 2021 Nov;135(6):2335-2345.; Butt, A.A., Guerrero, M.D., Canlas, E.B. et al. Evaluation of mortality attributable to SARS-CoV-2 vaccine administration using national level data from Qatar. Nat Commun 14, 24 (2023); Nafilyan, V., Bermingham, C.R., Ward, I.L. et al. Risk of death following COVID-19 vaccination or positive SARS-CoV-2 test in young people in England. Nat Commun 14, 1541 (2023); Mahase E. Covid-19: Study reports no significant increase in deaths after vaccination but raises questions over AstraZeneca's vaccine. BMJ. 2023 Mar 29;380:741. Of course, there are retractions, which have nothing to do with the documented reality: Vaccines Editorial Office. Expression of Concern: Walach et al. The Safety of COVID-19 Vaccinations-We Should Rethink the Policy. Vaccines 2021, 9, 693. Vaccines. 2021; 9(7):705; Vaccines Editorial Office. Retraction: Walach et al. The Safety of COVID-19 Vaccinations-We Should Rethink the Policy. Vaccines 2021, 9, 693. Vaccines. 2021; 9(7):729.

[45] Marty Makary (July 19, 2021), The Flimsy Evidence Behind the CDC's Push to Vaccinate Children, The Wall Street Journal.

[46] Sette A, Crotty S. Adaptive immunity to SARS-CoV-2 and COVID-19. Cell. 2021 Feb 18;184(4):861-880; Lineburg KE, Grant EJ, Swaminathan S, Chatzileontiadou DSM, Szeto C, Sloane H, Panikkar A, Raju J, Crooks P, Rehan S, Nguyen AT, Lekieffre L, Neller MA, Tong ZWM, Jayasinghe D, Chew KY, Lobos CA, Halim H, Burrows JM, Riboldi-Tunnicliffe A, Chen W, D'Orsogna L, Khanna R, Short KR, Smith C, Gras S. CD8+ T cells specific for an immunodominant SARS-CoV-2 nucleocapsid epitope cross-react with selective seasonal coronaviruses. Immunity. 2021 May 11;54(5):1055-1065.e5; Cohen KW,

457

Gates Foundation, J Stanton, T Gillespie, and J and E Nordstrom, which has many discrepancies and omissions from other very significant studies.[47]

We could say that due to the thinking of considering almost everything politically correct, many believe without further ado that it is impossible for such a blatant deviation from the analysis and application of science to happen in the West. But belief is not evidence, but authentic science.

As Allysia Finley wrote in a February 2023 *Wall Street Journal* article:

Linderman SL, Moodie Z, Czartoski J, Lai L, Mantus G, Norwood C, Nyhoff LE, Edara VV, Floyd K, De Rosa SC, Ahmed H, Whaley R, Patel SN, Prigmore B, Lemos MP, Davis CW, Furth S, O'Keefe J, Gharpure MP, Gunisetty S, Stephens KA, Antia R, Zarnitsyna VI, Stephens DS, Edupuganti S, Rouphael N, Anderson EJ, Mehta AK, Wrammert J, Suthar MS, Ahmed R, McElrath MJ. Longitudinal analysis shows durable and broad immune memory after SARS-CoV-2 infection with persisting antibody responses and memory B and T cells. medRxiv [Preprint]. 2021 Jun 18:2021.04.19.21255739; Wang Z, Muecksch F, Schaefer-Babajew D, Finkin S, Viant C, Gaebler C, Hoffmann HH, Barnes CO, Cipolla M, Ramos V, Oliveira TY, Cho A, Schmidt F, Da Silva J, Bednarski E, Aguado L, Yee J, Daga M, Turroja M, Millard KG, Jankovic M, Gazumyan A, Zhao Z, Rice CM, Bieniasz PD, Caskey M, Hatziioannou T, Nussenzweig MC. Naturally enhanced neutralizing breadth against SARS-CoV-2 one year after infection. Nature. 2021 Jul;595(7867):426-431; Gazit S, Shlezinger R, Perez G, Lotan R, Peretz A, Ben-Tov A, Herzel E, Alapi H, Cohen D, Muhsen K, Chodick G, Patalon T. Severe Acute Respiratory Syndrome Coronavirus 2 (SARS-CoV-2) Naturally Acquired Immunity versus Vaccine-induced Immunity, Reinfections versus Breakthrough Infections: A Retrospective Cohort Study. Clin Infect Dis. 2022 Aug 24;75(1):e545-e551; Lozano-Ojalvo D, Camara C, Lopez-Granados E, Nozal P, Del Pino-Molina L, Bravo-Gallego LY, Paz-Artal E, Pion M, Correa-Rocha R, Ortiz A, Lopez-Hoyos M, Iribarren ME, Portoles J, Rojo-Portoles MP, Ojeda G, Cervera I, Gonzalez-Perez M, Bodega-Mayor I, Montes-Casado M, Portoles P, Perez-Olmeda M, Oteo J, Sanchez-Tarjuelo R, Pothula V, Schwarz M, Brahmachary M, Tan AT, Le Bert N, Berin C, Bertoletti A, Guccione E, Ochando J. Differential effects of the second SARS-CoV-2 mRNA vaccine dose on T cell immunity in naive and COVID-19 recovered individuals. Cell Rep. 2021 Aug 24;36(8):109570; Cho, A., Muecksch, F., Schaefer-Babajew, D. *et al.* Anti-SARS-CoV-2 receptor-binding domain antibody evolution after mRNA vaccination. *Nature* 600, 517-522 (2021); Wei J, Matthews PC, Stoesser N, Maddox T, Lorenzi L, Studley R, Bell JI, Newton JN, Farrar J, Diamond I, Rourke E, Howarth A, Marsden BD, Hoosdally S, Jones EY, Stuart DI, Crook DW, Peto TEA, Pouwels KB, Walker AS, Eyre DW; COVID-19 Infection Survey team. Anti-spike antibody response to natural SARS-CoV-2 infection in the general population. Nat Commun. 2021 Oct 29;12(1):6250; Loyal L, Braun J, Henze L, Kruse B, Dingeldey M, Reimer U, Kern F, Schwarz T, Mangold M, Unger C, Dörfler F, Kadler S, Rosowski J, Gürcan K, Uyar-Aydin Z, Frentsch M, Kurth F, Schnatbaum K, Eckey M, Hippenstiel S, Hocke A, Müller MA, Sawitzki B, Miltenyi S, Paul F, Mall MA, Wenschuh H, Voigt S, Drosten C, Lauster R, Lachman N, Sander LE, Corman VM, Röhmel J, Meyer-Arndt L, Thiel A, Giesecke-Thiel C. Cross-reactive CD4[+] T cells enhance SARS-CoV-2 immune responses upon infection and vaccination. Science. 2021 Oct 8;374(6564):eabh1823; Sureshchandra S, Lewis SA, Doratt BM, Jankeel A, Coimbra Ibraim I, Messaoudi I. Single-cell profiling of T and B cell repertoires following SARS-CoV-2 mRNA vaccine. JCI Insight. 2021 Dec 22;6(24):e153201; Pugh J, Savulescu J, Brown RCH, *et al* The unnaturalistic fallacy: COVID-19 vaccine mandates should not discriminate against natural immunity *Journal of Medical Ethics* 2022;48:371-377; O Murchu E, Byrne P, Carty PG, De Gascun C, Keogan M, O'Neill M, Harrington P, Ryan M. Quantifying the risk of SARS-CoV-2 reinfection over time. Rev Med Virol. 2022 Jan;32(1):e2260. doi: 10.1002/rmv.2260; Riemersma KK, Haddock LA 3rd, Wilson NA, Minor N, Eickhoff J, Grogan BE, Kita-Yarbro A, Halfmann PJ, Segaloff HE, Kocharian A, Florek KR, Westergaard R, Bateman A, Jeppson GE, Kawaoka Y, O'Connor DH, Friedrich TC, Grande KM. Shedding of infectious SARS-CoV-2 despite vaccination. PLoS Pathog. 2022 Sep 30;18(9):e1010876.

[47] COVID-19 Forecasting Team. Past SARS-CoV-2 infection protection against re-infection: a systematic review and meta-analysis. Lancet. 2023 Mar 11;401(10379):833-842.

"Many liberals label themselves "pro-science" as if that's a political position. Then again, so many putatively scientific studies seem intended to promote progressive policies rather than advance scientific knowledge. Such studies then get amplified by the media and self-appointed experts on social media."[48]

Now, about the pharmaceutical companies' agreements to sell vaccines to different countries. Pfizer's agreement with Albania, for example, goes like this:

"Purchaser acknowledges and agrees that (i) Pfizer's efforts to develop and manufacture the Product are aspirational in nature and subject to significant risks and uncertainties, and (ii) the fact that any other drug or vaccine to prevent, treat or cure COVID-19 infection is successfully developed or granted authorization earlier than the granting of Authorization for the Product shall not change the current situation of urgent needs for prevention of the spread of the COVID-19 infection that poses serious threats to and harmful effects on the lives and health of the general public."[49]

In other words, Pfizer accepts that its own vaccine can cause "serious threats and harmful effects" in the contract with Albania, being that its product was "aspirational in nature," so it was "subject to significant risks and uncertainties." We also read on page 19, where it expands on the above:

"Purchaser acknowledges that the Vaccine and materials related to the Vaccine, and their components and constituent materials are being rapidly developed due to the emergency circumstances of the COVID-19 pandemic and will continue to be studied after provision of the Vaccine to Purchaser under this Agreement. Purchaser further acknowledges that the long-term effects and efficacy of the Vaccine are not currently known and that there may be adverse effects of the Vaccine that are not currently known. Further, to the extent applicable, Purchaser acknowledges that the Product shall not be serialized."[50]

Page 22, further states that, "Purchaser hereby agrees to indemnify, defend and hold harmless Pfizer, BioNTech, each of their Affiliates [...] from and against any and all suits, claims, actions, demands, losses, damages, liabilities, settlements, penalties, fines, costs and expenses [...] arising out of, relating to, or resulting from the Vaccine, including but not limited to any stage of design, development, investigation, formulation, testing, clinical testing, manufacture, labeling, packaging, transport, storage, distribution, marketing, promotion, sale, purchase, licensing, donation, dispensing, prescribing, administration, provision, or use of the Vaccine."[51]

The same is known about other Pfizer agreements with other countries, and also with Johnson & Johnson itself.

What about preventive measures to avoid contagion? We read in *The New York Times*:

---

[48] Allysia Finley (Feb. 19, 2023), The CDC's Long-Covid Deception, The Wall Street Journal.
[49] Contract Between Albania And Pfizer (Manufacturing And Supply Agreement), January 6, 2021, p. 7.
[50] Ibid, p. 19.
[51] Ibid, p. 22.

"The most rigorous and comprehensive analysis of scientific studies conducted on the efficacy of masks for reducing the spread of respiratory illnesses — including COVID-19 — was published late last month. Its conclusions, said Tom Jefferson, the Oxford epidemiologist who is its lead author, were unambiguous."[52]

As the column written by Bret Stephens rightly states, such observations do not emanate from just anywhere, as Jefferson and 11 colleagues conducted the study for Cochrane, "a British nonprofit that is widely considered the gold standard for its reviews of health care data."

The article further describes, "The conclusions were based on 78 randomized controlled trials, six of them during the Covid pandemic, with a total of 610,872 participants in multiple countries. And they track what has been widely observed in the United States: States with mask mandates fared no better against Covid than those without." We are also rightly reminded that "No study — or study of studies — is ever perfect. Science is never absolutely settled."

Here are some excerpts from an interview with one of the scientists involved in the study:

"There is just no evidence that they" — masks — "make any difference," he told the journalist Maryanne Demasi. "Full stop."

But, wait, hold on. What about N-95 masks, as opposed to lower-quality surgical or cloth masks?

"Makes no difference — none of it," said Jefferson.

What about the studies that initially persuaded policymakers to impose mask mandates?

"They were convinced by nonrandomized studies, flawed observational studies."

What about the utility of masks in conjunction with other preventive measures, such as hand hygiene, physical distancing or air filtration?

"There's no evidence that many of these things make any difference."

It is true that someone named Erin Kelley, writing from Washington, gave a response to the article noting that the study authors themselves wrote that they could not draw definitive conclusions for various reasons, such as the length of time the masks were used in the study group, to see how effective they were.[53] Now, the study is very extensive. According to it, wearing a mouth or face mask makes little or no

---

[52] Bret Stephens (February 21, 2023), The Mask Mandates Did Nothing. Will Any Lessons Be Learned, The New York Times. Note: unless otherwise noted, this is the same source.
[53] Erin Kelley (Feb. 22, 2023), Arguing About Mask Mandates, The New York Times.

difference in how many people get a flu-like or Covid-like illness.[54] What is also not considered is that the study found no evidence that the masks actually worked.

COVID-19 and 'the new normal'
With all this in mind, in November 2020, Pope Francis criticized:

"Yet some groups protested, refusing to keep their distance, marching against travel restrictions — as if measures that governments must impose for the good of their people constitute some kind of political assault on autonomy or personal freedom! Looking to the common good is much more than the sum of what is good for individuals. It means having a regard for all citizens and seeking to respond effectively to the needs of the least fortunate."[55]

That same month, COMECE called for solidarity and hope in Europe during the COVID-19 crisis; and appealed for the vaccine for the entire population once it became available.[56]

Also, in January 2021 during an interview, Pope Francis with the news program *TG5 Italia*, said:

"The ruling class has the right to have different points of view and to impose its own policy. But in this time we must play for unity, always [...] At this time -he added- there is no right to distance oneself from unity. Political struggle is a noble thing, but if politicians emphasize self-interest more than the common interest, they ruin things [...] At this time the whole ruling class has no right to say 'I'. We must say 'We' and seek unity in the face of the crisis [...] conflicts are necessary, but at this moment they must take a vacation. We must stress the unity of the country, of the Church, and of society."[57]

He also noted:

"I believe that morally everyone must take the vaccine [...] I do not understand why some say that this could be a dangerous vaccine [...] If the doctors are presenting this to you as a thing that will go well and doesn't have any special dangers, why not take it? There is a suicidal denialism that I would not know how to explain but today people must take the vaccine."[58]

It can be seen that the Pope pointed out that the right to defer is not right and that all should be united to get out of the crisis, criticizing the denialism in the face of a

---

[54] Jefferson T, Dooley L, Ferroni E, Al-Ansary LA, van Driel ML, Bawazeer GA, Jones MA, Hoffmann TC, Clark J, Beller EM, Glasziou PP, Conly JM. Physical interventions to interrupt or reduce the spread of respiratory viruses. Cochrane Database of Systematic Reviews 2023, Issue 1. Art. No.: CD006207.

[55] Pope Francis (Nov. 26, 2020), Pope Francis: A Crisis Reveals What Is in Our Hearts, The New York Times.

[56] Vatican News Editor (Nov. 18, 2020), EU Bishops call for solidarity and hope on path towards better future, Vatican News.

[57] Tgcom24 (January 10, 2021), Papa Francesco al Tg5: "Per la politica questo non è il momento di rompere l'unità," Tgcom24.

[58] Joshua J. McElwee (Jan. 11, 2021), Pope Francis suggests people have moral obligation to take coronavirus vaccine, National Catholic Reporter.

supposedly "safe" vaccine. With this, he reinforced the declaration he approved in December 2020 by the Congregation for the Doctrine of the Faith, which indicated that vaccination against COVID-19 is a moral obligation.[59]

In fact, by a decree signed on February 8, 2021, any Vatican employee who refused to take the vaccine without a valid medical reason would be fired.[60]

In the same month, the global Jesuit advocacy network for the COVID-19 vaccine quoted the February communiqué from the presidents of the six Jesuit conferences worldwide to President Biden and other world leaders: "The Society of Jesus is committed to engaging in advocacy at the local, national, and international levels with like-minded organisations to ensure that all individuals, no matter where they live, have access to the COVID-19 vaccine."[61]

In March, a consortium of Catholic media and experts was formed to combat misinformation about vaccines.[62]

The Hill reported in March 2021 that Pope Francis could be President Joe Biden's most important ally. One of the key points is that the pope has emphasized that humans should be vaccinated against COVID-19, which was then listed as the Biden administration's top priority.[63]

In fact, Joe Biden on April 6 praised partnerships between faith-based groups and community health centers to provide COVID-19 vaccines. He called the efforts to provide vaccines "an example of America at its finest [...] they're all meeting what Pope Francis calls the moral obligation - get vaccinated - something which he went on to say can save your life and the lives of others."[64]

Now, on May 6-8 of the same year, a Vatican health conference entitled "Unite to Prevent & Unite to Cure" was held, which was jointly organized by the Pontifical Council for Culture and Cura Foundation. It focused significantly on COVID-19 treatments and prevention but also provided a platform to promote vaccines produced by large pharmaceutical companies. Of the 114 speakers, Dr. Anthony Fauci, leader of the Trump and Biden administrations' response to COVID-19 and vaccination (director of the National Institute of Allergy and Infectious Diseases, National Institutes of Health), gave the opening talk, titled "Exploring the Mind, Body & Soul: How Innovation and Novel Delivery Systems Improve Human Health."[65] *Religion en Libertad* headlined "Anthony Fauci, el médico católico de formación jesuítica que asesora a Trump para frenar la pandemia" (Anthony Fauci, the Jesuit-trained Catholic

[59] Matt Hadro (April 27, 2021), White House: Pope Francis has said there's a 'moral obligation' to get vaccinated, Catholic News Agency.

[60] Nicole Winfield (Feb. 18, 2021), Anti-vax at the Vatican? You might lose your job, The Associated Press.

[61] ISN Staff (May 12, 2021), Global Jesuit Network Covid Vaccine Advocacy Continues as Biden Administration Appears Favorable, Ignatian Solidarity Network.

[62] Aleteia Editor (March 16, 2021), Medios católicos y expertos, unidos contra la desinformación sobre las vacunas, Aleteia.

[63] John Kenneth White (March 10, 2021), Pope Francis may be Joe Biden's most important ally, The Hill.

[64] Matt Hadro (April 27, 2021), White House: Pope Francis has said there's a 'moral obligation' to get vaccinated, Catholic News Agency.

[65] Edward Pentin (April 23, 2021), Vatican Health Conference: A Platform to Combat COVID-19 'Vaccine Hesitancy?', National Catholic Register.

doctor advising Trump to curb the pandemic).[66] Fauci praised the training he received from the Jesuits, which would have prepared him to deal with the pandemic.[67]

The conference was also attended by Dr. Francis Collins, director of the US National Institutes of Health. But also Stephen Bancel and Albert Bourla, the respective directors of Moderna and Pfizer.[68] Another speaker was David Feinberg, vice president of Google Health, who had committed $150 million to promote "COVID-19 vaccine education and equitable distribution to underserved communities," and more funds to other institutions, including WHO, to promote vaccination.

The Cura Foundation, through an e-mail, expressed its opinion on April 22 on the eve of the conference:

"The Catholic Church has come under scrutiny for questioning the use of the J&J vaccine but came out on the side of science saying it's better to get any vaccine — and that is the point of this gathering [...].
"In these difficult times of COVID," the email read, "international experts including Dr. Anthony Fauci, National Institute of Health's Dr. Francis Collins, Moderna and Pfizer CEOs, as well as religious leaders in Christianity, Judaism, Buddhism, and the Muslim faiths will be present as we grapple as a society with global health and being a unified global society."

Although the conference was not only about COVID-19 and vaccination but also about other diseases, the aforementioned focus is significant.

Other guests included Amy P. Abernethy, former principal deputy commissioner and acting chief information officer of the FDA. Chelsea Clinton, vice president of the Clinton Foundation.

Less than two months later, the Vatican's bioethics academy and the World Medical Association called for an all-out effort to combat vaccine hesitancy and correct the "myths and disinformation" that were holding back the fight against the coronavirus. The greatest concern came from third-world countries, which were wary of pharmaceuticals, as well as "fake news, myths and disinformation about vaccine safety, including among religious groups and some in the medical community."[69]

"They demanded that "all relevant stakeholders exhaust all efforts to... confront vaccine hesitancy by sending a clear message about the safety and necessity of vaccines and counteracting vaccine myths and disinformation."[70]

Also, in August, following mandates requiring all New York City employees to undergo SARS-CoV-2 vaccination, the Archdiocese of New York instructed its priests

---

[66] Carmelo López-Arias (April 11, 2020), Anthony Fauci, el médico católico de formación jesuítica que asesora a Trump para frenar la pandemia, Religión en Libertad; See also: James T. Keane (May 12, 2020), Dr. Anthony Fauci to Jesuit grads: 'Now is the time for us to care selflessly about one another', America Magazine.

[67] Ibid.

[68] Edward Pentin (April 23, 2021), Vatican Health Conference: A Platform to Combat COVID-19 'Vaccine Hesitancy?', National Catholic Register. Note: unless otherwise noted, this is the same source.

[69] Nicole Winfield (July 2, 2021), Vatican seeks all-out effort to combat vaccine hesitancy, The Associated Press.

[70] Ibid.

to refuse to sign religious exemption requests filed by Catholics opposed to such vaccinations. Cardinal Timothy Dolan quoted Pope Francis as saying that he made it very clear that it is morally acceptable to take any of the vaccines and that we have a moral responsibility to vaccinate. Chancellor John P. Cahill said that giving an exemption would contradict one of the pope's directives.[71] This is not surprising, since months ago at the Washington National Cathedral, a special event was organized to encourage people to get the COVID-19 vaccine, with Dr. Francis Collins and Dr. Anthony Fauci in attendance.

In late October 2021, the Biden administration said it would not commit to postponing the firing of military and civilian federal employees seeking religious exemptions from mandatory COVID-19 vaccination until their case is fully adjudicated. Although the White House denied the news, the truth is that the Safer Federal Workforce Task Force itself contradicted those statements.[72]

Michael Yoder, an attorney representing 20 federal employees who sued President Biden and members of his administration over an executive order mandating COVID-19 vaccination for federal employees, said:

"The Biden administration has shown an unprecedented, cavalier attitude toward the rule of law and an utter ineptitude at basic constitutional contours [...] This combination is dangerous to American liberty [...] Thankfully, our Constitution protects and secures the right to remain free from religious persecution and coercion. With this order, we are one step closer to putting the Biden administration back in its place by limiting government to its enumerated powers. It's time citizens and courts said no to tyranny. The Constitution does not need to be rewritten, it needs to be reread."[73]

Likewise, Francis urged journalists, scientists, and others in January of the new year, and we quote: "To be properly informed, to be helped to understand situations based on scientific data and not fake news, is a human right." And that there was spreading "a distortion of reality based on fear, falsified or invented news." *The New York Times* tells us of Francis' message: "He praised the Catholic consortium of media organizations, fact-checking websites and scientists for combating inaccurate information on vaccines, particularly online."[74]

Speaking to diplomats earlier this month, Francis stressed the importance of "the effort to immunize the general population as much as possible."[75]

Although there are many reactionary groups even among the Catholic Church who are ultra-right-wing, who were very much in favor of the late Benedict XVI, and who are against COVID-19 vaccines and restrictions to combat the spread of the virus (in

---

[71] Patrick Delaney (Aug. 4, 2021), Citing Pope Francis, NY archdiocese tells priests not to issue religious exemptions from jab, LifeSiteNews.
[72] Calvin Freiburger (Oct. 29, 2021), Biden White House refuses to say if it'll comply with judge's pro-religious exemption ruling, LifeSiteNews.
[73] Ibid.
[74] The New York Times (January 28/February 7, 2022), Coronavirus Pandemic Covid News: Pope Warns Against 'Infodemic', The New York Times.
[75] Ibid.

addition to being against Pope Francis and pro-Trump)[76] that does not negate the reality of the scientific evidence on the high -though not majority- risks of the COVID-19 vaccines. Nor do other aspects of the issue.

Employers required their employees to be vaccinated and risked being suspended or fired if they failed to do so.[77] It is not surprising that hundreds and even thousands of workers in different sectors of the U.S. labor force preferred to be suspended or even fired rather than get the COVID-19 vaccine.[78]

The *New Boston Post* reports on a measure that is also part of Catholic and Protestant teaching, albeit unacknowledged:

"At least one societal change resulting from the quarantine could do wonders to reinvigorate our national sense of family, faith, and community. Let's give serious thought to reinstating at least some of the time-honored Sunday closure laws, sort of a one-day-per-week modified stay-at-home request. Such action would rededicate our society to a regular day of rest, family meals, civic associations, and religious observance.

"By rededicating each Sunday as "a common day of rest," we would say that the life of America is much more than never-pausing commerce and ever-grinding bureaucracy. We would proclaim that the heart of the nation transcends consumerism and looms larger than even the biggest government. We would emphasize that the real value in a country comes not from its GNP or tax collections, but from families, faith, communities, that it comes from "We the people."[79]

Likewise, the Congregation of the Sisters of the Good Samaritan of the Order of St. Benedict, a female Catholic religious order of apostolic life and pontifical rights, also published an article where it points out that the presence and consequences of COVID-19 lead us to rethink our existence for a spiritual rebirth. He also stresses that "The C19 pandemic provides many with an opportunity to "slow down" and to rediscover the

---

[76] Tom Gjelten (May 8, 2020), Some See Plot To Create 'World Government' In Coronavirus Restrictions, National Public Radio; Crux Staff (Sept. 7, 2020), COVID deniers invoke Pope Benedict, burn image of Francis at Rome rally, Crux Catholic Media, Inc.

[77] Vimal Patel (Dec. 18, 2020/July 20, 2021), Employers Can Require Workers to Get Covid-19 Vaccine, U.S. Says, The New York Times; Jenny Gross (June 9/16, 2021), Yes, Your Employer Can Require You to Be Vaccinated, The New York Times; Haley Messenger (Aug. 3/Nov. 16, 2021), From McDonald's to Goldman Sachs, here are the companies mandating vaccines for all or some employees, NBC News; Jessica Mathews (Aug. 23/30, 2021), All the major companies requiring vaccines for workers, Fortune.

[78] Jesus Jimenez and Niraj Chokshi (June 7/8, 2021), Texas hospital workers suspended over mandatory vaccine policy, The New York Times; Andrea Hsu (Oct. 24, 2021), Thousands of workers are opting to get fired, rather than take the vaccine, National Public Radio; Howard Blume (Dec. 8, 2021), Nearly 500 L.A. Unified employees lose their jobs for failing to get COVID-19 vaccine, Los Angeles Times; Chantal Da Silva (Jan. 5, 2022), Mayo Clinic fires 700 workers who failed to comply with Covid vaccine mandate, NBC News; Emma G. Fitzsimmons (Feb. 14, 2022), N.Y.C. fires 1,430 workers, less than 1 percent of city employees, over a vaccine mandate..., The New York Times; Mary Kekatos and Aaron Katersky (Feb. 15, 2022), Nearly 1,500 NYC municipal workers fired for not being vaccinated against COVID, ABC News; Dave Muoio (Feb. 22, 2022), How many employees have hospitals lost to vaccine mandates? Here are the numbers so far, Fierce Healthcare; Andrea Hsu (Dec. 27, 2022), Thousands of workers were fired over vaccine mandates. For some, the fight goes on, National Public Radio; Rachel Tillman (Jan. 17, 2023), DOD 'not currently pursuing' back pay for service members fired over COVID vaccine refusal, Spectrum News NY1.

[79] Joseph Tortelli (April 1, 2020), If History Rhymes, New Boston Post.

restfulness and creativity that flows from keeping Sabbath." Walter Brueggemann is quoted in the article, who "notes that the Sabbath is much neglected in contemporary society."[80] The article continues:

"The Sabbath is about withdrawal from the anxiety system of Pharaoh and Caesar (still prevalent in various forms today). It is a refusal to let one's life be defined by busyness or production. How can this C19 period allow you more time to slow down and to recommit to the Sabbath? How can it connect you to the disadvantaged and vulnerable in your community?"[81]

The European Sunday Alliance thus called on March 3, 2021, on European Union political leaders "to put synchronised free time as a priority on the social policy agenda, especially "in times where the COVID-19 pandemic has accelerated existing challenges of digitalisation by intensifying work and extending working hours, thus putting a healthy work-life balance at risk for more people."[82]

A new post-COVID-19 world order led by the Vatican through the Great Reset
A 2020 review report by the Vatican's Dicastery for Promoting Integral Human Development published the following:

"The COVID-19 pandemic is the defining crisis of this generation, from which we can either emerge for the better or the worse. It has laid bare the inequities and injustices that threaten people's well-being, safety, and lives, and exacerbated an interconnected set of crises – economic, ecological, political, social – that disproportionately impact the poor and most vulnerable.

"As we move through recovery, we must ensure the cures for the immediate crises are steppingstones to a more just, inclusive, and integrated set of systems, and that a global, regenerative healing takes place to transform societies and our planet."[83]

The report highlights the Laudato Si' Business Roundtables, which to build an inclusive and sustainable regenerative economy, as an initiative of the Economy Task Force coordinated with NOW Partners, brought together leading business, academic, and community leaders from around the globe, guided by Laudato Si, to discuss how to reform the global economy in the post-COVID era. The Pope stressed his duty to use the current crisis as an opportunity to promote peace, social friendship to world leaders, and a change of mind and heart. Francis called for the creation of an international fund in a multilateral effort to help negotiate agreements between states to invest in effective security -peace-building efforts, poverty reduction, and health- for human development.

---

[80] Dr Peter Mudge (August 2020), COVID-19: an opportunity for cultivating a fresh approach to spirituality?, The Sisters of the Good Samaritan of the Order of St Benedict.
[81] Ibid.
[82] Alessandro Di Maio (March 3, 2021), The European Sunday Alliance releases statement on synchronised free time in the EU, COMECE.
[83] 2020 Year in Review: Vatican COVID-19 Commission *Preparing the Future*, Dicastery for Promoting Integral Human Development, p. 1.

Thus, as the recovery progresses, it is intended to produce a global, regenerative improvement that will transform societies and the planet.[84]

In October 2021, at the Autumn Assembly of COMECE (Commission of Bishops of the European Union), the Vatican's Cardinal Secretary of State, Pietro Parolin, also spoke about the recovery from COVID-19.[85]

Tedros Adhanom Ghebreyesus, head of WHO, wrote that the COVID-19 pandemic will change the world.

Klaus Schwab, German economist, businessman, as well as founder and executive chairman of the World Economic Forum (WEF), wrote a few years ago his book "The Fourth Industrial Revolution,"[86] where he addresses the issue of the new technological revolution that is bringing about the transformation of humanity through the convergence of digital, physical and biological systems; and what it may mean for the development of global society, with its opportunities and dilemmas. He said verbatim in 2020: "the pandemic represents a rare but narrow window of opportunity to reflect, reimagine, and reset our world." Therefore, he co-authored with economist Thierry Malleret *COVID-19: The Great Reset*.[87] That book describes the crossroads the world is at because of the challenges it has faced with COVID-19. This is something that will lead, according to the book, "to a better world: more inclusive, more equitable and more respectful of Mother Nature."[88] The book offers the idea that capitalism should be transformed so that companies stop focusing only on serving shareholders, and become custodians of society by creating value for customers, suppliers, employees, communities, as well as other stakeholders.[89] Such a plan is offered to be implemented through a series of multi-stakeholder partnerships that bring together the private sector, governments, and civil society in every area of global governance. The voice of government would be one among many. And while this sounds more democratic, it has its dangers: it translates into a worrying accumulation of corporate power over society and less to democratic institutions, however good the intentions may seem. Corporations become the official stakeholders in global decision-making. With this, the UN becomes a public-private institution. This would have real implications on the world stage for the organization of the food system, the governance of large technology companies, as well as the distribution of vaccines and medicines. Such companies, under this model, have no proven democratic regulation in the countries where it is already taking place, and drive their own commercial interests without oversight. Since the UN is immersed in this project, concerns have not been long in coming.[90]

Renowned journalist and social activist Naomi Klein, for example, has rightly pointed out:

---

[84] Ibid, pp. 7, 11, 8, 1.

[85] Alejandro Di Maio (October 30, 2020), COMECE Autumn Assembly 2020 - Cardinal Parolin on the Covid-19 recovery: "the Church in the frontline for a fairer and more solidary Europe," COMECE Press.

[86] Klaus Schwab, The Fourth Industrial Revolution (World Economic Forum, Geneva, Switzerland, 2016).

[87] Klaus Schwab, Thierry Malleret, COVID-19: The Great Reset (Forum Publishing, Edition 1.0, Geneva, Switzerland, 2020).

[88] Ibid.

[89] See until otherwise noted, to Ivan Wecke (Aug. 16, 2021), Conspiracy theories aside, there is something fishy about the Great Reset, openDemocracy.

[90] https://www.foodsovereignty.org/wp-content/uploads/2020/03/EN_Edited_draft-letter-UN-food-systems-summit_070220.pdf; accessed May 3, 2023.

"Through its highly influential Global Competitiveness Report, the WEF has played a leading role in the transnational campaign to liberate capital from all encumbrances (like robust regulation, protections for local industries, progressive taxation, and — heaven forbid — nationalizations). Long ago, however, Schwab realized that if Davos didn't add some do-gooding to its well-doing, the pitchforks that had started amassing at the foot of the mountain would eventually storm the gates [...].

The Great Reset is merely the latest edition of this gilded tradition, barely distinguishable from earlier Davos Big Ideas, from "Shaping the Post-Crisis World" (2009) to "Rethink, Redesign, Rebuild" (2010) to "The Great Transformation" (2012) and, who can forget, "Creating a Shared Future in a Fractured World" (2018). If Davos wasn't "seeking a better form of capitalism" to solve the spiraling crises Davos itself systematically deepened, it wouldn't be Davos."[91]

Naomi Klein goes on to tell us about Schwab:

"All kinds of dangerous ideas are lurking under its wide brim, from a reckless push toward more automation in the midst of a joblessness crisis, to the steady move to normalize mass surveillance and biometric tracking tools, to the very real (though not new) problem of Bill Gates's singular power over global health policy. The irony, though, is that the fact-Vitamix currently whirring around the Great Reset actually makes it harder to hold the Davos set accountable for any of this, since legitimate critiques have now been blended together with truly dangerous anti-vaccination fantasies and outright coronavirus denialism."[92]

Some of the Great Reset's supporters include U.S. President Joe Biden, Canadian Prime Minister Justin Trudeau, then German Chancellor Angela Merkel, and then Prince (now King) Charles of Great Britain.[93] They see it as a model for restoring capitalism; as a better reconstruction after the global pandemic and leading the world onto a greener, more sustainable path.

Pope Francis also raises the idea of a reset, with a series of initiatives along the same lines as Klaus Schwab; by telling us that:

"He has frequently expressed a wish for the world to take the opportunity to emerge better from the COVID crisis, including through his October 2020 social encyclical *Fratelli Tutti* (which the WEF read as proposing a reset similar to its own), his "Economy of Francesco" initiative in Assisi in November that proposed a "new economy" of "communal wealth," his U.N.-affiliated Global Compact for Education initiative, or the Vatican's collaboration with Mission 4.7, a U.N.-backed project that, like the Global Compact, aims to educate the world in sustainable lifestyles, gender equality and a culture of peace and nonviolence."

The Prefect of the Dicastery for Integral Human Development, Cardinal Peter Turkson, notes other manifest commonalities between the goals of the Great Reset initiative and those of Pope Francis with "The Vatican COVID-19 Commission,"

[91] Naomi Klein (Dec. 8, 2020), The Great Reset Conspiracy Smoothie, The Intercept.
[92] Ibid.
[93] Edward Pentin (Feb. 4, 2021), 'Great Reset' Plan Parallels Some of Pope's Initiatives - But There's a Crucial Difference, National Catholic Register. Note: unless otherwise noted, this is the same source.

whose motto is "Prepare the Future." Turkson stated that the Vatican wishes to remain open to initiatives such as the Great Reset; and that such openness and commitment has its origin in the call of the Second Vatican Council to be "witness" and show "solidarity with humanity." Turkson stresses, the *National Catholic Reporter* continues:

"The objective for us and from the point of view of Pope Francis is to reimagine a social order with more justice, equity, where social injustices are overcome," he said. This is why, he explained, his dicastery has "shared a lot of information with Davos, the U.N., about our approach," making it "very likely" that language of the Vatican and the WEF "now begins to be closer."

The World Economic Forum has mentioned Pope Francis' criticism of neoliberalism, and echoes his encyclical Fratelli Tutti:

"The story did not end the way it was meant to," Pope Francis wrote recently, deftly excommunicating about a half-century's worth of economic ideology.

"In a striking, 43,000-word-long encyclical published last Sunday, the pope put his stamp on efforts to shape what's been termed a Great Reset of the global economy in response to the devastation of COVID-19.

"The "story" he's referring to is neoliberalism, a philosophy espousing austerity, privatization, deregulation, unbridled markets, and relatively weak labour laws. While it's been faithfully told through innumerable economists and policy-makers since the 1970s, and put into practice in prominent ways, the pope believes this tale has now worn thin. He is not alone."[94]

Francis has written to Klaus Schwab on several occasions and in different years, thanking him for his efforts to improve a more just economy at the global level, and expressing the economic philosophy of the Holy See for the future of humanity.[95] Schwab has invited Pope Francis to participate in the Forum on several occasions, and although as of this writing he has not attended, in 2020 he sent Cardinal Peter Turkson.

Under Francis' leadership, the Holy See joined the Council of Inclusive Capitalism founded by Lynn Forester de Rothschild, who stated, "This Council will follow the warning from Pope Francis to listen to 'the cry of the earth and the cry of the poor' and

---

[94] John Letzing (October 9, 2020), Here's the pope's prescription for resetting the global economy in response to COVID-19, World Economic Forum.
[95] See, e.g., Francis (January 17, 2014), Message Of His Holiness Pope Francis To Prof. Klaus Schwab - Message of His Holiness Pope Francis to Prof. Klaus Schwab, Founder and Executive Chairman of the World Economic Forum Davos-Klosters (Switzerland), January 22-25, 2014. Klaus Schwab, Founder and Executive Chairman of the World Economic Forum Davos-Klosters (Switzerland), January 22-25, 2014; Message of His Holiness Pope Francis to the Executive Chairman of the "World Economic Forum" on the occasion of the Annual Gathering in Davos-Klosters [Davos, Switzerland, January 23-26, 2018] (Copyright © Dicastero per la Comunicazione - Libreria Editrice Vaticana, January 12, 2018); Message of the Holy Father Francis to Professor Klaus Schwab, Executive Chairman of the World Economic Forum [Davos, Switzerland, January 21-24, 2020] (Bulletin of the Holy See Press Office, January 15, 2020/Copyright © Dicastero per la Comunicazione - Libreria Editrice Vaticana).

answer society's demands for a more equitable and sustainable model of growth."[96] Previously it was the Council for Inclusive Capitalism with the Vatican (CICV). But cooperation with the Vatican remains strong, with the pope as a major advisor.

"The Council is led by a core group of global leaders, known as Guardians for Inclusive Capitalism, who meet annually with Pope Francis and Cardinal Turkson. These leaders represent more than $10.5 trillion in assets under management, companies with over $2.1 trillion of market capitalization, and 200 million workers in over 163 countries. The organization challenges business and investment leaders of all sizes to embrace the Council's guiding principles and make public commitments to act on them. These collective actions are intended to lead to systemic change by making capitalism a greater force for inclusivity and sustainability. [...].

"Speaking to the Guardians, Pope Francis said, "An economic system that is fair, trustworthy, and capable of addressing the most profound challenges facing humanity and our planet is urgently needed. You have taken up the challenge by seeking ways to make capitalism become a more inclusive instrument for integral human wellbeing."

"The Guardians have already committed to hundreds of measurable actions, and Council members will make ongoing commitments to continue to advance inclusive capitalism. They will be accountable for their public commitments and invite businesses around the world to join."[97]

The Coalition is also an offshoot of the Coalition for Inclusive Capitalism, which heeds Francis' call and which was also founded by Lynn Forester de Rothschild.

It is worth noting that important figures of the conservative Catholic clergy are against the Great Reset. Even traditionalist clerics and Catholic media see it as the establishment of a new world order against God and Christian values (Cardinals Raymond Leo Burke, Gerhard Müller, Archbishop Carlo Maria Viganò; LifeSiteNews, OnePeter5, etc.) However, these media also resort to conspiracy theories about the human future.

Other than this, Augusto Zampini-Davies, who is a priest and was Deputy Secretary of the Dicastery for Promoting Integral Human Development at the Vatican, said in October 2019:

"The world is on fire and the Church is determined to lead change. We have a historic opportunity to show that we are on the side of the oppressed, on the side of creation. We cannot sit back and watch everything being destroyed. Caring for the planet is not optional. If we are not part of the solution, we will be part of those who oppress

---

[96] Council for Inclusive Capitalism (Dec. 8, 2020), The Council for Inclusive Capitalism with the Vatican, A New Alliance Of Global Business Leaders, Launches Today, PR Newswire. See also Andrew Ross Sorkin, Jason Karaian, Michael J. de la Merced, Lauren Hirsch and Ephrat Livni (Dec. 8/31, 2020), The Pope Blesses Business Plans, The New York Times.
[97] Ibid.

and depredate it. Catholics have an advantage, which is the divine mandate to care for God's creation. It is not only a moral motivation, but one of faith."[98]

Note that another difference with the Great Reset is that the papal proposal establishes excessive state intervention;[99] even though it agrees with the more open service of business to humanity. As was the case when Zampini-Davies co-authored a World Economic Forum article.[100]

Through interviews with various members of the Society of Jesus, I was able to access confidential information from which we have learned that the Pope has tried to take advantage of the coronavirus crisis to establish a new global governance, led by the Holy See. As implausible as it may seem.

It was in August 2020, sometime after meeting with Pope Francis, that Argentine journalist and political analyst Gustavo Sylvestre, quoting the pope, said on television:

"Nobody is saved alone. This was launched a few days ago by Pope Francis, who begins to lead this new world economic order that must necessarily be installed in Argentina and the world; when this pandemic leaves us. When the world begins to rise from the ashes. And when, as a central element, solidarity and a new world economic order, must necessarily be set in motion. Nothing will be the same after this pandemic. [...] Why don't you listen to Pope Francis? He is really fabulous. He is beginning to lead the new world that is coming. Pope Francis.[101]

Fratelli Tutti

On his apostolic journey to the United Arab Emirates -February 3-5, 2019- Pope Francis and the Grand Imam of Al-Azhar Ahmad Al-Tayyeb, signed in Abu Dhabi the Document on Human Fraternity for World Peace and Living Together.[102] In the same document, it is especially emphasized:

"We, who believe in God and in the final meeting with Him and His judgment, on the basis of our religious and moral responsibility, and through this Document, call upon ourselves, upon the leaders of the world as well as the architects of international policy and world economy, to work strenuously to spread the culture of tolerance and of living together in peace; to intervene at the earliest opportunity to stop the shedding of innocent blood and bring an end to wars, conflicts, environmental decay and the moral and cultural decline that the world is presently experiencing.

---

[98] Victoria Isabel Cardiel C. (October 30, 2019), Augusto Zampini-Davies: «Estamos, por una vez, a la vanguardia», Alfa & Omega.

[99] Christopher Lamb (June 19, 2020), Vatican pushing for rethink of financial system post-Covid, The Tablet.

[100] Augusto Zampini Davies, Amy Goldman, Francois Bonnici (May 15, 2020), COVID-19 shows the need for radical change. Here's how faith leaders can help rebuild a better post-pandemic world, World Economic Forum.

[101] (April 5, 2020), Gustavo Sylvestre proclama el inicio del NOM liderado por el papa, Dilo Al Mundo: https://www.youtube.com/watch?v=XHbuNMD8tXU; accessed May 18, 2023.

[102] Document on "Human Fraternity for World Peace and Living Together (February 4, 2019), Dicasterio per la Comunicazione - Libreria Editrice Vaticana.

"We call upon intellectuals, philosophers, religious figures, artists, media professionals and men and women of culture in every part of the world, to rediscover the values of peace, justice, goodness, beauty, human fraternity and coexistence in order to confirm the importance of these values as anchors of salvation for all, and to promote them everywhere."[103]

Francis and Al-Tayyeb also indicated that they were promoting the document to "influential leaders, persons of religion all over the world, appropriate regional and international organizations, organizations within civil society, religious institutions and leading thinkers. They further pledge to make known the principles contained in this Declaration at all regional and international levels, while requesting that these principles be translated into policies, decisions, legislative texts, courses of study and materials to be circulated."[104]

They requested that the declaration be an invitation to reconciliation and fraternity among all believers, and even between believers and non-believers, as well as among all people of goodwill.[105]

Therefore, the project of the development of the Abrahamic Family House in Abu Dhabi, which embodies the historical relations between the three Abrahamic religions, namely Judaism, Christianity, and Islam, is being carried out. The project provides a platform for dialogue, understanding, and coexistence among them.[106]

UN Secretary-General António Guterres praised the statement.[107]

The document recalls Pope Paul VI's Declaration Nostra aetate of October 28, 1965, which was part of the Second Vatican Council.

Fratelli Tutti is the encyclical signed by Pope Francis in October 2020. It deals with issues of universal fraternity and social friendship. It is a dream for the future formation of humanity. Of the issues it addresses, it speaks against racism, support for immigration, interreligious relations, and the concept of the "Good Samaritan."[108] Likewise, he refers to the positive that fraternity offers to freedom and equality.[109] He speaks of the dignity of women, against the death penalty.[110] He calls for a form of global governance in solidarity that encompasses the above-mentioned.[111] And he criticizes populist and liberal regimes, as well as just war.[112]

In addition, he points out that private property is a secondary right since it should obey the universal distribution of goods, taking into account those who do not have them.[113] Francis does not tell us how he imagines an action to this proposal, but he

---

[103] Ibid, p. 3.

[104] Ibid, p. 6.

[105] Ibid, p. 7.

[106] PR Newswire (Sept. 21, 2019), As Part of Global Initiative to Promote Peace, Higher Committee of Human Fraternity Unveils Design for the Abrahamic Family House, PR Newswire.

[107] (February 4, 2021), La ONU celebra el Día de la Fraternidad Humana con un llamado a promover la tolerancia y el diálogo, Noticias ONU.

[108] Pope Francis, Encyclical Letter Fratelli tutti of the Holy Father Francis on Fraternity and Social Friendship (Dicastero per la Comunicazione - Libreria Editrice Vaticana, 2020), pp. 1, 2. 6, 11, 17-22, 24-27, 28, 30, 32, 34, 36, 38, 39, 44, 45, 59, 69, 73, 78, 17-23, 27, 43, 74.

[109] Ibid, p. 26, 27.

[110] Ibid, pp. 6, 7, 64-67.

[111] Ibid, p. 33.

[112] Ibid, pp. 10, 39, 40-42.

[113] Ibid, pp. 30, 31.

could refer to the fact that private property has a social purpose, that of sharing with the needy.[114]

Austen Ivereigh, biographer and personal friend of Pope Francis, said based on Fratelli Tutti: "The Pope is the spiritual director of this world in crisis."[115]

Although his encyclical wields correct and moral principles, Monsignor Carlo Maria Viganò spoke out on the matter:

"A cursory reading of the text of Fratelli tutti would give the impression that it was written by a Freemason [...] Everything that is said in it is inspired by a vague deism and philanthropy that have nothing Catholic about them.
[...]
This encyclical constitutes Bergoglio's ideological manifesto, his profession of Masonic faith, as well as his candidacy for the presidency of the universal religion, servant of the New World Order."[116]

Italian Freemasonry, as well as the Grand Lodge of Spain, celebrated Francis' encyclical because it supports the Masonic ideal of universal fraternity.[117] But Luis Argüello, the secretary general and spokesman for the Spanish Episcopal Conference, said in October 2020 that "it is neither an invention of the Enlightenment nor a Masonic proposal," and that it rather has very deep roots in the Gospel.[118]

COMECE said in a public statement on November 18, 2020:

"Many of us were worried that the European Union itself, as an economic, political, social, and cultural project, was at risk. We realized then, as Pope Francis said, that we are in the same boat and that we can only save ourselves by staying together.
[...]
"The future of the European Union does not depend only on economy and finances but also on **a common spirit and a new mindset**. This crisis is a spiritual opportunity for conversion. We must not simply devote all our efforts to returning to the "old normal" but take advantage of this crisis to bring about a radical change for the better. It forces to rethink and to restructure the present model of globalisation guaranteeing respect for the environment, openness to life, concern for the family, social equality, the dignity of workers and the rights of future generations. Pope Francis with his Encyclical *Laudato si'* has provided a compass for shaping a new civilization. In his new Encyclical *Fratelli tutti*, signed a few weeks ago on the tomb of Saint Francis of Assisi, he calls the whole of humanity to universal brotherhood and social friendship, not forgetting those on the margins, wounded and suffering. The

---

[114] Daniel Amiri (October 26, 2020), Misreading Francis on Private Property, Where Peter Is.

[115] Darío Menor (November 24, 2020), Austen Ivereigh: "El papa Francisco es el director espiritual de este mundo en crisis", Vida Nueva Digital: https://www.vidanuevadigital.com/2020/11/24/austen-ivereigh-el-papa-francisco-es-el-director-espiritual-de-este-mundo-en-crisis/; accessed April 23, 2023.

[116] Msgr. Carlo Maria Viganò (Oct. 6, 2020), Viganò sobre la encíclica Fratelli tutti: «daría la impresión de que fue escrita por un masón», Adelante la Fe.

[117] GOI (November 11, 2020), Italian Freemasonry also celebrates the encyclical Fratelli Tutti, Grande Oriente d'Italia.

[118] Fran Otero (October 29, 2020), Argüello: «La fraternidad no es un invento de la Ilustración o una propuesta masónica», Alfa & Omega. See on the pope's thinking on the subject a book interview with Austen Ivereigh: Pope Francis, Let Us Dream: The Path to a Better Future (Simon & Schuster, New York, 2020).

Principles of Catholic Social Teaching as human dignity and solidarity, like also the preferential option for the poor and sustainability, can be guiding principles to build up a different model of economy and society after the pandemic"[119]

But the statement continues:

"We assure all who lead and work in the European Institutions and Member States, that the Church is by your side in our common effort to construct a better future for our continent and the world. All initiatives that promote the authentic values of Europe will be supported by us. **We are hopeful that from this crisis we can come out stronger**, wiser, more united, exercising more solidarity, caring more for our common home, being a continent that pushes the whole world forward towards greater fraternity, justice, peace and equality."[120]

All of this seems to unconsciously echo the so-called "Cosimo Maestroianni"[121] or Cardinal Agostino Casaroli -the former Vatican Secretary of State under Pope John Paul II-[122] as recorded in *Windswept House*, by Jesuit Malachi Martin. Since he would work for the Catholic Church to accept the challenges of the new times, *regardless* of national sovereignties and lead the Holy See to accept its merger and cooperation with a kind of new world order: much like the encyclical Fratelli Tutti.[123]

---

[119] Message from the Presidents of the Bishops' Conferences of the European Union to the European Institutions and Member States: "Recovering Hope and Solidarity" (November 18, 2020), COMECE.
[120] Ibid.
[121] Malachi Martin, Windswept House: A Vatican Novel (Broadway Books, New York, 1996), pp. 131-140, 269, 273, 94, 95.
[122] WHO'S WHO IN "WINDSWEPT HOUSE": A KEY TO THE CHARACTERS IN FR. MALACHI MARTIN'S "WINDSWEPT HOUSE," TRADITIO Traditional Roman Catholic Network. Last Revision: 7/22/18.
[123] Malachi Martin, Windswept House: A Vatican Novel (Broadway Books, New York, 1996), pp. 77, 78.

CHAPTER
14

French Freemasonry and the
Holy See in the 21st Century

French Freemasonry and the Holy See in the 21st Century
The Freemasonry of the Grand Orient of France and other French Masonic lodges would be a challenge to the Holy See in foreign policy, particularly in Europe. Recalling chapters 1 and 2 we have considered in this essay.

France, in part of the 21st century, has supported the Catholic Church and embraced Freemasonry in a way that places both on a particular political plane and connects it with the papacy of Francis, where the influence of the Catholic Church was growing. Moreover, the Jesuits were playing an important role in the drama; and the very support of Pope Francis was been solicited in the acceptance of Freemasonry on the French Catholic plane. In fact, the cooperation of Macron's France with the papacy of Francis has been impressive. Let us see how it all begins.

Thus, from the years 2008-2010 and following, the famous Masonic obedience of the Grand Orient of France was very concerned about the very strong influence of religion on MEPs.[1] This was occurring as ethical issues such as abortion, stem cells, and others, became the subject of debate between supporters of a secular Europe and those who wish to see society shaped by their religious beliefs.

Marcel Conradt, Freemason and parliamentary assistant in 2008 to Socialist MEP Veronique De Keyser, denounced the assault of "lobbies and religious sects" in Europe. This was intended to influence legislation and decision-makers, particularly MEPs.

The influence of churches, as well as cults such as Scientology or the Raelian movement, was described, urging a Europe with God outside of politics.

However, special recognition was given to the churches, as the Lisbon Treaty guarantees them an "open, transparent and regular" dialogue with the institutions. Instead of "lobbyists," they are considered "partners" who are required to disclose their sources of funding.

Conradt criticized that the European Commission (José Barroso), the European Parliament (Jerzy Buzek), and the European Council (Herman Van Rompuy) were chaired by people with religious convictions. In addition to Ireland and Italy, other nations were eager to defend Catholicism. One indication of the tensions was the display of religious symbols in public buildings.

On February 3 of the same year -2010-, an Italian ultra-Catholic close to Pope Benedict XVI, attacked what he called, "a European plague of apostasy," while an Irish lobbyist lamented that the "right to equality comes at the expense of religious rights."

---

[1] Martin Pascal (February 17, 2010), La reconquista des francs-maçons, Le soir. Note: unless otherwise noted, this is the same source.

Another assembly of the Council of Europe was informed of the evident desire of the Catholic Church to move from influence to interference. In January, in fact, the apostolic nuncio in France asked parliamentarians to endorse one of their representatives for the post of judge at the European Court (Human Rights) in Strasbourg. Tempers flared over this recommendation.

Conradt stated, "It should be pointed out that there are other options for society." The Freemasons tried to unite their different schools of thought and give their opinions in front of the President of the European Commission in a more open way. Jean-Michel Quilladert, Past Grand Master of the Grand Orient of France, said about the transformation undertaken by Freemasonry on the European continent that, in 2008, they first got a meeting with José Barroso (European Commission). Present were the Grand Orient of France, the Feminine Grand Lodge of France, the Droit humain, and the Grand Orient of Portugal. They indicated to him that Europe owes its roots not only to Christianity but also to Greece and Rome, to the humanism of the Renaissance and the Enlightenment. They obtained representation for Masonic obediences and in defense of secularism in the Bepa, or advisory office of the president and the commission on politics; which previously was only for religious and spiritual groups. Quillardet further said, "When we organized an international Masonic meeting in Athens in 2008, Barroso had written us a message about the importance he attached to the contribution of Freemasonry to the history and integration of Europe."

But he pointed out that there was still a great battle to be fought since the churches were still very present. Therefore, the Grand Orient of France created a small organization in charge of organizing Masonic obediences throughout Europe. Thus creating a federation between Masonic obediences to speak with one voice. However, the challenge is that although many obediences have a strong spiritual current, they are nevertheless lagging in social matters, particularly in secularism.

A precedent to such a federation was the creation of the International Masonic Assembly in Strasbourg in 2007. With subsequent meetings in Greece and Turkey, among others.

Jean-Michel Quilladert concluded:

"Now it is necessary to impose the universalist conception of the Enlightenment, which implies extending the notion of European citizenship to the Jew, the black, the North African, the homosexual, the heterosexual, etc. We must come to understand that what unites us is a certain idea of man regardless of their ancestry."

Although Freemasonry establishes an obligation of perfect neutrality towards public authorities, an exchange of letters between the Grand National French Lodge (GLNF) and the then President of France, Nicolas Sarkozy in 2009, revealed its strong support for the Elysée government.[2]

But it was with Emmanuel Macron (May 2017) that Freemasonry would have a particular era, because of its well-known anti-clerical history and secularism.

Many Freemasons were seduced by Macron when he worked near the headquarters of the Grand Orient de France in June 2016, on rue Cadet.[3] The Freemasons

---

[2] François Koch (November 30, 2010), Quand des francs-maçons soutiennent l'Elysée, L'Express.
[3] Airy Routier (February 23, 2019), Quel est vraiment le poids des francs-maçons sous l'ère Macron, Challenges. Note: unless otherwise noted, this is the same source.

476

contributed a lot to Macron's coming to power. They had called for a massive vote against the conservative Marine Le Pen. Many Freemasons attended Macron's enthronement in front of the Louvre pyramid and were reinforced after the election, by the formation of a new government akin to Freemasonry, with Masonic brothers such as Gérard Collomb, Jean-Yves Le Drian or Jacques Mézard. Others in Macron's government are close to lodges or are Freemasons. However, many Freemasons were disillusioned when they saw a more top-down government during his first year in office, as well as his evident clericalism.

Although solid links between Alexandre Benalla, a member of the lodge Chevaliers de l'Espérance of the Grand National French Lodge (GLNF), and the soon-to-be ex-fellow advisor to Emmanuel Macron, Ismaël Emelien, trained at the Grand Orient trend Masonic school in Havas, are intriguing.

Macron chose as his Minister of Europe and Foreign Affairs Jean-Yves Le Drian (from May 2017 to May 2022). Le Drian is a Freemason and belongs to the Grand Orient of France.[4] He strongly supported Macron during his campaign and, under his tenure, would have to work particularly to "refound" Europe.[5] He is described as a "man of strategy and networks, the foreign minister would thus also rely on Freemasonry, of which he would be an active member." Since the higher one goes in the military hierarchy, the more Freemasons one finds, this would facilitate Le Drian's relations with the military chiefs. When he was a deputy, Le Drian belonged to the Parliamentary Fraternity, which gathers Masonic deputies and senators, of right and left, whatever the Masonic obedience.[6]

However, the Grand Orient of France has shown great concern about the rapprochement between Emmanuel Macron and the Catholic Church.[7] Being that Macron is a *Catholic* agnostic,[8] although he sympathizes with Masonic ideals. For example, the president's visit to the Lateran Basilica in Rome, where he would take possession of his title of "first and only honorary canon" and for his visit to Pope Francis at the Vatican at the end of June 2018.[9]

Also Macron's vision of the Catholic Church in his April 9, 2018 speech at the Collège des Bernardins to Catholics.[10] His speech was considered as a real attack on secularism; or an operation of seduction of Catholics. Macron called to repair the damaged link between Church and State. He invited the Church to get involved in the debate and the life of the city.[11]

Macron was invited to speak before the U.S. Congress, and, in his standing ovation speech on April 25, 2018, criticized Trump's policies as extreme nationalism; arguing

---

[4] Bernard Morvan (September 13, 2018), Franc-maçonnerie : il n'y a pas que Le Drian à en être..., Breizh-info.

[5] Olivier Drouin (May 17, 2017), Franc-maçonnerie, andouille, VTT... les petits secrets de Jean-Yves Le Drian, le nouveau ministre des Affaires étrangères, Capital.

[6] Breizh-info (March 3, 2016), Jean-Yves Le Drian franc-maçon. Maiwenn Raynaudon (Bretons) manque de curiosité, Breizh-info.

[7] Jean-Marie Guénois (June 25, 2018), Laïcité : Macron provoque des bisbilles chez les francs-maçons, Société.

[8] Adam Plowright (June 25, 2018), Vatican visit puts Macron's religious views in spotlight, AFP.

[9] Jean-Marie Guénois (June 25, 2018), Laïcité : Macron provoque des bisbilles chez les francs-maçons, Société.

[10] Ibid.

[11] Pierre-Hervé Grosjean (April 10, 2018), Abbé Grosjean : "Emmanuel Macron aux Bernardins, un discours qui engage," Figaro Vox.

that it was up to the United States to preserve the international order it had helped create. He also criticized the aggressive trade war the U.S. was waging, because it would destroy jobs, raise prices, and the middle class would have to pay. He also criticized Trump's withdrawal from the Paris Agreement on climate change. All in all, he considerably emphasized the virtues of the United States and its historical ties with France.[12]

Macron's first visit to the Vatican, taking into account that he was educated in a Jesuit school,[13] was cataloged by *La Croix* as a singular relationship between the French head of state and Catholics.[14] It occurred at the end of June 2018, where in an unusually long meeting with Pope Francis, the two discussed migration issues, the conflict in the Middle East and the future of European unity; secularism, interreligious dialogue, and environmental protection.[15]

At the end of the interview, Macron introduced the pope to the members of the delegation, among whom was Jean-Yves Le Drian.[16] Jean Landousies, a priest from Pontivy, was the pope's interpreter and has been a friend of Le Drian for many years.[17]

But the fears of French Freemasons would disappear in December 2018, being that the Grand Orient de France and the Grand National Lodge of France rekindled their ties with Emmanuel Macron because of his approach to other policies supported by the Freemasons.[18]

On January 15, 2019, the French Minister of the Interior, Christophe Castaner - a Freemason - invited to dinner the main French Masonic obediences: GODF, GLDF, GLNF, FFDH, GLAMF, GLFF, GLTSO, GLMF, GLCS and GLMU (which are the ones present at the Elysée Palace); to discuss the defense of secularism against the attempt to modify the structure of the 1905 Law of separation of State and Church.[19]

But Le Drian did not believe there was any threat, and he visited the Vatican in April of the same year. There, he spoke with the Secretary of State, Cardinal Pietro Parolin, as well as with Monsignor Paul Gallagher, Secretary for Relations with States. They discussed the fire that destroyed Notre Dame Cathedral and its reconstruction, as well as the resolution of international crises, and the major conflicts in the Middle East, Africa, and Central and South America. During his visit, Le Drian renewed Macron's invitation to the Pope to visit France.[20]

---

[12] Julie Hirschfeld-Davis (April 25, 2018), Macron Critiques Trump's Policies in Speech to Congress, The New York Times.

[13] Angelique Chrisafis (June 26, 2018), Macron meets Pope Francis for twice as long as Trump, The Guardian.

[14] Gauthier Vaillant (November 24, 2021), Emmanuel Macron et les catholiques, mains tendues et illusions perdues, La Croix.

[15] Angelique Chrisafis (June 26, 2018), Macron meets Pope Francis for twice as long as Trump, The Guardian. Ouest-France (June 26, 2018), Macron, le Pape, les Bretons et la mafia : Jean-Yves Le Drian raconte, Ouest-France; Megan McCluskey (June 26, 2018), The Pope and Emmanuel Macron Hug it Out in Photo After Remarkably Long Meeting, Time Magazine.

[16] Ouest-France (June 26, 2018), Macron, le Pape, les Bretons et la mafia : Jean-Yves Le Drian raconte, Ouest-France.

[17] Ouest-France (June 27, 2018), " Mafia " bretonne au Vatican : quand Jean-Yves Le Drian retrouve un ami d'enfance, Ouest-France.

[18] Challenges (Dec. 21, 2018), Macron renoue avec les francs-maçons et leur "pacte Girondin," Challenges.

[19] François Koch (January 15, 2019), Castaner dîne avec les Francs-Maçons, La Lumière.

[20] Nicolas Senèze (April 19, 2019), Jean-Yves Le Drian en visite au Vatican pour Pâques, La Croix; Vatican News (April 20, 2019), Jean-Yves Le Drian a rencontré le cardinal Pietro Parolin, Vatican News.

On COVID-19, Emmanuel Macron, who wants to figure as a leader in the international fight against it, held a conversation with Pope Francis on April 21, 2020; receiving his support for several of his initiatives.[21]

Subsequently, as foreign minister, Le Drian visited the Vatican in June, where he had a long meeting with Cardinal Secretary of State Pietro Parolin, as well as with the Secretary for Relations with States, Bishop Paul R. Gallagher. The talks were on Africa and the Middle East, as well as the post-COVID-19 world. On that subject, France and the Vatican "share the same concern for reconstruction based on multilateralism and solidarity." Le Drian reiterated the invitation made to the Vatican to participate in the third edition of the Peace Forum in November of that year on the construction of "a better world after the pandemic." All three agreed that the future vaccine against COVID-19 is a "common good of humanity." They also spoke of the importance of Europe's role in its recovery.[22]

Le Drian visited the Vatican again in early December to speak again with Parolin and Gallagher; discussing the Lebanese crisis and climate change. But he also reiterated that he was expecting the pope in France.[23]

Separately, both Pope Francis and Macron visited Iraq in March and August 2021, respectively, to bring hope, promote interreligious dialogue, and inspire the country's future.[24]

Macron visited the Pope again on November 26, 2021, where they spoke at length about climate change, the situation in Lebanon, the Middle East, Africa, COVID-19 and vaccines; and his upcoming presidency of the Council of the European Union. It should be noted that Le Drian was present in the French delegation.[25]

Another third visit took place on October 24, 2022, where they focused at length on the war in Ukraine and what actions would be best to end it; the Caucasus region, the Middle East, and Africa.[26]

It is no coincidence that Lebanon and Africa are the subjects of conversation between the Pope (a Freemason) and Macron and between Le Drian (a Freemason) and Pietro Parolin and Paul Gallagher. Le Drian has woven a very large network of influence, especially in Africa and the Middle East. Le Drian has a great familiarity with presidents from the African continent. He was particularly close to the late Idriss Déby Itno, who was president of Chad and a Freemason initiated into the Grand Orient of France in 1982. There are also Ali Bongo Ondimba, Denis Sassou Nguesso (DSN), Faustin Archange-Touadéra, Faure Essozimna Gnassingbé, or even Alpha Condé, all close to Le Drian and Freemasons. Others close to him are the Senegalese Macky Sall,

[21] Gauthier Vaillant (April 21, 2020), Coronavirus: Emmanuel Macron reçoit le soutien du pape dans ses initiatives internationales, La Croix.

[22] Nicolas Senèze (June 4, 2020), Jean-Yves Le Drian au Vatican : Covid-19, Afrique et Moyen-Orient au programme, La Croix.

[23] Cath-Info (Dec. 7, 2020), Jean-Yves Le Drian invite le pape François en France, Cath-Info.

[24] Thomas Reese (March 11, 2021), Pope Francis' pilgrimage to Iraq improves relations with Muslims; National Catholic Reporter; Courtney Mares (Aug. 31, 2021), French president visits Catholic church in Iraq damaged by ISIS; Catholic News Agency.

[25] Philip Pullella (Nov. 26, 2021), Pope tells Macron 'I'm still alive' during Vatican talks, Reuters.

[26] Loup Besmond de Senneville (October 25, 2022), Pope Francis and Emmanuel Macron compare visions of peace, La Croix.

the Ivorian Alassane Ouattara, the Congolese Denis Sassou Nguesso, and the Rwandan Paul Kagame.[27]

Similarly, on May 20, 2019, Loyola University of Congo, which belongs to the Jesuits, and Icam, signed in the presence of Le Drian an agreement providing for the creation of the Faculty of Engineering ULC-Icam. [28]

On Lebanon, in May 2021, Le Drian, together with a delegation, visited the Saint-Joseph University (USJ) of Beyrouth, to explore the rich heritage of the Oriental Library and check the progress of the rehabilitation works. The Rector and Vice-Chancellor briefed the delegation on the USJ and the Jesuit Quarter, including Saint Joseph's Church and the former cloister. Christian Taoutel, Director of the Department of History and International Relations, spoke about the Jesuit archives and their great contribution to writing on the history of Lebanon and the Middle East.[29]

It is worth noting that Pope Francis has visited, as of this writing, ten African countries.[30]

Le Drian is Breton, and historically according to the Freemasons themselves, a very large number of Masons who would be outstanding of the beginnings of Freemasonry in Brittany, if not all, passed through the Jesuit colleges of Quimper, then Brest. The influence of the Jesuits, it is said, would be only pedagogical;[31] as well as of mutual respect. Indeed, in 2017, the new provincial of the Jesuits in France, François Boëdec, is Breton.[32]

All these actions because, despite the insistence of many Masons such as those of the Grand Orient of France and other French Masonic obediences to take care of their relations with the Catholic Church, the exponential change that many Masons experienced due to the influence of Charles Riandey; the Mason who as we saw in Chapter 2 conspired with the Jesuits and French Catholicism in general to create a state Freemasonry, totalitarian and infiltrating the ideals of the rest of the Masons who were not legal in 1943: "It is enough to see today how many brothers and sisters are sympathizers of the extreme right and/or of an uninhibited right wing in our columns. The story of Charles Riandey should force us to be humble and vigilant concerning our values and above all, when looking at the dark side of the history of Freemasonry."[33]

In 2020, French Catholic Freemasons contacted the Vatican and even French Jesuits who support freemasonry:

"In 2020, the French lodges again approached the Vatican with a dossier full of testimonies from Catholic Freemasons underlining the compatibility of the two approaches: "I see my commitment to Freemasonry as an active complement and as a

---

[27] Jeune Afrique (July 4, 2021), Famille, chefs d'État, francs-maçons... Le Drian's very VIP network, from Paris to Abidjan, Jeune Afrique.

[28] EOF (June 20, 2019), L'Icam ouvre son 10ème campus à Kinshasa, Jésuites d'Europe Occidentale Francophone.

[29] USJ (May 6, 2021), H.E. Mr. Jean-Yves Le Drian at the Oriental Library, Université Saint-Joseph de Beyrouth.

[30] AFP (Jan. 26, 2023), Pope Francis' previous visits to Africa; Associated Press; Armani Syed (Feb. 3, 2023), The World Has Forgotten About the Conflict in South Sudan. Enter Pope Francis, Time Magazine.

[31] Jean François (January 19, 2017), JÉSUITES ET FRANCS-MAÇONS EN BRETAGNE ! LA RÉACTION, la Franc Maçonnerie au Coeur.

[32] Ouest-France (July 31, 2017), Le nouveau provincial des Jésuites est breton, Ouest-France.

[33] La Maçonne (October 20, 2016), Charles Riandey, antisémite ?, Overblog: https://lamaconne.over-blog.com/2016/10/charles-riandey-antisemite.html Accessed on February 4, 2024

way of putting my Catholic faith into practice. It was this complementarity that involved my partner in parish life, as my wife was a Mason." The Congregation for the Doctrine of the Faith refuses to reconsider.

[…]

The Jesuit Etienne Perrot, who takes a close interest in the question, considers however that today "a condemnation in principle is no longer appropriate, given the diversity of commitments and interpretations of Masonic symbols and rites." The Church looks at Freemasonry as if it were looking in a mirror: "It asks the Great Architect of the Universe [to whom Masons refer] to assume all the theological qualities of the Christian personal God as if a Catholic Mason could not invest it with a personal religious experience."

"In this sense, as a witness quoted in the report sent to Rome affirms, "Freemasonry in no way substitutes for ecclesial life, nor for the action of the sacraments, but can constitute a preparation of the whole being for the actualization in oneself of the Word, and of the interior communion with the Divine Word, which the sacraments will bring about"."[34]

The article continues:

"The Conference of Bishops of France has delegated Bishop Jean-Charles Descubes and Bishop Michel Dubost to meet between 2017 and 2020 with representatives of the regular French lodges (French National Grand Lodge; Traditional Grand Lodge and Symbolic Opera; Traditional and Modern Grand Lodge of France) to support their rapprochement with Rome and with the aim of accounting for the diversity of approaches referring to a personal God, compatible with the Christian faith."[35]

On November 8, 2023, Macron visited the Freemasons at the headquarters of the Grand Orient de France, to "demonstrate the Republic's recognition of the Grand Orient de France and what it represents in the history of our country," the Elysée stressed.[36] The *Le Point* article notes:

"For Emmanuel Macron, who deals with his relations with religious representatives, it is about strengthening ties with a family of thought that remains influential in the circles of power and of which he had deeply offended many of its members by promising to "repair the link" between the Catholic Church and the Republic, in his speech to the Christian community at the Collège des Bernardins in 2018. Many have not forgotten it."[37]

[34] Eclairages romands (June 1, 2021), Ces catholiques francs-maçons qui interpellent, L'Essentiel.
[35] Ibid.
[36] Jérôme Cordelier (November 8, 2023), Emmanuel Macron : opération séduction chez les francs-maçons, Le Point.
[37] Ibíd.

Reports *Le Journal du Dimanche*: "Inspired by faith, built by reason, Emmanuel Macron moves along a nuanced path that remains undescribed. One foot in the Bernardins, the other in the Grand Orient."[38]

Such developments are very revealing.

---

[38] Antonin André (November 8, 2023), [André] Emmanuel Macron, le président croyant chez les francs-maçons, Le Journal du Dimanche.

CHAPTER
15

Donald Trump and the resurgence of Christian fascism - part 2

The new age of fascism

"America First" is the slogan assiduously used by Trump, and it calls to mind some of the anti-Semitic sentiments in World War II for the extreme of national socialism.[1]

On a visit to Europe to commemorate the 100th anniversary of the end of World War I in November 2018, Trump insisted to White House Chief of Staff John F. Kelly, "Well, Hitler did a lot of good things." That comment came in the wake of an impromptu history lesson in which Kelly reminded the president which countries were on which side during the conflict, connecting the dots from World War I through World War II and all of Hitler's atrocities. Although spokeswoman Liz Harrington said that episode is fictional, several sources reporting the incident said Kelly "told the president that he was wrong, but Trump was undeterred"; arguing for Germany's economic recovery under Hitler in the 1930s.[2]

Citing Bender, *The Guardian* indicated that Kelly pressed again, arguing that the German people would have been better off in poverty than under the Nazi genocide. He told Trump that if his claim of the German economy under the Nazis after 1933 were true, "you cannot ever say anything supportive of Adolf Hitler. You just can't."[3]

Trump later canceled a visit to the U.S. cemetery at Aisne-Marne near Paris because he feared getting mussed up in the rain and because he didn't think it was important to honor Americans killed during the war. In a conversation with senior officials the morning of the visit, Trump said, "Why should I go to that cemetery? It's filled with losers." Similarly, in a separate conversation during that same trip, in referring to the more than 1800 Marines who died at Belleau Wood, he treated them as morons for being killed.[4]

Again speaking to Kelly on another occasion, Trump indicated, "You --- generals, why can't you be like the German generals?" After Kelly asked for clarification from the president, he responded, "The German generals in World War II." Kelly asked Trump if he knew that those generals "tried to kill Hitler three times and almost pulled it off"; to which Trump, dismissing Kelly's historically accurate description, insisted, "No, no, no, they were totally loyal to him." Kelly confirmed the narrative, describing in his own words, Trump's "unwillingness to accept that the American generals should

---

[1] Brian Bennett (Jan. 20, 2017), 'America First,' a phrase with a loaded anti-Semitic and isolationist history, Los Angeles Times.
[2] Martin Pengelly (July 7, 2021), Trump told chief of staff Hitler 'did a lot of good things', book says, The Guardian.
[3] Ibid.
[4] Jeffrey Goldberg (Sept. 3, 2020), Trump: Americans Who Died in War Are 'Losers' and 'Suckers,' The Atlantic.

not be loyal to him as the German generals were to the leader of Germany. And, again, I very definitely pointed out that they tried to kill him [Hitler] a number of times."[5]

Timothy Snyder, the renowned Yale University history professor, said of Trump:

"Often the move is to say: you're making a comparison to Hitler. It's not a perfect comparison, and therefore, let's throw all of history out.

Whereas what I would say is, of course, the comparison is not perfect. No comparison is ever perfect. History doesn't repeat. But history is this huge resource of patterns. It's a huge resource of structures. It's a way of trying to get your bearings in a moment like the present one, where we're really sure what's going on."[6]

Michael Moore, the American filmmaker, rightly comments that Germany was one of the world's greatest liberal democracies. It was the first country to have universal health care for all citizens. They read more books than in any other nation, and it was not unusual for every city to have a dozen newspapers: a robust freedom of the press.

They produced many films. They were very advanced in art, culture, and science. They were considered the most intelligent people in the world.

However, in November 1932, the Germans chose an Austrian immigrant to be their leader, but he had no political experience and did not speak like a normal politician. He said things clearly, which appealed to many, many citizens. He told jokes as well as stories.

He talked about putting Germany first. And when German soccer players disrespected the national anthem, they were punished.

He said he wanted to create jobs for all. He built roads and infrastructure. He used radio and television news very effectively. In 1935, he started his first television network; and they knew how to use fake news. For example, when they claimed that in a camp for Jews, they had the opportunity to continue their jobs, to give a positive image that everything was fine with them.

Likewise, people flocked to Hitler to listen to him.

A Jewish weekly newspaper in Germany published a front-page editorial advising that everyone should be calm: "Now that the Nazis are in power, we don't believe that Herr Hitler and his friends will do all the things that they promised. They won't suddenly take away the constitutional rights of German Jews. They won't lock us up in race ghettos, or unleash the murderous mobs on us. They can't do these things, because the constitution won't let them." In the United States, *The New York Times* held the same view in a January 31, 1933 article. They assured the American people that things would not be that bad. Because the German centrist party was helping to maintain the balance in the German parliament.

They even wrote articles claiming that "Hitler's anti-Semitism was not so genuine or violent as it sounded, and that he was merely using anti-Semitic propaganda as bait to catch masses of followers."

---

[5] Zoë Richards and Peter Nicholas (Aug. 8/9, 2022), Trump once complained that his generals weren't like Hitler's, book says, NBC News.

[6] Basel Hamdan, Tia Lessin (Producer) Michael Moore (Director). (2018), Fahrenheit 11/9. (State Run Films, Midwestern Films, LLC). Note: unless otherwise noted, this is the same source.

Ruth Ben-Ghiat, professor of history at New York University:

"When you track how people first reacted to Hitler and Mussolini, they said, oh, he's just insane. Or the classic thing is that the elite party, in this case the GOP: We're going to invite him into power [Trump], and then we're going to control him.

Over and over in history, what has happened is that these people get invited in, they legitimized. And then they take over the show."

Some examples. Come January 20, 2021, Trump prepared the papers for the 2020 re-election. He began holding rallies in several states, with his famous "Make America Great Again" campaign. But he spoke of the possibility of extending his presidency to more than eight years, or even 16. He expressed his admiration for Xi Jinping because he would be president for life in China, and that perhaps one day they would make such an attempt in the United States.

He congratulated Turkish President Erdogan on the referendum that granted him sweeping new powers.

He constantly ordered reporters uncomfortable for him to sit down or he told them to shut up. He cryptically joked about assassinating the press for promoting what he called *fake news*:

"The most dishonest groups of people I have ever met."

"But I would never kill them. I hate them. I would never kill them. I would never do that. Uh... Let's see. No. No, I wouldn't.

Wait, let's see, who... I want to find a friendly journalist.

Ben-Ghiat says of these statements, "These are what I call trial balloons. You throw out an idea that previously was unthinkable. Unthinkable in democracy, or unthinkable for human rights reasons. They float these ideas, they get them out there, and then the press does its job for him. Picks them up, amplifies them, circulates. And then it the thing. And it becomes part of the discourse.

And there's Trump was doing that with his rallies and his loyalty oaths."

On the corruption cases brought against him, it is curious that Trump criticized the fact that the United States still has a judge-based system. Ben-Ghiat points out that: "He knows what he's doing. It's the same thing that authoritarians and fascists have done in the past. You need to make sure that when charges of corruption or other wrongdoing come forth, nobody believes the judiciary. Intelligence services. The press."

"People don't care if he's lying. They believe in him, and that's more important than believing in the truth."

Trump declared from the Capitol steps, "From this day forward, a new vision will govern our land. From this day forward, it's going to be only America First. America First."[7] That message had galvanized a mass populist movement against U.S. involvement in the second European war, even as the German army swept through France and Belgium in 1940. A broad coalition of politicians and business leaders on

---

[7] Brian Bennett (Jan. 20, 2017), 'America First,' a phrase with a loaded anti-Semitic and isolationist history, Los Angeles Times. Note: unless otherwise noted, this is the same source.

the right and left joined the America First Committee, which grew to more than 800,000 members in opposition to President Franklin D. Roosevelt's support for France and Britain. But the committee was marred by anti-Semitic and pro-fascist rhetoric, as documented in the words of its principal leader, Charles Lindbergh.

"The "greatest danger" Jews posed to the U.S. "lies in their great ownership and influence in our motion pictures, our press, our radio, and our government," Lindbergh said."

Although Trump has spoken out against such pronouncements, the truth is that the parallels are striking. Brian Bennett documents Trump's words:

"Every decision on trade, on taxes, on immigration, on foreign affairs, will be made to benefit American workers and American families," Trump said in Friday's inaugural speech.

"We must protect our borders from the ravages of other countries making our products, stealing our companies, and destroying our jobs," he said."

Susan Dunn, a humanities professor at Williams College, points out that Lindbergh and other prominent members of America First believed that democracy was in decline and that fascism represented a new future. And indeed, Trump was gradually becoming more authoritarian in his presidency.[8]

He has a history of racism - although Ben Carson was in his administration - and discrimination against the disabled for more than four decades, which is well documented.[9]

Although he says he is not an isolationist, his dictatorial principles, which, Michael Anton, a member of Trump's security staff went so far as to externalize to justify it, cannot be overlooked.[10]

Jason Stanley, a renowned professor of philosophy at Yale, comments:

"Often, those who employ fascist tactics do so cynically – they do not really believe the enemies they target are so malign, or so powerful, as their rhetoric suggests. Nevertheless, there comes a tipping point, where rhetoric becomes policy. Donald Trump and the party that is now in thrall to him have long been exploiting fascist propaganda. They are now inscribing it into fascist policy."[11]

---

[8] Jeet Heer (January 23, 2017), Donald Trump Is Becoming an Authoritarian Leader Before Our Very Eyes, The New Republic; Andrew Gawthorpe (July 23, 2020), Trump is unleashing authoritarianism on US cities - just in time for the election, The Guardian.

[9] Adrienne Green, Cullen Murphy, Parker Richards (June 2019), An Oral History of Trump's Bigotry, The Atlantic.

[10] Publius Decius Mus (September 5, 2016), The Flight 93 Election, American Greatness; Jonathan Chait (February 2, 2017), America's Leading Authoritarian Intellectual Is Working for Trump, The New York Magazine; Michael Anton, After the Flight 93 Election: The Vote that Saved America and What We Still Have to Lose (Encounter Books, New York, 2019).

[11] Jason Stanley (December 22, 2021), America is now in fascism's legal phase, The Guardian. Note: unless otherwise noted, this is the same source.

Stanley continues:

"Despite its radical start, the Nazi party dramatically increased its popularity over many years in part by strategically masking its explicit antisemitic agenda to attract moderate voters, who could convince themselves that the racism at the core of Nazi ideology was something the party had outgrown. It represented itself as the antidote to communism, using a history of political violence in the Weimar Republic, including street clashes between communists and the far right, to warn of a threat of violent communist revolution. It attracted support from business elites by promising to smash labor unions. The Nazis portrayed socialists, Marxists, liberals, labor unions, the cultural world and the media as representatives of, or sympathizers with, this revolution. Once in power, they bore down on this message.
[...]
"The Nazis recognized that the language of family, faith, morality and homeland could be used to justify especially brutal violence against an enemy represented as being opposed to all these things. The central message of Nazi politics was to demonize a set of constructed enemies, an unholy alliance of communists and Jews, and ultimately to justify their criminalization."

Timothy Snyder stresses that "for violence to transform not just the atmosphere but also the system, the emotions of rallies and the ideology of exclusion have to be incorporated into the training of armed guards."

The viability of an extreme right-wing party in a democracy depends on offering an image that is defended as "moderate," sharing an ambiguous relationship with the extreme thinking and statements of its most explicit members.

Rachel Kleinfeld tells us that the legitimization of violence in the United States is seen when right-wing communities that approve of it believe that white "Christian" men are under cultural and demographic threat, and need to be defended. Donald Trump safeguards their way of life, which is threatened by the elimination of their national identity through "gender, racial and religious equality turning to a leader who promises a violent response."

Most alarming, Stanley comments, is that the United States was at the legal stage of fascism, as the International Center for Not for Profit Law, 45 states have considered 230 bills to criminalize protest, with the threat of violent rebellion by the left and blacks as justification.

"That this is happening at the same time that multiple electoral bills enabling a Republican state legislature majority to overturn their state's election have been enacted suggests that the true aim of bills criminalizing protest is to have a response in place to expected protests against the stealing of a future election (as a reminder of fascism's historical connection to big business, some of these laws criminalize protest near gas and oil lines)."

Donald Trump has emboldened different kinds of extreme right-wingers in the country with a deep nationalist ideal in wanting to close the borders, mistreating through foul language Latinos, Muslims, the left, socialists, and communists. He refuses to condemn in an evident and unambiguous manner the crimes and marches of neo-Nazi groups and the radical preaching of various evangelical preachers who are putting the United States on high ground, wanting to impose religion through the State.

Trump's countless inflammatory political rallies have ignited emotions and the more radical right on different fronts, through hateful language, contempt, and through the slogan, "America First."

The Washington Post documented:

"From the inauguration to his National Prayer Breakfast address to his provocative tweets, the president seems to speak just to his supporters. He regularly wields the language of violence and destruction against those who oppose his actions."[12]

Timothy Snyder of Yale University and Michael Moore:

"Michael Moore: Susan Sontag, she said, "We're just one 9/11 away from losing our democracy."

"Timothy Snyder: Yeah, I mean, I may be a bit more pessimistic.
I think we're zero 9/11s away. We have to think. We have to reflect. We have to think, "These are the kinds of things which happen in history."
Let's not trade the real freedom for fake safety. When there's a terrorist attack, the thing we have to mobilize for is not safety, but freedom."[13]

A Catholic-evangelical far-right under Trump
Johnnie Moore and Paula White, two members of Trump's evangelical advisory board, helped shape an executive order from the president establishing the White House Faith and Opportunity Initiative.

"There is a long list of progress we have made with this administration because we took our seat at the table," Moore told RNS. "We've provided consequential feedback on policy and personnel decisions particularly affecting religious liberty, judges, the right to life and foreign policy. We are also actively at work on issues like criminal justice reform, and when we've disagreed, we've had every opportunity to express our point of view."[14]

Moore mentioned on C-SPAN that the board "pays regular visits to the White House, which can start with policy briefings from West Wing staff and agency officials and end with impromptu visits to the Oval Office." He noted that the advisory board has a "pretty significant" influence in "directing or affecting" administration policy.

Trump said during a dinner at the White House on Aug. 27 of the same year to Religious Right leaders, including members of the Evangelical Advisory Board:

---

[12] David Beaver and Jason Stanley (Feb. 7, 2017), Unlike all previous U.S. presidents, Trump almost never mentions democratic ideals, The Washington Post.
[13] Basel Hamdan, Tia Lessin (Producer) Michael Moore (Director). (2018), Fahrenheit 11/9. (State Run Films, Midwestern Films, LLC).
[14] Rob Boston (October, 2018), All The Presidents' Men And Women: Members Of President Trump's Evangelical Advisory Board Are Hard At Work Changing Public Policy - But They'd Rather You Not Know About It, Church & State. Note: unless otherwise noted, this is the same source.

"America is a nation of believers" [...] "And tonight we're joined by faith leaders from across the country who believe in the dignity of life, the glory of God and the power of prayer. [...].

"We're here this evening to celebrate America's heritage of faith, family and freedom. As you know, in recent years, the government tried to undermine religious freedom. But the attacks on communities of faith are over. We've ended it. We've ended it. Unlike some before us, we are protecting your religious liberty."

Donald Trump expected advisory board members and others to provide support for his party in November and possibly break the law by defending candidates from the pulpit:

"This Nov. 6 election is very much a referendum on not only me, it's a referendum on your religion, it's a referendum on free speech and the First Amendment. It's a referendum on so much," Trump said.

"He added, "It's not a question of like or dislike, it's a question that they will overturn everything that we've done and they will do it quickly and violently. And violently. There is violence. When you look at Antifa, these are violent people.

"You have tremendous power," Trump continued. "You were saying, in this room, you have people who preach to almost 200 million people. Depending on which Sunday we're talking about. You have to hopefully get out and get people to support us. If you don't, that will be the beginning of ending everything that you've gotten. ... I just ask you to go out and make sure all of your people vote. Because if they don't... we're going to have a miserable two years and we're going to have, frankly, a very hard period of time. You're one election away from losing everything that you've gotten."

All over the world fascist-style movements are rising up under the banner of "Christ" to impose morality on world society as much as they can.[15]

Trump granted the Christian right veto and appointment power over key government positions, especially in the federal courts.[16]

He installed -at least until early 2020- 133 district court judges out of a total of 677; 50 appellate court judges out of a total of 179; and two Supreme Court justices. Almost all of the judges were selected by the Federalist Society and the Christian right.[17] Since Republicans know that the judiciary is one of the most effective governmental instruments of minority rule -There were already in November 2020, 220 federal judges, including 3 Supreme Court justices. Katherine Stewart tells us that it will be "one of his most devastating legacies" (of Trump), as "The prospect of further entrenching minority rule in the coming years will keep the alliance between Republicans and the religious right alive."[18]

---

[15] Rob Boston (May 1, 2019), They Want The Whole World In Their Hands: Through The World Congress Of Families, The Religious Right Is Building A Global Network, Church & State Magazine.

[16] Chris Hedges (Jan. 3, 2020), Onward, Christian fascists, Salon.

[17] Ibid.

[18] Katherine Stewart (Nov. 16, 2020), Trump or No Trump, Religious Authoritarianism Is Here to Stay, The New York Times.

Supreme Court supports a growing conservative religious agenda in the United States. They "appear eager to take on a subject at the heart of the country's culture wars."[19] Six of the nine Supreme Court justices are conservative Catholics: Chief Justice John Roberts and Justices Clarence Thomas, Samuel Alito, Amy Coney Barrett, Sonia Sotomayor, and Brett Kavanaugh.[20] Several of the justices have been involved in financial scandals.[21] *The Globalist* magazine stated in its article: "The U.S. Supreme Court: Now a Roman Catholic Institution?"

"Conservative Supreme Court Justices are making unaccountable and undemocratic decisions, much like the Vatican Congregation of the Doctrine of the Faith."[22]

Although the author, Terri Langstone, says it is not seriously argued that judges obey the Vatican, she points out:

"While the general teachings of the Church often are admirably Christian in essence, the Catholic Church certainly does not shy away from offering firm positions on temporal, earthly matters of governance and behavior as well.
[...]
"Despite ever stronger murmurs at the grass roots, there is no effective form of democratic input, nor is there a real opportunity for appeal of its decisions.
[...]
"The contemporary Republican Party resembles the male-dominated and elite-driven structure of the Roman Catholic Church.

"The party eschews participatory democracy and does not trust participation by common people in any significant manner."[23]

The author says that the basic reason for Republicans not wanting to rely more on Protestant judges lies in the structure of Protestantism, which, in contrast to Roman Catholicism, has much more democratic governing bodies. Being a bottom-up approach, something that indirectly influenced the structure of American political governing bodies.[24]

---

[19] Linda Greenhouse (September 12, 2019), Religious Crusaders at the Supreme Court's Gates, The New York Times.
[20] Alyssa Murphy (Oct. 28, 2020), 6 of the 9 Supreme Court Justices are Catholic - Here's a Closer Look, National Catholic Register.
[21] Joshua Kaplan, Justin Elliott and Alex Mierjeski (April 6, 2023), Clarence Thomas and the Billionaire, Pro Publica; Justin Elliott, Joshua Kaplan, Alex Mierjeski (June 20, 2023); Justice Samuel Alito Took Luxury Fishing Vacation With GOP Billionaire Who Later Had Cases Before the Court, Pro Publica; Jesse Eisinger and Stephen Engelberg (June 25, 2023), Behind the Scenes of Justice Alito's Unprecedented Wall Street Journal Pre-buttal, Pro Publica; Giulia Carbonaro (June 23, 2023), Amy Coney Barrett Faces Scrutiny Over Real Estate Deal With Religious Group, Newsweek; Heidi Przybyla (April 25, 2023), Law firm head bought Gorsuch-owned property, Politico; Paul Waldman (June 22, 2023), Welcome to the Supreme Court, where corruption has no meaning, The Washington Post; Jennifer Rubin (June 25, 2023), Sheldon Whitehouse was right all along: The Supreme Court is corrupt, The Washington Post.
[22] Terri Langston (May 6, 2021), The U.S. Supreme Court: Now a Roman Catholic Institution?," The Globalist.
[23] Ibid.
[24] Ibid.

An article by *Salon* entitled "The Supreme Court's right-wing Catholics are destroying true religious freedom," says of the separation of church and state, "this bold pillar of American democracy is rotting fast. It is under attack by theocrats, especially those who sit on our Supreme Court."[25]

The court, in fact, approved the constitutionality of a 40-feet-tall Latin cross on public land in Bladensburg, Maryland, as well as the funneling of public money to religious schools, thus forcing taxpayers to fund them.[26]

The Supreme Court in 2021 allowed a Catholic social services agency in Philadelphia to refuse to work with same-sex couples. But it also sided with those who sought to lift the virus restrictions on religious services.[27]

It reversed Roe v. Wade, ending abortion rights in the United States, and leaving it up to the states to decide. But the story of how it took place, considering that most of the Supreme is Catholic, happened months earlier. During the U.S. Conference of Catholic Bishops on June 18, 2021, 168 bishops voted for, 55 against, and 6 abstentions, on the approval of a document giving the green light to deny the Eucharist to public officials who favored abortion, euthanasia, and homosexual couples. Joe Biden holding the most visible public office.[28]

Pope Francis intervened directly to prevent a political and diplomatic conflict. He privately blamed the U.S. bishops who even hinted that they were going to excommunicate Biden.[29]

In September, Francis said publicly that it was a political and not a pastoral problem and, that "although "abortion is murder..., communion is not a prize for the perfect, communion is a gift, it is a gift."[30]

On May 3, 2022, *Politico* obtained an initial leaked draft of the Supreme Court's majority opinion, which suggested reversing Roe v. Wade; which Supreme Court Justice John Roberts confirmed.[31]

Biden and Democratic leader and House Speaker Nancy Pelosi were denied communion in some of the nation's parishes.[32]

Pelosi visited the Vatican in June 2022, and at a Mass presided over by the pope, she received communion without any problems.[33]

The document, approved by a majority of the bishops, was an exhortation to increase the attacks against abortion clinics, doctors, and health personnel. Strong pressure from some of the most conservative sectors, with the support of some bishops and cardinals who personally intervened appealing to the Christian conscience of some magistrates,

[25] Phil Zuckerman, Andrew L. Seidel (Sept. 14, 2021), The Supreme Court's right-wing Catholics are destroying true religious freedom, Salon.

[26] Linda Greenhouse (September 12, 2019), Religious Crusaders at the Supreme Court's Gates, The New York Times.

[27] Ian Prasad Philbrick (June 22, 2022), A Pro-Religion Court, The New York Times.

[28] Vicens Lozano, Vaticangate: El complot ultra contra el papa Francisco y la manipulación del próximo conclave (Roca Editorial, 2023), ob. cit.

[29] Ibid.

[30] Ibid.

[31] Josh Gerstein and Alexander Ward (May 2/3, 2022), Supreme Court has voted to overturn abortion rights, draft opinion shows, Politico.

[32] Vicens Lozano, Vaticangate: El complot ultra contra el papa Francisco y la manipulación del próximo conclave (Roca Editorial, 2023), ob. cit.

[33] Ibid.

made it possible to reverse Roe v. Wade[34] by a mostly Catholic court. It was left to each state to decide whether to uphold or prohibit abortion during pregnancy.

And that's because the Supreme Court began 2022 with its first full term with its new conservative majority (6-3) with a slate of decisions leaning decidedly to the right.[35] Reversing Roe v. Wade with Dobbs v. Jackson Women's Health Organization on June 24, was a landmark ruling in which Supreme Court Justice Clarence Thomas wanted to go further by urging the court to "reconsider all of this Court's substantive due process precedents." In response, Congress passed the Respect for Marriage Act to provide federal protections for same-sex marriage in a remarkable show of bipartisan support for LGBTQ rights.

Similarly, the Supreme Court sided with the public high school soccer coach who was suspended for praying after games. We already mentioned funding to religious schools.

The Court ruled unanimously in a Boston case that the city should allow a Christian flag to fly over City Hall while other flags of other groups are displayed.

They also overturned a New York law governing permits to carry guns.

Another very disturbing intervention was when in March they ruled to protect information about the CIA's black sites. We mentioned in one chapter that the black sites were clandestine torture sites as part of a covert clandestine campaign in the war on terror that had deep religious motivations in the style of a crusade against terrorism.

The court also restricted in June the ability of the US Environmental Protection Agency, or EPA, to control carbon emissions, claiming that the agency exceeded its authority.

By early 2023, the Court would hear the case of a Colorado website designer because she wanted to be respected for her right not to design same-sex marriage wedding websites.

Just in 2022, such a fruitful year for the Supreme Court's religious agenda, the public discovered that the Republican party is being swept up in the push for a Christian government. Doug Mastriano (state senator, retired Army colonel), three weeks before winning the Republican nomination for governor of Pennsylvania, addressed a far-right conference that mixed Christian beliefs with conspiracy theories. There he spoke about what he saw as America's true Christian identity and that it was time for Christians, together, to take back political power. He added that the separation of church and state was a myth.[36]

Likewise, Colorado Republican Representative Lauren Boebert received a standing ovation at the Cornerstone Christian Center after urging, "The church is supposed to direct the government, the government is not supposed to direct the church [...] I'm tired of this separation of church and state junk." While this was going on, there was a wave of action across the country promoting the cultural priorities of many conservative Christians. Some candidates admired the series of Supreme Court decisions as a sign that their mission was succeeding.[37]

---

[34] Ibid.

[35] Al Jazeera staff (Dec. 30, 2022), Five ways the US Supreme Court reshaped policy in 2022, Aljazeera. Note: unless otherwise noted, this is the same source.

[36] Elizabeth Dias (July 8/13, 2022), The Far-Right Christian Quest for Power: 'We Are Seeing Them Emboldened', The New York Times.

[37] Ibid.

492

Also in mid-January of that year, the Supreme Court agreed to consider a religious discrimination case because a former Pennsylvania postal carrier said he was not allowed to have Sundays off because of his religious beliefs.[38] Gerald Groff's attorneys -the former postal carrier in the case-, when they heard that the Supreme Court would weigh his case, argued that the time had come for the Court to "boost protections for religious workers."[39] That is, Sunday rest would make way for the Supreme Court to rule that on religious grounds, all those who wish to respect Sunday rest following their beliefs should have it respected by law. In an opinion essay by Linda Greenhouse in *The New York Times* titled, "The Latest Crusade to Place Religion Over the Rest of Civil Society," she expressed her opinion on that case. She noted that the "Federal civil rights law requires employers to accommodate their employees' religious needs unless the request would impose "undue hardship on the conduct of the employer's business."[40] For that reason, Gross' request in the past was disregarded, but that would be about to change:

"That isn't an idle prediction but rather the surely foreordained outcome of the new case the justices recently added to their calendar for decision during the current term. The appeal was brought by a conservative Christian litigating group, First Liberty Institute, on behalf of a former postal worker, Gerald Groff, described as a Christian who regards Sunday as a day for "worship and rest."
[...]
"The decision to hear his appeal brings the Supreme Court to a juncture both predictable and remarkable. It is predictable because Justices Samuel Alito, Clarence Thomas and Neil Gorsuch have all called for a case that would provide a vehicle for overturning a precedent that is clearly in tension with the current court's privileging of religious claims above all others."[41]

Linda Greenhouse continues a few paragraphs later:

"It may be just a coincidence, but the plaintiff who finally persuaded the justices to take his case is in fact, according to the joint statement of facts agreed to by the parties, "an evangelical Christian within the Protestant tradition." When the court doubtless rules for him later this term, the decision will not stand for a vindication of minority rights. It will instead signify the court's complete identification with the movement in the country's politics to elevate religion over all other elements of civil society."[42]

Finally, on June 29, the Supreme Court unanimously decided in Groff's favor, allowing millions of Americans to request Sunday off by law, if it represents a matter

---

[38] Aljazeera (Jan. 13, 2023), US Supreme Court to consider religious discrimination case, Aljazeera.

[39] Kelsey Dallas (January 13, 2023), Can you be forced to work on the Sabbath? The Supreme Court will soon weigh in, Deseret News.

[40] Linda Greenhouse (January 30, 2023), The Latest Crusade to Place Religion Over the Rest of Civil Society, The New York Times.

[41] Ibid.

[42] Ibid.

of faith for them[43] or the most popular Sabbath of universal Christianity. However, the law did not approve of the employee not working on Sundays regardless of the conditions of the job, as the *Associated Press* reported:

"In a unanimous decision the justices made clear that workers who ask for accommodations, such as taking the Sabbath off, should have their requests honored unless employers show that doing so would result in "substantial increased costs" to the business.

"The court made clear that businesses must cite more than minor costs — known as "de minimis" costs — to reject requests for religious accommodations at work."[44]

Ian P. Philbrick wrote in *The New York Times*, "The Supreme Court has become the most pro-religion it's been since at least the 1950s, and it appears to include the six most pro-religion justices since at least World War II."[45]

Reuters noted, "The conservative-majority U.S. Supreme Court has chipped away at the wall separating church and state in a series of new rulings, eroding American legal traditions intended to prevent government officials from promoting any particular faith."[46]

The ACLU indicated in July 2022, that "the conservative majority on the Supreme Court made it abundantly clear that there's little room for the separation of church and state in its regressive constitutional framework."[47] It has also indicated:

"For nearly 75 years, the court has recognized that both of the First Amendment's religion clauses are vital to protecting religious freedom: The Establishment Clause protects against governmental endorsement and imposition of religion, and the Free Exercise Clause ensures the right to practice your faith without harming others. No more. The court has increasingly treated the Establishment Clause as a historical footnote, threatening both the independence of religion and the religious neutrality of the state."[48]

Clarence Thomas, one of the Supreme Court justices who always attends Mass before his work, said in a 2018 commencement address at Christendom College, "I am decidedly and unapologetically Catholic."[49] Another justice, Samuel Alito, gave a July 2022 speech "for Notre Dame Law School's Religious Liberty Initiative in Rome." He

---

[43] Jessica Gresko (June 29, 2023), Supreme Court solidifies protections for workers who ask for religious accommodations, Associated Press; Lawrence Hurley (June 29, 2023), Supreme Court rules for Christian mail carrier who refused to work Sundays, NBC News; Peter Pinedo (June 29, 2023), Supreme Court rules in favor of Christian postal worker in unanimous religious freedom decision, Catholic News Agency.

[44] Jessica Gresko (June 29, 2023), The Supreme Court bolsters protections for workers who ask for religious accommodations, Associated Press.

[45] Ian Prasad Philbrick (June 22, 2022), A Pro-Religion Court, The New York Times.

[46] Lawrence Hurley and Andrew Chung (June 28, 2022), U.S. Supreme Court takes aim at separation of church and state, Reuters.

[47] Heather L. Weaver, Daniel Mach (July 6, 2022), The Supreme Court Benches the Separation of Church and State, ACLU News & Commentary.

[48] Ibid.

[49] Phil Zuckerman, Andrew L. Seidel (Sept. 14, 2021), The Supreme Court's right-wing Catholics are destroying true religious freedom, Salon.

lamented the significant rejection of religion by Western society, which for him justifies a total "fight against secularism." In this context, he referred, for example, to the revocation of the right to abortion. In other words, secularism is being combated by employing religious laws.[50]

For her part, Supreme Court Justice Amy Coney Barrett wrote that Catholic judges should not take any action that conflicts with the dogma of the Catholic Church. Instead of defending their secular oath when such a conflict arises, Barrett recommended that judges "conform their own behavior to the [Catholic] Church's standard." She has stated that her "legal career is but a means to an end… and that end is building the Kingdom of God." Phil Zuckermann and Andrew L. Seidel aptly wrote: "Our judges certainly have a right to their personal religious faith. But when they impose that faith on all of us, the wall of separation between church and state is truly undermined."[51]

It is unusual that *America*, the U.S. Jesuit magazine, sees it as positive that most of the judges are Catholic,[52] considering that the Society of Jesus supports secularism and the separation of Church and State. A few months earlier, the magazine pointed out that the Supreme Court should not try to solve all the moral problems of the country, although it recognizes that they exist.[53] It seems inconceivable until we know what the Jesuits have been proposing since the end of the Great War.

In turn, *America* published an *Associated Press* article quoting Clarence Thomas, where he states that religion should not conflict with politics, and use it as a means.[54] But Thomas had already told American lawyer and conservative legal activist Leonard Leo that Catholicism was the hope for the construction of a country's society and that it should take precedence.[55]

Precedents to the U.S. Capitol Attack on January 6, 2021

The spring of 2020, marks a huge assault on American democracy by President Donald Trump, who launched a series of pre-emptive attacks on the integrity of the national voting system. His supporters listened to him very seriously.

On Sept. 26, more than a month before voters went to the polls, at a rally outside Harrisburg, Pennsylvania, and after talking about voter fraud, Trump hinted that Congress could determine the winner of the presidential race, something not faced since the 19th century.[56]

---

[50] Kimberly Wehle (Aug. 10, 2022), The Supreme Court Wants to End the Separation of Church and State, Politico.

[51] Phil Zuckerman, Andrew L. Seidel (Sept. 14, 2021), The Supreme Court's right-wing Catholics are destroying true religious freedom, Salon.

[52] Allyson Escobar (Oct. 27, 2020), Why do Catholics make up a majority of the Supreme Court, America Magazine.

[53] The Editors (July 13, 2020), Editorial: The Supreme Court can't solve all our moral disputes. It shouldn't try, America Magazine.

[54] Sarah Burnette - Associated Press (September 17, 2021), Justice Clarence Thomas on when the law conflicts with his Catholic faith: 'You do your job and you go cry alone', America Magazine.

[55] Danny Hakim and Jo Becker (February 22, 2022/September 1, 2022), The Long Crusade of Clarence and Ginni Thomas, The New York Times Magazine.

[56] Aaron C. Davis, Hannah Allam, Devlin Barrett, Josh Dawsey, Amy Gardner, Shane Harris, Rosalind S. Helderman, Paul Kane, Dan Lamothe, Carol D. Leonnig, Nick Miroff, Ellen Nakashima, Ashley Parker, Beth Reinhard, Philip Rucker, and Craig Timberg (Oct. 31, 2021), Red Flags, The Washington Post. Note: unless otherwise noted, this is the same source.

Faced with this threat, in early August, House Speaker Nancy Pelosi quietly instructed members of her leadership team to initiate contingency plans in the event of a tie or dispute in the electoral college.

But on November 3, the results clearly showed that Joe Biden won the election. As election night drew to a close, Trump held up a paper with vote tallies, and in the early hours of the next morning, in danger of losing, Trump stood before his supporters in the East Room and fallaciously claimed the election was rigged. A whole series of lies were told about the alleged electoral fraud, driven with the help of secret donors working behind the scenes with NGOs promoting the electoral conspiracy, as shown in a series of documents where it is revealed that Trump was wanted to win at any cost.[57]

It is worth recalling that when the Democratic National Convention came to a close in August 2020, Democratic Congresswoman Alexandria Ocasio-Cortez, said, "Let's keep it real," she said. "We need to win in November." The election is about "stopping fascism in the United States. That is what Donald Trump represents."[58] During an interview with *The New Yorker* in February 2022, she externalized the grave danger that in ten years America will lose democracy, as there is a "specific attack on the right to vote across the United States, particularly in areas where Republican power is threatened by changing electorates and demographics. You have white-nationalist, reactionary politics starting to grow into a critical mass. What we have is the continued sophisticated takeover of our democratic systems in order to turn them into undemocratic systems, all in order to overturn results that a party in power may not like."[59]

When Trump claimed without any basis that he had won the election, he had also been influenced by Rudy Giuliani's conspiracy theories in this regard.[60] It was discovered that there was a whole plot to show false evidence that voter fraud was committed in favor of Biden, in addition to the fact that no evidence of voter fraud was found, as observed in the multiple and documented existing sources.[61]

---

[57] Murtaza Hussain (August 7, 2021), Secret Donors to Nonprofit Pushing Trump's "Big Lie" Election Conspiracy Revealed, The Intercept; Jane Mayer (August 2, 2021), The Big Money Behind the Big Lie, The New Yorker; Danny Hakim and Alexandra Berzon (June 8, 2022), A Big Lie in a New Package, The New York Times.

[58] Federico Finchelstein, Pablo Piccato, Jason Stanley (Aug. 20, 2020), Alexandria Ocasio-Cortez Is Right to Warn of "Fascism in the United States," The New Republic.

[59] David Remnick (Feb. 14, 2022), Is Alexandria Ocasio-Cortez an Insider Now?," The New Yorker.

[60] Bob Woodward, Robert Costa, Danger (Roca Editorial de Libros, 2021), ob. cit.

[61] Tessa Berenson (Nov. 20, 2020), Donald Trump And His Lawyers Are Making Sweeping Allegations Of Voter Fraud In Public. In Court, They Say No Such Thing, Time Magazine.; Richard Salame (August 20, 2020), Trump Team Fails to Cite Mail-in Election Fraud Cases in Court, The Intercept; Jane Mayer (August 9, 2021), The Big Money Behind the Big Lie, The New Yorker; Murtaza Hussain (August 7, 2021),Revealed: Secret Donors to Hub of Election Fraud Conspiracies, The Intercept; Danny Hakim and Alexandra Berzon (May 29/June 8, 2022), A Big Lie in a New Package, The New York Times; Cassandra Jaramillo (June 8, 2022), She Helped Create the Big Lie. Records Suggest She Turned It Into a Big Grift..., Reveal News; Cassandra Jaramillo (June 8, 2022), 6 Takeaways From Our Investigation Into a Prominent Voter Fraud Nonprofit, Reveal News; Cassandra Jaramillo (July 21, 2022), Group Behind '2000 Mules' Has Deep Ties to Ken Paxton, Reveal News; Josh Dawsey (Feb. 11, 2023),Trump campaign paid researchers to prove 2020 fraud but kept findings secret, The Washington Post; Shawn Boburg and Jon Swaine (Feb. 15, 2021), A GOP donor gave $2.5 million for a voter fraud investigation. Now he wants his money back, The Washington Post; Aaron Blake (Dec. 9, 2021), A conservative group debunks Trump's voter-fraud claims (yet again), The Washinton Post.

On the evening of the same date, November 7 at the White House, Trump made it clear that he wanted to believe there was evidence of voter fraud in order to remain in power:

"He asked, what's the plan? What's our plan in each state? What are our options? [...]

-Well, it's going to be a little tough," said an outside political adviser to Trump, David Bossie. We have to do it the right way, methodically, and the work is hard. We can fight and win, but it's going to be tough. It's going to be an uphill battle.

Bossie, a feisty and hardened politician, had been Trump's deputy campaign manager in 2016.

- Is that so? -Don't you think we should fight?

-No, not that," said Bossie. You have to fight for every legal ballot. [...]

- How do we find the 10,000 votes we need in Arizona? How do we find the 12,000 we need in Georgia? -Trump asked, "What about the military votes - are they all counted?"[62]

On Nov. 9, and meeting with Mike Pompeo, Gen. Mark Milley recalled a statement Trump made to *Breitbart News* in March 2019, when he said, "I can tell you I have the support of the police, the support of the military, the support of the bikers for Trump. I have the tough people, but they don't play it tough until they go to a certain point, and then it would be very bad, very bad." It sounded like a threat to Milley, and the general thought of the military, the police, the FBI, the CIA, other intelligence agencies, and the ministries of power, because often all the agencies mentioned had been used by despots. Pompeo told Milley that things were taking a dangerous turn for the republic.

On November 10, Gina Haspel, then the CIA director, called Milley at 8:10 in the morning. She believed Trump wanted to fire her, and said, "Yesterday was appaling," she told Milley. "We are on the way to a rightwing coup. The whole thing is insanity. He is acting out like a six-year-old with a tantrum."

"We're going to be steady," Milley repeated his mantra. "Steady as a rock. We're going to keep our eye on the horizon. Keep alert to any risks, dangers. Keep the channels open."

Milley and Pompeo were working for a peaceful transfer of presidential power.

"Milley arranged to speak at a Veterans Day celebration at the Army Museum on November 11.

"We do not take an oath to a king, or a queen," Milley told the crowd, "to a tyrant or a dictator. We do not take an oath to an individual. No, we do not take an oath to a country, a tribe, or a religion. We take an oath to the Constitution." He added, "Each of us will protect and defend that document, regardless of personal price."

After his speech, Secretary of the Army Ryan McCarthy said, "You've got about five hours" until Trump finds out and fires you."

---

[62] Bob Woodward, Robert Costa, Peril (Simon & Schuster, New York, 2023), ob. cit. Note: unless otherwise indicated, this is the same source.

Likewise, Virginia (Ginni) Thomas, the wife of Justice Clarence Thomas (both extremely conservative Catholics), urged White House Chief of Staff Mark Meadows to make relentless efforts to overturn the 2020 election. She also said that President Trump should not cave.[63] Reported *The Washington Post*, Thomas wrote to Meadows, "Help this great president stand firm, Mark!.... You are the leader, with him, who is defending America's constitutional government on the precipice. Most know Biden and the left is attempting the greatest heist in our history."

Come Nov. 10, after the news agencies had Biden winning by state vote totals, Thomas texted Meadows: "Help This Great President stand firm, Mark!!!...You are the leader, with him, who is standing for America's constitutional governance at the precipice. The majority knows Biden and the Left are attempting the greatest Heist of our History." Woodward and Costa continue:

"When Meadows wrote to Thomas on Nov. 24, the White House chief of staff invoked God to describe the effort to overturn the election. "This is a fight of good versus evil," Meadows wrote. "Evil always looks like the victor until the King of Kings triumphs. Do not grow weary in well doing. The fight continues. I have staked my career on it. Well at least my time in DC on it."

"Thomas replied: "Thank you!! Needed that! This plus a conversation with my best friend just now… I will try to keep holding on. America is worth it!"[64]

There were many additional text messages between the two.[65]

The New York Times Magazine reported that at the White House, Ginni Thomas was often off-limits, with access to President Trump and passing notes to the president about his priorities.[66] Ginni Thomas definitely believed that the election results were rigged. We read about one group in particular:

"The call to action was titled "Election Results and Legal Battles: What Now?" Shared in the days after the 2020 presidential election, it urged the members of an influential if secretive right-wing group to contact legislators in three of the swing states that tipped the balance for Joe Biden — Arizona, Georgia and Pennsylvania. The aim was audacious: Keep President Donald J. Trump in power.

"The group, the Council for National Policy, brings together old-school Republican luminaries, Christian conservatives, Tea Party activists and MAGA operatives, with more than 400 members who include leaders of organizations like the Federalist Society, the National Rifle Association and the Family Research Council. Founded in 1981 as a counterweight to liberalism, the group was hailed by President Ronald Reagan as seeking the "return of righteousness, justice and truth" to America."

[63] Bob Woodward and Robert Costa (March 24, 2022), Virginia Thomas urged White House chief to pursue unrelenting efforts to overturn the 2020 election, texts show, The Washington Post.
[64] Ibid.
[65] Ibid.
[66] Danny Hakim and Jo Becker (February 22, 2022/September 1, 2022), The Long Crusade of Clarence and Ginni Thomas, The New York Times Magazine. Note: unless otherwise noted, this is the same source.

That council was also notable for one of its newest leaders; Virginia Thomas herself, who assumed a prominent role on that council during the Trump years and in 2019. She joined the nine-member board of C.N.P. Action (Council for National Policy), an arm of the council that distributed in November 2020 the "action steps" document, which called on members to pressure Republican lawmakers to challenge election results and nominate alternative lists of electors. Had it succeeded, the plan would almost certainly have reached the Supreme Court, where Ginni Thomas' husband, Clarence Thomas as we noted, is a justice. Trump himself was already calling for that to happen, hoping that the Supreme Court would see the alleged "millions of votes [that] were cast illegally in swing states alone." Ginni Thomas also founded a group called Groundswell with the support of Stephen K. Bannon, the hard-nosed nationalist and former Trump adviser who holds a weekly meeting of influential conservatives, many among those working directly on issues coming before the Court. The Thomases' work has often intersected, "with Trump's three appointments reshaping the Supreme Court, her husband finds himself at the center of a new conservative majority poised to shake the foundations of settled law."

The New York Times Magazine continues:

"Many of the rally organizers and those advising Trump had connections to the Thomases, but little has been known about what role, if any, Ginni Thomas played, beyond the fact that on the morning of the March to Save America, as the rally was called, she urged her Facebook followers to watch how the day unfolded. "LOVE MAGA people!!!!" she posted before the march turned violent. "GOD BLESS EACH OF YOU STANDING UP or PRAYING!"

Although Thomas apparently did not foresee the march turning violent, she was involved in organizing the January 6, 2021 rally, which would lead to the assault on the Capitol, which, as we shall see, had a Christian-nationalist, violent undertone. On that day, the results in favor of Biden for the presidency would be certified in Congress.

In the face of Trump's refusal to accept the results, his enraged supporters and self-styled militias prepared for a fight.[67] There would be a march on November 14 in Washington, where Stewart Rhodes, founder of Oath Keppers, an anti-government organization who had said in September that "civil war is here, right now," because of the violence rocking Portland (Oregon), said he was willing to engage in violent acts if Trump invoked the Insurrection Act.

"Extremists associated with the Three Percenters planned to join the Oath Keepers on Nov. 14. Nicholas Fuentes, leader of the white-nationalist "Groyper" movement, and who was present at the deadly Unite the Right rally in Charlottesville in 2017, called on his allies to join him in Washington."

---

[67] Aaron C. Davis, Hannah Allam, Devlin Barrett, Josh Dawsey, Amy Gardner, Shane Harris, Rosalind S. Helderman, Paul Kane, Dan Lamothe, Carol D. Leonnig, Nick Miroff, Ellen Nakashima, Ashley Parker, Beth Reinhard, Philip Rucker, and Craig Timberg (Oct. 31, 2021), Red Flags, The Washington Post. Note: unless otherwise noted, this is the same source.

On the same day, as the night progressed, extremists and groups of counter-demonstrators began to fight, prompting police to separate the two sides. Several people were injured, including policemen.

Trump was the driving force throughout, instilling in his supporters that the election was rigged and that he was the rightful winner. The U.S. leader had already leaned on election officials in Georgia and Arizona with a slew of tweets and personal phone calls, trying to overturn the election results. So he would then move on to the strategy on January 6.

Days passed, and in the face of Trump's allegations and his insistence on reviewing the results in Georgia, a top official in the Georgia Secretary of State's office, Brad Raffensperger (R-Ga.), was jaded. He stood before television cameras at a Dec. 1 press conference at the state Capitol, saying:

"It. Has. All. Gone. Too. Far."

"Mr. President, it looks like you likely lost the state of Georgia," Sterling continued, and then added: "Stop inspiring people to commit potential acts of violence. Someone is going to get hurt. Someone's going to get shot. Someone is going to get killed."

On December 12, many hundreds of Proud Boys and others went to Washington DC to protest.

Katrina Pearson, Trump's campaign advisor, told the protesters, "This isn't over, this is just beginning." Trump expressed his admiration for the demonstration, regardless of the ultra-right and threatening tendencies of the protesters.

Former national security adviser Michael Flynn [who says there should be one religion and the church should be united with the state], who was urging the president to declare martial law and redo the election, urged the crowd, "There are still avenues [...] The courts aren't going to decide who the next president of the United States is going to be. We the people decide."

Violence broke out again.

On Dec. 19 Trump tweeted to his supporters, "Big protest in D.C. on January 6th. Be there, will be wild!" Some replied in the affirmative at a pro-Trump forum, stating that this was as close to revolt as it would get, and others stated about carrying guns.

As Jan. 6 approached, Trump stepped up his calls for action and pressure on Vice President Mike Pence, who was to preside over the joint session to certify the votes for Biden. The U.S. leader had a group of lawyers who argued that Pence could turn away electors from several states and overturn Biden's election. But that maneuver was unconstitutional. At a Jan. 4 rally in Georgia, Trump said he hoped Pence would support him; if not, he wouldn't like him very much. At these words, his supporters already knew who to target.

Going back to December, on the 20th, an informant called the FBI to warn that Trump supporters were discussing online how to sneak guns into Washington to attack police and arrest members of Congress the following month when the electoral college vote would be formalized. The informant also told the FBI that those planning the violence believed they had "orders from the President" Trump.

A few days later, Christian nationalists collaborated with Trump ahead of the January 6, 2021, Capitol attacks.[68] A fast-growing network of charismatic Christians called the New Apostolic Reformation (NAR), with "charismatic prophets," operated as Donald Trump's propagandists on alleged voter fraud. Figures within the White House were strategizing with NAR Christian leaders. They do not believe in the separation of church and state. It should be noted, that they "served as key mobilizers and participants in the events surrounding January 6." Indeed, as Matthew D. Taylor and Bradley Onishi tell us, "the events around the Capitol that day were the culmination of a months-long spiritual warfare campaign waged by charismatic Christians to see Trump reinstated for another term."

People working in the administration had suggested and instigated a "prophetic" tour in November 2020 on behalf of the president. Similarly, on December 29, as we have already indicated, Dutch Sheets, director of the NAR, and his team of "prophets," were staying at the Willard Hotel in Washington DC. A place that was the site of several "war rooms" supervised by Rudy Giuliani and Stephen Bannon. They had that same day a several-hour meeting inside the White House with Trump administration officials.

By those days, Donell Harvin, the head of intelligence for DC's office of homeland security, was growing more desperate by the month; as he and his team detected increasing signs that the president's supporters were planning violence when Congress convened to formalize the electoral college vote.[69] However, federal law enforcement did not seem to share their urgency. So on Saturday, January 2, 2021, he picked up the phone and called his counterpart in San Francisco, Mike Sena, before dawn. Sena listened in alarm. The office he commanded in Northern California was also inundated with political threats flagged by social media companies, some of which involved plans to disrupt the joint session or even hurt lawmakers on Jan. 6.

He organized a call for all regional homeland security offices (fusion centers), to find out what they were seeing. Sena expected a couple of dozen people to get on the line on Monday, but something similar had happened since September 11, 2001: the number of callers reached a hundred, then two hundred, then almost three hundred; with officials from almost all 80 regions, from New York to Guam. For the first time and from coast to coast, the centers were flashing red; the time, date, and place of concern being the same: 13:00 hours, U.S. Capitol, January 6.

After Harvin asked his counterparts to share what they saw, a flood of new warnings came in just minutes. Self-styled militias and additional extremist groups in the Northeast were circulating radio frequencies for use near the Capitol. Likewise, in the Midwest, violent men with criminal records were discussing traveling to Washington with guns.

So, 48 hours before the attack, Harvin did what he could: he invited the Federal Bureau of Investigation, the Department of Homeland Security, military intelligence, and other agencies to see real-time information as his team gathered it. He also asked

---

[68] Matthew D. Taylor and Bradley Onishi (Jan. 6, 2023), Evidence Strongly Suggests Trump Was Collaborating with Christian Nationalist Leaders Before January 6th, Religion Dispatches. Note: unless otherwise noted, this is the same source.

[69] Aaron C. Davis, Hannah Allam, Devlin Barrett, Josh Dawsey, Amy Gardner, Shane Harris, Rosalind S. Helderman, Paul Kane, Dan Lamothe, Carol D. Leonnig, Nick Miroff, Ellen Nakashima, Ashley Parker, Beth Reinhard, Philip Rucker, and Craig Timberg (Oct. 31, 2021), Red Flags, The Washington Post. Note: unless otherwise noted, this is the same source.

the city's health department to summon DC-area hospitals, urging them to prepare for a mass casualty event.

"Alerts were raised by local officials, FBI informants, social media companies, former national security officials, researchers, lawmakers and tipsters."

Pentagon leaders had considerable fear of widespread violence, and some feared that Trump would abuse the National Guard to remain in power.

Meanwhile, on Jan. 4, Gen. Mark A. Milley, chairman of the Joint Chiefs of Staff, suggested shutting down the city and revoking protest permits; and Christopher C. Miller, the acting secretary of defense, feared a bloody "Boston Massacre"-type altercation that far-right groups might exploit to claim they were being attacked by government terrorists.

Milley was frustrated by the lack of seriousness of the justice officials in the face of very little action on what might happen, as they did not think it would be that serious. He questioned why protesters would be allowed into the Capitol given the threats against Pelosi and McConnell, noting that extremists boasted on social media that they planned to come armed and attack lawmakers.

On the same day, Trump met with Mike Pence and John Eastman - then a professor and former dean of Chapman University Law School - in the Oval Office. Eastman "had written that Pence could exercise unprecedented powers over the certification process"; arguing that he could set aside electoral college votes and name Trump as the next president.

He noted that for lawmakers to further evaluate claims of fraud, Pence could delay the recount, which would nullify Biden's electoral advantage and allow Trump to win. Now, added to this, it is extremely troubling that Eastman, a right-wing Christian, makes an over-evaluation, a revisionism of the Establishment Clause (Separation of Church and State), where he pretends that there is no contradiction between the establishment of religious laws to protect believers and even Christian duties on those who do not believe and what the Clause dictates: for example, the obligation of every sect or religion to observe the Sabbath or Lord's Day, as happened with Vermont upon its admission as a new state in 1786.[70] In fact, according to Eastman, even as late as 2017, he indicated that the Establishment Clause should not prohibit state and local governments from establishing, literally, official state religions.[71] Eastman belongs to the powerful Federalist Society and is a devout ultra-conservative Catholic.[72]

The next day (January 5), Trump supporters gathered in Freedom Plaza, and across Washington DC, officials in charge of the country's security had different expectations of what would take place the following day.[73]

---

[70] John C. Eastman (Fall, 2000), We are a Religious People Whose Institutions Presuppose a Supreme Being, Nexus: A Journal of Opinion, Vol. 5, pp. 13-23.

[71] Teri Sforza (March 21, 2022), Was John Eastman, former Chapman legal scholar, trying to overthrow democracy, The Orange County Register.

[72] Tim Drake (Sept. 28, 2011), National Organization for Marriage Names John Eastman Chairman of the Board, National Catholic Register; Melanie Mason (June 26, 2022), John Eastman's long, strange trip to the heart of the Jan. 6 investigation, Los Angeles Times.

[73] Aaron C. Davis, Hannah Allam, Devlin Barrett, Josh Dawsey, Amy Gardner, Shane Harris, Rosalind S. Helderman, Paul Kane, Dan Lamothe, Carol D. Leonnig, Nick Miroff, Ellen Nakashima, Ashley Parker, Beth Reinhard, Philip Rucker and Craig Timberg (Oct. 31, 2021), Red Flags, The Washington Post.

Trump again pressed Pence to delay the vote to certify the election, but the vice president refused, although Trump did not appear discouraged.[74]

Then, Trump had a short conversation with Mike Pence, referring to the thousands of supporters who were near the White House supporting him and chanting with flags:

"They love me, he said.

Pence nodded. "Of course, they're here to support you," he said. "They love you, Mr. President."

"But," Pence added, "they also love our Constitution."

Trump grimaced.

That may be, Trump said, but they agree with him regardless: Pence could and should throw Biden's electors out. Make it fair. Take it back.

That is all I want you to do, Mike, Trump said. Let the House decide the election.

Trump was not ready to give up, especially to a man he maligned as "Sleepy Joe."

"What do you think, Mike?" Trump asked.

Pence returned to his mantra: He did not have the authority to do anything other than count the electoral votes.

"Well, what if these people say you do?" Trump asked, gesturing beyond the White House to the crowds outside. Raucous cheering and blasting bullhorns could be heard through the Oval Office windows.

"If these people say you had the power, wouldn't you want to?" Trump asked.

"I wouldn't want any one person to have that authority," Pence said.

"But wouldn't it almost be cool to have that power?" Trump asked.

"No," Pence said. "Look, I've read this, and I don't see a way to do it.

"We've exhausted every option. I've done everything I could and then some to find a way around this. It's simply not possible. My interpretation is: No.

"I've met with all of these people," Pence said, "they're all on the same page. I personally believe these are the limits to what I can do. So, if you have a strategy for the 6th, it really shouldn't involve me because I'm just there to open the envelopes. You should be talking to the House and Senate. Your team should be talking to them about what kind of evidence they're going to present."

"No, no, no!" Trump shouted.

"You don't understand, Mike. You can do this. I don't want to be your friend anymore if you don't do this."[75]

The conversation continued:

"You're not going to be sworn in on the 20th. There is not a scenario in which you can be sworn in on the 20th," Pence said. "We need to figure out how to deal with it, how we want to handle it. How we want to talk about it."

Trump seemed furious. The man who had acceded to Trump's every request, who had never publicly disagreed or criticized him once he became vice president, would not do him this final favor. The power he held over Pence for four years, the loyalty that seemed like an inherent character trait, seemed now to slip away by the second.

Trump's voice grew louder. You are weak. You lack courage.

---

[74] Ibid.
[75] Bob Woodward, Robert Costa, Peril (Simon & Schuster, New York, 2023), ob. cit.

"You've betrayed us. I made you. You were nothing," Trump said. "Your career is over if you do this."

Pence did not budge."[76]

That day, in a *suite* near Freedom Plaza at the Willard Hotel, Epshteyn was with Rudy Giuliani and Steve Bannon, lobbying Republicans via telephone to join forces with Trump on January 6 and block Biden's ratification.[77]

Assault on the Capitol on January 6, 2021

Late in the evening, because of rumors spread in the press that Vice President Pence was resisting pressure from the president, Trump ordered, without consulting Pence, a statement to be circulated stating that he and Pence were "total agreement that the Vice President has the power to act." In doing so, the president lied.[78]

Inside the Oval Office, there was the sound of Trump supporters gathered a couple of blocks away.[79] Trump gathered his team to listen, and tweeted that the thousands gathered, would not let them be robbed of "a landslide election victory." Trump then said he did not want law enforcement authorities to detain protesters, as had happened in November and December.

He tweeted to his followers, saying he would speak at 11 am the next day (January 6) at the Save America rally on the Ellipse, inviting them to arrive early. That morning, some of those present carried red flags, foreshadowing bloodshed. Police recovered several weapons at various sites in DC.

Then came a very large contingent of the Proud Boys who engaged in political violence; wearing body armor bulged, and wearing patches or gaiters with Confederate flags, Punisher skulls, and other extremist symbols.[80]

When people made way for them, a woman said, "Praise God!"[81]

Gathered all together on the Ellipse, Trump began speaking around noon to his supporters who shouted "USA!" repeatedly.[82] As he told them, "We will never give up. We will never concede." After the time had passed, he said, "I know that everyone here will soon be marching over to the Capitol building to peacefully and patriotically make your voices heard." However, near the end of his speech, he stated, "You will never take back our country with weakness. We fight like hell. And if you don't fight like hell, you're not going to have a country anymore."[83]

---

[76] Ibid.

[77] Ibid.

[78] Ibid.

[79] Aaron C. Davis, Hannah Allam, Devlin Barrett, Josh Dawsey, Amy Gardner, Shane Harris, Rosalind S. Helderman, Paul Kane, Dan Lamothe, Carol D. Leonnig, Nick Miroff, Ellen Nakashima, Ashley Parker, Beth Reinhard, Philip Rucker, and Craig Timberg (Oct. 31, 2021), Red Flags, The Washington Post. Note: unless otherwise noted, this is the same source.

[80] Jacqueline Alemany, Hannah Allam, Devlin Barrett, Emma Brown, Aaron C. Davis, Josh Dawsey, Peter Hermann, Paul Kane, Ashley Parker, Beth Reinhard, Philip Rucker, Marianna Sotomayor and Rachel Weiner (Oct. 31, 2021), Bloodsheed, The Washington Post. Note: unless otherwise noted, this is the same source.

[81] Ibid.

[82] Amna Nawaz, Maea Lenei Buhre, Lorna Baldwin, Sam Lane (June 9, 2022), Examining the sequence of events during the assault on the U.S. Capitol, PBS.

[83] AP (January 13, 2021), Transcript of Trump's speech at rally before US Capitol riot, Associated Press.

A Capitol Police officer reported at 12:29 p.m., that he heard a Taser weapon fired near the Senate; and four minutes later, the Park Police reported that they detained a person with a rifle on 17th Street, not far from where Trump was speaking at the rally.[84]

At 1:03 p.m., an unoccupied red pickup truck with Alabama plates containing numerous weapons, including an M4 carbine assault rifle, magazines of ammunition, and Molotov cocktail components, was found by Capitol Police.

As soon as Trump returned to the White House, he complained about the organization of the rally but also expressed himself endlessly about how great it was. Retreating to his private dining room just off the Oval Office, he turned on the huge flat-screen TV to see what would happen.

The horror was accelerating minute by minute after 1:10 pm. Protesters tore down security barricades. They beat the police and scaled granite walls. Then they smashed windows and doors to breach the Capitol, which was besieged by hundreds of pro-Trump protesters. As Trump watched on TV, he did nothing to stop them. *The Washington Post*:

"For 187 minutes, Trump resisted entreaties to intervene from advisers, allies and his elder daughter, as well as lawmakers under attack. Even as the violence at the Capitol intensified, even after Vice President Mike Pence, his family and hundreds of Congress members and their staffers hid to protect themselves, even after the first two people died and scores of others were assaulted, Trump declined for more than three hours to tell the renegades rioting in his name to stand down and go home."

Meanwhile, harrowing scenes of violence unfolded in and around the Capitol. Outside, "some rioters tried to reason with about 10 officers who were struggling to stand their ground on the building's steps. "This is not going to end well for you," one of them told the officers. "Look at the numbers. Just go now before it gets ugly. Just stand down." But the officers continued to struggle to restrain them. They were defeated within minutes, however, and the way to the doors was clear.

Inside the Capitol, some Republicans disputed the Arizona vote count. Soon the Senate would go into emergency recess, with each of them hiding to avoid violence.

Once inside, the demonstrators grabbed a news photographer, dragged him down a flight of stairs, and threw him over a wall. A police officer was kicked in the chest and then surrounded by a mob. Two rioters died of cardiac events.

A rioter paraded a Confederate battle flag through the Capitol.

Another police officer was injured, being sprayed in the face with chemicals. Another police officer was attacked with a flagpole. And then rioters broke in and began ransacking the Speaker's office. Another news photographer was also surrounded, pushed down, and stripped of his camera.

Then a rioter was shot and killed.

Rioters broke into the Senate chamber, stealing documents and posing for photographs around the dais. Sometime later, a fourth policeman was smashed in a doorway and beaten with his baton.

---

[84] Jacqueline Alemany, Hannah Allam, Devlin Barrett, Emma Brown, Aaron C. Davis, Josh Dawsey, Peter Hermann, Paul Kane, Ashley Parker, Beth Reinhard, Philip Rucker, Marianna Sotomayor and Rachel Weiner (Oct. 31, 2021), Bloodshed, The Washington Post. Note: unless otherwise noted, this is the same source.

Trump remained motionless and did absolutely nothing, despite rejecting violence in his tweets, he continued to encourage his followers to continue their fight.

Kevin McCarthy, then House Minority Leader (R-California) and a Trump supporter, called him saying, "You have to denounce this." But the president falsely told him that the rioters were antifa members, but McCarthy corrected him, saying they were actually supporters of him. To which Trump responded, "You know what I see, Kevin? I see people who are more upset about the election than you are. They like Trump more than you do."

Among the ten thousand gathered, there were demonstrators "wearing ballistic helmets, body armor and carrying radio equipment and military-grade backpacks."

Trump watched complacently on TV, despite reports he received of violence by protesters, and at 2:24 he tweeted pleased with the Capitol takeover.

For his part, Eastman, Trump's lawyer adviser for reversing the election, sent an email to Jacob, Pence's lawyer, accusing the vice president of causing the violence by refusing to block Biden's certification as the nation's president.

The leaders of the Senate and House of Representatives were also evacuated by the Capitol Police and taken to safety.

Several black legislators found it impossible to leave, especially given the parade of Confederate flags inside the Capitol and the horrible racist expressions.

Schumer and Pelosi issued a joint statement urging Trump to call off the riots.

"At the Pentagon, Miller, Gen. Mark A. Milley, chairman of the Joint Chiefs of Staff, and Army Secretary Ryan McCarthy huddled to discuss how to mobilize the Guard."

Finally, before 3 p.m., reinforcement units from federal and neighboring law enforcement arrived at the Capitol. Also, members of a DC police riot unit, officers from Prince George's County, Maryland, as well as officers from Montgomery County, Maryland, and Arlington County, Virginia.

At 2:52 pm, the first FBI SWAT teams arrived. Thus, there were a total of 520 federal agents in response to an urgent call from the Department of Justice.

With Miller's consent, shortly after 3 p.m., McCarthy approved a full mobilization of the DC National Guard.

Meanwhile, at the Capitol, the "QAnon Shaman," Jacob Anthony Chansley, shirtless and with his face painted, and who stood behind the desk wielding a megaphone, said, "Let's all say a prayer in this sacred space," while several others bowed their heads in thanksgiving for the opportunity to "do justice."

Afterward, one of them, Hodgkins, beat his chest twice with his right hand, holding the flag in his left hand. He then raised it in salute after the prayer and the group said "Amen!"

For his part, the president said that he was not to blame for what happened and that his supporters would not commit such violence. Several aides gathered just outside the Oval Office, hoping the president would see them and ask for advice, but he was in his private dining room.

Chris Christie, Trump's friend and advisor, was unable to reach him, so he tried to send him a message through television on ABC. Former White House adviser Kellyanne Conway and former communications director Alyssa Farah sent messages to the president through intermediaries. Farah communicated with Mark Meadows, her former boss, virtually begging the White House Cabinet to issue a statement or address the cameras if Trump did not. He wrote, "If someone doesn't say something, people will die." But Meadows did not respond.

As rioters broke through security barricades outside the Capitol, some of the president's most trusted advisors tried to persuade him to order his supporters to disperse. At 2:38 pm, Trump tweeted a message that did not have the effect: "Please support our Capitol Police and Law Enforcement. They are truly on the side of our Country. Stay peaceful!"

His daughter, Ivanka, tried to persuade him to use stronger language, but just when she thought she had him convinced, Meadows called her and said the opposite: "I need you to come back here. We've got to get this under control."

At 3:13 pm he tweeted, "I am asking for everyone at the U.S. Capitol to remain peaceful. No violence! Remember, WE are the Party of Law & Order – respect the Law and our great men and women in Blue. Thank you!"

But it didn't work, so several White House aides devised new strategies to get Trump to say what they thought he should communicate. He agreed to send two tweets drafted by Jason Miller in the president's style and taste:

"Bad apples, like ANTIFA or other crazed leftists, infiltrated today's peaceful protest over the fraudulent vote count. Violence is never acceptable! MAGA supporters embrace our police and the rule of law and should leave the Capitol now!"

"The fake news media who encouraged this summer's violent and radical riots are now trying to blame peaceful and innocent MAGA supporters for violent actions. This isn't who we are! Our people should head home and let the criminals suffer the consequences!"

But as the afternoon progressed, the rioters pounced with greater ferocity and in greater numbers.

Wyoming Republican Congresswoman Liz Cheney worked behind the scenes to ensure that the election tally was not tampered with. While in secure locations, she approached Rep. Hakeem Jeffries of New York, chairman of the Democratic caucus, and brought up the subject of Trump's impeachment: "Look, we have to move articles," she told her Democratic counterpart. "Immediately."

At 4:05 p.m., Biden appeared on television from Wilmington, Del., condemning in no uncertain terms the Capitol takeover, and saying it must stop.

Minutes later, at 4:17 pm, Trump posted a video on Twitter: he began his speech by saying that the election was fraudulent. He asked his supporters to go home, adding, "We love you. You're very special." When ten minutes later on TV the president's speech appeared, rioters attacked the police who were standing guard inside the arch of the west terrace of the Capitol. They beat several of the policemen, accompanied by curses. One of the officers was severely beaten.

But gradually, the Capitol Police with their reinforcements continued to advance through the violent containment and control of the insurgents. At 4:32 pm, permission was given to deploy the National Guard to the Capitol. At 5:40 about 150 members arrived for support. At 6:00 pm, a citywide curfew went into effect. But fights between police and rioters continued. Trump asked a minute later the insurrectionists to leave with love and peace, but not before insisting on the lie of electoral fraud.

Police and the National Guard were able to clear outside the Capitol and establish a security perimeter around the west side of the Capitol. At 7:00 pm, FBI and ATF agents completed the clearance of the Capitol by going room by room.

At 8:00 pm, the session resumed. Shortly before the time, Graham took Pence aside, telling him, "You're doing the right thing. I'm proud of you." And the two embraced.

Eastman, Trump's lawyer, sent at 9:00 pm an email to Jacob, Pence's lawyer, to try to convince him not to certify the results. Jacob ignored the email and the recount continued until the end (3:24 am), with Nancy Pelosi opening at 9:02 pm.

At 3:41 a.m., Senate Chaplain Barry Black closed the session with a prayer:

"We deplore the desecration of the United States Capitol building, the shedding of innocent blood, the loss of life and the quagmire of dysfunction that threaten our democracy. These tragedies have reminded us that words matter, and that the power of life and death is in the tongue."

Several extreme right-wing groups and the Christian and Catholic far-right in the January 6 manifestation

QAnon is a shadowy pro-Trump conspiracy theory, claiming that the then US president was up against a shadowy group of pedophiles in the Democratic Party. Supposedly, it would be a clique of Satan-worshipping pedophiles operating a global child sex trafficking ring. But the theory is far more bizarre than described.[85]

When Trump was asked in August 2020 if he believed in such a conspiracy theory, a theory pushed by Marjorie Taylor Greene, he replied, "She won by a lot. She comes from a great state." When asked again by *AP* reporter Jill Colvin if he specifically agreed with Greene's support of the QAnon conspiracy theory, Trump did not respond and gave way to another reporter.[86] Again, in mid-October of the same year, reporter Savannah Guthrie asked Trump to publicly reject the QAnon conspiracy theory as completely false, to which the president responded, "I know nothing about it. I do know they are very much against pedophilia. They fight it very hard, but I know nothing about it." Supporters of such a theory saw in the president's words a strengthened support for their position.[87]

"It's beyond words how much Donald Trump has elevated the domestic threat that is QAnon," said Rita Katz, the executive director of SITE. "I've never been more worried for U.S. democracy than I am now, and it's disturbing how much of this fear is coming from the president himself."[88]

Pro-QAnon rioters were part of the assault on the Capitol. But also neo-Nazis, people with Confederate flags, anti-government militia symbols, Proud-Boys, the Boogaloo movement, aspiring to start a second civil war; the Oath Keepers, also anti-

---

[85] Kevin Roose (Aug. 21, 2020), What is QAnon, the pro-Trump viral conspiracy theory, The New York Times.

[86] Annie Karni (Aug. 15, 2020/updated Sept. 1, 2020), Trump refrains from disavowing QAnon conspiracy, The New York Times.

[87] Craig Timberg (Oct. 16, 2020), Trump's comments on conspiracy theory are celebrated: 'This was the biggest pitch for QAnon I've ever seen', The Washington Post.

[88] Ibid.

government; the Kek Flags, a white supremacist ultra-right-wing group with a Nazi-like symbol; and others.[89]

So for example, it was perhaps in December 2020, when a man wearing sunglasses and a gaiter, wearing a T-shirt with the message "6MWE" (6 million were not enough) in Washington DC, was photographed with some members of the Proud Boys. Therefore, the subject most likely belonged to that group. A hateful image that undoubtedly established that it was not enough to kill six million Jews in WWII, but that more were needed.[90]

But at the January 6, 2021, assault on the Capitol, there were many other symbols of hate. For example, Robert Keith Packer wore a sweatshirt that read Camp Auschwitz. Work brings freedom. The phrase alludes to the infamous Auschwitz concentration camp, while "Work brings freedom" is a rough translation of the phrase that greeted Jewish prisoners arriving at the Nazi concentration camp.

The back of the sweatshirt read "Personal."[91] But there were many other extremist symbols from different ultra-right-wing camps, thus communicating hateful ideologies.[92]

However, Christian-nationalist symbols were the most prominent.

Prior to the Capitol Assault, there were some "prophecies" from far-right evangelists who predicted Trump would remain president for a second term, such as Pat Robertson, Kat Kerr, Paula White, Kris Vallotton, Jeremiah Johnson, Steve Schultz, Charlie Shamp, and others. With thousands and hundreds of thousands of followers.[93]

But also, there were well-known conservative Christian figures who claimed that the elections were fraudulent.[94]

However, perhaps the most prominent figure in questioning the election results was the aforementioned Ginni Thomas, the wife of Supreme Court Justice Clarence Thomas; both conservative Catholics. She revealed that she attended the January 6 rally at the Ellipse in Washington, but went home due to the cold; "disappointed and frustrated that there was violence."[95]

As a precursor to the assault on Capitol Hill, on December 12, 2020, in Washington DC, there was a large-scale interfaith prayer protest called the Jericho March, which brought together various factions of the religious right presenting the pantomime of the biblical Battle of Jericho as they prayed to "bring down the walls of the Deep State."[96]

---

[89] Laura E. Adkins and Emily Burack (January 7, 2021), Neo-Nazis, QAnon and Camp Auschwitz: A guide to the hate symbols and signs on display at the Capitol riots, Jewish Telegraphic Agency.

[90] Ben Sales (January 11, 2021), The '6MWE' shirt: How a photo that went viral after the Capitol siege is misleading, and why it matters, Jewish Telegraphic Agency.

[91] Ben Sales (Jan. 10, 2021), Capitol rioter in 'Camp Auschwitz' sweatshirt identified as Virginia man, Jewish Telegraphic Agency.

[92] Matthew Rosenberg and Ainara Tiefenthäler (Jan. 13, 2021), Decoding the Far-Right Symbols at the Capitol Riot, The New York Times; Mallory Simon and Sara Sidner (Jan. 11, 2021), Decoding the extremist symbols and groups at the Capitol Hill insurrection, CNN; Washington Post staff (Jan. 15, 2021), Identifying far-right symbols that appeared at the U.S. Capitol riot, The New York Times.

[93] Julia Duin (Nov. 16, 2020), The Charismatic Christians Prophesying Trump's Victory (And Not Backing Down), Religion Unplugged.

[94] Steve Rabey (June 28, 2022), 8 Christian Conservatives Who Promoted False Claims Of Rigged, Stolen Election, Religion Unplugged.

[95] Kevin Daley (March 14, 2022), EXCLUSIVE: Ginni Thomas Wants To Set the Record Straight on January 6, The Washington Free Beacon.

[96] Kathryn Joyce (Jan. 6, 2022), How Christian nationalism drove the insurrection: A religious history of Jan. 6, Salon. Note: unless otherwise noted, this is the same source.

Two federal government employees at the time were the organizers, presenting that day a fusion of charismatic evangelicalism, Christian Zionism, and right-wing Catholicism: with contemporary Christian music and worship and iconography of the Virgin of Guadalupe; a rendition of "Ave Maria"; "and the female pastor of a pro-cannabis church in New England wearing Catholic vestments while playing a Jewish shofar."

Eric Metaxas, the well-known evangelical radio broadcaster and a key figure in building an alliance between conservative evangelicals and Roman Catholics, hosted the event.

"Metaxas had become increasingly extreme throughout the Trump era. The week of the Jericho March rally, he told TurningPoint USA founder Charlie Kirk that the 2020 election was like "somebody is being raped or murdered... times a thousand," and that conservatives would need "to fight to the death, to the last drop of blood" to keep Trump in office."

Salon also indicated:

"That December rally featured several notable names on the Catholic right, including a bishop from Texas who refused to acknowledge Biden as president-elect, a nun who had delivered a fiery pro-Trump address at the 2020 Republican National Convention and, most prominently, Archbishop Carlo Maria Viganò [...]"

Salon echoed Trump's "Christian" supporters on January 6, 2021:

"In the Age of Trump, movement conservatism has metastasized or devolved into its purest form: American fascism, a form of religious politics taken to its most illogical extreme. Facts, truth and even the conception of reality itself are being replaced with lies, fictions, and fantasies that serve the American fascist movement and its leader."[97]

But likewise, evangelical speaker Lance Wallnau, who in 2016 compared Trump to the biblical figure of King Cyrus, who served as God's instrument to liberate the people of Israel, said, "This is the beginning of a Christian populist uprising. There's a backlash coming," he said. "And you're going to see this wrecking ball of a reformation hit the church as well... because it's going to divide between those who are awake and those that are asleep. ... There is a great awakening coming, and this is the spark that is starting it right now."[98]

As *Salon* highlights, not every speaker at the Jericho March was a traditional religious leader. A considered devout Christian and founder of the militia group Oath Keepers, Stewart Rhodes, attempted to influence police and members of the military that day to prepare to fight Chinese "proxies" in the nation, who he said were working to install Biden as their "puppet."

Also Trump's former national security adviser, Michael Flynn, just then pardoned by Trump for lying in federal investigations, was on hand with a bandana flag to speak to

---

[97] Chauncey Devega (Oct. 19, 2021), Religion scholar Anthea Butler on "White Christianity" and its role in fueling fascism, Salon.
[98] Kathryn Joyce (6 de enero, 2022), How Christian nationalism drove the insurrection: A religious history of Jan. 6, Salon. Nota: a menos que se indique lo contrario, es la misma fuente.

510

the crowd about spiritual warfare and lead them in an "Our Father." Flynn, who is an ultra-conservative Catholic, has declared that America should be one nation under God, with one religion.

For his part, Alex Jones, the host of the conspiracy theories and fantasy show *Infowars*, delivered what sounded like a sermon, proclaiming, "This is the beginning of the great revival before the Antichrist comes. World government, implantable microchips, Satanism — it's out in the open. The Bible is fulfilled, Revelation is fulfilled."

"And there was Ali Alexander, the bombastic founder of the Stop the Steal movement, who appeared frequently on stage alongside Metaxas, vowing that if Biden was installed as president, Alexander and his supporters would return to "occupy D.C. full of patriots," adding, "We can do all things through Christ who strengthens us."

"In the following weeks, Alexander repeatedly underscored the religious dimensions of his mission. In late December, he told the Epoch Times-affiliated NTD television network, "We are in a fight of good versus evil, of light versus the darkness, and a global order over sovereign citizens. ... I believe that this is a metaphysical fight and we are channeling all energy in heaven and on earth towards a favorable outcome."

Alexander, who was converting to Catholicism because the Catholic Church had been "infiltrated" by an "earthly [sic] order that works in concert with Satan himself against the Church," had said he was called to personally join the battle. For the return of the Jericho March on January 5, 2021, a day before the attack on the Capitol for the MAGA march on the 6th, Alexander spoke in a chant of "Victory or death" to the crowd.

"As public opinion polls and other research have repeatedly shown, white right-wing Christians, especially Protestant evangelicals, have pledged their loyalty to Donald Trump and his movement. Many view him as a literal prophet or savior: His evident immorality has been rationalized as somehow necessary to his prophetic role."[99]

Not surprisingly, it has been identified as "right-wing Christian terrorism."

During the assault on the Capitol, people with horns or shofars appeared, which in this context, would be a sign of battle as in the Old Testament, to overthrow "wickedness."

Likewise, there were imprecatory or curse prayers. For example, on that day they "were on a mission from God to go into the Capitol and get Nancy Pelosi, Mike Pence and other people they saw as enemies."

A huge wooden cross that was taken to the assault was seen in the context of prayer and to be used as the crusaders during the European Middle Ages.

Being "a central driving force," as *Salon* called it, Christian nationalism carried Jacob Chansley, with bare torso and Viking horns who stopped his fellow marauders in the Senate chamber praying, "Thank you Heavenly Father for gracing us with this opportunity... to send a message to all the tyrants, the communists and the globalists,

---

[99] Chauncey Devega (Oct. 19, 2021), Religion scholar Anthea Butler on "White Christianity" and its role in fueling fascism, Salon. Note: unless otherwise noted, this is the same source.

that this is our nation, not theirs [...] Thank you for filling this chamber with patriots that love you and that love Christ. Thank you for allowing the United States of America to be reborn."[100] Across the sea of protesters, both inside and outside the building, slogans on T-shirts and baseball caps proclaimed, "Jesus is my savior, Trump is my president"; "God, Guns, Trump"; and on a rough sweatshirt of a man who helped make the crude gallows erected on the Capitol lawn, "Faith, Family, Freedom." The gallows had handwritten notes, "Hang them high" and "In God We Trust."

Other demonstrators carrying giant portraits of Jesus and replicas of statues of the Infant of Prague sang about the blood of Jesus cleansing the U.S. Congress. One man sang songs of praise into a microphone connected to a stack of amplifiers.

A Catholic priest from Nebraska performed an "exorcism" at the Capitol building to banish the demon Baphomet, who, he said, was "dissolving the country" to "bring it back as something different." Another troublemaker was a cast member of a touring production of "Jesus Christ Superstar."

"Another, Leo Brent Bozell IV, came from a long line of Christian right activists: His father, L. Brent Bozell III, founded the right-wing Media Research Center and his grandfather, L. Brent Bozell Jr., wrote speeches for Joseph McCarthy and a manifesto for Barry Goldwater."

Jerome Copulsky, co-director of Uncivil Religion said on Jan. 6, "It was evident to anyone watching that there was this religious character to what was going on, both in the Trump movement writ large but particularly in the leadership of the 'Stop the Steal' movement"

Other demonstrators dressed as Captain Moroni, a legendary warrior from the Book of Mormon. Still others sang "Battle Hymn of the Republic" along with other demonstrators carrying Confederate flags.

Near the west entrance of the Capitol, some of the crowd were singing the first verse of the hymn "Amazing Grace." Then appeared the image of a lion's head, on which was engraved Trump's name; and underneath the mane was written "Proverbs 30:30," a biblical reference that expresses that the lion, as the strongest of animals, does not back down.[101]

There was at least one crucifix and a statue of the Virgin Mary. A sign with the words "The Truth Will Set You Free--Jesus"; and another that read "You Must Be Born Again."

Someone wore a cap that read: "God. Guns. Trump" with a cross in the middle. Also, someone was carrying a U.S. flag, which read at the top of the flag, "God. Guns." At the bottom: "Trump." In the middle of the flag, a cross and two rifles: one on each side of the cross.

A woman unfurled a white flag, which read "Proud American" at the top. On the bottom, "Christian." And in the center of it the Christian symbol of the fish, with the American flag as the background of the fish. Also, on January 6, a group of Dominican

---

[100] Kathryn Joyce (Jan. 6, 2022), How Christian nationalism drove the insurrection: A religious history of Jan. 6, Salon. Note: unless otherwise noted, this is the same source.

[101] Theodore Louis Trost (January 6, 2022), The Lion, The Crowd, and Amazing Grace, Uncivil Religion: January 6, 2021: https://uncivilreligion.org/home/the-lion-the-crowd-and-amazing-grace; accessed April 21, 2023.

nuns (not in communion with Rome) who supported Trump, marched that day with flags supporting the president around their necks.[102]

Someone else carried a message with the words, "GOD is Trying to Save this Country through Trump."[103]

Someone was carrying a yellow banner with a picture of Trump, with the decapitated head of Karl Marx in his left hand and in his right hand a sword.

Others carried painted Catholic images of the Virgin Mary and Jesus.[104]

Another sign said "Glory to God," while there was also a huge banner that said "Jesus 2020." Another sign had biblical references: "HEB 4:12, JER. 4:7, PSALM 67," which texts taken together, allude that the Word of God is the warrior to remove evil from the nations, which must surrender to God.

But there were many other Christian symbols; as well as chants and expressions of faith at the January 6, 2021 demonstrations against the Capitol.

The U.S. Conference of Catholic Bishops issued a strong condemnation of the assault on the Capitol, along with other prominent Catholic leaders in the country.[105] The problem is that despite that condemnation, the still-conservative U.S. Catholic clergy agree with the advancement of religious agendas in the United States. And not everyone thinks as they do about what happened on Capitol Hill.

Kevin McCarthy, then Speaker of the House of Representatives, provided Fox News' Tucker Carlson with tens of thousands of hours of video of the assault on the Capitol, causing the journalist to be selective and assemble a documentary that portrayed the assault as entirely peaceful.[106] Despite the many video evidence and testimonies of violence by many protesters.

We will see something else. On June 9, 2021, the January 6 committee to fully investigate what happened about the assault on the Capitol would begin. Many felt that American democracy was in grave danger. Adam Kinzinger and Liz Cheney were the only Republicans on the committee. Cheney said, "Tonight I say this to my Republican colleagues who are defending the indefensible: There will come a day when Donald Trump is gone, but your dishonor will remain." Republicans and conservative pro-Trump media outlets like Fox News, criticized and derided the committee, despite the powerful evidence presented of what happened. It was considered a partisan committee, by the Democratic party as a strategy to advance their political agenda, thus belittling the facts.[107]

Republican Congressman Adam Kinzinger, a member of the January 6 Commission, had said in March 2021, that "had there not been some of these kind of errant prophecies [...] This idea that, you know, God has ordained it to be Trump, I'm not sure January 6 would have happened like it did." But the final report on January 6, included

---

[102] Joyce Dalsheim, Gregory Starret (September 26, 2022), Christian nationalism is downplayed in the Jan. 6 report and collective memory, The Conversation.

[103] Ibid.

[104] https://uncivilreligion.org/home/media/icons-of-jesus-and-virgin-mary; accessed April 21, 2023.

[105] John Lavenburg (Jan. 7, 2021), Catholic leaders condemn violence by Trump supporters in D.C., Crux Catholic Media; Timothy Nerozzi (Jan. 8, 2021), Catholic Leaders Condemn Capitol Riot With Rare Display of Patriotism, Religion Unplugged.

[106] Alex Thomas (April 7, 2023), The Second January 6 Insurrection, The New Republic.

[107] Michael Kirk (Writer), Michael Kirk (Writer), & Mike Wiser (Director) (2022, September 6). Lies, Politics and Democracy (Season 41, Episode 1) [TV Series Episode]. Raney Aronson, David Fanning (Executive Producers), Frontline. Public Broadcasting Service (PBS).

no mention of the role of Christian nationalism in the fateful events of that day. The reason, as Amanda Tyler, executive director of the Baptist Joint Committee for Religious Liberty and who testified before the Jan. 6 committee, says, is that perhaps the reason is due-as seemed to be glimpsed from comments by committee member Liz Cheney-, that confronting Christian nationalism can be misconstrued as an attack on Christianity or Christians, but that this reasoning is far from the truth, as there are Christians and Christian groups who have clearly denounced Christian nationalism and continue to do so. Amanda Tyler rightly adds that Christian nationalism is a quest for power through politics and threatens American democracy.[108]

In 2022 and 2023, Trump was financially assisting defense lawyers for some of the Capitol assailants, claiming they had been treated unfairly and promising to pardon many of them if he was elected president again.[109]

Peril: the post-January 6 era

The forces that propelled Trump supporters to Capitol Hill have not faded. The following months saw renewed calls for scrutiny of the results and demands for more restrictive voting laws. Across the country, election officials received hundreds of threatening emails and phone calls.[110]

Trump refused to address those threats and insisted that the media failed to seek the truth about the 2020 election.[111]

Liz Cheney, "the third-highest ranking Republican in the House and the highest-ranking Republican woman in Congress," was one of the movers in the House of Representatives, who indicted Trump for his role in inciting insurrectionists against Capitol Hill to prevent ratification votes for Biden.[112] In a statement, she said:

"Much more will become clear in coming days and weeks, but what we know now is enough. The President of the United States summoned this mob, assembled the mob, and lit the flame of this attack. Everything that followed was his doing. None of this would have happened without the President. The President could have immediately and forcefully intervened to stop the violence. He did not. There has never been a greater betrayal by a President of the United States of his office and his oath to the Constitution. I will vote to impeach the President."[113]

She was one of ten Republicans who voted to oust Trump from the presidency. Since then, she has faced a backlash from her party, causing a serious rift.[114] Her father, Dick Cheney, had been concerned for her safety on January 6, when he heard Trump

---

[108] (Dec. 28, 2022), Christian Nationalism Conspicuously Absent From January 6 Report, MSNBC: https://www.youtube.com/watch?v=rgmY3yVBaMg; accessed July 2, 2023.
[109] Kristen Holmes (Dec. 2, 2022), Trump expresses support for Capitol rioters as he continues to embrace extremist groups, CNN; Shane Goldmacher and Maggie Haberman (May 11, 2023), Five Takeaways From Trump's Unruly CNN Town Hall, The New York Times.
[110] Philip Rucker, Jacqueline Alemany, Hannah Allam, Devlin Barrett, Emma Brown, Aaron C. Davis, Josh Dawsey, Peter Hermann, Paul Kane, Ashley Parker, Beth Reinhard, Marianna Sotomayor and Rachel Weiner (Oct. 31, 2021), Bloodshed, The Washington Post.
[111] Ibid.
[112] Leena Kim (May 6, 2021), Who Is House Republican Liz Cheney, Town & Country.
[113] Ibid.
[114] Ibid.

mention her in his speech in negative terms because she would ratify the votes.[115] Something that cost him a lot politically.

On January 8 of the same year, Mark Milley, chairman of the Joint Chiefs of Staff, received a phone call from Nancy Pelosi, the speaker of Congress and second in line to the president, after the vice president. She knows a lot about national security, military, and intelligence issues.[116] Part of the conversation goes like this:

"What precautions are available," Pelosi asked, "to prevent an unstable president from initiating military hostilities or from accessing the launch codes and ordering a nuclear strike?

"This situation of this unhinged president could not be more dangerous. We must do everything that we can to protect the American people from his unbalanced assault on our country and our democracy."

[...]

"I can tell you that we have a lot of checks in the system," Milley said. "And I can guarantee you, you can take it to the bank, that there'll be, that the nuclear triggers are secure and we're not going to do—we're not going to allow anything crazy, illegal, immoral or unethical to happen."

[...]

"But he just did something illegal, immoral and unethical and nobody stopped him. Nobody. Nobody at the White House. This escalated in the way it did because of the intent of the president. The president incited it and nobody in the White House did anything about it. Nobody in the White House did anything to stop him."

"I'm not going to disagree with you," Milley replied.

"So you're saying you're going to make sure it doesn't happen?" the speaker asked. "It already did happen. An assault on our democracy happened and nobody said, you can't do that. Nobody."

[...]

She continued, "Is there any reason to think that somebody, some voice of reason, could have weighed in with him? So for this, we are very, very affected by this. This is not an accident. This is not something that you go, well, now that's done, let's go from there. Let's move on. It ain't that. This is deep what he did. He traumatized the staff. He assaulted the Capitol and the rest of that. And he's not going to get away with it. He's not going to be empowered to do more."

[...]

"Madam Speaker, you have to take my word for it. I know the system and we're okay. The president alone can order the use of nuclear weapons. But he doesn't make the decision alone. One person can order it, several people have to launch it.

"Thank you, Madam Speaker."[117]

On the recommendation of his advisors, on January 13, Trump gave a public statement from the Oval Office, fearing impeachment against him as the provocateur of the assault on the Capitol:

[115] Mark Leibovich (June 21, 2021), Liz Cheney, once Republican royalty, is now a lone warrior, The New York Times.
[116] Bob Woodward, Robert Costa, Peril (Simon & Schuster, New York, 2023), ob. cit.
[117] Ibid.

"My fellow Americans," Trump said in the January 13 video, "I want to be very clear. I unequivocally condemn the violence that we saw last week. Violence and vandalism have absolutely no place in our country and no place in our movement."

He added, "Like all of you, I was shocked and deeply saddened by the calamity at the Capitol last week. I want to thank the hundreds of millions of incredible American citizens who have responded to this moment with calm, moderation, and grace. We will get through this challenge, just like we always do."

Before ending, Trump took a shot at "the efforts to censor, cancel, and blacklist our fellow citizens."

It seemed to be a wink to his supporters that even though he was reading this stiff presidential statement, he was with them in spirit."[118]

Republicans were appalled by what Trump did on January 6, which included his inaction to stop the assault on the Capitol or even condemn it.[119] Republican leaders clearly rebuked the president, including Mitch McConnell, Kevin McCarthy and Lindsey Graham.

Many of Trump's supporters treated Republican leaders as traitors, and some officials who condemned the president's actions received death threats. Soon that January, a second impeachment trial was opened against the U.S. president.

After Trump departed from the White House, Republican leaders were frightened that if he left, the party would fragment, as Trump felt betrayed by Republicans and threatened to create his party. Kevin McCarthy, Lindsey Graham, Ted Cruz, and many other Republican senators visited Trump at Mar-a-Lago in Florida to show their support.

And even Mitch McConnell said on television that he would support a second Trump nomination as the GOP nominee for the 2024 election.

Liz Cheney, who was in favor of impeachment against Trump, was ousted from the Republican leadership by Kevin McCarthy. Cheney indicated to the press that the Republican party was in a dangerous state, due to the lies of the former president.

Dangers on the horizon-1

"This is Donald Trump's America. We were warned over and over and over about it, and we ignored all of that. So here we are," said Charlie Sykes, conservative podcaster for *The Bulwark*.[120] Similarly, Mona Charen, a conservative columnist, expressed, "There were many, many signals throughout 2016 that this was not just a showman, but no, somebody who had definite authoritarian sympathies. And there was violence at his rallies that he openly encouraged. I mean, it wasn't a joke. [...] It was vertigo-inducing,

[118] Ibid.

[119] Michael Kirk (Writer), Michael Kirk (Writer), & Mike Wiser (Director) (2022, September 6). Lies, Politics and Democracy (Season 41, Episode 1) [TV Series Episode]. Raney Aronson, David Fanning (Executive Producers), *Frontline*. Public Broadcasting Service (PBS). Note: unless otherwise noted, this is the same source.

[120] Michael Kirk (Writer), Mike Wiser (Writer), & Michael Kirk (Director) (2021, January 26). Trump's American Carnage (Season 39, Episode 11) [TV Series Episode]. Raney Aronson, David Fanning (Executive Producers), *Frontline*. Public Broadcasting Service (PBS).

because it showed me that either I had gone crazy or everybody else had gone crazy."[121]

Mona Charen earned her conservative credentials in the Reagan administration. And she was surprised by what she was seeing among Republicans, as she also said, "I didn't know what world I was living in. It felt really Alice in Wonderland-esque. The things I thought were solid were not. And it was very disorienting."

Trump had said, "We're going to be so strong. We're going to be so tough. We're going to be so vicious. And we're going to knock them for a loop. We have no choice."

And while some Republicans publicly complained about him, most did not.

All in all, the yearning to turn America into a theocracy has not been stifled but has grown very strong. *The New York Times* reported that "Rituals of Christian worship have become embedded in conservative rallies, as praise music and prayer blend with political anger over vaccines and the 2020 election."[122]

No wonder, as Katherine Stewart pointed out on November 16, 2020, in *The New York Times*, despite Biden's November 2020 victory over Trump, religious authoritarianism is so powerful that it is here to stay. Many nationalist Christian conservative leaders believed the election in favor of Biden was fraudulent and wanted Trump to remain in office. The network is extremely powerful and works from the highest apexes down.[123]

"Trump's ideological vacuum, the more he is isolated and attacked, is led by the proto-fascist forces of the Christian right. This Christianized fascism, with its network of megachurches, schools, universities, and law schools and its vast radio and television empire, is a potent ally for a beleaguered White House. The Christian right has been organizing and preparing to take power for decades. If the nation suers another economic collapse, which is probably inevitable, another catastrophic domestic terrorist attack, or a new war, Trump's ability to force the Christian right's agenda on the public and shut down dissent will be dramatically enhanced."[124]

When Chris Hedges spent several hours at the end of two years of reporting with Fritz Stern and Robert O. Paxton, two of America's leading scholars of fascism, he could see clearly that the popular Christian right fit that picture very well. "Was it virulent enough and organized enough to seize power? Would it go to the ruthless extremes of previous fascist movements to persecute and silence dissent?"[125]

"The evangelicalism promoted by the Christian right is very different from the evangelicalism and fundamentalism of a century ago. The emphasis on personal piety that denied the old movement, the call to avoid the contamination of politics, has been

---

[121] Michael Kirk (Writer), Michael Kirk (Writer), & Mike Wiser (Director) (2022, September 6). Lies, Politics and Democracy (Season 41, Episode 1) [TV Series Episode]. Raney Aronson, David Fanning (Executive Producers), *Frontline*. Public Broadcasting Service (PBS). Note: unless otherwise noted, this is the same source.

[122] Elizabeth Dias and Ruth Graham (April 6/11, 2022), The Growing Religious Fervor in the American Right: 'This Is a Jesus Movement,' The New York Times.

[123] Katherine Stewart (Nov. 16, 2020), Trump or No Trump, Religious Authoritarianism Is Here to Stay, The New York Times.

[124] Chris Hedges, America: The Farewell Tour (Simon & Schuster, New York, 2018), ob. cit.

[125] Ibid.

replaced by Christian Reconstructionism, also called Dominionism. This new ideology is about taking control of all institutions, including the government, to build a "Christian" nation."[126]

In the face of all this, Chris Hedges sees clearly that this scenario will lead to a government dominated by the Christian Right, to impose the Ten Commandments, to silence any dissent that threatens its philosophy, to arrest and even kill... Especially since "Tens of millions of Americans are already hermetically sealed within this bizarre worldview."[127]

As Katherine Stewart rightly emphasized about American Christian nationalism, "We ignore the political implications for our democracy at our peril."[128]

Dominik Tarczyński is a far-right Polish politician, who spoke at the 2019 World Congress of Families in Italy, where religious leaders and ultra-conservative politicians from around the world gathered. There was a red cap on the podium next to him and it read "Make Europe Great Again."[129]

And it is under Trump, that the United States -observes Katherine Stewart-, "has become a flashing red beacon of hope for a new, global, religious, right-wing populist movement. It calls itself a "global conservative movement" and claims that it seeks to "defend the natural family," but is really about ending democracy and replacing it with faith-based authoritarian states. As "a kind of global holy war" that goes against global liberalism.[130]

For decades the religious ultra-right has been threatening to take control of the country. Due to the half-awakening of some Democrats and the media in general, more attention has been paid to it. But it is still not believed to be as serious as it seems. It may be too late when it comes to react. There has been solid literature on the dangers of Christian fascism for some years now, including what has happened with Donald Trump.[131]

In a dark Phoenix parking lot at a 2022 event, a group of people opened with a prayer, invoking God's "hedge of thorns and fire" to protect every person on site.[132] The microphone was passed to those who wanted to give testimony to whoever had

---

[126] Ibid.

[127] Ibid.

[128] Katherine Stewart (Nov. 16, 2020), Trump or No Trump, Religious Authoritarianism Is Here to Stay, The New York Times.

[129] Katherine Stewart, The Power Worshippers: Inside the Dangerous Rise of Religious Nationalism (Bloomsbury Publishing, New York, 2020), ob. cit.

[130] Ibid.

[131] Other books: Anne Nelson, Shadow Network: Media, Money, and the Secret Hub of the Radical Right (Bloomsbury Publishing Inc., New York, 2019); Kristin Kobes Du Mez, Jesus and John Wayne: How White Evangelicals Corrupted a Faith and Fractured a Nation (Liveright Publishing Corporation, New York, 2020); Jeff Sharlet, The Family: The Secret Fundamentalism at the Heart of American Power (HarperCollins, 2008); Sarah Posner, Unholy: How White Christian Nationalists Powered the Trump Presidency, and the Devastating Legacy They Left Behind (Random House, New York, 2020); Andrew L. Whitehead, Samuel L. Perry, Taking America Back for God: Christian Nationalism in the United States (Oxford University Press, 2020); Sheldon Whitehouse, The Scheme: How the Right Wing Used Dark Money to Capture the Supreme Court (The New Press, 2022); Andrew L. Seidel, American Crusade: How the Supreme Court Is Weaponizing Religious Freedom (Union Square & Co., New York, 2022).

[132] Elizabeth Dias and Ruth Graham (April 6/11, 2022), The Growing Religious Fervor in the American Right: 'This Is a Jesus Movement', The New York Times. Note: unless otherwise noted, this is the same source.

518

inspiring words to say "on behalf of our J-6 political prisoners." Referring to those arrested in connection with the attack on the Capitol and paying tribute to them one year later. While holding candles, the few dozen people gathered sang an a cappella song treasured by millions of believers who sing it on Sundays:

"Way maker, miracle worker, promise keeper Light in the darkness, my God That is who you are…"

A right-wing voter mobilization effort focused on dismantling electoral politics sponsored surveillance in the parking lot, where a few men armed with guns and accompanied by a German shepherd dog were smoking and talking about what they were watching on *Infowars*, the most famous conspiracy theories portal in the United States.

Gospel music is perhaps the most powerful element in these events.

During a post-election Trump rally in Michigan in April 2022, a local evangelist offered the following prayer, "Father in heaven, we firmly believe that Donald Trump is the current and true president of the United States." He prayed "in Jesus' name." The prayer was offered for precinct delegates to the upcoming Michigan Republican convention, endorsing Trump-endorsed candidates, naming them all, and drawing applause from the crowd.

"The infusion of explicitly religious fervor — much of it rooted in the charismatic tradition, which emphasizes the power of the Holy Spirit — into the right-wing movement is changing the atmosphere of events and rallies, many of which feature Christian symbols and rituals, especially praise music."

The *NYT* aptly comments, "Trump rallies are taking on the feel of worship events, from the stage to the audience."

It is not surprising that given Russian President Vladimir Putin's strong defense of Christian values, the Republican party is divided over the president and his attack on Ukraine.[133]

An additional motive for militant Christian nationalism is represented by former General Michael Flynn.[134] He has been touring the country since the late 2020s as the leader of a far-right movement that seeks to place "Christianity" at the center of the nation's civic life and institutions. Michelle R. Smith of the *Associated Press* wrote that Flynn:

"He's building a movement, headlining rallies that draw anti-vaxxers, election deniers and extremists from around the country. He's building alliances. He's made around 100 political endorsements for this year's elections."

He began by claiming, as did Trump, that the 2020 election results in Biden's favor were fraudulent. He went so far as to suggest that Trump could confiscate voting

---

[133] Ibid.

[134] Richard Rowley (Writer), & Richard Rowley (Director) (2022, October 18). Michael Flynn's Holy War (Season 41, Episode 2) [TV Series Episode]. Raney Aronson, David Fanning (Executive Producers), *Frontline*. Public Broadcasting Service (PBS). Note: unless otherwise noted, this is the same source.

machines. He proposed the idea of establishing martial law. What he called an ongoing coup d'etat.

He affirms that the country is in a battle against authentic civilization and wants to project its safeguard under the "banner of Christ;" in a proclaimed revival that he affirms has already begun. He has also expressed that, "We are a faith-based society, and that's in our DNA. It's in the DNA of the United States of America."

Flynn is regarded among his supporters as a martyr, a warrior, and an evangelist. He claims to be the absolute product of prayer, something with which his worst enemies, namely the left, the socialists, the Marxists, and the communists, are terrified. That vision would be traced to him from his childhood by an ultra-conservative Catholic education.

Flynn played a major role in the January 5, 2021 marches in Washington DC, one day before the insurrection on Capitol Hill.

When Liz Cheney asked him if he justified the violence that took place that day, as well as the peaceful transition of power in the United States, he declined to answer.

Smith tells us that, "After the insurrection, Flynn and those around him immediately began talking about the future and how to influence elections down to the local level."

She further adds that after the insurrection, Flynn moved to Florida, where he established the base of operations for a network of well-financed organizations, including America's Future, Resilient Patriot, Tower 1 LLC, as well as Digital Soldiers Media, which changed its name to Manasota Shores Real Estate.

America's Future was created in 1946 and is known for being very conservative and anti-communist.

Also, located in Sarasota County, The Hollow is one of the groups supported by Flynn. They emphasize their family activities. They even celebrate weddings. However, they also hold right-wing political events with extremists like the Proud Boys and offered gun training for children as young as 6 years old. Michael Flynn was often there.

The site has a large outdoor cross for worship services, which was Flynn's idea.

Victor Mellor, the owner of The Hollow, fears that the United States will become another Venezuela because of what he considers to be socialist and communist ideas. He was present with his son at the insurrection against the Capitol on January 6, 2021.

Mellor told *Frontline*, "The future America's going to look back at what's going on right now. This is what they're going to talk about. Maybe not even World War II. And I firmly believe that. We are at a testing stage of our country. We just are. We'll just see how the elections go, OK? If they try to steal it again, we will be at a new level of—will be unprecedented. And then, I'm glad I'm in Florida is all I have to say, OK?"

Many of the supporters of Christian nationalism are, in Hedges' words, "Christian fascists [that] stand in the pulpits of mega-churches and denounce Obama as the Antichrist."[135]

Add to that the work of Republican Congresswoman Marjorie Taylor Greene, who is a harsh conspiracy theorist and hate theorist, including against Jews, Democrats, and

---

[135] Chris Hedges, The Death of the Liberal Class (Capitán Swing Libros, S.L., Madrid, 2016), ob. cit.

520

others.[136] She declares herself to be deeply Christian, pro-life, pro-gun, pro-Trump.[137] She said in July 2022, "We need to be the party of nationalism and I'm a Christian, and I say it proudly, we should be Christian nationalists."[138]

Lauren Boebert is also a Republican congresswoman, who is a gun activist[139] and known to be part of the far right.[140] She also said in that year before a Colorado Springs crowd on a Sunday:

"The church is supposed to direct the government, the government is not supposed to direct the church."

"I'm tired of this separation of church and state junk. This is not in the Constitution, it was in a stinking letter and it means nothing like what they say it does."[141]

Greene and Boebert, along with Matt Gaetz, were part of the opposition votes to award the Congressional Gold Medal to the law enforcement officers who fought to defend the Capitol from attack. All supported Trump, and the votes for the no vote were too many.[142]

The New York Times reported in February of that year, that "An emboldened extremist wing flexes its power in a leaderless G.O.P." It adds that "With no dominant leader other than the deplatformed one-term president, a radical right movement that became emboldened under President Donald J. Trump has been maneuvering for more power."[143]

According to a February 2023 poll by the Public Religion Research Institute and the Brookings Institution that same month, more than half of Republicans support Christian nationalism, although most Americans do not adhere to Christian nationalism.[144] Many congregations and pastors are pro-Trump and want the establishment of a theocracy in America.[145]

---

[136] Lauren Gambino (Feb. 6, 2021), Who is the Republican extremist Marjorie Taylor Greene, The Guardian; Alan Fram, Brian Slodysko and Kevin Freking (Feb. 4, 2021), Divided House officially removes Rep. Marjorie Taylor Greene from committees, punishing far-right provocateur for violent, racist rhetoric, The Chicago Tribune.

[137] Ibid.

[138] Amanda Tyler (July 27, 2022), Opinion: Marjorie Taylor Greene's words on Christian nationalism are a wake-up call, CNN.

[139] Olafimihan Oshin (May 5, 2023), Boebert offers bill to repeal bipartisan gun control measures, The Hill.

[140] Jesse Paul (June 1, 2021), Lauren Boebert is known for her far-right Republican views. But Republicans alone didn't send her to Congress, The Colorado Sun.

[141] Amanda Taheri (June 29, 2022), Rep. Lauren Boebert Calls Separation of Church and State 'Junk,' Says Church Should Direct Government, People.

[142] Philip Bump (June 16, 2021), What's the unifying force behind the House's far-right 'nay' caucus, The Washington Post.

[143] Annie Karni and Mike Baker (Feb. 1, 2021), An emboldened extremist wing is flexing its power in a leaderless G.O.P., The New York Times.

[144] Ashley Lopez (Feb. 14, 2023), More than half of Republicans support Christian nationalism, according to a new survey, National Public Radio.

[145] John Burnett (Jan. 23, 2022), Christian nationalism is still thriving - and is a force for returning Trump to power, National Public Radio.

There is no doubt, as Ed Kilgore wrote in *Intelligencer*, that "Mixing Christianity with nationalism is a recipe for fascism."[146]

The Catholic Church in the United States has suffered the penetration of extreme right-wing conspiracy theories. We are talking about the conservative side, which is in the majority and a good sector has been affected. Moreover, media such as *OnePeter5*, *LifeSiteNews*, *The Remnant*, *Church Militant*, *Vatican Insider*, and others, who are traditionalist Catholics, yearn for a United States led by Trump or someone similar that will give strength to a union of Church and State to lead the world to surrender to a conservative Catholic Church and to a not distant future papacy that adheres to tradition. A pre-Vatican II Roman Catholic Church.

Kathryn Joyce wrote that "Catholicism's increasingly powerful political right reflects fringe America, fueled by paranoia, conspiracy, racism, and the threat of apocalypse."[147]

Many media outlets have shown their deep concern about Christian nationalism, which threatens to eliminate American democracy. For example, "A Christian Insurrection," as published by *The Atlantic*.[148] *Religious Dispatches* wrote of "Attack on the US Capitol Has Many Journos Finally Taking Evangelical Authoritarianism and Christian Nationalism Seriously."[149] Likewise the Council on Foreign Relations (CFR), with its article "The Rise of Christian Nationalism."[150] And there have been many other significant articles.[151] As well as a book profusely documenting concern about the role of American Catholic bishops and the far right.[152]

Leslie Cohen in *The Cairo Review of Global Affairs* indicated:

"Christian Nationalism in the United States is a movement on the rise. It can be defined as an ideology that merges Christian identity with notions of American patriotism, and seeks to establish an explicitly Christian government. Since the lead up to Donald Trump's presidential election in 2016, and particularly in the aftermath of the January 6, 2021 insurrection, Christian Nationalism has been emboldened"[153]

---

[146] Ed Kilgore (September 18, 2022), Mixing Christianity with Nationalism Is a Recipe for Fascism, Intelligencer.

[147] Kathryn Joyce (Oct. 30, 2020), Deep State, Deep Church: How QAnon and Trumpism Have Infected the Catholic Church, Vanity Fair.

[148] Emma Green (January 8, 2021), A Christian Insurrection, The Atlantic.

[149] Chrissy Stroop (Jan. 14, 2021), Attack on the US Capitol Has Many Journos Finally Taking Evangelical Authoritarianism and Christian Nationalism Seriously, Religion Dispatches.

[150] Andrew L. Whitehead (invited), Irina A. Faskianos (chair) (February 9, 2021), The Rise of Christian Nationalism, Council on Foreign Relations.

[151] Jack Jenkins (February 9, 2022), New report details the inuence of Christian nationalism on the insurrection, Religion News Service; Jack Jenkins (January 12, 2021), For insurrectionists, a violent faith brewed from nationalism, conspiracies and Jesus, Religion News Service; Morgan Lee (January 13, 2021), Christian Nationalism Is Worse Than You Think, Christianity Today.

[152] Mary Jo McConahay, Playing God: American Catholic Bishops and The Far Right (Melville House Publishing, Brooklyn, NY, 2023).

[153] Leslie Cohen (February 8, 2023), Fear and Power: Christian Nationalism in America, The Cairo Review of Global Affairs.

Salon:

"[...]religious leaders have used the rhetoric of faith to minimize and redirect responsibility for the violence of that day: whether it's people like Wallnau or South Carolina televangelist Mark Burns blaming "antifa soldiers" for perpetrating a false-flag operation to smear Trump supporters; Mike Huckabee suggesting, in email newsletters over the last six months, that Nancy Pelosi may have orchestrated the attack, and casting indicted Jan. 6 protesters as political prisoners; or former Vice President Mike Pence, in a December interview with the Christian Broadcasting Network, downplaying the very attack in which an angry mob called for his execution."[154]

For its part, *The New York Times Magazine* reported on the Thomases (Clarence and Ginni Thomas), regarding the assault on the Capitol:

"Ginni Thomas co-signed a letter in December calling for House Republicans to expel Representatives Liz Cheney and Adam Kinzinger from their conference for joining the Jan. 6 committee. Thomas and her co-authors said the investigation "brings disrespect to our country's rule of law" and "legal harassment to private citizens who have done nothing wrong," adding that they would begin "a nationwide movement to add citizens' voices to this effort."
"A few weeks later, the Supreme Court ruled 8 to 1 to allow the release of records from the Trump White House related to the Jan. 6 attack. Justice Thomas was the sole dissenter."[155]

Subsequently, the magazine indicates something alarming about Clarence Thomas, in conversation with his friend Leo, of the Federalist Society:

"Leo, a Catholic like the justice, first met him when he was clerking on the District of Columbia Circuit. Thomas, then a judge on that court, became a mentor. The justice has spent time at Leo's New England vacation home, is godfather to one of his children and has supported him through hardships, including the death of his 14-year-old daughter from spina bifida. The two men often discussed religion — Thomas once recommended he read "A History of Christianity" by Paul Johnson — and Leo says Justice Thomas saw parallels between how the church grew and how to build a body of conservative jurisprudence.

"It's very similar to what happened with the Catholic Church in the Middle Ages," he said of the justice's approach, adding that the church and its institutions "did their work during that time, laying the foundations for future Catholic thinking and Catholic thought to sort of grow the church and preserve its traditions. It happened quietly; it did not happen in the grand chambers of the Vatican, but it happened."[156]

---

[154] Kathryn Joyce (Jan. 6, 2022), How Christian nationalism drove the insurrection: A religious history of Jan. 6, Salon.
[155] Danny Hakim and Jo Becker (February 22, 2022/September 1, 2022), The Long Crusade of Clarence and Ginni Thomas, The New York Times Magazine.
[156] Ibid.

Dangers on the horizon-2

The Speaker of the U.S. House of Representatives, Mike Johnson, in November 2023 dismissed the validity of the wall of separation between Church and State. His ambition is to establish a government strongly influenced by biblical religious principles.[157]

Add to the above and more, a possible second term for Trump or another candidate aligned with his policies. Project 2025 is a plan to reshape the executive branch of the U.S. federal government to support Trump's agenda in the event of a Republican victory in the November 2024 presidential election. The Presidential Transition Project 2025 is organized by The Heritage Foundation and represents the effort of a broad and powerful coalition of conservative organizations united to ensure the success of the administration that begins in January 2025. The project claims it seeks to rescue America from the radical left and to put in its place a conservative, Judeo-Christian values-friendly administration. Its 920-page document, entitled Mandate for Leadership: The Conservative Promise, says on page 43 about the executive branch and its relationship to the president:

"The modern conservative President's task is to limit, control, and direct the executive branch on behalf of the American people. This challenge is created and exacerbated by factors like Congress's decades-long tendency to delegate its lawmaking power to agency bureaucracies, the pervasive notion of expert "independence" that protects so-called expert authorities from scrutiny, the presumed inability to hold career civil servants accountable for their performance, and the increasing reality that many agencies are not only too big and powerful, but also increasingly weaponized against the public and a President who is elected by the people and empowered by the Constitution to govern."[158]

Note that after critically pointing out the unlimited and uncontrolled use of executive power among the various agencies under its purview, the solution offered is to concentrate all that power on a single agent: the president. To use it "for the benefit of the people." The matter does not end there. Let's look at page 44 on how the president should assume that power:

"The great challenge confronting a conservative President is the existential need for aggressive use of the vast powers of the executive branch to return power—including power currently held by the executive branch—to the American people. Success in meeting that challenge will require a rare combination of boldness and self-denial: boldness to bend or break the bureaucracy to the presidential will and self-denial to use the bureaucratic machine to send power away from Washington and back to America's families, faith communities, local governments, and states.

Fortunately, a President who is willing to lead will find in the Executive Office of the President (EOP) the levers necessary to reverse this trend and impose a sound direction for the nation on the federal bureaucracy."[159]

---

[157] Ed Pilkington (Nov. 15, 2023), Speaker Mike Johnson calls separation of church and state 'a misnomer', The Guardian; Ronald Brownstein (Oct. 31, 2023), Mike Johnson symbolizes a new turn for the religious right, CNN.
[158] Paul Dans and Steven Groves (eds.), Mandate for Leadership: The Conservative Promise: Project 2025 (The Heritage Foundation, Washington, DC, 2023), p. 43.
[159] Ibid, p. 44.

524

This is not to say that abuses do not exist in various government agencies, but the solution does not lie in concentrating such power in the hands of a single individual. *Politico* rightly pointed out:

"They aim to defund the Department of Justice, dismantle the FBI, break up the Department of Homeland Security and eliminate the Departments of Education and Commerce, to name just a few of their larger targets. They want to give the president complete power over quasi-independent agencies such as the Federal Communications Commission, which makes and enforces rules for television and internet companies that have been the bane of Trump's political existence in the last few years."[160]

Project 2025's favorite Republican candidate is unquestionably Donald Trump. His allies have planned to use the federal government to punish critics and opponents if he wins a second term by appointing individuals he wants to punish or prosecute. His associates plan to potentially invoke the Insurrection Act on his first day in office to deploy the military against civilian protesters.[161]

He has said privately to advisers and friends that he wants the Justice Department to investigate former officials and allies who have become critical of him while in office.[162]

Much of the organization for a possible second term was unofficially outsourced to Project 2025, including draft executive orders to deploy the military to the nation under the Insurrection Act, according to someone involved in the conversations and internal communications, which were reviewed by *The Washington Post*. According to internal communications, such a proposal was identified as an immediate priority.[163]

In addition to all this, we read one of the points about initiatives based on the Christian faith to be promoted by the government:

"**Sabbath Rest.** God ordained the Sabbath as a day of rest, and until very recently the Judeo-Christian tradition sought to honor that mandate by moral and legal regulation of work on that day. Moreover, a shared day off makes it possible for families and communities to enjoy time off together, rather than as atomized individuals, and provides a healthier cadence of life for everyone. Unfortunately, that communal day of rest has eroded under the pressures of consumerism and secularism, especially for low-income workers.

Congress should encourage communal rest by amending the Fair Labor Standards Act (FLSA) to require that workers be paid time and a half for hours worked on the Sabbath. That day would default to Sunday, except for employers with a sincere religious observance of a Sabbath at a different time (e.g., Friday sundown to Saturday sundown); the obligation would transfer to that period instead. Houses of worship (to the limited extent they may have FLSA-covered employees) and employers legally required to operate around the clock (such as

---

[160] Michael Hirsh (Sept. 19, 2023), Inside the Next Republican Revolution, Politico.
[161] Isaac Arnsdorf, Josh Dawsey and Devlin Barrett (Nov. 6, 2023), Trump and allies plot revenge, Justice Department control in a second term, The Washington Post.
[162] Ibid.
[163] Ibid.

hospitals and first responders) would be exempt, as would workers otherwise exempt from overtime."[164]

Attorney Jonathan Berry, who wrote that section for Project 2025,[165] belongs to the Federalist Society.

Bettina Krause, the editor of *Liberty* magazine, wrote that policy proposals that repudiate the Constitution's limits on governance, "or which attempt to impose a religious orthodoxy or preference" are to be condemned. Such is the test where Project 2025 fails, she says, spectacularly.[166]

Against this backdrop, it is worth closing this chapter with the words of Anthea Butler, professor of religious studies and African studies at the University of Pennsylvania, when asked about American democracy in an interview:

"Imagine that American democracy is a patient in the hospital. If you were a type of religious figure — a priest, an imam, a rabbi or the like — what counsel would you be offering that patient in this dire moment?

"I will answer that question in the context of the Catholic tradition. In that faith tradition there is something called "extreme unction." This is when you are on your deathbed, and they come to you to give you a prayer. Before the changes of Vatican II, the priest also carried a little kit, which had what would be used for communion and other needs. If I were diagnosing democracy right now in America, it is in a state of extreme unction. American democracy is in its last moments and it is going to need a miracle to get up from that deathbed. I would whisper in that patient's ear right now that you had better decide to fight back or you are dead in the next 15 minutes. Your 15 minutes are about up."[167]

[164] Paul Dans and Steven Groves (eds.), Mandate for Leadership: The Conservative Promise: Project 2025 (The Heritage Foundation, Washington, DC, 2023), p. 589.
[165] Ibid, p. 581.
[166] Bettina Krause (January/February 2024), The Real Problem With "Project 2025," Liberty Magazine.
[167] Chauncey Devega (Oct. 19, 2021), Religion scholar Anthea Butler on "White Christianity" and its role in fueling fascism, Salon.

CHAPTER
16

Schism in the Catholic Church and the resistance against Pope Francis

Schism under Francis' papacy

"Bishop of Rome" reads the 2013 edition of the Pontifical Yearbook for Pope Francis. But his predecessor is defined as "supreme pontiff emeritus."[1]

From the beginning of his pontificate, Francis chose to call himself almost exclusively "bishop of Rome." Unlike him, on page 23 of the 2012 edition of the Annuario Pontificio, Benedict XVI, in addition to calling himself "bishop of Rome," is also called "Vicar of Jesus Christ, Successor of the Prince of the Apostles, Supreme Pontiff of the Universal Church, Primate of Italy, Archbishop and metropolitan of the Roman province, Sovereign of Vatican City-State, Servant of the Servants of God." However, in the 2013 Yearbook and on the same page, only "Francis / bishop of Rome" appears, with the other titles appearing on page 24 in the background.[2] Such a difference has marked most of his papacy in many ways.

Early on and over the years, Francis' papacy has concerned conservatives because of his radical style and the various changes in facets of Church doctrine.

He replaced Cardinal Gerhard Ludwig Müeller as prefect of the Sacred Congregation for the Doctrine of the Faith. Müeller was at odds with Francis' vision of a more inclusive church, criticizing the pope's Apostolic Exhortation Amoris Laetitia. Francis chose Jesuit Luis Ladaria Ferrer instead.[3] Some of the cardinals opposed to the pope are Müller, Raymond Leo Burke, Robert Sarah, and Walter Brandmüller. But there are also other prelates, such as Bishop Athanasius Schneider and Archbishop Carlo Maria Viganò. All of them also have in common that they supported the then US President Donald Trump, particularly because of his theocratic centrality over the country. Considered the champion of justice to return the Gospel to the world.

Pope Emeritus Benedict XVI was against some of Francis' attempts at doctrinal progressivism, which caused him deep discomfort. Thus, for example, when Pope Emeritus co-authored with Cardinal Robert Sarah - belonging to the conservative resistance against Francis - a book favoring priestly celibacy.[4] The pope reportedly called Archbishop Georg Gänswein, secretary to Benedict XVI and then prefect of

---

[1] Sandro Magister (May 23, 2013), Vatican Diary / The identity documents of the last two Popes, Settimo Cielo.

[2] Ibid.

[3] Maquita Peters (July 1, 2017), Pope Francis Replaces Conservative Top Theologian, The Two-Way.

[4] MDZ Mundo (January 13, 2020), Ratzinger contra Bergoglio: el tema que enfrenta a los dos Papas, MDZ.

Francis' papal household, to ask Benedict to retract his name from that book.[5] Someone important in the Curia said about Francis:

"He is soft on homosexuals, lesbians, and transsexuals. How dare he criticize the curia? He accuses us of suffering from spiritual Alzheimer's because his papacy is crumbling." He is angered by the rebuke he gave to the Cardinals four years ago, because of the "grave illness" that the rumors entailed. The pontiff declared: "Brothers, let us be on our guard against the terrorism of gossip."[6]

Progressives counted on Francis, while conservatives had Pope Emeritus Benedict XVI.[7] But Cardinal Walter Kasper once said "Francis is not a liberal, he is a radical: one who goes back to the roots. Liberal expectations are not part of his agenda."[8] We saw elsewhere that this is part of his ambiguity.

The Washington Post reported that there are deep divisions in the Catholic Church over the role taken on by Pope Francis.[9] Many conservatives reproach him for his criticism of capitalism, his rhetorical distancing from critical points of the culture war, and his efforts to liberalize the church's teachings on divorce. Even a Polish priest - Edward Staniek - prayed for his death if he did not change his heart. It is a conflict between the progressive followers of Pope Francis and the conservatives who sighed for Benedict XVI. Those are two different visions of the church's relationship with modernity. Ross Douthat, a Catholic and columnist for *The New York Times*, wrote "With more popes like Francis, Catholic truth will stand on a knife's edge."

The Synod of Bishops on the Family, convened in 2014 and 2015, revealed in its narrative the Jesuit pope's plan to alter Catholic teaching more profoundly than at the Second Vatican Council. The pope failed at least in the short term to organize the outcome of the synod. The main objective was to revise the church rule that forbids remarried Catholics to receive the Eucharist unless a church tribunal annuls it by declaring the first marriage invalid. Douthat states that:

"To toss out their traditional interpretation would set the church sliding down a slippery slope toward endorsing same-sex marriage, polygamy and "any stable, entangling commitment that fell outside the norms proposed by Catholic sexual teaching." Before you can recite a Hail Mary, ancient dogmas will crumble into a "theology of situations."

---

[5] Dorothy Cummings McLean (Jan. 15, 2020), Vatican insider: 'Furious' Francis demanded Benedict retract name from priestly celibacy book, LifeSiteNews.
[6] John Cornwell (February 16, 2019), Benedicto XVI vs Francisco I: la guerra oculta que divide al Vaticano, Vanity Fair.
[7] Ibid.
[8] Rubén Cruz (Nov. 13, 2019), Kasper: "El papa Francisco no es liberal, es radical", Vida Nueva Digital.
[9] Molly Worthen (May 18, 2018), A conservative Catholic's case against Pope Francis, The Washington Post. Note: unless otherwise noted, this is the same source.

Christopher Lamb, Rome correspondent for *The Tablet*, also explained:

"The theological attacks on Francis are now increasingly politicized with those voicing doctrinal concerns about the pope's teaching so often aligned with nationalist political agendas which run counter to everything this pontificate stands for."[10]

He adds, "For liberals, Francis is too conservative and for conservatives he's too liberal. The Pope is an old-fashioned Jesuit who can't be put into a box."[11] That is part of the ambiguity that characterizes him.

At least until 2020, 30% of the clergy, laity, and bishops of the world church are against the pope; and they are already trying to influence the next conclave.[12] The English-speaking public has been the most scandalized by his non-protocol and straightforward manner.[13]

But the theological attacks on Francis are increasingly politicized, often aligned with nationalist political agendas that run counter to everything his pontificate stands for.[14]

The Telegraph reported that "Even allies of Pope Francis admit there is a schism, if not a deep rift between conservatives and progressives at the highest levels of the Catholic Church."[15]

In September 2017, sixty-two disgruntled Catholics, including a retired bishop and a former Vatican bank chief, published an open letter accusing the pope of seven specific counts of teaching labeled heretical.[16]

Cardinal George Pell, who was chosen by Francis after his election as one of his eight advisory members on the reform of the Vatican bureaucracy (the Roman Curia) and other important Vatican positions, died in January 2023. In his will, he criticized the 2022 Synod's working document as a "potpourri"; as a New Age outpouring of goodwill where there is no mention of the Catholic faith or the New Testament. He further denounced in his testament that, "Commentators of every school, if for different reasons, with the possible exception of Father Spadaro, SJ, agree that this pontificate is a disaster in many or most respects; a catastrophe." He also criticized how Pope Francis was persecuting traditionalists, nuns, and even the legacy of Pope John Paul II in faith and morals; being "under systemic attack."[17] He wrote how Francis, pretending to carry out reforms, more or less veiledly defended corruption:

"Initially the Holy Father strongly backed the reforms. He then prevented the centralization of investments, opposed the reforms and most attempts to unveil corruption, and supported (then) Archbishop Becciu, at the centre of Vatican financial establishment. Then in 2020, the Pope turned on Becciu and eventually ten persons

---

[10] Charles Collins (April 29, 2020), 'Outsider Pope' faces resistance as he tries to reform the Church, author says, Crux Catholic Media.

[11] Ibid.

[12] Elena Magariños (May 14, 2020), Marco Politi: "El 30% del clero está en contra del papa Francisco", Vida Nueva Digital.

[13] Charles Collins (April 29, 2020), 'Outsider Pope' faces resistance as he tries to reform the Church, author says, Crux Catholic Media.

[14] Ibid.

[15] Nick Squires (Jan. 8, 2023), Pope Francis could be ousted in 'secret plan' by Vatican hardliners, The Telegraph.

[16] Andrew Brown (October 27, 2017), The war against Pope Francis, The Guardian.

[17] T. S. Flanders (Jan. 24, 2023), The Last Testament of Cardinal Pell, OnePeterFive.

were placed on trial and charged. Over the years, few prosecutions were attempted from AIF reports of infringements.

"The external auditors Price Waterhouse and Cooper were dismissed and the Auditor General Libero Milone was forced to resign on trumped up charges in 2017. They were coming too close to the corruption in the Secretariat of State."[18]

He stressed that after the Second Vatican Council, Church authorities often underestimated the hostile power of secularization, the world, the flesh, and the devil, especially in the West; overestimating the influence and strength of the Catholic Church.[19] Pell supported a pope who would bring order and a defense of church doctrine, in a document circulated to all cardinals in an attempt to raise awareness for the next conclave. [20]

Many claimed that Benedict XVI's death on December 31, 2022, would mark a new era for Pope Francis and predicted a major conservative backlash.[21] Days later, it was reported that a campaign was organized by Vatican hardliners to put Francis under such deep stress that he would have to resign. Archbishop Georg Gänswein, who for 19 years was Benedict XVI's personal secretary, would be one of the members of such a campaign, who in his soon-to-be-published memoir wrote that Benedict XVI was deeply hurt that Pope Francis would end the use of the traditional Latin Mass. And Gänswein has not held back in his criticism of the pope. Other highly critical members include Cardinals Raymond Burke and Gerhard Müller, the latter who authored the book *In Buona Fede. La religione nel XXI secolo* ("In Good Faith: Religion in the 21st Century") which was published in November 2022 and harshly criticizes the pope's pontificate. As well as the president of the U.S. Conference of Catholic Bishops Timothy Broglio and others.[22] Francis had already rebuked his critics for their defense of rigidity, and for not adapting to Western post-Christianity.[23]

In addition, the John Paul II Pontifical Institute, entrusted by Wojtyla in 1982 to Cardinal Carlo Caffarra, was threatened under Francis' papacy as it undermined the church's traditional teaching on the family and sexuality.

With Pope Francis, came the appointment of Archbishop Paglia as Grand Chancellor of the Institute, with whom the Institute's vision was slowly undermined and stealthily sabotaged. Life-long professors, such as Livio Melina, Jaroslaw Kupczak, and Stanislaw Grygiel, were dismissed in 2019.

They were replaced by theologians such as the priest Maurizio Chiodi, who supported artificial contraception. And in the spirit of Amoris Laetitia, he declared that under certain conditions same-sex couples could engage in sexual relations to strengthen their relationship.

---

[18] Ibid.

[19] Ibid.

[20] Sandro Magister (March 15, 2022), A Memorandum on the Next Conclave Is Circulating Among the Cardinals. Here It Is, L'Espresso.

[21] Ed. Condon (Jan. 19, 2023), 'Pope Francis unleashed' vs the 'conservative plot' - are either real?," The Pillar.

[22] Nick Squires (Jan. 8, 2023), Pope Francis could be ousted in 'secret plan' by Vatican hardliners, The Telegraph.

[23] Bradford Betz (Dec. 22, 2019), Pope Francis warns of 'rigidity,' says church must adapt or it will become increasingly irrelevant, Fox News.

Chiodi was accompanied at the Institute by priest Pier Davide Guenzi, another advocate of sexual relations between homosexual couples.

But in 2021, Monsignor Philippe Bordeyne, a distinguished moral theologian and rector of L'Institut Catholique de Paris, was elected as the new president of the Institute; and he favors the private blessing of homosexual unions.

More than one hundred and fifty students and alumni of the Institute signed a letter on July 24, 2019, pointing out that the recently approved bylaws would undermine the Institute's mission and identity.[24] But the president then reacted by defending the changes made.[25]

José Granados, a priest, said that the identity of the Institute was seriously threatened.[26]

Amid the controversy, Pope Emeritus Benedict XVI invited Monsignor Livio Melina to meet with him on August 1. The meeting took place. Melina had been president of the Institute from 2006-2019 until he was then dismissed following the promulgation of the new statutes.[27] *CNA* reported:

"The pope emeritus "wanted to receive Prof. Mons. Livio Melina at a private audience. After a long discussion of the recent events at the Pontifical Institute John Paul II, he granted his blessing, expressing his personal solidarity and assuring him of his closeness in prayer."[28]

But the ambiguities were running rampant. At the end of May 2015, Cardinal Secretary of State Pietro Parolin said the vote in favor of same-sex marriage in Ireland was a "defeat for humanity," adding that he was "deeply saddened by the result."[29]

For his part, Francis signed a decree issued on March 15, 2021, by the Congregation for the Doctrine of the Faith (CDF) stating that priests cannot bless homosexual unions.[30] Francis said that response was "not intended to be a form of unjust discrimination, but rather a reminder of the truth of the liturgical rite."[31]

The National Catholic Reporter stated:

"The Vatican's decree comes at a time when Catholics in Western Europe and the United States are increasingly accepting of LGBTQ relationships, with 61% of U.S. Catholics approving of gay marriage."[32]

---

[24] JD Flynn (July 26, 2019), Students say changes at Rome's JPII Institute undermine its mission, Catholic News Agency.

[25] CNA (July 30, 2019), After John Paul II Institute students publish letter, president defends changes, Catholic News Agency.

[26] JD Flynn (July 31, 2019), JPII Institute VP says school's identity is 'seriously threatened', Catholic News Agency.

[27] CNA (Aug. 5, 2019), Amid JPII Institute controversy, Benedict XVI meets with recently dismissed professor, Catholic News Agency.

[28] Ibid.

[29] Stephanie Kirchgaessner (May 26, 2015), Vatican says Ireland gay marriage vote is 'defeat for humanity', The Guardian.

[30] Christopher White (May 15, 2021), Vatican says priests can't bless gay couples. Why did Pope Francis approve this decree, National Catholic Reporter.

[31] BBC (May 10, 2021), German priests defy Vatican to bless gay couples, BBC News.

[32] Christopher White (May 15, 2021), Vatican says priests can't bless gay couples. Why did Pope Francis approve this decree, National Catholic Reporter.

In May, it was reported that priests in about 100 Catholic churches in Germany were blessing homosexual couples, in defiance of the decree.[33]

Love Wins, the German movement in favor of giving such a blessing, criticized the CDF document. Thousands of German priests and church employees signed a petition calling on the Church to extend such blessings, while some parishes displayed rainbow flags outside their churches.[34]

But Francis has supported civil-order homosexual unions.[35] He told Chilean sex abuse survivor Juan Carlos Cruz in 2018, "it doesn't matter that you are gay. God made you that way and he loves you the way you are, and it doesn't matter to me." Also in January 2021, he encouraged an Italian gay couple to raise their children as Catholics.[36]

James Martin, the Jesuit editor of *America* magazine, had said by the time of the CDF document that he feared the directive would incite "some LGBTQ Catholics to leave the Church, after years of feeling rejected and unwelcome."[37]

Pope Francis, as it became known in 2018, said "When in doubt, better not to let them in," to gay men at the Italian Bishops' Conference.[38]

Therefore, when he pointed out as unjust the criminalization of homosexuality by several governments, he also said that while homosexuality is a sin, so is to criticize homosexuals.[39]

Because of the remarks made to his statement, he then said he was quoting the catechism, that any relationship outside of marriage is a sin.[40] But his initial message does not seem to refer to that. Once again, one sees the ambiguity of his papacy to appeal to all.

A pope of controversies telling Biden that he can receive communion even though he promotes abortion. He told him that he is a good Catholic, but in turn has said that "For the Catholic faith, you cannot be pro-abortion and defend the environment."[41]

Conservative U.S. Catholic plot against Pope Francis
When asked about the dangers of sovereignism during an interview with the Italian daily *La Stampa* in August 2019, Francis responded:

---

[33] Ibid.

[34] Ibid; America (May 3, 2021), Catholic parishes in Germany to include gay and lesbian couples in planned 'blessing services for lovers', America.

[35] BBC (May 10, 2021), German priests defy Vatican to bless gay couples, BBC News.

[36] Christopher White (May 15, 2021), Vatican says priests can't bless gay couples. Why did Pope Francis approve this decree, National Catholic Reporter.

[37] Philip Pullella (March 17, 2021), Vatican ruling on same-sex couples prompts defiance, pain, confusion, Reuters.

[38] CNN Español (Jan. 26, 2023), El papa Francisco dijo que la homosexualidad es pecado pero "no es delito", CNN Español.

[39] Pablo Monroy (Jan. 25, 2023), "No es un delito. Sí, pero es pecado": Papa Francisco sobre la homosexualidad, Rolling Stone; see also Vatican News (Feb. 5, 2023), Pope: 'Entire world is at war and in self-destruction', Vatican News.

[40] Nicole Winfield (Jan. 28, 2023), Pope clarifies homosexuality and sin comments in note, Associated Press.

[41] Perfil (November 24, 2020), Papa Francisco: "No se puede estar a favor del aborto y defender el medio ambiente", Perfil.

"Sovereignty is an attitude of isolation. I am worried because you hear speeches that resemble Hitler's in 1934. "First us. Us.... Us"; these are scary thoughts. Sovereignism is closed-mindedness. A country must be sovereign, but not closed. Sovereignty must be defended, but relations with other countries, with the European Community, must also be protected and promoted. Sovereignty is an exaggeration that always ends badly: it leads to wars."[42]

Then, having been asked about populism, he said:

"It is the same thing. At the beginning I could not understand it, because, studying theology, I studied popularism, that is to say, the culture of the people: but one thing is that the people express themselves and another is to impose a populist attitude on the people. The people are sovereign (they have a way of thinking, of expressing themselves, of feeling, of evaluating), on the other hand, populisms lead us to sovereignisms: that suffix, "isms, never does any good."[43]

Undoubtedly, Francis was referring not only, but particularly to Donald Trump.

Many traditional American Catholics criticize Francis for his progressivism of Catholic orthodoxy, to which the pope explained that, "For me, it's an honor that Americans are attacking me."[44] And that while he does not want a schism, he is not afraid of it either.[45]

The Vatican editor of *Civiltà Cattolica*, the Jesuit Antonio Spadaro, as well as the editor of the Argentinean edition, Marcelo Figueroa -close collaborators of Francis-, wrote an article entitled "Evangelical Fundamentalism and Catholic Integralism: A surprising ecumenism."[46] They condemn the division of reality between absolute good and absolute evil. A trend radiated by George W. Bush after the terrorist attacks of September 11, 2001. Donald Trump was continuing the tradition but against a broader and more generic collective of "bad" and "very bad." Underlines the article:

"These stances are based on Christian-Evangelical fundamentalist principles dating from the beginning of the 20th Century that have been gradually radicalized. These have moved on from a rejection of all that is mundane – as politics was considered – to bringing a strong and determined religious-moral influence to bear on democratic processes and their results."

The authors indicate that the term "evangelical fundamentalism," can be assimilated into "evangelical right" or "theoconservatism."

And they condemn literal adherence to the Bible.

---

[42] Domenico Agasso Jr. (August 9, 2019), "El soberanismo me espanta, lleva a las guerras", La Stampa.
[43] Ibid.
[44] Inés San Martín (September 4, 2019), Pope Francis says 'it's an honor that Americans are attacking me', Cruz Catholic Media, Inc.
[45] Inés San Martín (September 11, 2019), On American critics, Pope says he doesn't want a schism but he's not afraid of it, Crux Catholic Media, Inc.
[46] Antonio Spadaro, Marcelo Figueroa (July 13, 2017), Evangelical Fundamentalism and Catholic Integralism: A surprising ecumenism, La Civiltà Cattolica. Note: unless otherwise noted, this is the same source.

The group the authors criticize indicates that threats to their understanding of the American way of life, include "modernist spirits, the black civil rights movement, the hippy movement, communism, feminist movements and so on."; as well as immigrants and Muslims.

"To maintain conflict levels, their biblical exegeses have evolved toward a decontextualized reading of the Old Testament texts about the conquering and defense of the "promised land," rather than be guided by the incisive look, full of love, of Jesus in the Gospels.

"Within this narrative, whatever pushes toward conflict is not off limits. It does not take into account the bond between capital and profits and arms sales. Quite the opposite, often war itself is assimilated to the heroic conquests of the "Lord of Hosts" of Gideon and David. In this Manichaean vision, belligerence can acquire a theological justification and there are pastors who seek a biblical foundation for it, using the scriptural texts out of context."

Such religious groups are mostly composed of "whites from the deep American South"; who are against the fight for climate change and *erroneously* believe in a literal understanding of the book of Genesis; thus promoting dominionism. They see in natural disasters an apocalyptic fulfillment, and prepare "for the imminent justice of an Armageddon." Any process of peace and dialogue would not be considered due to the paradigm described.

Steve Bannon, the then "chief strategist at the White House and supporter of an apocalyptic geopolitics" is criticized.

These groups want a theocracy, where the State is subjected to the Bible, "that is no different from the one that inspires Islamic fundamentalism."

It also reproaches "the passage from original puritan pietism, as expressed in Max Weber's The Protestant Ethic and the Spirit of Capitalism, to the "Theology of Prosperity" that is mainly proposed in the media and by millionaire pastors and missionary organizations with strong religious, social and political influence."

The authors point out that some electoral campaign messages and their semiotics were riddled with references to evangelical fundamentalism.

Finally, we note that the authors see "a strange form of surprising ecumenism is developing between Evangelical fundamentalists and Catholic Integralists brought together by the same desire for religious influence in the political sphere." What has been described conflicts with the objectives of Francis' pontificate:

"Francis radically rejects the idea of activating a Kingdom of God on earth as was at the basis of the Holy Roman Empire and similar political and institutional forms, including at the level of a "party."

In response to the article, there was a backlash, with accusations of anti-Americanism, and Archbishop Charles Chaput calling the authors "useful idiots." Thus evidencing a further rift between Pope Francis and American Catholics.[47] Indeed, not

---

[47] Jason Horowitz (Aug. 2, 2017), A Vatican Shot Across the Bow for Hard-Line U.S. Catholics, The New York Times; Archbishop Charles Chaput (July 18, 2017), A word about useful tools, Catholic Philly.

534

long after his election, Vatican ambassadors informed him to take special care in appointing bishops and cardinals in the United States; to which he replied, "I know that already."[48]

There are, says Tom Roberts, "a growing number of right-wing Catholic nonprofits with political motivations."[49] They have a prosperity gospel with a Catholic content and great strength, in the service of free-market capitalism. They are interested in joining forces with the U.S. Conference of Catholic Bishops.

The Napa Institute, one of the ultra-conservative Catholic organizations, sponsored a birthday soiree at the Rome residence of Cardinal James Harvey, an extreme right-wing American cleric. Present were Cardinals Raymond Burke, German Cardinal Ludwig Müller, Steve Bannon, who had invited Müller to Bannon's Washington headquarters - "Breitbart Embassy"-, and Cardinal Harvey.

Because there was a rise of the religious right from the evangelicalism provided by Reagan in the 1980s, the Catholic right is now growing and being well funded. It possesses greater strength being that "In the United States, Catholics constitute the largest and most organized Christian denomination and include Catholic parishes, schools and universities, and hospitals."

"The Napa Institute—with its mission, according to its tax forms, to "equip Catholic leaders to defend and advance the Catholic faith in the 'next America'"—is one of several Catholic nonprofits that have become forceful players within the church and at the intersection of religion and politics, and one of the most active."

Traditional-Catholic groups like the Knights of Columbus, who have given millions of dollars to the Vatican, make major charitable contributions and allocate funds for politically conservative think tanks, news agencies, and even the Federalist Society, which advocates for conservative judges. The main mastermind is an ultra-conservative Catholic, Leonard Leo, who has used many billions of dollars to advance conservative causes in the United States. Leo served as an advisor to the president on the choice of Catholic Supreme Court justices.[50] Leo controls a network of right-wing groups funded by dark money and wishes to mold the country under extreme right-wing Catholicism.[51] He belongs to the most conservative wing of the Catholic Church, namely Opus Dei, which was founded by the pro-Franco Spanish priest, Josemaría Escrivá de Balaguer.[52] For Opus Dei, there is no wall separating Church and State and Catholicism must reign supreme in government: under the pre-Vatican II ideology.

Supreme Court Justices John Roberts, Samuel Alito, Neil Gorsuch, Brett Kavanaugh, and Amy Coney Barrett are all Catholic.[53] The Catholic Information Center, founded

---

[48] Ibid.

[49] Tom Roberts (March 2019), The Rise of the Catholic Right, Sojourners. Note: unless otherwise noted, this is the same source. But see also Jason Horowitz (February 7, 2017), Steve Bannon Carries Battles to Another Influential Hub: The Vatican, The New York Times.

[50] Chris McGreal (September 4, 2022), Leonard Leo: the secretive rightwinger using billions to reshape America, The Guardian.

[51] Jay Michaelson (July 24, 2018), The Secrets Of Leonard Leo, The Man Behind Trump's Supreme Court Pick, Daily Beast.

[52] Matthew Fox (June 29, 2022), Supreme Court Judges Sharing an Opus Dei Seal of Approval, Daily Meditations with Matthew Fox.

[53] Ibid.

by McCloskey, an Opus Dei priest, "continue to have an outsize impact on policy and politics. It is the conservative spiritual and intellectual center that McCloskey had imagined and its influence is felt in all of Washington's corridors of power."[54]

William Barr, former U.S. Attorney General under Trump, is also a Roman Catholic and served on the board of the Catholic Information Center from 2014-2017, which is likewise known for being a hub for conservative intellectuals, Republican politicians, and other well-connected Catholics in Washington DC. [55]

Barr said at the University of Notre Dame on October 11, 2019, quoting in extenso:

"On the one hand, we have seen the steady erosion of our traditional Judeo-Christian moral system and a comprehensive effort to drive it from the public square.

"On the other hand, we see the growing ascendancy of secularism and the doctrine of moral relativism.

"By any honest assessment, the consequences of this moral upheaval have been grim. [...]
"We are told we are living in a post-Christian era. But what has replaced the Judeo-Christian moral system? What is it that can fill the spiritual void in the hearts of the individual person? And what is a system of values that can sustain human social life? [...]
"First is the force, fervor, and comprehensiveness of the assault on religion we are experiencing today. This is not decay; it is organized destruction. Secularists, and their allies among the "progressives," have marshaled all the force of mass communications, popular culture, the entertainment industry, and academia in an unremitting assault on religion and traditional values.

"These instruments are used not only to affirmatively promote secular orthodoxy, but also drown out and silence opposing voices, and to attack viciously and hold up to ridicule any dissenters. [...]
As Catholics, we are committed to the Judeo-Christian values that have made this country great."[56]

They have also supported the Koch brothers, of Koch Industries, who since the Reagan era especially, have favored the religious cause and the Republican Party.[57]

Legatus and the Acton Institute, which are also Catholic, are devoted to individualism, unfettered capitalism, and diminishing government services, especially for the poor and marginalized. Stephen Schneck, former director of the Catholic University of America's Institute for Policy Research and Catholic Studies, said, "I

---

[54] Joe Heim (Jan. 14, 2019), 'Quite a shock': The priest was a D.C. luminary. Then he had a disturbing fall from grace, The Washington Post.
[55] John Gehring (July 23, 2020), William Barr, nation's top lawyer, is a culture warrior Catholic, National Catholic Reporter.
[56] Justice News (Oct. 11, 2019), Attorney General William P. Barr Delivers Remarks to the Law School and the de Nicola Center for Ethics and Culture at the University of Notre Dame, Justice News.
[57] Chris McGreal (September 4, 2022), Leonard Leo: the secretive rightwinger using billions to reshape America, The Guardian.

think we're in a kind of brave new world where these groups really are setting themselves up as authorities above the authorities." The explosion of religious nonprofits is "something that leaked over of American politics."[58]

Conservative and international Catholic conspiracy against Pope Francis

"I believe that the role of this pope is extremely prophetic" - a Jesuit superior told me in his office, staring at his desk in 2013 - "[...] you will see the governments making their files because he is so revolutionary." He supported with examples, the fact that the dominant Western capitalism would be against this pope. The journalist Vicens Lozano comments:

"That the Argentine pontiff is not the Vatican, or rather, that he does not participate in the secular atmosphere and tradition that make up the courtly life in the palaces of the Holy See, has been quite evident since he was elected on March 13, 2013. The Argentine pope is not resigned to bowing to that way of acting. He fights every day, and in recent times even more vigorously, to transform, with successes, but also with mistakes, the institution of the Church. His goal is to turn it into a solid and stable ship that can navigate the changing waters of the 21st century. This has made him in the eyes of many a rebel..., an enemy."[59]

That same year, a Polish priest named Pawel said in St. Peter's Square with great irritation: "This pope is not and never will be our pope. We do not want him. He disgusts us. He is a communist, a heretic, and he wants to destroy the Holy Mother Church. Either we throw him out now or he will put an end to the Christian world that our ancestors have instilled in us. Neither God nor the faithful want him. Out, out!"

This happened when thousands of pilgrims filled St. Peter's Square shortly before Pope Francis appeared under the window of the Apostolic Palace for the Angelus prayer and the final blessing. Then, the gendarmes had to take the priest away, as he began to shout a series of insults that horrified his listeners.

When Jorge Bergoglio was elected as the new pope, Lozano tells us, "the darkest forces of the institution began to conspire, to boycott, to defame and to make life impossible for the new pontiff. The machinery to wear down the image and the pontificate of the Argentine pope was set in motion with a shocking eagerness, both inside and outside the Vatican. This telluric force has not stopped and will not stop."

Similarly, in June 2014, a prestigious emeritus professor of Canon Law at the ultra-conservative Pontificia Università della Santa Croce in Rome explained:

"He is not the holy father the Church needs. He is very popular, but he is not the right man to face the challenges that we Catholics have to face in a 21st century that presents itself as a triumph of the evil one to destroy the work of God. We cannot hide the fact that the Church needs to face a world that has become worldly, where vice and depravity are presented as something natural. Where the evil one is winning the battle with each passing day. Where doctrine, faith, and tradition are called into question even by many elements of the Church itself, who, captivated by relativism,

---

[58] Tom Roberts (March 2019), The Rise of the Catholic Right, Sojourners.
[59] Vicens Lozano, Vaticangate: El complot ultra contra el papa Francisco y la manipulación del próximo conclave (Roca Editorial, 2023), ob. cit. Note: unless otherwise indicated, this is the same source.

liberal aberrations, feminism, gender ideology, or false religions, betray the principles of God's work. Where heresy is transformed into doctrine, and our sacred institution into an NGO. Yes, Francis is not the holy father we need. He is an imposter to be fought, a man without the principles that believers demand."

Later, referring to what those who thought like him would do, he said, "We must eliminate evil as soon as it is detected. Afterwards, we will lament that it is too late."

It has been confirmed by various sources that the most ultra-conservative forces of the Catholic Church, collaborating with external forces of the same quality, are fighting to annul or even eliminate Pope Francis. Either by making him resign or even by alleged assassination attempts. But if this is not possible, to work at full speed "to prepare with great care the machinery of the future conclave." If necessary, use the fabrication of evidence to blackmail the cardinals to manipulate the outcome of the votes in favor of an ultra-conservative candidate, and thus reverse all the changes and reforms made by Francis.

The Titular Archbishop of Ulpiana and former Apostolic Nuncio to the United States (2011-2016), Carlo Maria Viganò, was denounced by journalist Emiliano Fittipaldi for his great greed, which he proved with documents and the testimonies of his brother, the Jesuit biblical scholar Lorenzo Viganò, as well as his sister Rossana.[60] Carlo and his brother broke off relations after an escalation of tensions in early 2009 over their inheritance, resulting in a civil lawsuit that Lorenzo filed against Carlo in Milan court.

After the death of their father in 1961, the eight siblings had decided to jointly manage an estate of several tens of millions of euros; but after the death of their brother Giorgio, Carlo Maria began to dispose of the vast majority of the money, without warning; stripping his siblings of their inheritance and leaving them crumbs compared to the hundreds of millions of euros in his possession.

Rossana also had to bring Archbishop Viganò in 2012 before the courts of the Swiss canton of Graubünden. Carlo Maria stole 900 million lire from her, leaving her no part of it.

The conflict ended in 2014 with a settlement in which the archbishop paid her 180,000 Swiss francs which she donated to a hospital in Tanzania where her daughter works.

A court sentenced Carlo Maria in October 2018 to pay his brother €1.8 million.

In addition, 3.8 million euros from the IOR - Vatican Bank - came into Carlo Maria's possession; but they were actually destined for charitable works and specifically for a monastery in Burundi.

Such actions do not seem to give moral value to his attempts to discredit Francis' papacy.

However, the rest of Carlo Maria's brothers came out to deny Lorenzo's accusations years ago with dates and names of judges. And they showed documentation; which adds to the archbishop's statements.[61]

---

[60] Nicolas Senèze, Lo scisma americano: Come l'America vuole cambiare Papa (Mondadori, 2020), ob. cit. Note: unless otherwise indicated, this is the same source.

[61] https://www.aldomariavalli.it/wp-content/uploads/2018/08/Il-comunicato-dei-fratelli-Vigano.pdf; accessed June 13, 2023; Edward Pentin (Dec. 3, 2018), Archbishop Viganò Addresses Dispute With Brother Over Family Inheritance, National Catholic Register; Steve Skojec (Dec. 3, 2018), Archbishop Viganò Breaks Silence About Family Legal Battle, OnePeter5.

Now, during Pope Francis' September 2015 visit to the United States, one of his purposes was to defuse tensions between the nation's Catholic Church and the Obama administration.[62] During a private conversation at the nunciature in Washington D.C., Francis agreed with Viganò to see Kim Davis, an official who was jailed for five days for refusing to issue marriage licenses to gay couples in Kentucky. The condition was that it be "in a completely confidential manner, out of the media's attention." But Viganò got careless and did it his way, so, much publicity was given to the meeting, which greatly irritated Francis, who fired Viganò as apostolic nuncio in the North American country.

Upon his return to Rome, Viganò could no longer have free use of the large representative apartment of two hundred and fifty square meters that he occupied in Santa Marta when he was secretary general of the Vatican, and that he had been allowed to keep even after leaving for Washington to serve as nuncio. Added to this was an internal investigation into his handling of the allegations against Monsignor John Nienstedt for sexual abuse.

Unemployed and retired in Milan, Viganò reconnected with the most conservative circles in the Church and most opposed to Francis; out of which have come his strong attacks against his pontificate. To find out what happened, let's look at the additional background: Timothy Busch, a conservative Catholic lawyer, businessman, and philanthropist, co-founded the Napa Institute, which is "a network that brings together wealthy donors, conservative Catholic bishops and Republican politicians."[63]

In October 2017, Napa sponsored an event at Catholic University titled "Good Profit," in homage to the book of the same name by Charles Koch, the right-wing billionaire of Koch Industries. Busch said that "The evangelization of our country is being done by private foundations, Catholic NGOs, like Napa and Legatus." These remain "tethered to the church through a bishop... But they have access to capital that the church doesn't."[64]

Busch has been associated with right-wing Catholic efforts to discredit Pope Francis. Using for example the accusations of Archbishop Carlo Maria Viganò, who had shared with Busch his letter denouncing Francis' role in the McCarrick case, which we will quote below.[65]

On June 29, 2018, Napa hosted an evening for some close friends at San Paolo Fuori le Mura, or St. Paul Outside the Walls, in Rome.[66] The event was officially meant to celebrate the anniversary of the episcopal ordination of U.S. Cardinal James Harvey, archpriest of that papal basilica. That summer evening, Cardinal Harvey, a prudent but effective opponent of Pope Francis, welcomed such figures as U.S. Cardinal Raymond Burke, a great enemy of Pope Francis, and Princess Gloria von Thurn and Taxis, the well-known German Catholic activist. The aristocrat was characterized as the soul of the traditionalist opposition to the pope. After having bet for a long time on Cardinal Marc Ouellet, who seems never to have wanted to back down from Jorge Mario

---

[62] Nicolas Senèze, Lo scisma americano: Come l'America vuole cambiare Papa (Mondadori, 2020), ob. cit. Note: unless otherwise indicated, this is the same source.
[63] John Gehring (Dec. 16, 2021), Napa, Koch funding sparks backlash from Notre Dame professors, National Catholic Reporter.
[64] Tom Roberts (March 2019), The Rise of the Catholic Right, Sojourners.
[65] Ibid.
[66] Nicolas Senèze, Lo scisma americano: Come l'America vuole cambiare Papa (Mondadori, 2020), ob. cit. Note: unless otherwise indicated, this is the same source.

Bergoglio, the German aristocrat now placed her hopes in Cardinal Gerhard Müller, "former bishop of Regensburg - fiefdom of the Thurn und Taxis - and later prefect of the Congregation for the Doctrine of the Faith, recently removed from office by Francis." The princess would have introduced him to her friend Steve Bannon before the two men met in the offices of *Breitbart news* in Washington.

Also present was Carlo Maria Viganò, with whom Gloria von Thurn and Taxis "recalls having "a fabulous conversation that gave birth to the hope of "an alarm signal that will awaken the Church."

"[...] in the following days, while the Napa Institute was organizing the annual meeting on the magisterium of John Paul II in California, Viganò began to have contact with some journalists close to the most conservative circles." Journalists from Italy, Canada, and the United States. Among the Italians were Aldo Maria Valli and Marco Tosatti. In the United States, Robert Moynihan; and in Canada, John-Henry Western. There was a document full of accusations against Pope Francis.

Tim Busch would participate in the genesis of Archbishop Viganò's text, telling *The New York Times* that "Viganò has done us a great service." He also said that "Viganò has dictated an agenda to us: we must follow this example and move forward."

Busch, who was on the board of the Papal Foundation for financial aid, on the occasion of the meeting organized on October 2, 2018, in Washington by the Napa Institute, complained about the lack of (moral) reform in the Vatican, "We cannot allow the Vatican to get it so cheaply." "If we don't tolerate it in our businesses, we can't tolerate it in our Church," but noting that he respects priests and bishops "to the extent that they respect business practice and business sense."

"On September 6, the Legatus group, created by Tom Monaghan, and of which Tim Busch is also a member, announces the suspension and placement in a trust account of the annual contribution to the Vatican, namely eight hundred and twenty thousand dollars according to the "Wall Street Journal": this is a relatively small amount compared to the five hundred million euros of the combined budgets of the Vatican City State and the Holy See, but indicative for other donors."

In late August 2018, Viganò published a letter highly critical of Francis' papacy, particularly over the case of former Cardinal Theodore McCarrick and U.S. Jesuit interests. In the 11-page letter, Viganò stressed "that corruption has reached the very top of the Church hierarchy," referring particularly to the McCarrick case. Viganò recounts that the apostolic nuncios in the United States, Gabriel Montalvo, and Pietro Sambi, immediately informed the Vatican of Archbishop McCarrick's grave immorality with seminarians and priests. All this, since the year 2000, under the pontificate of John Paul II.[67]

Viganò also wrote a note on documents entrusted to him as Delegate for Pontifical Representations, and on December 6, 2006, he wrote to his superiors, Cardinal Tarcisio Bertone and Substitute Leonardo Sandri, that the facts attributed to McCarrick were of

---

[67] Testimony by His Excellency Carlo Maria Viganò Titular Archbishop of Ulpiana Apostolic Nuncio. Rome, August 22, 2018, p. 1.

extreme gravity and vileness, and he recommended taking harsh measures.[68] But Viganò was not written to on the matter.[69]

Benedict XVI placed sanctions on McCarrick, which were later communicated to Francis, who for decades was a friend of McCarrick, who openly boasted of his travels and missions to various continents, despite Francis' knowledge of his case.[70]

The pope asked Archbishop Viganò about the Jesuits in the United States, to which he replied that they "had played a key role in secularizing the country's influential Catholic universities, and had often been in the forefront of an effort to change Catholic teaching in a direction not in keeping with the wishes of all the recent Popes — Paul VI, John Paul I, John Paul II, and Benedict XVI." He added that if the pope "could manage to reign in the order, reform it, and restore it to its former orthodox path, it would be a great gift to the Church in the United States and throughout the world."[71]

On the McCarrick case, in February 2019, the Vatican finally expelled the cardinal for sexual abuse.[72]

In November, Viganò said of Pope Francis' ministry: "We painfully acknowledge how divisive and destructive his ministry has been." He condemned the divinization of the Earth in the figure of Pachamama, which was held at St. Peter's and St. Mary's in Traspontina with the Pope's permission.[73] Viganò expressed:

"Faced with such a scenario, in which the very survival of the Catholic Church is seriously threatened; in the face of so many reprehensible actions and statements by the Supreme Pontiff, one hundred scholars have drafted a Declaration asking "respectfully for Pope Francis to publicly and without ambiguity to repent and to repair these outrages." I felt it was my duty to unite my own voice to theirs. In similar fashion, all bishops and cardinals of the Catholic Church should feel obliged to "address a fraternal correction to Pope Francis for these scandals."[74]

On May 7, 2020, conservative bishops signed a letter written by Viganò,[75] entitled "Appeal for the Church and the World," which stated that, "there are powers interested in creating panic among the world's population with the sole aim of permanently imposing unacceptable forms of restriction on freedoms, of controlling people and of tracking their movements." Further, "The imposition of these illiberal measures is a disturbing prelude to the realization of a world government beyond all control." Among the signatories were three cardinals: "Cardinal Joseph Zen, emeritus bishop of Hong Kong, Cardinal Janis Pujats, emeritus archbishop of Riga, Latvia, and Cardinal Gerhard Muller, former prefect of the Congregation for the Doctrine of the Faith." Eight bishops also signed the letter, among them the bishop of a U.S. diocese, Joseph Strickland of

---

[68] Ibid, p. 2.

[69] Ibid, p. 3. Note: unless otherwise indicated, from here on it is the same page.

[70] Ibid, p. 6. Note: Id.

[71] Letter #48, 2019: A New Church, Inside the Vatican.

[72] Chico Harlan (Feb. 16, 2019), Ex-cardinal McCarrick defrocked by Vatican for sexual abuse, The Washington Post.

[73] Archbishop Carlo Maria Viganò (Nov. 21, 2019), Abp Vigano: Pope is subjecting Church to 'powerful forces' that want world government, LifeSiteNews.

[74] Ibid.

[75] CAN staff (May 7, 2020), Cardinal Sarah says he did not sign letter claiming coronavirus exploited for one-world government, Catholic News Agency.

Tyler, Texas;[76] and Bishop Rene Gracida, bishop emeritus of Corpus Christi. Also included is the auxiliary bishop of Astana, Kazakhstan, Athanasius Schneider.[77]

Cardinal Sarah, prefect of the Vatican's Congregation for Divine Worship and the Sacraments, who is among the signatories, said he did not sign. He expressed that while he shared some of the concerns raised regarding restrictions on fundamental freedoms, he did not sign the letter; asking the authors of the petition not to mention it.[78] But Archbishop Carlo Maria Viganò indicated that Cardinal Sarah did sign it, but then called for his removal because it was not advisable, given the position he held at the Vatican.[79]

He spoke for the October 23-25, 2020 Catholic Identity Conference (the 24th) in Pittsburgh, Pennsylvania, addressing the crisis in the Catholic Church, specifically the connection between Vatican II and Pope Francis' revolution. It was entitled "How the Revolution of Vatican II serves the New World Order." The conference featured Catholics from the more conservative wing such as Michael Matt of the Catholic newspaper *The Remnant*. With talks by Steve Bannon, Bishop Athanasius Schneider, Steven Mosher, Abby Johnson, Dr. Peter Kwasniewski, Diane Montagna, Vatican correspondent for *LifeSiteNews*; Christopher Ferrara, Dr. John Raoy, as well as many more embodying the resistance against Pope Francis and the Jesuits. That group compared themselves to the Crusaders or Knights Templar of the 11th-13th centuries. They have called the resistance to the pope and secularism: "HOLY WAR: The Kingdom of Christ vs. the Great Reset."[80]

Now, about the speech of Viganò, who pointed out in part:

"We know that the *New World Order* project consists in the establishment of tyranny by Freemasonry: a project that dates back to the French Revolution, the Age of Enlightenment, the end of the Catholic Monarchies, and the declaration of war on the Church. We can say that the New World Order is the antithesis of Christian society, it would be the realization of the diabolical *Civitas Diaboli – City of the Devil –* opposed to the *Civitas Dei – City of God –* in the eternal struggle between Light and Darkness, Good and Evil, God and Satan."[81]

He referred to the so-called "Deep Church" as the church of Francis, and the Deep State as the U.S. Democratic Party. He indicated "For sixty years, we have witnessed the eclipse of the true Church by an anti-church." He also noted that *"Fratelli Tutti* seems to be a form of Vatican endorsement of the Democratic candidate, in clear opposition to Donald Trump, and come a few days after Francis refused to grant audience to Secretary of State Mike Pompeo in Rome. This confirms which side the *children of light* are on, and who the *children of darkness* are." He also said, "In these

[76] JD Flynn (May 13, 2020), Vatican, US Church leaders quiet on coronavirus 'world government' letter signed by bishops, Catholic News Agency.
[77] CAN staff (May 7, 2020), Cardinal Sarah says he did not sign letter claiming coronavirus exploited for one-world government, Catholic News Agency.
[78] Ibid.
[79] Marco Tosatti (May 8, 2020), SARAH SIGNS THE APPEAL, THEN REVOKES. THE WAY IT HAPPENED, STILUM CURIAE.
[80] Michael J. Matt (October 26, 2020), Archbishop Viganò Addresses the Catholic Identity Conference 2020 (Francis & the New World Order), The Remant Newspaper.
[81] Ibid. Emphasis from The Remnant Newspaper. Note: unless otherwise noted, this is the same source.

extraordinary times, we hear a conspirator – Cardinal Godfried Danneels – tell us that, since the death of John Paul II, the *Mafia of St. Gallen* had been plotting to elect one of their own to Peter's Chair, which later turned out to be Jorge Mario Bergoglio."

Continued:

"The theme of *brotherhood*, an obsession for Bergoglio, finds its first formulation in *Nostra Ætate* and *Dignitatis Humanae*. The latest Encyclical, *Fratelli Tutti*, is the manifesto of this Masonic vision, in which the cry *Liberté, Égalité, Fraternité* replaced the Gospel, for the sake of a unity among men that leaves out God. Note that the *Document on Human Fraternity for World Peace and Living Together* signed in Abu Dhabi on February 4, 2019 was proudly defended by Bergoglio with these words:

"From the Catholic point of view the document did not go one millimeter beyond the Second Vatican Council."
[...]
"It is no surprise, therefore, that the infamous *Grand Lodge of Spain*, after having warmly congratulated its paladin raised to the Throne, has once again paid homage to Bergoglio with these words:

["*The great principle of this initiatory school has not changed in three centuries: the construction of a universal brotherhood where human beings call themselves brothers to each other beyond their specific beliefs, their ideologies, the color of their skin, their social extraction, their language, their culture or their nationality. This fraternal dream clashed with religious fundamentalism which, in the case of the Catholic Church, led to harsh texts condemning the tolerance of Freemasonry in the 19th century.*] Pope Francis' latest encyclical shows how far the present Catholic Church is from its previous positions. In "Fratelli Tutti", the pope embraced the Universal Brotherhood, the great principle of modern Freemasonry."*

"The reaction of the *Grande Oriente of Italy* is not dissimilar:

"These are the principles that Freemasonry has always pursued and guarded for the elevation of Humanity."

Viganò's words were even labeled by Catholic media as "conspiracy theories about the coronavirus pandemic, the Marian apparition of Fatima and the Second Vatican Council."[82] Some of these themes, far from being "conspiracy theories," are very solidly documented facts. For example, when it is stated about Vatican Council II:

"Those arguments have been addressed and critiqued repeatedly by theologians and historians, including Benedict XVI, and in the mind of the Church's hierarchy, have been sufficiently refuted. Objections to the council's authority have long been rejected by the Church's authorities."[83]

---

[82] JD Flynn (July 1, 2020), Analysis: As Archbishop Viganò denounces Vatican II, the Vatican is not speaking, Catholic News Agency.
[83] Ibid.

But as we have seen in this book, there is nothing that addresses the deeper investigations of the subject, and which leaves no doubt about the conspiracy of the U.S. government of the day about Vatican II and Fatima, as we shall see in due course on the latter.

Viganò found from his personal study of Francis' pontificate, as a member of the Jesuit order at the head of the Catholic Church, that this represents the accomplishment of a plan dating back some 60 years, and perhaps even earlier. What he qualifies as a union with Freemasonry.[84]

He has referred to a worldwide conspiracy where the "deep church" and the "deep state" with the Jesuits as protagonists and leftist politicians are leading it.[85]

Viganò addressed the world summit "Truth over Fear: COVID-19, the Vaccine and the Great Reset," held in May 2021. He said about COVID-19, that it "as a pretext to sow terror amidst the population, thanks to the complicity of politicians, the media, doctors, and law enforcement." He refers to the control measures as "the fantasy world desired by the Great Reset, by the proponents of the New World Order, by the followers of the globalist sect. A transhuman world, in which algorithms born from sick, diabolical minds decide if you can leave the house, which treatments should be administered, which activities are allowed to continue, and which people have the right to work." He holds the ecclesiastical hierarchy responsible for following and promoting these measures and that this is "the New Infernal Order that is the prelude to the advent of the Antichrist and the end times."[86] We do not exactly adhere to his conspiracy theories seen as a "plandemic."

Now, about the papal encyclical Fratelli Tutti, Viganò referred to its content as: "The globalist and ecumenical pacifism of *Fratelli Tutti* envisions an earthly paradise that lays its foundations on refusing to recognize the Kingship of Christ over societies and the entire world."[87]

However, while Viganò is right about the hidden intentions of the Great Reset, he is not right about his support for Vladimir Putin and the Russian military in invading Ukraine, which the archbishop has supported. Viganò sees the Russian invaders as heroes of traditional Western values that are akin to traditional Catholicism, which he says, are under attack by the forces of the "deep state" in the United States, the European Union, and NATO; to install a New World Order based on a departure from those values, which is why he sees the war in Ukraine as justified.[88] Catholic media have criticized the Archbishop for his pro-Russian and anti-Ukrainian position.[89]

---

[84] Letter #48, 2019: A New Church, Inside the Vatican.

[85] Archbishop Carlo Maria Viganò (September 26, 2020), Corruption of the Best is The Worst: The Jesuits, The Church, & the Deep State, OnePeter5.

[86] Carlo Maria Viganò (May 8, 2021), TRUTH OVER FEAR: COVID-19, the Vaccine and the Great Reset, The Remnant Newspaper.

[87] John-Henry Western (Oct. 15, 2020), Viganò on Pope's 'brotherhood' encyclical: 'A manifesto in the service of the New World Order', LifeSiteNews.

[88] Msgr. Carlo Maria Viganò, Archbishop (March 7, 2022), Declaration of Msgr. Carlo Maria Viganò on the Russia-Ukraine Crisis, Stilum Curiae; Archbishop Carlo Maria Viganò (March 17, 2023), Viganò. Message to the International Congress of Russophiles (MIR), Stilum Curiae.

[89] Claire Giangravé (March 7, 2022), Viganò, Vatican critic, blames 'deep state' for Ukraine war, citing COVID-19 measures, Religion News Service; George Weigel (March 16, 2022), Archbishop Viganó and Colonel Grace-Groundling-Marchpole, First Things.

Powerful resistance against Pope Francis and the support for Trump

Carlo Maria Viganò strongly supported Donald Trump, as evidenced in his letter dated June 7, 2020, where we quote in extenso:

"Although it may seem disconcerting, the opposing alignments I have described are also found in religious circles. There are faithful Shepherds who care for the flock of Christ, but there are also mercenary infidels who seek to scatter the flock and hand the sheep over to be devoured by ravenous wolves. It is not surprising that these mercenaries are allies of the children of darkness and hate the children of light: just as there is a *deep state*, there is also a *deep church* that betrays its duties and forswears its proper commitments before God. Thus the *Invisible Enemy*, whom good rulers fight against in public affairs, is also fought against by good shepherds in the ecclesiastical sphere. [...]

"For the first time, the United States has in you a President who courageously defends the right to life, who is not ashamed to denounce the persecution of Christians throughout the world, who speaks of Jesus Christ and the right of citizens to freedom of worship. Your participation in the *March for Life*, and more recently your proclamation of the month of April as *National Child Abuse Prevention Month*, are actions that confirm which side you wish to fight on. And I dare to believe that both of us are on the same side in this battle, albeit with different weapons.

"For this reason, I believe that the attack to which you were subjected after your visit to the National Shrine of Saint John Paul II is part of the orchestrated media *narrative* which seeks not to fight racism and bring social order, but to aggravate dispositions; not to bring justice, but to legitimize violence and crime; not to serve the truth, but to favor one political faction. And it is disconcerting that there are Bishops – such as those whom I recently denounced – who, by their words, prove that they are aligned on the opposing side. They are subservient to the *deep state*, to globalism, to aligned thought, to the New World Order which they invoke ever more frequently in the name of a *universal brotherhood* which has nothing Christian about it, but which evokes the Masonic ideals of those who want to dominate the world by driving God out of the courts, out of schools, out of families, and perhaps even out of churches.

"The American people are mature and have now understood how much the mainstream media does not want to spread the truth but seeks to silence and distort it, spreading the lie that is useful for the purposes of their masters. However, it is important that the good – who are the majority – wake up from their sluggishness and do not accept being deceived by a minority of dishonest people with unavowable purposes. It is necessary that the good, the children of light, come together and make their voices heard. What more effective way is there to do this, Mr. President, than by prayer, asking the Lord to protect you, the United States, and all of humanity from this enormous attack of the Enemy? Before the power of prayer, the deceptions of the children of darkness will collapse, their plots will be revealed, their betrayal will be shown, their frightening power will end in nothing, brought to light and exposed for what it is: an infernal deception.

"Mr. President, my prayer is constantly turned to the beloved American nation, where I had the privilege and honor of being sent by Pope Benedict XVI as Apostolic Nuncio. In this dramatic and decisive hour for all of humanity, I am praying for you and also for all those who are at your side in the government of the United States. I trust that the American people are united with me and you in prayer to Almighty God.

"United against the *Invisible Enemy* of all humanity, I bless you and the First Lady, the beloved American nation, and all men and women of good will."[90]

Three days after this letter, Donald Trump wrote: "So honored by Archbishop Viganò's incredible letter to me. I hope everyone, religious or not, reads it!"[91]

America, the U.S. Jesuit magazine, said that Viganò was supporting Trump to stay in the limelight and should not be paid attention to. And that the archbishop was increasingly paranoid with conspiracy theories about Pope Francis, Vatican II "and many other enemies."[92] They also noted that:

"Archbishop Viganò's anti-Francis texts are often released in the United States in seeming coordination with a set of sympathetic publications and amplified by media outlets even further out on the political and ecclesial fringe."[93]

Since the epicenter of the resistance comes from the United States, as we have seen, there is a campaign to deteriorate the public image of Pope Francis and in a major confrontation against the Jesuits, because they want to return the papacy to the "glory" it had more than two hundred and twenty years ago, to be more exact. We have been able to verify that the papacy they desire is an intolerant one that does not respect freedom of conscience. Where the civil authorities submit to the dictates of the Church.

When Archbishop Viganò was asked the reason for his letter, he said that on August 14, 2011, Benedict XVI had told him:

"I would like to tell you that I have reflected and prayed with reference to your condition after the recent events. The sad news of the passing away of His Excellency Archbishop Pietro Sambi has confirmed in me the conviction that your providential position at this moment is the Nunciature in the United States of America. On the other hand, I am certain that your knowledge of this great country will help you to undertake the demanding challenge of this work, which in many ways will prove decisive for the future of the universal Church."[94]

Under this revelation, where it seems to be glimpsed that he wishes to use the United States as the bastion of Christianity and of a future right-wing and intransigent papacy, he went on to state: "My official assignment in that immense and beloved country has ended, but the challenge to which Pope Benedict referred to almost prophetically, and in which he chose to involve me, is still present more than ever; indeed, it has become

---

[90] Ibid.
[91] Michelle Boorstein (June 10, 2020), Trump praises Italian archbishop who urges him to fight 'deep state' protests, The Washington Post.
[92] James T. Keane (June 12, 2020), Archbishop Viganò is aligning with Trump to stay in the spotlight. Pay him no attention, America Magazine.
[93] Ibid.
[94] Archbishop Carlo Maria Viganò (Oct. 1, 2020), Archbishop Viganò: President Trump Has a "Decisive Mission" in the Current "Epochal Confrontation," OnePeter5.

546

ever more dramatic, taking on tremendous dimensions: the destiny of the world is being played out at this hour precisely on the American front."[95]

For Viganò, should Trump lose the presidential election, it would fail, according to his interpretation, the final kathèkon [withholder] (2 Thess. 2:6, 7), who prevents the "mystery of iniquity" and the dictatorship of the New World Order that won Bergoglio to the cause from being revealed and, therefore, would have an ally in the new president (Biden).[96]

Viganò emphasized that: "[...] the universal religion desired by the United Nations and Freemasonry has active collaborators at the highest levels of the Catholic Church who usurp authority and adulterate the Magisterium. They are opposing the Mystical Body of Christ, which is mankind's only ark of salvation, with the mystical body of the Antichrist, according to the prophecy of the Venerable Archbishop Fulton Sheen. Ecumenism, Malthusian environmentalism, pan-sexualism, and immigrationism are the new dogmas of this universal religion, whose ministers are preparing the advent of the Antichrist prior to the final persecution and the definitive victory of Our Lord."[97]

In mid-September -still in 2020- Viganò spoke of the connections between the 'deep state' and the 'deep church', and hinted that Trump would be re-elected in the November presidential election, saying that it would confirm that, "the Lord's right hand has done mighty things' as Psalm 117 reminds us."[98]

Around the same time, Cardinal Gerhard Müller, former prefect of the Vatican's Congregation for the Doctrine of the Faith, said about the United States and the future of the world vis-à-vis China in an interview with *Breitbart*:

"The outcome of the U.S. election will determine whether the U.S. remains the leading power in the world — for freedom and democracy [...].

"American Catholics, Christians of other denominations, and all people of faith must render an account to God over whom they make commander of the flagship of the free world," the cardinal said. "The world is looking to America because this fateful election will determine the future of democracy and human rights for decades to come."
[...]
"America secured human rights against the godless ideology of National Socialism/Fascism during World War II," he recalled. "And then the Cold War against the atheist communism of the Soviet Union was won only with the help and under the leadership of the United States."
[...]
"But every American must also know that his country is the world's number one power: militarily, scientifically and economically," he said. "And because the U.S. is the first power in the free world, it must also put a stop to the imperialist grip of a communist superpower that seeks world domination and allow the Chinese people and other oppressed peoples to enter the community and solidarity of free peoples."
[...]

[95] Ibid.
[96] Ibid.
[97] Ibid.
[98] John-Henry Western (Sept. 14, 2020), Archbishop Viganò hints he believes God will deliver the election to President Trump, LifeSiteNews.

"In this crucial election, it is vital that voters evaluate the candidates based on their willingness to do the right thing while in office," he said, "and according to Catholic teaching, not all issues have the same weight."

"Three points are decisive in the upcoming elections," the cardinal noted: "First, the 'yes' to life against abortion, second, freedom of religion against the mainstreaming of gender ideology, and third, the mission of the United States to defend democracy and human rights against dictatorships."[99]

The cardinal's support for Donald Trump is clear. But the irony is, Müller said in this interview, that "No government has the right to arbitrarily arrest and even torture its citizens, to brainwash them, to hold them in concentration camps, to murder them, to harvest their organs like spare parts and sell them on the world market." We say ironic because of what Trump envisions in the framework of intolerance and authoritarianism. But also because the main resistance against the papacy of Francis and the Jesuits, comes from very high-ranking clerics and others like those mentioned, who support the union of the Church with the State, as well as intolerance to error and support the death penalty....

Again, in an open letter to Trump dated October 25, 2020, and just days before the presidential election, Viganò wrote that he was addressing the U.S. president "at this hour in which the fate of the whole world is being threatened by a global conspiracy against God and humanity."[100]

"Daily we sense the attacks multiplying of those who want to destroy the very basis of society: the natural family, respect for human life, love of country, freedom of education and business. We see heads of nations and religious leaders pandering to this suicide of Western culture and its Christian soul, while the fundamental rights of citizens and believers are denied in the name of a health emergency that is revealing itself more and more fully as instrumental to the establishment of an inhuman faceless tyranny.

"A global plan called the **Great Reset** is underway. Its architect is a global élite that wants to subdue all of humanity, imposing coercive measures with which to drastically limit individual freedoms and those of entire populations. In several nations this plan has already been approved and financed; in others it is still in an early stage. Behind the world leaders who are the accomplices and executors of this infernal project, there are unscrupulous characters who finance the *World Economic Forum* and *Event 201*, promoting their agenda."[101]

---

[99] Thomas D. Williams, Ph.D. (Oct. 1, 2020), Vatican Cardinal: 'Future of Democracy' at Stake in U.S. Elections, Breitbart News.
[100] María Viganò, Carlo, Titular Archbishop of Ulpiana. Former Apostolic Nuncio to the United States of America. Open letter to the President of the United States of America Donald J. Trump. Sunday, October 25, 2020.
[101] Ibid.

More than twenty days later, on November 2, Viganò penned a prayer that was published in *The Remnant* and entitled: "Archbishop Viganò's Prayer for a Resurgence of Christianity in America and the Re-election of Donald Trump,"[102] where we quote in part:

"Almighty and Eternal God, King of Kings and Lord of Lords [...].

"Bless us, citizens of the United States of America; grant peace and prosperity to our Nation; illuminate those who govern us so that they may commit themselves to the common good, in respect for Your holy Law.

"Protect those who, defending the inviolable principles of the Natural Law and Your Commandments, must face the repeated assaults of the Enemy of the human race.
[...]
"Give courage to those who, in spiritual combat, fight the good fight as soldiers of Christ against the furious forces of the children of darkness.

"Keep each one of us, O Lord, in your Most Sacred Heart, and above all him whom Your Providence has placed at the head of our Nation.

"Bless the President of the United States of America, so that aware of his responsibility and his duties, he may be a knight of justice, a defender of the oppressed, a firm bulwark against Your enemies, and a proud supporter of the children of light.

"Place the United States of America and the whole world under the mantle of the Queen of Victories, our Unconquered Leader in battle, the Immaculate Conception. It is thanks to her, and through your Mercy, that the hymn of praise rises to you, O Lord, from the children whom you have redeemed in the Most Precious Blood of Our Lord Jesus Christ."[103]

Viganò also believes in the conspiracy theory that the presidential election was rigged.[104]

Amidst ultra-conservative plots against the pope and the realities of corruption in his entourage, we note that most U.S. bishops are against his papacy, and some have even been angered by some of his decisions.[105]

"In the elections for the various committees of the U.S. Conference of Bishops, candidates critical of the pope are systematically elected. Archbishop Paul Coakley of Oklahoma City, who had expressed "great respect for Viganò and his personal integrity," became chairman of the justice and human development committee. San Francisco Archbishop Salvatore Cordileone was elected by seniority to chair the

[102] Carlo Maria Viganò, Archbishop (Nov. 2, 2020), Archbishop Viganò's Prayer for a Resurgence of Christianity in America and the Re-election of Donald Trump, The Remant Newspaper.
[103] Ibid.
[104] Archbishop Carlo Maria Viganò (November 14, 2020), Million MAGA March.
[105] Nicolas Senèze, Lo scisma americano: Come l'America vuole cambiare Papa (Mondadori, 2020), ob. cit. Note: unless otherwise indicated, this is the same source.

committee on laity, marriage, family, life and youth. Puzzled by the turn of events, some in the Vatican no longer hesitate to speak of schism in the United States..."

The pope had addressed the problems of the U.S. bishops spiritually, when on October 24, 2018 in addressing them, he referred to "the politicians, religious and business authorities of the time" of Jesus, whose problems surrounded his disciples, and that the "imprint and wound that is carried over also within the episcopal communion, generating not precisely the healthy and necessary confrontation and tensions proper to a living organism, but division and dispersion." In this way, he pointed out that the character of the divisions afflicting the episcopate was evil. Much of the influence of the U.S. bishopric comes from wealthy Catholic donors to the U.S. Catholic Church.

Now, the *dark web* writes journalist Vicens Lozano, is "the paradise of swindlers, mafiosi, terrorists and criminals of all kinds." Where "the darkest interests and activities of society are hidden."[106] There you can find addresses where you can hire an assassin with total impunity, and get all kinds of false documents, as well as the strangest narcotic substances and even sex with minors. There, the journalist tells us:

"Camouflaged in the midst of all this horror, a kind of 21st century Dante's Inferno, many characters and organizations are hiding, preparing the current plots against Pope Francis. In that secret sphere I have found the forums and laboratories where some of the strategies are designed and managed to bring the extreme right to power and also to return the leadership of the Catholic Church to past times, in which the spirit of the most reactionary immobilism prevailed."

The following refers not only to the case of the United States, but also to many other countries in the world: Internet, and television media that embrace a small sector that objects to the Second Vatican Council, not only say that the Catholic tradition before the Council is the one that should govern, but automatically advocate, therefore, the defense and return of the State protecting and promoting the Catholic Church in every country of the world.

A second group is made up of lay people who are members or sympathizers of organized groups, as well as of international ultra-right-wing personalities. These are individuals and fundamentalist Catholic and other Christian denominations that increasingly enjoy broad popular support. They include white supremacists, climate change and Covid deniers, as well as xenophobes, racists, sexists, and homophobes. They regard Pope Francis as a potential enemy to be shot down, as they abhor his proclamations of support for immigration, respect for Islam, LGBT groups, women's rights, he's against the death penalty, the abuses of capitalism, and warnings against climate change.

But another sector, is those who collect and proliferate extensively all the statements provided by the rigorists, the neo-fascist groups and leaders, as well as the theologians and the most hidden and high-level strategists, who rarely show their faces and show themselves in public.

---

[106] Vicens Lozano, Vaticangate: El complot ultra contra el papa Francisco y la manipulación del próximo conclave (Roca Editorial, 2023), ob. cit. Note: unless otherwise indicated, this is the same source.

Media, intentionally and others out of ignorance (many of them prestigious and renowned), give the news and amplify them. And important media of much propaganda and fake news to manipulate public opinion. For example *Fox News*, and other Trump supporters.

Likewise, the more conservative academics and theologians have risen up in a war against Francis.

Steve Bannon, former White House strategist under Trump, is an avowed enemy of Pope Francis. He has two laboratories with dozens of experts in social networks and media that provide strategies and substantial financial means to the international ultra-right. He also provides key mechanisms to articulate a plot against the pope and to try to manipulate the next conclave that will elect his successor.

Bannon invited Viganò to speak on his program *The War Room* in 2021, where the two agreed that the pope is going in the opposite direction of what the Catholic Church should be. Bannon likewise agreed with the archbishop that Trump was the force to take back the Catholic Church from the Vatican itself.[107]

U.S. Cardinal Raymond Burke, one of the most vocal critics of Francis' papacy, reportedly met Stephen Bannon in April 2014 during the canonization of John Paul II at the Vatican. They met in one of the cardinal's anterooms, and bonded over their shared vision of the world, which they saw as "a prostrate West weakened by the erosion of traditional Christian values." *The New York Times* reported that in the Vatican, elements on the right saw Trump and the rise of Bannon as the hope for the change they craved.[108]

"Just as Mr. Bannon has connected with far-right parties threatening to topple governments throughout Western Europe, he has also made common cause with elements in the Roman Catholic Church who oppose the direction Francis is taking them. Many share Mr. Bannon's suspicion of Pope Francis as a dangerously misguided, and probably socialist, pontiff."[109]

It continues:

"Conservatives and traditionalists in the Vatican secretly pass around phony mock-ups of the Vatican's official paper, L'Osservatore Romano, making fun of the pope. Or they spread a YouTube video critiquing the pope and his exhortation on love in the family, "Amoris Laetitia," which many traditionalists consider Francis' opening salvo against the doctrine of the church. Set to the music of "That's Amore," an aggrieved crooner sings, "When will we all be freed from this cruel tyranny, that's Amoris" and "It's the climate of fear engineered for four years, that's Amoris."[110]

[107] Archbishop Carlo Maria Viganò (Jan. 4, 2021), TRANSCRIPT: Steve Bannon's 'War Room' interview with Abp. Viganò, LifeSiteNews.
[108] Jason Horowitz (February 7, 2017), Steve Bannon Carries Battles to Another Influential Hub: The Vatican, The New York Times.
[109] Ibid.
[110] Ibid.

Burke has been a champion for traditionalist Catholics in the United States.[111]

He was Bannon's best liaison with the Vatican until 2019 when he broke ties with the US strategist.[112] But it would have been a temporary estrangement already dissipated since both are needed in their cause against Francis. Bannon has been advising far-right figures in various European countries to raise political groups that go along with a form of government like the one exercised by Trump.

For Bannon, Pope Francis is a danger in the face of an eventual schism in the Catholic Church. But he has also externalized his desire to dethrone the pope. Stephen Bannon, Cardinal Raymond Burke, and Italian Interior Minister Matteo Salvini have a relationship that unites them against the leader of the Catholic Church.[113]

The US strategist presides over a laboratory in Rome and another in Belgium, where expert mass sociologists, publicists, and specialists in social networks work.[114] An article published by *El Mundo*, whose title is, translated in English: "Bannon and Salvini prepare the assault on Europe with the blessing of the conservative Catholic Church," highlights their plan to obtain the support of the most conservative wing of Catholicism, as well as the transnational sovereigntist movement of "The Movement," with which the strategist intends to conquer the European institutions.[115] Rome is the center of operations in Europe in the unification of the right-wing nationalist movements of Matteo Salvini's European Union and with the support of Bannon. Until 2018, "The Movement" has Marine Le Pen, the president of the far-right National Front (NF) in France, and could have representation in Germany, Austria, Poland, Belgium, and Holland. Supporting Salvini would be Cardinal Raymond Burke and his trump cards outside Europe appeared to be Trump and Vladimir Putin.[116] But Salvini is also sympathetic to Viktor Orbán's Hungary, with whom he has talked about an ultra-conservative union; and with Le Pen, a Catholic and ultra-conservative vision to expand in Europe is added.[117]

I am not aware if there is any link to Croatia, where there was a neo-Nazi march in Zagreb in February 2017, where American flags were waved in favor of Trump, with people dressed in black and chanting slogans used by the Ustasha regime of dictator Ante Pavelić during World War II.

The U.S. Embassy in Zagreb condemned the march.[118]

But it was repeated in April 2018 in Zagreb, and with the same representation. They were from the Autochthonous Croatian Party of Rights (AHSP) and its right-wing arm, the Croatian Patriotic Forces Club.[119]

---

[111] Ibid.

[112] Vicens Lozano, Vaticangate: El complot ultra contra el papa Francisco y la manipulación del próximo conclave (Roca Editorial, 2023), ob. cit.

[113] Barbie Latza Nadeau (June 20, 2018), Steve Bannon, Cardinal Burke, Minister Salvini, and the Plot to Take Down Pope Francis, The Daily Beast.

[114] Ana Rodríguez (June 13, 2023), Vicens Lozano: "Hay una guerra abierta contra las democracias y contra el papa", Faro de Vigo.

[115] Soraya Melguizo (Sept. 22, 2018), Bannon y Salvini preparan el asalto a Europa con la bendición de la Iglesia católica conservadora, El Mundo.

[116] Irene Savio (September 13/16, 2018), La tela de araña 'ultra': Mapa de las alianzas de Salvini en Europa (y fuera de ella), El Confidencial.

[117] Antonino Galofaro (January 24, 2019/June 10, 2023), Près de Rome, à l'école des souverainistes, Les Temps.

[118] AP (Feb. 27, 2017), US embassy condemns far-right march with US flag in Croatia, Associated Press.

For his part, on July 4, 2021, Pope Francis underwent a colon operation at the Gemelli Polyclinic in Rome, which served to spread rumors and speculations of all kinds.[120] In fact, several purpurates presaged an early conclave... That night, a dinner was held in a Vatican dependency, with bishops and cardinals of different nationalities, but all belonging to the most belligerent sector of the curia against Francis. Some, who considered the dinner as a plot against the pope, called it "the dinner of the crows." The Vatican secret services and the Gendarmerie know the list of those who attended, and the pope learned who is the high prelate of the Holy See who acted as organizer of the event. He has in recent years cooperated enthusiastically with U.S. cardinals and bishops who are designing a future for the Catholic Church contrary to what Francis wants. It was discussed that the pope was very ill and that it was necessary to force his resignation by any means necessary and to have everything ready when the cardinals were summoned to the Sistine Chapel. On the table, the names of future papal traditionalists were put, and groups working towards a future conclave from the United States, Italy, and Spain were activated.

But at the beginning of September, Francis told the Jesuit magazine *La Civiltà Cattolica*: "I am still alive. Although some would want me dead. I know that there were even meetings between prelates who thought the pope was more serious than he is. They were preparing the conclave."

Regarding the curia participants and other characters at the dinner, it can be described as: "A center of operations with close ties to neocon organizations and groups in the United States."

In the summer and autumn of 2022, Pope Francis' intramural enemies in the Vatican were looking to the future, as if the Argentine pope were no longer among them. However, Francis' closest friends denied it. But there were a minimum of six additional conspiratorial meetings within the Vatican until December of that year.

Thus, the years 2022-2023 generated doubts about the future of the pope, who "was rushing to complete reforms that had been stalled for years." The battles between conservatives and reformists were heating up, and little by little the opinion was growing that the "springtime" of changes and reforms initiated by the pope could soon become a mirage.

There were conspiratorial meetings planned in 2023, after the death of Benedict XVI on December 31 of the previous year. Vicens Lozano tells us:

"Many of these "crows" no longer even keep their manners or have any problem with being placed clearly in the camp of opposition to Bergoglio. They no longer even fear reprisals. They are so convinced of winning the game that they also have no doubt that immediately afterwards they will be rewarded with generosity by the new pontiff."

Francis knew that many important people inside and outside the Vatican, as well as the powerful media of the international right wing, were in preparation for the eventuality of his death or resignation from the papacy.

---

[119] Total Croatia (April 8, 2018), Far-Right Party Holds Rally, Expresses Support for Trump, Total Croatia News.
[120] Vicens Lozano, Vaticangate: El complot ultra contra el papa Francisco y la manipulación del próximo conclave (Roca Editorial, 2023), ob. cit. Note: unless otherwise indicated, it is the same source.

The pope's appearance in a wheelchair in May 2022 at a general audience, and at the funeral of Cardinal Angelo Sodano, again raised alarms. Already in June, he replaced it with a cane.

Sensational news was reported, such as that the pope was suffering from serious cancer and Alzheimer's disease.

"From the spring to the winter of 2022, and also at the beginning of 2023, there was a strong tension in the air. Everyone, at least within the Vatican, whatever their leanings, was already very clear that the period known as the "end of the pontificate" had begun. It was therefore evident that this way of proceeding on the part of those responsible for communications in the Holy See was part of the usual code of conduct in a pre-conclave environment."

In the context of the ultra-right-wing assault, particularly the so-called "Christian" assault on the Capitol on January 6, 2021, with divided voices in Catholicism and Evangelicalism, the Cardinal Archbishop of New York, Timothy Dolan, who does not hide his dislike of Pope Francis, shamelessly postulated himself to the College of Cardinals as the great elector of the future conclave. He had already sent in July 2020 to all the cardinals of the world, paying for it out of his pocket, a book that draws a portrait of the qualities that the next pope would have to have, written by George Weigel, who is very critical of Francis.

Dolan had participated in the campaign to discredit U.S. President Joe Biden.

A bishop from the most depressed areas of the United States, in the Mississippi basin, said of many Catholic bishops in the country, "They are against Biden because they are Trumpists and they will not stop until they destroy him with any excuse. They are against him and they want to erode the Holy Father as well."

A Spanish general in the reserve, about 70 years old and deep in the conspiracy, said, "Many lies are told about Hitler," he affirms, "but he did know how to defend our Christian civilization. He also referred to the dictator Francisco Franco, who murdered millions of Spaniards and emboldened the most aggressive Catholicism, as the "caudillo who continues to inspire my life."

This general is involved in a plan that seeks to bring about a new totalitarian regime not only in Spain but also to bring back an ultra-conservative pontiff to the Vatican. The center for them in international change is the leadership of the Vatican.

He has good friends in the Spanish police and in the Spanish CNI (Centro Nacional de Inteligencia/National Intelligence Center), who are nationalist and "Christian."

He is against and deeply despises homosexuals, atheists, communists and freemasons. Referring to communism, he says:

"We cannot tolerate that people who play the game of this dangerous ideology endanger the values we have as a race, as a religion, as sovereign nations. The arrival of Pope Francis, in addition to being illegitimate, as was the manipulation in the United States so that Donald Trump would lose the election, means the destruction of all the ideals for which we have fought."

With his conspiratorial friends, the general wants to return Europe to its "Christian" roots. Catholicism, to be more precise. And so, according to him, they must destroy "Masonic and relativistic globalism."

Before Bergoglio's election to the papacy in 2013, that same year, the general and others met in Madrid at a hotel along with two cardinals, five bishops, and a dozen priests, some deputies of Partido Popular (Popular Party), and leaders of Church organizations, as well as a few army officers to discuss the Catholic Church's problems with cases of corruption and sexual abuse by the clergy and conjure to fix the situation. There were also people from El Yunque, the Legionaries of Christ, Opus Dei, the Neocatechumenal Kikos, members of the Sodalicio de Vida Cristiana (Sodalitium Christianae Vitae), HazteOír, Asociación Española de Abogados Cristianos (Spanish Association of Christian Lawyers), Centro de Estudios Tomás Moro (Thomas More Study Center), the Catalans of E-Cristians, members of Asociación Católica de Propagandistas (Catholic Association of Propagandists), Heraldos del Evangelio (Heralds of the Gospel), in short... For years, they often met and have very close relations with representatives of these organizations in Europe, Latin America, and the United States.

They have established links with people and organizations mostly from France, Italy, Germany, Austria, and Poland. They believe that the pontiff who was closest to the time of Francis' papacy was John Paul II, who received the general once and supported all the aforementioned Catholic organizations.

In Italy, at a three-day meeting in mid-May 2021 in a mansion of a reputable Italian businessman near Ostia, there were very important people - twenty in all - among whom were four Italian cardinals who work in the Vatican, and one American who has become very famous, the general told Lozano. Most likely referring to Raymond Leo Burke, who is Francis' number one enemy and a Trump supporter.

There was a fellow officer of the Italian army; and there were also Silvio Berlusconi, Matteo Salvini, and Giorgia Meloni, the current Prime Minister of Italy since October 2022 and president of the European Conservatives and Reformists (ECR) group. Meloni is the leader of Fratelli d'Italia, the heir party of the party created by Italian dictator Benito Mussolini; and is supported by Matteo Salvini's League and Silvio Berlusconi's Forza d'Italia (now deceased).[121]

"Meloni **has been an ultra-right-wing militant since the age of 15**, when she joined the Youth Front of the Italian Social Movement, MSI, the party founded in 1947 by the survivors of the elite of the Italian Social Republic in northern Italy, under the guidance of Giorgio Almirante, a former minister of the Duce."[122]

After the Admiral's death, the MSI was dissolved and Meloni joined Gianfranco Fini's National Alliance, a continuation of the traditional Fascist movement.[123]

Meloni, who supports Spain's ultra-right-wing political party Vox, which has a lot of support as well as many Franco regime sympathizers among them, including its president Santiago Abascal,[124] said at a Vox rally in Marbella in June 2022:

---

[121] Gustavo Sierra (September 25, 2022), Quién es Giorgia Meloni, la neofascista que puede convertirse en la próxima primera ministra italiana, Infobae.

[122] Ibid. Author's emphasis.

[123] Ibid.

[124] Mariano Sánchez Soler, La familia Franco S.A.: Negocios y privilegios de la saga del último dictador de Occidente (Roca Editorial, 2019), ob. cit.; Mariano Sánchez Soler, Los ricos de Franco: Grandes magnates de la dictadura, altos financieros de la democracia (Roca Editorial de Libros, 2020), ob. cit.; Antonio Maestro, Franquismo S.A. (Ediciones Akal, S.A., 2019), ob. cit.

"There is no middle ground possible. Either you say yes, or you say no. Yes to the natural family, no to the LGTB lobbies. Yes to sexual identity, no to gender ideology. **Yes to the culture of life, no to the abyss of death.** Yes to the universality of the cross, no to Islamist violence. Yes to secure borders, no to mass immigration. Yes to the sovereignty of the peoples, no to the bureaucrats of Brussels. Yes to civilization, no to those who want to destroy it."[125]

Meloni has the strong support of Viktor Orbán, President of Hungary; and he also has friendship and support from nationalist leaders in Slovenia and Poland. He has connections with interest groups close to Putin.[126]

But going back to the meeting cited by the general in reserve, everyone's points coincided with Pope Francis.[127] The Italians have many people infiltrated in the curia, in the dicasteries and congregations, as well as in the security services of the Holy See and the Italian State.

They are all waiting for the moment to return to a neoconservative world, with a traditional papal ideology.

The Italian-Spanish confluence was followed by Portugal, Germany, Hungary, Austria...

The general has attended meetings in Paris, Marseille, or Lyon, in France, and has met with Mario Maréchel, the niece of the ultra-right and Catholic Marine Le Pen, and where in all of them there has been a presence of the episcopate, and characters linked to parish debate groups and elected officials of the extreme right of the French National Front, renamed by Marine Le Pen as Rassemblement National. Very active there are the members of the Cité Catholique, which sought from the beginning to form a national Catholic State. Vicens Lozano, in his very well-documented book that we have quoted, tells us:

"In Ecône I attended with the TV3 team to many skinhead demonstrations that gathered to accompany him. Hundreds of French and Spanish ultras, German and American neo-Nazis, wearing fascist symbols and raising their arms, made the Roman salute. The Lefebvrists, some of whom continue to defy Rome's control and deny the Holocaust and make proclamations against the Argentine pope, are present in France and are very active in the meetings where my interlocutor, the general, participates."

There have continued to be international meetings of these groups and many others, to change the papacy to an ultraconservative one. About Poland, as Lozano rightly says:

"We are talking about a Poland that practices repression against homosexuals, has harsh anti-immigration policies, and legislates against the most fundamental human rights. Even in August 2022, the vice-president of the government, Zbigniew Ziobro, promoted a collection of signatures to have the Penal Code amended to punish "making jokes" or "ridiculing" the Catholic Church with two years in prison."

---

[125] Gustavo Sierra (September 25, 2022), Quién es Giorgia Meloni, la neofascista que puede convertirse en la próxima primera ministra italiana, Infobae. Author's emphasis.
[126] Ibid.
[127] Vicens Lozano, Vaticangate: El complot ultra contra el papa Francisco y la manipulación del próximo conclave (Roca Editorial, 2023), ob. cit. Note: unless otherwise indicated, this is the same source.

They have had meetings with leaders of Ley y Justicia (Law and Justice) and with xenophobic and homophobic Catholic parish groups. Europa Christi is a very active party in Warsaw and is led by the director of Radio María in the country, priest Tadeusz Rydsyk. The general says that Rydsyk is very influential in Poland and that he is the political arm of the most reactionary sectors of the Polish Catholic Church. In addition, the priest is a tycoon who controls a commercial empire called Lux Veritatis; with a private university, a television channel, and a newspaper.

The ultimate goal of Europa Christi is "to forge a new European constitution based on the Gospel."

For its part, Orbán's Hungary has become the inspiration, the model for what they wish to achieve through a new papacy. Although Orbán is a Calvinist, he has a Catholic majority in the country. He cares for the national and Christian identity of the nation. The general says that Orbán designed the Hungarian electoral system to never lose any election, leading to his fourth mandate. He has prevented the arrival of immigrants and refugees. Trump had said of him, "Viktor Orbán has done an impressive job in many respects..., he is respected throughout Europe. Probably a little like me, a little controversial, but that's fine."

Orbán acts under his own rules, outside the European Union, with which he is at odds. He does not accept that the European peoples become a mixed race, he fights against gender ideology, homosexuality, abortion, divorce, and Muslim immigration. Add to the list of the general, that there are new laws that annul fundamental rights, that there are limitations to freedom of expression, modifications to the rule of law, destroying the main democratic values.

At the beginning of the year 2022, there was a meeting in Budapest, Hungary, with European and American ultra-conservative representatives. It was attended by Hungarian, Italian, French, German and Spanish politicians. There were also Republicans from the United States and Catholic priests, as well as attendees from other Christian denominations. There was unanimous praise for the Hungarian government, ratifying among those present that the country is a model for many things.

Hungary is mainly Catholic; at least 62%. Five percent are Protestant, 8 percent are Christians of other denominations, and 20 percent have no religion. They do not want the European Union or the United Nations.

Orbán has visited the pope in the Vatican, and the pope has visited Hungary, despite the differences between the two. So has Giorgia Meloni, who has met the pope twice.

For her part, Marjorie Taylor Greene, the far-right Republican U.S. Congresswoman, praised Orban in April 2022 for his election victory and his anti-LGBT+ law: "Congratulations to Viktor Orban on winning a victory well deserved!" tweeted Ms. Greene. "He's leading Hungary the right way and we need this in America."[128]

The CPAC, or Conservative Political Action Conference of America, which brings together conservative activists and U.S. elected representatives, held a conference in May 2022 in Budapest, Hungary, with Viktor Orbán as its keynote speaker.[129] The conference was also attended by Eduardo Bolsonaro, son of Brazil's then ultra-conservative president; and Santiago Abascal, leader of Spain's far-right Vox party. But

---

[128] Gino Spocchia (April 4, 2022), Marjorie Taylor Greene condemned for praising 'autocrat' Viktor Orban on election victory and anti-LGBT+ law, The Independent.
[129] Craig Unger (April 21, 2022), Why Is CPAC Having a Conference Next Month in Budapest?," The New Republic.

in recent months at the event, both Greene, Alex Jones and Tucker Carlson, ultra-conservative figures in their respective media, have spoken very positively of Orban's Hungary.[130] Indeed, the effect of Orban's speech, who said that we should "play by our own rules. The only way to win is to refuse to accept the solutions and the paths offered by others," was highly infusive on those present, including U.S. representatives. However, he criticized the use of conspiracy theories in the United States.[131]

Orban's U.S. admirers believe Hungary is a quasi-utopian model to be emulated in the United States.[132]

"Indeed, the parallels between the Hungarian and American right are explicit and many. Orbán, a self-described "illiberal" authoritarian, solidified his power through a canny mix of culture war and gerrymandering. He enacted a series of one-sided electoral reforms, brought the media under state control, and amended the constitution to better allow his party to exercise power. [...]
"If the American right does eventually follow Orbán's advice, mixing redistributive economic policies, voter suppression, and all-out culture war on marginalized groups in ways that prove broadly popular, we're in deep trouble."[133]

The actions of Ron De Santis, Republican governor of Florida, are a sign of the use of ultra-right-wing state power like the one ruling Hungary, and under the banner of Judeo-Christian values.[134] For CPAC Dallas 2022, Donald Trump, Ted Cruz, Marjorie Taylor Greene, and Hungarian PM Viktor Orbán would be among the speakers.[135] Orbán urged at that CPAC held in August, that Americans fight for the next presidential election to feature a president -we say in our words- who will impose the ultra-right on the nation's government.[136] He also pronounced:

"Victory will never be found by taking the path of least resistance," he said during one of the keynote slots of the three-day CPAC event. "We must take back the institutions in Washington and Brussels. We must find friends and allies in one another."[137]

The power that is aspired to, has gathered the figures of the ultra-right also in Washington and Tokyo.[138] The general says that "When we reach our goal, we will sound the trumpets of Jericho. The walls of corrupt democracy will fall, and order will be imposed in a natural way."

---

[130] Ibid.
[131] Noah Y. Kim (May 20, 2022), MAGA Makes the Pilgrimage to Authoritarian Hungary, Mother Jones.
[132] Ibid.
[133] Ibid. See also Philip Bump (March 23, 2022), That the American right hopes to emulate Hungary is telling, The Washington Post.
[134] Andrew Marantz (June 27, 2022), Does Hungary Offer a Glimpse of Our Authoritarian Future, The New Yorker. See also other articles of much interest: Justin Spike and Nicholas Riccardi (July 25, 2022), Embrace for Hungary's Orban deepens among US conservatives, Associated Press.
[135] Patrick Strickland (July 20, 2022), Trump, Ted Cruz, Marjorie Taylor Greene and Hungarian PM Viktor Orban Will Speak at CPAC Dallas, Dallas Observer.
[136] Paul J. Weber (August 4, 2022), Autocratic Hungarian leader Orban hailed by US conservatives, Associated Press.
[137] Ibid.
[138] Vicens Lozano, Vaticangate: El complot ultra contra el papa Francisco y la manipulación del próximo conclave (Roca Editorial, 2023), ob. cit. Note: unless otherwise indicated, this is the same source.

Before the Covid crisis erupted in 2019, there was a meeting in Washington DC that was hosted by the Trump administration. All the speakers cited the concept - and it was the most cited - of a "new world order." There were at the meeting, Catholic bishops, evangelical pastors, military from allied countries, representatives of political and religious organizations from around the world, and very important people from the world of international finance. At the meeting, strategies were defined, and the design of a society based on Christian values was developed. The papacy of Francis, who was pointed out by an important banker as one of the main enemies of capitalism, was also discussed.

The general called the assault on the Capitol heroic.

The ultra-conservative Catholics in the United States, who are working on one of the most important centers to stop Francis' papacy and its continuity, are working with their Red Hat Report. And they use the power of social networks.

Alexey Komov, of the Russian division of the World Congress of Families, and personal friend of Vladimir Putin, channels millions of rubles from the Kremlin to finance campaigns of the European ultra-right (Italy, France, Spain) and has connections in the Vatican.

Much of this is known to Pope Francis and his intelligence services or the Entity.

Because the curia holds back many of his reforms, the pope has had no choice but to approve them himself, without further ado. And to use unofficial channels also to get some help. Already in 2014, Francis had addressed himself very harshly to the curia, when he pointed out their many very serious faults: "not very exemplary" conduct, the fact of "feeling immune," "indispensable".., "incapable of admitting self-criticism," of "being mentally and spiritually immobile," of not working collectively, of "falling into the evil of rivalry and vainglory." [...] "The evil of indifference towards others," [...] "a double life, the fruit of the hypocrisy typical of the mediocre," [...] "the evil of gossip," the evil of deifying their bosses and accumulating material goods. [...] the evil of the funeral face and arrogance, of closed circles, and [...] the evil of worldly life and exhibitionism." Many came away sorrowful and crestfallen, and others very upset.

The Italian journalist and Vaticanist Marco Politti told Katholisch.de in 2022 that "Today, in the curia, twenty percent are openly in favor of the pope, ten percent are against him, and the remaining seventy percent are waiting for the next pope.

Burke has not been the only one to say that the pope has committed heresy, and encouraged disobedience. Although he claims not to be an enemy of the pope, in addition to criticizing him, he "organizes meetings and constantly pulls the strings of internal conspiracy." He also defies the pope by celebrating the Tridentine Mass in Latin.

Regarding attempts to discredit the pope or make him resign, a priest close to Francis told Lozano that the pope intended to resign when Providence tells him to. Unless his physical or mental health is no longer allied. But his intention was to resign until he has cemented changes that cannot be reversed.

About the conclave, one of the most powerful centers of operation to manipulate the upcoming conclave is located in the United States. The aforementioned Red Hat Report, which is managed by the association The Better Church Governance Group, was formed on September 30, 2018, on a terrace on the campus of the Catholic University of America, in Washington. It grew out of a circle of ultra-conservative American Catholic businessmen. But it also brought together influential people, such as

Republican politicians, some Trump administration officials, and owners of media holdings. But there were also famous journalists.

The project prepared meticulous dossiers to expose the most hidden details of the past and present of all cardinal electors to participate in the next conclave. It would record possible sexual and corruption scandals, criticisms received and the support of their defenders, denunciations, or if they have ever been subject to police investigation or court proceedings; or if they are homosexuals. The objective was to make an "audit" to promote the "transparency" of the Catholic Church and to make a cleanup, which would lead to discredit the possible candidates before the cardinal electors and to use blackmail if necessary so that an ultra-conservative pope was to be elected instead after Francis.

To spy on the cardinals, the promoters of the project recruited more than a hundred individuals, including academics, Catholic priests, university students, communication experts, journalists, sociologists, former CIA agents, and at least a dozen former FBI agents. There is also a very active intramural network - inside the Vatican - "made up of priests, bishops and high officials who collaborate with American investigators to collect personal data on priests." Similar groups also exist around the world, with good contacts with allied international espionage agencies, in cities where a cardinal-elector serves as a bishop or titular archbishop, and who are therefore key informants in the investigation. However, students and journalists also contributed by supplying data they obtained in their fieldwork. The academics and sociologists contrasted them so that the communication experts could then present them to the public. Vicens Lozano tells us that: "The final approval is given by director Nielsen, who emphasizes more or less some aspects of the personality and activity of the investigated cardinal."

An agent of the Entity, or Vatican intelligence service, informed journalist Lozano of two attempts on the life of Pope Francis: one by the Islamic State and another by the U.S. ultra-right and financed by it, involving an Italian and a Spanish priest on the life of Pope Francis.[139]

[139] EITB (March 10/14, 2023), Vicens Lozano: "Este Papa ha tocado muchos privilegios de mucha gente que no está dispuesta a perderlos", EITB; Vicens Lozano, Intrigas y poder en el Vaticano: Una crónica de los secretos y escándalos mejor guardados (Roca Editorial, 2022), ob. cit.

CHAPTER
17

A last papacy?

A U.S. pope or a pope sympathetic to the far-right?
The *Associated Press* published on February 17, 2013:

"Conventional wisdom holds that no one from the United States could be elected pope, that the superpower has more than enough worldly influence without an American in the seat of St. Peter."[1]

The article noted that after the abdication of Pope Benedict XVI, ecclesiastical analysts wondered whether these old assumptions were still valid, even if they were still being discarded. Especially when the election of a new pope occurred after a pontificate in which Americans played unusually prominent roles. Eleven American cardinals would vote in the conclave that would elect[2] Jorge Bergoglio as the next pope.
The *AP* article continues:

"The church has tried to keep the papacy separate from a reigning superpower for centuries, whether the Holy Roman Empire, France or Spain, according to the Rev. Thomas Reese [...].
But the role of the United States in the world today is what weighs most heavily against a American pope. The Vatican navigates complex diplomatic relations [...]An American pope could be perceived as acting in the interests of the United States instead of Catholics."[3]

New York Cardinal Timothy Dolan, however, was mentioned as one of the contenders for the papacy.[4]
The *Catholic Herald* reported in February 2013 that "it was impossible that we could ever have an American Pope. [...] The reasoning behind this, I seem to remember at the time, was that an American Pope would mean the Catholic Church being seen as aligned to the West when the Church had to steer a neutral course between the West and the Soviet bloc." But now that the bloc has disappeared, it is now argued that there cannot be an American pope, because "America is the world's only superpower"[5]
George Weigel noted for *Foreign Policy* in March 2013, that "in years past, there has always been an unwritten proscription on an American pope." The above, and we go on

---

[1] AP News (Feb. 17, 2023), Could the next pope come from the United States?," Associated Press.
[2] Ibid.
[3] Ibid.
[4] Ibid.
[5] Fr. Alexander Lucie-Smith (February 19, 2013), Is it time for an American Pope, Catholic Herald.

to quote, "because the United States is so powerful in the world, it should not have one of its sons rule the Church."[6] The article continues:

"In many ways, this is the obverse of American fears that John F. Kennedy would collude with the Vatican to bring the U.S. under the sway of the Holy See
[...]
Behind that power calculation against an American pope, there is the long-standing suspicion as well that Americans were prone to, well, "Americanism" as it was known in Church circles in the 19th and early 20th centuries. That is, Americans are given to individualism, private conscience, and a general lack of docility. No telling what might happen if a Yank put on that ring."[7]

However, Weigel says that this "superpower veto" is now inoperative."[8] Since the U.S. "is no longer seen as so dominant in world affairs that the Church should fear an American pope," Weigel says.[9]

Around the same time, *The Washington Post* published:

"A U.S. pope has long been viewed as a highly unlikely possibility, partly due to the nation's reputation as too informal in contrast with the heavily ritualized, even mystical Vatican culture. An even larger obstacle, experts on Catholicism say, is the image of the United States as a global superpower reputedly under the sway of Wall Street and the CIA and morally corrupted by Hollywood.
[...]
Now, even as a U.S. pope remains a long shot, the fact that it's such a subject of discussion points to dramatic changes both in the Catholic Church and in the perception of the United States's place in the world.
[...]
"Yet others familiar with the mind-set of cardinals say it will be hard to overcome the perception that the United States already has enough power and that our perspectives on topics such as income inequality and religious freedom are sheltered ones because these aren't life-and-death matters for us."[10]

According to *The Washington Post*, Jorge Mario Bergoglio, who was elected pope at the conclave of March 13, 2013, had among his contenders two North American cardinals, namely, Sean O'Malley of Boston (USA), and Marc Oullet, of Canada. The possibility that a North American could have been elected to the papacy was considered novel and surprising.[11]

Cardinal Joe Tobin of Detroit was seen as a possible candidate for the papacy at the next conclave. [12]

---

[6] Joe Wood (March 1, 2013), Could U.S. decline make possible an American pope?," Foreign Policy.
[7] Ibid.
[8] Ibid.
[9] Ibid.
[10] Michelle Boorstein (March 2, 2013), An American pope is an unlikely prospect - but more likely than last time, The Washington Post.
[11] Michelle Boorstein (March 22, 2019), American pope? Rare, leaked report from Pope Francis's election reveals who got votes, The Washington Post.
[12] Patricia Montemurri (April 1, 2018), Can Cardinal Joe, a native Detroiter, rise to become 1st American pope, Detroit Free Press.

562

Similarly, the *Catholic Herald* reported in 2022:

"For years, the consensus was that an American pope would never fly. Since the US overtook the British Empire as the world's pre-eminent political and economic power, the consensus has been that an American pontiff would concentrate too much power in one country, while a non-American head of the Catholic Church would offer some counterweight to US influence. Smarting Europeans and wary Latin Americans would, the consensus went, be especially wary of electing a pope from the US."[13]

But the report continues:

"But times change. Today, the US faces the prospect of relative decline, as the threat of war hangs over the country, not least from the People's Republic of China. While a heavy blow to US influence, this could open the door for an American pope, as Europeans and Latin Americans – as well as others from the Global South (already hugely represented among the College of Cardinals) – warm up to the idea.

"There is the prospect of a dark-horse candidate, such as conservative Cardinal Burke, or perhaps the newly-promoted Cardinal McElroy, but other front-runners could include Cardinal Sean O'Malley, Archbishop of Boston and a member of the Order of Friars Minor Capuchin, as well as Cardinal Timothy Dolan, the Archbishop of New York, both of whom scored relatively well in the 2013 vote which saw Pope Francis pave the way for a non-European pontiff.
[...]
"Perhaps most interesting is the implications a US pope would have for the faith in the US, given the rise of New Right Catholics and social media "trads". Whatever else, unlike in previous years, the chances of a US pope cannot be dismissed. Whether O'Malley or Dolan, or an outside runner, the odds are increasing."[14]

Catholic Herald published in August 2022 that for the past half-century, the Catholic Church has been wary of considering a U.S. pontiff, due to that country's superpower status and misgivings about excessive concentration of power.[15]

"Today, however, a relative decline in US power may play to the advantage of American clerics as that argument is starting to lose sway. Meanwhile, the election of a Latin American pope has perhaps heralded a new era of pontiffs who come from outside Europe."[16]

The U.S. Catholic Church, the one that was mostly in friction with Francis' papacy, would have perhaps as its main contender for the papacy Cardinal Raymond Leo Burke, the canon lawyer and former archbishop of St. Louis and the pope's No. 1 enemy. Thus, Burke's election would be a huge boost to conservative forces in the United States. Thus, he is often considered the de facto leader of American

---

[13] The Catholic Herald (September 1, 2022), Why not an American pope, The Catholic Herald.
[14] Ibid.
[15] Staff Reporter (Aug. 30, 2022), Cardinal Burke: the dark horse in the running to succeed Pope Francis, Catholic Herald.
[16] Ibid.

Catholicism, with enormous support and authority among conservative Catholics around the world. We would speak of him being the leading contender among the conservative cardinals.[17]

"While conservatism is swimming with the tide in central and eastern Europe, conservativism in the US is locked in a life-or-death struggle with liberalism." Although Francis chose many cardinals who would be electors at the next conclave, stressing that continuism is not entirely certain and considering that a different approach may be taken, given that the election of the pope has become somewhat less European.[18]

---

[17] Ibid.
[18] Ibid.

CHAPTER
18

The Secret - concealment about non-human intelligences

Sign, Grudge, and Blue Book projects

In June 1947, private pilot Kenneth Arnold saw a mysterious formation of glowing discs near Mount Rainier in Washington State. It was then that newspapers reported on "shining saucerlike disks" and the popular term "flying saucer" was born.[1]

Thus, in 1948, the U.S. Air Force began investigating such UFO reports, initiating Project Sign. But in the late 1940s, it was replaced by Project Grudge, which in turn became the famous Project Blue Book;[2] which was the code name for the systematic study of unidentified flying objects (UFOs) by the U.S. Air Force. This lasted from March 1952, until its cessation on December 17, 1969, by the Secretary of the Air Force.[3]

Project Blue Book was based at Wright-Patterson Air Force Base, Ohio. It obtained a total of 12,618 sightings of which 701 remained unidentified.[4] Blue Book was not unique and was almost always shrouded in secrecy.[5] The first document related to the beginnings of the Project was written and signed on September 23, 1947. Then, Nathan F. Twining, then commander of the Air Materiel Command, "suggested to the commanding general of the Army Air Forces, General Carl Spaatz, through Brigadier General George Schgulen, that "The phenomenon reported is something real and not visionary or fictitious." He recommended that "Headquarters, Army Air Forces issue a directive assigning a priority, security classification and Code Name for a detailed study of the matter."

Significant sighting cases and the U.S. government cover-up

Kevin Randle recounts that during the Project Sign period, there were dozens of allegedly unexplained cases in the summer of 1948, which were reported to the Wright Field Air Technical Intelligence Center at Dayton, Ohio.

Some of the Project Sign officers became convinced that there was no evidence that the flying saucers were of extraterrestrial origin, and they made an estimate of the situation; preparing a report with the best evidence they had, and sent it to General Hoyt S. Vanderberg, then Air Force chief of staff. Vanderberg, however, was not impressed with the evidence, said Capt. Edward Ruppelt, who eventually headed Blue

---

[1] Joseph A. Angelo, Jr, The Facts on File Dictionary of Space Technology (Facts on File, Inc., Revised Edition, New York, 2004), p. 441.
[2] Ibid.
[3] Ibid.
[4] Ibid.
[5] Kevin Randle, Project Blue Book: Exposed (Crossroad Press Trade Edition, 1997), ob. cit. Note: unless otherwise noted, this is the same source.

Book. After Vanderberg rejected the report, he ordered it declassified and later destroyed.

For his part, Dr. Michael Swords, who reviewed drafts of Ruppelt's original paper, outlined in an article published in the *International UFO Reporter* about those deletions: "[...] the people at ATIC decided that the time had arrived to make an Estimate of the Situation. The situation was 'UFOs; the estimate was that they were interplanetary!" Adding that:

"It was a rather thick document with a black cover and it was printed on legal-sized paper. Stamped across the front were the words TOP SECRET.

"It contained the Air Force's analysis of many of the incidents I have told you about plus many similar ones. All of them had come from scientists, pilots, and other equally credible observers, and each one was an unknown.

"It concluded that 'UFOs were interplanetary. As documented proof, many unexplained sightings were quoted. The original UFO sighting by Kenneth Arnold; the series of sightings from the secret Air Force Test Center, MUROC AFB; the F-51 pilot's observation of a formation of spheres near Lake Mead; The report of an F-80 pilot who saw two round objects diving toward the ground near the Grand Canyon; and a report by the pilot of an Idaho National Guard T-6 trainer, who saw a violently maneuvering black object.

"As further documentation, the report quoted an interview with an Air Force major from Rapid City AFB (now Ellsworth AFB) who saw twelve 'UFOs flying a tight diamond formation. When he first saw them they were high but soon they went into a fantastically high-speed dive, leveled out, made a perfect formation turn, and climbed at a 30 to 40-degree angle, accelerating all the time. The 'UFOs were oval-shaped and a brilliant yellowish-white.

"Also included was one of the reports from the AEC's Los Alamos Laboratory. The incident occurred at 9:40 A.M. on September 23, 1948. A group of people were waiting for an airplane at the landing strip in Los Alamos when one of them noticed something glint in the sun. It was a flat, circular object, high in the northern sky. The appearance and relative size were the same as a dime held edgewise and slightly tipped, about 50 feet away."

"The document pointed out that the reports hadn't actually started with the Arnold Incident. Belated reports from a weather observer in Richmond, Virginia, who observed a 'silver disc' thought his theodolite telescope; an F- 47 pilot and three pilots in his formation who saw a 'silvery flying wing,' and the English 'ghost airplanes' that had been picked up on radar early in 1947 proved the point. Although reports on them were not received until after the Arnold sighting, these incidents had all taken place earlier."

Because of Vanderberg's rejection, military officers and civilian technical intelligence engineers from Project Sign were called to the Pentagon to defend the Estimate but were unsuccessful. Soon after, they were reassigned, and "only the lowest grades in the project, civilian George Towles and Lieutenant H.W. Smith were left to write the 1949 Project Grudge document about the same cases." Randle claims that government authorities pointed out that the Estimate was a myth.

Sign's findings grouped the objects found into four classifications according to their configuration:

"1. Flying discs, i.e., very low aspect ratio aircraft.
"2. Torpedo or cigar shaped bodies with no wings or fins visible in flight.
"3. Spherical or balloon-shaped objects.
"4. Balls of light."

About Blue Book cases, let's look at some examples:

In McMinnville, Oregon, on May 11, 1950, Evelyn Trent was feeding her rabbits when she suddenly saw a metallic disc-shaped object hovering above her farm. She called her husband Paul, who, with his camera, subsequently took two photographs. Both said the object flew slowly overhead before abruptly speeding away. *Life* magazine published the case, making it a global sensation.[6]

A most amazing case occurred in 1951 when future NASA astronaut Gordon Cooper was training in Germany. Suddenly, with his squadron of fighter planes, he found himself chasing a large formation of silvery metallic flying disks, which they were unable to intercept, as the disks were flying very high and much faster. For the next two to three days, the objects flew over the base daily. They appeared at times in groups of four, and at other times as many as sixteen.[7]

The objects could maneuver and dodge at will, moving at varying speeds: sometimes very fast, sometimes slow. While other times they would stop dead in their tracks as squadrons of aircraft passed below them. "They came right over the air base at regular intervals all day long, generally heading east to west over central Europe"- Cooper wrote.[8]

Outside of chronological cases, for particular reasons, on November 2, 1957, in Levellan, Texas, witnesses reported seeing an egg-shaped glowing object about 60 meters long, landing on farms and roads, and observed from multiple locations. Both the Hockley County Sheriff, the Texas Department of Public Safety, and Reese Air Force Base officials saw the UFO.[9]

As the cars approached it, somehow, all the lights and car engines went out. After two hours, it took off vertically at an astonishing speed and disappeared.[10]

Cases similar to this one were reported in France and South America in 1954, including descriptions of creatures from these UFOs.[11]

Now, 24 to 36 hours after these sightings in Levelland, at the White Sands Experimental Area in New Mexico, very close to the Trinity Test Site where the first atomic bomb was detonated, military personnel observed a glowing egg-shaped object that apparently landed. Bill Haggert, public information officer at White Sands Experimental Area, reported that what they saw appeared to be the landing and takeoff of a controlled object from outer space.[12]

---

[6] Oregon Historical Quarterly (Oregon Historical Society, University of California, 2000), p. 208; Eden Dawn, Ashod Simonian, The Portland Book of Dates: Adventures, Escapes, and Secret Spots (Sasquatch Books, Seattle, WA, 2021), p. 67.
[7] Gordon Cooper with Bruce Henderson, Leap of Faith: An Astronaut's Journey into the Unknown (HarperTorch, New York, 2000), p. 91.
[8] Ibid.
[9] Kevin D. Randle, Levelland (Published independently, 2021), ob. cit.
[10] Ibid.
[11] Ibid.
[12] Larry Frascella, Jim Ledwith, Jordan Pease (Producer) James Fox (Director) (2020), The Phenomenon (Farah Films, 1091 Pictures).

On April 24, 1964, in Socorro, New Mexico, police officer Lonnie Zamora spotted a large cloud of smoke off the main road in the distance, so he went up in his patrol car to investigate. Upon arriving at the site, he saw a large white object sitting in the ravine in the area. His patrol's radio was not working, and he observed some silhouettes of beings as if they were walking around the object. They were the size of children and appeared to be dressed in white clothing. One of the beings turned its face looking at Lonnie, being about 15 meters away from each other. Then the beings entered the ship and it ignited, and a great flame came out just below the object, which rose about 6 to 9 meters, remaining suspended at that height, silent, and then departed.[13]

After the experience, Zamora went to the Catholic church to talk to the priest about what he observed.[14]

Then, an hour later and for the next several days, FBI officials, military, and Blue Book members documented the evidence found at the scene.[15]

Both the grass and the ground where the object had been were burned. Zamora identified one of the landing gear tracks, and there were four landing gear marks. They also noted two pairs of footprints. Zamora said he was told that many of these objects were seen throughout the state.[16] There were reports of witnesses seeing creatures around the country at the same time as the event witnessed by Zamora.[17]

Noting that Dr. J. Allen Hynek, astronomer and professor, was the senior consulting scientist for Project Blue Book hired by the Air Force, Jacques Vallée tells us: "Socorro was very similar to French cases that I had brought to Hynek's [Project Blue Book's scientific leader] attention. Checked by the police. Checked by the French Air Force. Where there were also occupants who were seen. Small beings, in connection with the object. I think that's what convinced him that there were UFO landings in the United States."[18]

For his part, Hynek, privately convinced of UFO reality, was pressured in March 1966 by Major Héctor Quintanilla, the director of Blue Book, to offer a debunking press release on the case of a spectacular landing in Michigan, which had hundreds of witnesses, including police officers. Hynek said it was due to swamp gas, thus following pressure from the Air Force to discourage public excitement, something Hynek later deeply regretted. There was outrage around the world over the swamp gas fiasco, leading Michigan Congressman Gerald Ford, who would later become the 38th president of the United States, to say that the Air Force's role in the case was irresponsible and that the phenomenon deserved serious scrutiny. For his part, Hynek felt used and displeased with the Air Force; and from that point on, his relationship with the Air Force and Quintanilla went into a rapid decline.[19]

In another case, on July 2, 1952, in Tremonton, Utah, Delbert Newhouse, a Navy photographer, saw about twelve flying saucers, which appeared to be made of some

[13] Kevin D. Randle, Encounter in the Desert: The Case for Alien Contact at Socorro (New Page Books, Wayne, NJ, 2018), ob. cit.

[14] Ibid.

[15] Ibid.

[16] Ibid.

[17] Ibid.

[18] Larry Frascella, Jim Ledwith, Jordan Pease (Producer) James Fox (Director) (2020), The Phenomenon (Farah Films, 1091 Pictures).

[19] Larry Holcombe, The Presidents and UFOs: A Secret History from FDR to Obama (St. Martin's Press, New York, 2016), ob. cit.

kind of polished metal. They were above him, and when he had his camera ready, they moved to a considerably greater distance; but he was able to record them performing various maneuvers.[20]

Commercial pilots William Nash and William Fortenberry, former Navy aviators with thousands of hours of flying experience, witnessed eight huge, bright red disks flying in formation over the Chesapeake Bay in Virginia on July 14, 1952. They traveled between nine thousand and nineteen thousand kilometers per hour.[21]

Five days later, on July 19, in Washington DC, seven unknown signals suddenly appeared on airport radar. Air traffic controllers at Andrews and Bolling Air Force Bases confirmed the objects as they flew through restricted airspace. Air Force F-94 interceptors took off to intercept them. While Albert M. Chop, the Pentagon press liaison, was in the radar room that night, the objects subsequently disappeared. But it started again the following weekend. Air Force pilot William Patterson, gave full speed to his Starfire jet (900 km/h), to try to intercept one of the bright objects, flying in the middle of three or four of them. He remarked in his radio communication to the ground, "They're closing in on me. What do I do?" Then the objects turned away from him and flew away. The next day, Air Force top brass hastily prepared the Pentagon's largest press conference since World War II. Present was General Roger Ramey, director of Air Force operations at the Pentagon. Capt. Edward Ruppelt of Project Blue Book; and Air Force intelligence director John Samford, who said, "Since 1947, we have received and analyzed between one and two thousand reports, that have come to us from all kinds of sources. Of this great mass of reports, we have been able adequately to explain the great bulk of them. [...] However, there have been a certain percentage of this volume of reports that have been made by credible observers of relatively incredible things. [...] We can say that the recent sightings are in no way connected with any secret development by any department of the United States."[22]

During the question-and-answer session with reporters, Samford suggested a 50-50 chance that it could be radar waves bouncing back from a thermal inversion. Ultimately, the Air Force treated the phenomenon as an atmospheric event that posed no threat to national security.[23]

Contrary to the above, ten days later, a radio report expressed itself on July 29, 1952, a letter from Robert L. Farnsworth, president of the American Rocket Society: "Robert L. Farnsworth, president of the American Rocket Society, urged defense officials not to permit our planes to fire at any flying saucers. He said this might alienate mankind from beings of far superior powers. Farnsworth believes that friendly contacts should be sought as long possible."[24]

It was then that a government cover-up of the reality of the so-called UFO phenomenon became evident. Behind the scenes, the CIA and the Air Force were concerned about the proximity of these unexplained objects in the vicinity of major U.S. defense installations.[25] The rising tide of UFO reports in 1952, prompted the Air

---

[20] Paul R. Hill, Unconventional Flying Objects: A Former NASA Scientist Explains How UFOs Really Work (Hampton Roads Publishing Company, Inc., Charlottesville, VA, 2014), ob. cit.
[21] Larry Frascella, Jim Ledwith, Jordan Pease (Producer) James Fox (Director) (2020), The Phenomenon (Farah Films, 1091 Pictures).
[22] Ibid.
[23] Ibid.
[24] Ibid.
[25] Ibid.

Force to contract with a renowned organization focused on contract research and development in the field of metals and materials science, the highly prestigious Battelle Memorial Institute, in Columbus, Ohio;[26] located just a stone's throw away from Wright-Patterson Air Force Base, Ohio.[27]

Historian Richard Dolan tells us that on Friday, November 21 of the same year, an Air Force review panel met at the ATIC (Air Technical Intelligence Center) for three days, and recommended forming a "higher court" to review the UFO issue.[28] H. Marshall Chadwell, deputy director of the CIA's Office of Scientific Intelligence, prepared a secret memo on December 2, 1952, for CIA Director Walter Bedell Smith, which stated:

"At this time, the reports of incidents convince us that there is something going on that must have immediate attention.... Sightings of unexplained objects at great altitudes and traveling at high speeds in the vicinity of major U.S. defense installations are of such nature that they are not attributable to natural phenomena or known types of aerial vehicles."[29]

Attached to this document was a memorandum from the National Security Council stating that the UFO problem had "implications for our national security," directing the CIA to "formulate, and carry out a program...to solve the problem of instant, positive identification of unidentified flying objects."[30] Two days later, the Intelligence Advisory Committee accepted a panel's proposal, recommending that the Director of Central Intelligence "enlist the services of selected scientists to review and appraise the available evidence in the light of pertinent scientific theories." Chadwell wanted it to be H. P. Robertson, who accepted the panel's assignment.[31] On December 12, another meeting was held at ATIC with representatives from the CIA, ATIC, and the Battelle Memorial Institute, a group that had been studying the UFO issue for some time, in Hynek's words, in "very great secrecy." When members of the group learned of the impending CIA-sponsored study, they sent an urgent letter, classified as secret, to the CIA through Blue Book. They wanted the next scientific panel postponed until they completed their own study. The memo was written by Battelle's director, Howard C. Cross, and in part, talked about simulating a wave of UFOs to see how people would react; but we don't know if the recommendation was carried out.[32] Let's see more about the document: Hynek and Jacques Vallée, a French-born astrophysicist and PhD in computer science, were close colleagues, and Hynek relied on Vallée to sort through the countless Project Blue Book files scattered around Hynek's house. There, Vallée discovered a letter dated January 9, 1953, that was so secret, that he had to appeal to the chief counsel of the Senate Defense Appropriations Committee, to get it declassified.

---

[26] Dr. J. Allen Hynek, The Hynek UFO Report (Sphere Books Limited, Great Britain, 1978), p. 21.

[27] Thomas J. Carey and Donald R. Schmitt, Roswell: The Ultimate Cold Case (New Pages Books, Newburyport, MA, 2020), ob. cit.

[28] Richard M. Doland, UFOs and the National Security State: Chronology of a Cover-up 1941-1973 (Hampton Roads Publishing Company, Inc., Charlottesville, VA, Revised Edition, 2002), ob. cit.; citing Durant 1953, Ruppelt 1956, 264.

[29] Ibid; citing Chadwell 1952b.

[30] Ibid; citing Good 1988, 335; Fawcett and Greenwood 1984, xiv; Randles 1988, 35; Hall 1988, 336-337.

[31] Ibid.

[32] Ibid.

The contents of the letter revealed that the UFO issue had been taken much more seriously than anyone had imagined. The document revealed "[...] a major operation, and expensive. [...] based on our experience to date analyzing several thousands of reports" working in parallel with Blue Book, unknown to all but a select few. The letter was signed by H. C. Cross, director of Exotic Metallurgy at Battelle National Laboratories. These people analyzed the facts, at great expense, with highly competent physicists and computer scientists. "Who are these people? What information did they have?"- asks Vallée.[33]

This tells us that the U.S. government knew much more about the subject than previously thought. On the other hand, Battelle could not delay the Robertson panel, and Battelle's Project Stork also published its own report called Blue Book Special Report Number 14.[34] But both were not faithful to the scientific evidence and said only what the Air Force wanted: dismissed that there was anything beyond the prosaic in the phenomenon.[35]

Dr. Hynek visited the Battelle Memorial Institute and asked to see its "carefully preserved" records, but was informed that they had been completely destroyed.[36]

Former Marine Air Corps Major Donald Keyhoe said of the concealment of the reality of the UFO phenomenon, "The Air Force is simply treating the American people like children. They don't trust them with the facts."[37]

Hynek recounts that over the years, the Pentagon operated through various instruments to support their position that all UFOs were misidentified natural phenomena or outright hoaxes. They did this through poorly presented statistics and overly careful wording, mentioning only generalities and not specific study results. If properly and completely presented, they would be in serious conflict with the public position held by the Air Force. Because of this, the results of that report were never presented. Their conclusion was that due to the subjectivity of the data, the results were "inconclusive."[38]

Both the Pentagon and the Air Force were trying to hide the truth and avoid explanation.[39] See below what Hynek reported on the 1953-1955 data:

"All cases evaluated as "Insufficient Information" were considered by Blue Book to be "Knowns"; all cases evaluated as "Possible Balloons" or "Probable Aircraft" were considered in the statistics as balloons and aircraft—the qualifying words "possible" or "probable" were dropped. Clearly, the "Insufficient Information" cases should have been excluded from the statistical computations altogether. Instead, these cases were treated statistically as if they had been solved! Thus, if the insufficient information

---

[33] Larry Frascella, Jim Ledwith, Jordan Pease (Producer) James Fox (Director) (2020), The Phenomenon (Farah Films, 1091 Pictures).

[34] Richard M. Doland, UFOs and the National Security State: Chronology of a Cover-up 1941-1973 (Hampton Roads Publishing Company, Inc., Charlottesville, VA, Revised Edition, 2002), ob. cit.; citing Cross 1953; UFO Magazine 1993.

[35] Ibid.

[36] Dr. J. Allen Hynek, The Hynek UFO Report (Sphere Books Limited, Great Britain, 1978), p. 275.

[37] Larry Frascella, Jim Ledwith, Jordan Pease (Producer) James Fox (Director) (2020), The Phenomenon (Farah Films, 1091 Pictures).

[38] Dr. J. Allen Hynek, The Hynek UFO Report (Sphere Books Limited, Great Britain, 1978), p. 253.

[39] Ibid, p. 259.

cases are removed from the 1952 total, the percentage of unknowns rises to 23 percent."[40]

Indeed, it was noted in excerpts from a Department of Defense Office of Public Information press release dated December 27, 1949:

"The Air Force said all evidence and analysis indicate that the reports of unidentified flying objects are the result of:
  1-misinterpretation of various conventional objects
  2-a mild form of mass hysteria
  3-or hoaxes."[41]

Hynek wrote, that during the last years of Project Blue Book, when the U.S. Air Force maintained its well-known "all is nonsense" approach, it became clear to the general public that reporting strange UFO cases to the Air Force made no sense as a serious scientific matter, but was apt to draw ridicule to those who reported their cases.[42]

Even if cases of "high strangeness" were reported, it was very difficult for them to pass through the channels and finally reach Blue Book. For example: "Reports of humanoids and of strange physical, physiological, or electromagnetic effects would almost always be "solved at local level," and not even be brought before a panel of consultants."[43]

Years later, on April 5, 1966, Congressional hearings were held with Dr. J. Allen Hynek and Air Force Secretary Harold Brown both testifying. Harold Brown, Secretary of the Air Force, said when asked, that it was not true that the Air Force was hiding anything about the phenomenon.[44]

When the 1966-1968 Air Force-funded Condon Committee, led by Dr. Edward Condon, was set up to investigate the phenomenon, it concluded that the case was solved in its 1,400-page report, but the report itself had extraordinary cases that remained unexplained.[45]

Contrary to these conclusions, years before, in 1964, The National Investigations Committee on Aerial Phenomena (NICAP), published a detailed report where extraordinary cases were addressed, with particularities such as the great speeds reached by the objects, the sighting of their occupants, electromagnetic effects of the phenomenon, the fibralvina or angel hair, and more.[46]

---

[40] Ibid.

[41] Ibid, p. 260.

[42] Ibid, p. 266.

[43] Ibid.

[44] Larry Frascella, Jim Ledwith, Jordan Pease (Producer) James Fox (Director) (2020), The Phenomenon (Farah Films, 1091 Pictures).

[45] Richard M. Doland, UFOs and the National Security State: Chronology of a Cover-up 1941-1973 (Hampton Roads Publishing Company, Inc., Charlottesville, VA, Revised Edition, 2002), ob. cit.

[46] Richard H. Hall (editor), The UFO Evidence (Unidentified Flying Objects) (The National Investigations Committee on Aerial Phenomena (NICAP), Washington, D.C., May, 1964).

A worldwide phenomenon

There is no doubt that the UFO phenomenon or UAP (Unidentified Anomalous Phenomenon) is a worldwide phenomenon. The vast majority of the world's nations have reported large numbers of cases, many of which are extraordinary. The number of sightings in the 20th and 21st centuries alone is extremely numerous, numbering in the thousands.

Let us look at some examples. On November 5, 1976, near Grenoble, France, multiple witnesses, including a senior French scientist, saw from different locations a very luminous, slightly flattened disk, white in the center and bluish-white on the periphery, surrounded by an intense green halo. It made sudden, rapid movements; and then disappeared at a very high speed.[47]

But three hours earlier, a similar object, leaving a trail, was seen about eighteen kilometers east of Rives; and two hours later, a bright disk was seen "by the civilian traffic controller in the tower of the military airport at Aulnat." A few minutes short of the Grenoble sighting, a few kilometers away-near Vienne-a witness saw a slightly flattened sphere, "whose light was similar to that of a very bright neon tube, with a fiery red-orange area underneath." The sphere was flying very fast.[48]

An FBI document dated July 18, 1947, reported flying saucer sightings in Mexico City, New Orleans, Philadelphia, New York, Boston, Halifax, Newfoundland, Paris, Milan, Bologna, Yugoslavia, and Albania.[49]

The CIA, echoing some French reports, described that on July 12, 1952, in Morocco, two policemen saw, during the night in Had Kourt, two elongated flying saucers followed by a trail of white light and traveling from north to south at high speed.[50]

The next day, on July 14, two Fedala residents reported seeing at 11:45 p.m., a blue-green spherical object, followed by a small luminous trail and moving at high speed, disappearing about 3 to 4 seconds later as if it had melted.[51]

And on July 15, a couple reported having observed at 9 a.m., and for about thirty seconds, a mysterious flying object traveling from Ifrane in the direction of Meknes.[52]

A surprising case in my country, Costa Rica, occurred at 8:56 am on July 26, 1995, over the Moravia area in the province of San José, when pilot Everardo Carmona was flying over the area with his T1-AL2 light aircraft, at about 7,000 feet, when he saw an egg-shaped object, golden and shiny in color and about the size of a soccer stadium, which passed under his aircraft.[53]

The object "produced electromagnetic effects in the navigation control equipment" at Tobías Bolaños Airport, where air traffic controller Javier Mayorga, also saw the glow caused by the object just over Moravia; so he told his colleague Gerardo Jiménez, also an air traffic controller, to use the binoculars to get a better look. He then saw a flying object traveling from east to west, which remained still for a few seconds, and then

---

[47] Vallee, J.F. (1998). Estimates of Optical Power Output in Six Cases of Unexplained Aerial Objects with De® ned Luminosity Characteristics 1, pp. 352, 353.

[48] Ibid, p. 354.

[49] U.S. FBI (July 18, 1947). "Flying saucers." Washington, DC: U.S. Government Printing Office.

[50] U.S. CIA (September 2, 1952). Military - Unidentified aircraft. Washington, DC: U.S. Government Printing Office, p. 1.

[51] Ibid.

[52] Ibid.

[53] Carlos Jimenez (August 3, 1995), Piloto y técnicos avistaron un enorme platillo volador, Diario Extra, p. 6.

moved again. Likewise, Vemer Piedra, the air traffic controller at Juan Santa María Airport, located in Alajuela, saw the same object.[54]

The director of Civil Aviation, Nelson Rodríguez, summoned the three air traffic controllers to give a full report of what happened. Subsequently, Jiménez and Mayorga recorded the event in the Tobías Bolaños Airport logbook.[55]

In South America, Argentina, at dusk on May 21, 1962, in Bahía Blanca, photographer Miguel Thomé of *La Nueva Provincia, was* on Chiclana Street when hundreds of people looked up at the sky to see a light twice as big as the full moon, which was already visible at 7:30 p.m. in the city. The object was unusually changing trajectory. Thomé got into the newspaper's jeep to look for a place with good visibility, and when he reached Don Bosco Street, he parked the car, as the object was approaching that place. The photographer took two photographs, including one when the object was about 50 centimeters in diameter. It then remained fixed in one place and, a moment later, turned sharply to the south and disappeared.[56]

On May 22, at dusk and again in Bahía Blanca, four pilots from the Comandante Espora Naval Air Base saw several unidentified objects. The chronicles of that event report that: "Pilot Marcelo Figueroa saw an orange object moving on an oscillating course, below the visible horizon." The pilots chased an oval-shaped luminous object for thirty-five minutes. Minutes later, pilot Roberto Wilkinson reported that his aircraft was illuminated by an object behind him, during which time his radio stopped working. The object then sped underneath and was lost from sight. Some witnesses also saw it from the control tower until it disappeared. The event, with additional witness data and luminous object landings, was recorded in a document from the U.S. Embassy to the U.S. State Department.[57]

Nevertheless, a high military command reported that in that month of 1962, a UFO crashed in the vicinity of the Puerto Belgrano Naval Base and military personnel recovered the craft and the non-human bodies from it. On the 22nd of the same month, the high command was summoned to the Military Hospital by the Navy doctor Constantino Núñez. There, the witness saw the two deceased bodies of the crashed object, which were small and with large heads.[58]

Núñez was sent to Bahía where he learned that arrangements were made for the transfer of the UFO and the bodies to the United States. Many details shared by the former military high command about his story have already been confirmed. And a report of that year from the newspaper *La Nueva Provincia*, tells that on May 22nd at night, shortly after the planes of Commander Espora took off in pursuit of one of the objects, "some truck drivers who were approaching Bahía Blanca, saw an object of great luminosity that they mistook for a train. When they noticed that there were no railroad tracks, they approached and saw charred remains and burnt grass. Technicians from Puerto Belgrano and the National Atomic Energy Commission of Argentina intervened."[59]

---

[54] Ibid.

[55] Ibid.

[56] Mariano Muñoz (February 12, 2021), La increíble investigación sobre la caída de un UFO en Puerto Belgrano, La Nueva.

[57] Ibid.

[58] Ibid.

[59] Ibid.

On April 2, 1966, an engineer from near Balwyn, Australia, was taking photographs in his mother's garden when a tremendous flash of light caught his eye. Looking up, he saw an object, which as an engineer, he knew was designed. It was shaped like a wide bell, with a circle in the center at the top of its dome; and in the center of its bottom, a small protruding circular base. The object looked metallic. It turned and subsequently went northward at extreme speed.[60]

Air Force officers showed up at his home, asking him about every detail of his experience. The officers had pictures of similar objects, as well as a book with pictures of certain things attached. They said that what he saw was an unidentified flying object.[61]

In Papua New Guinea in June 1959, an Australian missionary by the name of William Gill saw what he described as a large solid disk hovering just 60 meters above the ground; as he stood with 38 other people who also saw it. On top of the craft, there were four small occupants dressed in what looked like black diving suits, who were walking on top of it, and there was not the slightest noise.[62]

Gill and the others waved to the beings, who waved back in kind. This encounter lasted for several hours, after which the craft abruptly departed at incredible speed.[63]

In England, from December 26-28, 1980, outside the Woodbridge Royal Air Force facility, then used by the U.S. Air Force, near Rendlesham Forest in Suffolk, the most significant UFO incident in the country occurred. First, on the night of December 26, strange lights appeared on the horizon in what appeared to be a downed aircraft. U.S. servicemen John Burroughs and James Penniston were dispatched to the scene. As the two approached the target area, their radios failed, and the air itself felt electrically charged as they approached. Once they reached the area, there was a strange triangular craft on the ground, approximately three meters wide at its base. Penniston observed it closely, noting on its side some indecipherable pictorial glyphs. The object was very warm to the touch and it felt as if its electricity was bouncing around with increasing force, causing Penniston's mind to become "trapped," so he visualized a picture of zeros and ones.[64]

The following two nights, additional sightings occurred and were reported by U.S. Air Force Colonel Charles Halt, who took his group of military personnel with him to put an end to the confusion. The group noticed high levels of radioactivity where Burroughs and Penniston had seen the strange craft and three pit marks on the ground. Later, they noticed through the trees a light in the immediate area moving at high speed. As they looked up at the sky, they saw between four or five elliptical objects, moving at very high speed in sharp angular turns and as if performing some kind of grid search. One of the objects came in at high speed, stopping directly above the group, between three thousand to five thousand feet in altitude. The craft directed a concentrated beam of light, or laser beam toward the ground. Another of the objects

---

[60] Larry Frascella, Jim Ledwith, Jordan Pease (Producer) James Fox (Director) (2020), The Phenomenon (Farah Films, 1091 Pictures).

[61] Ibid.

[62] Ibid.

[63] Ibid.

[64] Nick Pope, John Burroughs, USAF, Ret., Jim Penniston, USAF, Ret., Encounter in Rendlesham Forest: The Inside Story of the World's Best-Documented UFO Incident (Thomas Dunne Books, New York, 2014), ob. cit.; Jim Penniston (USAF/Retired) and Gary Osborn, The Rendlesham Enigma: Book 1: Timeline (Copyright 2019 by Jim Penniston (USAF/Retired), and Gary Osborn), ob. cit.

directed similar beams of light toward Woodbridge Base, near the weapons depot, which worried the others. Eventually, the objects left and vanished.[65]

On January 13, 1996, the U.S. Air Force shot at a UFO that crashed six miles from the town of Varginha, southeastern Brazil.[66] Before its final crash, multiple witnesses spotted it at a very close distance, swaying and shaking, struggling to stay afloat and with white smoke billowing from the rear of the object. Carlos De Sousa witnessed the crash of the object, which was shaped like a submarine and similar in size to a school bus, but without windows. He went to look at the wreckage: one part intact, and pieces of metal like thin aluminum foil scattered in the field. Taking a piece of metal in his hand, he crumpled it and after releasing it, it returned to its original shape. Immediately, military and soldiers appeared and started shouting at him to leave, while an officer pointed at his face, so De Sousa left the place.

Witnesses saw the creatures in Varginha: they were small, very thin, with large red eyes, and emitted a terrible smell like sulfur.

Six miles from the crash site, the military set up a roadblock in a residential neighborhood. Various sources reported that the local fire department, which is under the control of the military police, captured one of the creatures in the morning. Another was captured near where some girls saw it later that afternoon. Officer Marco Chereze, who caught the creature, became ill and died shortly after it scratched him.

Vitório Pacaccini, a civilian UFO researcher, saw a 35-second film fragment of the creature that a senior officer showed him in 2012. The creature looked like it was about to die, and made a small bee-like sound. Also in 2014, the former sheriff of Varginha showed in his office to UFO investigator Patricia Fernandes Silva, a color photograph, shot on film and printed on Kodak paper where there were two creatures, one dead and the other crouched.

Regarding the wreckage of the object and the bodies of the creatures, some reported that they were taken to the United States by the U.S. Air Force.

We must point out that multiple anonymous military officers, seven in total, gave an account of the facts in video interviews with Pacaccini, who after denouncing a cover-up, had to flee to Italy due to death threats.

UFO crash retrieval and reverse engineering program

This "legend" began when on July 8, 1947, the *Roswell Daily Record* published on the front page that *RAAF Captures Flying* Saucer *On Ranch in Roswell Region.*[67] The RAAF was Roswell Army Air Field in New Mexico, in the southern United States.

The article indicated, went on to report that the intelligence office of the 509th Bombardment group in RAAF, announced that same day that they came into possession of a flying saucer. We read verbatim from the article:

---

[65] Ibid.

[66] James Fox and Marco Aurelio Leal (Producers) James Fox (Director) (2022), Moment of Contact (1091 Pictures/James Fox CE3 Productions); Michael Shellenberger (Oct. 29, 2022), People claim they saw aliens after UFO crash-landed in Brazil in 1996, documentary reveals, New York Post. Note: unless otherwise noted, these are the same sources.

[67] Roswell Daily Record (July 8, 1947), RAAF Captures Flying Saucer On Ranch in Roswell Region, Roswell Daily Record, Vol. 47, Number 99, p. 1. Note: unless otherwise noted, this is the same source.

"According to information released by the department, over authority of Maj. J. A. Marcel, intelligence officer, the disk was recovered on a ranch in the Roswell vicinity, after an unidentified rancher had notified Sheriff Geo. Wilcox, here, that he had found the instrument on his premises.

Major Marcel and a detail from his department went to the ranch and recovered the disk. It was stated.

After the intelligence office here had inspected the instrument it was flown to "higuer headquarters."

The intelligence office stated that no details of the saucer's construction or its appearance had been revealed."

The article relates, that around ten o'clock Wednesday night, two residents, Dan Wilmot and his wife, were apparently the only ones in Roswell who saw a bright object, in what they thought was an oval-shaped flying disk; like two inverted saucers and coming out of the sky from the southeast to the northwest at high speed, about 400-500 miles per hour; while they were both sitting on their porch at 105 South Penn.

In the last paragraph of the important article, we read that Wilmot was one of the most respected and trusted citizens of the city and that he had kept the story to himself in the hope that someone would tell of having seen one. But finally, he decided that he would give his testimony, which, a few minutes after he shared it, the RAAF announced that it had come into possession of a saucer.

The next day, however, the *Roswell Morning Dispatch*, published an article entitled *Army Debunks Roswell Flying Disk As World Simmers With Excitement*. The Army issued a report that it was only a weather balloon.[68] Similarly, the *Roswell Daily Record* published a front-page article titled *Gen. Ramey Empties Roswell Saucer*. Gen. Roger M. Ramey highlighted the weather balloon version.[69]

But several decades later, some researchers conducted an exceptional investigation when they discovered that the RAAF version was not true and that the original version was it: that a flying disk crashed in Roswell, New Mexico, in mid-June 1947.[70] Much metal debris was found at Mac Brazel's ranch. Witnesses said that the metal debris found at the crash site was very thin and extremely light. The debris could crumple in the hand but would return to its original state when released. Even when hit with a sledgehammer, the material did not dent, it always returned to its original state. Some of the debris had strange symbols on it. Military witnesses who were told to lie later revealed the truth in interviews with various investigators.[71]

Jesse Marcel, a lieutenant colonel in the Air Force, was ordered to change the version of the saucer, saying it was the remains of a weather balloon. But many years

[68] Roswell Morning Dispatch (July 9, 1947), Army Debunks Roswell Flying Disk As World Simmers With Excitement, Roswell Morning Dispatch, Vol. XXIII, No. 158,l, p. 1.
[69] Roswell Daily Record (July 9, 1947), Gen. Ramey Empties Roswell Saucer, Roswell Daily Record, Vol. 47, Number 100, p. 1.
[70] Don Berliner, Stanton T. Friedman, Crash at Corona: The U.S. Military Retrieval and Cover-Up of a UFO (Marlowe & Company, New York, Second Edition, 1994); Jesse Marcel, Jr. and Linda Marcel, The Roswell Legacy: The Untold Story of the First Military Officer at the 1947 Crash Site (New Page Books, Pompton Plains, NJ, 2009); Thomas J. Carey and Donald R. Schmitt, The Children of Roswell: A Seven-Decade Legacy of Fear, Intimidation, and Cover-Ups (The Career Press, Inc., 2016); Thomas J. Carey and Donald R. Schmitt, Roswell: The Ultimate Cold Case (New Pages Books, Newburyport, MA, 2020).
[71] Thomas J. Carey and Donald R. Schmitt, Roswell: The Ultimate Cold Case (New Pages Books, Newburyport, MA, 2020), ob. cit.

later, he revealed that it was a cover-up; and instead, the metallic debris strewn about the site was like nothing he had ever seen before.

A second crash site was found 40 miles from his ranch, on the plains of St. Augustine, where the undestroyed body of the flying disk, and small bodies, which did not look entirely human, were recovered. A firefighter in the area saw the bodies, but the military insisted he say nothing. Sgt. Melvin Brown also claimed to have witnessed the bodies. There were other apparent witnesses to the disk and the recovered bodies.

For example, on orders from Colonel William Blanchard, First Lieutenant Walter Haut, the base's public information officer, was responsible for issuing through the 509th Bombardment Group the press release to the world media early in the morning of July 8, 1947, that they had recovered a flying disk. That caused a nationwide stir, with a flurry of phone calls from all over the country, including overwhelming worldwide interest. But as noted above, by the end of the day the information was retracted.

Haut's daughter, Julie Shuster, asked her dad in the late 1970s about the events, but he said he only released the press release. Although Haut, a personal friend of Col. Blanchard, promised him not to talk about what would have really happened, Haut prepared a signed affidavit in 2002 to be opened after his death. Julie and Don Schmitt, one of the best Roswell researchers and a personal friend of Haut's, spoke to him about it. In it, he indicated that the first press release was accurate and that he saw the bodies and the craft bringing them. When Haut died in 2005, the affidavit was published in Witness to Roswell: Unmasking the Government's Biggest Cover-Up, by Don Schmitt and Thomas Carey.[72]

A teletype sent by the Dallas FBI Field Office, dated July 8, 1947, is entitled "Flying Disk, Information concerning," which was listed as urgent. The Eighth Air Force (Strategic Air Forces), advised that office that an object, apparently a flying disk, was recovered near Roswell, New Mexico, on the date of the teletype.[73] The report stated:

"The disc is hexagonal in shape and was suspended from a balloon by cable, which balloon was approximately twnty feet in diameter. [crossed out] further advised that the object found resembles a high altitude weather balloon with a radar reflector, but that telephone conversation between their office and Wright Field had not [crossed out] borne this belief. Disc and balloon being transported to Wright Field by special plane for examination."[74]

At that time, there were saucer-shaped weather balloons.[75] Note that the teletype indicates suspicions of what was the object found but without certainty about it.

A large number of first-hand witnesses, from the military to civilians, and other secondary and tertiary witnesses, totaling some 600 of them, reported that what was

<hr>

[72] Thomas J. Carey and Donald R. Schmitt, Witness to Roswell, Revised and Expanded Edition: Unmasking the Government's Biggest Cover-Up (New Page Books, Pompton Plains, NJ, Revised and Expanded Edition, 2009), ob. cit.

[73] FBI Dallas (July 8, 1947). Flying Disk, Information concerning, Washington, DC: U.S. Government Printing Office.

[74] Ibid. See also a: Government Records: Results of a Search for Records Concerning the 1947 Crash Near Roswell, New Mexico (Letter Report, 07/28/95, GAO/NSIAD-95-187).

[75] Medicman11 (April 1, 2022), USAF Type 17 Weather Balloon, Plane Encyclopedia: https://plane-encyclopedia.com/fake-aircraft/usaf-type-17-weather-balloon/ Accessed September 19, 2023.

recovered was a flying disk made of extremely light and strong metal and that when crumpled, it would return to its original shape.[76]

But an official Air Force report published in 1995, concluded in its 994-page report, that a Mogul balloon with test dummies was what crashed.[77] However, the report has a huge number of contradictions with the findings at the site.

Other investigations have indicated through apparently reliable witnesses, as well as a good deal of documentation, that what was found had a particular, but far from non-human, origin. The renowned American journalist, Annie Jacobsen, recounts the testimony of one of EG&G's elite engineers, who was a U.S. defense contractor that marketed materials and technical services for a wide variety of military installations.[78] Allegedly, the engineer was involved in an engineering project arising from the Roswell incident. Information from the incident was sent to Wright Field, later renamed Wright-Patterson Air Force Base in Ohio, where it remained until 1951. The data was sorted and moved to the Nevada Test Site, where it was received by the elite EG&G group. The Atomic Energy Commission was in command of the Roswell crash wreckage because it was the organization best equipped to manage a secret that could never be declassified.

EG&G engineers would have received the Roswell wreckage and set up a secret facility outside the perimeter of the Nevada Test Site, in a facility so far away that it would never be seen.

The five engineers were told they would be involved in the most clandestine and important engineering program since the Manhattan Project. Its leader would be Dr. Vannevar Bush, President Roosevelt's most trusted scientific advisor during World War II. The operation would have only one alphabetical designation, called S-4 or Sigma 4.

Engineers would have to figure out how to operate the flying disk, which had no tail or wings; and the fuselage was round, with a dome mounted on top. It had much more advanced technology than the U.S. Air Force was aware of, with puzzling propulsion techniques such as traveling at a very high speed and hovering in the air for a few moments. It also appeared very briefly on radar. None of these capabilities could be demonstrated while the aircraft was consigned to Wright-Patterson Air Force Base.

The engineers also had to figure out what happened to the crew members of the craft, who were the size of children about thirteen years of age; and that seeing them was a startling and disturbing experience. The crewmen were still alive, though comatose. Upon seeing them, they noticed that they had very large heads and their eyes were enormous.

It had been determined that the craft was sent by Stalin, the leader of the Soviet Union, as it had writing stamped in Russian characters on a ring inside. In addition, military intelligence agents believed that the flying disk was the work of two aeronautical engineers from the former Third Reich named Walter and Reimar Horten, who were then working for the Russian military services. Thanks to the scientists of Project Paper Clip, a project charged with bringing to the United States a huge number

---

[76] Ibid.

[77] The Roswell Report: Fact versus Fiction in the New Mexico Desert (Headquarters United States Air Force, 1995).

[78] Annie Jacobsen, Area 51: An Uncensored History of America's Top Secret Military Base (Little, Brown and Company, 2011), ob. cit. Note: unless otherwise noted, this is the same source.

of German scientists, engineers, and technicians, many of whom were members and some former leaders of the Nazi party, military intelligence investigators learned that Hitler was rumored to have developed a high-speed aircraft designed by the Horten brothers and shaped like a saucer. Even if Stalin did not have possession of the Horten brothers, he may have gained control of their prototypes and plans for advanced aircraft.

A Department of the Air Force document, dated October 28, 1947, four months after the Roswell incident and entitled "Intelligence Requirement on Flying Saucer Type Aircraft," defines a request from General George Schulgen, Chief, Air Intelligence Requirements Division, U.S. Army Air Forces Headquarters, Washington, D.C., about saucer-shaped aircraft.[79] In the document, he claimed that German scientists possessed better than average knowledge of the Horten brothers' work, asking where these scientists were and what their activity was then. He requested that they be contacted and questioned; as well as which Russian factories were building the Horten VIII design and why the Russians were building 1800 designs of that aircraft.

One of the items states, "Are any efforts being made to develop the Horten "Parabola" or modify this configuration to approximate an oval or disc?"

It also requested information on "any aircraft whose shape approximates that of an oval, disc, or saucer."

One of the aspects asked was about "Unusual fabrication methods to achieve extreme light weight and structural stability particularly in connection with great capacity for fuel storage." However, the document further states: "Aircraft would be characterized by lack of fuel systems and fuel storage place."

Additional aspects of interest were: "Special provisions such as retractable domes to provide unusual observation for the pilot or crew members."

"High altitude or high speed escapement methods."

The six-page document states: "An alleged "Flying Saucer" type aircraft or object in flight, approximating the shape of a disc, has been reported by many observers from widely scattered places, such as the United States, Alaska, Canada, Hungary, the Island of Guam, and Japan. This object has been reported by many competent observers, including USAF rated officers. Sightings have been made from the ground as well as from the air."

The aircraft was characterized by the absence of sound, except for a small resonance such as an occasional rumble when operating under super performance conditions. There is talk of "Extreme maneuverability and apparent ability to almost hover."

The shape of the vehicles approximated an oval or disk shape, sometimes with a dome on the surface.

The document also stresses the ability of the aircraft: "The ability to quickly disappear by high speed or by complete disintegration." As well as "The ability to suddenly appear without warning as if from an extremely high altitude."

It was also believed that the aircraft could be "of Russian origin, and based on the perspective thinking and actual accomplishments of the Germans." And that a Horten design could be the inspiration for these flying saucers. Even more, it was stressed that

---

[79] Department of the Air Force (28 October 1947). Intelligence Requirement on Flying Saucer Type Aircraft, Washington, DC: U.S. Government Printing Office. Note: unless otherwise noted, this is the same source.

the Russians came into possession of a German plant-building aircraft of Horten designs.

After months of searching for the Horten brothers, in November 1947, agents of the U.S. Counterintelligence Corps (CIC) received first-hand testimony from Fritz Wendel, a former Messerschmitt test pilot.[80] He noted that after the war, the Horten brothers were certainly working on a flying saucer or crescent-shaped aircraft at Heiligenbeil in East Prussia. The aircraft could travel up to about sixteen hundred miles per hour, by one or two pilots or by radio control.

On March 12, 1948, it was reported that the Horten brothers were found and interrogated by American agencies. The Horten indicated that it was quite possible that once the Russians occupied part of Germany, they recovered prototypes of various German aircraft, as well as the Horten IX at the Gotha Railway car factory.

In May of the same year, the headquarters of the European command issued a memorandum stating that Walter Horten acknowledged his contacts with the Russians.

Regarding the bodies found in the aircraft, the S-4 engineers were told that there were rumors that they were people kidnapped by Dr. Josef Mengele, the death doctor of the Auschwitz concentration camp and other places, who performed inconceivable surgical experiments on children, dwarfs and twins of Jewish and Gypsy origin, as well as people with severe deformities.

Apparently, shortly before the war ended in 1945, Stalin offered Mengele a laboratory where he could continue his work in eugenics, the so-called science of improving the human population by controlling reproduction to increase desired hereditary traits; in exchange for Mengele creating for him "a crew of grotesque, child-size aviators." Mengele did his part, but Stalin did not.

The leader of the USSR sent the aircraft with the surgically or biologically modified children to New Mexico in the hope that it would land there. He hoped that the children would come out of the aircraft and that people would think they were visitors from Mars. The Soviet leader's purpose would have been to produce scenes of panic among the American population.

The former IG&G engineer told Annie Jacobsen that then U.S. President Harry Truman did not want to reveal the truth so that everyone would know how terrible the Soviet dictator was because the American nation was doing the same thing to children beginning in 1951 through the Atomic Energy Commission at a secret government facility in the Nevada desert. All ostensibly to "give science a boost." Such a project would have extended at least into the 1980s.

In late July 2020, Jacobsen shared on her Twitter account a map of the Nevada test site, which her EG&G source marked with a red, hand-drawn "X" where the horrific operation occurred. Well-known Las Vegas investigative journalist George Knapp spoke to Annie Jacobsen about it years ago about some points of collating accounts, as Knapp knew the same source as Jacobsen; who wrote that perhaps one of them had disinformation, but without knowing who.

In July 2020, Knapp said in The Joe Rogan Experience podcast that a son of that source was a state senator, who told Knapp that he should talk to his father about UFOs and aliens. But that same ex-EG&G source told Knapp something very different than he told Jacobsen, claiming that on S-4 they had a being and aircraft of unknown origin.

---

[80] Annie Jacobsen, Area 51: An Uncensored History of America's Top Secret Military Base (Little, Brown and Company, 2011), ob. cit. Note: unless otherwise noted, this is the same source.

He also told him that he would record a video confessing what they had at S-4 for Knapp to reveal to the public. But after two or three years, the source changed his story. There was a congressional investigator named Richard D'Amato, who worked for Senator Robert Byrd. D'Amato oversaw black budget projects and became involved in the UFO case, traveling around the country and having numerous testimonies. He met with Knapp, who told him about the source who worked for EG&G, with whom D'Amato subsequently had multiple conversations. They both went to the EG&G founders for more information, resulting in a dead end. However, after this Congressional investigation, the source completely changed his story: the one heard by Jacobsen. He was probably threatened and faked a different story than Jacobsen to be published.[81]

On September 2022, Jacobsen posted on her Twitter account a photo of a SIGMA-4 Area 51 badge that belonged to Jim Freedman-accompanied by a photo of him with the badge-another former EG&G employee. Although he was not the same source of Jacobsen and Knapp, he knew him very well. Freedman would have witnessed a lot of things. He validated the information from Jacobsen's source.

More than a year earlier, in March 2021 and again on Twitter, Jacobsen shared another photo with the following message:

"From a reporting trip to Nevada: with Col. Slater, TD Barnes and Jim Freedman — discussing A-12 Oxcart @CIA Project 57, Area 25, Area 51, Area 52, UFO false flags, disinformation, and secrets.
"So many secrets. AREA 51"

Jacobsen shared a bit below:

"Freedman, who worked at AREA 51 on Special Projects, and who was also an EG&G nuclear weapons engineer, kept records of things locked away in blue boxes.

"I fact-checked names and dates and *other* things this way."

We must ask, did the former EG&G engineer tell George Knapp that what was recovered at Roswell was of unknown origin because Knapp was after information about UFOs and possible bodies of their non-human occupants, but switched the information to Jacobsen because her focus was otherwise? If so, what was the purpose of disinformation?

Or did that source receive threats after D'Amato's investigation and switch the story to Jacobsen, and then warn Jim Freedman as well? The latter seems to be the most accurate.

On the other hand, researcher and writer Nick Redfern proposes a theory similar to the Nazi one due to anonymous sources whose credentials he was supposedly able to verify, but the major difference with what Annie Jacobsen exposed, is that it was a U.S.

---

[81] Rogan, J. (Host) (2020, July 17). George Knapp & Jeremy Corbell (No. 1510) [YouTube podcast episode]. In *The Joe Rogan Experience*. Joerogan: https://www.youtube.com/watch?v=Hc6pbG4wICA 2:39:13.

government operation with Nazi scientists to cover up an operation.[82] More disinformation?

What is certain is that the Air Force documents at least show that the authorities suspected that the Russians were developing modified Horten technology in the shape of a saucer or oval; and that this could be the origin of the wreckage of the aircraft recovered in Roswell, New Mexico. We have no documents to prove that inside the craft there was an inscription with Cyrillic characters, specifically in Russian. At least the documentation does show that the origin of the wreckage of the aircraft and, surely by extension, the bodies of its passengers, was unknown.

But there is additional information that may shed further light on the origin of Roswell: Battelle National Laboratories had been contracted by Wright-Patterson to research the development of "self-healing metal," as evidenced in a 1948 report by Battelle.[83] Some scientists at that institute, revealed to researchers Donald Schmitt and Thomas Carey, that they had come to work with a "strange metal" with properties that made it recover its original shape (as witnessed in the Roswell accident), to try to decipher its properties. But they were never informed of the metal's provenance. Battelle began to develop a similar metal called Nitinol.[84] Researcher Anthony Braglia tells the story:

"In an interview conducted in the 1990s, former Wright-Patterson Air Force Base Brigadier General Arthur Exon confirmed the existence of the Roswell metal reports. Exon, the Base Commander of Wright-Patterson in the 1960s, related that he was privy to some of the details on the composition of the crash debris and the variety of tests that were performed on it. Astonishingly, Exon stated of the debris: "It was Titanium and some other metal they knew about, and the processing was somehow different." Of course, special "processing" of Titanium and the "other metal" that "they knew about" (Nickel) is required to create Nitinol."[85]

Another Battelle scientist by the name of Elroy J. Center, related to a close friend of the above authors, that in 1957 "when he worked at Battelle (1939-1957), he had worked on a 'piece' of a very unusual material that no one there was familiar with, which was inscribed with strange symbols which he called 'glyphs'." He also informed her that it was his understanding that the material was recovered from a UFO crash. Interestingly, Wright-Patterson Air Force Base is where one of the Roswell UFO sites is said to have been.[86]

---

[82] Nick Redfern, Body Snatchers in the Desert: The Horrible Truth at the Heart of the Roswell Story (Paraview Pocket Books, New York, NY, 2005); Nick Redfern, The Roswell UFO Conspiracy: Exposing A Shocking And Sinister Secret (Lisa Hagan Books, 2017).

[83] *Progress Report No. 2*, Battelle Institute, 1948; cited in Thomas J. Carey and Donald R. Schmitt, Roswell: The Ultimate Cold Case (New Pages Books, Newburyport, MA, 2020), ob. cit.

[84] Thomas J. Carey and Donald R. Schmitt, Roswell: The Ultimate Cold Case (New Pages Books, Newburyport, MA, 2020), ob. cit.

[85] Anthony Bragalia (May, 2009), ROSWELL DEBRIS CONFIRMED AS EXTRATERRESTRIAL: Lab Located, Scientists Named, UFO Explorations: https://www.ufoexplorations.com/roswell-debris-confirmed-as-et Accessed September 21, 2023.

[86] Thomas J. Carey and Donald R. Schmitt, Roswell: The Ultimate Cold Case (New Pages Books, Newburyport, MA, 2020), ob. cit.

A study published by Battelle in 1949 and obtained under the Freedom of Information Act by Billy Cox, refers to the mysterious metal on which scientists at the institute worked.[87]

Dr. Howard C. Cross was the metallurgical expert commissioned by Battelle to lead the analysis of the metals, as well as the principal in the Air Force's commissioned investigation of the UFOs by Battelle.[88] Was the nature of the strange metal of non-human origin?

In his latest book Forbidden Science, which is the fifth of the diaries of renowned UFO researcher Jacques Vallée, he recounts that a renowned astrophysicist, Dr. Eric Davis, spoke on two occasions in 2004 with former U.S. President George Bush Sr:

"Could that have been Nazi hardware?" Eric asked.

"Impossible," replied Bush. "The two topics were clearly separated. By that time (1947) all German secrets had been processed and filed away; they were not used as cover for anything else."[89]

It should be noted that the Roswell case resembles the 1996 crash in Varginha, Brazil, in at least three respects: the metal of both aircraft was very thin, and it could crumple and return to its original shape.

The beings, although not identical, were extremely similar in appearance and size.

And finally, the beings emitted a dreadful odor.[90]

As to the nature of what was found at Roswell and other sites, we await solid documentation that goes to the very root of the archives; as well as material evidence and analysis of what was found.

Now, it has been said of other apparent crashed aircraft of unknown origin and with bodies of small "non-human" beings all dead. We have already seen in this chapter several cases mentioned. Another, and one that has been much criticized, but then rigorously investigated by Scott and Suzanne Ramsey, is of an apparent 30-meter diameter saucer that crashed in Aztec, New Mexico, on March 25, 1948. Inside it had sixteen small bodies of beings of unknown or "non-human" origin; all dead.[91] The operation to remove the wreckage of the aircraft and the bodies was high security and was conducted by the Air Force and the 5th Army Division. The aircraft may have been transported to Los Alamos National Laboratory in New Mexico. It is rumored that it was later transported to Wright Patterson Air Force Base in Dayton, Ohio. The Ramsey husband and wife did a very convincing investigation, uncovering a cover-up by the U.S. government through the military and the private sector. They also uncovered an

---

[87] Second Progress Report Covering The Period September 1 to October 31, 1949 on Research and Development on Titanium Alloys: Contract No. 33 (038)-3736 to Wright-Patterson Air Force Base, Dayton, Ohio (Battelle Memorial Institute, October 31, 1949).

[88] Thomas J. Carey and Donald R. Schmitt, Roswell: The Ultimate Cold Case (New Pages Books, Newburyport, MA, 2020), ob. cit.

[89] Jacques Vallée, Forbidden Science 5, Pacific Heights: The Journals of Jacques Vallee 2000-2009 (Anomalist Books, Charlottesville, Virginia, 2023), ob. cit.

[90] Thomas J. Carey and Donald R. Schmitt, Witness to Roswell, 75th Anniversary Edition: Unmasking the Government's Biggest Cover-Up (New Page Books, Newburyport, MA, 2022), ob. cit.

[91] Scott Ramsey, Suzanne Ramsey, The Aztec UFO Incident: The Case, Evidence, and Elaborate Cover-up of One of the Most Perplexing Crashes in History (New Page Books/The Career Press, Inc., Wayne, NJ, 2016), ob. cit. Note: unless otherwise noted, this is the same source.

intense, extensive, and pervasive disinformation campaign against Silas Newton and Frank Scully, the first investigators in the case, but without getting so much closer to the facts of the aircraft and its bodies, as to smear their character. The Ramseys show extensive documentation in this regard, and that the sources Newton and Scully had were solid.

The Ramseys also obtained extraordinary documentation from the Air Force, such as a document dated October 9, 1950, describing an episode that took place on September 30, 1950, where we read the summary of the document with important clarifications by the Ramseys -a scan of it can be seen in their book-:

"The Army CID (Counter Intelligence Division) reported that a "sting operation" was staged at the Edelweiss Bar in the Melwyn Hotel in Denver. Actually, the Edelweiss Bar was next door to the Melwyn Hotel, and the bar was the setting where the FBI and the Army CID were trying to intercept the sale of photographs of the Aztec flying saucer. The seller was L.D. Mclaughlin, and the buyer was Mr. Cline from The Baltimore Sun. The FBI and the CID from Fifth Army Headquarters in Denver participated in the operation."[92]

The following are excerpts from the Air Force document:

"The Fifth Army Regional Office in Denver, Colorado reported the following information: On 30 September the Regional Office received a call from C.I.D, Denver, said that an XXXXX (Redacted), Melwyn Hotel, Denver, said that when he was at the Edelweiss Bar a man named XXXXX (Redacted) offered him $1,500 for the photographs he had taken of a flying saucer which had crashed near Aztec, New Mexico. XXXXX (Redacted) said that "Army Officials" had attempted to take the photographs of the crashed saucer away from him but that he had given them another roll of film. He said that XXXXX (Redacted) in some way found out about the photographs and offered him $1,500 for the photographs.

"On October 2, 1950 XXXXX (Redacted) was interviewed at the Fifth Army Regional Office in Denver. He then denied any knowledge of the flying saucer episode. The Regional Office commented that in spite of his denials his manner indicated that he had some knowledge of the incident or may have taken pictures of it."

Williams S. Steinman and Wendelle C. Stevens, shared in their work on the Aztec case, documents about the aircraft crash and many other related documents.[93]

As for the bodies, Detlev Wilf Bronk, one of the scientists who examined them with his team and was in charge of the report -Project Sign Report No. 13-, said:

"The bodies were all small, averaging 42 inches in lenght. The facial features strongly resembled mongoloid orientals in appearance, with large heads, large "slant" eyes, small noses and mouths. The average weight was around 40 pounds. They had very thin necks. Their torso was very small and thin. They had long and slender arms

---

[92] Ibid; citing Headquarters United States Air Force (9 October 1950). PURCHASE OFFER OF FLYING SAUCER PHOTOGRAPHS, Washington, DC: U.S. Government Printing Office.
[93] Williams S. Steinman, Wendelle C. Stevens, UFO Crash at Aztec: A Well Kept Secret (UFO Photo Archives, Tucson, Arizona, 1986), pp. 53-55, 77-83, 106-118, 125-129, 148-153, etc.

reaching the knees, with hands containing long and slender fingers with webbing between them. There didn't seem to be any reproductive organs. (One scientist suggested that these "aliens" might be manufactured or constructed).

Instead of blood, as we know it, they had a colorless liquid prevalent in the body, with no red cells. This liquid had a kind of ozone smell about it. They had no digestive system or GI tract, no alimentary or intestinal canal and no rectal point.

As the one scientist stated, "I got the impression that these alien beings were "constructed." These humanoid beings may have been clones produced through some very highly advanced genetic technology!"[94]

Generally, documents such as these are ignored and not very well-researched. But while I am unaware of other "reports" that give details of the anatomy of the beings, it should be noted that the claim that they may have been somehow constructed is apparently believed by those within the intelligence community, as stated by Dr. Garry Nolan, professor of pathology at Stanford University.[95]

A memorable case among other researchers occurred on December 9, 1965, when a bell-shaped object crashed in Kecksburg, Pennsylvania. Military officials tried to quarantine the crash site. A witness mentioned that noise was coming from inside the object, so someone opened the lid of the aircraft and fired into it, locking the lid in place. They then covered the object with a tarp and took it away in a vehicle. The official story says that nothing was recovered, but that is not the case, considering the presence of six people with long suits, shirts, ties, and no badges.[96]

Journalist Leslie Kean requested through FOIA - Freedom of Information Act - a box of documents on that case, but NASA reported that they were lost in 1987.[97]

Additional evidence of U.S. government interest in crashed aircraft of unknown origin was provided to George Koehler, another investigator in the Aztec case, who obtained information directly from Silas Newton. Koehler made a secret recording on March 31, 1950, of an interrogation of him by two members of AFOSI (Air Force Office Of Special Investigations) at their radio station KMYR in the Denver area.[98]

Such interrogation occurred a few weeks after the March 8, 1950 conference at the University of Denver on "Crash Retrievals" (C/R). A few months earlier, beginning in December 1949, a series of newspaper articles appeared "talking about crashed discs in the Mexico City and southwest areas, "midget" occupants, mystery metals that totally defied analysis, an acclimation program to prevent public hysteria, etc." "A similar 1947 recorded interrogation situation occurred after the Roswell crash retrieval, but the officers caught on," wrote Richard Geldreich, Jr. A copy of the recording was made for reporter Frank Scully.

[94] Ibid, pp.46, 48.

[95] (August 2, 2022), Dr Garry P Nolan UAP UFO Tucker Carlson Full Interview 03/08/2022, UAP Tracker: https://www.youtube.com/watch?v=T3sszdf_93w; accessed January 14, 2024. 35:23-37:15.

[96] Jackie Contreras (Editor), Adam Rzeplinski (Editor), Megan Winiarski (Editor), & Tim McNeela (Director) (2021, January 14). Alien Crash Secrets (Season 1, Episode 2) [TV series episode]. Michael Sorensen, Matthew Kelly, Andrew Nock (Executive Producers), *UFO Witness*. Anomaly Entertainment, Inc.

[97] Ibid.

[98] Richard Geldreich, Jr. (Nov. 2, 2022), Secret March 31, 1950 Recording of the AFOSI Interrogation of George Koehler, Medium: https://medium.com/@richgel99/secret-march-31-1950-recording-of-the-afosi-interrogation-of-george-koehler-70cc1ce160db Accessed September 20, 2023. Note: unless otherwise noted, hereafter is the same source.

The Ramsey husband and wife transcribed the same interrogation in their Aztec book, as they also came across the recording.[99] Another trigger, perhaps the most important of all, became the whirlwind caused by Frank Scully's book, Behind the Flying Saucers. It was not only a subject of investigation for AFOSI, but also for the U.S. Army Counter Intelligence Division (CID), the CIA, and the FBI.

Apparently, J.P. Cahn was one of the first to contact J. Edgar Hoover, director of the FBI, as well as Hollywood actor Bruce Cabot, suggesting that Scully's sources were worth investigating. The FBI was already on the trail of the Aztec incident, and they had a file on Silas Newton from the early 1930s that showed his character to be sound until their interest grew because of Scully's book.

Now, the special agents who interrogated Koehler, Hanson, and Unger, never denied or nodded to Koehler's incessant claims that the Air Force was engaged in a cover-up of the UFO phenomenon.

In addition, notes from Frank Scully's files (AHC Box 10 ff5) at the American Heritage Center reveal that one of Dr. G's men (a literary resource of a composite of eight scientists), was ordered to report quickly to the Pentagon. And that the Air Force chief of research questioned him for hours about everything he knew about the Aztec flying disk. At the end of the interview, he told him to forget everything he had ever said or heard about it.[100]

Consecutively, the Air Force chief of research told Robert Imanidt, a Lockheed Martin photographer, that he would talk "privately with what's going on saucer-wise at Lockheed."[101]

More original documents came to light decades ago, confirming that UFOs with the bodies of their occupants were recovered by the U.S. government. In the late 1970s, Arthur Bray, a former member of the Royal Canadian Air Force, got a document from the Canadian government entitled "Geo-Magnetics," which was written by Wilbert E. Smith, Senior Radio Engineer of the Canadian Ministry of Transport, dated November 21, 1950, and classified Top-Secret. It set out the beginning of a formal request to establish a Canadian government-sponsored UFO study to accumulate information on how flying saucers operate so that the technology discovered could be put to practical use for mankind. The document was downgraded from Top Secret to Confidential on September 15, 1969, under the stipulation that "It must never be disclosed to the public."[102]

"While in Washington attending the NARB conference, two books were released, one titled "BEHIND THE FLYING SAUCERS" by Frank Scully, and the other, "THE FLYING SAUCERS ARE REAL" by Donald Kehoe. Both books dealt mostly

---

[99] Scott Ramsey, Suzanne Ramsey, The Aztec UFO Incident: The Case, Evidence, and Elaborate Cover-up of One of the Most Perplexing Crashes in History (New Page Books/The Career Press, Inc., Wayne, NJ, 2016), ob. cit. Note: unless otherwise noted, this is the same source. To listen to the recording: (May 20, 2014), UFO Archives: Project Blue Book - George Koehler, UFO Archives: https://www.youtube.com/watch?v=mhP9Mr2bgvE Accessed September 20, 2023.
[100] Richard Geldreich, Jr. (July 2, 2023), Frank Scully's 1950's Private Notes Mention Informants at "Right Field" and Lockheed, Medium: https://medium.com/@richgel99/frank-scullys-1950-s-private-notes-mention-informants-at-right-field-and-lockheed-f0b3155bdd81 Accessed September 20, 2023.
[101] Ibid.
[102] Quoted in Williams S. Steinman, Wendelle C. Stevens, UFO Crash at Aztec: A Well Kept Secret (UFO Photo Archives, Tucson, Arizona, 1986), p. 305.

with the sightings of Unidentified Flying Objects and both books claimed that the flying objects were of extra-terrestrial origin and might well be Space ships from another planet. Scully claimed that the preliminary studies of one saucer which fell into the hands of the United States Government indicated that they operated on some hitherto unknown magnetic principles............

"I made discreet enquiries through the Canadian Embassy staff in Washington, who were able to obtain for me the following information:

"a. The matter is the most highly classified subject in the United States Government, rating higher even than the H-bomb.

"b. Flying saucers exist.

"c. Their modus operandi is unknown, but concentrated effort is being made by a small group headed by Doctor Vannevar Bush."[103]

The above document gives validity to the Aztec and Roswell cases. But digging deeper, after digging through the papers of the late Wilbert Smith, in the possession of his son, Smurl Smith, Arthur Bray found three notes under the title: "Notes on interview through Lt. Col. Bremner with Dr. Robert I. Sarbacher", dated September 15, 1950," a little over two months before the above memo.[104]

Dr. Robert Sarbacher was Director of Research at WEDD Laboratories, Dean of the Georgia Tech Graduate School; and a consultant to the U.S. Government's Research and Development Board (R&DB).[105]

Now, the notes reveal that Dr. Sarbacher told Wilbert Smith "that the facts in Scully's book were "substantially correct." After assuring him that flying saucers do exist, Sarbacher told him that they had not "been able to duplicate their performance." He pointed out that they did not originate on this planet, and that the subject "is classified two points higher than the H bomb. In fact, it is the most highly classified subject in the U.S. government at the present time."[106]

In a telephone conversation on July 31, 1983, Sarbacher told researcher William Steinman that Scully's story about the recovery of flying saucers was true and that he recalled conversing with Wilbert Smith in September 1950 at the Canadian Embassy in Washington, D.C.;[107] corroborating what was written in the memo.

More formally, Dr. Sarbacher wrote to William Steinman in a letter dated November 29, 1983, on letterhead under Washington Institute of Technology-Oceanographic and Physical Sciences, and Sarbacher as President and Chairman of the Board of Directors, from which we transcribe the main points:

"1. Relating to my own experience regarding recovered flying saucers, I had no association with any of the people involved in the recovery and have no knowledge regarding the dates of the recoveries. If I had I would send it to you.

---

[103] Ibid, p. 306.
[104] Ibid, p. 307.
[105] Ibid, p. 308.
[106] Ibid, p. 308, 310-313.
[107] Ibid, p. 318, cf. p. 314.

"2. Regarding verification that persons you list were involved, I can only say this:

"John von Neuman was definitely involved. Dr. Vannevar Bush was definitely involved, and I think Dr. Robert Oppenheimer also.

"My association with the Research and Development Board under Doctor Compton during the Eisenhower administration was rather limited so that although I had been invited to participate in several discussions associated with the reported recoveries, I could not personally attend the meetings. I am sure that they would have asked Dr. von Braun, and the others that you listed were probably asked and may or may not have attended. This is all I know for sure.

"3. I did receive some official reports when I was in my office at the Pentagon but all of these were left there as at the time we were never supposed to take them out of the office.
[...]
5. [...]
"I recall the interview with Dr. Brenner of the Canadian Embassy. I think the answers I gave him were the ones you listed. Naturally, I was more familiar with the subject matter under discussion, at that time. Actually, I would have been able to give more specific answers had I attended the meetings concerning the subject. You must understand that I took this assignment as a private contribution. We were called "dollar-a-year men." My first responsibility was the maintenance of my own business activity so that my participation was limited.

"About the only thing I remember at this time is that certain material reported to have come from flying saucer crashes were extremely light and very tough. I am sure our laboratories analysed them very carefully.
"There were reports that instruments or people operating these machines were also of very light weight, sufficient to withstand the tremendous deceleration and acceleration associated with their machinery. I remember in talking with some of the people at the office that I got the impression these "aliens" were constructed like certain insects we have observed on earth, wherein because of the low mass the inertial forces involved in operation of these instruments would be quite low.

"I still do not know why the high order of classification has been given and why the denial of the existence of these devices."[108]

A copy of that letter is preserved in the Archives and Special Collections of the University of Ottawa, Canada.[109]

---

[108] Ibid, pp. 324, 325.
[109] https://arcs-atom.uottawa.ca/index.php/letter-from-robert-i-sarbacher-to-mr-steinman Accessed January 26, 2024. Archives et collections spéciales/Archives and Special Collections Finding Aid - Arthur Bray fonds (30-003) (Generated by Archives et collections spéciales/Archives and Special Collections on January 9, 2023), p. 138.

Next, an FBI memorandum dated March 22, 1950, stated:

"An investigator for the Air Force stated that three so-called flying saucers had been recovered in New Mexico. They were described as being circular in shape with raised centers, approximately 50 feet in diameter. Each one was occupied by three bodies of human shape only 3 feet tall, dressed in metallic cloth of a very fine texture. Each body was bandaged in a manner similar to the blackout suits used by speed flyers and test pilots.

"According to Mr. HOWE'S informant, the saucers were found in New Mexico due to the fact that the Government has a very high-powered radar set-up in that area and it is believed the radar interferes with the controling mechanism of the saucers.

"No further evaluation was attempted by SA KURTZMAN concerning the above."[110]

That memo was written by the FBI's Washington DC field office chief, Guy Hottel; and then sent to J. Edgar Hoover, the agency's director. Although it is unconfirmed testimony that the agency never followed up on,[111] it should be noted that Hottel saw fit to send it to Hoover.

Additional information is available on Merlin Hansen, who was an industrial engineer and computer scientist; and who was involved in logistics, and communication systems; and was in charge of solving unusual problems and special project work.[112] Sadly he became involved in eugenics projects.

He also installed one of the first computers at Wright-Patterson Air Force Base in Ohio.

In 1950, Hansen made a deal to work for the government at the same air base. In one of his letters, he indicated that he was at Kecksburg from December 9-10, 1965, when he was taken away on an emergency basis for a few weeks. Other dates of his absence correspond with other UFO incidents not developed here: Socorro, New Mexico, in April 1964. In Montana, on March 16, 1967; and in Dexter, Michigan, on March 20, 1966.

Many years later, on the night Hansen would pass away, he told his son, "Dave... We are not alone. We are not alone." David Hansen indicated that as a son, he knew what his father was talking about.

Also, for decades, there has been an active campaign of misinformation and misinformation about the UAP phenomenon, particularly by the U.S. Air Force, Los Alamos National Laboratory, and other agencies. This is based on the reality of what

---

[110] Federal Bureau of Investigation (March 22, 1950). FLYNG SAUCERS INFORMATION CONCERNING, Washington, DC: U.S. Government Printing Office. See unredacted document in: John Greenewald (August 8, 2022), The "Guy Hottel" Memo and the Crashed Flying Saucers of New Mexico, March 22, 1950, The Black Vault: https://www.theblackvault.com/documentarchive/the-guy-hottel-memo-and-the-crashed-flying-saucers-of-new-mexico-march-22-1950/ Accessed September 20, 2023.
[111] News (March 25, 2013), UFOs And The Guy Hottel Memo, FBI News: https://www.fbi.gov/news/stories/ufos-and-the-guy-hottel-memo/ufos-and-the-guy-hottel-memo Accessed September 20, 2023.
[112] Adam Rzeplinski (Editor), Megan Winiarski (Editor), & Tim McNeela (Director) (2021, January 14). Alien High Tech (Season 1, Episode 3) [TV series episode]. Michael Sorensen, Matthew Kelly, Andrew Nock, Alex Byrnes, Cecile Bouchardeau Weiland (Executive Producers), *UFO Witness*. Anomaly Entertainment, Inc. Note: unless otherwise noted, this is the same source.

the government has been hiding for decades. We have, for example, the U.S. Air Force's tiresome deception of businessman Paul Bennewitz about the UFO phenomenon and hoaxes about false UFO appearances and cattle mutilations that were carried out by humans.[113] We also have the fabrication of documents from an alleged government organization called MJ-12 or Majestic 12, as reported by Richard Doty, a former Air Force special investigator who indicated that the FBI informed him that they found that someone at Los Alamos National Laboratory forged the documents so well known to the public.[114] Jacques Vallée says it is now known that the Majestic-12 document hoax began with Admiral Edward Burkhalter, then Chief of Naval Intelligence. His counterespionage staff would have forged authentic documents referring to a classified project in the 1950s, to deceive the Soviets about technological advances, as Dr. Eric Davis would have found out through his contacts.[115]

Despite that, it has been said that the documents would be based on the reality of such an organization. The purpose of planting the disinformation is not yet clear, although it is claimed that it is to sow ridicule about the phenomenon to attract disbelief about it and about an alleged government cover-up.

An additional example of a cover-up is the Phoenix lights event, which was witnessed by thousands of people on the night of March 13, 1997.[116] At the time, Frances Emma Barwood was a city councilwoman and vice mayor of Phoenix, Arizona. A reporter told her he wanted to talk to her about what happened and to see if anyone was investigating. When she returned to her office by Monday, her voicemail was full, with about seven hundred messages in which witnesses described seeing basically the same thing. So she started digging, but the investigation was halted by Arizona Governor Fife Symington.

Barwood appealed to the public to put pressure on the governor. So the phone calls to Symington were so many, that he had to make a public statement where he dismissed everything. Apparently, he was pressured to deny the existence of UFOs. Some time later he would admit that he saw the Phoenix lights.

Convinced more than ever of a cover-up, days later, Barwood received a phone call from a local veteran named Richard Curtis, who informed her that he had incontrovertible video evidence showing that the lights were part of an aircraft. Curtis promised to send a copy of the video evidence to the councilwoman's office. But when Curtis called back a week later, he asked Frances what she thought about the video, to which she replied that it had not yet reached her. Curtis then told her that men claiming to come from her office had arrived to pick it up. Frances told Curtis that she did not

---

[113] Greg Bishop, Project Beta: The Story of Paul Bennewitz, National Security, and the Creation of a Modern UFO Myth (Gallery Books, 2005); Mark Pilkington, Mirage Men: An Adventure into Paranoia, Espionage, Psychological Warfare, and UFOs (Skyhorse, First Edition, 2010); Roland Denning, Kypros Kyprianou, John Lundberg, Mark Pilkington (Producer) John Lundberg (Director). (2013), Mirage Men. (With Dog Eat Dog Films, Fellowship Adventure Group).

[114] George Knapp (Feb. 20, 2020), Former spy found himself accused, then cleared, twice in '80s MJ-12 leak, Mystery Wire.

[115] Jacques Vallée, Forbidden Science 5, Pacific Heights: The Journals of Jacques Vallee 2000-2009 (Anomalist Books, Charlottesville, Virginia, 2023), pp. 466, 467.

[116] Jackie Contreras (Editor), Adam Rzeplinski (Editor), Megan Winiarski (Editor), & Tim McNeela (Director) (2021, January 28). The Mothership Returns (Season 1, Episode 5) [TV Series Episode]. Alex Byrnes, Matthew Kelly, Andrew Nock, Michael Sorensen, Cecile Bouchardeau Weiland (Executive Producers), UFO Witness. Anomaly Entertainment, Inc. Note: unless otherwise noted, hereafter is the same source.

have men working in her office, but only three women. When she asked Curtis what the men looked like, he replied that they were in three-piece suits and hats. It was then the month of July when the temperature was very high.

Shortly thereafter, Curtis became very ill, and according to neighbors, he changed his medication and had a bad reaction, so he was taken by ambulance to the hospital and no one saw him again.

Barwood indicates that a private investigator found that her phone line had been tapped; and that it came from the government. When former FBI agent Ben Hansen asked Barwood if she had any idea who might be intercepting her calls, she replied, "Well, I was told a long time ago, that there's a government you see, and there's a shadow government. It's not elected officials, it's not hired officials. It's beyond that."

Richard Doty, a former Air Force special agent, was regularly tasked to cover up government secrets through the Air Force Office of Special Investigations (AFOSI) special investigation-counterintelligence division. He had been stationed at Area 51 in the 1980s. While civilian sightings were investigated by Project Blue Book, the real mysterious cases were handled by AFOSI. But its agents were sent to disinform people who had had a UFO sighting. He said there were manuals and a policy that stated exactly how they were to do it, such as discrediting people. And even though there were genuine UFO sightings and AFOSI was aware of them, they carried out their planned disinformation campaign.

"The beginning of the end"

Tom DeLonge, co-founder, co-vocalist, and guitarist of the rock band Blink-182 until 2015, said during an interview with *Papermag* magazine according to government sources:

"The CIA was very interested in the UFO civilian research groups, with the intention of being in control over all the research and the public awareness. It was a psychological operation. They were very scared of Americans being gullible and having Russia come in and repeat a *War of the Worlds* scenario. So the CIA said, "We better get in there and make everyone go crazy, but at least it's controlled, and when we're in charge we can slowly let people know the phenomenon is real, but, 'Don't worry – we've been building something secret to help protect us.'" It's a crazy thing, but it's real."[117]

Ralph Blumenthal, then a reporter for *The New York Times*, wrote an article published by the newspaper in April 2017, discussing a statistical book on UFO sightings that was written by Cheryl Costa, a former military technician and aerospace analyst, along with his wife Linda Miller Costa, a librarian at Le Moyne College-a private Catholic Jesuit university located in Syracuse, New York and a former librarian for the National Academy of Sciences, NASA, and the Environmental Protection Agency. Gordon G. Spear, professor emeritus of physics and astronomy at Sonoma

---

[117] Michael Tedder (Feb. 17, 2015), Blink-182 Co-Founder Tom DeLonge Goes Deep on UFOs, Government Coverups and Why Aliens are Bigger than Jesus, Papermag.

State University in California, wrote the foreword. The research showed that UFO sightings tripled since 2001 in the United States alone.[118]

The report describes sightings of flying circles, spheres, triangles, discs, ovals, and cigar shapes. A small percentage of the sightings defy prosaic explanations.[119]

The Costa's stated, "they have spotted U.F.O.s themselves and want to detoxify the subject." In addition to the fact that "We're doing scientific research," Cheryl Costa said. "What's crazy is not being willing to look at research."[120]

Just a few months after the article, on December 16, 2017, *The New York Times*, authored by Helene Cooper, Ralph Blumenthal, and Leslie Kean, published an article titled Glowing Auras and 'Black Money': The Pentagon's Mysterious U.F.O. Program.[121] It reports that $22 million was invested in the Advanced Aerospace Threat Identification Program (AATIP), which was a classified program and therefore funded by the kind of "black money" used for classified programs. According to Defense Department officials, program participants, and records obtained by the newspaper, for years the program investigated UFO reports. A military intelligence officer named Luis Elizondo was in charge of the program on the fifth floor of the Pentagon.

The obscure program, with portions still classified, began in 2007 and closed in 2012. It was initially funded largely at the behest of the late Senator Harry Reid, a Nevada Democrat and former Senate Majority Leader.

The program began after Bigelow piqued Reid's interest in UFOs in 2007 when he told him that a Defense Intelligence Agency official approached him to visit Bigelow's ranch (Skinwalker Ranch, in the state of Utah, which we will see later), where he conducted research.

Most of the $22 million went to the Las Vegas-based aerospace research firm Bigelow Aerospace, run by billionaire entrepreneur and longtime friend of Reid's, Robert Bigelow, who by the time of the article in *The New York Times*, was working with NASA to produce expandable spacecraft for human use in space.

Bigelow had said on CBS's "60 Minutes" program in May of the same year (2017), that he was "absolutely convinced" of the existence of extraterrestrials and that UFOs have visited planet Earth.

Working with Bigelow's company, the program produced documents describing sightings of aircraft moving at very high speeds with no visible signs of propulsion, or hovering with no apparent means of lift.

They also studied videos of encounters between unknown objects and U.S. military aircraft, such as that "of a whitish oval object, about the size of a commercial plane, chased by two Navy F/A-18F fighter jets from the aircraft carrier Nimitz off the coast of San Diego in 2004."

Bigelow's company used subcontractors for the research and modified buildings in Las Vegas to store metal alloys and other materials that Luis Elizondo and the program's contractors said were recovered from unidentified aerial phenomena. But

---

[118] Ralph Blumenthal (April 24, 2017), People Are Seeing U.F.O.s Everywhere, and This Book Proves It, The New York Times.

[119] Ibid.

[120] Ibid.

[121] Helene Cooper, Ralph Blumenthal, and Leslie Kean (Dec. 16, 2017), Glowing Auras and 'Black Money': The Pentagon's Mysterious U.F.O. Program, The New York Times. Note: unless otherwise noted, this is the same source.

they also studied people who claimed to have experienced physical effects from UFO encounters, so they examined them for physiological changes.

Harold E. Puthoff, an engineer who conducted ESP (extrasensory perception) research for the CIA in the past and also a contractor for the "AATIP" program, told the *Times* that they did not yet know the function of the materials that were found.

By 2009, Harry Reid became convinced that the program had made too many extraordinary discoveries.

A 2009 AATIP briefing by Luis Elizondo stated that "what was considered science fiction is now science fact," and that the United States was unable to defend itself against some of the technologies discovered.

Similarly, Elizondo stated that he and his government colleagues determined that the phenomena they studied did not appear to originate in any nation; and that: "That fact is not something any government or institution should classify in order to keep secret from the people."

With the program's funding exhausted in 2012, Elizondo continued the program in his Pentagon office with the help of Navy and CIA officials until October 2017, when he resigned protesting what he characterized as excessive secrecy and internal opposition to the program's efforts. But many sightings were also going unreported for fear of ridicule or stigmatization

Luis Elizondo joined Hal Puthoff and Christopher K. Mellon, former Deputy Assistant Secretary of Defense for Intelligence, in 2017 in a new commercial venture called TTSA or To The Stars Academy of Arts and Science, which began in October 2017 (after Elizondo's resignation) and whose goal was to raise funds for UFO research.

Tom DeLonge, the former guitarist and singer of the band Blink-182 is also the founder and CEO of TTSA.[122]

In an interview published in February 2015 in *Papermag*, DeLonge, who had been saying he was cooperating with government contacts about the reality of the UFO phenomenon, felt vindicated, since in his words, "now, NASA is holding symposiums on the inevitability of finding life in the universe. The Vatican is talking about, yes, there's life out there, and how it interferes or doesn't interfere with the church's view of existence."[123]

"[...] I've been involved in this for a long time. I have sources from the government. I've had my phone tapped. I've done a lot of weird stuff in this industry -- people wouldn't believe me if I told them. But this is what happens when you start getting on an email chains with hundreds of scientists from the Jet Propulsion Laboratory and different universities around the country, and you start outing seniors scientists from Lockheed Martin talking about the reality of this stuff, guys that hold 30 patents, guys that work underground out in the Nevada test sites in Area 51. It goes far beyond just saying, "Hey, that little light in the sky, that's a little green man." That doesn't lend the right gravity to the topic."[124]

---

[122] Derrick Bryson Taylor (September 26, 2019/June 3, 2021), How Blink-182's Tom DeLonge Became a U.F.O. Researcher, The New York Times.
[123] Michael Tedder (Feb. 17, 2015), Blink-182 Co-Founder Tom DeLonge Goes Deep on UFOs, Government Coverups and Why Aliens are Bigger than Jesus, Papermag. Note: unless otherwise noted, this is the same source.
[124] Ibid.

He said in September of the same year (2015), he was doing a project that he could not talk about and that it involved national security issues. He would fly to New Mexico to meet for the third time with the U.S. Air Force Space Command general. He added that the project involved something related to a conversation he had the same month with two Area 51 employees.[125]

In an interview for *Mic* in 2016, he explained of an alleged secret government control group about the most secret information on the UFO phenomenon and said that "the irony now is that I'm dealing with people from the modern version of whatever that group is called. It's a big deal." He adds, "I think there has been [alien] hardware, and whether by design or by accident, it's fallen in multiple countries."[126]

Referring to a franchise based on a series of fictional books - Sekret Machines - he was writing at the time based on what to him is an indication of information he obtained from the highest echelons of the U.S. military and intelligence community, he said that "we don't really call it 'aliens'" [...] "it's much more complex than that,"[127] and adding:

"[...] when you dive into this type of material, it's a lot more than just science and technology. It has to do with religion and cosmology and it has to do with politics and secrecy. So it's a pretty fantastic ride when you start studying this stuff. You'll find yourself trying to challenge your belief system. This project was a good way to bring it to the world in a more elevated way."[128]

During an interview already quoted, he also said: "The phenomenon has been around forever. All the ancient religions were written down based on witnessing this phenomenon in various forms. Governments of the world watched the phenomenon and tried to replicate the technology, but they did in secret. So the governments are fighting each other with these pieces of technology. But within those little skirmishes, the phenomenon is still here, and it's much more advanced. So in order to hide what the governments are building in secret, they blame it on spaceships and aliens [...] but it's all in an effort to hide what we're really building, something that is real but is exotic and esoteric, and it's all part of a plan. And as we find out that the phenomenon is real, they're hoping it won't be as bad as we thought it was, because we were scared along the way. It's a really complex game that's been played, especially since the '80s."[129]

DeLonge further adds:

"It's totally, universally accepted amongst the country's elite scientific establishments that there's life everywhere. The question is what kind, where, how'd they get here, what are they doing when they get here, and how do we communicate with them?

---

[125] Alternative Press Magazine (September 4, 2015), Tom DeLonge claims to be doing "really important things" with Area 51, Alternative Press Magazine.
[126] Kelly Dickerson (June 17, 2016), Tom DeLonge Took a Break From Blink-182 to Focus on UFOs, Mic.
[127] Ibid.
[128] Ibid.
[129] Michael Tedder (Feb. 17, 2015), Blink-182 Co-Founder Tom DeLonge Goes Deep on UFOs, Government Coverups and Why Aliens are Bigger than Jesus, Papermag.

That's when you start reading books about the mind and consciousness, and telepathy and ESP."[130]

When Tom DeLonge officially announced To The Stars Academy of Arts & Sciences (TTSA) on October 11, 2017, he did so from a stage in Seattle, introducing himself as president and CEO.[131] The team members consisted of Jim Semivan, one of TTSA's co-founders then recently retired from the CIA's Directorate of Operations after 25 years as an operations officer working in the U.S. and internationally.

The third co-founder was Dr. Hal Puthoff, a theoretical physicist who led the controversial CIA and Department of Defense research on "psychic spies" or remote viewing, defined as the alleged psychic ability to receive information or impressions of a person, object, place, or event from a great distance.

Another team member, Steve Justice, heading TTSA's aerospace division, had just finished a month as director of advanced systems at Lockheed Martin Skunk Works.

Also introduced as a member, Christopher Mellon, deeply aware of the mystery of UAPs (Unidentified Aerial Phenomena)[132] from his past investigations as a staff member of the Senate Intelligence Committee and his senior role as Deputy Assistant Secretary of Defense for Intelligence in the Department of Defense.

Each member of former infiltrators, possessing top-secret compartmented security clearances, then joined TTSA to campaign for UAP research and advocate for government transparency on the issue.

In a TTSA presentation, always on October 11, 2017, Jim Semivan said: "I think it's an opportunity for us to take certain topics, whether that's unidentified aerial phenomena or ESP or telepathy and really get to the bottom of this."[133]

Luis Elizondo also added: "In the last ten years we've come a long way in understanding our place here in this universe. There is physics that we do not quite yet understand, doesn't mean that is not real, just simply means that we do not have the capacity to understand those physics." [...] the fact is we may not necessarily be alone." With these words, Elizondo suggests that there is a non-human intelligence involved in UFOs/UAPs.[134]

Again, Semivan: "These things are real, these things are out there. They have been out there for a long time. They are not the provenance of the government or any government in the world. They belong to us. They're things that happen to people all the time, and they're things that we need to explore. And we need to finally get together to find out what this is all about." Semivan implies that the UAP phenomenon is not of human origin.[135]

DeLonge concludes by inviting the public "to help build a paradigm-shifting global movement [...] that will propel us forward and make us see that we are far more special and far more connected to each other than we ever could have imagined."[136]

---

[130] Ibid.

[131] Ross Coulthart, In Plain Sight: An investigation into UFOs and impossible science (HarperCollins Publishers, 2021), ob. cit. Note: unless otherwise noted, this is the same source.

[132] Today, unidentified anomalous phenomena.

[133] (Oct. 11, 2017), To The Stars Academy of Arts & Science, To The Stars*: https://www.youtube.com/watch?v=-gr-A4ebLeE; accessed July 31, 2023.

[134] Ibid.

[135] Ibid.

[136] Ibid.

TTSA's agenda strongly suggests that the phenomenon is not human and has the potential to unify humanity under a new consciousness.

A couple of weeks after the release of TTSA, Tom DeLonge was interviewed on *The Joe Rogan Experience* podcast. In the interview, he claimed that very high-level government officials informed him of the discovery of a new life form and recovered aircraft at the beginning of the Cold War. Secretly conversing with very high-ranking U.S. generals, spies, and aerospace executives, he was assured of a seven-decade history of contact with non-human intelligences.[137] As a result, DeLonge would go on to write a series of novels based on contacts with government and government contractors.

His first book, part of a successful series entitled *Sekret Machines*, that are two novels that combine inside knowledge of senior government officials and others about UFO and alien phenomena. For example, in his first volume co-written with A. J. Hartley, DeLonge tells in the preface, that he was at two meetings of a very high-level company that is a major U.S. defense contractor.[138] We know he is referring to members of Skunkworks, the Advanced Development Programs division of Lockheed Martin.[139] DeLonge spoke with Skunk Works' chief executive, Rob Weiss,[140] about the project in books and a documentary about *Sekret Machines*, which would help young people change their cynical view of the government and the Department of Defense.[141] Sekret Machines would be just that and much more.

DeLonge would receive an email from the director of Skunk Works, to meet with the Pentagon on a certain day and time to introduce him to someone who was "connected." DeLonge was introduced to two senior military commanders, including two U.S. Air Force generals, intelligence officers, high-ranking NASA bureaucrats, and senior White House officials. Then followed a meeting with "The General." The first thing the highly decorated general told him seemed frightening: "It was the Cold War [...] We found a life- form."[142]

Tom DeLonge told Joe Rogan that this was a green light from the black world of U.S. defense and intelligence to spread the U.S. government's impending disclosure of incredible UFO secrets. He was informed that the government has recovered aircraft of alien origin, as well as the bodies of their pilots; and that there is a secret effort to understand and master that technology and protect humanity from an imminent threat.

DeLonge would send the Skunk Works editor a draft foreword to his nonfiction book on UFOs, as part of his Sekret Machines series co-authored with researcher Peter Levenda. The foreword made a good impression on Rob Weiss, as DeLonge was now on his way to meeting other sources. One of the most impressive aspects of the book's content is that the foreword discusses, as journalist Ross Coulthart pointed out:

---

[137] Rogan, J. (Host). (2017, October). Tom DeLonge (No. 1029) [Audio podcast episode]. In *The Joe Rogan Experience*.Joerogan: https://open.spotify.com/episode/2ybsXdWAtxqLBdRByLb2YG
[138] A. J. Hartley, Tom DeLonge, Sekret Machines Book 1: Chasing Shadows (To The Stars, 2017), ob. cit.
[139] Tyler Rogoway (Dec. 1, 2019), Tom DeLonge's Origin Story For To The Stars Academy Describes A Government UFO Info Operation, The Drive.
[140] Giuseppe Macri (Oct. 27, 2016), Podesta Emails Show High-Level DOD, Hollywood Support for Tom Delonge's UFO Project, InsideSources, LLC.
[141] A. J. Hartley, Tom DeLonge, Sekret Machines Book 1: Chasing Shadows (To The Stars, 2017), ob. cit. Note: unless otherwise noted, this is the same source.
[142] Rogan, J. (Host). (2017, October). Tom DeLonge (No. 1029) [Audio podcast episode]. In *The Joe Rogan Experience*.Joerogan: https://open.spotify.com/episode/2ybsXdWAtxqLBdRByLb2YG

"Quite why that prologue helped open the door to the secret UAP gatekeepers is baffling because the version DeLonge eventually published is all about the aggressively debunked, hugely controversial (and potentially very frightening, if true) 'contactees and abductee aspect of the [UAP] phenomenon'. In SeKret Machines: Gods, Man & War, DeLonge and coauthor Peter Levenda suggest that it is possible to prove there are physical effects on UAP contactees and that those abducted (presumably by nonhuman intelligences/aliens?) show signs of post-traumatic stress disorder."[143]

During an interview for *GQ*, asked why he decided to start with a fiction novel, he replied, "The enormity of what's being told might hit people in a weird way if it was just laid on their lap all at once. It's better to go step by step to understand how we found these things and dealt with them."[144]

Now, to advance the project to inform the public, emails leaked by WikiLeaks between Tom DeLonge and John Podesta (2015-16), former Chief of Staff to former President Bill Clinton, and former advisor to then-President Barack Obama, but at the time of the emails, Hillary Clinton's campaign manager, reveal conversations between DeLonge and major television studios (February 23, 2016 email) and Hollywood, such as Scott Free, founded by Ridley Scott, responsible for the renowned production "The Martian." Allison Shearmur, producer of the then-upcoming installment of the Star Wars franchise "Rogue One: A Star Wars Story;" Imagine Entertainment, from director Ron Howard, Netflix, Amazon and VICE News, to develop a fictional television series based on DeLonge's novel "Sekret Machines: Chasing Shadows," to create 8-10 one-hour episodes that could be run on HBO.[145]

He told *Rolling Stone* magazine, in an article published April 27, 2016, that production of his multimedia effort comes from "sources within the aerospace industry and the Department of Defense and NASA."[146]

As for additional revelations to DeLonge, he has said that there "were UFO crashes in Nazi Germany, China, and Russia, all of which were covered up."[147]

"What was going on in secret, he claimed, was an international collaboration between countries to be prepared for The Others."[148]

He suggested that the supernatural "myths" about demons were related to the UFO/UAP phenomenon. He stated, "What you have is something that doesn't like man, and either feels jealous of, or has some kind of plan for what man is to be."[149]

John Podesta and Hillary Clinton herself agreed on this and informed the press on different occasions that if she were elected president, she would release everything there was about the UFO phenomenon to see what was out there.[150]

---

[143] Ross Coulthart, In Plain Sight: An investigation into UFOs and impossible science (HarperCollins Publishers, 2021), ob. cit.

[144] Tom DeLonge (April 2, 2016), Tom DeLonge Has Something Very Important to Tell You, GQ.

[145] Quoted in Grant Cameron, Managing Magic: The Government's UFO Disclosure Plan (CreateSpace Independent Publishing Platform, 2017), ob. cit.

[146] Patrick Doyle (April 27, 2016), Inside Tom DeLonge's UFO Obsession, Blink-182 Turmoil, Rolling Stone.

[147] Ross Coulthart, In Plain Sight: An investigation into UFOs and impossible science (HarperCollins Publishers, 2021), ob. cit.

[148] Ibid.

[149] Ibid,; quoting George Knapp, Coast To Coast AM, hour 3 at approximately 9:03.

The New York Times reported in late May 2019, that strange objects with no visible engine or infrared exhaust plumes that could reach 30,000 feet and supersonic speeds appeared almost daily from the summer of 2014 through March 2015, high in the skies over the U.S. East Coast. Lt. Ryan Graves, an F/A-18 Super Hornet pilot who was in the Navy for ten years, said, "These things would be out there all day;" and he reported his sightings to the Pentagon and Congress.[151]

The same newspaper reported in mid-May 2020, that, "Navy fighter pilots reported close encounters with unidentified aerial vehicles, including several dangerously close, in eight incidents between June 27, 2013, and Feb. 13, 2019, according to documents recently released by the Navy."[152]

Major revelations

The New York Times reported in a July 2020 article that the Pentagon was continuing its effort to investigate unidentified aerial phenomena through the Unidentified Aerial Phenomena Task Force or UAP Task Force (2017-2022).[153] Sen. Marco Rubio, a Florida Republican serving as acting chairman of the Senate Select Committee on Intelligence, told CBS he was especially concerned about reports of unidentified craft over U.S. military bases. And that they might be of Russian or Chinese origin or some other adversary. Luis Elizondo said that the program was part of the transparency in investigating the phenomenon; and that he and others from TTSA claimed "are convinced that objects of undetermined origin have crashed on earth with materials retrieved for study."

Former Senate Majority Leader Harry Read said he pushed for the earlier program - the AATIP - because "After looking into this, I came to the conclusion that there were reports — some were substantive, some not so substantive — that there were actual materials that the government and the private sector had in their possession." *The New York Times* continued:

"Eric W. Davis, an astrophysicist who worked as a subcontractor and then a consultant for the Pentagon U.F.O. program since 2007, said that, in some cases, examination of the materials had so far failed to determine their source and led him to conclude, "We couldn't make it ourselves."

Dr. Davis, who worked for Aerospace Corporation, a defense contractor, indicated in March 2020 in a classified briefing to a Department of Defense agency of recoveries of "retrievals from "off-world vehicles not made on this earth." He also provided

---

[150] The Conway Daily Sun (Dec. 31, 2015/Feb. 6, 2020), Clinton promises to investigate UFOs, The Conway Daily Sun; Amy Chozick (May 10, 2016), Hillary Clinton Gives U.F.O. Buffs Hope She Will Open the X-Files, The New York Times; Claire Landsbaum (March 4, 2016), Clinton Campaign Chairman: 'The American People Can Handle the Truth' About UFOs, Intelligencer; Eli Watkins (April 7, 2016), Clinton campaign chair: 'The American people can handle the truth' on UFOs, CNN; Abigail Tracy (June 3, 2016), Hillary Clinton's Campaign Chairman Can't Stop Talking About Aliens, Vanity Fair.
[151] Helene Cooper, Ralph Blumenthal and Leslie Kean (May 26, 2019), 'Wow, What Is That?' Navy Pilots Report Unexplained Flying Objects, The New York Times.
[152] Ralph Blumenthal and Leslie Kean (May 14/July 24, 2020), Navy Reports Describe Encounters With Unexplained Flying Objects, The New York Times.
[153] Ralph Blumenthal and Leslie Kean (July 23, 2020/June 3, 2021), No Longer in Shadows, Pentagon's U.F.O. Unit Will Make Some Findings Public, The New York Times. Note: unless otherwise noted, this is the same source.

classified briefings about unexplained object recoveries to Senate Armed Services Committee staff members on October 21, 2019; and to Senate Intelligence Committee staff members two days later.

Months later, the same newspaper reported that there were "official briefings — ongoing for more than a decade — for intelligence officials, aerospace executives and Congressional staff on reported U.F.O. crashes and retrieved materials."[154] He further reported that "Numerous associates of the Pentagon program, with high security clearances and decades of involvement with official U.F.O. investigations, told us they were convinced such crashes have occurred, based on their access to classified information. But the retrieved materials themselves, and any data about them, are completely off-limits to anyone without clearances and a need to know."[155]

Department of Defense sources within the research program stated that they had done numerous briefings and that they were based on facts, not beliefs.[156]

On May 28, 2019, *The Washington Post* published "UFOs exist and everyone needs to adjust to that fact," which pondered the possibility that they were of extraterrestrial origin.[157]

TTSA reported in August 2019, that multiple U.S. news outlets such as newscasts and newspapers, massively echoed the reality of UFOs.[158]

Luis Elizondo, in an interview with *GQ*, expressed that the technology demonstrated by the UAPs does not belong to any country, since it would be an undisclosed cover-up for 70 years; and that since the early 1950s and 1960s, there is government documentation describing objects like the Tic Tac, performing impressive and unknown maneuvers.[159] About this, Elizondo said on June 4, 2021, on CNN, that neither the United States, Russia, nor China, possesses this technology and that newly declassified documents describe the sighting of an object similar to a Tic Tac, as it turns out in a CIA report from 1953, where it is related that "Swedish airline pilots encountered a silver or white flying lozenge traveling at high speeds. You got, an FBI report from 1964 that details a UFO that typically looks like a butane tank. And then some Navy pilots say they have seen something like a flying Tic Tac." Because of this, Elizondo stated that other possibilities of the nature of the phenomenon must be addressed. And that technology has been tracked for at least 70 years.[160]

When Luis Elizondo, Tom DeLonge, and others on his team met years ago with former Italian military representatives and investigators, they told him they had a database of cases in Italy going back 70 years.[161]

---

[154] Ralph Blumenthal and Leslie Kean (July 28, 2020/June 3, 2021), Do We Believe in U.F.O.s? That's the Wrong Question, The New York Times.

[155] Ibid.

[156] Ibid.

[157] Daniel W. Drezner (May 28, 2019), UFOs exist and everyone needs to adjust to that fact, The Washington Post.

[158] (August 20, 2019), The Social and Political Impact of To The Stars Academy, To The Stars Academy of Arts & Science: https://www.youtube.com/watch?v=16_bAySUQfQ; accessed August 7, 2023.

[159] Charlie Burton (November 9, 2021), This man ran the Pentagon's secretive UFO programme for a decade. We had some questions, GQ.

[160] (June 5, 2021), Lue Elizondo on CNN - Why UAP/UFOs Aren't Human Technology, Random UFO Things: https://www.youtube.com/watch?v=qLWdvE0BQLo; accessed August 23, 2023.

[161] Ryan Carpenter, Conor Flynn, Peter Iannuccilli, Peter Schmuhl, Patricia Sunshine (Editors), & Joe Brisbois (Director) (2019, July 5). The Revelation (Season 1, Episode 6) [TV Series Episode]. Russell Binder (Executive Producers), *Unidentified: Inside America's UFO Investigation*. History Channel.

During his interview with *GQ*, he spoke of pilots who came close to one of these objects and later felt and looked burned and reddened for days, as if from a source of radiation from being near the object. Other pilots were hospitalized with symptoms indicative of microwave damage, so they had internal injuries and some brain morphology. Elizondo told of experiences of individuals who came very close to some UAP and strangely felt as if they had been there only five minutes, but when they looked at the clock half an hour had passed, and they only used five minutes of fuel. Elizondo said they believed that the reason for this probably has to do with space-time warping. And the closer someone gets to one of these vehicles, the more they can "begin to experience space time relative to the vehicle and the environment."[162]

Elizondo adds that the phenomenon could be interdimensional and not only the extraterrestrial hypothesis; and that it may have been on Earth for a very long time. They appear not only in the air but also underwater near nuclear technology. He expressed that Steven Spielberg's movie, *Close Encounters of the Third Kind*, is the one that comes closest to the reality of the UAP phenomenon, due to its characteristics and the way they were described, as observed in some classified American documents. As an example, he said, "The description of how they do right-angle turns at very fast velocity, the illumination, the shapes of some of these craft. [Steven] Spielberg definitely had somebody on the inside that was giving him information, for sure. I mean there's a lot of that movie that, if you know what you're looking at, is very, very close to real life."

Now we quote the late Harry Read, former Senate Majority Leader and initiator of AATIP, who in an interview with director James Fox, said that most of the U.S. government's holdings of UFO information have not seen the light of day. This, was after Fox told him about the account of former NASA astronaut Gordon Cooper, who claimed that with other witnesses, he observed a UFO landing in 1957 at Edwards Air Force Base. When he showed a recording to his superiors, agents in a courier plane from Washington took it there.[163]

Read also told *The New Yorker*, "I was told for decades that Lockheed had some of these retrieved materials," he said. "And I tried to get, as I recall, a classified approval by the Pentagon to have me go look at the stuff. They would not approve that. I don't know what all the numbers were, what kind of classification it was, but they would not give that to me."[164]

How much did Reid know about the nature of the phenomenon? When asked by Christopher Mellon if he shared the view that UFOs were extraterrestrial in origin, he replied, "I feel it would be.... from a congressional standpoint, it would affect my credibility if I started talking about..... am, everything I know."[165]

Let's consider again Eric Davis, who according to a memo he authored, on October 16, 2002, apparently met with Vice Admiral Thomas R. Wilson, Director of the

---

[162] Charlie Burton (November 9, 2021), This man ran the Pentagon's secretive UFO programme for a decade. We had some questions, GQ. Note: unless otherwise noted, this is the same source.

[163] Larry Frascella, Jim Ledwith, Jordan Pease (Producer) James Fox (Director) (2020), The Phenomenon (Farah Films, 1091 Pictures).

[164] Gideon Lewis-Kraus (April 30, 2021), How the Pentagon Started Taking U.F.O.s Seriously, The New Yorker.

[165] Ryan Carpenter, Conor Flynn, Peter Iannuccilli, Peter Schmuhl, Patricia Sunshine (Editors), & Joe Brisbois (Director) (2019, July 5). The Revelation (Season 1, Episode 6) [TV Series Episode]. Russell Binder (Executive Producers), *Unidentified: Inside America's UFO Investigation*. History Channel.

Defense Intelligence Agency, and who would have revealed to Davis his unveiling among Pentagon documents, of a UFO crash recovery and reverse engineering program.[166] It is a documented fact, as stated in the memo about his meeting with Wilson, that the Vice Admiral met with Dr. Edgard Mitchell, the sixth man to set foot on the Moon, Dr. Steven Greer, and Commander Willard Miller at the Pentagon on April 9, 1997. At the meeting, they talked to him about UFOs, MJ-12, Roswell, UFO crashes, "alien" bodies, etc.[167]

The rest of the Wilson-Davis memo, reveals other names mentioned by Tom Wilson, and there were many things he could not tell Davis because they were top secret. But he said he spoke personally at the facility (private space corporation) with the head of the UFO crash recovery and reverse engineering program, its safety director, and the company attorney, who refused to answer many of Wilson's questions. But he learned that that program was known to very few in the Pentagon, but they admitted that the craft they had was of non-human origin, but did not know where it came from.[168]

The memo was found in Dr. Edgard Mitchell's files after his death in February 2016.[169]

Although Tom Wilson vehemently denied that the meeting occurred,[170] further research has shed light on its very possible authenticity.[171]

To all this, about the questions to AATIP, TTSA, the UAP Task Force, Elizondo, Mellon, and others; and that this may be a disinformation campaign without a reality

---

[166] Eric Davis Meeting with Adm. Wilson (10/16/02):
https://www.congress.gov/117/meeting/house/114761/documents/HHRG-117-IG05-20220517-SD001.pdf Accessed September 24, 2023.

[167] Ibid, p. 1.

[168] Ibid, pp. 5-15.

[169] (Aug. 24, 2022), UFO & UAP 'Need to Know' News Documentary with Coulthart & Zabel | 7NEWS Spotlight: https://www.youtube.com/watch?v=pSZUBulON6I 42:14-44:38 Accessed Sept. 24, 2023.

[170] Ross Coulthart, In Plain Sight: An investigation into UFOs and impossible science (HarperCollins Publishers, 2021), ob. cit.

[171] Omega Point & The Hermetic Penetrator, Loose Threads (November 6, 2022): https://omega-point.medium.com/loose-threads-af8f652ee8cb /
https://www.dropbox.com/s/ugjn0isjcd8pfv7/PDF%20Loose%20Threads.pdf?dl=0 Accessed September 24, 2023.

about the phenomenon,[172] there are also some answers to those questions, although not many.[173]

Assessing all the available and unquestionable equivalent evidence, I believe that their claims are true.

An unnamed program has also been questioned: AAWSAP (Advanced Aerospace Weapon Systems Applications Program), which contained AATIP; and which conducted investigations of anomalous effects and/or paranormal phenomena on an obscure Utah ranch, called Skinwalker.

In the mid-1990s, Robert Bigelow wanted to manage an investigation at Skinwalker Ranch, as it is a hot sector for UAPs and other paranormal activity, so he assembled a group of experienced scientists with serious equipment to investigate the ranch 24-7; seeing several UAPs and paranormal events; but apparently nothing of a repetitive nature that would produce genuine scientific evidence.[174]

Bigelow managed his interest in such phenomena through BAASS/Bigelow Aerospace Advanced Space Sciences, which he founded in 2008.[175]

In a book called *Skinwalkers at the Pentagon*, co-written by James T. Lacatsky, the former director of AAWSAP, by Colm A. Kelleher and George Knapp, tells what happened there from scientific tests conducted at the site by the agency.[176] Before describing what happened there, let's say that the contents of the work were approved for publication by the Department of Defense Pre-Publication and Security Review Office on May 11, 2021. It further adds that the statements expressed in the brief are those of the authors and do not necessarily represent the official policy or position of the U.S. government's Department of Defense.

---

[172] John Greenewald (June 11, 2020), Inside The Pentagon's "Release" Of Three UFO Videos, The Black Vault; John Greenewald (May 22, 2021), Pentagon Now Admits AATIP Utilized UAP / UFO Reports, The Black Vault; John Greenewald (May 27, 2021), Pentagon Destroyed E-mails Of Former Intelligence Official Tied To UFO Investigation Claims, The Black Vault; John Greenewald (Dec. 20, 2021), History Channel's "Unidentified" and a Secret Meeting Between Intelligence Officials Running AATIP. Or... was it? The Black Vault; John Greenewald (February 24, 2023), How Secretly Filming a Counterintelligence Agent And Misrepresenting Classified Information Sparked An Official US Army Investigation, The Black Vault; John Greenewald (January 21, 2023), The Black Vault's AAWSAP/AATIP and Post 2017 UAP/UFO Timeline Project, The Black Vault; ; John Greenewald (June 23, 2023), Ex-DoD Intelligence Officer's UFO Claims Spark Security Concerns And Confusion, Pentagon Memos Reveal, The Black Vault; John Greenewald (June 28, 2023), Ep. #124 - Ex-DoD Intelligence Officer's UFO Claims Spark Security Concerns & Confusion, Pentagon Memos Reveal, The Black Vault; (June 23, 2023), Ex-DoD Intelligence Officer's UFO Claims Spark Security Concerns & Confusion, Pentagon Memos Reveal, The Black Vault Originals: https://www.youtube.com/watch?v=pSeQsFqRwAM; accessed August 16, 2023; Steven Greenstreet (Writer), & Steven Greenstreet (Director). (2022, May 12). The UFO Lie (Season 3, Episode 1) [TV Series Episode]. Warren Cohen (Executive Producer), New York Post.
[173] Tim McMillan (April 14, 2022), Sex, Lies, and UFOs: Pentagon's Head of Counterintelligence and Security Ousted, The Debrief; Bryan Bender (May 26, 2021), Ex-official who revealed UFO project accuses Pentagon of 'disinformation' campaign, Politico; Alexandra Villareal (May 28, 2021), Whistleblower who spoke out on UFOs claims Pentagon tried to discredit him, The Guardian.
[174] Larry Holcombe, The Presidents and UFOs: A Secret History from FDR to Obama (St. Martin's Press, New York, New York, 2016), ob. cit.; Colm A. Kelleher, Ph.D., and George Knapp, Hunt for the Skinwalker: Science Confronts the Unexplained at a Remote Ranch in Utah (Paraview Pocket Books, New York, NY, 2005), ob. cit.
[175] Ibid.
[176] James T. Lacatski, D.Eng., Colm A. Kelleher, Ph.D., and George Knapp, Skinwalkers at the Pentagon: An Insiders' Account of the Secret Government UFO Program (RTMA, LLC, Henderson, Nevada).

The government investigation reported numerous UFOs/UAPs at Skinwalker Ranch, especially above the ranch plateau; in an area called "the triangle," and in other parts of the site. There have been reports of what appear to be "portals" through which the UAPs enter and exit. And appearances of strange creatures and additional paranormal events. It has also been characterized by unusual electromagnetic signals where paranormal phenomena have occurred. This has resulted in radiation burns and even severe brain damage.[177]

The Debrief obtained documents from the AAWSAP program, where it was noted that they investigated the ranch and that the paranormal findings reported in Lacatsky's book were recorded in the program's reports.[178]

Journalist Steven Greenstreet has made a documentary series in The Basement Office where he tries to disprove that something paranormal happens at Skinwalker Ranch.[179] "The Secret of Skinwalker," a History Channel science series that has been running for four seasons since 2020, proves without a doubt that something paranormal is going on at the ranch, especially by appearances of UAPs, spheres of light, high radioactive readings, and physical effects such as those already mentioned.

While Greenstreet and others have pointed out serious doubts that some of the cases of what happens at the ranch are paranormal in scope; and in others, they are not so certain, they tend to ignore the most compelling evidence of what happens at the ranch, which goes beyond all prosaic explanations. However, additional first-hand evidence in other places allows me to conclude that what is reported in general is real.

In 2017, former President George W. Bush sensibly and hilariously said on Jimmy Kimmel's comedy show that he would say nothing about whether or not he knew about secret government documents about UFOs.[180] A little more than four years later, in April 2021, he again told Kimmel that if he knew the truth about the subject, he would never say anything.[181]

Barack Obama for his part, when asked by the same Kimmel in March 2015 about Area 51 and the UFO files to know everything that has happened on the subject, replied that he could not reveal anything.[182] More than five years later, in December 2021,

[177] Ibid.

[178] MJ Banias (Jan. 13, 2021), Shocking Documents Show Government Paid Millions to Chase Ufos and Werewolves, The Debrief.

[179] Steven Greenstreet (Writer), & Steven Greenstreet (Director) (2022, July 21). Skinwalker Ranch Part 1 (Season 3, Episode 2) [TV Series Episode]. Warren Cohen (Executive Producer), New York Post; Steven Greenstreet (Writer), & Steven Greenstreet (Director). (2022, August 25). Skinwalker Ranch Part 2 (Season 3, Episode 3) [TV Series Episode]. Warren Cohen (Executive Producer), New York Post; Steven Greenstreet (Writer), & Steven Greenstreet (Director). (2022, October 27). Skinwalker Ranch: Angels and Demons (Season 3, Episode 4) [TV series episode]. Warren Cohen (Executive Producer), New York Post; (December 28, 2022), Skinwalker Ranch: New Evidence of Paranormal Activity, UFOs, Ghosts (Part 4) | The Basement Office, New York Post: https://www.youtube.com/watch?v=Q9Kwv_p2Cww; accessed August 17, 2023; (April 18, 2023), Skinwalker Ranch: Judgment Day, camping on ranch alone & new revelations | The Basement Office, New York Post: https://www.youtube.com/watch?v=3Tsg0X4onCo; accessed August 17, 2023.

[180] (Mar. 3, 2017), Jimmy Kimmel Asks President George W. Bush to Reveal Government Secrets, Jimmy Kimmel Live: https://www.youtube.com/watch?v=XaNPO2o2XZk Accessed Sept. 22, 2023.

[181] (April 21, 2021), President George W. Bush on Friendship with Michelle Obama, Immigration, UFOs & Trump's Inauguration, Jimmy Kimmel Live: https://www.youtube.com/watch?v=ujAs1disEwg 7:06-8:26 Accessed September 22, 2023.

[182] (March 13, 2015), President Barack Obama Denies Knowledge of Aliens, Jimmy Kimmel Live: https://www.youtube.com/watch?v=EYzRY2XpLBk Accessed September 22, 2023.

Stephen Colbert asked him if he consulted during his tenure on the UFO issue, to which Obama replied, "Certainly I asked about it." To Colbert's question, "And?," Obama responded in turn, "Can't tell you. Sorry."[183]

Recovered and examined remains of 'UAPs' and additional revelations

In July 2019, TTSA announced the ADAM (Acquisition & Data Analysis of Materials) Research Project, which was an academic research program focused on samples of exotic materials from UFOs. Luis Elizondo said that they would try to find the most qualified specialists in the scientific field in the most reputable institutions to carry out scientific analysis including physical, molecular, and chemical examinations; and ultimately, nuclear analysis.[184]

He added that the ADAM Research Project has material from a variety of solid sources to examine,[185] and elsewhere, he indicated that the evidence shows something of such magnitude that it would eventually flow considerably to stimulate worldwide change.[186]

For his part, Dr. Jacques Vallée has been collecting UFO material for years, dating back to 1947.[187] The samples are examined in a state-of-the-art laboratory that makes it possible to observe the atomic structure, which is impossible to fake. Dr. Garry Nolan, a scientist and professor of pathology at Stanford University, says he has a Multi-parameter Ion Beam Imager device to analyze the debris down to its individual atoms.

As Nolan placed some of the metal samples in the vacuum chamber of his instrument, he was astonished to find that their composition was like no other known metal. "No matter where he looked in the sample's jumble of elements, whether magnesium, iron, nickel, or titanium, the ratio of isotopes didn't make sense."

Dr. Nolan further stated, "If you're talking about an advanced material from an advanced civilization, you're talking about something that I'll just call ultramaterial. Right. It's something which has properties where somebody is putting it together again at the atomic scale. We're building our world with 80 elements. Somebody else is building the world with 253 different isotopes."

Jacques Vallée adds: "This material was manufactured. It's not natural. It's not natural to the materials that we have around us, in the lab or on the Earth. It does not mean that it was necessarily made someplace in outer space. Just means that it was manufactured specially for a particular purpose that we don't understand, and we want to understand."

But about that technology, have there been attempts to access any of the referenced recovered aircraft? Garry Nolan explained in May 2023 at SALT iConnections New York, "I can say this: I was working with a group about seven, eight years ago and I literally got within a few weeks of gaining access to one of the... one of the objects, and

---

[183] (Dec. 1, 2020), Barack Obama knows the truth about space aliens, government UFO files | New York Post, New York Post: https://www.youtube.com/watch?v=vuRvdHXuk94 Accessed September 22, 2023.

[184] Derrick Bryson Taylor (September 26, 2019/June 3, 2021), How Blink-182's Tom DeLonge Became a U.F.O. Researcher, The New York Times.

[185] Ibid.

[186] (September 19, 2018), Observations On Potential UAP/UFO Material In Possession for The ADAM Research Project, To The Stars Academy of Arts & Science: https://www.youtube.com/watch?v=vP1v44NM9ls; accessed July 31, 2023.

[187] Larry Frascella, Jim Ledwith, Jordan Pease (Producer) James Fox (Director) (2020), The Phenomenon (Farah Films, 1091 Pictures). Note: unless otherwise noted, this is the same source.

when the people who didn't want us to gain access to it found out about it, they pulled some bureaucratic administrative tricks and snatched it away."[188]

Garry Nolan has been involved in the subject far more than imagined. Years ago, the CIA sought him out to review people who were exposed to UAPs and who had considerable damage to brain tissue - white matter disease - (Havana syndrome).[189]

According to Dr. Nolan, some reasons for the cover-up are that the government does not really know what the UAPs are; and that the U.S. has no control over its airspace.[190]

On the nature of the UAP phenomenon, in 2022 Nolan said in an interview with the renowned Australian journalist, Ross Coulthart: "[...] of all the people that I've spoken with on the inside there's very little unanimity about what it is, except for, that, whatever it is, appears to be so far advanced from us that it beggars our understanding. [...] I'm sure it's not human."[191]

Bills and laws for the declassification of programs on UAP technology, including their pilots

National Defense Authorization Act 2022

Regardless of the arguments for and against the nature of what was revealed, on April 2021, the Pentagon confirmed that the UFO photos and videos leaked to journalist Jeremy Corbell were real. It was revealed that military pilots photographed a sphere; a metallic "blimp"; an "acorn"; and a pyramidal object at night from the Navy's USS Russell. As well as a transmedia sphere that flew over the sea until it submerged.[192]

Likewise, the Pentagon provided a hearing before Congress in May 2022 on what they found about the UAP phenomenon; accompanied by some videos of spheres witnessed by air pilots, and without ruling out the extraterrestrial hypothesis.[193]

Two UAP reports were published (2021 and 2022), mentioning hundreds of cases and again without ruling out the extraterrestrial hypothesis.[194]

Additional provisions for declassification of information on what the government has on the subject of the UAPs were approved by Congress in the year 2022 in what is the National Defense Authorization Act. So we see, that section 1673 entitled "Unidentified Anomalous Phenomena Reporting Procedures," states that through the head of the Office and in consultation with the Director of National Intelligence, the Secretary of Defense establishes a secure mechanism to authoritatively notify any event related to unidentified anomalous phenomena/UAP. As well as, "any activity or program by a department or agency of the Federal Government or a contractor of such

---

[188] (May 22, 2023), "100%" Aliens Have Already Arrived -Dr. Garry Nolan & Alex Klokus | SALT iConnections New York: https://www.youtube.com/watch?v=e2DqdOw6Uy4 9:42-10:02 Accessed September 24, 2023.

[189] (Aug. 22, 2022), Out Of This World - By Ross Coulthart (by 7News Australia), sent5: https://www.youtube.com/watch?v=o0_z0FEEt4U 23:36-24:52. Accessed September 24, 2023.

[190] (Aug. 24, 2022), UFO & UAP 'Need to Know' News Documentary with Coulthart & Zabel | 7NEWS Spotlight: https://www.youtube.com/watch?v=pSZUBulON6I 37:07-37:23 Accessed Sept. 24, 2023.

[191] Ibid. 38:23-38:59.

[192] Duncan Phenix (April 9/21, 2021), Pentagon confirms leaked UAP photos and video are real, Mystery Wire.

[193] Jeffrey Kluger (May 17, 2022), Congress is Finally Taking UFOs Seriously, 50 Years After Its Last Hearing on the Mysterious Subject, Time Magazine.

[194] Preliminary Assessment: Unidentified Aerial Phenomena (June 25, 2021), Office of the Director of National Intelligence; 2022 Annual Report on Unidentified Aerial Phenomena, Office of the Director of National Intelligence.

a department or agency relating to unidentified anomalous phenomena, including concerning material retrieval, material analysis, reverse engineering, research and development, detection and tracking, developmental or operational testing, and security protections and enforcement."-it reads verbatim.[195]

Some very interesting sections of section 1683 on the establishment of the AARO (All-domain Anomaly Resolution Office), which supplanted the UAP Task Force, provide for the development of:

"[...] procedures to synchronize and standardize the collection, reporting, and analysis of incidents, including adverse physiological effects, regarding unidentified anomalous phenomena across the Department of Defense and the intelligence community, in coordination with the Director of National Intelligence, which shall be provided to the congressional defense committees, the congressional intelligence committees, and congressional leadership."[196]

The report to be submitted includes an investigation dating back to "January 1, 1945, and ending on the date on which the Director of the Office completes activities," thus including "include a compilation and itemization of the key historical record of the involvement of the intelligence community with unidentified anomalous phenomena;" as well as "any program or activity that was protected by restricted access that has not been explicitly and clearly reported to Congress." It also includes "successful or unsuccessful efforts to identify and track unidentified anomalous phenomena." Finally, referring to a government disinformation campaign: "any efforts to obfuscate, manipulate public opinion, hide, or otherwise provide incorrect unclassified or classified information about unidentified anomalous phenomena or related activities."[197]

Dr. Garry Nolan told Australian journalist Ross Coulthart, that he knows that within the U.S. government, there has been a long-standing active cover-up of the UAP phenomenon since at least 1947, the year of the Roswell incident in New Mexico: "Because I've spoken to the people who are about to come out and whistleblow on it," Nolan said.[198]

But let's continue with other subsections of section 1683 of the National Defense Authorization Act, where it highlights:

"(xii) An assessment of any health-related effects for individuals that have encountered unidentified anomalous phenomena.

"(xiii) The number of reported incidents, and descriptions thereof, of unidentified anomalous phenomena associated with military nuclear assets, including strategic nuclear weapons and nuclear-powered ships and submarines."[199]

---

[195] Public Law 117-263-23 Dec. 2022. Section 1673.
[196] Ibid, Section 1683.
[197] Ibid.
[198] (Aug. 22, 2022), Out Of This World - By Ross Coulthart (by 7News Australia), sent5: https://www.youtube.com/watch?v=o0_z0FEEt4U 22:04-22:55 Accessed September 24, 2023.
[199] Public Law 117-263-23 Dec. 2022. Section 1683.

It can be read further on the mention of "transmedium objects or devices," which are "observed to transition between space and the atmosphere, or between the atmosphere and bodies of wáter;" as well as "not immediately identifiable."[200]

It then defines "unidentified anomalous phenomena" as "airborne objects that are not immediately identifiable"; "transmedium objects or devices;" and "submerged objects or devices that are not immediately identifiable [...]."[201]

David Grusch

With the National Defense Authorization Act passed and signed by U.S. President Joe Biden in December 2022, much was going on behind the scenes.

In June 2023, *NewsNation*, a popular U.S. cable news channel, premiered an exclusive interview by journalist Ross Coulthart with a whistleblower named David Grusch, who worked for U.S. military intelligence.[202] The interview was presented as a "story that impacts every person on this planet," said Coulthart.

Grusch served for 14 years in the U.S. Air Force. He holds a bachelor's degree in physics from the University of Pittsburgh; and a master's degree with honors in Intelligence Studies from the American Military University, in addition to other studies.[203]

His last assignment was as a senior intelligence officer until April 2023, co-leading the UAP portfolio for the National Geospatial Intelligence Agency. Some of the most senior officials within the Department of Defense and the Intelligence Community used to call on him to advise them on some of the country's toughest targets.

But after 2019, he was invited to join the UAP Task Force; and he possessed the security clearances to go anywhere and ask anyone anything, being at one point very highly cleared. He said that during his work, the UAP Task Force was denied access to an extensive recovery program of several technical aircraft of non-human origin, some having crashed and others only found unharmed.

Grusch was approached by numerous former senior intelligence officers, some of whom he had known his entire career. They revealed to him the existence of a UFO crash retrieval and reverse engineering program, of which they supplied him with the name of the program. They also told him that they were part of the program, and supplied him with documents and other evidence.

Grusch claims that through intensive intelligence research, he and his team learned that this was not a cover-up disinformation operation for another program. However, their investigation was subsequently stonewalled, and their requests for access were denied.

He then reported the information gathered to the Inspector General of the intelligence community (Thomas A. Monheim) as well as to congressional authorities. Grusch promptly faced retaliation and attacks from higher levels, so he filed a whistleblower report with the respective authorities. For that reason and out of his

---

[200] Ibid.

[201] Ibid.

[202] (July 20, 2023), "We Are Not Alone: The UFO Whistleblower Speaks" - NewsNation / Need to Know - Aired 06/11/23, Need to Know: https://www.youtube.com/watch?v=gfZUA9DMzYQ Accessed September 22, 2023. Note: unless otherwise noted, this is the same source.

[203] David C. Grusch, SECURITY CLEARANCE: Active TOP SECRET//SCI with CI & LS Polygraph: https://docs.house.gov/meetings/GO/GO06/20230726/116282/HHRG-118-GO06-Bio-GruschD-20230726.pdf Accessed January 19, 2024.

sense of patriotism to the American people, he decided to make his testimony public on *NewsNation*.

Regarding the origin of the phenomenon, Grusch did not affirm that the crafts and non-human intelligence are extraterrestrial, since there is not enough evidence to affirm it; therefore, there are several hypotheses of their origin, such as the possibility that they are interdimensional beings and crafts, as described by quantum mechanics.

On the aircraft that have crashed, Grusch said their pilots have also been found dead. He has seen photographs of the evidence and has read reports on the subject. All the evidence was still classified at the time of this writing, so he could not show it to the public.

He also claimed that Roswell is real and that the first aircraft recovered crashed in 1933 in Magenta, Italy. It was a partially intact vehicle. An internal memo apparently from Mussolini's Italian secret services includes drawings of the UAP.

The government moved the craft to a secure air base in Italy for the remainder of the Fascist regime until 1944-45. Then, Pope Pius XII would have informed the American authorities what was in the possession of the Italians; and they would have ended up picking it up. So, certainly, Grusch mentions, the Vatican knows of the existence of non-human intelligences.

Grusch indicated that one reason for the cover-up of the non-human vehicle recovery and reverse engineering program is to secretly reverse engineer the technology to exploit it for military dominance. As happened in the 1950s and 1960s.

It was claimed that for decades there has been a behind-the-scenes Cold War between the United States, Russia, and China over exploiting this technology for military purposes.

David Grusch indicated that there have been cases where non-human intelligences have murdered human beings. But that would not necessarily mean that all such intelligences are malevolent.

The former intelligence agent wrote an internal document of his discoveries where he refers to agreements that risk putting the future of humanity in danger. He also made a veiled reference to the danger of an existing agreement between the United States and non-human intelligences. The document provided by Grusch and authorized for public release by the Department of Defense Office of Prepublication and Security Review, dated April 4, 2023, presents a summary of his resume as well as a summary of his findings. He indicated in this regard that in May 2022, he was the first government official in U.S. history to file a complaint to the Intelligence Community Inspector General (ICIG) about credible and detailed information he gathered as a member of the Unidentified (now Anomalous) Aerial Phenomena Task Force (UAPTF) about a publicly unknown Cold War for recovered and exploited physical material that has been raging under great noise for decades. Similarly, he noted that he disclosed this evidence under oath to the ICIG along with close colleagues and that they found the strength to come forward to support his claim. He adds that the ICIG found the testimony credible and urgent to Congress in July 2022, and a summary was immediately admitted to the Director of National Intelligence (DNI) and the Congressional Intelligence Committees. He traveled to DC to testify in a closed session on the matter.

It should be emphasized that Grusch was trained under extremely empirical training, requiring substantial empirical data to arrive at a high-confidence assessment.

Given his background, he stated that he did not believe that such a program was real, but after a serious investigation and the testimony of high-ranking officials who spoke to him, plus other people of great authority who closed their doors to him, very uncomfortable with his investigation, he corroborated the authenticity of the program.

There are even serious suspicions that people have been killed to protect the secret.

Grusch mentioned the existence of a sophisticated disinformation campaign directed at the American people that is extremely unethical and immoral.

He said he knew Dr. Sean Kirkpatrick, then director of AARO (All-domain Anomaly Resolution Office), which is the Pentagon office that investigates the UAP phenomenon, to whom a year earlier he told about the results of his research, but Kirkpatrick apparently did not follow up with Grusch, whom he had known for eight years.

Journalists Leslie Kean and Ralph Blumenthal, prepared an article published on June 5, 2023, by *The Debrief* on Grusch's account. Kean and Blumenthal named others who know Grusch: "Karl E. Nell, a recently retired Army Colonel and current aerospace executive who was the Army's liaison for the UAP Task Force from 2021 to 2022 and worked with Grusch there, characterizes Grusch as "beyond reproach." The article also mentions Jonathan Grey, "a generational officer of the United States Intelligence Community with a Top-Secret Clearance who currently works for the National Air and Space Intelligence Center (NASIC), where the analysis of UAP has been his focus." Grey worked for "Private Aerospace and Department of Defense Special Directive Task Forces."[204]

"The non-human intelligence phenomenon is real. We are not alone," Grey said. "Retrievals of this kind are not limited to the United States. This is a global phenomenon, and yet a global solution continues to elude us."[205]

Many media outlets, particularly U.S. and foreign newspapers, echoed Grusch's testimony. The list is staggering and would be impossible to cite here. For the most part, however, the mainstream media has remained silent.

Per David Grusch's testimony, a public hearing on UAPs was held on July 26, 2023, whose witnesses were former military officers Ryan Graves and David Fravor, when they were Navy pilots and witnessed first-hand UAPs over restricted airspace. The third witness was David Grusch.

At one point, he said that as part of their investigation, they interviewed 40 witnesses about the existence of the program.[206] It is also impossible to get a sense of the U.S. and foreign newspapers and television media that picked up on the hearing and its explosive testimony.

However, AARO's then-director, Dr. Sean Kirkpatrick, expressed his displeasure, saying the hearing was "insulting" to Defense Department and Intelligence Community officials who joined AARO.[207] Susan Gough, a spokeswoman at the Defense

[204] Leslie Kean and Ralph Blumenthal (June 5, 2023), Intelligence Officials Say U.S. Has Retrieved Craft of Non-Human Origin, The Debrief.
[205] Ibid.
[206] (July 26, 2023), House holds hearing on UFOs, government transparency | full video, CBS News: https://www.youtube.com/watch?v=SNgoul4vyDM 49:27-49:31 Accessed September 24, 2023.
[207] Nomaan Merchant and Tara Copp (July 28, 2023), The UFO congressional hearing was 'insulting' to US employees, a top Pentagon official says, AP.

Department, stated that the Pentagon has no information about any individual who has provided information about UAPs or any verifiable information about any program on possession or reverse engineering of extraterrestrial material in the past or currently.[208]

Kirkpatrick noted that AARO has yet to find if any, information on the existence of such a program. And that Grusch declined to speak with AARO.[209]

For their part, critical journalists such as Steven Greenstreet,[210] of *The New York Post* and Ken Klippenstein of *The Intercept*,[211] raised accusations against Grusch of "no evidence," and attempts to discredit him because of his past post-traumatic stress disorder while still serving as an intelligence officer; something unethical. But both have ignored, at least publicly, Grusch's central claim that he possesses evidence from the program and turned it over to the respective authorities for analysis and investigation. In fact, critics do not seem to have addressed that claim.

Still, many said they want to see evidence for Grusch's claims.[212]

Three journalists, Michael Shellenberger, Andrew Mohar, and Phoebe Smith, published an article in *Public* reporting that at least thirty whistleblowers of the UFO recovery and reverse engineering program, who work for the federal government; as well as government contractors, testified to the Office of the Inspector General of the Intelligence Community (ICIG), Thomas Monheim; to the Department of Defense Inspector General (DOD IG), or to Congress. But then they note that between 30-50 government employees or contractors were reported to have come to the AARO office to testify about the UAPs.[213]

Some of them provided "first-hand and second-hand reports of crash retrieval and reverse-engineering programs by US, Russian, and Chinese governments." Information has been provided on "the testing of materials obtained from retrieved craft; active and ongoing government disinformation operations; kinetic military action with UAPs; contact and collaboration with nonhuman intelligence (NHIs); and the successful reverse-engineering of a triangle-shaped craft with unconventional propulsion," the article's authors wrote.[214]

---

[208] Ibid.

[209] Ibid.

[210] (July 28, 2023), Congress UFO Hearing - It's even crazier than you think, New York Post: https://www.youtube.com/watch?v=EDyZvv3D3ws; accessed August 17, 2023; (August 9, 2023), UFO Hearing Insanity - Jeremy Corbell & George Knapp Influencing Congress on UFOs, New York Post: https://www.youtube.com/watch?v=FKtI91TdRjQ; accessed August 17, 2023.

[211] Ken Klippenstein (Aug. 9, 2023), UFO Whistleblower Kept Security Clearance After Psychiatric Detention, The Intercept.

[212] Richard Barlow (June 22, 2023), Is the Government Concealing UFO Craft *and* Dead Extraterrestrials?, BU today: https://www.bu.edu/articles/2023/ex-intelligence-official-us-government-ufo/ Accessed January 19, 2024; Alex Hawgood (October 5, 2023), Behind the scenes of a UFO whistleblower's odd visit to Capitol Hill, The Washington Post; Avi Loeb (December 5, 2023), New Physics or Misinformation?, Medium: https://avi-loeb.medium.com/new-physics-or-misinformation-d44b50185ed2 Accessed January 19, 2024.

[213] Michael Shellenberger, Andrew Mohar, and Phoebe Smith (Sept. 25, 2023), Dozens Of Government UFO Whistleblowers Have Given Testimony To Congress, Pentagon, And Inspectors General, Say Sources, Public.

[214] Ibid.

Whistleblowers of UFO crash retrieval and reverse engineering program

The *Daily Mail* made public on April 26, 2023, that attorney Daniel Sheehan, scientist Garry Nolan, and astrophysicist Hal Puthoff, were in contact with at least six former government officials - including a former director of the Defense Intelligence Agency - or military contractors who worked on crashed UFO recovery and reverse engineering who have spoken to members of Congress. Some of those witnesses briefed Senate committee staff dealing with military intelligence and did so even before the passage of the 2022 National Defense Authorization Act.[215]

The complainants were referred for an interview with AARO.[216]

Dr. Sean Kirkpatrick, in an interview with *ABC* in July 2023, noted, "We have interviewed almost 30 individuals who have come forward to testify. And of all of them, none have yet provided any verifiable information that would corroborate the claim that the U.S. government has these craft or has a reverse engineering program, either in the past or currently." [217]

In an article published by *Scientific American* on January 19, 2024, Kirkpatrick stated that after a year of arduous investigation by AARO, such programs do not exist: that is, that the U.S. government has nothing in its possession about UAPs or non-human biological remains, and therefore that such programs for recovery and reverse engineering of aircraft of non-human origin are non-existent. He indicated that AARO reviewed historical accounts coming from as far back as the 1940s and that one of his last acts before retiring from AARO was to sign Volume 1 of the AARO Historical Report.[218]

Kirkpatrick said that as director of AARO, he experienced up close and personal the erosion of a solid scientific foundation when it came to the UAPs, especially when it came to those who have made grand claims without solid evidence about what the U.S. does or does not possess. He regretted that AARO's efforts were ultimately overwhelmed by sensationalist and unsubstantiated claims that ignored contradictory evidence. Nonetheless, capturing the attention of policymakers and the public and prompted legislative battles that dominated the public narrative in favor of an apparent government cover-up of the UAP phenomenon.[219]

Dr. Sean Kirkpatrick's sincerity is distrusted because, after his tenure at AARO, he was chosen for Oak Ridge National Laboratory, which is managed by UT-Battelle LLC for the U.S. Department of Energy. Let's remember that Battelle's role decades ago in UFO/UAP research was very serious and that he actively participated in the U.S. Air Force's cover-up of the phenomenon; as well as debris from what crashed at Roswell.

Kirkpatrick works at Oak Ridge as Director of Technology for Defense and Intelligence Programs.

---

[215] Josh Boswell (April 26, 2023), EXCLUSIVE: Six whistleblowers who claim they worked on military UFO programs retrieving and analyzing crash material have come forward to spill their secrets to senior members of congress, Daily Mail.

[216] Ibid.

[217] Devin Dwyer, Tommy Brooksbank, and Jon Schlosberg (July 20, 2023), Extraterrestrial 'technical surprise' is a top concern, Pentagon UFO investigator says, ABC News.

[218] Sean Kirkpatrick (January 19, 2024), Here's What I Learned as the U.S. Government's UFO Hunter, Scientific American.

[219] Ibid.

For its part, Volume 1 of AARO's Historical Report was published on March 6, 2024.[220] But amazingly, AARO was satisfied with a simple "no" for an answer from the relevant authorities about the existence of UAP crash retrieval and reverse engineering programs: "AARO met with high-ranking officials, including executives and chief technology officers, of the named companies. All denied the existence of these programs, and attested to the truthfulness of their statements on the record."[221] Not only that, but it contains numerous very important historical errors and omissions about the reality of the phenomenon and what the government records, as well as exaggerated distortions of Project Blue Book findings.[222]

Robert Powell, a board member of the Scientific Coalition for UAP Studies, provided a very detailed critique on his Twitter account of the problems with the AARO report. Christopher Mellon did the same in *The Debrief*.[223]

Furthermore, on January 12, 2024, members of the House Oversight Committee on Capitol Hill met with Thomas Monheim, the Inspector General of the Intelligence Community (ICIG),[224] who had indicated that Grusch's allegations were "credible and urgent."

Reactions from congressmen were mixed. Florida Democratic Congressman Jared Moskowitz noted, "We've now made, I would say, progress on some of the claims Mr. Grusch has made in his complaint."

"Based on what we heard many of Grusch claims have merit!"

For his part, Republican Congressman Tim Burchette said, "I think everybody left there thinking and knowing that Grusch is legit."[225] Although he also added, dissatisfied with the information provided, that it was "more of the same."[226]

Illinois Democratic Rep. Raja Krishnamoorthi, "Let's just say that all of us were very interested in the substance of his [Grusch] claims, and unfortunately, I didn't get the answers that I was hoping for."[227]

[...]

"Mr. Grusch has made allegations that we're still trying to figure out the veracity of, and we haven't gotten the answers that we need [...] Unfortunately, I don't think that we're looking at the substance of his claims, and instead we're dancing around the procedural nature of his claims."[228]

---

[220] AARO (February, 2024), Report on the Historical Record of U.S. Government Involvement with Unidentified Anomalous Phenomena (UAP), Volume I, The Department of Defense All-domain Anomaly Resolution Office.

[221] Ibid, p. 32.

[222] Ibid, p. 11-21.

[223] Christopher Mellon (April 12, 2024), The Pentagon's New UAP Report Is Seriously Flawed, The Debrief.

[224] Matthew Phelan (January 12, 2024), Inside secret UFO briefing in DC: Congress finds 'many' claims about US government harboring aliens and spaceships 'have merit' after grilling top US spy watchdog, Daily Mail: https://www.dailymail.co.uk/sciencetech/article-12957317/US-spy-watchdog-tells-Congress-claims-UFOs-merit-secret-briefing-DC.html Accessed January 22, 2024.

[225] Ibid.

[226] Ellen Mitchell (January 12, 2024), Classified UFO briefing: House members emerge with mixed feelings, The Hill.

[227] Ibid.

[228] Kayla Guo and Julian E. Barnes (January 12, 2024), U.F.O.s Remain a Mystery to Lawmakers After Classified Briefing, The New York Times.

Anna Paulina Luna, R-Florida, indicated, "[...] I think that Grusch absolutely, if there was any doubt in anyone's mind that he isn't credible, I think that after leaving that, where I'm at is, I feel like he's a very credible witness."[229]

[...]

"It's just become evident that there is over-classification and that we are continually being stonewalled [...] We are authorizing money that is supposed to be spent on certain programs, and yet there is compartmentalization in which Congress doesn't have access to oversight in those programs. And that's a problem.[230]

Marco Rubio, Republican senator for the state of Florida, told *NewsNation* in late June 2023, that he has heard from first-hand witnesses who have held high positions within the U.S. government; and some of them with very high clearances, who claim that the government has in its possession a UFO crash retrieval and reverse engineering program. "We're trying to gather as much of that information as we can... And frankly, a lot of them are very fearful of their jobs... fearful of harm coming to them," Rubio added." While the senator said he saw no reason why the whistleblowers would lie, he indicated, "What I think we owe is just a mature, you know, understanding, listening and trying to put all these pieces together and just sort of intake the information without any prejudgment or jumping to any conclusions."[231]

Unidentified Anomalous Phenomena Disclosure Act of 2023

Just a few weeks after Grusch's *NewsNation* interview, and prior to the public hearing before Congress where Grusch, Ryan Graves, and David Fravor testified, Chuck Schumer, the U.S. Senate Majority Leader, introduced the proposed Unidentified Anomalous Phenomena Disclosure Act of 2023;[232] and historically unprecedented in the U.S. and worldwide. The bill called for the disclosure of technologies of unknown origin that are being reverse-engineered, as well as biological evidence of non-human intelligence, whether living or deceased, held by various government and private agencies.[233]

Let's look at some of the excerpts of some of the definitions and requirements of the bill. The first one, dealt with control authority: "The term ''controlling authority'' means any Federal, State, or local government department, office, agency, committee, commission, commercial company, academic institution, or private sector entity in physical possession of technologies of unknown origin or biological evidence of non-human intelligence."[234]

On the subsequent page, it defines: "The term "legacy 6 program" means all Federal, State, and local government, commercial industry, academic, and private sector endeavors to collect, exploit, or reverse engineer technologies of unknown origin or

[229] Matt Laslo (January 14, 2024), EXCLUSIVE — Rep. Luna: "this has been a long-term effort to really keep this information outside of the purview of Congress", Ask a Pol: https://www.askapol.com/p/exclusive-rep-luna-this-has-been Accessed April 10, 2024.
[230] Kayla Guo and Julian E. Barnes (January 12, 2024), U.F.O.s Remain a Mystery to Lawmakers After Classified Briefing, The New York Times.
[231] Joe Khalil, Liz Jassin (June 26, 2023), Rubio: Recent UFO whistleblower isn't the only one, NewsNation: https://www.newsnationnow.com/space/ufo/rubio-recent-ufo-whistleblower-isnt-the-only-one/ Accessed January 26, 2024.
[232] Unidentified Anomalous Phenomena Disclosure Act of 2023.
[233] Ibid.
[234] Ibid, p. 5.

examine biological evidence of living or deceased non-human intelligence that pre-dates the date of the enactment of this Act."[235] We further read, "The term "non-human Intelligence" means any sentient intelligent non-human lifeform regardless of nature or ultimate origin that may be presumed responsible for unidentified anomalous phenomena or of which the Federal Government has become aware."[236]

We read on page 7, that "public interest" means "the compelling interest in the prompt public disclosure of unidentified anomalous phenomena records for historical and Governmental purposes and for the purpose of fully informing the people of the United States about the history of the Federal Government's knowledge and involvement [...]."[237]

About technologies of unknown origin, on page 8 highlights:

"The term "technologies of unknown origin" means any materials or meta-materials, ejecta, crash debris, mechanisms, machinery, equipment, assemblies or sub-assemblies, engineering models or processes, damaged or intact aerospace vehicles, and damaged 16 intact ocean-surface and undersea craft associated with unidentified anomalous phenomena or in corporating science and technology that lacks prosaic attribution or known means of human manufacture."[238]

Page 11 reads: "The term "unidentified anomalous phenomena record" means a record that is related to unidentified anomalous phenomena, technologies of unknown origin, or non-human intelligence [...]."[239]

This bill required that: "Not later than 60 days after the date of the enactment of this Act, the Archivist shall commence establishment of a collection of records in the National Archives to be known as the "Unidentified Anomalous Phenomena Records Collection." Such collection would consist of copies of each Government record provided or funded by the Government relating to UAPs and, verbatim, "technologies of unknown origin, and non-human intelligence."[240]

Finally, we cite a plan for official government disclosure, as proposed by the bill, on pages 49 and 50:

"CONTROLLED DISCLOSURE CAMPAIGN PLAN.—With respect to unidentified anomalous phenomena records, particular information in unidentified anomalous phenomena records, recovered technologies of unknown origin, and biological evidence for non-human intelligence the public disclosure of which is postponed pursuant to section___06, or for which only substitutions or summaries have been disclosed to the public, the Review Board shall create and transmit to the President and to the Archivist a Controlled Disclosure Campaign Plan [...]."[241]

---

[235] Ibid, p. 6.
[236] Ibid.
[237] Ibid, p. 7.
[238] Ibid, p. 8.
[239] Ibid, p. 11.
[240] Ibid, p. 14.
[241] Ibid, pp. 49, 50.

Regarding the above paragraph, more detailed information on disclosure controlled by the U.S. government, which includes the incumbent U.S. President, can be found in section 11.[242]

Many and various well-known media outlets referred to the bill and captured the attention of many U.S. citizens and abroad.[243]

However, the bill, with good bipartisan support, faced a major roadblock in the Senate, as Schumer testified on December 4, 2023 on the Senate floor:

"[...] House Republicans are also attempting to kill another commonsense, bipartisan measure passed by the Senate, which I was proud to cosponsor… to increase transparency around what the government does and does not know about unidentified aerial phenomena."[244]

Schumer noted that credible sources told them that information about UAPs was being withheld from Congress: "We've also been notified by multiple credible sources that information on UAPs has also been withheld from Congress, which if true, is a violation of laws requiring full notification to the legislative branch."[245]

According to various sources, Rep. Mike Turner (R-Ohio), chairman of the House Intelligence Committee, and Rep. Mike Rogers (R-Alabama), chairman of the House Armed Services Committee, were "leading efforts to prevent any meaningful version of this provision from being added to the 2024 National Defense Authorization Act."[246] Both Republican senators receive money from powerful aerospace agencies that would be behind the concealment of certain aircraft of unknown origin. Which is why Schumer's bill was defeated after much pressure in Congress. The lack of transparency leaves questions about whether they are not hiding something about recovered non-human aircraft wreckage.[247]

However, some provisions of the law were approved for inclusion in the NDAA 2024.[248]

[242] Ibid, pp. 59-61.

[243] For example, see a: Josephine Walker (July 15, 2023), Senators move to require release of US government UFO records, Reuters; Mary Kay Linge (July 15, 2023), Schumer leads bipartisan push to reveal feds' secret UFO records, The New York Post; Thomas Kika (July 17, 2023), UFOs Are Bringing Democrats and Republicans Together, Newsweek; Marik von Rennenkampff (July 18, 2023), 'Non-human intelligence': Schumer proposes stunning new UFO legislation, The Hill.

[244] Marik von Rennenkampff (Dec. 5, 2023), Powerful members of Congress are dead-set on killing UFO transparency, The Hill.

[245] Stephanie Whiteside (Dec. 13, 2023), Schumer: Credible sources say UAP info kept from Congress, NewsNation.

[246] Marik von Rennenkampff (Dec. 5, 2023), Powerful members of Congress are dead-set on killing UFO transparency, The Hill.

[247] Kayla Guo (Dec. 14, 2024), Congress Orders U.F.O. Records Released but Drops Bid for Broader Disclosure, The New York Times.

[248] Eric Lagatta (December 18, 2023), Did America get 'ripped off'? UFO disclosure bill derided for lack of transparency, USA Today.

CHAPTER
19

Origins and intentions of the non-human phenomenon

Particularities of the phenomenon in the present time
Let's look briefly at the experiences of Kevin Day, a former U.S. Navy Chief Petty Officer, former TOPGUN air intercept controller and operations specialist, and Matthew Roberts, a former U.S. Naval Service member stationed aboard, who were among the witnesses to UAPs on the Navy ships Nimitz and Theodore Roosevelt, respectively. Both cases were reported by The New York Times.[1] An additional importance in both cases is that they have a very significant spiritual component.

Thus, in November 2004, Kevin Day was chief radar operator when the USS Nimitz case of a tic-tac object seen by military pilots took place.[2] Day observed a strange object over Catalina Island moving slowly and then at high speed, which changed direction and speed in defiance of the laws of physics.[3]

After that event, which was very well known, Day began to have nightmares; as of all kinds of natural disasters; something that he does not know why it happens to him, but somehow links it to what happened on the Nimitz.[4]

For its part, the USS Roosevelt group experienced UFO sightings from 2014 to 2015. And in early 2015, a co-worker of then-Navy petty officer Matthew Roberts showed him video taken by a fighter pilot of the "Gimbal" UFO, and he thought it changed shape. Watching that video disturbed him. When he returned home to Arlington, Virginia, his mind was still haunted by what he saw.[5]

As he slept in his bed, he felt "someone" grab his arm and wake him up, and he saw a shadowy figure with hands and head standing next to him. Next, a golden light began to illuminate the room from behind the figure, to which Matthew fainted. After opening

---

[1] Helene Cooper, Leslie Kean and Ralph Blumenthal (Dec. 16, 2017), 2 Navy Airmen and an Object That 'Accelerated Like Nothing I've Ever Seen,' The New York Times; Helene Cooper, Ralph Blumenthal, Leslie Kean (May 26, 2019), 'Wow, What Is That?' Navy Pilots Report Unexplained Flying Objects, The New York Times.

[2] Jackie Contreras (Editor), Adam Rzeplinski (Editor), Megan Winiarski (Editor), & Tim McNeela (Director) (2021, January 14). Secrets of the State (Season 1, Episode 1) [TV series episode]. Alex Byrnes, Michael Sorensen, Matthew Kelly, Andrew Nock, Cecile Bouchardeau Weiland (Executive Producers), *UFO Witness*. Anomaly Entertainment, Inc.

[3] Ibid.

[4] Ibid.

[5] Amanda Copeland (Editor), Nicole Diaz (Editor), Adam Rzeplinski (Editor), & Tim McNeela (Director) (2022, June 21). The Shapeshifter (Season 2, Episode 1) [TV series episode]. Alex Byrnes, Michael Sorensen, Matthew Kelly, Ismael Soto, Cecile Bouchardeau Weiland (Executive Producers), *UFO Witness*. Anomaly Entertainment, Inc.

his eyes, he saw a woman with blue-colored skin, and who was thicker than human but softer. She was about six feet tall, and a light radiated from the center of her body.[6]

It can be noted that the phenomenon has a deep mental and spiritual interaction.

Long-standing characteristics of the phenomenon

Chris Bledsoe, the most recognized experiencer of the UAP phenomenon and non-human intelligences, both by ordinary people and U.S. government agencies, says: "People have always seen what I've seen, it's just that the words for it vary according to the cultures and religions."[7]

He also wrote that, "The more I talked with Diana [Dr. Diana Pasulka] and learned about the history of world religions, the more certain I became that the phenomena were a worldwide and angelic presence."[8]

Jacques Vallée, astrophysicist and PhD in computer science, as well as a renowned researcher of the UFO/UAP phenomenon, tells us in his UFOlogy classic *Passport to Magonia*, that since ancient times, in widely diverse cultures, beings such as star gods, fairies, elves, goblins, and the celestial signs of lights and strange objects flying across the sky, have the same origin, but under different names and similar traditions. All these phenomena have spread to the present day.[9]

"It is in the literature of religion that flying objects from celestial countries are most commonly encountered, along with descriptions of the organization, nature, and philosophy of their occupants. Indeed, several writers have consistently pointed out that the fundamental texts of every religion refer to the contact of the human community with a "superior race" of beings from the sky."[10]

Jacques Vallée tells us that in 1575, Pierre Boaistuau (a French Renaissance humanist writer, and author of several informative compilations and discourses on various subjects):

"The face of heaven has been so often disfigured by bearded, hairy comets, torches, flames, columns, spears, shields, dragons, duplicate moons, suns, and other similar things, that if one wanted to tell in an orderly fashion those that have happened since the birth of Jesus Christ only, and inquire about the causes of their origin, the lifetime of a single man would not be enough."[11]

Vallée cites an edition of the work dated 1594 of what happened on December 5, 1577, at seven o'clock in the morning a few leagues from the German city of Tübingen:

---

[6] Ibid.

[7] Chris Bledsoe, UFO of GOD: The Extraordinary True Story of Chris Bledsoe (Chris Bledsoe, 2023), ob. cit.

[8] Ibid.

[9] Jacques Vallée, Passport to Magonia: On UFOs, Folklore, and Parallel Worlds (Contemporary Books, Chicago, 1993), ob. cit.

[10] Ibid, p. 3.

[11] Ibid, p. 7; quoting Pierre Bolastuau, Histoires Prodigieuses (C. Mace, Parfs: 1575).

618

"About the sun many dark clouds appeared, such as we are wont to see during great storms: and soon afterward have come from the sun other clouds, all fiery and bloody, and others, yellow as safran. Out of these clouds have come forth reverberations resembling large, tall and wide hats, and the earth showed itself yellow and bloody, and seemed to be covered with hats, tall and wide, which appeared in various colors such as red, blue, green, and most of them black.... It is easy for everyone to think of the meaning of this miracle, which is that God wants to induce men to amend their lives and make penance. May Almighty God inspire all men to recognize Him. Amen."[12]

Particularly between the 8th and 10th centuries, European legends abound in celestial prodigies; and books on magic and demonology relate supernatural beings to signs occurring in the sky.[13]

As we will see below, the figure of ancient female deities is closely related to UFO manifestations. The first goddess of the world was Inanna, who in Sumerian mythology was the goddess of love, beauty, sex, fertility, and war.[14] Inanna's priestesses were sacred sexual priestesses. One documented source tells us about the third millennium B.C. onwards, about the worship of that deity: "[...] written records of the Sumerians describe the goddess Inanna as the creator of the frame drum, along with all other musical instruments. The scriptures tell of Inanna's priestesses, who sang and chanted to the rhythms of round and square frame drums."[15]

Such drumming rituals, "were carried into the later worship of Ishtar, Asherah, Ashtoreth, Astarte, and Anat in Babylonia, Phoenicia, Palestine, and Assyria."[16] As can be seen, the same goddess passed into different ancient cultures and under very similar beliefs and forms of worship.

Dr. Betty De Shong Meador states: "Canaanite religious practices that bore a strong resemblance to those of Mesopotamia found their way into the Hebrew temples. Pillars of the goddess Asherah were erected in the sanctuary. The priestesses to the goddess actually lived in the temple."[17] About communication with the goddess, Layne Redmond stated:

"The drum was the means our ancestors used to summon the goddess and also the instrument through which she spoke. The drumming priestess was the intermediary between divine and human realms. Aligning herself with sacred rhythms, she acted as summoner and transformer, invoking divine energy and transmitting it to the community."[18]

---

[12] Ibid; citing Ibid (1594), p. 614.

[13] Ibid, p. 60.

[14] Diane Wolkstein, Samuel Noah Kramer, Inanna, Queen of Heaven and Earth: Her Stories and Hymns from Sumer (Harper & Row, 2009), ob. cit.

[15] Cheris Kramarae and Dale Spender (General Editors), Routledge International Encyclopedia of Women: Global Women's Issues and Knowledge (Routledge, New York, 2000), Volume 2, p. 427.

[16] Ibid.

[17] Betty De Shong Meador, Inanna, Lady of Largest Heart: Poems of the Sumerian High Priestess Enheduanna (University of Texas Press, 2002), p. 85.

[18] Layne Redmond (October 11, 2009), *When The Drummers Were Women, Drum! Magazine.*

Emil Jovanov and Melinda C. Maxfield state that many "oral traditions acknowledge that percussion in general, and rhythmic drumming in particular, facilitates communication with the spiritual world."[19]

Again, Layne Redmond indicates that "The use and basic constructions of the drums are so similar that they probably both grew from the same root techniques of altering consciousness."[20] And she wrote literally, that, "From the civilizations of Anatolia (Old Turkey), Mesopotamia, Egypt, Greece and Rome, the Goddess and the frame drum emerge as the core trance and mystical religious traditions."[21]

It was also believed that female deities could foretell the future. The bird goddess, who was said to have dominion over heaven, earth and the underworld, was the source of prophecy, thus giving her knowledge of the past and the future.[22] Later, "in Mesopotamia, Egypt, Cyprus, Crete, Anatolia, Greece, and Rome, priestesses of bird goddesses used the frame drum to enter the trance state from which they could divine the future."[23]

Cases of the "gods" in more modern times

On the night of September 14, 1994, in the Republic of Zimbabwe, several witnesses reported seeing a UFO in the sky that did not make any noise.[24]

Just two days later, on September 16, at Ariel School in Ruwa, Zimbabwe, some sixty-eight children saw two maroon-colored UFOs in the sky, both oval-shaped and silver and flying very slowly. They had blue, red, and yellow lights.

One of the aircrafts descended beyond the far edge of the playground, with four smaller crafts surrounding it. A being of small stature, with large head and eyes, dressed in a black suit, was on top of the UFO; and then descended and stood beside the aircraft.

Some of the witnesses said they received messages in their minds: that the beings thought that people were really hurting this planet and that we should not use so much technology. Another of the girls said that the message conveyed was that we don't take care of the planet, the environment, like cutting down trees, and that there will be no air and that people will die if they don't take care of themselves properly.

Dr. John Mack, a Pulitzer Prize-winning psychiatrist and Harvard University professor, took an interest in this case and for several days interviewed the children and investigated the case.

For the purposes of this section, a very interesting aspect of this case is that not far from the Ariel school, in Shumba Kuchiweyi, which is the traditional Custodian of the Cultural Heritage Valley, are the burial sites of the native ancestors of that place. There is the tomb of the royal chief. It is said that the "extraterrestrials" landed in the center

---

[19] Jonathan Berger and Gabe Turow (eds.), Music, Science, and the Rhythmic Brain: Cultural and Clinical Implications (Routledge, New York, 2011), p. 31; citing Crawley, 1912; Rouget, 1985; Eliade, 1964; Needham, 1979; Hart, 1990; Harner, 1990.

[20] Layne Redmond (October 11, 2009), When The Drummers Were Women, Drum! Magazine.

[21] Ibid.

[22] Layne Redmond, When The Drummers Were Women: A Spiritual History of Rhythm (Three Rivers Press, New York, 1997), p. 52.

[23] Ibid.

[24] Larry Frascella, Jim Ledwith, Jordan Pease (Producer) James Fox (Director) (2020), The Phenomenon (Farah Films, 1091 Pictures). Note: unless otherwise noted, this is the same source.

of the tombs; as well as in the center of the sacred rock shrines. Thus, the phenomenon is intertwined by the tombs of the chief, or the great ancestors of Zimbabwe.[25]

The story goes that the mysterious happenings have been going on at the site for decades.[26]

Likewise, in the Hebrew Bible, we read that the worship and sacrifices to the gods and Baal-peor (Num. 25:1-3), was related to sacrifices to the dead (Ps. 106:28). That was equivalent to offering sacrifices to demons (vs. 36-38; Deut. 32:17).

Similarly, a large, silver-colored, noiseless UFO was observed during a major earthquake in the town of Rio Blanco, Mexico, in 2017.[27] It then went north into the jungle; where many locals have observed strange objects in the area.

Venancio Osorio Ortiz, a resident of rural Rio Blanco, said that for centuries, his ancestors, the Aztecs, tell of seeing flying objects above the trees. He took samples from the jungle of a strange gelatinous substance, which is usually found where UAPs apparitions occur. About that substance, on August 7, 1994 in Oakvillle, Washington, a mysterious jelly fell from the sky as rain, covering 20 square miles; causing some flu-like symptoms in the population. Analysis by the Washington Department of Health determined that it was like nothing else on the planet.

For its part, deep in the jungle already indicated, there is a site from where these UFOs are produced, where there are ruins where the tribes of ancient civilizations lived. Whether they were Totonacs, Olmecs or Mayas.

These ruins preserve some carvings on their rocky walls; and inside an entrance to the site, there are engravings on the rocky ground, one of which shows a large head of a being, somewhat large eyes, with a mouth and nose.

South of the United States occurred the famous case of the Phoenix lights, in Arizona, on March 13, 1997. In the mountainous rocks of that area, there are engravings that seem to indicate that the Hohokam Indians may have observed UFOs and strange beings more than a thousand years ago.[28] Native residents in the basin between South Mountain and Las Estrellas have said they saw the Phoenix lights that night and have seen them for centuries.[29]

Again, it seems that the phenomenon is closely linked to ancient cultures and their gods.

Latin America, Costa Rica, on September 4, 1971, the Instituto Geográfico Nacional (National Geographic Institute) took an aerial photograph of Cote Lagoon, in Guatuso, in the province of Alajuela, showing a flying disk with a dome protruding from the

[25] Randall Nickerson (Producer) Randall Nickerson (Director) (2022), Ariel Phenomenon (String Theory Films).

[26] Ibid.

[27] Steve Mellon (Writer), Karin Hoving (Writer), & Jeffrey Daniels (Director) (2019, August 14). Declassified Breakthrough (Season 39, Episode 11) [TV Series Episode]. Emre Sahin, Sarah Wetherbee, Kelly McPherson, Jason Wolf (Executive Producers), Contact. A Red Arrow Studios Company, Karga Seven Pictures. Note: unless otherwise noted, this is the same source.

[28] Jeff Tober (Editor), Paul Cross (Editor), & Rob Blumenstain (Producer) (2008, December 10). Arizona Lights (Season 2, Episode 6) [TV Series Episode]. Jon Alon Walz, Michael Stiller (Executive Producers), UFO Hunters. Motion Picture Production, Incorporated.

[29] J. D. Seraphine (Producer) Amardeep Kaleka (Director) (2013), Sirius (Neverending Light Productions/Bayview Films).

center.[30] Its photographer, Sergio Loaiza, had from the age of five, experiences with UFOs and beings considered by him as coming from outer space.[31]

The Costa Rican volcanologist, Guillermo E. Alvarado, wrote concerning this case: "Several photographs and similar sightings have been reported in the surroundings of the Arenal Lagoon [35 km from Lake Cote]. In the Arenal Lake there is also reported a "monster" of three humps and about 15 m long, which according to Korsiak (1996) the Indians called Ahuizotl, and that for others it is a snake, the "sierpa," of about 30 m."[32]

Even today, sightings of lights and objects diving into the Cote Lagoon are still reported.

The Maleku Indians relate that for centuries, the lagoon has been considered sacred by the tribe, and that indigenous people from different Central American countries visited it on the occasion of special events. They have long believed that these objects, or gods, live there.

Countries in the region such as Mexico, Belize, Guatemala, Honduras, and many other Mesoamerican nations have ancient stories of star beings. Many Maya myths tell stories of sky people or sky gods who came to Earth, often in a luminous beam. Stories of giants, little people, and spirits became universal.[33]

Robert Morning Sky, a Hopi-Apache speaker, claimed that the Blue Men, or just "blues," were beings of small stature and translucent skin with large almond-shaped eyes.[34]

The Cherokee elders described a universe in which humans shared the world with other supernatural or non-human peoples.

Some say that the blues never disappeared, but decided to live underground. The story goes that a team of explorers, found in northern Arkansas a tunnel illuminated by greenish phosphorescence, finding nearly a mile underground a race of six to ten foot tall blue-skinned beings. "The beings possessed advanced technology and lived in massive underground cities."

Another case is the aforementioned Skinwalker Ranch, in Utah, whose current owner is Brandon Fugal and where for several years, a series of scientific experiments have been conducted, causing phenomena of unusual nature have manifested on multiple occasions through the appearance of UFOs, technical failures at particular times of the experiments, strange radiation peaks, etc.

The phenomenon has been witnessed through sudden temperature changes in the "House number 2" by means of traditional prayers performed by a rabbi to open the "doors" to other "entities."[35]

---

[30] Guillermo E. Alvarado Induni, Los volcanes de Costa Rica: Geología, historia, riqueza natural y su gente (Editorial Universidad Estatal a Distancia, San José, Costa Rica, Third edition, 2009. Reprint, 2011), p. 103.

[31] Kimberly Herrera (November 13, 2021), Un ovni sobre un lago en Costa Rica: La foto que hace 50 años cambió la vida a un cartógrafo, La Nación.

[32] Guillermo E. Alvarado Induni, Los volcanes de Costa Rica: Geología, historia, riqueza natural y su gente (Editorial Universidad Estatal a Distancia, San José, Costa Rica, Third edition, 2009. Reprint, 2011), p. 103; quoting at the end (García, 2008).

[33] Ardy Sixkiller Clarke, Sky People: Untold Stories of Alien Encounters in Mesoamerica (New Page Books, Pompton Plains, NJ, 2015), ob. cit.

[34] Ardy Sixkiller Clarke, Space Age Indians: Their Encounters with the Blue Men, Reptilians, and Other Star People (Anomalist Books, San Antonio, TX, 2019), ob. cit. Note: unless otherwise noted, this is the same source.

At the foot of the ranch plateau, local drummers provoked the sense of the presence of "someone" or "something" walking on the slope of the plateau; and the descent of two large spheres that penetrated the top of the plateau, practically on top of a stone building in the shape of a spiral.[36] This form is observed in petroglyphs in all parts of the world; which has been interpreted as a portal through which UFOs and beings of non-human origin manifest themselves.[37]

Ancient stories about star ancestors, in addition to coming from Mesopotamia, originate from Australian Aboriginal, Japanese, Celtic, Israeli, Native American, and other spiritual leaders throughout the world.[38]

The reason: prophecies or apparitions of such entities appearing as UFOs, dreams, and other physical encounters according to legends, show "how Earth's current crisis is part of a larger cosmic plan for the planet's transition into an enlightened age"[39]

Some groups claim to have direct contact with UFOs and their non-human occupants.[40]

"Satan," Lam, and 'modern' music

Aleister Crowley (1875-1947) was the founder of so-called modern Satanism.[41]

Crowley claimed to have contacted various Egyptian deities, such as Thoth, Horus, Set, and others, and to have written books under the inspiration of these spiritual entities and under the effects of drugs.[42] One of the many spiritual entities he invoked was a being called Lam, which is very similar to the classic "gray" that is identified in various UFO appearances and so-called "abductions." For Kenneth Grant, English occultist and Crowley's secretary initiated by him in the Ordo Templi Orientis (OTO), "Lam" is an "extraterrestrial" being; a statement that quickly spread throughout California.[43]

---

[35] Joe Lessard (Writer), Ken Warun (Writer), Mari Johnson (Director) (2021, May 25). There's No Place Like Homestead 2 (Season 2, Episode 4) [TV Series Episode]. Kevin Burns, (Executive Producer), *The Secret of Skinwalker Ranch*. Prometheus Entertainment for History. A&E Television Networks, LLC.

[36] Joe Lessard (Writer), Jason Shook (Writer), Mari Johnson (Director), & Hunter Bartholomew (Director) (2023, June 27). A Frequency Occurrence (Season 4, Episode 10) [TV series episode]. David Comtois, Kim Egan, Joe Lessard, Brandon Fugal, Joel Patterson, Matt Crocco, Jason Shook, Jennifer Wagman (Executive Producers), *The Secret of Skinwalker Ranch*. Prometheus Entertainment for History. A&E Television Networks, LLC.

[37] Joe Lessard (Writer), Mark Marinaccio (Writer), Mari Johnson (Director), & Hunter Bartholomew (Director) (2022, May 17). Inner Fear-ence (Season 3, Episode 3) [TV series episode]. David Comtois, Kim Egan, Joe Lessard, Brandon Fugal, Joel Patterson, Mark Marinaccio, Jennifer Wagman (Executive Producers), *The Secret of Skinwalker Ranch*. Prometheus Entertainment for History. A&E Television Networks, LLC.

[38] Nancy Red Star, Legends of the Star Ancestors: Stories of Extraterrestrial Contact from Wisdomkeepers around the World (Bear & Company, 2002), ob. cit.

[39] Ibid.

[40] Dr. Steven Greer (Producer) Michael Mazzola (Director) (2020), Close Encounters of the Fifth Kind (1091 Media/Star-Contact LLC); J. D. Seraphine (Producer) Amardeep Kaleka (Director) (2013), Sirius (Neverending Light Productions/Bayview Films).

[41] Roger Hutchinson, Aleister Crowley: The Beast Demystified (Mainstream Publishing Company, Edinburgh, 2006), ob. cit.

[42] Tobias Churton, Aleister Crowley: The Biography: Spiritual Revolutionary, Romantic Explorer, Occult Master and Spy (Watkins Publishing, London, 2011) ob. cit.

[43] Lynn Picknett & Clive Prince, The Stargate Conspiracy: The Truth about Extraterrestrial life and the Mysteries of Ancient Egypt (Berkley Publishing Group, Hudson Street, New York, 1999), ob. cit.

Recalling that since ancient civilizations have held ceremonies with the use of music to invoke their deities, Lon Millo DuQuette, American writer, lecturer, musician and occultist, wrote that on a cold spring night in 1910, Crowley discovered that through music and poetry performed in intense and ecstatic ways, used in a way that creates a tangible state of ecstasy, he noted a way to introduce Scientific Illumination and the Magick of Thelema [discovering and following the "True Will," a unique purpose and calling beyond ordinary desires, which includes ideas from occultism, yoga, and Eastern and Western mysticism (especially Kabbalah)]; for which he developed a dramatic ecstasy-inducing ritual that was publicly staged. Crowley called it the Eleusinian technique,[44] which were annual initiation rites in worship of the goddesses Demeter and Persephone held at Eleusis, near Athens, Greece. They united the worshiper with the god, which included promises of divine power and rewards in the afterlife.

The English magician died in Brighton, England, in 1947; "and was almost forgotten until the English rock musicians, who alone had the money and inclination to live as Crowley did, started reading about him years after his death."[45] John Symonds, Crowley's biographer, said that the magician elevated his hate "to the rank of a religion of world importance which, fifty years after his death, is beginning to interest the public, especially those who congregate around pop music."[46]

Just as Crowley used drugs, so did rock music. LSD is known to have had a decisive influence on the music of the 1960s.[47]

American historian and percussionist Layne Redmond wrote, for example, about rock music:

"At contemporary rock concerts we have all the trappings of ritual without the spiritual purposes. Flashing trance-inducing lights, loud rhythmic sound, chanted and sung words, but often with no higher purpose than to momentarily entertain or to glorify the individual performer. And no matter how much idolization some of these quite gifted musicians attain, they are often driven to attempt to fill the emptiness with drugs and alcohol."[48]

Many rock music groups have been admirers of Crowley's work, and many have had contact with what they call "extraterrestrial intelligence." For example, the Beatles are known to have resurrected Crowley; Paul and Linda McCartney are known to have had a fascination with the magician; but John Lennon and Yoko Ono were more open to his influence.[49] The Beatles, it has been said, "opposed oppression of all types, and they

---

[44] Lon Millo DuQuette, The Magick of Aleister Crowley: A Handbook of the Rituals of Thelema (Weiser Books, Boston, MA, 2003), p. 193.

[45] Stephen Davis, Led Zeppelin: Hammer of the Gods (Berkley Boulevard Books, New York, 1997), p. 109.

[46] John Symonds, The Great Beast: The Life of Aleister Crowley (Rider and Company, London, Great Britain. 1951), pp. 331, 332.

[47] Sheila Whiteley, Jedediah Sklower, Countercultures and Popular Music (Ashgate Publishing Company, Burlington, VT, 2014), 36.

[48] Layne Redmond (October 11, 2009), *When The Drummers Were Women, Drum! Magazine.*

[49] R. U. Sirius, Everybody Must Get Stoned: Rock Stars on Drugs (Citadel Press, 2012), ob. cit.

saw in Crowley one who had succeeded in throwing off the shackles of social convention."[50]

Sgt. Pepper's Lonely Hearts Club Band (1967) was the most anticipated piece of musical art in all of history. The album cover, designed by Peter Blake, was a collage of the Beatles' sixty-two most influential people. One of them was Aleister Crowley.[51]

When the Beatles released the album, critics and fans alike quickly found references to drugs.[52]

John Lennon lived in the legendary Dakota Building in New York City. At the beginning of the twentieth century, Aleister Crowley lived in the building, who performed several black magic rituals there. It was also inhabited at the time by horror film actor Boris Karloff, who was accused by neighbors of conducting countless seances. It was said that after his death, neighbors came face to face with ghostly figures, causing some of the tenants to flee the building in terror.[53]

Gerald Brossau Gardner, a high priest of the Wicca sect, also stayed in the building when he visited New York and is said to have performed magical rituals to invoke the occult forces of nature.[54]

Now, bearing in mind that music in ancient times was also used to invoke the gods and goddesses of the nations; and its link with today's musical entertainment, it is worth underlining the effects of music in invoking or attracting UFOs and their occupants. And also appearing to musicians who are not even making music. A truly intriguing account occurred on August 23, 1974, when Lennon was with May Pang in his apartment in the Dakota Building.[55]

Lennon was lying in bed when, looking out, he saw hovering over the adjacent building not more than a hundred feet away, a UFO with flashing lights at the bottom and a steady red light at the top. The object made no noise (the police and a newspaper confirmed the sighting as other witnesses reported it).[56] Lennon called May Pang, who also saw the same thing and reported: "As I walked out onto the terrace, my eye caught this large, circular object coming towards us. It was shaped like a flattened cone, and on top was a large, brilliant red light, not pulsating as on any of the aircraft we'd see heading for a landing at Newark Airport. When it came a little closer, we could make out a row or circle of white lights that ran around the entire rim of the craft - these were also flashing on and off. There were so many of these lights that it was dazzling to the mind."[57]

Pang recalls that Lennon told her he had seen other UFOs before that night.

The English musician thought about UFOs since he was a boy, and used to subscribe to the *British UFO Magazine* when he was in the Beatles. He also claimed to have been

---

[50] Scott Calef (editor), Led Zeppelin and Philosophy: All Will Be Revealed (Open Court Publishing Company, Chicago and La Salle, Illinois, 2009), p. 104.

[51] Lon Milo Duquette, The Magick of Aleister Crowley: A Handbook of the Rituals of Thelema (Weiser Books, Boston, MA, 2003), p. xiv.

[52] Tim Kasser, Lucy in the Mind of Lennon (Oxford University Press, New York, 2013), ob. cit.

[53] Alberto Granados, Historias imprescindibles para los amantes de los viajes: Una vuelta al mundo sorprendente y curiosa (Penguin Random House Grupo Editorial España, 2013), ob. cit.

[54] Ibid.

[55] Carlos Manuel Sánchez (December 8, 2017), *El triangulo amoroso de Lennon, XLSemanal*.

[56] Andy Warhol (November, 1974), *Interview/Interview with by/on John Lennon and/or Dr. Winston O'Boogie, Interview Magazine,* p. 11.

[57] Jeremy Allen (March 29, 2017), 11 pop stars who claim to have seen UFOs, BBC.

abducted by aliens as a child, living in the Liverpool suburb of Woolton. Pang said that Lennon felt the experience made him feel different from other people for the rest of his life.[58]

Likewise, the famous Israeli-British illusionist, Uri Geller, said that in the mid-1970s, when he was in Manhattan, John Lennon told him about another experience:

"One night he was lying in his bed in the Dakota building where he lived in New York and suddenly noticed an extremely bright light pouring in from around the edges of the bedroom door. It was so powerful, he thought it was someone aiming a searchlight through his apartment. He got up, crossed to the door and flung it open. The next thing he could remember was four thin-looking (bug-like) figures. He said that the figures came over to him as he just stood there. Two of them held his hands and the other two gently pushed his legs and he was gently guided into this tunnel of light. He was shown all of his life, just like watching a movie, and he told me it was the most outstandingly beautiful thing he'd ever seen."[59]

Lennon further told Geller: "Something happened. Don't ask me what. Either I've forgotten, blocked it out, or they won't let me remember. But after a while they weren't there and I was just lying on the bed, next to Yoko, only I was on the covers." But he also claimed that the beings gave him a very smooth, heavy golden metallic oval, about an inch wide. John gave it to Geller, telling him that "It's too weird for me. If it's my ticket to another planet, I don't want to go there." [60]

Both Lennon and Yoko were aware of the presence of a spirit in the Dakota, where they lived. But the musician was comfortable with the spirit: supposedly "Jessie Ryan," the late wife of Robert Ryan, an actor.[61] At the time, Yoko was deeply immersed in the occult.[62]

Other artists from the rock & roll world with experiences either to one extent or another with the UAP or "alien" phenomenon, are: Elton John, Madonna, Sting, Bob Dylan, Moby, Tina Turner, Dave Grohl, Dan Aykroyd, Reg Presley, Marc Bolan, Sun Ra, George Clinton, Merle Haggard, Willie Nelson, Deborah Harry, Lance Bass, Patti LaBelle, Judy Collins, Laurie Anderson, Jamiroquai, Jerry Garcia, Dave Davies, Sammy Hagar, Rick Wakeman, Nina Hagen, Olivia Newton-John, Ace Frehley, Cat Stevens, Phoebe Snow, Johnny Rotten, Marilyn Manson, Bill Haley, David Bowie, Sammy Hagar, and many more.[63]

Likewise, bands and other rock & roll musicians admired and inspired by Crowley were: the Rolling Stones,[64] Pink Floyd through Syd Barrett,[65] Led Zeppelin,[66] David

---

[58] (December 7, 2004), The night aliens called on Lennon, The Telegraph; Bryce Zabel (November 12, 2021), Did John Lennon Imagine His UFO Sighting, Medium: https://medium.com/on-the-trail-of-the-saucers/did-lennon-imagine-his-ufo-sighting-2694d87d27c0 Accessed January 24, 2024.

[59] Ibid.

[60] Ibid.

[61] L'Aura Hladik, Ghosthunting New York City (Clerisy Press, Cincinnati, OH, 2010), ob. cit.

[62] Albert Goldman, The Many Lives of John Lennon (Titivillus, 2018), ob. cit.

[63] Michael C. Luckman, Alien Rock: The Rock 'n' Roll Extraterrestrial Connection (Pocket Books, Simon & Schuster, Inc. 2005); Ken McLeod (2003), Space oddities: aliens, futurism and meaning in popular music, Popular Music, Volume 22/3, pp. 337-355; Sean Michaels (March 22, 2011), Van Halen's Sammy Hagar says his mind was infiltrated by aliens, The Guardian; Grant Cameron, Tuned-In: The Paranormal World of Music (Itsallconnected Publishing, Canada, 2018).

[64] Stephen Davies, Rolling Stones: Old Gods Never Die (Robinbook Editions, 2006), p. 281, 301.

Bowie,[67] Frank Zappa,[68] Black Sabbath,[69] Daryl Hall, Sting,[70] Steven Tayler of Aerosmith,[71] Raul Seixas, from Brazil, Ab-Soul,[72] and many others. This can explain a lot.

Music has been one of the most powerful, if not the most powerful popular means in the past and present centuries to shape consciences and bring about profound cultural, political, and spiritual changes.

Mickey Hart, drummer for the Grateful Dead band, born in the mid-1960s, wrote:

"The worldwide connection between percussion and ritual was alluded to everywhere [...] "Can't you see what's staring you in your face? Everywhere you look on the planet people are using drums to alter consciousness.""[73]

He further noted:

"It's hard to pinpoint the exact moment when I awoke to the fact that my tradition - rock and roll - did have a spirit side, that there was a branch of the family that had maintained the ancient connection between the drum and the gods."[74]

Just as fermented beverages and other substances modifying the mental functioning and state, facilitated with or without ceremonies the invocation to the gods, so it has happened in modern times with psychedelic drugs, whose experimentation since the 60's brought communications with non-human entities, which some catalogued as "extraterrestrials."[75]

It is no coincidence that the principles of antiquity that attracted "the gods" continue to work today.

[65] Julian Palacios, Syd Barrett & Pink Floyd (Plexus Publishing Limited, London, 2010), pp. 48, 49, 90.
[66] Stephen Davis, Led Zeppelin: The Hammer of the Gods (Ediciones Robinbook, s. l., Barcelona, 2008), p. 60, 98, 99, 132; Gary Lachman, Aleister Crowley: Magick, Rock and Roll, and the Wickedest Man in the World (Penguin Group, New York, 2014), ob. cit.; Scott Calef, Led Zeppelin and Philosophy: All Will Be Revealed (Open Court, Chicago and La Salle, Illinois, 2009), p. 95, 96; citing Aleister Crowley, Magick in Theory and Practice (Castle, 1991), p. 107.
[67] David Buckley, Strange Fascination: David Bowie: The Definitive Story (Virgin Books, London, 2005), p. 240.
[68] Tom Taylor (July 16, 2021), Frank Zappa's favorite books about the occult, Far Out.
[69] Scott McLennan (November 30, 2018), How "The Wickedest Man In The World" Influenced 6 Of Your Fave Artists, I Like Your Old Stuff.
[70] Peter Bebergal, Season of the Witch: How the Occult Saved Rock and Roll (Jeremy P. Tarcher/Penguin, New York, 2014), ob. cit.
[71] Eduardo Izquierdo, Aerosmith: La turbulenta historia de una de las bandas más espectaculares del Rock and Roll, auténticos iconos del Hard Rock (Ma Non Troppo, Barcelona, 2020), ob. cit.
[72] Andres Tardio (December 9, 2016), Ab-Soul Breaks Down the Inspirations & Revelations Behind 'Do What Thou Wilt', Billboard.
[73] Mickey Hart, Jay Stevens, Drumming at the Edge of Magic: A Journey Into the Spirit of Percussion (Grateful Dead Books, 1998), p. 28.
[74] Ibid, p. 212.
[75] Rick Strassman, M.D., DMT: The Spirit Molecule: A Doctor's Revolutionary Research into the Biology of Near-Death and Mystical Experiences (Park Street Press, Rochester, Vermont, 2001); Terence McKenna, Food of the Gods: The Search for the Original Tree of Knowledge: A Radical History of Plants, Drugs, and Human Evolution (Bantam, Reprint Edition, 1993); Terence Mckenna, The Archaic Revival: Speculations on Psychedelic Mushrooms, the Amazon, Virtual Reality, UFOs, Evolution, Shamanism, the Rebirth of the Goddess, and the End of History (Harper Collins, San Francisco, 1991).

Lynn E. Catoe, Library of Congress Bibliographer for the Science and Technology Department, stated in her 1969 report from the Science and Technology Division of the Library of Congress:

"A large part of the available UFO litel'ature is closely linked with mysticism and the metaphysical. It deals with subjects like mental telepathy, automatic writing, and invisible entities as well as phenomena like poltergeist manifestations and "possession." [...]
Many of the UFO reports now being published in the popular press recount alleged incidents that are strikingly similar to demoniac possession and psychic phenomena which have long been known to theologians and parapsychologists."[76]

Dr. Pierre Guerin, in the May 1979 *Flying Saucer Review*, stresses that: "According to the best testimony available, the UFOs can move equally well either by covering a trajectory through the air or by vanishing "on the spot" and then re-materializing at a distance, which behaviour is more akin to magic than to physics as we know it."[77] "[...] the fact that the modern ufonauts and the demons of past days are probably identical. These latter invariably made their appearance in precisely the sort of garb that the eyewitnesses of the period expected of them. But this chamaleon-effect [...] is a characteristic feature of the UFO phenomenon."[78] He also stated:

"And these Extraterrestrials are not coming here in order to *discover* us or to *study* us. All the indications suggest that they have known all about us since the very beginning, and we are lost if we waste our time in vain conjectures concerning the meaning of what they are doing: for example, why do they concoct for us these UFOs, which - with the exception of the saucer-shaped discs - are fashioned in the likeness of our own ideas at a given moment in time? Why do they so persistently and monotonously go on displaying for us these situations - frequently quite absurd ones - flying about over us, chasing us, vanishing into thin air, and - above all - *landing* here! All of which must have some meaning.
The problem is: What meaning? In any event, what is quite certain is that the phenomenon is active here, on our planet, *and active here as Master*. We can neither stop the phenomenon nor comprehend it, and we are well aware that its power totally defies not merely our technological possibilities *but probably our mental possibilities as well*."[79]

Thus, many of the manifestations of the phenomenon are what will have been called demonic for millennia. There is no doubt that the phenomenon prefers to form a spiritual consciousness that is close to their beliefs, whether they are good, bad, or a combination of both.

---

[76] Lynn E. Catoe, UFOs and Related Subjects: An Annotated Bibliography (The Library of Congress Science and Technology Division, 1969), p. iv.
[77] Dr. Pierre Guerin (May 1979), 'Thirty Years after Kenneth Arnold; A Summing Up of the UFO Situation', Flying Saucer Review, Vol. 25, N. 1, p. 13.
[78] Ibid, p. 14.
[79] Ibid.

"Somber" and future effects

Luis Elizondo, former director of AATIP, was asked on June 23, 2021 on Curt Jaimungal's legendary *Theories of Everything* (TOE) podcast, "If the general public knew or saw what you saw, what would the next week look like? How would the public react?"

"Somber. I think there would be this big exhale... for about a day. And then this turning inward and trying to reflect on what this means to us and our species and ourselves. [...] I think you would have some people perhaps turning to religion more so. You might have some people turning away from religion.

I think you're going to have at that point, the philosophical and theological questions... will be raised. And people will have some serious soul-searching to do no pun intended. And I don't think that's bad, by the way.

After referring to the religious field, he moved on to the scientific community and the unity of the human race:

"I think the scientific and academic community is going to have to take a real hard look at itself and see why it repeated the same mistakes it did when Galileo first proposed that the Earth was not the center of the solar system. [...] And then I think that, you know, maybe we start an international conversation and say, OK, we realize that there's some things out there that are probably way beyond our petty discrepancies we have with each other.

Maybe we really need to start working together on this. Realize that we are really a global family. Doesn't matter where you're from, or doesn't matter what your religion is, culture, your color, anything else. We are all brothers and sisters on this tiny little rock called Earth."[80]

Adding to his comment on "grim," he said on October 21 of that year always on the renowned podcast about the advanced nature of the phenomenon and the work of all mankind:

"Are we prepared to recognize that we're not at the top of the food chain, potentially, that we're not the alpha predator, that we're maybe somewhere in the middle? [...] What if it turns out that... there's another species that is, is even higher up that ladder than we are? Do we need the social institutions that we have today? Will we need governmental and religious organizations that we have today? If it turns out that there is something else or someone else that is technologically more advanced? And perhaps, from an evolutionary perspective, more advanced?

Have we've been wasting our time, all this time? Or are we doing exactly what what is supposed to be doing?

Are we, does it turn out that mankind is in fact, just another animal in the zoo? Or, because we thought of ourselves as a zookeeper before, but maybe we're just another exhibit inside the zoo? What would that mean to us? So when I say sombering and sobering, I mean, that is it, you know, there's gonna come a point in this conversation, where we're going to have to do a lot of reconcile with ourselves, whatever that

---

[80] (June 23, 2021), Luis Elizondo: UFOs, Skinwalker, Remote Viewing [Part 1], Theories of Everything with Curt Jaimungal: https://www.youtube.com/watch?v=aAmFlLfsZKM; accessed August 24, 2023.

means, from whatever philosophical background you have, this is going to impact every single one of us this same and yet equally knit differently. You know. Do we find ourselves in a situation where history may have to be rewritten. So that's what I meant."[81]

Elizondo told *TOE* that there are anecdotal reports that the phenomenon can disguise itself or take the form of an airplane, a 747 or that the occupants can be made to look like human beings.[82]

Some appear to be plasma and others are much larger and intelligently controlled. There seems to be information suggesting that others appear to be light and related to other UFO sightings.[83] Such components reflect a consciousness of a spiritual character.

Undoubtedly, the phenomenon changes forms according to its intentions to human beings when viewing them.

On the other hand, Elizondo noted that there are very convincing photographs that appear to show some sort of occupants. Exposure to UAPs can cause physiological as well as psychological effects. And that biological samples have been recovered from these objects.[84]

Dr. Garry Nolan said in an interview with Tucker Carlson in March 2022, that unless God intervened to make the bodies look like ours, that from an evolutionary perspective, it is impossible for them to have evolved to look like us. So it has been hypothesized from within the intelligence community, that the real phenomenon would send avatars, or biological robots to be the bait and see how we react to them.[85]

Jacques Vallée summarizes his conclusions on the nature of the phenomenon:

"[...] if you take the trouble to join me in the analysis of the modern UFO myth, you will see human beings under the control of a strange force 1 h3t is bending them in absurd ways, forcing them to play a role in a bizarre game of deception. [...]

"Let me summarize my conclusions thus far. UFOs are real. They are physical devices used to affect human consciousness. They may not be from outer space. Their purpose may be to achieve social changes on this planet, through a belief system that uses systematic manipulation of witnesses and contactees; covert use of various sects and cults; control of the channels through which the alleged "space messages" can make an impact on the public."[86]

As Vallée aptly wrote, these are the "Messengers of Deception".[87] Who or what is behind the phenomenon?

---

[81] (October 21, 2021), Luis Elizondo: Gov't Has Biological UFO Samples [Part 2], Theories of Everything with Curt Jaimungal: https://www.youtube.com/watch?v=wULw64ZL1Bg; accessed August 24, 2023.

[82] Ibid.

[83] Ibid.

[84] Ibid.

[85] (August 2, 2022), Dr Garry P Nolan UAP UFO Tucker Carlson Full Interview 03/08/2022, UAP Tracker: https://www.youtube.com/watch?v=T3sszdf_93w 36:02 38:39 Accessed September 25, 2023.

[86] Jacques Vallée, Messengers of Deception: UFO Contacts and Cults (Daily Grail Publishing, 2008), p. 21.

[87] Ibid, p. vi.

CHAPTER

20

The Holy See, non-human forces, and the future of humanity

Introduction

The Roman Catholic Church is a very powerful millennia-old political and religious institution. Windston Black effectively says that, "The Roman Catholic Church was arguably the most powerful institution of the Middle Ages in terms of its influence on the lives and beliefs of all Europeans from peasants to the Holy Roman Emperor, as well as in terms of its financial and landholdings."[1]

It has also been referred to by historians in similar ways: as "[...] the most permanent and most powerful organization of history - the Roman Catholic Church."[2] Also as "[...] the most powerful international player in medieval European life, the Catholic church."[3] We read that: "In the Middle Ages the Catholic Church became the most powerful entity in Europe. It was one of the largest landowners, asserted its right to crown and dethrone kings, and claimed ownership of the only set of keys to heaven."[4] We can read that: "[...] the Catholic Church became the most powerful institution of medieval period. The kings, queens and other leaders derived much of their power from their alliances with and protection of the Church."[5] Another serious historian recounts, "Nothing is a greater mystery than the Roman Catholic Church, by far the most enormous and most powerful religious body in the history of the world, and the most catholic or universal body in history, comprising more peoples and more traditions than any other world body, and the Catholic Church is truly unique in this universality."[6] Similarly, the Catholic Church became: "[...] the most powerful institution in the Western world during the Middle Ages. While the church lost much of its political power in modern times, it now has more than a billion members and continues to play a

---

[1] Winston Black, The Middle Ages: Facts and Fictions (ABC-CLIO, Santa Barbara, California, 2019), p. 153.

[2] George Burton Adams, Civilization During the Middle Ages: Especially in Relation to Modern Civilization (Charles Scribner's Sons, New York, 1903), p. 108.

[3] Anthony Musson (editor), Expectations of the Law in the Middle Ages (The Boydell Press, Woodbridge, 2001), p. 42.

[4] Joseph Early Jr, A History of Christianity: An Introductory Survey (B&H Publishing Group, Nashville, Tennessee, 2015), p. 149.

[5] Aly Abdel Razek Galaby, Amal Adel Abdrabo, Handbook of Research on Creative Cities and Advanced Models for Knowledge-Based Urban Development (IGI Global, Hershey, PA, 2021), p. 328.

[6] David Jasper and Dale Wright, with Maria Antonaccio and William Schweiker (eds.), Theological Reflection and the Pursuit of Ideals: Theology, Human Flourishing and Freedom (Ashgate Publishing, New York, 2016), ob. cit.

major role in the spiritual and intellectual life of the world today. It is also one of the largest landowners in the world."[7]

The question is, what relationship does the UAP phenomenon have with a country and institution that, as we have seen throughout this book, has so much influence and power in the moral, political and religious vision in this world? And what can we also say about the role of Freemasonry?

We saw in the previous chapter, that ultimately the UAP phenomena and the non-human forces that control them, are behind many of the ancient religious cultures, up to the present day. Personally, I do not believe that we can box every religion or religious movement as being influenced and even formed by the same non-human intelligences that have been the object of so much study by different experts and researchers; and this due to many reasons that for lack of space and for the purposes of this book, we will not comment here. But let us say for the moment, that historically, the Roman Catholic Church has experienced much of the influence of the phenomenon. Being this a country and a religious and political institution with so much influence in the world, it is worth asking ourselves to what extent the phenomenon is not interested in forming consciences through its influence; although it is not the only one.

Since the phenomenon is behind countless religions, whose traditions, reminiscences and forms we have to this day, we believe that the ecumenical movement led by the Roman Catholic Church, may be preponderant in this case. Moreover, remembering the powerful Masonic influence in the Vatican and considering that Freemasonry in the world embraces practically all the existing religions, whose members adhere to the same, history tells us, as we have seen, that the Roman Catholic Church has been the most influential in the ecumenical movement, not only but particularly under the leadership of the first pope of the Society of Jesus, the first pope who is a Freemason, as well as the first pope most involved and even in direct contact, at least in the past, with the non-human intelligences behind the UAP phenomenon, at such a preponderant moment in history: Why did Jorge Mario Bergoglio come to the papacy just when the most extraordinary moment in American and world history would arrive to reveal to humanity the existence of non-human intelligences? How is it that the two issues converged, just when in the world, especially in the United States and the Vatican, cultural differences, both conservative and progressive, are at a boiling point and threaten to radically transform them; and in the face of the conflagrations so threatening to world peace at this time?

Roman Catholicism leading especially the ecumenical movement; and with great influence of Freemasonry, couples many religions behind which the phenomenon has shaped them throughout history under different names, nicknames and "surnames." With an agenda to unite humanity, with celestial messages that Pope Francis assures are from God; from angels and non-human entities behind the UAPs.

I have learned through various inside sources, that the Vatican has had an interest in the subject of UAP and its occupants for a long time. Particularly during the papacy of Francis, it is believed that the phenomenon is behind every religion and that it comes from God. In this manner, the Vatican is trying to prepare the world for a future revelation.

---

[7] Cynthia Clark Northrup (editor), Encyclopedia of World Trade: From Ancient Times to the Present (Routledge, New York, 2015), Volumes 1-4, p. 793.

Let's look at the history we know about the influence of the UAP phenomenon in the Roman Catholic Church.

Supernatural events in the Catholic Church and the UFO phenomenon

Dr. Diana Walsh Pasulka, a professor of Religious Studies at the University of North Carolina Wilmington, is the author of several books. Recounting experiences of 19th century Catholic saints and mystics, she recounts that in the late 1800s, a young nun sleeping in her small cell in the convent where she resided was awakened by a glowing, flame-like object that seemed to emerge from the wall of her room and hover above her. She was terrified and told the other nuns and the community priest about the experience, but they did not believe her. Nevertheless, the events persisted. Discouraged and frightened, the nun persisted and convinced the Mother Superior of what had happened, so she sat next to the nun until the "flame" emerged from the wall and hovered over them. The Mother Superior was surprised, but determined that the flame was a soul in purgatory in need of prayers, so the next day she ordered the members of the convent to pray for the soul in purgatory.[8]

Pasulka wrote that this 19th century report is similar to another report of a floating ball of light. She quoted Dr. John Mack, a renowned Harvard University psychiatrist:

"When Melissa was in her early twenties she saw a ball of light come through the sliding doors of her apartment, "bounce around the room," go down the hall and into another room and "through a wall." She was with a friend, and they both ignored the phenomenon until Melissa said, "Wait a minute, the curtains are closed. It's not a light from a car going down the street." As Sheila related, "They followed the light around the room before it went back outside through the same sliding doors."[9]

Which is why, Pasulka tells us, "A common theme within these reports is the reference to a floating, shining object that seems to possess the ability to move through walls."[10]

Another similarity is the interpretation of attributing to the ball of light a metaphysical character, or beyond physical reality: the reports are framed in a description that assumes a supernatural origin.[11] While on the one hand the phenomenon is interpreted as a soul from purgatory, on the other hand, it is seen as an extraterrestrial being, in both cases being something entirely extraordinary.[12]

We are told verbatim that, "Further comparisons of supernatural events within the European Catholic tradition with modern reports of UFO events suggest other striking similarities." For example, people from both eras describe balls or luminous beings descending from the sky or passing through walls. These beings terrorize, poke and prod people with a dart-like instrument; assaulting them with a peculiar light and leaving them utterly transformed.[13]

---

[8] Diana Walsh Pasulka, From Purgatory to the UFO Phenomenon: The Catholic Supernatural Goes Galactic, in Jeffrey J. Kripal, Religion: Super Religion (Macmillan, New York, 2017), p. 375.
[9] Ibid; citing (Mack 2007, 1326 - 1329).
[10] Ibid.
[11] Ibid, pp. 375, 376.
[12] Ibid, p. 376.
[13] Ibid.

Another case is that of St. Teresa of Avila, a 16th century nun and Doctor of the Catholic Church; and the second is the contemporary account of Edward Carlos, a professor of fine arts whose case is reported in John Mack's Abduction: Human Encounters with Aliens. Both saw equally a small luminous being penetrating both of them with a sharp, piercing instrument, each experiencing the light in an extraordinary way.[14]

Teresa and Carlos also reported experiencing levitation, a process by which an object or body defies gravity and appears to float or fly. In the Catholic tradition, many mystics and saints are reported to have levitated.[15]

They attempted "to make sense of their experiences by trying to fit them into their own culture's interpretive framework, but this effort appears to present a struggle for them."[16] Thus, for Teresa the being of light was an angel, while for Edward it was just a being of light. But for John Mack her case was that of an extraterrestrial.[17]

Herbert Thurston, a Jesuit priest and scholar, studied numerous cases of Catholic mystics who generated a radiant form of light while praying. The examples are so numerous that Thurston was strongly inclined to believe that they were literal.[18]

Diana Pasulka describes and notes, "Placing Teresa's descriptions of her levitation beside modern reports of similar instances in the "UFO literature" is revealing. Carlos noted that he was taken up by a beam of light into the clouds and that while he was there he saw "the edge of a ship in the clouds" and multiple beings of light."[19]

He also notes: "Teresa's descriptions of her air travel are similar. A cloud appears, and then "the cloud rises to heaven, taking the soul with it, and begins to show it the features of the kingdom He has prepared for it. I do not know whether this is an accurate comparison, but in point of fact that is how it happens"[20]

Like Teresa, today non-mystical people see balls of light and glowing aerial objects.[21]

The Catholic Church, the authentic apparitions of Fatima and Freemasonry

It has been said that "the events of Fatima constituted the most exceptional "religious" event of the 20th century."[22] However, I agree more with Gerald O'Collins and Eamond Duffy that it was the Second Vatican Council.[23]

However, we will later see that both events are basically united by the content and spirit that shaped them both.

As for the first event, in 1917, three Portuguese shepherd children, Jacinta and Francisco Marto, as well as Lucia dos Santos, experienced the apparition of the "Virgin Mary," illuminated by a radiance of heavenly lights. Apparently, the "Virgen" told the

---

[14] Ibid, p. 379.

[15] Ibid, p. 383.

[16] Ibid, p. 379.

[17] Ibid, pp. 381, 382.

[18] Ibid, pp. 382, 383; citing Thurston 2013, 162.

[19] Ibid, p. 383; citing Mack 2007, 6859.

[20] Ibid; quoted in Cohen, 136.

[21] Ibid, p. 384.

[22] Joaquim Fernandes and Fina d'Armada, El Secreto de Fátima: La historia oculta de las misteriosas apariciones y la conspiración de los jesuitas (Ediciones Nowtilus S.l., April, 2007), p. 17.

[23] Gerald O'Collins, SJ, The Second Vatican Council: Message and Meaning (Michael Glazier Book/Liturgical Press, 2014), p. vii; Andrew Brown (October 11, 2012), How the second Vatican council responded to the modern world, The Guardian.

children three secrets about the destiny of the world. These contacts were followed by an unexplained aerial phenomenon that became popularly known as "The Miracle of the Sun": supposedly, thousands of frightened and crowded spectators saw the sun "dance" in Fatima, Portugal.[24]

By August, the apparitions at Fatima were uniting Catholics throughout Portugal.[25]

Thousands and thousands of the faithful made pilgrimages to Cova da Iria, in Fatima, on the 13th of each month in eager anticipation of the reappearance of the so-called "Our Lady."[26]

For its part, in previous chapters, we saw that in the 19th and 20th centuries, Freemasonry gained much political power and its ascendancy was attested in many countries in Europe and Latin America.[27] The same was true, of course, in the United States.

In Portugal, with the assassination of King Dom Carlos and his son Dom Felipe on February 1, 1918, the Freemasons came to power in the nation. When Dom Manuel II became king, he was overthrown by a revolution of Freemasons in 1910. They then began to persecute the Catholic Church, especially priests and religious, expelling the Cardinal Patriarch of Lisbon.

Assuming control of the government, in 1911 the Masons in office passed a severely anti-religious law; and Alfonso Costa, the leader of the Masons, boasted that in two generations Catholicism would be eliminated from Portugal. Thus the country was dominated by Freemasons, and thus with officials belonging to Freemasonry; and these huge gatherings of faithful Catholics were seen as a threat to their political power.[28] Fearing that it would encourage the Portuguese people to rise up and support the overthrown pro-Catholic monarchs, the Freemasons conspired to forcibly stop the meetings at Cova da Iria. Thus, Artur de Oliveira Santos, the administrator of the district of Vila Nova de Ourem, as well as founder-president of the Masonic Lodge of Vila Nova de Ourem, summoned the three child witnesses of the apparitions and their parents to appear before him on August 11 at the Vila Nova town hall, but only Lucia and her father attended. Having failed to convince Lucia to tell him the contents of the secret and to promise never to return to Cova da Iria, he told her and her father to leave, and threatened the children.

When the thirteenth day arrived, Santos kidnapped the three children and took them to the prison in Ourem. Confident that they would give in under pressure and confess to him that the apparitions in Cova were an "ecclesiastical conspiracy" designed to restore the monarchy, he tried to bribe them with money and expensive gifts, but it didn't work. So he threatened to throw them into a cauldron of boiling oil. However, none of this worked, so he let them go.

The "lady" appeared at noon in Cova da Iria, as she said she would.

---

[24] Joaquim Fernandes and Fina d'Armada, El Secreto de Fátima: La historia oculta de las misteriosas apariciones y la conspiración de los jesuitas (Ediciones Nowtilus S.I., April, 2007), p. 17.
[25] David Michael Lindsay, The Woman and the Dragon: Apparitions of Mary (Pelican Publishing Company, Gretna, Louisiana 2000), p. 130.
[26] Ibid.
[27] Father Andrew Apostoli, C.F.R., Fatima For Today: The Urgent Marian Message of Hope (Ignatius Press, San Francisco, 2010), ob. cit. Note: unless otherwise noted, this is the same source.
[28] David Michael Lindsay, The Woman and the Dragon: Apparitions of Mary (Pelican Publishing Company, Gretna, Louisiana 2000), p. 130. Note: unless otherwise noted, hereafter it is the same page.

But officially, it has been documented that at first there were apparitions of "angels," followed some time later by the apparition of the "Virgin Mary." That official account states that in the spring of 1916, the three children were with their families' sheep one day in Cabeco; when after eating lunch and briefly praying the rosary together, they began to play and a strong wind shook the treetops. Then they witnessed "a young man, about fourteen or fifteen years old, whiter than snow, transparent as crystal when the sun shines through it and of great beauty."[29]

Astonished and without saying anything, the "angel" said: "Do not be afraid. I am the Angel of Peace. Pray with me." Then he would have taught them to pray to God, Jesus and Mary, and then disappeared.[30]

A second apparition took place in the summer of that year; informing the children to pray more than they were accustomed to, and that Jesus and Mary had plans for them.[31]

The "angel" appeared to them once again.[32]

And such manifestations prepared the way for the apparition of the "Virgin Mary." The first of them occurred on May 13, 1917, when it was the liturgical celebration of Our Lady of the Blessed Sacrament.[33] The "lady" would have told them that she would appear above the oak tree on the 13th of each month until October.[34]

But as Andrew Basiago aptly pointed out, that "Whatever the truth, the Fatima apparitions were not properly investigated until sixty years later. The original records of the case remained locked away under guard for six decades in secret archives within the Fatima Shrine. The heavenly secrets in these archives contained what religion could not admit and what science could not explain."[35]

In 1978, two young Portuguese historians, Joaquim Fernandes and Fina d'Armada, were granted unprecedented access to the original archives of the case. For twenty-five years, they spent researching the actual facts of the Fatima case, digging deep into historical records; such as newspapers and magazines, weather reports and letters written by witnesses.[36]

The documents revealed that the children did not actually interact with an apparition of the Virgin Mary, but instead with a hologram of a luminous being, projected by a beam of light emitted by an object hovering above them. The researchers also interviewed witnesses who were among the youngest observers of the Fatima event, or, the "Miracle of the Sun." Both historians "identified many relevant connections between the enigmatic events that occurred at Fatima and numerous other episodes recorded in the strange and illustrious annals of the history of ufology. They established that there were many UFO cases before and after 1917 that unfolded in a manner similar to the events at Fatima."[37]

---

[29] Father Andrew Apostoli, C.F.R., Fatima For Today: The Urgent Marian Message of Hope (Ignatius Press, San Francisco, 2010), p. 22.

[30] Ibid, pp. 23, 24.

[31] Ibid, pp. 26, 27.

[32] Ibid, p. 31 et seq.

[33] Ibid, p. 33.

[34] Francis Johnston, Fatima: The Great Sign (TAN Books, 2010), ob. cit.

[35] Joaquim Fernandes and Fina d'Armada, El Secreto de Fátima: La historia oculta de las misteriosas apariciones y la conspiración de los jesuitas (Ediciones Nowtilus S.I., April, 2007), p. 17.

[36] Ibid, p. 18.

[37] Ibid, p. 19.

The Catholic Church would cover up the true nature of the Fatima apparitions in 1941, and presented them as Marian in order to reinforce Catholic orthodoxy.[38]

Four of the most important Portuguese newspapers predicted the events: -*Diário de Notícias* from Lisboa, on March 10, 1917, two months before the first appearance of May 13. *O Primeiro de Janeiro*, the most important newspaper of the time in Porto, published a front-page story dated two days before the May 13 event. Similarly, bulletins published on May 13 in two other Porto newspapers, *Jornal de Notícias* and *Liberdade*, announced that something big would happen on that date.[39] These predictions were the work of two groups of psychics who described themselves as "spiritualists;" based in the cities of Lisbon and Porto.[40] There is no trace of any connection between these groups and the children of the apparitions, nor with any kind of conspiracy.[41]

For example, on February 7, 1917, in one of the congregated "spiritualist" groups, one of the members received a message through "automatic writing":

"It is not for you to be judges. He who is to judge you would not like your prejudices. Have faith and be patient. It is not our custom to predict the future. The arcana of the future are impenetrable, although, at times, God allows a corner of the veil that covers it to move slightly. Have confidence in our prophecy. May 13th will be a day of great joy for good spirits everywhere. Have faith and be good. *Ego Sum Charitas* ("I am love"). You will always have your friends by your side, who will guide your steps and help you in your work. *Ego Sum Charitas.* The bright light of the Morning Star will illuminate the way.

"- Stella Matutina"[42]

The original Fatima records describe the "lady" who appeared to the shepherds as being approximately one meter tall.[43]

Father Manuel Marques Ferreira, in his notes on the Second Apparition;

"What she wore was: a white cloak that extended from her head to the end of the skirt, which was golden from the waist to the part below the two cords [there may have been a typographical error: "two cords instead of "from the two cords"] which crossed above and below and at the hem, everything was golden and together. The skirt was white and gold with cords, which crossed it vertically but only reached to the knees; the coat was white not gold, and had only two or three gold cords at the cuffs; she wore no shoes, but white stockings with nothing gold; at her neck she wore a gold chain from which hung a medallion."
"This medallion that hung, interpreted as a "ball" in 1922, will be transformed into the "Immaculate Heart of Mary" 20 years later in "Fatima two"..."[44]

---

[38] Ibid, p. 20.
[39] Ibid, p. 25.
[40] Ibid, pp. 25, 26.
[41] Ibid, p. 26.
[42] Ibid, p. 34.
[43] Ibid, p. 38.
[44] Ibid, pp. 202, 203.

Although the seers said that in one of the lady's hands was the broken heart of Mary surrounded by thorns, the original documents show that this certainty is not correct; for Lucia recorded that it was a sphere of light from which emanated an immense light that was projected towards the ground and towards the sky.[45]

But there were pre-appearances of another figure, which took place in 1915; but at that time Lucia was with other children: she saw a figure that seemed to be entirely wrapped in a white sheet, but the figure did not say anything. Lucia did not believe it was "Our Lady."[46] "She" appeared again in 1916, but this time approaching Lucia. They distinguished her features as those of a young man of about fourteen or fifteen years of age, who was whiter than snow and became transparent as crystal when the sun's rays touched "her." They described her as incredibly beautiful.[47]

Another girl named Carolina Carreira, had another apparition, but on July 28, 1917: she saw walking inside a stone fence a strange "child" between eight and eleven years old, near the same oak tree where the lady was appearing, and suddenly she seemed to hear inside her: "'Go there and pray three Hail Marys; 'go there and pray three Hail Marys'." But the "child" had long hair, so it could be a "girl" or "the lady."[48]

Portugal is a country of mystery, where the worship of female deities was common, such as the goddess Mora, who seduced men and killed them after obtaining what "she" wanted.[49]

Many apparitions qualified as "Marian" have occurred in Portugal, both before and after 1917.

And what about the miracle of the sun which occurred on October 13, 1917 before several thousand witnesses? They said they saw a cloud in front of the sun, which opened and from the opening a disk came down, which then rose back to the cloud; which then moved away and they saw a silver-colored disk, but not shiny or opaque.[50]

Engineer Mario Godinho, who was an eyewitness, said that the "star" was "magnetic," and like "unpolished glass."[51] Dr. Almeida Garrett said it was an opaque silver-colored disk. Even people who were 20 miles south of Fatima witnessed the phenomenon.[52]

Other witnesses reported seeing flickering lights around the disk. Still others said it was wider at the bottom. Several more claimed to have seen three occupants inside, waving to the people: some said they were Mary, Jesus, and Joseph. Father Goias, also an eyewitness, said that the disk changed its color to a tan color and that it was spinning.[53]

It has been estimated that the disc flew over the witnesses at a height of 50 meters or more. It made astonishing maneuvers before the terrified people present, who

[45] Ibid, pp. 137, 213.

[46] Ibid, pp. 82-85.

[47] Ibid, p. 88.

[48] Ibid, pp. 109-123.

[49] L. A. Marzulli (Producer) L. A. Marzulli (Director). (2018), Fatima 2 Strange Phenomenon (L. A. Marzulli).

[50] Ibid.

[51] Joaquim Fernandes and Fina d'Armada, El Secreto de Fátima: La historia oculta de las misteriosas apariciones y la conspiración de los jesuitas (Ediciones Nowtilus S.I., April, 2007), p. 62; citing Revista *Stella*, January 1962.

[52] L. A. Marzulli (Producer) L. A. Marzulli (Director). (2017), Fatima: The Miracle of the Sun or a Harbinger of Deception? (L. A. Marzulli).

[53] Ibid.

experienced physical effects, such as a buzzing of bees; as well as burns on the skin, particularly on the face, and psychological effects. Indeed, the children of Fatima had said that when these beings spoke, they always heard a buzzing sound in their heads. It is suspected to have to do with an electromagnetic field.[54]

Beholiel, a Jewish man who lived in Lisbon and worked in magazines and publications, took an impressive photograph showing the cone-shaped disk that was leaving a trail of smoke from the oak tree, rising vertically and then turning abruptly to the left.[55] It was shown to L. A. Marzulli, an American Christian researcher.

When the disc flew past, parts of cars broke off and the front windows of other cars shattered, as well as sudden combustion of gasoline.[56]

Dr. Geus said that there were no aircraft at that time in Portugal.[57]

Maria do Carmo Menezes, observed three figures "in the sun." And in the year 1918 she observed the fall of something called "fibralvina/angel hair,"[58] already mentioned briefly in this book as being common in UFO cases.[59] In fact, it fell on people in large quantities on October 13, 1917 and was photographed.[60] Fibralvina was seen in the case of the oval UFO that appeared in Oléron, France, on October 17, 1952; and from which small metallic spheres came out. The UFO left a large quantity of fibralvina or angel hair in a tree.[61] There is also the case occurred in the town of Évora in Portugal, on November 2, 1952, a little more than two weeks after the previous one, where a UFO appeared, followed by another one later, spherical above and in circular form below - but like a jellyfish, while it remained suspended for half an hour, when it left at great speed.[62] Fibralvina or "angel hair" is a luminous fiber which, according to laboratory tests, are filaments that do not withstand the temperature of the hands.[63] As soon as the incident occurred, gelatinous threads or angel hair began to appear throughout the region, leaving almost everything submerged in white.

For their part, military and scientists from the University of Lisbon began to collect samples for some tests and examinations. The results showed that it was a unicellular organism with unknown characteristics; about 4mm long and formed by tentacles made

---

[54] Ibid.

[55] L. A. Marzulli (Producer) L. A. Marzulli (Director) (2018), Fatima 2 Strange Phenomenon (L. A. Marzulli). Note: the photograph, number 13 in the archives of the official website of Fatima, kept by the Portuguese Catholic Church, is the same one, where the flying disk can be appreciated: https://www.fatima.pt/es/multimedia/images/19171013 Accessed January 29, 2024.

[56] Ibid.

[57] Ibid.

[58] Joaquim Fernandes and Fina d'Armada, El Secreto de Fátima: La historia oculta de las misteriosas apariciones y la conspiración de los jesuitas (Ediciones Nowtilus S.I., April, 2007), p. 212, 149; citing Doc. A Voz.

[59] Ibid, p. 149; citing Doc. A Voz.

[60] L. A. Marzulli (Producer) L. A. Marzulli (Director). (2017), Fatima: The Miracle of the Sun or a Harbinger of Deception? (L. A. Marzulli).

[61] Stan Seers, UFOs, the Case for Scientific Myopia (Vantage Press, 1983), p. 181.

[62] Zilke Lemmer (Writer), Dirk Michiels (Writer), Miranda Watts (Writer), & Kasia Uscinska and Matthew Wortman (Directors) (2012, November 27). Episode 3 (Season 1, Episode 3) [TV Series Episode]. Robert Strange (Executive Producer), UFO Europe: The Untold Stories. National Geographic. Note: unless otherwise noted, this is the same source.

[63] L. A. Marzulli (Producer) L. A. Marzulli (Director). (2017), Fatima: The Miracle of the Sun or a Harbinger of Deception? (L. A. Marzulli); Galán Vázquez (August 12, 2019), An extraterrestrial living being, captured and studied eighteen years ago, Medium. Note: unless otherwise noted, this is the same source.

up of parallel filaments connected by a gelatinous substance. At the beginning of its observation, its central body was yellow, the tentacles of an intense red; but the colors changed to a brownish yellow color that became darker and darker.

A very striking aspect was when the organism, which was on a glass surface in the laboratory, raised two of its tentacles trying to stop the glass plate that would be placed on top of it, as if it had consciousness not to be flattened. A scientist, Amaral, was the one who performed the analysis and made the discoveries.

In its interior, small bodies that had grown over time were visible. The observations lasted two years until the organism disintegrated.

Fibralvina is also common not only in UFO apparitions but also in apparitions of the "Virgin Mary" and "angels."[64]

As for cases similar to the Fatima UFO, on May 13, 1925, Luís António Carraça and other witnesses saw what appeared to be the sun at dawn, perfectly round but then changed its outline to an irregular formation, and then immediately appeared a series of dark-colored globules, rotating hastily back and forth around the sun.[65]

But there was also a typical "solar miracle" observed during a series of "Marian" apparitions in Baiturité, Brazil.[66]

And healings have been experienced as a result of these "Marian" apparitions. The being who appears is described as "Lady" and the connected witnesses are in these cases invariably women - in Portugal, except for Fatima (and Medjugorje) - and in addition: "they request the construction of chapels in specific places."[67] The phenomenon is inclined here to favor and strengthen Catholicism.

How did we go from the Fatima 1 version to Fatima 2, as Fina d'Armada and Joaquim Fernandes rightly point out? Well, the Jesuit Fathers José da Silva Aparicio, José Bernardo Gonçalves -Lucia's teachers-, Francisco Rodriguez, and La Chaize, in their respective turns, recognizing that the Masons expelled the Society of Jesus from Portugal in 1910, and due to the emerging Bolshevik Russia that threatened the desires of expansion of Catholicism, would have been the conspirators of the secret that consisted according to Lucia in "little words" (1917-1927), to two secrets (1927-1942); and in 1942 to three parts.[68]

It is not surprising, therefore, that the Belgian Jesuits detected an imposture in their supposed secrets.[69]

Very interesting in view of the real intentions of the phenomenon, is that on October 13, 1917, there were many conversions of heretics and agnostics to Catholicism.[70]

Other "Marian" apparitions have occurred in other parts of the world: Nigeria, Zeitoun, Egypt, between 1968 and 1969, and another on December 10, 2009, on top of a Coptic church, which was illuminated and accompanied by three luminous objects

---

[64] Stephen J. Spignesi, The UFO Book if Lists (Citadel Press, 2000), ob. cit.; Mara Faustino, Heaven and Hell: A Compulsively Readable Compendium of Myth, Legend, Wisdom, and Wit for Saints and Sinners (Grove/Atlantic, Incorporated, 2004), pp. 57, 58.

[65] Joaquim Fernandes and Fina d'Armada, El Secreto de Fátima: La historia oculta de las misteriosas apariciones y la conspiración de los jesuitas (Ediciones Nowtilus S.I., April, 2007), pp. 154, 155.

[66] Ibid, p. 176.

[67] Ibid, pp. 157-181.

[68] Ibid, pp. 63-69.

[69] Ibid, pp. 260-263.

[70] L. A. Marzulli (Producer) L. A. Marzulli (Director). (2018), Fatima 2 Strange Phenomenon (L. A. Marzulli).

suspended above. Also in Conyers, Georgia, in 1990. Ivory coast. Knock, Ireland in 2017.[71]

And just as "the virgin" appeared in the Mojave Desert (Our Lady of the Rocks) in 1989,[72] that desert also witnessed UFOs in 1989 and other paranormal phenomena continue.[73]

Later on, we will see other significant "Marian" apparitions.

Catholic Church's thoughts on the possibility of extraterrestrial life

During a morning Mass in May 2014, Pope Francis stated, "If an expedition of Martians arrives and some of them come to us and if one of them says: 'Me, I want to be baptized!', what would happen?"[74]

For the Roman Catholic Church, enriched by Greco-Roman philosophy, the question of the existence of other inhabited worlds began centuries ago. In the 13th century, Thomas Aquinas defended the existence of other worlds where there is life, and he began to understand its theological implications in his Third Book of Sentences.[75]

Likewise, John Buridan (1295-1363), a French priest and philosopher, wrote that affirming that there were no other inhabited worlds implied imposing limits on God's power, writing: "We hold from faith that just as God made this world, so he could make another or several worlds.[76]

An Italian Dominican friar named Giordano Bruno wrote in 1588 in his 5th dialogue in *Cause, Principle and Unity*:

"I can imagine an infinite number of worlds like the earth, with a Garden of Eden on each one. In all these Gardens of Eden, half the Adams and Eves will not eat the fruit of knowledge, but half will. But half of infinity is infinity, so an infinite number of worlds will fall from grace and there will be an infinite number of crucifixions."[77]

The 19th-century Jesuit Angelo Secchi (1818-1878), who directed the Observatory at the Jesuit Roman College (forerunner of the Vatican Observatory) and devised the first stellar classification system, thought there was life elsewhere in the universe. He did not consider this possibility a theological anomaly.[78]

Catholic thinkers were most concerned with the extraterrestrial question in the early part of the 20th century.[79] Astonished by the diversity and structure of the universe, Januarius De Concilio and Joseph Pohle used the astronomy of their time at the turn of

---

[71] Ibid.

[72] Lisa M. Bitel, Our Lady of the Rock: Vision and Pilgrimage in the Mojave Desert (Cornell University Press, 2015), ob. cit.

[73] Ron Felber, Mojave Incident: Inspired by a Chilling Story of Alien Abduction (Barricade Books, 2015), ob. cit.; M. L. Behrman, Mojave Mysteries (CreateSpace Independent Publishing Platform, 2016), ob. cit.

[74] Claire Giangravè (February 24, 2017), Could Catholicism handle the discovery of extraterrestrial life?," Crux Catholic Media.

[75] Ibid.

[76] Ibid.

[77] Ibid.

[78] John A. Coleman (February 25, 2013), Why is the Vatican Interested in the Search for Life in the Universe?," America Magazine.

[79] David Wilkinson, Science, Religion, and the Search for Extraterrestrial Intelligence (Oxford University Press, 2013), p. 148; citing Davis, 1960; Raible, 1960; Kleinz, 1960 ; Zubek, 1961; Vakoch, 2000; O'Meara, 2012: 86-7.

the century to present a series of arguments in favor of intelligent life on other planets at the end of the 19th century. Pohle's written work was very popular, and contributed to the formation of numerous thinkers. It was after the Second World War that he reawakened the interest of Catholic thinkers. David Wilkinson writes that: "From the 1950s onwards authors such as Domenico Grasso, Joaquin Salverri, Angelo Perego, Charles Davis, T. J. Zubek, John P. Kleinz, and Daniel C. Raible, on the basis of the immensity of the Universe, came to think that there must be extraterrestrial life."[80]

"[...] in 1962, the Executive Secretary of the American Rocket Society claimed that the 'liveliest speculation' about EIT came from Roman Catholic theologians (Harford, 1962: 19). It is therefore interesting to ask the question of why there was such openness among Roman Catholics." Speculations range from the influence of the Vatican Observatory to the fact that theological speculation was not restricted by the biblicism of so many Protestant churches; or whether it was due to openness to a world beyond human beings.[81]

The German Jesuit theologian, Karl Rahner, was also open to the existence of extraterrestrial life.[82]

Pierre Teilhard de Chardin, the renowned French Jesuit priest, as well as scientist, paleontologist, theologian, philosopher, and teacher, considered the possibility of life elsewhere in the cosmos.[83]

Closer to our time, Jesuit Monsignor Corrado Balducci, Vatican demonologist and exorcist, maintained until his death in 2008, that extraterrestrial life was a reality, including the vehicles in which they travel.[84] In an interview with Dr. Michael Hesemann in 1997, Balducci said again that UFOs were real and that contact does occur; that they were not angels.[85] He added that such a belief did not contradict Catholic doctrine.[86]

Likewise, Jesuit priest George Coyne, director of the Vatican Observatory from 1978 to 2006, also wondered:

"How could he be God and leave extraterrestrials in their sin? After all he was good to us. Why should he not be good to them? God chose a very specific way to redeem human beings. He sent his only Son, Jesus, to them and Jesus gave up his life so that human beings would be saved from their sin. Did God do this for extraterrestrials?"[87]

Argentine José Gabriel Fúnes, a Jesuit astronomer and director of the Vatican Observatory at the time, had said on May 13, 2008, that it was difficult to exclude the possibility of intelligent life elsewhere in the universe: "This is not in contrast with the

---

[80] Ibid, p. 149.

[81] Ibid.

[82] Ibid.

[83] Joel L. Parkyn, Exotheology: Theological Explorations of Intelligent Extraterrestrial Life (Pickwick Publications, Eugene, Oregon, 2021), ob. cit.

[84] Richard M. Dolan and Bryce Zabel, A.D. After Disclosure: When the Government Finally Reveals the Truth About Alien Contact (Red Wheel/Weiser, 2012), ob. cit.; Michael Baigent and Richard Leigh, The Inquisition (Penguin Books, 2000), ob. cit.

[85] Michael Hesemann, The Fatima Secret (Dell Publishing/Random House, Inc., New York, 2000), pp. 30, 31.

[86] Ibid, p. 31.

[87] Steven J. Dick, Many Worlds: New Universe Extraterrestrial Life (Templeton Foundation Press, Radnor, Pennsylvania, 2000), p. 187.

faith, because we cannot place limits on the creative freedom of God" [...] "To use St. Francis' words, if we consider earthly creatures as 'brothers' and 'sisters,' why can't we also speak of an 'extraterrestrial brother?'"[88]

Likewise, on the implications that the discovery of extraterrestrial life could have for Christian redemption, Funes cited the Gospel parable of the shepherd who left his flock of ninety-nine sheep to go in search of the one that was lost: "We who belong to the human race could really be that lost sheep, the sinners who need a pastor [...] God became man in Jesus in order to save us. So if there are also other intelligent beings, it's not a given that they need redemption. They might have remained in full friendship with their creator." He added that the incarnation and sacrifice of Christ was a unique and unrepeatable event. But he added that he was sure that, if necessary, God's mercy would be offered to extraterrestrials as well as to human beings.[89]

When in November 2013, I consulted with George Coyne about how belief in God might be affected given the possible finding of extraterrestrial life, and what the Holy See's position might be on that revelation and its impact in our world on people of faith and the rest of humanity, in response he shared with me a document he authored and which is in the public domain and others, where two paragraphs in particular jump out:

"The theological implications about God are getting ever more serious. Surely God is completely free to choose his methods. He certainly did not have to send his Son to us. But once he chose to do so, did he have to choose to redeem extraterrestrials in the same way? There is deeply embedded in Christian theology, throughout the Old and New Testament but especially in St. Paul and in St. John the Evangelist, the notion of the universality of God's redemption and even the notion that all creation, even the inanimate, participates in some way in his redemption.

"After this whole sequence of hypotheses, increasingly more difficult to make, theologians must accept a serious responsibility to rethink some fundamental realities within the context of religious belief. What is the human being? Could Jesus Christ, fully a human being, exist on more than one planet at more than one time? We are obviously very limited today in our ability to answer such questions. We cannot rely, even theologically, solely on God's revelation to us in the Scriptures and in the churches, since that revelation was to us and was received, therefore, in a very anthropocentric sense."[90]

What Coyne indicates is that written revelation would not be sufficient in the theological field to define the theological implications of the finding of extraterrestrial life, so we would have to enter into a new and more advanced definition of the humanity and mission of Jesus Christ, what it means to be human, and theology itself. Personally, I strongly believe that before we think about redefinitions of theology from a finding of a non-human intelligence more advanced than us, if there are presuppositions and assertions about theology that are wrong, that could lead to a

---

[88] CNS (May 22, 2008), Vatican astronomer says if aliens exist, they may not need redemption, Catholic News Service.
[89] Ibid.
[90] George V. Coyne, S.J.-VaticanObservatory, The Evolution of Intelligent Life on Earth and Possibly Elsewhere: Reflections from a Religious Tradition, p. 11; Steven J. Dick, Many Worlds: New Universe Extraterrestrial Life (Templeton Foundation Press, Radnor, Pennsylvania, 2000), p. 187.

wrong theological change on that basis. We must ask ourselves, what is the empirical and rational source/s for accepting theology as worthy of attention, and if serious, to what extent does the theological method adhere to what the sources provide for understanding God?

But let's move on: the aforementioned Jesuit theologian Karl Rahner, faced with the possibility of life elsewhere in the universe, admitted that, "in view of the immutability of God in himself and the identity of the *Logos* with God, it cannot be proved that a multiple incarnation in different histories of salvation is absolutely unthinkable."[91] Again, are there erroneous presuppositions in that statement? Guy Consolmagno, a Jesuit brother, American astronomer, planetary scientist, and director of the Vatican Astronomical Observatory since 2016, also wrote:

"Of course, if you are really eager to find a reference to extraterrestrials in the Bible, you can't do better than look at John 10: 14-16, the famous Good Shepherd passage: "I am the Good Shepherd. I know My own and My own know me, just as the Father knows Me and I know the Father. And I lay down My life for the sheep. I have other sheep that do not belong to this fold. I must bring them also, and they will listen to My voice. So there will be one flock, one shepherd." Perhaps it's not so far- fetched to see the Second Person of the Trinity, the Word, Who was present "In the beginning" (*John* 1: 1), coming to lay down His life and take it up again (*John* 10: 18) not only as the Son of Man but also as a Child of other races?"[92]

He said in 2010, that he was comfortable with the idea of baptizing an alien, but would do so "Only if they asked."[93]

Next, we quote Funes again:

"The discovery of intelligent life does not mean there's another Jesus," he said. "The incarnation of the son of God is a unique event in the history of humanity, of the universe."

He added: "If there was intelligent life (on another planet), I don't see that as a contradiction with the Christian faith."[94]

When astrophysicist and Jesuit priest Christopher Corbally of the Vatican's Mount Graham Observatory in Arizona was asked in 1994 if he would baptize an extraterrestrial, he said yes, but added ruefully, "I would first want to examine the theological data of their beliefs."[95]

---

[91] Claire Giangravè (February 24, 2017), Could Catholicism handle the discovery of extraterrestrial life?," Crux Catholic Media.

[92] Guy Consolmagno S.J., Intelligent Life in the Universe? Catholic belief and the search for extraterrestrial intelligent life (CTS Publications, Harleyford Road, London, 2005), p. 37.

[93] James Martin, S.J. (September 23, 2010), Vatican Astronomer Would Baptize Alien, America Magazine; Alok Jha (September 17, 2010), Pope's astronomer says he would baptize an alien if it asked him, The Guardian.

[94] Abby Ohlheiser (August 1, 2015), Why the Vatican doesn't think we'll ever meet an alien Jesus, The Washington Post.

[95] Jack Hitt (May 29, 1994), Would You Baptize an Extraterrestrial?, The New York Times Magazine, ob. cit.

Funes expressed himself somewhat differently from Corbally, mentioning the hypothesis that "we human beings might be the lost sheep, the sinners in need of a shepherd. God became man in Jesus to save us. In that case, even if there were other sentient life forms, they might not be in need of redemption. They could have stayed in full harmony with their Creator."[96]

Giuseppe Tanzella-Nitti, another Jesuit astronomer and theologian at the Vatican Observatory, has stated: "The last word on the question of ET life does not come from theology, but from science. The existence of intelligent life on other planets beyond Earth is neither required nor excluded by any theological argument. For theology, as for all humanity, all we can do is wait, patiently."[97]

But he also indicated:

"Every believer in God would certainly see any eventual meeting with a non-terrestrial civilization as an extraordinary experience. A believer would be fundamentally inclined to manifest a sense of respect in such an encounter, to recognize our common origin and the new possibility of better understanding the relationship between God and the whole of creation. A similar encounter, and perhaps the ensuing dialogue, would have a "religious" dimension in the more natural sense of the term. At the same time, it seems important to note that a believer who is respectful of the requirements of scientific reasoning would not be obliged to renounce his own faith in God simply on the basis of the reception of new, unexpected information of a religious character from extraterrestrial civilizations. In the first place, human reason itself would suggest the need to submit this new "religious content" coming from outside the Earth to an analysis of reasonableness and credibility (analogous to what we are accustomed to do when any religious content is proposed to us, on Earth); once the trustworthiness of the information has been verified, the believer should try to reconcile such new information with the truth that he or she already knows and believes on the basis of the revelation of the One and Triune God, conducting a re-reading inclusive of the new data, similar to that which would be applied in an ordinary interreligious dialogue."[98]

Malachi Martin, the famous Irish Jesuit priest and conservative, believed that extraterrestrials were monitoring our planet.[99]

What about some efforts to promote an analysis and study of the possibility of extraterrestrial life in the Vatican? For example, on November 6-10, 2009, a meeting sponsored by the Vatican Observatory and the Pontifical Academy of Sciences brought together 30 scientists from around the world for a study on astrobiology. Chris Impey, then director of the Steward Observatory and the Department of Astronomy at the University of Arizona, said they were very close to finding the answer to finding life in

[96] Claire Giangravè (February 24, 2017), Could Catholicism handle the discovery of extraterrestrial life?," Crux Catholic Media.

[97] Ted Peters with Martinez Hewlett, Joshua M. Moritz, and Robert John Russell, Astrotheology: Science and Theology Meet Extraterrestrial Life (Cascade Books, Eugene, Oregon, 2018), note 32, p. 66.

[98] Giuseppe Tanzella-Nitti, Extraterrestrial life, Interdisciplinary Encyclopedia of Religion and Science (Advanced School for Interdisciplinary Research (ADSIR), Pontifical University of the Holy Cross, 2008): https://inters.org/extraterrestrial-life Accessed September 7, 2023.

[99] (Feb. 2, 2020), Malachi Martin on Alien Life - "Aliens have been monitoring the Earth for at least 600 years," MalachiMartinAudio: https://www.youtube.com/watch?v=VKgQiT2vM80 Accessed Sept. 19, 2023.

the universe. Jonathan Lunine, then professor of planetary science and physics, also at the University of Arizona participated.[100] We are intrigued by his participation, as we will see later in this chapter.

"Funes said that even though the study week looked exclusively at scientific evidence and theories, it was "very important that the church is involved in this type of research" looking at life in the cosmos."[101]

The Italian newspaper *La Stampa*, published in May 2010 that a conference was held that month in the pontifical parish of Sant'Anna in the Vatican City, which brought together leading UFO experts to talk about extraterrestrials, where it was affirmed that the phenomenon is real. The conference was not organized by the Vatican, but it did popularize it.[102]

Another event to discuss the issue was held at the same Vatican parish on October 30, 2013 by the Italian organization CIFAS. [103]

CIFAS held similar events at the Vatican on other dates: on January 18, 2017;[104] on January 31, 2018;[105] in February 2019; February 12, 2020; and April 19, 2023.[106]

Also in February 2013, the Vatican Observatory Foundation sponsored a seminar on astrobiology, discussing from a scientific, philosophical and theological perspective the possibility of extraterrestrial life and its implications for the world.[107] In March 2014, the Vatican co-sponsored a science conference in Arizona, USA, where again the possibility of life elsewhere in the universe was discussed.[108]

George Coyne, who in the 1990s was director of the Vatican Astronomical Observatory, admitted to Dr. Steven M. Greer that UFOs and extraterrestrials were real.[109] Greer affirmed that in the Vatican, both the Society of Jesus and the Knights of Malta, have sectors that keep in the most absolute secrecy what they know about the UFO and "extraterrestrial" phenomena.[110]

Although it is true that Dr. Steven M. Greer tends to exaggerate too much, the statements provided seem to be close to reality.

---

[100] Carol Glatz (Nov. 11, 2009), Vatican discusses extraterrestrial life, Catholic News Service.
[101] Ibid.
[102] Giacomo Galeazzi (May 6, 2010), Alieni in Vaticano, La Stampa.
[103] https://www.cifas-italia.net/convegni.html;
https://www.centroufologiconazionale.net/documenti/doc.htm Accessed September 10, 2023.
[104] https://www.cifas-italia.net/2017-xenoling.jpg Accessed September 10, 2023.
[105] https://www.cifas-italia.net/paradigmi-2018.jpg Accessed September 10, 2023.
[106] https://www.cifas-italia.net/convegni.html Accessed September 10, 2023.
[107] John A. Coleman (February 25, 2013), Why is the Vatican Interested in the Search for Life in the Universe?," America Magazine.
[108] Megan Gannon (March 16, 2014), Is Alien Life Out There? Vatican Observatory Co-Hosts Science Conference in Arizona, Space: https://www.space.com/25060-vatican-observatory-alien-life-conference.html Accessed September 8, 2023.
[109] Steven M. Greer M.D., Hidden Truth: Forbidden Knowledge (ZTT Consulting, Lansing, MI, 2013), p. 217.
[110] Ibid, pp. 217, 218.

The people's advocate Daniel Sheehan and the Jesuits, the Vatican, and Project Blue Book

Take the case of the well-known constitutional and public interest lawyer, Daniel P. Sheehan, who has spent more than fifty years fighting the National Security State, since the Pentagon Papers and Iran-Contra scandals, as two of his most emblematic cases.[111] He then became a whistleblower and legal advisor to the Disclosure Project in 2001, a testimony we will quote shortly.[112]

According to Sheehan, since he felt contrary to the narrative that the UFO phenomenon is a threat, he indicated that "we have to come forward with a positive set of programs; a positive vision of this; and that's why I'm trying to help get the Vatican and the Jesuit order to become involved and and putting forth, you know, a discussion about the theological and philosophical challenges that this presents to us, but it's not a national security threat."[113]

Sheehan was an attorney for Luis Elizondo, the former director of AATIP, the Pentagon's UFO program for the Department of Defense before its successors (UAP Task Force and AARO). The attorney defended Elizondo on the Pentagon's denigrating role in AATIP.[114]

In order to better understand Sheehan's role on the UFO issue and the Vatican, we must go back to an episode under the Jimmy Carter administration.

Carter had promised that if he became president of the nation, he would reveal what the government knows about the UFO phenomenon.[115]

As president-elect of the United States (1977-1981), Carter began the process of getting the information disclosed. In his first briefing with then Director of Central Intelligence George H. W. Bush, where, according to Marcia Smith, Carter asked Bush for information about UFOs and extraterrestrial intelligence.[116] Bush denied him that information because it would reveal "sources and methods" of the country's intelligence-gathering resources, which were above Carter's top-secret clearance level as president-elect. The only way to be informed about it was on a "need to know" basis. But Bush told him that some of the information he wanted was in the National Archives and available for consultation.

By that time, Sheehan worked (1975-1985) as chief counselor for the U.S. Jesuit headquarters in Washington, D.C. in the office of National Social Ministry, which is

---

[111] Daniel Sheehan, The People's Advocate: The Life and Legal History of America's Most Fearless Public Interest Lawyer (Counterpoint, Berkeley, 2013); Robert J. Barnhart, Hadrien Majoie, Darren Patterson, Chip Story, DGZ60 (Producers) Michael Mazzola (Director). (2020), Close Encounters of the Fifth Kind. (The Orchard).

[112] Robert J. Barnhart, Hadrien Majoie, Darren Patterson, Chip Story, DGZ60 (Producers) Michael Mazzola (Director). (2020), Close Encounters of the Fifth Kind. (The Orchard).

[113] Ibid.

[114] Bryan Bender (May 26, 2021), Ex-official who revealed UFO project accuses Pentagon of 'disinformation' campaign, Politico.

[115] Larry Holcombe, The Presidents and UFOs: A Secret History from FDR to Obama (St. Martin's Press, New York, 2015), ob. cit.

[116] William J. Birnes & Joel Martin, UFOs and The White House: What Did Our Presidents Know and When Did They Know It? (Skyhorse Publishing, 2018), ob. cit. Note: unless otherwise noted, this is the same source.

their public policy office dealing with major political issues.[117] He served under the Superior General of the Jesuits, Pedro Arrupe.

In January 1977, Marsha Smith, Director of the Science and Technology Division of the Congressional Research Service of the Library of Congress, telephoned Sheehan. She had been informed by the Science and Technology Committee of the House of Representatives that President Jimmy Carter had contacted congressional staff to conduct a major investigation undertaken by the U.S. Congress. This, because George Bush Sr., as director of central intelligence, advised Carter "to go to the United States Congress, to the Science and Technology Committee of the House of Representatives, and ask them to undertake a process by means of which the Congress can get certain documents declassified." Carter wanted to know whether or not extraterrestrial intelligence exists, and "what percentage of these UFO sightings and reports that have been coming to the government have been investigated and is there any evidence indicating they might represent vehicles from an extraterrestrial civilization that are visiting our planet."

Thus, at Marsha Smith's request, Sheehan returned to Jesuit headquarters and spoke with Father William J. Davis, who was the Director of the National Social Ministry office in the Oregon Province of the Jesuits, and asked him whether or not he would consent to sign a letter from the National Headquarters of the Jesuits in the United States requesting documentation on the UFO phenomenon and on extraterrestrial life from the Vatican library Subsequently, the Jesuit in charge of the library was sent a formal letter and asked him if they, at the Jesuit headquarters, "could get access to that section of the Vatican library where the information about UFOs and extraterrestrial intelligence was." But about two weeks later they received a letter in reply saying that they could not have access to that information.

Sheehan and Davis were stunned, since the request came from the headquarters of the Jesuit order in the United States. With ten Jesuit provinces in the U.S., that's more than any other area of the world, so it's a pretty influential place, Sheehan says. And The U.S. Catholic Conference of Bishops was a major power in the Catholic world."

Therefore, they prepared a second, much more detailed letter, assuring them that Sheehan would personally go to Rome and inspect the documents, agreeing to abide by the conditions that would be established. However, two weeks later, they again received the reply that they could not access that section of the Vatican library.

Now, some six weeks later, Marsha Smith informed Sheehan that Project SETI (Search for Extraterrestrial Intelligence), the California Jet Propulsion Laboratory, recently saw its budget for the coming year cut in half. And the people at the lab asked him if he "would accompany them to the corresponding budget meetings." Sheehan recounts in his own words:

"Long story short: The budget was reinstated and the top fifty scientists at the Jet Propulsion Laboratory—as a thank you for any help I may have rendered—invited me to come to the JPL and to deliver a closed-door seminar on the theological implications of the search for extraterrestrial intelligence. I received permission to do this—the Jesuits were suddenly more interested in the subject. They were quite put

---

[117] Steven M. Greer, M.D., Unacknowledged: An Exposé of the World's Greatest Secret (A & M Publishing, L.L.C., West Palm Beach, FL, 2017), ob. cit. Note: unless otherwise noted, this is the same source.

off too by not being allowed to see this stuff at the Vatican library and began to suspect there was something there."

Subsequently, Sheehan telephoned Marsha Smith and said, "Look, if I'm going to get to go out and meet with the top fifty scientists of the Jet Propulsion Laboratory on the SETI project, I would like to, if I could, get access to the material that you're developing here for the president. That way, at least I'm informed." She proposed to Sheehan to make him a special assistant researcher for the Congressional Research Service on that specific project, and she asked him what he wanted to see in preparation for that seminar. The constitutional lawyer replied that he wanted to see the classified portions of Project Blue Book.

About a week later, Marsha informed him that they agreed and would send them to the Library of Congress the following Saturday, where he would be given a brief window of time to go in and review those files.

Sheehan had to go to the newly opened Madison Building in May, across Independence Avenue from the Library of Congress. There wasn't a single office set up, but there was no one there either.

He met a guard at the main entrance, where Sheehan identified himself. After the guard confirmed by phone that Sheehan was to be there, he escorted him to the basement and told him which room he was to be in. After he in the hallway, Sheehan came to a part where he saw two men waiting for him. After showing his ID to someone sitting at at a desk, he told Sheehan, "You're not going to be allowed to take your briefcase in there; you're not going to be allowed to take any notes, and you're only going to get about an hour in there." So the lawyer was left with only a yellow notepad under his arm.

Once inside, he saw a table with several beige-green boxes stacked on it. He thought that if he started reading documents he wouldn't get much, so he decided to look for photographs. He found a couple of boxes with film and a small projector and turned it on, but there was UFO stuff he had seen elsewhere, so he looked in some more boxes, in one of which there was a wrapper that said Top-Secret. And he said, "Beneath it was a canister of microfiche and a machine with a little hand crank. I threaded through the first microfiche… only it's more documents. The next… more documents… and more.

Finally I hit upon a microfiche of photographs… and there they were! I mean, there wasn't any doubt about what this was—this was a crashed UFO." He recounts in his own words:

"It was a winter scene; there was snow on the ground. There was a recovery team present. Two men were measuring the craft with a tape measure. From these black and white photographs you could see this big trench mark… like the ship had come through this field and the UFO had struck the side of this embankment. It had kind of nosed into it, so you couldn't quite see the bottom part. There was a dome on top. And there were little engraving marks on the side of it."

The lawyer continues his story:

"There was a close-up photograph of the section of the craft that had these symbols. I looked at it, then I turned around at the door of the room I was in to check on the guards… they weren't looking.

Quickly, I opened the yellow legal pad to its cardboard backing. Focusing the microfiche projection of the symbols onto the cardboard, I traced the entire long string of symbols that were there using my pen. And I was absolutely fastidious about it to make sure they were exact.

When I finished, I cranked the microfiche out of the projector and put everything away in the exact same spot where I had found it. Then I announced I was done."

Sheehan went back to Jesuit headquarters, straight to William Davis' office, and showed the cardboard to him. Sheehan never called Marsha Smith about what happened; nor did he tell the SETI people. He then comments:

"Marsha shared with me the findings from the Congressional Research Service report on the probability of extraterrestrial existence and the analysis of the UFO phenomenon. It opened right up with saying the Congressional Research Service, having reviewed unclassified and classified data, has come to the conclusion that there are at least two to six other highly, technologically-developed intelligent civilizations inside our galaxy. Just a simply stated fact; just like that. And this was the information provided to the president.

With regard to the UFOs, they pointed out that there were seven or eight different shapes of craft that were classically reported, with 20% credible, reliable accounts of vehicles that they concluded were not ours, and did not belong to the Soviet Union, and appeared to have technological capabilities that made it absolutely clear that they were of no known origin on this planet. Only they wouldn't go on to the next step… "Ergo, they must be from some other planet." They didn't say that in the report."

Although there are those who dispute this story,[118] the reality is that Sheehan has maintained his account to the present day.

Sheehan said in early October and late November 2023, that when José Gabriel Funes, being director of the Vatican Astronomical Observatory said in May 2008 that extraterrestrial life could exist, that he went to the Vatican and spoke personally with Johan Ickx, the director of the Vatican Archives about releasing the documents that the Vatican has on the UFO phenomenon and "extraterrestrial" life, but that he could not comment further.[119] He also spoke with Funes, to try to get them to share with the world. Funes told Sheehan, "Look Dan, we're not talking here about the discovery of some single cell life form under some frozen sea on some distant moon in some far off galaxy. We're talking about another highly intelligent, highly technologically developed but non-human species right here in our Milky Way galaxy. And this is what we have to start getting our people prepare for. And so this idea of how we're going to coordinate getting this information that has been kept secret for so long by these authorities like the Catholic Church."[120]

[118] Larry Holcombe, The Presidents and UFOs: A Secret History from FDR to Obama (St. Martin's Press, New York, 2015), ob. cit.
[119] (November 30, 2023), Controlled Or Catastrophic Disclosure w/ Daniel Sheehan, Engaging The Phenomenon: https://www.youtube.com/watch?v=2S5Iojd6v9s 1:08:53 onwards. Accessed January 30, 2024.
[120] (Oct. 3, 2023), The Government & UFO Secrecy: Live Updates from Washington, DC By Daniel Sheehan and Steve Bassett, RVMLResourceCenter: https://www.youtube.com/watch?v=sSpQsovx1_A 1:09:48 onward. Accessed January 30, 2024.

Coincidence or not, this effort began the year after the start of AATIP at the U.S. Department of Defense. Luis Elizondo had said that the Vatican took an interest in what the program was doing, years before the program's existence was made public.

Jorge Mario Bergoglio's influences on UFOs and non-human entities:
1. The Jesuit priest and astronomer Benito Segundo Reyna
The Jesuit priest Juan Antonio Bussolini, astronomer and director of the Cosmic Physics Observatory of San Miguel in Cordoba, Argentina, who died in 1966, was the first Argentine clergyman to speak about the possibility of life on other worlds and flying saucers.[121]

"Not three months ago, I sent to the spectroscopic laboratory of the Vatican, which specializes in aerolites, two curious specimens to be examined; one was a piece of semi-melted iron that had been given to me as a souvenir of one of the expeditions to Aconcagua of the ruined Link and which I considered a valuable specimen of a probable cosmic message; and another, some pumice residues of rare configuration, also given to this Observatory, with the certainty that they were the remains of a flying saucer that had been sighted by the Serranos of La Rioja and whose explosion I had witnessed. The examination of both specimens has already been carried out; the scientific communication reports that what I thought was a vulgar rubble and the Serranos rest... (a word which cannot be read in the magazine) flying saucer have turned out to belong to an aerolite which, according to an expert from the Smithsonian Institute in Washington, is of inestimable value."[122]

However, it was Benito Segundo Reyna, who was a Jesuit priest and astronomer who died in 1982, who was the most influential among them. He was also the best known religious UFO enthusiast of the time.[123]

Peruvian researcher Ricardo González, said that Benito Reyna had given conferences in Buenos Aires years before an event called "la huella del pajarillo" (the footprint of the little bird),[124] which refers to the following:

"On the night of January 9, 1986, on a farm near the Sierra del Pajarillo, Mrs. Esperanza, her sister Sara and their 12-year-old grandson, Gabriel, were playing cards. Suddenly, a powerful red light illuminated the room. They looked out and, seeing that it was moving over the hills, they ordered to close the windows and thought it was the 'bad light'," says Luz about the story that made the place famous.

"But the boy looked out twice: "He saw something like a flattened ball with windows, with a red light and a lighter one, plus lines of white lights. After that he never saw it again.

---

[121] Luis B. (November 9, 1954), Los Platos Voladores: El Gran Misterio del Siglo XX, Esto Es, Year II, No. 50, p. 7.

[122] Ibid.

[123] Alejandro Agostinelli, Invasores: Historias reales de extraterrestres en la Argentina (Sudamericana, 2012), ob. cit.

[124] (February 13, 2018), Ricardo González (Congress 2017, Capilla del Monte), Ricardo González Corpancho: https://www.youtube.com/watch?v=V9_GZTTp4GM 21:14 onwards. Accessed September 1, 2023.

"The next day uncle Manuel Gómez arrived and told them he had seen a black spot in the shape of an oval on the southeastern slope of Pajarillo. The track of burned grasses measured 70 by 120 meters, and was in the same place where they had seen the lights."[125]

In spite of the criticisms about the quality of the witnesses of that event and the nature of it,[126] what should be emphasized is that the Jesuit Benito Segundo Reyna, gave conferences before the footprint of the little bird in 1986, talking about "Witaicon," the name of a luminous entity that appeared before certain witnesses in the Uritorco Mountain. The researcher Guillermo Alfredo Terrera quotes him in one of his books (which one?), that Benito Segundo Reyna was closely linked to contactism.[127]

Carlos Alberto Segura, collaborator of the newspaper *La Vanguardia*, said that in one of Reyna's lectures given in 1969, he showed photographs of UFOs and gave examples of the activity of "extraterrestrial life" in the everyday world -Carlos was then Director of Culture of the Municipality-. At that time, an Italian company was building the Satellite Communications Ground Station between the El Volcán and La Vigilancia mountain ranges. Reyna asked Carlos to obtain a permit to visit the construction site, which he did not know it. When they were walking around the site, he said: "this is a place where in the early mornings -said the priest- the spectacle of the arrival of flying saucers and their wanderings must be extraordinary."[128]

Reyna was a mentor to Jesuit priest Jorge Mario Bergoglio, the current Pope Francis.[129] But at the time Reyna's hobby irritated his superiors, among them Jorge Bergoglio himself.[130]

[125] Diana Pazos (September 5, 2021), Misterio, historias de ovniS y energía en el Cerro Uritorco: cómo saltó a la fama por la enigmática Huella del Pajarillo: https://www.clarin.com/viajes/misterio-historias-ovnis-energia-cerro-uritorco-salto-fama-enigmatica-huella-pajarillo_0_at9Wdaa2h.html; accessed September 1, 2023. See for example the book: Sebastiano De Filippi, La Ciudad de la Llama Azul: Luces y sombras sobre el cerro Uritorco (Editorial Biblos, 2020).

[126] Fernando Jorge Soto Roland (January 10, 2023), "Una mentira piadosa". La «Huella del Pajarillo», entre la meteorología y el fraude, Factor-El Blog de Alejandro Agostinelli: https://factorelblog.com/2023/01/10/una-mentira-piadosa-huella-del-pajarillo-entre-la-meteorologia-y-el-fraude/ Accessed September 1, 2023.

[127] (February 13, 2018), Ricardo González (Congress 2017, Capilla del Monte), Ricardo González Corpancho: https://www.youtube.com/watch?v=V9_GZTTp4GM 21:42 onwards. Accessed September 1, 2023.

[128] (October 23, 2022), Del archivo de LV: Platos voladores en la sierra El Volcán, La Vanguardia.

[129] (February 13, 2018), Ricardo González (Congress 2017, Capilla del Monte), Ricardo González Corpancho: https://www.youtube.com/watch?v=V9_GZTTp4GM 21:42 onwards. Accessed September 1, 2023.

[130] Alejandro Agostinelli (December 5, 2023), Fabio Zerpa «científico», su papel menos convincente, Factor El Blog de Alejandro Agostinelli: https://factorelblog.com/2014/12/05/fabio-zerpa-cientifico-su-papel-menos-convincente/ Accessed September 18, 2023; Alejandro Agostinelli (June 28, 2013), Nunca estuvimos tan cerca de beatificar a Evita, Factor-El Blog de Alejandro Agostinelli: https://factorelblog.com/2013/06/28/evita-puede-ser-santa/ Accessed September 18, 2023.

2. Ángel Cristo Acoglanis, Pedro Romaniuk, Solari Parravicini, Pope Francis, UFOs and "extraterrestrials," and the future of the Roman Catholic Church

Two well-known Argentinean ufologists, Ángel Cristo Acoglanis and Pedro Romaniuk, knew Jorge Mario Bergoglio personally. Acoglanis claimed to receive messages from "extraterrestrials," which could be prophetic.

Jorge Bergoglio was interested in the mystic-esoteric subject, and according to multiple sources of the researcher and writer Ricardo González, Bergoglio was in Capilla del Monte, at the Hotel Roma to talk about UFO phenomena and contactism.[131] That area, Capilla del Monte, is an Argentine city and municipality north of Cordoba, where the aforementioned Uritorco mountain is located. There they talk about the mysterious "city of Erks," associated with Hindu beliefs in reincarnation, astral travel, UFO sightings and encounters with "extraterrestrials."[132]

According to Osvaldo Allie, owner of the Hotel Roma and who attended a meeting in the city of Cordoba in 1988 at the home of a mutual friend, Angel Acoglanis told Bergoglio that he would become pope. "Stop bothering!," Bergoglio replied forcefully; then Angel told Pedro Romaniuk: "He doesn't believe me that he is going to be pope."[133]

Romaniuk, who was a personal friend of Bergoglio, was also a personal friend of the "Nostradamus of America," the Argentine artist Benjamin Solari Parravicini, who died in 1974 and who also claimed to have been contacted by extraterrestrials.[134]

Let us briefly consider Parravicini's life: being a Catholic, he said that under the command of the spirit of Fray José de Aragón, as well as of other "incorporeal personalities," he made his prophetic drawings -more than a thousand-. But his supernatural experiences began in childhood. Justino, Benjamin's younger brother, told journalist Alejandro Agostinelli that "La Casona" or the mansion where Benjamin, his parents and siblings lived, was "a hotbed of strange phenomena, especially noises coming from Pelon's [Benjamín] room."[135]

One early morning, a bronze lamp rose "on its own" and crashed against the wall. And at times, the family felt "banging on the windows and shattering against the outside walls." Indeed, many eerie experiences occurred in Benjamín's bedroom.

As a child, he claimed to receive messages about simple matters and the future from fairies, goblins and elemental spirits.

One night, he dreamed that "Anita Parravicini," the spirit of his "late great-aunt," introduced him to "Saint Rita de Cassia" and "the Virgin of Guadalupe;" and that whatever he asked them for would be given to him. Later, Benjamín told the dream to his mother, who confirmed his aunt's devotion to the saint.

---

[131] (February 13, 2018), Ricardo González (Congress 2017, Capilla del Monte), Ricardo González Corpancho: https://www.youtube.com/watch?v=V9_GZTTp4GM 21:42 onwards. Accessed September 1, 2023.

[132] María Inés Palleiro (ed.), Narrativa: identidades y memorias (Editorial Dunken, Buenos Aires, 2005), pp. 56, 57.

[133] Gustavo Cairo and Roberto Villamil, Ángel Cristo Acoglanis: El portero de Erks (3R Ediciones, Buenos Aires, 2015), p. 160.

[134] Yohanan Diaz Vargas (May 2018), Francisco, el Papa ocultista, Año/Cero, Year XXIX Issue 05-334, pp. 24, 25.

[135] Alejandro Agostinelli (April 15, 2024), Vida del profeta que sigue Milei, Página 12. Nota: a no ser que se indique lo contrario, es la misma fuente.

Benjamín recounted that one night in 1936, when he entered his room with the lights off, "a very strong hand grabbed me by the neck and pulled me to the floor (...) I only managed to say: 'Oh, Jesus, my God'." Then he saw his Christ carved in wood shining, who said to him: "Faith in faith, hope in the plans, charity in the sentiments. Fulfill them and you will be saved." After that, in the bathroom, he saw bruises, marks and parquet wax on his forehead.

The voice spoke to him again the next night, instructing him to take a pad and pencil and write down what "he" was going to dictate. Parravicini said that "it was" the voice of "Fray José de Aragón" (1603-1667). Agostinelli tells:

"His "guardian angel" first began to dictate to him and then held his hand, while he watched as he wrote or drew. "Messages would come to me for various people. I gave them to them and, naturally, they took me for crazy." At first "I didn't understand them and I threw them away... I threw away so many! I had this inner struggle about their value and meaning, good and evil. For some of them are so rare they look demonic." He began to keep them when he noticed that the predictions were coming true. He envisioned world events, interplanetary visits and wrote surrealist plays inspired by science and spiritualism that today would be classified as science fiction, along the lines of Eduardo L. Holmberg (1852-1937)."

Agostinelli adds: "Benjamín did not want to have anything to do with spiritualism, perhaps because it was a religion frowned upon or associated with madness."

Parravicini claimed to have been abducted by them in an aircraft in June 1968. After that, he received "prophecies" about the future of Argentina, the Catholic Church, and the world;[136] of which we will discuss later.

How did his "abduction" occur? He said that in 1961 while he was sitting on a bench on the sidewalk on 9 de Julio Avenue in downtown Buenos Aires, he was abducted by an alien spacecraft when he was approached by two tall, pale-skinned, platinum-haired, whitish-eyedbeings. Parravicini and the beings were transported to a circular room after an enormous light covered them. The room, Parravicini notes, had luminous panels and a central tube in which the beings moved. One of the beings approached him and gave him a telepathic message: "You must preach love. Universe is harmony. We are watching you [human beings]. Your behavior is aggressive. We have many chosen ones. We will meet again." More than three hours later, Parravicini appeared on the same bench, at 18:40.[137]

Parravicini claimed that so-called "extraterrestrial beings" visited him many nights through dreams or voices. And "many of his psychographies speak of a future encounter of mankind with aliens, in tune with a growing movement of people calling for the declassification of NASA and Pentagon files."[138]

When he channeled, he would enter a trance state, and then "he would wake up with a message to transmit that he would accompany with a phrase and a drawing."[139]

---

[136] Fabio Zerpa, Benjamín Solari Parravicini, el Nostradamus de América: sus predicciones inéditas, experiencias psíquicas y psicografías proféticas (Ediciones Continente, 2004), pp. 179, 180.
[137] Fabio Zerpa, Benjamín Solari Parravicini, el Nostradamus de América: sus predicciones inéditas, experiencias psíquicas y psicografías proféticas (Ediciones Continente, 2004), ob. cit.
[138] (August 11, 2021), Las profecías de Benjamín Solari Parravicini se "actualizan" en pandemia, Clarín.
[139] Ibid.

With all this in mind, Bibiana Bryson, former student of Pedro Romaniuk and he Parravicini's psychographies, said in Edgardo Luis Stekar's podcast, that Bergog was a friend of Romaniuk for many years. And Bergoglio went to visit him in the hospital while he was convalescing from an illness.[140]

Bryson said the Jesuit priest Bergoglio knows a lot about the subject of extraterrestrials and is a great admirer of Parravicini.[141]

In fact, Bergoglio and political personalities, artists, writers, among others, participated in gatherings with Pedro Romaniuk in his house in Buenos Aires, where they talked about the UFO phenomenon, extraterrestrial life and the prophecies of Parravicini.[142]

Alfa Bidondo, an Argentine contactee with the UFO phenomenon, also said that Pedro Romaniuk told him that he used to meet with a group of friends in meetings at his house, and that on some of those occasions Jorge Mario Bergoglio attended. Bergoglio liked very much to talk about the reality of the Vatican, about life after death, about UFOs as something that was real, about the possibility of visits of extraterrestrial beings in various parts of the world today; but he was very interested in the psychographies of Parravicini that referred to the future of the Catholic Church. And Pedro Romaniuk possessed dozens of unpublished psychographies.[143]

Yohanan Díaz, a Mexican researcher, says that when he spoke to four of the attendees at the meetings at Pedro Romaniuk's house, they told him that people from politics, the artistic world, and those contacted by "extraterrestrials" arrived at these evening meetings, which could last until 5-6am.[144] Bidondo adds that the Argentinean congresswoman Elisa Carrió also attended.[145] He also added that there was interest in these topics on the part of other Argentinean clergymen close to Bergoglio.[146]

Those present offered their points of view on the topics mentioned, but Romaniuk was always the first to speak. Bergoglio listened attentively and thoughtfully to Pedro and the others, and said on one occasion: "Something important will happen with these prophecies that will be fulfilled over Argentina." A witness pointed out that they listened "to what Bergoglio said because he questioned everything, it seemed that he wanted to analyze the information." On one occasion, Pedro R. "explained to the future Pope the prophecies of Parravicini that referred to the collapse and subsequent renewal of the Church," but Bergoglio was especially interested in the psychographies that

[140] (March 26, 2013), 'El papa Francisco y su nexo con Parravicini', Podcast de Edgardo Luis Stekar en ivoox: https://www.ivoox.com/el-papa-francisco-su-nexo-parravicini-audios-mp3_rf_1899660_1.html 31:14-49:11. Accessed September 1, 2023.
[141] Ibid.
[142] Yohanan Diaz Vargas (May 2018), Francisco, el Papa ocultista, Año/Cero, Year XXIX Issue 05-334, pp. 24, 25.
[143] Ibid, pp. *24-25-27*; (August 2, 2015), ALFA BIDONDO: Contacto con "Seres del Tiempo" en Argentina., Yohanan Díaz Vargas I Reportero e Investigador: https://www.youtube.com/watch?v=3IwcQv5mtSI 57:29-1:08:07. Accessed September 1, 2023.
[144] Ibid; (May 11, 2018), CONTACTO ovni en este 11 de mayo de 2018 I ALFA BIDONDO., Yohanan Díaz Vargas I Reportero e Investigador: https://www.youtube.com/watch?v=7CgEA7aOylc 28:27. Accessed September 1, 2023.
[145] (May 30, 2018), ALFA BIDONDO I Historia FASCINANTE de un Contactado. ¡Tiene fotos y videos de "ELLOS"!, Yohanan Díaz Vargas I Reportero e Investigador: https://www.youtube.com/watch?v=4pPMAwzznZk 1:14:19. Accessed September 1, 2023.
[146] (August 2, 2015), ALFA BIDONDO: Contacto con "Seres del Tiempo" en Argentina., Yohanan Díaz Vargas I Reportero e Investigador: https://www.youtube.com/watch?v=3IwcQv5mtSI 57:29-1:08:07. Accessed September 1, 2023.

irch must go out to the streets." Such is one of the main ideals, we media, of the current Pope Francis since the beginning of his ᵧ.[147]

ormation from witnesses about these meetings, Díaz says that he ᵤme after Bergoglio was elected to the papacy under the name of y important personality of the Catholic Church in Argentina asked those ᵤ the gatherings: "Look, we are going to support the pope. He is Argentinean ᵤerefore we are going to support him;" and he asked them not to talk any more ᵤoout Bergoglio's participation in those meetings, in order to protect the pope's image.[148]

In fact, we consulted several solid Argentine sources who know first hand that these meetings took place, but prefer to remain silent about giving further details and Bergoglio's messages in these gatherings.

A source who was a friend of Romaniuk's assured me that even Argentine Masons are interested in the subject.

Now, for their part, some of the Argentine prelates and others close to Bergoglio who were interested in some of the issues discussed in Romaniuk's home may have been the Reverend Jose Antonio Lombardi and Don Eduardo Dentino, Pope Francis' spiritual advisor. In a blog, Lombardi shows some photographs of himself, in two of which he appears to be performing miraculous healings. In fact, the blog claims that he attends to "hundreds of people with various health problems." Other photographs show Lombardi in the town of Virrey del Pino, Route 3, km 41, on the grounds of the FICI (Fundación Instituto Cosmobiofísico de Investigaciones/ Cosmobiophysics Research Institute Foundation), founded by Pedro Romaniuk, which we will mention in due course. In fact, Lombardi appears in three photographs next to Pedro Romaniuk.[149]

But in another of the photographs, Lombardi appears in a photo with his friend Eduardo Dentino, "spiritual advisor to Pope Francis."[150] Dentino had some posts on his Facebook page about "a universal energy that is the same in the microcosm;" and that is defined as frequencies and waves that permeate everything. Apparently, this would give us human capabilities to discover what some once considered to be parapsychology. As for example, Dentino cites, there is "remote viewing," psychokinesis, as well as other psychic abilities. It should be noted that all of these concepts were believed by Romaniuk, whose legacy continues today at FICI.

A blog tells us about FICI, even though its official website no longer exists:

---

[147] See also Yohanan Díaz Vargas (May 2018), Francisco, el Papa ocultista, Año/Cero, Year XXIX Number 05-334, p. 25.

[148] (January 23, 2022), ALFA BIDONDO: Contacto con "Seres del Tiempo" en Argentina., MENSAJE IMPORTANTE I ¿LLEGÓ LA AYUDA? KILMER un ser del FUTURO está aquí. ¡ATENTOS! ALFA BIDONDO: https://www.youtube.com/watch?v=4zsMuxSYVIw 1:16:54-1:18:03. Accessed September 1, 2023; Yohanan Díaz Vargas (May 2018), Francisco, el Papa ocultista, Año/Cero, Year XXIX Number 05-334, p. 26.

[149] eltchanek (November 30, 2015). ORATORIO SAN CAYETANO - TEMPERLEY - PCIA. DE BUENOS AIRES - ARGENTINA. *Rvdo. JOSÉ A. LOMBARDI Blog.* http://joselombardi.blogspot.com/2015/11/ Accessed September 1, 2023.

[150] Ibid.

"FICI (Fundación Instituto Cosmobiofísico de Investigaciones) is one of the oldest independent institutions of Atomic, Paranormal and Extraterrestrial Research, founded by Pedro Romaniuk.

"Our objective is the scientific and spiritual diffusion with the aim of awakening Minds and Souls, and helping them to rise to the ideal Critical Levels for the achievement of a better world, of a Humanity governed by the Supreme Laws of Our Father Creator.

"The ultimate goal is the establishment of a system of community life that is as respectful, balanced, just and enriching as possible for the Planet and Humanity."[151]

FICI's Facebook page contains photographs of the facilities, where we can see a pyramid where activities on 'meditation and harmonization' take place inside. On the outside of the pyramid, there is a statue of the Virgin Mary (in other photographs on the Internet, paintings of Jesus can be seen inside a building). Another structure, called "Agujeros cósmico" ("Cosmic holes") is considered a gateway to the secrets of the universe. It has a large sign on its exterior that reads: "Virgen María Madre de la Nueva Argentina" ("Virgin Mary Mother of the New Argentina").

While a cubicle called "Cubículos alpedoides" ("alpedoid cubicles") is built in bakelite and suitable for "all kinds of intergalactic affairs."

A first-hand source documents:

"Within the nine thousand square meters of the property, there are four pyramidal structures, a barbecue area with a capacity for one thousand people, and the chapel, an oratory that condenses the main aspects of its faith. Right there Don Pedro [Romaniuk] tells me:

-There is Christ, the Virgin, Mohammed, Allah, Yahweh, David... That is ecumenism, that is what the Pope is asking for. We are all inhabitants of the Earth."[152]

For Romaniuk, "the imposing figure of the only Master of Masters, Christ Jesus, wrapped in a splendorous white robe and totally happy, smiling and joyful, who with his outstretched arms invites us to follow him, without fear, and to shelter under his divine protection."[153]

One of Romaniuk's several books refers to Jesus as the chief of the celestial teachers; of the extraterrestrials.[154]

This was very familiar to me, since from March 12-16, 2018, a conference entitled "Dawn of InterSpirituality" was held at Casa Siloé in Heredia, Costa Rica, where representatives of various religious denominations from different parts of the world gathered. Among them, friends and collaborators of Pope Francis himself. I attended as an observer on one of the days, and was present at the talk entitled, "The Face of Christ;" given by the priest Guillermo Marcó, former spokesman for the current Pope

[151] FICI Investigaciones (July, 2013). ¿QUIÉNES SOMOS?. *FICI INVESTIGACIONES Blog*. http://fici-investigaciones.blogspot.com/p/quienes-somo.html Accessed September 1, 2023.
[152] Ibid.
[153] Alejandro Agostinelli, Invasores: Historias reales de extraterrestres en la Argentina (Sudamericana, 2012), ob. cit.
[154] Pedro Romaniuk, Argentina, tierra bendita: discos voladores sobre América (Editorial Larín, 1986).

Francis when he had been the Archbishop of Buenos Aires. Marcó said at one point something that intrigued me at the time: "As our Venezuelan aboriginal friend here said, that up there are the gods of the heavens, and [Marcó added], the main one of them is Jesus."

In the face of such startling revelations, what do some of Benjamin Solari Parravicini's psychographies, in which the current pope has been so interested, have to say?

A psychography of Parravicini says especially: "Three popes, four councils, Catholics. The priesthood will leave the habit. The priesthood will speak of God in the streets. The sisters will go out to deliver Peace [1939]."

"In the first international trip that Pope Francis made in July 2013, to participate in the *XXVIII World Youth Day*, held in Rio de Janeiro, he said before more than three million young people on the Copacabana beach: "Do not be afraid to go and take Christ to any environment (...) The Church needs you, the enthusiasm and joy that characterizes you," because it is necessary that "the Church goes out to the streets," as Solari Parravicini had prophesied."[155]

Of the papacy, a psychography reads in part: "NEW POPE. What? Divergences!, the new Pope will be after arduous internal struggles. Two different lights, two truths, two problems. Confusion will advance and from it the unexpected will arise."[156] Here it seems to be referring to the internal intrigues that that provoked the resignation of Pope Benedict XVI.

A second psychography: "New era is coming! World in disguise. Perennial masquerade. The Church will surrender its bestowal to the resignation of the Papacy. And the new one will be young in ideas."[157]

González and Villamil tell us that "Psychographies speak, clearly, of a papal resignation and of a new pontiff who will be "young in ideas." It is difficult not to think about Francis' assumption..."[158]

Such new ideas would perhaps invoke, for reasons that we will mention, another psychography that clearly describes the Second Vatican Council: "The Papacy will have new norms. The bad of yesterday will cease to be so. The Mass will be Protestant, without being Protestant. The Protestants will be Catholics without being Catholics. The Pope will travel away from the Vatican and come to America, while humanity will fall." Von Wurmb, compiler of the psychographies, to whom Parravicini bequeathed them, comments: "[...] many years later the reforms brought about by the Ecumenical Council and the celebration of the Mass in vernacular languages were implemented, just as the Protestants do. The Pope not only travels the world, but for the first time in

---

[155] Yohanan Díaz Vargas (May 2018), Francisco, el Papa ocultista, Año/Cero, Year XXIX Issue 05-334, pp. 25, 26.

[156] Sigurd von Wurmb, Dibujos Proféticos Tomo 1: Benjamín Solari Parravicini: Una vida guiada desde el cosmos (Editorial Kier, S.A., 3rd ed., Buenos Aires, 2002), p. 96.

[157] Ibid, p. 97.

[158] Ricardo González, Roberto Villamil, El Enigma del Hombre Gris: Las profecías de Parravicini, Francisco y los secretos del Vaticano (ECIS Publicaciones, First Edition, Buenos Aires, June 2014), p. 159.

history he visits our American continent. Notwithstanding these belated efforts, "humanity will fall."[159]

A third psychography: "The world falls!... Rolls! But... Where does it go? New rules in the new papacy! Old rules withdrawn return! Leap year! Roman autumn! Retreat! Meditation. Peace."[160] It seems that the "new rules in the new papacy" refer to the pope who will be "young in ideas" of the first psychography we quoted about the papacy. If that is the message communicated, the phrase "old rules withdrawn return" would seem to indicate the return of a pre-Vatican II papacy. Is that the "Roman autumn" when "The world falls...""? And is that why there must be "Retreat! Meditation. Peace," in order to have peace again? It would be a papacy that does not respect freedom of conscience and religion.

Or does it mean that the return of that pre-Vatican II papacy will be after the "Roman autumn" when "The world falls," and that it will be part of the "Peace" solution?

Several of the prophecies about UFOs and extraterrestrial beings were:

"The seas will be invaded by beings from other worlds that will arrive in their amphibious boats. They will carry from the earth to Ganymede and its twin Europa algae, there it is needed as food, they lack great seas. They will arrive."[161]

"The UFO problem will be placed on the table and it will soon be put, that the truth must be elucidated before the end of the end. The scientist must move away from the infatuated blindness that blinds him. The young man will do it and... he will see" (1968).[162]

"Every Astral Craft is built with materials not yet known on Earth.
Its crafts are light, molded in one piece without any joint.
The Naviero is also enclosed in an entire seamless scaphandric garment and some transparent and blue.
Our fire to the maximum degree will not heat or pierce the consistency of both! [1960]."[163]

"In the face of constant visits from extraterrestrial pilots, science will deny, then doubt, and finally say: Truth! It is true and our sapience is left behind.
Centuries watch and contemplate us! [1940]"[164]
"At the end of Time, at the first hour of the hour, they will again descend to Earth from the Astropilots of yesterday, bearing words in warnings.
These blue beings will coexist on Earth with the blind man.

[159] Sigurd von Wurmb, Dibujos Proféticos Tomo 1: Benjamín Solari Parravicini: Una vida guiada desde el cosmos (Editorial Kier, S.A., 3rd ed., Buenos Aires, 2002), p. 9.
[160] Ibid, p. 97.
[161] Nicolás Hornos (February 26, 2023), The prophecies of Benjamín Solari Parravicini that speak of contact with extraterrestrials, MDZ Online: https://www.mdzol.com/sociedad/2023/2/26/las-profecias-de-benjamin-solari-parravicini-que-hablan-del-contacto-con-extraterrestres-317553.html Accessed February 1, 2024.
[162] (August 11, 2021), Las profecías de Benjamín Solari Parravicini se "actualizan" en pandemia, Clarín.
[163] Sigurd von Wurmb, Dibujos Proféticos Tomo II: Benjamín Solari Parravicini: Una vida guiada desde el cosmos (Editorial Kier, S.A., Buenos Aires, 2003), ob. cit.
[164] Ibid.

Their crafts will be stored in the high peaks of mountainous regions, inside their well-known craters.

The astral astropilot will do good to the Earth, without being warned!"[165]

"The blue Astral Naviero will prove the existence of God with arduous effort, for man will have forgotten Him for gold.

In real presence, the Naviero will speak telepathically of the great Universe, of planets and superior men, of astonishing civilizations and will say: "Everything is God's work!"

The Naviero will emphatically emphasize: "All is of God, as you are, Terrestrial man. Abandon now the "fetishism," the eagerness for new gods, new conductors and new religions; for they will not be.

Learn to be God's... and you shall be! [1960]"[166]

Parravicini also wrote about the arrival of the enigmatic "Gray Man," who would be a key character or a group of people, or a movement that would emerge in Argentina in the midst of a crisis and that would have repercussions in the world.[167]

It would be a new paradigm, a new man, who does not choose between black and white, between left and right.[168]

During a homily on May 12, 2014 in St. Peter's Square, Pope Francis would say, "If tomorrow an expedition of Martians comes here and one says: 'I want to be baptized,' what would happen? Martians, right? Green, with long noses and big ears, like in children's drawings. [...] When the Lord shows us the way, who are we to say: 'No, Lord, it is not wise! No, let's do it another way'? Who are we to close the doors?"[169]

Likewise, in October 2015, during an interview with journalist Caroline Pigozzi of *Paris Match* magazine, she asked Francis his opinion on the existence of extraterrestrial life, to which the pope replied that until now, scientific knowledge has always excluded that there are traces of other thinking beings in the universe, but he also admitted that in the past, science did not even contemplate the existence of the American continent.[170]

Alfa Bidondo, the aforementioned Argentine contactee from San Salvador de Jujuy in Argentina and who personally met Pedro Romaniuk, had a meeting with Pope Francis at the Vatican in August 2015:

"I asked him if he knew the ornate cross, which is the symbol that appears in many psychographies of Benjamín Solari Parravicini. It is the cross of the new era. I showed it to him, he touched it and blessed it. A smile clearly appeared on his face. He knew perfectly well what it was about. The Pope told me: 'I know it very well'."[171]

---

[165] Ibid.
[166] Ibid.
[167] Ricardo González, Roberto Villamil, El Enigma del Hombre Gris: Las profecías de Parravicini, Francisco y los secretos del Vaticano (ECIS Publicaciones, First Edition, Buenos Aires, June 2014), p. 152.
[168] (August 11, 2021), Las profecías de Benjamín Solari Parravicini se "actualizan" en pandemia, Clarín.
[169] Yohanan Diaz Vargas (May 2018), Francisco, el Papa ocultista, Año/Cero, Year XXIX Issue 05-334, p. 26.
[170] Ibid, p. 27; Elise Harris (October 15, 2015), Do aliens exist? Pope Francis tackles this (and other things) in new interview, Catholic News Agency.
[171] Ibid.

Bidondo indicates that the cross generates great energy, bringing great peace and protection to people, as well as healing to the sick.[172]

The Andes, home of "the gods": The Mapuches, the case of the Jesuits, Bergoglio and Solari Parravicini

The Argentine province of Neuquén is located in northwestern Patagonia. One of its boundaries lies to the west with Chile, largely on the criteria of the high peaks of the Andes Mountains.

Centuries ago, the Jesuits were interested in the Andes because they heard from the Mapuche tribes that the gods lived there. This was the time when the Spanish arrived in what is now South America.

The Jesuit missions in Chile, established in the 16th century, linked them with the Mapuche indigenous tribes, transforming their cultural and religious vision towards Catholicism, but fostering a cultural exchange.[173] It is known that the Mapuche Indians believed in the gods of the heavens. The Mapuches had the *machis* (a kind of shaman), as well as the kultrún; a ceremonial drum to invoke the gods of the sky and the spirits of the deceased. Ana Bacigalupo, a Peruvian anthropologist, tells us: "The *machi* are the intermediaries between the Mapuche world and the supernatural world and their protective spirits give them powers to fight evil spirits. They watch over the wellbeing of their patients and the community."[174]

The *tayil* is a chant that is believed to have been transferred by the gods to the *machis*, as well as "a means of transcendent communication for having the power to bring the gods and spirits down from the *wenumapu* [heaven] to earth [...]." They were the space gods. An instrument used by the *machi* to invoke the gods, as already mentioned, was the kultrún.[175] According to Desmadryl, it represents half of the universe and the power of the Ngenechén, god of the Mapuches.[176] Where did this deity come from according to their beliefs? From the *wenumapu* or heaven. We are told that: "In the archaic Mapuche culture, the rainbow acts as a parapet for the gods of the *wenumapu*, the upper heaven, when they visit the earth or decide to approach the atmosphere that humans breathe."[177]

[172] (August 2, 2015), ALFA BIDONDO: Contacto con "Seres del Tiempo" en Argentina., Yohanan Díaz Vargas I Reportero e Investigador: https://www.youtube.com/watch?v=3IwcQv5mtSI 57:29-1:08:07. Accessed September 1, 2023.

[173] Javiera Susana Jaque (2007), *Misiones Jesuitas en la Frontera de Arauco: Resistencia Misiones Jesuitas en la Frontera de Arauco: Resistencia Mapuche, Negociación y Movilidad Cultural en la Periferia Colonial Mapuche, Negociación y Movilidad Cultural en la Periferia Colonial (1593-1641)* (Publication No. 1115) [Doctoral dissertation, Washington University in St. Louis] Arts & Sciences Electronic Theses and Dissertations.

[174] Bacigalupo AM. La Voz del Kultrun en la Modernidad: Tradición y Cambio en La Terapéutica de Siete Machi Mapuche. Santiago: Editorial Universidad Católica de Chile, 2001; cited in Castellano Salas, Ángela. (2007). Guardiana del espíritu de un machi y sus sueños. Index de Enfermería, 16(57), 65-69. Retrieved February 02, 2024, from http://scielo.isciii.es/scielo.php?script=sci_arttext&pid=S1132-12962007000200014&lng=es&tlng=es.

[175] Jorge Hidalgo L., Virgilio Schiappacasse F., Hans Niemeyer F., Carlos Aldunate del S., Pedro Meger R. (editors), Etnografía. Sociedades indígenas contemporáneas y su ideología (Editorial Andres Bello, Santiago de Chile, 1996), p. 217.

[176] Jorge Dowling Desmadryl, Religión, chamanismo y mitologia mapuches (Editorial Universitaria, 1971), pp. 92, 95.

[177] Ziley Mora Penroz, Yerpun: El Libro Sagrado de la Tierra del Sur (Editorial Kushe, 2ª. ed., Concepción, Chile, 2001), p. 233.

Wenumapu is also defined as the land above or abode of the gods, beneficial spirits and ancestors.[178] It is "where the spirits of the people can be abducted."[179] Where Ngenechén, creator and dominator of humans and good spirits, resides. It is believed that the spirits (*pullü*) of the deceased come to the *wenumapu*.[180]

With all this in mind, in the 16th and 17th centuries, the Jesuits witnessed in South America strange lights in the sky traveling at great speeds. The researcher and writer, Dr. Antonio Las Heras, wrote that in the archives of the Society of Jesus, there are many such events that were registered during the conquest. He writes for example:

"In the reduction of San Ignacio de Ipané, on August 10, 1631, something strange and luminous was seen crossing the sky. Between 6 and 7 o'clock in the evening a *luminous globe* of strange grandeur was seen rising on the eastern side, which came flying without haste, but somewhat slowly, above the town, like a full moon."

"It emitted many sparks towards the East, and when it reached the western horizon line, it opened with greater light, which then went out, and after the time it took to recite a creed, it gave a tremendous burst as if it were *thunder*."[181]

There is a legend that tells that during the Jesuit reductions in Paraguay, the Society of Jesus gathered and hid a rich treasure in silver, gold, and others, which can be traced back to the 16-18th centuries and perhaps beyond; given some good historical documentation.[182] A testimony from the province of Jujuy, Argentina, from 1940, tells that apparently in the place called La Misión, in La Candelaria, the Jesuits left buried a large amount of silver, from where lights come out that witnesses have seen in the skies.[183] These lights were seen by the Mapuches.

It is said that in places where hidden treasures are found, there are always "walking" lights and people dressed in white.[184]

Multiple sightings of such lights have indeed been seen in Argentina.[185]

The Society of Jesus was also a fervent missionary order in the Neuquén area; and in fact, very extensively in Patagonia. Dr. María Andrea Nicoletti, Argentine historian:

"The Jesuit mission of Nahuel Huapi (1669-1717) and the Franciscan mission of Santa María del Pilar de Rainleuvú (1758-59) were developed in Northern Patagonia (Neuquén) as part of a missionary project planned by both religious orders in the Chilean Araucanía."[186]

---

[178] María Catrileo, Diccionario Lingüístico Etnográfico de la Lengua Mapuche (Ediciones Universidad Austral de Chile, Second Edition, 2017), ob. cit.

[179] Estudios filológicos, Edition 46 (Facultad de Filosofía y Letras, Universidad Austral de Chile, 2010), p. 180.

[180] Sonia Montecino Aguirre, Mitos de Chile: Enciclopedia de seres, apariciones y encantos (Editorial Catalonia, Santiago de Chile, 2017), ob. cit.

[181] Antonio Las Heras, O.V.N.I.S.: los extraterrestres entre nosotros (Rueda Ed., 1978).

[182] Alfredo Boccia Romañach, Sueño y realidad del Oro en el Nuevo Mundo: Los tesoros ocultos del Paraguay (Editorial Servilibro, Asunción, Paraguay, 2005), pp. 179, 180.

[183] Berta Elena Vidal de Battini, Cuentos y leyendas populares de la Argentina (Ediciones Culturales Argentinas, Bs. Aires, Argentina, 1984), Volume VII, p. 340, cf. 255.

[184] Ibid, 414, cf. 316.

[185] Ibid, 155, 164, 407, 417.

[186] Maria Andrea Nicoletti (2002), Jesuitas y franciscanos en las misiones de la Norpatagonia. Coincidencias y controversias en su discurso teológico, Anuario de Historia de la Iglesia, 11, pp. 215, 216.

Now, let's look at the 20th and 21st centuries. Neuquén has also been known for its many UFO sightings for decades. For example, a well-known professional from that city, under the pseudonym of Tito Del Bianco, said that lights in the sky are common in the province, but he also indicated other sightings: "I am referring specifically to machines that could be seen in broad daylight and I am talking about what happened in Neuquén in the early 1950s. [...]"[187]

Del Bianco tells several stories of his investigations. He noted, for example, that one day in 1952, his wife's father, who worked as an engine foreman at the Calf Cooperative, saw in the sky, along with other witnesses, a flying disc flying over the power plant in the middle of the day.

We also read that in 1955, at the height of Sarmiento Street, Tito observed, while suspended "clearly a flying disk of solid metallic appearance of about 30 meters in diameter."

Residents of Cerro Chapelco, as well as those who live or frequent Lake Lácar, always in Neuquén, have witnessed many anomalous celestial phenomena.

Precisely, the entire area of the Río Negro and Neuquén Valley "was the historic scene of sightings and close encounters, whose testimonies are recorded in neat folders of clippings."

This professional said that "the Neuquén sky is very special because there is a lot of 'UFO activity'" and that if you talk "with people about it you will always find testimonies, many people at some point in their lives have seen something of this nature at some time."

All this takes on greater importance, given two psychographies by the artist Benjamín Solari Parravicini, which refer to Neuquén. The first one is dated 1942 and presents a remarkable lighthouse, facing the rising sun and whose message reads: "-On the Argentinean Earth a new lighthouse... Neuquén!-"[188] This prediction seems to refer to the fact that a new hope will shine from Neuquén; logically for Argentina, but perhaps "it could be extended" to mankind.

In 1968, Parravicini added:

"At the end of the test. The South of Argentina will speak in triumph. There will be the birth of tomorrow. Neuquén will be the compass of compasses. The coast of Río Negro will speak of the great fishing and the cultivation of seaweed in its waters and the cultivation of fruit trees in its heights, Holy Cross, will be."[189]

Again, the province seems to be the object of a guiding "light" for Argentina; for a new dawn. That its aquatic and agricultural wealth would be an example of prosperity for the nation. And whose source would be the "Holy Cross": or Jesus and by extension, his atoning sacrifice.

---

[187] Santiago Rosa (May 5, 2023), Los primeros UFOs que se vieron en Neuquén, Diario LMNeuquén. Note: unless otherwise indicated, this is the same source.

[188] Benjamin Solari Parravicini, El Testamento Profético de Benjamín Solari Parravicini (Editorial Kier, S.A., Buenos Aires, Argentina, 2006), p. 160.

[189] LMNeuquén (July 16, 2021), Solari Parravicini: el Nostradamus argentino que predijo el COVID y describió a Neuquén como "faro para la humanidad," Diario LMNeuquén.

Since Parravicini's predictions largely consider a future revelation about UFOs and "extraterrestrials," and as we saw, since Neuquén is located in Patagonia and borders to the west with a large part of the Andes mountain range, another psychography by Parravicini from 1939 becomes important:

"Extraterrestrial beings will arrive on Earth again, they will arrive in different spaceships, from different planets and will inhabit the craters of the Andes and the Patagonian South. They will coexist with human life, they will be seen and talked to."[190]

An Argentine source who is a renowned researcher with many UFO cases to her credit, told me that "mountain chains, summits, mountains, peaks [...] are related to the phenomenon." The late speleologist Julio Goyen Aguado, who was the founder of the Centro Argentino de Espeleología (Argentine Center of Speleology) and who from scientific research discovered more than five hundred natural caverns in Argentina and the world,[191] was very interested in the UFO phenomenon. He told my source that: "The abode of the gods is the Andes Mountains."

Therefore, the importance given to Neuquén even in the 21st century, as having "prophetic" significance, does not seem to be accidental. The history of the last two decades tells us something very important: Alejandro Santana is a professional architect and sculptor, as well as a consecrated Catholic with a close relationship with different parts of the Argentine Church.[192] When the Salesians of Junín de los Andes, a city located in the southwest of the province of Neuquén, saw the Stations of the Cross made by the sculptor in the Cathedral of Bariloche, they proposed him to make it in the Cerro de la Cruz, in Junín de los Andes.[193]

Thus, in 1998, Santana moved with his family to that city, where he began the first model of the "Way of the Cross." The project was presented to the then Cardinal of Buenos Aires, Jorge Mario Bergoglio, who, when he saw the photographs of what was being conceived, said: "this is not a Way of the Cross but a Via Christi," which means "way of Christ," because it goes through the moments of Jesus' life.[194] Santana says: "Bergoglio saw the project and liked it. This Via Christi was baptized by the man who is now Pope Francis.[195] The work was almost entirely completed in 2017.

Most of the inhabitants of Junín de los Andes are of Mapuche origin, where the Catholic culture takes shape and coexists. Precisely, through its sculptures, the Vía Christi combines the communion between the Catholic culture and the Mapuche culture.[196] The sculptural work of the Via Christi of Junín de los Andes, which has 23

---

[190] Ibid.

[191] La Nación (November 9, 1999), Murió Julio Goyén Aguado, La Nación.

[192] LMNeuquén (March 26, 2017), El escultor que se consagró a expresar la fe religiosa, Diario LMNeuquén.

[193] Ibid.

[194] Ibid; CAPARROZ, Maximiliano José - SOTO, Ramón Ángel - SAPAG, Alma Liliana - PILATTI, Mario Alberto - DU PLESSIS, María Laura - BONGIOVANI, Pablo Fabián - LOZANO, Encarnación - MENQUINEZ, Lucía Corel - SIFUENTES, Gloria Beatriz - SAPAG, Luis Felipe - DOMÍNGUEZ, Claudio - KOOPMANN IRIZAR, Carlos Damián - MPN Block - GALLIA, Sergio Adrián - PADEN Block - SÁNCHEZ, Carlos Enrique - UP-UNA Block -. Letter to Mr. President. March 30, 2017, p. 2.

[195] LMNeuquén (March 26, 2017), El escultor que se consagró a expresar la fe religiosa, Diario LMNeuquén.

[196] Ibid.

stations in a 2.5 km route, reflects passages from the life of Christ, "accompanied by Mapuche indigenous faces and together with characters from the history of the town of Junín de los Andes."[197] We read from an important document:

"The Vía Christi Sculpture Park was created under this conception of Christ's path. Alejandro Santana meditated on it and thought of it in the form of a contemplative, and wanted it as a Christ that goes through the history of Latin America and Argentina. But this great work goes beyond that; it is a Christ that goes through the life of every man, always following the principles of *interculturalism and interreligiosity*, he united cultures through art, the symbology of each country, of each race and culture. This idea can be simplified in the motto that Alejandro Santana chose: *"That all may be one so that the world may believe."*[198]

The aforementioned 23 stations, with sculptures of twelve meters in stones and supported on a platform representing the sun, called "sunny," make up an extremely amazing journey through 22 hectares. Starting with the sculpture "God made man, to save us," passing through other events of the life and ministry of Christ: with his crucifixion and resurrection, until arriving at "Jesus and the miraculous fishing." But it culminates, finally, with the imposing Christ-Light, 52 meters long and 47 meters wide, which emerges from the earth and is made of glass; with lights that illuminate spectacularly at night.

While I am writing these words, station 24 has yet to be built, which will be the Apocalypse, the meeting with Mary.[199]

An inhabitant of Neuquén rightly said that the sculptures significantly resemble the images of Benjamín Solari Parravicini. In fact, Alejandro Santana himself, referring to the Christ-Light, said that its name is because "we wanted to give meaning to two prophecies in Junín de los Andes, one by Father Milanesio, who was the first missionary; and another by another prophet, Parravicini, who also made some drawings, and says: "Neuquén, lighthouse of the world."[200]

In the documentary on the Vía Christi (El Faro), the prophecy of the priest Domingo Milanesio (1843-1922) is introduced, who said: "Our mission in Junín de los Andes will be like a lighthouse that will spread its evangelical light for hundreds of miles around."[201] That message is on the outside of the Church Nuestra Señora de las Nieves y beata Laura Vicuña (Our Lady of the Snows and Blessed Laura Vicuña), in Junín de los Andes, which was founded by Milanesio, and whose parish was built around 1950.

---

[197] CAPARROZ, Maximiliano José - SOTO, Ramón Ángel - SAPAG, Alma Liliana - PILATTI, Mario Alberto - DU PLESSIS, María Laura - BONGIOVANI, Pablo Fabián - LOZANO, Encarnación - MENQUINEZ, Lucía Corel - SIFUENTES, Gloria Beatriz - SAPAG, Luis Felipe - DOMÍNGUEZ, Claudio - KOOPMANN IRIZAR, Carlos Damián - MPN Block - GALLIA, Sergio Adrián - PADEN Block - SÁNCHEZ, Carlos Enrique - UP-UNA Block -. Letter to Mr. President. March 30, 2017, p. 2.
[198] Ibid.
[199] Andrea Ventura (April 2, 2023), Semana Santa. El imponente Cristo que emerge de la tierra y su curiosa vinculación con el Papa Francisco, La Nación.
[200] (June 4, 2018), Con Alejandro Santana en el Via Christi de Junin de los Andes | Tripin Argentina, TripinTV: https://www.youtube.com/watch?v=y7ccH0l9BB8 Accessed February 2, 2024.
[201] Juan Olmos (Producer) Esteban "Mex" Hoffmann (Director) (2018), El Faro (Radio y Televisión del Neuquén/RTN).

The remodeling was also in charge of Santana, where the Mapuche and Catholic cultures are considerably combined.[202]

The exterior remodeling bears a strong resemblance to Parravicini's psychography of the lighthouse of Neuquén, as if this province were a lighthouse of the world: part of a future revelation of UFOs and their non-human occupants?

The prophecy of the then Cardinal Bergoglio

Several years back, *Río Negro*, a publication of Editorial Río Negro, reported that in 2007, according to unimpeachable sources, the Archbishop of Buenos Aires, Jorge Mario Bergoglio, referred to Elisa Carrió, Roberto Lavagna, and particularly to Eduardo Duhalde, a "prophecy" according to which there would be a social outbreak in Argentina in 2008. Bergoglio would have had a clairvoyance that consisted in the "appearance of corpses hanging from lighting columns, as well as deaths and gunshots."[203]

The Argentine newspaper *La Tribuna* reported:

"According to what several indisputable sources have told this newspaper, approximately a month and a half ago, former President Eduardo Duhalde met with Cardinal Jorge Bergoglio to discuss the current situation of the country. Unexpectedly, at a certain moment, the Cardinal spoke to the Buenos Aires leader about a "prophecy" referring to President Néstor Kirchner.

"To the visitor's astonishment, Bergoglio closed his eyes, raised his right hand and began to appear "possessed" while he related an apparent "clairvoyance" in which "corpses hanging from lighting columns, as well as deaths and gunshots" appeared. The apparent prophecy was about something that would supposedly happen in the year 2008 and, according to the religious man, it was necessary to do something to stop the possible reelection of Néstor Kirchner or the entrance of his wife to the presidency."[204]

This extraordinary information also appeared in the site "valoresreligiosos.com.ar," then directed by the priest Guillermo Marcó, former spokesman of Cardinal Bergoglio until December 2006.[205]

A close friend of former President Duhalde reported that Duhalde was hesitating to run in the October national elections because of the events "prophesied" by Bergoglio.

---

[202] (March 9, 2017), RTN - Iglesia Nuesta Señora de las Nieves y Laura Vicuña de Junín de los Andes, Radio y Televisión del Neuquén: https://www.youtube.com/watch?v=6B4eTGnpSrI Accessed February 2, 2024.

[203] Redacción (July 23, 2007), Insólita versión sobre profecías apocalípticas de Bergoglio, Río Negro: https://www.rionegro.com.ar/insolita-version-sobre-profecias-apocalipticas-de-bergoglio-XVHRN200771423631/ Accessed September 3, 2023.

[204] Tribuna Newsroom (July 4, 2007), Titulares del 5 de julio de 2007, Periódico Tribuna: https://periodicotribuna.com.ar/3025-titulares-del-5-de-julio-de-2007.html#sthash.nq7feq6L.dpuf Accessed September 3, 2023.

[205] Redacción (July 23, 2007), Insólita versión sobre profecías apocalípticas de Bergoglio, Río Negro: https://www.rionegro.com.ar/insolita-version-sobre-profecias-apocalipticas de-bergoglio-XVHRN200771423631/ Accessed September 3, 2023. Note: unless otherwise noted, this is the same source.

But Duhalde reportedly said: "Perhaps it is necessary to serve the homeland in such circumstances."

"Meanwhile Sergio Rubín, editor of "Valores religiosos," pointed out to "Río Negro" that "the rumor about the omen transmitted by Bergoglio "circulated a lot in political environments so we echoed it"; and added: "Initially it did not seem very serious to us, but as time went by speculations and comments were added which led us to soberly report what was said."

Bergoglio would have asked Duhalde to intervene to prevent the first lady's access to the Casa Rosada (presidential palace). It is no secret in Argentina that the now deceased Néstor Kirchner and his wife, Cristina Fernández de Kirchner, saw in Cardinal Jorge Bergoglio a very critical enemy of Néstor's presidency and Cristina's subsequent presidency.

The Archbishop of Buenos Aires reportedly told Duhalde: "You have the obligation that this does not happen, I ask you to do something."

A source from the Duhaldist heart told *Río Negro* that all this was only a rumor, attributed to "an operation of the government to place Bergoglio in the role of conspirator." Meanwhile, Lavagna's main advisor also dismissed the version, alluding that his political boss did not meet with the Archbishop and Cardinal, but also that "it is not his style to look for definitions of that style from a religious authority."

However, I was informed through various means about people who heard Duhalde on Radio 2 of Rosario explaining that vision of Bergoglio. Sources I am not allowed to name, reported that the same friend of the Archbishop of Buenos Aires, Pedro Romaniuk, told that Bergoglio had that vision.

Other sources say that in 2007 Jorge Bergoglio sent two of his military friends to Pedro Romaniuk's house to tell him about the vision and to ask him and his groups to pray.

We wonder if the politicians mentioned by *Río Negro* were part of the talks that took place in Pedro Romaniuk's house and with Bergoglio's assistance.

A certain source with key contacts told me of an Argentinean priest who worked for some years with Bergoglio in Argentina. He saw Bergoglio performing practices that, in his opinion, were witchcraft. We understand that it was part of the contact with certain non-human intelligences.

Dr. Edgard Mitchell, John Podesta, revelation, *extraterrestrial* contact, and the Vatican

Next, to further deepen the significance of this story, we will look at a larger context to further perceive the weight it possesses.

Under the context of the emails of John Podesta (former campaign manager of Hillary Clinton for the 2016 presidential election), which were leaked to the Wikileaks portal -cited in chapter 18-, we read that Dr. Edgar Mitchell, former astronaut and sixth man on the Moon in the Apollo 14 mission, communicated with John Podesta about the importance of the disclosure of the "extraterrestrial" contact to the American people. We will quote from some of these e-mails, which were sent through representatives to Podesta.

Let's start with a January 16, 2015 email from Dr. Mitchell, through his colleague Terese (Terri) Donovan Mansfield to Podesta, who was then in his last days of labors under the Barack Obama administration:

"Dear John,

"In learning that you will leave the Administration next month to work with Hillary Clinton, I write to suggest that Hillary talk with President Obama after Terri Mansfield and I meet with you to discuss Zero Point Energy and Disclosure.

"Best regards,

"Edgar

"Edgar D. Mitchell, ScD

"Chief Science Officer & Founder, Quantrek

"Apollo 14 astronaut

"6th man to walk on the Moon."[206]

By "Disclosure," as we will see in later messages to Podesta, Dr. Mitchell - always through Terri Mansfield - referred to what the U.S. government would publicly reveal about the reality of UFOs and "extraterrestrial" life.

At least two e-mails that we will cite, will not be placed in chronological order for reasons that will be discussed later.

But first, let's look at the rest of the emails, some quoted more partially than others, and whose sources we share at the bottom of the page.

First, Mitchell wrote to Podesta in a message dated January 21, 2015: "You will note the extreme timing of our request to meet with you, and the recent announcement that the US Air Force just released secret files of UFO reports cited in the Blue Book Project. [...] Let's get our meeting time and date set up ASAP so we can move forward on our unprecedented discussion concerning disclosure of our ETI from a contiguous universe and their connection to zero point energy for humanity."[207] Terri Mansfield wrote on her Twitter account that ETI are the very angels of God.

On April 7, Dr. Mitchell stated, "The urgency as I see it is to explain as much as possible to you and to President Obama about what we know for sure about our nonviolent ETI from the contiguous universe who are peacefully assisting us with bringing zero point energy to our fragile planet."[208]

[206] email for John Podesta strategy (c/o Eryn) from Edgar Mitchell (January 16, 2015): https://wikileaks.org/podesta-emails/emailid/58918 Accessed September 4, 2023.
[207] email for John Podesta (c/o Eryn) re Air Force disclosure (Jan. 21, 2015): https://wikileaks.org/podesta-emails/emailid/32937 Accessed Sept. 4, 2023.
[208] email for John Podesta (c/o Eryn) re Disclosure (April 7, 2015): https://wikileaks.org/podesta-emails/emailid/35713 Accessed September 4, 2023.

Later in his message, Mitchell thanked Podesta and a colleague of his named Eryn "for letting me know when you can share a Skype talk with Terri Mansfield and me."[209]

An April 30 email directly from Mansfield to Podesta on behalf of Dr. Mitchell tells us:

"[...] to request your Skype talk with him [Dr. Mitchell] ASAP regarding Disclosure and the difference between celestials [beings] in our own solar system and their restraint by those from the nonviolent contiguous universe.

"[...] His [Dr. Mitchell's] talk with you, John, is of great importance given the alternative of your not being aware of these key distinctions heralding either intergalactic warfare or peace.

"It is also imperative that after your talk with Edgar, he then speak directly with President Obama via Skype for historical purposes, about the same issue, while the President is still in office."[210]

In a message dated June 11, 2015:

"In ongoing requests for our Skype talk to discuss Disclosure and the difference between our contiguous universe nonviolent obedient ETI and the celestials of this universe, and because Hillary and Bill Clinton were intimates of Laurance Rockefeller who had an avid interest in ETI, I direct your attention to Scott Jones, PhD.

"In Scott's book Voices From the Cosmos, he describes himself as an octogenarian in full karmic payback made following 30 years in the military, half in combat arms and half in intelligence.

"He references you in his ETI matter, as well as the Catholic Church."[211]

He further added, "Disclosure is now top priority for ETI itself in protection of the people. Thank you for giving me 3 dates and times when you are available to Skype with Terri Mansfield and me about Disclosure and ETI."[212]

Another email from Dr. Mitchell via Terri Mansfield, dated August 18 to Podesta:

"Because the War in Space race is heating up, I felt you should be aware of several factors as you and I schedule our Skype talk.

"Remember, our nonviolent ETI from the contiguous universe are helping us bring zero point energy to Earth.

"They will not tolerate any forms of military violence on Earth or in space.

---

[209] Ibid.
[210] email for John Podesta re talk with Edgar Mitchell cc: Eryn (April 30, 2015): https://wikileaks.org/podesta-emails/emailid/27026 Accessed September 4, 2023.
[211] email for John Podesta (Eryn) from Edgar Mitchell re Skype (June 11, 2015): https://wikileaks.org/podesta-emails/emailid/44097 Accessed September 4, 2023.
[212] Ibid.

"The following information in italics was shared with me by my colleague Carol Rosin, who worked closely for several years with Wernher von Braun before his death.

"Carol and I have worked on the Treaty on the Prevention of the Placement of Weapons in Outer Space, attached for your convenience."[213]

Given this information, let's go back to an email to Podesta, again through Terri Mansfield, dated January 18, 2015, stating:

"As 2015 unfolds, I understand you are leaving the Administration in February.

"It is urgent that we agree on a date and time to meet to discuss Disclosure and Zero Point Energy, at your earliest available after your departure.

"My Catholic colleague Terri Mansfield will be there too, to bring us up to date on the Vatican's awareness of ETI."[214]

According to Mansfield and Dr. Mitchell, angels, or ETI, are extraterrestrial since their origin would not be on Earth. However, does the Vatican know anything else?

First and foremost, Dr. Edgar Mitchell's message goes on to indicate that another colleague of his was working on a new Space Treaty and cites Russian and Chinese involvement in this regard, but because of Russia's extreme interference in Ukraine, he believed they should seek another path to peace in space and ZPE/Zero Point Energy on Earth.

He indicated that he met "with President Obama's Honolulu childhood friend, US Ambassador Pamela Hamamoto" at the U.S. Mission in Geneva, where he was able to talk to her a bit about zero-point energy. He concludes, "I believe we can enlist her as a confidante and resource in our presentation for President Obama. I appreciate Eryn's assistance in working with Terri to set up our meeting."[215]

But an email written prior to all of the above, dated October 1, 2014, via Terri Mansfield to Eryn Hugs, who was acting on behalf of Podesta and where she referred to issues already mentioned, she expressed the following about the Vatican:

"Hugs Eryn,

"Dr. Edgar Mitchell asks that I write to Mr. Podesta and you requesting his meeting in Washington, DC with John to discuss Disclosure and zero point energy.

---

[213] email for John Podesta c/o Eryn re Space Treaty (attached) (Aug. 18, 2015): https://wikileaks.org/podesta-emails/emailid/1802 Accessed Sept. 4, 2023.
[214] email for John Podesta (c/o Eryn) from Edgar Mitchel re meeting ASAP (January 18, 2015): https://wikileaks.org/podesta-emails/emailid/1766 Accessed September 4, 2023.
[215] Ibid.

"As John is aware, more than 20 countries including the Vatican have released top secret papers discussing extraterrestrial incidents on Earth over many years. The US has NOT participated in Disclosure, yet."[216]

Which documents is Terri Mansfield referring to? Such "extraterrestrial" incidents, which include some twenty countries, could hardly be categorized as ETI or angels, according to the above definition. Therefore, it seems that the Vatican does not necessarily believe that the only beings of "extraterrestrial" origin are "angels," but also of another nature.

The email goes on to state that the following people would attend the proposed meeting with Dr. Mitchell: Mr. Dan Hill, a Catholic philanthropist; Dr. Michael Mansfield, retired Catholic Air Force Colonel; and Ms. Terri Mansfield, a Catholic consultant who was substituting Dr. Rebecca Wright for Dr. Mitchell on the subject. The reason for this was that, "Because of his own background as a Catholic, we feel it is imperative that John be aware of the Vatican's interest in ETI, Extraterrestrial Intelligence, and in sustainability for our planet." We can note the interest in influencing Podesta on the definition of ETI by appealing to Podesta's Catholic view of the Vatican's interest in that subject. But somehow, the sustainability of the planet is very likely, but not solely and necessarily, related to zero-point energy. The message continues:

"The Vatican has hosted global seminars on the repercussions of humans interacting with ETI, and how this will affect religion and consciousness.

"The Vatican's Observatory is located here in Arizona, and its top astronomers including Father Jose Funes and Brother Guy Consolmagno, who have met with Pope Francis, have publicly stated that God's creation could very well include OTHER intelligent life, and that would mean they are our "brothers".

Do Funes, Guy Consolmagno, and Pope Francis know more than they have claimed? Consolmagno said in an interview a few years back, "I believe [that extraterrestrial life exists], but I have no proof. It would make me very excited and it would make my understanding of religion deeper and richer in ways I can't yet predict, that's why it would be so exciting."[217] On the claims by David Grusch, the former U.S. intelligence agent and whistleblower about a cover-up by the U.S. government over a crash retrieval and reverse engineering program of UFOs and non-human pilots, Consolmagno comments that he doesn't believe it, unless the evidence is revealed.[218]

Funes has said "It is probable there was life and perhaps a form of intelligent life," Funes said. But, he cautioned: "I don't think we'll ever meet a Mr. Spock;" referring to

---

[216] email for John Podesta (c/o Eryn Sepp) from Apollo 14 astronaut Edgar Mitchell requesting meeting (October 1, 2014): https://wikileaks.org/podesta-emails/emailid/12127 Accessed September 4, 2023. Note: unless otherwise noted, this is the same source.

[217] Lee Speigel (Sept. 22, 2014), Will ET Be Here Soon? NASA Brings Scientists, Theologians Together To Prepare, The Hufftington Post: https://www.huffpost.com/entry/nasa-astrobiology-alien-search_n_5860714 Accessed September 28, 2023.

[218] Robert Duncan (September 26, 2023), Aliens, demons or PSYOPS? Catholics study, debate UFO allegations, Detroit Catholic.

a far superior intelligence.[219] Nevertheless, in October 2020, the *International Journal of Astrobiology* published the results of a research studying new probabilities of contact with extraterrestrial civilizations.[220] We know about the personal experiences on the subject from Pope Francis, but no more. We are in the dark, at least at the time of this writing. Mansfield wrote in her email to Podesta:

"We work with specific ETI from a contiguous universe. They are nonviolent and in complete obedience to God.

"Our ETI's connection to zero point energy is obvious in that their purpose is to guide Edgar's international Quantrek science team to apply their zero point energy research for humanity, to move away from the use of fossil fuels which are so deleterious to our fragile planet. Quantrek's science intuitive, Dr. Suzanne Mendelssohn, also a practicing Catholic, advises the Quantrek team as to the specific Tau neutrino which is the foundation for zero point energy, something CERN scientists have begun to study, as well as scientists all over the planet."[221]

We will shortly see that Dr. Suzanne Mendelssohn played a crucial role in Dr. Mitchell's "conversion," not least her contributions to the no-longer-existing Quantrek team.

The email concludes in part:

"Because of the recent demonstrations addressing the overwhelming issue of climate change, and President Obama's own concern, we feel the timing is perfect to meet with John to map out a plan involving Disclosure and zero point energy."

With the prediction that, after meeting with U.S. Ambassador Pamela Hamamoto at the UN Mission in Geneva on July 4 of that year, Mitchell "announced to Swiss media that he intends to return to the moon on a space ship fueled by zero point energy at age 100, in 16 years."

As a side note, Dr. Mitchell would have adhered to the beliefs of Terri Mansfield and Dr. Mendelssohn, being that he would have been completely obedient to God for Dr. Mendelssohn to help cure him with ETI frequencies, "to the complete satisfaction of his NYC oncologist."[222]

On the other hand, I was able to learn from recognized sources that there are important Catholic astronomers and astrophysicists in the United States at recognized Catholic universities who are well aware of what the Vatican knows about "extraterrestrial" intelligence and contact with these non-human entities.

---

[219] Abby Ohlheiser (August 1, 2015), Why the Vatican doesn't think we'll ever meet an alien Jesus, The Washington Post.

[220] Lares, Marcelo, Funes, José Gabriel and Gramajo, Luciana (2020) Monte Carlo estimation of the probability of causal contacts between communicating civilizations. International Journal of Astrobiology, 19 (5). pp. 393-405.

[221] email for John Podesta (c/o Eryn Sepp) from Apollo 14 astronaut Edgar Mitchell requesting meeting (October 1, 2014): https://wikileaks.org/podesta-emails/emailid/12127 Accessed September 4, 2023. Note: unless otherwise noted, this is the same source.

[222] http://www.terrimansfield.com/suzanne Accessed September 4, 2023.

Multiple sources well connected with the Vatican, whose names we keep anonymous for reasons we cannot reveal, have told me that the luminous spheres that appear frequently around the world are supposedly lower beings that reflect humans: some good and some bad. Another assertion is that apparently in "another megaverse," they are the ETIs or angels, who perfectly obey Christ and the Catholic Church. I have been told that these non-human intelligences are "Catholic," and that the world will soon know the "truth."

Dr. Diana Walsh Pasulka, Professor of Religious Studies at the University of North Carolina Wilmington and author, traveled to the Vatican with Tim Taylor, a respected scientist who worked at NASA. The two presented a photograph of their personal friend, Chris Bledsoe, who has frequently experienced the phenomenon of spheres of light, whose case they also told several Vatican representatives; apparently Jesuit scientists at the Vatican Observatory. The photograph was placed among the original books of Nicolaus Copernicus and Galileo Galilei.[223]

During their visit, Pasulka and Taylor had a meeting with Pope Francis and told him about Bledsoe's experiences with the UAP phenomenon, particularly with the luminous spheres. To this effect, the pope sent him a message through Diana Pasulka, telling him to be especially careful with the spheres, because they were angels, since if he [Bledsow] got too close to them, with no intention of harming, they could cause him physical harm. According to Francis, they could cause the stigmata, as happened to St. Francis of Assisi.[224]

An additional influence of Pope Francis on the spheres may have come from at least two psychographies by Benjamin Solari Parravicini. One from 1952, he wrote:
"Beings visible to our retina that travel on small fireballs, that penetrate houses and inhabit them... are already on earth."[225] A second one, from 1938, reads: "Circles of lights will appear flying on the heights, bringing strange beings from other planets. Yes, yes, they will be those who came to populate the earth, it will be said, and it will be well said. Yes, those who were called angels in the Old Testament, or the voice of Jehovah, they will be. And again they shall be seen and seen and heard."[226]

Francisco sent Bledsoe, through Diana Pasulka, photographs of some paintings of these luminous spheres with angels inside, and provoking the stigmata.[227]

According to historical records, and when looked at under the lens of medicine, St. Francis had the same effects as Chris Bledsoe-albeit without stigmata-which is rheumatoid arthritis.[228]

It should be noted that there was another Jesuit at the meeting with the pope who told the same story about the spheres.[229]

---

[223] (Jan. 3, 2021), #11 Chris Bledsoe & Bob McGwier - A Family of Experiencers Connected to the US Government, Project Unity: https://www.youtube.com/watch?v=j4iC5lek3Lo 28:21-30:5. Accessed Sept. 3, 2023.

[224] Ibid.

[225] Nicolás Hornos (February 26, 2023), Las profecías de Benjamín Solari Parravicini que hablan del contacto con extraterrestres, MDZ Online: https://www.mdzol.com/sociedad/2023/2/26/las-profecias-de-benjamin-solari-parravicini-que-hablan-del-contacto-con-extraterrestres-317553.html Accessed February 1, 2024.

[226] Ibid.

[227] (Jan. 3, 2021), #11 Chris Bledsoe & Bob McGwier - A Family of Experiencers Connected to the US Government, Project Unity: https://www.youtube.com/watch?v=j4iC5lek3Lo 28:21-30:5. Accessed Sept. 3, 2023.

[228] Ibid.

When the phenomenon seems to especially favor both ultra-conservative Catholicism and progressive Catholicism

Since the unidentified anomalous phenomenon appears to be highly capricious and deceitful, it is disturbing, given what has been going on with Roman Catholicism and Freemasonry for decades, that it favors Roman Catholicism under what is patently seen as a kind of "disguise" under a "positive agenda" in combination with highly questionable actions. All of this seems to be aimed at the formation of consciences to achieve a certain objective, which seems to be hidden from us. Therefore, I believe from the heart that we should not jump to a variety of conclusions about the true nature of the phenomenon. Who is really behind it?

Let's look at some examples in history of this favoritism.

1. The "Virgin of Revelation," "our Lady of Fatima," and Pope Pius XII's UFO apparitions

In addition to the apparitions of the Lady of Fatima, there have been many other apparitions of "the Virgin Mary" in the history of Catholicism, although not every testimony deserves trust. But let us look at several of which deserve special trust.

Thus, on April 12, 1947, Bruno Cornacchiola, a Protestant "Christian" belonging to the Seventh-day Adventist Church and who was extremely anti-clerical, intended to assassinate Pius XII.[230]

Cornacchiola was in the park with his three sons while he was preparing a low speech denying the existence of the Virgin Mary. One of his sons interrupted him, requesting his help in finding the game ball; and when he went in search of it, he found his son Gianfranco on his knees in front of the grotto, as if in a state of ecstasy and repeating the words, "Beautiful lady!" Seconds later, his other two sons fell to their knees, enraptured by the same vision and repeating the words, "Beautiful lady!"

Being overwhelmed by the strange mystical experience, Cornacchiola's eyes were filled with an intense ephemeral light, which then disappeared. Later: "He felt himself becoming weightless, ethereal, as if his spirit had been freed of his body. When he regained his sight, Bruno saw in the cave a woman of indescribable beauty, and clothed in radiant white. Her black hair was surrounded by a halo of brilliant golden light. Her dress was gathered by a rose-colored sash, and over her shoulders she wore a striking green mantle." These colors, as Cornacchiola explained years later, were meant to represent Mary's relationship with the Trinity, as well as the apparitions of Lourdes in France, Fatima in Portugal, and Rome in Italy.

Continuing with the apparition, at the feet of the "virgin" lay a black cloth with a shattered crucifix. In her right hand, she held a small gray book, and identified herself by saying: "I am the one that is of the Divine Trinity;" and then adding: "I am the Virgin of the Revelation." Addressing Cornacchiola, "she" indicated: "You persecute me—enough of it now! Enter into the true fold, God's Kingdom on earth. The Nine First Fridays of the Sacred Heart have saved you. You must be like the flowers which Isola picked; they make no protest, they are silent and do not rebel... With this dirt of sin, I shall perform powerful miracles for the conversion of unbelievers."

---

[229] (December 22, 2021), Episode 22: Bledsoe Said So | Bledsoe Said So, Bledsoe Said So: https://www.youtube.com/watch?v=6dO4dWjRRZs 26:42-27:28. Accessed September 3, 2023.
[230] ITV Staff (May 1, 2020), The Virgin of Revelation at Tre Fontane (Three Fountains), Inside the Vatican. Note: unless otherwise noted, this is the same source.

She also added: "Pray much and recite the Rosary for the conversion of sinners, of unbelievers and of all Christians."

Several years later, Cornacchiola's experience was key to Pope Pius XII, who early on learned of the apparition; for the *National Catholic Register* reported, that the apparition at Tre Fontane was informally approved by Pope Pius XII on October 5, 1947, when he blessed the statue of the "Virgin of Revelation" "with a procession from the Vatican to the grotto and gave permission for Cornacchiola to speak about the apparition."[231]

The actions of Pope Pius XII, influenced by the apparition, took place during the beginning of the Cold War that same year. As we saw elsewhere in this essay, hatred against the USSR was promoted; which was spearheaded by the Vatican when Pope Pius XII dispatched a statue of Our Lady of Fatima with "her message" on a "pilgrimage" around the world.[232] It was sent from country to country with governments of known integrity receiving it, with the aim of stirring up anti-Russian hatred. As the Cold War progressed, the statue passed through Europe, Asia, Africa, the Americas, and Australia, having passed through a total of fifty-three nations.[233]

In 1948, the American-Russian atomic race began. To strengthen the anti-Russian front, Pius XII ex-communicated any voter who supported the Communists. And soon after, American theologians expressed to the United States that it was their duty to use atomic bombs. In effect, American warmongers, led by prominent Catholics, were preparing for an atomic confrontation with Russia.[234]

On August 6, 1949, Attorney General and Catholic MacGrath spoke to the Catholic order of the Knights of Columbus at their convention in Oregon, urging Catholics to rise up and put on the armor of the Church militant in the battle to save Christendom.[235]

Now, in that same year, Bruno Cornacchiola, the visionary of "the Virgin of Revelation," was at the Vatican in audience with Pius XII.[236] Cornacchiola asked Pius XII for forgiveness for his past hatred of the Catholic Church; and confessed that at the time he had planned to take his life.

The words of "Our Lady" given to Cornacchiola for Pius XII were: "My body could not decay and did not decay. My Son and the angels took me to heaven." For the pope, this message and the testimony of Cornacchiola, was a heavenly sign for him from "Our Lady," since Pius XII was asking for confirmation "on how to clearly define the dogma of the Assumption," which he would do the following year or 1950, in his encyclical published on November 1 of that year.

That year, under direct instructions from the pope, the statue of Our Lady of Fatima was sent by plane, accompanied by the priest Arthur Brassard to go to the heart of the bear: Moscow. Once in the Russian capital, and with the warm approval of the

---

[231] Rachel Lanz (April 27, 2018), From Contemplating Murder to Honoring Mary: The Marian Apparition at Tre Fontane, National Catholic Register. Note: unless otherwise noted, this is the same source.
[232] Avro Manhattan, Vietnam: Why Did We Go? The shocking Story of the Catholic "Church's" Role in Starting the Vietnam War (Chick Publications, Chino, CA, 1984), pp. 30, 31.
[233] Ibid, p. 31.
[234] Ibid.
[235] Ibid, pp. 31, 33.
[236] Rachel Lanz (April 27, 2018), From Contemplating Murder to Honoring Mary: The Marian Apparition at Tre Fontane, National Catholic Register. Note: unless otherwise noted, this is the same source.

American ambassador, Admiral Kirk, the statue was solemnly placed in the church of the foreign diplomats: "To wait for the imminent liberation of Soviet Russia."[237]

Almost three years later, on October 29, 1950, and amid great turmoil, the statue of Our Lady of Fatima arrived in Rome after traveling through Europe. The next day, in a meeting with more than four hundred bishops, Pius XII announced his intention to define the dogma of the Assumption, maintaining that the Virgin Mary had been assumed not only spiritually into Heaven, but also bodily. Later the next day, the pope took a walk alone in the gardens behind the Vatican, where the statue of the Virgin of Fatima had been installed.[238]

"It was October 30, 1950," 2-days before the solemn definition of the Assumption, Pius XII says. The Pope was about to proclaim dogma of faith what the Church had always believed since the early centuries: the bodily taking up of the Virgin Mary at the end of her earthly life. [...] Towards four o'clock that afternoon, he went on his "usual walk in the Vatican gardens, reading and studying." [...] as he rose from the piazza of Our Lady of Lourdes "toward the top of the hill, on the tree-lined road next to the brick wall"; he lifted his eyes from the leaves. "I was struck by a phenomenon, which I never saw until then. The sun, which was still high enough, looked like a yellow opaque globe surrounded all around by a bright circle, "that I could stare at," without receiving the slightest trouble. With a light cloud in front." "The opaque globe - Pius XII continues in the note - moved slightly towards the external side, both turning and moving from left to right and vice versa. But inside the globe, there were clear and uninterrupted movements."[239]

The Pope affirmed having seen the same phenomenon again the following day, October 31, as well as on November 1, the day when the dogma of the Assumption was defined; but also on November 8.[240] He recalled having tried to witness the phenomenon on other days; "at the same time and with similar weather conditions, "to look at the sun to see if the same phenomenon appeared, but in vain; I could not stare, not even for a moment, the sight being immediately dazzled".[241]

There is no doubt that what Pope Pius XII saw was not "the sun," but an unidentified flying object in the shape of an oval and shining around him; it was rotating and moving from left to right in the sky.

Evidently, the phenomenon influenced the pope, for a year later, on October 13, 1951, he ordered a great celebration at the Shrine of Fatima. Cardinal Tedeschini solemnly revealed before more than a million faithful gathered there that the Virgin had visited the pope: "Pope Pius XII was able to witness the life of the sun [...] under the hand of Mary. The sun was agitated, all convulsed, transformed into a picture of life...

---

[237] Avro Manhattan, Vietnam: Why Did We Go? The shocking Story of the Catholic "Church's" Role in Starting the Vietnam War (Chick Publications, Chino, CA, 1984), p. 31.

[238] Randall Sullivan, The Miracle Detective: An Investigative Reporter Sets Out to Examine How the Catholic Church Investigates Holy Visions and Discovers His Own (Grove Press, New York, 2004), p. 178.

[239] Andrea Tornielli (May 12, 2017), Pius XII and Fatima, the secret note on the "miracle of the sun," La Stampa.

[240] Ibid.

[241] Ibid.

into a spectacle of celestial movement... in a transmission of silent but eloquent messages to the Vicar of Christ."[242]

This was the first time in the history of the Roman Catholic Church that a papal vision was announced during the lifetime of the reigning pontiff.[243]

Since we do not know the original "little words" of the Lady of Fatima to the three little shepherds, due to the concealment of the Jesuits, it is strange that "the lady" comes to confirm a lie to the reigning pontiff of the events indicated.

It is also worth asking whether the phenomenon supported a papacy that was particularly intransigent toward non-Catholics before and during World War II, particularly when the opportunity to do so presented itself.

2. The Garabandal apparitions, Spain

Many years before the events of Garabandal, Benjamin Solari Parravicini wrote in some of his psychographies:

"The visit of the Virgin will arrive in Spain on her day will be (1938)".[244]
"The Celestial Word will arrive to a Village in Spain and will be heard (1938)".[245]

"Praying on the rock of the miracle in Spain- the Virgin will arrive one day- she will arrive escorted by Gabriel- she will give the little peasant girls her hand and teach them her footsteps to follow. Christ will come down from that hand, Christ will be in Spain the 66 (1938)".[246]

The 66, which appears in many of his psychographies, has been recognized as an apparently unknown code.

It should be noted that from 1961 to 1965, four girls between the ages of 10 and 12: Conchita González, Mari Cruz González, Jacinta González, and Mari Loli Mazón, experienced the apparition of the "archangel St. Michael" and "the Virgin Mary" in San Sebastián de Garabandal, in northern Spain. [247]

The aforementioned girls experienced all kinds of ecstasies, being examined by doctors and undoubtedly showing that something supernatural was happening. While in ecstasy, they received the rosary from one of the many witnesses present, while they saw only "the Virgin;" and they mentioned the name of the person who gave it, without looking at those around them. Several prophecies took place: all exalting the triumph of Catholicism throughout the world through the "Immaculate Heart of Mary." The prophecies included a number of popes remaining for the beginning of the end times.[248] Although there were prophecies that were failed.

---

[242] Janice T. Connell, The Secrets of Mary: Gifts from the Blessed Mother (St. Martin's Press, New York, 2009), p. 125.
[243] Ibid.
[244] Carteri Clara (April, 1967), Conocimiento de la Nueva Era, No. 352, Buenos Aires.
[245] Carteri Clara (April, 1966), Conocimiento de la Nueva Era, No. 354, Buenos Aires.
[246] Carteri Clara (July, 1966), Conocimiento de la Nueva Era, No. 354, Buenos Aires.
[247] Juan José Isac, El Misterio de Garabandal (Liber Factory, Madrid, Spain, 2017), ob. cit.; Eusebio Garcia De Pesquera, Se fue con prisas a la montaña: Los hechos de Garabandal (1961-1965) (Published Independently, 2018), ob. cit.
[248] Ibid.

We ask ourselves again: why in apparitions such as those mentioned above, did "the Virgin or the lady," unlike in Fatima, identify herself with the Virgin and exalt the Catholic Church as the only Church and its victorious future kingdom?

It should be noted that the ancient inhabitants of the area of San Sebastian de Garabandal, already portrayed in caves in their cave paintings, giant beings from the stars. The different clans of the seven valleys of Cantabria met there thousands of years ago, as it was the most sacred place, so they called it Peña Sagra. There are witnesses who claim that it is common to observe strange lights streaking across the sky, as well as the presence of non-human beings.[249]

In fact, historian and writer Mariano Fernández Urresti tells us that during the apparitions of the "virgin" of Garabandal, in 1961-1965, many eyewitnesses witnessed balls of light, balls with a kind of tail.[250]

In other times, Third Phase, a group of UFO researchers who went to the big mountain of the town of Garabandal, witnessed very large spheres of light behind the mountain, which when descending, left the descent site burned.[251] In fact, a number of videos show spheres of light during the apparitions.[252]

Moreover, an additional detail jumps out about the visions of "the virgin" at Garabandal. Mari Loli Mazon, one of the visionaries of the apparitions, told Jose Luis Respuela, a veteran UFO investigator of Tercera Fase, that next to "the virgin" was a transparent sphere, and Mari asked "her", "Mother, what is that?" To which "she" replied, "That is what I come in."[253]

Conchita wrote about it in her diary in 1961:

"In one of the apparitions Loli and I came down from the pine trees with many people and we saw a thing like fire in the clouds that was also seen by people who were with us and those who were there. When that happened, Our Lady appeared to us and we asked her what it was.
She told us:
I have come on that."[254]

Also in that year, there was another celestial phenomenon that she described:

"Another day, Loli and I (it was the day of the Pilar) were looking at the Virgin when a star and a very large trail was seen below the Virgin's feet. Several people saw the star. We asked the Virgin what it meant, but she did not answer us."[255]

---

[249] (Dec. 26, 2023), Conexión entre aliens y religión | Extraterrestres: Ellos están entre nosotros, DMAX España: https://www.youtube.com/watch?v=xQLcQAqNhhM Accessed Feb. 1, 2024.
[250] Ibid.
[251] Ibid.
[252] (January 21, 2022), Punto Final Ovnis En Garabandal, Historias Reales 2: https://www.youtube.com/watch?v=g0odSZMNHQE 48:34-56:23 Accesado el 19 de abril, 2024.
[253] (Dec. 26, 2023), Conexión entre aliens y religión | Extraterrestres: Ellos están entre nosotros, DMAX España: https://www.youtube.com/watch?v=xQLcQAqNhhM Accessed Feb. 1, 2024.
[254] María Concepción González, Diario de Conchita de Garabandal (Nuestra Señora del Carmen de Garabandal, Inc., Lindenhurst, New York, 1980), p. 61.
[255] Ibíd.

A former priest, Eleuterio Bravo, who witnessed the apparitions of Garabandal as well as numerous paranormal events during the ten days he visited the place, says that Conchita told him that in the apparitions, one or several times, a luminous object or ball of fire appeared above "the virgin", who was asked what it was. "Her" answer was that it was the "vehicle" where they came (with "the angels").[256] Eleuterio adds that one of the apparitions was in a cemetery, where the girls said they talked to the dead.[257]

Eleuterio said that in 1969 he was contacted by "extraterrestrial beings from Andromeda." The same ones appeared to him again in 2012 when he and others saw a series of "extraterrestrial aircrafts" outside the house.[258]

3. The Medjugorje apparitions in Bosnia-Herzegovina

The apparitions of "the Virgin of Medjugorje" began on June 24, 1981 in Bosnia-Herzegovina and they continue to this day, with scientific data proving that a supernatural phenomenon is occurring in the region.[259] UFOs have been witnessed over that region.

The manifestations of ecstasies and prophecies on the site continually favor Catholicism as the only religion through which "the Virgin Mary" will save mankind that has turned away from her.[260]

Mario Danelon and Pietro Zorza explain:

"At the beginning, the signs that accompanied the apparitions and that would lead to conversion were rather of an external and visible nature. There were signs in the sun, signs of lights on the mountain of the Cross, fires on the hill of apparitions and around the church, with characteristics like those described by Moses in the Bible. Also the word MIR [peace] written in letters of fire in the sky of Medjugorje and the surrounding valleys."[261]

Gabriel Paulino, a Brazilian ufologist, writes that a woman named Draga told him that at the beginning of the apparitions in 1981, she went out to collect firewood near the mountain where the seers had their first apparition; and that she saw a UFO the size of the mountain. Paulino himself, along with two hundred other people, witnessed a huge crystal-clear globe moving in the sky. And in fact, about three weeks after the first apparition of Medjugorje, the visionaries went to the hill barefoot at the request of "the virgin," around 10:00 p.m. and being with about 40 people. They began to pray

---

[256] (31 de mayo, 2022), Apariciones de Garabandal: quiénes eran realmente? Entrevista a Eleuterio Bravo Parte 1, MVA Contacto Cuántico: https://www.youtube.com/watch?v=OF4irOrACg8 13:51 [48]-14:16 Accesado el 19 de abril, 2024.

[257] Ibid. 27:21-28:48

[258] Eleuterio Bravo Bravo, Plan Andrómeda: Fin de los tiempos (Ediciones Ende, 2014).

[259] Daniel Maria Klimek, Medjugorje and the Supernatural: Science, Mysticism, and Extraordinary Religious Experience (Oxford University Press, 2018), ob. cit.

[260] Ibid; Jesús García, Medjugorje: El libro definitivo para comprender por qué más de 30 millones de personas han acudido a un pequeño pueblo de Bosnia-Herzegovina (Libros Libres, 7th edition, 2012), ob. cit.

[261] Mario Danelon, Pietro Zorza, Testimonios sobre Medjugorje (Bonum, Buenos Aires, Argentina, 2007), p. 225.

and suddenly a great light appeared in the sky and a bright yellow "balloon" slowly descended towards the village.[262]

In Medjugorje fireballs have been observed coming from the top of Mount Križevac, the site of the apparitions.[263] It is reported that one ball of light flew overhead and disappeared in the bushes on the hillside. It appeared a second time down the slope towards the crowd and approached Ivan, one of the seers. The ball of light shone brightly three times before vanishing, after which Ivan went into ecstasy.[264]

On another occasion, around the cross located at the top of Mount Križevac, there appeared "immense lights over more than a kilometer around" it.[265] On another day, the cross began to rotate very rapidly, to the point that it "disappeared," only to reappear again.[266]

When the communist police imprisoned priest Jozo, a Medjugorje adherent, the guards witnessed strange lights in his cell at night. Jozo later said he was visited by "Our Lady."[267]

These are just a few of many examples that could be cited.

For its part, Tito's communist regime tried to discredit the apparitions and the visionaries.[268]

It is alleged that "the Virgin" intentionally chose Medjugorje - a largely Muslim region - whose apparitions were widely propagated by the Franciscan priest Zovko, who was sentenced for teaching children fascist greetings.[269]

In fact, considering the terrible and fateful scenes that occurred in Croatia during World War II, it is known that two Zovko friars from the region "were murderous ustashis who killed in the name of Our Lady."[270]

We noted in another chapter that the Balkan war in the 1990s between Croatia and Serbia, that both sides were moving under nationalistic sentiments. The Croatian government heavily favored Catholicism and the revival of ustasha pride among many. Priest Jozo met in 1992 with John Paul II at the Vatican, who told the priest that "I am with you. Protect Medugorje. Protect Our Lady's messages!"[271]

Missiles and mortar shells were launched against Medjugorje, but they all landed in the fields; for according to a Serbian newspaper, Yugoslav warplanes sent to destroy Medjugorje, could not drop their bombs because of a "strange silver fog" that formed over the area.[272] Was it the phenomenon protecting Medjugorje?

[262] Gabriel Paulino Junior (1 de abril 2007), Evidências de UFOs em Medjugorje, Revista UFO, Edición 132, ob. cit.

[263] Elizabeth Ficocelli, The Fruits of Medjugorje: Stories of True and Lasting Conversion (Paulist Press, New York/Mahwah, N.J., 2006), p. 138.

[264] Ibid, p. 42.

[265] Emmanuel Maillard, Medjugorje, el triunfo del corazón: La década de 1990 (Asociación Hijos de Medjugorje, 2010), ob. cit.

[266] Ibid.

[267] Ibid.

[268] Paolo Brosio, Il papa e Medjugorje. La Madonna "postina," gli intrighi del KGB e i vescovi di Mostar (Incontri) (Piemme, 2017), ob. cit.

[269] Krsto Skanata (Producer) Krsto Skanata (Director) (1993), Bog i Hrvati (Dunav Film).

[270] Ibid.

[271] Mirjana Soldo, My Heart Will Triumph (Catholic Shop, 2016), ob. cit.

[272] Ibid.

When the visionary Mirjana spoke to John Paul II in person, he showed absolute support for the apparitions and the message of Medjugorje as the hope of the world. And he asked Mirjana to take care of Medjugorje.[273]

John Paul II had been interested in Medjugorje from the beginning, and in fact he prayed to Virgin Mary to appear again on earth to help so many faithful to practice their faith freely in the communist countries. When he heard that "Virgin Mary" appeared in one of those countries, he believed that it was in answer to his request.[274]

On June 25, 1991, the tenth anniversary of the Medjugorje apparitions, war was declared in the former Yugoslavia, when Tudjman declared the independence of Croatia and referred to the Medjugorje apparitions as "a call to the Croatian people." The visionaries of Medjugorje did not support Tudjman's invocation because they were not nationalists. But why would "the Virgin" support John Paul II, who so severely pushed for the independence of Croatia, which was sheltered under the most intolerant Catholic nationalism?[275]

Tudjman visited Medjugorje in May 1993 and claimed that the Croatian revival was heralded by the apparitions of "the Virgin" in that region. Tudjman blamed Muslims in the region for the massacre of entire Croatian villages, for which he gave them persecution shortly after he visited Medjugorje. Muslim women and children were kicked and beaten by Croatian troops who drove them to the west bank. The men were transported in trucks to concentration camps, where fifteen thousand of them were imprisoned at the beginning of May.[276]

On the occasion of Pope John Paul II's visit to Croatia in 1994, the "Virgin Mary" said in Medjugorje on August 25: "Dear children! Today I am united with you in a special way, praying for the gift of the presence of my beloved son in your home land. Pray, little children, for the health of my dearest son, who is suffering, and whom I have chosen for these times. I pray and intercede before my Son, Jesus, so that the dream that your fathers had may be fulfilled. Pray, little children, in a special way, because Satan is strong and wants to destroy hope in your heart. I bless you. Thank you for having responded to my call."[277]

Many other "Marian" apparitions occurred in the 20th century, with many of them surrounding historical events that were then affecting the position of Catholicism in the world;[278] particularly in a state of intransigence.

If this is "the Virgin," she would be the supposed "mediatrix" before "Jesus Christ" in a future return. Parravicini wrote in one of his psychographics:

"Interplanetary crafts not visible to the human retina are traveling towards Earth. Their beings, equally non-visible, have always lived on our planet and they dwell in the Temples. Convents: religious and mystic homes of solitary life. They do so because they are equally mystical, meditative and try to impose faith.
They speak of Faith, Charity, hopes, and Love in purity.

---

[273] Ibid.
[274] Ibid.
[275] Randall Sullivan, The Miracle Detective (Grove Press, New York, 2004), ob. cit.
[276] Ibid.
[277] June Klins, I Have Come to Tell the World That God Exists: The Best of "The Spirit of Medjugorje" Volume III: 2005-2009 (AuthorHouse, Bloomington, IN, 2011), p. 266.
[278] Chris Maunder, Our Lady of the Nations: Apparitions of Mary in 20th-Century Catholic Europe (Oxford University Press, 1st edition, 2016), ob. cit.

"They preach the return of Christ and infinite peace by repeating:

"-It will be... It will be...!"[279]

4. Chris Bledsoe and the UAP phenomenon

We have mentioned Chris Bledsoe, who is a deeply religious family man as well as a successful North Carolina businessman; who was on the brink of the unthinkable after losing everything in the 2007 financial crisis; but also suffered from a debilitating chronic illness.[280]

On the night of January 8, 2007, when Bledsoe was fishing on the banks of the Cape Fear River with three co-workers and his teenage son, standing around a nighttime campfire, he decided to walk away from the group and desperately cried out for help to whoever was there. Sometime later, a fire appeared in the sky, as if swirling and shooting flames out of it. Climbing the hill, Chris spotted two fireballs hovering in the sky about forty-five feet in diameter. Then a third appeared.

Bledsoe's son Chris Jr., who accompanied him fishing, went in search of his father because he had been walking for a long time. As he walked along, he saw two red balls of glowing light, suspended above the ground. Chris Jr. was frightened and could not scream or move.

Meanwhile, his father returned to his fishing buddies, who told him that Chris Jr. was looking for him, so he went back to look for him. When Jr. heard his father, he was able to move and the two were reunited. Chris Jr. told his father that he had been gone all night, in response to his father telling him that he had been gone only twenty minutes. Both said they had seen UFOs, and Bledsoe wanted to see the phenomenon again every night of his life.

Chris Jr. complained about red-eyed creatures that had kept him from moving.

After the two joined the others at the campfire, what was to be an incredible night began, with multiple UFOs almost everywhere they went, of different colors and sizes; from large to small, and producing electromagnetic effects.

When they returned home, the family was absent because they were visiting other relatives, but Bledsoe witnessed several non-human entities in his backyard. One of them informed him that they were not there to harm him, but to help him.

Experiences of this type continued, and continue to this day; but mostly luminous spheres hovering in the sky.

He and his family were ostracized by the community for recounting his experiences. Although Chris Bledsoe was eventually "miraculously" cured of his illnesses, Junior had constant nightmares for months; screaming in the middle of the night, and hearing a strange sound, like helicopter rotors. Seeing shadowy figures in his bedroom staring at him.

His family has also experienced the phenomenon on several occasions.

Chris experienced dreams of apocalyptic visions of famine, plague, widespread destruction, and suffering that caused him to wake up screaming in the night. He felt those were warnings from non-human intelligence accompanying him.

---

[279] Sigurd Von Wurmb, Dibujos Profeticos: Benjamin Solari Parravicini la Voz de los Ovnis (Editorial Kier S.A., First Edition, Buenos Aires, 2003), pp. 22, 23.
[280] Chris Bledsoe, UFO of GOD: The Extraordinary True Story of Chris Bledsoe (Chris Bledsoe, 2023), ob. cit. Note: unless otherwise noted, this is the same source.

But he also had visions of the pyramids of Egypt.

Bledsoe and "the lady"

The most dramatic experience of these beings occurred one night when awakened by them, Bledsoe was led by them to the outside of the house.

Among the many things that happened to him, he finally saw a woman suspended in a circle of light, motionless and silent and gazing at him. Her beauty reassured him and his fear vanished. He found himself kneeling within the circle of light she emanated. Her feet were bare at his chin and pointing downward as she was suspended.

She wore a simple, shimmering robe that reached to her ankles, like an ancient priestess robe, with long sleeves that extended to her wrists and an unadorned collar.

It was also reminiscent of the robes of the goddesses in Roman sculptures and mosaics.

Her hair was blonde and her blue eyes were extremely dazzling. She was about five feet tall. She told him that he was to fulfill a mission to spread the message of the existence of non-human entities, and of the possible apocalyptic future for the Earth and peace. She made him see that the beings that appeared to him were guardians that she sent in fulfillment of her orders.

She also warned, "that there were forces at work to cast phenomena like this in a negative light, and that if this view won out, humanity would be set on a path to ruin." "A new knowledge must arrive. Mankind must awaken to it," she said.

Chris Bledsoe has shared his story and message at MUFON conferences, in a 2008 Discovery documentary, and at *Beyond Skinwalker Ranch*, where the spheres of light appeared, one of which snuck through the trees, coming within significant distance of where they were.[281]

Bledsoe was visited on numerous occasions, both officially and unofficially, by government agents, including the CIA, NASA, several professors, and MUFON.[282]

His case was investigated by AATIP and was known to Lue Elizondo, Tom DeLonge, NASA engineer Timothy Taylor, Dr. Harold Pufhoff who was part of AATIP, Colonel John B. Alexander; former senior CIA officer Jim Semivan, who is part of TTSA. Semivan began to have experiences with the phenomenon from his early years in the CIA, a career spanning 25 years.

Semivan had told an audience of more than a dozen people that "NASA, the CIA, the FBI, the NRO, the Vatican, and every division of the defense department had their hands in this" in the study of the UAP phenomenon. And that the "white house and other world leaders had been briefed on the events that took place on the very land we stood on."

---

[281] James Schwandt (Writer), & LeWalter R Fooks (Director) (2023, August 1). Chris Bledsoe (Season 1, Episode 8) [TV Series Episode]. David Carr, Mary Donahue, Brandon Fugal, Matthew Ginsburg, Tim Healy, Joel Patterson, Jennifer Wagman, Justin Christenson (Executive Producers), *Beyond Skinwalker Ranch*. Public Broadcasting Service (PBS). Note: unless otherwise noted, this is the same source.
[282] Chris Bledsoe, UFO of GOD: The Extraordinary True Story of Chris Bledsoe (Chris Bledsoe, 2023), ob. cit. Note: unless otherwise noted, this is the same source.

"The dead" warn of an assassination attempt on Pope Francis
One night while conducting an experiment, Chris and company heard from a small box attached to a digital recorder a voice urgently warning them that Pope Francis would be in danger in Philadelphia during his September 2015 visit to the United States.

On September 22, through a remote viewing exercise done with Bledsoe and another over the phone with Joseph McMoneagle, the 001 remote viewer and former member of the government's classified program for their remote viewing program, they yielded combined information that the Ben Franklin Bridge, which was closest to Pope Francis' speeches, seemed to fit what they had received. Someone contacted the CIA, whereupon "Security tightened on the Walt Whitman and Betsy Ross bridges, and vehicle traffic was completely shut down on the Ben Franklin Bridge."

After the pope visited Philadelphia, the attorneys general charged a local man with conspiring to assassinate the pope near the Ben Franklin Bridge. Bledsoe did not know if the arrest had anything to do with the information that was made available to the CIA.

International Organization for the Destiny of the World: the Vatican, Freemasons, military, prelates, politicians, others, and John Podesta
Luis Elizondo, the former director of AATIP, presented in April 2019, a list of foreign governments involved in the investigation of the UAP phenomenon, among which was the Vatican.[283] In June 2021, he said for *TOE* that he had recently traveled to Rome "and spoke to some very senior academics in the Vatican. They told me that in the 1600s, have you told people there was no such thing as aliens, that would be considered heresy because there is no limit to the dominion of God or the notion of God." It is in recent history that limitations have been placed on what God can and cannot do.[284] Some time later, he added that he spoke to some people at the Vatican, where "they describe these flaming Roman shields in the sky that would follow them from battlefield to battlefield, that they call the clipeus, which is the shape of the Roman shield."[285]

Let us look at an article that originally appeared in the Italian newspaper *Libero*, and which was written by journalist Enzo Amadori.[286] It was entitled, in its English translation: "It is called "International Organization for the Destiny of the World," which reads: "The club of the powerful who believe in extraterrestrials."[287] Occasionally, we will quote verbatim several of the details describing the organization.

It has or had its headquarters in Moscow, where the "Center for Information, Analysis and Situation Strategies" under the President of the Russian Federation,

---

[283] (April 5, 2019), AAPC 2019 Luis Elizondo Presentation, Scientific Coalition for UAP Studies: https://www.youtube.com/watch?v=6dO4dWjRRZs 28:50-31:42. Accessed September 3, 2023.

[284] (June 23, 2021), Luis Elizondo: UFOs, Skinwalker, Remote Viewing [Part 1], Theories of Everything with Curt Jaimungal: https://www.youtube.com/watch?v=aAmFlLfsZKM 33:23-33:51 Accessed August 24, 2023.

[285] (October 21, 2021), Luis Elizondo: Gov't Has Biological UFO Samples [Part 2], Theories of Everything with Curt Jaimungal: https://www.youtube.com/watch?v=wULw64ZL1Bg 34:11-36:25 Accessed August 24, 2023.

[286] It no longer appears on the Internet. But it appeared with important additions in *Affaritaliani*.

[287] Affaritaliani (August 16, 2016), Si chiama "Organizzazione internazionale per i destini del mondo," Affaritaliani. https://www.affaritaliani.it/politica/palazzo-potere/si-chiama-organizzazione-internazionale-per-i-destini-del-mondo-436648.html?refresh_ce Accessed September 4, 2023. Note: unless otherwise noted, this is the same source.

Vladimir Putin, was located. The organization's headquarters "is a futuristic building in the suburbs, with a large situation room and interactive maps showing the critical areas of the planet." Alexei Savin, a former lieutenant general in the reserve, is or was the head of the section dealing with UFOs.

This organization brought together "military, prelates, politicians, managers, professionals who are already part of other organizations or are linked by their membership in international Masonic lodges or institutions close to the Catholic Church." John Podesta was there.

The project involved such major cities as Washington, London, Beijing, Tel Aviv, and Rome.

Amadori in *Libero*, writes that the main common denominator of the attendees is the belief in a Creator and their conviction that there are other forms of intelligence in the universe.

Many of the members were convinced "that humanity is a kind of laboratory product of a superior extraterrestrial civilization, which for thousands of years has been watching over us." Its members rely on sacred texts, particularly some passages of the Bible to support their belief in the existence of life elsewhere in the universe. They quote the words of the Jesuit priest, Monsignor Corrado Balducci and Monsignor Gianfranco Basti, a "theologian and professor of philosophy of nature and science at the Pontifical Lateran University, and a former collaborator of the Italian Space Agency."

The Italian spokesman is the lobbyist and Mason Piergiorgio Bassi, who is "a public relations entrepreneur with excellent connections in the Vatican and politics." In fact, on his "Twitter" account - now X - he published two photographs: 1. Dated April 28, 2016, standing next to representatives of Islam, and next to Michael Heinrich Weninger, an Austrian Catholic priest mentioned in another chapter and who is a member of the Pontifical Council for Interreligious Dialogue. But it was reported years ago that he is also a Freemason and chaplain of three Austrian lodges.[288] 2. In another photograph, dated May 5, 2016, Bassi appears in a very good relationship with the Vatican's Cardinal Secretary of State, Pietro Parolin.

Bassi often traveled between Rome and Russia, thus facilitating communications and relations between Savin's men and the then director of the Vatican Observatory, Jesuit astronomer José Gabriel Funes.[289]

Thanks to Bassi, Monsignor Gianfranco Basti was then in the center of Moscow for these meetings. The report reads verbatim: "Bassi, sitting in his office in Rome, smiles at the reporter's skepticism: 'At this point, even one of the closest collaborators of the president of the United States thinks like us.'" Indeed, Bassi had recently met (this report is from August 2016) in Rome with John Podesta, then head of Hillary Clinton's election campaign. *Dagospia* news intercepted Bassi and Podesta at the Pariolino restaurant Pescheria Rossini. They discussed business, "but also confidential documents about the so-called Area 51 and the secrets about UFOs kept there."

---

[288] Cameron Doody (Feb. 15, 2020), Catholic Freemasons "certainly not" excommunicated, says Austrian member of Vatican interfaith dialogue body, Novena News.
[289] Affaritaliani (August 16, 2016), Si chiama "Organizzazione internazionale per i destini del mondo," Affaritaliani: https://www.affaritaliani.it/politica/palazzo-potere/si-chiama-organizzazione-internazionale-per-i-destini-del-mondo-436648.html?refresh_ce Accessed September 4, 2023. Note: unless otherwise noted, this is the same source.

Also, the group was working to get Barack Obama to address the issue.

Bassi additionally recalled that former Russian President Dmitry Medvedev had said, "Along with the briefcase with nuclear codes, the president is given a special 'top secret' folder. It contains information about aliens who have visited our planet..." But "according to some witnesses, Medvedev was joking"- Amadori pointed out, but Bassi indicated that he was very serious.

Savin's organization also believes in the possibility of changing the destiny of the world. The report continues: "At this point Bassi, an expert in Masonic and esoteric matters, introduces us to the "New Paradigm," the vision of a humanity ready to relaunch itself and eliminate social injustices with the help of the technological discoveries of extraterrestrial civilizations in energy, health and transportation." The article adds that: "The reporter's incredulous expression does not discourage Bassi, who states: "Thanks to relations with extraterrestrials in Russia they are able to predict future events, such as terrorist attacks, environmental disasters and political upheavals."

For its part, *Vatican News*, the information portal of the Holy See, referred to the deep contacts of Piergiorgio Bassi, who at one time "dealt with UFOs."[290] *Alfa & Omega* also referred to Bassi's Russian contacts.[291]

At the same time, a great deal of Catholic literature has been written about the possibility of extraterrestrial life.[292] According to a 2015 study, which was conducted by Joshua Ambrosius, a professor at the University of Dayton, USA, and published in *Space Policy*, both Catholics and non-Catholics in the country are the two groups most optimistic about the possibility of finding extraterrestrial life in the next forty years.[293]

What can we say about all of the above and where is it headed? Dr. Jacques Vallée, without mentioning Roman Catholicism, appropriately summarizes some conclusions in this way, fitting with the above:

"The eager anticipation of encounters with other intelligent beings would help in transcending local conflicts on this earth and in achieving within a single generation behavioral changes that might otherwise take hundreds of years to complete. If this is the contribution of the UFO phenomenon, then we are in fact dealing with one of history's major transitions."[294]

[290] Salvatore Cernuzio (January 14, 2023), Chaouqui y Ciferri en el juicio en el Vaticano. Becciu: un plan en mi contra, Vatican News.

[291] Editor (May 19, 2022), Puigdemont y dos emisarios rusos quisieron reunirse con Becciu, Alfa & Omega.

[292] José G. Funes, SJ (editor), La búsqueda de vida extraterrestre inteligente: Un enfoque interdisciplinario (Editorial Universidad Católica de Córdoba, 2023); Guy Consolmagno, SJ and Paul Mueller, SJ, Would You Baptize an Extraterrestrial?: . . . and Other Questions from the Astronomers' In-box at the Vatican Observatory (Image, New York, New York, 2014); Joel L. Parkyn, Exotheology: Theological Explorations of Intelligent Extraterrestrial Life (Pickwick Publications, Eugene, Oregon, 2021); Paul Thigpen, Extraterrestrial Intelligence and the Catholic Faith: Are We Alone in the Universe with God and the Angels? (TAN Books, Gastonia, NC, 2022); Jennifer Rosato and Alan Vincelette (eds.), Extraterrestrials in the Catholic Imagination: Explorations in Science, Science Fiction and Religion (Cambridge Scholars Publishing, 2021); Thomas F. O'Meara, Vast Universe: Extraterrestrials and Christian Revelation (Liturgical Press, Collegeville, Minnesota, 2012).

[293] Claire Giangravè (February 24, 2017), Could Catholicism handle the discovery of extraterrestrial life?, Crux Catholic Media.

[294] Jacques Vallée, Dimensions: A Casebook of Alien Contact (Contemporary Books, 1988), p. xiii.

Given the interesting backdrop of the current confrontation over the rise of the extreme Christian right in the United States and the world, as well as the progressive Catholicism of Pope Francis, what will the phenomenon finally do, given that everything points to its desire to unite the world under a "new humanity," but under a confusing cloak, which few want to see?

Made in United States
Troutdale, OR
11/29/2024

25440998R10381